From Beginning of Oral Language	**The Oral Tradition** Folktales Mythology Legends
1400s	**Early Books** Hornbooks Caxton's Printing Press — 1476
1500s	**Chapbooks Introduced** *Jack the Giant Killer*
1600s	**The Puritan Influence** *Spiritual Milk for Boston Babes in either England, Drawn from the Breasts of Both Testaments for Their Souls' Nourishment* John Bunyan's *Pilgrim's Progress*
1693	**View of Childhood Changes** John Locke's *Some Thoughts Concerning Education*
1697	**First Fairy Tales Written for Children** Charles Perrault's *Tales of Mother Goose*
1719	**Great Adventure Stories** Daniel DeFoe's *Robinson Crusoe* Jonathan Swift's *Gulliver's Travels* (1726)
1744	**Children's Literature: A True Beginning** John Newbery's *A Little Pretty Pocket Book* and *History of Little Goody Two Shoes*
1762	**Children Should Be Guided in Their Search for Knowledge** Jean Jacques Rousseau's *Emile*
1789	**Poetry About Children** William Blake's *Songs of Innocence*
Early 1800s	**The Romantic Movement in Europe** The Grimms' *German Popular Stories* including "Cinderella" and "Hansel and Gretel" Hans Christian Andersen's *Fairy Tales Told for Children*
1800s	**Illustrators Make Their Impact on Children's Books** Walter Crane's *The House That Jack Built* (1865) Randolph Caldecott's *The History of John Gilpin* (1878) Kate Greenaway's *Under the Window* (1878)
1860	**The Victorian Influence** Charlotte Yonge's *The Daisy Chain* and *The Clever Woman of the Family*

(continued on back endsheet)

THROUGH THE EYES OF A CHILD

THIRD EDITION

THROUGH THE EYES OF A CHILD

An Introduction to Children's Literature

DONNA E. NORTON

Texas A&M University

Merrill, an imprint of
Macmillan Publishing Company
New York

Collier Macmillan Canada, Inc.
Toronto

Maxwell Macmillan International Publishing Group
New York Oxford Singapore Sydney

About the cover and chapter openers: Children's literature enjoys the special enhancement of imaginative illustration that often tells the story on its own. For this new, full-color edition of *Through the Eyes of a Child,* it is appropriate to celebrate the special quality of children's literature with paintings designed specifically for the text. Working in watercolor, Anne Porterfield Vega illustrated each chapter's subject matter with a focus on children's unique viewpoints. On the cover, Ms. Vega's vision extends elements from the chapter openers to provide a composite landscape suggesting the limitless horizons of childhood imagination.

Administrative Editor: Sally B. MacGregor
Senior Developmental Editor: Linda James Scharp
Production Editor: Victoria M. Althoff
Art Coordinator: Vincent A. Smith
Photo Editor: Gail Meese
Text Designer: Cynthia Brunk
Cover Designer: Brian Deep

This book was set in Usherwood.

Printed in the United States of America

Macmillan Publishing Company
866 Third Avenue, New York, NY 10022
Collier Macmillan Canada, Inc.

Library of Congress Catalog Card Number: 90-60624

International Standard Book Number: 0-675-21144-1

Printing: 1 2 3 4 5 6 7 8 9 Year: 1 2 3 4

FOLLOWING THE COMPLETION of her doctorate at the University of Wisconsin, Madison, Donna E. Norton joined the College of Education faculty at Texas A&M University where she teaches courses in children's literature, language arts, and reading. Dr. Norton is the 1981–1982 recipient of the Texas A&M Faculty Distinguished Achievement Award in Teaching. This award is given "in recognition and appreciation of ability, personality, and methods which have resulted in distinguished achievements in the teaching and the inspiration of students." She is listed in *Who's Who of American Women, Who's Who in America,* and *Who's Who in the World.*

Dr. Norton is the author of two books in addition to this volume: *The Effective Teaching of Language Arts,* 3d ed. and *Language Arts Activities for Children,* 2d ed. She is on the editorial board of several journals and is a frequent contributor to journals and presenter at professional conferences. The focus of her current research is multicultural literature, comparative education, and literature-based reading programs. The multicultural research includes a longitudinal study of multicultural literature in classroom settings. This research is supported by grants from the Meadows Foundation and the Texas A&M Research Association. In conjunction with the research in comparative education, she developed a graduate course that enables students to study children's literature and reading instruction in England and Scotland and is evaluating educational programs in several Asian and European countries. She currently has a grant from GTE Foundation to develop institutes in children's literature and literacy.

Prior to her college teaching experience, Dr. Norton was an elementary teacher in River Falls, Wisconsin and in Madison, Wisconsin. She was a Language Arts/Reading Consultant for federally funded kindergarten through adult basic education programs. In this capacity she developed, provided in-service instruction, and evaluated kindergarten programs, summer reading and library programs, remedial reading programs, learning disability programs for middle school children, elementary and secondary literature programs for the gifted, and diagnostic and intervention programs for reading disabled adults. Dr. Norton's continuing concern for literature programs results in frequent consultations with educators from various disciplines, librarians, and school administrators and teachers.

CREDITS

TEXT EXCERPTS AND POEMS

Page 89, text excerpt from *The Goats* by Brock Cole. Copyright © 1987 by Brock Cole. Reprinted by permission of Farrar, Straus and Giroux, Inc.

Page 92, text excerpt from *Hatchet* by Gary Paulsen. Text, Copyright © 1987 by Gary Paulsen. Reprinted by permission of Bradbury Press, an Affiliate of Macmillan, Inc.

Page 93, text excerpt from *A Bag of Moonshine* by Alan Garner, © 1986. Reprinted by permission of Delacorte Press.

Pages 99, 101, 480, and 502, text excerpts from *No Hero for the Kaiser* by Rudolf Frank. Text © 1986 by Rudolf Frank. By permission of Lothrop, Lee & Shepard, a division of William Morrow & Co.

Page 99, text excerpt from *Darkness and the Butterfly* by Ann Grifalconi © 1987 by Ann Grifalconi.

Page 113, text excerpts from *On My Honor* by Marion Dane Bauer. Copyright © 1986 by Marion Dane Bauer. Reprinted by permission of Houghton Mifflin Company.

Page 114, text excerpts from pages 3, 9, 12, 19, 20, 22, 28, 46 and 52 *Sarah, Plain and Tall* by Patricia MacLachlan. Copyright 1985 by Patricia MacLachlan. All selections reprinted by permission of Harper & Row, Publishers, Inc.

Page 116, text excerpt from *Song and Dance Man* by Karen Ackerman. Copyright © 1988 by Karen Ackerman. Reprinted by permission of Alfred A. Knopf, Inc.

Page 116, text excerpt from *Tuck Everlasting* by Natalie Babbitt. Copyright © 1975 by Natalie Babbitt. Reprinted by permission of Farrar, Straus and Giroux, Inc.

Page 172, poems from *Chinese Mother Goose Rhymes* by Robert Wyndham, with the permission of Philomel Books. Copyright © 1968 by Robert Wyndham.

Page 187, text excerpt from *The Cat in the Hat* by Dr. Seuss. Copyright © 1957 by Random House. Used by permission.

Page 187, text excerpt from *Frog and Toad Are Friends*, written and illustrated by Arnold Lobel. Copyright © 1970 by Arnold Lobel. By permission of Harper & Row Publishers Inc. and World's Work Ltd.

Page 192, text excerpt from *No Such Things* by Bill Peet (New York: Houghton Mifflin, 1983).

Page 193, text excerpt from *A Baby Sister for Frances* by Russell Hoban, Courtesy of Harper & Row, Publishers, Inc.

Page 195, from *The Little House* by Virginia Lee Burton. Copyright © 1942 by Houghton Mifflin Co.

Page 196, text excerpt from *The 500 Hats of Bartholomew Cubbins* by Dr. Seuss. Copyright © 1938 by Vanguard Press. Used by permission.

Page 241, text excerpt from *British Folktales* by K. M. Briggs. Copyright © 1977 by Katharine Briggs. Reprinted by permission of A.P. Watt Ltd.

Page 252, text excerpt from *The Woman Who Married a Snake* by David Conger. Copyright © 1987 by David Conger. Reprinted by permission of Charles E. Tuttle Co.

Page 253, text excerpt from *The Chinese Mirror,* © 1988 by Mirra Ginsburg, text reprinted by permission of Harcourt Brace Jovanovich, Inc.

Page 258, text excerpted from "Gratitude" in *Aesop's Fables* by Tom Paxton. Copyright © 1988 by Tom Paxton. Reprinted by permission of William Morrow & Co.

Page 259, text excerpt reprinted with permission of Macmillan Publishing Company from *Doctor Coyote: A Native American Aesop's Fables* retold by John Bierhorst, pictures by Wendy Watson. © 1987 by John Bierhorst. Illus. Copyright © 1987 by Wendy Watson.

Page 266, text excerpt from *The Outlaws of Sherwood* by Robin McKinley. Copyright © 1988 by Robin McKinley. Reprinted by permission of Greenwillow Books (A Division of William Morrow & Co.).

Page 309, text excerpts from *Redwall* by Brian Jacques, © 1986 by Brian Jacques. Reprinted by permission of Philomel Books.

Page 324, text essay copyright © 1991, 1987, 1983, by Merrill Publishing Company. Reprinted by permission of Madeleine L'Engle.

Page 356, poem "Rainbow Writing" from Eve Merriam, *Rainbow Writing.* Copyright © 1976 by Eve Merriam (New York: Atheneum, 1976). Reprinted with the permission of Atheneum Publishers.

Pages 358 and 386, text excerpts from pp. 7-8 and 16-17 from *Pass the Poetry, Please!* by Lee Bennett Hopkins. Copyright © 1972 by Lee Bennett Hopkins. All selections reprinted by permission of Harper & Row, Publishers, Inc.

Page 361, poem "The Pickety Fence" from *Far and Few: Rhymes of Never Was and Always Is* by David McCord. Copyright © 1952 by David McCord. By permission of Little, Brown and Company.

Page 362, "Poem to Mud" from Zilpha Keatley Snyder, *Today Is Saturday.* Text copyright © 1969 by Zilpha Keatley Snyder (New York: Atheneum, 1969). Reprinted with the permission of Atheneum Publishers.

Page 362, poem "Don't Ever Seize a Weasel by the Tail" reprinted with permission of Macmillan Publishing Company, Inc. from *A Gopher in the Garden* by Jack Prelutsky. Copyright © by Jack Prelutsky, 1966, 1967.

Page 364, "Spill" from Judith Thurman, *Flashlight and Other Poems.* Copyright © 1976 by Judith Thurman (New York: Atheneum, 1976). Reprinted with the permission of Atheneum Publishers.

Page 364, poem "The Path on the Sea" from *The Moon is Like a Silver Sickle* by Miriam Morton. Copyright, © 1972 by Miriam Morton. Reprinted by permission of Simon & Schuster, a Division of Gulf & Western Corporation.

Page 364, poem "The Wind" reprinted by permission of Four Winds Press, an imprint of Macmillan Publishing Company, from *The Covered Bridge House and Other Poems* by Kaye Starbird. Copyright © 1979 by Kaye Starbird Jennison.

Page 365, text of "Mummy Slept Late and Daddy Fixed Breakfast" from *You Read to Me, I'll Read to You* by John Ciardi. Copyright © 1962 by John Ciardi. By permission of J. B. Lippincott, Publishers.

Page 368, poem "Dead Tree" from *Seeing Things: A Book of Poems,* written and designed by Robert Froman with lettering by Ray Barbar. Copyright © 1974 by Robert Froman. By permission of Thomas Y. Crowell, Publishers.

Page 369, poem "Forsythia" from *Concrete Poetry: A World View,* edited by Mary Ellen Solt. Copyright © 1968 by Mary Ellen Solt. Reprinted by permission of Indiana University Press.

Page 369, poem "The Sidewalk Racer" from *The Sidewalk Racer and Other Poems of Sports and Motion* by Lillian Morrison. Copyright © 1965, 1967, 1968, 1977 by Lillian Morrison. By permission of Lothrop, Lee & Shepard Books (A Division of William Morrow & Company).

Page 369, from Ann Atwood, *Haiku: The Mood of Earth.* Copyright © 1971 by Ann Atwood (New York: Charles Scribner's Sons, 1971). Reprinted with the permission of Charles Scribner's Sons.

Page 370, poem excerpt from "The Man in the Marmalade Hat Arrives" in *A Visit to William Blake's Inn,* text © 1981, 1980 by Nancy Willard, reprinted by permission of Harcourt Brace Jovanovich, Inc.

Page 371, poem "Eletelephony" from *Tirra Lirra* by Laura Richards. Copyright © 1960 by Hamilton Richards. By permission of Little, Brown and Company.

Page 371, poem "Ickle Me, Pickle Me, Tickle Me Too" from *Where the Sidewalk Ends* by Shel Silverstein (New York: Harper & Row, 1974).

Page 372, poem "Pumberly Pott's Unpredictable Niece" in *The Queen of Eene* by Jack Prelutsky. Text copyright © 1970, 1978 by Jack Prelutsky. By permission of Greenwillow Books (A Division of William Morrow & Company).

Page 372, poem "The Land of Ho-Ho-Hum" excerpted from the book *Laughing Time* by William Jay Smith. Copyright © 1953, 1955, 1956, 1957, 1959, 1968, 1974, 1977, 1980 by William Jay Smith. Reprinted by permission of Delacorte Press/Seymour Lawrence.

Page 373, poem "Bickering" from N. M. Bodecker, *Hurry, Hurry Mary Dear and Other Nonsense Poems.* Copyright © 1976 by N. M. Bodecker, A. Margaret K. McElderry Book. (New York: Atheneum Publishers, 1976) Reprinted with the permission of Atheneum Publishers.

Page 373, text of "Change" from *River Winding: Poems by Charlotte Zolotow.* Copyright © 1970 by Charlotte Zolotow. By permission of Thomas Y. Crowell, Publishers.

Page 373, from *Moonsong Lullaby* by Jamake Highwater. Copyright © 1981 by Jamake Highwater. Reprinted by permission of Lothrop, Lee & Shepard (A Division of William Morrow & Co.).

Page 374, text of "Frosted-Window World" from *In One Door and Out the Other: A Book of Poems* by Aileen Fisher. (Thomas Y. Crowell) Copyright © 1969 by Aileen Fisher. By permission of Thomas Y. Crowell, Publishers.

Page 374, poem from Byrd Baylor, *The Desert Is Theirs.* Text copyright © 1975 by Byrd Baylor (New York: Charles Scribner's Sons). Reprinted with the permission of Charles Scribner's Sons.

Page 376, poem, "Cicadas" from *Joyful Noise* by Paul Fleischman. Illustrated by Eric Beddows. Text © 1988 by Paul Fleischman. Illustrations © by Eric Beddows. All selections reprinted by permission of Harper & Row, Publishers, Inc.

Page 377, poem from Myra Cohn Livingston, "I Haven't Learned to Whistle," from *O Sliver of Liver and Other Poems.* Copyright © 1979 by Myra Cohn Livingston. A Margaret K. McElderry Book. Reprinted with the permission of Atheneum Publishers.

Page 377, poem "Barefoot" from *Still More Small Poems* by Valerie Worth. Copyright © 1976, 1977, 1978 by Valerie Worth. Reprinted by permission of Farrar, Straus and Giroux, Inc.

Page 378, poem "The Spelling Test" reprinted by permission of Four Winds Press, an imprint of Macmillan Publishing Company, from *The Covered Bridge House and Other Poems* by Kaye Starbird. Copyright © 1979 by Kaye Starbird Jennison.

Page 379, poem "The Grasshopper" from *One at a Time* by David McCord. Copyright © 1952 by David McCord. By permission of Little, Brown and Company.

Page 380, poem "Dreams" from *The Dream Keeper* by Langston Hughes (New York: Knopf, 1932).

Page 381, poem "Teenagers" reprinted with permission of Bradbury Press, an Affiliate of Macmillan, Inc. from *Waiting to Waltz: A Childhood* by Cynthia Rylant. Text, © 1984 by Cynthia Rylant.

Page 381, poem "The Furry Ones" from *Feathered Ones and Furry* by Aileen Fisher. Copyright © 1971 by Aileen Fisher. By permission of Thomas Y. Crowell, Publishers.

Page 381, poem "Macavity: The Mystery Cat" from *Old Possum's Book of Practical Cats,* © 1939 by T. S. Eliot and renewed 1967 by Esme Valerie Eliot, reprinted by permission of Harcourt Brace Jovanovich, Inc.

Page 382, poem "Snail" by John Drinkwater, © 1929 by John Drinkwater. Reprinted by permission of Samuel French, Inc.

Page 382, poem "Witchery" from *Halloween A B C* by Eve Merriam. Copyright © 1987 by Eve Merriam. All Rights Reserved. Reprinted by permission of Marian Reiner for the author.

Page 419, text excerpts from *After the Rain* by Norma Fox Mazer. Copyright © 1987 by Norma Fox Mazer. Reprinted by permission of Morrow Junior Books (A Division of William Morrow & Co.).

Page 422, text excerpt from *Dear Mr. Henshaw* by Beverly Cleary, illustrated by Paul O. Zelinsky. Copyright © 1983 by Beverly Cleary. Reprinted by permission of Morrow Jr. Books (A Division of William Morrow & Co.).

Page 424, text excerpt from *Good-Bye and Keep Cold* by Jenny Davis. Copyright © 1987 by Jenny Davis. Reprinted by permission of Orchard Books, a division of Franklin Watts, Inc.

Page 424, text excerpt from *The Moonlight Man* by Paula Fox. Copyright © 1986 by Paula Fox. Reprinted by permission of Bradbury Press, an Affiliate of Macmillan, Inc.

Page 442, text excerpts. Copyright © 1987 by Gillian Cross. All rights reserved. Reprinted from *Roscoe's Leap* by permission of Holiday House.

Page 480, text excerpt from *The Ruby in the Smoke* by Philip Pullman. Copyright © 1985 by Philip Pullman. Reprinted by permission of Alfred A. Knopf, Inc.

Page 494, text excerpt from *Sweetgrass* by Jan Hudson. Copyright © 1984 by Jan Hudson. Reprinted by permission of Orchard Books, a division of Franklin Watts, Inc.

Page 528, text excerpt from *The Village of Round and Square Houses* by Ann Grifalconi. Copyright © 1986 by Ann Grifalconi. By permission of Little, Brown and Company.

Page 542, text excerpts from *Scorpions* by Walter Dean Myers. Copyright © 1988 by Walter Dean Myers. All selections reprinted by permission of Harper & Row, Publishers, Inc.

Page 542, text excerpt from *Jump! The Adventures of Brer Rabbit,* © 1986 by Van Dyke Parks and Malcom Jones, reprinted by permission of Harcourt Brace Jovanovich, Inc.

Page 543, text excerpt from *The Tales of Uncle Remus: The Adventures of Peter Rabbit* by Julius Lester, introduction by Augusta Baker. Reprinted by permission of Dial Books and Augusta Baker Alexander.

Page 543, text excerpt from *Flossie and the Fox* by Patricia C. McKissack. Text © 1986 by Patricia C. McKissack. Reprinted by permission of the publisher, Dial Books for Young Readers.

Page 550, text excerpt reprinted with permission of Bradbury Press, an Affiliate of Macmillan, Inc. from *Buffalo Woman* by Paul Goble. Copyright © 1984 by Paul Goble.

Page 552, text excerpt from *Iktomi and the Boulder: A Plains Indian Story* by Paul Goble. Copyright © 1988 by Paul Goble. Reprinted by permission of Orchard Books, a division of Franklin Watts, Inc.

Page 555, text excerpt from *Knots on a Counting Rope* by Bill Martin, Jr. and John Archambault. Text © 1966 and 1987 by Bill Martin and John Archambault. Reprinted by permission of Henry Holt and Company, Inc.

Page 555, text excerpt from *Annie and the Old One* by Miska Miles. Text © 1971 by Miska MIles. By permission of Little, Brown and Company.

Page 558, text excerpt from *Chief Sarah: Sarah Winnemucca's Fight for Indian Rights* by Dorothy Morrison. Copyright © 1980 by Dorothy Morrison. Reprinted by permission of Oregon Historical Society.

Page 562, text excerpt from *My Aunt Otilia's Spirits* by Richard Garcia, copyright © 1987. Reprinted by permission of Children's Book Press.

Page 590, flap text excerpt from *The Flame of Peace* by Deborah Nourse Lattimore. Copyright © 1987 by Deborah Nourse Lattimore. All selections reprinted by permission of Harper & Row, Publishers, Inc.

Pages 612 and 619, text excerpts from *Lincoln: A Photobiography* by Russell Freedman. Copyright © 1987 by Russell Freedman. Reprinted by permission of Clarion Books, a Houghton Mifflin Company.

Page 618, text excerpt from *Benjamin Franklin: The New American* by Milton Meltzer. Copyright © 1988 by Milton Meltzer. Reprinted by permission of Orchard Books, a division of Franklin Watts, Inc.

Page 628, text excerpt from *Changes in the Wind: Earth's Shifting Climate,* © 1986 by Margery Facklam and Howard Facklam, reprinted by permission of Harcourt Brace Jovanovich, Inc.

Page 647, text excerpt from *Living in Polar Regions: A Cultural Geography* by Theodore A. Rees Cheney. Copyright © 1987 by Theodore A. Rees Cheney. Reprinted by permission of Franklin Watts, Inc.

PHOTOS

All photos copyrighted by the individuals or companies listed.

Constance Brown, p. 280

Tim Chapman, p. 592

Janet Gagnon, p. 460

Jack Hamilton, p. 387

Michael Hayman/Corn's Photo Service, pp. 391, 593

Charles Quinlan, pp. 206, 583

Anne E. Schullstrom, pp. 199, 283, 331, 339, 510

Paul M. Shrock, p. 515

Strix Pix, pp. 336, 517, 663

ILLUSTRATIONS

Pages 8, 95, 129, 257, 310, 367, and 427 courtesy of Lilly Library, Indiana University, Bloomington, Indiana

Page 57, advertisement appeared in *Jo's Boys and How They Turned Out* by Louisa M. Alcott. From the collection of Julia Estadt

Page 168, from *The Original Mother Goose's Melody,* as first issued by John Newbery, of London, about A.D. 1760. Reproduced in facsimile from the edition as reprinted by Isaiah Thomas, of Worcester, Mass, about A.D. 1785. Reissued by Singing Tree Press, Detroit, 1969.

Page 486, illustration by Richard Westall. *Do you dispute me slave!* From Sir Walter Scott, *Ivanhoe,* Vol. 1. Edinburgh, 1820. Frontispiece. Rare Books and Manuscripts Division. The New York Public Library, Astor, Lenox and Tilden Foundations

Page 627, reproduced from *The Story of Mankind* by Hendrik Willem van Loon, by permission of Liveright Publishing Corporation. Copyright 1921, 1926 by Boni & Liveright, Inc. Copyright renewed 1948 by Helen C. van Loon. Copyright renewed 1954 by Liveright Publishing Corporation. Copyright 1936, 1938, 1951, 1967 by Liveright Publishing Corporation. Copyright © 1972 by Henry B. van Loon and Gerard W. van Loon

Page 658, Figure 12–1, courtesy OCLC, Inc., Dublin, Ohio

DEVELOPMENT OF TEXTBOOK CONCEPT AND ORGANIZATION

Martha Barclay, Northern Iowa Area Community College; Delorys Blume, University of Central Florida; Robert O. Boord, University of Nevada, Las Vegas; N. Boraks, Virginia Commonwealth University; Maxine Burress, University of Wisconsin; Gertrude B. Camper, Roanoke College; Delila Caselli, Sioux Falls College; Virginia Chirbart, College of St. Benedict; Eileen Cunningham, St. Thomas Aquinas College; Douglas L. Decker, Virginia State University; Lois Elendine, Oklahoma Christian College; Marjorie L. Farmer, Pembroke State University; Kay E. Fisher, Simpson College; E. W. Freeman, Le Moyne-Owen College; Margaret Gunn, Delta State University; C. Hooker-Schrader, Longwood College; Louise M. Hulst, Dordt College; Betty Kingery, Westmar College; Eleanor W. Lofquist, Western Carolina University; Mary Maness, Bartlesville Wesleyan College; Charles Matthews, College of Charleston; Rita E. Meadows, Lakeland, Florida; D. D. Miller, University of Missouri—St. Louis: Dorothy Z. Mills, East Carolina University; Martha L. Morris, Indiana Central University; Joan S. Nist, Auburn University; Olga M. Santora, State University of New York; Ronnie Sheppard, Georgia College; Richard J. Sherry, Asbury College; Sidney W. Shnayer, California State University at Chico; Dorothy Spethmann, Dakota State College; John Stinson, Jr., Miami, Florida; Emilie P. Sullivan, University of Arkansas; Lola Jiles Sullivan, Florida International University; Marylin C. Teele, Loma Linda University; Barbara Townsend, Salisbury State College; Marion Turkish, William Paterson College; Linda Western, University of Wisconsin—Milwaukee; Marilyn Yoder, Grace College; Collette Zerba, Cardinal Stritch College.

PREFACE

THIS TEXT IS INTENDED for any adult who is interested in evaluating, selecting, and sharing children's literature. Its focus and organization are designed for children's literature classes taught in the departments of English, Education, and Library Science. *Through the Eyes of a Child* is written in the hope that adults who work with children and literature will discover and share with children the enchantment in books and will help children develop a lifetime appreciation for literature and a respect for our literary heritage. It is my hope that my own love for literature and enthusiasm for books will be transmitted to the reader of this text.

NEW TO THE THIRD EDITION

A major concern in preparing this edition, as well as the first two, was selecting from the thousands of books available. For the three editions, I personally read over eight thousand books. The ones discussed in this third edition were chosen for their quality of literature and to create a balance between new books and those that have passed the test of time or are considered classics. As in the first two editions, approximately twenty-five percent of the books included in each chapter were published within the two years preceding the publication of *Through the Eyes of a Child.* During the preparation of the third edition, each chapter was carefully screened for books that are no longer in print. The majority of these books have been replaced with selections that reflect current copyright dates. A few out-of-print books are included when they are the best examples for a specific discussion or when they are just too good to be ignored. Most of these books are still available in libraries.

Not only has the entire book been updated, but some chapters also have been reorganized to improve the clarity and exposition of topics. A number of important new topics are introduced, including a section in chapter 3 on involving children in understanding literary elements. This addition is especially important as educators are searching for ways to develop literature-based reading and language arts programs.

The Involving Children section of each genre chapter includes numerous approaches for bringing literature into the total curriculum. The multicultural chapter has been reorganized to reflect a procedure that allows university students to understand the foundations of the literature and the culture.

Within each chapter are current issues and new research information. Areas such as literary criticism and children's responses to text and illustration are emphasized.

The Instructor's Manual is a valuable teaching resource. It contains three types of test questions with an increased emphasis on testing higher order thinking skills. In addition to discussion questions and suggestions for using the text and its special features, an experienced children's librarian has added resources particularly useful to that profession.

HIGHLIGHTS

Two-Part Chapter Organization

This unique feature of the text, in chapter 3 and extending from chapter 5 through chapter 12, places the characteristics, history, and titles of each genre next to the appropriate strategies for involving children in that genre. Thus, genre and involvement can be taught together, sequentially, or independently. The involvement strategies have been field tested at the university, elementary, and secondary school levels, and during inservice training for teachers and librarians.

Emphasis on Criteria for Book Evaluation and Selection

Each chapter builds a model for evaluating and selecting books based upon literary and artistic characteristics that readers can then use themselves. The importance of child development in this process is also stressed.

Issues

Each chapter identifies important issues that are related to the genre or content of the chapter and are designed to introduce teachers, librarians, and parents to current concerns. Most of these issue highlights are referenced to current periodicals and professional journals and are written to encourage readers' contemplation and further investigation. For this reason, they are presented as open-ended discussions.

Flashbacks

Also included in each chapter, these illustrated features highlight important people, works, and events in the history of children's literature. They are designed to provide a more complete understanding of the genre.

Through the Eyes of . . .

Each chapter includes a personal statement by a well-known author, illustrator, publisher, or librarian, providing a special glimpse into that person's "view" of the creation of children's books.

Annotated Bibliographies of Children's Literature

These extensive bibliographies include readability by grade level and interest by age range.

Text Teaching Aids

Each part of the two-part chapters concludes with suggested activities designed to either foster adult understanding of or children's appreciation for the genre. Special web diagrams are used to highlight the interrelationships in literature, the many values of literature, and the multiple learning possibilities available. Webs are also used to illustrate the development of instructional activities and oral discussions about literature. The webbing process, according to my students, helps them clarify concepts, visualize relationships, and identify numerous values for sharing literature with children.

Chapter on Multicultural Literature

This material was organized as a separate chapter to make it more accessible to librarians, teachers, and students of children's literature. Information about the criteria for selection, the choice of literature, and the development of literature-related activities resulted from longitudinal research that was partially supported by Texas A&M Research Association and the Meadows Foundation of Dallas, Texas. Educators at national and state meetings have been especially emphatic when they recommended that this chapter remain as a strong content in this textbook.

Annual Update

Due to the many additions and changes in this field, I will prepare for adopters of *Through the Eyes of a Child* a list of the new children's books and award winners and the new professional publications, and a discussion of current issues or new developments in the field. This free update will be distributed by the publisher when requested by instructors who have adopted the text for their class.

ACKNOWLEDGMENTS

A massive project such as writing and publishing a children's literature text would not be possible without the enthusiasm, critical evaluation, suggestions, and hard work of many people. My appreciation is extended to my children's literature students, teachers, and librarians who discussed books with me, created enthusiasm for books, and shared books with children. The multicultural literature chapter was enhanced by research supported by the Meadows Foundation; work by research associates Sue Mohrmann, Blanche Lawson, and Charmaine Bradley; field testing in the Bryan, Texas, schools; teachers and librarians across Texas who took part in the research; and support by curriculum coordinators Barbara Erwin and Dana Marable. The children's librarians at the Houston Public Library and the Houston Library archives deserve a special thank-you. They discussed reactions to books, searched for hard-to-locate literature, and allowed me to check out hundreds of books at one time. My consulting with school districts such as Wheeling, Willamette, Skokie, and Glenview, Illinois, allowed me to work with teachers, students, and administrators as these districts develop and improve their own literature-based curricula.

The children's librarians at the Public Library of Columbus and Franklin County; Grandview, Ohio, Public Library; Bexley, Ohio, Public Library; and Westerville, Ohio, Public Library provided much assistance in locating numerous children's books.

I would like to thank the people at Merrill—Linda James Scharp, senior developmental editor, who spent a great deal of time guiding and coordinating the many facets of this project; Victoria Althoff, production editor, for her extra effort and persistent attention to detail during the production phase of this revision; Anne Vega for the extraordinary cover and chapter-opening artwork; Cindy Brunk for enhancing her original text design to make best use of color in this edition; Vincent Smith, for his diligence in coordinating art and photos; Gail Meese for photo editing; Michele Byers, Julie Enriquez, and Joyce Rosinger for their patience in pursuit of securing permissions; Ken Montavon and David Faherty for the excellent advertising and promotional support; and Jeff Johnston, vice-president and editor-in-chief.

My sincere appreciation is also extended to Ethel Ambrose, Ashley Bryan, Patricia Clapp, Beverly Cleary, Susanne Canavan, Tomie dePaola, Jean Fritz, Jamake Highwater, Hiram Howard, Madeleine L'Engle, Jack Prelutsky, Martin and Alice Provensen, and Jack Denton Scott for their contribution to this text. The insights, personal statements, and viewpoints of these publishers, librarian, authors and illustrators are especially rewarding in a textbook about children's literature.

I wish to thank Peter J. Fisher of the National College of Education, Richard Van Dongen of the University of New Mexico, Ramona S. Frasher of Georgia State University, Carol J. Fisher of the University of Georgia, Inga Kromann-Kelly of Washington State University, John Carney of the University of New Hampshire, Rosie Webb-Joels of the University of Central Florida, Dixie Turner of Olivet Nazarene College, Kankakee, Illinois, and Dorothy Smith of St. Mary's University, San Antonio, Texas for their suggestions for improving the second edition of *Through the Eyes of a Child*. Their efforts have been invaluable in ensuring an accurate, timely, and lively text. My gratitude also goes to Ethel N. Ambrose, Coordinator of Children's Services, Central Arkansas Library System for her work on updating, revising, and expanding the Instructor's Resource Manual that accompanies the text.

Finally, I wish to dedicate this book to my husband, Verland, and my children, Saundra and Bradley, for their constant support, immense understanding, and insightful viewpoints.

Donna E. Norton

CONTENTS IN BRIEF

CONTENTS

1

The Child and Children's Literature

2

The History of Children's Literature

3

Evaluating and Selecting Literature for Children

8

Poetry

9

Contemporary Realistic Fiction

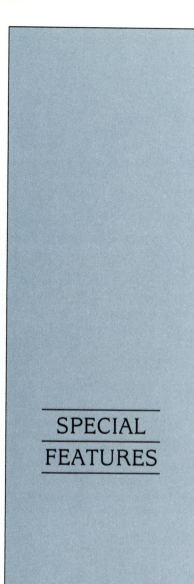

SPECIAL FEATURES

ISSUES

FLASHBACKS

THROUGH THE EYES OF . . .

EVALUATION CRITERIA

THROUGH THE EYES OF A CHILD

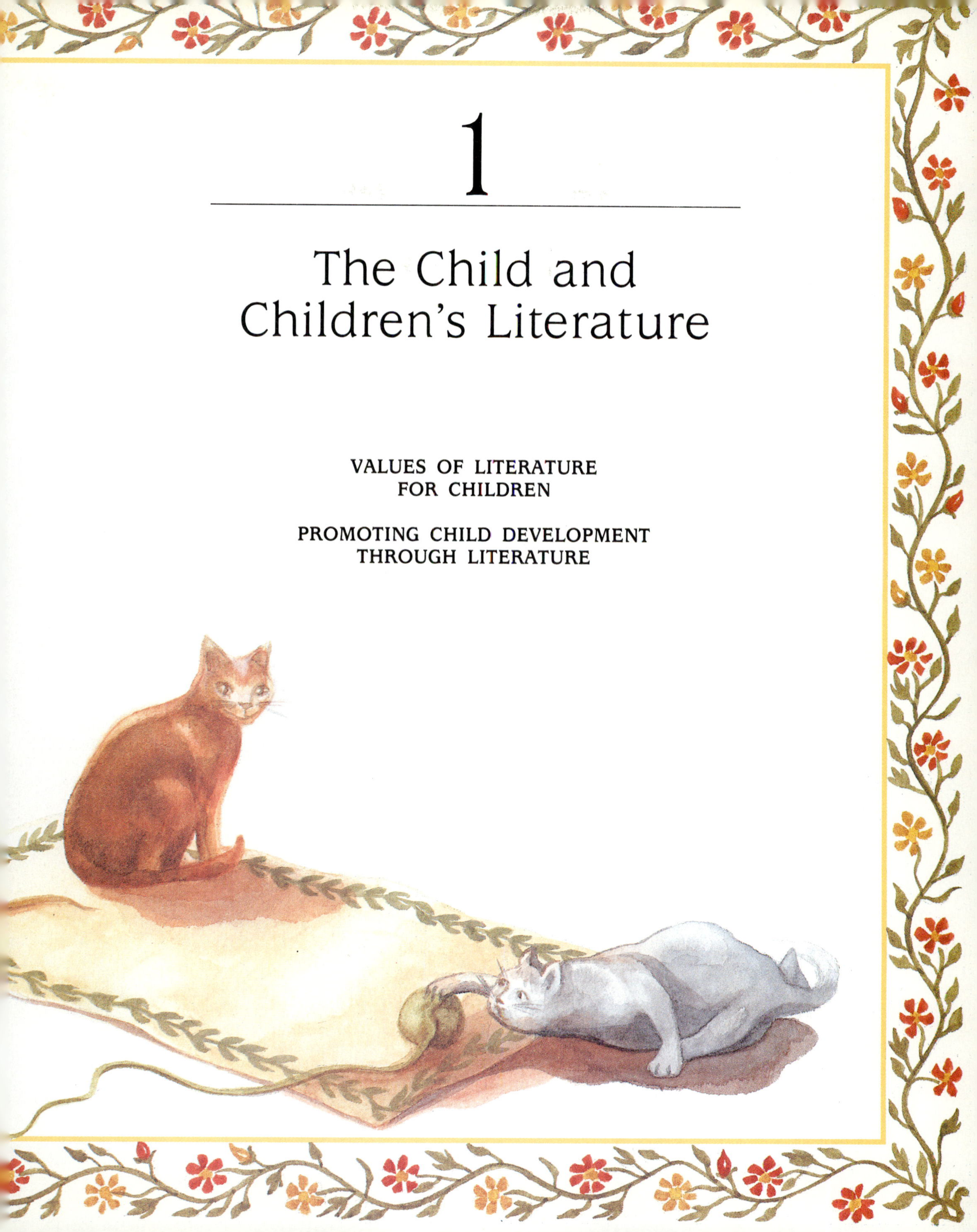

1

The Child and Children's Literature

VALUES OF LITERATURE FOR CHILDREN

PROMOTING CHILD DEVELOPMENT THROUGH LITERATURE

LITERATURE ENTICES, MOTIVATES, AND INSTRUCTS. It opens doors to discovery and provides endless hours of adventure and enjoyment. Children need not be tied to the whims of television programming nor wait in line at the theater in order to follow a rabbit down a hole into Wonderland, save a wild herd of mustangs from slaughter, fight in the Revolutionary War, learn about a new hobby that will provide many enjoyable hours, or model themselves after real-life people of accomplishment. These experiences are available at any time on the nearest bookshelf.

Adults have a responsibility to help children become aware of the enchantment in books. As Bernice Cullinan (8) suggests, "Books can play a significant role in the life of the young child, but the extent to which they do depends entirely upon adults. Adults are responsible for providing books and transmitting the literary heritage contained in nursery rhymes, traditional tales, and great novels" (p. 1). As you read this book, you will gain knowledge about literature so that you can share stimulating books and book-related experiences with children. This chapter introduces various values of literature for children in order to help you search for books that can play significant roles in children's lives. It also looks at the importance of considering children's stages of language, cognitive, personality, and social development when selecting literature for children and suggests books that reflect children's needs during different stages of the maturing process.

VALUES OF LITERATURE FOR CHILDREN

Following a rabbit down a rabbit hole or walking through a wardrobe into a mythical kingdom sounds like fun. There is nothing wrong with admitting that one of the primary values of literature is pleasure, and there is nothing wrong with turning to a book to escape or to enjoy an adventure with new or old book friends. Time is enriched, not wasted, when children look at beautiful pictures and imagine themselves in new places. When children discover enjoyment in books, they develop favorable attitudes toward them that usually extend into a lifetime of appreciation.

Books are the major means of transmitting our literary heritage from one generation to the next. Each new generation can enjoy the words of Lewis Carroll, Louisa May Alcott, Robert Louis Stevenson, and Mark Twain. Through the work of storytellers such as the Brothers Grimm, each generation can also experience the folktales originally transmitted through the oral tradition.

Literature plays a strong role in helping us understand and value our cultural heritage as well. Developing positive attitudes toward our own culture and the cultures of others is necessary for both social and personal development. Carefully selected literature can illustrate the contributions and values of the many cultures. It is especially critical to foster an appreciation of the heritage of the ethnic minorities in American society. A positive self-concept is not possible unless we respect others as well as ourselves; literature can contribute considerably toward our understanding and thus our respect.

The vicarious experiences of literature result in personal development as well as pleasure. Without literature, most children could not relive the European colonists' experiences of crossing the ocean and shaping a new country in North America; they could not experience the loneliness and fear of a fight for survival on an isolated island; they could not travel to distant places in the galaxy. Historical fiction provides children with opportunities to live in the past. Science fiction allows them to speculate about the future. Contemporary realistic fiction encourages them to experience relationships with the people and environment of today. Because children can learn from literature how other people handle their problems, characters in books can help children deal with similar problems, as well as understand other people's feelings.

Another value of literature is illustrated by a television interview with a high school sophomore who was a promising young scientist. When asked how he had become so knowledgeable, the boy replied, "I read a lot." For him, books had opened doors to new knowledge and interests. Don't educators and parents want such doors opened for all children? Hazel Rochman (18) maintains that children should read books set in many locations and times because if children read books that reflect their own views only, they miss the interesting diversity of the world.

Informational books relay new knowledge about virtually every topic imaginable, and they are available at all levels of difficulty. Biographies and autobiographies tell about the people who gained knowledge or made discoveries. Photographs and illustrations show the wonders of nature or depict the processes required to master new hobbies. Realistic stories from a specific time bring history to life. The use of concept books that illustrate colors, numbers, shapes, and sizes may stimulate the cognitive development of even very young children.

Any discussion about the values of literature must stress the role that literature plays in nurturing and expanding the imagination. Books take children into worlds that stimulate additional imaginative experiences when children tell or write their own stories and interact with each other during creative drama inspired by what they have read. Both well-written literature and illustrations, such as those found in picture books and picture storybooks, can stimulate aesthetic development. Children enjoy and evaluate illustrations and may explore artistic media by creating illustrations of their own.

PROMOTING CHILD DEVELOPMENT THROUGH LITERATURE

Research in child development has identified stages in the language, cognitive, personality, and social development of children. Not all children progress through these stages at the same rate, but all children do pass through each stage as they mature. Researchers associate developmental stages with children of certain ages, but these connections are approximate, not absolute. Specific developmental characteristics apply to many, but not all, children in a particular age group. The general characteristics of children at each developmental stage provide clues for appropriate literature. Certain books can benefit children during a particular stage of development, helping the children progress to the next stage. Understanding the types and stages of child development is useful for anyone who works with children.

Language Development

Literature has profound influences on children's language development. Chart 1–1 lists characteristics, implications, and books that are appropriate for language development.

Preschool Children. During their first few years, children show dramatic changes in language ability. Most children learn language very rapidly. They speak their first words at about one year of age; at about eighteen months, they begin to put words together in two-word combinations, called *telegraphic speech*. Speech during this stage of language development consists of nouns, verbs, and adjectives. It usually contains no prepositions, articles, auxiliary verbs, or pronouns. When children say "pretty flower" or "milk gone," they are using telegraphic speech. The number of different two-word combinations increases slowly, then shows a sudden upsurge around age two. Martin Braine (5) began recording the speech of three eighteen-month-old children. He reported that the cumulative number of different two-word combinations for one child in successive months was 14, 24, 54, 89, 350, 1,400, and 2,500+. This is a rapid expansion of speech in a very short time.

A longitudinal study conducted by Roger Brown (6) demonstrated how widely the rate of language development can vary from child to child. For example, one child successfully used six grammatical morphemes (the smallest meaning-bearing unit in a word) by the age of two years, three months; a second child did not master them until the age of three years, six months; and a third was four years old before reaching an equivalent stage in language development.

Speech usually becomes more complex by age three, when most children have added adverbs, pronouns, prepositions, and additional adjectives to their vocabularies. Children also enjoy playing with the sounds of words at this stage of language development. By age four, they produce grammatically correct sentences. This stage is a questioning one, during which language is used to ask why and how.

Literature and literature-related experiences can encourage language development in preschool children. Joanne Hendrick (12) recommends children's books and related activities to enhance language development. Book experiences in the home, at the library, and at nursery school can help children use language to discover the world, identify and name actions and objects, gain more complex speech, and enjoy the wonder of language. Many children first experience literature through picture books. Picture books help children give meaning to their expanding vocabularies. For example, children who are just learning to identify their hands and other parts of their bodies may find these parts in drawings of children. Parents of very young children may share Helen Oxenbury's excellent baby board books. (Board books are toy books made of cardboard for young children.) *Dressing*, for example, includes a picture of a baby's clothing, followed by a picture of the child dressed in those items. The illustrations are sequentially developed to encourage talking about the steps in dressing. Nancy Tafuri's board book *One Wet Jacket* follows the opposite

CHART 1–1
Language development

Characteristics	Implications	Literature Suggestions
Preschool: Ages Two–Three		
1 Very rapid language growth occurs. By the end of this period, children have vocabularies of about nine hundred words.	1 Provide many activities to stimulate language growth including picture books and Mother Goose rhymes.	Hayes, Sarah. *This Is the Bear.* Lobel, Arnold. *The Random House Book of Mother Goose.* Wells, Rosemary. *Max's Birthday.*
2 Children learn to identify and name actions in pictures.	2 Read books that contain clear, familiar action pictures; encourage children to identify actions.	Lindgren, Barbro. *Sam's Bath.* Oxenbury, Helen. *I Touch.* Steptoe, John. *Baby Says.* Wells, Rosemary. *Max's Breakfast.*
3 Children learn to identify large and small body parts.	3 Allow children to identify familiar body parts in picture books.	Berger, Terry, and Alice Kandell. *Ben's ABC Day.* Oxenbury, Helen. *Dressing.*
Preschool: Ages Three–Four		
1 Vocabularies have increased to about fifteen hundred words. Children enjoy playing with sound and rhythm in language.	1 Include opportunities to listen to and say rhymes, poetry, and riddles.	Emberley, Barbara. *Drummer Hoff.* Griego, Margot, et al. *Tortillitas Para Mama.* Hale, Sarah Josepha. *Mary Had a Little Lamb.* Rosen, Michael. *We're Going on a Bear Hunt.* Yolen, Jane. *The Three Bears Rhyme Book.*
2 Children develop the ability to use past tense but may overgeneralize the *ed* and *s* markers.	2 Allow children to talk about what they did yesterday; discuss actions in books.	Hill, Eric. *Spot Goes to School.* ———. *Spot's First Walk.* Keats, Ezra Jack. *The Snowy Day.* Weiss, Nicki. *Where Does the Brown Bear Go?*
3 Children use language to help find out about the world.	3 Read picture storybooks to allow children to find out about and discuss pets, families, people, and the environment.	Carle, Eric. *The Very Busy Spider.* Keller, Holly. *Geraldine's Big Snow.* Potter, Beatrix. *The Tale of Peter Rabbit.* Tafuri, Nancy. *Early Morning in the Barn.* Winter, Jeanette. *Come Out to Play.*
4 Speech becomes more complex, with more adjectives, adverbs, pronouns, and prepositions.	4 Expand the use of descriptive words through detailed picture books and picture storybooks. Allow children to tell stories and describe characters and their actions.	Barton, Byron. *Machines at Work.* Crews, Donald. *Freight Train.* ———. *Harbor.* Hill, Eric. *Spot Goes to the Beach.* Narahashi, Keiko. *I Have a Friend.*
Preschool: Ages Four–Five		
1 Language is more abstract; children produce grammatically correct sentences. Their vocabularies include approximately twenty-five hundred words.	1 Children enjoy books with slightly more complex plots. Ask them to tell longer and more detailed stories. They enjoy retelling folktales and can tell stories using wordless books.	Brett, Jan. *Goldilocks and the Three Bears.* McCully, Emily. *School.* McDermott, Gerald. *Tim O'Toole and the Wee Folk.* Wiesner, David. *Free Fall.* Zimmerman, H. Werner. *Henny Penny.*

CHART 1–1 (cont.)
Language development

Characteristics	Implications	Literature Suggestions
2 Children understand the prepositions *over, under, in, out, in front of,* and *behind.*	2 Use concept books or other picture books in which prepositions can be reinforced.	Bancheck, Linda. *Snake In, Snake Out.* Dodds, Dayle Ann. *Wheel Away!* Hutchins, Pat. *Rosie's Walk.* McMillan, Bruce. *Here a Chick, There a Chick.*
3 Children enjoy asking many questions, especially those related to *why* and *how.*	3 Take advantage of natural curiosity and find books to help answer children's questions. Allow them to answer each other's questions.	Barton, Byron. *Airport.* Hirschi, Ron. *Who Lives on . . . the Prairie?* Oppenheim, Joanne. *Have You Seen Birds?* Showers, Paul. *Look at Your Eyes.* Yabuuchi, Masayuki. *Whose Baby?*
Preschool—Kindergarten: Ages Five–Six		
1 Most children use complex sentences frequently and begin to use correct pronouns and verbs in present and past tense. They understand approximately six thousand words.	1 Give children many opportunities for oral language activities connected with literature.	Aardema, Verna. *Bringing Rain to Kapiti Plain.* ———. *Why Mosquitoes Buzz in People's Ears: A West African Tale.* Gag, Wanda. *Millions of Cats.* Grimm, Brothers. *Hansel and Gretel.* Hutchins, Pat. *The Very Worst Monster.* Lee, Dennis, *Jelly Belly: Original Nursery Rhymes.*
2 Children enjoy taking part in dramatic play and producing dialogue about everyday activities such as those at home and the grocery store.	2 Read stories about the home and community. Allow children to act out their own stories.	Hurd, Edith Thacher. *I Dance in My Red Pajamas.* Martin, Rafe. *Will's Mammoth.* Ryder, Joanne. *White Bear, Ice Bear.* Seuss, Dr. *And to Think That I Saw It on Mulberry Street.*
3 Children are curious about the written appearance of their own language.	3 Write chart stories using the children's own words. Have children dictate descriptions of pictures.	McCully, Emily Arnold. *Picnic.* Tejima, *Fox's Dream.* Willard, Nancy. *Night Story.*
Early Elementary: Ages Six–Eight		
1 Language development continues. Children add many new words to their vocabularies.	1 Provide daily time for reading to children and allow for oral interaction.	Bryan, Ashley. *The Cat's Purr.* Kellogg, Steven. *A Rose for Pinkerton.* Lewin, Hugh. *Jafta.* Ryder, Joanne. *Inside Turtle's Shell: And Other Poems of the Field.* Silverstein, Shel. *A Light in the Attic.*
2 Most children use complex sentences with adjectival clauses and conditional clauses beginning with *if.* The average oral sentence length is seven and one-half words.	2 Read stories that provide models for children's expanding language structure.	Burton, Virginia Lee. *The Little House.* de Paola, Tomie. *The Legend of the Bluebonnet.* Hodges, Margaret. *Saint George and the Dragon.* McCloskey, Robert. *Make Way for Ducklings.*

CHART 1–1 (cont.)
Language development

Characteristics	Implications	Literature Suggestions
Middle Elementary: Ages Eight–Ten		
1 Children begin to relate concepts to general ideas. They use connectors such as *meanwhile* and *unless.*	1 Supply books as models. Let children use these terms during oral language activities.	Nesbit, E. *Melisande.* Steptoe, John. *Mufaro's Beautiful Daughters: An African Tale.* Young, Ed. *Lon Po Po: A Red Riding Hood Story from China.*
2 The subordinating connector *although* is used correctly by 50 percent of children. Present participle active and perfect participle appear. The average number of words in sentence is nine.	2 Use written models and oral models to help children master their language skills. Literature discussions allow many opportunities for oral sentence expansion.	Brett, Jan. *Beauty and the Beast.* de Paola, Tomie. *The Quicksand Book.* Gilchrist, Theo. *Halfway up the Mountain.* Mayer, Marianna. *The Twelve Dancing Princesses.* Walter, Mildred Pitts. *Brother to the Wind.*
Upper Elementary: Ages Ten–Twelve		
1 Children use complex sentences with subordinate clauses of concession introduced by *nevertheless* and *in spite of.* Auxiliary verbs *might, could,* and *should* appear frequently.	1 Encourage oral language and written activities that permit children to use more complex sentence structures.	Corbett, W. J. *The Song of Pentecost.* L'Engle, Madeleine. *A Swiftly Tilting Planet.* Lunn, Janet. *Shadow in Hawthorn Bay.* McKinley, Robin. *The Hero and the Crown.* Paulsen, Gary. *Hatchet.* ———. *The Winter Room.* Yolen, Jane. *The Devil's Arithmetic.*

Sources: Bartel (2); Braga and Braga (4); Brown (6); Gage and Berliner (9); Hendrick (12); and Loban (14).

approach. In *One Wet Jacket,* each of the labeled pieces of clothing is taken off until the child is shown in the tub.

Young children also learn to identify actions in pictures, and enjoy recognizing and naming familiar actions, such as those in Eve Rice's *Oh, Lewis!* In this picture storybook, Lewis is going shopping with his mother, but first he must find his mittens and have his jacket zipped, his boots buckled, and his hood tied. Richard Scarry's *The Best Word Book Ever* and *My First Word Book* appeal to young children and provide practice in naming common objects.

Many excellent books allow children to listen to the sounds of language and experiment with these sounds. For example, children may sing along with the songs in *Go In and Out the Window,* which is produced by the Metropolitan Museum of Art. Rhyming books are especially appealing to young children. Both the colorful pictures and the rhyming words in Barbara Emberley's *Drummer Hoff* fascinate them. They love to join in with the rhyming elements, *parriage—carriage, farrell—barrel,* and *bammer—rammer*. Children may respond in both Spanish and English when they interact with the rhymes in *Tortillitas Para Mama* by Margot C. Griego et al.

Young children enjoy playing with language and interacting with nonsense words. The language in Margaret Mahy's *17 Kings and 42 Elephants* is reminiscent of Laura Richards's poem "Eletelephony" in her *Tirra Lirra, Rhymes Old and New*. Mahy's descriptions include elephants that have ears like "umbrellaphants," crocodiles that are as "rough as rockodiles," and birds that are "twangling trillicans."

Elementary-Age Children. Language development of course continues as children enter school and progress through the grades. Walter Loban (14) conducted the most extensive longitudinal study of language development in school-age children, examining the language development of the same group of over two hundred children from age five to age eighteen. He found that children's power over language increases through successive control over different forms of language, including pronouns, verb tenses, and connectors, such as *meanwhile* and *unless*.

Loban identified dramatic differences between children who ranked high in language proficiency and those who ranked low. The high group reached a level of oral proficiency in first grade that the low group did not attain until sixth grade and a level of written proficiency in fourth grade that the low group did not attain until tenth grade. Those who demonstrated high language proficiency excelled in the control of ideas expressed, showing unity and planning in both their speech and writing. These students spoke freely, fluently, and easily, using a rich vocabulary and adjusting the pace of their words to their listeners. They were attentive and creative listeners themselves, far outranking the low group in listening ability. The oral communication of those with low language proficiency was characterized by rambling and unpurposeful dialogue that demonstrated a meager vocabulary.

Children who were superior in oral language in kindergarten and first grade also excelled in reading and writing in sixth grade. They were more fluent in written language than were the low-ranked children, used more words per sentence, showed a richer written vocabulary, and were superior in using connectors and subordination to combine thoughts into complex forms of expression. Given the demonstrated connection between oral and written language skills, Loban concluded that teachers, librarians, and parents should give greater attention to developing children's oral language. Discussion should be a vital part of elementary school and library programs because it helps children organize ideas and make complex generalizations.

Books with repetitive language are excellent for enticing listeners to join in during oral reading. Mem Fox's *Hattie and the Fox* includes both cumulative plot development and repetitive refrains. The illustrations are excellent for predicting language because they show various features of the approaching fox. John Ivimey's *The Complete Story of the Three Blind Mice* includes repetitive

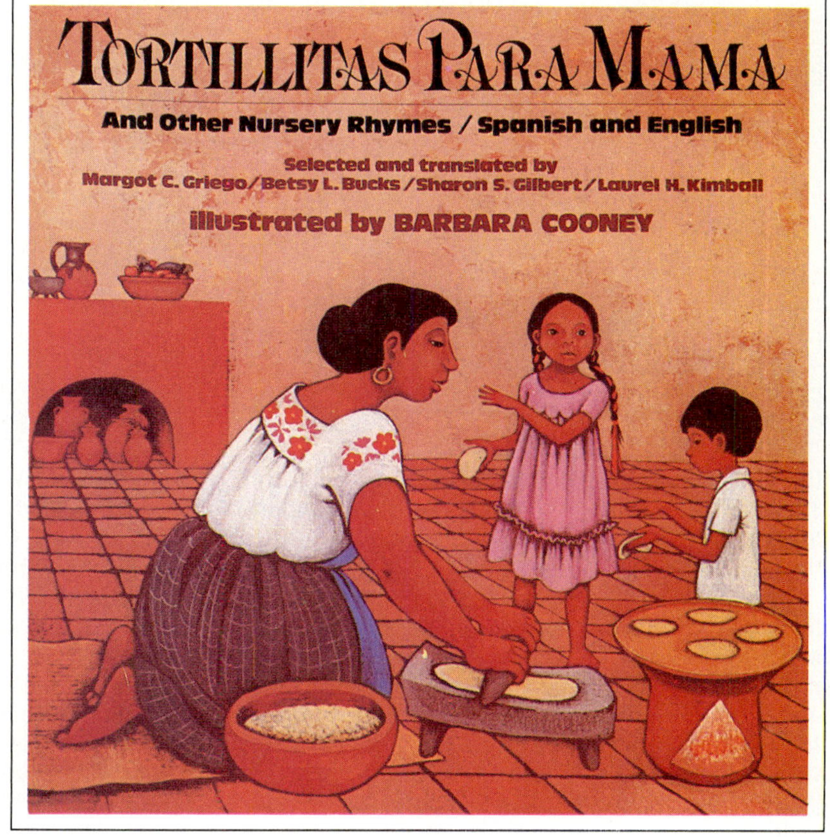

The loving environment captured by the illustrations and the accompanying nursery rhymes encourages language development. (From *Tortillitas Para Mama,* selected and translated by Margot C. Griego, Betsy L. Bucks, Sharon S. Gilbert, and Laurel H. Kimball. Illustrated by Barbara Cooney. Copyright © 1981 by Margot Griego, Betsy Bucks, Sharon Gilbert, Laurel Kimball. Copyright © 1981 by Barbara Cooney. Reproduced by permission of Holt, Rinehart and Winston, Publishers.)

FLASHBACK

THE ADVENTURES OF TOM SAWYER.

CHAPTER I.

"TOM!"

No answer.

"Tom!"

No answer.

"What's gone with that boy, I wonder? You TOM!"

No answer.

The old lady pulled her spectacles down and looked over them about the room; then she put them up and looked out under them. She seldom or never looked *through* them for so small a thing as a boy; they were her state pair, the pride of her heart, and were built for "style," not service—she could have seen through a pair of stove lids just as well. She looked perplexed for a moment, and hen said, not fiercely, but still loud enough for the furniture to hear:

THE ADVENTURES OF TOM SAWYER, WRITTEN BY Mark Twain (Samuel Clemens) in the late nineteenth century, was one of the first adventure stories that was truly American in tone. In both *Tom Sawyer* and *The Adventures of Huckleberry Finn,* Twain captured the human, cultural, and geographical influences that affected a boy's life in a certain era of American history. Twain wrote from his own experiences living in the town of Hannibal, Missouri—an environment in which boys could explore the countryside, fish in a leisurely flowing stream, swim in the Mississippi River, and plan all types of mischief.

Tom Sawyer portrays not only the free, adventurous life of childhood but also Tom's discoveries about himself and those around him. There is the horror of a churchyard murder that Tom and his friend Huckleberry Finn witness. There is the racial bias some characters express. Twain's characters exemplify both the best and the worst of human qualities.

Twain's books became popular reading with children who wanted adventure stories about believable people in real locations. The popularity of the American adventure story set in a definite region may be seen in a partial list of much-loved books written by Twain's contemporaries: Kate Douglas Wiggin's *Rebecca of Sunnybrook Farm* takes place in rural Maine; Thomas Aldrich, in *The Story of a Bad Boy,* places his characters in a New England town; and Noah Brooks's *The Boy Emigrants* is set in the Great Plains.

lines, rhyming language, and descriptive terms. This extended story, illustrated by Paul Galdone, allows readers to discover what caused the loss of the tails. This version even has a happy ending.

Wordless picture books are excellent stimulators for oral and written language. Emily Arnold McCully's *School* follows the exploits of the littlest mouse child, who discovers what happens during a real school day. Peter Collington's *The Angel and the Soldier Boy* provides an exciting adventure, in which an angel and a soldier rescue a coin from pirates and return it to a sleeping child. David Wiesner's *Free Fall* shows the adventures that are possible within dreams. More complex wordless books may stimulate the oral language of older children. John Goodall's *The Story of an English Village* shows the changes that occur in a village from the fourteenth century to the twentieth century.

Books with vivid language, similes, and metaphors stimulate language development and appreciation for literary style. For example, the text for Jane Yolen's *Owl Moon* is filled with figurative language. It personifies trees, dogs, and shadows.

For example, footprints in the snow "follow us," shadows "bumped after me," and cold places an "icy hand. . .palm-down on my back." Similes and metaphors produce vivid comparisons; voices in the night fade away "as quiet as a dream," snow is "whiter than milk in a cereal bowl," and an owl moves "like a shadow without a sound."

Literature is a crucial resource, providing both a model for language and a stimulation for oral and written activities. This text suggests a wealth of literature for use in the elementary grades: literature to be read aloud to children; literature to provide models for expanding language proficiency; and literature to stimulate oral discussion, creative dramatics, creative writing, and listening enjoyment.

Literature provides stimulation for the dramatic play and creative dramatics that inspire children in the primary grades to express themselves verbally with much enjoyment. For example, in Maurice Sendak's *Where the Wild Things Are,* Max gets into so much mischief when he is wearing his wolf suit that his mother sends him to his room without any supper. His vivid imagination turns the room into a forest inhabited by wild things. Max stays in the forest and becomes its king, but finally, he gets lonely and wants to return to the land where someone loves him. Children can relate to Max's experience and use it to stimulate their own wild experiences.

In Dr. Seuss's *And to Think That I Saw It on Mulberry Street,* Marco is another boy who uses his imagination when he is in a normal environment. The setting is the street on which Marco walks home from school. The only thing that Marco sees is a horse drawing a wagon, but this does not stifle his imagination. He envisions what he would like to see on plain old Mulberry Street. Imagination allows a boy to have an exciting adventure in his own yard in Rafe Martin's *Will's Mammoth*. A winter setting takes on new meaning for a boy in Joanne Ryder's *White Bear, Ice Bear*. Children enjoy using their imaginations and turning common occurrences into creative experiences.

Cognitive Development

Factors related to helping children remember, anticipate, integrate perceptions, and develop concepts fill numerous textbooks and have been the subject of both research and conjecture. Jean Piaget and B. Inhelder (17) maintained that the order in which children's thinking matures is the same for all, although the pace varies from child to child. Stimulation is also necessary for cognitive development. Children who grow up without a variety of experiences may be three to five years behind other children in developing the mental strategies that aid recall. Chart 1–2 lists books that can promote cognitive development in children.

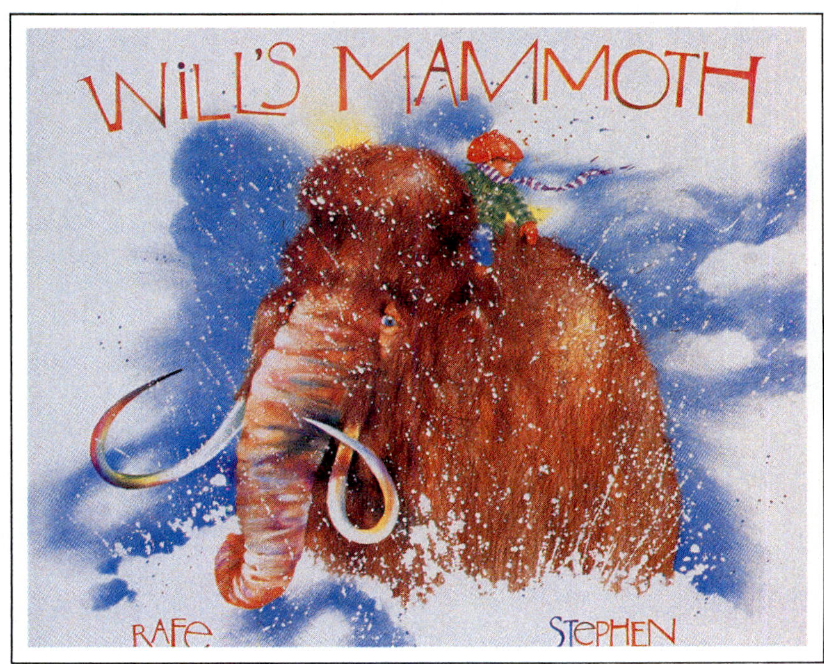

A boy turns a day in the snow into a very imaginative experience. Illustration by Stephen Gammell, reproduced with permission of G. P. Putnam's Sons from *Will's Mammoth* by Rafe Martin, illustrations copyright © 1989 by Stephen Gammell.

CHART 1–2
Cognitive development

Characteristics	Implications	Literature Suggestions
Preschool: Ages Two–Three		
1 Children learn new ways to organize and classify their worlds by putting together things that they perceive to be alike.	1 Provide opportunities for children to discuss and group things according to color, shape, size, or use. Use picture concept books with large, colorful pictures.	Hoban, Tana. *Of Colors and Things.* ———. *1, 2, 3.* ———. *Look! Look! Look!* ———. *What Is It?*
2 Children begin to remember two or three items.	2 Exercise children's short-term memories by providing opportunities to recall information.	Duke, Kate. *Bedtime.* Maris, Ron. *Are You There, Bear?*
Preschool: Ages Three–Four		
1 Children develop an understanding of how things relate to each other: how parts go together to make a whole, and how they are arranged in space in relation to each other.	1 Give children opportunities to find the correct part of a picture to match another picture. Use simple picture puzzles.	Emberley, Rebecca. *City Sounds.* Hoban, Tana. *Take Another Look.* Hutchins, Pat. *Changes, Changes.* Oxenbury, Helen. *I See.*
2 Children begin to understand relationships and classify things according to certain perceptual attributes that they share, such as color, size, shape, and what they are used for.	2 Share concept books on color, size, shape, and use. Provide opportunities for children to group and classify objects and pictures.	Aylesworth, Jim. *One Crow: A Counting Rhyme.* Carle, Eric. *My Very First Book of Colors.* de Brunhoff, Laurent. *Babar's Book of Color.* Hoban, Tana. *Shapes, Shapes, Shapes.*
3 Children begin to understand how objects relate to each other in terms of number and amount.	3 Give picture counting books to children. Allow them to count.	Bang, Molly. *Ten, Nine, Eight.* Carle, Eric. *My Very First Book of Numbers.* Christelow, Eileen. *Five Little Monkeys Jumping on the Bed.* Tafuri, Nancy. *Who's Counting?*
4 Children begin to compare two things and tell which is bigger and which is smaller.	4 Share and discuss books that allow comparisons in size, such as a giant and boy, a big item and a small item, or a series of animals.	Campbell, Rod. *Dear Zoo.* Voake, Charlotte. *Mrs. Goose's Baby.*
Preschool: Ages Four–Five		
1 Children remember to do three things told to them or retell a short story if the material is presented in a meaningful sequence.	1 Tell short, meaningful stories and allow children to retell them. Use flannelboard and picture stories to help children organize the story. Give practice in following three-step directions.	Galdone, Paul. *The Gingerbread Boy.* ———. *What's in Fox's Sack? An Old English Tale.* Stevens, Janet. *The House That Jack Built.*

CHART 1–2 (cont.)
Cognitive development

Characteristics	Implications	Literature Suggestions
2 Children increase their ability to group objects according to important characteristics but still base their rules on how things look to them.	2 Provide many opportunities to share concept books and activities designed to develop ideas of shape, color, size, feel, and use.	Carle, Eric. *My Very First Book of Shapes.* Hoban, Tana. *Circles, Triangles, and Squares.* ———. *Is It Red? Is It Yellow? Is It Blue?* Pluckrose, Henry. *Capacity.* ———. *Sorting.*
3 Children pretend to tell time but do not understand the concept. Things happen "now" or "before now."	3 Share books to help children understand sequence of time and when things happen, such as the seasons of the year and different times of the day or different days of the week.	Johnson, Angela. *Tell Me a Story, Mama.* Rockwell, Anne. *First Comes Spring.*
Preschool—Kindergarten: Ages Five–Six		
1 Children learn to follow one type of classification (such as color or shape) through to completion without changing the main characteristic partway through the task.	1 Continue to share concept books and encourage activities that allow children to group and classify.	Emberley, Ed. *Ed Emberley's ABC.* Giganti, Paul. *How Many Snails? A Counting Book.* Lobel, Arnold. *On Market Street.* Pluckrose, Henry. *Length.*
2 Children count to ten and discriminate ten objects.	2 Reinforce counting skills with counting books and other counting activities.	Carle, Eric. *My Very First Book of Numbers.* Dubanevich, Arlene. *Pigs in Hiding.* Knight, Hilary. *Hilary Knight's The Twelve Days of Christmas.* Magee, Doug. *Trucks You Can Count On.*
3 Children identify primary colors.	3 Reinforce color identification through the use of color concept books and colors found in other picture books.	Carle, Eric. *Let's Paint a Rainbow.* Ehlert, Lois. *Color Zoo.* Hutchins, Pat. *Changes, Changes.*
4 Children learn to distinguish between "a lot of" something or "a little of" something.	4 Provide opportunities for children to identify and discuss the differences between concepts.	Gág, Wanda. *Millions of Cats.* Zemach, Margot. *It Could Always Be Worse.*
5 Children require trial and error before they can arrange things in order from smallest to biggest.	5 Share books that progress from smallest to largest. Have children retell stories using flannelboard characters drawn in appropriate sizes.	Galdone, Paul. *The Three Billy Goats Gruff.* Zemach, Margot, *It Could Always Be Worse.*
6 Children still have vague concepts of time.	6 Share books to help children understand time sequence.	Fowler, Susi. *When Summer Ends.*

CHART 1–2 (cont.)
Cognitive development

Characteristics	Implications	Literature Suggestions
Early Elementary: Ages Six–Eight		
1 Children are learning to read; they enjoy reading easy books and demonstrating their new abilities.	1 Provide easy-to-read books geared to children's developing reading skills.	Griffith, Helen. *Alex and the Cat.* Lobel, Arnold. *Frog and Toad All Year.* ———. *Uncle Elephant.* Marshall, Edward. *Four on the Shore.* Seuss, Dr. *The Cat in the Hat.*
2 Children are learning to write and enjoy creating their own stories.	2 Allow children to write, illustrate, and share their own picture books. Use wordless books to suggest plot.	Van Allsburg, Chris. *The Mysteries of Harris Burdick.* Waber, Bernard. *The Snake: A Very Long Story.* Wiesner, David. *Free Fall.*
3 Children enjoy longer stories than they did when they were five because their attention spans are increasing.	3 Read longer storybooks to children, such as books in which the chapters can be completed in a short time.	Berenzy, Alix. *A Frog Prince.* Milne, A. A. *The House at Pooh Corner.* San Souci, Robert. *The Talking Eggs: A Folktale from the American South.* Van Allsburg, Chris. *The Polar Express.*
4 Children under seven still base their rules on immediate perception and learn through real situations.	4 Provide experiences that allow children to see, discuss, and verify information and relationships.	Bellville, Cheryl Walsh. *Rodeo.* Peters, Lisa Westberg. *The Sun, the Wind and the Rain.* Reiss, John J. *Shapes.* Simon, Seymour. *Meet the Computer.*
5 Sometime during this age, children pass into the stage that Piaget refers to as concrete operational. Children have developed a new set of rules, called groupings, so they don't have to see all objects to group; they can understand relationships among categories.	5 Provide opportunities for children to read and discuss concept books.	Anno, Mitsumasha. *Anno's Counting Book.* ———. *Anno's Math Games.* Blake, Quentin. *Quentin Blake's ABC.* Feelings, Muriel. *Moja Means One: Swahili Counting Book.* Hoban, Tana. *26 Letters and 99 Cents.*
Middle Elementary: Ages Eight–Ten		
1 Children's reading skills improve rapidly, although there are wide variations in reading ability among children within the same age group.	1 For independent reading, provide books at appropriate reading levels. Allow children opportunities to share their book experiences with peers, parents, teachers, and other adults.	Blume, Judy. *Tales of a Fourth Grade Nothing.* Cleary, Beverly. *Ramona and Her Father.* ———. *Ramona Quimby, Age 8.* Wilder, Laura Ingalls. *Little House in the Big Woods.*
2 Children's level of interest in literature may still be above their reading levels.	2 Provide a daily time during which children can listen to a variety of books being read aloud.	Burnett, Frances Hodgson. *The Secret Garden.* Grahame, Kenneth. *The Wind in the Willows.* Lewis, C. S. *The Lion, the Witch and the Wardrobe.* Martin, Eva, ed. *Canadian Fairy Tales.* White, E. B. *Charlotte's Web.*

CHART 1–2 (cont.)
Cognitive development

Characteristics	Implications	Literature Suggestions
3 Memory improves as children learn to attend to certain stimuli and ignore others.	3 Help children set purposes for listening or reading before the actual literature experience.	Malnig, Anita. *Where the Waves Break: Life at the Edge of the Sea.* Nance, John. *Lobo of the Tasaday.* Selsam, Millicent. *Mushrooms.*
Upper Elementary: Ages Ten–Twelve		
1 Children develop an understanding of the chronological ordering of past events.	1 Encourage children to read historical fiction and books showing historic changes to help them understand differing viewpoints and historical perspectives.	Forbes, Esther. *Johnny Tremain.* Meyer, Carolyn, and Charles Gallenkamp. *The Mysteries of the Ancient Maya.* Sattler, Helen. *Hominids: A Look Back at Our Ancestors.* Speare, Elizabeth. *The Sign of the Beaver.* Sutcliff, Rosemary. *Sun Horse, Moon Horse.* Yolen, Jane. *The Devil's Arithmetic.*
2 Children apply logical rules, reasoning, and formal operations to abstract problems.	2 Use questioning and discussion strategies to develop higher-level thought processes. Children enjoy more complex books.	*Beowulf.* Blumberg, Rhoda. *The Incredible Journey of Lewis & Clark.* Freedman, Russell. *Lincoln: A Photobiography.* Simon, Seymour. *Storms.*

Sources: Braga and Braga (4); Mussen, Conger, and Kagan (15); Piaget and Inhelder (17); and Shaffer (21).

According to child development authority David Shaffer (21), cognitive development "refers to the changes that occur in children's mental skills and abilities over time" (p. 306). Shaffer states, "[W]e are constantly attending to objects and events, interpreting them, comparing them with past experiences, placing them into categories, and encoding them into memory" (p. 306). Mussen, Conger, and Kagan (15) define cognition as the process involved in

> (1) perception—the detection, organization, and interpretation of information from both the outside world and the internal environment, (2) memory—the storage and retrieval of the perceived information, (3) reasoning—the use of knowledge to make inferences and draw conclusions, (4) reflection—the evaluation of the quality of ideas and solutions, and (5) insight—the recognition of new relationships between two or more segments of knowledge (pp. 234–235).

All of these processes are essential for success in both school and adult life. Each is also closely related to understanding and enjoying literature. Without visual and auditory perception, literature could not be read or heard; without memory, there would be no way to see the relationships among literary works and to recognize new relationships as experiences are extended. Literature is also important in stimulating cognitive development by encouraging the oral exchange of ideas and the development of thought processes. Children's literature is especially effective for developing the basic operations associated with thinking: (1) observing, (2) comparing, (3) classifying, (4) hypothesizing, (5) organizing, (6) summarizing, (7) applying, and (8) criticizing.

Observing. Colorful picture books are excellent means of developing observational skills in both younger and older children. Young children discover how many animals they can locate in *Keep Looking!* by Millicent Selsam and Joyce Hunt. Suse MacDonald's *Alphabatics* encourages young children to observe how the illustrator introduces a letter and within three or four drawings changes the letter to picture an object that begins with that letter. Pat Hutchins's *Which Witch Is Which?*

The detailed illustrations in *The Inside-Outside Book of Washington D.C.* provide an excellent source for observing. (From *The Inside-Outside Book of Washington D.C.* by Roxie Munro. Copyright © 1987 by Roxie Munro. Reproduced by permission of the publisher, Dutton Children's Books, a division of Penguin Books USA, Inc.)

increases observational skills as readers identify the twins according to their choices of colors, foods, and games. Mitsumasa Anno's humorous, detailed illustrations in *Anno's Aesop: A Book of Fables by Aesop and Mr. Fox* encourage children to search for various characters found in fables. Older children enjoy searching for art objects, literary and historical characters, and present-day personalities in Anno's detailed, wordless books, such as *Anno's Britain* and *Anno's U.S.A. Lentil,* by Robert McCloskey, contains excellent drawings of a midwestern town in the early 1900s: the town square, the houses on the streets, the interior of the schoolhouse, the train depot, and a parade. Single lines of text accompany each picture, but the details of the pictures show the life-styles and the emotions of the characters in the story.

Comparing. Picture books and other literature selections provide opportunities for comparing. For example, young children can compare the various attributes of the hats illustrated in Stan and Janice Berenstain's *Old Hat, New Hat*. The hats include ones that are heavy, light, loose, tight, flat, tall, big, small, shiny, frilly, fancy, silly, and lumpy. These new hats can also be compared with the old hat, still considered the best of all.

Wordless books are also excellent for comparisons. *Changes, Changes,* by Pat Hutchins, opens with a picture of two doll figures who have built a house from blocks. The book continues to illustrate their adventures: When the house catches on fire, they change the structure of the blocks to form a fire truck; the fire truck puts out the fire but causes an overabundance of water; the dolls then change the blocks into a boat and sail safely to shore; on shore they build a truck and then a train; finally, they reach their preferred location and rebuild their house of blocks. Children can compare the changes in this book by examining the pictures, deciding what is being built and why, and then describing the changes that occur between pictures. Because there is one difference between the second house and the original, they can make a final comparison. Children can make additional comparisons by building their own structures out of blocks and trying to change the purpose of the structures by using only the original blocks. They may compare the results of the forces in nature in Lisa Peters's *The Sun, the Wind and the Rain*.

Different artists' renditions of the same story provide opportunities for artistic comparisons. For example, there are several newly illustrated versions of Margery Williams's *The Velveteen Rabbit*, originally published in 1922, including those by Allen Atkinson, Michael Hague, and Ilse Plume. Versions of the popular folktale "Beauty and the Beast" include those illustrated in different styles by Warwick Hutton, Etienne Delessert, Jan Brett, and Michael Hague. Students can consider the impact of color, line, design, and media on the interpretation of the text, as well as evaluate the accuracy of the illustrations.

Older children can also use pictures to compare. They can make historical comparisons in John Goodall's *The Story of a Main Street*. In this wordless book, Goodall chronicles the same street from medieval through modern times. Upper-elementary children can compare the main characters, their struggles for survival, and their growing up in books such as Maia Wojciechowska's *Shadow of a Bull* and Elizabeth George Speare's *The Bronze Bow*. They can compare one author's depiction of characterization and survival in Gary Paulsen's *Hatchet* and *The Voyage of the Frog*. They can compare themes, characterizations, and person-against-self conflicts in Marion Dane Bauer's *On My Honor* and Paula Fox's *One-Eyed Cat*. They can compare Russell Freedman's depiction of Lincoln in *Lincoln: A Photobiography* with the depiction of Lincoln by other biographers.

Classifying. Children must be able to classify objects or ideas before seeing or understanding the relationships among them. Various concept books use different levels of abstractness to introduce children to such concepts as color, shape, size, and usefulness. Eric Carle allows children to match blocks of color with the color shown in an illustration in his *My Very First Book of Colors*; illustrates the colorful story of a chameleon who wants to change his appearance in *The Mixed-Up Chameleon*; and presents the eight basic colors, as well as simple addition and subtraction, in *Let's Paint a Rainbow*.

Roger Duvoisin's *See What I Am* is a more difficult color concept book. It introduces the primary colors and then mixes them to produce the secondary colors. The artist also shows how colors are used to make color illustrations in picture books.

Size concept books also vary in level of difficulty. Carle's *My Very First Book of Shapes* encourages children to match black shapes with similar shapes in color. John Reiss's *Shapes* presents shapes, their names, and their three-dimensional forms. Photographs in Tana Hoban's *Shapes, Shapes, Shapes* encourage children to search for circles, rectangles, and ovals.

Many other types of books can be used to develop children's classification skills. For example, after listening to the folktale "The Three Bears," children may classify the bears, porridge bowls, chairs, and beds according to their size, then identify which bear could best use a particular bowl, bed, or chair. (Flannelgraph characters and objects make classification more concrete for young children.) Stories can be classified using an animals category for wild animals or pets; a boy or girl category for the main character; or a category for settings such as country or city. For example, country and city settings may be compared in Rebecca Emberley's *City Sounds* and Jane Chelsea Aragon's *Winter Harvest*. Characteristics of a story can also be used for classification: realistic or unrealistic; likable or unlikable; happy or sad; and funny or serious. For example, children can compare the realistic and unrealistic qualities found in Patricia Lauber's *The News About Dinosaurs*, Henry Schwartz's *How I Captured a Dinosaur*, and Rafe Martin's *Will's Mammoth*.

Hypothesizing. Several illustrated books encourage younger children to hypothesize about what they will find when they turn the page. In *Look! Look! Look!*, Tana Hoban uses cut-out squares to reveal portions of pictures. The total picture appears on the page following the portions. At a more complex level, students must turn the page to verify the identity of a baby animal in Masayuki Yabuuchi's *Whose Baby!* or to determine the possible dialogue in Chris Van Allsburg's *The Z Was Zapped*.

Hypothesizing about the subject, plot, or characters in a story assists children in developing their cognitive skills and their interests. It also motivates them to read or listen to literature. For example, children can look at the cover illustration of Russell Hoban's *Nothing to Do* and guess what the book is about. In this story, Father gives Walter a "something-to-do stone." Children can guess what Walter will do with the stone and decide what they would do if they had a similar stone. Before reading Patricia Lauber's *The News About Dinosaurs,* children can speculate about the content of the text.

Descriptive chapter titles and titles to subsections of books are excellent stimuli for verbal or written speculations by older children. For example, before reading or listening to Martha Brenner's *Fireworks Tonight!,* children can discuss what information they believe will be in each of the following sections: "Triumph and Tragedy on the Fourth," "Protective Regulation," "Mischief and Misuse," and "How Safe Are Fireworks?" After reading each section, they can review the accuracy of their predictions.

Organizing. Young children have difficulty understanding concepts and sequences of time. Illustrated books for young children, such as Helen Oxenbury's *Dressing* and Kate Duke's *Bedtime,* show the sequential order related to familiar activities. For older children, Kathryn Lasky's *Sugaring Time* follows the sequential order in which maple syrup is collected and processed; William Jaspersohn's *Magazine: Behind the Scenes at Sports Illustrated* follows the production of a magazine.

Plot development in literature encourages children to learn forms of logical organization. After listening to or reading a literature selection, children can improve their abilities to put ideas into order by retelling the story or developing a creative drama based on the story. With their strong sequential plots and repetition of sequence and detail, folktales are especially appropriate for developing organizational skills. *The Little Red Hen* uses chronological order. The story progresses from the seed, to the planting, to the tilling, to the harvesting, to the baking, and finally to the eating. In *The Three Billy Goats Gruff,* the goats cross the bridge and confront the troll in ascending size, beginning with the small goat, proceeding to the medium goat, and ending with the large goat. The Yiddish folktale *It Could Always Be Worse* tells the story of a man discontented with his small, crowded hut. He takes his rabbi's advice and brings a series of larger and larger animals into his hut. When he finally clears out the animals, he appreciates his home.

Cumulative folktales reinforce the organization of the plot by repeating the sequence each time a new experience is added to the story. Paul Galdone uses this cumulative technique in the American folktale *The Greedy Old Fat Man*. The story establishes a pattern early, as the title character approaches a boy and girl with the threatening words, "I ate a hundred biscuits and drank a barrel of milk, and I'll eat you, too, if I can catch you!" (p. 3). Language and action are repeated as new victims are added to the list. By the time the greedy old man approaches a frisky squirrel, the

In addition to richly detailed full-page illustrations that depict different historical time periods, in *The Story of a Main Street,* John Goodall uses clever half-page illustrated inserts. The inserts overlay half of the full-page illustration, adding still more historical details and giving the reader a sense of movement and change on the street. (Reprinted by permission of Margaret K. McElderry Books, an imprint of Macmillan Publishing Company from *The Story of a Main Street* by John S. Goodall, copyright © 1987 John S. Goodall.)

sequence of the plot has become familiar: "I ate a hundred biscuits, I drank a barrel of milk, I ate a little boy, I ate a little girl, I ate a little dog, I ate a little cat, I ate a little fox, I ate some little rabbits, and I'll eat you, too, if I can catch you" (p. 22). The story ends in true folktale fashion: The squirrel outwits the greedy old fat man and the victims emerge unhurt.

"Why" tales also frequently depict a series of events to explain something. For example, Verna Aardema's *Why Mosquitoes Buzz in People's Ears: A West African Tale* describes the sequence of events that prevented the owl from waking the sun and bringing in a new day. Such folktales make excellent selections for flannelboard stories. When children retell the stories using the flannelgraphs or use the stories as the basis for creative drama, they develop and reinforce their organizational skills.

Summarizing. Summarizing skills can be developed with literature of any genre or level of difficulty. Children may summarize stories orally or in writing. Oral summaries may motivate other children to read the same book or story. After a recreational reading period in the classroom, library, or home, members of the group can retell a story, the part of the story they liked best, the most important information that they learned, the funniest part of the story, the most exciting part, and the actions of the character they admired the most or the least.

Summaries can be related to specific content. For example, children can summarize the most important historical information in Rhoda Blumberg's *The Incredible Journey of Lewis & Clark* and *Commodore Perry in the Land of the Shogun,* or the most important scientific information in Patricia Lauber's *Volcano: The Eruption and Healing of Mount St. Helens,* and in Necia H. Apfel's *Nebulae: The Birth & Death of Stars*.

Applying. Young children need many opportunities to apply the skills, concepts, information, or ideas in books. When they read concept books, for example, they should see and manipulate concrete examples, not merely look at pictures. Children who read Tana Hoban's *Twenty-Six Letters and Ninety-Nine Cents* can count and group objects. Children also can apply their counting skills when reading Paul Giganti's *How Many Snails? A Counting Book*.

Information books offer application opportunities, too. Numerous "how-to" books stimulate children's interests in hobbies, crafts, and sports. For example, students can apply the information found in Barbara Isenberg and Marjorie Jaffe's *Albert the Running Bear's Exercise Book* when they try the exercises discussed and illustrated in the book. Children can use *Cactus in the Desert,* by Phyllis Busch, as they grow their own cactus gardens. Jim Arnosky's *Flies in the Water, Fish in the Air* provides information on fishing as a sport; and Arnosky's *Sketching Outdoors in Summer* uses detailed sketches to show children how to draw. Children can both apply and compare when they read Barbara Reid's *Playing with Plasticine*. They can follow directions for making clay models and compare the models with the illustrations in Joanne Oppenheim's *Have You Seen Birds?*

Criticizing. Neither adults nor children should be required or encouraged to accept everything they hear or read without criticism. Children should be given many opportunities to evaluate critically what they read or hear. Children develop critical evaluation skills when they sense the appropriate-

ness, reliability, value, and authenticity of literature selections. Historical fiction selections are excellent for investigating and discussing the authenticity of plots, characters, and settings. Research indicates that the levels and types of questioning strategies used with children affect their levels of thinking and their development of critical evaluative skills.

Personality Development

Children go through many stages of personality development. They gradually learn to express emotions acceptably, experience empathy toward others, and develop feelings of self-esteem. According to child development authority Joanne Hendrick (12), children "pass through a series of stages of emotional development when basic attitudes are formed. Early childhood encompasses three of these: the stages of trust versus mistrust, autonomy versus shame and doubt, and initiative versus guilt" (pp. 103–104). Hendrick maintains that people who work with children must foster mental health in young children by providing many opportunities to develop healthy emotional attitudes. Slowly, with guidance, children learn to handle their emotions productively rather than disruptively. Expanded experiences, adult and sibling models, and personal success show positive ways of dealing with emotions.

Overcoming fears, developing trust, relinquishing the desire to have only one's own way, and learning acceptable forms of interaction with both peers and adults inevitably involve traumatic experiences. Progressing through the stages of personality development is part of the maturing process, and books can play a very important role in that process. Chart 1–3 lists books that can promote children's personality development.

Bibliotherapy is an interaction between a reader and literature. In bibliotherapy, the ideas inherent in the reading materials have a therapeutic effect upon the reader. Experts in child development frequently suggest bibliotherapy to help children through various times of stress. Joanne Bernstein's *Books to Help Children Cope with Separation and Loss* (3) provides an introduction to bibliotherapy and annotated bibliographies in various areas of childhood adjustment, such as hospitalization, loss of a friend, and parents' divorce.

Although most of the emotional problems young children experience are not so severe as coping with loss and separation, children must face numerous smaller crises that require personal adjustment. Literature can help children understand their feelings, identify with characters who experience similar feelings, and gain new insights into how others have coped with the same problems. According to Masha Rudman and Anna Pearce (19), "[B]ooks can serve as mirrors for children, reflecting their appearance, their relationships, their feelings and thoughts in their immediate environment" (p. 159). In addition, books can act as windows on the world, inviting children to look beyond themselves and to form bonds with characters and circumstances.

Joan Glazer (10) identifies four ways in which literature contributes to the emotional growth of children. First, it shows children that many of their feelings are common to other children and that those feelings are normal and natural. Second, it explores a feeling from several viewpoints, giving a fuller picture and providing a basis for naming it. Third, actions of various characters show options for ways of dealing with particular emotions. Fourth, literature makes clear that one person experiences many emotions and that these emotions sometimes conflict.

Fear and jealousy are emotions familiar to most children. Jealousy is a common reaction when a new baby comes into the home, for example. books about new babies can help children express their fears and realize that their parents still love them but that it is not unusual to feel fearful about a new relationship. Ezra Jack Keats's *Peter's Chair* shows how one child handles these feelings when he not only gets an unwanted baby sister but also sees his own furniture painted pink for the new arrival. Roslyn Banish's *Let Me Tell You About My Baby* explores various feelings that range from jealousy to acceptance. The main character in Marisabina Russo's *Waiting for Hannah* questions her mother about preparations made for her birth.

The text and illustrations in *Arthur's Baby* by Marc Brown follow an animal family as it prepares for a new baby. Arthur goes through very normal concerns as he worries about how the baby will change his life and then becomes jealous of the interest shown the baby. The story concludes as Arthur discovers that having a baby in the family is enjoyable. *New Baby* by Emily Arnold McCully is a wordless book that explores the feelings of the youngest mouse child when its parents have another baby.

In Jacqueline Martin's *Buzzy Bones and the Lost Quilt*, a mouse-child experiences troubled dreams when he loses his security quilt. An understanding uncle and numerous friends help him search for

CHART 1–3
Personality development

Characteristics	Implications	Literature Suggestions
Preschool: Ages Two–Three		
1 Children begin to think that they have an identity separate from that of other members of the family.	1 Help children understand that they are people who have their own identity and their own worth.	Duke, Kate. *Clean-up Day.* Holzenthaler, Jean. *My Hands Can.*
2 Children feel the need for security.	2 Hold a child during lap reading to add to a sense of security and enjoyment of books.	Carlstrom, Nancy. *Jesse Bear, What Will You Wear?* Lindgren, Barbro. *The Wild Baby.* Van Vorst, M. L. *A Norse Lullaby.*
Preschool: Ages Three–Four		
1 Children have developed a fairly steady self-concept; they identify themselves as "I" and have sets of feelings about themselves.	1 Children's self-concepts are affected by attitudes and behavior of those around them, so make them feel that others care about them, accept them, and think they are worthy.	Jonas, Ann. *When You Were a Baby.* Krauss, Ruth. *The Carrot Seed.* Pomerantz, Charlotte. *Flap Your Wings and Try.* Rylant, Cynthia. *Birthday Presents.* Wahl, Jan. *Humphrey's Bear.*
2 Children require warm and secure environments.	2 Share books with children in a warm atmosphere in classrooms, in libraries, or at home.	Adoff, Arnold. *Black Is Warm Is Tan.* Dabcovich, Lydia. *Sleepy Bear.* Hill, Eric. *Spot's Birthday Party.* McPhail, David. *The Dream Child.* Rice, Eve. *Benny Bakes a Cake.*
3 Children hide from unhappy situations by withdrawing, suggesting that problems don't exist, or blaming someone else.	3 Give special guidance to help children accept mistakes without decreasing their feelings of self-worth.	Cazet, Denys. *A Fish in His Pocket.*- Sharmat, Marjorie. *A Big Fat Enormous Lie.*
4 Children begin to become aware of their cultural heritage.	4 Children need to be proud of who they are, so provide literature to stress cultural contributions and the contributions of the home and neighborhood.	Adoff, Arnold. *Black Is Warm Is Tan.* Bunting, Eve. *The Wednesday Surprise.*
Preschool: Ages Four–Five		
1 Children continue to be egocentric; they talk in first person and consider themselves the center of the world.	1 Present literature in which children can identify with the character and the story.	Engel, Diana. *Josephina Hates Her Name.* Hest, Amy. *The Purple Coat.* Mark, Jan. *Fun.* Small, David. *Imogene's Antlers.* Vincent, Gabrielle. *Feel Better, Ernest!*
2 Children improve in their ability to handle their own emotions in productive ways.	2 Help children identify other ways to handle problems. Use literature to help them see how others handle their emotions.	Anholt, Catherine. *Truffles in Trouble.* Keats, Ezra Jack. *Peter's Chair.* McCully, Emily Arnold. *New Baby.* Naylor, Phyllis Reynolds. *Keeping a Christmas Secret.* Steig, William. *Spinky Sulks.* Viorst, Judith. *Alexander and the Terrible, Horrible, No Good, Very Bad Day.* Wagner, Jenny. *John Brown, Rose and the Midnight Cat.*

CHART 1–3 (cont.)
Personality development

Characteristics	Implications	Literature Suggestions
3 Fears of unknown situations cause children to lose confidence and to lose control of their emotions.	3 Help children understand what is new to them and help them feel comfortable with their ability to handle unknown situations. Read about and discuss new situations.	Anholt, Catherine. *Truffles Is Sick.* Carle, Eric. *Do You Want to Be My Friend?* Rockwell, Harlow. *My Dentist.* Rogers, Fred. *Going to the Doctor.* ———. *Going to Day Care.*
4 Children begin to respond to intrinsic motivation.	4 Children require good models for intrinsic motivation, so provide books as sources of models.	Bunting, Eve. *The Mother's Day Mice.* Vincent, Gabrielle. *Feel Better, Ernest!* Williams, Barbara. *Chester Chipmunk's Thanksgiving.*
5 Children require warm and secure environments.	5 Continue reading to children in a loving atmosphere.	Gammell, Stephen. *Wake Up, Bear . . . It's Christmas!* Larrick, Nancy. *When the Dark Comes Dancing: A Bedtime Poetry Book.*
Preschool—Kindergarten: Ages Five–Six		
1 Children are usually outgoing, sociable, and friendly.	1 Read stories showing outgoing, sociable, and friendly characteristics in the main characters.	Flournoy, Valerie. *The Patchwork Quilt.* Johnson, Angela. *Tell Me a Story, Mama.* Marshall, James. *George and Martha One Fine Day.* Small, David. *Eulalie and the Hopping Head.*
2 Children are quite stable and adjusted in their emotional life; they are developing self-assurance and confidence in others.	2 Encourage children to develop self-assurance and confidence in others. Provide opportunities for children to expand self-assurance—it is closely related to self-worth.	Brandenberg, Aliki. *The Two of Them.* Day, Alexandra. *Frank and Ernest Play Ball.* Hadithi, Mwenye. *Crafty Chameleon.* Ormerod, Jan. *Sunshine.* Purdy, Carol. *Least of All.* Seuss, Dr. *Oh, the Places You'll Go!*
3 Children require warmth and security in adult relationships even though self-assurance increases.	3 Continue to provide warm relationships through a close association during story time.	Brown, Margaret Wise. *The Runaway Bunny.* Ernst, Lisa Campbell. *When Bluebell Sang.* Hest, Amy. *The Crack-of-Dawn Walkers.* Murphy, Jill. *Peace at Last.* Zolotow, Charlotte. *My Grandson Lew.*
Early Elementary: Ages Six–Eight		
1 Children are not so emotionally stable as before; they show more tension and may strike out against a teacher or parent.	1 Help children discover acceptable ways to handle their tensions. Read stories to illustrate how other children handle their tensions.	Ehrlich, Amy. *Leo, Zack, and Emmie.* Jukes, Mavis. *Like Jake and Me.* Khalsa, Dayal Kaur. *I Want a Dog.* Preston, Edna Mitchell, and Rainey Bennett. *The Temper Tantrum Book.*

CHART 1–3 (cont.)
Personality development

Characteristics	Implications	Literature Suggestions
2 Children seek independence from adults but continue to require warmth and security from the adults in their lives.	2 Provide opportunities for children to demonstrate independence; allow them to choose books and activities for sharing. Supply books in which characters develop independence.	Cleary, Beverly. *Ramona Quimby, Age 8.* Greene, Carol. *Hinny Winny Bunco.* Porte, Barbara. *Harry in Trouble.* Stanek, Muriel. *All Alone After School.* Wallace, Ian. *Chin Chiang and the Dragon's Dance.* Williams, Vera B. *Something Special for Me.*
Middle Elementary: Ages Eight–Ten		
1 The personality characteristic of cooperation is highly valued by fourth graders but declines in later grades.	1 Encourage literature activities that allow for cooperation; provide books stressing cooperation as the theme.	Baylor, Byrd. *The Best Town in the World.* Goffstein, M. B. *Family Scrapbook.*
2 Children have fewer fears about immediate and possible dangers but may have strong fears about remote or impossible situations, such as ghosts, lions, and witches.	2 Use literature selections describing children's fears for discussion and developing understanding of unrealistic fears.	Brittain, Bill. *The Wish Giver.* Johnston, Tony. *Four Scary Stories.*
Upper Elementary: Ages Ten–Twelve		
1 Many children have internalized their control; they believe that they are in control of what happens and assume personal responsibility for their successes and failures.	1 Reinforce responsibility, organizing, and making decisions. Provide books that illustrate the development of internalized control.	Cleary, Beverly. *Dear Mr. Henshaw.* Fine, Anne. *My War with Goggle-Eyes.* Fox, Paula. *One-Eyed Cat.* Hughes, Dean. *Family Pose.* MacLachlan, Patricia. *The Facts and Fictions of Minna Pratt.* ———. *Sarah, Plain and Tall.* Shura, Mary Francis. *The Search for Grissi.*
2 Children value independence as a personality trait.	2 Supply literature to illustrate developing independence for both male and female characters.	O'Dell, Scott. *Island of the Blue Dolphins.* Park, Ruth. *Playing Beatie Bow.* Sperry, Armstrong. *Call It Courage.* Staples, Suzanne Fisher. *Shabanu: Daughter of the Wind.* Voigt, Cynthia. *Dicey's Song.* ———. *A Solitary Blue.*
3 Rapid changes in physical growth may cause some children to become self-conscious and self-critical; others may be preoccupied with their appearance.	3 Provide stories of other children who experience problems growing during this time.	Cleaver, Vera, and Bill Cleaver. *Me Too.* Paterson, Katherine. *Come Sing, Jimmy Jo.*

Sources: Hendrick (12); Mussen, Conger, and Kagan (15); and Sarafino and Armstrong (20).

ISSUE

Challenges to Theories of Human Development

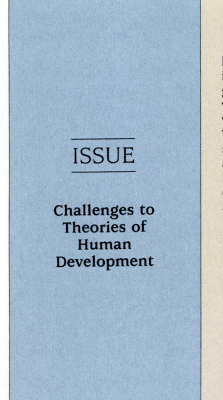

IS THERE A GENDER ISSUE in studies related to children's moral development? Is there a gender issue in studies related to children's language and communication development and to children's visual-spatial development? Was Piaget incorrect when he stated that children under the age of seven or eight do not have a grasp of cause-and-effect relationships? These are a few of the current developmental issues discussed in both the scientific and the popular press.

Several researchers are questioning Kohlberg's and Piaget's assertions about the social and moral development of children. Carol Gilligan contends that the developmental models of Kohlberg and Piaget "equate male development with child development"[1] and thereby ignore female development. Kohlberg, for example, based his hierarchy of moral development on a twenty-year study of eighty-four males. Gilligan's research, which involved both female and male subjects, indicated that females and males develop different value systems due to traditional gender roles that assign females the primary responsibility for taking care of others' needs. Females develop a "morality of responsibility," which stresses the importance of maintaining relationships and considering other people's feelings and points of view (roughly equivalent to Kohlberg's Stage 3). Males learn to place more value on competitive self-assertion and develop a "morality of rights," which considers rules more important than relationships (roughly equivalent to Kohlberg's Stages 5 and 6).

The implications of the gen-

the quilt. After the tattered quilt is found, the friends create a new quilt that includes pieces from the old one. Thus, books can help children anticipate and prepare themselves for situations that frighten them.

Many children fear going to school for the first time or moving into a new school or neighborhood. Eric Carle's *Do You Want to Be My Friend?*, Miriam Cohen's *Will I Have a Friend?*, and Rosemary Wells's *Timothy Goes to School* present heroes who successfully cope with this problem. Harlow Rockwell has written and illustrated *My Doctor* and *My Dentist* to help answer young children's questions about the procedures and equipment used during physical checkups. Older children have many of their questions answered in James Howe's *The Hospital Book*. Barbara Greenberg's *The Bravest Babysitter* illustrates the common childhood fear of thunder and storms. This story reverses the normal situation: when the babysitter becomes frightened during a thunderstorm, the younger child tries to distract the fearful older one.

Literature provides children with many examples of how to cope with feelings of anger. Many children have days when absolutely nothing goes right. Books can act as stimuli for discussing how children handled or could have handled similar situations. Young children, for example, can certainly identify with Judith Viorst's Alexander in *Alexander and the Terrible, Horrible, No Good, Very Bad Day* or with Patricia Giff's Ronald in *Today Was a Terrible Day*. Edna Mitchell Preston and Rainey Bennett's *The Temper Tantrum Book* shows that even animals can have tantrums, and the animals explain what makes them angry. The book can prompt children to share what makes them angry and how they deal with this problem.

Literature can play a dramatic role in helping children develop positive and realistic self-concepts. Infants do not think of themselves as individuals. Between the ages of two and three, children slowly begin to realize that they have identities separate from those of other members of the family. By age three, with the assistance of warm, loving environments, most children have developed a set of feelings about themselves; they consider themselves "I."

Egocentric feelings continue for several years, and children consider themselves the center of the

der differences between the Kohlberg and the Gilligan theories of moral development are highlighted by John West and Davele Bursor.[2] These educators argue that counselors or anyone else who works with children should understand gender differences in moral development and should be able to use these differences when counseling either girls or boys during the decision-making process.

Studies reported by Jo Durden-Smith and Diane Desimone[3] also question theories of language and cognitive development that are based primarily on male subjects. These authors report results from brain research that suggest sex-related differences between males and females. They outline brain research studies demonstrating female superiority in verbal skills, fine-motor coordination, and response to emotional content. These studies suggest that the left hemisphere and its abilities develop faster in girls than in boys. In contrast, males demonstrate superiority in visual-spatial skills and in mathematical and mechanical tasks. Consequently, some researchers conclude that the right hemisphere and its abilities develop faster in boys than in girls.

The ages of children in Piaget's pre-causal level are also being challenged. Maya Pines[4] reports on research by psychologists such as Rochel Gelman and Thomas Shultz, which shows that children as young as three or four have an understanding of cause and effect.

As might be expected, these studies, the interpretations of these studies, and the implications of these studies are highly controversial. Both Janet Shibley Hyde[5] and Mary Roth Walsh[6] identify these earlier studies as controversial in their discussions of issues related to the psychology of women. Students of children's literature and child development may read the conflicting theories and discuss the implications.

[1]Gilligan, Carol. *In a Different Voice: Psychological Theory and Women's Development*. Cambridge, Mass.: Harvard Univ. Press, 1982.

[2]West, John D., and Davele E. Bursor. "Gilligan and Kohlberg: Gender Issue in Moral Development." *Humanistic Education and Development* 22 (June 1984): 134–142.

[3]Durden-Smith, Jo, and Diane Desimone. *Sex and the Brain*. New York: Arbor House, 1983.

[4]Pines, Maya. "Can a Rock Walk?" *Psychology Today* 17 (November 1983): 46–52.

[5]Hyde, Janet Shibley. *Half the Human Experience: The Psychology of Women*. Lexington, Mass.: D. C. Heath and Co., 1985.

[6]Walsh, Mary Roth, ed. *The Psychology of Women: Ongoing Debates*. New Haven, Conn.: Yale University Press, 1987.

universe. If the development of self-esteem is to progress positively, they need to know that their families, friends, and the larger society value them. Aliki Brandenberg's *The Two of Them,* for example, develops a strong relationship between a girl and her grandfather. This relationship helps her accept his eventual death and become responsible for an orchard they both loved.

Books also show children that it is all right to be different from their families. Jan Mark's *Fun* shows that a boy who prefers quiet, contemplative activities can be happy living with an active, boisterous mother and father.

Books that stress creative problem solving are especially valuable for the personal development of young children. Denys Cazet's *A Fish in His Pocket* follows a young bear as he accidently causes the death of a fish, discovers a solution to the problem, and concludes a satisfactory ending to his dilemma. In Dayal Kaur Khalsa's *I Want a Dog,* a young girl finds a way to show her parents that she will be ready to take care of a dog when she is old enough to own a pet. Her solution, to practice taking care of a roller skate as if it were a dog, is both novel and humorous. In Amy Hest's

Illustrations of realistic situations provide a preview of a visit to a doctor. (From *The Checkup* by Helen Oxenbury. Copyright © 1983 by Helen Oxenbury. By permission of Dial Books for Young Readers, a Division of E. P. Dutton, Inc.)

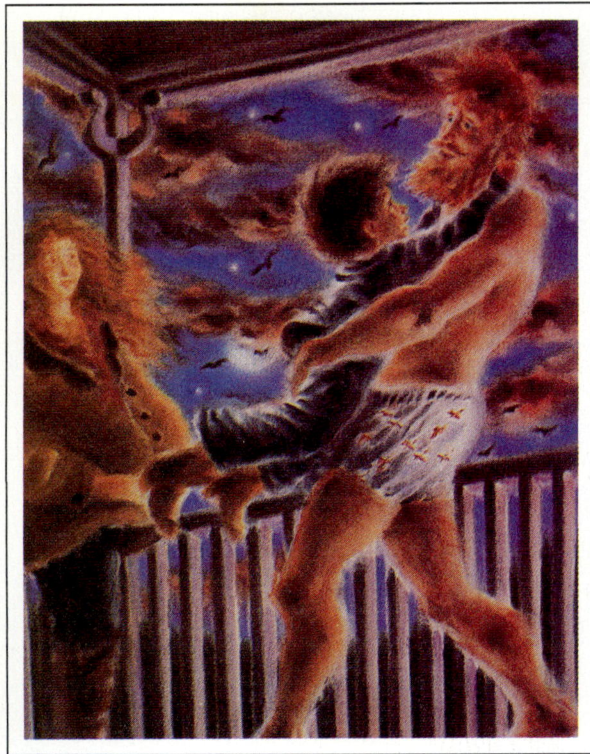

Illustrations and text develop understanding between a boy and his stepfather. (From *Like Jake and Me* by Mavis Jukes. Pictures by Lloyd Bloom. Illustrations copyright © 1984 by Lloyd Bloom. By permission of Alfred A. Knopf, Inc.)

The Purple Coat, a young girl finds a way to have the purple coat she wants and still have the navy blue coat preferred by her mother. The reversible coat results when Gabrielle and her grandfather work on the problem together. The six-year-old main character in Carol Purdy's *Least of All* is tired of always being told that she is not big enough to work on the farm. In this story set in turn-of-the-century Vermont, the heroine surprises everyone and proves that she is big enough to contribute to the family. In a satisfying conclusion, she teaches herself to read and then teaches her family. In Eve Bunting's *The Wednesday Surprise,* a girl teaches her grandmother to read. In Tomie dePaola's *The Art Lesson* a boy discovers that he can retain his individual beliefs about art and still comply with the teacher's requirements.

Several excellent books for older children are based on the themes of overcoming problems. In Scott O'Dell's *Island of the Blue Dolphins* a girl survives alone on an island off the coast of California. She is not rescued for eighteen years and must overcome loneliness, develop weapons that violate a taboo of her society, and create a life for herself. Gary Paulsen's *Hatchet* follows a boy as he learns about personal and physical survival in the Canadian wilderness. *Call It Courage,* by Armstrong Sperry, is another survival book. In this book, a boy must overcome his fear of the sea before he can return home.

All children must feel pride in their accomplishments and cultural heritage and must develop positive sex-role identifications. Those who have developed positive feelings of self-worth will be able to assume responsibility for their own successes and failures. Literature can help young children discover the capabilities they have and realize that acquiring some skills takes considerable time. For example, in Ezra Jack Keats's *Whistle for Willie,* Peter tries and tries to whistle. After considerable practice, he finally learns this skill. Books such as Jean Holzenthaler's *My Hands Can* help children realize they can do many things.

Positive attitudes toward one's heritage can be reinforced through reading about the contributions of the people who belong to it. In addition books can provide excellent role models and illustrate that both males and females can function successfully in many different roles.

Levels of reading achievement may influence feelings of self-worth. Alexander and Filler (1, pp. 6–7) reviewed research in the area of reading achievement and self-concept development and concluded that (1) low self-concepts may result when children feel that they are poor readers or are evaluated as poor readers by respected peers, parents, and/or teachers; (2) children who believe that others consider them unsuccessful readers may refuse to make an effort or decide that they hate reading or find it boring; (3) if children believe that they are poor readers, they may in fact become poor readers; and (4) positive self-concepts lead children to further success in reading, while negative self-concepts encourage even greater failure in the future.

Personality development in children is extremely important. If children do not understand themselves and believe that they are important, how can they value anyone else? Many literary selections and literature-related experiences reinforce positive personality development. Such experiences include reading orally in a warm and secure environment, discussing and acting out various roles from literature, and simply enjoying a wide variety of literature.

Social Development

According to David Shaffer (21), socialization "is the process by which children acquire the beliefs, values, and behaviors deemed significant and appropriate by the older members of their society" (p. 560). Shaffer identifies three ways that socialization serves society: (1) as a means of regulating children's behavior and controlling their undesirable or antisocial impulses, (2) as a way to promote the personal growth of the individual, and (3) as a means to perpetuate the social order. Chart 1–4 lists books that can promote the social development of children.

Socialization. Socialization is said to occur when children learn the ways of their groups so that they can function acceptably within them. Children must learn to exert control over aggressive and hostile behavior if they are to have acceptable relationships with family members, friends, and the larger community. These acceptable relationships require an understanding of the feelings and viewpoints of others. Quite obviously, socialization is a very important part of child development. Understanding the processes that influence social development is essential for anyone who works with children. Researchers have identified three processes influential in the socialization of children.

First, reward or punishment by parents and other adults reinforces socially acceptable attitudes and behaviors and discourages socially unacceptable ones. For example, a child who refuses to share a toy with another child may be deprived of the toy, while appropriate sharing may be rewarded with a hug and a favorable comment.

Second, observation of others teaches children the responses, behaviors, and beliefs considered appropriate within their culture. Children learn how to act and what to believe by imitating adults and peers. For example, a girl may learn about gender distinctions in our culture by observing and trying to copy her mother's role in the family. Children also observe what other members of the family fear and how members of their group react to people who belong to different racial or cultural groups.

The third process, identification, may be the most important for socialization. It requires emotional ties with models. Children's thoughts, feelings, and actions become similar to those of people they believe are like them.

Children's first relationships usually occur within the immediate family, then extend to a few friends in the neighborhood, to school, and finally to the broader world. Literature and literature-related activities can aid in the development of these relationships by encouraging children to become sensitive to the feelings of others. For example, Ann Herbert Scott's *Sam* is very unhappy when the members of his family are too busy to play with him. When they realize what is wrong, they remember to include Sam in their activities. The four-year-old in Eve Rice's *Benny Bakes a Cake* helps his mother in the kitchen but faces disappointment when his dog eats the cake.

Overcoming problems related to sibling rivalry is a frequent theme in children's books and is one that children can understand. In Charlotte Zolotow's *Big Brother,* a little sister is constantly teased by her older brother. In *Stevie,* by John Steptoe, Robert is upset when his mother takes care of a child from another family, but he discovers that he actually misses Stevie when he leaves.

Patricia Lee Gauch's *Christina Katerina and the Time She Quit the Family* is a humorous story

The main character develops feelings of self-worth through his drawings. Illustration by Tomie dePaola. Reprinted by permission of G. P. Putnam's Sons from *The Art Lesson* copyright © 1989 by Tomie dePaola.

CHART 1–4
Social development

Characteristics	Implications	Literature Suggestions
Preschool: Ages Two–Three		
1 Children learn to organize and represent their world; they imitate actions and behaviors they have observed.	1 Encourage children to role-play so they can begin to take others' points of view and learn about other behavior.	Carle, Eric. *The Mixed-up Chameleon.* Oxenbury, Helen. *Family.* Steptoe, John. *Baby Says.*
2 Children transform things into make-believe: a yardstick may be a horse.	2 Provide objects and books that suggest creative interpretations.	Hutchins. Pat. *Changes, Changes.* Lionni, Leo. *Let's Make Rabbits.*
Preschool: Ages Three–Four		
1 Children begin to realize that other people have feelings, just as they do.	1 Encourage children to talk about how they felt when something similar happened to them; provide books that show feelings.	Alexander, Martha. *Nobody Asked Me If I Wanted a Baby Sister.* Keats, Ezra Jack. *Peter's Chair.* Winthrop, Elizabeth. *Bear and Mr. Duck.*
2 Children enjoy playing together and develop strong attachments to other children.	2 Encourage the growing social skills of sharing, taking turns, and playing cooperatively.	Cohen, Miriam. *Best Friends.* Hoban, Russell. *Best Friends for Frances.* Lindgren, Barbro. *Sam's Ball.*
3 Children begin to enjoy participating in group activities and group games.	3 Let children be both leaders and followers during group activities after reading a book.	Bulla, Clyde. *Keep Running, Allen!* Oxenbury, Helen. *First Day at School.* Scott, Ann Herbert. *Sam.*
4 Children begin to identify others' feelings by observing facial expressions.	4 Encourage children to become sensitive to their own and others' feelings by talking about the feelings that accompany different facial expressions in books.	Berger, Terry. *I Have Feelings.* Bonsall, Crosby. *It's Mine!—A Greedy Book.* Henkes, Kevin. *Jessica.* Hoban, Russell. *The Little Brute Family.* Hutchins, Pat. *Where's the Baby?*
Preschool: Ages Four–Five		
1 Children start to avoid aggression when angry and to look for compromises. They are, however, frequently bossy, assertive, and prone to using alibis.	1 Praise children for talking out anger, help them to calm down and talk about the situation, direct them toward finding solutions. Choose books in which aggression is avoided.	Vincent, Gabrielle. *Smile, Ernest and Celestine.* Viorst, Judith. *I'll Fix Anthony.* Zolotow, Charlotte. *The Quarreling Book.*
2 Children begin to understand consequences of good and bad and may engage in unacceptable behavior to elicit reactions.	2 Explain actions in terms that children understand. Let children discuss alternative actions.	Galdone, Paul. *The Little Red Hen.* Hadithi, Mwenye. *Crafty Chameleon.*
3 Children seldom play alone, but they begin to work by themselves.	3 Encourage persistence; let children work at something until it is completed to their satisfaction. This is crucial for problem solving and self-directed learning.	Burton, Virginia Lee. *Mike Mulligan and His Steam Shovel.* Carle, Eric. *The Very Busy Spider.*

CHART 1–4 (cont.)
Social development

Characteristics	Implications	Literature Suggestions
4 Children increase their awareness of the different roles people play—nurse, police officer, grocery clerk, man, woman, etc.	4 Provide opportunities to meet different kinds of people through real life and books; encourage dramatic play around different roles.	Barton Byron. *I Want to Be an Astronaut.* Klein, Norma. *Girls Can Be Anything.* Oxenbury, Helen. *The Checkup.* Rockwell, Harlow. *My Doctor.* Zolotow, Charlotte. *William's Doll.*
5 Children exhibit unreasonable fears, such as fear of the dark, thunder, and animals.	5 Help children overcome fears by sharing experiences of others who had fears but overcame them.	Bunting, Eve. *Ghost's Hour, Spook's Hour.* Greenberg, Barbara. *The Bravest Babysitter.*
Preschool—Kindergarten: Ages Five–Six		
1 Children like to help parents around the house; they are developing dependable behavior.	1 Allow children to be responsible for jobs that they can realistically complete. Read stories about children helping.	Rice, Eve. *Benny Bakes a Cake.* Rylant, Cynthia. *When I Was Young in the Mountains.* Williams, Vera B. *A Chair for My Mother.*
2 Children protect younger brothers and sisters and other children.	2 Let children help and read to younger children, encourage them to become aware that they are growing into independent people. Share reasons why all people need security.	Howe, James. *There's a Monster Under My Bed.* Hughes, Shirley. *Dogger.* Schwartz, Amy. *Anabelle Swift, Kindergartner.*
3 Children are proud of their accomplishments; they take pride in going to school and in their possessions.	3 Encourage a feeling of self-worth: praise accomplishments, encourage children to share school and home experiences, and allow them to talk about their possessions.	Fassler, Joan. *Howie Helps Himself.* Schwartz, Amy. *Anabelle Swift, Kindergartner.* Udry, Janice. *What Mary Jo Shared.*
4 Children continue to show anxiety and unreasonable fear.	4 Help children overcome their fears and anxieties; stress that these are normal.	Sharmat, Marjorie. *The Best Valentine in the World.* Waber, Bernard. *Ira Says Goodbye.* ———. *Ira Sleeps Over.* Wells, Rosemary. *Timothy Goes to School.*
5 Children enjoy playing outside on their favorite toys, such as tricycles and sleds.	5 Provide opportunities for play, discussions about play, reading and drawing about outside play, and dictating stories about outside play.	Keats, Ezra Jack. *The Snowy Day.* McLeod, Emilie Warren. *The Bear's Bicycle.* Martin, Rafe. *Will's Mammoth.*
6 Children enjoy excursions to new places and familiar ones.	6 Plan trips to zoos, fire stations, historic sites, and such. Read about these places, encourage children to tell about family trips.	Griffith, Helen V. *Grandaddy's Place.* Stock, Catherine. *Sophie's Knapsack.*
7 Children enjoy dressing up, role playing, and creative play.	7 Provide opportunities for children to dress up and play different roles. Read stories that can be used for creative play.	Aardema, Verna. *Who's in Rabbit's House?* Cauley, Lorinda Bryan. *Goldilocks and the Three Bears.* Hadithi, Mwenye. *Greedy Zebra.* Ichikawa, Satomi. *Nora's Castle.*

CHART 1–4 (cont.)
Social development

Characteristics	Implications	Literature Suggestions
Early Elementary: Ages Six–Eight		
1 Children may defy parents when they are under pressure; they have difficulty getting along with younger siblings.	1 Encourage children to become more sensitive to family needs and to talk and read stories about similar situations. Direct children toward finding solutions.	Blume, Judy. The *One in the Middle Is the Green Kangaroo.* Flournoy, Valerie. *The Patchwork Quilt.* Hoberman, Mary Ann. *Mr. and Mrs. Muddle.* Ness, Evaline. *Sam, Bangs, and Moonshine.* Sendak, Maurice. *Where the Wild Things Are.*
2 Children want to play with other children but frequently insist on being first.	2 Encourage children both to lead and follow, read books in which children overcome similar problems.	Kellogg, Steven. *Best Friends.* Udry, Janice May. *Let's Be Enemies.*
3 Children respond to teachers' help or praise. They try to conform and please teachers.	3 Allow children to share work and receive praise. Show and tell is especially enjoyable for six- and seven-year-olds. Praise their reading and sharing of books.	Lobel, Arnold. *Frog and Toad All Year.* Schwartz, Alvin. *There Is a Carrot in My Ear and Other Noodle Tales.* Van Leeuwen, Jean. *More Tales of Oliver Pig.*
4 Children enjoy sitting still and listening to stories read at school, at home, or in the library.	4 Provide frequent storytelling and story-reading times.	de Paola, Tomie. *The Clown of God.* Fleischman, Sid. *The Scarebird.* Isele, Elizabeth. *The Frog Princess.* Steptoe, John. *The Story of Jumping Mouse.* Turkle, Brinton. *Do Not Open.*
5 Children have definite inflexible ideas of right and wrong.	5 Discuss attitudes and standards of conduct in books.	Friedman, Ina R. *How My Parents Learned to Eat.* Lobel, Arnold. *Grasshopper on the Road.* Schotter, Roni. *Captain Snap and the Children of Vinegar Lane.* Wild, Margaret. *Mr. Nick's Knitting.*
6 Children are curious about differences between boys and girls.	6 Ask children questions about differences between boys and girls and where babies come from. Provide books that help answer such questions.	Andry, Andrew, and Steven Schepp. *How Babies Are Made* (plants and animals). Isenbart, Hans-Heinrich. *A Duckling Is Born.* Sheffield, Margaret, and Sheila Bewley. *Where Do Babies Come From?* (human).
Middle Elementary: Ages Eight–Ten		
1 Concepts of right and wrong become more flexible; the situation in which the wrong action occurred is taken into consideration.	1 Provide experiences and books to help children relate to different points of view; they begin to realize there are different attitudes, values, and standards from those their parents stress.	Branscum, Robbie. *The Saving of P.S.* Callen, Larry. *Who Kidnapped the Sheriff? Tales from Tickfaw.* Fritz, Jean. *The Double Life of Pocahontas.* Goble, Paul. *The Girl Who Loved Wild Horses.*

CHART 1–4 (cont.)
Social development

Characteristics	Implications	Literature Suggestions
2 Children begin to be influenced by their peer groups.	2 Read and discuss books in which peer groups become more important; these groups can influence attitudes, values, and interests.	Alcock, Vivien. *The Trial of Anna Cotman.* Allard, Harry. *Miss Nelson Is Missing.* Delton, Judy. *Kitty in the Middle.*
3 Children's thinking is becoming socialized; children can understand other people's points of view. They feel that their reasoning and solutions to problems should agree with others.	3 Provide many opportunities for children to investigate differing points of view. Literature is an excellent source.	Byars, Betsy. *The Animal, the Vegetable, and John D. Jones.* Margolis, Richard J. *Secrets of a Small Brother.* Monjo, F. N. *The Drinking Gourd.* Peet, Bill. *Bill Peet: An Autobiography.* Sandin, Joan. *The Long Way to a New Land.*
Upper Elementary: Ages Ten–Twelve		
1 Children have developed racial attitudes; low-prejudiced children increase in perception of nonracial characteristics; high-prejudiced children increase in perception of racial characteristics.	1 Provide literature and instructional activities to develop multiethnic values and stress contributions of ethnic minorities.	Adoff, Arnold. *All the Colors of the Race.* ———. *Malcolm X.* Highwater, Jamake. *Anpao—An American Indian Odyssey.* Paulsen, Gary. *Dogsong.* White, Florence. *Cesar Chavez: Man of Courage.*
2 Children want to do jobs well instead of starting and exploring them; feelings of inferiority and inadequacy may result if children feel that they cannot measure up to their own personal standards.	2 Encourage expansion of knowledge in high-interest areas; provide books in these areas; provide assistance and encouragement to allow children to finish jobs to meet their expectations.	Arnosky, Jim. *Sketching Outdoors in Summer.* Cobb, Vicki, and Kathy Darling. *Bet You Can't! Science Impossibilities to Fool You.*
3 Children have a sense of justice and resist imperfections in the world.	3 Read and discuss stories where people overcome injustice, improve some aspect of life, or raise questions about life.	Arnold, Caroline. *Saving the Peregrine Falcon.* Barry, Scott. *The Kingdom of Wolves.* Lasky, Kathryn. *The Night Journey.* Lowry, Lois. *Number the Stars.* Riskind, Mary. *Apple Is My Sign.* Yates, Elizabeth. *Amos Fortune, Free Man.*
4 Peer groups exert strong influences on children; conformity to parents decreases and conformity to peers increases in social situations. Children may challenge their parents.	4 If differences between peer and family values are too great, children may experience conflicts. Provide literature selections and discussions to help.	Brooks, Bruce. *The Moves Make the Man.* Byars, Betsy. *The Cybil War.* Greenberg, Jan. *The Iceberg and Its Shadow.* Lisle, Janet Taylor. *Afternoon of the Elves.*

CHART 1–4 (cont.)
Social development

Characteristics	Implications	Literature Suggestions
5 Children have developed strong associations with gender-typed expectations: Girls may fail in "masculine" tasks; boys in "feminine" tasks.	5 Provide books and discussions that avoid sex-stereotyped roles; emphasize that both sexes can succeed in many roles.	Cleary, Beverly. *A Girl from Yamhill: A Memoir.* Facklam, Margery. *Wild Animals, Gentle Women.* Fox, Mary. *Women Astronauts: Aboard the Shuttle.* Paige, David. *A Day in the Life of a Marine Biologist.* Tobias, Tobi. *Arthur Mitchell.* Yates, Elizabeth. *My Diary—My World.*
6 Boys and girls accept the identity of the opposite sex. Girls more than boys begin to feel that marriage would be desirable.	6 Provide books that develop relationships with the opposite sex; such books interest girls especially.	Cole, Brock. *The Goats.* Cooper, Susan. *Seaward.* L'Engle, Madeleine. *A Ring of Endless Light.* Lunn, Janet. *The Root Cellar.* MacLachlan, Patricia. *The Facts and Fictions of Minna Pratt.*

Sources: Braga and Braga (4); Mussen, Conger, and Kagan (15); Piaget and Inhelder (17); and Shaffer (21).

about what happens to a child when she decides she cannot tolerate her family. In Gauch's text, her understanding family allows her to change her name, live in a divided part of the house, and basically do anything she chooses. She eventually decides that being separated from the family is not pleasant. Cynthia Rylants's *Birthday Presents* develops strong, loving parent-child relationships as the parents tell their young daughter stories about her previous birthdays. Helen V. Griffith's *Grandaddy's Place* explores developing relationships between a girl and her grandfather.

Many books for preschool and early-primary children deal with various emotions related to friendship. Best friends may have strong attachments with each other, as shown in Miriam Cohen's *Best Friends* and Russell Hoban's *Best Friends for Frances*. In contrast, they may also experience problems, as Crosby Bonsall demonstrates in *It's Mine!—A Greedy Book*. In this book, best friends quarrel when one of them wants to play with the other's toys. Jim Judkis's photographs in Fred Rogers's *Making Friends* show friends interacting during many types of activities. It also explores difficult emotions, such as jealousy and anger.

Social development includes becoming aware of and understanding the different social roles people play. One of the greatest contributions made by literature and literature-related discussions is the realization that both boys and girls can succeed in a wide range of roles. Books that emphasize nonstereotyped sex roles and achievement are excellent models that can stimulate discussion. For example, Margery Facklam's *Wild Animals, Gentle Women* includes information on the lives and contributions of eleven women who have studied animal behavior. The author also shows how a student can prepare for this profession.

Some books also stress the nonstereotyping of emotions. Charlotte Zolotow's *William's Doll,* a book for young children, relates a young boy's experiences when he wants a doll. His brother and neighbor consider him a sissy; his father buys him masculine toys. His grandmother finally explains that it is perfectly all right for boys to have dolls.

Becoming aware of different views about the world is important in socialization, and literature can help accomplish this. Children may sympathize with the Native American girl who loves her family but longs for a free life among the wild horses in *The Girl Who Loved Wild Horses* by Paul Goble. They may also understand the slave's viewpoint and the consequences of prejudice when they read F. N. Monjo's *The Drinking Gourd*. Older children discover the consequences of prejudice when they read Mildred Taylor's *Let the Circle Be Unbroken* or Belinda Hurmence's *A Girl Called Boy*.

Contemporary realistic fiction presents many different viewpoints on issues familiar to children today. These issues include divorce (Judy Blume's *It's Not the End of the World*); religious nonconformity (Robbie Branscum's *The Saving of P.S.*); and environmental concerns (Mel Ellis's *The Wild Horse Killers*).

Moral Development. Acquiring moral standards is an important part of each child's social development. Preschool children start to develop concepts of right and wrong when they identify with their parents and with parental values, attitudes, and standards of conduct. The two-year-old knows that certain acts are wrong. According to Piaget and Inhelder (17), children younger than seven or eight have rigid and inflexible ideas of right and wrong, which they have learned from their parents. Piaget and Inhelder suggest that between the ages of eight and eleven a considerable number of changes occur in the moral development of children. At this time, children start to develop a sense of equality and to take into account the situation in which a wrong action occurs. Children become more flexible and realize that there are exceptions to their original strict rules of behavior; at this time, their peer groups begin to influence their conduct.

Lawrence Kohlberg (13) defines the stages of moral judgment of adults and children according to the choices made when two or more values conflict. Kohlberg considers the moral decisions that are made as well as the reasons the decisions are chosen when he identifies the stages in moral development. At Stages 1 and 2, Kohlberg's "preconventional" level, a child responds to external, concrete consequences. During Stage 1, a child chooses to be good, or to obey rules in order to escape physical punishment. During Stage 2, a child obeys or conforms in order to obtain rewards. Kohlberg's stages and children's ages cannot be equated because some people progress more rapidly through the sequence. However, Stages 1 and 2 apparently dominate most children's behavior during the primary years.

At Stages 3 and 4, Kohlberg's "conventional" level, a child is concerned with meeting the external social expectations of family, group, or nation. During Stage 3, a child desires social approval and consequently makes decisions according to the expectations of people who are important to the child. Stage 4 has a law-and-order orientation; a child conforms because of a high regard for social order and for patriotic duty. Although one stage builds on another and the transition between stages is gradual. Stage-3 behaviors usually begin in the upper elementary grades, and Stage-4 behaviors usually emerge in adolescence.

Stages 5 and 6 (which may be incorporated into a single stage) are at the "postconventional," autonomous, or principled level. At this level, a person establishes his or her own moral values. At Stage 5, a person responds to equal rights and consequently avoids violating the rights of others. At Stage 6, an individual conforms to his or her inner beliefs in order to avoid self-condemnation. Kohlberg estimates that only 25 percent of the population moves on in late adolescence or adulthood to a morality of equal rights, justice, and internal commitment to the principles of conscience.

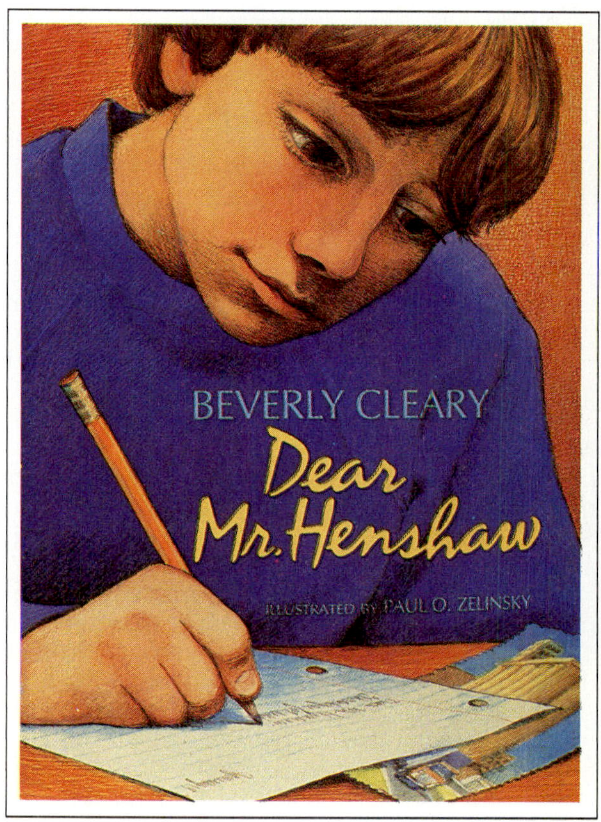

Writing to an author helps a boy accept his parents' divorce. (From *Dear Mr. Henshaw*, by Beverly Cleary, illustrated by Paul O. Zelinsky. Copyright © 1983 by Beverly Cleary. By permission of Morrow Jr. Books, a division of William Morrow and Company.)

THROUGH THE EYES OF A JOURNAL PUBLISHER

Tapping Professional Resources

SUSANNE F. CANAVAN and HIRAM HOWARD own Christopher-Gordon Publishers, Inc., publishers of the children's literature journal *The New Advocate* as well as professional books for educators.

FOR MANY EDUCATORS, journals represent important professional resources. These diverse publications keep them in touch with many different parts of their fields. Journals offer educators the opportunities to examine the in-progress work of researchers; to take one-on-one tours of colleagues' classrooms thousands of miles or whole cultures away; and to consider differing viewpoints on various "hot topics." They may also inspire, frustrate, or motivate. Journals invite involvement, either emotionally or intellectually.

If journals have a mission, or focus, (and most do have at least a general editorial policy), it is the vision of the editor, within the framework of parameters established jointly with the publisher, and not that of the publisher that should be the driving force. *The New Advocate* is fortunate to have Joel Taxel as its editor. His integrity and vision have been primary forces in establishing and maintaining the journal's quality. Since the journal exists in a changing world, readership needs evolve. We all need to be constantly aware of change—not for itself, but as a reflection of the dynamic nature of education in general and children's literature in particular. This is not always easy, but it is something that has to be dealt with in any publishing endeavor.

The New Advocate intentionally does not examine research; rather it focuses on enrichment in experience and practice and on using children's books effectively and with enjoyment in

Kohlberg suggested that a Stage 7 in moral development is the highest level of ethical and religious thinking. He refers to this stage as one of qualitatively new insight and perspective, in which a person experiences wholeness—a union with nature, a deity, and the cosmos. Although Kohlberg recognizes Stage 7 as an aspiration rather than as a complete possibility, he maintains that Stage-7 behaviors support individuals through experiences of suffering, injustice, and death.

Children's literature contains numerous moments of crisis, when characters make moral decisions and contemplate the reasons for their decisions. Although Kohlberg does not apply his stages of moral development to children's literature, both Donna Norton (16) and Cheryl Gosa (11) have developed such applications. Norton used Kohlberg's stages of moral development for evaluating the moral decisions of characters in biographical literature. Gosa maintains that Kohlberg's stages are appropriate as guidelines for categorizing and evaluating the moral decisions of characters in realistic fiction. If adults expect children to understand the decision-making process of characters in a story, Gosa asserts, they should be aware of the level of the decision that the characters are making and consider whether or not the children are at a stage when they can appreciate that decision. Otherwise, she contends, "fiction containing. . .high level decisions [will be] meaningless for early character development. . .and beyond the level of their readers" (p. 530).

Students of children's literature may find it valuable to consider the stages of moral decisions represented by the characters in children's books when selecting literature for use with children. Chart 1–5 identifies Kohlberg's stages of moral development and lists decisions made by characters in books written for children from approximately age four through age twelve. As can be seen from the chart, the only book in this group that relies on Stage-6 decision-making processes is *Jacob Have I Loved,* which was written for older

the classroom. Our readers particularly like articles by and about children's writers and illustrators (so do we), particularly pieces that offer some insights into the creative process, some glimpses behind the scenes as it were. Readers also respond to concept and theme pieces, in which issues such as censorship, the role of reading tests, or cultural literacy are discussed. *The New Advocate* welcomes thoughtful teachers' insights and experiences in practical reflections.

With journals, it is possible to have a much closer relationship with readers than with books. If we were to try to characterize reader response to *The New Advocate,* the words that come immediately to mind are *personal* and *stimulating*. On the one hand, it's lovely to hear how much people enjoy certain articles or issues, but we'll also find out as quickly if something is not to their liking. What's good about this, though, is that the journal can be responsive to these likes and dislikes. And, we want to hear from people because it helps us do our jobs better.

In all our years of publishing, we have never experienced such immediate or enthusiastic feedback. We have talked to people who read each issue cover to cover, making copious notes in the margin. Some school districts personnel have told us that they regularly xerox copies of articles to hand out to teachers, while others purchase single copies or subscriptions for their school libraries. It's very gratifying to know that the journal is being used and to be told how helpful it is.

Publishing a journal is nothing like publishing a book. It is always immediate, ongoing, and persistent. It is never *not* a part of our thinking. Since we are likely to be working on more than one issue at a time, juggling multiple (sometimes conflicting) priorities is part of everyday life. Most readers rarely are aware of this behind-the-scenes activity. *The New Advocate* has enabled us to feel much closer to educators, to be more closely involved, which is not such a bad thing. And as a couple of English literature majors, the journal has been fun too. We're proud to be the publishers.

readers. Stage-7 decisions were not found in the books. Decision-making processes may be used for discussions in which children consider the options open to the characters and ways they might have responded in similar circumstances.

Suggested Activities for Understanding the Child and Children's Literature

- ☐ Listen to the language of several children who are the same age. Do you notice any differences in their language development? Are these differences similar to those identified by Walter Loban (14, p. 7)?
- ☐ Select several books, such as Eve Rice's *Oh Lewis,* to encourage young children to identify familiar actions in books. Share these with a few preschool children and let them interact orally with the text.
- ☐ Ask several children how school and reading literature could be made more enjoyable. Compare the responses of students in different grades.
- ☐ Select several books that you believe would stimulate children's language development. Present the books and your rationales for choosing them.
- ☐ With a group of your peers, compile a list of picture books that would be useful when developing one of the following cognitive skills: observing, comparing, hypothesizing, organizing, summarizing, applying, and criticizing. Share your findings with your class.
- ☐ Read several books in which young children must overcome such problems as jealousy, fear, or anger. Compare the ways the authors have allowed the children to handle their problems. Do the feelings seem normal and natural? Is more than one aspect of a feeling developed? Are options shown for handling each emotion?

CHART 1–5
Decision making in realistic fiction

Kohlberg's Stages of Moral Development	Ages 4–7 *Send Wendell* by Genevieve Gray	Ages 6–8 *Benjie on His Own* by Joan M. Lexau	Ages 8–10 *Tales of a Fourth Grade Nothing* by Judy Blume	Ages 10+ *Jacob Have I Loved* by Katherine Paterson
1 **Premoral Level** *Stage I:* A punishment and obedience orientation. Rules are obeyed to avoid punishment.		Benjie obeys the big boys; he turns his pockets out to show them he has no money; he is very frightened.	Three-year-old Fudge eats to avoid punishment. Nine-year-old Peter believes Fudge would behave if he were punished. Father allows Fudge in commercial to keep his firm's account.	
Stage II: Naive instrumental hedonism. A child conforms in order to obtain rewards.			Peter obeys his mother and tricks Fudge so they can go to lunch. Fudge stops complaining when he gets popcorn. Peter's puppy is a reward for his good behavior.	
2 **Level of Morality of Conventional Role Conformity.** *Stage III:* A good-boy morality of maintaining good relations. A child conforms to avoid disapproval.	Six-year-old Wendell happily goes on errands because he loves Mama and likes to help her.	Benjie does not want his grandmother to walk him home after school but he puts up with it, Benjie promises to be good while his grandmother is in the hospital.	Peter does not want to share his room but knows there is no point in arguing with his mother. Peter says thank you for a gift he does not like.	Louise takes off her dirty overalls rather than argue with her grandmother.
Stage IV: An authority maintaining morality. A child conforms to avoid censure by authorities and resulting guilt.	Wendell's self-esteem increases as his uncle recognizes his worth. He now says he is busy and suggests they send someone else.			
3 **Level of Morality of Self-Accepted Principles.** *Stage V:* A morality of contract. A duty is defined in terms of contract and general avoidance of violation of the rights of others.		Benjie wants to ask his grandmother to wait for him but does not because he knows it would worry her. Benjie laughs because he knows his grandmother is trying to cheer him up.		Louise expects her teacher to defend and explain her position. She is surprised and hurt when he does not. Louise does not talk back to her grandmother because such behavior is disrespectful to those who are older.
Stage VI: A morality of individual principles of conscience. A child conforms to avoid self-condemnation.				Louise suggests that Christmas be cancelled because people are suffering and dying in World War II. Her classmates object; they do not understand her principles.

References

1 Alexander, J. Estill, and Ronald Claude Filler. *Attitudes and Reading*. Newark, Del.: International Reading Assn., 1976.

2 Bartel, Nettie. "Assessing and Remediating Problems in Language Development." In *Teaching Children with Learning and Behavior Problems,* edited by Donald Hammill and Nettie Bartel. Boston: Allyn & Bacon, 1975.

3 Bernstein, Joanne. *Books to Help Children Cope with Separation and Loss*. New York: Bowker, 1977.

4 Braga, Laurie, and Joseph Braga. *Learning and Growing: A Guide to Child Development*. Englewood Cliffs, N.J.: Prentice-Hall, 1975.

5 Braine, Martin. "The Ontogeny of English Phrase Structure: The First Phase." In *Readings in Language Development,* edited by Lois Bloom. New York: John Wiley, 1978.

6 Brown, Roger. *A First Language/The Early Stages*. Cambridge, Mass.: Harvard Univ. Press, 1973.

7 Burke, Eileen M. *Early Childhood Literature: For Love of Child and Book*. Boston: Allyn & Bacon, 1986.

8 Cullinan, Bernice E. "Books in the Life of the Young Child." In *Literature and Young Children,* edited by Bernice Cullinan and Carolyn Carmichael. Urbana, Ill.: National Council of Teachers of English, 1977.

9 Gage, N. L., and David C. Berliner. *Educational Psychology*. Chicago: Rand McNally, 1979.

10 Glazer, Joan. *Children's Literature for Early Childhood*. Columbus, Ohio: Merrill, 1981.

11 Gosa, Cheryl. "Moral Development in Current Fiction for Children and Young Adults." *Language Arts* 54 (May 1977): 529–536.

12 Hendrick, Joanne. *The Whole Child*. 4th ed. Columbus, Ohio: Merrill, 1988.

13 Kohlberg, Lawrence. *Essays on Moral Development: The Philosophy of Moral Development*. New York: Harper & Row, 1981.

14 Loban, Walter. *Language Development: Kindergarten Through Grade Twelve*. Urbana, Ill.: National Council of Teachers of English, 1976.

15 Mussen, Paul Henry, John Janeway Conger, and Jerome Kagan. *Child Development and Personality*. New York: Harper & Row, 1979.

16 Norton, Donna. "Moral Stages of Children's Biographical Literature: 1800s–1900s." *Vitae Scholasticae*. (Fall 1986).

17 Piaget, Jean, and B. Inhelder. *The Psychology of the Child*. New York: Basic Books, 1969.

18 Rochman, Hazel. "Booktalking: Going Global." *The Horn Book* (January–February 1989): 30–35.

19 Rudman, Masha Kabakow, and Anna Markus Pearce. *For Love of Reading: A Parent's Guide to Encouraging Young Readers from Infancy Through Age 5*. Mount Vernon, N.Y.: Consumers Union, 1988.

20 Sarafino, Edward P., and James W. Armstrong. *Child and Adolescent Development*. Glenview, Ill.: Scott, Foresman, 1980.

21 Shaffer, David R. *Developmental Psychology: Childhood and Adolescence*. 2d ed. Pacific Grove, Calif.: Brooks/Cole, 1989.

CHILDREN'S LITERATURE*

Aardema, Verna. *Bringing the Rain to Kapiti Plain*. Illustrated by Beatriz Vidal. Dial, 1981.
———. *Who's in Rabbit's House?* Illustrated by Leo and Diane Dillon. Dial, 1977.
———. *Why Mosquitoes Buzz in People's Ears: A West African Tale*. Illustrated by Leo and Diane Dillon. Dial, 1975.
Adoff, Arnold. *All of the Colors of the Race*. Illustrated by John Steptoe. Lothrop, Lee & Shepard, 1982.
———. *Black Is Warm Is Tan*. Harper & Row, 1973.
———. *Malcolm X*. Crowell, 1970.
———, ed. *My Black Me: A Beginning Book of Black Poetry*. Dutton, 1974.
Ahlberg, Janet, and Allen Ahlberg. *Peek-a-boo!* Viking, 1981.
Alcock, Vivien. *The Trial of Anna Cotman*. Delacorte, 1990.
Alexander, Lloyd. *Westmark*. Dutton, 1981.
Alexander, Martha. *Nobody Asked Me If I Wanted a Baby Sister*. Dial, 1971.
———. *Out! Out! Out!* Dial, 1968.
Allard, Harry. *Miss Nelson Is Missing*. Illustrated by James Marshall. Houghton Mifflin, 1977.
Andry, Andrew, and Steven Schepp. *How Babies Are Made*. Time-Life, 1968.
Anholt, Catherine. *Truffles in Trouble*. Little, Brown, 1987.
———. *Truffles Is Sick*. Little, Brown, 1987.
Anno, Mitsumaso, ed. *Anno's Aesop: A Book of Fables by Aesop and Mr. Fox*. Orchard, 1989.
———. *Anno's Britain*. Philomel, 1982.
———. *Anno's Counting Book*. Crowell, 1977.
———. *Anno's Italy*. Collins, 1980.
———. *Anno's Math Games II*. Philomel, 1989.
———. *Anno's U.S.A.* Philomel, 1983.
Apfel, Necia H. *Nebulae: The Birth & Death of Stars*. Lothrop, Lee & Shepard, 1988.
Aragon, Jane Chelsea. *Winter Harvest*. Illustrated by Leslie Baker. Little, Brown, 1988.
Arkhurst, Joyce Cooper. *The Adventures of Spider*. Illustrated by Jerry Pinkney. Little, Brown, 1964.
Arnold, Caroline. *Saving the Peregrine Falcon*. Photographed by Richard R. Hewett. Carolrhoda, 1985.
Arnosky, Jim. *Flies in the Water, Fish in the Air*. Lothrop, Lee & Shepard, 1986.
———. *Freshwater Fish and Fishing*. Four Winds, 1982.

*Most of these titles are annotated and discussed in depth in later chapters.

———. *Sketching Outdoors in Summer*. Lothrop, Lee & Shepard, 1988.
Asian Cultural Centre for UNESCO. *Folktales from Asia for Children Everywhere*. 1977, 1978, 1979.
Ayal, Ora. *Ugbu*. Harper & Row, 1979.
Aylesworth, Jim. *One Crow: A Counting Rhyme*. Illustrated by Ruth Young. Lippincott, 1988.
Banchek, Linda. *Snake In, Snake Out*. Crowell, 1978.
Bang, Molly. *Ten, Nine, Eight*. Greenwillow, 1983.
Banish, Roslyn. *Let Me Tell You About My Baby*. Harper & Row, 1988.
Barry, Scott. *The Kingdom of Wolves*. Putnam, 1979.
Barton, Byron. *Airport*. Crowell, 1982.
———. *I Want to Be an Astronaut*. Crowell, 1988.
———. *Machines at Work*. Crowell, 1987.
Bauer, Marion Dane. *On My Honor*. Houghton Mifflin, 1986.
Baylor, Byrd. *The Best Town in the World*. Scribner's Sons, 1983.
Bellville, Cheryl Walsh. *Rodeo*. Carolrhoda, 1985.
Benjamin, Carol Lea. *The Wicked Stepdog*. Crowell, 1982.
Bennett, Jill. *Tiny Tim: Verses for Children*. Illustrated by Helen Oxenbury. Delacorte, 1982.
Beowulf. Translated by Kevin Crossley-Holand. Illustrated by Charles Keeping. Oxford Univ. Press, 1984.
Berenstain, Stan, and Janice Berenstain. *Old Hat, New Hat*. Random House, 1970.
Berenzy, Alix. *A Frog Prince*. H. Holt, 1989.
Berger, Terry. *I Have Feelings*. Human Science, 1971.
———, and Alice Kandell. *Ben's ABC Day*. Lothrop, Lee & Shepard, 1982.
Bess, Clayton. *Story for a Black Night*. Houghton Mifflin, 1982.
Blake, Quentin. *Quentin Blake's ABC*. Knopf, 1989.
Blumberg, Rhoda. *Commodore Perry in the Land of the Shogun*. Lothrop, Lee & Shepard, 1985.
———. *The Incredible Journey of Lewis & Clark*. Lothrop, Lee & Shepard, 1987.
Blume, Judy. *Are You There, God? It's Me, Margaret*. Bradbury, 1970.
———. *It's Not the End of the World*. Bradbury, 1972.
———. *The One in the Middle Is the Green Kangaroo*. Bradbury, 1981.
———. *Tales of a Fourth Grade Nothing*. Dutton, 1972.
Bonsall, Crosby. *It's Mine—A Greedy Book*. Harper & Row, 1964.
Brandenberg, Aliki. *The Two of Them*. Morrow, 1979.

Branscum, Robbie. *The Saving of P.S.* Doubleday, 1977.
Brenner, Martha. *Fireworks Tonight!* Hastings House, 1983.
Brett, Jan. *Beauty and the Beast.* Clarion, 1989.
———. *Goldilocks and the Three Bears.* Dodd, Mead, 1987.
Briggs, Raymond. *The Snowman.* Random House, 1978.
British Museum of Natural History. *Man's Place in Evolution.* Cambridge, 1981.
Brittain, Bill. *The Wish Giver.* Illustrated by Andrew Glass. Harper & Row, 1983.
Brooks, Bruce. *The Moves Make the Man.* Harper & Row, 1984.
Brown, Marc. *Arthur's Baby.* Little, Brown, 1987.
Brown, Margaret Wise. *The Runaway Bunny.* Harper & Row, 1972.
Bryan, Ashley. *The Cat's Purr.* Atheneum, 1985.
Bulla, Clyde. *Keep Running, Allen!* Crowell, 1978.
Bunting, Eve. *Ghost's Hour, Spook's Hour.* Illustrated by Donald Carrick. Houghton Mifflin, 1987.
———. *The Mother's Day Mice.* Illustrated by Jan Brett. Clarion, 1986.
———. *The Wednesday Surprise.* Illustrated by Donald Carrick. Clarion, 1989.
Burnett, Frances Hodgson. *The Secret Garden.* Illustrated by Tasha Tudor. Lippincott, 1909, 1962.
Burningham, John. *The Rabbit.* Crowell, 1975.
———. *The Snow.* Crowell, 1975.
Burton, Virginia Lee. *Mike Mulligan and His Steam Shovel.* Houghton Mifflin, 1939.
———. *The Little House.* Houghton Mifflin, 1942.
Busch, Phyllis. *Cactus in the Desert.* Crowell, 1979.
Byars, Betsy. *The Animal, the Vegetable, and John D. Jones.* Illustrated by Ruth Sanderson. Delacorte, 1982.
———. *The Cybil War.* Viking, 1981.
Callen, Larry. *Who Kidnapped the Sheriff? Tales from Tickfaw.* Illustrated by Stephen Gammell. Little, Brown, 1985.
Campbell, Rod. *Dear Zoo.* Four Winds, 1982.
Carle, Eric. *Do You Want to Be My Friend?* Crowell, 1971.
———. *Let's Paint a Rainbow.* Philomel, 1982.
———. *The Mixed-up Chameleon.* Crowell, 1975.
———. *My Very First Book of Colors.* Crowell, 1974.
———. *My Very First Book of Numbers.* Crowell, 1974.
———. *My Very First Book of Shapes.* Crowell, 1974.
———. *The Very Busy Spider.* Putnam, 1985.
Carlstrom, Nancy. *Jesse Bear, What Will You Wear?* Illustrated by Bruce Degen. Macmillan, 1986.
Cauley, Lorinda Bryan. *Goldilocks and the Three Bears.* Putnam, 1981.
Cazet, Denys. *A Fish in His Pocket.* Watts, 1987.
Chorao, Kay. *The Baby's Lap Book.* Dutton, 1977.
Christelow, Eileen. *Five Little Monkeys Jumping on the Bed.* Clarion, 1989.
Cleary, Beverly. *Dear Mr. Henshaw.* Illustrated by Paul O. Zelinsky. Morrow, 1983.
———. *A Girl from Yamhill: A Memoir.* Morrow, 1988.
———. *Ramona and Her Father.* Illustrated by Alan Tiegreen. Morrow, 1977.
———. *Ramona Quimby, Age 8.* Morrow, 1981.
Cleaver, Vera, and Bill Cleaver. *Me Too.* Lippincott, 1973.
Cobb, Vicki, and Kathy Darling. *Bet You Can't! Science Impossibilities to Fool You.* Illustrated by Martha Weston. Lothrop, Lee & Shepard, 1980.
Cohen, Miriam. *Best Friends.* Macmillan, 1971.
———. *Will I Have a Friend?* Macmillan, 1971.
Cole, Brock. *The Goats.* Farrar, Straus & Giroux, 1987.
Collington, Peter. *The Angel and the Soldier Boy.* Knopf, 1987.
Conly, Jane Leslie. *Racso and the Rats of NIMH.* Harper & Row, 1986.
Cooper, Susan. *Seaward.* Atheneum, 1983.
Corbett, W. J. *The Song of Pentecost.* Illustrated by Martin Ursell. Dutton, 1983.
Crews, Donald. *Freight Train.* Greenwillow, 1978.
———. *Harbor.* Greenwillow, 1982.
Cristini, Ermanno, and Luigi Puricelli. *In the Pond.* Alphabet, 1984.
Dabcovich, Lydia. *Sleepy Bear.* Dutton, 1982.
Dallinger, Jane. *Grasshoppers.* Photographed by Uko Sato. Lerner, 1981.
Day, Alexandra. *Frank and Ernest Play Ball.* Scholastic, 1990.
de Brunhoff, Laurent. *Babar's Book of Color.* Random House, 1984.
Delessert, Etienne. *Beauty and the Beast.* Creative Education, 1984.
Delton, Judy. *Kitty in the Middle.* Dell, 1980.
de Paola, Tomie. *The Art Lesson.* Putnam's, 1989.
———. *The Clown of God.* Harcourt Brace Jovanovich, 1978.
———. *Fin M'Coul: The Giant of Knockmany Hill.* Holiday House, 1981.
———. *The Hunter and the Animals: A Wordless Picture Book.* Holiday House, 1981.
———. *The Legend of the Bluebonnet.* Putnam, 1983.
———. *Pancakes for Breakfast.* Harcourt Brace Jovanovich, 1978.
———. *The Quicksand Book.* Holiday House, 1977.
Dodds, Dayle Ann. *Wheel Away!* Illustrated by Thatcher Hurd. Harper & Row, 1989.
Dubanevich, Arlene. *Pigs in Hiding.* Four Winds, 1983.
Duke, Kate. *Bedtime.* Dutton, 1986.
———. *Clean-up Day.* Dutton, 1986.
Duvoisin, Roger. *See What I Am.* Lothrop, Lee & Shepard, 1974.
Ehlert, Lois, *Color Zoo.* Lippincott, 1989.
Ehrlich, Amy. *Leo, Zack and Emmie.* Dial, 1981.
Ellis, Mel. *The Wild Horse Killers.* Holt, Rinehart & Winston, 1976.
Emberley, Barbara. *Drummer Hoff.* Illustrated by Ed Emberley. Prentice-Hall, 1967.
Emberley, Ed. *Ed Emberley's ABC.* Little, Brown, 1978.
Emberley, Rebecca. *City Sounds.* Little, Brown, 1989.
Engel, Diana. *Josephina Hates Her Name.* Morrow, 1989.
Ernst, Lisa Campbell. *When Bluebell Sang.* Bradbury, 1989.
Facklam, Margery. *Wild Animals, Gentle Women.* Harcourt Brace Jovanovich, 1978.
Fassler, Joan. *Howie Helps Himself.* Illustrated by Joe Lasker. Whitman, 1975.
Feelings, Muriel. *Moja Means One: Swahili Counting Book.* Illustrated by Tom Feelings. Dial, 1971.
Fine, Anne. *My War with Goggle-Eyes.* Little, Brown, 1989.
Fleischman, Sid. *The Scarebird.* Greenwillow, 1988.
Flournoy, Valerie. *The Patchwork Quilt.* Illustrated by Jerry Pinkney. Dial, 1985.
Forbes, Esther. *Johnny Tremain.* Illustrated by Lynd Ward. Houghton Mifflin, 1943.
Fowler, Susi. *When Summer Ends.* Illustrated by Marisabina Russo. Greenwillow, 1989.
Fox, Mary. *Women Astronauts: Aboard the Shuttle.* Messner, 1984.
Fox, Mem. *Hattie and the Fox.* Illustrated by Patricia Mullins. Bradbury, 1987.
Fox, Paula. *One-Eyed Cat.* Bradbury, 1984.
Freedman, Russell. *Lincoln: A Photobiography.* Houghton Mifflin, 1987.

Friedman, Ina R. *How My Parents Learned to Eat*. Illustrated by Allen Say. Houghton Mifflin, 1987.
Fritz, Jean. *The Double Life of Pocahontas*. Illustrated by Ed Young. Putnam, 1983.
———. *Make Way for Sam Houston*. Illustrated by Elise Primavera. Putnam, 1986.
Gág, Wanda. *Millions of Cats*. Coward-McCann, 1928.
Galdone, Paul. *The Amazing Pig: An Old Hungarian Tale*. Houghton Mifflin, 1981.
———. *Cinderella*. McGraw-Hill, 1978.
———. *The Gingerbread Boy*. Seabury, 1975.
———. *The Greedy Old Fat Man*. Houghton Mifflin, 1983.
———. *The Little Red Hen*. Houghton Mifflin, 1973.
———. *Puss in Boots*. Houghton Mifflin, 1976.
———. *The Three Billy Goats Gruff*. Houghton Mifflin, 1973.
———. *What's in Fox's Sack? An Old English Tale*. Clarion, 1982.
Galler, Helga. *Little Nerino*. Neugebauer, 1982.
Gammell, Stephen. *Wake Up, Bear. . . It's Christmas!* Lothrop, Lee & Shepard, 1981.
Gauch, Patricia Lee. *Christina Katerina and the Time She Quit the Family*. Illustrated by Elise Primavera. Putnam, 1987.
George, Jean Craighead. *My Side of the Mountain*. Dutton, 1975.
Giff, Patricia. *Today Was a Terrible Day*. Viking, 1980.
Giganti, Paul, Jr. *How Many Snails? A Counting Book*. Illustrated by Donald Crews. Greenwillow, 1988.
Gilchrist, Theo. *Halfway up the Mountain*. Lippincott, 1978.
Ginsburg, Mirra. *How the Sun Was Brought Back to the Sky*. Macmillan, 1975.
Goble, Paul. *The Girl Who Loved Wild Horses*. Bradbury, 1978.
———. *Iktomi and the Berries*. Watts, 1989.
Goffstein, M. B. *Family Scrapbook*. Farrar, Straus & Giroux, 1978.
Goodall, John S. *Paddy Under Water*. Atheneum, 1984.
———. *The Story of an English Village*. Atheneum, 1979.
———. *The Story of a Main Street*. Macmillan, 1987.
Grahame, Kenneth. *The Wind in the Willows*. Illustrated by E. H. Shepard. Scribner's Sons, 1908, 1940.
Gray, Genevieve. *Send Wendell*. Illustrated by Symeon Shimin. McGraw-Hill, 1974.
Greenberg, Barbara. *The Bravest Babysitter*. Dial, 1977.
Greenberg, Jan. *The Iceberg and Its Shadow*. Farrar, Straus & Giroux, 1980.
Greene, Carol. *Hinny Winny Bunco*. Illustrated by Jeanette Winter. Harper & Row, 1982.
Gretz, Susanna. *The Bears Who Went to the Seaside*. Follett, 1973.
Griego, Margot C., Betsy L. Bucks, Sharon S. Gilbert, and Laurel H. Kimball. *Tortillitas Para Mama*. Illustrated by Barbara Cooney. Holt, Rinehart & Winston, 1981.
Griffith, Helen V. *Grandaddy's Place*. Illustrated by James Stevenson. Greenwillow, 1987.
Grimm, Brothers. *Hansel and Gretel*. Retold by Rika Lesser. Illustrated by Paul O. Zelinsky. Dodd Mead, 1984.
Hadithi, Mwenye. *Crafty Chameleon*. Illustrated by Adrienne Kennaway. Little, Brown, 1987.
———. *Greedy Zebra*. Illustrated by Adrienne Kennaway. Little, Brown, 1984.
Hague, Kathleen, and Michael Hague. *The Man Who Kept House*. Harcourt Brace Jovanovich, 1981.
Hague, Michael. *Beauty and the Beast*. H. Holt, 1983.
Hale, Sarah Josepha. *Mary Had a Little Lamb*. Illustrated by Tomie de Paola. Holiday, 1984.
Hall, Lynn. *Danza!* Scribner's Sons, 1981.
Hayes, Sarah. *This Is the Bear*. Illustrated by Helen Craig. Lippincott, 1986.
Henkes, Kevin. *Jessica*. Greenwillow, 1989.
Hest, Amy. *The Crack-of-Dawn Walkers*. Illustrated by Amy Schwartz. Macmillan, 1984.
———. *The Purple Coat*. Illustrated by Amy Schwartz. Four Winds, 1986.
Highwater, Jamake. *Anpao—An American Indian Odyssey*. Harper & Row, 1980.
Hill, Eric. *Spot's Birthday Party*. Putnam, 1981.
———. *Spot's First Walk*. Putnam, 1981.
———. *Spot Goes to the Beach*. Putnam, 1985.
———. *Spot Goes to School*. Putnam, 1984.
Hirschi, Ron. *Who Lives on. . .the Prairie?* Photographs by Galen Burrell. Putnam, 1989.
Hoban, Russell. *Best Friends for Frances*. Harper & Row, 1976.
———. *The Little Brute Family*. Macmillan, 1966.
———. *Nothing to Do*. Harper & Row, 1964.
Hoban, Tana. *Circles, Triangles, and Squares*. Macmillan, 1974.
———. *Is It Red? Is It Yellow? Is It Blue?* Greenwillow, 1978.
———. *Look Again!* Macmillan, 1971.
———. *Look! Look! Look!* Greenwillow, 1988.
———. *Of Colors and Things*. Greenwillow, 1989.
———. *1, 2, 3*. Greenwillow, 1984.
———. *Round & Round & Round*. Greenwillow, 1983.
———. *Shapes, Shapes, Shapes*. Greenwillow, 1986.
———. *Take Another Look*. Greenwillow, 1981.
———. *Twenty-Six Letters and Ninety-Nine Cents*. Greenwillow, 1987.
———. *What Is It?* Greenwillow, 1984.
Hoberman, Mary Ann. *Mr. and Mrs. Muddle*. Illustrated by Catharine O'Neill. Little, Brown, 1988.
Hodges, Margaret. *Saint George and the Dragon*. Illustrated by Trina Schart Hyman. Little, Brown, 1984.
Holzenthaler, Jean. *My Hands Can*. Dutton, 1978.
Howe, James. *The Hospital Book*. Photos by Mal Warshaw. Crown, 1981.
———. *There's a Monster Under My Bed*. Atheneum, 1986.
Hughes, Dean. *Family Pose*. Atheneum, 1989.
Hughes, Shirley. *Dogger*. Bodley Head, 1977.
Hurd, Edith Thacher. *I Dance in My Red Pajamas*. Illustrated by Emily Arnold McCully. Harper & Row, 1982.
Hurmence, Belinda. *A Girl Called Boy*. Clarion, 1982.
Hutchins, Pat. *Changes, Changes*. Macmillan, 1971.
———. *Rosie's Walk*. Macmillan, 1968.
———. *The Very Worst Monster*. Greenwillow, 1985.
———. *Where's the Baby?* Greenwillow, 1988.
———. *Which Witch Is Which?* Greenwillow, 1989.
Hutchinson, Veronica. *Henny Penny*. Little, Brown, 1976.
Hutton, Warwick. *Beauty and the Beast*. Atheneum, 1985.
Ichikawa, Satomi. *Nora's Castle*. Putnam, 1986.
Isele, Elizabeth. *The Frog Princess*. Illustrated by Michael Hague. Crowell, 1984.
Isenbart, Hans-Heinrich. *A Duckling Is Born*. Photographed by Othmar Baumli. Putnam, 1981.
Isenberg, Barbara, and Marjorie Jaffe. *Albert the Running Bear's Exercise Book*. Illustrated by Diane de Groat. Clarion, 1984.
Ivimey, John. *The Complete Story of the Three Blind Mice*. Illustrated by Paul Galdone. Clarion, 1987.
Jaspersohn, William. *Magazine: Behind the Scenes at Sports Illustrated*. Little, Brown, 1983.

Johnson, Angela. *Tell Me a Story, Mama*. Illustrated by David Soman. Watts, 1989.
Johnston, Tony. *Four Scary Stories*. Putnam, 1978.
Jonas, Ann. *When You Were a Baby*. Greenwillow, 1982.
Jukes, Mavis. *Like Jake and Me*. Illustrated by Lloyd Bloom. Knopf, 1984.
Keats, Ezra Jack. *Peter's Chair*. Harper & Row, 1967.
———. *Regards to the Man in the Moon*. Four Winds, 1982.
———. *The Snowy Day*. Viking, 1962.
———. *Whistle for Willie*. Viking, 1964.
Keller, Holly. *Geraldine's Big Snow*. Greenwillow, 1988.
Kellogg, Steven. *Best Friends*. Dial, 1986.
———. *A Rose for Pinkerton*. Dial, 1981.
Kennedy, Richard. *Amy's Eyes*. Illustrated by Richard Egielski. Harper & Row, 1985.
Khalsa, Dayal Kaur. *I Want a Dog*. Clarkson, 1987.
King-Smith, Dick. *Pigs Might Fly*. Illustrated by Mary Rayner. Viking, 1982.
Klein, Norma. *Girls Can Be Anything*. Dutton, 1975.
Knight, Hilary. *Hilary Knight's The Twelve Days of Christmas*. Macmillan, 1981.
Konigsburg, E. L. *Journey to an 800 Number*. Atheneum, 1982.
Kraus, Robert. *Leo the Late Bloomer*. Illustrated by Jose Aruego. Windmill, 1971.
Krauss, Ruth. *The Carrot Seed*. Harper & Row, 1945.
Langstaff, John. *Oh, A-Hunting We Will Go*. Atheneum, 1974.
Larrick, Nancy. *When the Dark Comes Dancing: A Bedtime Poetry Book*. Putnam, 1983.
Lasky, Kathryn. *The Night Journey*. Warne, 1981.
———. *Sugaring Time*. Photographs by Christopher G. Knight. Macmillan, 1983.
Lauber, Patricia. *The News About Dinosaurs*. Bradbury, 1989.
———. *Volcano: The Eruption and Healing of Mount St. Helens*. Bradbury, 1986.
Lee, Dennis. *Jelly Belly: Original Nursery Rhymes*. Harper & Row, 1985.
L'Engle, Madeleine. *A Ring of Endless Light*. Farrar, Straus & Giroux, 1980.
———. *A Swiftly Tilting Planet*. Farrar, Straus & Giroux, 1978.
Lewin, Hugh. *Jafta*. Illustrated by Lisa Kopper. Carolrhoda, 1983.
Lewis, C. S. *The Lion, the Witch, and the Wardrobe*. Macmillan, 1951.
Lexau, Joan. *Benjie on His Own*. Dial, 1970.
Lindgren, Barbro. *Sam's Ball*. Illustrated by Eva Eriksson. Morrow, 1983.
———. *Sam's Bath*. Illustrated by Eva Eriksson. Morrow, 1983.
———. *The Wild Baby*. Illustrated by Eva Eriksson. Greenwillow, 1981.
Lionni, Leo. *Let's Make Rabbits*. Pantheon, 1982.
Lisle, Janet Taylor. *Afternoon of the Elves*. Watts, 1989.
Lobel, Arnold. *Frog and Toad All Year*. Harper & Row, 1976.
———. *Grasshopper on the Road*. Harper & Row, 1978.
———. *On Market Street*. Illustrated by Anita Lobel. Greenwillow, 1981.
———, ed. *The Random House Book of Mother Goose*. Random House, 1986.
———. *Uncle Elephant*. Harper & Row, 1981.
Lowry, Lois. *Anastasia Again!* Houghton Mifflin, 1981.
———. *Number the Stars*. Houghton Mifflin, 1989.
Lunn, Janet. *The Root Cellar*. Scribner's Sons, 1983.
———. *Shadow in Hawthorn Bay*. Scribner's Sons, 1986.
McCloskey, Robert. *Lentil*. Viking, 1940.
———. *Make Way for Ducklings*. Viking, 1941.
———. *Time of Wonder*. Viking, 1957.
McCully, Emily Arnold. *New Baby*. Harper & Row, 1988.
———. *Picnic*. Harper & Row, 1984.
———. *School*. Harper & Row, 1987.
MacDonald, Suse. *Alphabatics*. Bradbury, 1986.
McDermott, Gerald. *Tim O'Toole and the Wee Folk*. Viking, 1990.
McKinley, Robin. *The Hero and the Crown*. Greenwillow, 1984.
MacLachlan, Patricia. *The Facts and Fictions of Minna Pratt*. Harper & Row, 1988.
———. *Mama One, Mama Two*. Illustrated by Ruth Lercher Bornstein. Harper & Row, 1982.
———. *Sarah, Plain and Tall*. Harper & Row, 1985.
McLeod, Emilie Warren. *The Bear's Bicycle*. Little, Brown, 1975.
McMillan, Bruce. *Here a Chick, There a Chick*. Lothrop, Lee & Shepard, 1983.
McPhail, David. *The Dream Child*. Dutton, 1985.
Magee, Doug. *Trucks You Can Count On*. Dodd Mead, 1985.
Magnus, Erica. *Old Lars*. Carolrhoda, 1984.
Mahy, Margaret. *Seventeen Kings and Forty-Two Elephants*. Illustrated by Patricia MacCarthy. Dial, 1987.
Malnig, Anita. *Where the Waves Break: Life at the Edge of the Sea*. Photographed by Jeff Rotman. Carolrhoda, 1985.
Margolis, Richard J. *Secrets of a Small Brother*. Illustrated by Donald Carrick. Macmillan, 1984.
Maris, Ron. *Are You There, Bear?* Greenwillow, 1985.
Mark, Jan. *Fun*. Illustrated by Michael Foreman. Viking Kestrel, 1988.
Marshall, Edward. *Four on the Shore*. Illustrated by James Marshall. Dial, 1985.
Marshall, James. *George and Martha One Fine Day*. Houghton Mifflin, 1978.
Martin, Eva, ed. *Canadian Fairy Tales*. Illustrated by Laszlo Gal. Douglas & McIntyre, 1984.
Martin, Jacqueline. *Buzzy Bones and the Lost Quilt*. Illustrated by Stella Ormai. Lothrop, Lee & Shepard, 1988.
Martin, Rafe. *Will's Mammoth*. Illustrated by Stephen Gammell. Putnam, 1989.
Mayer, Marianna, ed. *The Twelve Dancing Princesses*. Illustrated by K. Y. Craft. Morrow, 1989.
Metropolitan Museum of Art. *Go in and out the Window*. H. Holt, 1987.
Meyer, Carolyn, and Charles Gallenkamp. *The Mystery of the Ancient Maya*. Atheneum, 1985.
Milne, A. A. *The House at Pooh Corner*. Illustrated by E. H. Shepard. Dutton, 1928, 1956.
Monjo, F. N. *The Drinking Gourd*. Harper & Row, 1969.
Moore, Clement Clarke. *The Night before Christmas*. Illustrated by Tomie de Paola. Holiday House, 1980.
Munro, Roxie. *The Inside-Outside Book of Washington D.C.* Dutton, 1987.
Murphy, Jill. *Peace at Last*. Dial, 1980.
Nance, John. *Lobo of the Tasaday*. Pantheon, 1982.
Narahashi, Keiko. *I Have a Friend*. Macmillan, 1987.
Naylor, Phyllis Reynolds. *Keeping a Christmas Secret*. Illustrated by Lena Shiffman. Atheneum, 1989.
Nesbit, E. *Melisande*. Illustrated by P. J. Lynch. Harcourt Brace Jovanovich, 1989.
Ness, Evaline. *Sam, Bangs, & Moonshine*. Holt, Rinehart & Winston, 1966.
Oakley, Graham. *The Church Mice in Action*. Atheneum, 1982.
———. *Hetty and Harriet*. Atheneum, 1982.
O'Dell, Scott. *Island of the Blue Dolphins*. Houghton Mifflin, 1960.
Oppenheim, Joanne. *Have You Seen Birds?* Illustrated by Barbara Reid. Scholastic, 1986.
Ormerod, Jan. *Sunshine*. Lothrop, Lee & Shepard, 1981.
Oxenbury, Helen. *The Checkup*. Dial, 1983.

———. *Dressing*. Simon & Schuster, 1981.
———. *Family*. Simon & Schuster, 1981.
———. *First Day at School*. Dial, 1983.
———. *Friends*. Simon & Schuster, 1981.
———. *I Can*. Random House, 1986.
———. *I See*. Random House, 1986.
———. *I Touch*. Random House, 1986.
———. *Playing*. Simon & Schuster, 1981.
———. *Working*. Simon & Schuster, 1981.
Paige, David. *A Day in the Life of a Marine Biologist*. Photographed by Roger Ruhlin. Troll Associates, 1981.
Park, Ruth. *Playing Beatie Bow*. Atheneum, 1982.
Paterson, Katherine. *Come Sing, Jimmy Jo*. Lodestar, 1985.
———. *Jacob Have I Loved*. Crowell, 1980.
Paulsen, Gary. *Dogsong*. Bradbury, 1985.
———. *Hatchet*. Bradbury, 1987.
———. *The Winter Room*, Orchard, 1989.
———. *The Voyage of the Frog*. Orchard, 1989.
Peet, Bill. *Bill Peet: An Autobiography*. Houghton Mifflin, 1989.
Peters, Lisa Westberg. *The Sun, the Wind and the Rain*. Illustrated by Ted Rand. H. Holt, 1988.
Pluckrose, Henry. *Capacity*. Photographed by Chris Fairclough. Watts, 1988.
———. *Length*. Photographed by Chris Fairclough. Watts, 1988.
———. *Sorting*. Photographed by Chris Fairclough. Watts, 1988.
Pomerantz, Charlotte. *Flap Your Wings and Try*. Illustrated by Nancy Tafuri. Greenwillow, 1989.
Porte, Barbara. *Harry in Trouble*. Illustrated by Yossi Abolafin. Greenwillow, 1989.
Potter, Beatrix. *The Tale of Peter Rabbit*. Warne, 1902, 1986.
Preston, Edna Mitchell, and Rainey Bennett. *The Temper Tantrum Book*. Penguin, 1976.
Purdy, Carol. *Least of All*. Illustrated by Tim Arnold. Macmillan, 1987.
Rabe, Berniece. *The Balancing Girl*. Illustrated by Lillian Hoban. Dutton, 1981.
Raskin, Ellen. *The Westing Game*. Dutton, 1978.
Reid, Barbara. *Playing with Plasticine*. Morrow, 1988.
Reiss, John J. *Numbers*. Bradbury, 1971.
———. *Shapes*. Bradbury, 1974.
Rice, Eve. *Benny Bakes a Cake*. Greenwillow, 1981.
———. *Oh, Lewis!* Macmillan, 1974.
Richards, Laura E. *Tirra Lirra, Rhymes Old and New*. Illustrated by Marguerite Davis. Little, Brown, 1955.
Riskind, Mary. *Apple Is My Sign*. Houghton Mifflin, 1981.
Rockwell, Anne. *First Comes Spring*. Harper & Row, 1985.
Rockwell, Harlow. *My Dentist*. Greenwillow, 1975.
———. *My Doctor*. Macmillan, 1973.
Rogers, Fred. *Going to Day Care*. Photographed by Jim Judkis. Putnam, 1986.
———. *Going to the Doctor*. Photographed by Jim Judkis. Putnam, 1986.
———. *Making Friends*. Photographed by Jim Judkis. Putnam, 1987.
Rose, Anne. *As Right As Right Can Be*. Dial, 1976.
Rosen, Michael, ed. *We're Going on a Bear Hunt*. Illustrated by Helen Oxenbury. Macmillan, 1989.
Russo, Marisabina. *Waiting for Hannah*. Greenwillow, 1989.
Ryder, Joanne. *Inside Turtle's Shell: And Other Poems of the Field*. Illustrated by Susan Bonners. Macmillan, 1985.
———. *White Bear, Ice Bear*. Illustrated by Michael Rothman. Morrow, 1989.
Rylant, Cynthia. *Birthday Presents*. Illustrated by Sucie Stevenson. Orchard, 1987.
———. *A Blue-Eyed Daisy*. Bradbury, 1985.
———. *When I Was Young in the Mountains*. Illustrated by Diane Goode. Dutton, 1982.
Sandin, Joan. *The Long Way to a New Land*. Harper & Row, 1981.
San Souci, Robert. Retold by *The Talking Eggs: A Folktale from the American South*. Illustrated by Jerry Pinkney. Dial, 1989.
Sattler, Helen Roney. *Hominids: A Look Back at Our Ancestors*. Lothrop, Lee & Shepard, 1988.
Scarry, Richard. *Richard Scarry's The Best Word Book Ever*. Western, 1963.
———. *My First Book*. Random House, 1986.
Schlee, Ann. *Ask Me No Questions*. Holt, Rinehart & Winston, 1982.
Schotter, Roni. *Captain Snap and the Children of Vinegar Lane*. Illustrated by Marcia Sewall. Watts, 1989.
Schwartz, Alvin. *There Is a Carrot in My Ear and Other Noodle Tales*. Illustrated by Karen Ann Weinhaus. Harper & Row, 1982.
Schwartz, Amy. *Annabelle Swift, Kindergartner*. Orchard, 1988.
Schwartz, Henry. *How I Captured a Dinosaur*. Illustrated by Amy Schwartz. Watts, 1989.
Scott, Ann Herbert. *Sam*. Illustrated by Symeon Shimin. McGraw-Hill, 1967.
Selsam, Millicent. *Mushrooms*. Photographed by Jerome Wexler. Morrow, 1986.
———. *Tyrannosaurus Rex*. Harper & Row, 1978.
Selsam, Millicent, and Joyce Hunt. *Keep Looking!* Illustrated by Normand Chartier. Macmillan, 1989.
Sendak, Maurice. *Where the Wild Things Are*. Harper & Row, 1963.
Seuss, Dr. *And to Think That I Saw It on Mulberry Street*. Vanguard, 1937.
———. *The Cat in the Hat*. Beginner, 1957.
———. *Oh, the Places You'll Go!* Random House. 1990.
Sharmat, Marjorie. *The Best Valentine in the World*. Illustrated by Lilian Obligado. Holiday House, 1982.
———. *A Big Fat Enormous Lie*. Dutton, 1978.
Sheffield, Margaret, and Sheila Bewley. *Where Do Babies Come From?* Knopf, 1973.
Showers, Paul. *Look at Your Eyes*. Crowell, 1962.
Shura, Mary Francis. *The Search for Grissi*. Illustrated by Ted Lewin. Dodd Mead, 1985.
Silverstein, Shel. *A Light in the Attic*. Harper & Row, 1981.
Simon, Seymour. *Meet the Computer*. Illustrated by Barbara and Ed Emberley. Harper & Row, 1985.
———. *Storms*. Morrow, 1989.
Skorpen, Liesel M. *His Mother's Dog*. Harper & Row, 1978.
Small, David. *Eulalie and the Hopping Head*. Macmillan, 1982.
———. *Imogene's Antlers*. Crown, 1985.
Speare, Elizabeth George. *The Bronze Bow*. Houghton Mifflin, 1961.
———. *The Sign of the Beaver*. Houghton Mifflin, 1982.
Sperry, Armstrong. *Call It Courage*. Macmillan, 1940.
Stanek, Muriel. *All Alone After School*. Illustrated by Ruth Rosner. Whitman, 1985.
Staples, Suzanne Fisher. *Shabanu: Daughter of the Wind*. Knopf, 1989.
Steig, William. *Spinky Sulks*. Farrar, Straus & Giroux, 1988.
Steptoe, John. *Baby Says*. Lothrop, Lee & Shepard, 1988.
———. *Mufaro's Beautiful Daughters: An African Tale*. Lothrop, Lee & Shepard, 1987.
———. *Stevie*. Harper & Row, 1969.
———. *The Story of Jumping Mouse*. Lothrop, Lee & Shepard, 1984.
Stevens, Janet. *The House That Jack Built*. Holiday House, 1985.

Stock, Catherine. *Sophie's Knapsack*. Lothrop, Lee & Shepard, 1988.
Sutcliff, Rosemary. *Sun Horse, Moon Horse*. Illustrated by Shirley Felts. Dutton, 1978.
Tafuri, Nancy. *Early Morning in the Barn*. Greenwillow, 1983.
———. *One Wet Jacket*. Greenwillow, 1988.
———. *Two New Sneakers*. Greenwillow, 1988.
———. *Who's Counting?* Greenwillow, 1986.
Taylor, Mildred. *Let the Circle Be Unbroken*. Dial, 1981.
———. *Roll of Thunder, Hear My Cry*. Dial, 1976.
Tejima. *Fox's Dream*. Philomel, 1987.
Tobias, Tobi. *Arthur Mitchell*. Illustrated by Carol Byard. Crowell, 1975.
Turkle, Brinton. *Do Not Open*. Dutton, 1981.
Udry, Janice May. *Let's Be Enemies*. Harper & Row, 1961.
———. *What Mary Jo Shared*. Whitman, 1966.
Van Allsburg, Chris. *The Mysteries of Harris Burdick*. Houghton Mifflin, 1984.
———. *The Polar Express*. Houghton Mifflin, 1985.
———. *The Z Was Zapped*. Houghton Mifflin, 1987.
Van Leeuwen, Jean. *More Tales of Oliver Pig*. Dial, 1981.
Van Vorst, M. L. *A Norse Lullaby*. Illustrated by Margot Tomes. Lothrop, Lee & Shepard, 1988.
Vincent, Gabrielle. *Feel Better, Ernest!* Greenwillow, 1988.
———. *Smile, Ernest and Celestine*. Greenwillow, 1982.
Viorst, Judith. *Alexander and the Terrible, Horrible, No Good, Very Bad Day*. Illustrated by Ray Cruz. Atheneum, 1972.
———. *I'll Fix Anthony*. Harper & Row, 1969.
Voake, Charlotte. *Mrs. Goose's Baby*. Little, Brown, 1989.
Voight, Cynthia. *Building Blocks*. Atheneum, 1984.
———. *Dicey's Song*. Atheneum, 1982.
———. *A Solitary Blue*. Atheneum, 1983.
Waber, Bernard. *Ira Says Goodbye*. Houghton Mifflin, 1988.
———. *Ira Sleeps Over*. Houghton Mifflin, 1972.
———. *The Snake: A Very Long Story*. Houghton Mifflin, 1978.
Wagner, Jenny. *John Brown, Rose, and the Midnight Cat*. Bradbury, 1978.
Wahl, Jan. *Humphrey's Bear*. Illustrated by William Joyce. H. Holt, 1987.
Wallace, Ian. *Chin Chiang and the Dragon's Dance*. Atheneum, 1984.
Walter, Mildred Pitts. *Brother to the Wind*. Illustrated by Diane and Leo Dillon. Lothrop, Lee & Shepard, 1985.
Weiss, Nicki. *Where Does the Brown Bear Go?* Greenwillow, 1989.
Wells, Rosemary. *Max's Birthday*. Dial, 1985.
———. *Max's Breakfast*. Dial, 1985.
———. *Timothy Goes to School*. Dial, 1981.
White, E.B. *Charlotte's Web*. Harper & Row, 1952.
———. *Stuart Little*. Harper & Row, 1945.
White, Florence M. *Cesar Chavez: Man of Courage*. Garrard, 1973.
Wiesner, David. *Free Fall*. Lothrop, Lee & Shepard, 1988.
Wild, Margaret. *Mr. Nick's Knitting*. Illustrated by Dee Huxley. Harcourt Brace Jovanovich, 1988.
Wilder, Laura Ingalls, *The First Four Years*. Illustrated by Garth Williams. Harper & Row, 1971.
———. *Little House in the Big Woods*. Harper & Row, 1932.
———. *These Happy Golden Years*. Harper & Row, 1943.
Willard, Nancy. *Night Story*. Illustrated by Ilse Plume. Harcourt Brace Jovanovich, 1986.
Williams, Barbara. *Chester Chipmunk's Thanksgiving*. Dutton, 1978.
Williams, Margery. *The Velveteen Rabbit: Or How Toys Became Real*. Doubleday, 1922, 1958.
———. *The Velveteen Rabbit*. Illustrated by Ilse Plume. Godine, 1982.
———. *The Velveteen Rabbit*. Illustrated by Michael Hague. Holt, Rinehart & Winston, 1983.
———. *The Velveteen Rabbit*. Illustrated by Allen Atkinson. Knopf, 1984.
Williams, Vera B. *A Chair for My Mother*. Greenwillow, 1982.
———. *Something Special for Me*. Greenwillow, 1983.
Winter, Jeanette. *Come Out to Play*. Knopf, 1986.
Winthrop, Elizabeth. *Bear and Mrs. Duck*. Illustrated by Patience Brewster. Holiday House, 1988.
Wojciechowska, Maia. *Shadow of a Bull*. Illustrated by Alvin Smith. Atheneum, 1964.
Yabuuchi, Masayuki. *Whose Baby?* Philomel, 1985.
Yates, Elizabeth. *Amos Fortune, Free Man*. Aladdin, 1950.
———. *My Diary—My World*. Westminister, 1981.
Yolen, Jane. *The Devil's Arithmetic*. Viking Kestrel, 1988.
———. *The Lullaby Songbook*. Illustrated by Charles Mikolaycak. Harcourt Brace Jovanovich, 1986.
———. *Owl Moon*. Illustrated by John Schoenherr. Philomel, 1987.
———. *The Three Bears Rhyme Book*. Illustrated by Jane Dyer. Harcourt Brace Jovanovich, 1987.
Young, Ed. Trans. by *Lon Po Po: A Red Riding Hood Story from China*. Philomel, 1989.
Zemach, Margot. *It Could Always Be Worse*. Farrar, Straus & Giroux, 1977.
Zimmerman, H. Werner. *Henny Penny*. Scholastic, 1989.
Zolotow, Charlotte. *Big Brother*. Illustrated by Mary Chalmers. Harper & Row, 1966.
———. *My Grandson Lew*. Illustrated by William Pène du Bois. Harper & Row, 1974.
———. *The Quarreling Book*. Illustrated by Arnold Lobel. Harper & Row, 1963.
———. *William's Doll*. Illustrated by William Pène du Bois. Harper & Row, 1972.

2

The History of Children's Literature

MILESTONES IN THE HISTORY OF CHILDREN'S LITERATURE

CHILDREN AND THE FAMILY IN CHILDREN'S LITERATURE

MANY PEOPLE ARE SURPRISED TO DIScover that childhood has not always been considered an important time of life. When students of children's literature look at the beautiful books published to meet children's needs, interests, and reading levels, many are amazed to learn that not too long ago books were not written specifically for children. Changes in printing technology provided affordable books, but more important were changes in social attitudes toward children. When society looked upon children as little adults who must rapidly step into the roles of their parents, children had little time or need to read books relevant to a nonexistent childhood. When childhood began to be viewed as a special part of the human life cycle, literature written specifically for children became very important.

Within the context of human history as a whole, the history of children's literature is very short. Neither early tales told through the oral tradition nor early books were created specifically for children. When children's books were eventually written, they usually mirrored the dominant cultural values of their place and time. Thus, a study of children's literature in Western Europe and North America from the fifteenth century through contemporary times reflects both changes in society as a whole and changes in social expectations of children and the family.

Literature researchers view children's literature as a viable vehicle for studying social values and changing attitudes. Karen J. Winkler (43) maintains that the 1970s and 1980s have been characterized by an ever-increasing interest in the scholarly study of children's literature as an index to the social attitudes of a particular time. Robert Gordon Kelly's (19) "Mother Was a Lady: Self and Society in Selected American Children's Periodicals, 1865–1890," Mary Lystad's (27) *From Dr. Mather to Dr. Seuss: Two Hundred Years of American Books for Children,* and Ruth M. Phelps's (33) "A Comparison of Newbery Award Winners in the First and Last Decade of the Award (1922–31 and 1976–85)" are examples of such research. The increasing number of doctoral dissertations that critically evaluate certain aspects of children's literature also suggests the current importance of children's literature as a research subject. For example, from the 1930s until 1970, approximately two hundred dissertations covered topics related to children's literature. In contrast, the 1970s alone produced nearly eight hundred such dissertations. Several of these studies suggest the interrelatedness of social, cultural, and economic factors and the story themes and values presented in children's literature of a certain period.

MILESTONES IN THE HISTORY OF CHILDREN'S LITERATURE

This chapter first considers some milestones in the development of children's literature, then it looks at changing views of children and the family as reflected in early books for children and in more contemporary stories. Chart 2–1 provides a brief overview of the historical milestones.

The Oral Tradition

Long before the recorded history of humanity, family units and tribes shared their group traditions and values through stories told around the campfire. On every continent around the globe, ancient peoples developed folktales and mythologies that speculated about human beginnings, attempted to explain the origins of the universe and other natural phenomena, emphasized ethical truths, and transmitted history from one generation to the next. When hunters returned from their adventures, they probably told about the perils of the hunt and hostile encounters with other tribes. Heroic deeds were certainly told and retold until they became a part of a group's heritage. This tradition has existed since the first oral communication among human beings and goes back to the very roots of every civilization on earth. These tales were not told specifically to children, but children were surely present—listening, watching, learning, and remembering.

The various native peoples of North America developed mythologies expressing their reverence for the rolling prairies, lush forests, ice floes, deserts, and blue lakes of their continent. In Latin and South America, storytellers of the Yucatan Peninsula and the Andes chronicled the rise of Maya, Aztec, and Inca empires, wars of expansion, and eventually, the Spanish conquest of their homelands. Across Africa, highly respected storytellers developed a style that encouraged audiences to interact with storytellers in relating tales of dramatic heroes, personified animals, and witty tricksters. In the extremely ancient cultures of Asia, from Mesopotamia to Japan, early myths and folktales were eventually incorporated into the complex mythologies and philosophical tenets of Taoism, Confucianism, Hinduism, and Buddhism. In Europe, the earliest oral traditions of the Celts,

CHART 2–1
Historic milestones in children's literature

—	The Oral Tradition "Beowulf" "Jack the Giant Killer"
1400s	Early Books Hornbooks Caxton's Printing Press—1476
1500s	The Introduction of Chapbooks "Jack the Giant Killer"
1600s	The Puritan Influence *Spiritual Milk for Boston Babes in either England, drawn from the Breasts of both Testaments for their Souls' Nourishment* *Pilgrim's Progress*
1693	A View of Childhood Changes John Locke's *Some Thoughts Concerning Education*
1697	First Fairy Tales Written for Children Charles Perrault's *Tales of Mother Goose*
1719	Great Adventure Stories Daniel Defoe's *Robinson Crusoe* Jonathan Swift's *Gulliver's Travels*
1744	Children's Literature: A True Beginning John Newbery's *A Little Pretty Pocket Book* and *History of Little Goody-Two Shoes*
1762	Guidance of Children in Their Search for Knowledge Jean Jacques Rousseau's *Emile*
1789	Poetry About Children William Blake's *Songs of Innocence*
1800s	The Romantic Movement in Europe The Brothers Grimm Hans Christian Andersen
1800s	The Impact of Illustrators on Children's Books Walter Crane Randolph Caldecott Kate Greenaway
1860	The Victorian Influence Charlotte Yonge's *The Daisy Chain* and *The Clever Woman of the Family*
1850–1900	Childhood Seen as an Adventure, Not a Training Ground for Adulthood Fantasy Lewis Carroll's *Alice's Adventures in Wonderland* Edward Lear's *A Book of Nonsense* Adventure Robert Louis Stevenson's *Treasure Island* Howard Pyle's *The Merry Adventures of Robin Hood* Jules Verne's *Twenty Thousand Leagues under the Sea* Real People Margaret Sidney's *The Five Little Peppers and How They Grew* Louisa May Alcott's *Little Women* Johanna Spyri's *Heidi*

Franks, Saxons, Goths, Danes, and many other groups eventually influenced one another as a result of human migration, trade, and warfare; and the mythologies of ancient Greece and Rome became widely influential as the Roman Empire expanded over much of the continent.

The European oral tradition, according to Robert Leeson (22), reached its climax in the feudal era of the Middle Ages. What are often called *castle tales* and *cottage tales* provided people with literature long before those tales were widely accessible in writing or print. The ruling classes favored poetic epics about the reputed deeds of the lord of the manor or his ancestors. In the great halls of castles, minstrels or bards accompanied themselves on lyres or harps while singing tales about noble warriors, such as Beowulf and King Arthur, or ballads of chivalrous love in regal surroundings, such as those found in the French version of Cinderella.

Around cottage fires or at country fairs, humbler people had different heroes. Storytellers shared folktales about people much like the peasants themselves; people who daily confronted servitude, inscrutable natural phenomena, and unknown spiritual forces. In these tales, even the youngest or poorest person had the potential to use resourcefulness or kindness to go from rags to riches and live "happily ever after." Often, such achievement required outwitting or slaying wolves, dragons, malevolent supernatural beings, or great lords.

By whatever name they were known—bards, minstrels, or devisers of tales—the storytellers of medieval Europe were entertainers: If they did not entertain, they lost their audiences or even their meals and lodging. Consequently, they learned to tell stories that had rapid plot development and easily identifiable characters. These storytellers also possessed considerable power. Sir Philip Sidney (37), a sixteenth-century English poet, described storytellers as able to keep children away from their play and old people away from their chimney corners. Whether woven from imagination or retold from legends and stories of old, a storyteller's tales could influence the people who heard them. Thus, if a minstrel's story offended or discredited a lord, the minstrel could be punished. By the end of the fourteenth century, feudal authority sought to control the tales being told and often jailed storytellers who angered either a ruler or the church.

Today, many early European folktales, myths, and legends are considered ideal for sharing with children, but this was not the attitude of feudal Europe. Storytellers addressed audiences of all ages. A child was considered a small adult who should enter into adult life as quickly as possible, and stories primarily for young people were considered unnecessary. Consequently, the stories about giants, heroes, and simpletons that relieved the strain of adult life also entertained children. These favorite tales, which had been told and retold for hundreds of years, were eventually chosen for some of the first printed books in Europe.

The hornbook, which was used for instruction, usually contained the alphabet, numerals, and the Lord's Prayer. (Photo courtesy of The Horn Book, Inc.)

Early Printed Books

Prior to the mid-1400s, the literary heritage of Europe consisted of the oral tradition and parchment manuscripts laboriously handwritten by monks and scribes. Manuscript books were rare and costly, prized possessions of the nobles and priests, who were among the few Europeans able to read and write. To the extent that these books were meant for the young, they were usually designed to provide instruction in rhetoric, grammar, and music for the children privileged enough to attend monastery schools. Children were rarely trusted with the books themselves, and usually wrote on slates as monks dictated their lessons.

A significant event occurred in the 1450s, when the German Johannes Gutenberg discovered a practical method for using movable metal type, which made possible the mass production of books. After learning the printing process in Germany, William Caxton established England's first printing press in 1476. The use of printing presses led to the creation of hornbooks, which were printed sheets of text mounted on wood and covered with translucent animal horn. Hornbooks were used to teach reading and numbers. The books were in the shape of a paddle. They usually included the alphabet, a syllabary, numerals, and the Lord's Prayer.

Hornbooks remained popular into the 1700s, when the battledore, a lesson book made of folded paper or cardboard, became more prevalent. Like hornbooks, battledores usually contained an alphabet, numerals, and proverbs or prayers.

When William Caxton opened his printing business in 1476, most of the books used with children were not written for their interest. Instead, books for children adhered to the sentiment that young readers should read only what would improve their manners or instruct their minds. *Caxton's Book of Curtesye,* first printed in 1477 (14), contained directions for drawing readers away from vice and turning them toward virtue. Verses guided readers toward personal cleanliness (comb your hair, clean your ears, clean your nose but don't pick it), polite social interactions (look people straight in the face when speaking, don't quarrel with dogs), suitable reverence in church (kneel before the cross, don't chatter), and correct table manners (don't blow on your food or undo your girdle at the table).

The majority of books Caxton published were not meant to be read by children, but three of his publications are now considered classics in chil-

This lesson book, or battledore, was made from folded paper or cardboard. (Courtesy of The Horn Book, Inc.)

dren's literature. In 1481, Caxton published the beast fable *Reynart the Foxe* (The History of Reynard the Fox), a satire of oppression and tyranny. This tale of a clever fox who could outwit all his adversaries became popular with both adults and children.

Caxton's most important publication may be *The Book of the Subtyle Historyes and Fables of Esope* (The Fables of Aesop), which Caxton translated from a manuscript by the French monk Machault in 1484. These fables about the weaknesses of people and animals were popular with readers of various ages and are still enjoyed by children. F. J. Harvey Darton (10) maintains that Caxton's version of Aesop, "with infinitely little modernization, is the best text for children today" (p. 10). Caxton's publication in 1485 of Sir Thomas Malory's *Le Morte d'Arthur* (The Death of Arthur) preserved the legendary story of King Arthur and his knights, which has been published since in many versions suitable for young readers.

Caxton's translations, standardization of English, and literary style had a major impact upon English literature, according to Jane Bingham and Grayce Scholt (5). At least eight of Caxton's books are mentioned in the "Famous Prefaces" volume of *The Harvard Classics* (23). Cornelia Meigs et al. (31) also stress Caxton's importance in creating the first printed books in the English language. In outward form, these books were of a standard not easily equaled. The ample pages, the broad margins, and the black-letter type that suggested manuscript contributed to their beauty, dignity, and worthiness to be England's first widespread realization of her own literature.

Caxton's books were beautiful, but too expensive for the common people. Soon, however, peddlers (or "chapmen") were selling crudely printed chapbooks for pennies at markets and fairs, along with ribbons, patent medicines, and other wares. Customers could also go directly to a printer and select from large uncut sheets of as many as sixteen pages of text, which then were bound into a hardcover book.

Some of the first chapbooks were based on ballads, such as "The Two Children in the Wood," and traditional tales, such as "Jack the Giant Killer." According to Lou J. McCulloch (29), the content of chapbooks fell into the following categories: religious instruction, interpretations of the supernatural, romantic legends, ballad tales, and historic narratives. John Ashton's (3) *Chap-Books of the Eighteenth Century* includes religious titles, such as "The History of Joseph and His Brethren"

From the sixteenth to the nineteenth century, peddlers sold inexpensive chapbooks in Europe and North America. (From *Chap-Books of the Eighteenth Century* by John Ashton. Published by Chatto and Windus, 1882. From the John G. White Collection, Cleveland Public Library.)

and "The Unhappy Birth, Wicked Life, and Miserable Death of the Vile Traytor and Apostle Judas Iscariot"; traditional tales, such as "Tom Thumb" and "A True Tale of Robin Hood"; and supernatural tales, such as "The Portsmouth Ghost."

Chapbooks were extremely popular in both England and the United States during the 1700s, but their popularity rapidly declined during the early 1800s. McCulloch (29) maintains that they were especially important as forerunners to many modern literary forms: children's books, western tales, and even comic books.

The Puritan Influence

According to Jane Bingham and Grayce Scholt (5), political upheaval, religious dissent, and censorship all affected English literature in the 1600s. As printing increased and literacy spread, the British monarchy realized the power of the press. In 1637, it decreed that only London, Oxford, Cambridge, and York could have printing establishments.

The beliefs of the Puritans, dissenters from the established Church of England who were growing in strength and numbers in England and North America, also influenced literature of the period. Puritans considered the traditional tales about giants, fairies, and witches found in chapbooks to be impious and corrupting. They urged that children not be allowed to read such materials and instead be provided with literature to instruct them and reinforce their moral development. Puritans expected their offspring to be children of God first and foremost. Bernard J. Lonsdale and Helen K. Macintosh (26) describe:

> Family worship, admonitions from elders, home instruction, strict attendance at school, and close attention to lessons all were aimed at perpetuating those ideals and values for which the parents themselves had sacrificed so much. To the elders, the important part of education was learning to read, write, and figure. Only literature that would instruct and warn was tolerated. (p. 161)

Awesome titles for books that stressed the importance of instructing children in moral concerns were common in Puritan times. In 1649, the grandfather of Cotton Mather (the Puritan who was so influential during the Salem witch-hunts in New England) wrote a book called *Spiritual Milk for Boston Babes in Either England, Drawn from the Breasts of Both Testaments for Their Souls' Nourishment*. In 1671, the leading Puritan writer, James Janeway, published a series of stories about children who had led saintly lives until their

The New England primer taught both Puritan ideals and the alphabet. (From *The New England Primer, Enlarged*, Boston, 1727 edition. From the Rare Books and Manuscript Division, The New York Public Library, Astor, Lenox, and Tilden Foundations.)

deaths at an early age. His *A Token for Children, Being an Exact Account of the Conversion, Holy and Exemplary Lives, and Joyful Deaths of Several Young Children* was meant not for enjoyment, but to instruct Puritan children in moral development.

The most influential piece of literature written during this period was John Bunyan's *The Pilgrim's Progress from this world, to that which is to come. Delivered under the similitude of a Dream. Wherein is discovered, the manner of his setting out, his dangerous journey and safe arrival at the Desired Country*, or *Pilgrim's Progress*, published in England in 1678. While moral improvement was this book's primary purpose, *Pilgrim's Progress* also contained bold action that appealed to both children and older readers, some of whom adopted it for its entertainment, as well as religious, value. Bunyan's hero, Christian, experiences many perilous adventures as he journeys alone through the Slough of Despond and the Valley of Humiliation in his search for salvation. Characters such as Mr. Valiant-for-Truth and Ignorance appear in such settings as the Valley of the Shadow of Death, the Delectable Mountains, and the Celestial City. Christian acquires a companion, Faithful, who is executed in the town of Vanity Fair. Then another companion, Hopeful, helps him fight the giant Despair and finally reach his goal.

Pilgrim's Progress and the *Spiritual Milk for Boston Babes in Either England* were required reading for colonial children in North America. Another important book in colonial homes was *The New England Primer,* a combination alphabet and catechism designed to teach Puritan ideals. The primer was written in such a way that spiritual instruction was the main theme. The primer appeared around 1690 and was printed in hundreds of editions until 1830. According to Cornelia Meigs et al. (31), the powerful influence of the primer lasted so long because in that era "the chance of life for young children was cruelly small" (p. 114), and spiritual preparation for an early death was thus imperative.

John Locke's Influence on Views of Childhood

In a social environment that viewed children as small adults and expected them to behave accordingly, few considered that children might have interests and educational needs of their own. The Puritans and other Calvinist Christians believed that everyone was born predestined to achieve either salvation or damnation. Thus, all must spend their lives attempting to prove predestined worthiness to be saved.

The English philosopher John Locke, however, envisioned the child's mind at birth as a *tabula rasa,* a blank page on which ideas were to be imprinted. In *Some Thoughts Concerning Education* (25), published in 1693, Locke stressed the interrelatedness of healthy physical development and healthy mental development, and he advocated milder ways of teaching and bringing up children than had been recommended previously. According to John Rowe Townsend (40), Locke believed that children who could read should be provided with easy, pleasant books suited to their capacities—books that encouraged them to read and rewarded them for their reading efforts but that did not fill their heads with useless "trumpery" or encourage vice.

Locke found a grave shortage of books that could provide children with pleasure or reward, but he did recommend *Aesop's Fables* and *Reynard the Fox* for the delight they offered children and the useful reflections they offered the adults in children's lives. Locke's attitude was quite enlightened for his time. It provided a glimmer of hope that children might be permitted to go through a period of childhood rather than immediately assume the same roles as their parents. While seventeenth-century European and North American culture contained few books appropriate for children, a realization dawned that children might benefit from books written to encourage their reading.

Charles Perrault's Tales of Mother Goose

An exciting development in children's literature occurred in seventeenth-century France. Charles Perrault, a gifted member of the Academie Française, published a book called *Contes de ma*

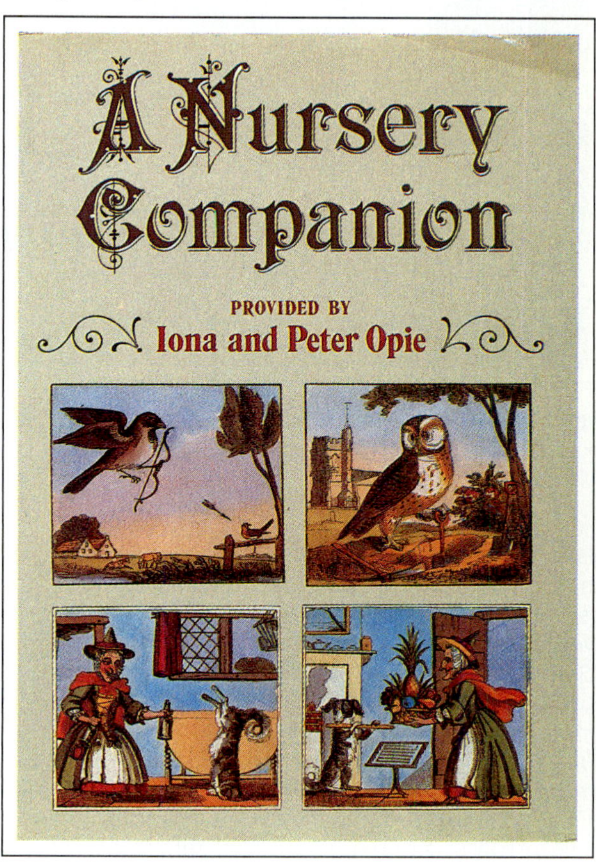

A Nursery Companion is a collection of Mother Goose rhymes that were published in the early 1800s from *A Nursery Companion* by Iona and Peter Opie. Published by Oxford University Press 1980.

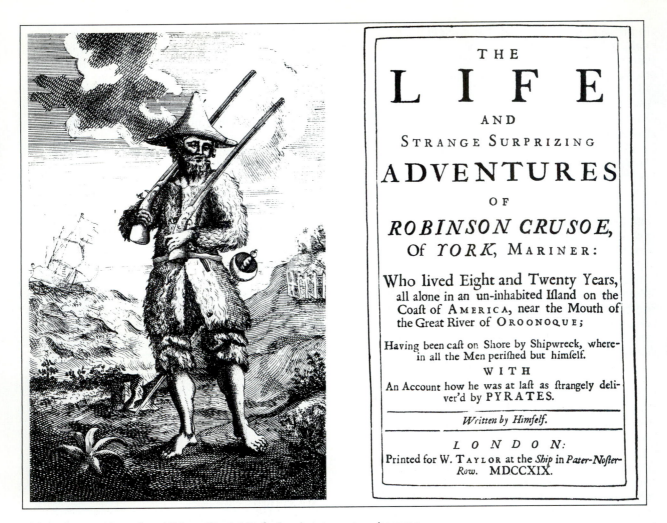

THE

LIFE

AND

STRANGE SURPRIZING

ADVENTURES

OF

ROBINSON CRUSOE,

Of *YORK*, MARINER:

Who lived Eight and Twenty Years, all alone in an un-inhabited Iſland on the Coaſt of AMERICA, near the Mouth of the Great River of OROONOQUE;

Having been caſt on Shore by Shipwreck, wherein all the Men periſhed but himſelf.

WITH

An Account how he was at laſt as ſtrangely deliver'd by PYRATES.

Written by Himſelf.

LONDON:

Printed for W. TAYLOR at the *Ship* in *Pater-Noſter-Row.* MDCCXIX.

Although not written for children, Daniel Defoe's adventure story became popular with eighteenth-century children. (Courtesy of Lilly Library, Indiana University, Bloomington, Indiana.)

Mère l'Oye (Tales of Mother Goose). The stories in this collection were not those normally referred to as Mother Goose rhymes today. Instead, they were well-known fairy tales, such as "Cinderella," "Sleeping Beauty," "Puss in Boots," "Little Red Riding Hood," and "Blue Beard." Perrault did not create these tales; he retold stories from the French oral tradition that had entranced children and provided entertainment in the elegant salons of the Parisian aristocracy for generations.

Perrault was one of the first writers to recognize that fairy tales have a special place in the world of children. Readers can thank Perrault or, as many scholars (32) now believe, his son Pierre Perrault d'Armancour, for collecting these tales, which have been translated and retold by many different contemporary writers and illustrators of children's books. At last, entertainment was written for children rather than adopted by them because nothing else was available.

The Adventure Stories of Defoe and Swift

Two adventure books that appeared in the early eighteenth century were, like virtually all literature of the time, written for adults, but these two were quickly embraced by children. A political climate that punished dissenters by placing them into prison molded the author of the first great adventure story, *Robinson Crusoe,* which was published in 1719. Daniel Defoe was condemned to Newgate Prison after he wrote a fiery pamphlet responding to the political and religious controversies of his time. However, Defoe wrote constantly, even while in jail.

Defoe was motivated to write *Robinson Crusoe* when he read the personal accounts of a Scottish sailor, Alexander Selkirk, who had been marooned on one of the Juan Fernandez Islands, located off the coast of Chile. This Scottish sailor had deserted ship after a disagreement with the captain and had lived alone on the island for four years before he was discovered by another ship and brought back to England. Defoe was so captivated by Selkirk's experience that he wrote an adventure story to answer his questions about how a person might acquire food, clothing, and shelter if shipwrecked on an island.

The resulting tale appeared first in serial publication and then in a book. Children and adults enjoyed the exciting and suspenseful story. The book was so influential that thirty-one years after Defoe's death, French philosopher Jean Jacques Rousseau, the founder of modern education, said that *Robinson Crusoe* would be the first book read by his son, Emile.

According to Brian W. Alderson (2) *Robinson Crusoe* reflects an era in Western history when people had begun to believe in the natural goodness of human beings uninfluenced by corruption in the world around them. *Robinson Crusoe* became and remained so popular that it stimulated a whole group of books written about similar subjects, which came to be known as Robinsonades. The most popular Robinsonade was Johann Wyss's *The Swiss Family Robinson*.

The second major adventure story written during the early eighteenth century also dealt with the subject of shipwreck. Jonathan Swift's *Gulliver's Travels,* published in 1726, described Gulliver's realistic adventures with strange beings encountered in mysterious lands: tiny Lilliputians, giant Brobdingnagians, talking horses, and flying islands. Swift wrote *Gulliver's Travels* as a satire for adults. Children, however, thought of the story as an enjoyable adventure and adopted Gulliver as a hero.

These adventure stories must have seemed truly remarkable to children otherwise surrounded by literature written only to instruct or to moralize. The impact of these eighteenth-century writers is still felt today, as twentieth-century children enjoy versions of the first adventure stories.

Newbery's Books for Children

The 1740s are commonly regarded as the time when the idea of children's books began in Europe and North America (40). New ways of thought emerged as the middle class became larger and strengthened its social position. Because more people had the time, money, and education necessary for reading, books became more important. Middle-class life also began to center on the home and family rather than on the marketplace or the great houses of nobility. With this growing emphasis on family life, a realization began that children should be children rather than small adults.

Into this social climate came John Newbery, an admirer of John Locke and an advocate of a milder way of educating children. Newbery was also a writer and publisher, who began publishing a line of books for children in 1744 with *A Little Pretty Pocket Book*. "Although his work reflected the didactic tone of the time," say Jane Bingham and Grayce Scholt (5), "his books were not intended to be textbooks. Their gilt-paper covers, attractive pages, engaging stories and verses—and sometimes toys which were offered with the books—provided 'diversion' for children of the English-speaking world" (p. 86). *A Little Pretty Pocket Book* included a letter from Jack the Giant Killer written to both instruct and entertain children. Modern readers would not consider this early book for children very entertaining compared with books written to amuse today's children, but it must have been revolutionary for its time. In 1765, Newbery published a more famous book, *History of Little Goody Two-Shoes,* a fictitious story by Oliver Goldsmith.

Newbery's company, set up in London, became a success. His accomplishments are often attributed to his bustling energy, his interest in literature and writers, his love for children, and his taking note of children's tastes as measured by the popularity of their favorite chapbooks. Newbery's publications included *Nurse Truelove's New Year's Gift, Mother Goose, Tom Thumb's Folio,* and old favorites, such as *Aesop's Fables, Robinson Crusoe,* and *Gulliver's Travels*. Because of Newbery's success, publishers realized that there was indeed a market for books written specifically for children. It is fitting that the coveted award given annually to the outstanding author of a children's literature selection bears Newbery's name.

Rousseau's Philosophy of Natural Development

While John Locke had advocated a milder and more rational approach to educating children, Jean Jacques Rousseau recommended a totally new approach. Locke believed that children should be led in their search for knowledge, but Rousseau believed that they should merely be accompanied. Rousseau maintained that children could and should develop naturally, with gentle guidance from wise adults who could supply necessary information. Margaret C. Gillespie (15) maintains:

> [A]t a time when the major emphasis was on sharpening the muscles of the mind and filling it to the brim with all the knowledge in the world it could absorb, Jean Jacques Rousseau's exhortations to "retournez à la nature" had a strong impact on the complacency of educators. (p. 21)

In his *Emile,* published in 1762, Rousseau described stages of children's growth, stressing the importance of experiences in harmony with children's natural development physically and mentally. Rousseau's stages progressed from early sensory motor development, through a concrete learning period, into a period where intellectual conceptualization was possible. As mentioned, Rousseau believed that Daniel Defoe's *Robinson Crusoe* was the most important piece of literature because it emphasized the necessity of using one's own ideas to cope with one's environment. Rousseau's impact on parents' attitudes toward children was "forceful and unmistakable," says Gillespie. "Now children were looked upon as 'little angels' who could do no wrong. They were permitted to be children rather than 'little adults'. They became the center of the educational scene rather than satellites around the curriculum" (p. 23).

William Blake's Poetry About Children

The English poet William Blake, who is credited with writing verses as if a child had written them, published his *Songs of Innocence* in 1789 and his *Songs of Experience* in 1794. F. J. Harvey Darton (10) characterizes Blake in the spiritual sense as "a child happy on a cloud, singing and desiring such songs as few but he could write" (p. 179). Blake's often quoted poem that introduces *Songs of Innocence* provides readers an opportunity to visualize this happy child (the punctuation and spelling are from the engraved first edition cited in Darton, 1932):

Introduction

Piping down the valleys wild
Piping songs of pleasant glee
On a cloud I saw a child.
And he laughing said to me.

Pipe a song about a Lamb:
So I piped with merry chear,
Piper pipe that song again—
So I piped, he wept to hear.

Drop thy pipe thy happy pipe
Sing thy songs of happy chear.
So I sung the same again
While he wept with joy to hear.

Piper sit thee down and write
In a book that all may read—
So he vanish'd from my sight.
And I pluck'd a hollow reed

And I made a rural pen,
And I stain'd the water clear,
And I wrote my happy songs,
Every child may joy to hear.

The Fairy Tales of Andersen and the Brothers Grimm

Sir Walter Scott's novels about the Middle Ages, enthusiasm for Gothic architecture, lyrical ballads, and Rousseau's philosophy of a return to nature typified the Romantic Movement in late-eighteenth-century Europe. This atmosphere encouraged an interest in folk literature.

In the early 1800s, two German scholars, Jacob and Wilhelm Grimm, became interested in collecting folktales that reflected the ancient German language and tradition. In researching their subject, the brothers listened to tales told by Dortchen and Gretchen Wild; the Wilds' maid, Marie; a farmer's wife called Frau Viehmännin; and other storytellers from throughout Germany. Although scholars disagree about how exactly the Brothers Grimm transcribed the tales they heard, Bettina Hürlimann (18) maintains that the brothers

> did not just write down what they heard. Even for the first edition they did a lot of revising, comparing with other sources, and trying to find a simple language which was at the same time full of character. With time and with later editions it became clear that Jacob, the more scholarly, tried to keep the tales in the most

> simple, original form, more or less as they had heard them, and that Wilhelm, more of a poet, was for retelling them in a new form with regard to the children. (p. 71)

The Grimms' first edition of tales, published in 1812, contained eighty-five stories, including "Cinderella," "Hansel and Gretel," "Little Red Riding Hood," and "The Frog Prince." According to Hürlimann, the second edition, published in 1815, was designed more specifically for children, with illustrations and a minimum of scholarly comment on the tales it contained.

In 1823, the tales collected by the Brothers Grimm were translated into English and published under the title *German Popular Stories*. Since that time, artists in many countries have illustrated such tales as "Snow White and the Seven Dwarfs," "Rumpelstiltskin," and "The Elves and the Shoemaker," which have become part of our literary heritage.

Most of the published folktales and fairy tales discussed thus far were written down by either Charles Perrault or the Brothers Grimm. The stories had been told in castles and cottages for many generations. Hans Christian Andersen, however, is generally credited with being the first to create and publish an original fairy tale, using his own experiences to stimulate his writing. "The Ugly Duckling," "The Little Mermaid," and "The Red Shoes" are among Andersen's famous stories.

Andersen was born to a poor but happy family in Odense, Denmark. His cobbler father shared stories with him and even built a puppet theater for Andersen. Even when his father died and it seemed that Andersen would have to learn a trade, Andersen retained his dream of becoming an actor. During these poverty-stricken years, he

German Popular Stories, such as this 1826 edition, introduced the Grimms' folktales to English-speaking children. (Courtesy of Lilly Library, Indiana University, Bloomington, Indiana.)

tried to forget his troubles by putting on puppet shows and telling stories to children.

Because Andersen wanted to write stories and plays, he returned to school to improve his writing skills. While there, he suffered from cruel jokes about his looks; he was thin and had large feet and a large nose. (Doesn't this sound like a theme for one of his fairy tales?)

In 1828, when Andersen was twenty-three, he began to write stories and poems. Five years later, he was recognized as a promising writer by the Danish government, whose financial support allowed him to travel and write about his experiences. When his *Life in Italy,* a rather scholarly work, was published, Andersen at last started to make money. His next book was far different; it was the first of his famous fairy tale books, and it was written in the same colloquial language used to tell stories.

When *Fairy Tales Told for Children* was published, a friend told Andersen that his *Life in Italy* would make him famous but his fairy tales would make people remember him forever. Although Andersen did not believe his fairy tales were as good as his other books, he enjoyed writing them and produced a new fairy tale book each Christmas as a gift to children of all ages. When Andersen was sixty-two, he was invited back to Odense, the town in which he had known happiness, poverty, and sadness. This time, however, he was the honored guest at a celebration that lasted for an entire week.

Andersen's fairy stories are still popular; newly illustrated versions are published every year. These colorful picture-book versions, as well as tales in anthologies, are still enjoyed by children of many ages.

Early Illustrators of Children's Books

The identity of the first picture book for children is debated. Eric Quayle (34) identifies *Kunst und Lehrbüchlein* (Book of Art and Instruction for Young People), published in 1580 by the German publisher Sigmund Feyerabend, as the "first book aimed at the unexplored juvenile market" (p. 11). The detailed, full-page woodcuts showing European life were the work of Jost Amman. Of particular interest are the pictures of a young scholar reading a hornbook and of a child holding a doll.

Johann Amos Comenius, a Moravian teacher and former bishop of the Bohemian Brethren, is usually credited with writing the first non-alphabet picture book that strove to educate children. Bettina Hürlimann (18) describes Comenius as a great humanist, who wanted children to observe God's creations—plants, stars, clouds, rain, sun, and geography—rather than memorize abstract knowledge. In order to achieve this goal, Comenius took children out of the conventional classrooms and into the natural world. He then wrote down their experiences in simple sentences, using both Latin and the children's own language. He published these simple sentences and accompanying woodcuts in 1658 as *Orbis Pictus* (Painted World). Educational historian Ayers Bagley (4) identifies allegorical meanings in the illustrations and text. According to Bagley, Comenius saw true understanding, right action, and correct speech as important contributors to the attainment of wisdom.

A typical woodcut from *Orbis Pictus,* the first picture book for children. (A reprint of the *Orbis Pictus* has been published by Singing Tree Press, Gale Research Company, Detroit, Michigan.)

Scholars disagree about whether Comenius drew the illustrations for *Orbis Pictus* himself or whether he instructed artists in their execution. Jane Bingham and Grayce Scholt (5) credit the woodcuts in the 1658 edition to Paul Kreutzberger and the wood engravings in the 1810 American edition to Alexander Anderson. Whoever the artist was, Hürlimann emphasizes that "the pictures are in wonderful harmony with the text, and the book was to become for more than a century the most popular book with children of all classes" (p. 67).

Most book illustrations before the 1800s, especially those in the inexpensive chapbooks, were crude woodcuts. If color was used, it was usually hand applied by amateurs who filled in the colors according to a guide. Thomas Bewick is credited with being one of the earliest artists to illustrate books for children. His skillfully executed woodcuts graced *The New Lottery Book of Birds and Beasts,* published in 1771, and *A Pretty Book of Pictures for Little Masters and Misses; or Tommy Trip's History of Beasts and Birds,* published in 1779.

Three nineteenth-century English artists had enormous impact on illustrations for children's books. According to Ruth Hill Viguers (12) in the introduction to Edward Ernest's *The Kate Greenaway Treasury,* the work of these artists "represents the best to be found in picture books for children in any era: the strength of design and richness of color and detail of Walter Crane's pictures; the eloquence, humor, vitality, and movement of Randolph Caldecott's art; and the tenderness, dignity, and grace of the very personal interpretation of Kate Greenaway's enchanted land of childhood" (p. 13).

Walter Crane's *The House That Jack Built,* published in 1865, was the first of his series of toy books, the name used for picture books published for young children. These books, engraved by Edmund Evans, are credited with marking the beginning of the modern era in color illustrations. From 1865 through 1898, Crane illustrated over forty books, including folktales, such as *The Three Bears* and *Cinderella,* and alphabet books, such as *The Farmyard Alphabet* and *The Absurd ABC.*

Many of Crane's illustrations reflect his appreciation of Japanese color prints. Crane (9) specified this appreciation in lectures that he gave before the Society of Arts in 1889, when he stated that Japanese art was "a living art, an art of the people, in which traditions and craftsmanship were unbroken, and the results full of attractive variety, quickness, and naturalistic force" (p. 133).

Randolph Caldecott's talent was discovered by Edmund Evans, the printer. Caldecott's illustrations for *The History of John Gilpin,* printed by Evans in 1878, demonstrated his ability to depict robust characters, action, and humor. (The Caldecott Medal for children's book illustration, named for the artist, is embossed with the picture of Gilpin galloping through an English village.) Caldecott's lively and humorous figures jump fences, dance to the fiddler, and flirt with milkmaids in such picture books as *The Fox Jumps over the Parson's Gate, Come Lasses and Lads,* and *The Milkmaid.*

Caldecott's picture books are now reissued by Frederick Warne. Brian Alderson's (1) *Sing a Song of Sixpence* provides a pictorial history of English picture books and Randolph Caldecott's art.

Randolph Caldecott's illustrations suggest action and vitality. (From *The Hey Diddle Diddle Picture Book* by Randolph Caldecott. Reproduced by permission of Frederick Warne & Co., Inc., Publishers.)

Kate Greenaway was one of the early influential illustrators. Her name is now attached to the Kate Greenaway medal for outstanding illustrators in Great Britain.

Printer and engraver Edmund Evans also encouraged and supported the work of Kate Greenaway. Delighted by Greenaway's drawings and verses, Evans printed her first book, *Under the Window,* in 1878. It was so successful that 70,000 English editions and over 30,000 French and German editions were sold.

Greenaway continued illustrating books that reflected happy days of childhood and the blossoming apple trees and primroses that had dotted the English countryside of her youth. In a letter to her friend John Ruskin, Greenaway described her view of the world:

> I go on liking things more and more, seeing them more and more beautiful. Don't you think it is a great possession to be able to get so much joy out of things that are always there to give it, and do not change? What a great pity my hands are not clever enough to do what my mind and eyes see, but there it is! (12, p. 19)

Other picture books illustrated by Greenaway include *Kate Greenaway's Birthday Book* (1880), *Mother Goose* (1881), *The Language of Flowers* (1884), and Robert Browning's *Pied Piper of Hamelin* (1880). Greenaway's name, like Caldecott's, has been given to an award honoring distinguished artistic accomplishment in the field of children's books. The Kate Greenaway Medal is given annually to the most distinguished British illustrator of children's books.

By the late 1800s, when Crane, Caldecott, and Greenaway began drawing for children, European and North American attitudes toward children were also changing. According to Frederick Laws (21), these three artists

> were under no public compulsion to be morally edifying or factually informative. Children were no longer supposed to be "young persons" whose taste would be much the same whether they were five or fifteen. So long as they pleased children, artists were free; indeed, Crane wrote that "in a sober and matter-of-fact age Toybooks afford perhaps the only outlet for unrestricted flights of fancy open to the modern illustrator who likes to revolt against the despotism of facts" (p. 318)

This brief discussion of illustrators does not mention all of the artists who made contributions in the nineteenth century, but it does outline the relatively short history of children's book illustration. Chart 2–2 summarizes some milestones in the illustration of children's books from the fifteenth century into the early twentieth century.

The Victorian Influence

English-speaking people identify the reign of Great Britain's Queen Victoria, from 1837 to 1901, with a distinct social epoch, the Victorian Age, although so-called Victorian social influences certainly preceded and followed the queen's life. The rise of a highly competitive industrial technology, the growth of large cities and the decline of rural traditions, an emphasis on strictly controlled social behavior and Christian piety, and a romantic focus on home and family are factors usually associated with the Victorian Age in Europe, North America, and elsewhere. The increasingly prosperous middle and upper classes began to view childhood sentimentally, as an even more special stage in the human life cycle, while children of the working poor labored many hours a day in mines and factories.

Walter Crane's illustrated texts, characterized by subdued colors, strong design, and rich detail, are credited with marking the beginning of the modern era in color illustrations. (From *The Baby's Own Aesop*. Reproduced by permission of the Department of Special Collections, Research Library, University of California, Los Angeles.)

Fred Raymond Erisman (11) has concluded that American children's literature of the late nineteenth and early twentieth centuries chiefly reflected upper-middle-class values, although it fell into two main categories: fiction and nonfiction. Nonfiction was realistic, dealing with the social, technological, and biographical concerns of an urban society. Fiction presented the ideal values

CHART 2–2
Milestones in the history of children's illustration

1484	William Caxton, *Aesop's Fables,* contained over one hundred woodcuts.
1658	Johann Amos Comenius, *Orbis Pictus* (Painted World), considered by many to be the first picture book for children.
1771	Thomas Bewick, *The New Lottery Book of Birds and Beasts.*
1784	Thomas and John Bewick, *The Select Fables of Aesop and Others.*
1789	William Blake, *Songs of Innocence.*
1823	George Cruikshank, translation of Grimms' *Fairy Tales.*
1853	George Cruikshank, *Fairy Library.*
1865	John Tenniel, illustrations for Lewis Carroll's *Alice's Adventures in Wonderland.*
1865	Walter Crane, *The House That Jack Built,* the first of the toy books engraved by Evans.
1878	Randolph Caldecott, *The Diverting History of John Gilpin,* the first of sixteen picture books.
1878	Kate Greenaway, *Under the Window.*
1883	Howard Pyle, *Robin Hood.*
1900	Arthur Rackham, illustrations for Grimms' *Fairy Tales.*
1901	Beatrix Potter, *The Tale of Peter Rabbit.*
1924	E. H. Shepard, illustrations for A. A. Milne's *When We Were Very Young.*
1933	Kurt Wiese, illustrations for Marjorie Flack's *The Story of Ping.*
1933	E. H. Shepard, illustrations for Kenneth Grahame's *The Wind in the Willows.*
1937	Dr. Seuss, *And to Think That I Saw It on Mulberry Street.*

FLASHBACK

MRS. EWING'S STORIES.
H. Paterson
"What's your name, boy?"—PAGE 247.
JAN OF THE WINDMILL.
A STORY OF THE PLAINS.
By Mrs. EWING. Price, $1.00.
ROBERTS BROTHERS, Publishers,
BOSTON

JULIANA HORATIA EWING WAS ONE OF THE MOST prolific authors of the Victorian period. Many of her popular tales for children first appeared in such English periodicals as *The Monthly Packet* and *Aunt Judy's Magazine for Young People*. Her first book, *Melchior's Dream and Other Stories,* was published by the Society for the Promotion of Christian Knowledge in 1862. Among her other books were *Mrs. Overtheway's Remembrances* (1869), *Jan of the Windmill* (1876), *Brothers of Pity, and Other Tales* (1882), *Jackanapes* (1884), and *Daddy Darwin's Dovecot* (1884). The last two books were illustrated by Randolph Caldecott.

Literary critics considered Mrs. Ewing's writing to be among the best of the time. Their comments also reflected typically Victorian concerns and values. For example, a critic for the *Worcester Spy* described Mrs. Ewing as a genius whose writing touched the heart, excited tender and noble emotion, encouraged religious feeling, and deepened the scorn for the mean and the cowardly. This same critic recommended that children read Mrs. Ewing's stories because they nourished everything that was lovely in children's characters. Mrs. Ewing's "refining" and "ennobling" stories were popular for many years, remaining in print until the 1930s.

of the well-to-do, implying that these were the typical American values.

Robert Gordon Kelly's (20) research also reveals that American children's literature in the nineteenth century presented children with an ideal concept of selfhood for emulation. As well, it indicated unresolved tensions about America's growing cities, a beginning emphasis on the responsibilities of a cultural elite, and changing ideas about childhood. According to Kelly, the "gentleman and lady" in children's literature "offered models for negotiating the difficult and precarious passage from childhood to adulthood as well as for moderating the economic competition . . . that was the most important social fact of American life" (p. 42). Children's literature encouraged the young to confront a dog-eat-dog world with courage, temperance, prudence, courtesy, self-reliance, and presence of mind. "So great was the emphasis on self-control," says Kelly, "that one author warned that carelessness is worse than stealing" (p. 41).

Kelly identifies two typical story patterns in children's literature of the period. In the *ordeal,* a child loses the protection and influence of parents or other adults for a short time. Circumstances force the child to act decisively; the situations described often seem contrived to emphasize sound character rather than sound reasoning. The child demonstrates the expected behaviors and then returns to the safety of the family and is justly rewarded.

The heroine of "Nellie in the Light House," published in an 1877 edition of *St. Nicholas* magazine, is the seven-year-old daughter of a lighthouse keeper. When her father goes to the mainland for supplies, the housekeeper is called away to nurse a neighbor, the housekeeper's husband collapses from a stroke, a storm causes high winds, and the beacon light is extinguished. Alone, Nellie must overcome her fear and find a way to rekindle the beacon. She remembers a hymn her mother sang to her and rekindles the light, which then saves her father, who is caught in the storm.

In the second type of story, *change of heart,* a child who has not yet reached the ideal of self-discipline and sound moral character realizes the need for improvement. In "Charlie Balch's Metamorphosis," which appeared in an 1867 edition of the *Riverside Magazine for Young People,* the hero is a sullen and lazy boy who has withdrawn into himself after his mother's death. His father sends him to a boarding school, where he joins a rough crowd of boys. Charlie realizes the errors of his ways during a sermon, and the rest of the story places him in situations that test his resolution for a change of heart. By the end of the story, Charlie has a cheerful disposition and better manners.

Charlotte Yonge was a prolific author of children's literature. She wrote about the large families so common in Victorian times; her own childhood had involved close ties with her brother and many cousins. Conversations among the people in her extended family later provided her with realistic settings and dialogue for her fiction. Yonge's stories also reflect the pronounced Christian ethic of the Victorian period.

In Yonge's *The Daisy Chain,* for example, a husband and wife become missionaries in the Loyalty Islands. In typical Victorian fashion, Yonge's fiction portrays females as inferior to males. In *The Daisy Chain,* the hero's sister is advised not to compete with her brother at the university because a woman cannot equal a man scholastically. In *The Clever Woman of the Family,* published in 1865, the heroine thinks for herself, but whenever there is a disagreement between her ideas and those of a man, she must adhere to the superior wisdom of a brother, father, or husband.

Myra Stark (39) maintains that the Victorian Age was in the grip of an ideology that viewed women as either wives and mothers or failed wives or mothers. Stark declares:

> Woman was the center of the age's cult of the family, "[t]he angel in the house," tending to the domestic altar. She was viewed as man's inferior—less rational, weaker, needing his protection; but at the same time, she was exalted for her spirituality, her moral influence. Man was the active one, the doer; woman was the inspirer and the nurturer. The spheres of work in the world and in the home were rigidly divided between the sexes. (p. 4)

Consequently, most Victorian literature for children directed middle- and upper-class girls and boys into the rigidly distinct roles expected of them as adults.

Robert MacDonald's analysis of illustrations in the boys' magazine *Chums* defines the masculine role model found in Victorian illustrations. MacDonald (28) states that by

> repetition and emphasis, a vocabulary of patriotic images was developed and exploited, which for a generation of British males dramatized the myth of Empire. The primary motifs of these illustrations defined manhood, race, and individual action: manhood shown in the heroics of courageous soldiers or brave frontiersmen; lessons of race demonstrated by the examples of barbarous natives or uncivilized Dutchmen; and the complicated relationship between choice and duty set forth as an insistent expectation that the wars of school led to the games of war. A close relationship was established between the world of boys and the world of men. (p. 33)

Some Victorian authors were sensitive to the realities of life for poor children. In 1862, the English poet Elizabeth Barrett Browning wrote of the woes of these children in her poem, "The Cry of the Children," describing the weeping of children in mines and factories while other children played. Another famous English author of the period, Charles Dickens, aroused the Victorian conscience to the plight of unfortunate children, such as the fictional orphan in *Oliver Twist*.

Reissues of lesser-known books and stories published during the Victorian period provide opportunities for further study. For example, *What I Cannot Tell My Mother Is Not Fit for Me to Know* is a collection of stories, poems, and songs selected by Gwladys and Brian Rees-Williams (35) from texts published in the nineteenth century. Andrew Tuer's *Stories from Forgotten Children's Books* (41) is a facsimile edition of a book published in 1898.

Fantasy, Adventure, and Real People

As the world was changing, views of childhood were changing, too. Emphases in children's literature mirrored the new attitudes and world developments. Childhood was becoming, at least for middle- and upper-class children, a more carefree and enjoyable period of life, and this change was reflected in the increase in fantasy stories for children. As adventurers explored unknown areas of the world, their experiences inspired new adventure stories. Also, the characters of specific families and localities were captured in the growing popularity of literature about ordinary people, places, and events in sometimes extraordinary circumstances.

Fantasy. By the mid-1800s, the puritanical resistance to fantasy in children's literature was on its way toward extinction in most segments of European and North American society. Children had been reading and enjoying the folktales of Perrault and the Brothers Grimm, and Andersen's stories had been translated into English. More and more educators and parents believed that literature should entertain children rather than merely instruct them.

According to Raymond Chapman (8), fantasy created a world where fears could be projected onto impossible creatures of the imagination while a child remained safe. Although growing to maturity seemed dangerous, the happiest people acquired new knowledge while retaining childlike qualities. Brian W. Alderson (2) describes the creation of one of the landmarks in fantasy and nonsense:

> One summer's day on the river at Oxford [England] a thirty-year-old lecturer in mathematics at Christ Church was taking the three daughters of his Dean, Edith, Lorina, and Alice, out for a row. His name was Charles Lutwidge Dodgson. The day was hot and the children wanted to have a story told them, a thing they had come to expect from Mr. Dodgson. So the young lecturer complied, his mind relaxing in the drowsy heat and his thoughts, which did not tire so easily, following paths of their own making. (p. 64)

The paths led directly down the rabbit hole and into adventures in Wonderland with the Cheshire Cat, the Queen of Hearts, and the Mad Hatter. The story told that afternoon in 1862 made such an impression on Alice that she pestered Dodgson to write it down. He wrote it for her, gave it to her as a gift, and, after it had been thoroughly enjoyed by many people, published it for others under the pseudonym Lewis Carroll.

According to Cornelia Meigs et al. (31), the revolutionary nature of Lewis Carroll's *Alice's Adventures in Wonderland* and *Through the Looking Glass* when compared with earlier books written for children is due to "the fact that they were written purely to give pleasure to children. . . . Here . . . for the first time we find a story designed for children without a trace of a lesson or moral" (p. 194).

Edward Lear, the other great writer of fantasy for children in the nineteenth century, created absurd and delightful characters in nonsense verses. Lear's *A Book of Nonsense* appeared in 1846, his *More Nonsense* in 1872. *Nonsense Songs, Botany and Alphabets,* published in 1871, contained Lear's "Nonsense Stories," "Nonsense Geography," "Natural History," and "Nonsense Alphabets." *Laughable Lyrics* (1877) included the nonsense verses "The Quangle-Wangle's Hat,"

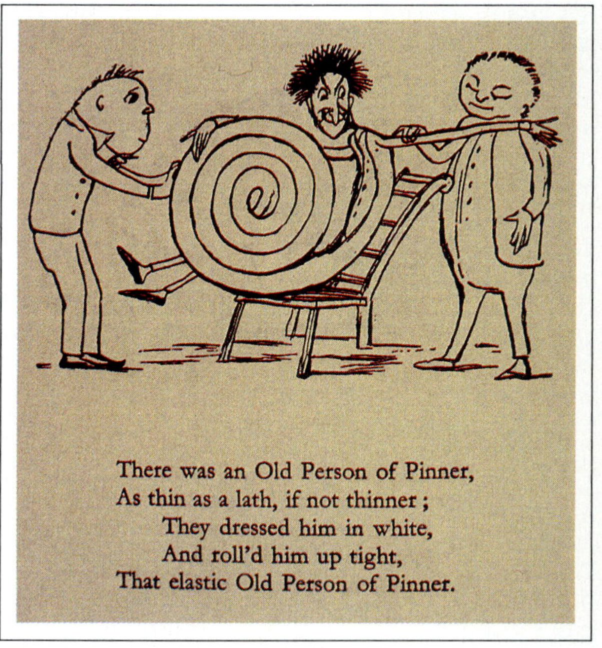

There was an Old Person of Pinner,
As thin as a lath, if not thinner;
They dressed him in white,
And roll'd him up tight,
That elastic Old Person of Pinner.

Edward Lear's illustrations heightened the humor of his limericks. (From *A Book of Nonsense* by Edward Lear. Published by Heinrich Hoffman, 1846. Courtesy of Lilly Library, Indiana University, Bloomington, Indiana.)

The illustrations and text for *Alice's Adventures in Wonderland* were designed to give pleasure, not to teach a lesson. (Illustration by John Tenniel. From *Alice's Adventures in Wonderland* by Lewis Carroll. Published by Macmillan and Co., 1865. Courtesy of Lilly Library, Indiana University, Bloomington, Indiana.)

"The Dong with the Luminous Nose," and "The Youghy-Bonghy-Bo."

Lear's work, like Carroll's, was popular with both young and adult readers. Today, both writers are often quoted and enjoyed as much as they were when their works were created.

Adventure. Europeans and North Americans were having many real-life adventures in the nineteenth century. Explorers were seeking the North Pole, Florence Nightingale was pioneering for female independence as a director of nursing in the Crimean War, and a railroad was being constructed across the United States. If a person could not go to a remote region and overcome the perils lurking there, the next best adventure was the vicarious one offered through books.

Robert Louis Stevenson was the master of the adventure stories written during this time. When *Treasure Island* was published, it was considered the greatest adventure story for children since *Robinson Crusoe*. Brian W. Alderson (2) agrees that Stevenson had the greatest influence on children's literature after Daniel Defoe.

Stevenson was born in Edinburgh, Scotland, the son of a lighthouse engineer. When he was a young boy, his father told him bedtime tales filled with "blood and thunder," and his nurse told him stories of body snatchers, ghosts, and martyrs. As an adult, Stevenson traveled to many lands, but he still loved the lochs, islands, and misty forests of his home. Stevenson's early experiences are evident in his two most famous adventure stories, *Treasure Island* and *Kidnapped*.

Treasure Island had an interesting beginning. While trying to entertain his stepson, Stevenson drew a watercolor map of an island, then followed his drawing with the now famous story of pirates, buried treasure, and a young boy's adventures.

Both *Treasure Island* and *Kidnapped* have the ingredients of outstanding adventure literature: action, mystery, and pursuit and evasion in authentic historical settings. Stevenson believed that an adventure story should have a specific effect on its readers: It should absorb and delight them, fill their minds with a kaleidoscope of images, and satisfy their nameless longings. According to Bernard J. Lonsdale and Helen K. Macintosh (26), Stevenson believed that Robinson Crusoe's discovering a footprint on his lonely beach, Achilles's shouting against the Trojans, and Ulysses's bending over his great bow were culminating moments that have been printed in the mind's eye forever. In addition, according to Brian W. Alderson (2), Stevenson believed that children and adults should demand such moments in their literature, and Stevenson achieved that quality in tales of "treasure and treachery . . . the comings and goings of . . . pirates, the ominous hints of the fearful events which are to come" (p. 257).

While Robert Lewis Stevenson wrote of pirates and buried treasure in the not-so-distant past, Howard Pyle took readers back to the Middle Ages to fight evil, overcome Prince John's injustice, and have a rollicking good time in the green depths of Sherwood Forest. Pyle's *The Merry Adventures of Robin Hood,* published in 1883, retold the old English ballad about Robin Hood, Little John, Friar Tuck, and the other merry men who robbed the rich to give to the poor and constantly thwarted the evil plans of the Sheriff of Nottingham. Here was swashbuckling entertainment that also provided children with a glimpse of an early period in European history.

The Industrial Revolution, the invention of the steam engine, and the prevalent feeling of new possibilities always just around the corner laid the groundwork for a new kind of adventure story in the last half of the nineteenth century. Jules Verne's science fiction adventure stories can certainly be classified as another benchmark in children's literature. Verne envisioned submarines, guided missiles, and dirigibles long before such things were possible. His first science fiction book, *Five Weeks in a Balloon,* was published in France in 1863. His two most famous books, *Twenty Thousand Leagues under the Sea,* published in 1869, and *Around the World in Eighty Days,* published in 1872, have also been immortalized on film. Consequently, the heroes of these books, Captain Nemo and Phileas Fogg, are well known to both readers and movie fans.

Verne admired the work of an earlier author, Daniel Defoe, and Verne's *The Mysterious Island,* published in 1875, was written because of Verne's interest in *Robinson Crusoe*. Verne's genius can be seen in the popularity of his works even today, after his glorious inventions have become reality. Verne's detailed descriptions are so believable they seem as modern now as they did when they were published in the 1800s. The popularity of Verne's literature also caused other authors to write science fiction and to expand the new genre.

Real People. During the later nineteenth and early twentieth centuries, the local-color story came into its own. Realistic situations and people are the setting and subject of such stories, in which place, plot, and characters are tightly integrated. According to James H. Fraser (13), "This integration, which reveals the complex involvement of human, cultural, and geographical influences, produces a rich literature—peculiarly rich for the student of American culture, and extraordinarily rich for the young persons fortunate enough to read it" (p. 55). The diversity of American geography and people are found in books like Edward Eggleston's *The Hoosier School Boy* (rural Indiana), Thomas Bailey Aldrich's *The Story of a Bad Boy* (a New England seafaring town), Kate Douglas Wiggin's *Rebecca of Sunnybrook Farm* (rural Maine), Mark Twain's *Huckleberry Finn* (Mississippi River towns), and Frances Courtenay Baylor's *Juan and Juanita* (the Southwest). Fraser maintains that these local-color stories also transmit a conservative, traditional view of American life to the next generation. Their characters are "carry-overs from an earlier age," an agrarian, preindustrial age, which the stories sentimentalize for their modern readers (p. 59).

The greatest American writer of realistic adventure in this period was Mark Twain (Samuel Clemens). While Robert Lewis Stevenson was writing about adventures on far-off islands, Twain was immortalizing life on the Mississippi River before the Civil War. Twain grew up in the river town of Hannibal, Missouri, where he lived many of the adventures about which he later wrote. He explored the river, raided melon patches, and used a cave as a rendezvous to plan further adventures and mischief with his friends. These adventures made Tom Sawyer and Huckleberry Finn come alive for many adventure-loving chil-

Mark Twain wrote adventures about life in the Mississippi River environment in which he himself had grown up. (From *Adventures of Huckleberry Finn* by Mark Twain. Published by Charles L. Webster and Co., 1885. Courtesy of Lilly Library, Indiana University,

ISSUE

Are the Writings of Mark Twain Racist?

THE WRITINGS OF MARK Twain (Samuel Clemens), especially the *Adventures of Huckleberry Finn,* were under protest in the 1980s because of Twain's depictions of black people. Those who suggest that the *Adventures of Huckleberry Finn* should be banned or rewritten point to the numerous uses of the word *nigger* and instances in which black Americans are stereotyped rather than presented as individual, well-rounded characters.

Twain might find this 1980s protest ironic; in the 1880s, he was accused of going too far in advancing the cause of human equality and justice. Robert Scott Kellner,[1] a recognized Twain scholar, believes, however, that "a close examination of Twain's writing reveals an element of satire in his seemingly racist language, a satire directed at the reader who would choose to agree with the stereotyped image. Twain's language and imagery about the blacks in his stories work together as a mirror in which bigoted readers ultimately see themselves."

Kellner stresses that in the relationship between Huckleberry Finn and Jim, Twain makes clear that a black man is capable of earning a trust that withstands the pressures of an anti-black heritage—that he can give love and loyalty, strive for physical emancipation, and be a wise father figure for a misinformed boy. As you read Twain's work, consider whether it reflects a belief in the inequality of human beings or whether it suggests that people of all races share a common humanity.

[1]Kellner, Robert Scott. "Defending Mark Twain." *The Eagle*. Bryan-College Station, Texas (April 11, 1982): 1D.

dren. Twain's heroes did not leave the continent, but they did have exciting adventures on a nearby island, return in time to hear plans for their own funerals, and then attend those momentous occasions. Characters such as Injun Joe, Aunt Polly, Tom Sawyer, Becky Thatcher, and Huckleberry Finn still provide reading pleasure for children and adults.

Many American books in the Victorian era took the family as their subject, and series stories dealing with the everyday lives of large families became popular. Margaret Sidney, for example, wrote a series of books about the five little Peppers. The first book, *The Five Little Peppers and How They Grew,* published in 1881, was followed by *The Five Little Peppers Midway* and *The Five Little Peppers Grown Up*.

Louisa May Alcott's account of family life in *Little Women,* published in 1868, is so real that readers feel they know each member of the March family intimately. This book showing the warm relationships and everyday struggles in a family of meager means is actually about Alcott's own family.

In many ways, Alcott's life was quite different from the usual Victorian model, which accounts for the ways in which *Little Women* was ahead of its time. Alcott's father believed in educating his daughters. Consequently, Alcott was first educated at home by her father and then sent to the district school. Later, she went to Boston to earn a living as a writer so that her family would not have to support her. She wrote constantly, publishing her early melodramatic stories in magazines. Alcott left Boston to nurse her sister during a terminal illness. (This incident became Beth's illness and subsequent death in *Little Women*.) During the Civil War, Alcott left home to nurse soldiers until poor health forced her to return to her family.

In 1867, a publisher asked Alcott to write a book for girls, and she decided to write about her own family. The resulting book, *Little Women,* was an overwhelming success. Readers enjoyed the inti-

CHART 2–3
Notable authors of children's literature

1477	William Caxton, *Caxton's Book of Curtesye*
1484	William Caxton, *The Fables of Aesop*
1485	William Caxton, *Le Morte d'Arthur*
1678	John Bunyan, *Pilgrim's Progress*
1698	Charles Perrault or Pierre Perrault d'Armancour, *Tales of Mother Goose*
1719	Daniel Defoe, *Robinson Crusoe*
1726	Jonathan Swift, *Gulliver's Travels*
1744	John Newbery, *A Little Pretty Pocket Book*
1789	William Blake, *Songs of Innocence*
1812	First volume of Grimm Brothers' fairy tales, *Kinder-und Hausmärchen*
	Johann Wyss, *Swiss Family Robinson*
1820	Sir Walter Scott, *Ivanhoe: A Romance*
1823	Clement G. Moore, *A Visit from St. Nicholas*
1826	James Fenimore Cooper, *The Last of the Mohicans*
1843	Charles Dickens, *A Christmas Carol*
1846	Edward Lear, *A Book of Nonsense*
	Hans Christian Andersen's fairy tales in English translations
1851	John Ruskin, *King of the Golden River*
1856	Charlotte Yonge, *The Daisy Chain*
1862	Christina Georgina Rossetti, *Goblin Market*
1863	Charles Kingsley, *The Water Babies*
1865	Lewis Carroll, *Alice's Adventures in Wonderland*
	Mary Elizabeth Mapes Dodge, *Hans Brinker, or the Silver Skates, a Story of Life in Holland*
1868	Louisa May Alcott, *Little Women*
1870	Thomas Bailey Aldrich, *The Story of a Bad Boy*
1871	George MacDonald, *At the Back of the North Wind*
1872	Jules Verne, *Around the World in Eighty Days*
1873	*St. Nicholas: Scribner's Illustrated Magazine for Girls and Boys,* edited by Mary Mapes Dodge
1876	Mark Twain, *The Aventures of Tom Sawyer*
1877	Anna Sewell, *Black Beauty*
1880	Margaret Sidney, *The Five Little Peppers and How They Grew*
1881	Joel Chandler Harris, *Uncle Remus; His Songs and Sayings: The Folklore of the Old Plantation*
1883	Howard Pyle, *Merry Adventures of Robin Hood of Great Renown, in Nottinghamshire*
	Robert Louis Stevenson, *Treasure Island*
1884	Johanna Spyri, *Heidi; Her Years of Wandering and Learning*
1885	Robert Louis Stevenson, *A Child's Garden of Verses*
1886	Frances Hodgson Burnett, *Little Lord Fauntleroy*
1889	Andrew Lang, *The Blue Fairy Book*
1892	Carlo Collodi, *The Adventures of Pinocchio*
	Arthur Conan Doyle, *The Adventures of Sherlock Holmes*
1894	Rudyard Kipling, *The Jungle Books*
1901	Beatrix Potter, *The Tale of Peter Rabbit*
1903	L. Leslie Brooke, *Johnny Crow's Garden*
	Kate Douglas Wiggin, *Rebecca of Sunnybrook Farm*
	J. M. Barrie, *Peter Pan; or The Boy Who Would Not Grow Up*
1904	Howard Garis, *The Bobbsey Twins; or Merry Days Indoors and Out* (There are over seventy books in the series.)
1908	Kenneth Grahame, *The Wind in the Willows*
1911	Frances Hodgson Burnett, *The Secret Garden*
1913	Eleanor H. Porter, *Pollyanna*
1918	O. Henry, *The Ransom of Red Chief*
1921	Hendrik Willem Van Loon, *The Story of Mankind* (One of the first informational books attempting to make learning exciting; first Newbery Medal, 1922)
1922	Margery Williams Bianco, *The Velveteen Rabbit*
1924	A. A. Milne, *When We Were Very Young*
1926	A. A. Milne, *Winnie-the-Pooh*
1928	Wanda Gág, *Millions of Cats*
	Carl Sandburg, *Abe Lincoln Grows Up*
1929	Rachel Field, *Hitty, Her First Hundred Years*
1932	Laura Ingalls Wilder, *Little House in the Big Woods*
	Laura E. Richards, *Tirra Lirra: Rhymes Old and New*
1933	Jean de Brunhoff, *The Story of Babar*
1937	Dr. Seuss, *And to Think That I Saw It on Mulberry Street*
	John Ronald Reuel Tolkien, *The Hobbit*
1939	James Daugherty, *Daniel Boone*
1940	Armstrong Sperry, *Call It Courage*
	Doris Gates, *Blue Willow*
1941	Lois Lenski, *Indian Captive, The Story of Mary Jemison*
	Robert McCloskey, *Make Way for Ducklings*
1942	Virginia Lee Burton, *The Little House*
1944	Robert Lawson, *Rabbit Hill*
1946	Esther Forbes, *Johnny Tremain*
1947	Marcia Brown, *Stone Soup*
1950	Beverly Cleary, *Henry Huggins*
1951	Olivia Coolidge, *Legends of the North*
1952	Lynd Ward, *The Biggest Bear*
	E. B. White, *Charlotte's Web*
	David McCord, *Far and Few*
1953	Mary Norton, *The Borrowers*
1954	Rosemary Sutcliff, *The Eagle of the Ninth*
1955	L. M. Boston, *The Children of Green Knowe*
1957	Else Holmelund Minarik, *Little Bear*
1958	Jean Fritz, *The Cabin Faced West*
	Elizabeth George Speare, *The Witch of Blackbird Pond*
1959	Leo Lionni, *Little Blue and Little Yellow*
	Jean George, *My Side of the Mountain*

CHART 2–3 (cont.)
Notable authors of children's literature

1960	Michael Bond, *A Bear Called Paddington*
	Scott O'Dell, *Island of the Blue Dolphins*
1961	C. S. Lewis, *The Lion, the Witch, and the Wardrobe*
1962	Ronald Syme, *African Traveler, The Story of Mary Kingsley*
	Madeleine L'Engle, *A Wrinkle in Time*
	Ezra Jack Keats, *The Snowy Day*
1964	Louise Fitzhugh, *Harriet the Spy*
	Irene Hunt, *Across Five Aprils*
	Lloyd Alexander, *The Book of Three*
1967	John Christopher, *The White Mountains*
	E. L. Konigsburg, *Jennifer, Hecate, MacBeth, William McKinley and Me, Elizabeth*
	Virginia Hamilton, *Zeely*
1969	John Steptoe, *Stevie*
	William H. Armstrong, *Sounder*
	Theodore Taylor, *The Cay*
	Vera and Bill Cleaver, *Where the Lilies Bloom*
	William Steig, *Sylvester and the Magic Pebble*
1970	Betsy Byars, *Summer of the Swans*
	Judy Blume, *Are You There God? It's Me, Margaret*
1971	Arnold Lobel, *Frog and Toad Are Friends*
	Muriel Feelings, *Moja Means One: Swahili Counting Book*
	Robert Kraus, *Leon, the Late Bloomer*
1972	Judith Viorst, *Alexander and the Terrible, Horrible, No Good, Very Bad Day*
1973	Doris Smith, *A Taste of Blackberries*
1974	Janet Hickman, *The Valley of the Shadow*
1975	Lawrence Yep, *Dragonwings*
1976	Mildred Taylor, *Roll of Thunder Hear My Cry*
1977	Jamake Highwater, *Anpao: An Indian Odyssey*
	Patricia Clapp, *I'm Deborah Sampson: A Soldier in the War of the Revolution*
	Katherine Paterson, *Bridge to Terabithia*
	Margaret Musgrove, *Ashanti to Zulu: African Traditions*
1978	Tomie de Paola, *The Clown of God*
1979	José Aruego and Ariane Dewey, *We Hide, You Seek*
1981	Nancy Willard, *Visit to William Blake's Inn*
1982	Nina Bawden, *Kept in the Dark*
	Laurence Pringle, *Water: The Next Great Resource Battle*
	Cynthia Ryland, *When I Was Young in the Mountains*
1984	Paula Fox, *One-Eyed Cat*
1985	Rhoda Blumberg, *Commodore Perry in the Land of the Shogun*
1986	Jean Fritz, *Make Way for Sam Houston*
1987	Russell Freedman, *Lincoln: A Photobiography*
1988	Paul Fleishman, *Joyful Noise: Poems for Two Voices*
1989	Janet Taylor Lisle, *Afternoon of the Elves*
1990	Dr. Seuss, *Oh, the Places You'll Go!*

mate details of a warm, loving, and very human family. The most popular character, Jo, shares many characteristics with Alcott herself. Jo is courageous, warm, and honest, but she has a quick temper that often gets her into difficulty. She also leaves home to earn a living as a writer and help support her family. *Little Women* was so popular that in 1869 Alcott wrote a sequel, *Little Women, Part II*. She also wrote other favorites, such as *An Old-Fashioned Girl, Little Men,* and *Eight Cousins*.

One very popular realistic story published in the nineteenth century had a setting foreign to most readers of its English translation. Mountains that climb into the sky, sheepherders, tinkling bells, rushing streams, flower-strewn meadows, a hut with a bed of fresh hay, and the freedom to wander in delightful Swiss surroundings were found in Johanna Spyri's *Heidi,* published in Switzerland in 1880 and translated into English in 1884. Spyri based her book on her own childhood experiences in the Swiss Alps, which may help explain its realistic appeal. According to Virginia Haviland (16):

> In an era when so much children's literature was burdened with dead dialogue and moral content, the freshness of this story must have come as a breath of mountain air; today, Heidi holds her own with carefree heroines of any of the best modern children's books because she is real. (p. 79)

Actual experience in a foreign land was not the only basis an author had for providing a believable setting. Mary Mapes Dodge used research and imagination to provide credible background and characters in *Hans Brinker, or the Silver Skates, A Story of Holland*. Readers in the Netherlands accepted this story as authentic in 1865, even though Dodge had never visited their country.

Space does not allow a complete discussion of all the books written for children or written for adults and read by children in earlier eras of our history. Chart 2–3 lists some previously discussed

literature that bring the world of children's books into the twentieth century.

CHILDREN AND THE FAMILY IN CHILDREN'S LITERATURE

Attitudes toward the place for children in the family have changed considerably over time. Before the Middle Ages, children were not greatly valued, and infanticide was a regular practice. During the Middle Ages, poor children shared the poverty and hard work of their parents, while children from the upper class and nobility spent most of their childhood separated from their families, receiving instruction and training in the roles they would assume as adults. Not until relatively recently has childhood become the time for the close family interaction that we are familiar with today.

Books written for children or adopted by children over the last few centuries have usually reflected views of childhood and the family typical of their time. Researchers are increasingly viewing children's literature as an important source of information about these changing attitudes. In *Fifteen Centuries of Children's Literature: An Annotated Chronology of British and American Works in Historical Context,* Jane Bingham and Grayce Scholt (5) consider the historical background of children's books, including attitudes toward and treatment of children, discuss the development of children's books, and provide an annotated chronology of children's books. Robert Gordon Kelly (19), in *Mother Was a Lady: Self and Society in Selected American Children's Periodicals, 1865–1890,* considers the social values reflected in children's stories of the late nineteenth century. Mary Lystad (27) considers the sociology of children's books over two centuries in *From Dr. Mather to Dr. Seuss: Two Hundred Years of American Books for Children*.

Other researchers have analyzed children's literature over time: Jean Duncan Shaw (36) has studied themes in children's books published between 1850 and 1964; Alma Cross Homze (17) has analyzed the changing interpersonal relationships depicted in realistic fiction published between 1920 and 1960; and Mary Cadogan and Patricia Craig (6) have looked at the changing role of females in *You're a Brick, Angela! A New Look at Girls' Fiction from 1839 to 1975*. Studies of more

ISSUE

Changing Issues Affecting Children's Book Publishing in the Twentieth Century

TWENTIETH-CENTURY American publishers of children's books, like publishers in all historical periods, must respond to the issues of the times. Ann Durell identifies some of these changing issues in two articles published in *The Horn Book.*[1,2]

According to Durell, the 1950s was a time when publishing was fun because the rules were clear-cut. The taboos of the early 1900s were still in place: no lying or stealing unless suitably punished, no drinking, and no bad language. Racial prejudice was evidenced by the controversy that greeted Garth Williams's black and white couple in *The Rabbits' Wedding*.

In the late 1950s, the library market took on new significance, as Russia launched Sputnik and our educational system came under attack. Books were considered means of improving education. Durell categorizes the 1960s as a time of rapidly expanding school libraries in the United States. Title II of the Elementary and Secondary School Act mandated funds for the purchase of nontextbooks for schools. The sales of both nonfiction and easy-to-read book titles and the expansion of school libraries increased rapidly.

New issues affected the publishing trade, however, as the country was polarized by the Vietnam War and the new demands of the Great Society. The all-white world of children's books was challenged; editors started searching for black au-

recent historical periods include John Rowe Townsend's (40) analysis of the relationships between generations depicted in the literature of the 1950s and the 1960s, Carolyn Wilson Carmichael's (7) analysis of social values reflected in contemporary realistic fiction, and Beverly Young's (44) analysis of female protagonists in literature of the 1930s, the 1950s, and the 1970s.

Unsurprisingly, a prominent theme in children's literature has been the relationships of children within the family. Changing views about children and the family over time necessarily reflect other social attitudes as well. The following time periods reflect the publication dates of a few popular American children's books in eras otherwise not easily demarcated by precise years. All these books are available today. The older books have been published in reproductions by Garland Publishing Company of New York and London.

The Child and the Family, 1856–1903

An emphatic sense of duty to God and parents, the rise of the public school and Sunday School movements, and the beginning of a belief that children are individuals in their own right are among the characteristics of the Victorian era identifiable in children's literature of the time. Much Victorian children's literature stresses the development of conscience, the merit of striving for perfection, and the male and female roles exemplified by family members. Illuminating examples of the social attitudes of this period may be drawn from Charlotte Yonge's *The Daisy Chain* (1856), Louisa May Alcott's *Little Women* (1868), Thomas Bailey Aldrich's *The Story of a Bad Boy* (1870), Margaret Sidney's *Five Little Peppers and How They Grew* (1880), and Kate Douglas Wiggin's *Rebecca of Sunnybrook Farm* (1903). (See also Chart 2–4.)

While these books have their differences, all of them stress the importance of accepting responsibility, whether for one's family, the poor and unfortunate, or one's self-improvement. For example, the older children in *The Daisy Chain* assume the task of raising the younger children when their mother dies; their greatest concerns are instilling Christian goodness in their siblings and living up to their father's wishes. Likewise, the children in *Little Women* and *Five Little Peppers and How They Grew* feel responsible for their siblings and their mothers. Rebecca, in *Rebecca of*

thors. For the most part, however, children's books did not reflect the social upheavals of the time.

The 1970s introduced literature that reflected the social upheavals. Reactions to two children's books in the early 1970s exemplify the changing times. When a white author won the Newbery Medal for writing about a black family (*Sounder*), protests intensified editors' searches for authors and illustrators who represented ethnic minorities. Mickey's nudity in Maurice Sendak's *In the Night Kitchen* resulted in actions ranging from covering the nudity before the book was placed on the shelf to actual banning of the book.

As the 1970s continued, concern about the sex roles portrayed in children's books increased; lists of taboos in children's books were reduced; and books reflected ethnic minorities more positively. Durell emphasizes the paradox created by these changes and the new pressures exerted on publishers. On the one hand, the only criterion for allowing books to be published was positive portrayal of females, minority groups, senior citizens, and the handicapped. On the other hand, groups demanding conservative standards insisted on returning to the 1950s taboos. Consequently, censorship, but for different reasons, became an issue on both sides.

Interestingly, one of the issues affecting book publishing in the 1990s is related to the growing financial success of children's trade book publishing. Eden Ross Lipson[3] discusses the impact of giant corporations, which buy out publishing houses and then try to make the publishing companies as profitable as possible. Consequently, there are concerns that mass market favorites may overshadow quality children's books.

[1]Durrell, Ann. "There Is No Happy Ending: Children's Book Publishing—Past, Present, and Future," Part 1. *The Horn Book* 58 (February 1982): 23–30.
[2]Durell, Ann. "There Is No Happy Ending: Children's Book Publishing—Past, Present, and Future," Part 2. *The Horn Book* 58 (April 1982): 145–50.
[3]Lipson, Eden Ross. "The Little Industry That Could," Part 2. *The New York Times Magazine*. (December 3, 1989): 20–21, 50, 52.

CHART 2–4
Social values, family life, and personal relationships, 1856–1903

	BOOK, AUTHOR, DATE, SETTING				
	Charlotte Yonge. *The Daisy Chain.* 1856, 1868. Rural England. Middle class.	**Louisa May Alcott. *Little Women.* 1868. New England city suburb; Large gardens, quiet streets.**	**Thomas Bailey Aldrich. *The Story of a Bad Boy.* 1870. New Orleans then to small New Hampshire town.**	**Margaret Sidney. *Five Little Peppers and How They Grew.* 1880. Poverty level. United States.**	**Kate Douglas Wiggin. *Rebecca of Sunnybrook Farm.* 1903. Small New England town.**
SOCIAL VALUES					
Dignity of Human Beings	Concern for family members. Some poor described as uncivilized. Wanted to improve role of poor by building church.	More important to have personal dignity, self-respect, and peace than wealth. Concern for the ill and the poor.	In New Orleans Tom kicked a "negro boy" who was in his way. Tom believed Indians scalp children. In New Hampshire household, aunt and servant were friends. No social criticism mentioned.	Peppers were proud and believed they had a good life, although they were poor.	Prejudice stated by neighbor against being "dark complected." Aunt Miranda disowned her sister when she married against her wishes. Rebecca respected many people.
Acceptance of Responsibility	Duty to tend to poor. Founded and taught in school for poor. Each member accepted responsibility to younger siblings after mother's death.	Duty to poor; gave their Christmas breakfast to a poor family. Strong duty to family.	Main character did not dwell on unhappy events in story but believed in accepting reality.	Each member expressed responsibility for siblings and mother. Polly almost ruined her eyes sewing for mother when Polly had measles.	Rebecca worked hard to complete the academy in three years instead of four.
Belief in Equality of Opportunity	Boys had advanced education. Girls not expected to understand mathematical concepts. Girls trained to guide family. Poor children worked at early ages.	Girls were educated but not at the university. Males attended university.	Stressed Puritan ethic of diligence and common sense. Veneer of well being. Main character thought all adults had money when they wanted it.	Family said their ship would come in and hard times would be over.	Rebecca thought boys could do more exciting things than girls. Teacher stressed that girls could have a profession. Brother hoped to become a doctor.
Ambition	Charity, humility, devotion to good works. Development of Christian goodness.	Heroine, Jo, wanted to write. Other sisters: drawing, music. Work ethic stressed by son-in-law.	Males should learn "manly arts" and become self-reliant. Tom did not want to be lowest in his class. No single drive expressed by the main character.	Members wanted to help mother. Polly wanted to play the piano. Ann wanted their ship to come in. To be "good."	Rebecca wanted an education to help her family. To become a writer.
Obedience to Law, Patriotism	Respect stated for military profession.	Mother encouraged her husband to serve in the Union army. Mother devoted time to Soldiers Aid Society.	Generally, yes. Boys escaped from jail so father would not learn about their prank. Military experience held in high esteem.	No disrespect stated.	No disrespect stated.
Importance of Education and Knowledge	Both sexes read many books. Read Bible in Greek and English. Males attended university. Asked not to use slang.	Jo loved Aunt March's large library. They all read. Felt humiliated when punished at school. Father described as scholar. Jo asked not to use slang.	Gained enjoyment and escaped by reading. Attended boys' academy. Wanted to be promoted to higher position in class.	Polly wanted to learn. Wealthy cousins had tutor. Wealthy old gentleman promised to educate Polly.	Reading gave pleasure. Education could make it possible to improve one's position in life. Rebecca respected intelligence.

CHART 2–4 (cont.)
Social values, family life, and personal relationships, 1856–1903

	BOOK, AUTHOR, DATE, SETTING				
	Charlotte Yonge. *The Daisy Chain.* 1856, 1868. Rural England. Middle class.	**Louisa May Alcott. *Little Women.* 1868. New England city suburb; Large gardens, quiet streets.**	**Thomas Bailey Aldrich. *The Story of a Bad Boy.* 1870. New Orleans then to small New Hampshire town.**	**Margaret Sidney. *Five Little Peppers and How They Grew.* 1880. Poverty level. United States.**	**Kate Douglas Wiggin. *Rebecca of Sunnybrook Farm.* 1903. Small New England town.**
SOCIAL VALUES (cont.)					
Respect for Adult Authority	Children wanted to live up to their father's wishes and ideals. Asked mother's permission at home.	Children wanted their parents' acceptance. Looked up to a "noble" mother and turned to the "quiet scholar" who helped them during "troublesome times."	Respected adults but did not always ask permission. Tom did not mention something when he knew grandfather would disapprove.	Children always respected their widowed mother. Jasper wanted his father's respect.	Rebecca respected knowledge of English teacher and sought her advice.
FAMILY LIFE					
Description	Warm, close, and self-sufficient. Family center of heroine's existence. Cleanliness of home considered a virtue.	Warm, filled with laughter and singing. Children made their own fun; played "Pilgrim's Progress" and acted out plays. At 9:00, stopped work and sang before going to bed.	Family and main character generally cheerful and affectionate. "Old Puritan austerity cropped but once a week." Main character interacted more with friends as they put on plays, formed a club, attended school, and played pranks.	Close, happy family who told stories and expressed love and concern for each other. Boys argued with new cousins.	Rebecca had a happy-go-lucky family led by father who had difficulty making money. Two aunts led a very conservative life.
Religion, Stability	Stressed responsibility for raising good and holy children. Family read Bible and discussed meaning of Sunday services.	Father asked his wife to pray for the girls each evening. They turned to God to help them overcome troubles and temptations.	Nutter house had been in the family nearly one hundred years. Attic with its treasures was symbolic of the long residence of one family. Sundays were solemn. Attended church, read Bible, and ate cold meals.	Stable because of closeness but grew up under considerable pressure. Expressed great respect for minister.	Contrasts drawn between the two families. Rebecca's parents moved often. Aunts lived in the same home as their father.
Numbers in Family	Eleven children, Father, Mother (died early in story).	Four girls. Mother. Father (away in Army in Part 1).	One child living with grandfather in the north. Parents living in New Orleans.	Five children, widowed mother.	One of seven children. Father died, mother had difficulties.
Extended Family	Prim, middle-aged governess. Nurse. Servants.	Housekeeper.	Grandfather. Maiden aunt. Servant.	Wealthy old gentleman, his son, his daughter, and her children.	Two spinster sisters Rebecca lived with them.
Relationships Within Family	Definite male and female roles. Children relied upon mother in the home. Father, head of household. Children respected each other.	Mother guided the heart. Father guided the soul. Father, head of family. Strong ties among sisters. Oldest sister's gentle advice influenced her sisters.	Grandfather understood boy; he had once run away to sea. Grandfather showed pride when Tom won fight with a bully who harassed smaller boys.	Everyone pampered Phronsie, the pretty baby in the family. Phronsie and Polly brought changes in others' lives because of the influence of their personalities.	Aunt Jane was warmer and more understanding. Aunt Miranda was strict, head of household and respected traditional values.

CHART 2–4 (cont.)
Social values, family life, and personal relationships, 1856–1903

	BOOK, AUTHOR, DATE, SETTING				
	Charlotte Yonge, *The Daisy Chain,* 1856, 1868. Rural England. Middle class.	**Louisa May Alcott, *Little Women,* 1868. New England city suburb; Large gardens, quiet streets.**	**Thomas Bailey Aldrich, *The Story of a Bad Boy,* 1870. New Orleans then to small New Hampshire town.**	**Margaret Sidney, *Five Little Peppers and How They Grew,* 1880. Poverty level. United States.**	**Kate Douglas Wiggin, *Rebecca of Sunnybrook Farm,* 1903. Small New England town.**
PERSONAL RELATIONSHIPS AND FEELINGS					
Independent Male or Female	Mother: at home, gentle power, strong authority. Father: skillful, clever, sensitive but showed vexation and sarcasm. Ethel: secretly kept up with brother's classical studies.	Jo: didn't want to grow up to be a lady. Jo: wanted to do something extraordinary. Jo: said her quick temper and restless spirit got her in trouble. Mother: managed household while husband was away.	Grandfather lived at ease on money invested in shipping. A maiden sister managed the household with her brother and servant. Tom had freedom to explore the countryside. Tom stressed male need to "learn to box, to ride, to pull an oar, and to swim."	Mother made family decisions but often had no idea about how they would manage. Boys got into more trouble than girls.	Rebecca was "plucky," "dauntless," and "intelligent." Aunt Miranda was strong-willed, managed their lives. Rebecca usually self-reliant.
Dependent Male or Female	Mother: reserved and shrinking from society. Males made major decisions. Girls clung to males.	Mother: worried about guiding children to meet husband's ideals. Children turned to parents for guidance. Beth: too bashful to attend school.	Girls attended separate school and were graduated by "a dragon of watchfulness." Pony's vanities compared to female "weaknesses."	Mother eventually accepted help from a wealthy gentleman who brought the family out of poverty. Polly, although plucky, often fainted.	Aunt Jane infrequently spoke out against Miranda. Aunts wanted dependent, obedient child.
Problems	Concerned with not living up to parents' expectations and God's desire. Love of glory considered a temptation.	Overcoming problems that led to "sweetness of self-denial and self-control."	Problems allowed main character to consider his moral code. When he disobeyed something usually went wrong.	Concerned with being good. Problems connected with survival in poverty.	Tried to live up to the traditional behavioral ideals of a strict aunt and Rebecca's desire to be "respectably, decently good."
Friendships	Mainly with family members or people in own class.	Greatest among sisters. Neighbor boy.	A group of boys at the academy. The Centipede Club—all boys. Tom and older seaman. Aunt and female servant were friends.	Mainly each other in the family. A wealthy boy who rescued Phronsie and was impressed with the warm family. Phronsie and the wealthy gentleman whom she changed.	Rebecca was friendly. Liked many adults and children. They also liked her.

Sunnybrook Farm, feels this responsibility to such an extent that she completes four years of work at the academy in three years so that she can earn a living and help educate her siblings.

The characters in these books respect adult authority. Children strive to live up to their parents' ideals or want the acceptance and respect of their parents. The protagonist in *The Story of a Bad Boy* may not always ask or follow his grandfather's advice, but he admits that he deserves the terrible things that usually happen to him when he disobeys.

Respect for authority is underscored by the characteristic religious emphasis in these books. In *The Daisy Chain,* family members read the Bible together, discuss the meaning of the minister's sermons, debate the relative importance of the temptations in their lives, and organize a church and school for the poor. In *Little Women,* the family members receive strength from prayer and Bible reading. In *The Story of a Bad Boy,* Sundays are solemn days, in which the family attends church, reads the scriptures, and eats food prepared the day before. The five little Peppers voice

May Alcott's illustrations for her sister Louisa May Alcott's *Little Women* reinforce the vision of a warm, loving Victorian family. (Illustration by May Alcott. From *Little Women or, Meg, Jo, Beth and Amy* by Louisa M. Alcott. Published by Roberts Brothers, 1868. Courtesy of Lilly Library, Indiana University, Bloomington, Indiana.)

considerable admiration for the clergy and want to become "good." Rebecca of Sunnybrook Farm's aunt, like her father before her, is an influential member of her church.

Family life in these books reiterates the definite social roles assigned to males and females in the Victorian era. Females usually run the household and make decisions related to everyday life, but the husband and father is usually the undisputed head of the family. The author may even state this fact point-blank, so there is no misunderstanding on the part of the reader—as Louisa May Alcott does in *Little Women*:

> To outsiders, the five energetic women seemed to rule the house, and so they did in many things; but the quiet scholar, sitting among his books, was still the head of the family, the household conscience, anchor, and comforter: to him the busy, anxious women always turned in troublous times, finding him, in the truest sense of those sacred words, husband and father. (p. 294)

Males and females attend separate schools in *The Story of a Bad Boy,* and only male characters attend the university in *The Daisy Chain* and *Little Women*. Education may also stress different objectives for males and females. Yonge's heroine in *The Daisy Chain* completes her brother's school assignments, but is not expected to understand mathematical concepts. Aldrich's hero wants training in manly arts, such as boxing, riding, and rowing. In contrast, drawing, writing, and music are desired accomplishments for the females in *Little Women,* piano lessons are sought by the oldest female Pepper, and writing is Rebecca's desire.

Considerable insights about the children and families in these books are gained by viewing the problems that the heroes and heroines experience. Many of these problems involve attempts to abide by the period's standards of moral rectitude. Yonge's heroine strives to raise her family and help the poor. She works to keep the youngest baby an "unstained jewel" until the baby returns to her mother. She and her brother also face the problems associated with providing spiritual guidance to the poor. Many of Jo's problems in *Little Women* are related to controlling her "unfeminine" high energy and self-assertiveness. Jo looks to her pious mother for guidance in how to be "good."

> Jo's only answer was to hold her mother close, and, in the silence which followed, the sincerest prayer she had ever prayed left her heart without words; for in that sad, yet happy hour, she had learned not only the bitterness of remorse and despair, but the sweetness of self-denial and self-control; and, led by her mother's hand, she had drawn nearer to the Friend who welcomes every child with a love stronger than that of any father, tenderer than that of any mother. (p. 103)

Rebecca of Sunnybrook Farm also confronts problems caused by the conflicts between her own high-spirited nature and adults' strict expectations about a young girl's behavior. She also experiences personal misgivings when her actions do not live up to her desire to be good. The advantages of these conflicts, however, are stated by Rebecca's English teacher at the academy: "Luckily she attends to her own development. . . . In a sense she is independent of everything and everybody; she follows her saint without being conscious of it." The problems Thomas Bailey Aldrich creates for his protagonist allow the "bad" boy to consider and strengthen his own moral code. Although he has several unhappy and even disastrous experiences, the boy does not dwell upon them, believing that they have caused him to become more manly and self-reliant.

Overcoming problems related to poverty and growing up without a father are major concerns of the Pepper children, but Margaret Sidney has their mother encourage them in this way: "You keep on a-tryin', and the Lord'll send some way; don't you go to botherin' your head about it now . . . it'll come when it's time." The family's financial problems are finally solved when a wealthy old gentleman invites them to share his home.

The Child and the Family, 1938–1960

The 1900s brought considerable change to the lives of American children. Many states passed child labor laws, John Dewey's influential theories encouraged a more child-centered educational philosophy, the quality and extent of public education improved, and religious training placed less emphasis on sinfulness and more emphasis on moral development and responsibility toward others. Children's literature reflected these changes, and children's book publishing expanded to meet the needs of an increasingly literate youthful population. Optimism was a keynote in the twentieth-century "Age of Progress," and, especially after World War II, "children's book editors saw a bright future for the children of this country and the world" (30, p. 89).

This optimism is reflected in the views of the children and families depicted in American children's books of the late 1930s through the beginning of the 1960s. John Rowe Townsend's (40) conclusions about depictions of family life in children's literature of the 1950s apply to earlier literature as well: Children live in stable communities, where most children are happy and secure, the older generations are wise and respected, and the generations follow one another into traditional social roles in an orderly way.

The following books, written by award-winning authors, characterize the social values, the stability of family life, and the types of personal relationships depicted in children's literature of this period: Elizabeth Enright's *Thimble Summer* (1938), Eleanor Estes's *The Moffats* (1941), Sydney Taylor's *All-of-a-Kind Family* (1951), and Madeleine L'Engle's *Meet the Austins* (1960). (See also Chart 2–5.) The families in these books live in different locations around the United States and range from lower to upper-middle class, but the values they support are similar. The characters admire and emulate the traditional family model of breadwinning father, housewife mother, and their children, living together in one place for a number of years.

Family members have happy and secure relationships with one another, complemented by mutual respect, warmth, and humor. The actions of the Moffats express confidence and trust in the family unit. The children in *All-of-a-Kind Family* cannot imagine what it would be like not to have a family. In *Meet the Austins,* Vicky is pleased because her mother looks just the way she believes a mother should look.

Religious values are suggested in these stories by Sunday school attendance, preparation for the sabbath, or prayers before meals. Dignity is stressed. The family in *Thimble Summer* brings an orphan boy into its home on trust without checking his background. The parents in *All-of-a-Kind Family* tell their children to accept people and not ask them about their personal lives. The Austin family feels empathy for others' problems, and the parents include their children in serious discussions.

Patriotism is strong in all books, and the law is respected. Education is considered important; children enjoy reading, go to school with the expectation that it will increase their understanding, and finish their homework before playing. Families prize even small collections of books. The work ethic is a powerful force in the lives of these families. Children talk about saving their money to buy a farm, a mother takes in sewing to keep the family together, and a father works long hours, saving for the day when he can make life better for his family. Children respect adult wisdom and authority; they obey rules, minding their teachers and complying with parental desires. Children also enjoy listening to their elders tell about their own experiences.

Unsurprisingly, given their secure lives and confident adherence to established social standards, the children in these books have few emotional problems. They usually feel good about themselves and other family members. Their actions suggest dependence upon the family for emotional stability, but independence in their daily experiences, as they move without fear around the neighborhood, city, or countryside.

CHART 2–5
Social values, family life, and personal relationships, 1938–1960

	BOOK, AUTHOR, DATE, SETTING			
	Elizabeth Enright, *Thimble Summer*, 1938. Rural Wisconsin farm.	**Eleanor Estes, *The Moffats*, 1941. Middle-sized New England city. Poor family.**	**Sidney Taylor, *All-Of-A-Kind Family*, 1951. New York, East Side (1912). Jewish family.**	**Madeleine L'Engle, *Meet the Austins*, 1960. Country home. Father M.D.**
SOCIAL VALUES				
Dignity of Human Beings	An orphan boy was given love and respect of the family.	They trusted each other and strangers. They expected strangers to give them help when they were lost.	You accept people. "You don't ask them about their personal lives."	Family felt empathy toward others' problems. Children included in serious discussions.
Acceptance of Responsibility	Children accepted farm chores without complaining.	Older members responsible for younger brothers and sisters. Joe felt terrible when he lost coal money, and his mother would need to work late. He searched until he found it.	Child felt responsible for lost library book; her sisters offered their few pennies. They tried to avoid household chores. A promise was considered important.	Consideration for others was essential. One child could not disrupt the family.
Belief in Equality of Opportunity	Father believed his daughter could be the farmer in the family.	Family worked together. Males and females did many things together. Positive mood.	Father believed his work and savings would make it possible to have a better life.	Yes. Aunt Elena was a well-known concert pianist.
Ambition	Strong work ethic: Children talk about saving money to buy a farm.	Mother worked hard to keep family. Took in sewing. Traded sewing for free dancing lessons.	Father wanted more for his family than he could give them. Worked and saved for the day he could make their lives better.	Scientific experiments were considered important. Education was important.
Obedience to Law, Patriotism	Yes. No conflicts mentioned.	Nine-year-old always walked cautiously by police chief's house; never stood on his lawn.	Father did not want the U.S. flag placed on the floor.	Family rules were stressed.
Importance of Education and Knowledge	Reading important to the girls as a means of escape.	Five-year-old Rufus looked forward to school. "Go to school or be a dunce." All children had dancing lessons.	Great excitement because Friday was library day. Books were treasured.	Homework was to be finished before playing. Grandfather collected books.
Respect for Adult Authority	Children respected parents. Enjoyed listening to friends, great-grandmother tell stories about her life.	Girl worried about mimicking new superintendent of schools. Mother: "Do as the teacher says." Mother was voice of authority; they went to her to ask questions.	Children obediently followed parents. Called themselves "Mama's children."	"When daddy speaks that way we hop." Children did not want their parents to come home and find work not finished.
FAMILY LIFE				
Description	Very happy and secure family. Garnet had a nice mother and a nice family. Considerable trust of others.	Family was happy and secure in their relationships, although their rented house had a "for sale" sign on it. Mother didn't really share children's experiences but listened to them.	Happy secure family: a "gentle, soft" father; a loving, but strong mother. After five girls, father cried with happiness when boy was born.	Spontaneous family love. Mutual respect and understanding. Warmth and humor. Strong father who made them accept the consequences when they didn't do their homework.
Religion, Stability	Families had lived in the valley for generations. No strong religious emphasis.	Worked together for good of the family, even when Rufus had scarlet fever and they were quarantined. Went to Sunday school.	Very stable; could not imagine what it would be like not to have a family. Law of the Sabbath carefully observed.	Strong family ties. Sunday school and church important. Family prayed before meals and at other times in their day.
Numbers in Family	Three children. Mother. Father.	Four children. Widowed mother.	Six children. Father. Mother.	Four children. Father. Mother.
Extended Family	Brought an orphan boy to work on farm without checking I.D.		Mother's brother was a frequent visitor.	Orphaned ten-year-old daughter of a friend.

CHART 2–5 (cont.)
Social values, family life, and personal relationships, 1938–1960

	BOOK, AUTHOR, DATE, SETTING			
	Elizabeth Enright, *Thimble Summer*, 1938. Rural Wisconsin farm.	**Eleanor Estes, *The Moffats*, 1941. Middle-sized New England city. Poor family.**	**Sidney Taylor, *All-Of-A-Kind Family*, 1951. New York, East Side (1912). Jewish family.**	**Madeleine L'Engle, *Meet the Austins*, 1960. Country home. Father M.D.**
FAMILY LIFE (cont.)				
Relationships Within Family	Strong, trusting. Slight brother and sister friction.	Had fun together. Humorous experiences. Mother was supportive and loving. Not critical except about getting clothes dirty.	Mother planned games for children to make them enjoy dusting. Children were proud of their mother; wanted to introduce her to new librarian.	Children disagreed with each other but always made up. Father and mother talked over family problems with children.
PERSONAL RELATIONSHIPS AND FEELINGS				
Independent Male or Female	Independent female who loved her family. Hitchhiked to town without fear. Angry when brother suggested she do women's work.	Children could travel around town. Always found their way back.	Strong mother who took care of the family. Father owned his own business: a "junk shop." Children hid their candy from their mother.	Children were individual thinkers.
Dependent Male or Female		They relied upon each other and upon their mother to answer questions.	Children gave in to firm mother.	Vicky believed her older brother always knew what to say and could get her out of difficulties. Family depended on each other.
Types of Problems	No real problems.	Their house was for sale, and they accepted the possibility of moving. Some problems because of family illness or need for money. Problems overcome in humorous ways.	No major problems. Saved for lost library book, hid candy.	Maggy, an orphaned girl, was disturbed because she had never known love. Problems centered around helping her make adjustments.
Friendships	Next-door girl whose family had lived there for generations.	Family members. Neighbors. They made friends with strangers around town.	Very close to each other: no other children mentioned. Neighborhood peddlers and librarian were friends.	Children close friends. Uncle Douglas always understood them and knew how to make them feel good about themselves.

The Child and the Family, 1969–1989

Researchers who have analyzed children's literature over time have identified the 1960s, 1970s, and 1980s as decades in which traditional social, family, and personal values appeared to be changing. Alma Cross Homze (17) found that in the late 1950s, adult characters in children's books were becoming less authoritarian and critical in their relationships with children, while children were becoming more outspoken, independent, and critical of adults. John Rowe Townsend (40) later concluded that children's literature of the 1960s suggested an erosion of adult authority and a widening of the generation gap. When Beverly Young (44) compared female protagonists of the 1930s, the 1950s, and the 1970s, she concluded that the characters became increasingly protest-oriented.

Binnie Tate Wilkin (42) connects these trends in the children's literature of the 1960s and 1970s with changing "educational, social and political, and economic concerns" (p. 21), citing as examples the civil rights movements, protest marches, and assassinations of the period. Wilkin says:

> Almost all levels of society were challenged to respond to the activism. Book publishers responded with new materials reflecting dominant concerns. Distress about children's reading problems, federal responses to urban unrest, the youth movements, new openness about sexuality, religious protest, etc. were reflected in children's books. (p. 21)

In 1981, polls quoted by John F. Stacks (38) showed that about 20 percent of Americans still expressed belief in most of the traditional values of hard work, family loyalty, and sacrifice, while the majority of respondents embraced only some of those values, doubted that self-denial and moral rectitude were their own rewards, and held tolerant views about abortion, premarital sex, remaining single, and not having children. Still, Stacks concluded that people who believed in traditional values were becoming an increasingly vocal group that "could set to a significant degree the moral tone for the 1980s" (p. 18). Other research indicates that the American family has experienced far more continuity than change over the last fifty years. Norman Lobsenz (24) reports findings from the study *Middletown Families: 50 Years of Change and Continuity* showing that marriage is still viewed as important, although divorce is widely accepted; many wives and mothers have jobs, but they still do most of the housework and child care; and many married couples see more of their relatives than they do of their friends.

Comparison of children's literature written between the 1930s and the early 1960s with children's literature written in the 1970s and 1980s reveals both similarities and differences between the characterizations of the American family in the two periods. Many books still portray strong family ties and stress the importance of personal responsibility and human dignity, but the happy, stable unit of the earlier literature is often replaced by a family in turmoil as it adjusts to a new culture, faces the prospects of surviving without one or both parents, handles the disruption resulting from divorce, or deals with an extended family, exemplified by grandparents or a foster home. Later literature also suggests that many acceptable family units do not conform to the traditional American model.

While many children's books could be selected for this discussion, the following books contain some of the diverse attitudes toward family and children in the period from 1969 to 1989: Vera and Bill Cleaver's *Where the Lilies Bloom* (1969), Marilyn Sachs's *The Bears' House* (1971), Norma Klein's *Mom, the Wolf Man, and Me* (1972), Betsy Byars's *The Night Swimmers* (1980), and Paula Fox's *The Moonlight Man* (1986). (See also Chart 2–6.) While children in the literature of the 1940s and 1950s had few personal and emotional problems, children between 1969 and 1989 may have considerable responsibility and may experience emotional problems as they try to survive. The strongest character in *Where the Lilies Bloom* attempts to hold the family together, but she discovers that she needs people outside her immediate family. The oldest boy in *The Bears' House* tries to organize his family, while his nine-year-old sister escapes into the imaginative world of a dollhouse family. The heroine of *Mom, the Wolf Man, and Me* fears her life will change if her mother marries. Characters in *The Night Swimmers* must look after themselves while their father works. The daughter in that book feels unappreciated, is jealous of a brother's attachment to a new friend, and realizes that the family needs help. Her personal problems increase because she is unsure of her place in the family. The main character in *The Moonlight Man* must accept her father and his behavior as well as her parents' divorce.

Characters in the literature of this period may express concern about equal opportunities and question respect for the law, education, and adult authority. The children in *The Bears' House* are afraid to ask for assistance because they fear authorities will separate the family and place them in foster homes. This book illustrates a stereotypical attitude toward education: Before the father leaves, he calls the oldest boy a sissy because he likes to read books rather than take part in sports. In *Mom, the Wolf Man, and Me,* the mother is a successful photographer and allows the daughter to accompany her on women's rights and peace marches.

The strongest story related to the dignity of human beings and acceptance of responsibility is Vera and Bill Cleaver's *Where the Lilies Bloom*. This story is about the proud, independent mountain people who earn their livings through wildcrafting (the gathering of wild plants for human use). Before the father dies, he asks his daughter to keep the family together without accepting charity and to instill in the children pride in having the name Luther.

An opposite condition is found in *The Bears' House,* where the father deserts his children and sick wife. The children want to stay together so much that they apply for welfare and lie to the authorities about their parents. The father in *The Night Swimmers* works evenings, wants to write country music lyrics, and says that fatherhood is a burden. His daughter is responsible for her younger brothers. The father in *The Moonlight Man* is an alcoholic, and when his daughter says, "See you," as she leaves him, he whispers, "Not if

CHART 2–6
Social values, family life, and personal relationships, 1969–1989

	BOOK, AUTHOR, DATE, SETTING				
	Vera and Bill Cleaver, *Where the Lilies Bloom*, 1969. Smoky Mountains. Poor wildcrafters.	**Marilyn Sachs, *The Bears House*, 1971. Poor city neighborhood.**	**Norma Klein, *Mom, The Wolf Man, and Me*, 1972. Middle class.**	**Betsy Byars, *The Night Swimmers*, 1980. Suburbs.**	**Paula Fox, *The Moonlight Man*, 1986.**
SOCIAL VALUES					
Dignity of Human Beings	Father took pride in family name of Luther; wanted to instill pride in family. Wanted to keep family together and not accept charity.	Father deserted the family. Children felt a strong longing to stay together. Applied for welfare.	Daughter sometimes bragged about her illegitimacy to see people's reactions. A best friend did not ask about her father.	Children believed people "run you off" their property to make you feel so bad that you won't come back.	Father does not believe in himself; he is also an alcoholic.
Acceptance of Responsibility	Fourteen-year-old promised her father she would keep family together. Kept her older sister from marrying their neighbor.	Strong responsibility for each other. Oldest boy schemed to keep them together. Nine-year-old Fran Ellen had strong attachment for the baby.	Mother had a nontraditional schedule. They were not constrained by time and other more conventional family living styles. Mother responsible for care of daughter.	Father let his daughter take over responsibility for the family. Father expressed feelings about burdens related to fatherhood: he would rather write lyrics.	Father does not get Catherine to school when he promises. Daughter lies to cover her father's actions.
Belief in Equality of Opportunity	Father stressed that you don't thank people who put you in bondage. You hate them or get out.	No. Fran Ellen was positive that she didn't have a chance of winning.	Mother was a professional photographer. Took her daughter on marches for women's rights and peace.	The children felt they could grow up and have their dreams. Didn't say how they would do it.	Father believed that it is the battle within yourself that causes the problems with opportunity.
Ambition	Daughter wanted to overcome her ignorance and keep the family together.	To survive together as a family.	Profession important to mother.	Children wanted to do things that rich people did. Father wanted a hit recording. Retta wanted to grow up and be important.	Daughter attends private school but is overcome by her father's problems.
Obedience to Law, Patriotism	Father disliked people in authority who might place him in bondage.	They were afraid of the law; it would separate their family and place them in a foster home.	Strong feelings against war.	Children waited until wealthier family had gone to bed and then swam in their pool. They knew they were trespassing.	Father seems to attract less desirable friends. Mother says he always had a "streak of lawlessness."
Importance of Education and Knowledge	Daughter knew books would give her answers that she wanted.	Father considered Fletcher a sissy because he read books all the time. Mother defended Fletcher; he was something special.	Not stressed.	Not stressed.	Father has considerable knowledge. Mother is excited about visiting the Lake Country, the home of Wordsworth.
Respect for Adult Authority	Children respected their father. Tried to do his wishes.	Children expressed fear of adults in power.	Eleven-year-old had frank discussions with her mother. Some disagreement.	Children's father paid little attention to his children. The older sister tried to manage her brothers, not always successfully.	Daughter discovers that her father's promises are not to be taken seriously. She gains new respect for her mother. Father likes to "go against things."

CHART 2–6 (cont.)
Social values, family life, and personal relationships, 1969–1989

	BOOK, AUTHOR, DATE, SETTING				
	Vera and Bill Cleaver, *Where the Lilies Bloom*, 1969. Smoky Mountains. Poor wildcrafters.	**Marilyn Sachs, *The Bears House*, 1971. Poor city neighborhood.**	**Norma Klein, *Mom, The Wolf Man, and Me*, 1972. Middle class.**	**Betsy Byars, *The Night Swimmers*, 1980. Suburbs.**	**Paula Fox, *The Moonlight Man*, 1986.**
FAMILY LIFE					
Description	A proud independent family who learned to gather medicinal plants on slopes of Smokey Mountains.	Father deserted them; mother was sick. The children argued and expressed fear of separation.	Mother and daughter had enjoyable relationship; they had fun together.	Father was a country singer who worked at night. Daughter was responsible for two boys. She considered herself social director. She tried to manage their lives and boys rebelled. She was hurt because she felt unappreciated.	Father and mother are divorced. Father is an alcoholic. Daughter takes care of her father.
Religion, Stability	Long-time mountain resident.	Unstable. Religion not mentioned.	Mother did not set household schedule. They enjoyed this freedom. They were Jewish but never talked about it.	They had moved from old neighborhood and friends. Neighbors disapproved of a father who wore rhinestones and high-gloss boots and let his children "run loose at night like dogs." Religion not mentioned.	Daughter is at boarding school. Father is unreliable. Mother lived in same apartment; mother remarried.
Numbers in Family	Four children. Father died early in the story.	Five children. Sick mother. Father deserted.	One child. Mother.	Three children. Father. Mother had died.	One child.
Relationships Within Family	Strong family ties.	Love between Fran Ellen and baby. Argued but tried to stay together. Mother ineffectual.	Daughter loved her unconventional life with her unmarried mother. Mother, daughter had frank discussions.	Father rarely interfered with or helped children. Retta learned her role model as a mother from T.V. Boys expected her to act like T.V. and grocery-store mothers.	Father cannot rely on himself, so others cannot rely on him. Daughter discovers Mother's strength and the meaning of love.
Extended Family			Mother's boyfriend lived with them on weekends.		Both father and mother have remarried.
PERSONAL RELATIONSHIPS AND FEELINGS					
Independent Male or Female	Mary Call was very resourceful. Found a way to earn money wildcrafting.	Children decided to look after themselves.	Mother had strong character. Daughter self-assured but worried about possible changes in their lives.	Retta planned exciting experiences like swimming at night in a private pool five blocks from house. She learned to cook from school cafeteria and watching T.V. commercials.	Catherine was very resourceful.
Dependent Male or Female	The children were dependent upon fourteen-year-old Mary who tried to hold family together.	Fran Ellen sucked her thumb. Worried about the baby. Escaped in her imagination to a dollhouse. Mother dependent.		Retta knew she had problems with the house and the boys. Didn't know what to do about them.	Catherine wanted to understand her parents and to have a father who resembled her hopes for a father.

CHART 2–6 (cont.)
Social values, family life, and personal relationships, 1969–1989

	BOOK, AUTHOR, DATE, SETTING				
	Vera and Bill Cleaver, *Where the Lilies Bloom,* 1969. Smoky Mountains. Poor wildcrafters.	**Marilyn Sachs, *The Bears House,* 1971. Poor city neighborhood.**	**Norma Klein, *Mom, The Wolf Man, and Me,* 1972. Middle class.**	**Betsy Byars, *The Night Swimmers,* 1980. Suburbs.**	**Paula Fox, *The Moonlight Man,* 1986.**
PERSONAL RELATIONSHIPS AND FEELINGS (cont.)					
Types of Problems	After father died, they tried to survive as a family. Mary discovered that she needed other people.	Tried to overcome problems related to parents' desertion and illness. Emotional problems: nine-year-old tried to solve her own problems.	Daughter feared how her life might change if her mother married.	Tried to raise a motherless family when father worked at night and slept in daytime. Conflicts showed difficulty for a young girl trying to find her own place in the family.	Catherine spends her vacation with her alcoholic father. She must grow to understand and accept him for himself.
Friendships	People could not trust friends when they had secrets.	No friends at school; they teased Fran Ellen.	Daughter's best friend was a boy whose father was a rabbi. He never asked her questions about her father.	One boy took pride in a male friend; he tried not to share friend with family.	Father/daughter relationships are stressed.

I see you first" (p. 179). Clearly, children's literature now presents a greater range and more realistic representations of family diversity.

Suggested Activities for Understanding the History of Children's Literature

- ☐ Investigate the life and contributions of William Caxton. What circumstances led to his opening a printing business in 1476? Why were *Reynart the Fox, The Book of the Subtyle Historyes and Fables of Esope,* and *Le Morte d'Arthur* considered such important contributions to children's literature?
- ☐ Compare the literary quality of William Caxton's books with the literary quality of a reproduced chapbook. Why have chapbooks been identified as forerunners of children's books, western tales, and comic books?
- ☐ Trace the development of the hornbook from its introduction in the 1400s until it was superseded by the battledores in the 1700s. Consider any changes in these two types of lesson books and how they have influenced the development of children's literature.
- ☐ Read John Bunyan's *Pilgrim's Progress*. Identify the characteristics that would make it acceptable Puritan reading. Compare these characteristics with the characteristics of books that would appeal to children.
- ☐ Choose a tale published by Charles Perrault in his *Tales of Mother Goose,* such as "Cinderella," "Sleeping Beauty," "Puss in Boots," "Little Red Riding Hood," "Blue Beard," or "Little Thumb." Compare the language and style of Perrault's early edition with the language and style in a twentieth-century version of the same tale. What differences did you find? Why do you believe they were made?
- ☐ Select one of the Robinsonades published after the successful publication of Daniel Defoe's *Robinson Crusoe*. Compare the plot development, characterization, and setting with those of Defoe's text.
- ☐ Investigate the impact of John Newbery's publications on the history of children's literature.
- ☐ Compare the backgrounds, possible motivations, and probable recording techniques of Jacob and Wilhelm Grimm with those of Charles Perrault. Can you identify any reasons for the possible differences between or similarities in their tales?
- ☐ Choose one of the following great nineteenth-century English artists who made an impact on children's illustrations: Kate Greenaway, Walter Crane, or Randolph Caldecott. Read biographical information and look at exam-

ples of their illustrations. Share your information and reactions with your literature class.

- ☐ Read a Victorian novel such as Charlotte Yonge's *The Daisy Chain*. Identify how the book reflects Victorian values, such as fortitude, temperance, prudence, justice, self-reliance, and strong family ties.
- ☐ Read Mark Twain's *Adventures of Tom Sawyer* or *Huckleberry Finn*. Consider the controversy about racism in Twain's work. How would you evaluate Mark Twain's writing for the nineteenth century with writing for the twentieth century?

References

1 Alderson, Brian. *Sing a Song of Sixpence*. New York: Cambridge University Press, 1986.

2 Alderson, Brian W., ed. and trans. *Three Centuries of Children's Books in Europe*. Cleveland: World, 1959.

3 Ashton, John. *Chap-Books of the Eighteenth Century*. London: Chatto & Windus, 1882.

4 Bagley, Ayers. *An Invitation to Wisdom and Schooling*. Society of Professors of Education Monograph Series, 1985.

5 Bingham, Jane, and Grayce Scholt. *Fifteen Centuries of Children's Literature: An Annotated Chronology of British and American Works in Historical Context*. Westport, Conn.: Greenwood, 1980.

6 Cadogan, Mary, and Patricia Craig. *You're a Brick, Angela! A New Look at Girls' Fiction from 1839 to 1975*. London: Gollancz, 1976.

7 Carmichael, Carolyn Wilson. "A Study of Selected Social Values as Reflected in Contemporary Realistic Fiction for Children," East Lansing, Mich.: Michigan State University, 1971, University Microfilm No. 71–31.

8 Chapman, Raymond. *The Victorian Debate: English Literature and Society 1832–1901*. New York: Basic Books, 1968.

9 Crane, Walter. *The Decorative Illustration of Books, Old and New*. London: Bell & Sons, 1896; Bracken Books, 1984.

10 Darton, F. J. Harvey. *Children's Books in England: Five Centuries of Social Life*. New York: Cambridge University Press, 1932, 1966.

11 Erisman, Fred Raymond. "There Was a Child Went Forth: A Study of St. Nicholas Magazine and Selected Children's Authors, 1890–1915," Minneapolis: University of Minnesota, 1966, University Microfilm No. 66–12.

12 Ernest, Edward. *The Kate Greenaway Treasury*. Cleveland: World, 1967.

13 Fraser, James H., ed. *Society and Children's Literature*. Boston: Godine, 1978.

14 Furnivall, Frederick J., ed. *Caxton's Book of Curtesye*. London: Oxford University Press, 1868.

15 Gillespie, Margaret C. *Literature for Children: History and Trends*. Dubuque, Iowa: Brown, 1970.

16 Haviland, Virginia. *Children and Literature: View and Reviews*. Glenview, Ill.: Scott, Foresman, 1973.

17 Homze, Alma Cross. "Interpersonal Relationships in Children's Literature, 1920 to 1960," University Park, Pa.: Pennsylvania State University, 1963, University Microfilm No. 64–5366.

18 Hürlimann, Bettina. "Fortunate Moments in Children's Books." In *The Arbuthnot Lectures, 1970–1979,* compiled by Zena Sutherland. Chicago: American Library Association., 1980, pp. 61–80.

19 Kelly, Robert Gordon. "Mother Was a Lady: Self and Society in Selected American Children's Periodicals, 1865–1890," Iowa City, Iowa: University of Iowa, 1970, University Microfilm No. 71–5770.

20 Kelly, Robert Gordon. "Social Factors Shaping Some Nineteenth-Century Children's Periodical Fiction." In *Society and Children's Literature,* edited by James H. Fraser. Boston: Godine, 1978.

21 Laws, Frederick. "Randolph Caldecott." In *Only Connect: Readings on Children's Literature,* edited by Sheila Egoff, G. T. Stubbs, and L. F. Ashley. 2d ed. Toronto: Oxford University Press, 1980.

22 Leeson, Robert. *Children's Books and Class Society*. London: Writers & Readers, 1977.

23 Lenaghan, R. T., ed. *Caxton's Aesop*. Cambridge, Mass.: Harvard University Press, 1967.

24 Lobsenz, Norman. "News from the Home Front." *Family Weekly* (August 2, 1981): 9.

25 Locke, John. "Some Thoughts Concerning Education." In *English Philosophers,* edited by Charles W. Eliot. Harvard Classics, vol. 37. New York: Villier, 1910.

26 Lonsdale, Bernard J., and Helen K. Macintosh. *Children Experience Literature*. New York: Random House, 1973.

27 Lystad, Mary. *From Dr. Mather to Dr. Seuss: Two Hundred Years of American Books for Children*. Boston: G. K. Hall, 1980.

28 MacDonald, Robert. "Signs from the Imperial Quarter: Illustrations in *Chums,* 1892–1914." *Children's Literature* 16 (1988): 31–55.

29 McCulloch, Lou J. *An Introduction to Children's Literature: Children's Books of the 19th Century*. Des Moines, Iowa: Wallace-Honestead, 1979.

30 McElderry, Margaret. "The Best Times, the Worst Times, Children's Book Publishing 1917–1974." *The Horn Book,* (October 1974): 85–94.

31 Meigs, Cornelia, Elizabeth Nesbitt, Anne Thaxter Eaton, and Ruth Hill. *A Critical History of Children's Literature: A Survey of Children's Books in English*. New York: Macmillan, 1969.

32 Muir, Percy. *English Children's Books, 1600 to 1900*. New York: Praeger, 1954.

33 Phelps, Ruth M. "A Comparison of Newbery Award Winners in the First and Last Decade of the Award (1922–31 and 1976–85). Miami University, 1985, DAI 47: 453A.
34 Quayle, Eric. *The Collector's Book of Children's Books*. New York: Clarkson N. Potter, 1971.
35 Rees-Williams, Gwladys, and Brian Rees-Williams, eds. *What I Cannot Tell My Mother Is Not Fit for Me to Know*. New York: Oxford University Press, 1981.
36 Shaw, Jean Duncan. "An Historical Survey of Themes Recurrent in Selected Children's Books Published in America Since 1850," Philadelphia: Temple University, 1966, University Microfilm No. 67-11, 437.
37 Sidney, Sir Philip. *An Apologie for Poetrie*. London: 1595.
38 Stacks, John F. "Aftershocks of the 'Me' Decade." *Time* (August 3, 1981): 18.
39 Stark, Myra. *Florence Nightingale*. New York: Feminist Press, 1979.
40 Townsend, John Rowe. *Written for Children: An Outline of English-Language Children's Literature*. New York: Lippincott, 1975.
41 Tuer, Andrew W. *Stories from Forgotten Children's Books*. London: Leadenhall Press, 1898; Bracken Books, 1986.
42 Wilkin, Binnie Tate. *Survival Themes in Fiction for Children and Young People*. Metuchen, N.J.: Scarecrow, 1978.
43 Winkler, Karen J. "Academe and Children's Literature: Will They Live Happily Ever After?" *Chronicle of Higher Education* (June 15, 1981).
44 Young, Beverly. "The Young Female Protagonist in Juvenile Fiction: Three Decades of Evolution." Washington State University, 1985, DAI 46: 3276A.

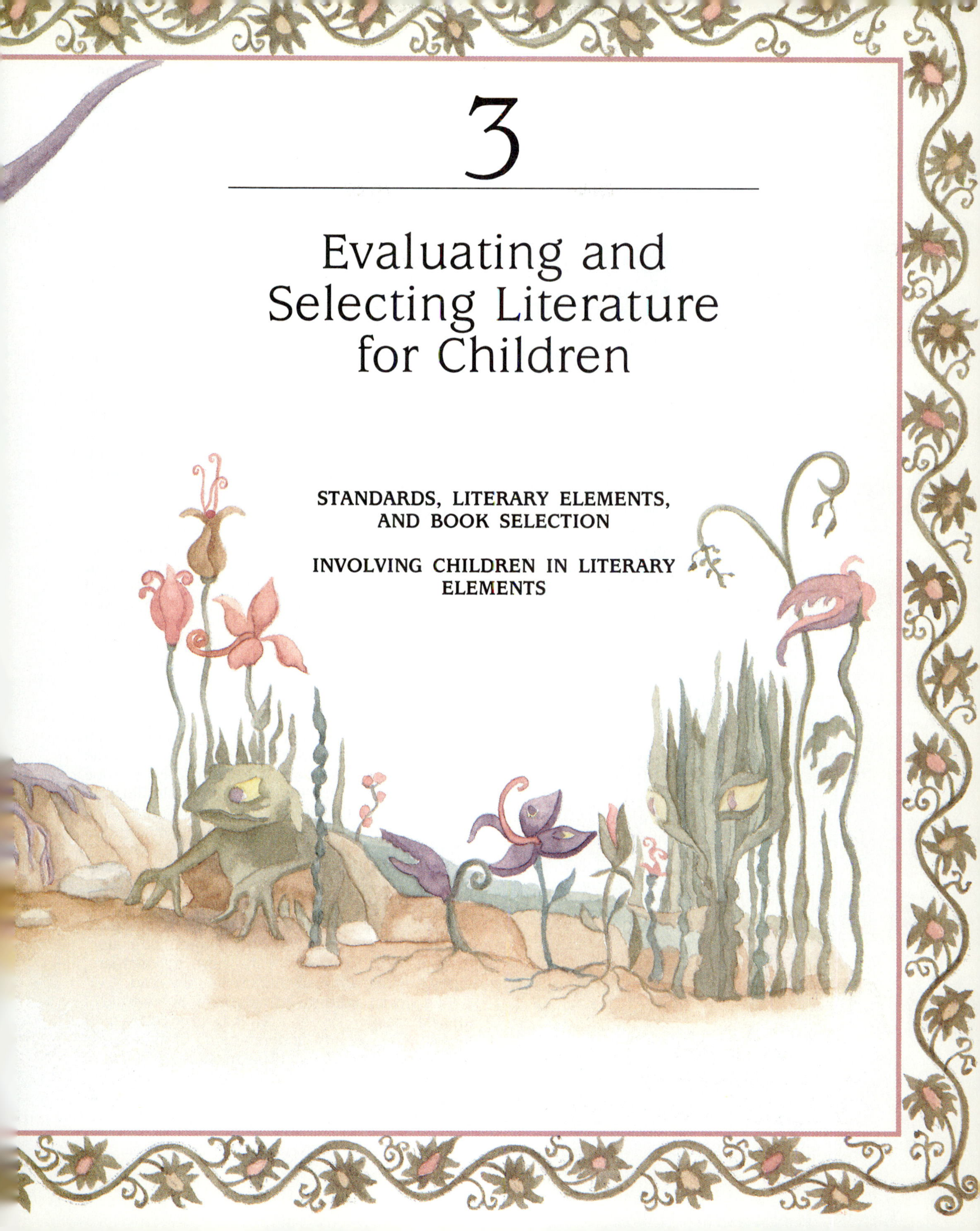

3

Evaluating and Selecting Literature for Children

STANDARDS, LITERARY ELEMENTS, AND BOOK SELECTION

INVOLVING CHILDREN IN LITERARY ELEMENTS

Standards, Literary Elements, and Book Selection

STANDARDS FOR EVALUATING BOOKS

LITERARY ELEMENTS

STEREOTYPES

THE RIGHT BOOK FOR EACH CHILD

THE CHILD AS CRITIC

BECAUSE THOUSANDS OF BOOKS HAVE been published for children, selecting books appropriate to the needs of children can be difficult. Teachers and librarians, who share books with groups of children as well as with individual children, should select books that provide balance in a school or public library. The objectives of literature programs also affect educators' selections of children's books.

According to Helen Huus (12), a literature program should have five objectives. First, a literature program should help students realize that literature is for entertainment and can be enjoyed throughout their lives. Literature should cater to children's interests as well as create interests in new topics. Consequently, educators must know these interests and understand ways to stimulate new ones.

Second, a literature program should acquaint children with their literary heritage. To accomplish this, literature should foster the preservation of knowledge and allow its transmission to future generations. Therefore, educators must be familiar with fine literature from the past and share it with children.

Third, a literature program should help students understand the formal elements of literature and lead them to prefer the best that our literature has to offer. Children need to hear and read fine literature and to appreciate authors who not only have something to say but also say it extremely well. Educators must be able to identify the best books in literature and share these books with children.

Fourth, a literature program should help children grow up understanding themselves and the rest of humanity. When children identify with literary characters who confront and overcome problems like their own, they learn ways to cope with their own problems. Educators should provide literature that introduces children to people from other times and nations, and that encourages children to see both themselves and their world in a new perspective.

Fifth, a literature program should help children evaluate what they read. Literature programs should extend children's appreciation of literature and their imaginations. Therefore, educators should help students learn how to compare, question, and evaluate the books they read.

If children are to gain enjoyment, knowledge of their heritage, recognition and appreciation of good literature, and understanding of themselves and others, they need balanced selections of literature. A literature program should include classics and contemporary stories, fanciful stories as well as realistic ones, prose as well as poetry, biographies, and books containing factual information. In order to provide this balance, educators need to know about many kinds of literature.

This text provides a wide knowledge of numerous types of books written for children. This chapter looks at standards for evaluating books written for children. It presents and discusses the literary elements of plot, characterization, setting, theme, style, and point of view. It also discusses children's literature interests, characteristics of literature found in books chosen by children, and procedures to help children evaluate literature.

STANDARDS FOR EVALUATING BOOKS

According to Jean Karl (13), in true literature, "there are ideas that go beyond the plot of a novel or picture-book story or the basic theme of a nonfiction book, but they are presented subtly and gently; good books do not preach; their ideas are wound into the substance of the book and are clearly a part of the life of the book itself" (p. 507). In contrast, Karl maintains that mediocre books overemphasize their messages or they oversimplify or distort life; mediocre books contain visions that are too obvious and can be put aside too easily.

Ruth Kearney Carlson (3) points out that use of inferior books underestimates children, especially slow learners and poor readers, whom adults too often assume have no interest in stimulating ideas. According to Carlson, poor and mediocre books "have commonplace, dully written pages," they "seldom take strong stands for certain causes," and they "build laziness in young readers" (p. 18). If literature is to help develop children's potentials, merit rather than mediocrity must be part of children's experiences with literature. Both children and adults need opportunities to evaluate literature. They also need supporting context to help them make accurate judgments about quality.

Literary criticism provides guidelines for evaluating children's literature. Paul Heins (10) maintains that critics must be acquainted with the best children's literature of the past and present. In fact, he says, no real criticism can occur unless "judgments are being made in a context of literary knowledge and of literary standards" (p. 76). Concern with the place of a book in a larger historical or aesthetic context and with its structure, technical subtlety, and overall literary integrity is not just dry analysis; it is part of "the joy of discovering the skill of the author" (p. 82).

Mary Kingsbury (15) builds a strong rationale for high-quality criticism that describes, compares, and judges literary texts. According to Kingsbury, critics must interpret a text accurately by understanding what the author is doing with language, contrast and compare a book with other books and with various book reviews, and then make their own judgments as objectively as possible. Kingsbury emphasizes the importance of both reading and writing literary criticism.

Northrop Frye, Sheridan Baker, and George Perkins (5) identify five focuses of all literary criticism, two or more of which are usually emphasized in an evaluation of a literary text:

> (1) The work in isolation, with primary focus on its form, as opposed to its content; (2) its relationship to its own time and place, including the writer; the social, economic, and intellectual milieu surrounding it; the method of its printing or other dissemination; and the assumptions of the audience that first received it; (3) its relationship to literary and social history before its time, as it repeats, extends, or departs from the traditions that preceded it; (4) its relationship to the future, as represented by those works and events that come after it, as it forms a part of the large body of literature, influencing the reading, writing, and thinking of later generations; (5) its relationship to some eternal concept of being, absolute standards of art, or immutable truths of existence. (p. 130)

The relative importance of each of the areas to a particular critic depends on the critic's degree of concern with the work itself, the author, the subject matter, and the audience.

Book reviews and longer critical analyses of books in the major literature journals are valuable sources for librarians, teachers, parents, and other students of children's literature. As might be expected from the five focuses of Frye, Baker, and Perkins, reviews emphasize different aspects of evaluation and criticism. Phyllis K. Kennemer (14) identified three categories of book reviews and longer book analyses: (1) descriptive, (2) analytical, and (3) sociological. Descriptive reviews report factual information about the story and illustrations of a book. Analytical reviews discuss, compare, and evaluate literary elements (plot, characterization, setting, theme, style, and point of view), the illustrations, and relationships with other books. Sociological reviews emphasize the social context of a book, concerning themselves with characterizations of particular social groups, distinguishable ethnic characteristics, moral values, possible controversy, and potential popularity.

Although a review may contain all three types of information, Kennemer concludes that the major sources of information on children's literature emphasize one type of evaluation. For example, reviews in the *Bulletin of the Center for Children's Books* tend to be descriptive, but they also mention literary elements. Reviews in *Booklist, The Horn Book, Kirkus Reviews,* and *The School Library Journal* chiefly analyze literary elements. *The School Library Journal* places the greatest emphasis on sociological analysis of any source Kennemer studied.

Reading and discussing excellent books, as well as analyzing book reviews and literary criticism, can increase one's ability to recognize and recommend excellent literature for children. Those of us who work with students of children's literature are rewarded when for the first time, people see literature with a new awareness, discover the techniques an author uses to create a believable plot or memorable characterizations, and discover that they can provide rationales for why a book is excellent, mediocre, or poor. Ideally, reading and discussing excellent literature help each student of children's literature become a worthy critic, what Mary Kingsbury (15) defines as one "who offers us new perspectives on a text, who sees more in it than we saw, who motivates us to return to it for another reading" (p. 17).

The plot structure of *The Canterbury Tales* follows the oral tradition. (The Franklin from *The Canterbury Tales* by Geoffrey Chaucer, selected, translated and adapted by Barbara Cohen, illustrated by Trina Schart Hyman. Text ©1988 by Barbara Cohen. Illustration ©1988 by Trina Schart Hyman. Reprinted by Lothrop, Lee & Shepard Books [A division of William Morrow & Company.])

LITERARY ELEMENTS

The focus of this chapter is literary elements. The chapter looks at the ways in which authors of children's books use plot, characterization, setting, theme, style, and point of view to create memorable stories.

Plot

Plot is important in stories, whether the stories reflect the oral storytelling style of Chaucer's *The Canterbury Tales* or the complex interactions in a mystery. When asked to tell about a favorite story, children usually recount the plot, or plan of action. Children want a book to have a good plot: enough action, excitement, suspense, and conflict to develop interest. A good plot also allows children to become involved in the action, feel the conflict developing, recognize the climax when it occurs, and respond to a satisfactory ending. Children's expectations and enjoyment of conflict vary according to their ages. Young children are satisfied with simple plots that deal with everyday happenings, but as children mature they expect and enjoy more complex plots.

Following the plot of a story is like following a path winding through it as the action develops naturally. If the plot is well developed, a book should be difficult to put down unfinished; if the plot is not well developed, the book will not sustain interest or will be so prematurely predictable that the story ends long before it should. The author's development of this action assists children in their enjoyment of the story.

Developing the Order of Events. Readers expect a story to have a good beginning, one that introduces the action and characters in an enticing way; a good middle section, one that develops the conflict; a recognizable climax; and an appropriate ending. If any element is missing, children consider a book unsatisfactory and a waste of time. Authors have several approaches for presenting the events in a credible plot. In children's literature, events usually happen in chronological order. The author reveals the plot by presenting the first happening, followed by the second happening, and so forth, until the story is completed. Illustrations reinforce the chronological order in picture storybooks for younger children.

In *I Want to Be an Astronaut,* for example, Byron Barton follows a child on a space mission that proceeds from taking off in a shuttle, to flying in outer space, to working on a space mission, to walking in space, to building a factory in orbit, and finally to returning to Earth. In *Stringbean's Trip to the Shining Sea,* a book for slightly older children, Vera Williams uses messages and pictures on postcards and snapshots to show the order of events as two brothers travel from Kansas to the Pacific Ocean.

Very strong and obvious chronological order is found in cumulative folktales. Actions and characters are related to each other in sequential order, and each is mentioned again when new action or a new character is introduced. Children who enjoy the cumulative style of the nursery rhyme "The House That Jack Built" also enjoy a similar cumulative rhythm in Verna Aardema's *Bringing the Rain to Kapiti Plain: A Nandi Tale*.

The American folktale "The Greedy Old Fat Man," retold and illustrated in book form by Paul Galdone, is developed totally on the cumulative approach. As the greedy man encounters each prospective victim, he repeats his previous actions. Finally, the man restates all of his previous encounters. This repetition is effective with young children, as it encourages them to join in during the storytelling and allows them to anticipate the cumulative style of the folktale. Cumulative, sequential action may also be developed in reverse, from last event to first, as in Verna Aardema's *Why Mosquitoes Buzz in People's Ears*.

Authors of biographies frequently use chronological life events to develop plot. Jean Fritz, for example, traces the life of a famous president and constitutional leader in *The Great Little Madison*. In *Lincoln: A Photobiography,* Russell Freedman begins with Lincoln's childhood and continues through his life as president. Dates in both texts help readers follow the chronological order.

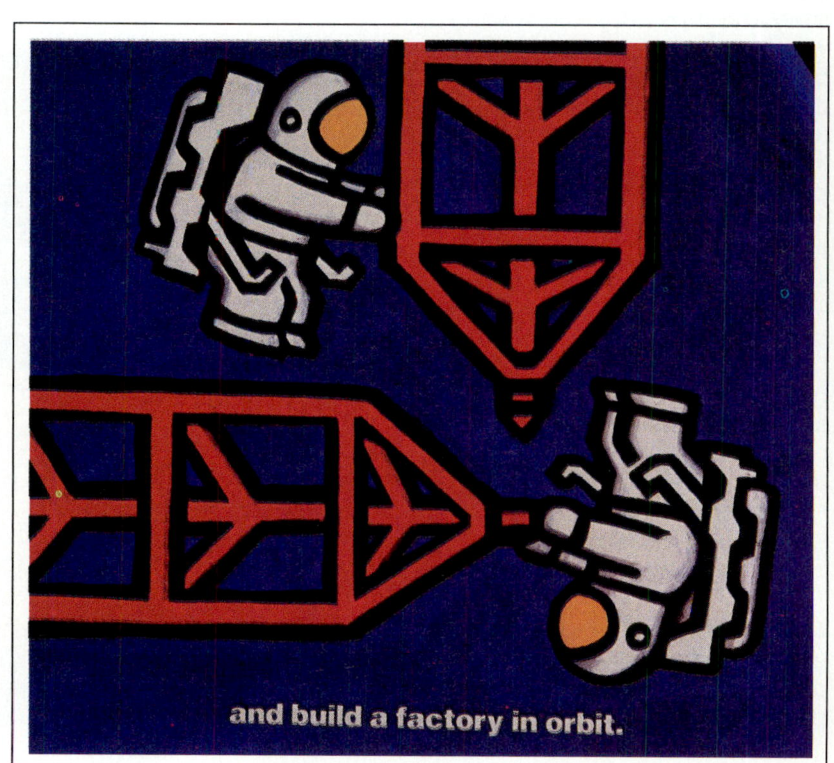

The events follow the sequential order of space missions in *I Want to Be an Astronaut* by Byron Barton. (Selected illustration from *I Want to Be an Astronaut* by Byron Barton, (Crowell) copyright, 1988 by Byron Barton. Reprinted by permission of Harper & Row Publishers, Inc.)

A story's events also may follow the maturing process of the main character. In *The Clown of God,* Tomie de Paola introduces a small beggar boy who is happy because he has the wonderful gift of being able to juggle. His fortune changes as time passes, and he even juggles before royalty. Years go by and the juggler becomes old and unable to perform. He is rejected by the crowd and wearily heads home. His journey ends in church, where he performs his final juggling act. This magnificent performance results in his death but also causes a miracle.

Books written for older readers sometimes use flashbacks in addition to chronological order. At the point when readers have many questions about a character's background or wonder why a character is acting in a certain way, the author interrupts the order of the story and reveals information about a previous time or experience. Robert C. O'Brien uses flashbacks effectively in *Mrs. Frisby and the Rats of NIMH.* When the readers and Mrs. Frisby are wondering why the rats were taken to the laboratory, how their intelligence was drastically increased, how they escaped from the laboratory, and how rat society was developed, the wise rat Nicodemus says, "To answer that I would have to tell you quite a long story about us, and NIMH, and Jonathan, and how we came here" (p. 97). After flashbacks answer the questions necessary for logical plot development, the chronological order continues. Because this technique is more complex than simple chronological order, it is not usually used in the shorter plots written for young children.

Patricia MacLachlan, however, uses flashbacks to provide background information in a picture storybook for young children, *Mama One, Mama Two*. The plot begins as a young foster child has difficulty sleeping. The reasons for her separation from her mother, her love for her mother, and her hopes for the future are developed as she and her foster mother share a warm bedtime story. In this case, young children can understand the use of the flashback and identify with its contents. In *Tell Me a Story, Mama,* Angela Johnson uses a similar storytelling technique to provide information about the mother when she was a young girl.

Developing Conflict. Excitement in a story occurs when the main characters experience a struggle or overcome conflict. Conflict is the usual source of plots in literature. According to Rebecca J. Lukens (16), children's literature contains four kinds of conflict: (1) person-against-person, (2) person-against-society, (3) person-against-nature, and (4) person-against-self. Plots written for younger children usually develop only one kind of conflict, but many of the stories for older children use several conflicting situations.

Person Against Person. One person-against-person conflict young children enjoy is the tale of that famous bunny, *Peter Rabbit,* by Beatrix Potter. In this story, Peter's disobedience and greed quickly bring him into conflict with the owner of the garden, Mr. McGregor, who has sworn to put Peter into a pie. Excitement and suspense develop as Peter and Mr. McGregor proceed through a series of life-and-death encounters. Mr. McGregor chases Peter with a rake, Peter becomes tangled in a gooseberry net, and Mr. McGregor tries to trap him inside a sieve. Knowledge of Peter's possible fate increases the suspense of these adventures. The excitement intensifies each time Peter narrowly misses being caught, and young readers' relief is great when Peter escapes for good. Children also sympathize with Peter when his disobedience results in a stomachache and a dose of camomile tea.

Conflicts between animals and humans, or animals and animals, or humans and humans are common in children's literature, including many

Illustrations and plot relate a humorous conflict between a seven-year-old and her father. (Illustration by Allan Tiegreen from *Ramona and Her Father* by Beverly Cleary. Copyright © 1975, 1977 by Beverly Cleary. By permission of William Morrow and Company.)

popular folktales. Both Little Red Riding Hood and the three little pigs confront a wicked wolf. Cinderella and Sleeping Beauty are among the fairytale heroines mistreated by stepmothers, and Hansel and Gretel are imprisoned by a witch. Josepha Sherman's *Vassilisa the Wise: A Tale of Medieval Russia* develops conflict between a clever and courageous female and an arrogant prince. The heroine saves her husband's life by proving that she is wiser than the prince. Alix Berenzy's *A Frog Prince* tells the familiar story through the frog's point of view. The frog overcomes conflicts with a princess, two trolls, and a witch before he finds a more suitable mate, a beautiful frog princess.

Folktales from many lands develop plots in which animals come into conflict with one another and are either rewarded for courage, loyalty, or intelligence or punished for foolishness, wickedness, or ignorance. In Priscilla Jaquith's *Bo Rabbit Smart for True: Folktales from the Gullah,* one humorous conflict involves Bo Rabbit's tricking a whale and an elephant into a pulling contest.

A humorous person-against-person conflict provides the story line in Beverly Cleary's *Ramona and Her Father*. Seven-year-old Ramona's life changes drastically when her father loses his job and her mother must work full-time. Ramona's new time with her father is not as enjoyable as she had hoped it would be, however. Her father becomes tense and irritable as his period of unemployment lengthens. When his smoking increases, Ramona decides that his life is in danger and devises a plan to save him. Her campaign includes hanging signs around the house and planting "no smoking" notes in the form of fake cigarettes in her father's pockets. Ramona and her father survive their experience and by the end of the story have returned to their normal, warm relationship.

Katherine Paterson develops a more complex person-against-person conflict for older children in *Jacob Have I Loved*. In this story, one twin believes she is like the despised Esau in the Old Testament, while her sister is the adored favorite of the family. The unhappy heroine's descriptions of her early experiences with her sister, her growing independence as she works with her father, and her final discovery that she, not her sister, is the strong twin create an engrossing plot and memorable characters.

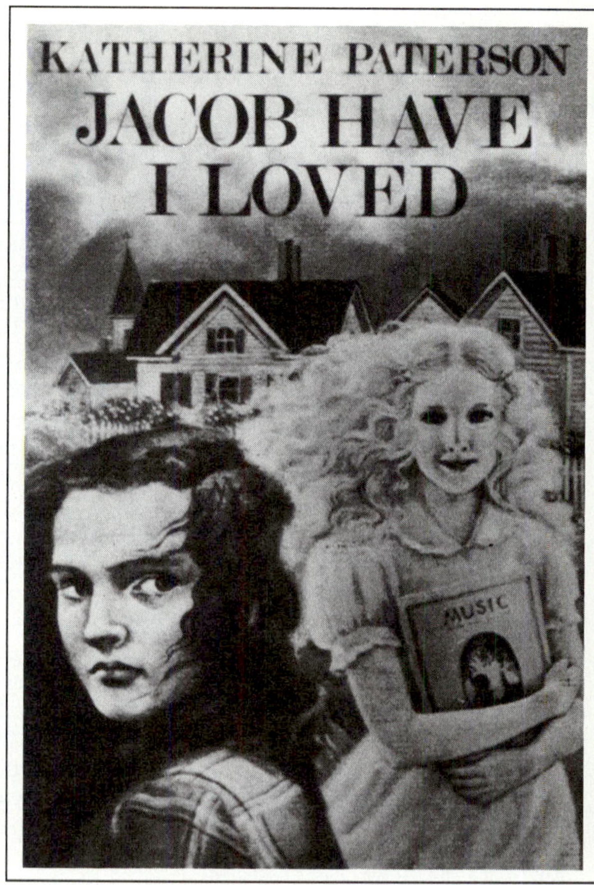

Complex person-against-person conflict develops between twin sisters in *Jacob Have I Loved* by Katherine Paterson. (Jacket by Kinoko Craft [Thomas Y. Crowell Co.] Copyright © 1980 by Katherine Paterson.)

Person Against Society. Conflicts also develop when the main character's actions, desires, or values differ from those of the surrounding society. This society may consist of groups of children who cannot tolerate children who are different from themselves. In Brock Cole's *The Goats,* a boy and a girl who are considered social outcasts by their peers at camp are stripped of their clothing and marooned on a deserted island. The author reveals the social attitudes of this camp when girls are classified as queens, princesses, dogs, and real dogs. The girl on the island is considered a real dog. Cole reveals the feelings of the children through their ordeal when he uses terms such as *they* and *them* to identify the society. When the girl wants the boy to leave her, his actions, thoughts, and dialogue reveal the strength of his dislike for the society that placed him in this isolation: " 'I'm afraid. Maybe you'd better go without me.' 'No,' he said. He didn't try to explain. He knew he was

THROUGH THE EYES OF A CHILDREN'S LIBRARIAN

Connecting Children and Books

A librarian specializing in working with children and their families for thirty years, ETHEL N. AMBROSE currently serves as the Coordinator of Children's Services, Central Arkansas Library System, Little Rock, Arkansas. (Drawn from a telephone interview, March 28, 1990, by Linda James Scharp.)

EVEN IN THIS AGE OF technology, I maintain that having a burning desire to bring people and books together in a meaningful way is the most important prerequisite for a successful career as a children's librarian. While a basic understanding of computer automation is necessary, I would never trade a person's sensitivity to people for an affinity for computers.

The best educational experience for an aspiring librarian for children is a broad-based liberal arts education. There has to be a knowledge base on which to build. The computer companies can train you to use the latest equipment, and technological changes require retraining every two to five years. A liberal arts background is a solid foundation forever.

In addition, children's librarians have always needed to be good managers, because they have always had to survive in an economy of scarcity and build collections under severe budget constraints. We have the largest historical collection of children's books in our state, due to the careful management by librarians for the past ninety-five years.

How does one select books and build a collection? I believe in responding to the needs of our readers and aiming for balance. By doing extensive breakdowns of circulation patterns, we can determine areas of demand and respond to them. However, it is important to exercise some patience in the selection process. One should not recommend purchase of a new book based on a single review, but make every attempt to examine the book itself. If this is not possible, then it is important to seek information from a variety of resources and not become dependent upon a single source.

At our libraries, we still select books "the old-fashioned way." Each of us reads several books and shares the information at monthly meetings. This is a great way to combine in-service training for staff and to cross-check our recommendations for purchase.

It is important to compare books of like genre or topic and select only the best. Children's librarians can feel pressured to order books the same way adult books are ordered. Col-

afraid to leave her alone, but even more important, it wouldn't be good enough. He wanted them both to disappear. To disappear completely" (p. 16).

Children's books often portray person-against-society conflicts that result from being different from the majority in terms of race, religion, or physical characteristics. Judy Blume's *Blubber* shows the cruelty to which a fat child is subjected by her peers. In Brent Ashabranner's collection of biographies, *To Live in Two Worlds: American Indian Youth Today,* contemporary Native American youths describe the conflicts facing them as they try to adjust to white society while retaining aspects of their own culture. For the conflict between person and society in such books to be believable, the social setting and its values must be presented in accurate detail.

Numerous survival stories set in wartime develop person-against-society conflicts. In Uri Orlev's *The Island on Bird Street,* the conflict is between a Jewish boy and the society that forces him to live in fear, loneliness, and starvation rather than surrender. In Jane Yolen's *The Devil's Arithmetic,* the conflict develops in a time-warp story, when a contemporary Jewish girl finds herself back in the 1940s. Her previously safe world changes to the violent world of the Holocaust. The

lections for children and adults need to be developed differently—adults are set in their reading habits, children are still in the process of becoming readers.

In responding to need of children, it is important to remember that children's choices for the most part are made based on the books adults make available to them. Therefore, while I consider lists that have been voted on by children, I try to keep in mind that they can vote only for books that are available to them.

However, the true measure of success of a collection is circulation. How do you get the books into the hands of children and their parents? I think it is important to have a mindset that escapes the four walls of the library building itself.

Librarians have to develop a realistic profile of the community to aid in book selection. I encourage my branch librarians to take neighborhood walks. How many laundromats are there? Medical facilities? Child care sites? Census information and statistics kept by health care providers can help round out this profile.

Our library system continues a program that began with federal funding in the '60s, and our bookmobiles visit seventy-five child care centers on an every-other-week schedule. That exemplifies our efforts to connect children and books!

Another specific program that our library system sponsors in conjunction with the community support of the Junior League of Little Rock is the *Reading Aloud Renaissance*. This ongoing program is designed to help prevent illiteracy by having adults (Junior League committee members) read aloud to school children in grades K–6 in four local elementary schools on a regular schedule—two and one-half hours per week at each school. We coordinate with principals and teachers on selection of materials so that classroom teachers can provide follow-up discussions. We have compiled a reading list for use by both parents and teachers.

Reading: The Key to the Dream was another read-aloud project co-sponsored by the library, schools and churches. Any group could receive a "Read-In" packet by calling the library. The packet contained suggestions for preparing to read aloud, a book list focused on Black History Month, a name tag, and background information on the program's theme. The theme was based on Dr. Martin Luther King, Jr.'s belief that a better world is achievable through education, and that literacy is the key to the dream.

A local art center sponsored a program of readings by authors whose art was represented in a traveling art exhibit. They did not schedule regular classes, but provided this activity on a walk-in basis. Thousands of children participated in this read-aloud program.

You cannot be bashful. It is important to seek out someone in the local media who is interested in children and cultivate publicity for your library programs fifty-two weeks a year.

Finally, let me say that well-honed management skills, creative programming, and garnering publicity cannot substitute for being a reader yourself. Read. Then share your enthusiasm for reading by connecting children and their families to books!

vivid descriptions, fear, and personal reactions to losing friends while in a concentration camp reveal the nature of the society.

Person Against Nature. Nature—not society or another person—is the antagonist in many memorable books for older children. When the author thoroughly describes the natural environment, readers vicariously travel into a world ruled by nature's harsh laws of survival. This is the case in Jean Craighead George's *Julie of the Wolves*. Miyax, a thirteen-year-old Eskimo girl also called by the English name Julie, is lost and without food on the North Slope of Alaska. She is introduced lying on her stomach, peering at a pack of wolves. The wolves are not her enemy, however. Her adversary is the vast cold tundra that stretches for hundreds of miles without human presence, a land so harsh that no berry bushes point to the south, no birds fly overhead so that she can follow, and continual summer daylight blots out the North Star that might guide her home:

> No roads cross it; ponds and lakes freckle its immensity. Winds scream across it, and the view in every direction is exactly the same. Somewhere in this cosmos was Miyax; and the very life in her body, its spark and warmth, depended upon these wolves for survival. And she was not so sure they would help. (p. 6)

The constant wind; the empty sky; and the cold, deserted earth are ever present as Miyax crosses the Arctic searching for food, protecting herself from the elements, and making friends with the wolves, who bring her food. The author encourages readers to visualize the power and beauty of this harsh landscape and to share the girl's sorrow over human destruction of this land, its animals, and the Eskimo way of life.

Another book that pits a young person against the elements of nature is Armstrong Sperry's *Call It Courage*. The hero's conflict with nature begins when the crashing, stormy sea—"a monster livid and hungry"—capsizes Mafatu's canoe during a hurricane, and his mother drowns:

> Higher and higher it rose, until it seemed that it must scrape at the low-hanging clouds. Its crest heaved over with a vast sigh. The boy saw it coming. He tried to cry out. No sound issued from his throat. Suddenly the wave was upon him. Down it crashed. Chaos! Mafatu felt the paddle torn from his hands. Thunder in his ears. Water strangled him. Terror in his soul. (p. 24)

The preceding quote makes clear that there are two adversaries in the story: The hero is in conflict with nature and also in conflict with himself. The two adversaries are interwoven in the plot as Mafatu sails away from his island in order to prove that he is not a coward. Each time the boy wins a victory over nature, he also comes closer to his main goal, victory over his own fear. Without that victory, he cannot be called by his rightful name Mafatu, "Stout Heart," nor can he have the respect of his father, his Polynesian people, and himself.

Authors who write strong person-against-nature conflicts use many of the techniques shown in the quotes by George and Sperry. Personification gives human actions to nature, vivid descriptions show that characters are in a life-and-death struggle, sentences become shorter to show increasing danger, and actions reveal that characters know that they are in serious conflict with nature.

Person Against Self. In *Hatchet,* Gary Paulsen creates person-against-self and person-against-nature conflicts for his major character, thirteen-year-old Brian. These two major conflicts are intertwined throughout the book. For example, Paulsen creates an excellent transition between unconsciousness at the end of chapter three and consciousness at the beginning of chapter four. In the following quote, notice how Paulsen ties together the two most destructive experiences in Brian's life: the plane crash that could have killed him and the secret about his mother that caused his parents' divorce.

> Without knowing anything. Pulling until his hands caught at weeds and muck, pulling and screaming until his hands caught at last in grass and brush and he felt his chest on land, felt his face in the coarse blades of grass and he stopped; everything stopped. A color came that he had never seen before, a color that exploded in his mind with the pain and he was gone, gone from it all, spiraling out into the world, spiraling out into nothing. Nothing. (p. 30, end of chapter 3)
>
> The Memory was like a knife cutting into him. Slicing deep into him with hate. The Secret. (p. 31, beginning of chapter 4)

Symbolically, the secret is the first thing Brian remembers after waking from unconsciousness. Paulsen reveals the destructive nature of the secret through flashbacks, as Brian's memory returns, and through comparisons between the hate that cut him like a knife and the sharp pain caused by the crash. As Brian gains confidence and ability to survive in the Canadian wilderness, he gains understanding about his parents' conflict and ability to face his own person-against-self conflict.

While few children face the extreme personal challenges described in *Hatchet, Call It Courage,* and *Julie of the Wolves,* all children must overcome fears and personal problems while growing up. Person-against-self conflict is a popular plot device in children's literature. Authors of contemporary realistic fiction often develop plots around children who face and overcome problems related to family disturbances. For example, the cause of the person-against-self conflict in Carol Lea Benjamin's *The Wicked Stepdog* is a girl's fear that she is losing her father's love. By describing the heroine's initial reactions to her new stepmother and her feelings about her father's actions, the author develops Louise's personal conflicts. The first-person narrative provides insights into Louise's changing attitudes as she overcomes feelings of fear and jealousy.

Lying is a problem that often gets children into difficulty. In *Sam, Bangs & Moonshine,* by Evaline Ness, Sam does not mean to do any harm with her fibs, but they do cause her problems and almost cost her friend's life. Sam convinces her friend Thomas that she has a mermaid mother and a baby kangaroo. Thomas believes the story and goes out to Blue Rock to search for Sam's mother and the kangaroo. Unfortunately, the tide almost covers the rock before Thomas is rescued. When

Sam realizes what she has done, her father asks her to tell herself the difference between real and "moonshine." She discovers that the mermaid mother, the baby kangaroo, and a dragon-drawn chariot are all "flummadiddle." Her father, her cat Bangs, and her friend Thomas are the real things. Sam overcomes her person-against-self conflict as she learns that there is good as well as bad moonshine.

In the modern fantasy, *The Hero and the Crown,* Robin McKinley develops two types of conflict. There is the conflict encountered as the heroine, Aerin, begins her quest and battles the forces of evil. Of equal importance, however, is her person-against-self conflict as she questions her birthright, searches for answers to her heritage, and finally accepts who she is even though the price is more than she imagined. The resolutions of the two conflicts are intertwined: acceptance of self and destruction of evil are both part of the climax and the conclusion of the book.

These plots do not rely on contrivance or coincidence. They are credible to young readers because many of the same conflicts occur in the children's own lives. Credibility is an important consideration in evaluating plot in children's books. Although authors of adult books often rely on considerable tension or sensational conflict to create interest, writers of children's books like to focus on the characters and the ways they overcome problems.

Characterization

A believable, enjoyable story needs main characters who seem lifelike and who develop throughout the story. Characterization is one of the most powerful of the literary elements whether the story is a contemporary tale in which characters face realistic problems, or an adaptation of classic literature such as *Tales from Shakespeare* retold for children by Charles and Mary Lamb. According to Nancy Bond (2), "the writer uses imagination and human experience to create three-dimensional characters—characters with pasts, futures, parents, siblings, hopes, fears, sorrows, happiness. At the same time that the writer shows us individuals, he or she is showing us our common humanity, inviting identification and involvement" (p. 299).

The characters we remember fondly from our childhood reading usually have several sides; like real people they are not all good or all bad, and they change as they confront and overcome their problems. Laura, from various Laura Ingalls Wilder's "Little House" books, typifies a rounded character in literature. She is honest, trustworthy, and courageous, but she can also be jealous, frightened, or angry. Her character not only is fully developed in the story but also changes during its course.

One child who enjoyed Wilder's books described Laura this way: "I would like Laura for my best friend. She would be fun to play with but she would also understand when I was hurt or angry. I could tell Laura my secrets without being afraid she would laugh at me or tell them to someone else." Any writer who can create such a friend for children is very skilled at characterization.

Strong characterization from Shakespeare's plays are available in a version for children. (From *Tales from Shakespeare* by Charles and Mary Lamb with sundry pictures and illuminations both in color and in line by Elizabeth Shippen Green Elliott. Reproduced by permission of Children's Classics, Crown Publishers.)

How does an author develop such a memorable character? How can an author show the many sides of the character as well as demonstrate believable change as this character matures? According to Charlotte S. Huck, Susan Hepler, and Janet Hickman (11), the credibility of a character depends upon the writer's ability to reveal the full nature of the character, including strengths and weaknesses. Huck, Hepler, and Hickman say that an author can achieve such a three-dimensional character by describing the character's physical appearance, recording the conversations of the character, revealing the character's thoughts, revealing the perceptions of other characters, and showing the character in action (p. 20).

In *Call It Courage,* Armstrong Sperry uses all of these methods to reveal Mafatu's character and the changes that occur in him as he overcomes his fears. Sperry first tells readers that Mafatu fears the sea. Then, through narration, Sperry shows the young child clinging to his mother's back as a stormy sea and sharks almost end both their lives. Mafatu's memories of this experience, revealed in his thoughts and actions, make him useless in the eyes of his Polynesian tribe, as Sperry reveals through the dialogue of other characters: "That is woman's work. Mafatu is afraid of the sea. He will never be a warrior" (p. 12).

The laughter of the tribe follows, and Sperry then describes Mafatu's inner feelings:

> Suddenly a fierce resentment stormed through him. He knew in that instant what he must do: he must prove his courage to himself, and to the others, or he could no longer live in their midst. He must face Moana, the Sea God—face him and conquer him. (p. 13)

Sperry portrays Mafatu's battle for courage through a combination of actions and thoughts: terror and elation follow each other repeatedly, as Mafatu lands on a forbidden island used for human sacrifice, then dares to take a ceremonial spear even though doing so may mean death; confronts a hammerhead shark that circles his raft, then overcomes his fear and attacks the shark to save his dog. Mafatu celebrates a final victory when he kills the wild boar, whose teeth symbolize courage. Mafatu's tremendous victory over fear is signified by his father's statement of pride: "Here is my son come home from the sea. Mafatu, Stout Heart. A brave name for a brave boy" (p. 115).

In *The Moves Make the Man,* Bruce Brooks develops character through basketball terminology. Brooks introduces this concept through the words of Jerome Foxworthy, a talented black student, who expresses these thoughts about his own character:

> Moves were all I cared about last summer. I got them down, and I liked not just the fun of doing them, but having them too, like a little definition of Jerome. Reverse spin, triple jump, reverse dribble. . . . These are me. The moves make the man, the moves make me, I thought, until Mama noticed they were making me something else. (p. 44)

Brooks uses contrasting attitudes toward fake moves in basketball to reveal important differences between Jerome and Bix Rivers, a talented but disturbed white athlete.

This textbook discusses many memorable characters in children's literature. Some of these characters—such as the faithful spider Charlotte and a terrific pig named Wilbur, in E. B. White's *Charlotte's Web*—are old favorites, who have been capturing children's imaginations for decades. Others—such as Max in Maurice Sendak's *Where the Wild Things Are* and Karana in Scott O'Dell's *Island of the Blue Dolphins*—are more recent arrivals in the world of children's books. Authors of picture storybooks, historical fiction, science fiction and fantasy, and contemporary realistic fiction have all created characters who are likely to be remembered long after the details of their stories have been forgotten.

Setting

The setting of a story—its location in time and place—helps readers share what the characters see, smell, hear, and touch, as well as makes characters' values, actions, and conflicts more understandable. Whether a story takes place in the past, present, or future, its overall credibility may depend on how well plot, characterization, and setting support one another. Different types of literature—picture storybooks, fantasy, historical fiction, and contemporary realistic fiction—have their own requirements so far as setting is concerned. When a story is set in an identifiable historical period or geographical location, details should be accurate and both plot and characterization should be consistent with what actually occurred or could have occurred at that time and place.

In some books, setting is such an important part of the story that the characters and plot cannot be developed without understanding the time and place. In other stories, however, the setting provides only a background. In fact, some settings are so well known that just a few words

FLASHBACK

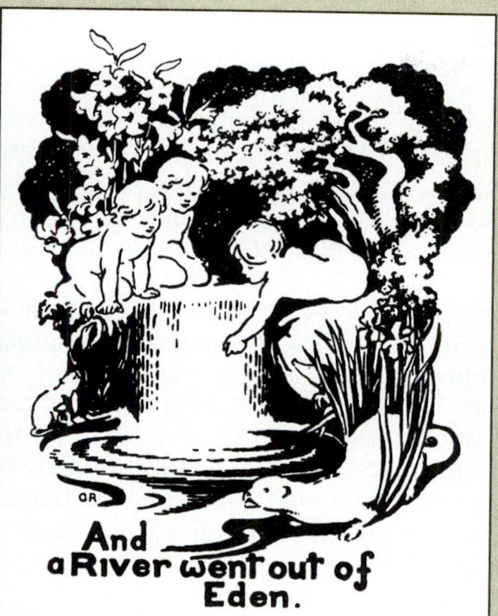

GRAHAM ROBERTSON'S FRONTISPIECE FOR Kenneth Grahame's 1908 edition of *The Wind in the Willows* suggests an idyllic woodland setting for an animal fantasy. It also hints that all may not go well if the inhabitants leave this Eden.

Grahame's description of the river, the river bank, the changing seasons, the wild wood, and the wide world helps the reader to visualize, and enter into, his story's location. Descriptions of wandering streams, whispering reeds and willows, and smells of marshlands also create a mood in which animal characters have the freedom to explore an enticing environment.

Other settings, however, are less desirable, settings that go beyond the river bank. In the wild wood, weasels, sloats, and foxes attack the peaceful inhabitants of the river bank. Beyond the wild wood is the wide world that may also entice some characters away from Eden into danger. Grahame creates the feeling, however, that that alien world does not really matter to the characters who enjoy living on the isolated river bank.

place readers immediately into the expected location. "Once upon a time," for example, is a mythical time in days of yore when it was possible for magical spells to transform princes into beasts or to change pumpkins into glittering carriages. Thirty of the thirty-seven traditional fairy tales in Andrew Lang's *The Red Fairy Book* begin with "Once upon a time." Magical spells cannot happen everywhere; they usually occur in "a certain kingdom," "deep in the forest," in "the humble hut of a wise and good peasant," or "far, far away, in a warm and pleasant land." Children become so familiar with such phrases—and the imaginative visualizations of a setting that such phrases trigger—that additional details and descriptions are not necessary.

Even a setting that is described quite briefly, however, may serve several different purposes. It may create a mood, provide an antagonist, establish historical background, or supply symbolic meanings.

Setting as Mood. Authors of children's literature and adult literature alike use settings to create moods that add credibility to characters and plot. Readers would probably be a bit skeptical if a vampire appeared in a sunny American kitchen on a weekday morning while a family was preparing to leave for school and work. The same vampire would seem more believable in a moldy castle in Transylvania at midnight.

The epic story of Attila the Hun, a famous invader of Eastern Europe in the fifth century A.D. could be told as historical fiction, with a setting that emphasizes accuracy of geographical and biographical detail. In *The White Stag,* Kate Seredy chose a mythical approach to telling the story of how a migratory Asiatic people reached their new homeland in what became Hungary. Gods, moon-maidens, and a supernatural animal are among the characters in this story, and Seredy uses setting to create a mood in which such beings seem natural. The leader of the tribe stands before a sacrificial altar in a cold, rocky, and barren territory, waiting to hear the voice of the god Hadur, who will lead his starving people to the promised land.

At this time, the white stag miraculously appears to guide the Huns in their travels—through "ghost hours" onto grassy hills covered with white

The illustrations create a nostalgic look at childhood in *In Coal Country.* (From *In Coal Country* by Judith Hendershot, illustrated by Thomas B. Allen. Illustration copyright © 1987 by Thomas B. Allen. Reprinted by permission of Alfred A. Knopf.)

birch trees, where they hear a brook tinkling like silver bells and a breeze that sounds like the flutes of minstrels. Readers expect magic in such a place, and they are not disappointed to see "Moonmaidens, those strange changeling fairies who lived in white birch trees and were never seen in the daylight; Moonmaidens who, if caught by the gray-hour of dawn, could never go back to fairyland again; Moonmaidens, who brought good luck . . ." (p. 34).

The setting becomes less magically gentle when Attila is born. Attila's father has just challenged his god, and the result is terrifying:

> Suddenly, without warning it [the storm] was upon them with lightning and thunder that roared and howled like an army of furious demons. Trees groaned and crashed to the ground to be picked up again and sucked into the spinning dark funnel of the whirlwind. (p. 64)

This setting introduces Attila, the "Scourge of God," who in the future will lead his people home, with the help of the white stag.

In the preceding quotes, notice how Seredy uses descriptive words that create the mood. Through word choice and ability to paint pictures with words, authors of excellent literature create moods that range from happy and nostalgic to frightening and forbidding.

Setting as Antagonist. Setting can be an antagonist in plots based on person-against-society or person-against-nature conflict. The descriptions of the Arctic in Jean Craighead George's *Julie of the Wolves* are essential. Without them, readers would have difficulty understanding the life-and-death peril facing Miyax. These descriptions make it possible to comprehend Miyax's love for the Arctic, her admiration of and dependence on the wolves, and her preference for the old Eskimo ways.

In *Witch of Blackbird Pond,* by Elizabeth George Speare, a Puritan colony in colonial New England is the setting as well as the antagonist of newcomer Kit Taylor, whose colorful clothing and carefree ways immediately conflict with the standards of an austere society. Careful depiction of the colony's strict standards of dress and behavior helps readers understand why the Puritans accuse Kit of being a witch.

Setting as Historical Background. Accuracy in setting is extremely important in historical fiction and in biography. The actions of the characters and the conflict in the story may be influenced by the time period and the geographical location. Unless authors describe settings carefully, children cannot comprehend unfamiliar historical periods or the stories that unfold in them. *A Gathering of Days,* by Joan W. Blos, is an example of historical fiction that carefully depicts setting—in this case, a small New Hampshire farm in the 1830s. Blos brings rural nineteenth-century America to life through descriptions of little things, such as home remedies, country pleasures, and country hardships.

Blos describes in detail the preparation of a cold remedy. The character goes to the pump for water, blows up the fire, heats a kettle of water over the flames, wrings out a flannel in hot water, sprinkles the flannel with turpentine, and places it on the patient's chest. Blos describes discipline and school life in the 1830s. Disobedience can result in a thrashing. Because of their sex, girls are excused from all but the simplest arithmetic. Readers vicariously join the characters in breaking out of the snow with a team of oxen, tapping the maple sugar trees, and collecting nuts. Of this last experience, the narrator says, "O, I do think, as has been said, that if getting in the corn and potatoes are the prose of a farm child's life, then nutting's the poetry" (p. 131).

In *Number the Stars,* set in Copenhagen during the 1940s, Lois Lowry develops a fictional story around the actions of the Danish Resistance. Actions of King Christian add to the historical accuracy of the time period. In addition to developing historically accurate backgrounds, Lowry develops the attitudes of the Danish people. Consequently, readers understand why many Danes risked their lives to relocate the Jewish residents of Denmark.

Make Way for Sam Houston, by Jean Fritz, places the biographical character into a carefully developed historical setting. Because this is a true story, Fritz describes two important types of historical setting. She depicts the physical environments associated with the nineteenth-century political hero as he moves from plantation Virginia to rural Tennessee to political Washington and finally to frontier Texas. Within these environments, Fritz develops the relationships between Sam Houston and the political figures of the time, such as Andrew Jackson, who influenced Sam's life. The historical period comes to life through Houston's descriptions of the everyday aspects of the environment and through dialogues between Houston and the real people who lived during that time.

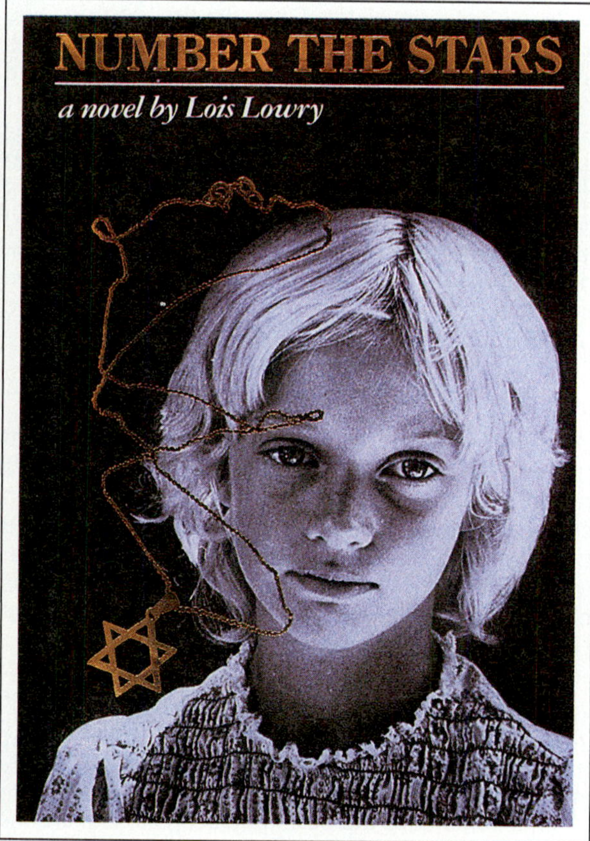

Lois Lowry develops a setting that is historically accurate for World War II Denmark. (From *Number the Stars* by Lois Lowry, copyright 1989. Reproduced with permission of Houghton Mifflin Co.)

The authors of historical fiction and biography must not only depict the time and location but also be aware of values, vocabulary, and other speech patterns consistent with the time and location. To do this, the authors must be immersed in the past and do considerable research. Joan Blos researched her subject at the New York Public Library, libraries on the University of Michigan campus, and the town library of Holderness, New Hampshire. She also consulted town and county records in New Hampshire and discussed the story with professional historians. Lois Lowry visited Copenhagen and researched documents about the leaders of the Danish Resistance. Jean Fritz referred to manuscripts and unpublished correspondence in the archives collections of the University of Texas and the Texas Baptist Historical Association.

Setting as Symbolism. Settings often have symbolic meanings that underscore what is happening in the story. Symbolism is common in traditional folktales, where frightening adventures and magical transformations occur in the deep, dark woods, and splendid castles are the sites of "happily ever after." Modern authors of fantasy and science fiction for children often borrow such symbolic settings from old folktales in order to establish moods of strangeness and enchantment, but authors of realistic fiction also use subtly symbolic settings to accentuate plot or character development.

In one children's classic, *The Secret Garden,* by Frances Hodgson Burnett, a garden that has been locked behind a wall for ten years symbolizes a father's grief after the death of his wife, his son's illness, and the emotional estrangement of the father and son from each other. The first positive change in the life of a lonely, unhappy girl occurs when she discovers the buried key to the garden and opens the vine-covered door:

It was the sweetest, most mysterious-looking place anyone could imagine. The high walls which shut it in were covered with the leafless stems of climbing roses which were so thick that they were matted together. (p. 76)

Finding the garden, working in it, and watching its beauty return bring happiness to the girl, restore health to the sick boy, and reunite the father and son. The good magic that causes emotional and physical healing in this secret kingdom is symbolized by tiny new shoots emerging from the soil and the rosy color that the garden's fresh air brings to the cheeks of two pale children.

In a more recent book, Katherine Paterson's *Bridge to Terabithia,* a secret kingdom in the woods symbolizes the "other world" shared by two young people who do not conform to the values of rural Virginia. The boy, Jess, would rather be an artist than follow the more masculine aspirations of his father, who accuses him of being a sissy.

A boy and girl create a secret kingdom in which they can escape the problems of the real world. (Illustration by Donna Diamond from *Bridge to Terabithia* by Katherine Paterson. Copyright © 1977 by Katherine Paterson. A Newbery Medal winner. By permission of Thomas Y. Crowell, Publishers.)

Schoolmates taunt the girl, Leslie, because she loves books and has no television. Jess and Leslie find that they have much in common, so they create a domain of their own, in which a beautiful setting symbolizes their growing sense of comradeship, belongingness, and self-love.

Even the entrance to their secret country is symbolic: "It could be a magic country like Narnia, and the only way you can get in is by swinging across on this enchanted rope" (p. 39). They grab the old rope, swing across the creek, and enter their stronghold, where streams of light dance through the leaves of dogwood, oak, and evergreen, fears and enemies do not exist, and anything they want is possible. Paterson develops credible settings as Jess and Leslie go from the world of school and home to the world that they make for themselves in Terabithia.

A dilapidated house, with its uncared-for backyard, becomes a symbolic setting in Janet Taylor Lisle's *Afternoon of the Elves*. In this setting, two girls, Hillary and Sara-Kate, make discoveries about each other and the importance of accepting people who are different. The girls work together in a miniature village that Sara-Kate maintains was built by elves. Like Paterson, Lisle creates two credible settings: (1) Hillary's normal world of school and home and (2) the almost otherworld existence of a yard that is entered through a thick hedge. Like many other authors of books that have symbolic settings, Lisle relates the setting to the theme.

Theme

The theme of a story is the underlying idea that ties the plot, characters, and setting together into a meaningful whole. When evaluating themes in children's books, consider what the author wanted to convey about life or society and whether that theme is worthwhile for children. A memorable book has a theme—or several themes—that children can understand because of their own needs. Laurence Perrine (20) states:

> There is no prescribed method for discovering theme. Sometimes we can best get at it by asking in what way the main character has changed in the course of a story and what, if anything, the character has learned before its end. Sometimes the best approach is to explore the nature of the central conflict and its outcome. Sometimes the title will provide an important clue. (p. 110)

Authors of children's books often directly state the theme of a book, rather than imply it, as they commonly do in books for adults. Theme may be stated by characters or through the author's narrative.

Theme Revealed by Changes in Characters. In *The Whipping Boy*, Sid Fleischman develops the theme that friendship is important. Fleischman shows how the main characters change in their attitudes toward each other. For example, the names that the main characters call each other progress from hostility to comradeship. At the beginning of the story, Jemmy thinks of the prince as "Your Royal Awfulness." Likewise, the prince refers to Jemmy as "Jemmy-from-the-Street" and "contrary rascal." As the story develops, and the two characters learn to respect and admire each other, Jemmy refers to the prince as "friend" and the Prince calls himself "Friend-o-Jemmy's."

In *Darkness and the Butterfly*, Ann Grifalconi develops the theme that we can, and must, overcome our fears. Grifalconi reveals the theme by describing Osa's actions as she moves from fearing the dark to seeing beauty in the night. In this book for younger children, the theme is stated by Osa when she excitedly exclaims, "I can be as brave as the butterfly. . . . SEE? I'm not afraid of the dark anymore" (unnumbered).

Theme and the Nature of Conflict. Stories set in other time periods frequently develop themes by revealing how the main characters respond to conflicts caused by society. For example, Rudolf Frank's *No Hero for the Kaiser*, set in World War I, develops several antiwar themes. Frank develops the harsh nature of war by exploring the actions and responses of a boy who is unwittingly drawn into battle. Through the viewpoint of the boy, Frank reveals that it takes more courage not to fight than to fight, that it is important to respect oneself, and that "guns never go off by themselves" (p. 13). Frank reinforces these themes through symbolism, similes, and contrasts. The contrasts are especially effective as Frank compares the same soldiers at home and on the battlefield and contrasts peacetime and wartime meanings for such terms as *bull's-eye, shot*, and *field*.

Janet Lunn's main character in *Shadow in Hawthorn Bay*, a historical novel set in 1800s Canada, discovers that prejudice is a harmful force and that it is important to respect one's own beliefs. The impact of prejudice is explored when the main character, a girl with second sight, leaves Scotland and arrives in a community where her abilities are feared, not honored. Prejudice is a harmful force in other historical fiction, such as Elizabeth George Speare's *The Witch of Blackbird Pond*, Paula Fox's *The Slave Dancer*, Carol Carrick's *Stay Away from Simon!*, Uri Orlev's *The Island on Bird Street*, and Mildred D. Taylor's *Roll of Thunder, Hear My Cry*.

The Theme of Personal Development. Literature offers children opportunities to identify with other people's experiences and thus better understand their own growing up. Consequently, the themes of many children's books deal with developing self-understanding. Gretchen Purtell Hayden (8) concluded that the following themes related to personal development are predominant in children's books that have received the Newbery Medal: difficulties in establishing good relationships between adults and children, the need for morality to guide one's actions, the importance of support from other people, an acceptance of oneself and others, a respect for authority, the ability to handle problems, and the necessity of cooperation.

The difficulty of establishing good relationships between adults and children is developed in a humorous way in Beverly Cleary's *Ramona and Her Father*. Cleary indicates that Ramona usually has a good relationship with her parents, but it rapidly deteriorates when her father loses his job. Ramona confronts new difficulties in getting along with adults who are worried and frustrated. Cleary describes Ramona's efforts to help her family and Ramona's frustration when her actions do not work out as she hopes. For example, after the cat destroys a jack-o'-lantern the family has made together, her father mistakenly thinks Ramona's sadness is due to the loss of the pumpkin: "Didn't grown-ups think children worried about anything but jack-o-lanterns? Didn't they know children worried about grown-ups?" (p. 85).

In Robert O'Brien's *Mrs. Frisby and the Rats of NIMH*, a group of superior rats search for a moral code to guide their actions. They have studied the human race and do not wish to make the same mistakes, but they soon realize how easy it is to slip into dishonest behavior. Some equipment they find allows them to steal electricity, food, and water from human society, which then makes their lives seem too easy and pointless. Eventually, the rats choose a more difficult course of action,

Superior rats consider the morality of their actions in a complex plot. (Illustration by Zena Bernstein from *Mrs. Frisby and the Rats of NIMH* by Robert C. O'Brien. Copyright © 1971 by Robert C. O'Brien. [New York: Charles Scribner's Sons, 1971]. Reprinted with the permission of Atheneum Publishers.)

moving into an isolated valley and working to develop their own civilization.

One book that develops the importance of support from another human being is Theodore Taylor's *The Cay*. When Phillip and his mother leave Curaçao in order to find safety in the United States, their boat is torpedoed by a German submarine. Phillip, a white boy, and a black West Indian named Timothy become isolated first on a life raft and then on a tiny Caribbean island. Their need for each other is increased when Phillip becomes blind after a blow to the head and must, in spite of his racial prejudice, rely on Timothy for his survival. Phillip's superior attitudes gradually vanish, as he becomes totally dependent on another person. When Phillip is finally rescued, Phillip treasures the way a wonderful friend has helped change his life for the better.

The Cay also stresses the theme of accepting oneself and others, as does Joan W. Blos's *A Gathering of Days,* in which Catherine experiences injustice for the first time when she and her friends secretly help a runaway slave. Catherine learns to respect authority as well when after years of responsibility for her widowed father and little sister, she must trust and obey her new stepmother.

Many children's books deal in some way with the necessity of overcoming problems. Characters may overcome problems within themselves or in their relationships with others, or problems caused by society or nature. Memorable characters face their adversaries, and through a maturing process, they learn to handle their own difficulties. Handling problems may be as dramatic and planned as Mafatu's search for courage in Armstrong Sperry's *Call It Courage* or may result from accident, as in Theodore Taylor's *The Cay*. In Katherine Martin's *Night Riding,* the conflicts, and the resulting maturing process, begin with the arrival of new neighbors. In this book, eleven-year-old Prin discovers the dark secrets kept by sexually abused children. In Colby Rodowsky's *Sydney, Herself,* Sydney learns to accept herself, her mother, and her heritage. In Evaline Ness's *Sam, Bangs & Moonshine,* Sam must overcome her tendency to lie. Katherine Paterson has Jess and Leslie cross *The Bridge to Terabithia* in order to overcome the difficulties of being nonconformists in the rest of their everyday lives.

The theme of cooperation is developed in Jean Craighead George's *Julie of the Wolves* when Miyax must make friends with frightening animals and a harsh environment in order to survive. Cooperation within the family and within the larger community is a theme throughout Laura Ingalls Wilder's "Little House" books about pioneers on the American frontier.

Style

Authors have a wide choice of words to select from and numerous ways to arrange words in order to create plots, characters, and settings and to express themes. Many authors use words and sentences in creative ways. To evaluate style, read a piece of literature aloud. The sound of a story should appeal to your senses and be appropriate to the content of the story. The language should enhance the plot development, bring the characters to life, and create a mood.

The Girl Who Loved Wild Horses, by Paul Goble, was a Children's Choice selection. The most frequent reason that children give for choosing this book is the author's use of language. Goble chooses his words carefully. He uses precise verbs and similes to evoke a landscape of cliffs and canyons, beautiful wild horses, and the high-spirited Indian girl who loves them. One stallion's eyes are "cold stars," while his floating mane and tail are "wispy clouds." During a storm, the horses gallop "faster and faster, pursued by thunder and lightning. . . . like a brown flood across hills and through valleys" (p. 12 unnumbered).

Figurative language also enhances characterization, plot, and setting in Jan Hudson's *Sweetgrass,* a historical novel about the Blackfeet, set on the Canadian prairies. Early in the story, for example, sweet berries symbolize a young girl's happiness and hopes: "Promises hung shimmering in the future like glowing berries above sandy soil as we gathered our bags for the walk home" (p. 12). Later, the same girl's acceptance of a disillusioning reality is symbolized again by berries, which are then bitter.

Frank's figurative language in *No Hero for the Kaiser* reinforces the antiwar themes developed within the story. In the following quote, Frank first uses contrasts to show the changing nature of terms previously understood and then uses simile to reveal the destructiveness of cannons:

> Jan could not help remembering that among those invisible men called enemies there was his own father. His own father was in the field and his father's son was in the field. Why could they not tend the field together as before? Because this field that the soldiers were taking was not a field at all. A real field does not kill, a field lies at peace under God's sun, rain, and wind, a field is where things grow. He had caught the military in a lie. The soldiers were sent into a field of deceit. Like huge wolves the four cannon of the Seventh Battery went "into the field," across Polish fields, deeper and deeper into Russia, and behind them walked the gunners. (p. 46)

Authors may also select words and sentence structures with rhythms that evoke different moods. Armstrong Sperry creates two quite different moods for Mafatu in *Call It Courage*. As Mafatu goes through the jungle, he is preoccupied and moves at a leisurely pace. Sperry uses long sentences to develop this mood: "His mind was not in this business at all: he was thinking about the rigging of his canoe, planning how he could strengthen it here, tighten it there" (p. 77). This dreamy preoccupation changes rapidly as Mafatu senses danger. Sperry's verbs become harsh and his sentences short and choppy as Mafatu's tension builds: "The boar charged. Over the ground it tore. Foam flew back from its tusks. The boy braced himself" (p. 78).

Many of the stories young children enjoy contain repetition of words, phrases, or sentences. Repetition is especially appealing because it encourages children to join in. It provides a pleasing rhythm in *When I Was Young in the Mountains,* by Cynthia Rylant. The author introduces her memories of Grandfather's kisses, Grandmother's cooking, and listening to frogs singing at dusk with "When I was young in the mountains," a phrase that adds an appropriate aura of loving nostalgia to the experiences that she describes.

Point of View

Several people may describe a single incident in different terms. The feelings they experience, the details they choose to describe, and their judgments about what occurred may vary because of their backgrounds, values, and other perspectives. Consequently, the same story may change drastically when told from another point of view. How would Peter Rabbit's story be different if Beatrix Potter had told it from the viewpoint of the mother rabbit? How would Armstrong Sperry's *Call It Courage* differ if told from the viewpoint of a Polynesian tribesman who loves the sea rather than from the viewpoint of a boy who fears it?

An author has several options when selecting point of view. A first-person point of view speaks through the "I" of one of the characters. An author who wishes to use a first-person narrative must decide which character's actions and feelings should influence the story. An objective point of view lets actions speak for themselves. The author describes only the characters' actions, and readers must infer the characters' thoughts and feelings.

An omniscient point of view tells the story in the third person, with the author talking about "they," "he," or "she." The author is not restricted to the knowledge, experience, and feelings of one person. The feelings and thoughts of all characters can be revealed. When using a limited omniscient point of view the author concentrates on the experience of one character, but has the option to be all-knowing about other characters. (A limited omniscient point of view, focusing on one character, may help an author clarify conflict and actions that would be less understandable if a first-person narrative were used.)

Although no point of view is preferred for all children's literature, an author's choice can affect how much children of certain ages believe and enjoy a story. Contemporary realistic fiction for children age eight and older often uses a first-person point of view or a limited omniscient point of view that focuses on one child's experience. Older children often empathize with one character if they have had similar experiences.

In *The Wicked Stepdog,* Carol Lea Benjamin introduces her first-person narrator through these thoughts: "I think most parents are pretty phony. Take my dad for example" (p. 1). The actions in the story are then interpreted through the view-

ISSUE

Evaluation of Children's Literature: Literary Merit Versus Popularity Versus Social Significance

CHILDREN'S LITERATURE is evaluated by not only children but also literary critics, teachers, librarians, parents, and publishers. Jean Karl[1] maintains, "[T]he informed bookstore and the informed bookstore purchaser of children's books have always been in a minority" (p. 506). Questions related to literary quality, social philosophy, and suitability of content are debated along with the potential and proven ability of a book to attract children's interest.

The evaluation criteria used for book awards, criticism, and recommendations for book purchases frequently reflect the standards of diverse groups. The adult-selected award winners—exemplified by the Newbery Medal, Caldecott Medal, Notable Children's Books, and Boston Globe-Horn Book Award—suggest that literary value should be the primary consideration when choosing books for children. In contrast, the various readers' choice awards, which are compiled from the preferences of young readers, imply that the popularity of the books among children should be the essential consideration. A third position, represented by groups such as the Council of Interracial Books for Children, suggests that books should be evaluated according to values that stem from child development and psychology, cultural pluralism, and aesthetic standards.

The selection standards reflected by these three positions

point of that twelve-year-old character. Likewise, Beverly Cleary's popular Ramona stories are told from the viewpoint of a precocious seven- or eight-year-old child.

The consistency of point of view encourages readers to believe in the characters and plot development of a story. Such belief is especially crucial in modern fantasy, where readers are introduced to imaginary worlds, unusual characters, and magical incidents. A writer may describe a setting as if it were being viewed by a character only a few inches tall. To be believable, however, the story cannot stray from the viewpoint of the tiny character. The character's actions, the responses of others toward the character, and the setting must be consistent.

Stereotypes

Consider stereotypes when evaluating literature for young children. Educators and other concerned adults strongly criticize stereotypical views of both race and sex. Of particular concern are literary selections that inadequately represent minority groups and females or that represent them in insensitive or demeaning ways.

Teachers, librarians, and parents may confront a shortage of high-quality stories about members of racial and ethnic minority groups, of works by authors who write from a minority perspective, and of materials that depict the literary, cultural, and historical influence of minorities. However, children's literature should present honest, authentic pictures of different people and their cultural and historical contributions.

When evaluating literature about minorities, for example, keep the following questions in mind: Are black, Native American, Hispanic, and other minority characters portrayed as distinct individuals, or are they grouped in one category under depersonalizing clichés? Does the author recognize and accurately portray the internal diversity of minority cultures? Is a minority culture respected or treated as inferior? Does the author accurately describe the values, behavior, and environment of characters who are members of minority groups? Are illustrations realistic and authentic? Research indicates that if stereotypical attitudes are to change, reading of positive multicultural literature must be followed by discussions or other activities that allow interaction between children and adults.

may or may not identify the same books as literature worthy of sharing with children. The merits of each type of evaluation are debated in professional literature, in college classrooms, and during professional conferences. Reviewers of children's books may emphasize one or more of these positions when they evaluate new books or compile lists of recommended books. It is helpful to identify any particular bias of a reviewer so that you can interpret and use recommendations to meet your own needs.

Carolyn Bauer and LaVonne Sanborn[2] maintain that both literary quality and popularity are important. They suggest that books that have won both types of awards deserve considerable emphasis. Children do enjoy some books with literary value. From a list of 193 books that won readers' choice awards, Bauer and Sanborn identified 39 that were also literary merit award winners. Of these, *Mrs. Frisby and the Rats of NIMH, The Mouse and the Motorcycle, Old Yeller, Rascal,* and *The Trumpet of the Swan* have each won four readers' choice awards. Authors Beverly Cleary, George Selden, and E. B. White each have written two titles that have won awards for literary value and popularity.

Increased sensitivity to the values expressed in books may result in debates about the merit of previously acclaimed literature. For example, Walter Edmonds's *The Matchlock Gun* won the Newbery Medal in 1942, but it was criticized in the 1970s because of insensitive descriptions of Native Americans.

When evaluating literature and reading literature critiques, you should consider each selection standard. Does the book have literary merit? Is it popular? Is it socially significant?

[1]Karl, Jean E. "What Sells—What's Good?" *The Horn Book* 63 (July/August 1987): 505–508.

[2]Bauer, Carolyn J., and LaVonne H. Sanborn. "The Best of Both Worlds: Children's Books Acclaimed by Adults and Young Readers." *Top of the News* 38 (Fall 1981): 53–56.

Sexism in children's literature also requires adults to evaluate children's books with care. Masha Kabakow Rudman (22) states:

> Books for children have reflected societal attitudes in limiting choices and maintaining discrimination. Most traditional books show females dressed in skirts or dresses even when they are engaged in activities inappropriate for this sort of costume. Illustrations also have conventionally placed females in passive observer roles, while males have been pictured as active. Studies have demonstrated time and time again that illustrations confirm the subordinate, less valued role for the female, while stressing the active, adventuresome, admirable role of the male. . .When a female is permitted to retain her active qualities, it is usually made clear to the reader that she is the notable exception and that all the other girls in the story are "normal." (p. 105)

Some children's books also stereotype males in ways that limit the options of boys to express a wide range of feelings and interests. Books should treat all characters as individuals. A book that groups all males or all females together and makes insulting remarks about either sex as a whole is sexist. However, you must read an entire book before you reach this decision, because you should not judge isolated quotes out of context.

THE RIGHT BOOK FOR EACH CHILD

Because of developmental stages, children have different personal and literary needs at different ages. Children in the same age group or at the same stage of development also have diverse interests and reading abilities that you must consider. Understanding why and what children read is necessary in order to help them select materials that stimulate their interests and enjoyment. John T. Guthrie (7) investigated why adults read, but his results apply to children as well. Guthrie concluded that the two most important reasons for reading were to obtain general knowledge and to gain relaxation and enjoyment.

Jeanne S. Chall and Emily W. Marston (4) found that the most powerful determinants of adult reading are accessibility, readability, and interest. These factors also influence children's reading habits and preferences. If developing enjoyment through literature is a major objective of your reading program for children, you must make available many excellent books, consider children's reading levels, and know how to gain and use information about children's reading interests.

Accessibility

Literature must be readily accessible if children are to read at all. In order to know what books interest them, gain knowledge of their heritage, recognize and appreciate good literature, and understand themselves and others through literature, children must have opportunities to read and listen to many books. As suggested, a literature program for children should include a wide variety of high-quality literature, both old and new. Unfortunately, studies show that children do not have enough opportunities to read literature in school. Roger Poole (21) surveyed schools in England and reported, "[F]indings of the research show that teachers do not make much use of quality narrative" (p. 179). Rebecca Barr and Marilyn Sadow (1) analyzed American schools and found "little reading of literary selections other than those available in the basal program" (p. 69).

A survey by Susan Swanton (24) showed that gifted students owned more books and used public libraries more than did other students. Fifty-five percent of the gifted students Swanton surveyed identified the public library as their major source of reading material, as opposed to only 33 percent of the other students, most of whom identified the school library as their major source for books. Thirty-five percent of the gifted children owned more than one hundred books. Only 19 percent of other students owned an equal number of books. Swanton made the following recommendations for cooperation between public libraries and schools:

1. Promote students' participation in summer reading programs that are sponsored by public libraries.
2. Inform parents about the value of reading aloud to children, giving children their own books, and parents as role models for developing readers.
3. Encourage school librarians to do book talks designed to entice children into reading.
4. Provide field trips to public libraries.
5. Advertise public library programs and services.
6. Make obtaining the first library card a special event.

Readability

According to Jeanne S. Chall and Emily W. Marston (4), readability is another major consideration in choosing literature for children. A book must conform to a child's reading level in order for the child to read independently. Children become frustrated when books contain too many words they don't know. A child is able to read independently when able to pronounce about 98–100 percent of the words in a book and to answer 90–100 percent of the comprehension questions asked about it. Reading abilities in any one age group or grade level range widely, so adults working with children must provide, and be familiar with, an equally wide range of literature. Many children have reading levels lower than their interest levels. Thus, they need many opportunities to listen to, and otherwise interact with, fine literature.

Books listed in the annotated bibliographies at the end of chapters in this book are identified by grade-level of readability, although a book will not be readable to every child in the grade indicated. See Appendix E for a readability graph and directions for computing readability.

Interest

You can learn about children's interests from studies of children's interests and interest inventories. You should consider information gained from each source.

For many years, researchers have investigated factors related to the leisure reading habits and interests of children at different age levels. Vincent Greaney (6) identified some of these factors. First, American and British studies indicate that the time and amount of leisure reading varies with age. Children at the end of primary school read the most, after which a decline in leisure reading occurs among all but high-ability readers. Second, girls read more books than boys do, although boys read more nonfiction. Third, children from working-class homes do not read as much as those from higher socioeconomic backgrounds. Finally, the amount of leisure reading and the level of student achievement are directly related; good students read more and read higher-quality materials.

Research indicates that children's reading interests are also influenced by their reading ability.

Susan Swanton's (24) survey comparing gifted students with students of average ability reports that gifted children prefer mysteries (43 percent), fiction (41 percent), science fiction (29 percent), and fantasy (18 percent). In contrast, the top four choices for students of average ability were mysteries (47 percent), comedy/humor (27 percent), realistic fiction (23 percent), and adventure (18 percent). Gifted students indicated that they liked "science fiction and fantasy because of the challenge it presented, as well as its relationship to Dungeons and Dragons" (p. 100). Gifted students listed Judy Blume, Lloyd Alexander, J. R. R. Tolkien, and C. S. Lewis as favorite authors. Average students listed Judy Blume, Beverly Cleary, and Jack London.

While this information can provide some general ideas about what subjects and authors children of certain ages, sexes, and reading abilities prefer, do not develop stereotyped views about children's preferences. Without asking questions about interests, for example, there is no way to learn that a fourth-grade boy is a Shakespeare buff, since research into children's interests does not indicate that a fourth-grader should like Shakespeare's plays. A first-grade girl's favorite subject was dinosaurs, which she could identify by name. Discovering this would have been impossible without an interview; research does not indicate that first-grade girls are interested in factual, scientific subjects. These two cases point to the need to discover children's interests before helping them select books. Informal conversation is one of the simplest ways to uncover children's interests. Ask a child to describe what he or she likes to do and read about. Usually, you should record the information when working with a number of children.

You can develop interest inventories in which students answer questions about their favorite hobbies, books, sports, television shows, and other interests. Write down the answers of young children, but let older children read questionnaires themselves and write their own responses. Interest inventories may include some of the questions asked in Chart 3–1. Make changes according to the age levels of the children involved. You may discover additional information if you ask children why they like certain books. The findings of an interest inventory can help you help children select books and extend children's enjoyment of literature.

When considering interests and selecting literature, remember that children of different ages may be interested in the same books but for different reasons. Michael Tunnell (25) describes how readers from age eight through adulthood enjoy Natalie Babbitt's *Tuck Everlasting*. Tunnell says that eight-year-olds enjoy the carefully foreshadowed plot, twelve-year-olds identify with Winnie's rites of passage, fifteen-year-olds empathize with Winnie's final decision, and adults appreciate Babbitt's craft as a writer.

Educators should remember that many children need to be led into reading and enjoying books that are beyond their normal interests. Perry Nodelman (18) warns:

> Children who experience nothing but conventional books do quickly learn to be intolerant of the unconventional. That's a pity, because being able to respond to more unusual or more complicated books makes one's life more interesting, one's knowledge of the world deeper and subtler, one's tolerance and humility greater. Being capable of enjoying just about anything is certainly a good place to start; but children deserve better than beginnings so that they will become more than just beginners, in reading, in understanding literature, and in understanding the subtle complexities of life. (p. 38)

THE CHILD AS CRITIC

Children are the ultimate critics of what they read, and you should consider their preferences when evaluating and selecting books to share with them. For the last few years, a joint project of the International Reading Association and the Children's Book Council has allowed approximately 10,000 children from around the United States to evaluate children's books published during a given year. Each year, their reactions are recorded, and a research team uses this information to compile a list called "Children's Choices" in the following categories: beginning independent reading, younger children, middle grades, older readers, informational books, and poetry. This very useful annotated bibliography is published each year in the October issue of *The Reading Teacher,* and it may be obtained from the Children's Book Council, 67 Irving Place, New York, NY 10003.

A look at these lists of children's favorites also gives an understanding of the characteristics of books that appeal to children. In order to identify characteristic elements found in the Children's

CHART 3–1
An informal interest inventory

1 Do you have a hobby? _____
If you do, what is your hobby? _____
2 Do you have a pet? _____
What kind of a pet do you have? _____
3 What is your favorite book that someone has read to you? _____
4 What kinds of books do you like to have read to you?

real animals _____	picture books _____
real children _____	information books _____
science fiction _____	mysteries _____
funny stories _____	fairy tales _____
sports stories _____	poetry _____
true stories _____	historical fiction _____
fantasy animals _____	science books _____
family stories _____	adventures _____

5 What is your favorite book that you have read by yourself? _____
6 What kinds of books do you like to read by yourself? (Similar to 4) _____
7 What sports do you like? _____
8 Who are your favorite sports stars? _____
9 What do you do when you get home from school? _____
10 What do you like to do on Saturday? _____
11 Do you like to collect things? _____
What do you like to collect? _____
12 What are your favorite subjects in school? _____
13 Would you rather read a book by yourself or have someone read it to you? _____
14 Name a book you read this week. _____
15 Where would you like to go on vacation? _____
16 Do you go to the library? _____
If you do, how often do you go? _____
Do you have a library card? _____
17 Do you watch television? _____
18 If you do, what kinds of programs do you like?

comedies _____	cartoons _____
sports _____	westerns _____
animal programs _____	music _____
family stories _____	game shows _____
educational TV _____	mysteries _____
true stories _____	detective shows _____
specials _____	science fiction _____
news _____	other _____

19 Name your favorite television programs. _____
20 Who are your favorite characters on TV? _____
21 Name several subjects you would like to know more about. _____
_____

Choices, Sam Leaton Sebesta (23) evaluated the books listed and tried to discover if their characteristics were different from those of books not chosen by children. His evaluation produced the following conclusions:

1 Plots of the Children's Choices are faster paced than those found in books not chosen as favorites.
2 Young children enjoy reading about nearly any topic if the information is presented in detail. The topic itself may be less important than interest studies have indicated; specifics rather than topics seem to underlie children's preferences.
3 Children like detailed descriptions of settings; they want to know exactly how a place looks and feels before the main action occurs.

4 One type of plot structure does not dominate Children's Choices. Some stories have a central focus with a carefully arranged cause-and-effect plot; others have plots that meander with unconnected episodes.
5 Children do not like sad books.
6 Children seem to like some books that explicitly teach a lesson, even though critics usually frown on didactic literature.
7 Warmth was the most outstanding quality of books children preferred. Children enjoy books in which the characters like each other, express their feelings in things they say and do, and sometimes act selflessly.

Sebesta believes that this information should be used to help children select books and to stimulate reading and discussions. For example, you can draw children's attention to the warmth, pace, or descriptions in a story in order to encourage involvement with the story.

The various Children's Choices lists also suggest particular types of stories that appeal to young readers. The beginning independent reading category contains comical stories about more or less realistic family situations, humorous animal stories, stories that develop emotional experiences, action-filled fantasies, traditional stories, counting books, rhymes, and riddles. The younger reader category includes realistic stories about families, friends, school, and personal problems; animal stories; fantasies; fast-paced adventures; folktales; and humorous stories. Stories chosen by children in the middle grades include realistic stories about sibling rivalry, peer acceptance, fears, and not conforming to stereotypes; fantasies; stories of suspense; and humorous stories. Popular informational books include factual and nonsensical advice about human health, factual information about animals, and biographical information about sports stars. Popular poetry includes collections by Judith Viorst, Shel Silverstein, and William Cole.

Children choose books from a wide variety of genres. Some are on highly recommended lists of children's books; others are not. Many educators and authorities on children's literature are concerned about the quality of books children read. If children are to improve their ability to make valid judgments about literature, they must experience good books and investigate and discuss what it is about books that make them memorable. Young children usually just enjoy and talk about books, but older ones can start to evaluate what they do and do not like about literature.

One sixth-grade teacher encouraged her students to make literary judgments and to develop a list of criteria for selecting good literature (19). The motivation for this literature study began when the students wondered what favorite books their parents might have read when they were in the same grade. To answer this question, the children interviewed their parents and other adults, asking them which books and characters were their favorites. They listed the books, characters, and number of people who recommended them on a large chart.

Each student then read a book that a parent or another respected adult had enjoyed. (Many adults also reread these books.) Following their reading, the children discussed the book with the adult, considering what made or did not make the book memorable for them. At this time, the teacher introduced the concepts of plot, characterization, setting, theme, and style. The children searched the books they had read for examples of each element. Finally, they listed questions to ask themselves when evaluating a book:

Questions to Ask Myself When I Judge a Book

1 Is this a good story?
2 Is the story about something I think could really happen? Is the plot believable?
3 Did the main character overcome the problem, but not too easily?
4 Did the climax seem natural?
5 Did the characters seem real? Did I understand the characters' personalities and the reasons for their actions?
6 Did the characters in the story grow?
7 Did I find out about more than one side of the characters? Did the characters have both strengths and weaknesses?
8 Did the setting present what is actually known about that time or place?
9 Did the characters fit into the setting?
10 Did I feel that I was really in that time or place?
11 What did the author want to tell me in the story?
12 Was the theme worthwhile?
13 When I read the book aloud, did the characters sound like real people actually talking?
14 Did the rest of the language sound natural? (19, p. 390)

A review of these fourteen evaluative questions shows how closely they correspond to the criteria that should be used in evaluating the plot, characterization, setting, theme, and style found in literature.

Research shows that children have preferences in the books they choose. Other research indicates that children also have preferences about how and when books should be read to them. Alicia Mendoza (17) reports the results of a survey of 520 elementary school children ranging in age from five to thirteen. The following recommendations, taken from Mendoza's longer report, highlight the importance of reading books to children and the preferences of children during those listening experiences. First, children throughout elementary grades enjoy having books read to them. Consequently, parents and teachers should read to children frequently. Second, during conferences with parents, teachers should emphasize the importance of reading to children at home. Third, role models are important, so both parents should read to children. Fourth, because children enjoy listening to stories in groups, teachers should encourage parents to make reading at home a group activity. Fifth, parents and teachers should provide opportunities for children to read to other children. Sixth, children should have opportunities to select the books read to them or read by them to others. Seventh, children like information about a book before it is read to them. They should be told who the author is and be given a brief summary of the plot, characters, and setting. Finally, children like and should be given an opportunity to discuss books and to read books after the books are read aloud.

When children are encouraged to share, discuss, and evaluate books, and given opportunities to do so, they are able to expand their reading enjoyment and to select worthwhile stories and characters. Sharing and discussion can take place in the library, classroom, or home.

Suggested Activities for Adult Understanding of the Selection and Evaluation of Children's Literature

- ☐ Compare the plots of several books written for younger children with plots in books written for older children. Compare the ways in which events are ordered, the ways in which the conflicts are developed, the amounts of suspense or tension, and the climaxes of the stories.
- ☐ Find examples of person-against-person, person-against-self, person-against-society, and person-against-nature conflicts in children's literature. Do some books develop more than one type of conflict? What makes the conflict believable? Share these examples with your class.
- ☐ Read one of Laura Ingalls Wilder's "Little House" books. Do you agree with the child who said she would like the character Laura for her best friend? How has the author developed Laura into a believable character? Give examples of techniques Wilder uses to reveal Laura's nature.
- ☐ Compare the main character in a fairy tale such as "Cinderella" or "Snow White" with the main character in a book such as Patricia Clapp's *I'm Deborah Sampson,* Scott O'Dell's *Island of the Blue Dolphins,* or Armstrong Sperry's *Call It Courage*. Describe each character. Does the character change in the course of the story? How does the author show that change?
- ☐ Find descriptions of settings that (1) are used to create a mood, (2) develop conflict, (3) are symbolic, and (4) describe a historical period. What is the importance of each setting? Close your eyes and try to picture the setting. If it is realistic, what did the author do to make it so? If it does not seem realistic, what is wrong? How would you improve it?
- ☐ Investigate themes found in children's literature published during the 1960s, 1970s, and 1980s. Which ones are most common? Can you draw any conclusions about the social, cultural, and economic influences of the times? Make a time line to summarize the results.
- ☐ Find several examples of writing in which the author's style has created a specific image. Read each selection to an audience. How does the audience respond to the author's style?
- ☐ Review the books in the most recent list of Children's Choices. What are some characteristics of books chosen by younger, middle elementary, and older readers?

References

1 Barr, Rebecca, and Marilyn W. Sadow. "Influence of Basal Programs on Fourth-Grade Reading Instruction." *Reading Research Quarterly* 24 (Winter 1989): 44–71.

2 Bond, Nancy. "Conflict in Children's Fiction." *The Horn Book* 60 (June 1984): 297–306.

3 Carlson, Ruth Kearney. "Book Selection for Children of a Modern World." In *Developing Active Readers: Ideas for Parents, Teachers, and Librarians,* edited by Dianne L. Monson and Day Ann K. McClenathan. Newark, Del.: International Reading Association, 1979, pp. 16–29.

4 Chall, Jeanne S., and Emily W. Marston. "The Reluctant Reader: Suggestions from Research and Practice." *Catholic Library World* 47 (February 1976): 274–275.

5 Frye, Northrop, Sheridan Baker, and George Perkins. *The Harper Handbook to Literature*. New York: Harper & Row, 1985.

6 Greaney, Vincent. "Factors Related to Amount and Type of Leisure Time Reading." *Reading Research Quarterly* 15 (1980): 337–357.

7 Guthrie, John T. "Why People (Say They) Read." *The Reading Teacher* 32 (March 1979): 752–755.

8 Hayden, Gretchen Purtell. "A Descriptive Study of the Treatment of Personal Development in Selected Children's Fiction Books Awarded the Newbery Medal." Detroit: Wayne State University, 1969, University Microfilm No. 70–19,060.

9 Heins, Paul. "Coming to Terms with Criticism." In *Crosscurrents of Criticism: Horn Book Essays 1968–1977*. Boston: The Horn Book, 1978, pp. 82–87.

10 Heins, Paul. "Out on a Limb with the Critics: Some Random Thoughts on the Present State of the Criticism of Children's Literature." In *Crosscurrents of Criticism: Horn Book Essays 1968–1977*. Boston: The Horn Book, 1978, pp. 72–81.

11 Huck, Charlotte S., Susan Hepler, and Janet Hickman. *Children's Literature in the Elementary School*. New York: Holt, Rinehart & Winston, 1987.

12 Huus, Helen. "Teaching Literature at the Elementary School Level." *The Reading Teacher* 26 (May 1973): 795–801.

13 Karl, Jean E. "What Sells—What's Good?" *The Horn Book* 63 (July/August 1987): 505–508.

14 Kennemer, Phyllis K. "Reviews of Fiction Books: How They Differ." *Top of the News* 40 (Summer 1984): 419–421.

15 Kingsbury, Mary. "Perspectives on Criticism," *The Horn Book* 60 (February 1984): 17–23.

16 Lukens, Rebecca J. *A Critical Handbook of Children's Literature*. Glenview, Ill.: Scott, Foresman, 1986.

17 Mendoza, Alicia. "Reading to Children: Their Preferences," *The Reading Teacher* 38 (February 1985): 522–527.

18 Nodelman, Perry. "Which Children? Some Audiences for Children's Books." *The Horn Book* 63 (January/February 1987): 35–40.

19 Norton, Donna E. *The Effective Teaching of Language Arts*. 3d ed. Columbus, Ohio: Merrill, 1989.

20 Perrine, Laurence. *Literature: Structure, Sound, and Sense*. 4th ed. San Diego: Harcourt Brace Jovanovich, 1983.

21 Poole, Roger. "The Books Teachers Use." *Children's Literature in Education* 17 (Fall 1986): 159–180.

22 Rudman, Masha Kabakow. *Children's Literature: An Issues Approach*. 2d ed. New York: Longman, 1984.

23 Sebesta, Sam Leaton. "What Do Young People Think About the Literature They Read?" *Reading Newsletter,* no. 8. Rockleigh, N.J.: Allyn & Bacon, 1979.

24 Swanton, Susan. "Minds Alive: What and Why Gifted Students Read for Pleasure." *School Library Journal* 30 (March 1984): 99–102.

25 Tunnell, Michael O. "Books in the Classroom." *The Horn Book* 63 (July/August 1987): 509–511.

Involving Children in Literary Elements

INVOLVING CHILDREN IN PLOT

INVOLVING CHILDREN IN CHARACTERIZATION

INVOLVING CHILDREN IN SETTING

INVOLVING CHILDREN IN THEME

INVOLVING CHILDREN IN STYLE

WHETHER DEVELOPING A LITERATURE program, developing literature-based reading instruction, or sharing literature on a one-to-one basis, remember the dual roles of literature: providing enjoyment and developing understanding. If you want children to love and appreciate literature, provide them with a varied selection of fine literature and give them many opportunities to read, listen to, share, and discuss literature.

Throughout, this children's literature text involves children with various genres of literature in exciting ways. Chapter 5 involves children in picture books through reading books aloud, sharing nursery rhymes and wordless books, and developing appreciation for illustrations. Chapter 6 involves children in traditional literature through storytelling, comparing folktales from different countries, investigating folktales from a single country, and developing creative dramatizations through folklore. Chapter 7 involves children in modern fantasy through developing artistic interpretations, identifying traditional elements in fantasy, and interacting with science fiction. Chapter 8 involves children in poetry through movement, choral speaking, music, and writing. Chapter 9 involves children in contemporary realistic fiction through interacting with survival literature and using webbing in guided discussions. Chapter 10 involves children in historical fiction through evaluating historical fiction, simulating time periods, and developing creative dramatizations. Chapter 11 involves children in multicultural literature by developing activities that enhance children's appreciation for black, Native American, Hispanic, and Asian literature. Chapter 12 involves children in biographies and informational books by using the biographies in creative interpretations, evaluating different versions of biographies, and evaluating scientific literature. Through these activities, children learn to both appreciate and understand various genres of literature. This section of Chapter 3 focuses on developing children's appreciation of and understanding for the literary elements of plot, characterization, setting, theme, and author's style.

INVOLVING CHILDREN IN PLOT

According to David Booth (2) and Kaile Kukla (5), creative drama interpretations based on story texts help children expand their imaginations, stimulate their feelings, enhance their language, and clarify their concepts. Through the playmaking process, children discover that plot provides a framework, that there is a beginning in which the conflict is introduced, that there is a middle that moves the action toward a climax, and that there is an ending with a resolution to the conflict.

Geraldine Siks (11) believes that nursery rhymes are excellent for introducing both younger and older children to the concept that a story has several parts—a beginning, a middle, and an end. The simple plots in many nursery rhymes make them ideal for this purpose. "Humpty Dumpty" contains three definite actions that cannot be interchanged and still retain a logical sequence: (1) a beginning—"Humpty Dumpty sat on a wall," (2) a middle—"Humpty Dumpty had a great fall," and (3) an end—"All the king's horses and all the king's men couldn't put Humpty Dumpty together again." Children can listen to the rhyme, identify the actions, discuss the reasons for the order, and finally act out each part. Encourage them to extend their parts by adding dialogue or characters to beginning, middle, or ending incidents. Other nursery rhymes illustrating sequential plots include "Jack and Jill," "Pat-a-Cake, Pat-a-Cake, Baker's Man," and "Rock-a-Bye Baby."

After children understand the importance of plot structure in nursery rhymes, they may proceed to folktales, such as "Three Billy Goats Gruff," in which there is also a definite and logical sequence of events. Teachers may divide the children according to the beginning incidents, middle incidents, and ending incidents. After each group practices its part, the groups can be put together into a logical whole. To help children learn the importance of order, have them rearrange the incidents. They will discover that if the ending incidents are enacted first, the story is over and there is no rising action and increasing conflict.

Diagramming plot structures is another activity that helps children appreciate and understand that many stories follow a structure in which the characters and the problems are introduced at the beginning of the story, the increasing conflict rises

The rhyme "Humpty Dumpty" contains three definite actions that cannot be interchanged and still retain a logical sequence.

until a climax is reached and the turning point is identified, and the conflict ends. Have children listen to or read stories and then discuss and identify the important incidents in plot development. For example, the important incidents in plot development from Dianne Snyder's *The Boy of the Three-Year Nap* are placed on the plot diagram in Figure 3–1.

With their easily identified plot incidents, many folktales are excellent for plot diagramming. Additional stories that have this characteristic include John Steptoe's *Mufaro's Beautiful Daughters: An African Tale,* Paul Zelinsky's retelling of the Grimms' *Rumpelstiltskin,* Selina Hastings's *Sir Gawain and the Loathly Lady,* and Antonia Barber's *The Enchanter's Daughter*. Most of the conflicts in these stories result because the characters are in conflict with outside forces, such as another person.

Stories in which the conflict results because characters must overcome problems within themselves may also be placed on plot diagrams. Caron Lee Cohen (3) identifies four major components in the development of person-against-self conflicts: (1) problem, (2) struggle, (3) self-realization, and (4) achievement of peace or truth. Cohen states, "The point at which the struggle wanes and the inner strength emerges seems to be the point of self-realization. The point leads immediately to the final sense of peace or truth that is the resolution of the quest" (p. 28). Literature selections such as Marion Dane Bauer's *On My Honor,* in which the author develops struggles within the main characters, are good for this type of discussion and plot diagramming. In this plot structure, identify (1) the problem and the characters, (2) the incidents that reflect increasing struggle with self, (3) the point of self-realization, and (4) the point at which the main character attains peace or truth. Because person-against-self conflicts are frequently complex, educators may lead students in the identification of significant incidents and ask them to provide support for their beliefs that these are major struggles.

For example, in *On My Honor,* the problem results for Bauer's character, Joel, because he betrays his parents' trust and swims with his friend in a treacherous river. The struggle continues as Joel feels increasing guilt, tries not to accept his friend's disappearance and probable death, and blames his father for allowing the two boys to go on a bike ride in the first place. Self-realization begins when Joel admits that Tony drowned and realizes that his father is not the cause of his

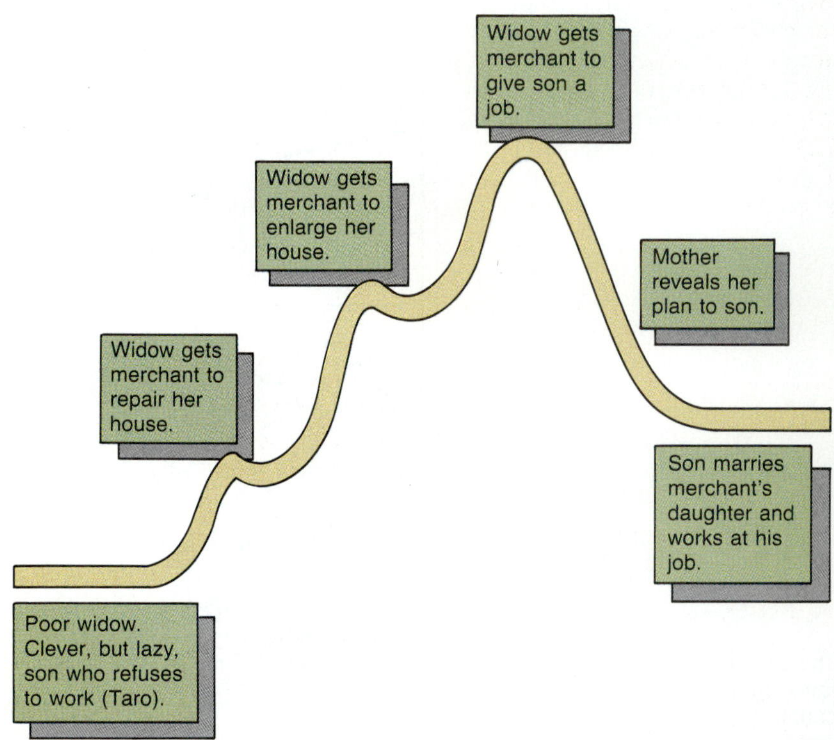

FIGURE 3–1
Plot diagram for Dianne Snyder's *The Boy of the Three-Year Nap*

problem: "But even as he slammed through the door and ran up the stairs to his room, he knew. It wasn't his father he hated. It wasn't his father at all. He was the one. . . . Tony died because of him" (p. 81).

Peace and truth begin, although the seriousness of the problem does not allow complete resolution. After Joel sobbingly tells his father the whole truth, he feels "tired, exhausted, but tinglingly aware" (p. 89). Even though there cannot be a total resolution of the conflict, because Joel's father cannot give him the reassurance he desires or take away his pain, Joel forgives his father and asks him to stay in the room until he falls asleep.

Students may compare Bauer's person-against-self conflict and plot with that of Paula Fox in *One-Eyed Cat*. (See Chapter 9.) Additional person-against-self conflicts for older students include Cynthia Rylant's *A Fine White Dust,* a traumatic conflict in which a thirteen-year-old boy becomes involved with an unscrupulous traveling evangelist and struggles to understand his own beliefs, and Janet Lunn's *Shadow in Hawthorn Bay,* a historical novel in which the protagonist must overcome her fears and gain the insight she needs to believe in herself.

Although many of the books with person-against-self conflicts are written for older students, several books may be used with younger students. For example, Arthur Yorinks's *Hey, Al* is a picture storybook in which Al and his dog Eddie overcome dissatisfaction and decide that "Paradise lost is sometimes Heaven found" (p. 27, unnumbered). Evaline Ness's *Sam, Bangs & Moonshine* is a picture storybook in which the main character faces the consequences of her lies.

INVOLVING CHILDREN IN CHARACTERIZATION

Authors of books with notable characters develop three-dimensional personalities that allow readers to gain insights into the strengths, weaknesses, pasts, hopes, and fears of the characters. You can help students understand how authors develop characters by discussing books in which the authors use several techniques for developing characterization discussed earlier. You may also help students understand the often complex nature of inferencing about characters by modeling activities in which you show the students how to analyze evidence from the text and to speculate about the characters.

Identifying Characterization

Students may search for examples in which an author reveals a character through such techniques as narration, thoughts, dialogue, and actions. Have the students list examples in which each of these techniques is used and identify what each example reveals about the author's technique. Have the students summarize what they know about a specific character and discuss whether the characterization is flat or rounded.

A group of students led by Diana Vrooman (12) used this approach to identify and discuss the characterization of Sarah in Patricia MacLachlan's *Sarah, Plain and Tall*. First, Vrooman introduced the story and reviewed the techniques that authors may use to develop characters. Second, she listed on the board the techniques that MacLachlan uses to reveal Sarah's character in *Sarah, Plain and Tall*. Third, she read the first chapter to the students and asked them to identify the examples in the chapter and to stipulate what they learned about Sarah from those examples. Fourth, she asked the students to complete the search for evidence of characterization by identifying examples found in the remaining chapters. Finally, she asked the students to summarize Sarah's characterization and defend whether or not they believed that Sarah was a rounded character.

Chart 3–2 shows a few of the characterizations and proofs for Sarah. Through the narration, the students discovered that Sarah was independent, plain, tall, loved by animals, kind, homesick, intelligent, and educated. Through the thoughts of others, they discovered that Sarah was dependable, hardworking, and homesick. Through the character's conversations with others they learned that Sarah was particular, educated, proficient, confident, poetic, versatile, and independent. Through Sarah's actions, they learned that she was understanding, adventurous, homesick, hardworking, foresighted, playful, and independent.

The students concluded that Sarah was a fully developed, three-dimensional character. In addition, they discovered the techniques that authors use to develop such well-rounded characters. The same book may be used to analyze the characterization of the young boy, Caleb, or the young girl, Anna.

Modeling Inferencing

Some of MacLachlan's characterizations in *Sarah, Plain and Tall* are stated, while others are implied. Students frequently need considerable assistance

CHART 3–2
Revealing characterization

Author's Technique	Characterization	Evidence
Narration	Plain and tall	"She was plain and tall." (p. 19)
	Loved by animals	"The dogs loved Sarah first." (p. 22)
	Loved animals	"The sheep made Sarah smile. . . . She talked to them." (p. 28)
	Intelligent	"Sarah was quick to learn." (p. 52)
Thoughts about the character	Loved the sea	Anna thought: "Sarah loved the sea, I could tell." (p. 12)
	Homesick	Anna thought: "Sarah was not smiling. Sarah was already lonely." (p. 20)
The character's actions	Adventurous	Sarah answers an advertisement asking for a wife. (p. 9)
	Sense of humor	When Sarah finished describing seals, she barked like one. (p. 27)
	Hardworking	Sarah learned how to plow the fields. (p. 33)
Dialogue	Strong	"I am strong and I work hard." (p. 9)
	Independent	Papa tells Sarah that the cat will be good in the barn. (p. 19) Sarah tells Papa that the cat will be good in the house.
	Confident	"I am fast and I am good." (p. 46)

in analyzing implied characterizations. Researchers such as Laura Roehler and Gerald Duffy (10) and Christine Gordon (4) have developed modeling approaches that place an adult in an active role with students and that show the adult's thought processing to the students. Modeling is an effective way to help students understand characterization in literature (8). The following activity shows the modeling process with Patricia MacLachlan's *Sarah, Plain and Tall.*

Requirements for Effective Reasoning. Effective characterization inferencing requires that readers go beyond the information an author provides in a text. Readers must use clues from the text to hypothesize about a character's emotions, beliefs, actions, hopes, and fears. Readers must also be aware that authors develop characters by dialogue between characters, narration, a character's thoughts or the thoughts of others about the character, and the character's actions.

Introduction to Inferencing. Review characterization by asking the students to identify how authors develop three-dimensional, believable characters. Share examples of each type of characterization as part of this review. Also explain to the students that in this modeling activity, they will listen to you ask a question, answer the question, provide evidence from the story that supports the answer, and share the reasoning process that you used to reach the answer. Tell the students that after they have listened to you proceed through the sequence, they will use the same process to answer questions, identify evidence, and explore their own reasoning processes. As part of this introduction, discuss the meanings of *evidence* and *reasoning*. Encourage the students to identify evidence about a character in literature and to share how they would use this evidence.

The Importance of Inferencing to Students. Ask the students to explain why it is important to be able to make inferences about characters in literature. Encourage the students to discuss how understanding characterization makes a story more exciting, enjoyable, and believable.

An Introduction to the Story. There are two important settings in *Sarah, Plain and Tall*: (1) the pioneer setting in one of the prairie states and (2) the pioneer setting in Maine. To identify the students' understandings of these locations and time periods, ask the students to pretend that they are sitting on the front porch of a cabin in one of the prairie states in the 1800s, to look away from the cabin, and to describe what they see. Make sure that they describe prairie grass, wheat fields, few trees, a dirt road, and flat or gently rolling land. Ask them to tell the colors they see. Then, ask them to turn around and describe what they see through the open door of the cabin. Again, make sure that they describe a small space, a fireplace, and characteristic furnishings, such as wooden chairs and a wooden table.

The Maine setting is also important to this story because Sarah's conflict results from love of a very different setting. Ask the students to pretend that they are sitting on the coast of Maine, to look out at the ocean, and to describe what they see. Ask them to turn toward the land and describe the setting. Ask them to discuss the differences between the prairie and the Maine coast and to consider whether the differences in these settings could cause conflicts for a character.

The First Modeling Example. Read orally from the beginning of the book through the line, "That was the worst thing about Caleb," on page 5. Ask, "What was Anna's attitude toward her brother Caleb when he was a baby?" Answer, "Anna disliked her brother a great deal. We might even say she hated him." Provide the evidence. Say, "Anna thinks that Caleb is homely, plain, and horrid smelling. Anna associates Caleb with her mother's death." Provide the reasoning that you used to reach the answer. For example, "The words Anna uses, especially *horrid*, are often associated with things we do not like. I know from the reference to the happy home that Anna loved her mother. When she says her mother's death was the worst thing about Caleb, I believe that she blamed him for the death."

The Second Modeling Example. At this point, verify that the students understand the procedure. If they do not, continue by completely modeling another example. If the students understand the process, let them join the discussion by providing an answer, the evidence, and the reasoning. It is advisable to have the students jot down brief answers to the questions, evidence, and reasoning; these notes will increase the quality of the discussion that follows each question.

The next logical discussion point occurs at the bottom of page 5. Read through the line, "And Papa didn't sing." Ask the question, "What is Anna really telling us about her inner feelings?" Ask the students to answer the question. They will provide answers similar to this one: "She believes that nothing can replace her lost mother and that the home will not be happy again." Ask the students to provide evidence, such as, "The author tells us that the relatives could not fill the house. The days are compared to long, dark winter days. The author states that Papa did not sing." Ask the students to provide reasoning, such as, "The author created a very sad mood. We see a house filled with relatives that do not matter to Anna. I know what long, dark, winter days are like. I can visualize a house without singing. I think Anna is very unhappy and it may take her a long time to get over her loss."

Continue this process, having the students discuss the many instances of implied characterization in the book. The letters written by Sarah to Mr. Wheaton (p. 9), to Anna (pp. 9–10), and to Caleb (p. 11) are especially good for inferencing about the characters because students need to infer what was in the letters written by Anna and Caleb. To help the students infer the contents of the letters, ask the students to write the letters themselves.

Longer stories, such as *Sarah, Plain and Tall,* lend themselves to discussions according to chapters. Students may read and discuss several chapters each day. After each session, however, ask the students to summarize what they know about Sarah, Anna, Caleb, and Papa. Ask them, "What do you want to know about these characters?"

INVOLVING CHILDREN IN SETTING

Believable settings place readers in geographic locations and time periods that they can see, hear, and even feel. In literature, authors use settings for four purposes: (1) designing appropriate moods, (2) developing antagonists, (3) creating historical and geographical backgrounds, and (4) suggesting symbolic interpretations.

Settings That Create Moods

Authors use settings to create moods. Through word choices and the visual pictures created by words, authors create moods that range from humorous and happy to frightening and foreboding. Comparing words and illustrations in a text helps students understand and evaluate the appropriateness of a mood. For example, students can discuss the frightening, eerie mood created by

Marcia Brown's illustrations for Blaise Cendrars's *Shadow* and examine the influence of words, such as *prowler,* and descriptions, such as "teeming like snakes," in Cendrars's poem. Likewise, they can compare the equally frightening moods created by Charles Keeping's stark, black lines and Alfred Noyes's sinister and disastrous text in the narrative poem "The Highwayman."

Additional literature that develops frightening moods through both illustrations and texts include Eve Merriam's *Halloween ABC* and Jan Plenkowski's *Haunted House*. Texts for older readers, such as Barbara Rogasky's *Smoke and Ashes: The Story of the Holocaust* and Toshi Maruki's *Hiroshima No Pika,* show students that both texts and photographs or illustrations can create very serious moods.

Teachers may use illustrated texts, such as *Song and Dance Man,* to show students very different moods. Stephen Gammell's illustrations create a warm, happy mood as children watch their beloved grandfather re-create the joyful days of his youth. The transition from a common, dreary, crowded attic to an uncommon experience is enhanced by the artist's drawing of a brightly colored, shadowy shape. From this point on, both the children and their grandfather seem to be transported to the joyful dazzling days when Grandfather was a vaudeville entertainer. Karen Ackerman's text supports the mood as Grandfather's voice "is as round and strong as a canyon echo, and his cheeks get rosy as he sings" (p. 14, unnumbered), as he tells jokes and "slaps his knee and laughs until his eyes water" (p. 19, unnumbered), and as the children "laugh so hard, the hiccups start" (p. 21, unnumbered).

Additional literature selections that develop warm, happy moods through both illustrations and text are Cynthia Rylant's *When I Was Young in the Mountains,* Eve Bunting's *The Wednesday Surprise,* Catherine Stock's *Sophie's Knapsack,* Alexandra Day's *Frank and Ernest Play Ball*, and Valerie Flournoy's *The Patchwork Quilt*. Funny, even absurd, moods are created in both the text and illustrations of Catharine O'Neill's *Mrs. Dunphy's Dog,* Mary Ann Hoberman's *Mr. and Mrs. Muddle,* and Patricia Polacco's *Meteor!*

Authors of fantasy frequently prepare their readers for the fantastical experiences to come by creating settings and moods in which fantasy seems possible. Sharing and discussing introductions to fantasies allows students to appreciate and understand the techniques that authors use to prepare them for both fantasy and conflict. For example, read and discuss the following introduction to Natalie Babbitt's *Tuck Everlasting*:

> The road that led to Treegap had been trod out long before by a herd of cows who were, to say the least, relaxed. It wandered along in curves and easy angles, swayed off and up in a pleasant tangent to the top of a small hill, ambled down again between fringes of bee-hung clover, and then cut sidewise across a meadow. Here its edges blurred. It widened and seemed to pause, suggesting tranquil bovine picnics: slow chewing and thoughtful contemplation of the infinite. And then it went on again and came at last to the wood. But on reaching the shadows of the first trees, it veered sharply, swung out in a wide arc as if, for the first time, it had reason to think where it was going, and passed around.
>
> On the other side of the wood, the sense of easiness dissolved. The road no longer belonged to the cows. It became, instead, and rather abruptly, the property of people. And all at once the sun was uncomfortably hot, the dust oppressive, and the meager grass along its edges somewhat ragged and forlorn. On the left stood the first house, a square and solid cottage with a touch-me-not appearance, surrounded by grass cut painfully to the quick and enclosed by a capable iron fence some four feet high which clearly said, "Move on—we don't want you here." So the road went humbly by and made its way, past cottages more and more frequent but less and less forbidding, into the village. But the village doesn't matter, except for the jailhouse and the gallows. The first house only is important; the first house, the road, and the wood. (pp. 5–6)

After you read this introduction, have the students consider the effect of the contrasts used by Babbitt, the influence of personification, and the impact of such wordings as "tranquil bovine picnics," "veered sharply," "touch-me-not," and "grass cut painfully to the quick." Have the students speculate about the changing mood in the introduction and the type of story that might follow. Of course, have them read the story to verify their predictions.

Settings That Develop Antagonists

Authors of both historical fiction and contemporary adventure stories frequently develop plots in which nature or society is the antagonist. Vivid descriptions of either nature or society are essential if readers are to understand why and how the setting has created conflicts or even life-and-death perils.

Sharing and discussing quotations will help students identify and appreciate vivid descriptions. Kevin Crossley-Holland's *Storm* is written for young readers. The author, however, vividly describes a fearful storm and a young girl who both fears the storm and faces her fears of a ghostly creature who supposedly roams the English marshlands. Crossley-Holland uses personification and metaphor to develop believable settings. For example, Crossley-Holland says that the storm "whistled between its salty lips and gnashed its sharp teeth" (p. 14) and "gave a shriek" (p. 27). Other elements in nature respond. The moon "seemed to be speeding behind grey lumpy clouds, running away from something that was chasing it" (p. 23). The young girl, Annie, responds in ways that suggest fear: "Annie felt a cold finger slowly moving from the base of her spine up to her neck, and then spreading out across her shoulders" (p. 12) and she swayed in the saddle as she "thought she could bear it no longer—the furious gallop, the gallop of the storm, the storm of her own fears" (p. 35). By the end of the story, Annie has faced her fears of both the storm and the ghost.

In *Call It Courage*, Armstrong Sperry uses personification to give human actions to the sea and decreasing sentence lengths to show increasing danger. Have your students search for vivid descriptions throughout the book.

After students discuss such examples, encourage them to find additional quotations in which nature is depicted through vivid descriptions, to share the quotations, and to tell why they believe that nature is the antagonist. Vivid descriptions of nature as an antagonist are found in Gary Paulsen's *Hatchet*, Farley Mowat's *Lost in the Barrens*, Scott O'Dell's *Island of the Blue Dolphins*, and Jean Craighead George's *Julie of the Wolves*.

It is more difficult for students to understand the setting if society, and not nature, causes the conflict because the students must understand both the larger societal attitudes and the reasons that the characters are in conflict with those attitudes. Thematic studies that allow students to read from several genres are usually best for developing understanding about complex subjects, such as anti-Semitism or slavery. In thematic studies, have students use nonfictional sources to authenticate the settings in historical fiction. For example, a series of books about the Holocaust might include nonfiction, biography, historical fiction, and even time-warp fantasy. Beginning with Barbara Rogasky's nonfictional *Smoke and Ashes: The Story of the Holocaust*, students can discover the historical background of the time period, the roots of anti-Semitism, the development of ghettos and concentration camps, and the tragic consequences. Have the students read Milton Meltzer's nonfictional *Rescue: The Story of How Gentiles Saved Jews in the Holocaust* to provide historical background about heroic people who risked their own lives to save the lives of other people. Next, have the students read Albert Marrin's biographical text, *Hitler*. Pages 17–20 are especially revealing. Within these pages, Marrin discusses the roots of Hitler's anti-Semitism and his developing hatred. For example:

> Once Adolph began to hate, it became harder and harder to stop hating. From the age of nineteen, his hatred deepened, grew stronger, until it passed the bounds of sanity. He had only to hear Jews mentioned, to see them or think he saw them, to lose self-control. . . . One day, he vowed, he'd get even with them. They'd pay, every last one of them, for the humiliation they'd caused him. (p. 20)

Have the students read Uri Orlev's historical fiction, *The Island on Bird Street*, Lois Lowry's historical fiction about the Danish resistance, *Number the Stars*, and Jane Yolen's time-warp story, *The Devil's Arithmetic*. Then, have the students use the background information from the first three books to evaluate the authenticity of the settings that cause so much conflict in the fictional books.

You may use a similar approach to develop understandings of settings that reflect slavery and racism. This study might include Milton Meltzer's nonfictional text, *The Black Americans: A History in Their Own Words*; Virginia Hamilton's biographical story, *Anthony Burns: The Defeat and Triumph of a Fugitive Slave*; Belinda Hurmence's time-warp fantasy, *A Girl Called Boy*; and Mildred D. Taylor's historical fiction story set in the depression, *Roll of Thunder, Hear My Cry*. Again, use the nonfictional texts to authenticate the conflicts in the historical fiction.

Settings That Develop Historical and Geographical Backgrounds

Settings in historical fiction and biography should be so integral to the story and so carefully developed that readers are encouraged to imagine the sights, sounds, and even smells of the environment. For example, have groups of students choose one of the settings developed in Elizabeth George Speare's *The Sign of the Beaver*, such as the log cabin, the wilderness, or the Penobscot village. Lead them to discover as much information as possible about the sights, sounds, and even tastes associated with that environment. Have them identify and analyze quotations that describe the setting.

A group analyzing the log cabin will discover that the cabin was built with an axe but without any nails (p. 38); is located in a clearing with wilderness all around it (p. 1); is one room constructed from spruce logs, cedar splints, and pine boughs (pp. 1, 3); is without windows (p. 3); is sparsely furnished with shelves, two stools, puncheon table, and pine bed (p. 122); and is heated and lighted by a temporary and dangerous log chimney (pp. 3, 124). The only reading material in the cabin is the Bible and *Robinson Crusoe* (pp. 29–30). By identifying luxuries that Matt longs for, students discover that he is without candles and lamplight (p. 124). By identifying objects that he makes for himself and for his mother, they discover the ruggedness and isolation of this 1700s wilderness.

Students enjoy creating maps and illustrations depicting well-defined settings. Have students use details from historical fiction or fantasy to draw maps, homes, or other settings. Carefully crafted fantasy worlds provide considerable evidence for map locations and show the importance of settings in creating believable worlds. For example, after students read J. R. R. Tolkien's *The Hobbit,* ask them to draw maps of Middle Earth. C. S. Lewis's *The Lion, the Witch and the Wardrobe* includes detailed information about Narnia. Likewise, Lewis Carroll's *Alice's Adventures in Wonderland* provides descriptions of Wonderland.

After students have read literature with well-developed settings, divide them into groups and ask each group to draw a map so that visitors to the land would be able to travel. Ask the students to defend their map locations by providing evidence from the literature. After the maps are completed, ask each group to share its map with the larger group and to defend why it placed landmarks in specific places.

Two sources provide interesting stimulation for these drawing tasks. Alberto Manguel and Gianni Guadalupi's *The Dictionary of Imaginary Places* (6) includes maps and descriptions of numerous fantasy worlds. Rosalind Ashe and Lisa Tuttle's *Children's Literary Houses: Famous Dwellings in Children's Fiction* (1) includes interpretations of the homes found in Frances Hodgson Burnett's *The Secret Garden,* T. H. White's *The Sword in the Stone,* Esther Forbes's *Johnny Tremain,* Louisa May Alcott's *Little Women,* and several other famous literature sources.

Settings That Are Symbolic

According to Laurence Perrine (9), a literary symbol "is something that means more than what it is. It is an object, a person, a situation, or some other item that has a literal meaning in the story but suggests or represents other meanings as well" (p. 196). Perrine maintains that to understand and interpret symbolism, readers must be aware of the following four requirements: (1) The story must furnish clues that details are to be taken symbolically, (2) the symbolic meaning must be established and supported by the context of the story, (3) an item must suggest a meaning that is different from its literal meaning, and (4) a symbol may have more than one meaning.

Settings in literature frequently meet these requirements for symbolism. For example, the easiest symbolic setting for students to understand is probably the once-upon-a-time setting found in folktales. Readers know that "once upon a time" means much more than long ago. When readers close their eyes, they often visualize deep woods or majestic castles, where enchantment, magic, and heroic adventures are expected. Folktale settings are excellent introductions to symbolic settings.

Authors of other types of literature also use symbolic settings to develop understandings of plots, characters, and themes. Frances Hodgson Burnett's *The Secret Garden* is one of the best literature selections for showing the importance of symbolic settings. Students can trace parallel changes that take place in the garden and the people living in Misselthwaite Manor. For example, the English setting begins in a cold, dreary mansion surrounded by gardens that are dormant from winter. The characters are equally unresponsive. Mary is "the most disagreeable-looking child ever seen. . . . She had a little thin face and a little thin body, thin light hair and a sour expression" (p. 1). Colin is a disagreeable invalid, Mr. Craven is still in mourning for his dead wife, and Colin and his father are estranged. The setting and the people begin to change after Mary finds the door to the secret garden. Finding the key to the garden is the symbolic turning point, after which the characters and the garden are slowly nurtured back to both physical and emotional health.

As students trace the parallel changes in both the garden and the people, they may ask themselves the following questions: Why does the author focus attention on a garden that has been locked and mostly uncared for for ten years? What is the significance of a key that opens a door? What are the relationships between the changing people and what happens to the garden? Why does the author draw parallels between nurturing a garden and healing people both physically and emotionally? Does the garden meet Perrine's requirements for symbolism in literature? Is the garden a good symbolic setting for both characterization and plot development? Why or why not?

Students may explore the symbolism of gardens in other books. For example, in Philippa Pearce's *Tom's Midnight Garden,* Tom receives both personal understanding and healing from the garden. Even when he is ill, he steals downstairs into the garden, and "there the feverishness of his chill always left him, as though the very greenness of trees and plants and grass cooled his blood" (p. 101). In Joan Phipson's *The Watcher in the Garden,* the garden has a benevolent power; it provides a sanctuary that protects an old man who loves it and it heals an emotionally disturbed girl.

INVOLVING CHILDREN IN THEME

Students need many opportunities to read and discuss literature in order to identify controlling ideas or central concepts in stories. Themes are difficult because they are frequently implied rather than directly stated. Students learn about themes, however, by studying the actions of characters, analyzing the central conflict, and considering the outcome of a story. When looking for theme, it is important to consider how the main character changes in the story, what types of conflict are found in the story, what actions are rewarded or punished, and what the main character has learned as a result of the conflict. Even the title may provide clues to the theme.

The following sequence of events develops an understanding of theme in Ann Grifalconi's *Darkness and the Butterfly*. First, explain to the students that theme is the controlling idea or central concept in a story. Themes often reveal important beliefs about life, and a story may contain more than one theme. When searching for theme, ask, "What is the author trying to tell us that would make a difference in our lives?" Review some of the ways that authors reveal themes, such as through conflict, the characters' actions, the characters' thoughts, the outcome of the story, the actions that are rewarded or punished, and narrative. In addition, the title and illustrations may provide clues.

Next, read orally *Darkness and the Butterfly*. Ask the students, "What is the author trying to tell us that would make a difference in our lives?" They will probably identify two important themes: (1) It is all right to have fears; we all may have fears that cause us problems and (2) we can and must overcome our fears.

After the students have identified the themes, ask them to listen to the story a second time. This time, ask them to search for proof that the author is developing these themes. Their discussion and evidence probably will include some of the following examples:

1 It is all right to have fears; we all may have fears that cause us problems.
- **a** The illustrations show contrasts between the beauty of the world in the day, which is without fear, and the monsters that surface in Osa's mind at night.
- **b** The actions of the mother show that she is understanding. She even gives beads to help Osa feel less fearful.
- **c** The actions of Osa show that she is a normal child during the day but a fearful child at night.
- **d** The wise woman tells Osa that she was once afraid, " 'specially at night!"

2 We can and must overcome our fears.
- **a** The author tells the story of the yellow butterfly, the smallest of the small, as it flies into the darkness.
- **b** The butterfly story is based on an important African proverb, "Darkness pursues the butterfly."
- **c** The wise woman tells Osa, "You will find your own way."
- **d** The wise woman compares finding your way to the wings of the butterfly.
- **e** The dream sequence reveals the beauties of the night.
- **f** The actions of the butterfly show that it is not afraid.
- **g** Osa reveals her own self-realization: "I can go by myself. I'm not afraid anymore."
- **h** The author states that Osa, the smallest of the small, "found the way to carry her own light through the darkness."

i The butterfly symbolizes that the smallest, most fragile being in nature can light up the darkness, trust the night, and not be afraid.
j The title of the book is *Darkness and the Butterfly*.

Folktales, with their easily identifiable conflicts and characterizations, are excellent for developing understanding of theme. For example, when searching for themes in John Steptoe's *Mufaro's Beautiful Daughters,* students discover that greed and selfishness are harmful and that kindness and generosity are beneficial. Considerable evidence in the story reflects these themes. This is especially true at the conclusion of the conflict. The kind and generous daughter becomes queen, and the greedy and selfish daughter becomes a servant to the queen.

INVOLVING CHILDREN IN STYLE

Many of the discussions and activities related to plot, characterization, and setting emphasize an author's style. By selecting words that create visual images and arranging the words to create moods or increase tension, authors show the power of carefully chosen words and sentence structures. When reading carefully crafted stories, you may not even notice the techniques that authors use. When you read aloud a carefully crafted story and one that is not so well developed, however, the differences become obvious. In this section, we look at developing students' appreciation for personification through narrative stories and for pleasing style.

Personification

Many of the most enjoyable books read to and by younger children develop characterizations through personification. This is probably so believable because children tend to give human characteristics to their pets and toys. Personification is an excellent introduction to style for younger children because the texts that include personification of objects and animals often are reinforced through illustrations that also personify the subjects.

Virginia Lee Burton's *The Little House* provides an enjoyable introduction to personification. As you read appropriate pages to the students, ask them: What pronoun is used when the author talks about the house? What actions can the house do that are similar to your actions? What feelings does the house express that are similar to your feelings? What causes the house to have each of these feelings? When have you had similar feelings? How do the illustrations help you understand the house's feelings and character? After the students have discussed the answers to these questions, share with them that the author is giving the house human feelings and behaviors through both the text and the illustrations.

Extend this understanding of personification in *The Little House* by asking the students to use pantomime or creative drama to enact the feelings expressed in the book. For example, have them listen to the text being read and pantomime the feelings expressed by the house. Have them create conversations that might occur between the house and her country or city neighbors. Have them tell the story from the point of view of one of the other objects found in the story.

Use similar discussions with books in which toys are personified, such as Anthony Browne's *Gorilla* and Margery Williams's *The Velveteen Rabbit*. Books in which animals are personified include Mary Ann Hoberman's *Mr. and Mrs. Muddle,* Diana Engel's *Josephina Hates Her Name,* Rosemary Wells's *Max's Chocolate Chicken,* and Lillian Hoban's *Arthur's Great Big Valentine*.

Pleasing Style

Jette Morache (7) recommends that older students collect and share quotations from literature that they find pleasing or that support other literary elements, such as characterization and theme. Morache recommends that while working in groups, students find quotes that illustrate a certain technique, compare and discuss the quotes chosen by their group and other groups, compile a page of quotes that they find particularly appealing, and develop a list of qualities that make a "quotable quote." This type of activity is appropriate for developing appreciation for any of the literary elements discussed in this chapter. Students can find quotes to support characterization, setting, and theme.

Quotes also can emphasize specific literary techniques, such as personification, symbolism, simile, or metaphor. Older students might read Henry Wadsworth Longfellow's "Hiawatha" and Jamake Highwater's *Moonsong Lullaby* and *Anpao: An American Indian Odyssey* to find examples of personification in nature. Jan Hudson's *Sweetgrass* is filled with symbolism, similes, and metaphors.

Cynthia Voigt's *Dicey's Song* has many references to music, a sailboat, and a tree as symbols.

Suggested Activities for Children's Understanding of Literary Elements

- ☐ Choose a book and develop a plot diagram that shows a person-against-person or a person-against-self conflict.
- ☐ Choose a story that reveals characterization through a variety of techniques. Identify those techniques, the evidence of the characterization, and the character traits revealed. Share your findings with your class.
- ☐ Develop a modeling activity that demonstrates modeling inferencing of characterization. Share the modeling activity with a group of children or your class.
- ☐ Choose settings that create moods, antagonists, historical backgrounds, or symbolism. Develop a list of books and references from books that could be used to help students understand these important purposes for setting.
- ☐ Choose a book and trace the author's development of theme. Share your book and activity with a child or your class.
- ☐ Working in a group, develop a list of "quotable quotes" and a list of qualities that make quotes memorable. Defend the quotations and the qualities that make them memorable.

References

1. Ashe, Rosalind, and Lisa Tuttle. *Children's Literary Houses: Famous Dwellings in Children's Fiction*. New York: Facts on File, 1984.
2. Booth, David. "Imaginary Gardens with Real Toads: Reading and Drama in Education." *Theory into Practice* 24 (1985): 193–198.
3. Cohen, Caron Lee. "The Quest in Children's Literature." *School Library Journal* 31 (August 1985): 28–29.
4. Gordon, Christine J. "Modeling Inference Awareness Across the Curriculum." *Journal of Reading* 28 (February 1985): 444–447.
5. Kukla, Kaile. "David Booth: Drama as a Way of Knowing." *Language Arts* 64 (January 1987): 73–78.
6. Manguel, Alberto, and Gianni Guadalupi. *The Dictionary of Imaginary Places*. Illustrated by Graham Greenfield and James Cook. New York: Macmillan, 1980.
7. Morache, Jette. "Use of Quotes in Teaching Literature." *English Journal* 76 (October 1987): 61–63.
8. Norton, Donna E. *The Effective Teaching of Language Arts*. 3d ed. Columbus, Ohio: Merrill, 1989.
9. Perrine, Laurence. *Literature: Structure, Sound, and Sense*. 4th ed. San Diego: Harcourt Brace Jovanovich, 1983.
10. Roehler, Laura, and Gerald G. Duffy. "Direct Explanation of Comprehension Processes." In *Comprehension Instruction*, edited by Gerald G. Duffy, Laura R. Roehler, and Jana Mason. New York: Longman, 1984, pp. 265–280.
11. Siks, Geraldine. *Drama with Children*. New York: Harper & Row, 1983.
12. Vrooman, Diana. "Characterization Techniques in *Sarah, Plain and Tall*." College Station: Texas A&M University, 1989.

CHILDREN'S LITERATURE

Aardema, Verna. *Bringing the Rain to Kapiti Plain: A Nandi Tale*. Illustrated by Beatriz Vidal. Dial, 1981 (I:5–8 R:6). A cumulative tale from Kenya tells how a herdsman brings rain to the parched land.

———. *Why Mosquitoes Buzz in People's Ears*. Illustrated by Leo and Diane Dillon. Dial, 1975 (I:5–9 R:6). A cumulative African folktale tells the humorous reason for mosquitoes' buzzing.

Ackerman, Karen. *Song and Dance Man*. Illustrated by Stephen Gammell. Knopf, 1988 (I:3–8 R:4). Grandfather recreates the magic of vaudeville for his grandchildren.

Alcott, Louisa May. *Little Women*. Little, Brown, 1868 (I:10+ R:7). This classic story tells about a loving family.

Andersen, Hans Christian. *The Wild Swans*. Retold by Amy Ehrlich. Illustrated by Susan Jeffers. Dial, 1981 (I:7–12 R:7). Finely detailed illustrations develop a fantasy setting.

Ashabranner, Brent. *To Live in Two Worlds: American Indian Youth Today*. Photographs by Paul Conklin. Dodd, Mead, 1984 (I:10+ R:7). Indian youth tell about their own lives.

Babbitt, Natalie. *Tuck Everlasting*. Farrar, Straus & Giroux, 1975 (I:8–12 R:6). A fantasy story about everlasting life.

Barber, Antonia. *The Enchanter's Daughter*. Illustrated by Errol Le Cain. Farrar, Straus & Giroux, 1987 (I:6–9 R:5). A young woman outwits an enchanter to regain her past life.

Barton, Byron. *I Want to Be an Astronaut*. Crowell, 1988 (I:2–6). Very large pictures show the work of astronauts.

Bauer, Marion Dane. *On My Honor*. Clarion, 1986 (I:10+ R:4). A boy faces guilt when his friend drowns.

Benjamin, Carol Lea. *The Wicked Stepdog*. Crowell, 1982 (I:9–12 R:4). A twelve-year-old girl believes she has lost her father when he remarries.

Berenzy, Alix. *A Frog Prince*. H. Holt, 1989 (I:6–10 R:6). In a twist on a folktale, a frog searches for a suitable mate.

Blos, Joan W. *A Gathering of Days*. Scribner, 1979 (I:8–14 R:6). The fictional journal is about a thirteen-year-old girl's life on a farm in New Hampshire in 1830.

Blume, Judy. *Blubber*. Bradbury, 1974 (I:10+ R:4). A girl becomes the victim in peer conflict.

I = Interest by age range.
R = Readability by grade level.

Brooks, Bruce. *The Moves Make the Man*. Harper & Row, 1984 (I:10+ R:7). Basketball develops understanding between a black boy and a white boy.

Browne, Anthony. *Gorilla*. Watts, 1983 (I:3–8 R:4). A toy gorilla comes to life for a young girl.

Bunting, Eve. *The Wednesday Surprise*. Illustrated by Donald Carrick. Clarion, 1989 (I:3–9 R:5). A girl teaches her grandmother to read.

Burnett, Frances Hodgson. *The Secret Garden*. Illustrated by Tasha Tudor. Lippincott, 1911, 1938, 1962 (I:8–12 R:7). A garden that hasn't been seen by anybody for ten years works its magic spell on a lonely girl, a sick boy, and an unhappy father.

Burton, Virginia Lee. *The Little House*. Houghton Mifflin, 1942 (I:3–7 R:3). A house is strong but needs love as it becomes dilapidated and lonely over the years.

Carrick, Carol. *Stay Away from Simon!* Illustrated by Donald Carrick. Clarion, 1985 (I:7–10 R:3). A mentally retarded boy helps two children realize his worth.

Carroll, Lewis. *Alice's Adventures in Wonderland*. Illustrated by John Tenniel. Macmillan, 1866; Knopf, 1984 (I:8+ R:6). A classic is presented in a facsimile edition.

Cendrars, Blaise. *Shadow*. Illustrated by Marcia Brown. Scribner, 1982 (I:all). A highly illustrated version of an African poem is about the world of spirits.

Chaucer, Geoffrey. *The Canterbury Tales*. Retold by Barbara Cohen. Illustrated by Trina Schart Hyman. Lothrop, Lee, & Shepard, 1988 (I:8+ R:5). Chaucer's tales are adapted for young readers.

Clapp, Patricia. *I'm Deborah Sampson: A Soldier in the War of the Revolution*. Lothrop, Lee & Shepard, 1977 (I:9+ R:6). Deborah disguises herself as a man and fights in the war.

———. *Witches' Children: A Story of Salem*. Lothrop, Lee & Shepard, 1982 (I:9+ R:6). A small group of girls creates witchcraft hysteria.

Cleary, Beverly. *Ramona and Her Father*. Illustrated by Alan Tiegreen. Morrow, 1977 (I:7–12 R:6). A warm and humorous story about Ramona, a second-grader, who tries to help her father through a trying period after he loses his job.

———. *Ramona Quimby, Age 8*. Illustrated by Alan Tiegreen. Morrow, 1981 (I:7–12 R:6). A humorous story is about how a third-grader helps her family when her father returns to college.

Cole, Brock. *The Goats*. Farrar, Straus & Giroux, 1987 (I:8+ R:5). Two children are marooned on an island by their peers at camp.

Crossley-Holland, Kevin. *Storm*. Illustrated by Alan Marks. Heinemann, 1985 (I:6–12 R:5). A girl faces her fear and gets a doctor for her sister.

Dabcovich, Lydia. *Sleepy Bear*. Dutton, 1982 (I:3–6 R:1). Illustrations and text follow a bear as he hibernates and wakes up in the spring.

Day, Alexandra. *Frank and Ernest Play Ball*. Scholastic, 1990 (I:5–8 R:5). The two characters provide a humorous look at baseball.

dePaola, Tomie. *The Clown of God*. Harcourt Brace Jovanovich, 1978 (I:all R:4). A legend about a juggler who offers the gift of his talent and the miracle that results.

Engel, Diana. *Josephina Hates Her Name*. Morrow, 1989 (I:5–8 R:4). An alligator child discovers pride in her name.

Fleischman, Sid. *The Whipping Boy*. Illustrated by Peter Sis. Greenwillow, 1986 (I:8+ R:5). A prince and his whipping boy exchange places.

Flournoy, Valerie. *The Patchwork Quilt*. Illustrated by Jerry Pinkney. Dial, 1985 (I:5–8 R:4). Constructing a quilt brings a family together.

Forbes, Esther. *Johnny Tremain*. Illustrated by Lynd Ward. Houghton Mifflin, 1943 (I:10+ R:6). A silversmith's apprentice survives early Revolutionary wartime in Boston.

Fox, Paula. *The Slave Dancer*. Illustrated by Eros Keith. Bradbury, 1973 (I:12+ R:7). In 1849, a fife player experiences the misery of the slave trade.

Frank, Rudolf. *No Hero for the Kaiser*. Translated from the German by Patricia Crampton. Illustrated by Klaus Steffens. Lothrop, Lee & Shepard, 1986 (I:10+ R:7). A historical fiction is set in World War I.

Freedman, Russell. *Lincoln: A Photobiography*. Clarion, 1987 (I:8+ R:6). Abraham Lincoln's life is carefully documented.

Fritz, Jean. *The Cabin Faced West*. Illustrated by Feodor Rojankousky. Coward, McCann, 1958 (I:7–10 R:5). A young girl whose family has moved West dreams of going back home until she begins to see the frontier with new eyes.

———. *The Great Little Madison*. Putnam, 1989 (I:10+ R:6). The life of the fourth president is presented in a biography.

———. *Make Way for Sam Houston*. Illustrated by Elise Primavera. Putnam, 1986 (I:9+ R:6). The biography is of a nineteenth-century hero.

———. *Traitor: The Case of Benedict Arnold*. Putnam, 1981 (I:8+ R:5). The book tells the life of a man who chose the British cause in the Revolutionary War.

Galdone, Paul. *The Greedy Old Fat Man*. Houghton Mifflin, 1983 (I:4–7 R:5). An American folktale is told in cumulative form.

George, Jean Craighead. *Julie of the Wolves*. Illustrated by John Schoenherr. Harper & Row, 1972 (I:10–13 R:7). An Eskimo girl lost on the North Slope of Alaska survives with the help of wolves.

Goble, Paul. *The Girl Who Loved Wild Horses*. Bradbury, 1978 (I:6–10 R:5). An American Indian girl loves wild horses, joins them in a flight during a storm, and finally goes to live with them.

Grifalconi, Ann. *Darkness and the Butterfly*. Little, Brown, 1987 (I:4–8 R:4). A young African girl learns not to fear the darkness.

Grimm, Brothers. *Rumpelstiltskin*. Retold and illustrated by Paul O. Zelinsky. Dutton, 1986 (I:all R:5). A miller's daughter is helped to spin gold by a little man who demands her first-born child.

Hamilton, Virginia. *Anthony Burns: The Defeat and Triumph of a Fugitive Slave*. Knopf, 1988 (I:9+ R:6). The biography of a slave from 1839–1854.

Hastings, Selina, retold by. *Sir Gawain and the Loathly Lady*. Illustrated by Juan Wijngaard. Lothrop, Lee & Shepard, 1985 (I:9–12 R:6). A legend tells about one of King Arthur's knights.

Highwater, Jamake. *Anpao: An American Indian Odyssey*. Illustrated by Fritz Scholder. Lippincott, 1977 (I:12+ R:5). Anpao journeys across the history of Native American traditional tales.

———. *Moonsong Lullaby*. Photographs by Marcia Keegan. Lothrop, Lee & Shepard, 1981 (I:all). A personified nature poem was inspired by ancient Native American stories.

Hoban, Lillian. *Arthur's Great Big Valentine*. Harper & Row, 1989 (I:5–7 R:2). An "I Can Read Book" tells about a monkey and his sister.

Hoberman, Mary Ann. *Mr. and Mrs. Muddle*. Illustrated by Catharine O'Neill. Little, Brown, 1988 (I:3–8 R:4). A humorous story tells about two animals who disagree.

Hudson, Jan. *Sweetgrass*. Tree Frog, Philomel, 1984, 1989 (I:10+ R:4). A young Blackfoot girl grows up during the winter of the smallpox epidemic in 1837.

Hurmence, Belinda. *A Girl Called Boy*. Houghton Mifflin, 1982 (I:10+ R:6). A black girl goes back in time to 1853 and experiences slavery.

Jaquith, Priscilla. *Bo Rabbit Smart for True: Folktales from the Gullah*. Illustrated by Ed Young. Philomel, 1981 (I:all R:6). Four tales from the islands off the Georgia coast.

Johnson, Angela. *Tell Me a Story, Mama*. Illustrated by David Soman. Watts, 1989 (I:3–7 R:4). A mother tells her daughter stories about when she was young.

Konigsburg, E. L. *Journey to an 800 Number*. Atheneum, 1982 (I:10+ R:6). A boy's life-style and ideas change drastically when he accompanies his father and a camel act.

Lamb, Charles, and Mary Lamb, retold by. *Tales from Shakespeare*. Illustrated by Elizabeth Shippen Green Elliott. Crown, 1988 (I:8+). Shakespeare's plays are retold for younger readers.

Lang, Andrew. *The Red Fairy Book*. Illustrated by H. J. Ford and Lancelot Speed. McGraw-Hill, 1967 (I:all R:6). This is a recent edition of the classic fairy tale book first published in 1890.

Lewis, C. S. *The Lion, the Witch and the Wardrobe*. Illustrated by Pauline Baynes. Macmillan, 1950 (I:9+ R:7). Four children enter Narnia through a wardrobe.

Lisle, Janet Taylor. *Afternoon of the Elves*. Watts, 1989 (I:10+ R:5). Two children gain understanding as they work on a miniature village.

Lowry, Lois. *Number the Stars*. Houghton Mifflin, 1989 (I:8–12 R:5). A ten-year-old girl helps the Danish Resistance.

Lunn, Janet. *Shadow in Hawthorn Bay*. Scribner's Sons, 1986 (I:10+ R:5). A girl with second sight experiences prejudice in 1800s Canada.

McKinley, Robin. *The Hero and the Crown*. Greenwillow, 1984 (I:10+ R:7). Aerin faces the forces of evil during a quest.

MacLachlan, Patricia. *The Facts and Fictions of Minna Pratt*. Harper & Row, 1988 (I:7–12 R:4). A girl learns to appreciate herself and her family.

———. *Mama One, Mama Two*. Illustrated by Ruth Lercher Bornstein. Harper & Row, 1982 (I:5–7 R:2). A foster mother shares a story about a girl's real mother.

———. *Sarah, Plain and Tall*. Harper & Row, 1985 (I:7–10 R:3). A frontier family longs for a mother.

Marrin, Albert. *Hitler*. Viking Kestrel, 1987 (I:10+ R:7). A biographer emphasizes Hitler's rise to power, his victories, and his final defeat.

Martin, Katherine. *Night Riding*. Knopf, 1989 (I:11+ R:6). In the 1950s, a young girl meets a neighbor who is being sexually abused.

Maruki, Toshi. *Hiroshima No Pika*. Lothrop, Lee, & Shepard, 1982 (I:8–12 R:4). The consequences of the Hiroshima bombing are shown in an illustrated text.

Meltzer, Milton. *Rescue: The Story of How Gentiles Saved Jews in the Holocaust*. Harper & Row, 1988 (I:10+ R:6). A nonfictional source describes heroism.

———, ed. *The Black Americans: A History in Their Own Words 1619–1983*. Crowell, 1984 (I:10+). Short excerpts written by people in history.

Merriam, Eve. *Halloween ABC*. Illustrated by Lane Smith. Macmillan, 1987 (I:all). Illustrations and poems about Halloween.

Mowat, Farley. *Lost in the Barrens*. Illustrated by Charles Geer. McClelland & Stewart, 1956, 1984 (I:9+ R:6). A Cree Indian boy and his friend are lost in Northern Canada.

Ness, Evaline. *Sam, Bangs & Moonshine*. Holt, Rinehart & Winston, 1966 (I:5–9 R:3). Sam's imagination almost costs a friend his life.

Noyes, Alfred. *The Highwayman*. Illustrated by Charles Keeping. Oxford, 1981 (I:10+). Strong black-and-white drawings complement the mood of the poem.

O'Brien, Robert C. *Mrs. Frisby and the Rats of NIMH*. Illustrated by Zena Bernstein. Atheneum, 1971 (I:8–12 R:4). Mrs. Frisby, a mouse, asks for help from a superior group of rats who are able to read.

O'Dell, Scott. *Island of the Blue Dolphins*. Houghton Mifflin, 1960 (I:10+ R:6). A girl survives alone on an island for eighteen years.

O'Neill, Catharine. *Mrs. Dunphy's Dog*. Viking, 1987 (I:3–8 R:4). A humorous text results from misinterpretations.

Orlev, Uri. *The Island on Bird Street*. Translated by Hillel Halkin. Houghton Mifflin, 1984 (I:10+ R:6). A twelve-year-old Jewish boy survives World War II in Warsaw.

Paterson, Katherine. *Bridge to Terabithia*. Illustrated by Donna Diamond. Crowell, 1977 (I:10–14 R:6). Terabithia is the special kingdom of a boy who wishes to be an artist and a girl different from the rest of her classmates.

———. *Jacob Have I Loved*. Crowell, 1980. (I:10 R:6). A girl overcomes the belief that her younger twin sister has stolen her birthright.

Paulsen, Gary. *Hatchet*. Bradbury, 1987 (I:10+ R:6). A thirteen-year-old boy learns personal and physical survival in the Canadian wilderness.

Pearce, Philippa. *Tom's Midnight Garden*. Illustrated by Susan Einzig. Lippincott, 1958 (I:8+ R:6). In a time-warp story, a boy goes back to a garden in an earlier time.

Phipson, Joan. *The Watcher in the Garden*. Atheneum, 1982 (I:10+ R:7). A garden has a strange influence on an older man, a girl, and a disruptive boy.

Pienkowski, Jan. *Haunted House*. Dutton, 1979 (I:all). Movable pictures show the ghostly inhabitants.

Polacco, Patricia. *Meteor!* Dodd, Mead, 1987 (I:6–10 R:7). A humorous fictional account tells of the reactions of a town when a meteor falls to earth.

Potter, Beatrix. *A Treasury of Peter Rabbit and Other Stories*. Avenel, 1979 (I:2–7 R:5). Peter has an unhappy experience in Mr. McGregor's garden.

Raskin, Ellen. *The Westing Game*. Dutton, 1978 (I:10–14 R:5). Sixteen heirs are invited to solve the riddle surrounding the death of an eccentric millionaire.

Rodowsky, Colby. *Sydney Herself*. Farrar, Straus & Giroux, 1989 (I:11+ R:6). A journal helps a girl make discoveries about herself.

Rogasky, Barbara. *Smoke and Ashes: The Story of the Holocaust*. Holiday House, 1988 (I:10+ R:6). A history tells of the Holocaust.

Rylant, Cynthia. *A Fine White Dust*. Bradbury, 1986 (I:10+ R:6). A thirteen-year-old boy faces challenges to his religious beliefs.

———. *When I Was Young in the Mountains*. Illustrated by Diane Goode. Dutton, 1982 (I:4–7 R:3). A young girl remembers special childhood experiences such as her grandmother's corn bread and going to the swimming hole.

Schlee, Ann. *Ask Me No Questions*. H. Holt, 1982 (I:10+ R:6). Two children discover the harsh reality of nineteenth-century England when they learn about hundreds of children who live in an asylum.

Sendak, Maurice. *Where the Wild Things Are*. Harper & Row, 1963 (I:4–8 R:6). A room turns into an imaginative world.

Seredy, Kate. *The White Stag*. Viking, 1937; Puffin, 1979 (I:10–14 R:7). An epic story tells of the Huns and Magyars as they migrate from Asia to Europe.

Sherman, Josepha, retold by. *Vassilisa the Wise: A Tale of Medieval Russia*. Illustrated by Daniel San Souci. Harcourt Brace Jovanovich, 1988 (I:6–10 R:5). A clever and courageous female outwits the prince.

Snyder, Dianne. *The Boy of the Three-Year Nap*. Illustrated by Allen Say. Houghton Mifflin, 1988 (I:4–9 R:4). A Japanese tale tells about a lazy son and his resourceful mother.

Speare, Elizabeth George. *The Sign of the Beaver*. Houghton Mifflin, 1983 (I:8–12 R:5). A boy survives in a frontier cabin after an Indian friend teaches him survival techniques.

———. *The Witch of Blackbird Pond*. Houghton Mifflin, 1958 (I:9–14 R:4). Kit Tyler leaves her island home and rapidly comes into conflict with the Puritan way of life in colonial New England.

Sperry, Armstrong. *Call It Courage*. Macmillan, 1940 (I:9–13 R:6). A Polynesian boy travels alone in an outrigger canoe to overcome his fear of the sea.

Steptoe, John. *Mufaro's Beautiful Daughters: An African Tale*. Lothrop, Lee & Shepard, 1987 (I:all R:4). An African folktale has some Cinderella elements.

Stock, Catherine. *Sophie's Knapsack*. Lothrop, Lee & Shepard, 1988 (I:3–8 R:4). A young girl has a camping experience with her parents.

Taylor, Mildred D. *Roll of Thunder, Hear My Cry*. Dial, 1976 (I:10+ R:6). A black Mississippi family in 1933 experiences humiliating and frightening situations but retains its pride and independence.

Taylor, Theodore. *The Cay*. Doubleday, 1969 (I:8–12 R:6). A prejudiced young white boy and a black West Indian are shipwrecked on a barren Caribbean island.

Tolkien, J. R. R. *The Hobbit*. Houghton Mifflin, 1938 (I:9–12 R:6). Bilbo Baggins, a hobbit, joins forces with dwarfs in a quest to overthrow the evil dragon.

Voigt, Cynthia. *Dicey's Song*. Atheneum, 1982 (I:10+ R:5). Dicey learns about her own possibilities as she takes care of her brothers and sister.

Wells, Rosemary. *Max's Chocolate Chicken*. Dial, 1989 (I:2–6). Two rabbits share an Easter experience.

White, E. B. *Charlotte's Web*. Illustrated by Garth Williams. Harper & Row, 1952 (I:7–11 R:3). Charlotte saves Wilbur's life.

White, T. H. *The Sword in the Stone*. Collins, 1938 (I:10+ R:7). This is the story of Arthur before he became king.

Wilder, Laura Ingalls. *Little House in the Big Woods*. Harper & Row, 1932 (I:8–12 R:6). The first book in a series is about family life on the American frontier, told from a girl's viewpoint.

Williams, Margery. *The Velveteen Rabbit*. Illustrated by William Nicholson. Doubleday, 1958 (I:6–9 R:5). A toy rabbit is given life after he faithfully serves a child.

Williams, Vera B. *Stringbean's Trip to the Shining Sea*. Illustrated by Vera B. Williams and Jennifer Williams. Greenwillow, 1988 (I:5–10). Postcards and illustrations show a summer vacation.

Yolen, Jane. *The Devil's Arithmetic*. Viking Kestrel, 1988 (I:8+ R:5). In a time-warp story, a Jewish girl finds herself in World War II.

Yorinks, Arthur. *Hey, Al*. Illustrated by Richard Egielski. Farrar, Straus & Giroux, 1986 (I:all). A janitor discovers that his home is better than he thinks.

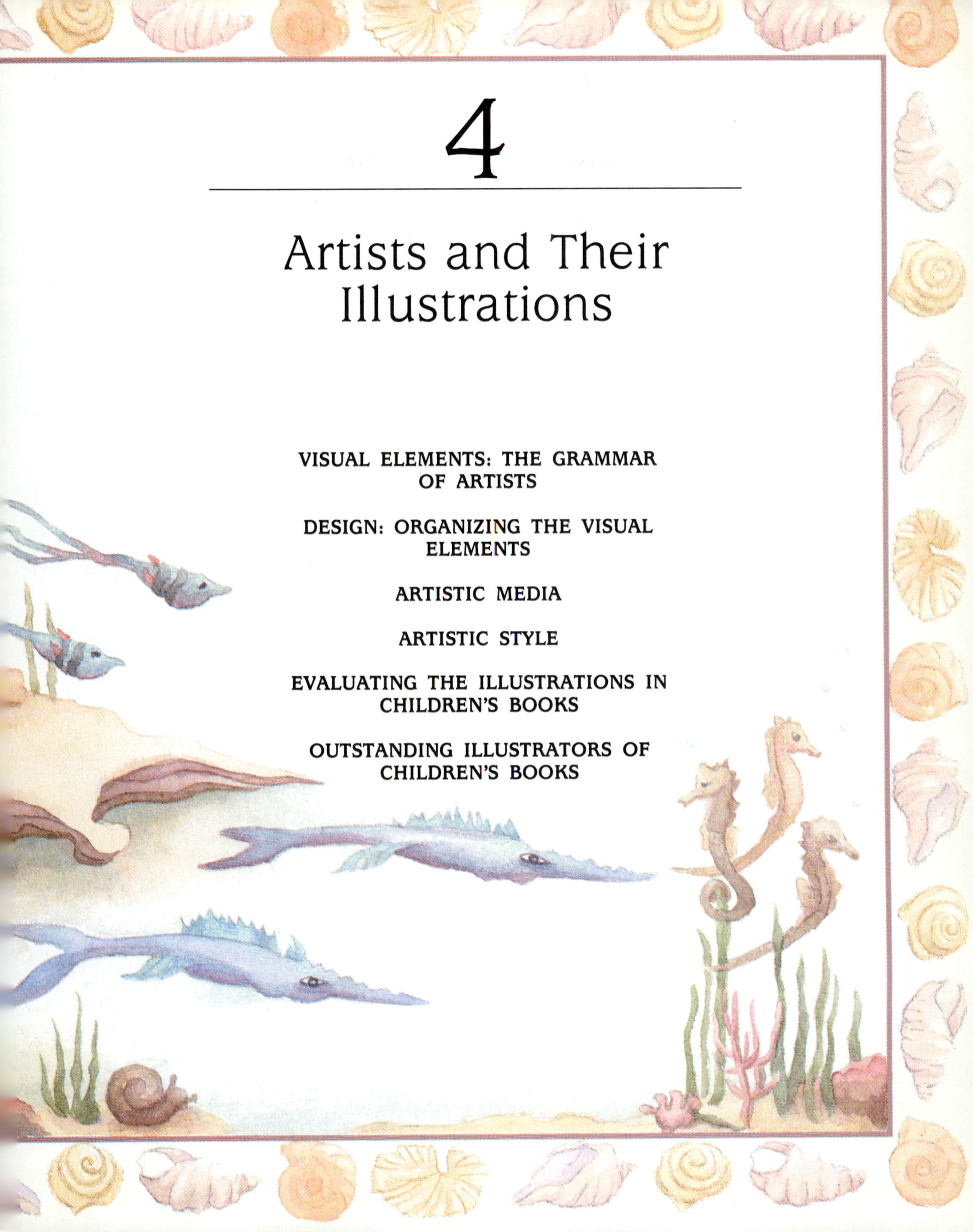

4

Artists and Their Illustrations

VISUAL ELEMENTS: THE GRAMMAR OF ARTISTS

DESIGN: ORGANIZING THE VISUAL ELEMENTS

ARTISTIC MEDIA

ARTISTIC STYLE

EVALUATING THE ILLUSTRATIONS IN CHILDREN'S BOOKS

OUTSTANDING ILLUSTRATORS OF CHILDREN'S BOOKS

MANY YOUNG CHILDREN MENTION THE illustrations when asked what attracted them to a book. The bright colors of an East African setting may entice children into searching for camouflaged animals. Jagged lines and dark colors may excite them with the prospect of dangerous adventures, while delicate lines and pastel colors may set them to dreaming about fairyland. The textures in illustrations may invite children to "feel" a bear's fur or an eagle's feathers. In these and many other ways, illustrations are integral to picture books for young children. Outstanding artists illustrate books for older children—such as Laura Ingalls Wilder's Little House series—but in such books, the text can stand on its own. In picture books, however, the illustrations join the text in telling the stories.

This chapter discusses the visual elements, media, and styles used by illustrators of all books for children, but it focuses on the special requirements of picture books. It suggests criteria for evaluating illustrations in picture books, provides examples of high-quality books, and looks at several outstanding illustrators to see how they create memorable picture books.

VISUAL ELEMENTS: THE GRAMMAR OF ARTISTS

This chapter considers the ways in which an illustrator creates an appropriate visual representation of an author's words. A writer creates a compelling story by arranging words; an artist arranges visual elements to create a picture that will complement the writer's story. Edmund Burke Feldman (5) maintains that "a visual grammar based on artistic usage" (p. 218) consists of the elements of line, color, shape, and texture. An artist who organizes these elements into a unified whole creates a visual design that conveys meaning.

Line

Artists use line to suggest direction, motion, energy, and mood. Lines can be thin or wide, light or heavy, feathery or jagged, straight or curved. According to Edmund Burke Feldman, line is the most crucial visual element for several reasons:

1. Line is familiar to virtually everyone because of experience with drawing and writing.
2. Line is definite, assertive, intelligible (although its windings and patternings may be infinitely complex); it is precise and unambiguous; it commits the artist to a specific statement.
3. Line conveys meaning through its identification with natural phenomena.
4. Line leads the viewer's eye and involves the viewer in the line's "destiny."
5. Line permits us to do with our eyes what we did as children getting to know the world: handle objects and feel their contours. When handling an object we trace its outlines with our fingers. In our growth toward maturity, the outlines of things eventually become more important to us than their color, size, or texture as means of identifying them.

Feldman's discussion of the relationship between line and natural phenomena is especially interesting to people involved with children and the illustrations found in literature for them. Experiences with common natural phenomena may help children relate more meaningfully to works of art. Vertical lines, for example, look like trees in a windless landscape or like people who stand rather than move. Consequently, they suggest lack of movement.

Horizontal lines, such as the surface of a placid lake or a flat horizon, suggest calm, sleep, stability, and an absence of strife. Most young children use a horizontal baseline in their drawings to convey the idea of the firm ground upon which they walk.

Vertical lines and horizontal lines joined at right angles depict artificial elements that differ considerably from the natural world of irregular and approximate shapes. Two vertical lines connected by a horizontal line at the top give the feeling of a solid, safe place: a doorway, house, or building.

In contrast, diagonal lines suggest loss of balance and uncontrolled motion—unless they form a triangle that rests on a horizontal base, which suggests safety. In both human design and nature, jagged lines have connotations of breakdown and destruction. Consequently, jagged lines suggest danger.

People see curved lines as fluid because of their resemblance to the eddies, whirlpools, and concentric ripples in water. Because of this, circles and curved lines seem less definite and predictable than do straight lines.

In *The Girl Who Loved Wild Horses,* Paul Goble uses line effectively to depict the natural setting of a Native American folktale, as well as to enhance the mood and plot. Goble introduces readers to the main character as she goes down to the river at

FLASHBACK

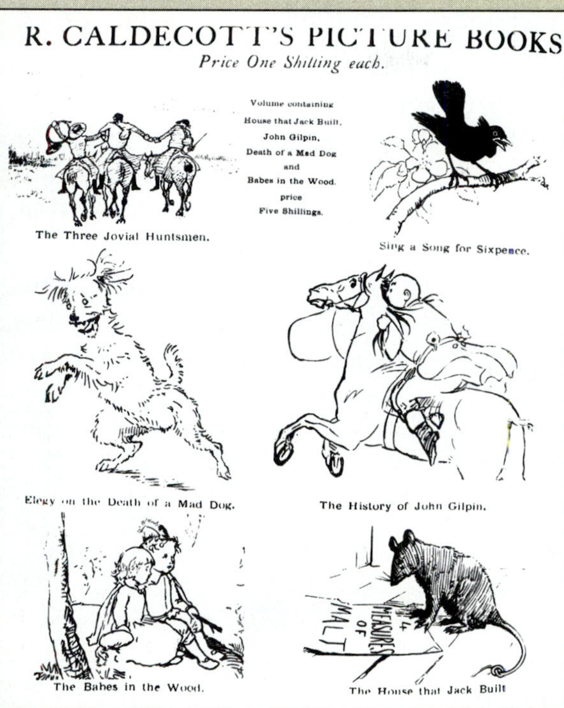

R. CALDECOTT'S PICTURE BOOKS
Price One Shilling each.
Volume containing
House that Jack Built,
John Gilpin,
Death of a Mad Dog
and
Babes in the Wood.
price
Five Shillings.
The Three Jovial Huntsmen.
Sing a Song for Sixpence.
Elegy on the Death of a Mad Dog.
The History of John Gilpin.
The Babes in the Wood.
The House that Jack Built
4 MEASURES OF MALT

ILLUSTRATOR RANDOLPH CALDECOTT IS credited with being the forefather of the modern picture book for children. Caldecott's illustrations had an enormous impact on children's book publishing in nineteenth-century England. His expert use of line created robust characters depicting humor, vitality, and action.

The books illustrated in this flashback are from a series of sixteen picture books, or toy books, illustrated by Caldecott. William Cowper's *The History of John Gilpin* was published in 1878. The Caldecott Medal for excellence in illustrating children's books is embossed with a picture from this book. The remaining five books shown here were published between 1879 and 1900.

Caldecott illustrated books by the top writers, including Juliana Horatia Ewing (*Jackanapes*) and Washington Irving (*Old Christmas, Washington Irving's Sketch Book*). Caldecott's toy books, however, signaled the beginning of the high-quality picture books that were eventually available for children.

sunrise to watch the wild horses. The illustration shows a calm, nonthreatening scene. The lines of the horses' legs are vertical, since the horses are quietly drinking from the river. The calm is enhanced by the reflections in the water; not even a ripple breaks the tranquillity.

On the next page, the girl rests in a meadow close to home. Goble illustrates the triangular shapes of teepees sitting securely on the ground. The text relates, however, that a rumble of thunder can be heard while the girl sleeps. The outlines of the clouds suggest this break in a peaceful afternoon: they are still rounded, but are also heavy, with protrusions jutting into the sky.

Movement in the story and the illustrations becomes more pronounced as lightning flashes and the horses rear and snort in terror. Sharp lines of lightning extend from black, rolling clouds to the ground. Even the lines of the plants are diagonal, suggesting the power of the dangerous wind as the horses gallop away in front of the storm. When night falls and the storm is over, the tired girl and horses stop to rest. Goble illustrates the hills with vertical lines connected by horizontal lines, suggesting the new feeling of safety and shelter under the moon and the stars.

In contrast to Paul Goble's depiction of familiar natural phenomena, the soft, delicate lines of Marcia Brown's illustrations for Charles Perrault's *Cinderella* create a mood and setting suggestive of a mythical kingdom that could exist only "once upon a time." The drawing of Cinderella's fairy godmother transforming her into a beautiful princess has an ethereal quality, as if the scene were floating on air. Because these illustrations seem to be almost as diaphanous and changeable as clouds, viewers are not surprised when a pumpkin turns into a coach and a rat becomes the driver of the coach. Even the illustrated architecture has a magical quality. Delicately curved windows, softly flowing draperies, and graceful pillars provide fitting backgrounds for a favorite fairy tale.

In an instant the herd was galloping away like the wind. She called to the horses to stop, but her voice was lost in the thunder. Nothing could stop them. She hugged her horse's neck with her fingers twisted into his mane. She clung on, afraid of falling under the drumming hooves.

Line and color combine to create a feeling of impending danger and terror. Notice the heavy black clouds with circular lines and jagged lightning. The diagonal lines of the horses' legs and manes complement the mood. (From the book *The Girl Who Loved Wild Horses* by Paul Goble. Reprinted with permission of Bradbury Press, Inc., an affiliate of Macmillan. Copyright © 1978 by Paul Gobel.)

Charles Keeping's illustrations for Alfred Noyes's ghost poem, *The Highwayman,* create quite a different mood. Stark black lines create ghostly, terrifying subjects and suggest the sinister and disastrous consequences in the tale.

Even invisible lines, or suggestions of lines, have considerable impact in illustrations. Lyn Ellen Lacy (8) emphasizes the role of vertical and horizontal invisible lines as directional influences. For example, when analyzing pages 43–44 in Robert McCloskey's *Make Way for Ducklings,* Lacy states:

> Tethered to a top coat button, the whistle manages to fly behind Michael like a free pixie spirit. It points in the direction opposite Michael's intended hasty path. Literally, it points toward the townscape; figuratively, it points our way back into the picture in case we missed something. We do not then turn the page too soon, but instead we follow the whistle's path of gesture along an invisible line, back into the maze of buildings whose vertical lines have a downward thrust to the sidewalk. This underlying structure in the picture is a gentle reminder that there are minute spots on the sidewalk. McCloskey did not want us to miss them. (p. 47)

These minute spots prove to be mother duck and her ducklings. As you look at the illustrations in picture books, try to locate invisible lines and consider the importance of these lines in the impact of the illustrations.

Color

Combining line and color is perhaps the most common way that artists convey mood and emotion in a picture book. Many feelings about color are associated with natural phenomena. Reds, yellows, and oranges are most associated with fire, sun, and blood, and they usually have warm or hot connotations: friendliness, high energy, or anger. Blues, greens, and some violets are most associated with air, water, and plant life; their coolness or coldness can suggest moods and emotions ranging from tranquillity to melancholy.

To evaluate an illustrator's use of color, adults may consider how well the color language of the artist conveys or complements the mood, characterization, setting, and theme the writer develops in words. Marcia Brown's use of delicate line in her illustration of Charles Perrault's *Cinderella* is enhanced by her choice of colors. Soft pastels bring a shimmering radiance to the fairy-tale quality of the pictures. If she had chosen bright colors, the mood could have been destroyed. In contrast, Paul Goble uses bright colors and black, in addition to strong line, to illustrate a desert setting and the tension and movement of animals and forces of nature in *The Girl Who Loved Wild Horses*.

Color can depict the total mood of a story. In *Ox-Cart Man,* Barbara Cooney visually translates Donald Hall's gentle story about a quieter time in American history by using pastels and muted hues of darker colors. Cooney portrays the hills of rural New England in the early 1800s as gentle curves of green, gray, and blue. The deep rusts, blues, and greens of the clothing look authentic for the time period.

Cooney's color choices also show the passing of time. When the farmer begins his journey over hills and past villages, the whole countryside is aflame with the rusts and oranges of fall; by the time he reaches Portsmouth, the trees have only a few brown leaves. As he returns home, a soft, brown land awaits the first snowfall. The scene turns white in winter, then soft greens cover the hills before the trees explode with white and pink apple blossoms.

Many readers of this book mention its feeling of tranquillity. One child said the pictures made her feel homesick; she had lived in an area that had hills, valleys, quiet farms, and distinct seasons.

The artist's choice of rich colors and costuming detail capture a humorous royal environment. (From *KING BIDGOOD'S IN THE BATHTUB,* text copyright © by Audrey Wood, illustrations copyright © 1985 by Don Wood. Reprinted by permission of Harcourt Brace Jovanovich, Inc.)

Color and line draw the reader's attention to the farmer and the ox. (From *The Ox-Cart Man* by Donald Hall, illustrated by Barbara Cooney. Illustrations copyright © 1979 by Barbara Cooney Porter. Reprinted by permission of Viking Penguin, Inc.)

Cooney creates a similar mood through color in her illustrations for *Island Boy,* which she also wrote.

Blues and greens emphasize the cold northern setting in Michael Rothman's illustrations for Joanne Ryder's *White Bear, Ice Bear*. Frosty whites and shades of blue and green are equally effective in Dan Guravich's photographs for Downs Matthews's *Polar Bear Cubs*. The colors in both texts reinforce the cold winds, creaking ice, and blowing blizzards.

Warm, bright colors evoke the sun and heat of East Africa and the high energy of its wildlife in Jose Aruego and Ariane Dewey's *We Hide, You Seek*. The artists first researched animals living in Africa, then drew pictures that show the animals' spots, stripes, patterns, and colors in the natural environment, where camouflage helps the animals when they need to hide. Reddish-brown vines camouflage the giraffe's reddish-brown markings; tigers' markings make them hard to see against tree limbs; and yellow and green birds look just like leaves covered with sunlight. When the artists reveal the animals out of hiding, they use color to expose differences between the animals and their environment. The camouflages encourage children to search for the hidden animals before they turn the page to discover their locations. The mother of a two-year-old said that her son was so excited by this book that he woke her up at midnight to read it again. This child appreciated the color used as a puzzle for him to solve.

Artists may use changes in color to depict contrasts in moods within a book. For example, in Tejima's illustrations for *Fox's Dream,* the frozen, icy forest of Fox's isolation is depicted by black-and-white illustrations, while the spring of Fox's happy dreams and memories is colored in warm yellows and rich browns.

Likewise, Donald Carrick's illustrations for Eve Bunting's *Ghost's Hour, Spook's Hour* show how color may be used to create moods. The dark shades used in the early illustrations develop and reinforce the scary environment and the young boy's fear of the dark. When the father rescues his frightened son, the father is shown in an open doorway that has a warm yellow background. The warm yellows are retained as the boy is comforted by his parents and joins them in the big couch bed.

The colors in Thomas Allen's illustrations for Judith Hendershot's *In Coal Country* are appropriate for a story about growing up in a 1930s Ohio coal mining town. The impressionistic pastel and charcoal illustrations create the feeling of a landscape observed through a combination of coal dust and nostalgia.

Artists may also use contrasts in illustrations to create drama and enhance plot. Helen Oxenbury's illustrations for Michael Rosen's *We're Going on a Bear Hunt* alternate between black and white and color. On the pages with black-and-white illustrations, the characters chant the portion of the bear hunt they are about to experience. The color illustrations show the family swishing through long grass, splashing across a river, squishing in mud, and stumbling through a dark forest.

Shape

Lines join and intersect to suggest shapes, and areas of color meet to produce shapes. Organic shapes, irregular and curving, are common in nature and in handmade objects. Geometric shapes—exact, rigid, and often rectangular—usually have mechanical origins. As discussed in relation to line, different shapes have different connotations. Illustrators may use organic, free-form shapes to convey anything from receptivity and imagination to frightening unpredictability; while they may use geometric shapes in illustrations to connote complexity, stability, assertion, or severity (11).

Gerald McDermott, illustrator and author of *Arrow to the Sun,* uses traditional Native American patterns of line and color to create shapes that draw readers into a desert world where humans, nature, and spiritual forces intertwine. Rich yellow, orange, and brown rectangles depict the pueblo home of the people. This building constructed by humans from natural materials is separated by a black void from the circular orange and yellow sun, which is the people's god. The people worship this god in the kiva, a circular ceremonial chamber. A rectangular ray from the sun to the pueblo represents the spark of life that becomes the sun god's earthly son. He is illus-

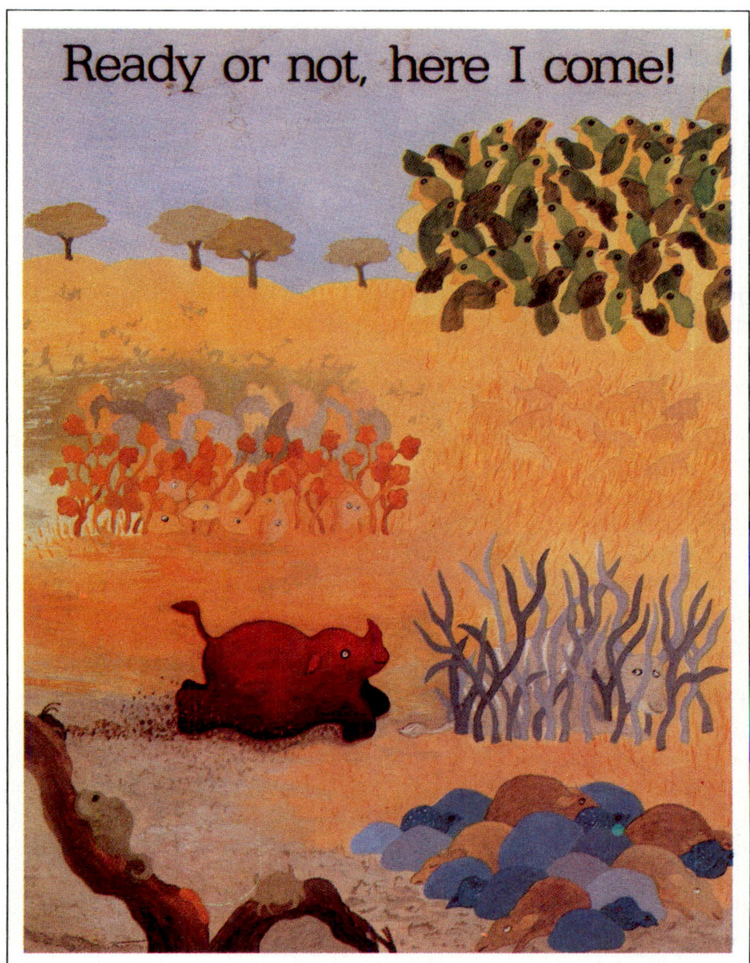

Warm, vivid colors, including red, yellow, and orange, are appropriate for an African setting. The color contrasts help readers locate hidden animals. (Illustration "Ready or not, here I come!" from *We Hide, You Seek* by Jose Aruego and Ariane Dewey. Copyright © 1979 by Jose Aruego and Ariane Dewey. Reprinted by permission of Greenwillow Books [A Division of William Morrow & Company].)

Vivid colors and simple shapes attract the attention of readers in this wordless picture book. (Reprinted with permission of Macmillan Publishing Co., Inc. from *Changes, Changes* by Pat Hutchins. Copyright © 1971, Pat Hutchins.)

trated as a black and yellow rectangle, while his mother's form has a more circular appearance. Black and yellow rectangles predominate in the illustrations until the son decides to search for his father and takes on the sun's power as well as the rainbow of colors available to the sun. He returns to earth as an arrow, and his people, now illustrated in all the colors he has brought with him, celebrate with the dance of life.

A person's shape says much about a person's self-image. In *Crow Boy,* Taro Yashima uses line and color to create shapes that emphasize a small boy's growth from fright and alienation to self-confidence. Yashima first draws the boy as a small, huddled shape isolated from his classmates in white space. As an understanding teacher helps Crow Boy become more self-assured, his shape on the page becomes larger, more outreaching, and closer to the shapes of other characters. Yashima also stresses Crow Boy's transformation by outlining his new form with shades of white that suggest shimmering light.

An illustrator's selection of shape is another way to emphasize the mood of a picture and story. According to illustrator Uri Shulevitz (23), two areas are related to shape and mood: (1) the overall form of an illustration if viewed as a silhouette (with no interior details) and (2) the edges of the picture, which can be hard, soft, jagged, or straight. Shulevitz states that symmetrical picture shapes, such as rectangles, squares, circles, and ovals, are calm and solid, while asymmetrical picture shapes are unbalanced, irregular, and dynamic. He maintains that these shapes and picture edges should be used in keeping the desired mood of a story.

To evaluate the impact of shape on mood in illustrated books, analyze several recent award-winning books and books on the Children's Literature Association's touchstone list. Consider Stephen Gammell's illustrations for Karen Ackerman's *Song and Dance Man,* John Schoenherr's illustrations for Jane Yolen's *Owl Moon,* Ed Young's illustrations for *Lon Po Po: A Red-Riding Hood Story from China,* and Richard Egielski's illustrations for Arthur Yorinks's *Hey, Al.* Earlier illustrated books on the touchstone list include Robert McCloskey's *Make Way for Ducklings,* Dr. Seuss's *The 500 Hats of Bartholomew Cubbins,* L. Leslie Brooke's *Johnny Crow's Garden,* Kate Greenaway's *A—Apple Pie,* Walter Crane's *Baby's Opera,* and Wanda Gág's *Millions of Cats*. Do the shapes reinforce and enhance the moods of these texts?

Texture

Looking at an object for the first time, a child usually wants to touch it in order to know exactly how it feels. Experience in touching rough bark, smooth skin, sharp thorns, and soft fur enables children later to imagine how something feels without actually touching it. Book illustrators manipulate such visual elements as line, color, and shape to create textural imagery that satisfies curiosity about how something feels.

Brian Wildsmith's ABC illustrates objects and animals in ways that visually communicate their textures. The short dark lines projecting from the outside of a nest look like rough twigs, while a solid deep purple conveys the softness inside the nest. In another picture, short curling lines of white, green, and black evoke the texture of a yak's fur. Children touch this picture to see if it is real.

Geometric shapes and sunny colors give a powerful feeling to a Native American tale from the southwestern United States. (From *Arrow to the Sun* by Gerald McDermott. Reprinted by permission of Viking Penguin, Inc.)

Owls with soft-textured feathers and big round eyes, peacocks ablaze with color, and roosters ready to fight are all found in Celestino Piatti's *The Happy Owls*. Piatti's forms are simple, and contrasts within the forms create highly satisfactory visual designs. The owls, for example, have fronts consisting of white feathers on brown backgrounds, and wings and backs of brown, blue, and green feathers. In contrast, their eyes are large circular white orbs with red centers that stare directly at viewers. Two thicknesses of black line assist in developing texture, form, and contrast. The owls' bodies and eyes are outlined with wide black lines, while the lines in the feathers are finer and more delicate. Leonard Baskin's illustrations of northern birds and animals for Ted Hughes's *Under the North Star* convey the fluffiness of a snowy owl's camouflaging feathers, the powerful musculature beneath a grizzly bear's thick fur, and the crisp tension in the wings of an eagle poised for flight.

Frequently, illustrators who depict the wonders of nature show a considerable amount of texture in their illustrations. When drawing the illustrations for Yolan's *Owl Moon,* John Schoenherr re-created the texture and the mood of the woods outside his own studio windows (20). Viewers can vicariously feel the textures of tree trunks, snow-covered landscapes, small animals peeking from behind trees, and the ultimate owl. Tejima's use of line in *Fox's Dream* creates a fox with a heavy winter fur. Steptoe's illustrations in *The Story of Jumping Mouse* use line and shades of black and white to create textures ranging from sharp spikes on cacti to delicate petals on flowers. A child's response to Kenneth Lilly's illustrations in Joyce Pope's *Kenneth Lilly's Animals: A Portfolio of Paintings* shows how effective texture can be in an informational book. The child did not want to put the book away because, "I was there with the animals. I kept touching the Koala bears to see if they were real."

DESIGN: ORGANIZING THE VISUAL ELEMENTS

Design, or composition, is the way in which an artist combines the visual elements of line, color, shape, and texture into a unified whole. When an

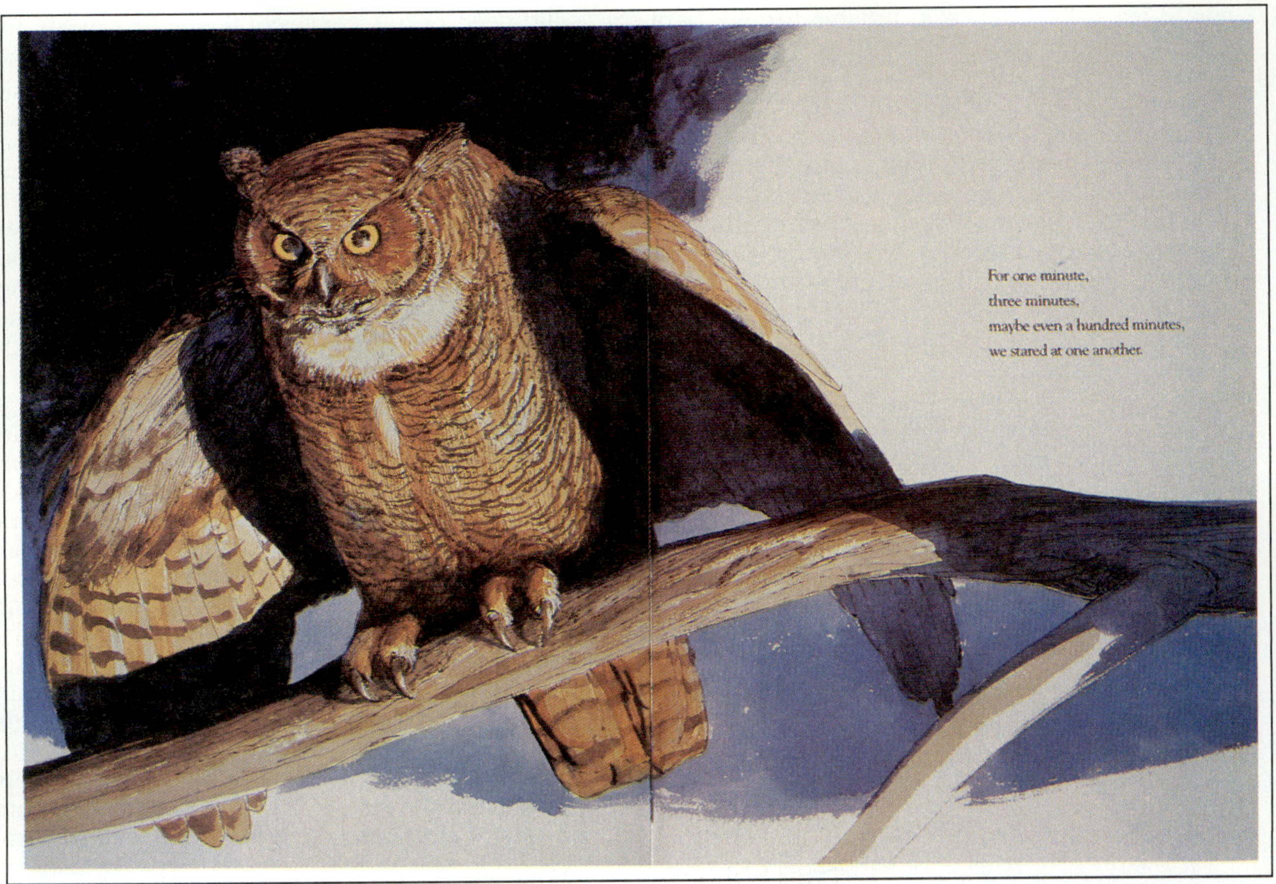

For one minute,
three minutes,
maybe even a hundred minutes,
we stared at one another.

Lines and color re-create the texture of an owl. (From *Owl Moon* by Jane Yolen. Illustrated by John Schoenherr, text copyright 1987, by Jane Yolen, illustrations © 1987 by John Schoenherr. Reprinted by permission of Philomel books.)

illustration has an overall unity, balance, and sense of rhythm, viewers experience aesthetic pleasure; when the design is weak, viewers often feel that they are looking at an incomplete, incoherent, or boring picture.

Illustrators of children's books emphasize certain characters, develop main ideas, and provide background information. They also organize their illustrations so that viewers can identify the most important element in a picture and follow a visual sequence within the picture. Artists show dominance in their work (5) by emphasizing size (the largest form is seen first), contrasting intense colors (an intense area of warm color dominates an intense area of cool color of the same size), placing the most important item in the center, using strong lines to provide visual pathways, and emphasizing nonconformity (a viewer's eye travels to an item that is different). When evaluating illustrations in children's books, consider whether or not dominant images are consistent with those of the story.

Tomie de Paola achieves balance through symmetry in his illustrations for Clement Moore's *The Night before Christmas*. The strong vertical lines of the central fireplace are reinforced by stockings hanging beneath the mantle, candles on the mantle, rows of trees in a picture over the mantle, and the legs of a chair and a table in the room. To the left and the right of the fireplace, portraits face the center of the illustration, where Santa stands on the hearth. For further emphasis, Santa's beard and the fur on his jacket are strikingly white against the rich reds and greens of the room.

Both authors and illustrators of children's books use repetition for emphasis. In illustrations, repetition can create rhythms and provide visual pathways. Virginia Lee Burton's illustrations are excellent examples of this technique. Burton's background in ballet and interest in the spatial concepts of dance may help account for her success in capturing rhythm and movement on paper (7). In *The Little House,* for example, Burton shows the house sitting on a hill with trees on either side. A row of trees follows the curve of several hills behind the house. On each hill are progressively smaller trees, houses, people, and animals. Beyond the last curving line of trees, the text tells us, lies the city that will soon spread out and surround the Little House with traffic and skyscrapers.

Page design can provide a unifying quality. Several artists develop visual continuity by framing text pages and/or illustrations. Trina Schart Hyman frames each text page in Margaret Hodges's *Saint George and the Dragon* with drawings of plants that are indigenous to the British Isles. In Barbara Cohen's adaptation of Chaucer's *Canterbury Tales,* Hyman borders the illustrations with rich gold designs. Laszlo Gal borders each illustration in Eva Martin's *Canadian Fairy Tales* with lightly penciled sketches of objects chosen from the appropriate story. In *Hiawatha's Childhood,* derived from Henry Wadsworth Longfellow's famous poems, artist Errol LeCain unifies the text by bordering each page with the tall birch trees shown in the cover illustration. Helen Davie uses Native American designs to add authenticity to the borders in Barbara Esbensen's *The Star Maiden*.

The artist's use of contrasting color and line creates the feeling of textures in nature. (Illustration by Keizaburo Tejima, reprinted with permission of Philomel Books from *Fox's Dream* © 1985 by Keizaburo Tejima.)

In addition to providing unifying qualities, page design should reflect the level of formality portrayed by the text. Lyn Ellen Lacy (8) emphasizes the importance of choosing levels of formality or informality that are in harmony with the intent of the text. Lacy identifies five levels of formality in book and page design. As you look at total book design, analyze the impact and the appropriateness of each of the levels of formality. First, text placed opposite illustrations on adjacent pages is considered the most formal arrangement. *Saint George and the Dragon,* by Margaret Hodges, has such an arrangement. Each text page is blocked in black type and surrounded by a formal border. To add to this formal feeling, each illustrated page is also bounded by a consistent border. The resulting text provides the formal feeling of a traditional legend. Likewise, in Arnold Lobel's *Fables,* the text and illustrations are carefully balanced on facing pages and appear within a border.

Second, text positioned above or beneath illustrations is considered formal. The text for Sid Fleischman's *The Scarebird* is consistently placed under Peter Sis's illustrations. Notice how texts such as *The Scarebird* and Donald Hall's *Ox-Cart Man* still appear formal but not so formal as *Saint George and the Dragon* and *Fables*.

Third, text shaped with irregular boundaries to fit inside, between, around, or to the side of the illustrations is considered informal. For example, notice how the text is shaped in Virginia Lee Burton's *The Little House* or in Wanda Gág's *Millions of Cats*.

Fourth, text combined with two or more arrangements is very informal. Julian Sheer's *Rain Makes Applesauce* is a good example of a very informal arrangement. The text is printed in different forms, colors, and sizes, and it appears to be part of Marvin Bileck's illustrations. This level of informality seems appropriate for a nonsense poem.

De Paola achieves balance through symmetry. Notice the lines of the trees in the painting over the fireplace, the pictures on each side of the fireplace, and the fireplace decorations. (Copyright © 1980 by Tomie de Paola. Reprinted from *The Night Before Christmas* by permission of Holiday House, Inc.)

Repetition and line provide a visual pathway and suggest movement. (Illustration by Virginia Lee Burton from *The Little House*. Copyright 1942 by Virginia Lee Demetrios. Copyright renewed 1969 by George Demetrios. Reprinted by permission of Houghton Mifflin Company.)

Finally, lack of text, such as in wordless books, is considered the most informal. Rafe Martin's text and Stephen Gammell's illustrations in *Will's Mammoth* provide such a level of informality. Text introduces an imaginary experience, but the words are printed in different sizes and colors. The illustrations then continue the story wordlessly. The story concludes with text again written in different sizes and colors. This combination is appropriate for a text that encourages imaginative play.

Page design influences reader response and may add to conflict. For example, Perry Nodelman (16) describes how changes in page design influence the response of readers:

> [W]hen the text has usually appeared below the pictures and suddenly appears above one, the rhythm of our response to the events we are learning about changes. In Steig's *The Amazing Bone,* for instance, the words usually appear under the pictures, so that we would logically view the pictures and then read the words. But in moments of intense action there are two pictures on each page, with words either above them or below them or both; and in moments of intense emotion, when Pearl is in serious danger or, at the end, when she returns happily home, the words tend to appear above the pictures. We usually look at a page from the top down, and because of their inherently attractive nature, we tend to look at pictures first, then read words. When Steig puts the words above the pictures, therefore, he puts us in an ambivalent state: should we read first or look first. This ambivalence adds tension to the tense moments of his book. (p. 55)

As you look at page design, consider the different responses that are possible.

ARTISTIC MEDIA

The elements of line, color, shape, and texture are expressed through the materials and techniques an artist uses in illustrating a book. Ink, wood, paper, paint, and other media can create a wide variety of visual effects. Artist Harry Borgman (1) indicates a few of the possibilities in stating his own preferences:

> If I want a bright, translucent wash tone, I would either use watercolor or dyes. For an opaque paint that is water resistant, I would use acrylics. If I want to draw a line that will dissolve a bit when water is washed over it, I would use a Pentel Sign pen. (p. 113)

Borgman's remarks suggest the importance of an illustrator's choosing the media and artistic techniques most appropriate for conveying the mood, characterization, and setting in a particular story.

The artist frames each illustration with sketches of objects found in the fairy tale. (© by Laszlo Gal 1984 from *Canadian Fairy Tales,* published as *Tales from the Far North.*)

Lines and Washes

Many illustrations discussed in this chapter rely on lines drawn in ink to convey meaning and develop the mood. For example, the crisp lines and repetition in Wanda Gág's pen-and-ink drawings help the reader visualize and believe in a world inhabited by *Millions of Cats,* each of which has special qualities appealing to an old man.

Ink is a versatile medium. It may be applied with brush, sponge, cloth, or even the artist's fingers, as well as with pen. According to Norman Laliberté and Alex Mogelon (9), what often emerges is "a terribly direct, strong, and uncompromising statement of the nature of our time and the talent of the artist. The very character of ink is challenging, demanding and a spur to experimentation and creativity. It is a bold form of expression, sparkling clean because it is so definite and positive" (p. 43).

In most cases, the author's words inspire the illustrator, but Tom Feelings's sensitive drawings of children inspired the accompanying poetry written by Nikki Grimes in *Something on My Mind.*

When he heard the owls at midnight,
Hooting, laughing in the forest,
"What is that?" he cried in terror;
"What is that," he said, "Nokomis?"
And the good Nokomis answered:
"That is but the owl and owlet,
Talking in their native language,
Talking, scolding at each other."

Birch trees frame the sides of each illustration and provide a continuity of both setting and design. (From *Hiawatha's Childhood* by Henry Wadsworth Longfellow. Illustrations by Errol LeCain. Illustrations copyright © 1984 by Errol LeCain. Reprinted by permission of Farrar, Straus & Giroux, Inc.)

Feelings's black-and-white drawings portray the loneliness, fear, sorrow, and hope that children experience while growing up. The backgrounds in the illustrations are also superb. Heavy black wrought-iron gates, lighter picket fences, an old Victorian house, and apartment-house steps provide believable settings and atmospheres for children's wishful thinking.

Artists also use varying qualities of pen-and-ink line to convey emotions corresponding to characterizations in books. Ray Cruz's drawings for Judith Viorst's *Alexander and the Terrible, Horrible, No Good, Very Bad Day* communicate the essence of a boy who experiences unhappy and frustrating emotions. The scowling expressions and hair on end convey the spirit of a boy who has lost his best friend and doesn't have any dessert in his lunch box.

Varying shades of water-thinned ink, sparely drawn figures, and textured paper suggest a traditional Japanese setting appropriate for Sumiko Yagawa's *The Crane Wife*. Illustrator Suekichi Akaba's traditional Japanese painting techniques complement the story of a transformed crane who rewards a poor farmer for his care, but returns to animal form when the young man becomes greedy and breaks his promise.

Watercolors, Acrylics, Pastels, and Oils

Watercolor can be applied in various ways—from thin, transparent washes to thick pigments. The choice depends upon the effect the artist wishes to create. Boris Zvorykin uses gouache, a method of painting with opaque watercolors, to evoke the rich colors of traditional costume and a magical

Strong line and repetition in pencil-and-ink drawings complement a story. (Illustration by Wanda Gág from *Millions of Cats*. Copyright 1928; renewed 1956, by Wanda Gág. Reprinted by permission of Coward, McCann & Geoghegan, Inc.)

setting in *The Firebird and Other Russian Fairy Tales,* edited by Jacqueline Onassis.

Tomie de Paola's illustrations for Shirley Rousseau Murphy's *Tattie's River Journey* exemplify the effect of opaque tempera paint applied over colored inks. De Paola proceeded from a detailed pencil drawing, to an application of brown-black inks, to painting with colored inks, and finally to an application of opaque tempera. Some of the illustrations take on a three-dimensional quality, as areas of colored ink show through the paint.

The effects of three color media—watercolors, pastels, and acrylics—are seen in Leo and Diane Dillon's illustrations for Margaret Musgrove's

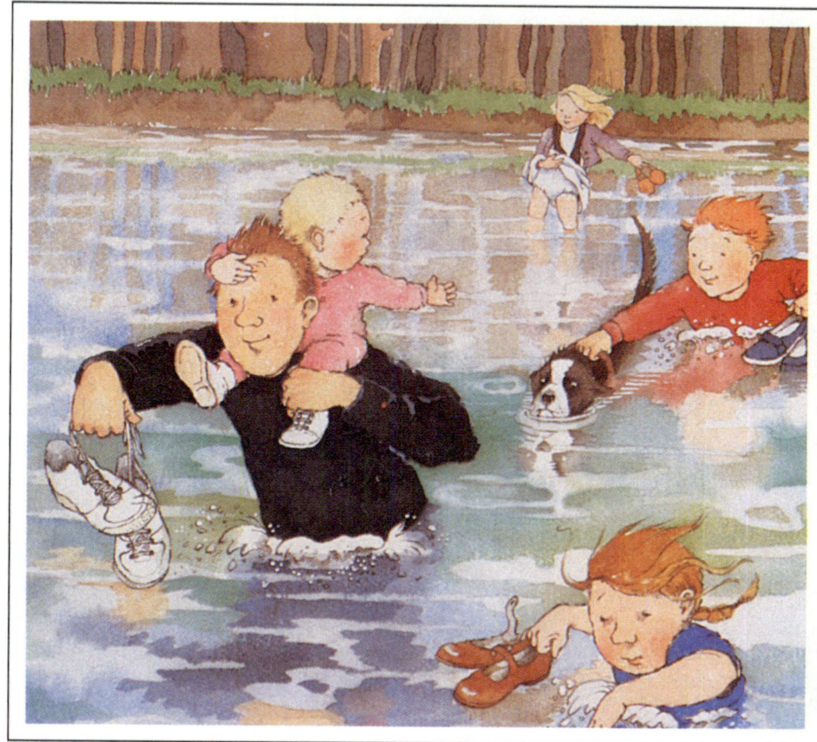

Watercolors contrast with charcoal sketches to create an exciting text. (From *We're Going on a Bear Hunt* retold by Michael Rosen, illustrated by Helen Oxenbury, copyright © 1989 by Michael Rosen, illustrations copyright © 1989 by Helen Oxenbury. Reproduced by permission of Margaret K. McElderry Books, an imprint of Macmillan Publishing Company.

Ashanti to Zulu: African Traditions. Vibrantly colored jewelry and designs on artifacts contrast with the soft shades of the flowing garments. The river in the illustration that depicts the Lozi people is so transparent that the bottom of the boat shimmers through the water. In other pictures, the sky vibrates with heat from the sun, or jewel-like tones express the breathtaking beauty of exotic birds and plants.

Full-page oil paintings create a somber mood in Paul O. Zelinsky's illustrations for *Hansel and Gretel*, as told by the Brothers Grimm. Zelinsky's woods are menacing, where evil is likely to exist. The rich highlights that are possible with oil are shown in Zelinsky's illustrations for *Rumpelstiltskin*.

Dark, somber tones in full-page oil paintings create an appropriately menacing setting for a dramatic folktale. (From *Hansel and Gretel*. Illustrated by Paul O. Zelinsky and retold by Rika Lesser. Illustrations copyright © 1984 by Paul O. Zelinsky.)

Woodcuts

Woodcuts are among the oldest artistic media in both Western and Eastern culture. In the fifteenth century, the black-and-white woodcuts of the German artist Albrecht Dürer brought this medium to a new level of sophistication in Europe. The first printed books, including the earliest books for children, were illustrated with black-and-white woodcuts. Later, Japanese artists pioneered in the creation of full-color woodcuts that inspired other artists in Europe and North America, such as the famous French artist Paul Gauguin.

To create a woodcut, an artist draws an image on a block of wood and cuts away the areas around the design. After rolling ink onto this raised surface, the artist presses the woodblock against paper, transferring the image from the block to the paper. Color prints require a different woodblock for each color in the picture. Woodcuts can be printed in colors with varying degrees of transparency, and the grain and texture of the wood can add to the effect of the composition.

The strong lines and bold colors of woodcuts create a simplicity often desired by illustrators of folktales. Gail Haley used woodcuts to illustrate her version of an African folktale *A Story, a Story*, in which the grain of the wood replicates the texture of native huts and communicates the earthy nature of a traditional setting. The strong lines possible with woodcuts are found in Michael McCurdy's illustrations for his adaptation of the Russian folktale, *The Devils Who Learned to Be Good*.

Blair Lent's *Bayberry Bluff* is an example of cardboard cuts. The technique is similar to woodcuts and linoleum cuts, except that the designs are cut into thick cardboard with single-edged razor blades.

Collage

Collage—a word derived from the French word *coller*, meaning "to paste" or "to stick"—is a recent addition to the world of book illustration. Pasting and sticking are exactly what artists do when using this technique. Any object or substance that can be attached to a surface can be used to develop a design. Artists may use cardboard, paper, cloth, glass, leather, metal, wood, leaves, flowers, or even butterflies. They may cut up and rearrange their own paintings or use paint and other media to add background. When photographically repro-

Corporal Farrell
brought the barrel,
Private Parriage
brought the carriage,
but Drummer Hoff
fired it off.
SULTAN

Strong lines of the woodcuts and bold colors enhance the traditional quality of this cumulative tale. (From the book *Drummer Hoff* by Barbara Emberly. Illustrated by Ed Emberley. Copyright © 1967 by Edward R. Emberley and Barbara Emberley. Used by permission of the publisher, Prentice-Hall Inc., Englewood Cliffs, N.J. 07632.)

duced in a book, collages still communicate texture.

Eric Carle, a popular artist of picture books for young children, is known for his striking, colorful storybooks. *The Very Hungry Caterpillar* won the American Institute of Graphic Art's award for 1970. Carle develops his collages through a three-step process. He begins by applying acrylic paints to tissue paper. Then, he uses rubber cement to paste the paper into the desired designs. Finally, he applies colored crayon to provide accents. In *Eric Carle's Animals Animals,* tissue-paper collage creates a dazzling array of animals. In addition to brightly colored collage illustrations, Carle's most recent books include pop-ups and other features that encourage children to interact. In *The Honeybee and the Robber,* readers work tabs that move a honeybee's wings, stinger, and tongue.

Another artist who illustrates primarily with collage is Ezra Jack Keats. In *Peter's Chair,* lace looks realistic as it cascades from the inside of a cloth-covered bassinet. On the same page, pink wallpaper with large flowers provides the background for the baby sister's room. Keats also combines paints and collage in his illustrations, a combination effectively used in *The Trip*. These illustrations have a three-dimensional quality appropriate for a story about a boy who builds his old neighborhood within a box and then visits it in his imagination. Photographs are used in the collage illustrations in Keats's *Regards to the Man in the Moon*. These illustrations suggest the diversity that can be found in one medium.

Marcia Brown uses collage and paint to match the mood of Blaise Cendrars's *Shadow*. Brown's strong, dark images of the nighttime forest and her wispy ghosts strongly reinforce the spell cast by a storyteller in Cendrars's text.

A heavily textured look results when an artist uses leaves, wood, grasses, shells, and fur in collage illustrations. In *Where the Forest Meets the Sea,* Jeannie Baker combines many natural and artificial substances to create a glorious rain forest in North Queensland, Australia. The collage encourages readers to feel vicariously the textures of the forest and the forest animals.

ARTISTIC STYLE

Every artist has a style that distinguishes his or her artistic vision from that of other artists, serving as a signature of the distinct individual. Numerous individuals, however, gravitate toward similar ways of making visual statements through the use of line, color, shape, and texture. The many different styles of visual art identified by art critics

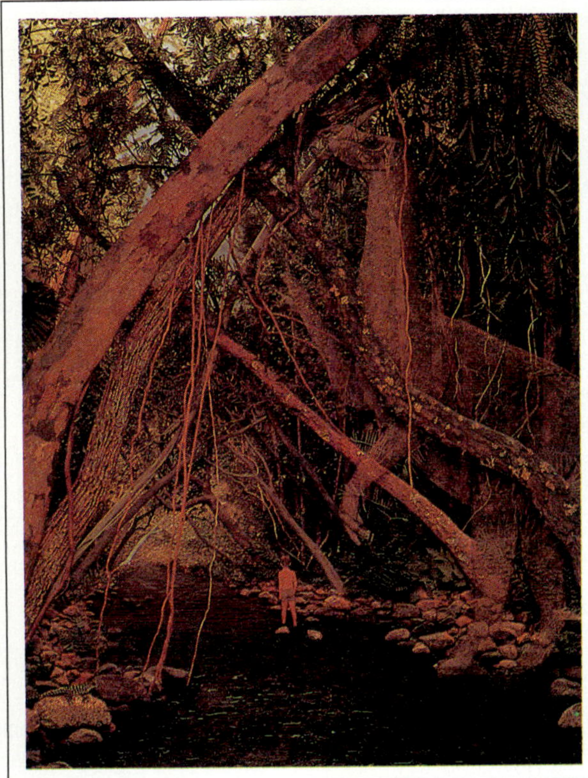

Natural and artificial materials create a strong feeling of texture. Illustration from *Where the Forest Meets the Sea* by Jeannie Baker. Copyright 1987 by Jeannie Baker. Reproduced by permission of Greenwillow Books, a division of William Morrow & Co.

and historians are too complex for this text to discuss in detail. For our purposes, however, we may consider two very general categories of artistic style, the *representational* and the *abstract*.

Representational Art

Representational art, sometimes also called realistic art, depicts subjects as they are seen in everyday life. Representational artists do not necessarily attempt to create photographically exact images of their subjects. Instead, they create compositions that clearly refer to people, objects, or natural phenomena in realistic ways. Many of the paintings and sculptures most familiar to us, such as Leonardo da Vinci's *Mona Lisa* and Auguste Rodin's *The Thinker* are representational in style.

Since the first books for children were illustrated, the pictures in most children's books have been representational, as examples show throughout this text. Realistic imagery helps children identify with and learn more about things in their environments, giving them familiar bases from which to expand their understandings of the world. In Susan Jeffers's line-and-wash illustrations for *Three Jovial Huntsmen,* for example, children can easily identify a leaf on the tip of a dog's tongue and two humans walking through the woods. At the same time, Jeffers's use of line encourages children to extend their visual perceptions in order to discover three deer hidden among the trees.

Lynd Ward's illustrations for *The Biggest Bear* are excellent examples of the use of representational art to create the details of a realistic story. Readers can almost feel the rough shingles and unpainted siding on the buildings, and the wheat looks ripe enough to harvest. When the bear cub runs in to claim the mash prepared for the

Collage and paint combine to create a shadowy, supernatural setting. (Illustration from *Shadow* by Marcia Brown. Illustrations © 1982 Marcia Brown. Reprinted with the permission of Charles Scribner's Sons.)

chickens, several frightened chickens look as if they will fly off the page.

Author-illustrator Holling Clancy Holling combines imaginative fiction with factual information in beautifully illustrated books that take their themes from North American history and geography. Holling's detailed realistic illustrations draw older children into both new adventure and new learning. In *Paddle-to-the-Sea,* a Native American boy in the Canadian wilderness carves a wooden canoe and "paddle person," which he launches on a journey from Lake Superior to the Atlantic Ocean. *Seabird* is an ivory gull carved by a young sailor on a whaling vessel. The gull accompanies several generations of one American family on their ocean voyages around the world. In each book, full-page realistic paintings in color encourage readers to enter the different settings of the story, while detailed black-and-white drawings on the text pages show, for example, how a sawmill turns logs into boards and how volcanoes in an ocean create islands.

Modern book illustrators, like most twentieth-century artists, have been profoundly influenced by stylistic innovations that have occurred over the last hundred years. Nineteenth-century French artist Claude Monet was among those who initiated a new approach to representational art, known as impressionism (originally a derogatory term applied by a disapproving contemporary critic). These artists departed from the tradition of representing the world in complex detail. Instead, they focused on the play of light over objects in the natural environment. Usually working from outdoor subjects, they experimented with breaking up colors and shapes to create an *impression* of the scintillating, changeable quality of light (17, p. 294).

Photographs of Monet's paintings and Monet's actual garden in Christina Bjork and Lena Anderson's *Linnea in Monet's Garden* permit comparisons between impressionistic drawings and natural settings. Four paintings of the bridge in Monet's garden, painted between 1899 and 1923, show how Monet's interpretation of light changed as his eyesight failed.

Thomas Locker's oil paintings for *Where the River Begins* reveal impressionist influences on this modern artist. Locker's magnificent landscapes shimmer with sunlight emerging through mist, the moon illuminating rushing water, and the reflection of sunset on billowing clouds.

Expressionism, a later stylistic development in representational art, uses visual elements to express an artist's deepest inner feelings. Expressionist paintings by such artists as Vincent van Gogh and Edvard Munch reverberate with the rhythm of intense emotion expressed through emphatic color, texture, and movement of line. Such art begins to move away from the representational into the more abstractly symbolic. (Later twentieth-century artists such as Jackson Pollock developed a style known as abstract expressionism.)

An oil painting reflecting impressionist style depicts a sunset landscape and a tranquil mood. (From *Sailing with the Wind* by Thomas Locker, copyright © 1986 by Thomas Locker. Reprinted by permission of the publisher, Dial Books for Young Readers.)

Expressionistic influences are vividly evident in Toshi Maruki's illustrations for her book *Hiroshima No Pika* (The Flash of Hiroshima). Maruki's uses of color and shape reinforce the emotional impact of horrific devastation, as a mother and child experience the aftereffects of the atomic bomb. Swirling red flames pass over the forms of fleeing people and animals. Black clouds cover the forms of huddling masses and destroyed buildings. A more realistic rendering of this holocaust would probably be far less powerful.

Leonard Fisher's expressionistic paintings complement the mood of Myra Livingston's poems in *A Circle of Seasons*. Whites and pinks suggest apple blossoms and dogtooth violets. Greens and yellows symbolize the warming sun, the rain, and awakening earth in spring. Hot sun reds, watery blues, and corn-ripened yellows seem appropriate for paintings accompanying summer poems, while the changing moods of autumn are suggested by oranges, reds, and shimmering frost against a dark blue sky. In winter paintings, white squares against shades of blue and purple suggest ice crystals and snowflakes converging on a bleak winter world. The wintery mood is enhanced as hoarfrost, icicles, and frosted windowpanes gleam in silvery needle shapes against a dark blue background.

Abstract Art

Some abstract art takes ordinary things as its subject but emphasizes certain characteristics of a subject by changing or distorting the usual image. Pablo Picasso's abstract paintings, for example, reduce people and familiar objects to angular forms and shifting planes. The work of other modern artists has become so abstract—focusing on pure form and representing no actual person, place, or thing—that art experts describe it as nonrepresentational. For example, Piet Mondrian's famous geometrical compositions in oil show the artist's attempts at visual statements that are "objective, impersonal, and universal" in their implications (17, p. 39).

The elimination of representational images characteristic of abstract art (14, p. 208) is evident in Beverly Brodsky McDermott's illustrations for *The Golem,* a Jewish legend about a rabbi who uses a magic spell to create a man out of clay. McDermott (12) says

> As I explored the mysteries of the Golem, an evolution took place. At first, he resembled something human. Then he was transformed. His textured body became a powerful presence lurking in dark corners, spilling out of my paintings. In the end he shatters into pieces of clay-color and returns to the earth. All that remains is the symbol of silence. (Foreword)

Both expressionist and abstract influences are apparent in Leo Lionni's illustrations. Lionni uses watercolor, textured collage, and thickly painted surfaces to recreate the feeling of a watery world in *Swimmy*. This is not a realistic world of easily discernible water plants and animals. Seaweed has the texture of painted doilies, and fish are only suggestive outlines. Vivid colors and strong shapes predominate in Lionni's *Pezzettino,* the story of a small orange shape who is convinced that he is a piece of someone else. Pezzettino's search takes him to larger shapes composed of many smaller squares of solid color.

a forest of seaweeds growing from sugar-candy rocks...

Muted colors and irregular shapes suggest an underwater kingdom. (Illustration by Leo Lionni from *Swimmy,* by Leo Lionni. Copyright © 1968 by Leo Lionni. Reprinted by permission of Pantheon Books, a division of Random House, Inc.)

Janice Hartwick Dressel (4) presents arguments for and against using abstract art in children's books. She concludes that exposing children to such sophisticated, symbolical art may encourage higher levels of thinking and enhance aesthetic response to all art.

EVALUATING THE ILLUSTRATIONS IN CHILDREN'S BOOKS

The collaborative process of creating a picture book for children makes special demands on an artist. Even when the illustrator and the author are the same person, the artist is a partner to the writer and must place his or her talents in the service of a certain story. Consider the following criteria when evaluating the illustrations in picture books for children:

1 The illustrator's use of visual elements—line, color, shape, texture—and of certain artistic media should complement the development of plot, characterization, setting, and theme in the text.
2 The design of the illustrations—individually and throughout an entire book—should reinforce the text and convey a sense of unity that stimulates aesthetic appreciation in viewers.
3 The artistic style chosen by the illustrator should enhance the author's literary style.
4 The illustrations should help the readers anticipate the unfolding of a story's action and climax.
5 The illustrations should convincingly delineate and develop the characters.
6 The illustrations should be accurate in historical, cultural, and geographical detail, and they should be consistent with the text.

Three-dimensional paper constructions provide depth for the illustrations. (From *Sing a Song of People* by Lois Lenski, and illustrated by Giles Laroche. Illustrations copyright 1987 by Giles Laroche. Reproduced with permission from Little, Brown and Company.)

OUTSTANDING ILLUSTRATORS OF CHILDREN'S BOOKS

A close look at several artists reveals the wide range of excellence in children's book illustration and the ways in which individuals fluent in artistic grammar create visual narratives that appeal to young children. The artists discussed in this chapter use the elements of line, color, shape, and texture to create memorable illustrations that highlight the moods of the texts. These illustrations provide numerous opportunities for both children and adults to interact with visual elements and to improve their appreciation of art.

Nancy Ekholm Burkert

According to Michael Danoff (2), Nancy Ekholm Burkert "is an artist whose work is rooted in the particulars of nature. Her drawings capture the specifics of the natural world with awe-inspiring precision and clarity. For her, the natural world is as miraculous as any realm of fantasy. . . . In her eyes, currents of the metaphysical flow through the particulars of the physical world; the natural is one with the super-natural" (p. 1).

Burkert uses pen, brush, and colored inks to express natural rhythms in a realistic style. Before illustrating *Snow White and the Seven Dwarfs,* a book-length version of the folktale told by the Brothers Grimm, Burkert visited Germany's Black Forest and read books about the Middle Ages. Consequently, Burkert's Snow White walks through a mysterious forest that viewers can almost smell and feel as sunlight filters down through the trees. The dwarfs' house is historically authentic in every detail: carved wood, pewter utensils, woven rugs, and a warm fireplace. (Burkert researched the details of this house at the Unterlinden Museum in Colmar, West Germany.) Realistic as these illustrations are, they also create a setting in which magic spells and poisoned apples do not seem out of place.

Burkert's detailed line and delicate color create a suitably magical mood in her illustrations for Eva LeGalliene's translation of Hans Christian Andersen's *The Nightingale*. The text tells that the emperor lives in a beautiful palace, built of finest porcelain, but so fragile that one must move carefully so as not to disturb it. In Burkert's illustrations, soft pink and white blossoms covering the trees and mist rising gently from the sea are the background for the detailed drawings of the palace. Burkert creates a unity for the whole

ISSUE

Are Children's Book Illustrators Creating Books for Adults Rather Than for Children?

ERIC A. KIMMEL[1] CONTENDS that a noticeable trend in children's literature is "the appearance of a growing number of exotically illustrated, high-priced picture books that appear to be far too unusual or sophisticated to attract many children" (p. 41). In this category of picture books he identifies Wayne Anderson's *Ratsmagic;* Chris Van Allsburg's *The Garden of Abdul Gasazi* and *Jumanji;* Molly Bang's *The Grey Lady and the Strawberry Snatcher;* Graham Oakley's *Magical Changes;* David Macauley's *Unbuilding;* most of Harlin Guin's books; and Maurice Sendak's *Outside Over There*.

Kimmel argues that books such as these are being written and illustrated to appeal to adult critics rather than to children. He speculates that children will ignore these books in favor of books by Ezra Jack Keats, Leo Lionni, and Tomie de Paola and books such as Virginia Lee Burton's *Mike Mulligan and His Steam Shovel,* Robert McCloskey's *Blueberries for Sal,* and Maurice Sendak's *Where the Wild Things Are*.

Students of children's literature may look at these books, talk to librarians about children's preferences, and share the books with children. How do children of different ages respond to the pictures and the text? Does the way in which adults share illustrated books with children affect how children respond to them? What do children like about the pictures and the text? What do you like about the pictures and the text?

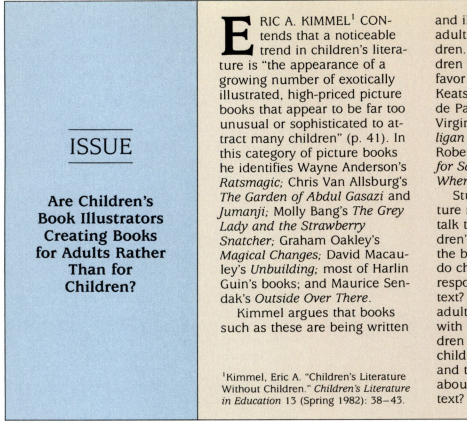

[1]Kimmel, Eric A. "Children's Literature Without Children." *Children's Literature in Education* 13 (Spring 1982): 38–43.

book by illustrating pages of text with blossoms, branches, and plants that gently curve around the margins.

Barbara Cooney

Barbara Cooney's illustrations for Donald Hall's *Ox-Cart Man* use gentle colors and rounded shapes to evoke the peaceful countryside of early nineteenth-century New England. Cooney creates the same mood in *Island Boy*; soft colors and curved landscapes add to the feeling of an unhurried way of life in which a young boy can explore the joys of his New England home. In Cooney's illustrations for *Chanticleer and the Fox,* however, bold black lines create a strutting, vain rooster in the earlier portion of the book and a frightened, humble one as the story reaches its climax in the life-and-death struggle between Chanticleer and his enemy, the fox.

Cooney is skilled in using artistic techniques that best complement a particular text. Her illustrations for Margot Griego et al.'s *Tortillitas Para Mama* re-create the varied settings associated with Spanish nursery rhymes. Warm browns depict the interior of a Mexican home, cool blues warmed by the shining moon suggest a village by the water, and warm fuchsia pinks reflect the warmth of a mother and father sharing a quiet time with their baby. Cooney uses Aztec colors to capture the settings in her illustrations for John Bierhorst's *Spirit Child: A Story of the Nativity*. The colors range from the strong reds and yellows used to depict volcanic eruptions and the dead land to the softer greens used to create a gentler setting for Mary and Jesus.

Color also creates an appropriate mood in Cooney's illustrations for Delmore Schwartz's *"I Am Cherry Alive," the Little Girl Sang*. Shades of gold depict the pleasure and well-being of a little girl who is observing a tree covered with autumn leaves, while a blue mood is reflected in a mist-covered valley seen by the light of a pale moon.

Tomie de Paola

Tomie de Paola has illustrated, or written and illustrated, over one hundred books, including traditional folktales from Italy, Scandinavia, and Mexico; informational books; realistic fiction; and Bible stories. De Paola's illustrations for *The Clown of God* reveal the influence of two pre-Renaissance artists, Giotto and Fra Angelico, whose simplicity and strength of line de Paola admires: "I almost reduce features to a symbol. And yet I think of my faces as good and warm. I try to show expression in very few lines" (6, p. 299). For *The Clown of God,* de Paola first penciled in the lines, then went over the sketches with raw sienna waterproof ink, a second brown pencil line, and brown ink. He completed the artwork with watercolors.

Strong, simple lines are also very important in de Paola's *Songs of the Fog Maiden*. The addition of cool blues and greens creates a mood in which a fog maiden could easily move from her day garden to her night one and accomplish magic along the way.

De Paola emphasizes that his great love of folk art is a strong element in his work. Consequently, he was inspired by the early works of Alice and Martin Provensen (18). Strong feelings of Americana are found in de Paola's *An Early American Christmas*. Many of de Paola's illustrations and texts reflect his belief that children and adults should be exposed to the rich heritage of ethnic folktales. In his illustrations for texts such as *The Legend of the Bluebonnet, The Legend of the Indian Paintbrush,* and numerous folktales from various European countries, de Paola combines folk art and folktale.

De Paola (6) also values his theater experience and makes use of it in his illustrations: "There are so many ways picture books are like theater-scenes, settings, characterization. A double page spread can be like a stage" (p. 300). De Paola's illustrations often have the symmetry of stage settings, with actions that appear to take place in front of a backdrop. *Giorgio's Village,* for example, a pop-up book that re-creates an Italian Renaissance village, is itself a stage-like setting in which windows open and tabs allow movement.

Other books show the influence of films. In *Watch Out for the Chicken Feet in Your Soup,* the action in the story and illustrations starts before the title page, which becomes part of both the narrative and the action. In these and other ways, de Paola's large body of work demonstrates his belief that children should be exposed to many types of visual imagery.

Leo and Diane Dillon

Leo and Diane Dillon's strong interest in the folklore of traditional peoples is evident in their beautifully illustrated, award-winning books. Their work reflects careful research into the decorative motifs of various cultures and helps re-create and preserve traditional ways of life.

The text for Mildred Pitts Walter's *Brother to the Wind* is rich in folklore, symbols, and dreams. The Dillons use light and dark, pastels, and deep colors to show the contrast between a boy's mythical quest to fly and the earthbound unbelievers who are sure he will fail. In one illustration, the wind, which makes it possible for the boy to

Emeke was so happy and excited he almost forgot to thank Good Snake as he hurried back to his goats.

Good Snake called after him. "Be sure you find the bark and bamboo before the rains come."

Turtle laughed. "He, he, he. Beware! Things without wings don't fly."

The dark heavy clouds threatened to overflow. Emeke hurried toward his goats, wondering how he would find bark and bamboo before it rained. He touched the rock and remembered: *The rock will help you.*

Contrasts between almost transparent colors and deeper shades enhance the mythical quality of a fantasy. Illustration by Leo and Diane Dillon from *Brother to the Wind* by Mildred Pitts Walter. Text copyright © 1985 by Mildred Pitts Walter. Illustration copyright © 1985 by Diane and Leo Dillon. By permission of Lothrop, Lee, & Shepard Books (a division of William Morrow & Company).

THROUGH THE EYES OF AN ILLUSTRATOR

Illustrating and Books

TOMIE DE PAOLA, illustrator of over one hundred books and winner of the Caldecott honor award, discusses early art experiences and the importance of doodling.

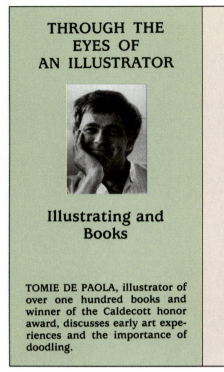

I AM A DOODLER. IN FACT, I *love* to doodle. I always have. I keep pads of scratch paper and black and red fine-line markers by the telephones, at my drawing table, on my desk, in my carry-on bag when I fly; and when I was teaching, I never went to a meeting (faculty, committee, etc.) without my handy pad and markers.

Growing up, coloring books were absent from our house . . . at least, in my room. My tools were plain paper, pencils, and my trusty Crayolas. After all, I was going to be an artist when I grew up. And besides, my own drawings and doodles seemed to be far more interesting to me, and those around me, than the simple coloring book images. (My mother also admitted recently that plain paper was lots cheaper.)

I learned at an early age that there was a definite difference between out-in-out drawing and serious doodling. A drawing had more structure, more direction. A definite idea was usually the beginning of a drawing. For example, I might say, "I think I will do a drawing of a girl ice skating, wearing a fancy Ice Follies-type costume." (Yes, the Ice Follies were around way back then.) Then the problem would be to try to do a drawing that coincided with my original idea or vision.

Doodles were (and are) totally different. I would just put pencil to paper and see what

fly, is a transparent woman whose color and shape blend into the pale cloudy sky. Viewers are given the impression that only they and the boy, not the doubting villagers, can see the wind.

The Dillons also use shades of black and white to contrast myth and reality in the illustrations for Virginia Hamilton's *The People Could Fly: American Black Folk Tales*. Their illustrations for Verna Aardema's *Why Mosquitoes Buzz in People's Ears* re-create the mood and setting of a traditional African folktale. In every case, careful research preceded the Dillons' illustrations.

Susan Jeffers

Susan Jeffers emphasizes texture and motion of line to convey differences between reality and fantasy in her realistic but magical illustrations. Her skilled use of line is especially apparent in her illustrations for Hans Christian Andersen's *The Wild Swans*. Strong lines depict forest, hillside, and stormy sea. More delicate, cross-hatched lines depict the sunshine and plants within the fragrant cedar grove. When a beautiful fairy enters the girl's dreams to guide her in freeing her brothers, Jeffers contrasts the reality of the characters sleeping on the ground and the fairyland of the palace in the clouds. The girl herself is in warm greens and browns, while the fairy and the fairy castle are almost transparent blues and grays.

Jeffers uses variety of line to depict similar distinctions of nature and the mythical spirit world in her illustrations for Henry Wadsworth Longfellow's *Hiawatha*. Other books in which Jeffers develops mood and setting through detailed line drawings include Robert Frost's *Stopping by Woods on a Snowy Evening,* the Grimms' *Hansel and Gretel,* Eugene Field's *Wynken, Blynken and Nod,* and Charles Perrault's *Cinderella,* adapted by Amy Ehrlich.

Ezra Jack Keats

Ezra Jack Keats combines collage, paint, and empathy for children's needs and emotions in compositions that portray inner-city life. Sometimes this environment is peaceful, as in *The Snowy Day,* where Keats uses brilliantly white torn paper to convey the snow covering chimneys and rooftops as Peter looks out on a fresh, white world. Later, shadowy blue footprints bring the text and the illustrations together, asking readers to look at Peter's footprints in the snow. Simple, rounded shapes depict snowbanks, and buildings are rect-

happened. All sorts of interesting images would result. I might start out not really concentrating on my doodle but on what else I was doing at the time. Talking on the phone was a very good activity for doodling. Late at night under the covers with a flashlight and listening to the radio was another activity that produced more terrific doodles—some actually on sheets rather than on paper. The "state of the art" doodles of this early period, though, appeared as if by magic on my arithmetic papers. There would be columns of figures copied from the blackboard and before I knew it, the paper would be covered with pictures with no room for the answers. My teachers—well, at least, a few of them—were *not* amused. They warned me. I'd never learn to add, subtract, multiply, etc. They were right, but for me as an artist, the doodling proved to be a far more important activity. I was able to buy a calculator with a royalty check, and now, I have an accountant.

"Meeting doodles," especially faculty meeting doodles, proved to be among the most valuable for me. It was during a college faculty meeting that was about the same issues the previous dozen meetings had been about, that "Strega Nona" appeared on my pad. I didn't know who she was at that moment, but a few months on my studio wall, and she soon let me know all about herself.

I've just opened a drawer and found some doodles that were done several years ago. (I stash doodles in different drawers so they can show up later and surprise me. My assistant saves all the phone-call doodles for me. My mother and an old friend both have doodles of mine in special drawers, waiting for the day they can cash in on them.)

The newfound doodles are on the wall of my studio. There is a rather fetching sheep and two classy cats, dressed to kill. Who knows . . . someday . . . . But remember! You read about them here first!

angles of color in the background. Peter's simple, red-clad figure stands out against the snowy background.

Keats evokes quite a different mood with collage and paint in *Goggles!* Here, two children confront harsher realities, as they try to escape from bigger boys who want their possessions. The colors are dark, and the collages include thrown-away items that one might find in back alleys. Keats shows the frightening big boys as almost featureless. In one picture, a hole in a piece of wood frames the scene as the two small boys look through it and plan how to get home. In other books—such as *Louie, The Trip,* and *Peter's Chair*—illustrations by Keats complement the loneliness, daydreams, or jealousy described in the text.

Joseph Schwarcz (21) believes that children respond to books by Keats, such as *Apt. 3,* because

> the illustrations dramatize the lyrical mood, probably also making it more easily accessible for the younger reader. The gestures and postures of the people in the story are down to earth, outspoken. The important visual motifs are the ones we know well. The apartment building is muddy and ugly. The large shapes of the boys, painted from a close angle, evoke intimacy. From the beginning there is visual metaphor. (p. 188)

Robert Lawson

It is highly unusual for one person to win both the Caldecott Medal for excellence in children's book illustration and the Newbery Award for excellence in children's literature. Author-illustrator Robert Lawson was the first person to achieve this distinction. Lawson's philosophy about illustrating children's books suggests the reasons for his success. According to Annette H. Weston (24), Lawson believed that adults should not condescend to children in either word or picture. Rather than having limited tastes or understanding, Lawson felt, children are actually less limited than adults: "They are, for a pitifully few short years, honest and sincere, clear-eyed and open minded. To give them anything less than the utmost that we possess of frankness, honesty and sincerity is, to my mind, the lowest possible crime" (24, p. 257).

Lawson's illustrations are both witty and honest. He researched Spanish landscapes, architecture, bullfighting, and costumes before illustrating Munro Leaf's *The Story of Ferdinand.* His black-and-white line drawings strongly complement an amusing story about the problems connected with being different, as a young bull prefers smelling flowers to preparing to fight in the bullring. At one point in the story, for example, Lawson uses powerful black lines to show Ferdinand finally acting like a fierce and energetic bull; but this occurs only because Ferdinand sits on a bee. Lawson's drawings ably convey the variety of emotions in the story, whether they are experienced by human characters or by Ferdinand himself. The matador struts with pride, the picadores cringe in terror, and Ferdinand simply sits in the ring refusing to fight until he can return to his favorite tree and flowers.

Robert McCloskey

Robert McCloskey's illustrations present the real world of boys, girls, families, and animals. Detailed black-and-white drawings depict the settings in most of his books, although McCloskey also uses color to evoke the essence of an island susceptible to forces of nature in *Time of Wonder*. In that book, McCloskey's watercolors first depict a serene world. When gentle rain approaches, the painting is so transparent that the first thing seen is a thin mist descending. Later, diagonal lines of raindrops break the surface of the peaceful water, and light fog surrounds two children as they experience the whispering sound of growing ferns. The island is not always serene, however. A hurricane bends the lines of the trees, as the illustrations themselves almost move on the page. McCloskey's use of line is so compelling that Lyn Ellen Lacy (8) uses page-by-page discussion of *Make Way for Ducklings* and *Time of Wonder* to analyze line in Caldecott Award-winning books.

Black-and-white drawings illustrate McCloskey's delightful *Blueberries for Sal*. The child, whether stealing berries from a pail or mistakenly following a mother bear instead of her own mother, looks as if she could walk right off the page.

Clare Turlay Newberry

Re-creating the many moods and motions of cats requires both a remarkable understanding of feline temperament and careful observation. Children often say that Clare Turlay Newberry must have watched cats for a long time in order to draw them so realistically and lovingly. The children are correct. In *Drawing a Cat* (15), Newberry explains that because cats do not stay in the same position for long, the artist must spend many hours observing and must draw hundreds of sketches before successfully capturing cats as she does in her humorous books.

Newberry's cat illustrations—such as the totally believable *Widget*—suggest the feeling of fur. Widget's fur is fluffy when she is calm and contented, but it stands on end in sharp spikes when danger in the form of a teddy bear or a dog named Pudge threatens her well-being. These effects result from painting with charcoal-gray watercolor on wet paper, then adding details with

The artist's black-and-white illustrations create a moment of surprise for human and animal characters. (Illustrations by Robert McCloskey from *Blueberries for Sal*. Copyright 1948, © renewed 1976 by Robert McCloskey. Reprinted by permission of Viking Penguin Inc.)

Maurice Sendak was inspired by the watercolors in William Blake's paintings in creating his illustrations for this book. (Illustrations from *Outside over There* by Maurice Sendak. Copyright © 1981 by Maurice Sendak. By permission of Harper & Row, Publishers, Inc.)

crayons after the paper is dry. While Newberry's illustrations are in grays, blacks, and browns, they forcefully demonstrate the text's characterization of the animals.

Alice and Martin Provensen

Color, symmetry, and effective use of space are noteworthy elements in the work of Alice and Martin Provensen. Recent illustrations by the Provensens, whose collaborative efforts include more than fifty books, reflect the world in earlier times or worlds of fantasy. The Provensens create a feeling of flying through space in their book about the first flight across the English Channel, *The Glorious Flight Across the Channel with Louis Bleriot, July 25, 1909*. Consecutive illustrations proceed from a close-up of the plane before it soars to a wide-angle view of the small plane surrounded by clouds and sky. The corresponding text reveals that Louis Bleriot is alone, lost in a world of swirling fog. The illustrators' use of space and color reinforces this mood of danger and exhilaration.

The impact of symmetry in design is felt in several of the Provensens' illustrations for Nancy Willard's *A Visit to William Blake's Inn: Poems for Innocent and Experienced Travelers*. In one illustration, for example, the Wonderful Car hovers over buildings that provide a visual center for the car; the steps of the flying vehicle lead viewers toward the passengers; and the two smaller sets of propeller blades balance the larger center blade.

Other books demonstrating the Provensens' skill in re-creating historical periods include *Birds, Beasts and the Third Thing: Poems by D. H. Lawrence; A Peaceable Kingdom; The Shaker Abecedarius; Shaker Lane;* and *Leonardo da Vinci*.

Maurice Sendak

Time magazine has called Maurice Sendak "the Picasso of children's books." Sendak's artistic versatility in using color, line, and balance to create evocative moods and settings is evident in the many books he has illustrated or written and illustrated, including Janice Udry's *The Moon Jumpers*. One of Sendak's primary aims in illustrating a text is to make "the pictures so organically akin to the text, so reflective of its atmosphere, that they look as if they could have been done in no other way. They should help create the special world of the story . . . creating the air for a writer" (13, p. 352).

This special relationship between text and illustration may be most apparent in Sendak's *Outside Over There* and *Where the Wild Things Are*. Sendak (3) has described the steps he took in creating the illustrations for *Outside Over There,* which he considers his best and most significant children's book. One of his first concerns was drawing ten-year-old Ida holding a baby. In order to produce realistic body postures, he made photographs of a child holding a baby. The baby kept slipping out of the child's arms, so that the clothes on both children drooped and became disheveled. These effects of body movements are replicated in the book's illustrations. Sendak referred to watercolors by the British poet and artist William Blake for inspiration in choosing colors that communicate the story's setting, mood, and characterization:

> The colors belong to Ida. She is rural, of the time in the country when winter sunsets have that certain yellow you never see in other seasons. There's a description of women's clothing, watered silk, and that's what those skies are like—moist, sensuous, silken, almost transparent—the color I copied in the cape Ida wears and in other things showing up against soft mauve, blue, green, tan—all part of the story's feeling. (p. 46)

The illustrations for *Where the Wild Things Are* are totally integrated with the text and play a crucial role in plot development and characterization, as well as setting. When Max is banished to his room for bad behavior, the room gradually becomes the kingdom of the wild things, with trees growing naturally out of the bedposts and the shag rug turning into grass. As the plot progresses, the illustrations cover more and more of the page; when Max becomes king of the wild things, six pages of illustrations are uninterrupted by text. Sendak's use of line creates a believably mischievous boy and humorous but forceful wild things with terrible rolling eyes and horrible gnashing teeth.

Similarities in illustrations may be found between Sendak's illustrations for *Outside over There* and *Dear Mili,* a tale by Wilhelm Grimm. Selma Lanes's *The Art of Maurice Sendak* (10) provides biographical information as well as examples from Sendak's numerous books. Sendak's *Posters by Maurice Sendak* (22) provides examples from many occasions. The posters also show how important wild things are in Sendak's art.

Peter Spier

In Peter Spier's illustrations, carefully drawn lines re-create each stone in the London Bridge, express the movement and tension of a battle at sea, fill Noah's ark with animals, or present the changing American scene in authentic historical detail.

Symmetry of design directs viewers toward the distant garden. (Illustration by Chris Van Allsburg from *The Garden of Abdul Gasazi*. Copyright 1979 by Chris Van Allsburg. Reprinted by permission of Houghton Mifflin Company.)

A clock struck midnight as
the elves roared their approval.
Santa handed the bell to me,
and I put it in my bathrobe
pocket. The conductor helped
me down from the sleigh.
Santa shouted out the reindeer's
names and cracked his whip.
His team charged forward and
climbed into the air. Santa
circled once above us, then
disappeared in the cold, dark
polar sky.

The glowing colors and contrasts between light and dark are appropriate for a children's fantasy. (Illustrations from *The Polar Express* by Chris Van Allsburg, copyright 1985 by Chris Van Allsberg. Reproduced with permission from Houghton Mifflin Co.)

Children find new details each time they look at Spier's *Noah's Ark.* Comparing an early drawing with a later one, for example, reveals that two snails are the last animals to board the ark and the last animals to leave. *The Fox Went Out on a Chilly Night* shows a country setting of farms, covered bridges, cemeteries, town squares, and colonial buildings. Spier illustrates the origins of our national anthem in *The Star-Spangled Banner,* with the drama and color of rockets glaring in the sky. All of Spier's illustrations are based on considerable research and touring of historic sites.

Spier uses pen-and-ink and full-color wash illustrations in a series of village books designed in the shape of buildings, such as supermarkets, schools, and fire stations. The detailed drawings in these books stimulate discussion as young children identify familiar objects and compare Spier's village with their own communities.

Chris Van Allsburg

Chris Van Allsburg's *The Garden of Abdul Gasazi, Jumanji,* and *The Mysteries of Harris Burdick* demonstrate the effectiveness of black-and-white illustrations. Both line and subtle shading focus attention along a visual pathway in the illustrations for *The Garden of Abdul Gasazi.* In one picture, the main character is framed by a central doorway. On either side of the doorway, a bright statue against dark leaves points down a black tunnel toward the circle of white. This circle represents the garden in which the story line develops. Such symmetry is one way artists create balance in their designs.

Van Allsburg's illustrations for *The Wreck of the Zephyr* are examples of the artist's use of line to create movement and of his use of line and color to convey mood. As the story begins, rolling waves and billowing dark clouds suggest movement and the ominous forces of angry sea and sky. Later, the mood changes to fantasy, and the artist uses color to create a calm sea sparkling with light, a fantasy harbor town seen through shadows, soft clouds tinged with sunset, and a star-studded sky. Compare Van Allsburg's use of line and shading in his black-and-white illustrations with his use of line and color in *The Wreck of the Zephyr, The Polar Express,* and *Swan Lake* (retold by Mark Helprin).

In *The Polar Express,* line creates the furry textures of lean wolves roaming the dark forests and the feathery texture of newly fallen snow. Even Santa Claus's beard and mittens seem to have texture. Van Allsburg's use of contrasting light and dark colors and shadings is especially effective. Moonlight focuses attention on the boy in his darkened bedroom, train windows glow with warmth as the train winds through cold forests and up snow-covered mountains, and city lights stream from windows to pierce the darkness.

Suggested Activities for Understanding Artists and Their Illustrations

- ☐ With some of your peers, select one of the following criteria for evaluating the illustrations and narrative portions of a picture book, find books that clearly exemplify the criteria, and share them with the class:
  - **a** The illustrations help readers anticipate both the action of the story and the climax (for example, Richard Egielski's illustrations for Arthur Yorinks's *Hey, Al* or Maurice Sendak's illustrations for *Where the Wild Things Are*).
  - **b** The pictures help create the basic mood of the story (for example, Paul Goble's *The Girl Who Loved Wild Horses* or Marcia Brown's illustrations for Charles Perrault's *Cinderella*).
  - **c** The illustrations portray convincing characters (for example, Taro Yashima's *Crow Boy*).
  - **d** All pictures are accurate and consistent with text (for example, Barbara Cooney's illustrations for Donald Hall's *Ox-Cart Man*).
- ☐ Consider the ways in which lines are related to natural phenomena. Look carefully at the illustrations in several books. Are there examples in which vertical lines suggest lack of movement, horizontal lines suggest calmness or an absence of strife, vertical and horizontal lines connected at the top suggest stability and safety, diagonal lines suggest motion, and jagged lines symbolize danger?
- ☐ Select a fairy tale, such as "Cinderella" or "Snow White," that has been illustrated by several artists. Compare the artists' use of line, color, and shape to create mood and setting.
- ☐ Read the narrative portion of several picture storybooks. Evaluate whether or not the dominant images in the illustrations complement the emphasis in the texts. Choose an example that complements the text and one that does not. Share the examples and your rationales for choosing them with the class.
- ☐ With a group of your peers, select one medium available to artists, such as woodcuts, collage, inks, watercolors, acrylics, pastels, and so forth. Investigate how different artists use the medium in picture-book illustrations. Share your findings with the class.
- ☐ With some of your peers, investigate how artists use representational and abstract artistic styles. Consider the styles used by the illustrators of several picture books. In each case, does the style complement the intended mood of the text? Share your findings with the class.
- ☐ Choose an outstanding illustrator of children's books. Find as many of the illustrator's works as you can. Analyze the artist's use of the elements of art—line, color, shape, and texture—and the various media and styles used by the artist. Compare the books. Does the artist use a similar style in all works, or does the style change with the subject matter of the text? Compare earlier works with later ones. Are there any changes in the use of artistic elements, style, or media?
- ☐ Read a book about an illustrator, such as the San Diego Museum of Art's *Dr. Seuss from Then to Now* (19), Selma Lanes's *The Art of Maurice Sendak* (10), or Bill Peet's *Bill Peet's Autobiography*. How has the work of the illustrator changed? What motivated the illustrator to work in children's book illustration? What impact has the illustrator had on young readers? If possible, discover how the illustrator's background influenced his or her work.

References

1 Borgman, Harry. *Art and Illustration Techniques*. New York: Watson-Guptill, 1979.

2 Danoff, Michael. Quoted in *The Art of Nancy Ekholm Burkert*, edited by David Larkin. New York: Harper & Row, 1977.

3 Davis, Joann. "Trade News: Sendak on Sendak." As told to Jean F. Mercier. *Publishers Weekly* (April 10, 1981): 45–46.

4 Dressel, Janice Hartwick. "Abstraction in Illustration: Is It Appropriate for Children?" *Children's Literature in Education* 15 (Summer 1984): 103–112.

5 Feldman, Edmund Burke. *Varieties of Visual Experience*. New York: Abrams, 1972.

6 Hepler, Susan Ingrid. "Profile, Tomie de Paola: A Gift to Children." *Language Arts* 56 (March 1979): 269–301.

7 Kingman, Lee. "Virginia Lee Burton's Dynamic Sense of Design." *Horn Book* 46 (October 1970): 449–460.

8 Lacy, Lyn Ellen. *Art and Design in Children's Picture Books: An Analysis of Caldecott Award-Winning Illustrations*. Chicago: American Library Association, 1986.

9 Laliberté, Norman, and Alex Mogelon. *The Reinhold Book of Art Ideas*. New York: Van Nostrand Reinhold, 1976.
10 Lanes, Selma. *The Art of Maurice Sendak*. New York: Abradale Press, 1980.
11 MacCann, Donnarae, and Olga Richard. *The Child's First Books: A Critical Study of Pictures and Texts*. New York: Wilson, 1973.
12 McDermott, Beverly Brodsky. *The Golem*. Philadelphia: Lippincott, 1976.
13 Moritz, Charles. *Current Biography Yearbook*. New York: Wilson, 1968.
14 Munro, Thomas. *Form and Style in the Arts: An Introduction to Aesthetic Morphology*. Cleveland: Case Western Reserve, 1970.
15 Newberry, Clare Turlay. *Drawing a Cat*. London: The Studio Limited, 1940.
16 Nodelman, Perry. *Words About Pictures*. Athens: University of Georgia Press, 1988.
17 Preble, Duane. *Art Forms*. New York: Harper & Row, 1978.
18 Rudman, Masha Kabakow. "People Behind the Books: Illustrators." In *Children's Literature: Resource for the Classroom,* edited by Masha Kabakow Rudman. Needham Heights, Mass.: Christopher Gordon, 1989.
19 San Diego Museum of Art. *Dr. Seuss from Then to Now*. New York: Random House, 1986.
20 Schoenherr, John. "Caldecott Medal Acceptance." *Horn Book* 64 (July/August 1988): 457–459.
21 Schwarcz, Joseph. *Ways of the Illustrator: Visual Communication in Children's Literature*. Chicago: American Library Association, 1982.
22 Sendak, Maurice. *Posters by Maurice Sendak*. New York: Harmony Books, 1986.
23 Shulevitz, Uri. *Writing with Pictures: How to Write and Illustrate Children's Books*. New York: Watson-Guptill, 1985.
24 Weston, Annette H. "Robert Lawson: Author and Illustrator." *Elementary English* 47 (January 1970): 74–84.

CHILDREN'S LITERATURE

Aardema, Verna. *Why Mosquitoes Buzz in People's Ears*. Illustrated by Leo and Diane Dillon. Dial, 1975 (I:5–9 R:6) An African cumulative tale tells the humorous reason for mosquitoes' buzzing.

Ackerman, Karen. *Song and Dance Man*. Illustrated by Stephen Gammell. Knopf, 1988 (I:3–8 R:4). Grandpa re-creates the magic of vaudeville for his grandchildren.

Andersen, Hans Christian. *The Nightingale*. Retold by Eva LeGalliene. Illustrated by Nancy Ekholm Burkert. Harper & Row, 1968 (I:6–12 R:8). The fairy tale is beautifully illustrated.

———. *The Wild Swans*. Retold by Amy Ehrlich. Illustrated by Susan Jeffers. Dial, 1981 (I:7–12 R:7). Finely detailed illustrations develop a fantasy setting.

Anno, Mitsumasa. *Anno's Britain*. Philomel, 1982 (I:all). A wordless book illustrates a traveler's journey throughout Great Britain.

———. *Anno's Italy*. Collins, 1980 (I:all). A wordless book illustrates a traveler's journey throughout Italy.

Aruego, Jose, and Ariane Dewey. *We Hide, You Seek*. Greenwillow, 1979 (I:2–6). Colors and lines create a camouflage book that allows children to look for hidden animals.

Baker, Jeannie. *Where the Forest Meets the Sea*. Greenwillow, 1988 (I:4–10). An Australian forest comes to life through the collage technique.

Baker, Olaf. *Where the Buffaloes Begin*. Illustrated by Stephen Gammell. Warne, 1981 (I:8+ R:7). Illustrations with soft, irregular shapes add power to a Native American legend.

Bemelmans, Ludwig. *Madeline*. Viking, 1939, 1977 (I:4–9 R:5). Madeline lives in Paris with eleven other little girls and has an appendectomy.

———. *Madeline in London*. Viking, 1961, 1977 (I:4–9 R:3). Madeline and eleven little girls visit London.

Bierhorst, John, trans. *Spirit Child: A Story of the Nativity*. Illustrated by Barbara Cooney. Morrow, 1984 (I:8–10 R:6). Pre-Columbian style illustrations accompany an Aztec story.

Bjork, Christina. *Linnea in Monet's Garden*. Illustrated by Lena Anderson. Farrar, Straus & Giroux, 1987 (I:all R:6). Photographs show Monet's paintings and garden.

I = Interest by age range.
R = Readability by grade level.

Brooke, L. Leslie. *Johnny Crow's Garden*. Warne, 1903, 1986 (I:all). A personified animal tale is considered a classic in children's book illustration.

Brown, Marcia. *Once a Mouse*. Scribner's Sons, 1961 (I:3–7 R:6). Woodcuts provide powerful illustrations for a fable from India.

Bunting, Eve. *Ghost's Hour, Spook's Hour*. Illustrated by Donald Carrick. Clarion, 1987 (I:2–7 R:2). A boy experiences fear when the lights go out and he cannot find his parents.

Burton, Virginia Lee. *The Little House*. Houghton Mifflin, 1942 (I:3–7 R:3). Repetition creates a sense of rhythm in illustrations.

Carle, Eric. *Catch the Ball*. Philomel, 1982 (I:3–6). A string attached to a ball encourages vocabulary development in children.

———. *Eric Carle's Animals Animals*. Philomel, 1989 (I:3–9). Collage illustrations accompany an anthology of poetry.

———. *The Honeybee and the Robber: A Moving/Picture Book*. Philomel, 1981 (I:3–6). A brightly colored pop-up allows children to move the wings of a bee and a butterfly.

———. *Let's Paint a Rainbow*. Philomel, 1982 (I:3–6). Rainbow colors help children learn eight basic colors.

———. *The Very Hungry Caterpillar*. Crowell, 1971 (I:2–7). A colorful collage picture book presents the life cycle of a caterpillar, who eats his way through the pages.

Cendrars, Blaise. *Shadow*. Illustrated by Marcia Brown. Scribner's Sons, 1982 (I:all). A highly illustrated version of an African poem is about the world of spirits.

Chaucer, Geoffrey. *Canterbury Tales*. Adapted by Barbara Cohen. Illustrated by Trina Schart Hyman. Lothrop, Lee & Shepard, 1988 (I:8+). Illustrations are framed in a formal manner.

Cooney, Barbara. *Chanticleer and the Fox*. Adapted from Geoffrey Chaucer. Crowell, 1958 (I:5–10 R:4). Chanticleer the rooster and a sly fox trick each other.

———. *Island Boy*. Viking Kestrel, 1988 (I:3–8 R:3). Text and illustrations show an earlier time on a New England island.

———. *The Little Juggler*. Adapted and illustrated by Cooney. Hastings, 1982 (I:all). An orphan offers his juggling talent as a Christmas gift to the Virgin Mary.

Crane, Walter. *Baby's Opera*. Warne, 190?, Simon & Schuster, 1981 (I:all). This is a reprint of a classic in illustration.

Crossley-Holland, Kevin. *Beowulf*. Illustrated by Charles Keeping. Oxford, 1982 (I:10+ R:6). Strong lines depict the power of a heroic character.

de Paola, Tomie. *Big Anthony and the Magic Ring*. Harcourt Brace Jovanovich, 1979 (I:5–9 R:3). Big Anthony uses Strega Nona's magic ring to turn himself into a handsome young man.

———. *Charlie Needs a Cloak*. Prentice-Hall, 1973 (I:3–6 R:4). A simple information book tells in a humorous way how a shepherd shears sheep, cards and spins wool, weaves and dyes the cloth, and then sews a cloak.

———. *The Clown of God*. Harcourt Brace Jovanovich, 1978 (I:all R:4). A legend tells about a juggler and a miracle.

———. *An Early American Christmas*. Holiday House, 1987 (I:4–7 R:6). A text and illustrations depict Christmas with a New England family living in the early 1800s.

———. *The Friendly Beasts: An Old English Christmas Carol*. Putnam, 1981 (I:3–8 R:2). The Christmas carol is illustrated in large colorful drawings.

———. *Giorgio's Village*. Putnam, 1982 (I:all). A pop-up book illustrates an Italian Renaissance village.

———. *Helga's Dowry: A Troll Love Story*. Harcourt Brace Jovanovich, 1977 (I:5–9 R:4). Helga leaves the world of trolls to earn a dowry.

———. *The Legend of the Bluebonnet*. Putnam, 1983 (I:all R:6). In a Commanche tale, unselfish actions are rewarded.

———. *The Legend of the Indian Paintbrush*. Putnam, 1987 (I:all R:6). A Native American tale tells about the beginning of a wildflower.

———. *Songs of the Fog Maiden*. Holiday House, 1979 (I:3–8 R:5). The fog maiden lives in a castle between the sun and the cold.

———. *Watch Out for the Chicken Feet in Your Soup*. Prentice-Hall, 1974 (I:3–7 R:2). Joey is embarrassed by his grandmother's old-fashioned ways until his friend shows great admiration for her.

———. *When Everyone Was Fast Asleep*. Holiday House, 1976 (I:3–8 R:6). The fog maiden's cat brings two children out into an enchanted night.

Emberley, Barbara. *Drummer Hoff*. Illustrated by Ed Emberley. Prentice-Hall, 1967 (I:3–7 R:6). A cumulative rhyme depicts in woodcuts all the people associated with firing a cannon.

Esbensen, Barbara. *The Star Maiden*. Illustrated by Helen Davie. Little, Brown, 1988 (I:all). Illustrations reinforce the Ojibway origins of the tale.

Fatio, Louise. *The Happy Lion*. Illustrated by Roger Duvoisin. McGraw-Hill, 1954 (I:3–7 R:7). A lion who lives in a zoo discovers that people aren't so friendly when he visits them in town.

Field, Eugene. *Wynken, Blynken and Nod*. Illustrated by Susan Jeffers. Dutton, 1982. The classic poem appears in a newly illustrated edition.

Fleischman, Sid. *The Scarebird*. Illustrated by Peter Sis. Greenwillow, 1988 (I:7+ R:4). An old man's loneliness is changed by friendship.

Frost, Robert. *Stopping by Woods on a Snowy Evening*. Illustrated by Susan Jeffers. Dutton, 1978 (I:all). This is a highly illustrated version of the poem.

Gág, Wanda. *Millions of Cats*. Coward, McCann, 1928 (I:3–7 R:3). An old woman's desire for a pretty cat results in a fight among trillions of cats.

———. *Snow White and the Seven Dwarfs*. Coward, McCann, 1938 (I:5–9 R:6). This is the popular fairy tale.

———. *Tales from Grimm*. Coward, McCann, 1936 (I:6–9 R:4). Sixteen tales from Grimm include "Hansel and Gretel," "Rapunzel," and "The Frog Prince."

Goble, Paul. *The Girl Who Loved Wild Horses*. Bradbury, 1978 (I:6–10 R:5). An American Indian girl loves wild horses, joins them in a flight during a storm, and finally goes to live with them.

Greenaway, Kate. *A—Apple Pie*. Castle, 1979 (I:all). This is a reissue of a classic in illustration.

Griego, Margot C., Betsy L. Bucks, Sharon S. Gilbert, and Laurel H. Kimball. *Tortillitas Para Mama and Other Spanish Nursery Rhymes*. Illustrated by Barbara Cooney. Holt, Rinehart & Winston, 1981 (I:3–7). Nursery rhymes appear in Spanish and English.

Grimes, Nikki. *Something on My Mind*. Illustrated by Tom Feelings. Dial, 1978 (I:all). Beautifully illustrated poems tell about the joys, fears, hopes, and sorrows of growing up.

Grimm, Brothers. *Hansel and Gretel*. Illustrated by Susan Jeffers. Dial, 1980 (I:5–9 R:6). Illustrations convey the dark mood of this classic folk tale.

———. *Hansel and Gretel*. Retold by Rika Lesser. Illustrated by Paul O. Zelinsky. Dodd, Mead, 1984 (I:all R:6). The folktale appears in another beautifully illustrated version.

———. *Little Red Riding Hood*. Illustrated by Trina Schart Hyman. Holiday House, 1983 (I:6–9 R:7) Richly bordered text pages add to the visual effect.

———. *Rumpelstiltskin*. Retold and illustrated by Paul O. Zelinsky. Dutton, 1986 (I:all). Oil paintings add a glowing mood to the tale.

———. *Snow White and the Seven Dwarfs*. Illustrated by Nancy Ekholm Burkert. Farrar, Straus & Giroux, 1972 (I:7–12 R:6). Carefully researched illustrations complement this fairy tale.

Grimm, Wilhelm. *Dear Mili*. Translated by Ralph Manheim. Illustrated by Maurice Sendak. Farrar, Straus & Giroux, 1988 (I:all R:6). This story was found in a letter written in 1816.

Haley, Gail E. *A Story, a Story*. Atheneum, 1970 (I:6–10 R:6). An African tale tells about a spider man's bargain with Sky God.

Hall, Donald. *Ox-Cart Man*. Illustrations by Barbara Cooney. Viking, 1979 (I:3–8 R:5). Subtle illustrations complement a tale about a New England farmer in the early 1800s.

Hamilton, Virginia. *The People Could Fly: American Black Folktales*. Illustrated by Leo and Diane Dillon. Knopf, 1985 (I:9+ R:6) Black-and-white illustrations reinforce the folktale quality of the book.

Helprin, Mark. *Swan Lake*. Illustrated by Chris Van Allsburg. Houghton Mifflin, 1989 (I:all R:8). The text is a retelling of the classic ballet.

Hendershot, Judith. *In Coal Country*. Illustrated by Thomas Allen. Knopf, 1987 (I:5–9 R:3). The artist and author depict growing up in an Ohio coal town.

Hodges, Margaret. *Saint George and the Dragon*. Illustrated by Trina Schart Hyman. Little, Brown, 1984 (I:9+ R:7). The classic tale is beautifully illustrated.

Holling, Holling Clancy. *Paddle-to-the-Sea*. Houghton Mifflin, 1941 (I:7–12 R:4). A Native American boy carves a canoe and places it where it will flow into Lake Superior.

———. *Seabird*. Houghton Mifflin, 1948 (I:7–12 R:4). A carved gull travels with several generations of one family.

Hughes, Ted. *Under the North Star*. Illustrated by Leonard Baskin. Viking, 1981 (I:all). Poems about northern animals come with realistic illustrations.

Jeffers, Susan. *Three Jovial Huntsmen*. Bradbury, 1973 (I:4–8). The nursery rhyme is highly illustrated.

Keats, Ezra Jack. *Apt. 3*. Macmillan, 1974 (I:3–8 R:3). A young boy and a blind man interact in a rundown apartment building.

———. *Dreams*. Macmillan, 1974 (I:3–8 R:3). Everyone dreams about Robert's handmade mouse.

———. *Goggles!* Macmillan, 1969 (I:5–9 R:3). Two boys escape from bullies.

———. *Louie*. Greenwillow, 1975 (I:3–8 R:2). Other children surprise Louie with a puppet.

———. *Peter's Chair*. Harper & Row, 1967 (I:3–8 R:2). Peter overcomes jealousy about a new baby sister.

———. *Regards to the Man in the Moon*. Four Winds, 1981 (I:4–8 R:3). Two children build a spaceship out of junk and take an imaginary ride.

———. *The Snowy Day*. Viking, 1962 (I:2–6 R:2). Peter experiences a great snowfall.

———. *The Trip*. Greenwillow, 1978 (I:3–8 R:2). Louie is lonesome in a new neighborhood.

Krauss, Ruth. *A Hole Is to Dig*. Illustrated by Maurice Sendak. Harper & Row, 1952 (I:2–6 R:2). Illustrations of children depict children's definitions for such things as brothers, mud, and mountains.

Lawrence, D. H. *Birds, Beasts and the Third Thing: Poems by D. H. Lawrence*. Illustrated by Alice and Martin Provensen, Viking, 1982 (I:all). Illustrations depict English scenes from Lawrence's youth.

Lawson, Robert. *Ben and Me*. Little, Brown, 1939 (I:7–11 R:6). Amos Mouse tells the story of his friend Benjamin Franklin.

———. *Rabbit Hill*. Viking, 1944 (I:7–11 R:7). Will the new humans on the hill be friends or enemies to the animals that live there?

Leaf, Munro. *The Story of Ferdinand*. Illustrated by Robert Lawson. Viking, 1936 (I:4–10 R:6). Ferdinand proves that he'd rather smell the flowers than fight the matador.

Lear, Edward, and Ogden Nash. *The Scroobious Pip*. Illustrated by Nancy Ekholm Burkert. Harper & Row, 1968 (I:all). The humorous poem is beautifully illustrated.

LeGalliene, Eva. *The Nightingale*. A retelling of Hans Christian Andersen's tale. Illustrated by Nancy Ekholm Burkert. Harper & Row, 1965 (I:6–12 R:8). An emperor learns that a live nightingale is preferable to a jeweled mechanical bird.

Lenski, Lois. *Sing a Song of People*. New York: Little, Brown, 1987.

Lent, Blair. *Bayberry Bluff*. Houghton Mifflin, 1987 (I:3–8 R:6). A town evolves from a tenting community to elaborately decorated houses.

Lionni, Leo. *Alexander and the Wind-up Mouse*. Pantheon, 1969 (I:3–6 R:3). A real mouse envies a lovable windup mouse.

———. *A Color of His Own*. Random House, 1975 (I:2–7 R:5). In an animal fable, the chameleon looks for his own color.

———. *Pezzettino*. Pantheon, 1975 (I:2–6 R:3). Pezzettino, or Little Piece, is so small that he believes he must be a piece of someone else.

———. *Swimmy*. Pantheon, 1963 (I:2–6 R:3). A little fish learns about the marvels of the sea.

Livingston, Myra Cohn. *A Circle of Seasons*. Illustrated by Leonard Everett Fisher. Holiday House, 1982 (I:all). Poems look at the four seasons.

Lobel, Arnold. *Fables*. Jonathon Cape, 1980 (I:all). Literary fables are created by the author.

Locker, Thomas. *Where the River Begins*. Dial, 1984 (I:all). Full-page paintings complement a search for the source of a river.

Longfellow, Henry Wadsworth. *Hiawatha*. Illustrated by Susan Jeffers. Dial, 1983 (I:all). The poem is beautifully illustrated.

———. *Hiawatha's Childhood*. Illustrated by Errol LeCain. Farrar, Straus & Giroux, 1984 (I:all). Excerpts appear from Longfellow's longer poem.

McCloskey, Robert. *Blueberries for Sal*. Viking, 1948 (I:4–8 R:6). A little girl mistakes a bear for her mother.

———. *Lentil*. Viking, 1940 (I:4–9 R:7). Lentil saves a homecoming celebration.

———. *Make Way for Ducklings*. Viking, 1941 (I:4–8 R:4). A city park provides a safe home for the ducklings.

———. *One Morning in Maine*. Viking, 1952 (I:4–8 R:3). Sal and her family live on an island.

———. *Time of Wonder*. Viking, 1957 (I:5–8 R:4). A family confronts a hurricane on its island.

McCurdy, Michael. *The Devils Who Learned to Be Good*. Little, Brown, 1987 (I:6–9 R:6). Wood engravings illustrate a Russian tale.

McDermott, Beverly Brodsky. *The Golem*. Lippincott, 1976 (I:9–14 R:5). Illustrations capture the magic spell that creates the Golem from a lump of clay.

McDermott, Gerald. *Arrow to the Sun*. Viking, 1974 (I:3–9 R:2). Strong shapes and colors complement a Native American tale.

———. *Sun Flight*. Four Winds, 1980 (I:all R:6). Daedalus the master craftsman and his son construct wings and escape from Crete.

MacLachlan, Patricia. *The Sick Day*. Illustrations by William Pène Du Bois. Pantheon, 1979 (I:2–7 R:2). Father and Emily entertain each other when they get sick.

Martin, Eva. *Canadian Fairy Tales*. Illustrated by Laszlo Gal. Douglas & McIntyre, 1984 (I:7–16 R:4). Fairy tales are illustrated in realistic detail.

Martin, Rafe. *Will's Mammoth*. Illustrated by Stephen Gammell. Putnam, 1989 (I:2–7). A child has a make-believe ride on a mammoth.

Martin, Sarah Catherine. *The Comic Adventures of Old Mother Hubbard and Her Dog*. Illustrated by Tomie de Paola. Harcourt Brace Jovanovich, 1981 (I:3–7). One nursery rhyme is humorously illustrated.

Maruki, Toshi. *Hiroshima No Pika*. Lothrop, Lee & Shepard, 1982 (I:8–12 R:4). A powerfully illustrated story reveals the horror of the atomic bomb.

Matthews, Downs. *Polar Bear Cubs*. Photographs by Dan Guravich. Simon & Schuster, 1989 (I:4–10 R:4). The photographs and text follow two bear cubs and their mother.

Moore, Clement. *The Night Before Christmas*. Illustrated by Tomie de Paola. Holiday House, 1980 (I:all). The popular poem is brightly illustrated.

Mosel, Arlene. *Tikki Tikki Tembo*. Illustrated by Blair Lent. Holt, Rinehart & Winston, 1968 (I:5–9 R:7). A Chinese folktale explains why Chinese children now have shorter names.

Murphy, Shirley Rousseau. *Tattie's River Journey*. Illustrated by Tomie de Paola. Dial, 1983 (I:5–8 R:5). A flood takes Tattie, her house and her animals to a new location.

Musgrove, Margaret. *Ashanti to Zulu: African Traditions*. Illustrated by Leo and Diane Dillon. Dial, 1976 (I:7–12). Traditions of twenty-six African peoples are presented in alphabetical order.

Newberry, Clare Turlay. *Marshmallow*. Harper & Row, 1942 (I:2–7 R:7). Oliver the cat has a new rabbit roommate.

———. *Widget*. Harper & Row, 1958. (I:2–7 R:6). Realistic drawings capture the image of a cat.

Noyes, Alfred. *The Highwayman*. Illustrated by Charles Keeping. Oxford, 1981 (I:10+). Strong black-and-white drawings complement the mood of the poem.

Onassis, Jacqueline, ed. *The Firebird and Other Russian Fairy Tales*. Illustrated by Boris Zvorykin. Viking, 1978 (I:8–14 R:3). Four Russian fairy tales are retold in a beautifully illustrated edition.

Peet, Bill. *Bill Peet's Autobiography*. Houghton Mifflin, 1989 (I:all R:5). This text is highlighted with numerous drawings by Peet.

Perrault, Charles. *Cinderella*. Adapted by Amy Ehrlich. Illustrated by Susan Jeffers. Dial, 1985 (I:5–8 R:4). Large, detailed illustrations accompany a simplified version of the fairy tale.

———. *Cinderella*. Illustrated by Marcia Brown. Harper & Row, 1954 (I:5–8 R:5). Fine lines suggest the mood of the fairy tale.

Piatti, Celestino. *The Happy Owls*. Atheneum, 1964 (I:3–7 R:4). The owls try to explain why they are happy; a group of fowls does not understand.

Pope, Joyce. *Kenneth Lilly's Animals: A Portfolio of Paintings*. Illustrated by Kenneth Lilly. Lothrop, Lee & Shepard, 1988 (I:all). Textured paintings add to the appeal of an informational book.

Provensen, Alice, and Martin Provensen. *The Glorious Flight Across the Channel with Louis Bleriot, July 25, 1909*. Viking, 1983 (I:all R:4). An account of the first flight across the English Channel is highly illustrated.

———. *Leonardo da Vinci*. Viking, 1984 (I:all R:8). A pop-up book describes Leonardo da Vinci's accomplishments.

———. *A Peaceable Kingdom: The Shaker Abecedarius*. Viking, 1978 (I:all). A Shaker ABC is newly illustrated.

———. *Shaker Lane*. Viking, 1987 (I:5–9 R:3). Illustrations show changing society along a street.

Ransome, Arthur. *The Fool of the World and the Flying Ship*. Illustrated by Uri Shulevitz. Farrar, Straus & Giroux, 1968 (I:6–10 R:6). Lines and warm colors focus attention in a Russian tale about a simple lad who overcomes enormous obstacles.

Rosen, Michael. *We're Going on a Bear Hunt*. Illustrated by Helen Oxenbury. Macmillan, 1989 (I:2–6). Large illustrations accompany a favorite story for young children.

Ryder, Joanne. *White Bear, Ice Bear*. Illustrated by Michael Rothman. Morrow, 1989 (I:3–8 R:4). In an imaginative story, a young boy changes into a polar bear.

Scheer, Julian. *Rain Makes Applesauce*. Illustrated by Marvin Bileck. Holiday House, 1964 (I:3–8). The illustrations combine with a poetic text.

Schwartz, Delmore. *"I Am Cherry Alive," The Little Girl Sang*. Illustrated by Barbara Cooney. Harper & Row, 1979. An illustrated poem is about a little girl who is celebrating being alive.

Sendak, Maurice. *In the Night Kitchen*. Harper & Row, 1970 (I:5–7). A young child dreams himself into a night world.

———. *Outside over There*. Harper & Row, 1981 (I:5–8 R:5). Goblins steal a baby sister.

———. *Where the Wild Things Are*. Harper & Row, 1963 (I:4–8 R:6). Max is very mischievous and very imaginative.

Seuss, Dr. *The 500 Hats of Bartholomew Cubbins*. Vanguard, 1938 (I:4–9 R:4). A bewitched hat keeps reappearing.

Shannon, George. *Dance Away*. Illustrated by Jose Aruego and Ariane Dewey. Greenwillow, 1982 (I:2–6). Line and color complement the repetitive language as a rabbit outwits a hungry fox.

Simon, Seymour. *Jupiter*. Morrow, 1985 (I:all R:7). Photographs enhance this informational book.

Singer, Isaac B. *Zlateh the Goat*. Illustrated by Maurice Sendak. Harper & Row, 1966 (I:6–10 R:6). This is a collection of Jewish folktales.

Spier, Peter. *The Erie Canal*. Doubleday, 1970 (I:all). The folk song is illustrated.

———. *The Fox Went Out on a Chilly Night*. Doubleday, 1961. (I:all). The folk song is highly illustrated.

———. *London Bridge Is Falling Down!* Doubleday, 1967 (I:5–12). The nursery rhyme is illustrated in detail.

———. *My School*. Doubleday, 1981 (I:3–7). Activities are associated with a school.

———. *Noah's Ark*. Doubleday, 1977 (I:3–9). This is a detailed, almost wordless book.

———. *The Pet Store*. Doubleday, 1981 (I:3–7). Drawings detail a pet store.

———. *The Star-Spangled Banner*. Doubleday, 1973. (I:8+). Our national anthem is illustrated.

———. *Tin Lizzie*. Doubleday, 1975 (I:7–12 R:6). Illustrations cover the history of an old car.

———. *The Toy Shop*. Doubleday, 1981 (I:3–7). Drawings detail a toy store.

Steig, William. *The Amazing Bone*. Farrar, Straus & Giroux, 1976 (I:6–9 R:5). A pig and a talking bone escape from robbers and a hungry fox.

Steptoe, John. *The Story of Jumping Mouse*. Lothrop, Lee & Shepard, 1984 (I:all R:4). Steptoe's illustrations convey the softness of a butterfly's wing and the sharpness of bristling cacti in this Great Plains Indian legend about a mouse who wanted to visit the far-off land.

Tejima, Keizaburo. *Fox's Dream*. Philomel, 1987 (I:all). A fox's dream transforms the icy winter woods.

Udry, Janice May. *The Moon Jumpers*. Illustrated by Maurice Sendak. Harper & Row, 1959 (I:3–9 R:2). Colors create a mood as children go out to play in the moonlight.

Van Allsburg, Chris. *The Garden of Abdul Gasazi*. Houghton Mifflin, 1979 (I:5–8 R:5). A boy has a magical experience in a magician's garden.

———. *Jumanji*. Houghton Mifflin, 1981 (I:5–8 R:6). An unusual game creates a jungle environment.

———. *The Mysteries of Harris Burdick*. Houghton Mifflin, 1984. (I:all). Pictures encourage children to solve mysteries.

———. *The Polar Express*. Houghton Mifflin, 1985 (I:5–8 R:6). Glowing illustrations accompany an original Christmas story.

———. *The Wreck of the Zephyr*. Houghton Mifflin, 1983 (I:5–8 R:6). A boy tries to become the greatest sailor in the world.

Viorst, Judith. *Alexander and the Terrible, Horrible, No Good, Very Bad Day*. Illustrated by Ray Cruz. Atheneum, 1972 (I:3–8 R:6). Nothing goes right for Alexander.

Walter, Mildred Pitts. *Brother to the Wind*. Illustrated by Diane and Leo Dillon. Lothrop, Lee & Shepard, 1985 (I:all R:3). An original story set in Africa tells about a young boy who wishes to fly.

Ward, Lynd. *The Biggest Bear*. Houghton Mifflin, 1952 (I:5–8 R:4). A boy wants a bearskin to hang on his barn.

Wildsmith, Brian. *Brian Wildsmith's ABC*. Watts, 1963 (I:3–6). A word and a picture are shown for each letter.

———. *Hunter and His Dog*. Oxford, 1979 (I:3–7 R:3). A hunting dog cares for wounded ducks.

Willard, Nancy. *A Visit to William Blake's Inn: Poems for Innocent and Experienced Travelers*. Illustrated by Alice and Martin Provensen. Harcourt Brace Jovanovich, 1981 (I:all). Poems describe a menagerie of guests.

Wood, Audrey. *King Bidgood's in the Bathtub*. Illustrated by Don Wood. Harcourt Brace Jovanovich, 1985 (I:6–9 R:1). The story tells of a humorous predicament.

Yagawa, Sumiko. *The Crane Wife*. Translated by Katherine Paterson. Illustrated by Suekichi Akaba. Morrow, 1981 (I:all R:6). A traditional Japanese tale expresses the dangers of greed.

Yashima, Taro. *Crow Boy*. Viking, 1955 (I:4–8 R:4). A lonely outcast at school gains respect and self-confidence.

———. *Umbrella*. Viking, 1958 (I:3–7 R:7). Momo receives an umbrella for her third birthday and then waits impatiently for the rain to come.

Yolen, Jane. *Owl Moon*. Illustrated by John Schoenherr. Philomel, 1987 (I:all). A poetic story follows father and son as they search for owls in the winter woods.

Yorinks, Arthur. *Hey, Al*. Illustrated by Richard Egielski. Farrar, Straus & Giroux, 1986 (I:all). A janitor discovers that his home is better than he thinks.

Young, Ed, translated by. *Lon Po Po: A Red-Riding Hood Story from China*. Philomel, 1989 (I:all R:5). The girls outwit the wolf in this version.

Zolotow, Charlotte. *Mr. Rabbit and the Lovely Present*. Illustrated by Maurice Sendak. Harper & Row, 1962 (I:3–8 R:2). With the help of a rabbit, a little girl searches for a gift for her mother's birthday.

A B C

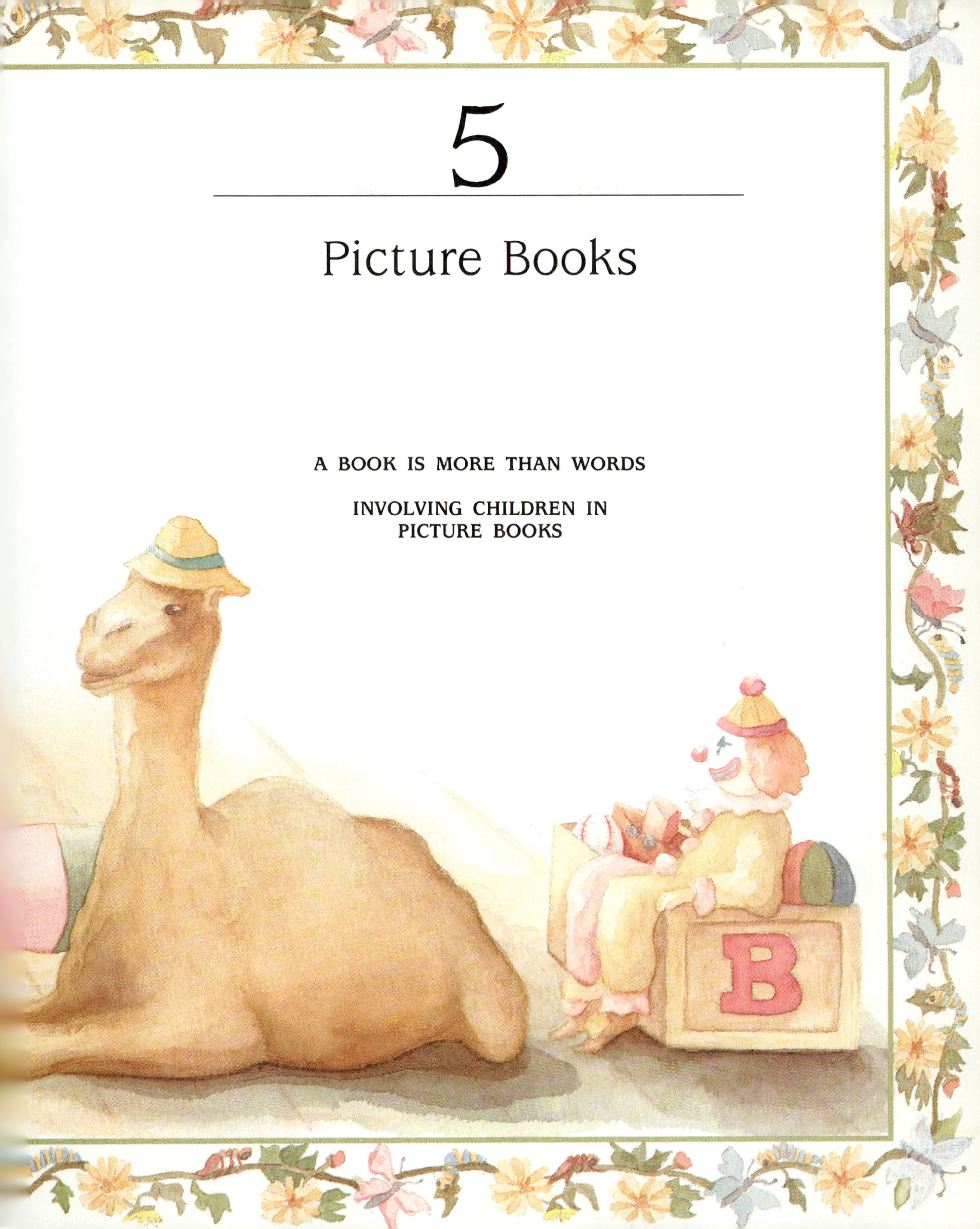

5

Picture Books

A BOOK IS MORE THAN WORDS

INVOLVING CHILDREN IN PICTURE BOOKS

A Book Is More Than Words

THE THOUGHT OF A CHILD, A LAP, AND A picture book arouses warm feelings and recollections in many adults. When a loving adult provides opportunities for a child to experience the enchantment found in picture books, both the child and the adult benefit.

The books included in the genre of picture books have many values in addition to pleasure. The rhythm, rhyme, and repetition in nursery rhymes stimulate language development as well as auditory discrimination and attentive listening skills in young children. Alphabet books reinforce ability to identify letter/sound relationships and help expand vocabularies. Concept books enhance intellectual development by fostering understanding of abstract ideas. Wordless books encourage children to develop their observational skills, descriptive vocabularies, and abilities to create stories characterized by logical sequence. Illustrations found in picture books stimulate sensitivity to art and beauty. Well-written picture storybooks encourage children to appreciate literary style. All of these values give picture books very important roles in children's development.

WHAT A PICTURE BOOK IS

Most children's books are illustrated, but not all illustrated children's books are what we call picture books. As Perry Nodelman (6) pointed out, picture books "communicate information or tell stories through a series of many pictures combined with relatively slight texts or no texts at all" (p. VII, preface).

Zena Sutherland and Betsy Hearne (9) stress that in picture books, the illustrations are as important as the text or even more important than the text. Because children respond to stories told visually as well as verbally, some picture books are quite effective with no words at all. Many picture books, however, maintain a balance between the illustrations and the text, so that neither is completely effective without the other.

Thus the term *picture books* covers a wide variety of children's books, ranging from Mother Goose books and toy books for very young children to picture storybooks with plots that satisfy more experienced, older children. Many of the picture books discussed in this chapter rely heavily upon illustrations to present content. In some, each scene or rhyme is illustrated. Other books, with more complex verbal story lines, are not so dependent upon pictures to develop their plots.

Many picture books have a characteristic not shared by other children's books: The writer and the illustrator may be the same person. Well-known artists often create picture books. This chapter emphasizes authors, or author-illustrators, and their literature.

EVALUATING PICTURE BOOKS

Because the text and the illustrations in picture books should complement each other, consider the relationships between the words and pictures when evaluating a picture book. Betsy Hearne (4) recommends that evaluators also "think complexity versus clutter, originality versus banality, loving versus cute, strong versus ponderous, and deepened versus decorated. Think of what you'd like to hang on the wall of your mind" (p. 577). The following questions can help you select high-quality picture books for children.

1 Are the illustrations accurate, and do they correspond to the content of the story?
2 Do the illustrations complement the setting, plot, and mood of the story?
3 Do the illustrations enhance characterization?
4 Do both the text and illustrations avoid stereotypes of race and sex?
5 Will the plot appeal to children?
6 Is the theme worthwhile?
7 What is the purpose for sharing this book with children or recommending that they read it?
8 Are the author's style and language appropriate for the children's interests and age levels?
9 Are the text, the illustrations, the format, and the typography in harmony?

Educators, researchers, and authorities in children's literature are increasingly interested in children's responses to picture books and in the characteristics of picture books that appeal to children. You should consider children's own evaluations when selecting picture books to share with children.

Peggy Whalen-Levitt (10) emphasizes the roles that a child's age and experience play in determining the child's response to a picture book. The first interactions of a very young child with a picture book are largely physical, as the child investigates the size, shape, texture, and moving parts of the unfamiliar object. The child may stick the book into his or her mouth to become acquainted with it or turn the pages even if the book is upside down. With adult guidance, the child soon learns the specific purposes and pleasures associated with books and responds to the symbolic nature of books, focusing on the content of the pictures and connecting illustrated objects and concepts with the sounds and names given to them. The child quickly begins to assume that books will contain stories.

As a sense of time develops, a child begins to see connections among past, present, and future in pictures and text and to expect that a story will have a beginning, a middle, and an end. Finally, after considerable time and experience with both books and everyday living, a child evaluates book text and illustrations in terms of his or her own view of reality and his or her own feelings and desires. Thus, different types of books and book-related experiences are appropriate for children at different ages and stages of development.

Patricia Cianciolo (2) identified four major factors that influence how a child perceives and evaluates the illustrations in picture books: (1) the child's age and stage of cognitive and social development; (2) the way in which an adult has (or has not) prepared the child for the experience with a picture book; (3) the child's emotional state of readiness; and (4) the number of times the child looks at the illustrations.

Cianciolo's analysis of picture books listed in the Children's Choices also reveals that children prefer illustrations that depict here-and-now situations, fantasies of all kinds, and humorous exaggerations and slapstick; illustrations that are colorful and add more detail to the text's descriptions of characters, action, and setting; and illustrations that are drawn in either a realistic or a cartoon-like style. Such preferences may help adults select picture books for children, but Cianciolo stresses that adults can and should also use books and book-related activities to teach children "how to be more evaluative and discriminating in their selections" (p. 28).

MOTHER GOOSE

Mother Goose rhymes are the earliest literature enjoyed by many young children; the rhymes, rhythms, and pleasing sound effects of these jingles appeal to young children, who are experimenting with their own language patterns, and aid children's language development. A brief review of the basic characteristics of nursery rhymes indicates why children enjoy them, as well as why they encourage language development in children.

FLASHBACK

Mother GOOSE's Melody. 37

JACK and *Gill*
Went up the Hill,
To fetch a Pail of Water;
Jack fell down
And broke his Crown,
And *Gill* came tumbling after.

Maxim.

The more you think of dying, the better you will live.

ARISTOTLE'S

38 Mother GOOSE's Melody.

ARISTOTLE'S STORY.

THERE were two Birds ſat on a Stone,
Fa, la, la, la, lal, de; [one,
One flew away, and then there was
Fa, la, la, la, lal, de;
The other flew after,
And then there was none,
Fa, la, la, la, lal, de;
And ſo the poor Stone
Was loft all alone,
Fa, la, la, la, lal, de.

This may ſerve as a Chapter of Conſequence in the next new Book of Logick.

AN EARLY EDITION of Mother Goose rhymes, *The Original Mother Goose's Melody,* was first printed in London by John Newbery in 1760. (The first known English nursery rhyme book for children, *Tommy Thumb's Song Book for All Little Masters and Misses,* was published in London in 1744.) Many experts believe that the poet and author Oliver Goldsmith collected the rhymes and prepared them for the press.

Thomas Carnan, John Newbery's stepson, secured the copyright for the Newbery Mother Goose in 1780. The rhymes, which contained maxims or morals, were popular in both Great Britain and North America. Soon after the American Revolution, Isaiah Thomas of Worcester, Massachusetts, copied many of Newbery's books, including *The Original Mother Goose's Melody*. In the early 1800s, the printers Munroe and Francis of Boston published a Mother Goose edition that closely resembled John Newbery's version.

Appealing Characteristics

The rhythm in many nursery rhymes almost forces children to react. For example, children may clap their hands or jump up and down to the rhythm of this jingle:

Handy dandy, Jack-a-Dandy
Loves plum cake and sugar candy;
He bought some at a grocer's shop
And out he came, hop, hop, hop.

Rhyme is another aspect of many nursery verses that children enjoy. Rhyming words, such as *dandy* and *candy, shop* and *hop,* invite children to join in and add the rhyming word or make up their own rhymes. Rhymes enhance the adventures of many favorite characters: "Little Miss Muffet sat on a tuffet"; "Jack and Jill went up the hill"; "Bobby Shafto's gone to sea, Silver buckles on his knee." Many verses rhyme at the end of each line, but some verses also use internal rhyming elements: "Hickory, dickory, dock, the mouse ran up the clock"; "Rub, a dub, dub, three men in a tub." To test the influence of these rhyming verses, ask older children to share one of their favorite Mother Goose rhymes. They can probably say several although they may not have heard or recited them for years.

Children also respond to the repetition of sounds in a phrase or line of a nursery rhyme. Alliteration, the repetition of an initial consonant in consecutive words, creates phrases that children enjoy repeating just to experience the marvelous feelings that result from the repetition of beginning sounds: "One misty, moisty, morning"; "Sing a song of sixpence"; "Diddle, diddle dumpling." Sentences that contain a great deal of alliteration become tongue twisters. Children love the challenge of this jingle:

Peter Piper picked a peck of pickled peppers.
A peck of pickled peppers Peter Piper picked.
If Peter Piper picked a peck of pickled peppers,
Where's the peck of pickled peppers Peter Piper picked?

Humor is another great appeal of Mother Goose verses for children.

Hey, diddle, diddle!
The cat and the fiddle,
The cow jumped over the moon;
The little dog laughed
To see such sport,
And the dish ran away with the spoon.

This verse is an example of hyperbole, the use of exaggeration for effect, which is common in Mother Goose rhymes. Children appreciate exaggerated, ridiculous situations, such as an old woman's living in a shoe with so many children she doesn't know what to do, a barber's trying to shave a pig, or Simple Simon's going for water with a sieve:

He went for water with a sieve,
But soon it ran all through:
And now poor Simple Simon
Bids you all adieu.

Both good and bad little girls and boys live in Mother Goose land. In fact, the same children may be both good and bad, and these characters have a strong appeal for young children, who are also good and bad at different times. Nursery rhymes often depict good children as going to bed when they should. Little Fred is one ideal child:

When little Fred went to bed,
He always said his prayers,
He kissed mamma and then pappa,
And straightway went upstairs.

Good children are also kind to animals:

I like Little Pussy,
Her coat is so warm,
And if I don't hurt her
She'll do me no harm;
So I'll not pull her tail,
Nor drive her away,
But Pussy and I
Very gently will play.

Not all children, however, are so nice to animals:

Ding, dong, bell,
Pussy's in the well!
Who put her in?
Little Tommy Green.
Who pulled her out?
Little Johnny Stout.
What a naughty boy was that,
To try to drown poor pussy cat,
Who never did him any harm.
But killed the mice in his father's barn!

Animals themselves may also portray naughty behavior in nursery rhymes. The raven is certainly bad when he attacks a farmer and his daughter who are riding a mare:

A raven cried croak! and they all tumbled down,
Bumpety, bumpety, bump!
The mare broke her knees, and the farmer his crown,
Lumpety, lumpety, lump!
The mischievous raven flew laughing away,
Bumpety, bumpety, bump!
And vowed he would serve them the same the next day,
Lumpety, lumpety, lump!

While nursery rhymes may not explicitly state which behavior is good or bad, children have no difficulty identifying which is which and empathizing with the characters that display it.

Collections

The many different collections of Mother Goose rhymes contain more or less the same verses, but their formats, sizes, and illustrations are quite different. Some editions contain several hundred verses in large-book format, while others have fewer verses and are small enough for a young child to hold. Some editions have illustrations reminiscent of eighteenth-century England, while others have modern illustrations. Many adult students in American university classes prefer the Mother Goose editions with settings in the England of the 1600s and 1700s—either reissues of the original early editions or editions first published in the twentieth century.

Two popular early editions, John Newbery's *The Original Mother Goose's Melody* and Kate Greenaway's *Mother Goose: Or, the Old Nursery Rhymes,* continue to be reissued. Newbery's edition may be of greater interest to adults than to children (the text contains a history of Mother Goose), although many older children enjoy looking at the early orthography in Newbery's edition and comparing the verses and illustrations with twentieth-century editions, which do not share Newbery's tendency to add a moral to the close of each nursery rhyme. In Newbery's edition, for example, "Ding, dong, bell, the cat is in the well," is followed by this maxim: "He that injures one threatens a Hundred" (p. 25).

TOMMY was a silly boy.
"I can fly," he said;
He started off, but very soon
He tumbled on his head.
His little sister Prue was there,
To see how he would do it;
She knew that, after all his boast,
Full dearly Tom would rue it!
KG

Kate Greenaway was an influential illustrator of children's books in the 19th century. (From *Kate Greenaway's Mother Goose*, copyright © 1988. Reprinted by permission of Dial Books for Young Readers.)

The edition illustrated by the well-known author-illustrator Kate Greenaway was first published in 1881. Greenaway's book is a small text suitable for sharing with one child. She illustrates the nursery rhymes with pictures of delicate children that appeal to the sentiments of most readers.

Collections assembled by Iona and Peter Opie provide older children and adults with an opportunity to examine early illustrated versions of Mother Goose. *A Nursery Companion* is a large, highly illustrated collection of nursery rhymes originally published in the early 1800s. The *Oxford Nursery Rhyme Book* contains 800 rhymes categorized according to contents. Black-and-white woodcuts, from both earlier editions and newly created works, illustrate this large volume. An informative preface and a list of sources for the illustrations increase the usefulness for those who wish to study early editions of nursery rhymes. *Tail Feathers from Mother Goose: The Opie Rhyme Book* is a collection of lesser-known rhymes, many of which are previously unpublished. The rhymes are illustrated by contemporary artists. *The Glorious Mother Goose,* a collection of Mother Goose rhymes by Cooper Edens, is another source for analyzing earlier illustrations. The text is illustrated with works by such artists as Randolph Caldecott, Walter Crane, and Kate Greenaway.

Marguerite De Angeli's Book of Nursery and Mother Goose Rhymes is a twentieth-century edition. It contains illustrations of appealing children in nineteenth-century English settings. In the foreword to her book, De Angeli describes how her illustrations were influenced by her English grandfather, who read nursery rhymes aloud to her when she was a child. De Angeli's illustrations show the flowering fields, blossoming hedgerows, stone walls, castles, and cobblestone streets of an earlier, rural England, with smiling, frolicking children reminiscent of Kate Greenaway's. This large book contains 376 rhymes. Several verses are printed on each page.

Arnold Lobel's *Gregory Griggs and Other Nursery Rhyme People* contains rhymes about lesser-known characters, such as Theophilus Thistle, the successful thistle sifter; Gregory Griggs, who had twenty-seven different wigs; Charley, Charley, who stole the barley; Michael Finnegan, who grew a long beard right on his chinnigan; and Terence McDiddler, the three-stringed fiddler. The language and strong rhyming patterns in these verses make the book appropriate for reading aloud. The humorous, nonsensical rhymes are enriched by Lobel's pastel illustrations. Each rhyme is illustrated with a large picture, making it especially good for sharing with a group of children. Lobel's *The Random House Book of Mother Goose* is a collection of 306 rhymes. The illustrations emphasize Lobel's ability to create humorous situations in pictures.

The placement of illustrations next to the matching nursery rhyme, the large-page format, and the humorous folk-art illustrations make *Tomie dePaola's Mother Goose* especially appealing to younger children. The series of pictures that accompany multiple verses illustrate the sequential development in longer rhymes, such as "Simple Simon." The plots of some of the rhymes are extended through the illustrations. For example, the illustrations accompanying "Jack and Jill" show the actions on a marionette stage.

Wallace Tripp's humorously illustrated *Granfa' Grig Had a Pig and Other Rhymes Without Reason from Mother Goose* depicts many of the characters as animals. The series of pictures that illustrate some longer rhymes may stimulate oral language activities, especially those developing sequential order.

Picture Books That Illustrate One Rhyme or Tale

Children often want to know more about their favorite nursery rhyme characters. The humor and simple plots found in nursery rhymes lend themselves to expansion into picture storybook format. Picture storybook versions of Mother Goose rhymes may stimulate creative interpretations, as children think about what might happen if they expanded and illustrated the plots in other nursery rhymes. Each verse of Sarah Josepha Hale's *Mary Had a Little Lamb* has several full-page color illustrations of nineteenth-century farm and school settings by Tomie dePaola.

Humorous illustrations and large-book format provide an appealing volume for young children. (Illustration reprinted by permission of G. P. Putnam's Sons from *Tomie dePaola's Mother Goose*. Copyright © 1985 by Tomie dePaola.)

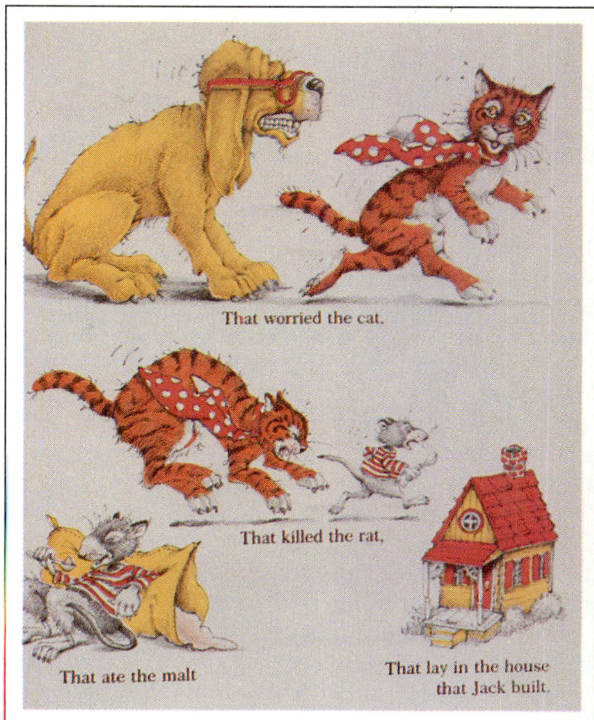

The illustrator enhances the language of a cumulative tale by repeating the illustrations. (Illustrations copyright © 1985 by Janet Stevens. Reprinted from *The House That Jack Built* by permission of Holiday House.)

Janet Stevens enhances the cumulative quality of *The House That Jack Built* by repeating the illustrations as well as the text. As the cumulative tale progresses, smaller versions of the brightly colored, humorous illustrations are repeated with each additional character.

Two illustrated texts reflect the authors' and illustrators' desires to extend story lines beyond those found in Mother Goose rhymes. John Ivimey's text and Paul Galdone's illustrations for *The Complete Story of the Three Blind Mice* reveal how the mice lost their sight as well as tails. This version has a happy ending, as the mice regain their sight and tails and become "three wise mice." Sarah Hayes's text and Charlotte Voake's illustrations for *Bad Egg: The True Story of Humpty Dumpty* show the egg challenging both horses and men to sit on the wall.

Susan Ramsay Hoguet's *Solomon Grundy* extends the nursery rhyme through historical illustrations. The illustrations allow readers and viewers to visualize what life was like in the United

States at an earlier time. This Solomon Grundy is born in 1836 and is buried in 1910 near the church in which he was christened.

Nursery Rhymes in Other Lands

Traditional nursery rhymes and jingles for children are found in many different lands. The language and style may differ from the English Mother Goose, but the content of all nursery rhymes is amazingly alike. Nursery rhymes everywhere tell about good and bad children, wise and foolish people, animals, and nature. The multicultural nature of nursery rhymes is emphasized with a collection of Chinese nursery rhymes that were adapted and illustrated by Demi. The rhymes in *Dragon Kites and Dragonflies* are illustrated with drawings that depict an ancient culture. Illustrations show kites, emperors, dragons, boats, dancers, weavers, acrobats, and pagodas.

Robert Wyndham has translated Chinese nursery rhymes into English versions that are designed to appeal to English-speaking readers and listeners. *Chinese Mother Goose Rhymes* are about dragons, Buddhas, carriage chairs, the Milky Way, and lady bugs, which seem to fascinate children of many nationalities. Each of the sprightly rhymes is shown in both English and Chinese, with a simple, colorful drawing to illustrate it. Turning games and nonsense words are well represented, as they are in English nursery rhymes.

> Gee lee, gu lu, turn the cake,
> Add some oil, the better to bake.
> Gee lee, gu lu, now it's done;
> Give a piece to everyone. (p. 40 unnumbered)

N. M. Bodecker has translated and illustrated Danish nursery rhymes in *It's Raining, Said John Twaining*. Wooden shoes and royalty are common characters in the Danish verses. Like English verses, Danish nursery rhymes use rhyming elements, tongue-twisting nonsense words, and riddles. The names of some characters in the rhymes, such as Skat Skratterat Skrat Skrirumskrat, appeal to the love of young children for nonsense and alliterative sounds. Each rhyme in this book is illustrated with a colorful, full-page picture.

Margot C. Griego et al. have collected nursery rhymes and lullabies from Mexico and Spanish-

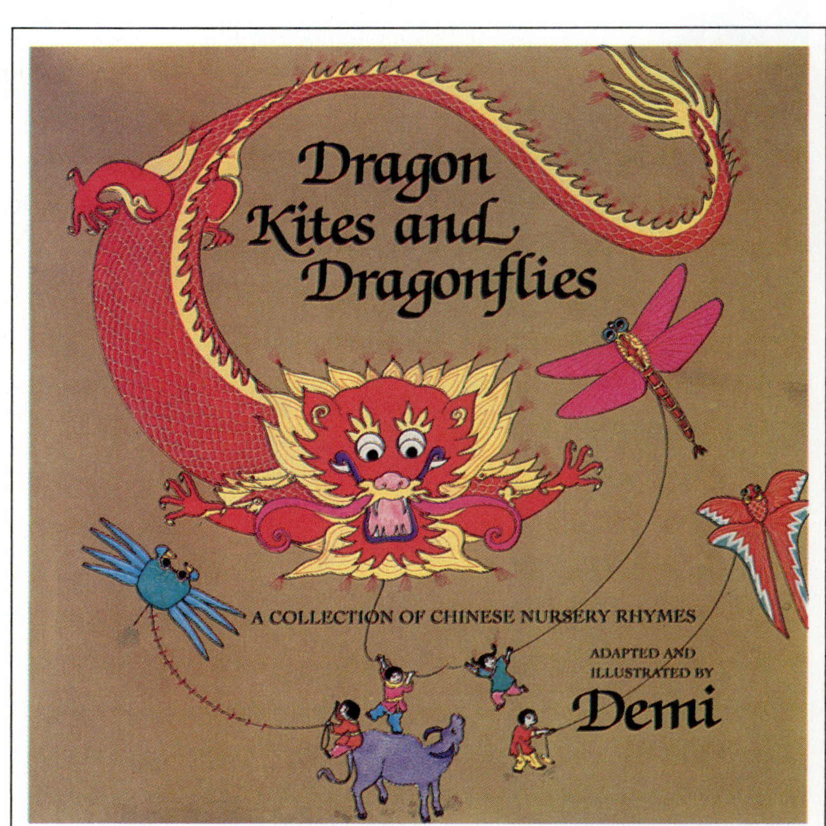

The illustrations reinforce the Chinese settings for the nursery rhymes. (Cover illustration from *Dragon Kites and Dragonflies* copyright © 1986 by Demi. Reprinted by permission of Harcourt Brace Jovanovich, Inc.)

speaking communities in the United States. *Tortillitas Para Mama and Other Spanish Nursery Rhymes* contains finger plays, counting rhymes, and clapping rhymes written in both Spanish and English.

Nursery rhymes from many nations are important contributions to our cultural heritage. They foster the self-esteem and language skills of the children who are members of ethnic minorities in the United States and help all American children appreciate the values and contributions of cultures other than their own.

TOY BOOKS

An increasing number and variety of toy books, including board books, pop-up books, flap books, cloth books, and plastic books, entice young children into interacting with stories, developing their vocabularies, counting, identifying colors, and discussing book content with adults. These books are valuable additions to children's literature because they stimulate the language, cognitive, personal, and social development of preschool children. They also provide happy experiences with books that, ideally, extend into later childhood and adulthood. Board books range in content from identifying a baby's clothing to describing typical experiences at school or in a doctor's office.

Some of Helen Oxenbury's board books are especially appropriate for younger children. In five appealing books in a series, *Dressing, Family, Friends, Playing,* and *Working,* each page contains an easily identifiable picture of a baby's actions as he or she gets dressed, interacts with family members, or accomplishes a new skill. Another book by Oxenbury, *I Hear,* identifies sounds within the environment.

Oxenbury's "Out-and-About Books" are excellent for slightly older children, who are curious about and sometimes fearful of the world outside their homes. For example, *The Checkup* presents a humorous account of a child's visit to a doctor. All of Oxenbury's books should stimulate discussion about activities that are important in the lives of most children.

Board books help children understand their expanding experiences and environments. A series of board books that uses familiar items and one simple object per page is illustrated by Zokeisha. *Things I Like to Eat, Things I Like to Look At, Things I Like to Play With,* and *Things I Like to Wear* enhance vocabulary identification of familiar objects. Nancy Tafuri uses a similar approach in *One Wet Jacket* and *Two New Sneakers*.

Three "Sam" board books, written by Barbro Lindgren and illustrated by Eva Eriksson, encourage language development through identification of objects and discussion of actions. In these books, a young boy takes a bath, plays with friends, and experiences accidents at home. A humanized rabbit provides similar subjects for discussion and enjoyment in *Max's Bath, Max's Bedtime, Max's Birthday,* and *Max's Breakfast,* which are by Rosemary Wells.

Kate Duke's board book *What Bounces?* encourages experimentation, while *The Playground* (also by Kate Duke) stimulates identification of playground equipment and discussion of actions. *Anno's Faces,* by Mitsumasa Anno, encourages identification of fruits and vegetables and experimentation with facial expressions. In *Anno's Faces,* children can move plastic strips with frowns or smiles across the illustrations. Several board books develop concepts related to counting and seasonal changes. For example, *Max's Toys: A Counting Book,* by Rosemary Wells, develops simple concepts related to numbers. *Mouse House Months,* by Helen Craig, shows a tree as it goes through its seasonal changes.

Pop-up books may introduce children to beloved storybook characters, tell simple stories, or create fascinating three-dimensional settings. *The Peter Rabbit Pop-Up Book* is based on Beatrix Potter's classic story, and Margaret Wise Brown's *The Goodnight Moon Room: A Pop-Up Book* introduces settings from popular fiction. Jan Pienkowski's *Haunted House* uses pop-up and flap techniques to create the detailed setting of a house inhabited by ghostly characters.

Eric Carle's bright, colorful illustrations and pop-up techniques enhance a simple story line in *The Honeybee and the Robber: A Moving Picture Book*. The plot follows a honeybee as she encounters a bird, a fish, and a frog who all wish to eat her for breakfast. Children enjoy making a bee move her wings, a bear cross his eyes, and a flower open its petals.

Flap books and other mechanical books encourage children to interact with the text as they speculate about what is under a flap and then open it to discover whether they were correct. Eric Hill has written and illustrated an excellent series of flap books for preschool children. *Where's Spot?,* for example, revolves around a dog's full dinner bowl and discovering where the dog could be. Children join Spot's mother as they open a door

THROUGH THE EYES OF AN ILLUSTRATOR TEAM

Creating Picture Books

ALICE and MARTIN PROVENSEN, whose work has won the New York *Times* Best Illustrative Children's Book award, the Brooklyn Museum's Art Books for Children Citation, and the Caldecott honor award, discuss the challenges of illustrating a new manuscript.

OUR WORK IS CONCENtrated on book illustration and starting each new book is still, after having worked together for thirty-seven years, an exhilarating experience. It is not surprising that there are so many husband and wife teams in the children's book field. Our marriages must surely have been enhanced by the enchantment of this shared experience. In addition to the actual illustration of a book, there is much craft, much measuring, calculation and minutiae and many decisions in its making. It is a welcome thing to have a reliable, able, sympathetic (if sometimes critical) person working alongside.

Publishing a book is in many ways similar to producing a movie or a play. It is not done by one person. The illustrator's part in its production has most in common with the actor's performance. We approach each new book as a new role and have never developed a style or mannerisms that would suit every text.

A brilliant player, such as Alec Guinness, creates a new persona for each new part he plays, trying to find the inner and outer guise which will best express the texture of the character and the meaning of the play. Each new role presents him with a new challenge. For us, each new manuscript does the same.

The illustrator's task if one really is an *illustrator* (that is to say "illuminator") is to do the text full justice, trying as the actor does, to find the right line, the right tone and rhythm, and the right spirit with which to bring a manuscript written or edited for children to the fulfillment of its intended purpose—a children's book.

Before we begin our search for what we hope will be this inevitable "rightness" in the fin-

Costumes and occupations in the illustrations show the Shaker influence of American children's literature. (From *A Peaceable Kingdom*, illustrated by Alice and Martin Provensen. Copyright © 1978 by Alice and Martin Provensen. Reprinted by permission of Viking/Penguin Inc.)

or lift a covering in search of Spot. Each opening reveals a different animal. The lettering of Hill's books is large and clear against a white background, and the illustrations are both colorful and humorous. Young children return many times to rediscover what is behind each flap.

Tana Hoban's *Look! Look! Look!* uses square openings on black pages to reveal small portions of the colored photograph on the next page. A child can guess what the object is and then turn the page to see if he or she is correct.

Robert Crowther has designed two mechanical books that help children develop concepts related to the alphabet and counting. *The Most Amazing Hide-and-Seek Alphabet Book* has clear capital and lower-case letters that conceal an object beginning with the letter. *The Most Amazing Hide-and-Seek Counting Book* uses pictures that rotate or lift to uncover objects for counting.

Cloth and plastic books help stimulate the language development of very young children while helping them identify colors, sounds, and

ished illustrations, we try to choose a format (shape) for the book which will be suitable for the subject matter and the age group of its readers. Then, too, there is the length of the book (the number of pages), based not only on the length of the manuscript but also on the size of the type used, the number of lines on each page, the size and number of illustrations, all again relating to the age level of its audience and increasingly the cost of its production, to be considered.

At this stage we often have several and separate opinions about what the appearance of the finished book should be. We work toward the solution by making rough layouts and actually constructing crude dummies. It is now that the first rough sketches, by either of us, are drawn. We decide which scenes or characters are the most important, which will make the most vital pictures, which, in the case of a narrative manuscript, will forward the story line and in the case of diverse subject matter, as in a Mother Goose book, how the pages can be designed to unify the text visually.

It is always easy to find the wrong solutions. The right ones emerge through a process of experimentation, but once we have decided on a format, ordered the type set, agreed on what the spirit and appearance of the book should be, we try to set aside our individual egos and place our individual drawing styles and painting skills to the service of that image.

We have been given the opportunity to draw Bibles and books of nonsense, warriors and lions, mythological landscapes and modern city streets. We have illustrated alphabet books and music books, cookbooks and books of poetry and yet are always astonished and pleased to discover how much there is still to be done.

ELEPHANT, Badger,
Pelican, Ox,

familiar everyday objects. In *I Can—Can You?*, Peggy Parish asks children to demonstrate their physical accomplishments, from touching their toes to putting away their toys.

The numerous toy books discussed here and listed in the children's literature at the end of the chapter indicate a trend toward publishing more books for very young children. A visit to a bookstore or a search through publishers' catalogues will show even more available texts. *Booklist*, the journal for the American Library Association, regularly reviews toy books as part of its coverage of children's books.

ALPHABET BOOKS

Alphabet books have long been used to help young children identify familiar objects, as well as letters and sounds. The objects pictured in alphabet books should be easy for children to identify and should not have more than one commonly used name. For example, since young children often call a rabbit a bunny, *rabbit* might not be the best choice for illustrating the letter *r* in an alphabet book for very young children. If letter/sound identification is a major concern, the letters and corresponding illustrations should be easily identifiable. If young children use the book independently, the pages should not be cluttered with numerous objects that could confuse letter/sound identification.

When adults share alphabet books with older children, however, pages rich with detail and numerous objects may help children develop their observational and discussion skills. A child's age and the educational objectives are basic considerations when evaluating any alphabet book. Some alphabet books are most appropriate for young children, while others contain enough detail or historical insight to interest even older children.

Early Alphabet Books

Like Mother Goose rhymes, alphabet books were among the first books published for children. Some early alphabet books have been reissued, and some new books are reminiscent of earlier texts. One very early ABC rhyme, "History of an Apple Pie," tells how "B bit it," "C cut it," and so forth, until the end of the alphabet and the pie. In 1886, Kate Greenaway illustrated the pie's alphabetical history in *A—Apple Pie,* and her original woodblock designs have been used in a reissue of this charming text.

Ruth Baldwin's *One Hundred Nineteenth-Century Rhyming Alphabets in English* contains a version of "History of an Apple Pie," as well as other early alphabets. The 296 pages of this large book are filled with colorful reproductions of nineteenth-century pictures and verses. Each rhyme is identified according to title, illustrator, publisher, and date of publication.

Alice and Martin Provensen have illustrated another early ABC, *A Peaceable Kingdom: The Shaker Abecedarius*. The Shaker alphabet book was first published in the Shaker Manifesto of July 1882 under the title "Animal Rhymes." According to Richard Barsam (1), it was written to teach reading. While Shaker teachers were strict disciplinarians, singing and dancing were part of the children's school life. The rhyme and rhythm of these verses must have appealed to Shaker children, as they appeal to children today. The Provensens' charming illustrations show people engaged in typical Shaker occupations, wearing the dress of an earlier time in American history. Such historical alphabet books give contemporary children a valuable sense of what life was like in the past, as they share a reading and learning experience that children in earlier eras also enjoyed.

Animal Themes

The animal theme in the Shaker alphabet book is still very popular. Contemporary animal alphabet books range in complexity: Some show one letter and a single animal for each entry; some have a single letter, a single animal, and a rhyming phrase; some have very descriptive phrases with each letter; and some develop an integrated story in alphabetical order.

Bert Kitchen's *Animal Alphabet* is a book that at first glance seems simple. Each page in this large, handsome text contains a crisp black capital letter and an animal that climbs, hangs onto, sits upon, or peeks out from behind the letter. Even older readers may have difficulty guessing the identities of the animals. Answers in the back of the book

The letters of the alphabet are shown in animals. (From *Animal Alphabet* by Bert Kitchen. Copyright © 1984 by Bert Kitchen. Reprinted by permission of Dial Books.)

In this alphabet book for younger children, the illustrator uses collage to depict each letter and accompanying objects. (Illustration from *ABC* by Elizabeth Cleaver. Copyright © 1985 Elizabeth Cleaver. Reprinted with the permission of Atheneum Publishers, Inc.)

reveal jerboas, newts, and umbrella birds in addition to frogs, lions, and elephants.

Ed Emberley's ABC is a more complex book that is appropriate for slightly older children. It not only shows each letter but also demonstrates, in a series of four pictures, how each letter is formed. This book is worthwhile to share with children as they learn to print letters, and it can motivate them to develop their own alphabet books.

Interaction with text is also encouraged in Arthur Geisert's *Pigs from A to Z*. In this detailed text, each letter and accompanying illustration is introduced by one or two sentences. Full-page illustrations depict pigs performing the accompanying actions. Within each illustration are hidden several examples of the specific letter as well as the letter that precedes and follows the letter. The book concludes with a key so that readers may verify the locations of the letters within the picture puzzle.

Mary Beth Owens's *A Caribou Alphabet* is unusual because the illustrations and alphabetical order reveal information about one of the large wild animals. The text begins "A caribou's antlers can grow mighty large/Bulls spar in the autumn to see who's in charge" (unnumbered). Each page continues with a letter, an illustration, and a rhyming text that highlights a word beginning with that letter.

Books for young children may use alphabetical order to develop a story line. Wanda Gág's *The ABC Bunny* is an older alphabet book still popular with young children, who follow the alphabetical adventures of the bunny after a falling apple wakes him up in his snug bed.

Other Alphabet Books

Anno's Alphabet: An Adventure in Imagination is a beautifully illustrated book by Mitsumasa Anno. The title is an excellent introduction to what is in store for observant readers. Large, simple objects suggest the beginning sound of each large letter, but Anno has also cleverly entangled numerous objects into the black-and-white border circling each page. For example, the *B* pages are bordered

Detailed illustrations may enhance understanding of concepts and development of oral discussion skills. (From *On Market Street,* by Arnold Lobel. Illustrated by Anita Lobel. Text copyright © 1981 by Arnold Lobel, Illus. copyright © 1981 by Anita Lobel. By permission of Greenwillow Books [A Division of William Morrow & Co.])

with beanstalks in which are entwined buttons, bees, bells, and birds. Children enjoy discovering these picture puzzles and searching for the hidden objects.

Brightly colored collages provide the visual focus in Elizabeth Cleaver's *ABC*. Letters and words that begin with each letter are printed on a white background. Each facing page contains a collage depicting the letter and objects that begin with that letter. Poetry associated with individual letters provides the controlling element in Barbara Lalicki's *If There Were Dreams to Sell*.

A buying excursion in an old-fashioned market provides an enjoyable trip through the alphabet in Arnold Lobel's *On Market Street,* illustrated by Anita Lobel. The child buys gifts from the shopkeepers: apples, books, clocks, doughnuts . . . and finally zippers. The colorful illustrations help children develop concepts as they see and discuss the goods offered for sale. Lois Ehlert's *Eating the Alphabet: Fruits and Vegetables from A to Z* is another theme approach to introducing the alphabet to young children.

Suse MacDonald's *Alphabatics* is an extremely creative alphabet book. The illustrator uses a series of pictures that proceed from the original letter to an object that represents the letter. For example, the A proceeds from a drawing of a capital A, to an A tilted on blue waves, to an A upside down on the waves, to an A turned into an ark, and finally to an ark filled with animals. This book can be used to motivate children's drawings of similar examples.

The Z Was Zapped by Chris Van Allsburg also encourages interaction between the text and readers. Van Allsburg presents the alphabet in the form of a twenty-six act play. Each act is a letter being treated to some action that begins with that sound. For example, the play is introduced with the letter *A* as it is bombarded with falling rock. The reader must turn the page to discover that Act 1 is "The A was in an Avalanche." Involvement is enhanced because readers must turn the page to discover the author's text. Teachers report that the book encourages writing as students create their own descriptions of each act.

Eve Merriam's *Halloween ABC,* an alphabet poetry book for older students, uses the ABC format to introduce poems about Halloween topics. For example, the *K* page has an illustration of the letter *K* and a key. The accompanying poem is about a key that opens a mysterious gate that in turn leads to adventure. This poem is another selection that may stimulate writing. Students may write a second verse to the key poem to reveal what happens when they find the key that spells "Follow me." Rhythmic verse also provides the focus for Bill Martin, Jr. and John Archambault's ABC, *Chicka Chicka Boom Boom*.

Several alphabet books are designed to provide information to older students rather than to teach letter/sound relationships to younger ones. Two award-winning books present information about African life. Margaret Musgrove's *Ashanti to Zulu: African Traditions,* vividly illustrated by Leo and Diane Dillon, depicts the customs of twenty-six African peoples. *Jambo Means Hello: Swahili Alphabet Book,* by Muriel Feelings, introduces Swahili words and customs. These beautiful books can encourage children of all cultural backgrounds to learn more about African people.

COUNTING BOOKS

Counting books, like alphabet books, are often used for specific educational purposes. To develop one-to-one correspondence and ability to count sequentially from one through ten, a counting book should contain easily identifiable numbers and corresponding objects. Effective number books for young children usually show one large number, the word for the number, and the appropriate number of objects—all on one page or facing pages. The actual number represented should be quite clear. For example, one star showing five points may be a poor choice for depicting the number five, since children may not understand that five, not one, is being depicted.

Books that stimulate the manipulation of concrete objects are especially useful. For example, a counting book showing the number two and two blocks might encourage a young child to count two real blocks. One very simple counting book for young children, Eric Carle's wordless *My Very First Book of Numbers,* is designed so that children can easily match numbered squares with their corresponding illustrations.

Counting books for young children may stimulate language development and interaction with the text. In *Roll Over!* Mordicai Gerstein uses a nursery rhyme, fold-out flaps, and humorous illustrations to involve children in counting the number of people in a bed. In Molly Bang's *Ten, Nine, Eight* a black father and child observe objects seen in the room and then say a rhythmic counting lullaby that proceeds backward from ten to one until the drowsy child is ready for bed. Eileen Christelow also uses the text of a nursery rhyme in *Five Little Monkeys Jumping on the Bed* to develop a counting book that proceeds backward from five to zero. In Nancy Tafuri's *Who's Counting?* children are encouraged to develop concepts related to the numbers one through nine.

Merle Peek's *The Balancing Act: A Counting Song* appeals to young children. The illustrations and text proceed from one elephant to ten elephants. The lines "They thought it was such an amusing stunt/that they called in another elephant" are repeated each time another elephant balances on the piece of string. With the count of ten, the elephants drop into a safety net. Jim Aylesworth's *One Crow: A Counting Rhyme,* another book for young children, presents numbers and farm scenes set in summer and winter. The numbers are presented in rhyming text, such as "Three puppies romp/and wag little tails./Summer breeze billows/the wash like sails." Paul Giganti's *How Many Snails? A Counting Book* encourages

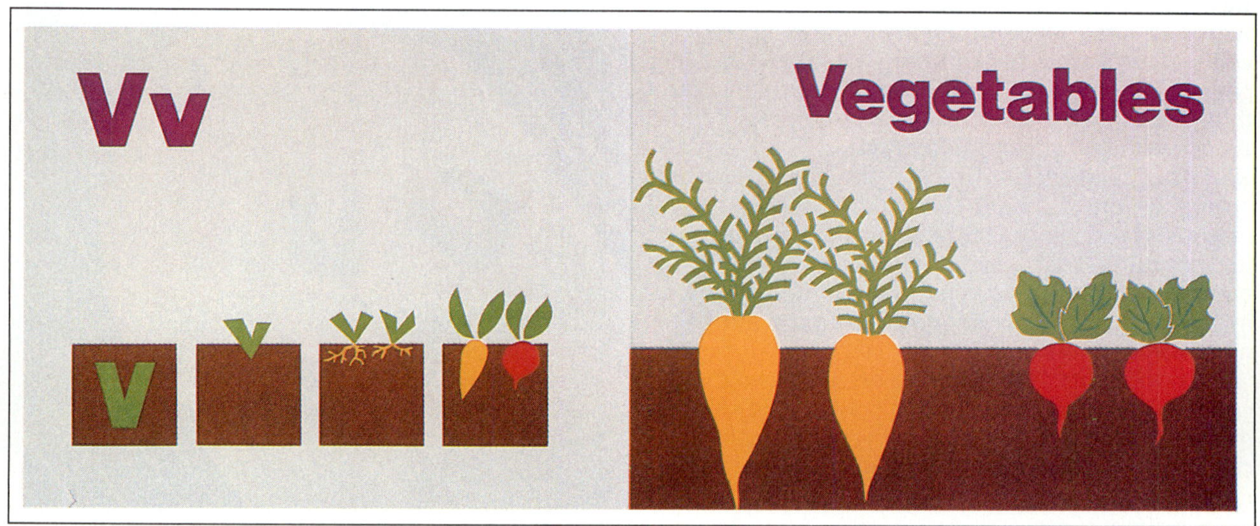

Changing formations show an object that begins with a letter in Suse MacDonald's *Alphabatics*. Reprinted by permission of Bradbury Press an affiliate of Macmillan, Inc. from *Alphabatics* by Suse MacDonald. Copyright © 1986 by Suse MacDonald.

interaction with the text as children count not only objects but also objects with specific characteristics. For example, readers are asked how many clouds are on a two-page spread. Next, they are asked how many clouds are big and fluffy and gray. Olivier Dunrea's *Deep down Under* encourages counting from one to ten and identifying various creatures that dig under the ground.

Counting books for older children may develop the concept of numbers, addition, or subtraction, or they may encourage children to search for many groups of the same number on a single page. You should consider children's abilities in order to select books of appropriate difficulty.

Mitsumasa Anno presents the numbers one through ten and the concepts of addition and subtraction in *Anno's Counting House*. On alternating double pages Anno shows the interiors and exteriors of two houses. In the old house, ten people are preparing to move. Then only nine people are in the old house and one is in the new house. The process continues until the new house is furnished. *Anno's Math Games II* includes numerous picture puzzles and mathematical concepts.

Count and See and *26 Letters and 99 Cents,* by Tana Hoban, are simple counting books with easy-to-identify number concepts that also extend to sets and higher numbers. In *Count and See,* each number, its corresponding written word, and a circle or circles illustrating the number appear in white on a black background. On the opposite page, a photograph illustrates the number with things found in the environments of many children: one fire hydrant, two children, . . . twenty watermelon seeds, . . . forty peanuts shown in groups of ten, . . . and one hundred peas shown in pods of ten each. The book could also be used for counting and grouping concrete items or making counting books that use the items shown in the pictures. (Counting and grouping aid cognitive development.)

26 Letters and 99 Cents may be used as either a counting book or an alphabet book. Read in one direction, the illustrations and text emphasize counting. By turning the book the other way, readers have an alphabet book.

In a slightly more complex book, Doug Magee uses photographs of a large tractor-trailer truck to introduce the parts of a truck and to reinforce counting. The photographer uses black-and-white photographs of truck parts in *Trucks You Can Count On* to illustrate the numbers one through ten. The wheels of the truck provide the concrete examples for counting to eighteen.

Hilary Knight's The Twelve Days of Christmas may also be used as a counting book. The humorous illustrations show the gifts given on each of the twelve days. Older children can count the accumulated objects on the final two-page spread. There are twelve lords a-leaping, twenty-two ladies dancing, thirty fiddlers fiddling . . . and twelve partridges in pear trees.

Handtalk Birthday: A Number & Story Book in Sign Language by Remy Charlip, Mary Beth Miller, and George Ancona is an unusual story. It is about a surprise party for a deaf woman. Photographs show the characters using sign language as the lady guesses the contents of her presents and the guests question her about her age.

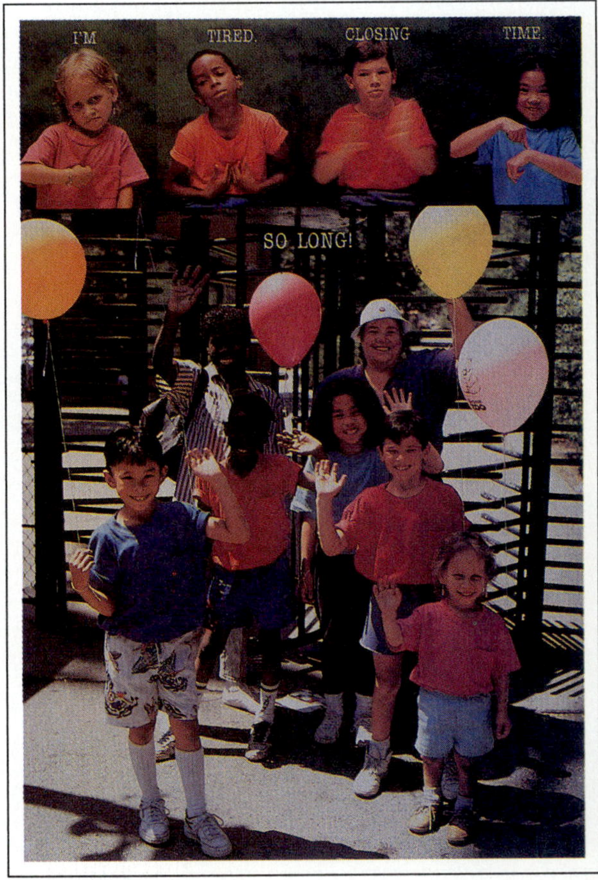

Children use sign language to describe their trip to the zoo. (From *Handtalk Zoo* by George Ancona and Mary Beth Miller. Photographs copyright © 1989 by George Ancona. Reprinted by permission of Four Winds Press, an Imprint of Macmillan Publishing Company.)

This unusual counting book depicts East African culture. (From *Moja Means One,* by Muriel Feelings. Illustrated by Tom Feelings. Illustrations copyright © 1971 by Tom Feelings. Used by permission of Dial Press.)

Muriel Feelings's *Moja Means One: Swahili Counting Book* is the counting-book partner to her Swahili alphabet book. Each two-page spread provides a numeral from one to ten, the Swahili word for the number, a detailed illustration (by Tom Feelings) that depicts animal or village life in Africa, and a sentence describing the contents of the illustration. This book may be more appropriate for stimulating interest in an African culture or providing information for older children than for presenting number concepts to younger children.

CONCEPT BOOKS

Many of the books recommended for use in stimulating the cognitive development of children are concept books. These books rely on well-chosen illustrations to help children grasp both relatively easy concepts, such as red and circle, and more abstract concepts (which may be difficult for children to comprehend), such as prepositions (*through,* for example) and antonyms (*fast* and *slow,* for example). Like counting books, concept books come in various degrees of difficulty, so teachers should consider a child's level of understanding when selecting concept books.

Numerous books have been designed to help young children learn basic concepts, such as colors and shapes. Eric Carle's *My Very First Book of Colors* is a simple, wordless book that asks a child to match a block of color with the picture of an object illustrated in that color. In *Of Colors and Things,* Tana Hoban uses both colors and photographs of objects to invite children to search for matching colors. In *Circles, Triangles, and Squares,* Hoban uses large black-and-white photographs to show common shapes in everyday objects. In *Shapes, Shapes, Shapes,* she uses photographs to depict such shapes as circles, rectangles, and ovals.

In *Snake In, Snake Out,* Linda Banachek presents spatial concepts humorously, as an old woman tries to chase a friendly snake out of her house. In *Over, Under, Through, and Other Spatial Concepts,* Tana Hoban uses photographs that show children jumping *over* fire hydrants, walking *under* outstretched arms, and crawling *through* large pipes.

Authors have tackled the challenge of explaining opposites, too. Hoban uses photographs in other excellent concept books, such as *Big Ones, Little Ones,* in which mother and baby animals convey the meanings of *big* and *little*. In *Push-Pull, Empty-Full: A Book of Opposites,* Hoban uses photographs to develop the meanings of such antonyms as *wet* (a puddle in the street) and *dry* (leaves on the street). Peter Spier's *Fast-Slow, High-Low: A Book of Opposites* is more detailed and complex. It shows, for example, many empty and full things, such as balloons, toothpaste tubes, flower vases, buses, and refrigerators. To illustrate such terms as *straight* and *crooked,* Bruce McMillan uses photographs of captivating baby chicks in *Here a Chick, There a Chick*.

A series of books written by Henry Pluckrose and photographed by Chris Fairclough emphasizes such concepts as *Length, Capacity,* and *Sorting*. These books use the photographs to show each concept developed in the text. Bruce McMillan's *Super Super Superwords* uses photographs to illustrate comparative words, such as *long, longer,* and *longest*. In the photographs, kindergarten children effectively demonstrate the meanings.

Donald Crews familiarizes children with various concepts in *Freight Train*. The cars of the train are different colors, and the movement of the train *across* trestles, *through* cities, and *into* tunnels encourages understanding of spatial concepts and of opposites, such as *darkness* and *daylight*. Trains fascinate many young children, and children eagerly learn concepts while enjoying the colors, movements, and sounds developed in this book.

Gail Gibbons develops specialized vocabulary and concepts in *Trains*. Large, colorful illustrations show historical changes in trains and depict specific types of trains and railroad cars. The illustrations are labeled to show such features as couplers, open hopper cars, boxcars, tank cars, dining cars, and Pullman cars. Byron Barton's *Machines at Work* also provides large illustrations, which show bulldozers digging and trucks loading and dumping.

Susi Gregg Fowler's text and Marisabina Russo's illustrations in *When Summer Ends* encourage children to identify happenings that are appropriate for each season. Anne Rockwell helps children understand seasonal changes and appropriate activities for each season in *First Comes Spring,* while Mitsumasa Anno encourages children to identify fruits and vegetables in *Anno's Faces*. In *City Sounds* and *Jungle Sounds,* Rebecca Emberley encourages children to listen for and to make appropriate sounds.

Nancy Tafuri encourages concept and language development with large illustrations of animals in her almost wordless book *Early Morning in the Barn*. Masayuki Yabuuchi helps children identify terminology and understand relationships between baby animals and their parents in *Whose Baby?* In addition, Yabuuchi encourages children to hypothesize about animal identity in *Whose Footprints?* These concept books and others offer

The illustrations show the concept developed in the text. (From *Here a Chick, There a Chick* by Bruce McMillan copyright © 1983 by Bruce McMillan. Reprinted by permission of Lothrop, Lee and Shepard [A division of William Morrow & Co.])

ISSUE

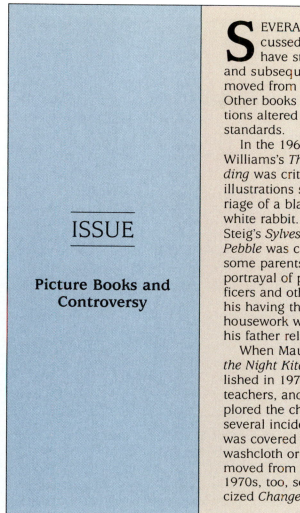

Picture Books and Controversy

Several books discussed in this chapter have stirred controversy and subsequently been removed from library shelves. Other books have had illustrations altered to meet specific standards.

In the 1960s, Garth Williams's *The Rabbit's Wedding* was criticized because the illustrations showed the marriage of a black rabbit and a white rabbit. In 1969, William Steig's *Sylvester and the Magic Pebble* was criticized because some parents objected to his portrayal of pigs as police officers and others objected to his having the mother do housework while Sylvester and his father relaxed.

When Maurice Sendak's *In the Night Kitchen* was published in 1970, some parents, teachers, and librarians deplored the child's nudity. In several incidents, the nudity was covered with a drawn-on washcloth or the book was removed from the shelf. In the 1970s, too, some people criticized *Changes, Changes*, by Pat Hutchins, because the man has a more active role than does the woman: He drives and decides what to make from the blocks, while the woman pulls the train whistle and hands him the blocks.

One book not discussed in this chapter illustrates the changing sensitivities of Americans toward certain social issues. Helen Bannerman's *Little Black Sambo* (1899) was popular for many years. Eventually, however, many people considered the crudely drawn features of the characters and the story line to be offensive, and the book was taken off many library shelves.

As you evaluate picture books, consider which books might be controversial and the reasons for the controversy. Does controversy change with the times? What subjects might have caused controversy in picture books published in the 1950s, 1960s, 1970s, 1980s, or 1990s? Are those subjects still controversial? Are any new areas of controversy developing today?

children pleasure as well as important learning experiences.

WORDLESS BOOKS

In a new type of picture book, the illustrations tell the whole story, without the addition of words. Children enjoy the opportunity to provide the missing text for wordless books—an excellent way of developing their oral and written language skills. Dorothy Strickland (8) maintains, "[E]xperiences with books that are thoughtfully planned to promote active verbal exchanges of ideas will have lasting positive effects upon both the communicative mode and the cognitive structure of the child" (p. 53). Wordless books stimulate creative thinking and enhance visual literacy abilities, as children watch the pages for clues to the action. Wordless books are especially valuable because they allow children of different backgrounds and reading levels to enjoy the same book.

Wordless books have various degrees of detail and plot complexity. Some contain considerable detail, while others do not. Some develop easily identifiable plots, while others can be interpreted in many different ways. Some are large, making them appropriate for sharing with a group, while others are small, easily held by one child or one adult with a child in the lap. You should consider all these characteristics when choosing wordless books for children of different ages, reading levels, and interests.

Henrik Drescher's *The Yellow Umbrella* is a small-format book designed for individual viewing or lap sharing. The detailed illustrations follow a mother and baby monkey as they retrieve a yellow umbrella in a zoo, sail away to the ocean, float along a river into their homeland, find the father monkey, and use the umbrella to shield their obviously happy home on top of a palm tree. The impact of the umbrella is enhanced by the two-tone illustrations, which encourage the eye to focus on the bright yellow umbrella.

Pat Hutchins's *Changes, Changes* is a simple wordless book that appeals to children in preschool and kindergarten who enjoy building with blocks. The illustrations show two wooden dolls building a house of blocks, coping with a fire by turning the house into a fire truck, solving the problem of too much water by building a boat, reaching land by constructing a truck, and eventually rebuilding their home. The large and colorful pictures make actions easily identifiable. The book stimulates oral language, as well as problem solving and manipulation of children's own blocks.

In Jan Ormerod's *Sunshine,* a child wakes up her parents and helps them prepare for their day. The action-filled color illustrations can stimulate oral discussions, creative dramatics, and writing.

Realistic humor is a popular theme of wordless books for young children. A series of wordless books by Mercer Mayer shows the humorous adventures of a boy, a dog, and a frog. *Frog Goes to Dinner*—the most detailed book in the series and, to many children, the funniest—illustrates the humorous disruptions that can occur if a frog hides in a boy's pocket and accompanies a family to a very fancy restaurant. Each of Mayer's books is small, just the right size for individual enjoyment or for sharing with an adult. The illustrations are expressive and contain sufficient detail to stimulate language development and enjoyment.

Several wordless books develop plots involving the antics of animals from the world of fantasy. John S. Goodall's *Paddy Under Water* follows Paddy Pork as he dives underwater and discovers a sunken ship. Emily Arnold McCully's *Picnic* follows a family of mice as they jubilantly go on a picnic, unhappily discover a small mouse is missing, and joyfully reunite the whole family. McCully's *School* and *New Baby* follow the same family of mice as they experience two common occurrences. The illustrations depict enough plot to stimulate the creation of narrative even by older children.

Peter Collington's *The Angel and the Soldier Boy* is a large-format book that can be viewed and discussed by groups of students. The wordless plot follows the actions in a young girl's dream. Her toy soldier and angel come to life and challenge the pirates who rob the girl's piggy bank, capture the soldier, and return to their ship on top of the piano. The illustrations include enough detail to enhance storytelling.

The sequential organization and detail of the illustrations provide a story line that stimulates language development. (Illustration on unnumbered page 11 from *Picnic* by Emily Arnold McCully. Copyright © 1984 by Emily Arnold McCully. Reprinted by permission of Harper & Row, Publishers, Inc.)

Another dream sequence forms the plot in David Wiesner's *Free Fall.* This beautifully illustrated, wordless book takes the dreamer on a fantasy as he explores uncharted lands. Interestingly, many of the objects that seem so real in his dream are by his bed when he awakes.

Some wordless books are exceptional because of their detail. John Goodall's *Story of a Main Street* encourages historical comparisons and analysis as older students trace the evolution of an English town from medieval to contemporary times. When developing observational skills, students may focus on differences in architecture, clothing, and transportation. Goodall shows that the market square location is the same even though the times change. The times include medieval, Elizabethan, Restoration, Georgian, Regency, Victorian, Edwardian, and modern. This text is similar to Goodall's *The Story of an English Village*. In *The Story of the Seashore*, Goodall traces the history of seaside holidays through different time periods.

Peter Spier's *Noah's Ark* is another excellent picture book. The only words occur at the beginning of the book. The pictures show the building of the ark, the boarding of all the animals, the long wait, and the starting of life again on the land, which is plowed and cultivated. These pictures contain so much detail that a child can discover something new each time he or she reads the book.

Several beautifully illustrated wordless books by Mitsumasa Anno also encourage oral discussion and storytelling by older children. The detailed drawings in *Anno's Journey,* for example, are the result of the artist's travels through the countryside, villages, and larger towns of Europe. Anno adds to the enjoyment by suggesting that readers look for certain details in the pictures, such as paintings and characters from children's literature. The pictures are detailed enough to keep even adults occupied. *Anno's Italy* and *Anno's Britain* follow a similar approach and encourage children to identify historical and literary characters. *Anno's Flea Market* captures the spirit of a busy market square in an old, walled city.

One enticing, almost wordless book is Chris Van Allsburg's *The Mysteries of Harris Burdick*. A title and a one-line caption precede each picture. In the introduction to the book, Van Allsburg asks readers to provide the missing stories. Teachers and librarians report that the illustrations contain enough elements of mystery and fantasy to motivate excellent oral and written stories.

Many wordless books are ideal for promoting oral language development. Others, however, are so obscure in story line that children may be frustrated when asked to tell the story. When choosing wordless books, consider the following questions:

1. Is there a sequentially organized plot that provides a framework for children who are just developing their own organizational skills?
2. Is the depth of detail appropriate for the age level of the children? (Too much detail will overwhelm younger children, while not enough detail may bore older ones.)
3. Do the children have enough experiential background to understand and interpret the illustrations? Can they interpret the book during individual reading or is adult interaction necessary?
4. Is the size of the book appropriate for the purpose? (Larger books are necessary for group sharing.)
5. Will the subject appeal to the children?

The illustrations show the dream world of the boy in *Free Fall* by David Wiesner. Copyright © 1988 by David Wiesner. Reprinted by permission of Lothrop, Lee and Shepard Books, a division of William Morrow & Co.

The varied levels of complexity found in wordless books indicate that wordless books are appropriate for young children as well as more advanced ones. This same complexity, however, means that adults must select the materials carefully.

EASY-TO-READ BOOKS

Easy-to-read books are designed to be read by children with beginning reading skills. These beginner books serve as transitions between basal readers and library trade books. Like picture storybooks, these books contain many pictures designed to suggest the story line. Unlike picture storybooks, however, their vocabulary is controlled so that young readers can manage independently. Controlling the vocabulary to fit the needs of beginning readers may result in contrived language; it is quite difficult to write stories that sound natural if all the words must be selected from the easiest level of readability.

Authors, teachers, and librarians use several different readability formulas to determine the approximate level of reading skill required to read a book. The Fry Readability Formula (3), for example, measures the reading level by finding the average number of sentences and syllables per 100 words. These averages are plotted on a graph that identifies the corresponding grade level for the book. (This technique is explained in Appendix E.) Readability experts assume that easier books have shorter sentences and more monosyllabic words. As the reading level becomes higher, the sentences become longer and multisyllabic words become more numerous.

Comparing the readability of easy-to-read books and other picture storybooks illustrates the difference between the two types of books. A 100-word selection from one popular easy-to-read book, Dr. Seuss's *The Cat in the Hat,* showed sixteen sentences and 100 syllables for those 100 words. The sentences were very short and all words were of one syllable. Plotting these two findings on the Fry graph indicates a first-grade reading level. In contrast, a picture storybook also written for first-grade interests by Dr. Seuss, *And to Think That I Saw It on Mulberry Street,* has seven and one-half sentences and 126 syllables in a 100-word selection. This book's reading level is fifth grade. While both books appeal to children of about the same age, children themselves usually read the first book, while adults usually read the second to children.

Even though easy-to-read books may not meet all standards for literary quality, they do meet the needs of beginning readers. Because children need experiences with books that allow them to reinforce their reading skills independently and develop pride in their accomplishments, you should include easy-to-read books in every book collection for primary-age children. Easy-to-read books are also helpful to students who need successful experiences in remedial reading classes. Because of their controlled use of language and sentence structure, easy-to-read books are less appropriate for adults to read aloud to children, although children may enjoy reading them aloud to appreciative adults.

Animal antics appeal to young children, and many favorite easy-to-read books have animals as

Humorous illustrations enhance an unexpected experience in a favorite easy-to-read book. (From *The Cat in the Hat,* by Dr. Seuss. Copyright © 1957 by Dr. Seuss. Reprinted by permission of Random House, Inc.)

the main characters. In Dr. Seuss's *The Cat in the Hat,* a cat amazes and entertains two children when he balances a fish bowl, a carton of milk, and a cake simultaneously. Seuss's humorous illustrations and rhyming dialogue appeal to children. The cat emphasizes this enjoyment:

> Look at me!
> Look at me!
> Look at me Now!
> It is fun to have fun
> But you have to know how. (p. 8)

Arnold Lobel has written and illustrated several enchanting easy-to-read books. The soft brown and green illustrations in Lobel's stories about Frog and Toad re-create the atmosphere of a woodland setting and show the friendship felt by these two characters. In *Frog and Toad Are Friends,* Frog tries to entice Toad out of his home in order to enjoy the new spring season. Children enjoy Toad's reactions when Frog knocks on the door:

> "Toad, Toad," shouted Frog,
> "wake up. It is spring!"
>
> "Blah," said a voice
> from inside the house.

In Lobel's *Grasshopper on the Road,* a curious insect decides to follow a winding country lane just to discover where it leads. Lobel's characterization is fuller than that found in many easy-to-read books. Lobel has the grasshopper encounter other rural inhabitants and then try to change their behaviors.

Helen V. Griffith develops a memorable animal character with feelings similar to those of her youthful readers in *Alex and the Cat*. When the dog is dissatisfied with himself, he attempts to be a cat, a wolf, and a rescuer of baby birds. After his adventures, he concludes that he is better off being himself, a house pet. Other easy-to-read books with stories of animals that appeal to children include Syd Hoff's *Chester* and *Sammy the Seal* and Bernard Wiseman's *Morris Goes to School* and *Morris Has a Cold*.

Easy-to-read books are also designed to appeal to special interests—mysteries, sports, science, history and magic, for example. Crosby Bonsall's gang of boy private eyes solves several mysteries, including *The Case of the Scaredy Cats,* in which girls invade the boys' private-eye clubhouse and prove that they are just as good as the boys. Short, scary stories are found in both Edward Marshall's *Four on the Shore* and Alvin Schwartz's *In a Dark, Dark Room*.

Soft woodland colors and animals with human characteristics combine in a memorable easy-to-read book. (From *Grasshopper on the Road,* written and illustrated by Arnold Lobel. Copyright © 1978 by Arnold Lobel. By permission of Harper & Row, Publishers, Inc.)

PICTURE STORYBOOKS

A characteristic common to many picture books discussed thus far is the use of illustrations to present all or most of the content of a book. Reliance on pictures is especially crucial in concept books, counting books, a majority of the alphabet books, and all wordless picture books. Many of these books do not have continuous story lines; instead, the illustrations are grouped according to common themes or are presented in numerical or alphabetical sequence.

Picture storybooks, however, contain many illustrations but also develop strong story lines in text. In a well-written picture storybook, the text and narrative complement each other, so children cannot deduce the whole story merely by viewing the pictures. The illustrations are integral to the story line; they enhance the actions, settings, and characterizations (7).

Elements in Picture Storybooks

When adults think about enjoyable book experiences shared by adults and children during story hour or at bedtime, they usually remember picture storybooks. Childhood would be less exciting without friends like Mike Mulligan, Frances the badger, and Ferdinand the bull. What makes some books so memorable for both children and adults? Originality and imagination are crucial in outstanding picture books, but so are strong plot, characterization, setting, style, and humor.

Originality and Imagination. A man and his dog discover that "Paradise lost is sometimes Heaven found"; a boy gets his wishes from a charge card company, whose machine goes mad; and a child's bedroom becomes the kingdom of wild things. Some adults never lose touch with the dreams, fears, and fantasies of childhood. As authors of picture storybooks for children, they are able to create imaginative new worlds, in which the impossible becomes both real and believable.

In *Hey, Al,* Arthur Yorinks's plot helps a janitor and his dog find a more satisfying way of life. Through experience in a beautiful location, where they do not need to work, they discover that beautiful places can have dangerous secrets.

In *The Wish Card Ran Out!,* James Stevenson gives his hero wishes by creating a spoof on credit cards. Charlie is unhappy when he does not get a baseball glove for his birthday, but then he finds a lost "International Wish" card issued by a big corporation that took over from wishing wells and fairy godmothers.

A child's imagination structures the delightful story in Maurice Sendak's *Where the Wild Things Are*. Only in such fantasy can young children who have been disciplined turn their rooms into kingdoms inhabited by other wild things like themselves and then return home in safety before their suppers get cold.

Picture storybooks and their accompanying illustrations are filled with many imaginative episodes. They provide hours of enjoyment and are excellent for stimulating children's imaginations during creative play, storytelling, and creative writing.

Plot. The short attention spans of children who read or hear picture storybooks place special demands on plot development. The plots of picture storybooks are usually simple, clearly devel-

The original plot suggests that beautiful places may be dangerous. (Illustrations from *Hey, Al* by Arthur Yorinks. Illustrated by Richard Egielski. Illustrations copyright © 1986 by Richard Egielsky. Reprinted by permission of Farrar, Straus & Giroux, Inc.)

oped, and brief. They involve few subplots or secondary characters. Such plots usually allow young children to become involved with the action, identify the problem, and solve it rapidly.

For example, in the first three pages of Maurice Sendak's *Where the Wild Things Are,* children know that Max is in so much trouble that he has been sent to bed without supper. Even though the thirty-seven words used thus far do not reveal what Max has done, the pictures explain his problems. Children see him standing on books, hammering nails into the wall, and chasing the dog with a fork. The plot is swiftly paced, and children rapidly join Max in his imaginary world, as the room becomes wilder and wilder.

Sendak introduces additional conflict and excitement when Max encounters the wild things and overcomes them with a magic trick. Children empathize with Max when he has played long enough, sends his new subjects off to bed, and returns home to his mother's love and his supper. The author uses only thirty-eight words to tell what happens between the time Max leaves the wild things and returns home. This book is an excellent example of the important relationship between illustrations and plot development; the illustrations become larger and larger as the drama increases and then become smaller again as Max returns to his everyday life.

It is interesting to compare Sendak's illustrations and Richard Egielski's illustrations for *Hey, Al.* Both illustrators increase their illustrations' sizes as conflict develops, use two-page spreads at the height of interest, and include considerable information about characters and setting within the illustrations.

Other picture books deal with children's problems in more realistic plots. In *Like Jake and Me,* Mavis Jukes portrays the strained relationship between Alex and his big, powerful stepfather Jake, who refuses to allow Alex to help with various chores. When a large, hairy spider crawls into Jake's clothes, Alex discovers that even a powerful, ex-rodeo cowboy can be afraid, and Jake discovers that even a small boy can provide assistance.

Whether a plot is based on fantasy or realism, it usually involves a rapid introduction to the action, a fast pace, and a strong, emotionally satisfying climax. In *The Patchwork Quilt,* Valerie Flournoy develops a warm, emotionally satisfying plot that follows the construction of a family quilt. The quilt gradually draws the members of the family together, as they remember past experiences associated with scraps of material, help Grandma sew, and marvel over the completed masterpiece, which reveals the family's life story. In Kathryn O. Galbraith's *Laura Charlotte*, a mother tells her daughter a story about an elephant that she had as a child. She then gives the elephant to her daughter. In Patricia Polacco's *Thunder Cake*, a grandmother and her granddaughter assemble a special cake as the thunderstorm grows nearer. These actions help the girl realize that she is brave enough to face the storm.

Characterization. The characters in picture storybooks must have specific traits that make them appealing to young children and that meet the demands of the short format. Since a short story does not allow for the fully developed characters that older children and adults prefer, the characters in picture storybooks must experience situations and emotions immediately familiar and credible to the children.

Maurice Sendak, for example, did not need to describe Max, the wild things, or the rumpus that takes place between them. His illustrations show these effectively. Likewise, Stephen Gammell's illustrations for Karen Ackerman's *Song and Dance Man* re-create the magic of vaudeville and express the love between grandchildren and their grandfather.

Any child can understand the feelings of Judith Viorst's hero in *Alexander and the Terrible, Horrible, No Good, Very Bad Day*. Alexander wakes up with gum in his hair, does not get a prize in his cereal when everyone else does, receives reprimands from his teacher, loses his best friend, has a cavity filled by the dentist, gets into trouble for making a mess in his dad's office, has to eat lima beans for dinner, and is ignored by the cat, who goes to sleep with his brother. In this book, as in most picture storybooks, the illustrations supplement the characterizations in the text by showing the characters' actions and reactions.

Children can understand stories about loneliness and friendship. In *The Scarebird,* Sid Fleischman creates a story of friendship between a lonely older farmer and his creation of a lifelike scarecrow and then between the farmer and an equally lonely and homeless young farm worker. As the human friendship increases, the farmer takes needed objects from the scarecrow and gives them to the boy. In *Captain Snap and the Children of Vinegar Lane,* Roni Schotter's characters use friendship and thoughtfulness to change the life of a lonely older man.

Children and an old man develop a warm relationship. (From *Captain Snap and the Children of Vinegar Lane* by Roni Schotter, illustrated by Marcia Sewall. Copyright © 1989 by Roni Schotter, illustrations copyright © 1989 by Marcia Sewall. Reprinted by permission of Orchard Books.)

Many storybooks for children contain animal characters that act and speak like humans. Margaret Wise Brown's *The Runaway Bunny* uses a credible little bunny to demonstrate a child's need for independence and love. The dialogue between the mother rabbit and the bunny stresses the bunny's desire to experience freedom by running away. Each time he suggests ways that he could run away, however, the mother rabbit counters with actions she would take to get him back. The love between the two animals is visible in both the dialogue and pictures, and the bunny decides it would be better to stay with the mother who loves him.

In *Ernest and Celestine's Picnic, Feel Better Ernest!,* and *Smile, Ernest and Celestine,* Gabrielle Vincent uses animal characters to portray easily identifiable emotions, such as excitement, dejection, resentment, jealousy, and acceptance. Young children can empathize with Celestine when, for example, rain spoils her picnic, but her friend Ernest saves the day with some make-believe sunshine.

Setting. In picture storybooks, as in all literature, setting is used to establish the location of a story in time and place, create a mood, clarify historical background if necessary, provide an antagonist, and emphasize symbolic meaning. Picture storybooks, however, strongly rely on illustrations to serve these functions of a setting. Many books, such as Judith Viorst's *Alexander and the Terrible, Horrible, No Good, Very Bad Day,* Valery Flournoy's *The Patchwork Quilt,* and Vera Williams's *Something Special for Me* take place in the familiar contemporary world of television sets, blue jeans, and shopping centers. Other books take place in locations or times unfamiliar to the readers.

Even though Ian Wallace's *Chin Chiang and the Dragon's Dance* has a contemporary setting, children might have difficulty visualizing it without illustrations depicting the Oriental section of Vancouver, British Columbia. Ronald Himler's illustrations for Byrd Baylor's *The Best Town in the World* show how important illustrations are for illuminating time and place in picture storybooks. The brief poetic text alone cannot describe the details of a turn-of-the-century general store, the warmth created by a kerosene lamp, and the many activities associated with a picnic celebration in the days when a picnic was a major social event. James Stevenson's *July* takes readers back to summer visits to grandparents fifty years ago. Likewise, the early Yorkshire setting for James Herriot's *Moses the Kitten* would be almost incomprehensible to young children without Peter Barrett's illustrations. Jon Agee's illustrations for *The Incredible Painting of Felix Clousseau* develop the background of an earlier Paris. Ted Rand's illustrations for Gloria Rand's *Salty Sails North* shows the northern Pacific coastline, while the illustrations in Catherine Stock's *Armien's Fishing Trip* show an African coastal village.

Toshi Maruki's dramatically expressive illustrations for *Hiroshima No Pika* (The Flash of Hiroshima) clarify the horrifying nature of the story's antagonist and the mood as seven-year-old Mii confronts the consequences of atomic warfare on August 6, 1945. The choice of colors is especially dramatic. Swirling red flames pass over fleeing people and animals. Black clouds cover huddling masses and destroyed buildings. The illustrations suggest both the setting as antagonist and a destructive, frightening mood.

In *The Wreck of the Zephyr,* Chris Van Allsburg uses his illustrated settings to create a light mood, subtly mixing reality and make-believe. A boy who dreams of becoming the best sailor in the world experiences a calm sea sparkling with light and a star-studded night disturbed only by a magical ship flying through the sky. The illustrations in all such worthy picture storybooks enhance the times, places, conflicts, and moods of the stories.

Style. Because a picture storybook contains so few words, its author must select those words very carefully. A storybook must also be designed to catch children's attention and stimulate their interest when adults read the story aloud. Adults can evaluate the effectiveness of a storybook's style by reading it orally to themselves or to a child.

Folktales are popular with children because they tend to use repetition. When folktales were retold by word of mouth rather than in print, repetition made the stories easier to remember. Today, repetition in both folktales and contemporary stories attracts children's attention and impresses the structure and content of the story upon their memories. Young children also enjoy repetition, because it provides them opportunities to join in with the dialogue.

In *The Witch's Hat,* Tony Johnston repeats both rhyming sounds and entire phrases. For example, "It was a magic pot, in case you forgot" is repeated after each incident with the enchanted hat. When adults read this book aloud, children quickly chime in with the repeated phrase.

Authors of picture storybooks also repeat a single word in a sentence to create stronger impressions when the books are read aloud. African folktales, for example, sometimes repeat words several times. In Gail E. Haley's *A Story, a Story,* the Sky God describes Ananse, the tiny spider man, as "so small, so small, so small." Similar use of repetition conveys the impression of a dancing fairy and rain on a hornet's nest. Verna Aardema uses this form of repetition to make a strong statement stronger in *Why Mosquitoes Buzz in People's Ears*. When a mother owl finds her dead baby, she is "so sad, so sad, so sad." The night that doesn't end is described as "long, long, long."

Young children enjoy listening to words that create vivid images. In the preface to *A Story, a Story,* Gail Haley says that many African words are found in the book and asks readers to listen carefully to the sounds so they can tell what the words mean. Haley uses many unknown words to describe the movements of animals. A python slithers "wasawusu, wasawusu, wasawusu" down a rabbit hole; a rabbit bounds "krik, krik, krik" across an open space; and sticks go "purup, purup" as they are pulled out of the iguana's ears.

Careful word choice also creates evocative moods in well-written picture storybooks. In *The Seeing Stick,* Jane Yolen creates a mood of wonder as Hwei Ming, the unhappy, blind daughter of a Chinese emperor, "sees" her father for the first time:

> She reached out and her fingers ran eagerly through his hair and down his nose and cheek and rested curiously on a tear they found there. And that was strange, indeed, for had not the emperor given up crying over such things when he ascended the throne? (p. 19 unnumbered)

Humor. Selecting and sharing books that contribute to merriment is a major goal of any literature program. Research shows that humorous literature is particularly effective in attracting children to the pleasures of reading and writing. Many elements in picture storybooks can cause children to laugh out loud. An investigation by Sue Anne

Martin (5) concluded that humor in books awarded the Caldecott Medal had five general sources: (1) word play and nonsense, (2) surprise and the unexpected, (3) exaggeration, (4) the ridiculous and caricature, and (5) superiority.

Word Play and Nonsense. Theodor Geisel, better known as Dr. Seuss, is one of the most popular authors of books for children and an undisputed authority on word play and nonsense. Dr. Seuss's characters often make up totally new words and names to describe the animals found in their imaginations. In *If I Ran the Zoo,* Gerald McGrew's imaginary zoological garden contains an elephant-cat, a bird known as a Bustard, a beast called Flustard, and bugs identified as thwerlls and chugs. Of course, no one could find such animals in the usual jungles, so Gerald must search for them in Motta-fa-Potta-fa-Pell, in the wilds of Nantasket, and on the Desert of Zind. Children enjoy not only the nonsense found in the rhyming text but also the nonsensical illustrations of these strange animals.

Bill Peet's nonsense rhymes and nonsensical illustrations in *No Such Things* appeal to children. Peet uses both internal and end-of-line rhyming to create text such as the following:

The blue-snouted Twumps feed entirely on weeds,
And along with the weeds they swallow the seeds.
Eating seeds causes weeds to sprout on their backs,
Till they look very much like walking haystacks. (p. 5)

Margaret Mahy creates equally enjoyable nonsense in *17 Kings and 42 Elephants,* as "Tinkling tunesters, twangling trillicans,/Butterflied and fluttered by the great green trees" (unnumbered). Patricia MacCarthy's illustrations support these nonsense words.

Surprise and the Unexpected. Margot Zemach's *It Could Always Be Worse: A Yiddish Folktale* is an excellent example of the unexpected found in many picture storybooks. If a man lived in a small one-room hut with his wife and six children, and living conditions became so miserable that he went to the rabbi for advice, how might the rabbi respond to the problem? Children are certainly surprised when the rabbi suggests that the man bring his chickens, a rooster, and a goose into the hut. When conditions do not improve, the rabbi suggests adding the goat and the cow to the group. When life in the hut becomes so difficult that the rabbi suggests that the animals leave the hut immediately, the poor man discovers that the hut is actually quite roomy and peaceful.

Wilson Gage also uses irony to create the unexpected. In *Cully, Cully and the Bear,* a hunter discovers that the bear he's after is chasing him. The hunter decides that he does not need a bearskin and that, in fact, the ground is softer than any bearskin rug. Irony provides an unexpected conclusion in Frank Asch and Vladimir Vagin's *Here Comes the Cat!* The text and illustrations lead readers to believe that the cat will harm the mice. Instead, the cat brings cheese and the mice repay this friendship with combing and milk.

Surprise occurs in Jon Agee's *The Incredible Painting of Felix Clousseau* when the paintings come to life. Chaos takes place and imprisonment of the artist results until a dog in one of the paintings captures a jewel thief. The unexpected also occurs in Mem Fox's *Night Noises*—the frightening night noises are caused by family members who are coming to give a surprise birthday party for the grandmother.

Exaggeration. Children's imaginations are often filled with exaggerated tales about what they can do or would like to do. In James Stevenson's *Could Be Worse!,* however, the grandfather is the one who exaggerates. Grandpa does and says the same things day after day. Whenever anyone complains, Grandpa responds, "Could be worse." When he overhears his grandchildren commenting on his dull existence, he tells them what happened to him the previous evening: He was captured by a large bird and dropped in the mountains, where he encountered an abominable snowman. Then he crossed a burning desert, escaped from a giant animal, landed in the ocean, and finally returned home on a paper airplane. After the grandchildren hear his story, they respond with his favorite expression, "Could be worse!" Stevenson uses similar exaggeration and characterization in *There's Nothing to Do.*

Patricia Polacco uses exaggeration to develop her humorous *Meteor!* After a meteor lands on a farm, the whole town exaggerates the power of the meteor. Individuals claim it gives the ability to play a trumpet, create a marvelous recipe, and even see extraordinary distances. The book is humorous because readers know that such an incident might really happen.

The Ridiculous and Caricature. The consequences of having antlers suddenly appear on a young girl's head provides the humor in *Imogene's Antlers,* in which author David Small caricatures the ridiculousness of some people's fears. To extend the humor, the story concludes with another what-if: The antlers disappear, but an even more beautiful appendage replaces the antlers.

Foolishness and ridiculous situations may change to wisdom, as shown in Eric Kimmel's *The Chanukkah Tree*. In this Jewish tale, the people of Chelm believe a peddler when he sells them a Christmas tree as "[a] Chanukkah tree. From America. Over there Chanukkah trees are the latest thing" (unnumbered). The townspeople decorate the tree with potato latkes and candles. The only star they can find for the top is on a door, so the whole door is placed on top of the tree. When they discover that they have been duped by the peddler, they are at first unhappy. Later birds take sanctuary on the tree during a snowstorm, and the people discover that their tree is not so ridiculous: The potato latkes fed the birds, the candles warmed them, and the door protected them.

Superiority. Some humorous picture storybooks gratify the desire of young children to be superior to everyone else for a change or to easily overcome their problems. When a town simpleton surpasses not only his clever brothers but also the czar of the land, the result is an unusual tale of humorous superiority. Arthur Ransome's *The Fool of the World and the Flying Ship* is a Russian tale. In it, the good deeds performed by a simple lad allow him to obtain a flying ship, discover companions who have marvelous powers, overcome obstacles placed in his path by the czar, win the hand of the czar's daughter, and live happily ever after.

A singing cow solves her problems by using superiority against a greedy human in Lisa Campbell Ernst's *When Bluebell Sang*. When the cow and the farmer become tired of being taken advantage of by a talent agent, the cow hides herself among a herd of cows, where the agent cannot identify her without her dress, hat, and shoes.

Typical Characters and Situations in Outstanding Picture Storybooks

Children's picture storybooks include stories about people in disguise as animals, talking animals with human emotions, personified objects, humans in realistic situations, and humorous and inventive fantasies. This section discusses stories by some outstanding writers of books on these subjects.

People Disguised as Animals. Many children's stories with animal characters are so closely associated with human life-styles, behavior patterns, and emotions that it is difficult to separate them from stories with human characters. If these stories were read without reference to the illustrations or to a specific type of animal, children might assume that the stories are about children and adults like themselves. These stories may be popular with children because the children can easily identify with the characters' emotions and the actions.

Russell Hoban's Frances the badger, for example, lives in a nice house with her two parents, loves bread and jam, and feels jealous when she gets a new baby sister. Children identify with Frances when, in *Bread and Jam for Frances,* she refuses to eat anything but her two favorite foods. Hoban has her parents, like good human parents, carefully guide Frances into her decision that eating only bread and jam is boring and that trying different foods is pleasant.

In *A Baby Sister for Frances,* the young badger decides to run away from home when her mother becomes busy with the new baby. She packs a lunch to take with her on her journey, but goes only as far as the next room, from which she looks longingly at her parents and her sister. In this warm story, Hoban shows how Frances's need for her family helps her overcome her jealousy and decide to accept the new arrival. The warmth is expressed in Hoban's choice of language.

> Big sisters really have to stay
> At home, not travel far away,
> Because everybody misses them
> And wants to hug-and-kisses them.
> (p. 26 unnumbered)

In *Leo the Late Bloomer,* Robert Kraus develops a credible character through experiences shared by many children: Leo, a young tiger, cannot read, write, draw, talk, or even eat neatly. One of Leo's parents worries, while the other suggests that Leo is merely a late bloomer. Kraus uses repetition to emphasize Leo's problem as the seasons go by: "But Leo still wasn't blooming." A satisfactory ending results in both the text and illustrations as Leo finally discovers that he can do everything he couldn't do before, and a happy father and mother hear their happy child declare, "I made it!"

Fears and experiences that result in temporary unhappiness are popular causes of conflict in stories about animals disguised as people. The young character in Jacqueline Martin's *Buzzy Bones and Uncle Ezra* fears the wind. In a satisfying ending, Martin allows her character to discover that wind, in the right circumstances, can also provide considerable pleasure. David McPhail uses a temporary unhappy experience to create a happy ending in *Fix-It*. A bear, who could easily be a young child, cries when the television does not work. After successive disappointments, her mother reads a book to try to calm the unhappy Emma. Emma discovers that reading is so much fun that she stays with the book rather than returning to the television.

In Gabrielle Vincent's *Feel Better, Ernest!* the young mouse character faces the problems of looking after a sick adult. The messy kitchen, the search for the doctor, the worry, and the concluding happiness when the adult is well make this story very human.

Talking Animals with Human Emotions. In other animal stories, the animals live in traditional animal settings, such as meadows, barnyards, jungles, and zoos. The animals in these stories display some animal traits, but they still talk like humans and have many human feelings and problems.

The main character in Munro Leaf's *The Story of Ferdinand* lives in a meadow with his mother and other cattle. Leaf develops contrasts between Ferdinand, who sits under his favorite cork tree smelling the flowers, and the bulls who run, jump, and butt their heads together practicing for the bullring. The theme of the story is relevant to any human child: All individuals should be themselves, and being different is not wrong. Leaf allows Ferdinand to remain true to his individual nature. When he is taken to the bullring, he merely sits and smells the flowers.

In Leo Lionni's *Tillie and the Wall,* the characters are common field mice. However, curiosity about what is on the other side of the wall causes one mouse to be celebrated by the others.

Jean de Brunhoff uses a variety of emotional experiences to develop characters and plots in the various Babar books. Emotionally, Babar grows up; grieves when his mother dies; runs away to the city; returns to the jungle, where he is crowned king; and raises a family.

In Roger Duvoisin's *Petunia,* a goose becomes conceited when she finds a book and believes that merely carrying it around gives her wisdom. Petunia's advice creates an uproar in the barnyard when she maintains that firecrackers discovered in the meadow are candy and thus good to eat. Her true wisdom begins when she discovers that books have words and that she will need to learn to read if she really wants to be wise.

Louise Fatio also takes her main character beyond the world he knows. *The Happy Lion* develops problems when he leaves his zoo cage to visit his good friends in town. To his wonderment, they respond with fright, screams, and running rather than with the "bonjour" he had expected.

Many young children like a combination of fast, slapstick adventure and an animal with easily identifiable human characteristics, such as Hans Rey's *Curious George*. Readers are introduced to this comedic monkey as he observes a large yellow hat lying on the jungle floor. His curiosity gets the better of him, he is captured by the man with the yellow hat, and his adventures begin. The text and illustrations develop one mishap after another, as George tries to fly but falls into the ocean; grabs a bunch of balloons and is whisked away by the wind; and is finally rescued again by the man with the yellow hat. These rapid verbal and visual adventures bring delight to young children, who are curious about the world around them and would like to try some of the same activities.

Other picture storybooks with animal characters satisfy children's desires for absurd situations, flights of fancy, and magical transformations. In William Steig's *Sylvester and the Magic Pebble,* for example, a young donkey accidentally changes himself into a rock and must figure out how to communicate with his grieving parents and return to his donkey form.

Personified Objects. The technique of giving human characteristics to inanimate objects is called personification. Children usually see nothing wrong with a house that thinks, a doll that feels, or a steam shovel that responds to emotions. Virginia Lee Burton, a favorite writer for small children, is the highly skilled creator of things that have appealing personalities and believable emotions. In Burton's *Katy and the Big Snow,* an extraordinary red tractor named Katy responds to calls for help from the chief of police, the postmaster, the telephone company, the water department, the hospital, the fire chief, and the airport. "Sure," she says, and digs the town of Geoppolis out from a big snow two stories deep. When such real city departments believe in her, it is easy for the readers to believe in her also.

In *Mike Mulligan and His Steam Shovel,* also by Burton, Mike's best friend is a large piece of machinery named Mary Anne, and a suspenseful story unfolds as the two friends try to dig the basement of Popperville's town hall in only one day. *The Little House* is a heroine who is strong and also needs love, as a growing city encroaches upon her and she becomes dilapidated and lonely. The house proceeds, like a real person, through a series of emotions until she is moved away from the city and happily settles down on a new foundation, where "once again she was lived in and taken care of" (p. 39).

In Leo Lionni's *Alexander and the Wind-up Mouse,* a windup toy mouse and a real mouse become friends. Like many children who want to be something else and then decide they would rather be themselves, the real mouse is envious of the lovable windup mouse and wishes to be transformed into a play mouse until he learns that the windup mouse is to be discarded. Then the real mouse uses his wish to transform his friend into a real mouse. Themes related to self-discovery and the need for love are common in picture storybooks. These themes relate to children's personal and social development.

Humans in Realistic Situations. Young children enjoy stories about other children who share their concerns, problems, and pleasures. The numerous books written and illustrated by Ezra Jack Keats, for example, have plots, characters, and pictures that easily draw young children into the private worlds of other children. One of Keats's realistic heroes is *Louie,* a shy boy who usually does not talk to anyone. He responds to a puppet when the neighborhood children present a show, however, and a warm feeling results when the children give the puppet to him. In another book, Louie is very lonely when his family moves to a new neighborhood. He solves his problems in *The Trip* by building a model of his old neighborhood and going on an imaginative adventure with his old friends. In *Regards to the Man in the Moon,* other children tease Louie because his father is a junk dealer. His father's advice—that Louie build a spacecraft from junk—and his own imagination allow Louie and a friend to experience flight into outer space. When the other children hear of these adventures, they want to take part in them also.

While Keats's books usually have inner-city settings, the settings created by another well-known children's author are usually the country or the coast of Maine. Robert McCloskey stresses warm family relationships in books such as *Blueberries for Sal.* This delightful story allows readers to share the berry-picking expeditions of a human mother and daughter and an adult bear and her cub. McCloskey develops drama when the youngsters get mixed up and start following the wrong parents. He provides a satisfying ending as both children are reunited with their mothers.

Loving relationships are popular themes in many picture storybooks for young children. In *The Crack-of-Dawn Walkers,* Amy Hest develops a loving relationship between a grandfather and granddaughter by describing the pleasure that they enjoy during their early morning walks. The relationship between a grandmother and a granddaughter forms the plot in Eve Bunting's *The Wednesday Surprise.* In an unusual ending, the seven-year-old teaches her grandmother to read and surprises the family. An aunt and her nephew share close after-dark activities in Sharon Phillips Denslow's *Night Owls.* The many happy experiences suggest warm relationships and joys in sharing.

Vera Williams's *A Chair for My Mother* shows that even a young child can help her mother fulfill a dream. After a fire destroys the family's furniture, Williams's heroine earns money to help fill the large coin jar that represents her mother's and grandmother's desire: a new, soft, comfortable chair. This goal is not easily reached, however; both mother and daughter must work together.

Mother and son share feelings about a dead grandfather in Charlotte Zolotow's *My Grandson Lew.* When six-year-old Lewis wakes up and informs his mother that he misses his grandfather, they remember together the grandfather's "eye hugs," scratchy beard, strong arms, and tobacco smell. The necessity of working together is also the theme developed by George Ella Lyon in *Come a Tide.* The author develops the theme as the family flees high water and then cleans up the mess.

The growth of love and understanding between a young boy and a very old family member is the theme of Sharon Bell Mathis's *The Hundred Penny Box.* Michael develops an important relationship with his Great-great-aunt Dew, who moves into his home with an old box containing a penny for every year of her long life. This is one of many picture storybooks, such as those of Ezra Jack Keats, that share with children of all backgrounds the warm relationships in nonwhite families. Arnold Adoff's *Black Is Brown Is Tan* tells the story of two children, their black mother and white father, and their loving grandmothers from both sides of the family.

Of course, young children also confront problems in their families, including sex-role biases. In Charlotte Zolotow's *William's Doll,* a young boy wants a doll to hug, cradle, and play with. His brother calls him a creep, and his neighbor calls him a sissy. His father tries to interest him in "masculine" toys and brings him a basketball and an electric train. William enjoys both toys but still wants a doll. When his grandmother visits, he explains his wish to her, shows her he can shoot baskets, and tells her that his father does not want him to play with a doll. Grandmother understands William's need, buys him a baby doll, and then explains to William's upset father that William wants and needs a doll so that he can practice being a father just like his own father. Tomie dePaola deals with a similar situation in *Oliver Button Is a Sissy*. Such books can reassure children that there is nothing wrong with nonstereotypic behavior.

Picture storybooks increasingly present the real experiences of children with special educational needs or disabilities. These books tend to show that children with special needs are similar to other children. One appealing book is Jeanne Whitehouse Peterson's *I Have a Sister, My Sister Is Deaf*. Peterson tells in poetic form what it was like to grow up with a sister who plays the piano by feeling the rumble of the chords, climbs monkey bars, stalks deer by watching movements in the grass, lip-reads, and enjoys life. Bernard Wolf's *Anna's Silent World* takes readers into the world of a happy deaf child as she learns to talk, read, join her classmates for stories and playground fun, and enjoy Saturday with her family and friends. Teachers report that this book helps sensitize children to the needs and feelings of the physically disabled.

Humorous and Inventive Fantasies. Dr. Seuss is one of the most popular authors of books for children. In his many outlandish stories, he develops characters who are original and humorous and who talk in a style that children enjoy. In *The 500 Hats of Bartholomew Cubbins,* both conflict and humor result when the king orders a peasant to remove his magical hat. Every time Bartholomew tries to remove one hat, another hat appears. When the number reaches 157 hats, the magicians cast a spell:

> Dig a hole five furlongs deep,
> Down to where the night snakes creep,
> Mix and mold the mystic mud,
> Malber, Balber, Tidder, Tudd. (p. 31 unnumbered)

As the hats begin to number in the hundreds, the king threatens Bartholomew with execution. Then hat number 500 is so beautiful that the king offers to buy it for 500 gold pieces. With that offer, the spell is broken and a rich Bartholomew returns home.

Several of Seuss's characters face moral issues. In *Horton Hatches the Egg,* Horton the elephant remains 100 percent faithful to his promise to hatch a lazy bird's egg in spite of leering bystanders and other unpleasant experiences. He gains his reward when the egg hatches and is an elephant-bird.

Chris Van Allsburg's *Jumanji* begins with a realistic scene involving two children who are asked to keep the house neat until their parents return with guests. Bored, the children make a mess with their toys and then go to the park, where they find instructions for a jungle adventure game that cannot be ended until one player reaches the golden city. When the children take the game home, they realize the consequences of the rules. A lion appears on the piano and chases one of them around the house. Other jungle animals and jungle-related action enter the scene each time the children frantically throw the dice. Van Allsburg ends the story on a note of suspense and speculation. The children return the game, but two other children, who are notorious for never reading directions, pick up the game and run through the park.

John Burningham develops a humorously unlikely situation in *Avocado Baby*. At first, the weakling baby of weakling parents refuses to eat. Then, he eats an avocado and the parents are forced to put "Beware of the Baby" on the gate. The baby demonstrates his strength by carrying a piano upstairs, breaking his cot, and outmatching bullies.

Fantastic occurrences also form the plot of Trinka Noble's *The Day Jimmy's Boa Ate the Wash*. That a boy might have a pet boa constrictor is not too farfetched, but catastrophes occur when Jimmy takes his pet along on a class trip to a farm. After several plot twists, Jimmy goes home carrying a new pet pig under his arm and the farmer's wife happily knits a sweater for the boa.

Picture storybooks can provide adults and children with many sharing experiences. The elements in outstanding picture books enhance children's enjoyment through originality, imaginative plots, sympathetic characterization, humor, and interesting style.

Suggested Activities for Adult Understanding of Picture Books

- ☐ Choose several different editions of Mother Goose that contain the same nursery rhymes. Compare the artists' interpretations of these characters—for example, the illustrations of Jack Sprat found in *Marguerite De Angeli's Book of Nursery and Mother Goose Rhymes,* Cooper Eden's *The Glorious Mother Goose,* Kate Greenaway's *Mother Goose,* and Wallace Tripp's *Granfa' Grig Had a Pig.*
- ☐ Select a common animal or object that often appears in books for children. Find several picture books that develop a story about that animal or object. Compare the ways the different artists depict the animals through the illustrations, and the ways the writers describe the animals and develop plots about them.
- ☐ Select several alphabet books appropriate for young children and for older children. Evaluate each group of books, then share the books, your rationales, and your evaluations with the class.
- ☐ Find examples of rhythm, rhyme, repetition of sounds, and hyperbole in Mother Goose.
- ☐ Select several wordless books appropriate for stimulating oral language development in young children and several that are more appropriate for use with older children. Compare their details and plots.
- ☐ Begin a collection of nursery rhymes from other lands that illustrate the universal nature of children and unique characteristics of the people living in these countries.
- ☐ Find examples of humor in picture storybooks. Look for word play and nonsense, the unexpected, exaggeration, the ridiculous, and superiority.
- ☐ Choose a picture storybook that develops characters through the illustrations. Try to depict this same characterization through narration. Compare the lengths of the two stories.

References

1 Barsam, Richard. *A Peaceable Kingdom: The Shaker Abecedarius.* New York: Viking, 1978.

2 Cianciolo, Patricia J. "A Look at the Illustrations in Children's Favorite Picture Books." In *Children's Choices: Teaching with Books Children Like,* edited by Nancy Roser and Margaret Frith. Newark, Del.: International Reading Association, 1983.

3 Fry, Edward. "Fry's Readability Graph: Clarifications, Validity, and Extension." *Journal of Reading* 21 (December 1977): 249.

4 Hearne, Betsy. "Picture Books: More Than a Story." *Booklist* 30 (December 1, 1983): 577–578.

5 Martin, Sue Anne Gillespi. "The Caldecott Medal Award Books, 1938–1968: Their Literary and Oral Characteristics as They Relate to Storytelling." Detroit, Mich.: Wayne State University, 1969. University Microfilm No. 72–16, 219.

6 Nodelman, Perry. *Words About Pictures.* Athens: University of Georgia Press, 1988.

7 Norton, Donna E. "Genres in Children's Literature: Identifying, Analyzing, and Appreciating." In *Children's Literature: Resource for the Classroom,* edited by Masha Kabakow Rudman. Norwood, Mass.: Christopher-Gordon, 1989.

8 Strickland, Dorothy S. "Prompting Language and Concept Development." In *Literature and Young Children,* edited by Bernice Cullinan. Urbana, Ill.: National Conference of Teachers of English, 1977.

9 Sutherland, Zena, and Betsy Hearne. "In Search of the Perfect Picture Book Definition." In *Jump Over the Moon: Selected Professional Readings,* edited by Pamela Barron and Jennifer Burley. New York: Holt, Rinehart & Winston, 1984.

10 Whalen-Levitt, Peggy. "Making Picture Books Real: Reflections on a Child's-Eye View." In *The First Steps: Best of the Early CHLA Quarterly,* compiled by Patricia Dooley. Lafayette, Ind.: Purdue University, Children's Literature Association, 1984.

Involving Children in Picture Books

SHARING MOTHER GOOSE WITH CHILDREN

SHARING ALPHABET BOOKS WITH CHILDREN

USING PICTURE BOOKS THAT ENCOURAGE INTERACTION BETWEEN CHILDREN AND TEXTS

SHARING WORDLESS BOOKS WITH CHILDREN

READING TO CHILDREN

USING PICTURE STORYBOOKS TO STIMULATE DEVELOPMENT IN CHILDREN

DEVELOPING AESTHETIC SENSITIVITY IN CHILDREN

ACTIVITIES POSSIBLE WITH PICTURE STORYBOOKS

TO TRULY SHARE PICTURE BOOKS, YOU must care enough to select books and prepare book-related activities that children find stimulating and enjoyable. Picture-book experiences involve sharing nursery rhymes that stimulate oral language development and dramatization; alphabet, counting, and concept books that develop basic knowledge and discussion skills; wordless books that encourage children to find objects in pictures, make predictions, tell their own stories, or write creatively; picture storybooks ideal for reading aloud; illustrations that encourage aesthetic sensitivity; and picture books of all sorts that encourage children to join in with songs and movement. Whatever the book, if it is worth sharing, the sharing experience is worth thoughtful preparation. This section discusses a few of the many ways you can use picture books to enhance personal development in children.

SHARING MOTHER GOOSE WITH CHILDREN

Mother Goose rhymes are natural means of stimulating language development and listening appreciation in very young children. Linda Gibson Geller (4), who strongly endorses the use of nursery rhymes with young children, maintains that nursery rhymes popular with preschool children have one or more of the following characteristics: a simple story line, a simple story line that encourages finger play, a story in song with repeated chorus, a verse with nonsense words, a description of daily actions, and a choral reading in which children join in with the rhyming words.

Even two- and three-year-olds thoroughly enjoy and respond to the rhyme, rhythm, and nonsense found in nursery rhymes. Because passive listening may not encourage language development, adults must create experiences that motivate children to interact with the verses in enjoyable ways. Once children have heard the simpler Mother Goose rhymes several times, they usually can help you finish the verses by filling in missing words or rhyming elements: "Jack and Jill, went up the ——— to fetch a pail of water. Jack fell down, and broke his ———, and Jill came tumbling after." In addition to providing enjoyment during shared experience, this activity encourages auditory discrimination and attentive listening, skills necessary for later successes in reading and language arts.

Mother Goose rhymes stimulate language development and enjoyment when shared with an appreciative child.

You may also insert an incorrect word into a rhyme familiar to children and have children correct the error. Children especially enjoy this exercise when the nursery rhyme book has large, colorful illustrations in which the children can point out what is wrong with your version. For example, say, "Jack be nimble, Jack be quick, Jack jump over a pumpkin," or "Little Boy Blue come blow your horn. The pig's in the meadow, the chick's in the corn." Many children also enjoy making up their own incorrect versions.

Books such as Joanna Cole and Stephanie Calmenson's *Miss Mary Mac: And Other Children's Street Rhymes* help children become involved in the rhythmic elements of rhyme. This collection includes hand-clapping, ball-bouncing, and counting rhymes.

Young children enjoy creative play and spontaneously dramatize many of their favorite rhymes. Dramatization allows children to explore body movements, develop their senses, expand their imaginations and language development, and experiment with characterization (15). One of the first adult-led creative drama activities recommended for beginning school-age children encourages development of a sense of movement and interpretation of a situation without the use of words. Read or tell various nursery rhymes while children pretend to be each character in the rhyme and perform the actions expressed in the verses. Following each line, allow enough time for the children to act out each part. Children especially enjoy acting out such action rhymes as "Little Miss Muffet," "Jack Be Nimble," and "Hey Diddle Diddle."

After children have experiences with a number of roles in nursery rhymes, lead them in the development of cooperative pantomimes. For example, "Little Miss Muffet" has two characters, a girl and a spider, while "Hey Diddle Diddle" has four. Have the children form small groups and informally interact with others as they pantomime the actions. A child or a group of children can also pantomime the actions of a nursery rhyme character while another child or group guesses the identity of the character.

Nursery rhymes that children have memorized can be used for choral-speaking arrangements, even though the children may not have developed reading skills. Chapter 8 suggests ways to stimulate oral language and appreciation through choral speaking.

You can also use nursery rhymes with five- through eight-year-olds to stimulate creative dramatic skills in pantomime and role playing, to introduce the concept of plot development, to expand children's interpretive skills through choral speaking, and to encourage children's own storytelling.

You can encourage children to expand upon one of their favorite nursery rhymes, as do several delightful picture books devoted to one rhyme—such as Janet Stevens's *The House That Jack Built,* Sarah Hayes's *Bad Egg: The True Story of Humpty Dumpty,* and John Ivimey's *The Complete Story of the Three Blind Mice*. Other Mother Goose rhymes that lend themselves to extended oral, written, or artistic versions are "Old Mother Hubbard," "Old King Cole," and "Simple Simon." After sharing one of these books or rhymes with children, ask the children if there are any Mother Goose characters they would like to know more about.

A discussion with first graders, for example, revealed that several children wanted to know what it would be like to live in a pumpkin. They talked about how they might decorate its interior, what they could do inside a pumpkin, and how neighbors might react to a pumpkin in the neighborhood. They dictated their story to the teacher and then divided it into separate sentences, each written and illustrated on tagboard by one child, then placed in the classroom library. This book was read by many children and because one of the most popular picture storybooks in the classroom. When more children created their own books, the children's librarian developed a library display of both commercially published Mother Goose books and books printed and illustrated by the children.

Even sixth-graders can benefit from activities related to Mother Goose rhymes. In one sixth-grade class, students were discussing their favorite early childhood stories and wondered whether Mother Goose had been a real person. This question led to library research and debate. The search led to conflicting answers. Some sources indicated that the original Mother Goose was Dame Goose of Boston. Another resource said that she was goose-footed Bertha, wife of Robert II of France. Still others referred to Charles Perrault's *Tales of Mother Goose,* published in 1697. Many others stated that there never was a Mother Goose. Following this research, members of the class chose the version they favored and debated the issue with one another.

Several of the children's sources indicated that some Mother Goose rhymes were based upon the lives of real people. The children found this idea fascinating, and they wondered who or what incident might have been the basis of "Little Miss Muffet," "Little Jack Horner," or "Humpty Dumpty." A search for possible personages and situations resulted in the information shown in Chart 5–1. (Please note that the authenticity of these connections between Mother Goose personages and real situations is not verifiable. The activity, however, proved fascinating to the students involved and increased their literary and historical awareness.) Finally, the children wrote their own Mother Goose rhymes about people and situations in the news or in history, which acquainted them with unfamiliar ideas, beliefs, and customs of the past and present.

University students in children's literature classes have developed other stimulating ways of using Mother Goose with older children. For example, they have had children compare the illustrations in different editions of Mother Goose, discuss their personal responses to the illustrations, discover more information about art media used by illustrators, demonstrate certain techniques to a group, and illustrate their own picture books to be shared with younger children.

SHARING ALPHABET BOOKS WITH CHILDREN

The most common way to share an alphabet book with children is to read it to them or have them identify the objects in the pictures to reinforce letter/sound relationships. According to John Warren Stewig (17), however, alphabet books can and should also be used for developing visual literacy (the ability to look analytically at a picture and interpret it) and verbal literacy (the ability to talk clearly about one's observations, comparisons, and reactions). Stewig recommends a three-step sequence of activities using the illustrations in alphabet books: (1) have children describe the object in a picture, (2) have them compare two different objects, and (3) have them say which picture they prefer and why. Since alphabet books are illustrated and written at several levels of complexity, this activity may be used with children of various ages.

Stewig's activities can be used, for example, with three alphabet books, appropriate for young children, that contain different types of illustrations of butterflies: (1) *Brian Wildsmith's ABC,* (2) *Ed Emberley's ABC,* and (3) Marcia Brown's *All Butterflies: An ABC*. During a discussion of these three books, use the following sequence in order to increase visual and verbal literacy in children. First, ask the children to look at each picture and to describe what the artist has drawn in the picture, what colors are used in the picture, how large the butterfly is, what the butterfly is doing, where the butterfly is in the picture, and so forth. Second, ask the children to compare the illustrations of butterflies in the three alphabet books, focusing the discussion on similarities and differences in size, color, and setting and on which butterfly seems most real. Third, have the children tell which picture they prefer and why.

It is important to allow children to think about and articulate their own reasons for choosing a picture. This requires careful leadership, because an adult's opinion should not be used to sway children into forming an opinion. One child preferred the Wildsmith butterfly because it had beautiful purple and pink colors and resembled one he had painted that his mother had had framed. Another child preferred Marcia Brown's butterflies because when she looked at them, she felt as if she were walking in a beautiful meadow and watching the butterflies flying up ahead of her. A third child liked Emberley's butterfly because it was part of a humorous picture and she liked the idea of a butterfly's sharing an experience with a bear and a bird. Each child had valid reasons.

To increase language skills further, have children pretend they are one of the butterflies and tell a story about what they would do if they were that butterfly. Also, have the children paint butterfly pictures to increase aesthetic and visual skills.

Suse MacDonald's *Alphabatics* is excellent for encouraging children to describe how the illustrations proceed from a letter to an object that begins with that letter. Children enjoy experimenting with letters to see if they can create their own alphabatics.

USING PICTURE BOOKS THAT ENCOURAGE INTERACTION BETWEEN CHILDREN AND TEXTS

Several books for young children encourage them to find hidden objects or to predict what is going to happen next. Young children love to play "I spy" and look for hidden objects in pictures. Actively involving children in story experiences stimulates their language development, cognitive development, and enjoyment.

Familiar folktale and nursery rhyme characters are hiding in the illustrations of Janet and Allen Ahlberg's *Each Peach Pear Plum: An I-Spy Story*. The two lines that precede each picture tell who is in the picture; the text also suggests a hidden figure. Children enjoy searching the pastel watercolor drawings for such favorites as Tom Thumb, Mother Hubbard, Cinderella, the three bears, Jack and Jill, and Robin Hood. Children, not adults, should locate the hidden characters.

Another excellent book for interaction and discovery is *We Hide, You Seek,* by Jose Aruego and Ariane Dewey. Children miss a great deal of potential enjoyment if adults read the twenty-six words of the text without encouraging the children to find and identify the animals in the pictures, which tell the story of what happens when a group of African animals challenges a rhino to a game of hide and seek. The artists have camouflaged the animals so well that children must search for spotted leopards and giraffes hidden in the bush, reptiles and birds hidden in the desert, alligators and birds hidden in the swamp, zebras and lions camouflaged on the plains, and hippos and crocodiles hidden in the river.

Tana Hoban's *Take Another Look* and *Look! Look! Look!* encourage children to make predictions. These fascinating books allow the readers to peek through a hole and see a portion of the photograph on the following page. Children can tell what they think a picture is, and why, before turning the page to see if their prediction is correct. The effectiveness of such books depends in part on your ability to stimulate children's active participation, whether they are reading or listening, sitting in your lap, or sitting in a small group.

SHARING WORDLESS BOOKS WITH CHILDREN

Wordless books are ideal for encouraging language growth, stimulating intellectual development, motivating creative writing, developing text for reading, and evaluating language skills. Consider children's ages and the complexity of plot or details when choosing wordless books. Some wordless books have considerable detail, which stimulates observational skills and descriptive vocabularies; others are more appropriate for encouraging understanding and interpretation of sequential plot.

CHART 5–1
Mother Goose personages

Mother Goose Rhyme	Personages	Situations
There was an old woman who lived in a shoe.	Parliament James VI of Scotland and I of England	Geographic location of Parliament. England had many people. This disliked monarch was not English, but Parliament told the people to get along as well as they could.
Old King Cole was a merry old soul.	Third century—King Cole	He was a brave and popular monarch.
Humpty Dumpty sat on a wall.	Richard III—1483	The "usurper" when he lay slain upon Bosworth Field.
I love sixpence, pretty little sixpence.	Henry VII—1493 Charles of France	Miserliness of Henry resulted in public jest. French ruler pacified Henry with £149,000 when Henry signed the treaty of Etaples.
Little Jack Horner sat in a corner eating his Christmas pie.	Jack Horner, an emissary of the Bishop of Glastonbury	Jack lived at Horner Hall and was taking twelve deeds to church-owned estates to Henry VII. The deeds were hidden in a pie. On his way, he pulled out the deed to Mells Park estate and kept it.
Sing a song of sixpence, a pocket full of rye. Four and twenty blackbirds baked in a pie When the pie was opened, The birds began to sing; Wasn't that a dainty dish To set before a king? The King was in the counting house Counting out his money The Queen was in the pantry Eating bread and honey; The maid was in the garden, Hanging out the clothes, When down flew a blackbird, And snipped off her nose.	Henry VIII The friars and monks The friars and monks Henry VIII Henry VIII Katherine of Aragon Anne Boleyn Anne Boleyn, Cardinal Wolsey, and the royal headsman.	Henry's humming over the confiscated revenues from the friars' rich grainfields. The title deeds to twenty-four estates owned by the church were put into a pie and delivered to Henry VIII. The monks put their choicest treasures in chests and hid them in a lake. Henry picked the deeds he wanted and bestowed others as payment. Henry was counting his revenues. She was eating the bread of England, spread with Spain's assurances that the King could not divorce her. Anne had dainty frocks from France and was smiling at the King in the garden of Whitehall Palace. Cardinal Wolsey broke Anne's engagement to Lord Percy. After Anne married Henry VIII, the royal headsman executed Anne—1563.
To market, to market to buy a fat pig.	Henry VIII	Henry VIII declared himself head of the Church of England to obtain a divorce from Catherine of Aragon.

CHART 5–1
Mother Goose personages (cont.)

Mother Goose Rhyme	Personages	Situations
Needles and pins, needles and pins, When a man marries his trouble begins.	Katherine Howard and Henry VIII	After her marriage to Henry, she introduced pins from France to the English court. Ladies had to begin a separate allowance for this luxury.
Punch and Judy fought for a pie; Punch gave Judy a sad blow in the eye.	Punch—England Judy—France	England and France fought over Italy.
Little Boy Blue	Cardinal Wolsey	The cardinal was too busy with pleasant dreams about his fame to be aware of danger.
Hey diddle, diddle, The cat and the fiddle.	The cat—Queen Elizabeth I—1561	Queen Elizabeth played with her ministers as if they were mice. She liked to dance.
A frog he would a-wooing go,	Duke of Anjou and Queen Elizabeth I—1577	A satire about the wooing of forty-nine-year-old Elizabeth by the twenty-three-year-old French prince.
I saw a ship a sailing, A sailing on the sea,	Sir Francis Drake	Drake brought back potatoes and other foods that were introduced to England.
Mistress Mary, quite contrary. How does your garden grow?	Mary Queen of Scots and her royal maids	She wore flashing jewels and gowns from Paris.
Little Miss Muffet sat on a tuffet Eating her curds and whey; When along came a spider, and sat down beside her,	Mary Queen of Scots John Knox	At eighteen (1560), she was made monarch of Scotland. She laughed with her maids. John Knox denounced the frivolous Mary from the pulpit of St. Giles.
Little Bo-Peep has lost her sheep.	Mary Queen of Scots	Tells about Mary's problems as the clans rose and prepared for battle.
Jack Sprat could eat no fat, His wife could eat no lean.	Charles I Henrietta Maria of France	After their marriage, they each went their heedless ways and plundered England.
Yankee Doodle came to town, Riding on a pony; He stuck a feather in his hat, and called it macaroni.	Prince Rupert of the Palatinate, Royalist General of the Civil Wars—1653	Prince Rupert had a large following; he could lead men and showed great endurance. The feather signified that the wearer was one of his soldiers. Rupert could steal into an enemy's camp and take the horses.

Stimulating Cognitive and Language Development

Shelley L. Knudsen Lindauer (11) states that perhaps one of the most important roles of wordless books is promoting and refining language skills through creative expression. Wordless books lend themselves to a creative approach to storytelling by children. Masha Rudman (14) believes, "[W]ordless books can help children use books to foster their storytelling skills" (p. 199). Rudman maintains that this goal is reached by helping children write stories to accompany the pictures. In addition, teachers may use wordless books to write stories that children may then read. This final use for wordless books is especially important for using literature during literature-based reading instruction.

Literature is valuable in promoting cognitive development in children. Several skills associated with the thinking process—observing, comparing, and organizing—can be developed through the use of wordless books. Children can describe what is happening in each picture and the details that they observe, compare pictures or changes that occur, and organize their thoughts into sequentially well-organized stories. Describing, comparing, and storytelling also help children expand their vocabularies.

Children can describe the action in each detailed picture in Peter Spier's *Noah's Ark,* for example, as they follow the building of the ark; the loading of food, utensils, and animals; the problems that develop inside the ark; and the final landing and starting of life anew. One group of seven-year-olds did the following:

1 Identified animals they recognized in a two-page spread showing animals boarding the ark.
2 Described the color, size, mode of travel, and natural habitat of the animals.
3 Identified humorous details in the illustrations.
4 Identified Noah's problems and suggested possible causes and solutions.
5 Speculated about Noah's feelings as he tried to rid the roof of too many birds, dealt with a reluctant donkey, and finally closed the doors of the ark.
6 Thought of descriptive words for the animals, such as *slithering* for snakes, *leaping* for frogs, and *lazy brown* for monkeys.
7 Compared the positions of the snails in the illustrations at the beginning of the book and at the end.
8 Chose one picture each and told or wrote a detailed description of the picture.

Mercer Mayer's humorous wordless book *Frog Goes to Dinner* encourages before-and-after comparisons. People are enjoying a leisurely meal in one picture, for example, and in the next are experiencing the disruptions caused by Frog. A first grader made the following comparison when he discussed two pictures of the band:

> The band was playing beautifully. They had their eyes closed and were enjoying the music. All of a sudden the frog jumped in the saxophone. Now the saxophone player tried to play but couldn't. His face puffed out and he looked funny. The other players jumped. The frog made the drum player fall into his drum. The horn player thought it was funny.

Stephen Gammell's illustrations in the wordless portion of Rafe Martin's *Will's Mammoth* encourage children to describe Will's imaginary experiences while playing in the snow. You also may use the book to stimulate children to describe their own imaginary lives.

Mitsumasa Anno's wordless books help develop observational skills in older children. *Anno's Journey, Anno's Italy,* and *Anno's Britain* contain fascinating details that can be discovered during a visual trip through Europe. At the end of the books, there are lists of details that readers should look for, such as characters from folktales and well-known paintings or people.

Motivating Writing and Reading

With their colorful illustrations, wordless books are ideal for motivating children to write or dictate captions, compose group stories, and write individual stories. After children have composed group stories or written individual stories, they may read their own creations.

Dictation of Picture Captions. Many younger children enjoy having their parents or teachers write down their brief descriptions of the pictures in wordless books. First, have the children look at a book and discuss it. Then write exactly what the child dictates about the picture. If reading readiness is also a goal, repeat each word as you write it. When the captions are finished, you and the children should read them in sequence while the children follow the illustrations and the printing. You can also mix up the captions and ask the children to put them in sequential order. Wordless books that are simple enough for young children and also have a plot development that encourages children to dictate sequentially ordered sentences or picture captions include Peter Collington's *The Angel and the Soldier Boy,* Henrik Drescher's *The Yellow Umbrella,* Martha Alexander's *Out! Out! Out!,* Pat Hutchins's *Changes, Changes,* and Mercer Mayer's various book adventures with Boy, Dog, and Frog.

Dictation of Group or Individual Stories. Educators in reading and language arts, such as Roach Van Allen (20) and Russell Stauffer (16), recommend the use of language experiences that stimulate children's oral language and writing by exploring ideas and expressing feelings. These experiences in turn provide the content for group and individual stories composed by children and recorded by adults, who then used these stories for reading instruction.

Many teachers introduce students to the language experience approach to literature through group chart stories. These activities are appropriate for all age groups, but they are used most as reading-readiness or early reading activities in kindergarten or first grade. Usually, an entire group (guided by the teacher) writes a chart story after a shared motivational experience, such as a field trip, an art project, a film, music, or a story. Many of the wordless books discussed in this text provide excellent sources for motivational activities.

If you use a wordless book to motivate the writing of a chart story, first share the book with the group. Following oral discussion, have the children dictate the story, as you record it on posterboard, the chalkboard, or large sheets of newsprint, repeating each word aloud. (Some teachers identify each child's contribution to the chart story by placing the child's name after the contribution.) It is essential that children be able to see each word as it is written. As you write the chart story, children will see that sentences flow from the top to the bottom on a page, follow a left-to-right sequence, begin with capital letters, and end with periods. Following completion of the chart story, read the whole story. Then, ask the children to reread the story with you. Following this experience, some individual children may choose to read the whole story aloud while others may choose to read only their own contributions.

Place wordless books and their accompanying chart stories in areas easily accessible to children, so that the children can enjoy reading the stories by themselves. Some teachers tape record the children's reading of the chart stories and then place the recordings, the chart stories, and the wordless books in a listening center. The stories may also be read to children in other classes, or added to the library. (For additional information on using the language experience method, see Russell Stauffer [16] and Roach Van Allen [20].)

You can also use sequentially developed wordless books to teach children how to tell or write stories with stronger plots and sequential order. John Goodall's *The Adventures of Paddy Pork* contains more plot development than most wordless books. When the book was used with a group of fourth graders, the primary purpose was to encourage them to write a sequentially developed story. The teacher first shared the book orally with the children. They discussed the setting, the characters in the story, and events that probably occurred. The teacher encouraged the children to give their own interpretations of the pictures and then to share their reasons for those interpretations. The children then wrote their own stories to accompany the pictures in the book.

Picnic, School, and *New Baby* by Emily Arnold McCully provide opportunities for children to write dialogue, describe settings, develop conflicts and characterizations, and discuss themes. David Wiesner's *Free Fall* encourages children to write various interpretations of a fanciful dream. University students report that Chris Van Allsburg's *The Mysteries of Harris Burdick* is one of the most enticing nearly wordless books for older elementary students. Children can speculate about each fantasy in Van Allsburg's book, write their own stories, and share the stories with other children, who may have had different interpretations. Because there is no correct answer, children may choose to write more than one story about a single picture.

READING TO CHILDREN

An adult who reads to children accepts an opportunity and a responsibility for sharing a marvelous experience. Kay Vandergrift (21) states this dual role very well:

Through reading aloud, the reader re-creates for children not only their own world seen through other eyes but leads them also to worlds beyond the eye. Reading aloud is a way to let children enter, vicariously, into a larger world—both real and fanciful—in company with an adult who cares enough to take them on the literary journey. (p. 11)

Values of Reading to Children

There is probably no better way to interest children in the world of books than to read to them. Listening to books read aloud is a way for children to learn that literature is a form of pleasure. Without parents, librarians, or other adults, a very young child would not experience nursery rhymes or such stories as Beatrix Potter's *Peter Rabbit*, and younger elementary children would not experience the marvelous verses and stories of A. A. Milne or enter the joyous world of Dr. Seuss. For children just struggling to learn to read, a book may not be a source of happiness. In fact, books actually arouse negative feelings in many children. Being read to helps beginning readers develop an appreciation for literature that they could not manage with their own reading abilities.

The pleasure of the listening experience usually motivates children to ask for a book again or to read it themselves. Very young children may ask for a book to be reread so many times that they memorize it and then feel proud of being able to "read" it. When a teacher reads a particularly enjoyable selection to children in an elementary classroom, the children tend to check out all copies of that book in the class or school library. Michael Tunnell and James Jacobs (19) report in a research review of literature-based programs that "daily reading aloud from enjoyable trade books has been the key that unlocked literacy growth" for many students (p. 475).

Another value of reading aloud is the improvement it often brings to related areas, such as reading achievement, language development, and vocabulary development. A study by Dorothy Cohen (3) demonstrated that the vocabulary and reading scores of seven-year-olds who listened to books read aloud for twenty minutes each day improved significantly. Cohen's results are not surprising. Listening to and discussing stories give children opportunities to learn new meanings of familiar words, new synonyms for known words, and new words and concepts.

Reading aloud to children also improves their readiness for formal reading instruction. According to Mary Jett-Simpson (7):

Parents are the most important resource for developing readiness for formal reading instruction. Parents can

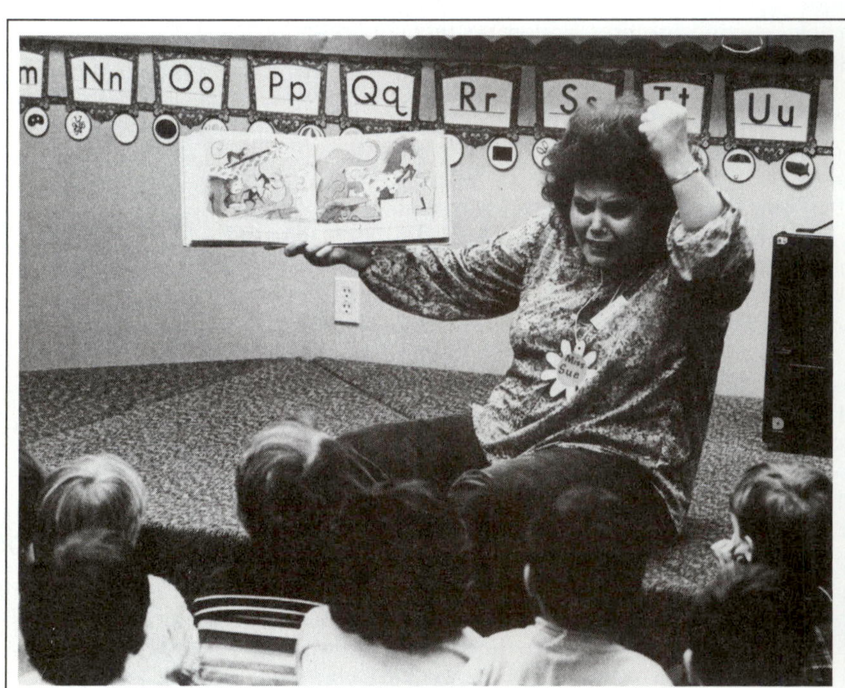

Sharing stories in the classroom or library allows children to discover the pleasure in books.

establish an attitude toward reading by giving books an important place in their own daily lives as well as in the lives of their children. (p. 73)

Jett-Simpson maintains that the most powerful sharing technique available for a parent is to set aside twenty to thirty minutes each evening to hold and read to a child. In order to gain the benefits from reading, you must select appropriate literature, prepare the selection carefully, and read with enthusiasm and enjoyment.

Choosing the Books

An appropriate book for reading aloud depends, of course, upon the ages of the children, their interests, the need to balance the types of literature presented, the number of children who will share the listening experience, and the quality of the literature. A book selected for reading aloud should be worthy of the time spent by the readers and the listeners. It should not be something picked up hurriedly to fill in time.

The style and the illustrations are both considerations when choosing books to read aloud. The language in A. A. Milne's *Winnie the Pooh* and Dr. Seuss's *The 500 Hats of Bartholomew Cubbins* appeals to young listeners. Likewise, young children enjoy illustrations that are integral to the story. For example, illustrations in Robert McCloskey's *Lentil* help children visualize a midwestern town in the early 1900s, and the illustrations in Maurice Sendak's *Where the Wild Things Are* bring Max's exceptional adventure to life. Other books, such as Arthur Yorinks's *Hey, Al* and Jane Yolen's *Owl Moon*, have such beautiful illustrations that they should be chosen to encourage aesthetic appreciation.

Children's ages, attention spans, and levels of reading ability are also important when selecting stories to be read aloud. The books chosen should challenge children to improve their reading skills and increase their appreciation of outstanding literature. The numerous easy-to-read books should usually be left for children to read independently. Young children respond to short stories; in fact, the four- or five-year-old may benefit from several short story times a day rather than a twenty- or thirty-minute period. Books such as Michael Rosen's *We're Going on a Bear Hunt*, Pat Hutchins's *The Wind Blew*, Robert Kraus's *Leo the Late Bloomer*, and Margaret Mahy's *17 Kings and 42 Elephants* are short and have colorful pictures. *We're Going on a Bear Hunt* uses repetitive language to encourage children to join in during reading. *The Wind Blew* uses rhyming words to tell its story. *Leo the Late Bloomer* relates the problems of a young tiger who cannot talk, eat, or read correctly until all at once, when he finally blooms. *17 Kings and 42 Elephants* includes both delightful nonsense text and humorous illustrations.

As children enter kindergarten and advance into first grade, they begin to enjoy longer picture storybooks with more elaborate plots. Robert McCloskey's *Make Way for Ducklings* and the various Dr. Seuss books are favorites with beginning elementary school children. Books such as William Steig's *Caleb & Kate* and Graham Oakley's *The Church Mice Adrift* have enough plot development to appeal to second-grade children.

By the time children reach the third grade, they are ready for stories read a chapter at a time. (A reading period should not end in the middle of a chapter.) Third graders usually enjoy E. B. White's *The Trumpet of the Swan, Charlotte's Web,* and *Stuart Little*. Fourth and fifth graders often respond to books like Madeleine L'Engle's *A Wrinkle in Time* and C. S. Lewis's *The Lion, the Witch and the Wardrobe*. Armstrong Sperry's *Call It Courage* and Esther Forbes's *Johnny Tremain* often appeal to sixth- and seventh-grade students. (These books will be discussed in later chapters.)

Reading to children should not end in the elementary grades. Without enjoyable oral listening experiences, many older children are not exposed to good literature because they cannot read it independently. Mary Kimmell and Elizabeth Segel (8) have compiled an annotated list of books that are appropriate for reading aloud to older children.

Preparing to Read Aloud

Many adults mistakenly believe that children's stories are so simple that there is no need for an adult to read a selection before reading it to children. Ramon R. Ross (13) states his view to the contrary with considerable force: "If I were to lay down for you one single cardinal rule that must never be broken, it would be that you never, *never* read a story aloud to an audience unless you have first read it aloud to yourself" (p. 207). Many embarrassing situations, such as being unable to pronounce a word or selecting an inappropriate book, can be avoided if you first read the story silently—in order to understand it, identify the sequence of events, recognize the mood, and identify any problems with vocabulary or concepts—and then read it aloud in order to practice pronunciation, pacing, and voice characterization. Adults with little or no experience in reading to children can listen to themselves on tape recorders. You should also decide how to introduce the story and what type of discussion or other activity, if any, to use following the reading.

The Reading Itself

What makes the story hour a time of magic or an insignificant part of the day? Research conducted by Linda Lamme (9) concludes that in addition to an enthusiastic reader and a carefully selected story, the following factors contribute to the quality of a reading performance:

1 *Child involvement*. Child involvement, including reading parts of a selection with an adult, predicting what will happen next, and filling in missing words, is the most influential factor during oral reading.
2 *Eye contact*. Eye contact between the reader and the audience is essential.
3 *Expression*. Adults who read with expression are more effective than those who read monotonously. Good oral readers try to put variety into their voices, but pitch should be neither too high nor too low, and volume should be neither too loud nor too soft.
4 *Pointing*. Readers who point to meaningful words or pictures in a book as they read are better oral readers than those who merely read the story and show the pictures.
5 *Knowledge of the story*. Adults who know the story and do not need to read the text verbatim are more effective during a presentation.
6 *Large and appealing books*. Readers who select picture books large enough for the children to see and appealing enough to hold their interest or elicit their comments are most effective.
7 *Grouping*. Grouping children so that all can see the pictures and hear the story is important.
8 *Highlighting*. Adults who highlight the words and language of a story by making the rhymes apparent, discussing unusual vocabulary words, and emphasizing repetition are better readers.

You should consider all of these factors when preparing for an oral presentation and when actually reading a story to an audience of children. Properly prepared, you can take children on a much-appreciated literary journey.

USING PICTURE STORYBOOKS TO STIMULATE DEVELOPMENT IN CHILDREN

Child development authority Barbara Borusch (1) maintains that adults can use picture storybooks to stimulate language, cognitive, moral, and social development in children, as well as to motivate interest in other books.

Robert McCloskey's *Time of Wonder*, for example, describes a family's experiences on an island in Maine. The natural setting of the story can encourage children to expand their vocabularies and can help them to understand such concepts as porpoise, gull, barnacle, bay, island, and driftwood. McCloskey's vivid language and figures of speech can acquaint children with new ways of experiencing and describing what they see and hear in the world around them: rustling leaves, heavy stillness, slamming rain, and gentle wind, as soft as a lullaby. As choppy waves indicate the approaching storm, McCloskey gives children many opportunities to observe the sharp contrasts in nature. Sharing the book with children can help them apply these observational powers to their own everyday lives.

Members of the family in *Time of Wonder* prepare for the hurricane and endure it together. Discussing the similarities and differences between the island before the hurricane and after it, between islands in different parts of the world, and between the island in the book and the children's own environment also can enhance children's cognitive development. Children can be encouraged to observe storms in their own environment and to describe the changes that result, using vocabulary that best conveys the color, sound, size, and time of such experiences. Also, children can evaluate the responsibilities and the possible feelings of each family member and consider what they or their families might feel and do under similar circumstances.

One of the most valuable things about picture storybooks such as *Time of Wonder* is the potential to motivate children to seek out other reading experiences. In this case, children may want to read or listen to other fictional or informational books about the Maine coast, storms, weather, coastal regions, water recreation, treasures from the sea, and water birds and other wildlife.

DEVELOPING AESTHETIC SENSITIVITY IN CHILDREN

If the word *aesthetic* denotes sensitivity to art and beauty, then looking at the beautiful illustrations in children's books must be aesthetic. Aesthetic sensitivity is important, according to H. S. Broudy (2), because "it is a primary source of experience on which all cognition, judgment, and action depend. It furnishes the raw material for concepts and ideals, for creating a world of possibility" (p. 636). Broudy believes that aesthetic experiences are so vital that they should be considered basic in children's education. He further believes that the best way to improve aesthetic sensitivity in children is to have them experiment with various artistic media themselves.

Linda Leonard Lamme and Frances Kane (10) also maintain that children learn to appreciate the artistic media used in book illustrations when they are given the stimulation and time to become actively involved in making their own illustrations. Some artistic media are too complex for very young children, of course, but Lamme and Kane believe that collage is an ideal medium for stimulating creative interpretations of literature and developing fine motor skills. In the process of making their own collages and reacting to the collages in book illustrations, children can also improve their vocabularies and oral discussion skills. Ezra Jack Keats, Leo Lionni, and Jeannie Baker are among the well-known illustrators of children's books who use collage. Adults can use works of such artists first to enlighten themselves and then as sources of material for children to discuss and compare. (Jeannie Baker's collage illustrations for *Where the Forest Meets the Sea* are fine sources of inspiration for both adults and children because Baker uses many different textures to create large, colorful pictures.)

Based on their work with young children, Lamme and Kane recommend use of the following sequence when introducing children to collage:

1. Encourage children to experiment with the collage technique by having them tear and cut shapes and pictures from plain paper or magazines and then paste the shapes onto another piece of paper.
2. Provide opportunities for children to experience different textures in the world around them and then use those textures in collages. Have the children take a texture exploration walk, for example, during which they feel and describe the textures of tree bark, leaves, grass, flowers, sidewalks, building materials, fabrics, paper, foods, and so forth. After they have experienced and discussed various textures, have them collect items with different textural qualities, then use the items in charts and texture collages. Encourage the children to touch and carefully look at their collage experiments and discuss their reactions to different texture combinations.
3. Have the children create their own collages or series of collages using as many different textures as they wish. Then, ask them to share these illustrations with one another, along with accompanying stories or descriptions.
4. Share with the children a picture book illustrated with collage. While reading the story and showing the children the pictures, ask the children to recognize the collage technique, discuss the feelings produced by each collage object and why they think the illustrator chose a certain material to represent it, and describe the texture they would feel if they could touch the original collage. Let them decide whether or not the collage illustrations make the story better.

Some picture book illustrations combine other artistic media with collage. Ezra Jack Keats's illustrations for *Maggie and the Pirate* are brightly colored combinations of collage and painting, while his *Regards to the Man in the Moon* uses bits of photography in the collages. Keats's *The Trip* even illustrates a young boy working with various colors and shapes of paper as he creates his own neighborhood within a box. This book can stimulate experimentation with both collage and painting.

Experimenting with simple cartoon techniques is another way that children can begin to develop their artistic skills and aesthetic sensitivities. Cartoons are very popular with children, who greatly enjoy watching Charles Schultz's "Peanuts" characters on television or reading about them when Schultz's cartoon books are available in the library. Well-known cartoonists, such as Syd Hoff (5, 6), have written books describing how they draw cartoons and illustrate picture storybooks for children—how they depict the different expressions on people's faces, show movement and various physical characteristics, and draw animals.

After experimenting with their own cartoons, children can look with new understanding and appreciation at picture storybooks illustrated by well-known cartoonists, such as Syd Hoff's easy-to-read book *Sammy the Seal,* James Stevenson's *Could Be Worse!* and *Grandaddy's Place* (by Helen V. Griffith) and William Steig's *Caleb & Kate* and *Spinky Sulks*. Have the children discuss how well the cartoons complement the text and compare the effectiveness of cartoons and other types of book illustration. Also have the children write stories and illustrate them with cartoons. Children enjoy creating their own cartoon books or creating a newspaper format that combines cartoons drawn by all of the children in a group.

ACTIVITIES POSSIBLE WITH A PICTURE STORYBOOK

The recommendations of this chapter for ways to share picture books with children are only a few of the possible ways of creating stimulating and enjoyable experiences with books. The following list (12) shows the varied activities that teachers, librarians, and other adults have developed around Maurice Sendak's *Where the Wild Things Are*.

1 *Appreciative listening*. Read the story to children; share the pictures and your enthusiasm.
2 *Oral language*. After reading the book, discuss with the children how they might also daydream like Max and make themselves heroes or heroines in a story. What activities would they dream about? Where would they go? What would they do? Ask the children to pantomime their dreams.
3 *Oral language and art interpretation*. Have the children create masks depicting the wild things and perform a creative drama of the story and other adventures that Max might have during another visit to the fantasy land.
4 *Oral language and art interpretation*. Have the children create puppets of the wild things and depict their adventures through a puppet production.
5 *Art interpretation*. At one time in his career, Maurice Sendak constructed papier-mâché models of storybook characters. Have the children select a favorite Sendak character and make a papier-mâché model.
6 *Art interpretation*. Maurice Sendak once designed window displays for new books. Have a group of children design a bulletin board as if it were a window display advertising *Where the Wild Things Are*.
7 *Art interpretation and oral language*. Ask the children to design a colorful poster to convince other people to buy and read Sendak's book.
8 *Art interpretation and oral language*. Have the children create a travel poster or travel brochure that advertises Max's fantasy land or that illustrates a new fantasy land of their own. The poster should be designed to convince others that they would enjoy visiting the fantasy land.
9 *Appreciative listening and creative writing*. Maurice Sendak enjoys listening to the music of Mozart, Beethoven, and Wagner while he works. Have the children listen to a recording of one of these composers, describe what they visualize as they listen, and draw a series of pictures stimulated by the listening experience. Have them write stories that accompany the pictures.
10 *Picture/mood interpretation*. Older children may also discover the relationship between the illustrations and text achieved by Sendak's book. Encourage older children to look carefully at the illustrations while reading or listening to the text. Discuss the enlargement of illustrations as the plot advances. Use the following quote from an interview with Sendak (22, p. 23) to stimulate the discussion:

> One of the reasons why the picture book is so fascinating is that there are devices to make the form itself more interesting. In *Where the Wild Things Are* the device is really a matching of shapes. I used it to describe Max's moods pictorially: his anger, which is more or less normal in the beginning; its expansion into rage; then the explosion of fantasy as a release from that particular anger; and finally the collapse of that, when the fantasy goes and it's all over. The smell of food brings Max back to reality and he's a little boy again. A book is inert. What I try to do is animate it, and make it move emotionally.

After children have discussed the pictorial devices that Sendak uses to animate the text, encourage them to use illustrations to animate their own writing.

11 *Motivation and enjoyment*. Create a Maurice Sendak reading center in the classroom or school library. In the center, place books written and illustrated by Sendak, books written by other authors and illustrated by Sendak, and any Sendak-motivated stories written and illustrated by children. Decorate the center with posters, papier-mâché characters, puppets, and other artwork created by children. Encourage the children to use the center.

While these activities are related to one book, they suggest the multiple experiences that could accompany many picture storybooks. Another source for developing activities around a single book or single illustrator is John Stewig's series, *Reading Pictures: Exploring Illustrations with Children* (18). This series includes activities to accompany illustrated texts by Marcia Brown, Nonny Hogrogian, Ezra Jack Keats, and Gerald McDermott. Remember, however, that children's enjoyment of books and reading is the major goal. Books can be shared and savored without planning any accompanying activities.

Suggested Activities for Children's Appreciation of Picture Books

- ☐ Choose a book of nursery rhymes appropriate for sharing with young children. Share the book with a child and encourage the child to interact with the rhymes by supplying missing words, making up rhyming games, or role-playing the characters found in the nursery rhymes.
- ☐ Choose several nursery rhymes that have a definite beginning, middle, and end. Use these rhymes with children to help them develop an understanding of plot development.
- ☐ Select several alphabet books that are appropriate for encouraging visual and verbal literacy. Develop a series of questions to encourage children to describe the pictures, compare the pictures, and evaluate their personal preferences for the pictures. Share the alphabet books and questions with a group of children.
- ☐ Select a wordless book appropriate for use with young children and another wordless book with enough detail for use with older children. Carefully plan an activity that encourages children to interact with each book. Share the books with the two different age groups, and compare the responses received from each group.
- ☐ Select a picture storybook appropriate for reading aloud to children. Prepare the story for reading, and share the book with a group of children or a peer group.
- ☐ Compile a list of picture storybooks appropriate for sharing with five-, six-, seven-, and eight-year-old children.
- ☐ Choose an art medium used to illustrate children's books. Research the methods used by illustrators who use that medium. Develop a series of activities that allow children to experience and experiment with the medium, create their own illustrations, and discuss literature illustrations that use the medium.
- ☐ Compile a list of picture book illustrators and their illustrations to stimulate an understanding of collage, cartoons, and other artistic media.
- ☐ Choose a picture book that illustrates a nursery song, animal song, or holiday song. Plan an activity that encourages children to sing, accompany the song with rhythm instruments, play a singing game, or play a counting game. Share the activity with a group of children or a peer group.
- ☐ Choose a children's picture storybook, other than Maurice Sendak's *Where the Wild Things Are,* and list various activities based on the book.

References

1 Borusch, Barbara. Personal correspondence with author, December 1, 1980.

2 Broudy, H. S. "How Basic Is Aesthetic Education? or Is It the Fourth R?" *Language Arts* 54 (September 1977): 631–637.

3 Cohen, Dorothy. "The Effect of Literature on Vocabulary and Reading Achievement." *Elementary English* 45 (February 1968): 209–213, 217.

4 Geller, Linda Gibson. *Wordplay and Language Learning for Children*. Urbana, Ill: National Council of Teachers of English, 1985.

5 Hoff, Syd. *How to Draw Cartoons*. New York: Scholastic, 1975.

6 Hoff, Syd. *Jokes to Enjoy, Draw, and Tell*. New York: Putnam, 1974.

7 Jett-Simpson, Mary. "Parents and Teachers Share Books with Young Children." In *Developing Active Readers: Ideas for Parents, Teachers and Librarians,* edited by Dianne L. Monson and Day Ann K. McClenathan. Newark, Del.: International Reading Association, 1979.

8 Kimmel, Mary, and Elizabeth Segel. *For Reading Out Loud*. New York: Dell, 1983.

9 Lamme, Linda Leonard. "Reading Aloud to Young Children." *Language Arts* 53 (November/December 1976): 886–888.

10 Lamme, Linda Leonard, and Frances Kane. "Children, Books, and Collage." *Language Arts* 53 (November/December 1976): 902–905.

11 Lindauer, Shelley L. Knudsen. "Wordless Books: An Approach to Visual Literacy." *Children's Literature in Education* 19 (1988): 136–142.

12 Norton, Donna. *Language Arts Activities for Children*. Columbus, Ohio: Merrill, 1989.

13 Ross, Ramon R. *Storyteller*. 2d ed. Columbus, Ohio: Merrill, 1980.

14 Rudman, Masha Kabakow. "Children's Literature in the Reading Program." In *Children's Literature: Resource for the Classroom,* edited by Masha Kabakow Rudman. Norwood, Mass.: Christopher-Gordon, 1989, 177–205.

15 Siks, Geraldine. *Drama with Children*. New York: Harper & Row, 1977.

16 Stauffer, Russell. *The Language-Experience Approach to the Teaching of Reading*. New York: Harper & Row, 1980.

17 Stewig, John Warren. "Alphabet Books: A Neglected Genre." *Language Arts* 55 (January 1978): 6–11.

18 Stewig, John Warren. *Reading Pictures: Exploring Illustrations with Children*. New Berlin, Wis.: Jenson, 1988. (There are four different titles in the series: *Marcia Brown, Nonny Hogrogian, Ezra Jack Keats,* and *Gerald McDermott*.)

19 Tunnell, Michael, and James S. Jacobs. "Using 'Real' Books: Research Findings on Literature Based Reading Instruction." *The Reading Teacher* 42 (March 1989): 470–477.

20 Van Allen, Roach. *Language Experiences in Communication*. Boston: Houghton Mifflin, 1976.

21 Vandergrift, Kay. "Reading Aloud to Young Children." In *Using Literature with Young Children,* edited by Leland B. Jacobs. New York: Columbia University, Teachers College, 1974.

22 Wintle, Justin, and Emma Fisher. *The Pied Pipers: Interviews with the Influential Creators of Children's Literature*. New York: Paddington, 1974.

CHILDREN'S LITERATURE

MOTHER GOOSE

Bodecker, N. M. *It's Raining, Said John Twaining*. Atheneum, 1973 (I:4–7). Fourteen Danish nursery rhymes are translated and illustrated.

Cole, Joanna, and Stephanie Calmenson. Compiled by. *Miss Mary Mac: And Other Children's Street Rhymes*. Illustrated by Alan Tiegreen. Morrow, 1990 (I:4–8). This text is a collection of 100 traditional rhymes.

De Angeli, Marguerite. *Marguerite De Angeli's Book of Nursery and Mother Goose Rhymes*. Doubleday, 1954 (I:4–7). A large book contains 376 nursery rhymes and illustrations with early English settings.

De Forest, Charlotte B. *The Prancing Pony: Nursery Rhymes from Japan*. Illustrated by Keiko Hida. Walker/Weatherhill, 1968 (I:5–10). Translations of traditional Japanese nursery rhymes were collected by Tasuku Harada.

Demi. *Dragon Kites and Dragonflies*. Harcourt Brace Jovanovich, 1986 (I:all). Twenty-two Chinese nursery rhymes are illustrated with Chinese drawings.

dePaola, Tomie. *Tomie dePaola's Mother Goose*. Putnam, 1985 (I:2–6). The large format and folk art make this a very appealing edition.

Edens, Cooper, ed. *The Glorious Mother Goose*. Atheneum, 1988 (I:all). This is a collection of rhymes illustrated by artists from the past.

Greenaway, Kate. *Mother Goose: Or, the Old Nursery Rhymes*. Warne, 1881 (I:3–7). A small Mother Goose is illustrated with charming Greenaway children.

Griego, Margot C., Betsy L. Bucks, Sharon S. Gilbert, and Laurel H. Kimball. *Tortillitas Para Mama and Other Spanish Nursery Rhymes*. Illustrated by Barbara Cooney. Holt, Rinehart & Winston, 1981 (I:3–7). Nursery rhymes appear in Spanish and English.

Hale, Sara Josepha. *Mary Had a Little Lamb*. Illustrated by Tomie dePaola. Holiday House, 1984 (I:3–7). The nursery rhyme is highly illustrated.

Hayes, Sarah. *Bad Egg: The True Story of Humpty Dumpty*. Illustrated by Charlotte Voake. Little, Brown, 1987 (I:2–6 R:3). An extended version explains why Humpty Dumpty fell.

Hoguet, Susan Ramsay. *Solomon Grundy*. Dutton, 1986 (I:3–7). Illustrations depict Solomon Grundy's life in early American history.

Ivimey, John. *The Complete Story of the Three Blind Mice*. Illustrated by Paul Galdone. Clarion, 1987 (I:2–8). A rhyming story extends information about the song.

Jeffers, Susan. *Three Jovial Huntsmen*. Bradbury, 1973 (I:4–7). Muted colors show hundreds of animals peeking out at three hunters who are unable to find them.

Lobel, Arnold. *Gregory Griggs and Other Nursery Rhyme People*. Greenwillow, 1978 (I:4–7). Thirty-four lesser-known nursery rhymes tell about humorous predicaments.

______. *The Random House Book of Mother Goose*. Random House, 1986 (I:2–6). A collection of 306 nursery rhymes is highly illustrated.

Marshall, James. *James Marshall's Mother Goose*. Farrar, Straus & Giroux, 1979 (I:3–7). Large humorous illustrations accompany each of the thirty-three nursery rhymes.

Martin, Sarah Catherine. *The Comic Adventures of Old Mother Hubbard and Her Dog*. Harcourt Brace Jovanovich, 1981 (I:3–7). A humorously illustrated edition contains one nursery rhyme.

Miller, Mitchell. *One Misty Moisty Morning*. Farrar, Straus & Giroux, 1971 (I:3–7). A small collection of the more unusual nursery rhymes is illustrated with soft pencil drawings.

Newbery, John. *The Original Mother Goose's Melody*. Reissue. Gale, 1969 (I:all). This is one of the early Mother Goose collections.

Opie, Iona, and Peter Opie. *A Nursery Companion*. Oxford University Press, 1980 (I:all). A collection of twenty-seven early British nursery rhymes appears with the original colored illustrations.

______. *The Oxford Nursery Rhyme Book*. Illustrated by Joan Hassall. Oxford University Press, 1955, 1984 (I:all). A collection of eight hundred rhymes and songs is illustrated with black-and-white woodcuts.

______. *Tail Feathers from Mother Goose: The Opie Rhyme Book*. Little, Brown, 1988 (I:all). A collection of mostly previously unpublished rhymes is illustrated by many artists.

Pearson, Tracey Campbell. *Old MacDonald Had a Farm*. Dial, 1984 (I:3–6). Humorous illustrations and music accompany the rhyme.

Rounds, Glen. *Old MacDonald Had a Farm*. Holiday House, 1989 (I:3–6). Bold pictures accompany the musical rhyme.

I = Interest by age range.
R = Readability by grade level.

Spier, Peter. *London Bridge Is Falling Down*. Doubleday, 1967 (I:all). Each line of the nursery rhyme and song is illustrated in detailed drawings.

Stevens, Janet. *The House That Jack Built*. Holiday House, 1985 (I:2–5). The cumulative nursery rhyme is developed into a humorously illustrated story.

Tarrant, Margaret. *Nursery Rhymes*. Crowell, 1978 (I:3–7). Forty-eight popular nursery rhymes are illustrated with traditional drawings.

Tripp, Wallace. *Granfa' Grig Had a Pig and Other Rhymes Without Reason from Mother Goose*. Little, Brown, 1976 (I:4–8). Humorous animal drawings illustrate 121 nursery rhymes in a large-book format.

Tudor, Tasha. *Mother Goose*. Walck, 1972 (I:3–7). Seventy-seven popular Mother Goose rhymes are illustrated in a small-book format.

Watson, Wendy. Compiled by. *Wendy Watson's Mother Goose*. Lothrop, Lee & Shepard, 1989 (I:5–8). This is a large collection of Mother Goose.

Wyndham, Robert. *Chinese Mother Goose Rhymes*. Illustrated by Ed Young. World, 1968; Philomel, 1982 (paperback) (I:4–7). Traditional Chinese rhymes are translated into English.

Zuromskis, Diane. *The Farmer in the Dell*. Little, Brown, 1978 (I:3–6). Colorful eighteenth-century pictures illustrate the song.

TOY BOOKS

Anno, Mitsumasa. *Anno's Faces*. Philomel, 1989 (I:2–6). Children can add facial expressions to fruits and vegetables.

Beisner, Monika. *A Folding Alphabet Book*. Farrar, Straus & Giroux, 1981 (I:4–6). In a long folded book, animals and other objects form the letters.

Bonforte, Lisa. *Farm Animals*. Random House, 1981 (I:2–4). A board book illustrates and describes common farm animals.

Brown, Margaret Wise. *The Goodnight Moon Room: A Pop-Up Book*. Illustrated by Clement Hurd. Harper & Row, 1984 (I:2–4). A combination of flaps and pop-ups encourages children to interact with the text.

Campbell, Rod. *Dear Zoo*. Four Winds, 1982 (I:2–4). Illustrations encourage children to hypothesize about the contents of a crate.

Carle, Eric. *Catch the Ball*. Philomel, 1982 (I:3–6). A string attached to a ball encourages children's vocabulary development.

_______. *The Honeybee and the Robber: A Moving Picture Book*. Philomel, 1981 (I:3–6). Brightly colored pop-ups allow children to move the wings of a bee and a butterfly.

_______. *Let's Paint a Rainbow*. Philomel, 1982 (I:3–6). A rainbow helps children learn the eight basic colors.

Craig, Helen. *Mouse House Months*. Random House, 1981 (I:3–6). A miniature foldout board book follows a tree through the seasons and shows a scene for each month.

Crowther, Robert. *The Most Amazing Hide-and-Seek Alphabet Book*. Viking, 1978 (I:3–6). In a mechanical book, each letter conceals an object that begins with that letter.

_______. *The Most Amazing Hide-and-Seek Counting Book*. Viking, 1981 (I:3–6). Colorful pages have pictures that pull, lift, or rotate to introduce counting.

dePaola, Tomie. *Giorgio's Village*. Putnam, 1982 (I:all). An Italian Renaissance village pops up.

Duke, Kate. *Clean-up Day*. Dutton, 1986 (I:1–3). A guinea pig helps in this board book.

_______. *The Playground*. Dutton, 1986 (I:1–3). Playground equipment is highlighted in this board book.

_______. *What Bounces?* Dutton, 1986 (I:1–3). A young guinea pig experiments with things that bounce.

Hill, Eric. *Spot Goes to School*. Putnam, 1984 (I:2–4). A flap-book encourages readers to discover a dog's activities at school.

_______. *Spot's Birthday Party*. Putnam, 1982 (I:2–4). In a "lift the flap" book, a dog plays hide-and-seek with the guests at his party.

_______. *Spot's First Walk*. Putnam, 1981 (I:2–4). Readers discover what a dog sees on his walk when they lift each flap.

_______. *Where's Spot?* Putnam, 1980 (I:2–4). Children search for a missing dog under the flaps.

Hoban, Tana. *Look! Look! Look!* Greenwillow, 1988 (I:3–6). Readers look through square cut-out spaces and hypothesize about what is in photographs.

Johnson, John E. *The Sky Is Blue, the Grass Is Green*. Random House, 1980 (I:2–4). This is a cloth color-concept book.

Lindgren, Barbro. *Sam's Ball*. Illustrated by Eva Eriksson. Morrow, 1983 (I:2–4). A boy and a cat learn to play together.

_______. *Sam's Bath*. Illustrated by Eva Eriksson. Morrow, 1983 (I:2–4). A boy puts many toys and his dog into the bathtub.

_______. *Sam's Lamp*. Illustrated by Eva Eriksson. Morrow, 1983 (I:2–4). A boy falls when he tries to reach a lamp.

Oxenbury, Helen. *The Car Trip*. Dial/Dutton, 1983 (I:2–4). A young boy enjoys a car ride even though he gets sick from eating too much.

_______. *The Checkup*. Dial/Dutton, 1983 (I:2–5). A young boy creates confusion when he visits a doctor.

_______. *Dressing*. Wanderer Books, 1981 (I:1–3). A board book shows step-by-step dressing.

_______. *Family*. Wanderer Books, 1981 (I:1–3). A board book shows a baby with a family.

_______. *First Day of School*. Dial/Dutton, 1983 (I:2–5). A girl experiences her first day at nursery school.

_______. *Friends*. Wanderer Books, 1981 (I:1–3). A board book illustrates a baby and friends.

_______. *I Can*. Random House, 1986 (I:1–3). A board book illustrates simple actions.

_______. *I Hear*. Random House, 1986 (I:1–3). This board book illustrates sounds in the environment.

_______. *I See*. Random House, 1986 (I:1–3). A child interacts with objects in the environment.

_______. *I Touch*. Random House, 1986 (I:1–3). A child touches objects.

_______. *Playing*. Wanderer Books, 1981 (I:1–3). A board book shows a baby playing.

_______. *Working*. Wanderer Books, 1981 (I:1–3). A board book shows familiar work.

Parish, Peggy. *I Can—Can You?* Illustrated by Marylin Hafner. Greenwillow, 1980 (I:1–3). A plastic book demonstrates accomplishments.

Pienkowski, Jan. *Haunted House*. Dutton, 1979 (I:all). A spooky house comes to life behind flaps and in pop-ups.

Potter, Beatrix. *The Peter Rabbit Pop-Up Book*. Warne, 1983 (I:3–8). This pop-up version creates a detailed setting for young children.

Roosevelt, Michele Chopin. *Animals in the Woods*. Random House, 1981 (I:2–4). One or two sentences describe pictures of woodland animals.

Scarry, Richard. *Richard Scarry's Lowly Worm Word Book*. Random House, 1981 (I:1–3). A worm demonstrates familiar objects, such as bath, body parts, and food.

Spier, Peter. *My School*. Doubleday, 1981 (I:3–7). Activities are associated with school.

______. *The Pet Store*. Doubleday, 1981 (I:3–7). Detailed drawings depict a pet store.

______. *The Toy Shop*. Doubleday, 1981 (I:3–7). Detailed drawings depict a toy store.

Tafuri, Nancy. *One Wet Jacket*. Greenwillow, 1988 (I:1–3). Items are taken off a child before she takes a bath.

______. *Two New Sneakers*. Greenwillow, 1988 (I:1–3). This book highlights items that a child puts on.

Wells, Rosemary. *Max's Bath*. Dial, 1985 (I:1–3). A young rabbit becomes stained when he takes juice and sherbet into the tub.

______. *Max's Bedtime*. Dial, 1985 (I:1–3). A young rabbit prepares for bed.

______. *Max's Birthday*. Dial, 1985 (I:1–3). A young rabbit enjoys his birthday.

______. *Max's Breakfast*. Dial, 1985 (I:1–3). A humorous book is about a young rabbit's breakfast.

______. *Max's First Word*. Dial, 1979 (I:2–4). A board book is for young children.

______. *Max's New Suit*. Dial, 1979 (I:2–4). This is a short board book story.

______. *Max's Ride*. Dial, 1979 (I:2–4). This is a humorous board book.

______. *Max's Toys: A Counting Book*. Dial, 1979 (I:2–4). This is a simple counting board book.

Zokeisha. *Things I Like to Eat*. Simon & Schuster, 1981 (I:1–3). One familiar food appears per page.

______. *Things I Like to Look At*. Simon & Schuster, 1981 (I:1–3). Pictures of familiar objects encourage language development.

______. *Things I Like to Play With*. Simon & Schuster, 1981 (I:1–3). Colorful pictures of familiar toys appeal to young children.

______. *Things I Like to Wear*. Simon & Schuster, 1981 (I:1–3). Illustrations help young children identify names of clothing.

ALPHABET BOOKS

Anno, Mitsumasa. *Anno's Alphabet: An Adventure in Imagination*. Crowell, 1975 (I:5–7). A wordless alphabet book shows a single letter on one page and a single object beginning with that letter on the opposite page.

Azarian, Mary. *A Farmer's Alphabet*. Godine, 1981 (I:5–8). Woodcuts present images of rural Vermont.

Baldwin, Ruth M. *One Hundred Nineteenth-Century Rhyming Alphabets in English*. Southern Illinois University, 1972 (I:all). A collection of older alphabets appeals to all readers.

Bayer, Jane. *A, My Name Is Alice*. Illustrated by Steven Kellogg. Dial, 1984 (I:3–7). Illustrations accompany the jump-rope rhyme.

Berger, Terry, and Alice S. Kandell. *Ben's ABC Day*. Lothrop, Lee & Shepard, 1982 (I:3–6). A child's familiar activities illustrate each letter.

Brown, Marcia. *All Butterflies: An ABC*. Scribner, 1974 (I:3–7). Two-word phrases that also correspond with two letters of the alphabet are illustrated on each double page.

Cleaver, Elizabeth. *ABC*. Atheneum, 1985 (I:3–7). A small book illustrates several items for each letter.

Ehlert, Lois. *Eating the Alphabet: Fruits and Vegetables from A to Z*. Harcourt Brace Jovanovich, 1989 (I:3–6). An ABC book develops around food.

Eichenberg, Fritz. *Ape in a Cape: An Alphabet of Odd Animals*. Harcourt Brace Jovanovich, 1952 (I:3–8). Each page presents one letter, a rhyming phrase about the illustration, and one large picture.

Emberley, Ed. *Ed Emberley's ABC*. Little, Brown, 1978 (I:5–8). An amusing alphabet shows the formation of the letters and an animal representation for each letter.

Feelings, Muriel. *Jambo Means Hello: Swahili Alphabet Book*. Dial, 1974 (I:all). A beautiful book uses the Swahili alphabet and drawings depicting the Swahili culture.

Gág, Wanda. *The ABC Bunny*. Coward, McCann, 1933 (I:3–6). A bunny has numerous adventures related to letters of the alphabet.

Geisert, Arthur. *Pigs from A to Z*. Houghton Mifflin, 1986 (I:all). Letters are hidden in the illustrations.

Greenaway, Kate. *A—Apple Pie*. Warne, 1886 (I:3–8). The old rhyme was first referenced in 1671.

Hague, Kathleen. *Alphabears: An ABC Book*. Illustrated by Michael Hague. Holt, Rinehart, & Winston, 1984 (I:3–7). Illustrations of teddy bears depict letters.

Hoban, Tana. *A, B, See!* Greenwillow, 1982 (I:4–6). Photographs illustrate objects that begin with the uppercase letters.

Kitchen, Bert. *Animal Alphabet*. Dial, 1984 (I:all). Unusual animals accompany each letter of the alphabet.

Lalicki, Barbara. *If There Were Dreams to Sell*. Illustrated by Margot Tomes. Lothrop, Lee & Shepard, 1984 (I:all). Poetry selections accompany each letter of the alphabet.

Lear, Edward. *An Edward Lear Alphabet*. Illustrated by Carol Newsom. Lothrop, Lee & Shepard, 1983 (I:3–7). This text is a newly illustrated version of Lear's famous nonsense rhyme.

Lobel, Arnold. *On Market Street*. Illustrated by Anita Lobel. Greenwillow, 1981 (I:4–7). Tradespeople show their wares from A to Z.

MacDonald, Suse. *Alphabatics*. Bradbury, 1986 (I:all). A series of pictures change a letter into an object that represents the letter.

Martin, Bill, Jr., and John Archambault. *Chicka Chicka Boom Boom*. Simon & Schuster, 1989 (I:4–8). The ABC's are presented through rhythmic verse.

Mendoza, George. *Norman Rockwell's Americana ABC*. Dell, 1975 (I:all). Norman Rockwell paintings illustrate each letter of the alphabet.

Merriam, Eve. *Halloween ABC*. Illustrated by Lane Smith. Macmillan, 1987 (I:6–12). Poems about Halloween are sequenced according to the alphabet.

Musgrove, Margaret. *Ashanti to Zulu: African Traditions*. Illustrated by Leo and Diane Dillon. Dial, 1976 (I:7–12). Traditions and customs from twenty-six African tribes are presented in alphabetical order.

Nicholson, William. *An Alphabet*. Wofsy, 1975 (I:all). A copy of an alphabet first published in 1897 is illustrated with different occupations.

Niland, Deborah. *ABC of Monsters*. McGraw-Hill, 1978 (I:3–6). A small humorous alphabet shows monsters doing funny things at a monster party.

Owens, Mary Beth. *A Caribou Alphabet*. Dog Ear, 1988 (I:all). Letters show actions and characteristics of caribou.

Provensen, Alice, and Martin Provensen. *A Peaceable Kingdom: The Shaker Abecedarius*. Viking, 1978 (I:all). This book is a newly illustrated edition of alphabet animal rhymes first published in the Shaker Manifesto of July 1882.

Tudor, Tasha. *A Is for Annabelle*. Walck, 1954 (I:3–7). Verses and illustrations relate to playing with a doll.

Van Allsburg, Chris. *The Z Was Zapped*. Houghton Mifflin, 1987 (I:all). Letters form a twenty-six-act play.

Wildsmith, Brian. *Brian Wildsmith's ABC*. Watts, 1962 (I:3–6). A word and a picture are included for each letter.

COUNTING BOOKS

Anno, Mitsumasa. *Anno's Counting Book*. Crowell, 1977 (I:3–7). Large, detailed drawings of landscapes illustrate each number.

______. *Anno's Counting House*. Philomel, 1982 (I:3–7). Cut-out windows show ten little people who demonstrate counting, adding, and subtracting.

______. *Anno's Math Games*. Philomel, 1989 (I:5–10). The illustrations and text show picture puzzles and mathematical recreations.

Aylesworth, Jim. *One Crow: A Counting Rhyme*. Illustrated by Ruth Young. Harper, 1988 (I:2–5). Groupings of animals represent the numbers.

Bang, Molly. *Ten, Nine, Eight*. Greenwillow, 1983 (I:3–6). A charming number game counts objects backward.

Carle, Eric. *My Very First Book of Numbers*. Crowell, 1974 (I:3–6). In this simple matching book, the child matches black squares with appropriate illustrations.

______. *The Very Hungry Caterpillar*. Crowell, 1971 (I:2–7). A colorful collage book shows the life cycle of a caterpillar.

Charlip, Remy, Mary Beth, and George Ancona. *Handtalk Birthday: A Number & Story Book in Sign Language*. Four Winds, 1987 (I:all). Vocabulary and numbers are shown through photographs of people using sign language.

Christelow, Eileen. *Five Little Monkeys Jumping on the Bed*. Clarion, 1989 (I:2–6). An illustrated text accompanies a counting rhyme.

Dunrea, Olivier. *Deep Down Under*. Macmillan, 1989 (I:3–7). Creatures that dig under the ground show numbers from one to ten.

Feelings, Muriel. *Moja Means One: Swahili Counting Book*. Illustrations by Tom Feelings. Dial, 1971 (I:all). Numbers from one through ten are shown in numbers, written in Swahili, and illustrated with scenes of Africa.

Gerstein, Mordicai. *Roll Over!* Crown, 1984 (I:3–6). A counting nursery rhyme uses various animals.

Giganti, Paul. *How Many Snails? A Counting Book*. Illustrated by Donald Crews. Greenwillow, 1988 (I:3–6). This is a combination counting and concept book.

Hoban, Tana. *Count and See*. Macmillan, 1972 (I:4–7). Photographs illustrate numbers.

______. *26 Letters and 99 Cents*. Greenwillow, 1987 (I:4–7). This is a combination alphabet and number book.

Hutchins, Pat. *The Doorbell Rang*. Greenwillow, 1986 (I:5–8). Math concepts develop as children divide cookies.

Kitchen, Bert. *Animal Numbers*. Dial, 1987 (I:all). This book is similar to the earlier *Animal Alphabet*.

Knight, Hilary. *Hilary Knight's The Twelve Days of Christmas*. Macmillan, 1981 (I:all). A bear gives his friend the gifts listed in the English folk song.

Magee, Doug. *Trucks You Can Count On*. Dodd, Mead, 1985 (I:3–8). Counting involves the parts of a large tractor-trailer.

Peek, Merle. *The Balancing Act: A Counting Song*. Clarion, 1987 (I:3–6). A counting song proceeds from one to ten.

Reiss, John J. *Numbers*. Bradbury, 1971 (I:4–7). Objects illustrate number concepts with large numbers shown in sets of five or ten.

Tafuri, Nancy. *Who's Counting?* Greenwillow, 1986 (I:3–6). Viewers follow a dog through the development of the concepts one through nine.

CONCEPT BOOKS

Ahlberg, Janet, and Allan Ahlberg. *The Baby's Catalogue*. Little, Brown, 1982 (I:2–6). Pictures and accompanying labels are categorized according to daily events and common objects.

Anno, Mitsumasa. *Anno's Faces*. Philomel, 1989 (I:3–7). Children can learn to identify different fruits and vegetables.

Banchek, Linda. *Snake In, Snake Out*. Illustrated by Elaine Arnold. Crowell, 1978 (I:3–7). Eight words related to spatial concepts are presented through the story of an old woman and a snake.

Barton, Byron. *Machines at Work*. Crowell, 1987 (I:2–6). Very large and colorful illustrations show construction equipment.

Carle, Eric. *The Grouchy Ladybug*. Crowell, 1971 (I:4–7). A ladybug progresses through the day from six in the morning to six at night.

______. *The Mixed-up Chameleon*. Crowell, 1975 (I:2–6). A chameleon that wishes to be other animals takes on different colors.

______. *My Very First Book of Colors*. Crowell, 1974 (I:3–6). Nine colors shown in half-page blocks are matched with illustrations.

______. *My Very First Book of Shapes*. Crowell, 1974 (I:4–7). Children match black shapes with similar shapes represented in color illustrations.

Crews, Donald. *Carousel*. Greenwillow, 1982 (I:4–8). Illustrations take readers on a carousel ride.

______. *Freight Train*. Greenwillow, 1978 (I:3–7). Colors, cars on a freight train, and concepts such as *through, daylight,* and *darkness* are developed.

______. *Harbor*. Greenwillow, 1982 (I:3–7). Children discover names of harbor ships as they go in and out of the harbor.

Dubanevich, Arlene. *Pigs in Hiding*. Four Winds, 1983 (I:3–6). An almost wordless book encourages children to search for the pigs.

Emberley, Ed. *Ed Emberley's Picture Pie: A Circle Drawing Book*. Little, Brown, 1984 (I:all). Color illustrations show how to make pictures from circles and portions of circles.

Emberley, Rebecca. *City Sounds*. Little, Brown, 1989 (I:2–7). This book includes urban sounds.

______. *Jungle Sounds*. Little, Brown, 1989 (I:2–7). This book presents quiet as well as noisy sounds.

Fowler, Susi Gregg. *When Summer Ends*. Illustrated by Marisabina Russo. Greenwillow, 1989 (I:3–7). A young girl and her mother discuss the seasons.

Gibbons, Gail. *Trains*. Holiday House, 1987 (I:4–7). Illustrations are labeled to show different types of cars and railroad functions.

Hoban, Tana. *Big Ones, Little Ones*. Greenwillow, 1976 (I:2–7). Big and little are illustrated in photographs of mother and baby zoo animals.

______. *Circles, Triangles, and Squares*. Macmillan, 1974 (I:4–8). Shapes are found in everyday objects.

______. *Dig, Drill, Dump, Fill.* Greenwillow, 1975 (I:5–10). Photographs present the world of heavy machinery.

______. *Look! Look! Look!.* Greenwillow, 1988 (I:3–6). Readers look through square cut-out spaces and hypothesize about what is in photographs.

______. *Of Colors and Things.* Greenwillow, 1989 (I:3–6). The illustrations encourage children to match colors.

______. *Over, Under, Through and Other Spatial Concepts.* Macmillan, 1973 (I:3–7). Photographs illustrate spatial concepts.

______. *Push–Pull, Empty–Full: A Book of Opposites.* Macmillan, 1972 (I:3–7). Photographs illustrate the meanings of antonyms.

______. *Round & Round & Round.* Greenwillow, 1983 (I:2–7). Color photographs illustrate round objects found in the environment.

______. *Shapes, Shapes, Shapes.* Greenwillow, 1986 (I:3–8). Photographs illustrate various shapes in the environment.

______. *Take Another Look.* Greenwillow, 1981 (I:4–8). Viewers look at an object through a circular cutout, guess what it is, and turn the page to see if they are correct.

Kalan, Robert. *Blue Sea.* Illustrated by Donald Crews. Greenwillow, 1979 (I:3–7). Large illustrations of fish show size concepts.

McMillan, Bruce. *Here a Chick, There a Chick.* Lothrop, Lee & Shepard, 1983 (I:3–6). Photographs illustrate opposites.

______. *Super Super Superwords.* Lothrop, Lee & Shepard, 1989 (I:3–7). Concepts are related to adjectives.

Pluckrose, Henry. *Capacity.* Photographs by Chris Fairclough. Watts, 1988 (I:4–8). Photographs show experiments with how much things hold.

______. *Length.* Watts, 1988 (I:4–8). Photographs show how to measure.

______. *Sorting.* Watts, 1988 (I:4–8). Photographs show different ways to sort.

Rockwell, Anne. *First Comes Spring.* Crowell, 1985 (I:3–6). Seasonal changes, activities, and appropriate clothing are shown through the life of a young bear.

Sattler, Helen. *Train Whistles.* Illustrated by Giulio Maestro. Lothrop, Lee & Shepard, 1985 (I:3–9). Text and illustrations explain the meanings of signals used by train whistles.

Spier, Peter. *Fast-Slow, High-Low: A Book of Opposites.* Doubleday, 1972 (I:5–10). Numerous detailed pictures illustrate opposites.

Tafuri, Nancy. *Early Morning in the Barn.* Greenwillow, 1983 (I:2–5). An almost wordless book illustrates the journey of three chicks as they explore the barnyard.

Yabuuchi, Masayuki. *Whose Baby?* Philomel, 1985 (I:2–4). Pictures of animal babies are followed by pictures of adult parents.

______. *Whose Footprints?* Philomel, 1985 (I:2–4). Pictures of animal footprints are followed by pictures of the animals that make the prints.

WORDLESS BOOKS

Alexander, Martha. *Bobo's Dream.* Dial, 1970 (I:3–7). Bobo dreams that he becomes large and rescues his master's football from a group of bigger boys.

______. *Out! Out! Out!* Dial, 1968 (I:3–7). A little boy coaxes a bird out of a house by creating a trail of cereal.

Anno, Mitsumasa. *Anno's Britain.* Philomel, 1982 (I:all). The illustrations follow a traveler through Great Britain.

______. *Anno's Flea Market.* Bodley Head, 1984 (I:all). Hundreds of items are seen in the flea market of an old city.

______. *Anno's Italy.* Collins, 1980 (I:all). Illustrations take the viewer on a trip through Italy.

______. *Anno's Journey.* Philomel, 1978 (I:6–12). Illustrations record the journey of the artist through the countryside, small towns, and cities of Europe.

______. *Topsy-Turvies—Pictures to Stretch the Imagination.* Walker/Weatherhill, 1970 (I:all). Children are instructed to decide what the little men are doing in the pictures.

Briggs, Raymond. *The Snowman.* Random House, 1978 (I:3–7). A snowman comes to life and takes his young creator on a tour of strange lands.

Carle, Eric. *Do You Want to Be My Friend?* Crowell, 1971 (I:3–7). A mouse searches for a friend.

Collington, Peter. *The Angel and the Soldier Boy.* Knopf, 1987 (I:3–7). A wordless book adventure has a boy angel and a solider as protagonists and pirates as antagonists.

dePaola, Tomie. *The Hunter and the Animals: A Wordless Picture Book.* Holiday House, 1981 (I:5–9). Forest animals convince the hunter to break his gun.

______. *Pancakes for Breakfast.* Harcourt Brace Jovanovich, 1978 (I:3–7). The procedures for making pancakes are shown in this humorous, wordless book.

Drescher, Henrik. *The Yellow Umbrella.* Bradbury, 1987 (I:all). A small wordless book follows the adventures of two monkeys and one yellow umbrella.

Goodall, John. *The Adventures of Paddy Pork.* Harcourt Brace Jovanovich, 1968 (I:5–9). A pig named Paddy leaves home and joins the circus.

______. *Paddy Goes Traveling.* Atheneum, 1982 (I:5–9). Paddy Pork has an adventure on the beach.

______. *Paddy Under Water.* Atheneum, 1984 (I:5–9). Paddy discovers a treasure chest.

______. *Story of a Main Street.* Macmillan, 1987 (I:all). This wordless book traces the same street from medieval through contemporary times.

______. *The Story of an English Village.* Atheneum, 1979 (I:all). Changes occur in an English village from the fourteenth century to the twentieth century.

______. *The Story of the Seashore.* Macmillan, 1990 (I:all). The illustrations provide an historical review.

Hutchins, Pat. *Changes, Changes.* Macmillan, 1971 (I:2–6). Two doll figures create different things out of blocks.

Keats, Ezra Jack. *Clementina's Cactus.* Viking, 1982 (I:all). The illustrations allow readers to explore the desert.

McCully, Emily Arnold. *New Baby.* Harper & Row, 1988 (I:3–8). This wordless book tells about the influence of a baby on a mouse family.

______. *Picnic.* Harper & Row, 1984 (I:3–7). A young mouse is lost on the day of the family picnic.

______. *School.* Harper & Row, 1987 (I:3–8). This wordless book tells about the mouse family introduced in *Picnic.*

Mayer, Mercer. *A Boy, a Dog, a Frog, and a Friend.* Dial, 1971 (I:5–9). The frog's son accompanies the boy and the dog when they find a turtle. The turtle tricks them but then becomes a friend.

______. *A Boy, a Dog and a Frog.* Dial, 1967 (I:5–9). A boy and a dog try unsuccessfully to catch a frog.

______. *Frog Goes to Dinner.* Dial, 1974 (I:6–9). Boy secretly puts Frog into his pocket and takes him along when the family goes to a fancy restaurant.

______. *Frog, Where Are You?* Dial, 1969 (I:5–9). Boy and Dog search for the missing Frog.

______, and Marianna Mayer. *One Frog Too Many.* Dial, 1975 (I:5–9). Frog becomes jealous when Boy receives a new frog for his birthday.

Ormerod, Jan. *Sunshine*. Lothrop, Lee & Shepard, 1981 (I:4–8). A child wakes up and helps her parents leave the house on time.

Spier, Peter. *Noah's Ark*. Doubleday, 1977 (I:3–9). Detailed illustrations accompany Jacobris Revius's poem *The Flood*.

Van Allsburg, Chris. *The Mysteries of Harris Burdick*. Houghton Mifflin, 1984 (I:all). Mystery and fantasy pictures encourage readers to plot their own stories.

Wiesner, David. *Free Fall*. Lothrop, Lee & Shepard, 1988 (I:all). A boy has a fantasy dream.

EASY-TO-READ BOOKS

Benchley, Nathaniel. *Oscar Otter*. Illustrated by Arnold Lobel. Harper & Row, 1966 (I:5–9 R:2). Oscar gets lost and is chased by a fox, a wolf, and a moose.

______. *Small Wolf*. Illustrated by Joan Sandin. Harper & Row, 1972 (I:6–10 R:3). A Native American family moves west from Manhattan Island in order to avoid conflict with European colonists.

Bonsall, Crosby. *The Case of the Cat's Meow*. Harper & Row, 1965 (I:5–9 R:2). The Wizard Private Eyes try to solve the mystery of Mildred the missing cat.

______. *The Case of the Scaredy Cats*. Harper & Row, 1971 (I:5–9 R:1). Girls prove that girls are as good as boys.

Brenner, Barbara. *Wagon Wheels*. Illustrated by Don Bolognese. Harper & Row, 1978 (I:6–9 R:1). The true story of Ed Muldie and his family as they move from Kentucky to Kansas in 1878.

Bulla, Clyde Robert. *Daniel's Duck*. Illustrated by Joan Sandin. Harper & Row, 1979 (I:6–9 R:2). Daniel lives in the mountains of Tennessee and admires his neighbor's talent for carving.

Bunting, Eve. *The Big Red Barn*. Illustrated by Howard Knotts. Harcourt Brace Jovanovich, 1979 (I:6–9 R:2). Craig's grandpa teaches him to accept changes in his life.

Chenery, Janet. *The Toad Hunt*. Illustrated by Ben Shecter. Harper & Row, 1967 (I:5–9 R:2). An entertaining information book tells about toads and frogs.

Ehrlich, Amy. *Leo, Zack and Emmie*. Dial, 1981 (I:5–8 R:2). A girl affects the friendship of two boys.

Flower, Phyllis. *Barn Owl*. Illustrated by Cherryl Pape. Harper & Row, 1978 (I:5–8 R:1). This science book describes the barn owl's hunting methods.

Gage, Wilson. *Squash Pie*. Illustrated by Glen Rounds. Greenwillow, 1976 (I:5–8 R:3). This humorous story is about a farmer who plants squash because he wants squash pie.

Gray, Genevieve. *How Far, Felipe?* Illustrated by Ann Grifalconi. Harper & Row, 1978 (I:6–9 R:2). A history book tells the story of Felipe and his donkey when they join Colonel Anzos's caravan in 1775 and travel to California.

Griffith, Helen V. *Alex and the Cat*. Illustrated by Joseph Low. Greenwillow, 1982 (I:5–8 R:1). A dog tries to realize his great dreams, but discovers that he is better off as a house pet.

Hoff, Syd. *Chester*. Harper & Row, 1961 (I:5–8 R:1). Chester is a wild horse who wants to belong to someone.

______. *Sammy the Seal*. Harper & Row, 1959 (I:5–8 R:1). Sammy lives in a zoo, but wants to see what it would be like on the outside.

Hopkins, Lee Bennett (ed.). *Surprises*. Illustrated by Megan Lloyd. Harper & Row, 1984 (I:5–9). This is a collection of short poems for beginning readers.

Kessler, Leonard. *Kick, Pass, and Run*. Harper & Row, 1966 (I:5–8 R:1). Football is explained in simple terms.

Leeuwen, Jean Van. *More Tales of Oliver Pig*. Dial, 1981 (I:5–7 R:2). Oliver has further adventures.

______. *Tales of Oliver Pig*. Illustrated by Arnold Lobel. Dial, 1979 (I:5–7 R:2). Oliver the pig has five short adventures.

Lobel, Arnold. *Frog and Toad All Year*. Harper & Row, 1976 (I:5–8 R:1). Frog and Toad have some funny adventures throughout the various seasons of the year.

______. *Frog and Toad Are Friends*. Harper & Row, 1970 (I:5–8 R:1). Frog and Toad are seen in five short stories.

______. *Frog and Toad Together*. Harper & Row, 1972 (I:5–8 R:1). These five short stories are about the adventures of Frog and Toad.

______. *Grasshopper on the Road*. Harper & Row, 1978 (I:5–8 R:2). Grasshopper sets out on a trip and meets some insects who don't like to do something different every day.

______. *Owl at Home*. Harper & Row, 1975 (I:5–8 R:2). Five stories explore Owl's adventures.

______. *Uncle Elephant*. Harper & Row, 1981 (I:5–8 R:2). Uncle Elephant takes care of his nephew when the parents are lost at sea.

Marshall, Edward. *Four on the Shore*. Illustrated by James Marshall. Dial, 1985 (I:5–9 R:1). Four boys tell ghost stories.

Ryder, Joanne. *Fireflies*. Illustrated by Don Bolognese. Harper & Row, 1977 (I:6–9 R:1). This book tells the life cycle of a firefly in words and pictures.

Schwartz, Alvin. *In a Dark, Dark Room*. Illustrated by Dirk Zimmer. Harper & Row, 1984 (I:6–9 R:2). This book contains seven scary stories.

Seuss, Dr. *The Cat in the Hat*. Random House, 1957 (I:4–7 R:1). A very unusual cat causes both amusement and mischief when he entertains two bored children on a rainy day.

______. *The Cat in the Hat Comes Back*. Random House, 1958 (I:4–7 R:1). The cat returns and brings with him little cats A through Z.

Wiseman, Bernard. *Morris Goes to School*. Harper & Row, 1970 (I:5–8 R:1). Morris Moose cannot count so he decides to go to school.

______. *Morris Has a Cold*. Dodd, Mead, 1978 (I:5–8 R:1). Boris Bear tries to help Morris Moose get rid of a cold.

PICTURE STORYBOOKS

Aardema, Verna. *Why Mosquitoes Buzz in People's Ears*. Illustrated by Leo and Diane Dillon. Dial, 1975 (I:5–9 R:6). This is a cumulative African folk tale.

Ackerman, Karen. *Song and Dance Man*. Illustrated by Stephen Gammell. Knopf, 1988 (I:3–8 R:4). Grandpa re-creates the magic of vaudeville.

Adoff, Arnold. *Black Is Brown Is Tan*. Illustrated by Emily Arnold McCully. Harper & Row, 1973 (I:3–7). A happy family with a black mother and a white father share experiences.

Agee, Jon. *The Incredible Painting of Felix Clousseau*. Farrar, Straus & Giroux, 1988 (I:5–8 R:4). Paintings come to life in an early Paris setting.

Ahlberg, Janet, and Allen Ahlberg. *Each Peach Pear Plum: An I-Spy Story*. Viking, 1978 (I:3–7). Two short lines on each page suggest what the reader should find in a picture.

______. *Peek-a-boo!* Viking, 1981 (I:2–6). A baby peeks through an opening on a page to discover the family's activities.

Ahnolt, Catherine. *Truffles Is Sick*. Little, Brown, 1987 (I:2–5 R:2). A young pig discovers that being sick has its advantages.

Aruego, Jose, and Ariane Dewey. *We Hide, You Seek*. Greenwillow, 1979 (I:2–6). A rhino plays hide-and-seek with many camouflaged African animals.

Asch, Frank, and Vladimir Vagin. *Here Comes the Cat!* Scholastic, 1989 (I:all). A bilingual story, written in Russian and English, shows what happens when a cat visits mice.

Baker, Jeannie. *Where the Forest Meets the Sea*. Greenwillow, 1988 (I:4–10 R:5). An Australian forest comes to life through the collage technique.

Baylor, Byrd. *The Best Town in the World*. Illustrated by Ronald Himler. Scribner's Sons, 1983 (I:all). The poetic text presents a nostalgic view of a small town.

Brown, Marc. *Arthur's Baby*. Little, Brown, 1987 (I:3–6 R:3). Arthur adjusts to a new baby.

Brown, Marcia. *Shadow*. Scribner's Sons, 1982 (I:all). This is a highly illustrated version of an African poem.

Brown, Margaret Wise. *The Runaway Bunny*. Rev. ed. Illustrated by Clement Hurd. Harper & Row, 1972 (I:2–7 R:6). A beautiful children's story emphasizes the need for both independence and love.

Bunting, Eve. *Ghost's Hour, Spook's Hour*. Illustrated by Donald Carrick. Clarion, 1987 (I:2–7 R:2). A boy experiences fear when the lights go out and he cannot find his parents.

_______. *The Mother's Day Mice*. Illustrated by Jan Brett. Clarion, 1986 (I:3–6). Mice search the woods for perfect gifts.

_______. *The Wednesday Surprise*. Illustrated by Donald Carrick. Clarion, 1989 (I:3–9 R:5). A seven-year-old girl teaches her grandmother to read.

Burningham, John. *Avocado Baby*. Crowell, 1982 (I:3–6 R:4). A weakling baby becomes strong after eating an avocado.

_______. *The Snow*. Crowell, 1975 (I:2–5). A small boy plays outside with his mother.

Burton, Virginia Lee. *Katy and the Big Snow*. Houghton Mifflin, 1943, 1971 (I:2–6 R:4). Katy the strongest crawler tractor saves a town after a heavy snowfall.

_______. *The Little House*. Houghton Mifflin, 1942 (I:3–7 R:3). A house is strong but needs love as it becomes dilapidated and lonely over the years.

_______. *Mike Mulligan and His Steam Shovel*. Houghton Mifflin, 1939 (I:2–6 R:4). Mary Anne the steam shovel proves that she can dig in one day more than one hundred men can dig in a week.

Carle, Eric. *The Secret Birthday Message*. Crowell, 1972 (I:3–7). Basic shapes are shown in a birthday message.

Carlstrom, Nancy White. *Jesse Bear, What Will You Wear?* Illustrated by Bruce Degen. Macmillan, 1986 (I:3–6). A rhyming text follows a young bear's activities.

Cazet, Denys. *A Fish in His Pocket*. Watts, 1987 (I:3–6 R:4). A young bear resolves the problem of a dead fish.

de Brunhoff, Jean. *The Story of Babar*. Random House, 1933, 1961 (I:3–9 R:4). In this original story, Babar eventually becomes the king of the elephants.

_______, and Laurent de Brunhoff. *Babar's Anniversary Album: 6 Favorite Stories*. Random House, 1981 (I:3–9 R:4). This album contains *The Story of Babar, The Travels of Babar, Babar the King, Babar's Birthday Surprise, Babar's Mystery,* and *Babar and the Wully-Wully*.

Denslow, Sharon Phillips. *Night Owls*. Illustrated by Jill Kastner. Bradbury, 1990 (I:4–8 R:4). An aunt and her nephew share memorable experiences.

dePaola, Tomie. *The Clown of God*. Harcourt Brace Jovanovich, 1978 (I:all R:4). A legend about a juggler and a miracle.

_______. *An Early American Christmas*. Holiday House, 1987 (I:4–7 R:6). The book shows a Christmas with a New England family living in the early 1800s.

_______. *Haircuts for the Woolseys*. Putnam, 1989 (I:2–6 R:4). A family of sheep are clipped and then saved from the cold by sweaters knitted from the wool.

_______. *Nana Upstairs & Nana Downstairs*. Putnam, 1973 (I:3–7 R:6). Tommy has two beloved grandmothers: a great-grandmother upstairs and a grandmother downstairs.

_______. *Oliver Button Is a Sissy*. Harcourt Brace Jovanovich, 1979 (I:5–8 R:2). Other boys call Oliver a sissy because he likes to dance, read books, and dress in costumes.

_______. *The Quicksand Book*. Holiday House, 1977 (I:5–9 R:4). A humorous story discusses the composition of quicksand and how to rescue someone who falls into quicksand.

_______. *Strega Nona's Magic Lessons*. Harcourt Brace Jovanovich, 1982 (I:5–9 R:6). Disaster results when Big Anthony tries to use Strega Nona's magic.

_______. *Too Many Hopkins*. Putnam, 1989 (I:2–6 R:4). A family of rabbits tries to plant a garden.

DeWitt, Jamie. *Jamie's Turn*. Illustrated by Julie Brinckloe. Raintree, 1984 (I:6–9 R:3). In a true story, a boy saves his stepfather's life.

Duvoisin, Roger. *Petunia*. Knopf, 1950 (I:3–6 R:6). Petunia, the silly goose, learns that she has to do more than carry a book to gain wisdom.

Emberley, Barbara. *Drummer Hoff*. Illustrated by Ed Emberley. Prentice-Hall, 1967 (I:3–7 R:6). A cumulative rhyme depicts all of the people associated with firing a cannon.

Engel, Diana. *Josephina Hates Her Name*. Morrow, 1989 (I:5–8 R:4). An alligator child discovers pride in her name.

Ernst, Lisa Campbell. *When Bluebell Sang*. Bradbury, 1989 (I:4–8 R:5). A singing cow overcomes her problems by reverting to animal behavior.

Fatio, Louise. *The Happy Lion*. Illustrated by Roger Duvoisin. McGraw-Hill, 1954 (I:3–7 R:7). A lion who lives in a zoo discovers people are not so friendly when he goes to town to visit them.

Fleischman, Paul. *Rondo in C*. Illustrated by Janet Wentworth. Harper & Row, 1988 (I:all). The artist shows a student's piano recital.

Fleischman, Sid. *The Scarebird*. Illustrated by Peter Sis. Greenwillow, 1988 (I:5–9 R:5). A lonesome farmer creates a scarecrow for a friend until he makes friends with a homeless boy.

Flournoy, Valerie. *The Patchwork Quilt*. Illustrated by Jerry Pinkney. Dial, 1985 (I:5–8 R:4). The sewing of a family quilt develops close family memories.

Fox, Mem. *Hattie and the Fox*. Illustrated by Patricia Mullins. Bradbury, 1987 (I:3–7). In a cumulative tale, a hen tries to convince farm animals about approaching danger.

_______. *Night Noises*. Illustrated by Terry Denton. Harcourt Brace Jovanovich, 1989 (I:3–8 R:5). Night noises turn out to be pleasant rather than scary.

Gág, Wanda. *Millions of Cats*. Coward, McCann, 1929 (I:3–7 R:3). A little old woman's desire for a pretty cat results in a fight between trillions of cats.

Gage, Wilson. *Cully, Cully and the Bear*. Illustrated by James Stevenson. Greenwillow, 1983 (I:4–6 R:2). In a humorous tale, a hunter goes after a bearskin to make his house more comfortable.

Galbraith, Kathryn O. *Laura Charlotte*. Illustrated by Floyd Cooper. Putnam's 1990 (I:4–6 R:4). A mother tells her daughter about her own childhood experiences.

Gammell, Stephen. *Wake Up Bear . . . It's Christmas!* Lothrop, Lee & Shepard, 1981 (I:5–8 R:4). A Christmas story is accompanied by humorous illustrations.

Gauch, Patricia Lee. *Christina Katerina and the Time She Quit the Family.* Illustrated by Elise Primavera. Putnam, 1987 (I:4–8 R:6). A young girl discovers that there are more important things than doing only what pleases her.

Gerstein, Mordicai. *The Room.* Harper & Row, 1984 (I:6–8 R:3). Text and illustrations follow the occupants of a room over many years.

Griffith, Helen V. *Grandaddy's Place.* Illustrated by James Stevenson. Greenwillow, 1987 (I:4–8 R:4). A young girl learns to appreciate her grandfather and her grandfather's rural home.

Hadithi, Mwenye. *Crafty Chameleon.* Illustrated by Adrienne Kennaway. Little, Brown, 1987 (I:4–8 R:5). An original story tells why the crocodile and the leopard do not bother the chameleon.

Haley, Gail E. *A Story, a Story.* Atheneum, 1970 (I:6–10 R:6). In an African tale, Ananse the spider man bargains with the Sky God.

Henkes, Kevin. *Jessica.* Greenwillow, 1989 (I:3–6 R:5). A girl has an imaginary friend.

Herriot, James. *Moses the Kitten.* Illustrated by Peter Barrett. St. Martin's, 1984 (I:all R:5). A young kitten finds a home on a Yorkshire farm.

Hest, Amy. *The Crack-of-Dawn Walkers.* Illustrated by Amy Schwartz. Macmillan, 1984 (I:5–8 R:3). A young girl develops a close relationship with her grandfather.

Hoban, Russell. *A Baby Sister for Frances.* Illustrated by Lillian Hoban. Harper & Row, 1964 (I:5–8 R:4). Frances the badger has a new baby sister, and things just aren't the same.

———. *A Bargain for Frances.* Illustrated by Lillian Hoban. Harper & Row, 1970 (I:4–8 R:2). This easy-to-read book tells the story of Frances and her friend Thelma.

———. *Best Friends for Frances.* Illustrated by Lillian Hoban. Harper & Row, 1969 (I:4–8 R:4). Frances discovers that her little sister is a lot of fun and can also be a best friend.

———. *Bread and Jam for Frances.* Illustrated by Lillian Hoban. Harper & Row, 1964 (I:4–8 R:4). Frances wants bread and jam, not eggs or anything else that is new.

———. *Nothing to Do.* Illustrated by Lillian Hoban. Harper & Row, 1964 (I:4–8 R:4). When Walter Possum complains that he has nothing to do, Father solves his problem.

Hoberman, Mary Ann. *Mr. and Mrs. Muddle.* Illustrated by Catharine O'Neill. Little, Brown, 1988 (I:3–8 R:4). In a humorous story, two animals disagree.

Hughes, Shirley. *Alfie Gives a Hand.* Lothrop, Lee & Shepard, 1983 (I:3–6 R:4). When he helps a friend, Alfie discovers that he no longer needs his security blanket.

Hurd, Edith Thacher. *I Dance in My Red Pajamas.* Illustrated by Emily Arnold McCully. Harper & Row, 1982 (I:3–7 R:3). A girl and her visiting grandparents form a warm relationship.

Hutchins, Pat. *Happy Birthday, Sam.* Greenwillow, 1978 (I:3–6 R:4). Grandpa's birthday present allows Sam to reach various items.

———. *Where's the Baby?* Greenwillow, 1988 (I:3–6 R:4). A monster baby leaves tracks.

———. *The Wind Blew.* Macmillan, 1974 (I:3–6 R:4). A short, rhyming story tells with colorful pictures what happened when the wind blew objects away from people.

Johnston, Tony. *The Witch's Hat.* Illustrated by Margot Tomes. Putnam, 1984 (I:4–8 R:2). Repetitive language enhances a story about a hat that turns itself into various creatures.

Jonas, Ann. *When You Were a Baby.* Greenwillow, 1982 (I:2–5 R:2). The author reminds children about things they could not do as babies but can do as growing children.

Joyce, William. *Dinosaur Bob and His Adventures with the Family Lazardo.* Harper & Row, 1988 (I:5–9 R:5). A friendly dinosaur accompanies a family home from Africa.

Jukes, Mavis. *Like Jake and Me.* Illustrated by Lloyd Bloom. Knopf, 1984 (I:6–9 R:4). An incident with a spider brings a boy and his stepfather closer together.

Keats, Ezra Jack. *Dreams.* Macmillan, 1974 (I:3–8 R:3). Robert makes a mouse at school, and everyone else dreams his mouse saves Archie's cat from a dog.

———. *Goggles!* Macmillan, 1969 (I:5–9 R:3). Archie and Willie outwit bullies and reach home safely.

———. *A Letter to Amy.* Harper & Row, 1968 (I:3–8 R:3). Peter writes a birthday party invitation to his friend Amy.

———. *Louie.* Greenwillow, 1975. (I:3–8 R:2). Louie responds to a puppet in a play and later is given the puppet by the children who put on the show.

———. *Maggie and the Pirate.* Four Winds, 1979 (I:4–8 R:3). A "pirate" steals Maggie's pet cricket.

———. *Peter's Chair.* Harper & Row, 1967 (I:3–8 R:2). Peter overcomes jealousy when his furniture is painted for his new baby sister.

———. *Pet Show!* Macmillan, 1972 (I:4–8 R:2). Beautiful bright colors and collages illustrate a children's pet show.

———. *Regards to the Man in the Moon.* Four Winds, 1981 (I:4–8 R:3). Two children build a spaceship from junk and fuel it with their imaginations.

———. *The Trip.* Greenwillow, 1978 (I:3–8 R:2). Louie constructs a shoe box scene so he can visit his friends.

Kellogg, Steven. *A Rose for Pinkerton.* Dial, 1981 (I:4–8 R:3). In a humorous story, a girl chooses a kitten as a friend for her Great Dane.

———. *Tallyho, Pinkerton!* Dial, 1982 (I:4–8 R:3). Rose the Great Dane and her owner go on a hilarious trip to the woods.

Khalsa, Dayal Kaur. *I Want a Dog.* Clarkson, 1987 (I:4–7 R:5). A girl pretends a roller skate is a dog to practice caring for a pet.

Kimmel, Eric A. *The Chanukkah Tree.* Illustrated by Giora Carmi. Holiday House, 1988 (I:5–9 R:5). A peddler convinces the people of a town that they need a special tree.

Kraus, Robert. *Leo the Late Bloomer.* Illustrated by Jose and Ariane Aruego. Windmill, 1971 (I:2–6 R:4). A large, colorful picture book tells the story of a young tiger who can't do anything right.

Leaf, Munro. *The Story of Ferdinand.* Illustrated by Robert Lawson. Viking, 1936 (I:4–10 R:6). A mild-mannered bull intended for the bullring manages instead to "be himself."

Lenski, Lois. *Sing a Song of People.* Illustrated by Giles Laroche. Little, Brown, 1987 (I:4–10). This is an illustrated poem about the city.

Lent, Blair. *Bayberry Bluff.* Houghton Mifflin, 1987 (I:3–8 R:6). A town evolves from a tenting community to elaborately decorated houses.

Lindgren, Barbro. *The Wild Baby Goes to Sea.* Adapted from the Swedish by Jack Prelutsky. Illustrated by Eva Eriksson. Greenwillow, 1983 (I:2–6). A story in rhyme tells about an imaginative child and a box.

Lionni, Leo. *Alexander and the Wind-up Mouse*. Pantheon, 1969 (I:3–6 R:3). A real mouse learns it's better to be real than to be a toy.

______. *The Biggest House in the World*. Pantheon, 1968 (I:3–6 R:7). A small snail decides it's better to be himself than to be the biggest in the world.

______. *Tillie and the Wall*. Knopf, 1989 (I:2–7 R:4). A mouse discovers what is on the other side of the wall.

Lyon, George Ella. *Come a Tide*. Illustrated by Stephen Gammell. Orchard, 1990 (I:5–8 R:5). High water causes a family to work together.

McAfee, Annalena. *Kristy Knows Best*. Illustrated by Anthony Browne. Knopf, 1988 (I:4–8). Fantasy material is written in rhyme while realistic material is written in prose.

Macaulay, David. *Why the Chicken Crossed the Road*. Houghton Mifflin, 1987 (I:5–9 R:6). A chicken causes a series of fantastic events.

McCloskey, Robert. *Blueberries for Sal*. Viking, 1948 (I:4–8 R:6). A bear cub and a young girl get mixed up and start following the wrong mothers.

______. *Lentil*. Viking, 1940 (I:4–9 R:7). Lentil saves the homecoming when Old Sneep tries to wreck the welcome.

______. *Make Way for Ducklings*. Viking, 1941 (I:4–8 R:4). A city park provides a safe home for the ducklings.

______. *One Morning in Maine*. Viking, 1952 (I:4–8 R:3). Sal and her family experience the joys of living on an island.

______. *Time of Wonder*. Viking, 1957 (I:5–8 R:4). A family explores an island in the spring, during a hurricane, and after the storm has passed.

McKissack, Patricia C. *Nettie Jo's Friends*. Illustrated by Scott Cook. Knopf, 1989 (I:5–9 R:5). A girl faces a dilemma when she cannot take her doll to a wedding.

McPhail, David. *Fix-It*. Dutton, 1984 (I:3–7 R:2). An emergency develops when the television does not function.

Mahy, Margaret. *17 Kings and 42 Elephants*. Illustrated by Patricia MacCarthy. Dial, 1987 (I:3–8). A nonsense poem is illustrated with cardboard cuts.

Marshall, James. *George and Martha One Fine Day*. Houghton Mifflin, 1978 (I:3–8). Two hippos have a thoroughly delightful day as they walk on a tightrope and visit an amusement park.

Martin, Bill, and John Archambault. *Up and Down on the Merry-Go-Round*. Illustrated by Ted Rand. Holt, Rinehart & Winston, 1988 (I:3–8). This is a rhyming story.

Martin, Jacqueline Briggs. *Buzzy Bones and the Lost Quilt*. Illustrated by Stella Ormai. Lothrop, Lee & Shepard, 1988 (I:4–8 R:6). A mouse-child is distraught after losing his quilt.

______. *Buzzy Bones and Uncle Ezra*. Illustrated by Stella Ormai. Lothrop, Lee & Shepard, 1984 (I:3–8 R:6). A young mouse overcomes his fear of the wind.

Martin, Rafe. *Will's Mammoth*. Illustrated by Stephen Gammell. Putnam, 1989 (I:2–8). In an almost wordless book, a young boy has an imaginary experience while playing in the snow.

Maruki, Toshi. *Hiroshima No Pika*. Lothrop, Lee & Shepard, 1982 (I:10+ R:4). A family experiences the atomic bomb on August 6, 1945.

Mathers, Peter. *Theodor and Mr. Balbini*. Harper & Row, 1988 (I:5–9 R:5). A man discovers that he has a talking dog.

Mathis, Sharon Bell. *The Hundred Penny Box*. Illustrated by Leo and Diane Dillon. Viking, 1975 (I:6–9 R:3). Young Michael becomes friends with his Great-great-aunt Dew and learns about the old box in which she keeps a penny for every year of her life.

Mayer, Mercer. *There's a Nightmare in My Closet*. Dial, 1969 (I:3–7 R:3). A young boy decides to get rid of his nightmare by confronting the monster.

Narahashi, Keiko. *I Have a Friend*. Macmillan, 1987 (I:2–6+ R:3). A small boy has a shadow for a friend.

Naylor, Phyllis Reynolds. *Keeping a Christmas Secret*. Illustrated by Lena Shiffman. Atheneum, 1989 (I:3–7 R:3). A four-year-old boy reveals a secret and then redeems his action.

Ness, Evaline. *Sam, Bangs & Moonshine*. Holt, Rinehart & Winston, 1966 (I:5–9 R:3). Sam almost costs a friend his life.

Newberry, Clare. *Barkis*. Harper & Row, 1938 (I:3–8 R:6). A new birthday puppy at first causes problems because two children do not want to share him.

______. *Marshmallow*. Harper & Row, 1942 (I:2–7 R:7). Oliver the cat is introduced to a new roommate, a rabbit.

Noble, Trinka Hakes. *The Day Jimmy's Boa Ate the Wash*. Illustrated by Steven Kellogg. Dial, 1980 (I:5–8 R:4). Havoc results when a boy drops his pet boa constrictor in the hen house.

Oakley, Graham. *The Church Mice Adrift*. Atheneum, 1977 (I:5–10 R:6). The church cat saves the church mice from an invasion of rats.

______. *The Church Mice in Action*. Atheneum, 1982 (I:5–10 R:7). The church mice enter Sampson in a cat show.

______. *The Church Mice Spread Their Wings*. Atheneum, 1975 (I:5–10 R:6). Sampson and the mice discover that nature is not so placid.

______. *The Church Mouse*. Atheneum, 1972 (I:5–10 R:6). Arthur lives peacefully and enjoyably in a church.

______. *Hetty and Harriet*. Atheneum, 1982 (I:5–10 R:6). A discontented hen and her meek friend leave the security of their barnyard for a series of adventures.

Peet, Bill. *Cyrus the Unsinkable Sea Serpent*. Houghton Mifflin, 1975 (I:5–9 R:7). A not-so-fierce sea serpent rescues a sailing ship from squalls and pirates.

______. *The Gnats of Knotty Pine*. Houghton Mifflin, 1975 (I:5–9 R:6). Gnats save the forest animals during hunting season.

______. *How Droofus the Dragon Lost His Head*. Houghton Mifflin, 1971 (I:5–9 R:5). A good, kind dragon befriends a poor family.

______. *No Such Things*. Houghton Mifflin, 1983 (I:4–8 R:6). Nonsense words and creatures combine to make humorous reading.

Peterson, Jeanne Whitehouse. *I Have a Sister, My Sister Is Deaf*. Illustrated by Deborah Ray. Harper & Row, 1977 (I:3–8 R:1). The author shares her enjoyable experiences with her deaf sister.

Polacco, Patricia. *Meteor!* Dodd, Mead, 1987 (I:6–10 R:7). Humorous fiction tells the reactions of a town when a meteor falls to earth.

______. *Thunder Cake*. Philomel, 1990 (I:5–8 R:5). A grandmother helps her granddaughter overcome fear of storms.

Porte, Barbara Ann. *Harry in Trouble*. Illustrated by Yossi Abolafia. Greenwillow, 1989 (I:3–7 R:2). A boy learns that other people also lose possessions.

Provensen, Alice, and Martin Provensen. *Shaker Lane*. Viking, 1987 (I:5–9 R:3). Illustrations show changing society along Shaker Lane.

______. *The Year at Maple Hill Farm*. Atheneum, 1978 (I:4–9 R:3). Large illustrations and text trace the seasons of the year.

Purdy, Carol. *Least of All.* Illustrated by Tim Arnold. Macmillan, 1987 (I:5–8 R:5). The youngest girl in the family proves that she can be important when she learns to read.

Rand, Gloria. *Salty Sails North.* Illustrated by Ted Rand. Holt, 1990 (I:5–8 R:4). A dog and its owner explore the Pacific coastline.

Ransome, Arthur. *The Fool of the World and the Flying Ship.* Illustrated by Uri Shulevitz. Farrar Straus & Giroux, 1968 (I:6–10 R:6). A humble Russian lad manages to marry the czar's daughter.

Rayner, Mary. *Garth Pig and the Ice Cream Lady.* Atheneum, 1977 (I:5–9 R:4). A wolf uses an ice cream truck to capture a pig.

Rey, Hans. *Curious George.* Houghton Mifflin, 1941, 1969 (I:2–7 R:2). George begins his slapstick adventures when he leaves the jungle with the man who has a yellow hat.

Rosen, Michael. *We're Going on a Bear Hunt.* Illustrated by Helen Oxenbury. Macmillan, 1989 (I:2–7). Repetitive language appeals to children.

Rylant, Cynthia. *Mr. Griggs' Work.* Illustrated by Julie Downing. Watts, 1989 (I:4–8 R:5). A post office worker is reminded of his work when he is not in the office.

Schatell, Brian. *Farmer Goff and His Turkey Sam.* Lippincott, 1982 (I:4–7 R:5). A prize-winning turkey who performs tricks runs away and wins a pie-eating contest.

Schotter, Roni. *Captain Snap and the Children of Vinegar Lane.* Illustrated by Marcia Sewall. Orchard, 1989 (I:5–9 R:5). Children are surprised after they help a hermit who is ill.

Schwartz, Amy. *Annabelle Swift, Kindergartner.* Orchard, 1988 (I:4–7 R:4). A girl faces kindergarten.

Schwartz, Henry. *How I Captured a Dinosaur.* Illustrated by Amy Schwartz. Orchard, 1989 (I:5–8 R:5). An eight-year-old girl finds a dinosaur while on a camping trip.

Sendak, Maurice. *In the Night Kitchen.* Harper & Row, 1970 (I:5–7). A young child dreams that he is in the world of the night kitchen.

______. *Seven Little Monsters.* Harper & Row, 1977 (I:5–8). An illustrated account of the actions of Sendak's monsters.

______. *The Sign on Rosie's Door.* Harper & Row, 1960 (I:5–9 R:2). Rosie pretends she's a singer and tries to stage a show.

______. *Where the Wild Things Are.* Harper & Row, 1963 (I:4–8 R:6). Max's vivid imagination turns his room into a forest inhabited by wild things.

Seuss, Dr. *And to Think That I Saw It on Mulberry Street.* Vanguard, 1937 (I:3–9 R:5). A young boy imagines all the fantastic things that could be on his street.

______. *Did I Ever Tell You How Lucky You Are?* Random House, 1973 (I:4–10 R:3). Many things are worse than sitting on a prickly cactus.

______. *Dr. Seuss's Sleep Book.* Random House, 1962 (I:4–10 R:5). Dr. Seuss gives readers a humorous "Who's-Asleep-Score."

______. *The 500 Hats of Bartholomew Cubbins.* Vanguard, 1938 (I:4–9 R:4). Bartholomew has a bewitched hat that keeps reappearing as he tries to take off his hat before the King.

______. *Horton Hatches the Egg.* Random House, 1940, 1968 (I:3–9 R:4). Horton replaces lazy Mayzie on her nest and finally hatches an elephant bird.

______. *Hunches in Bunches.* Random House, 1982 (I:6–10 R:4). A young boy has problems deciding on his hunches.

______. *I Can Lick 30 Tigers Today!* Random House, 1969 (I:4–10 R:4). This text contains several short stories.

______. *If I Ran the Zoo.* Random House, 1950 (I:4–10 R:3). A boy searches in odd places for some unusual animals.

Sharmat, Marjorie Weinman. *The Best Valentine in the World.* Illustrated by Lilian Obligado. Holiday House, 1982 (I:3–7 R:4). A fox believes his friend has forgotten to make him a valentine.

Sis, Peter. *Rainbow Rhino.* Knopf, 1987 (I:4–8 R:4). Four animals discover that home is the best place.

Skorpen, Liesel Moak. *His Mother's Dog.* Illustrated by M. E. Mullin. Harper & Row, 1978 (I:4–9 R:5). Jealousy results over a dog and a new baby.

Small, David. *Eulalie and the Hopping Head.* Macmillan, 1982 (I:4–7 R:5). A toad and her daughter find an abandoned doll in the woods.

______. *Imogene's Antlers.* Crown, 1985 (I:5–8 R:6). A young girl wakes up wearing antlers.

Spier, Peter. *Bored—Nothing to Do!* Doubleday, 1978 (I:3–9). When two boys become bored, they build and fly their own airplane.

______. *The Legend of New Amsterdam.* Doubleday, 1979 (I:all). Illustrations and text about the city of New Amsterdam (New York) in the 1660s.

______. *Oh, Were They Ever Happy!* Doubleday, 1978 (I:4–9). Children surprise their parents when they paint the house.

______. *The Star-Spangled Banner.* Doubleday, 1973 (I:8+). The words of the national anthem are illustrated in accurate detail from history.

Steig, William. *The Amazing Bone.* Farrar, Straus & Giroux, 1976 (I:6–9 R:3). A pig and a talking bone escape from robbers and a hungry fox.

______. *Caleb & Kate.* Farrar, Straus & Giroux, 1977 (I:6–9 R:3). Caleb the carpenter goes to sleep in the woods and is changed into a dog by Yedida the witch.

______. *Farmer Palmer's Wagon Ride.* Farrar, Straus & Giroux, 1974 (I:6–9 R:5). The pig and his donkey have one misfortune after another.

______. *Spinky Sulks.* Farrar, Straus & Giroux, 1988 (I:3–7 R:5). A sulky boy discovers that his family is really trying to help him.

______. *Sylvester and the Magic Pebble.* Simon & Schuster, 1969 (I:6–9 R:5). A magical pebble causes a donkey to turn into a rock.

Stevenson, James. *Could Be Worse!* Greenwillow, 1977 (I:5–9 R:3). Grandpa tells his grandchildren a whopper.

______. *July.* Greenwillow, 1990 (I:5–8 R:4). A book of memories takes readers back to summer visits at grandparents' home.

______. *Monty.* Greenwillow, 1979 (I:5–9). Three animals boss an alligator as he takes them across the river.

______. *The Sea View Hotel.* Greenwillow, 1978 (I:5–10 R:3). The story of a mouse at a resort, with cartoon-like illustrations.

______. *There's Nothing to Do.* Greenwillow, 1986 (I:5–9 R:3). Humor and exaggeration characterize this story.

______. *We Can't Sleep.* Greenwillow, 1982 (I:4–8 R:4). Grandpa tells a story when Louie and Mary Anne cannot sleep.

______. *The Wish Card Ran Out!* Greenwillow, 1981 (I:6–10 R:4). Cartoon illustrations enhance a spoof on credit cards.

Stock, Catherine. *Armien's Fishing Trip.* Morrow, 1990 (I:5–8 R:4). A boy sounds the alarm when a fisherman is swept overboard.

Thiele, Colin. *Farmer Schulz's Ducks*. Illustrated by Mary Milton. Harper & Row, 1988 (I:4–9 R:6). In an Australian story, a young girl solves the problem of how to keep the ducks safe when they cross the road.

Turkle, Brinton. *Do Not Open*. Elsevier-Dutton, 1981 (I:4–7 R:4). A monster pops out of a bottle marked "Do not open."

Turner, Ann. *Heron Street*. Illustrated by Lisa Desimini. Harper & Row, 1989 (I:5–9 R:5). Urbanization causes problems for the birds.

Ungerer, Tomi. *The Beast of Monsieur Racine*. Farrar, Straus & Giroux, 1971 (I:5–9 R:5). A strange beast steals prized pears and becomes a friend of Monsieur Racine.

Van Allsburg, Chris. *Jumanji*. Houghton Mifflin, 1981 (I:5–8 R:6). An unusual game creates a jungle environment.

———. *The Polar Express*. Houghton Mifflin, 1985 (I:5–8 R:6). A boy has an unusual adventure when he meets Santa Claus.

———. *The Wreck of the Zephyr*. Houghton Mifflin, 1983 (I:5–8 R:6). A boy tries to become the greatest sailor in the world.

Vincent, Gabrielle. *Ernest and Celestine's Picnic*. Greenwillow, 1982 (I:3–5 R:4). Ernest and Celestine have a picnic even though it is raining.

———. *Feel Better, Ernest!* Greenwillow, 1988 (I:3–5 R:4). Celestine helps when Ernest becomes ill.

———. *Smile, Ernest and Celestine*. Greenwillow, 1982 (I:3–5 R:4). Celestine experiences jealousy when she finds Ernest's pictures.

Viorst, Judith. *Alexander and the Terrible, Horrible, No Good, Very Bad Day*. Illustrated by Ray Cruz. Atheneum, 1972 (I:3–8 R:6). A boy experiences a series of bad incidents.

Voake, Charlotte. *Mrs. Goose's Baby*. Little, Brown, 1989 (I:2–6). The baby is really a chicken.

Waber, Bernard. *Ira Says Goodbye*. Houghton Mifflin, 1988 (I:3–8 R:4). This story about the moving away of a best friend has a happy ending.

———. *The Snake: A Very Long Story*. Houghton Mifflin, 1978 (I:3–8). Collages of scenery and a traveling snake provide an around-the-world adventure.

Wagner, Jenny. *John Brown, Rose and the Midnight Cat*. Illustrated by Ron Brooks. Bradbury, 1978 (I:4–8). A dog fears that a cat will disturb his life in the home of a nice widow.

Wallace, Ian. *Chin Chiang and the Dragon's Dance*. Atheneum, 1984 (I:6–9 R:7). A young boy gains self-confidence and his grandfather's respect when he performs the Dragon's Dance.

Ward, Lynd. *The Biggest Bear*. Houghton Mifflin, 1952 (I:5–8 R:4). A boy searches for a bear because he wants a bearskin for the outside of his barn.

Wayland, April Halprin. *To Rabbittown*. Illustrated by Robin Spowart. Scholastic, 1989 (I:3–8 R:5). A young child interacts with rabbits in a fantasy world.

Wells, Rosemary. *A Lion for Lewis*. Dial, 1982 (I:3–7 R:4). Lewis, the youngest child, discovers a way to gain his big brother's and sister's attention.

———. *Timothy Goes to School*. Dial, 1981 (I:4–7 R:4). Timothy Raccoon goes through many trials during his first week in school.

Wild, Margaret. *Mr. Nick's Knitting*. Illustrated by Dee Huxley. Harcourt Brace Jovanovich, 1989 (I:4–8 R:4). This book develops the theme of friendship.

Willard, Nancy. *Simple Pictures Are Best*. Illustrated by Tomie dePaola. Harcourt Brace Jovanovich, 1977 (I:5–9). Two characters frustrate a photographer when they keep adding items that they want included in a photograph for their wedding anniversary.

Williams, Barbara. *Chester Chipmunk's Thanksgiving*. Illustrated by Kay Charao. Dutton, 1978 (I:3–7). Chester wants to share Thanksgiving with his friends, but they are all busy.

Williams, Jay. *Everyone Knows What a Dragon Looks Like*. Illustrated by Mercer Mayer. Four Winds, 1976 (I:5–10). The Great Cloud Dragon saves a town.

Williams, Vera. *A Chair for My Mother*. Greenwillow, 1982 (I:3–7 R:6). A young girl helps save money for a new chair.

———. *Something Special for Me*. Greenwillow, 1983 (I:3–7 R:6). Rosa uses coins in a jar to buy a birthday present.

Willis, Val. *The Secret in the Matchbox*. Illustrated by John Shelley. Farrar, Straus & Giroux, 1988 (I:5–8 R:5). A matchbox reveals a dragon.

Winthrop, Elizabeth. *Bear and Mrs. Duck*. Illustrated by Patience Brewster. Holiday House, 1988 (I:3–6 R:2). A bear at first experiences fear when he has a babysitter.

Wolf, Bernard. *Anna's Silent World*. Lippincott, 1977 (I:5–10 R:6). A deaf girl experiences school and spends time with friends.

Yolen, Jane. *Owl Moon*. Illustrated by John Schoenherr. Philomel, 1987 (I:all). A boy and his father search for owls in the woods.

———. *The Seeing Stick*. Illustrated by Remy Charlip and Demetra Maraslis. Crowell, 1977 (I:5–8 R:6). In ancient China, an old man helps a blind girl by carving pictures on a stick.

Yorinks, Arthur. *Hey, Al*. Illustrated by Richard Egielski. Farrar, Straus & Giroux, 1986 (I:all R:5). A janitor discovers that his home is better than he thinks.

Zemach, Margot. *It Could Always Be Worse: A Yiddish Folktale*. Farrar, Straus & Giroux, 1976 (I:5–9 R:2). A rabbi advises a man who lives in a crowded hut.

Zolotow, Charlotte. *My Grandson Lew*. Illustrated by William Péne du Bois. Harper & Row, 1974 (I:5–8 R:2). Lewis and his mother share some beautiful memories about Lewis's grandfather who died four years before.

———. *The Quarreling Book*. Illustrated by Arnold Lobel. Harper & Row, 1963 (I:4–8). The day starts out all wrong when a father forgets to kiss his wife good-bye.

———. *William's Doll*. Illustrated by William Péne du Bois. Harper & Row, 1972 (I:4–8 R:4). William's desire for a doll results in various responses from his family.

6

Traditional Literature

OF CASTLE AND COTTAGE

INVOLVING CHILDREN IN TRADITIONAL LITERATURE

Of Castle and Cottage

OUR TRADITIONAL LITERARY HERITAGE

TYPES OF TRADITIONAL LITERATURE

VALUES OF TRADITIONAL LITERATURE FOR CHILDREN

FOLKTALES

FABLES

MYTHS

LEGENDS

ENCHANTED SWANS WHO REGAIN HUMAN form because of a sister's devotion, a brave boy who climbs into the unknown world at the top of a beanstalk, witches, warriors, supernatural animals, royal personages, and humans—all are brought to life in traditional literature. Such literature contains something that appeals to all interests: humorous stories, magical stories, and adventure stories. The settings of the stories are as varied as the enchanted places in the human imagination and as the geography of our world, from scorching deserts to polar icecaps. Regardless of location or subject, such tales include some of the most beloved and memorable stories of everyone's childhood. This chapter discusses the nature of our traditional literary heritage—its basic forms and themes, and what it has to offer children.

OUR TRADITIONAL LITERARY HERITAGE

The quest for traditional literary heritage takes students of children's literature to times before recorded history and to all parts of the world. Tales of religious significance allowed ancient people to speculate about their beginnings. Mythical heroes and heroines from all cultures overcame supernatural adversaries to gain their rewards. Stories of real people who performed brave deeds probably gratified the rulers of ancient tribes. Similarities in the types of tales and in the narrative motifs and content of traditional stories from peoples throughout the world constitute tangible evidence, according to folklorist Stith Thompson (23), that traditional tales are both universal and ancient.

Every social class has cultivated the art of storytelling, which reflects the culture, natural environment, and social contacts of the storyteller and the audience. For example, storytellers who earned their livings in medieval European castles related great deeds of nobility. The English court heard about King Arthur, Queen Guinevere, and the Knights of the Round Table, and the French court heard stories of princely valor, such as "The Song of Roland." In ancient China, stories for the ruling classes often portrayed benevolent dragons, symbols of imperial authority.

Commoners in medieval Europe lived lives quite different from those of the nobility, and the traditional stories of the commoners differed accordingly. The stories peasants told one another reflected the harsh, unjust, and often cruel circumstances of their existence as virtual slaves to the nobles. A common theme in their folktales is overcoming social inequality to attain a better way of life. In many tales, a poor lad outwits a nobleman, wins his daughter in marriage, and gains lifelong wealth. This theme is found in "The Flying Ship," a Russian tale; "The Golden Goose," a German tale; and "The Princess and the Glass Hill," a Norwegian tale.

Other traditional stories, such as the English "Jack the Giant Killer," tell of overcoming horrible adversaries with cunning and bravery. The peasants in these stories are not always clever. The consequences of stupidity are emphasized, for example, in the Norwegian tale "The Husband Who Has to Mind the House" and in the Russian tale "The Falcon Under the Hat." In place of the benevolent imperial dragon, the tales of early China's common people often involved cruel and evil dragons, whose power the heroines or heros overcame.

In early times, everyone in society, old and young, heard the same tales. The Puritans of seventeenth-century England and its colonies considered folktales about giants, witches, and enchantment to be immoral for everyone. They maintained that children in particular should hear and read only what instructed them and reinforced their moral development. Other social groups in Europe and North America felt differently, however. In 1697, the Frenchman Charles Perrault published a collection of folktales called *Tales of Mother Goose,* which included "Cinderella" and "Sleeping Beauty."

Over one hundred years later, the Romantic movement in Europe generated enthusiasm for exploring folklore to discover more about the roots of European languages and traditional cultures. In Germany, the Brothers Grimm carefully collected and transcribed oral tales from the storytellers themselves. These tales have been retold or adapted by many contemporary writers. Perrault and the Brothers Grimm thus brought new respect to traditional tales and ensured their availability for all time. Their work influenced collectors in other countries, as well as writers of literature.

By the end of the nineteenth century, European and North American societies generally considered childhood a distinct, necessary, and valuable stage in the human life cycle. Improved technology created more leisure hours for the middle and upper classes and a need for literature to entertain children. Traditional literature became a valuable part of the childhood experience. Today, folk literature is considered an important part of every child's cultural heritage. It is difficult to imagine the early childhood and elementary school years of American children without "The Little Red Hen," "The Three Bears," and "Snow White and the Seven Dwarfs." The literary experiences of older children would not be complete without tales of Greek and Norse mythology.

TYPES OF TRADITIONAL LITERATURE

Traditional tales have been handed down from generation to generation by word of mouth. In contrast to a modern story, a traditional tale has no identifiable author. Instead, storytellers tell what they have received from previous tellers of tales. Folklorists and others interested in collecting and analyzing traditional literature do not always agree about how to categorize and define different types of traditional tales. This text discusses four types of traditional tales—folktales, fables, myths, and legends—drawing on definitions recommended by folklorist William Bascom (4). Chart 6–1 summarizes and clarifies the differences among folktales, fables, myths, and legends, providing examples of each type of traditional literature.

Folktales

According to Bascom, folktales are "prose narratives which are regarded as fiction. They are not considered as dogma or history, they may or may not have happened, and they are not taken seriously" (p. 4). Because the tales are set in any time or place, they seem almost timeless and placeless. Folktales usually tell the adventures of animal or human characters. They contain common narrative motifs—such as supernatural adversaries (ogres, witches, and giants), supernatural helpers, magic and marvels, tasks and quests—and common themes—such as reward of good and punishment of evil. (Not all themes and motifs are found within one tale.) Subcategories of folktales include cumulative tales, humorous tales, beast tales, magic and wonder tales, *pourquoi* tales, and realistic tales.

Cumulative Tales. Tales that sequentially repeat actions, characters, or speeches until a climax is reached are found among all cultures. Most cumulative tales give their main characters—whether animal, vegetable, human, or

CHART 6–1
Characteristics of folktales, fables, myths, and legends

Form and Examples	Belief	Time	Place	Attitude	Principal Characters
Folktale	*Fiction*	*Anytime*	*Anyplace*	*Secular*	*Human or Nonhuman*
1. "Snow White and Seven Dwarfs" (European)	fiction	"once upon a time"	"in the great forest"	secular	human girl and dwarfs
2. "The Crane Wife" (Asian)	fiction	long ago	"in a faraway mountain village"	secular	human man, supernatural wife
3. "Why Mosquitoes Buzz in People's Ears" (African)	fiction	"one morning"	in a forest	secular	animals
Fable	*Fiction*	*Anytime*	*Anyplace*	*Secular/ Allegorical*	*Animal or Human*
1. "The Hare and the Frog" (Aesop)	fiction	"once upon a time"	on the shore of a lake	allegorical	animals
2. "The Tyrant who Became a Just Ruler" (Panchatantra—India)	fiction	"in olden times"	in a kingdom	allegorical	human king
Myth	*Considered Fact*	*Remote Past*	*Other World or Earlier World*	*Sacred*	*Nonhuman*
1. "The Warrior Goddess: Athena" (European)	considered fact	remote past	Olympus	deities	Greek goddess
2. "Zuñi Creation Myth" (Native American)	considered fact	before and during creation	sky, earth, and lower world	deities	Creator Awonawilona, Sun Father, Earth Mother
Legend	*Considered Fact*	*Recent Past*	*World of Today*	*Secular or Sacred*	*Human*
1. "King Arthur Tales" (European)	considered fact	recent past	Britain	secular	king
2. "The White Archer" (Native American)	considered fact	recent past	land of Eskimos	secular	Indian who wanted to avenge parents' death

inanimate object—intelligence and reasoning ability. Adults often share these stories with very young children because the structure of cumulative tales allows children to join in as each new happening occurs. A runaway baked food is a popular, culturally diverse subject for cumulative tales. It is found not only in the German "Gingerbread Boy" but also in a Norwegian version, "The Pancake"; an English version, "Johnny Cake"; and a Russian version, "The Bun." In each of these tales, the repetition builds until the climax. Other familiar cumulative tales include the English "Henny Penny"; "The Fat Cat," a Danish tale; and "Why Mosquitoes Buzz in People's Ears," an African tale.

Humorous Tales. Folktales allow people to laugh at themselves as well as at others, an apparently universal pleasure. In tales such as the Russian "The Peasant's Pea Patch," the humor results from absurd situations or the stupidity of the characters. Human foolishness resulting from unwise decisions provides the humor and a moral in the

English folktale "Mr. and Mrs. Vinegar" and in the Norwegian tale "The Husband Who Has to Mind the House."

Beast Tales. Beast tales are among the most universal folktales, being found in all cultures. For example, the coyote is a popular animal in Native American tales, while the fox and wolf are found in many European tales. The rabbit and the bear are popular characters in the folktales of black culture in the United States. Beasts in folktales often talk and act quite like people. In some stories, such as "The Bremen Town Musicians," animal characters use their wits to frighten away robbers and claim wealth. In other tales, such as "The Three Billy Goats Gruff," animals use first their wits and then their strength to overcome an enemy. Still other animals win through industrious actions, such as those found in "The Little Red Hen." Tales about talking animals may show the cleverness of one animal and the stupidity of another.

Magic and Wonder Tales. The majority of magic and wonder tales contain some element of magic. The fairy godmother transforms the kind, lovely, mistreated girl into a beautiful princess ("Cinderella"), the good peasant boy earns a cloth that provides food ("The Lad Who Went to the North-wind"), a kindhearted simpleton attains a magical ship ("The Fool of the World and the Flying Ship"), or the evil witch transforms the handsome prince into a beast ("Beauty and the Beast"). Magic can be good or bad. When it is good, the person who benefits has usually had misfortune or is considered inferior by a parent or society. When it is bad, love and diligence usually overcome the magic—as in the German tale "The Six Swans" and the Norwegian tale "East of the Sun and West of the Moon."

Pourquoi Tales. *Pourquoi* tales—or "why" tales, in an English translation of the French word—answer a question, or explain how animals, plants, or humans were created and why they have certain characteristics. For example, why does an animal or a human act in a certain way? Kathleen Arnott's (1) *Animal Folk Tales Around the World* contains several stories that are characteristic of this type of tale. "Why Siberian Birds Migrate in Winter," for example, tells why some birds migrate away from Siberia in the winter and why some birds stay behind and struggle to stay alive until spring. A West Indies folktale in this collection tells "Why You Find Spiders in Banana Bunches," and an American tale suggests "Why Rabbits Have Short Tails." Marcos Kurtycz's and Ana Garcia Kobeh's *Tigers and Opossums* presents six animal tales from Mexico that explain why the hummingbird is richly dressed, why the opossum has a hairless tail, and why the bat flies only at night, among other things. Children enjoy these tales and like to make up their own *pourquoi* stories about animal or human characteristics.

Realistic Tales. The majority of folktales include supernatural characters, magic, or other exaggerated incidents. A few tales, however, have realistic plots and involve people who could have existed. One such tale, "Dick Whittington," tells about a boy who comes to London looking for streets paved with gold. He doesn't find golden streets, but he does find work with an honest merchant, and eventually wins his fortune. Some versions of this story suggest that at least parts of it are true. A Dick Whittington was lord mayor of London.

Fables

Fables are brief tales in which animal characters that talk and act like humans indicate a moral lesson or satirize human conduct. For example, in the familiar "The Hare and the Tortoise," the hare taunts the tortoise about her slow movements and boasts about his own speed. The tortoise then challenges the hare to a race. The hare starts rapidly and is soon far ahead, but he becomes tired and, in his confidence, decides to nap. Meanwhile, the tortoise, keeping at her slow and steady pace, plods across the finish line. When the hare awakens, he discovers that the tortoise has reached the goal. The moral of this fable is that perseverance and determination may compensate for lack of other attributes.

Myths

According to William Bascom (4), myths are "prose narratives which, in the society in which they are told, are considered to be truthful accounts of what happened in the remote past. They are accepted on faith; they are taught to be believed; and they can be cited as authority in answer to ignorance, doubt, or disbelief. Myths are the embodiment of dogma; they are usually sacred; and they are often associated with theology and ritual" (p. 4). Myths account for the origin of the world and humans; for everyday natural phenomena, such as thunder and lightning; and for human emotions and experiences, such as love and death. The main characters in myths may be animals, deities, or humans. The actions take place in an earlier world or another world, such as the underworld or the sky. Many ancient Greek myths, for example, explain the creation of the world, the creation of the gods and goddesses who ruled from Mount Olympus, and the reasons for natural phenomena. The myth about Demeter and Persephone, for example, explains seasonal changes.

Legends

Legends, William Bascom (4) says, are "prose narratives which, like myths, are regarded as true by the narrator and his audience, but they are set in a period considered less remote, when the world was much as it is today. Legends are more often secular than sacred, and their principal characters are human" (p. 4). Many legends embroider the historical facts of human wars and migrations, brave deeds, and royalty. Legends from the British Isles tell about Robin Hood, the protector of the poor in the Middle Ages, who may have been an actual person. Legends from France tell about the miraculous visions of Joan of Arc, who led French armies into battle against the English. Legends from Africa describe how the prophet Amakosa saved the Juba people from extinction.

VALUES OF TRADITIONAL LITERATURE FOR CHILDREN

Traditional literature helps children understand the world and identify with universal human struggles. It also provides pleasure.

Understanding the World

Traditional tales help children improve their understanding of the world, as Ruth Kearney Carlson (9) outlines in eight respects. First, according to Carlson, traditional tales help children better understand the nonscientific cultural traditions of early humanity. Greek and Roman myths, for example, tell how early Europeans explained the mysteries of creation, human nature, and natural phenomena through the powers of gods, giants, and demons. These myths were taken so seriously that religions grew up around them. In addition to providing lively entertainment, traditional tales fill readers with admiration for the people who developed such answers for unanswerable questions.

Second, traditional tales show the inter-relatedness of various types of stories and narrative motifs. For example, the tale of a girl who loses her mother, acquires a jealous or evil stepmother, is mistreated (but remains gentle and kind), and finally receives rewards for her goodness is found in folk literature everywhere. Scholars have identified more than nine hundred versions of the Cinderella tale worldwide. While these stories have different characters, settings, and types of enchantment, their underlying themes are the same.

Third, children learn about cultural diffusion as they observe how different versions of a tale are dispersed. Anyone who has tried to categorize traditional literature according to country of origin is amazed at the similarity found among tales from different countries. Classifying the geographic location of a tale can be difficult if the author retelling it does not specify the source of the translation. The similarities among tales indicate movement of people through migration and conquests. They also emphasize that humans throughout the world have had similar needs and problems. Some folktales from different countries are almost identical. For example, the German tale "The Table, the Donkey and the Stick," is very similar to the Norwegian tale "The Lad Who Went to the North Wind." While researching animal tales, Kathleen Arnott (1) discovered that "almost every country has its traditional trickster, such as the fox in Palestine and the mouse-deer in Malaysia; its stupid, easily fooled creature, such as the bear in Lapland or the giraffe in West Africa; and its benevolent, good-natured animal, such as the kangaroo in Australia" (introduction). The tales are very similar, although the animals and the settings are characteristic of the countries in which they are told.

Fourth, traditional tales help children develop an appreciation for the culture and art of different countries. If the author who retells a tale retains authentic cultural detail and the illustrator carefully researches the culture before picturing its natural environment and customs, children gain appreciation for the social realities and cultural contributions of a country. Nancy Ekholm Burkert's illustrations for Randall Jarrell's version of the Grimms' *Snow White and Seven Dwarfs* reflect research into German history and culture. Paul O. Zelinsky studied seventeenth-century Dutch paintings before illustrating Rika Lesser's version of *Hansel and Gretel*. Suekichi Akaba used a traditional Japanese painting technique when illustrating Sumiko Yagawa's retelling of *The Crane Wife*.

Fifth, traditional tales provide factual information about different countries—information about geography, government, family patterns, food, celebrations, likes, and dislikes. For example, far from being an endangered species, wolves were numerous in medieval Europe and greatly feared by a largely rural population—as the German tale "Little Red Riding Hood" and the Hungarian tale "One Little Pig and Ten Wolves" demonstrate. In *Where the Buffalos Begin,* Olaf Baker shows the economic and spiritual importance of the buffalo to the traditional Native Americans of the Great Plains. Contrasts in weather and geography are evident when children compare the warm lands of Arabian folktales with the icy settings of Norse mythology.

Sixth, traditional tales familiarize children with the many languages and dialects of cultures around the world. The names in traditional tales from different countries fascinate children. They enjoy hearing stories about Russian Maria Morevna, the beautiful Tsarevna; Vietnamese Tam, the girl who lived in the Land of Small Dragon; and Mazel and Shlimazel, who have a wager in the Yiddish folktale. Many tales include language or dialects characteristic of a country or time period. Howard Pyle's *The Story of King Arthur and His Knights* contains dialogue suggesting early English: "Sir Knight, I demand of thee why thou didst smite that shield. Now let me tell thee, because of thy boldness, I shall take away from thee thine own shield, and shall hang it upon yonder apple-tree, where thou beholdest all those other shields to be hanging" (p. 44). Reading this prose may be difficult even for older elementary children, but children enjoy hearing it when an adult reads it to them.

Seventh, traditional tales provide marvelous stimulation for creative drama, writing, and other forms of artistic expression. When children listen to traditional tales and then interact with their own imaginations, they gain respect for the people who created such tales.

Finally, traditional tales encourage children to realize that people from all over the world have inherent goodness, mercy, courage, and industry. In a Chinese tale, a loving brother rescues his sister from a dragon; in a German tale, a sister suffers six years of ordeals in order to bring her brothers back to human form. A Jewish folk character works hard to cultivate fig trees that may benefit his descendants but not himself, while the Norse Beowulf's strength of character defeats evil monsters.

Identifying with Universal Human Struggles

In *The Uses of Enchantment: The Meaning and Importance of Fairy Tales,* Bruno Bettelheim (5) provides strong rationales for using traditional tales with children. In his psychoanalytic approach to traditional tales, Bettelheim claims that nothing is so enriching as traditional literature. To reinforce this claim, he argues that traditional tales allow children to learn about human progress and possible solutions to problems. Because tales state problems briefly, children can understand them. In addition, traditional tales subtly convey the advantages of moral behavior. Children learn that struggling against difficulties is unavoidable, but they can emerge victorious if they directly confront hardships.

Traditional tales present characters who are both good and bad. According to Bettelheim, children gain the conviction that crime does not pay. The simple, straightforward characters in traditional tales allow children to identify with the good and reject the bad. Children empathize with honorable characters and their struggles, learning that while they may experience difficulty or rejection, they too will be given help and guidance when needed.

Joyce Thomas (22) emphatically supports the use of traditional tales with children. She states, "To deny fairy tales to children or to allow only those with 'acceptable' morals and innocuous fantasy is to retard their psychological and imaginative growth and expression" (p. 111).

Pleasure

Traditional literature is extremely popular with children. In particular, folktales—with their fast-paced, dramatic plots and easily identifiable good and bad characters—are among the types of literature most appealing to young audiences. Although folktales may appeal primarily to young children, children of various ages and interests find them enjoyable. Animal tales, such as "The Three Little Pigs," "The Little Red Hen," and "The Three Bears," have been illustrated in picture-book format for young children, while fairy tales, such as "Beauty and the Beast," are of interest to upper-elementary school children.

F. André Favat (12) reviewed the relevant research and reached the following conclusions about interest in folktales among children of different ages:

1 Children between the ages of five and ten—or roughly from kindergarten through the fifth grade—are highly interested in folktales, whether they select books or are presented with books and asked for their opinions.
2 This interest follows a curve of reading preference—that is, children's interest in folktales emerges at a prereading age and gradually rises to a peak between the approximate ages of six and eight. It then gradually declines.
3 Concurrent with the decline in interest in folktales emerges an interest in realistic stories.

Favat maintains that the characteristics of folktales correspond with the characteristics Jean Piaget ascribed to children. First, children believe that objects, actions, thoughts, and words can exercise magical influence over events in their own lives. Folktales are filled with such occurrences, as spells turn humans into animals, or vice versa, and humble pumpkins become gilded coaches.

Second, children believe that inanimate objects and animals have consciousness much like that of humans. In folktales, the objects and animals in folktales that speak or act like people are consistent with children's beliefs.

Third, young children believe in punishment for wrongdoing and reward for good behavior. Folktales satisfy children's sense of justice. The good Goose Girl, for example, is rewarded by marrying the prince, and her deceitful maid is punished harshly.

Fourth, the relationship between heroes and heroines and their environments is much the same as the relationship between children and their own environments. Children are the center of their universes, while heroes and heroines are the centers of their folktale worlds. For example, when Sleeping Beauty sleeps for a hundred years, so does the whole castle.

FOLKTALES

Many folktales have similar characteristics and motifs. The folktales discussed in this section have many similarities in plot, characterization, setting, theme, and style. They also reflect cultural differences. Chart 6–2 summarizes some of these similarities and differences by comparing tales from several cultures. This section looks at British, French, German, Norwegian, Russian, Jewish, Asian, African, and North American tales. You may analyze other tales from each culture to identify common characteristics.

Characteristics

Because folktales differ from other types of literature, they have characteristics related to plot, characterization, setting, theme, and style that may differ from other types of children's stories.

Plot. Conflict and action abound in folktales. The nature of the oral tradition made it imperative that listeners be brought quickly into the action. Consequently, even in written versions, folktales immerse readers into the major conflict within the first few sentences. For example, the conflict in Paul Galdone's *The Little Red Hen* is between laziness and industriousness. The first sentence introduces the animals who live together in a little house. The second sentence introduces the lazy cat, dog, and mouse. The third sentence introduces the industrious hen and the conflict. The remainder of the story develops the conflict between the lazy animals and the industrious fowl. The conflict is resolved when the hen eats her own baking and doesn't share it with her lazy friends.

Similarly, in "The Three Billy Goats Gruff," the goats want to get to the other side of the bridge in order to eat the grass in a pasture, but they quickly discover that a troll lives under the bridge. The tension increases as each goat approaches the bridge, confronts the troll, and convinces the troll to allow him to cross. This cannot go on indefinitely; the largest billy goat and the troll must settle their differences. The conflict reaches a climax when the largest goat knocks the troll off the bridge and crosses to the other side. The goats eat happily ever after.

Conflict between characters representing good and characters representing evil is typical of folktales. Even though the odds are uneven, the hero overcomes the giant in "Jack the Giant Killer," the girl and boy outsmart the witch in "Hansel and Gretel," the intelligent animal outwits the ogre in "Puss in Boots," and a brother saves his sister from a dragon in "The Golden Sheng."

Actions that recur in folktales have been the focus of several researchers. Vladimir Propp (20) analyzed one hundred Russian folktales and identified thirty-one recurring actions that account for the uniformity and repetitiveness of folktales. While not all tales included all actions, actions

CHART 6–2
Comparisons of folktales from different cultures

Culture and Examples	Protagonist—Main Character	Portrayal of Hero or Heroine	Portrayal of Other Characters	Setting
British "Jack the Giant Killer"	Simple peasant lad	The lad is brave and is clever enough to outwit the villain.	The giants are evil. The king is weak.	Mountain cave
French "Sleeping Beauty"	Adolescent princess (about fifteen)	The prince is "pursued by love and honor" and is valiant.	The fairy is wicked. The father cannot protect his daughter.	Castle with a series of rooms similar to Versailles.
German "Hansel and Gretel"	Boy and girl (a woodcutter's children)	Hansel is caring, but Gretel is clever enough to outwit the witch.	The stepmother is uncaring. The father is weak. The witch is wicked.	Forest
Norwegian "The Lad Who Went to the North Wind"	Simple peasant lad	The lad is simple but honest.	The north wind is powerful. The mother is scolding. The innkeeper is dishonest and greedy.	Rural Far North
Russian "The Fool of the World and the Flying Ship"	Simple, young peasant	The young peasant is foolish but kindhearted.	The czar is dishonorable. The four companions have great powers.	Rural countryside and the czar's palace
Jewish "Mazel and Schlimazel"	Poor peasant	The bungler does poorly until good luck intercedes.	The spirit of good luck is happy and attractive. The spirit of bad luck is slumped and angry.	King's court and the countryside
Chinese "The Golden Sheng"	Poor adolescent girl	The boy grows up very rapidly.	The girl is helpless. The dragon is evil and cruel.	Rural
African "How Spider Got a Thin Waist"	Tricky and greedy spider	The greedy spider does not work; instead, he plays in the sun.	The villagers are hardworking.	Forest and village
Native American "The Fire Bringer"	Young Paiute Indian boy	The boy is concerned about his people.	The coyote is intelligent. The runners are swift.	Mesa and mountain

CHART 6–2 (cont.)

Culture and Examples	Intended Audience	Dominant Plot	Qualities Admired	Conclusion or Indication of Character's Fate
British "Jack the Giant Killer"	Common people	The hero is sent to rid the kingdom of giants.	Intelligence and bravery	Happy ending. The hero is rewarded with knighthood when the villains are slain.
French "Sleeping Beauty"	Nobility	A threatened girl is rescued by a prince.	Beauty, wit, grace, dancing, and singing	Happy ending. The prince and princess are married.
German "Hansel and Gretel"	Common people	Abandoned children outwit a wicked witch.	Caring and cleverness	Happy ending. The children are rewarded with jewels after the witch is burned to death.
Norwegian "The Lad Who Went to the North Wind"	Common people	The hero sets out to retrieve a lost object.	Honesty and kindness	Happy ending. The boy beats the innkeeper and is rewarded with magical objects.
Russian "The Fool of the World and the Flying Ship"	Common people	A simple boy sets out on a quest. He is aided by a magical ship and companions.	Kindness and honesty	Happy ending. The peasant marries royalty.
Jewish "Mazel and Schlimazel"	Common people	A simple boy is accompanied by good luck and then bad luck on a series of quests.	Diligence, honesty, sincerity, and helpfulness	Happy ending. The hero marries the princess and eventually becomes the wisest of prince consorts.
Chinese "The Golden Sheng"	Common people	A young boy goes on a quest to save his sister from a dragon.	Helpfulness, diligence, and loyalty	Happy ending. After the dragon whirls himself to death, the brother and sister return to their mother.
African "How Spider Got a Thin Waist"	Common people	The spider tries to get food without working.	Industriousness	Unhappy ending. The greedy spider gets a thin waist.
Native American "The Fire Bringer"	Common people	A boy and a coyote set out to get fire for the Paiutes.	Intelligence, swiftness, and bravery	Happy ending. The boy and the coyote are honored.

occurred in the same sequence in most tales. More importantly, Propp discovered that similar patterns were apparent in non-Russian tales. Propp concluded that consistency of action in folktales does not result from the country of origin. Instead, consistency results from the fact that tales remain true to the folk tradition.

F. André Favat (12) summarized Propp's findings and analyzed French and German tales according to their actions. The following list of recurring sequential actions that may be found in various combinations is adapted from Favat. In some tales, females are the primary actors, but most folktales, reflecting the values and social realities of their times and places of origin, assign actions primarily to male characters.

1 One family member leaves home.
2 The hero or heroine is forbidden to do some action.
3 The hero or heroine violates a forbidden order.
4 The villain surveys the situation.
5 The villain receives information about the victim.
6 The villain attempts to trick or deceive the victim in order to possess the victim or the victim's belongings.
7 The victim submits to deception and unwittingly helps the enemy.
8 The villain causes harm or injury to a member of a family.
9 One family member either lacks something or desires to have something.
10 A misfortune or lack is made known; the hero or heroine is approached with a request or command; and he or she is allowed to go or is sent on a mission.
11 The seeker agrees to, or decides upon, a counteraction.
12 The hero or heroine leaves home.
13 The hero or heroine is tested, interrogated, or attacked, which prepares the way for him or her to receive a magical agent or a helper.
14 The hero or heroine reacts to the actions of the future donor.
15 The hero or heroine acquires a magical agent.
16 The hero or heroine is transferred, delivered, or led to the whereabouts of an object.
17 The hero or heroine and the villain join in direct combat.
18 The hero or heroine is marked.
19 The villain is defeated.
20 The initial misfortune or lack is eliminated.
21 The hero or heroine returns.
22 The hero or heroine is pursued.
23 The hero or heroine is rescued from pursuit.
24 The hero or heroine, unrecognized, arrives home or in another country.
25 A false hero or heroine presents unfounded claims.
26 A difficult task is proposed to the hero or heroine.
27 The task is resolved.
28 The hero or heroine is recognized.
29 The false hero/heroine or the villain is exposed.
30 The hero or heroine is given a new appearance.
31 The villain is punished.
32 The hero or heroine is married and ascends to the throne.

Many of the folktales discussed in this chapter contain various combinations of these actions. All folktales have similar endings, just as they have similar beginnings and plot development, and most tales end with some version of "and they lived happily ever after."

Characterization. Folktale characters are less completely developed than are characters in other types of stories. Oral storytellers lacked the time to develop fully rounded characters. Thus, characters in folktales are essentially symbolic and flat—that is, they have a limited range of personal characteristics and do not change in the course of the story. A witch is always wicked, whether she is the builder of gingerbread houses in the German tale "Hansel and Gretel" or the fearsome Baba Yaga in the Russian "Maria Morevna." Other unchangeably evil characters include giants, ogres, trolls, and stepmothers.

Characters easily typed as bad are accompanied by those who are always good. The young heroine is fair, kind, and loving. The youngest son is honorable, kind, and unselfish even if he is considered foolish. Isaac Bashevis Singer's *Mazel and Shlimazel, or the Milk of the Lioness* demonstrates characteristic differences between good and bad characters: Mazel, the spirit of good luck, is young, tall, and slim, with pink cheeks and a jaunty stride; Shlimazel, the spirit of bad luck, is old, pale-faced, and angry-eyed, with a crooked red nose, a beard as gray as a spider's web, and a slumping stride.

Folktales usually establish the main characters' natures early on, as Charles Perrault does in the first paragraph of "Cinderella: or The Little Glass Slipper":

> There was once upon a time, a gentleman who married for his second wife the proudest and most haughty woman that ever was known. She had been a widow, and had by her former husband two daughters of her own humor, who were exactly like her in all things. He had also by a former wife a young daughter, but of an unparalleled goodness and sweetness of temper, which she took from her mother, who was the best creature in the world. (*Histories or Tales of Past Times,* p. 73)

Children easily identify the good and bad characters in folktales. This easy identification of heroes and heroines, as well as lively action, may account for the popularity of folktales with young children.

Setting. Setting in literature includes both time and place. The time in folktales is always the far-distant past, usually introduced by some version of "once upon a time." The first line of a folktale usually places listeners into a time when anything might happen. A Russian tale, "The Firebird," begins "Long ago, in a distant kingdom, in a distant land, lived Tsar Vyslar Andronovich." Native American folktales may begin with some version of "when all was new, and the gods dwelt in the ancient places, long, long before the time of our ancients." A French tale is placed "on a day of days in the time of our fathers," while a German tale begins "in the olden days when wishing still helped one." These introductions inform listeners that enchantment and overcoming obstacles are possible in the tales about to unfold.

The symbolic settings found in many folktales are not carefully described because there is no need for description. One knows immediately that magic can happen in the great forest of the Grimms' "Snow White and the Seven Dwarfs" or in the great castle of Madame de Beaumont's version of "Beauty and the Beast." The title of a Romanian tale, "The Land Where Time Stood Still," establishes a setting where the imagination will accept and expect unusual occurrences.

The introduction that places the folktale in the far-distant past may also briefly sketch the location. A Chinese tale, "The Cinnamon Tree in the Moon," suggests a nature setting, "where not even a soft breeze stirs the heavens and one can see the shadows in the moon." After introducing such settings, folktales immediately identify the characters and develop the conflict.

Theme. Folktales contain universal truths and reflect the values of the times and societies in which they originated, many of which are still honored today. The characters, their actions, and their rewards develop themes related to moral and material achievement. Good overcomes evil; justice triumphs; unselfish love conquers; intelligence wins out over physical strength; kindness, diligence, and hard work bring rewards. The tales also show what happens to those who do not meet the traditional standards. The jealous queen is punished, the wicked stepsisters are blinded by birds, the foolish king loses part of his fortune or his daughter, and the greedy man loses the source of his success or his well-being.

The universality of these themes suggests that people everywhere have responded to similar ideals and beliefs. Consider, for example, the universality of the theme that intelligence is superior to physical strength. The hero in the English "Jack the Giant Killer" outwits the much larger and less intelligent giant. In the African tale "A Story, a Story," Spider outwits a series of animals and wins his wager with the being who controls stories. The hero in the Jewish "The Fable of the Fig Tree" is rewarded because he considers the long-range consequences of his actions. The heroine in the Chinese "The Clever Wife" uses her wits to bring the family power.

In contrast, another universal theme is that foolishness causes the loss of possessions. In an English tale, "Mr. and Mrs. Vinegar" lose their possessions because of foolish actions. In a German tale, "The Fisherman and His Wife," the couple returns to a humble position because of foolish choices and greed. The Russian characters in "The Falcon Under the Hat" lose their possessions because of foolish actions. These themes are found in traditional literature around the world.

Style. Charles Perrault, the famed collector of French fairy tales in the seventeenth century, believed "that the best stories are those that imitate best the style and the simplicity of children's verses" (13, p. viii). Such style permits few distracting details or unnecessary descriptions. Simplicity is especially apparent in the thoughts and dialogues of characters in folktales: They think and talk like people. For example, the dialogue in the Grimms' "The Golden Goose" sounds as if the listener were overhearing a conversation. The little old gray man welcomes the first son with "Good morning. Do give me a piece of that cake you have got in your pocket, and let me have a draught of your wine—I am so hungry and thirsty."

The clever, selfish son immediately answers, "If I give you my cake and wine I shall have none left for myself; you just go your own way." Disaster rapidly follows this exchange.

When Dullhead, the youngest, simplest son, begs to go into the woods, his father's response reflects his opinion of his son's ability: "Both your brothers have injured themselves. You had better leave it alone; you know nothing about it." Dullhead begs hard, and his father replies, "Very well, then—go. Perhaps when you have hurt yourself, you may learn to know better." This German folktale is filled with rapid exchanges as Dullhead is rewarded with the golden goose and moves humorously on toward his destiny with the king and the beautiful princess.

The language of folktales is often enriched with simple rhymes and verses. In "Jack and the Beanstalk," the giant chants:

> Fee, fi-fo-fum,
> I smell the blood of an Englishman,
> Be he alive, or be he dead,
> I'll have his bones to grind my bread.

The enchanted frog from the Grimms' "The Frog King" approaches the door of the princess with these words:

> Princess! Youngest princess!
> Open the door for me!
> Dost thou not know what thou saidst to me
> Yesterday by the cool waters of the fountain?
> Princess, youngest princess!
> Open the door for me!

Likewise, the witch asks Hansel and Grethel:

> Nibble, nibble, gnaw,
> Who is nibbling at my little house?

As the story nears its end, another rhyme asks the duck for help:

> Little duck, little duck, dost thou see
> Hansel and Grethel are waiting for thee?
> There's never a plank or bridge in sight,
> Take us across on thy back so white.

The simple style, easily identifiable characters, and rapid plot development make folktales appropriate for sharing orally with children.

Motifs

Kind or cruel supernatural beings, magical transformations of reality, and enchanted young people who must wait for true love to break spells that confine them are all elements that take folktales out of the ordinary and encourage people to remember and repeat the tales. Folklorists have identified hundreds of such elements, or motifs, found in folktales.

Although a folktale may be remembered for one dramatic story element, most tales have multiple elements. Consider the following motifs in "Jack and the Beanstalk": (1) the hero makes a foolish bargain, (2) the hero acquires a magical object, (3) a plant has extraordinary powers, (4) the ogre repeats "fee-fi-fo-fum," (5) the ogre's wife hides the hero, (6) the hero steals a magical object from the ogre, (7) the magical object possesses the power of speech, and (8) the hero summons the ogre.

Researchers use motifs to analyze and identify the similarities in tales from various cultures. Some motifs are practically universal, suggesting similar thought processes in people living in different parts of the world. Other motifs help trace a tale's diffusion from one culture to another or identify a common source. Chart 6–3 summarizes the discussion of motifs and demonstrates that folktales from many parts of the world contain the same motifs. The search for common motifs is enlightening and rewarding for children as well as adults. Some of the most common of the many motifs in folktales are supernatural beings; extraordinary animals; and magical objects, powers, and transformations.

Supernatural Adversaries and Helpers. Supernatural beings in folktales are usually either adversaries or helpers. The wicked supernatural beings, such as ogres and witches, may find heroines or heroes, entice them into their cottages or castles, and make preparations to feast upon them. In contrast, the encounter with the evil being may be the result of an unlucky chance meeting, as in "Hansel and Gretel," or the main character may deliberately seek out the adversary, as in the Chinese tale "Li Chi Slays the Serpent." Luckily, the intended victims usually outwit the adversaries. In addition to being evil, supernatural adversaries are usually stupid; consequently, they are overcome by characters who use wit and trickery.

Supernatural helpers support many folklore heroes and heroines in their quests. Seven dwarfs help Snow White in her battle against her evil stepmother. A supernatural old man causes hardships to the selfish older brothers and rewards the generous younger brother in the Russian tale "The Fool of the World and the Flying Ship." The same motif is found in tales from western Asia, eastern Europe, and India.

CHART 6–3
Common motifs in folktales from different cultures

Common Motif	Culture	Folktale
Supernatural Adversaries		
Ogre	England	"Jack the Giant Killer"
Ogress	Italy	"Petrosinella"
Troll	Norway	"Three Billy Goats Gruff"
Giant	Germany	"The Valiant Little Tailor"
Dragon	China	"The Golden Sheng"
Witch	Africa	"Marandenboni"
Supernatural Helpers		
Fairies	France and Germany	"The Sleeping Beauty"
Fairy godmother	Vietnam	"The Land of Small Dragon"
Jinni	Arabia	"The Woman of the Well"
Cat (fairy in disguise)	Italy	"The Cunning Cat"
Deceitful or Ferocious Beasts		
Wolf	Germany	"The Wolf and the Seven Little Kids"
Wolf	France	"Little Red Riding Hood"
Wolf	England	"The Three Little Pigs"
Wild hog, unicorn and lion	United States	"Jack and the Varmints"
Magical Objects		
Cloak of invisibility	Germany	"The Twelve Dancing Princesses"
Magical cloth	Norway	"The Lad Who Went to the North Wind"
Magical lamp	Arabia	"Aladdin and the Magic Lamp"
Magical mill	Norway	"Why the Sea Is Salt"
Magical Powers		
Granted wishes	Germany	"The Fisherman and His Wife"
Wish for a child	Russia	"The Snow Maiden"
Humans with extraordinary powers	Mexico	"The Riddle of the Drum"
Humans with extraordinary powers	Russia	"The Fool of the World and the Flying Ship"
Magical Transformations		
Prince to bear	Norway	"East of the Sun and West of the Moon"
Prince to beast	France	"Beauty and the Beast"
Bird to human	Japan	"The Crane Wife"
Human to animal	United States (Native American)	"The Ring in the Prairie"

Extraordinary Animals. Whether cunning or stupid, deceitful or upstanding, extraordinary animals are popular characters in the folktales of all cultures. In the English and French versions of "Little Red Riding Hood," the wolf plays the role of ogre, deceives a child, and is eliminated. In Japanese folklore, the fox has a malicious nature. It can assume human shape, and it has the power to bewitch humans. Tricky foxes and coyotes are important characters in Black American and Native American folktales as well.

Some extraordinary animals are loyal companions and helpers to deserving human characters. The cat in the French "Puss in Boots" outwits an ogre and provides riches for his human master. The German version of "Cinderella" collected by the Brothers Grimm contains no fairy godmother; instead, white doves and other birds help Cinderella complete the impossible tasks her wicked stepmother requires.

Magical Objects, Powers, and Transformations. The possession of a magical object or power is crucial in many folktales. When all seems lost, the hero may don the cloak of invisibility and follow "The Twelve Dancing Princesses" to solve a mystery and win his fortune, or the heroine's loving tears may fall into her true love's eyes and save him from blindness, as in "Rapunzel."

Folktale characters often obtain magical objects in extraordinary manners, lose them or have them stolen, and eventually recover them. This sequence occurs in the Norwegian "The Lad Who Went to the North Wind," in which a boy goes to the North Wind demanding the return of his meal, is given a magical object, loses it to a dishonest innkeeper, and must retrieve it. The dishonest innkeeper is eventually punished. In folktales, stealing a magical object often results in considerable problems for the thief.

Magical spells and transformations are also common in folktales around the world. The spell of a fairy godmother turns a pumpkin into a golden coach, and the spell of a witch puts a princess to sleep for a hundred years. One of the most common transformation motifs is the transformation of a prince into an animal ("The Frog Prince") or a beastlike monster ("Beauty and the Beast"). A gentle, unselfish youngest daughter usually breaks the enchantment when she falls in love with the animal or beast. In a Basque tale, the beast is a huge serpent; a Magyar Hungarian tale has the prince transformed into a pig; and a Lithuanian tale tells of a prince who becomes a white wolf. "The Crane Wife," a Japanese folktale, contains another example of the transformation from animal to human, as a poor farmer gains a wife when a wounded crane he cares for transforms herself into a lovely woman.

Many Native American tales include humans who are transformed into animals. "The Ring in the Prairie," a Shawnee Indian tale, includes transformations of humans and sky dwellers: A human hunter transforms himself into a mouse to capture a girl who descends from the sky, and the sky dwellers secure part of an animal and are transformed into that specific animal. Many of the Native American transformation stories suggest close relationships between humans and animals.

Folktales from the British Isles

British folktales about ogres, giants, and clever humans were among the first stories published as inexpensive chapbooks in the 1500s. Joseph Jacobs collected the tales, and in 1890, he published over eighty of them as *English Fairy Tales*. In 1892, Jacobs published a collection of Celtic fairy tales. These books, in reissue or modern editions, are still available today. The number of possible folktales from the British Isles is further emphasized when we read Katharine Briggs's *Dictionary of British Folk-Tales* (7), which was originally published in four volumes and 2,558 pages. The fast plots and unpromising heroes of British tales are popular with children. For example, the various "Jack tales"—including "Jack the Giant Killer" and "Jack and the Beanstalk"—develop plots around villainous ogres or giants who terrorize a kingdom and the heroes who overcome their adversaries with trickery and cleverness rather than magical powers.

Other villains in British folktales play adversarial roles similar to those of giants and ogres. For example, "Three Little Pigs" must outwit a wolf, and a young girl is frightened by "The Three Bears." In *What's in Fox's Sack? An Old English Tale,* retold and illustrated by Paul Galdone, the villain is a sly fox who manages to get a boy into his sack. A clever woman outsmarts the fox by placing a large bulldog inside the sack. The mother goat in "Grey Goat," retold in Alan Garner's *A Bag of Moonshine,* saves her three kids by killing the fox.

In addition to clearly defined good and bad characters, repetitive language in many British folktales appeals to storytellers and listeners. In "The Three Little Pigs," the wolf threatens, "I'll huff

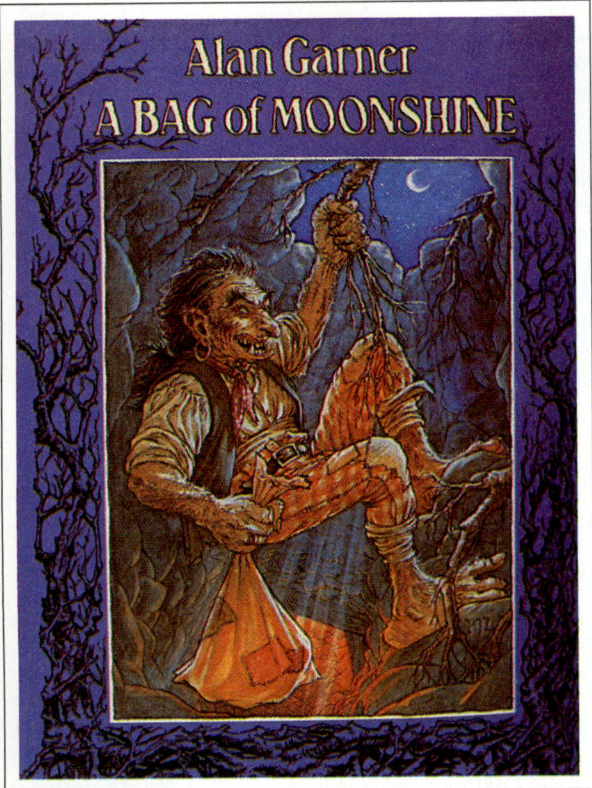

Ogres and giants play key roles in many of these tales set in the British Isles. (From *A Bag of Moonshine* by Alan Garner. Illustrated by Patrick James Lynch. Copyright © 1986 by Alan Garner. Illustrations copyright © 1986 by Patrick James Lynch. Reprinted by permission of Delacorte Press.

and I'll puff and I'll blow your house in," and the pig replies, "Not by the hair on my chinny chin chin." "The Three Bears" repeats chairs, bowls of porridge, and beds, and the three bears' questions: Who has been sitting in my chair? Who has been eating my porridge? Who has been sleeping in my bed? Several versions of this folktale appeal to young children. Lorinda Bryan Cauley's *Goldilocks and the Three Bears* has compelling illustrations. Paul Galdone's *The Three Bears,* which may be used to develop size concepts, has pictures that differentiate sizes of bears, bowls, beds, and chairs. James Marshall's *Goldilocks and the Three Bears* frolic in humorous illustrations. Jan Brett's *Goldilocks and the Three Bears* includes large, detailed illustrations on pages bordered with objects and characters from the story.

British folk literature is filled with tales that stress human foolishness, making a point about human foibles. In the Scottish tale "Master Above All Masters," found in David Buchan's *Scottish Tradition: A Collection of Scottish Folk Literature,* a wealthy tailor desires grander and longer names for himself, his family, and his possessions. One night, the house catches on fire, and the manservant rushes up the stairs calling:

"Arise, Master above all Masters,
Put on thy Stuntifiers,
Waken Madame for the Dame
And Sir John the Greater,
For Old Killiecraffus
Has gone to the top of Montaigo,
And if you don't apply to the Well of Strathfountain
The whole Castle of Kilmundy
Will be burned in twa minutes" (p. 56)

By the time the servant finishes calling the long list of acquired names and titles, the house is ablaze, and only the people escape.

The consequences of greed, a universal motif in folktales from many countries, are found in Susan Cooper's *The Silver Cow: A Welsh Tale*. In this tale, the magic people, the Tylwyth Teg, send a marvelous cow out of Bearded Lake as a reward for a young boy's music. The greed of the boy's father causes the cow and her offspring to return to the lake, where they are turned into water lilies. In Gwyn Jones's "Where Arthur Sleeps," found in *Welsh Legends and Folk-Tales,* and in "The Slumber King," found in Kevin Crossley-Holland's *British Folk Tales,* a greedy young man is thrown out of a cave filled with gold and silver and must return home with nothing.

An impossible task created by foolish boasting is a motif in Harve Zemach's *Duffy and the Devil,* a Cornish tale resembling "Rumpelstiltskin." An inefficient maid named Duffy misleads her employer about her spinning ability and makes an agreement with the devil, who promises to do the knitting for three years. At the end of that time, she must produce his name or go with him. When the time arrives, the squire goes hunting and overhears the festivities of the witches and the devil as the little man with the long tail sings this song:

Tomorrow! Tomorrow! Tomorrow's the day!
I'll take her! I'll take her! I'll take her away!
Let her weep, let her cry, let her beg, let her pray—
She'll never guess my name is . . . Tarraway! (p. 30 unnumbered)

Thus, Duffy learns the magic name and cheats the devil from claiming her soul. The importance of a secret name is reflected in folktales from many cultures. In the English version of "Rumpelstiltskin," the name is Tim Tit Tot; a Scottish secret name is Whuppity Stoories; a tale from Nigeria is "The Hippopotamus called Isantim."

A Cinderella-type story is found in several British folktales. In "Tattercoats," recorded by Joseph Jacobs in *More English Fairy Tales,* the heroine is mistreated by her grandfather, who mourns his daughter's death in childbirth and rejects the child who survived, and by the grandfather's cruel servants. In this British version, the prince invites her to attend the ball even though she is dressed in her rags. Only after she is at the ball does the gooseherd transform her into a beautifully dressed lady. Kevin Crossley-Holland's "Mossycoat," found in his *British Folk Tales,* is also mistreated by servants before she marries the young master.

In *Princess Furball,* retold by Charlotte Huck, the Cinderella-type heroine is at first ignored by her father, the king, and then promised in marriage to an ogre. Unlike many of the Cinderella tales, this heroine does not rely on magic to overcome obstacles. Instead, she relies on her own ingenuity. She demands and receives three gowns and a coat made from one thousand kinds of fur as a bridal gift from her father, but in order to escape the marriage, she runs away. Later, she is captured by a young king from a neighboring kingdom. At the castle, she becomes a servant to the servants. In this role she sweeps ashes, washes dishes, and fetches wood. When the king gives a ball, Furball wears one of her gowns, attends the ball, and dazzles the king. These actions continue through three balls, until a ring she is wearing shows the king that she is the girl that he loves.

One of the shortest British Cinderella-type stories is "Ashey Pelt," found in Katharine Briggs's *British Folktales*. In this variant, a black ewe provides the dress and horses for the girl to attend a party. It is also the black ewe who warns the prince that the stepsisters have been trimming their feet to fit into the silk slipper:

> Nippet foot and clippet foot
> Behind the king's son rides
> But bonny foot and pretty foot
> Is with the cathering hides.

The tales ends, "So he rode back and found her among the cows, and he married her, and if they live happy, so may you and me" (p. 21).

Folktales from Ireland are filled with fairies, leprechauns, and other little people. Many tales, such as "Connla and the Fairy Maiden," found in Joseph Jacob's *Irish Fairy Tales,* show the power of supernatural beings over humans. Jacob's "Guleesh," found in *Celtic Fairy Tales,* shows that the fairies do not always outwit people. A young man races with the "sheehogues," tricks those fairy hosts out of a captured princess, and breaks a spell so that the princess can speak. This tale has an ending characteristic of Irish folk literature:

> But I heard it from a birdeen that there was neither cark nor care, sickness nor sorrow, mishap nor misfortune on them till the hour of their death, and may the same be with me, and with us all! (p. 25)

Peasants rather than royalty are usually the heroes and heroines in folktales of the British Isles. Consequently, readers or listeners can learn much about the problems, beliefs, values, and humor of common people in early British history. Themes in British folktales suggest that intelligence wins over physical strength, that hard work and diligence are rewarded, and that love and loyalty are basic values for everyone.

French Folktales

The majority of French folktales portray splendid royal castles rather than humble peasant cottages. Charles Perrault, a member of the Académie Française, collected and transcribed many of these tales. In 1697, he published a collection of folktales called *Tales of Mother Goose,* which included "Cinderilla" (original spelling), "Sleeping Beauty," "Puss in Boots," "Little Red Riding Hood," "Blue Beard," "Little Thumb," "Requet with the Tuft," and "Diamond and the Toads." These stories had entertained children and adults of the Parisian aristocracy and, consequently, are quite different from tales that stress wicked, dishonest kings being outwitted by simple peasants. A new edition of Perrault's tales, *The Glass Slipper: Charles Perrault's Tales of Time Past,* includes eight tales highlighted by elegant illustrations, which capture the formality of the early French court.

Many illustrators and translators of French fairy tales depict royal settings. For example, Marcia Brown's *Cinderella* (based on Charles Perrault's version) is quite different from the German version. Cinderella has a fairy godmother who grants her wishes. A pumpkin is transformed into a gilded carriage, six mice become beautiful horses, a rat becomes a coachman with an elegant mustache, and lizards turn into footmen who are complete with fancy livery and lace. Cinderella is dressed in a beautiful gown, which is embroidered with rubies, pearls, and diamonds. This version also has the magical hour of midnight, when everything returns to normal. Perrault's *Cinderella* contains stepsisters who are rude and haughty,

ISSUE

Are "Cinderella" and Similar Traditional Tales Sexist?

Puritans in England and the United States considered many of the traditional tales too violent to be shared with children. Today, the tales are being attacked by groups who consider the actions of the beautiful, often helpless females, and the clever, handsome princes who rescue them to be sexist. Ethel Johnston Phelps believes the image of the good, obedient, meek, and submissive heroine is harmful and should be altered. She has published two books that depict brave and clever heroines: *Tatterhood and Other Tales*[1] and *The Maid of the North*.[2] *Time* magazine's review of these books concludes: "Though Phelps celebrates females who have brains and energy, her feminist lens at times distorts the drama beneath the surface of the folk tales."[3]

In defense of this criticism, the *Time* writer provides two examples. In "The Twelve Huntsmen," Phelps has the prince collapse at the appropriate moment; in the original story, the girl demonstrates this

but they are not as cruel as they are in the German version. Cinderella even finds it possible to forgive them:

> Now her stepsisters recognized her. Cinderella was the beautiful personage they had seen at the ball! They threw themselves at her feet and begged forgiveness for all their bad treatment of her. Cinderella asked them to rise, embraced them and told them she forgave them with all her heart. She begged them to love her always. (p. 27)

Cinderella not only forgives them but also provides them with a home at the palace and marries them to the lords of the court. Brown's illustra-

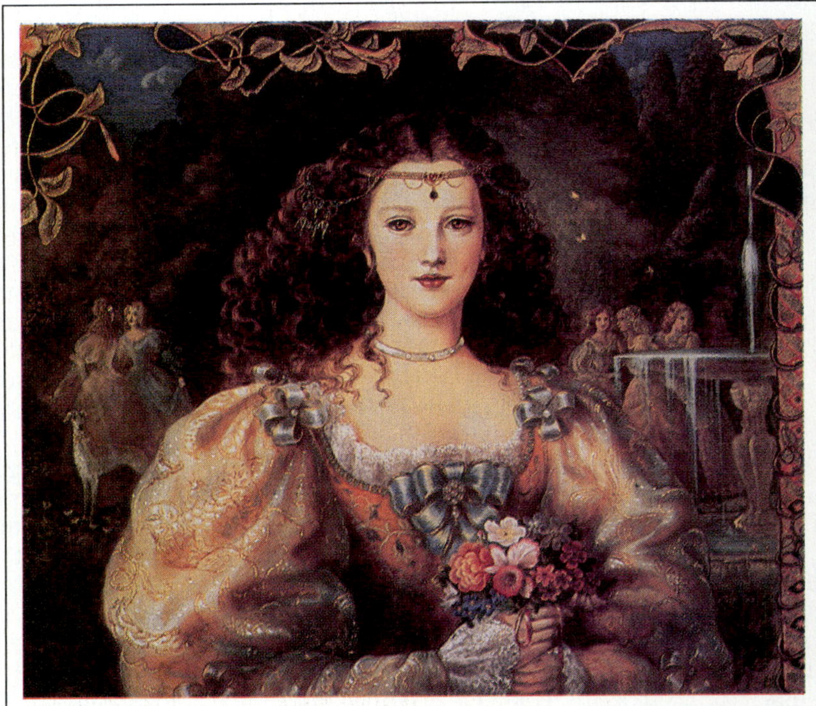

The tale of enchanted princesses emphasizes a regal setting. (From *Twelve Dancing Princesses* retold by Marianna Mayer. Illustrated by K. Y. Craft. Text © 1989 by Marianna Mayer. Illustrations © 1989 by K. Y. Craft. Reprinted by permission of Morrow Junior Books, a division of William Morrow & Co.)

behavior. In "The Maid of the North," Phelps changes the dialogue from the original, in which the maid fends off a suitor by describing the disadvantages of leaving home to join a stranger's household. In Phelps's version, the maid expresses this viewpoint against marriage: "A wife is like a house dog tied with a rope. Why should I be a servant and wait upon a husband?"

Should these stories be rewritten to reflect changing attitudes of the times, or will rewriting distort the value of traditional tales? Are children harmed by the male and female stereotypes developed in traditional literature? If stories are tampered with, will children lose their identification with characters like themselves, who are often bewildered and feel like underdogs in traditional tales?

Writing on a related subject of the advisability of reshaping folktales, Susan Hepler[4] states, "New twists and role reversals delight children familiar with the original versions of folktales." She also declares, however, "authors, illustrators, and publishers owe it to their audiences to make it absolutely clear when they alter the original content and/or tamper with the spirit of a tale" (p. 154).

[1]Phelps, Ethel Johnston. *Tatterhood and Other Tales*. New York: Feminist Press, 1978.

[2]Phelps, Ethel Johnston. *The Maid of the North*. New York: Holt, Rinehart & Winston, 1981.

[3]"Sexes: Feminist Folk and Fairy Tales." *Time* (July 20, 1981): 60.

[4]Hepler, Susan. "Fooling with Folktales: Updates, Spin-offs, and Roundups." *School Library Journal*. 36 (March 1990): 153–154.

tions, drawn with fine lines and colored with pastels, depict a kingdom where life in the royal court is marvelous.

The French version of "The Sleeping Beauty" suggests traditional French values. Seven good fairies bestow the virtues of intelligence, beauty, kindness, generosity, gaiety, and grace on the infant princess. David Walker's version of *The Sleeping Beauty* shows his background in theatrical set and costume design. His illustrations create the feeling of a stage setting, especially as his fairies dance lightly across the great hall of the castle.

Diane Goode has translated and illustrated an edition of Madame de Beaumont's *Beauty and the Beast*. Meant originally for the wealthy classes in French society, de Beaumont's tale begins with the traditional "Once upon a time," but it provides descriptions tailored for an aristocratic audience. For example, Beauty enjoys reading, playing the harpsichord, and singing while she spins. When she enters the beast's castle, he provides her with a library, a harpsichord, and music books. Goode's illustrations create the magical settings in which Beauty eventually loves the beast for his virtue, although he lacks good looks and wit. Beauty's moral discrimination permits the beast's transformation back into a handsome prince.

Jan Brett's version of *Beauty and the Beast* includes illustrations that Brett modeled after work of Walter Crane. The tapestries in the illustrations include messages and show the people in the castle before they were enchanted.

Warwick Hutton's shorter version of *Beauty and the Beast* is not aimed at the wealthy classes. His Beauty is the youngest daughter of a merchant who has had bad luck. Unlike her ill-tempered and resentful older sisters, she looks on the bright side of their situation and tries to keep her family happy.

French folktales contain more enchantment than do tales from other countries. The motifs in these tales include fairy godmothers, other fairies, remarkable beasts who help their young masters, unselfish girls who break enchantments, and deceitful beasts.

German Folktales

The following words bring to mind one of the most popular childhood tales:

> Mirror, mirror on the wall.
> Who is the fairest of them all?

German folktales—whether they are about enchanted princesses and friendly dwarfs, clever animals, or poor but honest peasants—are among the most enjoyed folktales in the world. Their accessibility to modern audiences is owed to the work of Wilhelm and Jacob Grimm, German professors who researched the roots of the German language through the traditional tales, which had been told orally for generations. The Grimms asked village storytellers throughout Germany to tell them tales. Then, they wrote down the stories and published them as *Kinder-und Hausmärchen*. The stories ultimately were translated into many

Four illustrations of a familiar tale show the impact of the pictures on the moods of the story. *A,* The formal border and illustrations create a traditional mood in the illustrations from *Little Red Riding Hood* by Trina Schart Hyman, copyright © 1983 by Trina Schart Hyman. Reprinted by permission of Holiday House. *B,* The black and white photographs suggest a frightening mood in Rita Marshall's illustrations for *Little Red Riding Hood,* copyright, © 1983 from Charles Perrault's story edited by Ann Redpath and Etienne Delessert. Reprinted by permission of Creative Education, Inc. *C,* James Marshall's cartoon illustrations add a humorous context to *Red Riding Hood*. Copyright © 1987 by James Marshall. Reproduced by permission of the publisher, Dial Books for Young Readers. *D,* Dark colors and frightened girls suggest the dangerous nature of the tale in *Lon Po Po: A Red-Riding Hood Story from China* translated and illustrated by Ed Young, copyright, © 1989 by Ed Young. Reprinted by permission of Philomel Books.

A

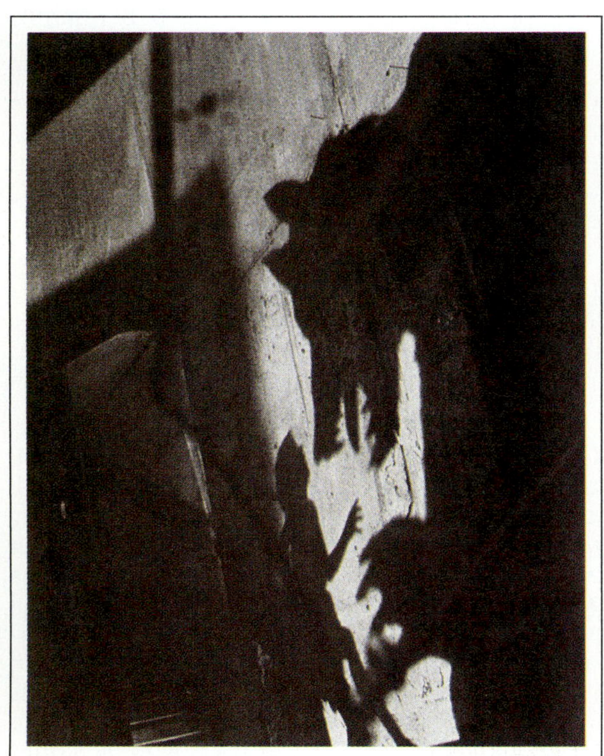

B

C

languages and became popular in Europe, North America, and elsewhere.

A wolf is the villain in several German folktales that young children enjoy. Wolves in these tales are cunning and dangerous, and they receive just punishments. In Anne Rogers's version of the Grimms' *The Wolf and the Seven Little Kids,* the mother goat specifically warns her children about the deceitful wolf: "He may try to disguise himself, but you'll know him by his gruff voice and his black feet" (p. 1). After the wolf has tricked and eaten the kids, the mother goat cuts him open, saves her children, and places rocks inside the wolf. When awakened, the wolf feels terrible, loses his balance, and falls into the well.

Paul Galdone's version of *Little Red Riding Hood* is particularly appropriate for younger children. Little Red Riding Hood is traveling through the woods to visit her grandmother. On the way, she stops to chat with a sly wolf, who then hurries ahead of her, gobbles up Grandmother, and does the same thing to Little Red Riding Hood when she arrives. In this version, the huntsman rescues Grandmother and Red Riding Hood from inside the wolf and places stones in the wolf's stomach.

Trina Schart Hyman's version of this tale is more involved and appropriate for older children. In addition to the story, Hyman stresses the importance of a moral in the Grimms' folktales. The incident with the dangerous wolf teaches Red Riding Hood a lesson: "I will never wander off the forest path again, as long as I live. I should have kept my promise to my mother."

Quite a different mood is created by James Marshall's humorous text and cartoon-type illustrations in his version of *Red Riding Hood*. The last page even includes a crocodile. Little Red Riding Hood has learned her lesson, however, and refuses to speak to him.

Shang listened through the door.
"Po Po," she said, "why is your
voice so low?"
"Your grandmother has caught a
cold, good children, and it is dark
and windy out here. Quickly open
up, and let your Po Po come in," th
cunning wolf said.
Tao and Paotze could not wait.
One unlatched the door and the
other opened it. They shouted, "Po
Po, Po Po, come in!"
At the moment he entered the
door, the wolf blew out the candle.
"Po Po," Shang asked, "why did
you blow out the candle? The room
is now dark."
The wolf did not answer.

Not all animals in German folklore are as fearsome as the wolf. For example, "The Bremen Town Musicians," old animals about to be de-

D

stroyed by their owners, have humorously appealing human qualities. In Hans Fischer's version of this tale, *The Traveling Musicians,* the donkey, hound, cat, and rooster set out to seek their fortunes as musicians. They give only one concert, but it is sufficient to frighten away a band of robbers, whose house and treasures they claim for themselves. Fischer's illustrations add to the humor of the text. Ilse Plume's softly colored illustrations for another version of this tale suggest the gentle nature of the animals and the setting, a sunlit forest. Josef Palecek's illustrations for *The Bremen Town Musicians* provide brightly colored, humorous characters.

Poor peasants and penniless soldiers are common heroes in German folklore. The peasant may not be cunning, but he is usually good. In "The Golden Goose," for example, the youngest son is even called Simpleton. When his selfish brothers leave home, their parents give each one a fine, rich cake and a bottle of wine, which they refuse to share with anyone. The despised Simpleton, however, is generous with the cinder cake and sour beer his parents give him. His kind heart is rewarded when he acquires a golden goose with magical powers that allow him to marry a princess. In Barbara Rogasky's retelling of *The Water of Life,* two prideful and treacherous older brothers are punished, while the kind and generous youngest brother is rewarded. Both of these tales contain many of the actions that Vladimir Propp (20) discovered to be recurrent in folktales.

Hansel and Gretel is the classic tale of an evil witch, a discontented and selfish mother, an ineffectual father, and two resourceful children. Rika Lesser's story with Paul O. Zelinsky's illustrations provides a rich retelling of this favorite tale.

Many of the best-loved German folktales are stories of princesses who sleep for a hundred years, have wicked stepmothers, and are enchanted by witches. One lovely version of the Grimms' "Snow White" is translated by Randall Jarrell and illustrated by Nancy Ekholm Burkert. Burkert undertook considerable research in German museums and visited the Black Forest before creating her drawings for *Snow White and the Seven Dwarfs,* which portrays every aspect of the mystical forest, the dwarfs' cottage, and the wicked stepmother's secret tower room.

The German version of "Cinderella" in *The Complete Brothers' Grimm Fairy Tales* differs somewhat from the French rendering of this tale in both detail and mood. A bird in the hazel tree growing by her mother's grave, not a fairy godmother, gives Cinderella a dress made of gold and silver and satin slippers for the ball. When Cinderella is successfully united with the prince, no softness of heart leads her to forgive her cruel stepsisters. On her wedding day, the sisters join the bridal procession; but doves perched on Cinderella's shoulders peck out the sisters' eyes.

The elegance of courtly life is reflected in tales such as *The Twelve Dancing Princesses.* Kinuko Craft's paintings re-create beautiful costumes, glorious gardens, and magical settings in Marianna Mayer's retelling of this magical tale.

Breaking enchantments through unselfish love is another common theme in German folklore. In the Grimms' "The Six Swans," the heroine can restore her brothers to human form only by sewing six shirts out of starwort. She cannot speak during the six years required for her task and suffers many ordeals before she is successful. The same theme and a similar plot are found in Elizabeth Crawford's translation of the Grimms' "The Seven Ravens."

Nonny Hogrogian's version of the Grimms' "The Devil with the Three Golden Hairs" contains many of the characteristics of German folktales. A poor, brave boy is rewarded; a wicked, greedy king is punished; a kind miller cares for the boy; a beautiful princess is rewarded; the devil's grandmother uses enchantment to help the boy; and the devil is outwitted. Common folktale motifs in this tale include a physical sign of luck, a quest, the importance of threes (three hairs, three questions), and magical transformations. The text concludes with a characteristic moral: "The youth, together with his bride, lived well and reigned well, for he who is not afraid can even take the hairs from the devil's head and conquer the kingdom."

After reading a number of German folktales first recorded by Jacob and Wilhelm Grimm, you may approach the challenge of Wilhelm Grimm's *Dear Mili,* which was illustrated by Maurice Sendak. What is the origin of the tale recently found in a letter written to a young girl in 1816? Is it part of the oral tradition collected by this famous recorder of German folktales, or did Grimm use characteristics of traditional tales to write his own literary folktale?

German folktales are ideal candidates for storytelling. Their speedy openings, fast-paced plots, and drama keep listeners entertained for story after story. In these tales, adversaries include devils, witches, and wolves. The good-hearted youngest child is often rewarded, but selfishness,

Bright, jeweled tones suggest magical abilities of an unusual fish in this German folktale. Illustration from *The Fisherman and His Wife* by the Brothers Grimm, translated by Elizabeth Shub, illustrated by Monika Laimgruber. Copyright © 1978 by Artemis Verlag. Reprinted by permission of Greenwillow Books (A Division of William Morrow & Company).

greed, and discontent are punished. The noble character frequently wins as a result of intervention by supernatural helpers, and magical objects and spells are recurring motifs.

Norwegian Folktales

Pat Shaw Iverson (15) states, "[I]f Norway were to show the world a single work of art which would most truly express the Norwegian character, perhaps the best choice would be the folktales, published for the first time more than a hundred years ago and later illustrated by Erik Werenskiold and Theodor Kittelsen" (p. 5). Collected by Norwegian scholars Peter Christian Asbjörnsen and Jörgen E. Moe, these folktales were published under the title *Norwegian Folk Tales* in 1845. Asbjörnsen and Moe's interest in collecting the traditional tales of the Norwegian people was stimulated by reading the Grimms' *Kinder-und Hausmärchen*. They were also inspired by the national renaissance then sweeping Europe. Folklore and folk music were excellent sources for studying early Norwegian traditions and history.

Claire Booss (6), a collector of the folktales of northern peoples, believes that climatic and geographic extremes created hardy, courageous, and independent people and that the folktales of these people reflect a strong sense of wonder, a fierce loyalty to ideals, and a great sense of humor. Booss also maintains that extremes inspire stories with the power to delight, haunt, and terrify.

It is interesting to compare Norwegian story elements with those of other European cultures. Consider, for example, Mercer Mayer's version of "East of the Sun and West of the Moon." The story elements in this tale are similar to those in the French "Beauty and the Beast" and other tales of human enchantment and lost loves: An enchanted human demands a promise in return for a favor; the promise is at first honored; the maiden disenchants the human; he must leave because she does not honor her promise; she searches for him, and she saves him finally.

The adversaries and helpers in this tale reflect a northern climate and culture. The human is enchanted by a troll princess who lives in a distant, icy kingdom. The loving maiden receives help from, among others, Father Forest, who understands the body of earth and stone; Great Fish, who knows the blood of salt and water; and North Wind, who understands the mind of the earth, the moon, and the sun. The gifts each helper gives the maiden allow her to overcome the trolls and free the prince. A tinderbox makes it possible to melt the ice encasing the youth, a shot from the bow and arrow causes the troll princess to turn to wood, and reflections in the fish scale cause the remaining trolls to turn to stone. Mayer's illustrations of snowy winters, creatures frozen in ice, icy mountains, and tree-covered landscapes also evoke northern settings.

Mayer's version of this tale differs from Claire Booss's version in *Scandinavian Folk & Fairy Tales,* in which a white bear offers a family riches if its youngest daughter is allowed to live in his castle. Nancy Willard's *East of the Sun & West of the Moon: A Play* provides another interesting comparison. As seen in the song that the woodcutter's daughter sings as she goes to the bear's palace, Willard develops a style that is very appropriate for oral presentations:

> When you go through the forest at midnight,
> and your friends and relations are few,
> just remember the crow and the cricket
> are twice as nervous as you.

Norwegian folktale collections provide many excellent stories for retelling. Several favorites are found in Virginia Haviland's *Favorite Fairy Tales Told in Norway*. Young children love to listen to, and dramatize "Three Billy Goats Gruff." Another favorite for storytelling and creative drama is "Taper Tom," whose hero is the characteristic youngest son. Tom sits in a chimney corner amusing himself by grubbing in the ashes and splitting tapers for lights. His family laughs at his belief that he can win the hand of the princess in marriage and half of the kingdom by making the princess laugh.

With the assistance of a magical golden goose who does not relinquish anyone who touches her, Tom forms a parade of unwilling followers: an old woman, an angry man who kicks at the woman, a smithy who waves a pair of tongs, and a cook who runs after them waving a ladle of porridge. At the sight of this ridiculous situation, the sad princess bursts into laughter. Tom wins the princess and half of the kingdom. Compare this tale with the Grimms' "The Golden Goose."

The humor in Erica Magnus's *Old Lars* results from another ridiculous situation. An old farmer hitches his horse to a sleigh, goes up to the mountains to gather wood, overloads the sleigh so much that the horse cannot pull the load, and empties the sleigh so that the horse can return home. The old man is satisfied, however. He has accomplished enough work for one day.

Norwegian folktales help children appreciate Norwegian traditions as well as provide children with pleasure and excitement. Themes suggest the rewarding of unselfish love and the punish-

Humor is developed through exaggeration and ridiculous situations. (From *Old Lars,* by Erica Magnus. Copyright © 1984 by Erica Magnus Thomas. Reproduced by permission of the publisher, Carolrhoda Books, Inc., 241 First Avenue North, Minneapolis, MN 55401.)

ment of greed. The sharp humor, the trolls, and the poor boys who overcome adversity are all excellent elements for storytelling.

Russian Folktales

Heroes and heroines who may be royalty or peasants; settings that reflect deep snows in winter, dark forests, the wooden huts of peasants, the gilded towers of palaces, and villains such as the long-nosed witch Baba Yaga and dishonest nobility or commoners are found in Russian folktales. Two types of folktales are common in traditional Russian literature: (1) short, merry tales characterized by rapid, humorous dialogue and plots that become absurd before things improve and (2) serious stories of enchantment and magic.

A merry tale that appears in picture storybook format for young children is Guy Daniels's *The Peasant's Pea Patch*. The tale builds upon the absurd acts of a foolish person and suggests that the remedy for a problem may be worse than the problem. This peasant feeds honey and vodka to the cranes that eat his peas, waits until they are asleep, ties them to his cart, and tries to drag them home. When the cranes awake, they take the peasant on a wild ride through the sky. The peasant attempts to solve this problem with another foolish act. He cuts the rope binding him to the cranes and plunges into a treacherous quagmire. When a strong duck lands on his head, he grabs the duck, and it frees him from the quagmire. His problems continue, however, in adventures with a bear and beehives. At the end, he limps home.

Many Russian folktales are complex stories of quests, longing, and greed. Arthur Ransome's *Old Peter's Russian Tales* includes such quest tales as "The Fire-bird, the Horse of Power and the Princess Vasilissa." In many of the quests, generosity and kindness are rewarded and greed and foolishness are punished. Michael McCurdy's *The Devils Who Learned to Be Good,* a good-versus-evil tale, includes common Russian motifs: a generous old soldier, and supernatural objects given to reward generosity and used to gain riches and outwit evil spirits. An even stronger and more complex good-versus-evil theme is developed in Carole Kismaric's *The Rumor of Pavel and Paali: A Ukrainian Folktale*. In this tale, the protagonist and antagonist are twin brothers who wager about people's beliefs in the powers of good and evil. Although the forces of evil win in the first phase of the tale, good finally overcomes.

Many of the characteristics of Russian folktales are found in Elizabeth Isele's retelling of "The Frog." The tale develops typical folktale characterizations. A ruler requires a quest of his three sons, the youngest brother receives the best prize, an enchanted princess is wise, and supernatural helpers give objects with magical powers or wise advice. Folktale motifs include a quest, the importance of three, tasks to prove worth, magical transformations, punishment for lack of patience, magical objects, and rewards for kindness. The moral of the story is that lack of patience is punished, while kindness and perseverance are rewarded.

Universal folktale themes found in Russian folktales include a desire for children, developed in a story about a childless couple who create "The Snow Maiden," and hatred of a beautiful child by her stepmother and stepsisters, developed in "Vassilissa the Fair," a Russian version of the Cinderella story. The latter tale and six others are collected in Aleksandr Nikolaevich Afanaséz's *Russian Folk Tales,* with illustrations by Ivan Bilibin, the late nineteenth-century Russian illustrator, who depicts traditional costumes and early Russian settings.

Alexander Pushkin was one of the first Russian writers to transcribe the orally transmitted folktales of his century. Patricia Tracy Lowe has translated and retold several of these stories in picture storybook formats, including *The Tale of Czar Saltan, or the Prince and the Swan Princess* and *The Tale of the Golden Cockerel*. These two tales reflect the importance of keeping promises and the consequences of jealousy and greed. Another tale of good versus evil and the consequences of jealousy and greed is Yūzō Otsuka's *Suho and the White Horse: A Legend of Mongolia*.

The familiar theme of kindness rewarded and the motifs of magical powers and foolish but kindhearted peasants are found in Arthur Ransome's *The Fool of the World and the Flying Ship*. The czar has offered his daughter's hand in marriage to anyone who can build a flying ship. Kindness to an old man provides an aspiring peasant with a magical ship. Companions with extraordinary powers also aid the peasant in his quest. This tale implies that the czar does not want a peasant to marry his daughter.

In various tales, the Russian witch Baba Yaga may be an evil, child-eating villain or a respecter of human spirit who rewards courage. In Maida Silverman's rendition of "Anna and the Seven Swans," Baba Yaga has characteristics similar to

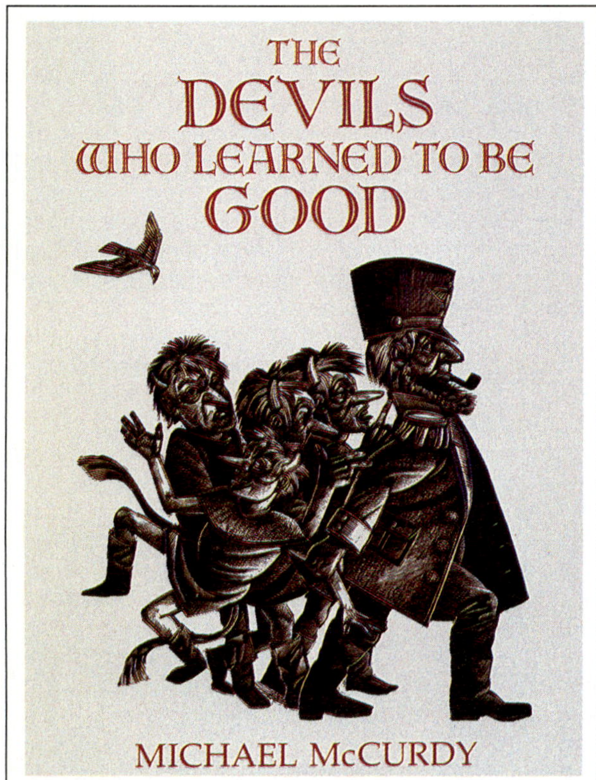

The woodcuts enhance the traditional story line in *The Devils Who Learned to Be Good* by Michael McCurdy, copyright © 1987 by Michael McCurdy. Reprinted by permission of Little, Brown and Company.

the witch in "Hansel and Gretel" as told by the Brothers Grimm. She steals children and intends to eat her human hostages. Quite a different Baba Yaga is portrayed in Elizabeth Isele's retelling of "The Frog Princess." The witch listens attentively to the prince's problem, respects him, and provides him with the information that makes his quest successful.

Russian protagonists may be strong and resourceful females. Josepha Sherman's retelling of *Vassilisa the Wise* shows that a clever and courageous female is able to outwit the prince and save her unwise husband from the prince's dark dungeon.

These and many other Russian folktales reflect a vast country containing numerous cultures. Talent, beauty, and kindness are appreciated and rewarded. People must pay the consequences for foolish actions, greed, broken promises, and jealousy. Humor suggests the universal need to laugh at oneself and others.

Jewish Folktales

According to Charlotte Huck, Susan Hepler, and Janet Hickman (14), Jewish folktales "have a poignancy, wit, and ironic humor that is not matched by any other folklore" (p. 285). Wit and humor are found in Margot Zemach's *It Could Always Be Worse*. This Yiddish folktale relates the story of nine unhappy people who share a small one-room hut. The father desperately seeks the advice of the rabbi, who suggests that he bring a barnyard animal inside. A pattern of complaint and advice continues until most of the family's livestock is in the house. When the rabbi tells the father to clear the animals out of the hut, the whole family appreciates its large, peaceful home.

Isaac Bashevis Singer's *Mazel and Shlimazel, or the Milk of a Lioness* is longer and more complex. It pits Mazel, the spirit of good luck, against Shlimazel, the spirit of bad luck. To test the strength of good luck versus bad, the two spirits decide that each of them will spend a year manipulating the life of Tam, a bungler who lives in the poorest hut in the village. As soon as Mazel stands behind Tam, he succeeds at everything he tries. He fixes the king's carriage wheel and is invited to court, where he accomplishes impossible tasks. Even Princess Nesika is in love with him.

Just as Tam is about to complete his greatest challenge successfully, Mazel's year is over, and an old, bent man with spiders in his beard stands beside Tam. With one horrible slip of the tongue encouraged by Shlimazel, Tam is in disfavor and condemned to death. Shlimazel has won. But wait! Mazel presents Shlimazel with the wine of forgetfulness, which causes Shlimazel to forget poor Tam. Mazel rescues Tam from hanging and helps Tam redeem himself with the king and marry the princess. Tam's success is more than good luck, however: "Tam had learned that good luck follows those who are diligent, honest, sincere and helpful to others. The man who has these qualities is indeed lucky forever" (p. 42).

Singer's *When Shlemiel Went to Warsaw & Other Stories* contains several folktales that reflect both human foibles and folklore themes. For example, "Shrewd Todie & Lyzer the Miser" pits foolish, greedy actions against cunning and trickery. To his discomfort, the miser learns that "if you accept nonsense when it brings you profit, you must also accept nonsense when it brings you loss" (p. 12). Singer's *The Golem* is a tale about human hopes for a better world and the realities of human limitations. There is a strong message that human attempts to play god are bound to reflect human imperfections. Jewish folktales suggest that sincerity, unselfishness, and true wisdom are rewarded. The tales reflect people who face and overcome dissatisfaction and realize the dangers of excessive power.

Asian Folktales

Asian folktales, like other folktales, portray the feelings, struggles, and aspirations of common people; depict the lives of the well-to-do; and reflect the moral values, superstitions, social customs, and humor of the times and societies in which they originated. Like medieval Europe, ancient Asia contained societies in which royalty and nobles led lives quite different from those of peasants. Females had less freedom and social influence than males. Asian tales tell about the rich and the poor, the wise and the foolish, mythical quests, lovers, animals, and supernatural beings and powers, motifs common to all folklore, but they also reflect the customs and beliefs of specific cultures.

Chinese Folktales. Traditional Chinese sayings (24) suggest Chinese values and philosophical viewpoints expressed in Chinese folktales over the centuries. For example:

A teacher can open the door, but the pupil must go through it alone.
The home that includes an old grandparent contains a precious jewel.

According to Louise and Yuan-hsi Kuo (16), Chinese tales often develop universal themes and contain roguish humor. Respect for ancestors, ethical standards, and conflict between nobility and commoners are popular topics in Chinese tales.

A dislike for imperial authority is evident in several Chinese equivalents to the cottage tales of medieval European peasants. In these tales, the dragon, the symbol of imperial authority, is usually evil and is overcome by a peasant's wit. "The Golden Sheng," included in Louise and Yuan-hsi Kuo's *Chinese Folk Tales,* tells the story of a little girl captured by a malevolent flying dragon:

Your sister is suffering; your sister is suffering,
In the evil dragon's cave.
Tears cover her face;
Blood stains her back;
Her hand drills the rock.
Your sister is suffering; your sister is suffering. (p. 18)

A common folktale theme, reward for unselfish action, and a common folktale motif, a magical object, allow the girl's brother to rescue her and dispose of the beast. En route, the brother moves a dangerous boulder out of the path and is rewarded with a dazzling golden sheng. The sheng creates a melodious sound when blown into, and the sound is so hypnotic that earthworms, lizards, and even dragons are forced to dance. While the dragon whirls, the brother and sister escape.

A very different dragon characterization is found in "Green Dragon Pond" in He Liyi's *The Spring of Butterflies and Other Chinese Folktales*. According to the tale, "From the very beginning to the end, this dragon did no harm, but only good deeds. For this reason, the villagers around Malong peak lived a happy life" (p. 119). In this tale of transformation, the dragon changes himself into a man and plays chess with an old monk who lives in the temple by the pond. The story has an unhappy ending because of the carelessness of the dragon and the monk, not because the dragon is cruel.

Marilee Heyer's *The Weaving of a Dream* reveals rewarded behavior: bravery, unselfish love, understanding, respect for one's mother, faithfulness, and kindness. In contrast, disrespect for one's mother and selfishness are punished. This tale also shows the power of a dream and the perseverance that may be required to gain the dream. Ed Young's translation of *Lon Po Po: A Red-Riding Hood Story from China* shows that the cleverness of the eldest daughter and the cooperation of the three sisters are powerful enough to outwit the intentions of the evil wolf.

Numerous tales in *The Spring of Butterflies and Other Chinese Folktales* reveal the consequences of kindness, humor, and greed. Moss Roberts's large collection, *Chinese Fairy Tales and Fantasies,* is divided into tales about enchantment and magic, folly and greed, animals, women and wives, ghosts and souls, and judges and diplomats. Laurence Yep's *The Rainbow People* is a collection of twenty Chinese folktales from Chinese Americans in the United States. The text is divided according to tales about tricksters, fools, virtues and vices, Chinese America, and love. Yep has included introductory comments for each of the sections.

Japanese Folktales. Chinese culture influenced Japanese culture, and many Japanese tales are similar to the Chinese. Dragons, for example, are common in tales from both countries. The tiger, usually considered a symbol of power (19), is a creature often found in Japanese tales. Davis Pratt and Elsa Kula's *Magic Animals of Japan* contains short stories about these and other animals —including the fox, either a symbol of abundance or a mischiefmaker able to transform himself, and the cat, a symbol of friendliness and prosperity.

Japanese folktales reflecting respected values and disliked human qualities include Patricia Newton's *The Five Sparrows: A Japanese Folktale,* the story of a woman who is richly rewarded after caring for an injured sparrow. A greedy neighbor in this tale is punished after she intentionally injures three birds in order to demonstrate her caring qualities and gain rewards.

Momoko Ishii's retelling of *The Tongue-Tied Sparrow* also uses sparrows to develop the theme that kindness is rewarded and greed is punished. In this tale, a kind old man befriends a sparrow and then seeks the sparrow's forgiveness after his angry wife snips the sparrow's tongue. The old man is rewarded for his kindness with a chest full of treasures. When his greedy wife seeks the sparrow, she is rewarded with a chest full of giant toads and snakes.

Cranes, like sparrows, are frequently important in Japanese folktales. Anne Laurin's *The Perfect Crane* suggests the desirability of friendship between humans and supernatural creatures. In this story, a lonely magician develops a strong friendship with a crane that he creates from rice paper. Molly Bang's *The Paper Crane* has a similar theme. A hungry man rewards a restaurant owner with a paper crane that can be brought to life by clapping hands, and this attraction creates many customers for the business.

Dianne Snyder's *The Boy of the Three-Year Nap* has a strong female protagonist who outwits her lazy son. The tale is a humorous match of wits. The lazy son tries to trick a wealthy merchant into letting him marry his daughter. His mother, however, shows that she is the equal of the son. She not only convinces the merchant to repair and enlarge her house but also tricks her son into getting a job.

Compassion is a valued characteristic in Jane Hori Ike and Baruch Zimmerman's *A Japanese Fairy Tale.* In this tale about a beautiful girl and an ugly man, the girl discovers "that she had been made beautiful because Manakata had taken upon himself the ugliness that was intended for her" (unnumbered). The story has a happy ending. The two are married and begin "a life together of perfect peace and harmony."

Other Asian Folktales. The Asian Cultural Centre for UNESCO has published a series of five books called *Folk Tales from Asia for Children Everywhere.* The series contains stories from many Asian countries. For example, a story from Burma, "The Four Puppets," stresses the harm that wealth and power can bring if they are not tempered with wisdom and love. "The Carpenter's Son," a tale from Afghanistan, is similar to the Arabian story of Aladdin and his magic lamp.

Additional collections of tales are Muriel Carrison's *Cambodian Folk Stories from the Gatiloke* and David Conger's *Many Lands, Many Stories: Asian Folktales for Children.* Carrison's text is a collection of fifteen tales that are divided according to scoundrels and rascals, kings and lords, and foolishness and fun. The introduction provides useful information. For example, folktales of the Gatiloke were used by Cambodian Buddhist monks as sermons to reveal right and wrong behavior. The introduction includes information about the Buddha and the Buddhist values reflected in the tales. It also gives a history of Cambodian Buddhist folktales.

Conger's text is a collection of stories from China, India, Japan, Korea, and Thailand. Conger has retold the tales with a storyteller's voice, and he interprets the tales for young readers. For example, in "The Woman Who Married a Snake" the human mother of a snake child wants her son to have a bride and a marriage festival. When she asks her husband to find a wife for the snake child, the storyteller reveals, "In India and in other countries in the East, young people don't choose the people they marry. Their fathers choose for them. Well, Godly's wife wanted him to do his duty as a father and find a wife for their son. But how was Godly supposed to find a wife for a snake?" (p. 36). Again, the storyteller intervenes with information as Godly asks, " 'What am I to do? Go to the underworld and ask Vasuki the serpent king for his daughter?' In India it was believed that a great snake king named Vasuki lives deep underground" (p. 36).

A Vietnamese version of the Cinderella tale develops motifs common in other versions and culturally related adaptations. *In the Land of Small Dragon,* rendered by Ann Nolan Clark, includes

The characters of a supernatural man and an old whaler combine to make a tall tale about whaling. (From *John Tabor's Ride* by Edward C. Day, illustrated by Dirk Zimmer. Copyright © 1989 by Edward C. Day, illustrations copyright 1989 by Dirk Zimmer. Reprinted by permission of Alfred A. Knopf, Inc.)

familiar motifs: the death of the mother, a cruel stepmother and stepsister, a persecuted heroine, magical assistance, a difficult task, meeting a prince, and proof of identity. The text and the illustrations strongly reflect the Vietnamese origins of the story, however. For example, one of the father's two wives is the wicked adversary; the girl's tasks include working in the rice paddies and separating rice from husks; the girl's fairy godmother gives her jeweled *hai* (slippers); and the prince is an emperor's son. As shown by the following description of the maiden, the language makes this story a good choice for sharing orally:

> Tam's face was a golden moon,
> Her eyes dark as a storm cloud,
> Her feet delicate flowers
> Stepping lightly on the wind.
> No envy lived in her heart,
> Nor bitterness in her tears. (p. 2)

Mirra Ginsburg's *The Chinese Mirror* is a Korean folktale about humorous consequences when a group of people see themselves in a mirror for the first time. They cannot convince each other that each one sees something else in the mirror until the mirror is broken into a hundred shiny splinters. Then, "that was the end of the stranger who looked at the traveler, the young beauty from China, the wrinkled old crone, the neighbor's grandpa, the nasty brat who stole pebbles, and the big fat bully who hurt little boys" (unnumbered).

Both Errol LeCain and Andrew Lang have published picture storybook versions of the Aladdin tale. It is one of several Arabian tales, collected in the original *The Thousand Nights and a Night,* supposedly told by Scheherazade to King Shahryar of Baghdad in her effort to keep from being beheaded.

Many folktales from India are included in a series of animal stories traditionally known as the *Panchatantra*. The original tales were moralistic and included reincarnations of the Buddha. English translations, however, usually delete the morals and the references to the Buddha. Consequently, the stories, some of which are included in Nancy DeRoin's *Jakata Tales,* have characteristics of folktales. Virginia Haviland's *Favorite Fairy Tales Told in India* is a fine source for other Indian folktales.

Eastern folktales contain such universal motifs as reward for unselfishness, assistance from magical objects, cruel adversaries, and punishment for dishonesty. The tales also emphasize the traditional values of the specific people: homage is paid to ancestors, knowledge and cleverness are rewarded, and greed and miserly behavior are punished.

African Folktales

African folktales are characterized by a highly developed oral tradition. Repetitive language and styles that encourage interaction with the storyteller make them excellent choices for sharing with children. Many of the stories are "why" tales. Such tales explain animal and human characteristics. Verna Aardema's *Why Mosquitoes Buzz in People's Ears* uses cumulative language to explain the buzz. *The Third Gift,* by Jan Carews, explains how the Jubas acquired work, beauty, and imagination. Personified animals, often tricksters, are popular subjects. The hare, the tortoise, and Ananse the spider use wit and trickery to gain their objectives. Chapter 11, "Multicultural Literature," discusses other tales that reflect traditional values of African peoples.

North American Folktales

Many North American folktales have roots in the cultures of other parts of the world or have been influenced by written literature and characters created by professional writers. Consequently, identifying tales that began in a specifically North American oral tradition is often difficult or impossible.

Folklorists identify four types of folktales found in North America: (1) Native American (and Native Canadian) tales that were handed down over centuries of tribal storytelling; (2) folktales of black Americans that reflect African and European themes but that were changed as slaves faced difficulties in a new land; (3) variants of European folktales containing traditional themes, motifs, and characters that were changed to meet the needs of a robust, rural North America; and (4) boisterous, boastful tall tales that originated on this continent.

Native American Folktales. Native American tales are usually considered the only traditional tales truly indigenous to the United States. Any study of the traditional literature of native peoples in North America reveals not one group of folktales, but tales different from region to region and tribe to tribe, although most Native American folktales have things in common.

Many of the traditional tales reveal why or how animals obtained specific characteristics. For example, Margaret Hodges's *The Fire Bringer* retells the Native American story about how coyotes received their markings and how a certain tribe obtained fire. Likewise, William Toye's *The Loon's Necklace* explains how the loon received its characteristic markings.

Animal trickster tales are popular in Native American culture, as elsewhere. The tricksters are often ravens, rabbits, or coyotes that have powers of magical transformation. Heroes and heroines may also use transformation in undertaking their quests. In *Arrow to the Sun: A Pueblo Indian Tale,* for example, a boy becomes an arrow as he searches for his father, the sungod.

The importance of folktales for passing on tribal beliefs is revealed in Olaf Baker's *Where the Buffaloes Begin*. A young Native American of the Great Plains learns from a tribal storyteller about a sacred spot where the buffaloes rise out of a lake. After he finds the lake, he waits quietly in the night. As he waits, he hears the words of the storyteller singing in his mind:

Do you hear the noise that never ceases?
It is the Buffaloes fighting far below.
They are fighting to get out upon the prairie.
They are born below the Water but are fighting for the Air.
In the great lake in the Southland where the Buffaloes begin! (p. 20)

The diversity of Native American cultures, customs and folktales is illustrated in Jamake Highwater's *Anpao: An Indian Odyssey*. Highwater's book emphasizes the importance of traditional tales in transmitting Native American culture. Chapter 11, "Multicultural Literature," discusses these tales and others.

Black American Folktales. Many black American folktales reflect both an African origin and an adaptation to a new environment and the harsh reality of slavery. For example, a rabbit trickster who triumphs over more powerful animals is popular in African folklore. He is also one of the most popular characters in tales collected from black people on southern plantations. This character's popularity with black Americans was probably related to the experience of slavery. Cunning, wit, and deception were often the only weapons available against oppression. (The tortoise and Ananse the spider play similar trickster roles.) The trickster Br'er Rabbit is famous in the black American folktales collected by Joel Chandler Harris in nineteenth-century Georgia and published as *Uncle Remus and His Friends* (1892) and *Told by Uncle Remus* (1905).

In 1981, Priscilla Jaquith published similar tales collected from black people living on the Sea Islands off the coasts of Georgia and South Carolina. The tales in *Bo Rabbit Smart for True: Folktales from the Gullah* are excellent examples of the infusion of later culture, language, and environment into tales from other places and earlier times. African words, such as *cooter* for tortoise, combine with Elizabethan English and dialect from the provinces of Great Britain, such as *bittles* for victuals. In the African tradition, the stories repeat key words to increase their significance: "Alligator, Miz Alligator and all the little alligators slither into the field, KAPUK, kapuk, kapuk, kapuk, kapuk, kapuk, kapuk, kapuk." These stories about a small, clever rabbit who outsmarts other animals, such as whales and elephants, are

THROUGH THE EYES OF AN AUTHOR

Traditional Native American Tales

Expert in traditional Native American literature and culture and a collector of traditional tales, JAMAKE HIGHWATER, author of *Anpao: An American Indian Odyssey,* discusses his feelings and beliefs.

IN A VERY REAL SENSE, I am the brother of the fox. My whole life revolves around my kinship with four-legged things. I am rooted in the natural world. I'm two people joined into one body. The contradiction doesn't bother me. But people always assume the one they're talking to is the only one there is. That bothers me. There is a little of the legendary Anpao in me, but also a little of John Gardner. I stand in both those worlds, not between them. I'm very much a twentieth-century person, and yet I'm traditional Northern Plains Indian.

I've always had an enormous regard for the intellect. Still, I like to go home to my people, who are in touch with the beginning of things. At home, people are carpenters; some are poets, painters, and teachers; some work on construction jobs. They are people who perceive the importance of small things that are easily missed by those of us who move much too quickly.

I came to terms with the solemn aspects of life very early. I was always among Indians, for we traveled the powwow circuit. I was always listening to some older person telling stories. They are nameless to me now, and countless, because there were so many. I was introduced to the Indian world as children in my tribe were in the 1870s, when we were a nomadic people. I was rootless yet connected to a vital tradition. The elders talked to me and gave me a sense of the meaning of my existence.

I talk and think as a poet, but I don't want to perpetuate the romantic notion of the Indian as watching chipmunks his entire life [and] waiting to see which side of the tree the moss grows on.

For the Indian, art is not reserved for a leisure class, as it is in Anglo society. It is part of our fundamental way of thinking. We are an aesthetic people. Most primal people are. We represent a constant chord that's been resounding ever since man began. While those Cro-Magnon people in the caves of southern France (at least according to Western mentality) should have been out worrying about the great likelihood that they wouldn't survive, they were building scaffolds fifty or sixty feet high and with tiny oil lamps were painting the ceilings of their caves with marvelous magical images. These images were an implicit and important part of their lives. For us, this aesthetic reality is a continuous process. The kiva murals of the Hopi and the Mimbres pottery rival the finest accomplishments of Western art. This idea of life as art is part of being Indian. It's not quaint or curious or charming. It's fundamental, like plowing a field. There's great beauty in plowing a field.

I think Indians have become a metaphor for a larger idea. We are building bridges toward cultures. Some people in white society are also building bridges toward us, and they sometimes join together. That means that it's possible for everyone to find the Indian in himself. It's a kind of sensibility that I'm talking about.

Drawn from an interview with Jane B. Katz, 1980.

exciting to young children. The stories in Jaquith's and Harris's collections have motifs in common.

Other black American tales about a trickster rabbit are found in West Virginia. Though not as powerful as his adversaries, the rabbit is more intelligent, and he manages to outwit them. Some of these stories, such as Jaquith's version of "Alligator's Sunday Suit," contain a serious moral: "Don't go looking for trouble, else you might find it." Such morals are often found in black American folklore. These tales and other tales are discussed in chapter 11, Multicultural Literature.

Variants of European Tales. The traditional literatures of the United States and Canada contain many variants of traditional European folktales. European settlers from England, France, and elsewhere brought their oral traditions with them. Then, they adapted the stories to reflect a new environment. Consequently, many North American folktales involve familiar European themes, motifs, and characters in settings that portray the unknown wilderness and harsh winters confronted by the early colonizers of North America. The only indigenous Canadian traditional literature comes from the Native Canadian and Inuit peoples.

Eva Martin's *Canadian Fairy Tales* contains twelve French-Canadian and English-Canadian variations of traditional European tales. Ti-Jean tales contain several familiar story elements. The lazy fellow kills one thousand flies with one blow, uses his wits to capture a unicorn and steal a giant's seven-league boots, and eventually marries the princess. In the Canadian variant of "Beauty and the Beast," the enchanted beast is female and the prince stays in her castle. William Hooks's *Moss Gown* is an adaptation of the English Cinderella tale. It also contains elements of King Lear and the plantation south.

The best-known North American variants of European tales belong to the Jack cycle. In these tales, a seemingly nonheroic person overcomes severe obstacles and outwits adversaries. The American "Jack and the Varmits," for example, is similar to the English "The Brave Little Tailor." In keeping with the European tradition, the American Jack is rewarded by a king. Instead of a giant, Jack must overcome a wild hog, a unicorn, and a lion. The influences of rural America are found in both the setting and language. The lion, who was killing cattle, horses, and humans, came over the mountains from Tennessee. Both the king and Jack speak in frontier dialect. Gail E. Haley's *Jack and the Bean Tree* is an Appalachian variant of "Jack and the Beanstalk."

Tall Tales. Boastful frontier humor is found in North American tall tales. These tales reflect the hardships of settlers, who faced severe climatic changes, unknown lands, and people whose lives reflected strange cultures. Exaggerated claims in tall tales—such as those found in Walter Blair's *Tall Tale America: A Legendary History of Our Humorous Heroes*—declare that the American soil is so rich that fast-growing vines damage pumpkins by dragging them on the ground; that frontier people are so powerful they can lasso and subdue cyclones; and that the leader of the river boaters can outshoot, outfight, outrun, and outbrag everyone in the world.

The North American heroes and heroines who faced extremes in weather, conquered humans and beasts, and subdued the wilderness are not the godlike heroes and heroines of European mythology. Instead, their lives reflect the primitive virtues of brute force, animal cunning, and courage. The characters and situations in tall tales reflect frontier idealism. People are free to travel. They live self-sufficient lives and are extremely resourceful.

American tall tales contain fictional heroes and heroes based on real people. Hard-working, persevering characters—such as Johnny Appleseed, who considered it his mission to plant apple trees across the country—demonstrate duty and endurance. Boisterous, bragging roughnecks—such as Davy Crockett, Calamity Jane, and Paul Bunyan—perform otherwise impossible feats, outshooting a thousand enemies or conquering mighty rivers and immense forests. Other characters—such as the steel-driving man, John Henry—reflect a country that was changing from a rural and agricultural way of life to an urban and mechanized one. *John Tabor's Ride,* by Edward C. Day, reflects the whaling industry and the yarns told by whalers in New England.

You may find additional information about the folklore associated with Davy Crockett by reading *The Tall Tales of Davy Crockett: The Second Nashville Series of Crockett Almanacs 1839–1841,* which is published by the University of Tennessee Press. In the introduction to the text, Michael Lofaro (18) states that Crockett's heroic death increased his image as a boasting, brawling backwoodsman. Lofaro continues:

FLASHBACK

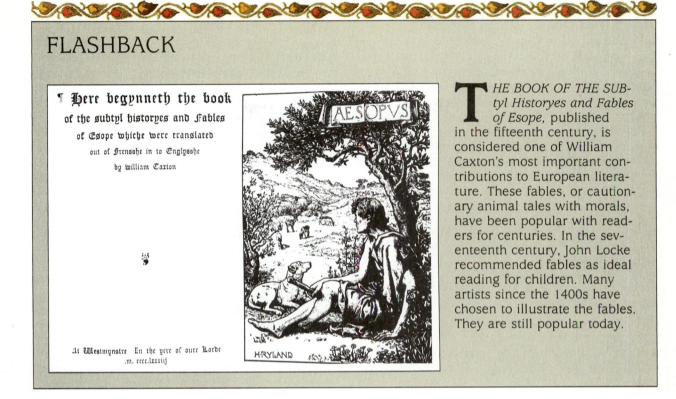

¶ Here begynneth the book
of the subtyl historyes and Fables
of Esope whiche were translated
out of Frensshe in to Englysshe
by william Caxton

At Westmynstre In the yere of oure Lorde
.m. cccc.lxxxiij

The Book of the Subtyl Historyes and Fables of Esope, published in the fifteenth century, is considered one of William Caxton's most important contributions to European literature. These fables, or cautionary animal tales with morals, have been popular with readers for centuries. In the seventeenth century, John Locke recommended fables as ideal reading for children. Many artists since the 1400s have chosen to illustrate the fables. They are still popular today.

The "wretched caricatures" soon became fantastic tall tales in the popular comic almanacs that bore Crockett's name. In these works Davy once again "assumed the character drawn for him by others"; it was, however, a character no longer bounded by the achievements of a mortal man, but only by the imagination. (p. x)

FABLES

Legend credits the origin of the fable in Western culture to a Greek slave named Aesop, who lived in the sixth century B.C. Aesop's nimble wit supposedly got Aesop's master out of numerous difficulties. Aesop may not have been one person, however. Several experts attribute the early European fables to various sources. Fables are found worldwide; the traditional literatures of China and India, for example, contain fables similar to Aesop's. Whatever their origins, fables are excellent examples of stories handed down over centuries of oral and written literary tradition.

Characteristics of Fables

According to R. T. Lenaghan (17) in his introduction to *Caxton's Aesop,* fables have the following characteristics: (1) they are fiction in the sense that they did not really happen, (2) they are meant to entertain, (3) they are poetic, with double or allegorical significance, and (4) they are moral tales, usually with animal characters. In fables, animals usually talk and behave like humans and possess other human traits. Fables are short, and they usually have not more than two or three characters. These characters perform simple, straightforward actions that result in a single climax. Fables also contain human lessons expressed through the foibles of personified animals.

The characteristics of fables apparently appealed to traditional storytellers around the world. In fifteenth-century England, fables were among the first texts that William Caxton printed on his newly created printing press. Lenaghan credits the popularity of fables to their generic ambiguity. They could be used as entertaining stories, teaching devices, or sermons. They could also reach people of various degrees of intelligence, be bluntly assertive or cleverly ironic, and be didactic or skeptical. Storytellers could emphasize whatever functions they chose.

The continuing popularity of fables led Randolph Caldecott to create his own edition of Aesop in the nineteenth century. *The Caldecott Aesop,* first published in 1883 and reissued in 1978, provides modern readers with an opportunity to enjoy fables accompanied by hand-colored drawings of a great illustrator of children's books. Caldecott's illustrations show first the animals in a fable, then the people replacing the animals. Sir Roger L'Estange's seventeenth-century translation of *Aesop's Fables* is also available in a reissued text.

Contemporary Editions of Fables

Fables are popular subjects for modern storytellers and illustrators. Young children like the talking animals and the often humorous climaxes. Authors and illustrators of fables for young children sometimes expand fables into longer, more detailed narrative stories. In *The Tortoise and the Hare,* Janet Stevens expands the story line of the fable by including the exercises Tortoise undertakes to prepare for the race and the actions of Tortoise's friends as they try to deter Hare. In *The Town Mouse and the Country Mouse,* Lorinda Bryan Cauley's illustrations and text provide details associated with the different life-styles of the two main characters. Stevens uses a similar approach in her picture storybook version of Aesop's *The Town Mouse and the Country Mouse*.

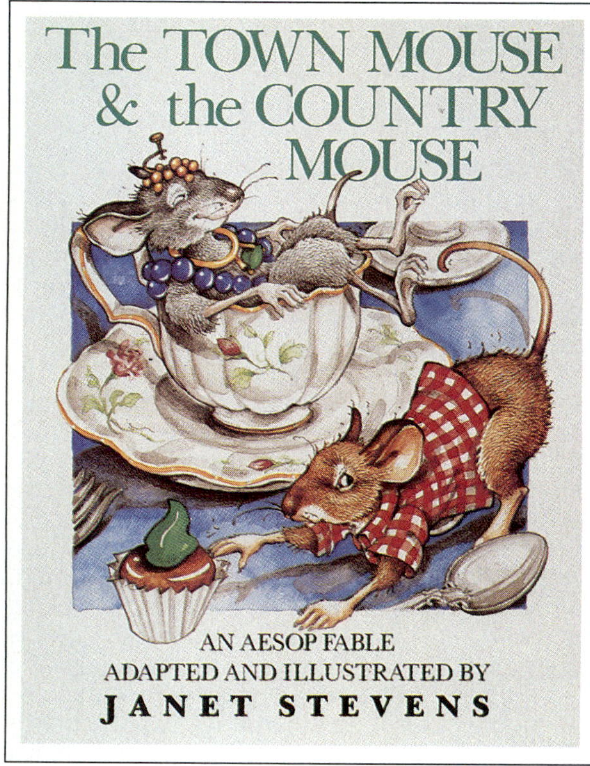

The author has expanded on a fable to create a picture storybook in *The Town Mouse & the Country Mouse,* adapted and illustrated by Janet Stevens.

Numerous collections of Aesop's fables have been compiled and illustrated for slightly older children, too. It is interesting to compare the various editions to see how the fables have been interpreted and illustrated. Anne Terry White's edition of Aesop contains forty fables. She introduces them by saying that Aesop made his animals behave like humans to make a point without hurting the feelings of great and powerful leaders, who could be cruel to a slave.

White's fables (complemented by Helen Siegle's woodcuts) are in simple narrative form. The descriptions and dialogue among the talking beasts are easily accessible to contemporary children. For example, in "The Lion and the Mouse," White describes the capture of the mouse in this way:

> Bang! The Lion clapped his paw to his face and felt something caught. It was furry. Lazily he opened his eyes. He lifted up one side of his huge paw just a little bit to see what was under it and was amazed to find a Mouse. (p. 5)

White gives a moral to each fable in this collection. The moral of "The Lion and the Mouse" is simply stated:

> Little friends may prove to be great friends.

Tom Paxton retells fables in verse in his *Aesop's Fables*. Paxton describes the incident in which the mouse is captured as follows:

> He ran over the lion, who awoke with a roar:
> "Who's treating my back like the jungle floor?"
> He grabbed the poor mouse by his poor little tail.
> "Oh, please, Mister Lion, I swear without fail,
> If you'll please just release me, I promise someday
> The debt will be one that I'll gladly repay."
> The proud lion laughed and let the mouse go. (unnumbered)

The moral of this fable is presented in verse form in the last two lines:

> Yes, sometimes the weak and sometimes the strong
> Must help each other to save right from wrong. (unnumbered)

Contemporary versions of fables differ in the illustrator's style as well as the author's style. Heidi Holder's *Aesop's Fables* contains detailed, elegant paintings surrounded by equally detailed borders. Michael Hague's *Aesop's Fables* is illustrated with full-page paintings in somber, earthy tones. Charles Santore's *Aesop's Fables* is a large-format text with dramatic full-page illustrations that range from earthy tones to the most vivid colors found in nature. Fulvio Testa's *Aesop's Fables* also follows each fable with a full-page illustration. Each illustration is framed with a colorful design.

An interesting cross-cultural comparison of both texts and illustrations may be made with John Bierhorst's *Doctor Coyote: A Native American Aesop's Fables*. Bierhorst identifies both Spanish-Aztec and ancient Latin connections. Bierhorst states:

> The Aztec Aesop's was adapted in the 1500s by one or more Indian retellers, using a now-lost Spanish collection of the standard fables. All of these, however, can be traced to Latin and Greek manuscripts of late classical and medieval times. Compared with the originals, the Aztec variants differ mainly in the cast of characters, which includes Coyote and Puma, two of the best-known animal tricksters in Native American folklore. (author's note, unnumbered).

Wendy Watson's illustrations reflect settings in New Mexico.

Other interesting comparisons can be made between contemporary versions of Aesop and versions published in earlier centuries. The language, spellings, and illustrations in these various editions differ widely. Some were intended for adults; others specifically for children. Older children can learn more about their literary heritage by comparing and discussing various versions of these ancient stories.

With a castle in the background, a detailed drawing creates an elegant setting for a fable. (From *Aesop's Fables*, by Heidi Holder. Copyright © 1981 by Heidi Holder. Reproduced by permission of Viking Penguin Inc.)

MYTHS

Every ancient culture made up stories that answered questions about the creation of the earth, the origins of people, and the reasons for natural phenomena. The Greeks called these explanations *mythos*, which means tales or stories. Today people sometimes use the word *myth* to describe any story they consider to be untrue. However, in literary terms, a myth is a story containing fanciful or supernatural incidents intended to explain nature or tell about the gods and demons of early peoples (2). In the distant past, as in some traditional cultures today, the stories were taken as fact made sacred by religious belief. The supernatural characters in the myths were considered divine. They controlled the forces of nature on earth and ruled the sun, moon, stars, and planets. Many of them had their own temples, where people worshipped them with prayer and sacrifice to win their favor.

Myths live on in contemporary literature and provide an understanding of the rich cultural heritage we have acquired from ancient civilizations all over the world. Greek, Roman, and Norse mythology have been most influential in Western culture. Many terms used in those mythologies are also found in modern language, such as our names for the planets and for the days of the week. Children find these stories exciting and become interested in this rich literary heritage.

Joseph Campbell (8) argues that myths are powerful literature and should be read and understood by everyone. He believes that four functions related to myths are as important today as they were in earlier times. The functions are (1) a mystical one that allows people to experience the awe of the universe, (2) a cosmological one that shows the shape and mystery of the universe, (3) a sociological one that supports and validates a certain social order, and (4) a pedagogical one that teaches people how to live.

Jane Yolen (25) identifies several ways in which myths are valuable to children. Myths provide children with knowledge about ancestral cultures and allow the children to look at other cultures from the inside out. Myths are models for belief; they are serious statements about existence. They provide a framework for understanding the things that other people did or thought. Myths are tools for understanding and expanded expression. They offer new dimensions for imagination and suggest ways for children to gain insights from their daydreams. Myths also provide means of introducing children to literary allusions: An author describing something as being "as swift as Diana" or "as mighty as Zeus" is alluding to characteristics of gods.

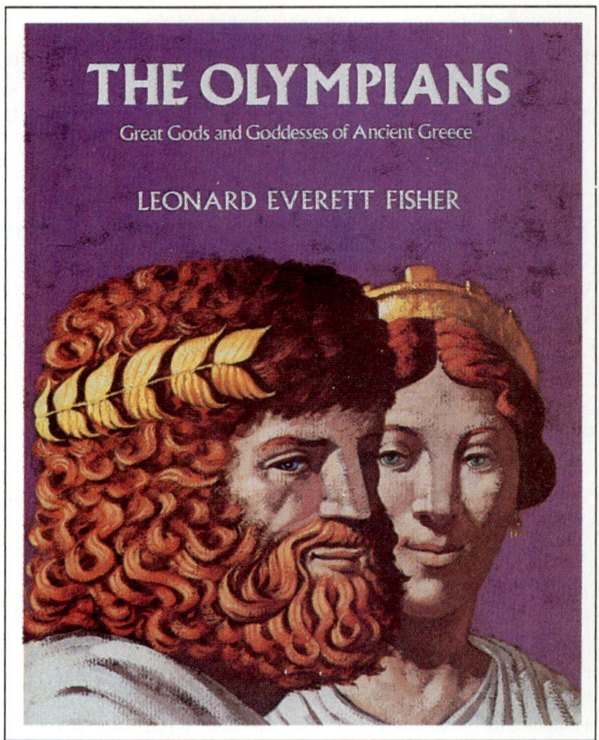

Fisher's illustrations and text provide an introduction to the Greek gods and goddesses. (From *The Olympians: Great Gods and Goddesses of Ancient Greece* by Leonard Everett Fisher. Copyright © 1984 by Leonard Everett Fisher. All rights reserved. Reprinted by permission of Holiday House.)

Greek and Roman Mythology

Probably, the best-known myths in Western culture originated in ancient Greece. When the Romans conquered Greece, they adopted many Greek myths, applying them to their own equivalent deities. In order to understand these stories, Helen Sewell (21) says that one must be acquainted with ancient Greek ideas about the structure of the universe. The Greeks believed that the universe had been created out of unorganized matter called *chaos,* swirling and transparent vapor. Form and shape resulted in *order* and *cosmos*. The Greeks believed that the first things formed out of chaos were the gods: *Gaia* (meaning earth; *terra* is the Roman name) and *Ouranos* (meaning sky; *Uranus* is the Roman name) (2). From the offspring of female Gaia and male Ouranos emerged the remaining Greek gods and goddesses, who lived on Mount Olympus (an actual mountain in Greece) and frequently came into the human world.

The Greeks believed that the earth was flat and circular and that their own country was the center. Around the earth flowed the river Ocean. The dawn, the sun, and the moon were supposed to rise out of the eastern ocean, driven by gods and giving light to gods and mortals. The majority of the stars also rose out of and sank into this ocean.

The Greeks believed that the northern part of the earth beyond the mountains was inhabited by a race of people called *Hyperboreans*. In these mountains were the caverns from which came the piercing north winds that sometimes chilled Greece. On the south lived the Ethiopians, whom the gods favored; on the west lay the Elysian Plain, where mortals favored by the gods were transported to enjoy immortality. Roman myths drew essentially the same picture.

Although mythology and folktales contain similar motifs and themes, myths include Bascom's requirements for setting, time, attitude, and principal characters. Chart 6–4 compares points in Edna Barth's version of the myth *Cupid and Psyche* and the Norse folktale "East of the Sun and West of the Moon."

The plot in the two tales is similar: A young girl breaks a promise, her loved one leaves, she searches for him, and she overcomes obstacles or performs tasks before they are reunited. The

CHART 6–4
A comparison of a myth and a folktale

"Cupid and Psyche"	"East of the Sun and West of the Moon"
Setting	
Mount Olympus, Greece	Any kingdom
Time	
In a remote past, when gods and goddesses dwelt on the earth	Once upon a time
Attitude	
Sacred—worship of the deity was required or punishment resulted	Secular
Principal Characters	
Venus (the goddess of love)	Transformed human boy
Cupid (the son of Venus)	Human girl
Psyche (a mortal girl who becomes immortal	Troll princess

principal characters differ in important characteristics, however. Psyche, a beautiful mortal princess, is the object of a goddess's anger and jealousy. She later falls in love with a god, performs tasks stipulated by the goddess, and requires intervention from the most divine ruler, Jupiter.

Edna Barth (3) sees strong religious significance in the Cupid and Psyche myth. The myth, she reminds us, originally represented the progress of the human soul as it travels toward perfection. Symbolized by Psyche, the soul originated in heaven, where all is love, which is symbolized by Cupid. The soul is then condemned for a period of time to wander the earth and undergo hardship and misery. If the soul proves worthy, it is returned to heaven and reunited with love.

Circumstances surrounding the creation of the gods and goddesses, their places within the Olympian family, the consequences of their varied personality traits, and their accomplishments create exciting tales and enjoyable reading for children. Chart 6–5 lists Greek and Roman gods and goddesses, their accomplishments, their powers, and texts that include myths about these deities.

Contemporary versions of Greek and Roman myths vary widely in terms of author's style, complexity of text, and illustration. Consider these factors when choosing myths to share with children of various ages and interests. Eight- or nine-year-olds, for example, enjoy Edna Barth's *Cupid and Psyche*. Barth's rendition of this myth is appropriate for children who enjoy such folktales as "Beauty and the Beast" and "East of the Sun and West of the Moon."

Children also enjoy Gerald McDermott's book-length version of the Daedalus myth, *Sun Flight*. McDermott's text for this myth about a mortal punished for attempting to rival the gods is based on his animated film. This film won the Zellerbach Award for Films as Art at the San Francisco International Film Festival. McDermott uses bold colors for the setting of Crete as the father and son fashion their wings. The final flight sequence of the story is told through the illustrations. In this sequence, McDermott changes the colors from the blues and greens of the initial flight of Icarus, to orange and red as Icarus nears the sun, to reds and browns as Icarus falls in flames, and back to greens as Icarus is engulfed by the waves.

Leonard Everett Fisher's *Theseus and the Minotaur* has bold, full-page illustrations to accompany his version of the story of a brave youth who slays an evil monster. Warwick Hutton's *Theseus and the Minotaur* is illustrated with watercolor paintings that are especially effective in the depiction of the tragic return of the hero.

Many older children enjoy longer, more developed versions of the myths. You may wish to compare Ian Serraillier's version of the Daedalus myth with McDermott's and Penelope Farmer's versions. Serraillier's *A Fall from the Sky* includes the reasons for Daedalus's jealousy, his trial, and his attempts to escape judgment. The intervention of the goddess Athena and symbolization of the partridge are also included in the more complex version.

Doris Gates develops stories with fast-paced plots and language that suggests word pictures. Her style reads well and her books are excellent

CHART 6–5
Greek and Roman gods and goddesses*

Name	Accomplishments	Powers	Examples of Texts
Zeus (Jupiter)	Ruler of Mount Olympus King of deities and humans	Used lightning to gain control of the universe.	Gates's *Lord of the Sky: Zeus*
Hera (Juno)	Queen of deities and humans Goddess of marriage and childbirth	Protected married women	Bulfinch's *A Book of Myths*
Athena (Minerva)	Goddess of wisdom, war, and handicrafts	Established rule of law Gave olive tree to mankind Protected cities	Gates's *The Warrior Goddess: Athena*
Apollo (Apollo)	God of Sun Patron of truth, music, medicine, and archery	Established the oracle (prophets who gave advice)	Gates's *The Golden God: Apollo* Bulfinch's *A Book of Myths*
Artemis (Diana)	Goddess of moon and the hunt Mighty archer and hunter	Guarded animals, nature, and women	Bulfinch's *A Book of Myths*
Aphrodite (Venus)	Goddess of love and beauty: Flowers sprang up where she walked	Had power to beguile gods Gave birth to Fear and Terror	Gates's *Two Queens of Heaven: Aphrodite and Demeter*
Demeter (Ceres)	Goddess of crops	Gave grain and fruit Caused famine when Hades took her daughter to the underworld	Coolidge's *Greek Myths* Gates's *Two Queens of Heaven: Aphrodite and Demeter*
Hermes (Mercury)	Divine messenger of the gods Trickster who was named god of commerce, orators, and writers	Protected flocks, cattle, and mischief makers	Gates's *The Golden God: Apollo*
Poseidon (Neptune)	God of the sea and earthquakes	Gave horses to humans Answered voyagers' prayers	*D'Aulaires' Book of Greek Myths*
Dionysus (Bacchus)	God of wine, fertility, the joyous life, and hospitality	Gave Greece the gift of wine	Bulfinch's *A Book of Myths* Coolidge's *Greek Myths*
Ares (Mars)	God of war	Caused the evils and sufferings of war	*D'Aulaires' Book of Greek Myths*
Hephaestus (Vulcan)	God of fire and artisans	From his forges, he produced Pandora, the first mortal woman Created mechanical objects	*D'Aulaires' Book of Greek Myths*
Eros (Cupid)	God of love (son of Venus)	Shot arrows at people to make them fall in love.	Barth's *Cupid and Psyche* Richardson's *The Adventures of Eros and Psyche*

*Roman names in parentheses.

for sharing orally. For example, her description of the creation of Athena in *The Warrior Goddess: Athena* seems appropriate:

> She sprang from the head of Zeus, father of gods. Born without a mother, she was fully grown and fully armed. Her right hand gripped a spear, while her left steadied a shield on her forearm. The awful aegis, a breast ornament bordered with serpents, hung from her neck, and from her helmeted head to her sandaled feet she was cloaked in radiance, like the flash of weaponry. So the great goddess Athena came to join the family of gods on high Olympus, and, of all Zeus's children, she was his favorite. (p. 11)

Older children can contrast this description by Gates with her description of the creation of the goddess of love and beauty in *Two Queens of Heaven: Aphrodite and Demeter*:

> There appeared a gathering of foam on the water. It resembled the white spindrift that trails behind a great wave as it breaks. But this form did not trail. It formed itself into a raft rising and falling with the sea. Suddenly a woman's figure appeared atop the raft balancing on slender feet. She was young and beautiful beyond anything in human form the sun had ever shone on. (pp. 9–10)

Versions of myths told by Olivia Coolidge, Charles Kingsley, and Padraic Colum are also good choices for older children. Virginia Hamilton's *In the Beginning: Creation Stories from Around the World* includes twenty-five creation stories from varied cultures.

Norse Mythology

A far different group of gods and heroes existed in the Norse universe of ice, glaciers, and cold mountains. The harsh conditions of the far North helped form the Norse people and their legends. According to Kevin Crossley-Holland (11), recurring strains in Norse mythology include a strong sense of fate that governs the lives of both gods and humans; a heroic bond between characters that is characterized by physical and moral courage, loyalty, and a willingness to take vengeance; a belief in omens; an ironic wit; a restless spirit of adventure; and a keen sense of wonder in the natural world and a close identification with nature. Unsurprisingly, Norse mythology tells that a frost giant was the first being created on earth.

Norse mythology influenced subsequent oral and written literature in northern Europe. Shakespeare was influenced by an old Norse tale when he wrote Hamlet; J. R. R. Tolkien, a professor of Anglo-Saxon literature at Oxford University, relied on his knowledge of the northern sagas

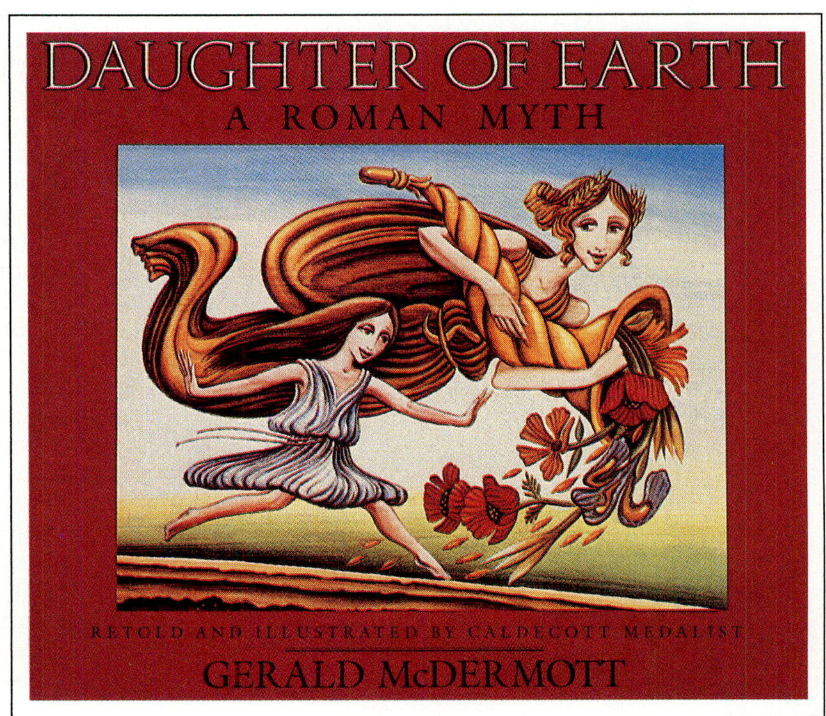

Highly illustrated versions of myths, such as this story about the goddess Ceres and her daughter Proserpina, provide introductions to mythology for young readers. (From *Daughter of Earth: A Roman Myth,* retold and illustrated by Gerald McDermott. Copyright © 1985 by Gerald McDermott. Used by permission of Delacorte Press.)

when he wrote *The Hobbit* and *The Lord of the Rings*.

The tales of the northern gods and goddesses were collected during the twelfth and thirteenth centuries from the earlier oral tradition. These original tales formed two volumes, the *Elder* and the *Younger Edda*. These texts are now the sources for most of our knowledge about Norse mythology. According to Olivia Coolidge (10), Norse mythology maintains that the earth began when a frost giant, Ymer, came out of swirling mists. The shifting particles formed a great cow, whose milk nourished Ymer. As time went by, sons and daughters were also created out of the mists. Gods took form when the cow began to lick the great ice blocks that filled the mists. As she licked, a huge god appeared. When he stood up, his descendants were formed from his warm breath.

The frost giants were evil, so the gods vowed to destroy them. A mighty battle resulted between the gods and the frost giants, with the gods finally overpowering the giants. Ymer was destroyed, and the remaining giants fled into the outer regions and created a land of mists and mountains. The mightiest of the gods, Odin, looked at the dead frost giant, Ymer, and suggested that the gods use his body to make a land where they could live. They formed Ymer's body into the round, flat earth, and on its center, they built mountains to contain their home, Asgard. Ymer's skull was used to form the great arch of heaven; his blood was the ocean, a barrier between the earth and giantland. The gods stole sparks from the fiery regions to light the stars, and they built chariots in which they placed sun and moon spirits to ride over the earth.

"The Hammer of Thor" is an excellent choice for storytelling. (From *Legends of the North*, by Olivia Coolidge. Copyright © 1951 and © renewed 1979 by Olivia E. Coolidge. Reprinted by permission of Houghton Mifflin Co.)

Padraic Colum portrays the strong moral code of Odin in his version of "The Building of the Wall," found in *The Children of Odin*. Even though a protective wall is built around Asgard, Odin grieves:

> But Odin, the Father of the Gods, as he sat upon his throne was sad in his heart, sad that the Gods had got their wall built by a trick, that oaths had been broken, and that a blow had been struck in injustice in Asgard. (p. 12)

Olivia E. Coolidge's *Legends of the North* is an excellent source of stories about the Norse gods and goddesses who lived on earth in the mighty citadel of Asgard and the heroes and heroines who lived under their power. In "The Apples of Idun," the divine beings often walked on earth because the mighty Odin believed they should know their realm intimately, in stone, flower, and leaf.

In Coolidge's text, Thor, the god of war, strides around with red hair bristling and fierce eyes ablaze. Sometimes, he rides in his chariot drawn by red-eyed goats, which are as shaggy and fierce as their master.

One humorous selection from this book is "The Hammer of Thor." In this story, Thor searches loudly for his missing hammer. Children probably feel close to Thor as he responds in exasperation when Freyja, the goddess of beauty, asks him where he put it. He shouts, "If I knew where I put it, I should not be looking for it now" (p. 35).

Thor discovers that the giant Thyrm has stolen the hammer and wants Freyja as ransom. When the goddess vehemently refuses to become the giant's bride, the suggestion is made that Thor dress up as a bride and go to giantland to retrieve his own hammer. After considerable argument, the huge god dresses in gown and veil to cover his fierce eyes and bristling beard, and accompanied by the impish Loki, he leaves for giantland.

Mighty Thor remains quiet as the wedding feast progresses, and fast-witted Loki answers the giant's questions and calms his suspicions. Finally, Thor is able to touch his hammer as the wedding ceremony begins. This is what he has been waiting for; he regains his hammer, overpowers the giant, removes his skirts, and leaves for home.

Thor's courage, loyalty, and willingness to take vengeance are recurring strains found in this mythology. The humor and action in this tale make it excellent for storytelling. Other enjoyable Norse tales suitable for sharing with children include Ingri and Edgar Parin D'Aulaire's *Norse Gods and Giants* and Kevin Crossley-Holland's *The Faber Book of Northern Legends*.

LEGENDS

The great legends in traditional literature are closely related to mythology. Many of these legends have been transmitted over the centuries in the form of epics. Epics are long narrative poems about the deeds of traditional or historical human heroes and heroines of high station. Two of the better-known Greek epics are *The Iliad* and *The Odyssey*. *The Iliad* is an account of the Trojan War. *The Odyssey* reports the journey of Odysseus (Ulysses in Latin) as he defeats the Cyclops, overcomes the song of the sirens, and manages to survive ten long years of hazardous adventures. Gods, goddesses, and other supernatural beings play important roles in such epics, but the focus is human characters.

"Beowulf," the story of a human warrior, is usually considered the outstanding example of Norse epic poetry. Beowulf's struggle against evil has three main episodes. First, Beowulf fights and kills the monster Grendel. Second, Beowulf dives to the depths of a pool and attacks Grendel's mother, She. Third, Beowulf fights the dragon Firedrake and is mortally wounded.

Versions of this epic are available in both narrative and poetic form. One version, which the author Robert Nye calls a new telling, is written in narrative form for younger readers. In this version, Beowulf is strong, but he is also good—loyal, courageous, and willing to take vengeance. His characterization epitomizes the heroic code found in Norse myths. A combination of heroic deeds and honorable characteristics make it possible for his good name to live after him. For example, Nye describes the hero as having real strength. It "lay in the balance of his person—which is perhaps another way of saying that he was strong because he was good, and good because he had the strength to accept things in him which were bad" (p. 25). His good is so powerful that it is felt by the evil monsters and is instrumental in their defeat.

Fate, a strong code of honor, and a willingness to avenge wrong are emphasized in Kevin Crossley-Holland's version of *Beowulf*. Crossley-Holland develops the importance of fate as Beowulf ponders the outcome of his forthcoming struggle with the monster Grendel: "Who knows? Fate goes always as it must" (p. 11) and "If a man is brave enough and not doomed to die, fate often spares him to fight another day" (p. 13). The importance of fate is reemphasized after Beowulf's victory, as King Hrothgar declares: "Beowulf, bravest of men, fate's darling! Your friends are fortunate, your enemies not to be envied" (p. 34).

Crossley-Holland develops a strong code of honor when Beowulf refuses to use a sword or a shield because the monster fights without weapons. Crossley-Holland combines honor and vengeance as Beowulf cries that he will avenge the Danes, the people who gave refuge to his father. Honor and vengeance are also part of the monster's code, and Beowulf is pleased when he discovers: "There is honor amongst monsters as there is honor amongst men. Grendel's mother came to the hall to avenge the death of her son" (p. 25). The conclusion emphasizes Beowulf's heroic characteristics: "They said that of all kings on earth, he was the kindest, the most gentle, the most just to his people, the most eager for fame" (p. 46).

Many of the heroes and heroines in epic legends reflect a strong sense of goodness as they overcome various worldly evils. The line between legend and myth is often vague, however. The early legends usually enlarged upon the lives of religious figures, such as martyrs and saints. In more recent times, legends developed around royal figures and folk heroes and heroines. Chart 6–6 shows similarities and differences between myth and legend.

We consider the tales of King Arthur to be legends rather than myths because they are stories primarily about humans rather than supernatural beings and because historical tradition maintains that King Arthur actually existed in fairly recent times. Tales of this legendary British king were so popular in early England that Sir Thomas Malory's *Morte d'Arthur* was one of the first books published in England.

Another early version of the tale is Howard Pyle's *The Story of King Arthur and His Knights*.

CHART 6–6
Similarities and differences between myth and legend

Myth: "The Birth of Athena"	Legend: "Tales of King Arthur"
Belief	
Told as factual—the birth of a goddess	Told as factual—the life of a British chieftain of the fifth–sixth century
Setting	
Mount Olympus, Greece	British Isles
Time	
In a remote past, when gods and goddesses dwelt on the earth	In the time of kings and knights, within a recognizable world
Attitude	
Sacred—Athena (a goddess) sprang from the head of Zeus (father of the gods)	Sacred—a quest for the Holy Grail Secular—King Arthur established the Round table and was the leader of the knights
Principal Characters	
Nonhuman—the goddess assists heroes and heroines in quests	Human—the king does not have supernatural powers

The first section of Pyle's version, "The Book of King Arthur," reveals how Arthur removed the sacred sword from a stone signifying that he was rightful King of England, claimed his birthright, wed Guinevere, and established the Round Table. The second section, "The Book of Three Worthies," tells about Merlin the magician, Sir Pellias, and Sir Gawaine. The original version of this book, with Pyle's illustrations, has been reissued. Other editions of Arthurian legends include Rosemary Sutcliff's *The Sword and the Circle: King Arthur and the Knights of the Round Table, The Light Beyond the Forest,* and *The Road to Camlann: The Death of King Arthur*.

Selina Hastings's *Sir Gawain and the Loathly Lady* retells one of the Arthurian legends in a picture-book format. Characteristically, the tale includes a challenge, a quest, enchantment, and a promise demanded by the code of chivalry. Juan Wijngaard's illustrations capture both the evil menace of the black knight and the ancient splendor of Arthur's court.

Another legendary figure in English culture is Robin Hood, the hero of Sherwood Forest. Stories about Robin Hood were told orally for centuries and were mentioned in manuscripts as early as 1360. Legend suggests that this figure was born Robert Fitzooth, Earl of Huntingdon, in Nottinghamshire, England, in 1160. According to the tales, he was a great archer. He and his band of outlaws poached the king's deer, robbed the rich, and gave money to the poor.

Stories of Robin Hood are popular with children. Movies and television plays have been produced about his adventures. Howard Pyle's *The Merry Adventures of Robin Hood* and the shorter version, *Some Merry Adventures of Robin Hood,* provide visions of what it would be like to live "in merry England in the time of old" and to interact with Little John, Maid Marian, Friar Tuck, the Sheriff of Nottingham, and King Richard of the Lion's Heart. Children enjoy comparing the various editions and describing the strengths and weaknesses of each. For this purpose, even the Walt Disney movie that presents Robin Hood as a fox, Little John as a bear, and Prince John as a lion adds to a lively discussion, especially about characterization.

The Outlaws of Sherwood is Robin McKinley's interpretation of the Robin Hood legend. McKinley has created a vivid and readable story that includes both a castle-versus-cottage conflict and romanticism of the original time period. For example, through the words of Alan-a-Dale, she shows the conflict between the outlaws and their wealthier antagonists:

Indeed, perhaps I have heard of this band for enough of time that I have written a ballad or two about them; a ballad or two received well enough at market day among the yeoman farmers and goodwives, but not so well among those who live in great castles and feel the need to have an eye to their own wealth. (p. 71)

Again, through Alan-a-Dale's words, she expresses the romantic vision of the period: " 'I love a lady,' Alan-a-Dale said, and his voice lifted and fell so that he almost sang it. 'I love a lady . . . fair and pure as dawn, as the first bud of a rose-tree in spring' " (p. 72). This text is good for reading and for making comparisons among Robin Hood legends.

The hero in Margaret Hodges's adaptation of the English legend, *Saint George and the Dragon* exemplifies the characteristics found in legendary heroes. He is noble, courageous, and willing to avenge a wrong. Another contemporary version of a European legend is Nina Bawden's *William Tell*. Kate Seredy's *The White Stag* tells how the Hun-Magyar tribes migrated into Eastern Europe and created Hungary.

The Hawaiian Islands provide the setting for Marcia Brown's *Backbone of the King: The Story of Pakáa and His Son Ku*. The characters display the qualities of other legendary heroes. Bravery, honor, and willingness to avenge a wrong characterize the chief, a trusted supervisor to the king, who is unjustly wronged and then brought back to honor through the brave actions of his son.

Legends help children understand the conditions of times that created a need for brave and honorable men and women. These tales of adventure stress the noblest actions of humans. In legends, justice reigns over injustice. Children can feel the magnitude of the oral tradition as they listen to these tales, so reading legends aloud is the best way to introduce them to children.

Suggested Activities for Adult Understanding of Traditional Literature

- ☐ Read the stories included in Charles Perrault's *Tales of Mother Goose* and some tales collected by the Brothers Grimm. Note similarities and differences in the characterizations, settings, and actions. Describe the people for whom you believe the stories were originally told.

Page design is enhanced by plain-colored borders on illustrated pages and drawings of plants and scenes bordering text pages. (From *Saint George and the Dragon*. Retold by Margaret Hodges and illustrated by Trina Schart Hyman. Illustration copyright © 1984 by Trina Schart Hyman.)

- ☐ Choose a professional group that has been interested in researching and interpreting traditional literature (such as early Christian scholars, folklorists, psychologists, or anthropologists). Investigate this group's interpretations of several folktales.
- ☐ Read a cumulative tale, a humorous tale, a beast tale, a magic and wonder tale, a *pourquoi* tale, and a realistic tale. Compare the characterizations, settings, themes, and styles.
- ☐ Choose a common theme found in folktales, such as that in Cinderella or in trickster stories. Find examples of similar stories in folktales from several countries. What are the similarities and differences? How do the stories develop cultural characteristics?
- ☐ Choose an animal often found in traditional literature. Read stories that include the animal, choosing stories from cultures throughout the world. Is the animal revered or despised? How would you account for this?
- ☐ Select a country and several traditional tales from that country. Choose stories for which illustrators conducted extensive research before completing the drawings. Share your discoveries about the fine arts of the country with the class.
- ☐ Find examples of settings, plot developments, or characterizations found in literature from different countries. Discuss any similarities and differences with the class.
- ☐ Choose three folktales from different countries. Compare the actions developed in the three tales.
- ☐ Choose several folktales that are not compared in Chart 6–2. Following a similar format, analyze the tales.
- ☐ Read a fable in *Caxton's Aesop* and in *The Caldecott Aesop*. Compare these versions of the fables with a modern version. Are there differences in writing style, language, spelling, and illustrations between the earlier and later versions? If there are, what do you believe is the reason for the differences? Share the versions with a child. How does the child respond to each version?
- ☐ Select numerous folktales from one country. Investigate the information you can learn about the culture, people, and country with your peers. Share your findings with the class.
- ☐ Compare the versions of creation and the characteristics of gods and goddesses in Greek and Norse mythology. Why do you believe differences exist?
- ☐ Choose a folktale, fable, myth, and legend. Develop a chart similar to Chart 6–1 to compare the four types of stories.

References

1 Arnott, Kathleen. *Animal Folk Tales Around the World*. New York: Walck, 1970.

2 Asimov, Isaac. *Words from the Myths*. Boston: Houghton Mifflin, 1961.

3 Barth, Edna. *Cupid and Psyche*. Boston: Houghton Mifflin, 1976.

4 Bascom, William. "The Forms of Folklore: Prose Narratives." *Journal of American Folklore* 78 (January/March 1965): 3–20.

5 Bettelheim, Bruno. *The Uses of Enchantment: The Meaning and Importance of Fairy Tales*. New York: Knopf, 1976.

6 Booss, Claire. *Scandinavian Folk & Fairy Tales*. New York: Avenel Books, 1984.

7 Briggs, Katharine. *Dictionary of British Folk-Tales*. 4 volumes. London: Routledge & Kegan Paul, 1970–1971.

8 Campbell, Joseph. *The Power of Myth*. New York: Doubleday, 1988.

9 Carlson, Ruth Kearney. "World Understanding Through the Folktale." In *Folklore and Folk Tales Around the World,* edited by Ruth Kearney Carlson. Newark, Del.: International Reading Association, 1972.

10 Coolidge, Olivia E. *Legends of the North*. Boston: Houghton Mifflin, 1951.

11 Crossley-Holland, Kevin. *The Faber Book of Northern Legends*. Boston: Faber & Faber, 1983.

12 Favat, F. André. *Child and Tale: The Origins of Interest*. Urbana, Ill.: National Council of Teachers of English, 1977.

13 Hearn, Michael Patrick. Preface to *Histories or Tales of Past Times,* by Charles Perrault. New York: Garland, 1977.

14 Huck, Charlotte S., Susan Hepler, and Janet Hickman. *Children's Literature in the Elementary School*. New York: Holt, Rinehart & Winston, 1987.

15 Iverson, Pat Shaw, trans. *Norwegian Folk Tales*. New York: Viking, 1960.

16 Kuo, Louise, and Yuan-hsi Kuo. *Chinese Folk Tales*. Millbrae, Calif.: Celestial Arts, 1976.

17 Lenaghan, R. T., ed. *Caxton's Aesop*. Cambridge: Harvard University Press, 1967.

18 Lofaro, Michael A. *The Tall Tales of Davy Crockett: The Second Nashville Series of Crockett Almanacs, 1839–1841*. Knoxville: University of Tennessee Press, 1987.

19 Pratt, Davis, and Elsa Kula. *Magic Animals of Japan*. Berkeley, Calif.: Parnassus, 1967.

20 Propp, Vladimir. *Morphology of the Folktale*. Translated by Laurence Scott. Austin, Tex.: University of Texas, 1968.

21 Sewell, Helen. *A Book of Myths, Selections from Bulfinch's Age of Fable*. New York: Macmillan, 1942.

22 Thomas, Joyce. "The Tales of the Brothers Grimm: In the Black Forest." In *Touchstones: Reflections on the Best in Children's Literature*, edited by Perry Nodelman. West Lafayette, Ind.: Children's Literature Association, 1987, 104–117.

23 Thompson, Stith. *The Folktale*. Berkeley: University of California Press, 1977.

24 Wyndham, Robert. *Tales the People Tell in China*. New York: Messner, 1971.

25 Yolen, Jane. "How Basic Is Shazam?" *Language Arts* 54 (September 1977): 645–651.

Involving Children in Traditional Literature

TELLING STORIES

COMPARING FOLKTALES FROM DIFFERENT COUNTRIES

INVESTIGATING FOLKTALES FROM A SINGLE COUNTRY

INITIATING CREATIVE DRAMATICS

INTERPRETING TRADITIONAL IMAGES IN ART

TRADITIONAL TALES ARE AMONG THE most memorable that children experience in literature. With their well-defined plots, easily identifiable characters, rapid action, and satisfactory endings, the tales lend themselves to enjoyable experiences. This section explores ways to recapture the oral tradition through telling stories, comparing folktales from different countries, investigating folktales from a single country, initiating creative dramatizations, and interpreting traditional images in art.

TELLING STORIES

Learning the ancient art of oral storytelling is well worth the effort in the pleasure that it affords both the teller and the audience. John Warren Stewig (13) lists three important reasons to include storytelling in childhood experiences. First, storytelling helps children understand the oral tradition of literature. In the past, children were initiated into their literary heritage through storytelling. Unhappily, this experience does not often occur today. Second, storytelling allows an adult the opportunity to bring children into the literary experience. Free from dependence on a book, a storyteller can use gestures and actions to involve children in the story. Third, when an adult tells a story, children understand that it is a worthy activity and are stimulated to try telling stories themselves.

Choosing a Story

The most important factor in choosing a story is selecting one that is really enjoyable. A narrator should enjoy spending time preparing a story and should retell it with conviction and enthusiasm.

Storytelling demands an appreciative audience. A storyteller must be aware of the interests, ages, and experience of the listeners involved. Young children have short attention spans, so story length must be considered when selecting a tale. Children's ages also should influence the subject matter of a tale. Young children like stories about familiar subjects, such as animals, children, or home life. They respond to the repetitive language in cumulative tales and enjoy joining in when such stories as "Henny Penny" reach their climax. Simple folktales, such as "The Three Bears," "The Three Little Pigs," and "The Three Billy Goats Gruff," are excellent to share with young children. Children from roughly ages seven through ten enjoy folktales with longer plots, such as those collected by the Brothers Grimm. "Rapunzel" and "Rumpelstiltskin" are favorites. Other favorites include such Jewish folktales as "It Could Always Be Worse." Older children enjoy adventure tales, myths, and legends.

Folktales have several characteristics that make them appropriate for storytelling: strong beginnings that bring listeners rapidly into the fast-paced action; several characters with whom listeners easily identify; climaxes that are familiar to children; and satisfactory endings. These characteristics suggest worthwhile criteria for selecting tales.

Storytellers should also consider the mood they wish to create, whether it be humorous and lighthearted or serious and scary. If, for example, you want to choose a story appropriate for Halloween, then mood is important. Even the site for storytelling may affect the mood and story selection. Assume, for example, that a group of people is sitting on high rocks overlooking Lake Superior. The wind is causing the waves to crash with a mighty roar onto the rocks below. When the people look out over the lake, they can see only a wide stretch of water. No humans are in sight. The view to the north is one of thick forests, ferns, and distant waterfalls. The Norse myth, "The Hammer of Thor," from Olivia E. Coolidge's *Legends of the North* seems ideal for this setting.

Preparing the Story for Telling

Storytelling does not require memorization, but it does require preparation. Certain steps will help you prepare for an enjoyable experience. Ramon Royal Ross (11) recommends the following sequence of steps:

1 Read the story aloud several times. Try to get a feeling for its rhythm and style, so that your retelling will be faithful to the original interpretation.

2 Think of the major actions of the story and try to find where one action or bit ends and another begins. These bits will help you form an outline to follow in telling the story.

3 Develop a sense of the characters in the story. Envision the characters—the clothes they wear, their shapes and sizes, unusual features, personality traits, their speech, their mannerisms, and the like.

4 Think through the setting of the story. A storyteller should be able to draw a map showing where the story took place.

5 Look for phrases to incorporate into the story when you tell it. Read the story again. What phrases and language patterns should you use to tell the story?

6 Begin telling parts of the story aloud, testing different ways to say the same words. Your intonation should agree with the meaning you hope to convey.

7 Plan gestures that add to the story. Once you have decided the gestures, practice them in front of a mirror.

8 Prepare an introduction and a conclusion for the story. Give background information, share information about hearing the story for the first time, or share an object related to the story.

9 Finally, practice the entire story. Time the telling at each practice. Record the story on audiotape. Play it back and listen for voice qualities to be cultivated and others to be discarded. Again, practice in front of a mirror, noting your posture, gestures, and general impression.

Sharing the Story with an Audience

Because you have spent considerable time in preparation, you should present the story effectively. However, you can enhance your presentation by creating an interest in the story, setting a mood, creating an environment where children can see and hear you, and presenting the story with effective eye contact and voice control. You may use book jackets, giant books, miniature books, travel posters, art objects, puppets, or music to stimulate children's interest in the story. A librarian or teacher who regularly tells stories to large groups of children can use any of these methods so that children will look forward to the story hour.

Colorful book jackets from folktales or myths not only entice children but also help set a mood for storytelling. For example, you might develop a display around the book jacket for Elizabeth Isele's *The Frog Princess*. In addition to the book jacket illustrated by Michael Hague, you could display a toy frog, a piece of linen, a container of flour, a toy duck, a toy hare, a small wooden chest, an egg, and a needle. Your accompanying questions might include the following: How could a frog make it possible for a prince to become the ruler of the country? How could a piece of linen and a container of flour allow a princess to prove her worth? What would you do if you had to find a needle that was inside an egg, that was inside a duck, that was inside a hare, that was inside a chest?

Stories about giants lend themselves to displays of large books. One librarian drew huge figures of giants and beanstalks on large sheets of tagboard and then placed the sheets together to form a gigantic book that stimulated interest in "Jack and the Beanstalk." Likewise, drawings of a huge hammer stimulated interest about Thor when the librarian prepared a Norse myth for telling. The giant books worked well in these cases. The children speculated about the size or strength of anyone who could read such a large book. Miniature books stimulated children's interest before another story hour when "Tom Thumb" was the story. The storyteller used other tiny objects, many formed out of clay, that would be appropriate for a little person.

If the story has an identifiable location, travel posters can stimulate interest and provide background information. They are especially appealing when used with folktales from other countries. Travel posters showing ancient English sites might introduce an oral telling of either Barbara Cohen's or Selina Hastings's adaptations of Geoffrey Chaucer's *Canterbury Tales*. You may use travel posters about Greece and Italy with Greek and Roman mythology. Travel posters showing Norwegian fjords and mountains can accompany Norse myths, while posters showing the Black Forest and old European castles are appropriate for "Snow White and the Seven Dwarfs" and "Sleeping Beauty."

Objects from the story or from the country that is the setting of the story can also increase children's interest. Dolls, plates, figurines, stuffed animals, and numerous other everyday objects and curios can add to the story hour.

After interest is high, concentrate on setting the mood for story time. Many storytellers use story-hour symbols. For example, if a small lamp is the symbol for story hour, children know that when the lamp is lit, it is time to listen. Music can also be a symbol; a certain record, music box tune, piano introduction, or guitar selection can introduce story hour. These techniques are usually effective, since children learn to associate them with enjoyable listening experiences. Donna E. Norton (7, p. 383) has the following suggestions for telling the story:

1 Find a place in the room where all children can see and hear the presentation.
2 Either stand in front of the children or sit with them.
3 Select an appropriate introduction. Use a prop, tell something about the author, discuss a related event, or ask a question.
4 Maintain eye contact with the children. This engages them more fully in the story.
5 Use appropriate voice rate and volume for effect.
6 While telling the story, use a short step or shift in footing to indicate a change in scene or character or to heighten the suspense. If seated, lean forward or away from the children.
7 After telling the story, pause to give the audience a chance to soak in everything you said.

Mary Ann Paulin (9) includes sample storytelling programs in her *Creative Uses of Children's Literature*. These programs include story introductions, texts, and follow-up suggestions.

Using Feltboards to Share Folktales

Storytelling does not require any props. In fact, some of the best storytellers use nothing except their voices and gestures to recapture the plots and characters found in traditional tales. Most storytellers, however, enjoy adding variety to their repertoire. Children also enjoy experimenting with different approaches to storytelling; the flannelboard or feltboard lends itself to storytelling by both adults and children.

A feltboard is a rectangular, lightweight board covered with felt, flannel cloth, or lightweight indoor-outdoor carpeting. This board acts as the backdrop for figures cut from felt, pellon, or other material backed with Velcro. Felt or pellon figures will cling directly to a feltboard, while any object, even leather, wood, or foam rubber will adhere to the felt if first backed with a small square or strip of Velcro. Other materials, such as yarn or cotton balls, will also cling to a feltboard and may be used to add interest and texture to a story.

Stories that lend themselves to feltboard interpretations have only a few major characters, plots that depend upon oral telling rather than physical action, and settings that do not demand exceptional detail. These characteristics are similar to those already stipulated for the simple folktales that young children enjoy. Pleasing stories to retell on the feltboard include the folktales "Three Billy

FIGURE 6–1
Stories that lend themselves to feltboard interpretations have only a few major characters, plots that depend on oral telling rather than physical action, and settings that do not demand exceptional detail.

Goats Gruff," "The Three Bears," "The Gingerbread Boy," and "Henny Penny." Stories should include actions that can be shown on the board. In addition, the number of figures should not overwhelm the board (See Figure 6–1).

Consider the Norwegian folktale "The Three Billy Goats Gruff." First, use simple cut-outs or objects to represent the characters. The three goats range in size from a small goat to a great big goat with curved horns. The ugly old troll has big eyes and a long, long nose. You can show the setting easily: a bridge crossing a stream and green grass on the other side of the bridge. You can illustrate the action effectively: each goat can go "Trip, trap! Trip, trap!" over the bridge. The troll can challenge each goat with "Who's that tripping over my bridge?" You can also illustrate the climax easily: the big billy goat knocks the troll off the bridge and continues to cross to the other side. The plot develops sequentially from a small billy goat, to a medium-sized billy goat, and finally to a great big billy goat.

The English folktale "The Donkey, the Table, and the Stick" is another story that is effective for feltboard production. Children enjoy seeing the magic donkey produce gold coins when his ear is pulled and they laugh over the poor lad's exasperation as nothing happens when he pulls and pulls the common donkey's ear. They are enthusiastic about the table that can produce turkey, sausages, and other good things. They laugh when the storyteller tries to get the ordinary table to produce food. Finally, they are overjoyed when the magic stick beats the evil innkeeper. You can use feltboard characters to show these actions effectively.

Cumulative tales are excellent for feltboard presentations. As you introduce each new character, place it on the feltboard. Have the children join the dialogue as "The Fat Cat," for example, encounters first the gruel, then the pot, the old woman, Skahottentot, Skilinkenlot, five birds, seven dancing girls, the lady with the pink parasol, the parson, and the woodsman.

Through such presentations, children learn about sequential order and improve their language skills. Using feltboard stories with children, you will often find that the children either ask if they can retell the stories or make up their own feltboard stories to share. If you provide feltboards and materials, children naturally enjoy telling stories in this manner. Whether you tell a story to one child or to a group, storytelling is well worth the effort of preparation and presentation. Watching children as they respond to a magical environment and then make their own efforts as storytellers will prove to you that storytelling should be included in every child's experience.

COMPARING FOLKTALES FROM DIFFERENT COUNTRIES

Understanding how various types of traditional stories are related, becoming aware of cultural diffusion, and learning about different countries are values gained from traditional literature. One way to help children gain these values is to compare folktales from different countries.

Comparing Different Versions of the Same Folktale

Many older children are fascinated to discover that some tales appear in almost every culture. The names vary, magical objects differ, and settings change, but the basic elements of the story remain the same. Over nine hundred versions of the Cinderella story have been found throughout the world. Mary Ann Nelson (6) claims that there are over five hundred European versions. Jane M. Bingham and Grayce Scholt (1) and Elinor P. Ross (10) suggest that older children should investigate the motifs in these tales. Compile questions such as the following with the children's assistance to guide their search and discovery:

1 What caused Cinderella to have a lowly position in the family?
2 What shows that Cinderella has a lowly position in the household?
3 How is Cinderella related to other household members?
4 What happens to keep Cinderella away from the ball?
5 How does Cinderella receive her wishes or transformation?
6 Where does Cinderella meet the prince?
7 What is the test signifying the rightful Cinderella?
8 What happens to the stepsisters?

Sources for comparisons include Mary Ann Nelson's (6) anthology, Bingham and Scholt's (1) synopses of twelve variants of the Cinderella story, Sutherland and Livingston's anthology (14), and folklore collections from around the world. Chart 6–7 represents some key variants found in Cinderella tales from different countries.

After children have read, listened to, and discussed many Cinderella tales, their investigations may agree with conclusions found in Bingham and Scholt's research. These investigators (1) compared twelve Cinderella tales and concluded the following:

1 The menial position of the heroine is usually shown by describing the impossible tasks she is asked to do. These tasks reflect the culture of the story.
2 Supernatural powers aid the heroine. Many powers relate to the dead mother: She returns in the form of an animal, or a tree appears over her grave.
3 The magical clothes of the transformed heroine are usually elegant and appropriate for the culture: gold and silver, or Indian dress of leather and beads.
4 The hero and heroine usually meet in places that are important to the culture: a ball, a theater, a church, or a wigwam.
5 The male figure has an elevated position in society. He is of noble birth in the majority of the tales, but the Chinese tale describes him as a scholar.
6 Seven of the twelve tales include cruel stepmothers. The heroine also has to contend with cruel stepsisters or sisters.
7 Eight tales have some form of shoe test for identifying Cinderella. A Japanese version requires the heroine to compose a song; a Native American version asks the heroine to identify what the chief's sledstrings and bowstrings are made of.
8 In five of the twelve tales, the wicked stepmother or stepsisters meet violent ends.
9 All the tales reflect the societies that produced them. Native American tales refer to wigwams, moccasins, and bowstrings; Japanese stories refer to kimonos, rice, and oni.

Other tales are also suitable for comparisons. P. T. Travers (15) has included five versions of the Sleeping Beauty tale and one of her own translations in *About the Sleeping Beauty*. This collection contains her own version, which has Arabian roots; "Dornroschen or Briar-Rose," from the Grimms' *Household Tales;* "La Belle au Bois Dormant, or The Sleeping Beauty in the Wood," from Charles Perrault; "Sole, Luna, e Talia or Sun, Moon, and Talia," from the Italian *The Pentamerone of Giambattista Basile;* "The Queen of Tubber Tintye," from *Myths and Folklore of Ireland;* and "The Petrified Mansion," from *Bengal Fairy Tales*. "Little Red Riding Hood" (8) and "The Lad Who Went to the North Wind" also have many variants. Linda Western's "A Comparative Study of Literature Through Folk Tale Variants" (16) is another source of different versions of tales.

A search for variant versions of a tale encourages children to develop an understanding of the

CHART 6–7
Variations found in Cinderella stories from different countries

Origin	Cause of Lowly Position	Outward Signs of Lowly Position	Cinderella's Relationship to Household	How She Receives Wishes	What Keeps Her from Social Occasion	Where She Meets the Prince	Test of Rightful Cinderella	What Happens to Stepsisters
French Perrault, "Cinderilla"	Mother died. Father remarried.	Sitting in ashes. Vilest household tasks.	Stepdaughter to cruel woman. Unkind stepsisters.	Wishes to fairy godmother.	(Ball) No gown. Family won't let her go.	Castle ball. Beautifully dressed.	Glass slipper.	Forgiven. Live in palace. Marry lords.
German Grimm, "Cinderella"	Mother died. Father remarried.	Wears clogs, old dress. Sleeps in cinders. Heavy work.	Stepdaughter to cruel woman. Cruel stepsisters.	Wishes to bird on tree on mother's grave.	(Ball) Must separate lentils.	Castle ball. Beautifully dressed.	Gold slipper.	Blinded by birds.
English "Tattercoats"	Mother died at her birth. Grandfather blames her.	Ragbag clothes. Scraps for food.	Despised granddaughter. Hated by servants.	Gooseherd plays pipe.	(Ball) Grandfather refuses.	In forest. Dressed in rags.	None.	Grandfather weeps. Hair grows into stones.
Vietnamese "In the Land of Small Dragon"	Mother died. Father's number two wife hates her.	Collects wood. Cares for rice paddies.	Stepdaughter to hateful woman. Hated by half-sisters.	Fairy. Bones of fish.	(Festival) Must separate rice from husks.	Festival. Beautifully dressed.	Jeweled slipper *(hai)*.	Not told.
Chinese "Beauty and Pock Face"	Mother turned into cow.	Straightens hemp. Hard work.	Stepdaughter to cruel woman. Cruel stepsister.	From bones of mother in earthenware pot.	(Theater) Straighten hemp. Separate sesame seeds.	Theater. Scholar picks up shoe from road.	Walks on eggs. Climbs ladder of knives. Jumps into oil.	Roasted in oil.
Micmac—Native American "Little Burnt Face"	Mother died.	Burned face, Ragged garments.	Despised by two jealous sisters.	The Great Chief's sister changes her.	She must make her own dress.	Wigwam by the lake.	Describe the Great Chief.	Sent back to wigwam in disgrace.

impact of cultural diffusion on literature. Children also realize that each culture has placed the tale in a context that reflects the society of the storyteller and the audience.

Analyzing Variants of a Folktale

Variants of folktales, especially those that changed as the original audiences moved to new lands, are especially interesting for developing the understanding that folktales frequently change as storytellers adjust to their new environments. In addition, if tales still retain the original motifs and themes, you may use the variants to help students analyze possible sources of the original tales. As a logical extension of a comparative study of Cinderella tales for upper-elementary and middle-school students, use William H. Hooks's *Moss Gown* to analyze variations on themes and motifs, to search for references to time and place, and to speculate about the country of origin.

To begin, provide some background knowledge gained from other sources of literature and from geography. First, furnish a knowledge of Cinderella-type elements by having the children read many variants of the Cinderella story. This activity can help children understand that most Cinderella-type stories have such characteristics as a girl who is given the hardest tasks, a helper with supernatural powers, and an occasion that the girl wants to attend. Supply a knowledge of the English versions of Cinderella through "Tattercoats" and "*Mossycoat*" to help the children understand how the English Cinderella stories differ from those in other countries. Also, give the children at least a brief introduction to Shakespeare's *King Lear* to help them identify these elements in the story. A King Lear story written for children is included in E. Nesbit's *Beautiful Stories from Shakespeare* and Charles and Mary Lamb's *Tales from Shakespeare*. William H. Hooks's *Moss Gown* is a variant collected from the tidewater section of North Carolina. Conse-

CHART 6–8
An analysis of William H. Hooks's *Moss Gown*

Cinderella elements found in Moss Gown:
A helper with supernatural powers.
A gown that changes to rags.
A girl who is given the hardest kitchen work.
An heir who holds a dance.
A heroine who cannot attend the dance because she lacks a dress.
A supernatural being who casts a spell and provides a dress.
An order that must be obeyed.
A handsome heir who dances with the heroine only.
An heir who searches for the heroine.
An heir and a heroine who marry.

King Lear elements found in Moss Gown:
A question asked to prove love.
A father who rejects youngest and most loving daughter's declaration.
A father who wanders after cruel treatment by elder daughters.
A youngest daughter who eventually proves her love for her father.

References to time and place found in Moss Gown:
A great plantation.
A "snow-white house, pillared with eight marble columns on every side" (p. 5).
A reference to fine fields.
A reference to riding and hunting in the murky, mysterious swamp.
A reference to black-green cypress treetops.
A reference to gray Spanish moss.
French words used in the Carolinas to cast a powerful, magical spell.
A party that is called a frolic.

Evidence that the original storytellers came from English backgrounds:
King Lear elements show knowledge of Shakespeare, an English author.
There are similarities to the British Cinderella. For example, in "Tattercoats," servants mistreat a girl, and a man of wealthy position loves the girl even though she is dressed in rags.

quently, there are references to the environment and to the southern plantations of an earlier time.

After providing these background understandings, ask the children to listen to or to read Hooks's *Moss Gown*. Ask them to search for (1) Cinderella elements, (2) King Lear elements, (3) references to time and place, and (4) evidence of the European country the early storytellers came from. From this activity, the children will discover evidence that is similar to the information in Chart 6–8.

After completing this task, ask the children to speculate about why *Moss Gown* has a happy ending and not the tragic ending of *King Lear*. They will probably decide that the Cinderella theme requires a happy ending. Consequently, the storytellers needed to find a way for the heroine and her father to live happily. Compare the themes in both *King Lear* and *Moss Gown* for an interesting and lively discussion. Additional variants for this type of activity include Gail E. Haley's *Jack and the Bean Tree*, an Appalachian variant of "Jack and the Beanstalk"; John Bierhorst's *Doctor Coyote: A Native American Aesop's Fables*, a Spanish-Aztec variant; and Eva Martin's *Canadian Fairy Tales*, a collection that includes Canadian variants from French, German, and English sources.

INVESTIGATING FOLKTALES FROM A SINGLE COUNTRY

Children can learn a great deal about a country and its people by investigating a number of traditional tales from that country. Such an investigation also increases understanding of the multicultural heritage of this country and develops understanding of, and positive attitudes toward, cultures other than one's own.

This fact was made clear when a group of fifth-grade children was studying folktales to learn more about the people of other countries. They were reading and discussing Russian folktales at a time when relationships between the Soviet Union and the United States were strained. As they read the tales, especially the merry ones, with their rapid, humorous dialogues and absurd plots, the children decided that the people who could invent and enjoy those stories must be similar to themselves. They realized that they were laughing at the same stories that brought humor to children in the Soviet Union.

During the sharing of folktales, the children commented, for example, that Jewish folktales often stress the unselfish desire for a better world or reward sincerity and wisdom. They were also impressed by the fact that the Chinese "Cinderella" married a scholar and not a nobleman. Through the folktales, they learned to respect the values of the people who created them.

Another fifth-grade class conducted a successful folktale study on one country. The web in Figure 6–2 uses traditional tales from China to analyze personal values, important symbols, and disliked human qualities in the Chinese culture. It also looks at supernatural beings. Finally, it lists stimulating activities and motivating introductions for the study of the traditional tales. The children first listened to, read, and discussed folktales from China. Objects displayed throughout the room stimulated interest. A large red paper dragon met the children as they entered the room. Other objects included joss sticks (incense), lanterns, Chinese flutes, a tea service, fans, statues of mythical beasts, lacquered boxes and plates, silk, samples of Chinese writing, a blue willow plate, jade, and pictures of artwork, temples, pagodas, people, and animals. Many Chinese folktales were displayed on the library table. In the background, a recording of Chinese music played. The chalkboard contained a message, written in Chinese figures, welcoming the children to China. The students looked at the displays, listened to the music, tried to decipher the message, and discussed what they saw and heard. They located China on a map and on a globe. Then, they listed questions about China—questions about the people, country, values, art, music, food, houses, animals, and climate.

The teacher read aloud some of the foreword to Louise and Yuan-hsi Kuo's *Chinese Folk Tales* (3). She asked the students to close their eyes and imagine the scene, to listen carefully, and then to tell whether the following scene took place in modern times or many centuries ago.

> But suddenly the room echoes with an ear-splitting clash of cymbals and the sonorous boom of a drum and in the street below our window prances a splendid lion. The sound of cymbals and the beat of drums have been heard incessantly since early morning and are merely a prelude to a major part to come: a procession with gay silk banners flying, votive offerings of barbecued pigs . . . golden brown and saffron, cartloads heaped with fruit, red-colored eggs and other delicacies, giant joss sticks, candles and lanterns. A magnificent dragon, gyrating and performing with vigor and intensity to the rapid beat of a drum, will bring the procession to a climax. Throngs crowd the doorways, line the path, as excited onlookers join the ranks to mingle with those on

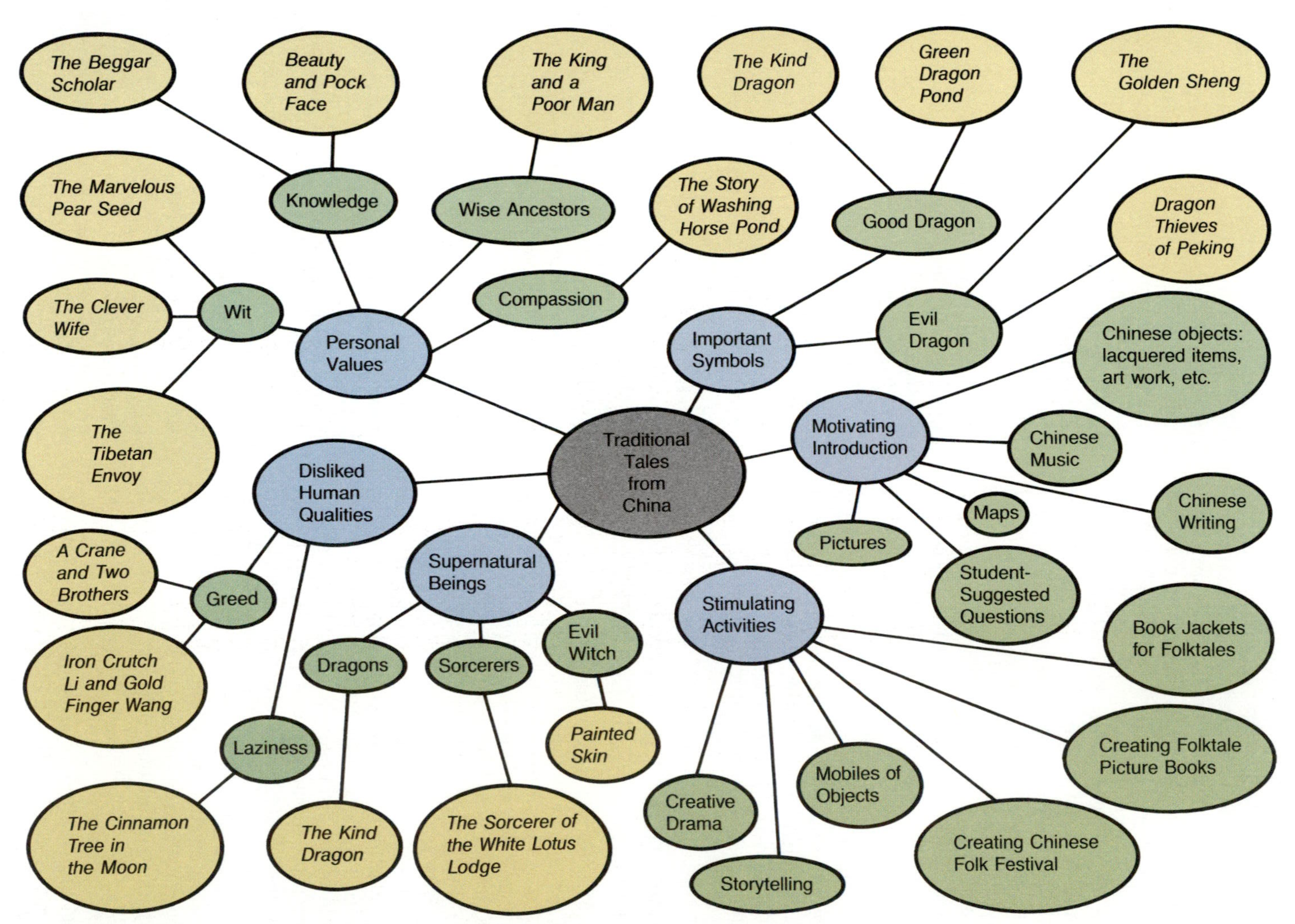

FIGURE 6–2
A fifth-grade study of Chinese folktales

their way to the temple . . . journey's end. This is the day of days . . . the grand finale of five days of celebration in homage to T'ien Ho, the Heavenly Goddess of the Sea . . . she who will bestow blessings on all who worship her, and protect them for the entire year. (p. 7)

After listening to the selection, the children speculated about the time period and gave their reasons for choosing either ancient or modern times. Many children were quite surprised to hear that the festival was held in modern Hong Kong. This discussion led to reading Chinese folktales in order to learn more about the Chinese people and a heritage that still influences people.

Next, the teacher shared several of her favorite Chinese folktales with the children. They included Marilee Heyer's *The Weaving of a Dream: A Chinese Folktale,* Margaret Mahy's *The Seven Chinese Brothers,* and several tales from He Liyi's *The Spring of Butterflies and Other Chinese Folktales.* The selections included "The Tibetan Envoy," which shows the importance of wit and intelligence; "The Story of Washing Horse Pond," which shows the importance of compassion for others; "The King and a Poor Man," which shows the importance of wise ancestors; and "A Crane and Two Brothers," which shows dislike for greed. She also provided brief introductions to other tales to stimulate the children's interest in reading the tales. The children then chose tales to read independently. As they read, they considered their questions about China. Consequently, when they discovered information about the culture and the people, they jotted the information down so that they could share it with the class.

After collecting considerable information, the children discussed ways of verifying whether or not the information was accurate. They compared the information with library reference materials and magazines, such as *National Geographic.* They also invited to the classroom several visitors who were either Chinese or had visited China.

The students used their knowledge about the people, culture, and literature of China in their own art, creative drama, and writing. They drew travel posters as well as book jackets and illustrations for folktales. They also made mobiles of folk-literature objects. One artistic activity was to create picture storybooks from single folktales. The children chose a favorite tale not already in picture-book format, illustrated it with drawings, and bound the pages together. Because many of the published picture books contained information about the origins of their tales, the children included similar information inside their own front covers. Because published book jackets often tell about the illustrator and the research to provide authentic pictures, the students' books contained this information. The children told about themselves and the ways they prepared for their drawing assignments. They described the mediums they used for their illustrations. Then, they shared their books with one another and other classes and proudly displayed the books in the library.

The class also chose some stories for creative drama. The teacher divided the class into groups according to favorite folktales. Each group then chose a method for sharing the story with the rest of the class. Some groups re-created the stories as plays, others chose puppetry, and one group used pantomime with a narrator who read the lines.

The children invited their parents to attend a Chinese folktale festival. The children shared their art projects, picture storybooks, new information, and creative dramas with an appreciative audience.

This unit about one country led to an interest in folktales from other countries. The children next read folktales from Japan and other Asian countries. They discovered the similarities among many of these tales, especially in the symbolic animals found in both Chinese and Japanese tales. The children went on to detect Chinese influence on non-Asian writers when they read the beautiful version of Hans Christian Andersen's *The Nightingale,* illustrated by Nancy Ekholm Burkert.

The discovery of similar mythical animals led to another interesting search through folklore. The teacher read Winifred Miller's article "Dragons—Fact or Fantasy?" (5) and the children discovered that both Chinese and Japanese folktales had good and evil dragons; good dragons, a representation of Han nobility, were found in folktales told to ruling classes, but folktales about the common people referred to dragons as evil. With the teacher's guidance, the students accomplished many of the activities suggested by Miller's article.

Folktales lend themselves well to many activities. Teachers and librarians will find many ways to increase world understanding through literature.

INITIATING CREATIVE DRAMATICS

Folklore is a natural source of materials for storytelling. It also stimulates creative drama. Elizabeth Cook (2) maintains that the most excit-

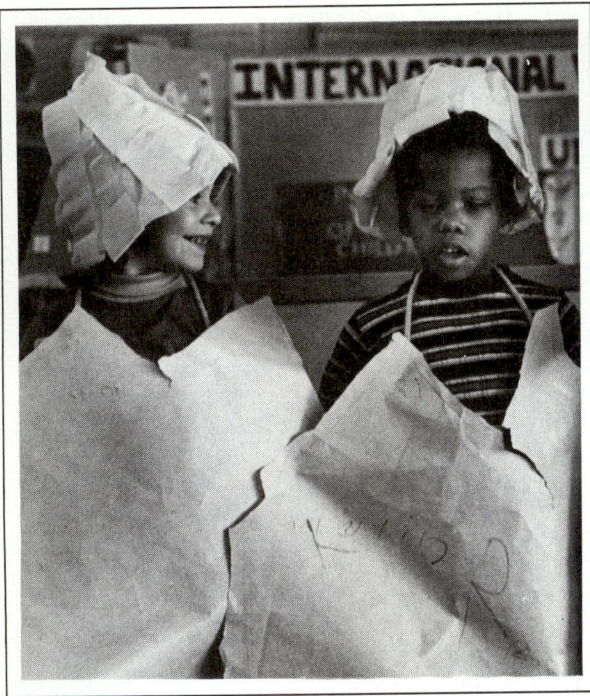

Folklore may encourage children to act out their favorite stories.

ing ways of retelling traditional tales are through drama, either in movement alone or in movement accompanied by words. Children can mime many sequences as you read to them. They can act out individual parts, or groups of children can recreate their own versions of the tales.

Pantomime

Pantomime is creative drama in which an actor plays a part with gestures and actions without using words. According to Geraldine Siks (12), pantomime should be part of a planned drama curriculum. In such a curriculum, children learn to experiment with body movement, use their senses, stimulate their imaginations, develop language and speech, and understand and use characterization. The first pantomime experiences of children usually include activities in which they learn to relax and to experiment with different ways to move their bodies. After children have ideas about what their bodies can express, pantomiming folktales can help them interpret various actions and emotions.

Familiar folktales young children enjoy are excellent for pantomime. For example, children can pretend to be each character in Paul Galdone's *The Three Bears* as you read the story aloud. Children can pretend to be as small as the wee bear, average size for the middle-sized bear, and huge for the great big bear. As bears, they can prepare their porridge, sit in their chairs, lie in their beds, and walk in the woods. Then, as Goldilocks, they can show curiosity as they peep into the window and then through the keyhole. They can cautiously enter the bears' home. They can react to porridge that is too hot, too cold, and just right. They can show discomfort as they try to climb into the great big chair, sink into the too soft chair, and then rock comfortably in the little chair until they surprisingly crash to the floor. They can show similar reactions to the three beds.

As bears, the children can return to the house, demonstrate outrage over the ideas that somebody has been tasting their porridge, somebody has been sitting in their chairs, and somebody has been lying in their beds. Finally, they can return to the character of Goldilocks as she awakens, sees the bears, and dashes into the woods. The experience allows children to develop believable characterizations through body movements. Other folktales that young children like to pantomime are "The Three Little Pigs," "The Three Billy Goats Gruff," and "The Little Red Hen."

When children start to enjoy longer folktales, use these many tales as sources of materials for pantomime. Children can put on their cloaks of invisibility and tiptoe behind "The Twelve Dancing Princesses" as the princesses descend the winding stairs. They can stop in fright as they accidentally step on the long dress of a princess. They can walk in wonderment through the silver forest, gold forest, and diamond forest. As prince and princess, they can dance gracefully through the night and then sleepily climb the winding stairs.

Because many magical tales show vivid contrasts between good and evil characters, children can form pairs and play opposing or complementary roles. "Cinderella" has scenes between good and evil characters: Cinderella and her stepmother, or Cinderella and her stepsisters. There are also scenes between evil characters and evil forces: the stepmother and stepsisters plot to leave Cinderella at home, force her to work, or try to fit their feet inside the slipper. Also, children can pantomime the opposing characters of good and bad luck in Isaac Bashevis Singer's Jewish tale *Mazel and Shlimazel, or the Milk of the Lioness.*

Scenes from Greek and Norse mythology are excellent for older children to pantomime. Children can enact Psyche's search for Cupid; Jason's search for the golden fleece; Persephone's descending into the underground world of Hades; Apollo's trailing across the sky in his sun chariot; and Thor's frantically searching for his missing hammer, dressing as a bride, and retrieving his hammer from the giant Thrym. Quite different movements and expressions are necessary to depict gods, goddesses, heroes, and heroines found in Greek and Norse mythology. Acting out scenes through pantomime helps children understand the qualities of these traditional folklore characters and appreciate the language found in the myths.

Creative Interpretations

As children pantomime stories such as "The Three Bears" or *Mazel and Shlimazel,* they usually want to add words and create their own plays. It is a natural extension of pantomime to add "Somebody has been sitting in my chair" or to create a dialogue in which the hero tries to convince the baroness that she should lend him her pig. Pantomiming provides a foundation for other creative activities; it allows children to experience the movement and emotion of the story and characters before they try to work with dialogue. Stories used to stimulate pantomime can also be used for creative interpretations requiring words. Folklore meets Barbara M. McIntyre's (4) criteria for stories that are appropriate for dramatization. They should (1) have ideas worth sharing, (2) involve conflict, (3) include action in the development of the plot, (4) contain characters who seem real, and (5) have situations in which interesting dialogue can be developed. The folktales discussed in this chapter qualify in all of these areas.

Folklore can be used to stimulate creative dramatizations in two ways. The stories themselves can be re-created, or the stories can serve as stimulators to help children create new interpretations. Usually, children begin by acting out stories that are close to the original in plot and characterization. As they become more secure, they enjoy making up new stories or creating additional ones about a character. Whatever the purpose for using the folktales, however, you must guide children's dramatizations in a sequence of steps:

1 *Stimulate children's interest in the story.* For example, for "The Golden Goose," a third-grade teacher placed a yellow toy goose, a dry crust of bread, and a bottle of sour liquid in front of the class. She then asked the children if they thought they could acquire a fortune and a beautiful princess if they had those objects. She let them try to think of ways they might accomplish this miracle. The children decided that a little magic might help.

2 *Present the story so that the children will have a foundation to draw upon in creating their dramatization.* The teacher next told the story of "The Golden Goose," using the toy goose, the stale bread, and the sour liquid to assist her. This time, however, as the stale bread was transformed, she had a pastry to take its place, and as the sour liquid was changed, she had a jug of sweet grape juice to exchange.

3 *Guide the children's planning and presentation of their creative dramatization.* The teacher encouraged the class to talk about their favorite characters in the story. She then asked them to improvise the actions of each character in various scenes in the story—the despised and mistreated Dummling (or Simpleton, depending upon the version used), his parents, and his brothers: for example, Dummling's sharing his food with the old man, cutting down the trees, and discovering the golden goose.

The children discussed which actions they would like to include in the play and what sequence of events they would use. They decided to use the goose, the bread, the liquid, the pastry, and the grape juice as props. After the children were satisfied with the sequence and who should play each role (at least for the first time), they acted out the story with encouragement from the teacher when necessary. They did not try to memorize lines. Instead, they improvised the general mood. They put on their production several times so that they could play various roles and take turns being the audience.

4 *Help the children evaluate their presentation.* The teacher encouraged the children to discuss the good things about their play: Why did they feel sorry for Dummling? How did the older brothers show that they thought they were brighter than Dummling? What did they do so that the children did not feel sorry for their bad luck? What did the old man do to let them know he was very old? Why did they laugh at Dummling? The children made many positive comments about their play. Then they talked about how they could improve the presentation.

A Christmas Festival, or Winter Holiday Celebration

Gallant knights show off their skills in tests of archery and outdoor games; the great hall is decorated with mistletoe; the Yule log is on the fire; plum puddings, wild boar, and roasted venison cover the banquet tables; and minstrels and storytellers prepare to enchant the holiday merrymakers. Books say this is how the Christmas season was celebrated in the days of King Arthur. Books also say that in the 1800s, groups of Cornish young people traveled from house to house performing the play *Duffy and the Devil*. Children in a fifth-grade class combined these two English holiday traditions to develop their own Christmas festival. (This can be called a winter holiday celebration to avoid referring to Christmas.)

To prepare for the festival, the fifth-graders chose English folktales and parts of heroic tales that could be told to a gathering of people. They included readings from King Arthur and Robin Hood along with "The Marriage of Sir Gawain," and the folktales "Jack the Giant Killer," "Mr. and Mrs. Vinegar," and "The Donkey, the Table, and the Stick."

They developed Harve Zemach's *Duffy and the Devil* into a creative dramatization to add to the traditional setting. To assist the children in developing the play, the teacher used steps similar to those for "The Golden Goose." After the teacher shared the story with the class, she asked the children to talk about their favorite parts and characters. The children improvised Squire Lovel of Trovel's unhappily observing his old housekeeper Jone; the old woman's chasing Duffy with a broom; Duffy's convincing Squire Lovel that she is a marvelous housekeeper; and numerous other scenes from the story. Then, they discussed the actions and scenes they would like to include in their dramatization. The group decided to retain the flavor of the early English language in the story. While they did not completely memorize their parts, they did use such words as *bufflehead, clouts, whillygogs,* and *whizamagees*. Next, they chose players, practiced the sequence, and discussed what they liked about the play and ways that it could be improved.

On the day of the festival, the children decorated the room like an Old English hall. Each class member had some part of the festival: introducing a ballad or folktale and giving a little information about it, reading a heroic tale, telling a folktale, or being in the play *Duffy and the Devil*. Both guests and children thoroughly enjoyed the festival. All agreed that the oral tradition was alive in that fifth-grade class.

The Way of Danger: The Drama of Theseus

During a study of Greek mythology, one university student developed a creative dramatization around the adventures of the Greek hero Theseus. With a group of fifth-grade students, she read Ian Serraillier's *The Way of Danger: The Story of Theseus* and other myths about Theseus. The children located the settings for Theseus's adventures and plotted his travels on a map.

Next, with guidance, the group outlined the life of Theseus into the major scenes they wished to portray. Then, they dramatized their story. The outline in Chart 6–9 resulted from their planning.

Additional Ways to Use Traditional Literature for Creative Dramatics

Mythology and other traditional literature are filled with tales that lend themselves to creative interpretations. Following are a few ideas that children's literature students, classroom teachers, and librarians have performed successfully:

1 Following the reading of King Midas, a group of children performed the story. Later, the children divided into groups and chose an object other than gold as an obsession. Each performed the King Midas story as if every-

CHART 6–9
The Life of Theseus

I. *Theseus as a boy*
   A. Aethra and Aegeus (his mother and father)
   B. Theseus and Aethra (his mother)
   C. Theseus and Pittheus (his grandfather)
II. *Theseus journeys to Athens*
   A. He meets the Club-bearer
   B. He meets the Foot-washer
   C. He meets the Stretcher
III. *Theseus meets his father, the king*
   A. He encounters Medea, the sorceress
   B. He is remembered by his father
IV. *Theseus and the Minotaur*
   A. Theseus travels to Crete
   B. He encounters Minos, the wicked king
   C. Ariadne saves Theseus from the Minotaur
   D. Theseus returns to Athens

thing the king touched turned to an object such as ice cream, chocolate, or money.

2 A teacher read the Greek myth about Meleager to students, omitting the part where the queen burns the fire that kills Meleager. The teacher guided the children in developing a court trial for the purpose of identifying Meleager's killer, including a judge, defense lawyers, prosecution lawyers, witnesses, suspects, and a jury. The class conducted a trial, and the lawyers elicited stories from each witness and suspect. Each player developed a story according to the facts presented in the literature. The jury members discussed their opinions, provided rationales, and then voted on who they believed was the guilty person. After the court trial, the teacher shared the real ending of the story with the group.

3 After reading myths about Poseidon, the ancient Greek god of the sea, children became interested in his challenge to Athena, the warlike goddess of wisdom and patron of the city of Athens. Poseidon wanted to rule Athens. The gods, however, decided that the city should be awarded to whichever of them could produce the gift most useful to mortals. Athena gave mortals the olive tree and thereby won the contest. The students accomplished several creative activities motivated by this myth. They debated which gift was the most useful, Poseidon's or Athena's; they developed short plays showing the desirability of each; and they created other challenges and acted out the results.

4 After reading Cohen's or Hastings's adaptation of Geoffrey Chaucer's *Canterbury Tales,* including the prologue, in which Cohen introduces the contest for the best oral tale, the students created their own pilgrimage to Canterbury. Thus, they prepared and told stories that might have been told during that time period.

5 After reading Margot Fonteyn's *Swan Lake* and enjoying Trina Shart Hyman's illustrations that accompany Fonteyn's written interpretation of the ballet, the students added movement to the words and created their own ballet.

INTERPRETING TRADITIONAL IMAGES IN ART

Traditional tales, especially those that have not been written in simplified language, are filled with passages that evoke visual images. Such tales can

Children enjoy making a gingerbread house after listening to "Hansel and Gretel."

inspire young artists to re-create the birth of the Greek goddess Aphrodite out of the foaming, shimmering sea; to depict the sacred lake where a Native American boy waits for the buffalo to appear; or to portray the cave of an evil flying dragon, where a Chinese girl is held captive.

Allowing children to experience the artistic moods of traditional literature through paints, chalk, or crayons helps the children extend their enjoyment. For example, you could use the Norse tale "The Valkyrie" from Olivia E. Coolidge's *Legends of the North* to stimulate children to draw or paint pictures in shades of the hottest colors. To aid the children, ask the following questions: What are the dancing flames that attract Sigurd to venture toward the glowing horizon? What is the circling pillar of smoke? Have robbers burned a citadel? Has a dragon breathed fire on the farmlands of a great king? Such questions help children to interpret Sigurd's adventures. As you read a passage such as the following, have the children close their eyes and try to visualize color and mood, and then express the images in color on paper:

> By dawn Sigurd could hear the hissing of the fire. Greyfell picked his way with care over the hot faces of the rock, which were bathed in a bright red light. The flames made a ring of flickering points, now sinking, now flaring, now parting, now shooting out over the sides of the mountain as though caught in a sudden wind. (p. 105)

Folktales, fables, myths, and legends contain scenes, characters, and story lines that are excellent stimuli for artistic expression. The tales encourage children to create imaginary worlds in chalk, paint, and other media.

Suggested Activities for Children's Understanding of Traditional Literature

- ☐ Choose a folktale of interest, prepare the story for telling, and share the story with one child or a group of children.
- ☐ Select a cumulative tale, such as "The Gingerbread Boy," or a simple folktale, such as "The Three Bears," and prepare it as a feltboard story. Share the story with one child or a group.
- ☐ Select a folktale that has many versions from diverse cultures. For example, "Sleeping Beauty" is found in many cultures. What questions should you ask children when they investigate the tales? Develop a chart similar to the one in the text for Cinderella. What are the key similarities and differences? How do the tales reflect the culture? List the conclusions that you and the children made from the folktales.
- ☐ With a peer group, select a country to investigate. Develop a list of appropriate traditional tales and a list of related examples of art, music, and so forth. Design some activities to help children develop an understanding of the country.
- ☐ Choose a folktale that has rapid action appropriate for pantomiming. Lead a peer group or a group of children through the pantomime.
- ☐ Lead a peer group or a group of children through the four steps described in this chapter for developing creative interpretations: (1) stimulating interest, (2) presenting the story, (3) guiding the planning and presentation of the creative dramatization, and (4) helping the group evaluate the presentation.
- ☐ Compile a file of creative writing ideas motivated by traditional literature.
- ☐ Select a story from traditional literature that evokes visual images. Share the selection with a child, and encourage the child to interpret the story using paints, chalk, or crayons.
- ☐ Compile a file of folktales that contain vivid word pictures. Discuss ways to use these tales to help children interpret the moods through art.

References

1 Bingham, Jane M., and Grayce Scholt. "The Great Glass Slipper Search: Using Folk Tales with Older Children." *Elementary English* 51 (October 1974): 990–998.

2 Cook, Elizabeth. *The Ordinary and the Fabulous: An Introduction to Myths, Legends, and Fairy Tales*. 2d ed. Cambridge: University Press, 1976.

3 Kuo, Louise, and Yuan-hsi Kuo. *Chinese Folk Tales*. Millbrae, Calif.: Celestial Arts, 1976.

4 McIntyre, Barbara M. *Creative Drama in the Elementary School*. Itasca, Ill.: Peacock, 1974.

5 Miller, Winifred. "Dragons—Fact or Fantasy?" *Elementary English* 52 (April 1975): 582–585.

6 Nelson, Mary Ann. *A Comparative Anthology of Children's Literature*. New York: Holt, Rinehart & Winston, 1972.

7 Norton, Donna E. *The Effective Teaching of Language Arts*. Columbus, Ohio: Merrill, 1989.

8 Norton, Donna E. "Folklore and the Language Arts." In *Language Arts Instruction and the Beginning Teacher,* edited by Dale Johnson and Carl Personke. Englewood Cliffs, N.J.: Prentice-Hall, 1987.

9 Paulin, Mary Ann. *Creative Uses of Children's Literature*. Hamden, Conn.: Library Professional Pubs., 1985.

10 Ross, Elinor P. "Comparison of Folk Tale Variants." *Language Arts* 56 (April 1979): 422–426.

11 Ross, Ramon Royal. *Storyteller*. 2d ed. Columbus, Ohio: Merrill, 1980.

12 Siks, Geraldine. *Drama with Children*. New York: Harper & Row, 1977.

13 Stewig, John Warren. "Storyteller: Endangered Species?" *Language Arts* 55 (March 1978): 339–345.

14 Sutherland, Zena, and Myra Cohn Livingston. *The Scott, Foresman Anthology of Children's Literature*. Glenview, Ill.: Scott, Foresman, 1984.

15 Travers, P. T. *About the Sleeping Beauty*. Illustrated by Charles Keeping. New York: McGraw-Hill, 1975.

16 Western, Linda. "A Comparative Study of Literature Through Folk Tale Variants." *Language Arts* 57 (April 1980): 395–402.

CHILDREN'S LITERATURE

FOLKTALES

African—Black

See Chapter 11.

American—Native American

See Chapter 11.

Asian

Asian Cultural Centre for UNESCO. *Folk Tales from Asia for Children Everywhere.* Book Three. Weatherhill, 1976 (I:8–12 R:6). Stories are from Afghanistan, Burma, Indonesia, Iran, Japan, Pakistan, Singapore, Sri Lanka, and Vietnam.

———. *Folk Tales from Asia for Children Everywhere.* Book Four. Weatherhill, 1976 (I:8–12 R:6). Folktales are from Bangladesh, Cambodia, India, Korea, Laos, Malaysia, Nepal, Philippines, and Thailand.

———. *Folk Tales from Asia for Children Everywhere.* Book Five. Weatherhill, 1977 (I:8–12 R:6). Stories are from India, Philippines, Pakistan, Japan, Malaysia, Burma, and Iran.

Bang, Molly. *The Paper Crane.* Mulberry Books, 1987 (I:8+ R:5). A paper crane brings success.

Carrison, Muriel. *Cambodian Folk Stories from the Gatiloke.* Tuttle, 1987 (I:8+ R:7). A collection of tales originated in the teachings of Buddhist monks.

Clark, Ann Nolan. *In the Land of Small Dragon.* Illustrated by Tony Chen. Viking, 1979 (I:7–12 R:7). This is a Vietnamese variation of Cinderella.

Conger, David. *Many Lands, Many Stories: Asian Folktales for Children.* Illustrated by Ruth Ra. Tuttle, 1987 (I:8+ R:5). Fifteen folktales are identified by their countries of origin.

de Roin, Nancy. *Jakata Tales.* Houghton Mifflin, 1975 (I:7–9 R:5). This text includes animal tales from India.

Ginsburg, Mirra, ed. *The Chinese Mirror.* Illustrated by Margot Zemach. Harcourt Brace Jovanovich, 1988 (I:5–8 R:4). A mirror causes confusion in a Korean folktale.

Haviland, Virginia. *Favorite Fairy Tales Told in India.* Illustrated by Blair Lent. Little, Brown, 1973 (I:8–10 R:5). This is a collection of characteristic tales.

Hearn, Lafcadio. *The Voice of the Great Bell.* Retold by Margaret Hodges. Illustrated by Ed Young. Little, Brown, 1989 (I:7+ R:6). A girl gives her life for her father in a Chinese tale.

Heyer, Marilee. *The Weaving of a Dream: A Chinese Folktale.* Viking, 1986 (I:8+ R:5). This is a retelling of "The Chuang Brocade."

Hyun, Peter, ed. *Korea's Favorite Tales and Lyrics.* Illustrated by Dong-il Park. Tuttle/Seoul International, 1986 (I:5–10 R:6). This is a collection of folktales, poems, and stories.

Iké, Jane, and Baruch Zimmerman. *A Japanese Fairy Tale.* Warne, 1982 (I:5–8 R:5). A man takes the disfiguration of his future wife.

Ishii, Momoko. *The Tongue-Cut Sparrow.* Translated by Katherine Paterson. Illustrated by Suekichi Akaba. Dutton, 1987 (I:7–10 R:6). A kind man and a greedy wife receive quite different rewards.

Lang, Andrew. *Aladdin and the Wonderful Lamp.* Illustrated by Errol LeCain. Viking, 1981 (I:7–9 R:6). Deep color and ornamentation appropriately illustrate a tale from *The Arabian Nights.*

Laurin, Anne. *The Perfect Crane.* Illustrated by Charles Mikolaycak. Harper & Row, 1981 (I:5–9 R:6). A Japanese tale tells about the friendship between a magician and the crane he creates from rice paper.

Lee, Jeanne M. *Legend of the Milky Way.* Holt, Rinehart & Winston, 1982 (I:6–9 R:5). A heavenly princess and her earthly husband are transformed into stars.

Louie, Ai-Lang. *Yeh Shen: A Cinderella Story from China.* Illustrated by Ed Young. Philomel, 1982 (I:7–9 R:6). This ancient Chinese tale has many similarities with versions from other cultures.

Mahy, Margaret. Retold by. *The Seven Chinese Brothers.* Illustrated by Jean and Mou-Sien Tseng. Scholastic, 1990 (I:5–8 R:4). Watercolors complement the traditional tale.

Mosel, Arlene. *The Funny Little Woman.* Illustrated by Blair Lent. Dutton, 1972 (I:5–8 R:5). A little woman pursues a rice dumpling and is captured by wicked people.

Newton, Patricia Montgomery. *The Five Sparrows: A Japanese Folktale.* Atheneum, 1982 (I:5–8 R:6). Kindness is rewarded and greed is punished.

Philip, Neil, ed. *The Spring of Butterflies and Other Folktales of China's Minority Peoples.* Translated by He Liyi. Illustrated by Pan Aiqing and Li Zhao. Lothrop, Lee & Shepard, 1986 (I:9+ R:6). These tales are from northwestern China.

I = Interest by age range.
R = Readability by grade level.

Pratt, Davis, and Elsa Kula. *Magic Animals of Japan*. Parnassus, 1967 (I:8–12 R:7). These are tales of the fabled creatures of Japan.

Roberts, Moss. *Chinese Fairy Tales and Fantasies*. Pantheon, 1979 (I:10 R:6). A collection of tales tells about enchantment, greed, animals, women, ghosts, and judges.

Snyder, Dianne. *The Boy of the Three-Year Nap*. Illustrated by Allen Say. Houghton Mifflin, 1988 (I:all R:6). A Japanese woman tricks her lazy son into working.

Yagawa, Sumika, ed. *The Crane Wife*. Translated by Katherine Paterson. Illustrated by Suekichi Akaba. Morrow, 1981 (I:7–10 R:6). A husband loses his wife when he breaks his promise.

Yep, Laurence. *The Rainbow People*. Illustrated by David Wiesner. Harper & Row, 1989 (I:9+ R:6). Twenty Chinese folktales were collected from Chinese Americans.

Young, Ed. Translated by. *Lon Po Po: A Red-Riding Hood Story from China*. Philomel, 1989 (I:all R:5). The girls outwit the wolf in this version of the tale.

British (United Kingdom)

Brett, Jan. *Goldilocks and the Three Bears*. Dodd, Mead, 1987 (I:3–7 R:6). This is a highly illustrated version of the folktale.

Briggs, Katharine. *British Folktales*. Pantheon, 1977 (I:all). An adult anthology also provides many sources for children.

Buchan, David, ed. *Scottish Tradition: A Collection of Scottish Folk Literature*. Routledge & Kegan Paul, 1984 (I:9+ R:5). A large adult collection provides selections for oral sharing.

Cauley, Lorinda Bryan. *The Cock, the Mouse, and the Little Red Hen*. Putnam, 1982 (I:3–6 R:4). The repetitive language appeals to young children.

———. *Goldilocks and the Three Bears*. Putnam, 1981 (I:3–7 R:4). Large colorful illustrations appeal to children.

Chaucer, Geoffrey. *Canterbury Tales*. Adapted by Barbara Cohen. Illustrated by Trina Schart Hyman. Lothrop, Lee & Shepard, 1988 (I:8+ R:6). Four tales include the prologue and an introduction.

———. *The Canterbury Tales*. Retold by Selina Hastings. Illustrated by Reg Cartwright. Holt, Rinehart & Winston, 1988 (I:8+ R:5). This volume includes seven tales.

Cooper, Susan. Retold by. *The Silver Cow: A Welsh Tale*. Illustrated by Warwick Hutton. Atheneum, 1983 (I:5–8 R:5). A cow and her offspring return to the lake because of a farmer's greed.

Crossley-Holland, Kevin. *British Folk Tales*. Watts, 1988 (I:8+ R:5). A large collection of tales includes sources and notes.

de Paola, Tomie. *The Friendly Beasts: An Old English Christmas Carol*. Putnam, 1981 (I:3–9). The Bethlehem setting is depicted in this folk song.

Galdone, Paul. *The Little Red Hen*. Seabury, 1973 (I:3–7 R:3). The industrious hen won't share her cake with her lazy friends.

———. *The Three Bears*. Seabury, 1972 (I:3–7 R:5). The traditional tale is illustrated with large, humorous pictures.

———. *The Three Sillies*. Houghton Mifflin, 1981 (I:3–7 R:2). Colorful, humorous illustrations add to this tale about a man's search for three people sillier than his future in-laws.

———. *What's in Fox's Sack? An Old English Tale*. Clarion, 1982 (I:3–7 R:2). A fox is outsmarted by a woman who puts a bulldog in his bag.

Garner, Alan. *Alan Garner's Book of British Fairy Tales*. Illustrated by Derek Collard. Delacorte, 1985 (I:9–12 R:6). Twenty-one tales include some that are not familiar.

———. *A Bag of Moonshine*. Illustrated by Patrick James Lynch. Collins, 1986 (I:5–9 R:4). A collection contains twenty-two folktales.

Glassie, Henry, ed. *Irish Folktales*. Viking, 1987 (I:all). An adult source has many tales that may be shared with children.

Godden, Rumer. *The Dragon of Og*. Illustrated by Pauline Baynes. Viking, 1981 (I:9–12 R:6). A Scottish tale tells about the new lord who refuses to give bullocks from his herd to the dragon.

Huck, Charlotte. Retold by. *Princess Furball*. Illustrated by Anita Lobel. Greenwillow, 1989 (I:6–10 R:6). The Cinderella-type character in this tale does not rely on magic.

Jacobs, Joseph. *Celtic Fairy Tales*. Illustrated by John D. Batten. David Nutt, 1890; reissued 1968 (I:9+ R:6). This is a selection of Celtic, Irish, and Gaelic tales.

———. *Irish Fairy Tales*. Illustrated by John D. Batten. David Nutt, 1889; Castle, 1984 (I:9 R:6). Twenty-six tales from Celtic Ireland.

———. *More English Fairy Tales*. David Nutt, 1894 (I:all R:6). The English collector includes more tales.

Jones, Gwyn. *Welsh Legends and Folk-Tales*. Oxford, 1955, Puffin, 1982 (I:9+ R:7). This is a collection of over thirty Welsh tales.

Kellogg, Steven. *Chicken Little*. Morrow, 1985 (I:5–8 R:5). This is a humorous, modern version of the tale, with cars, trucks, and helicopters.

Marshall, James. *Goldilocks and the Three Bears*. Dial, 1988 (I:3–8 R:5). Humorous illustrations add to the folktale.

Zemach, Harve. *Duffy and the Devil*. Illustrated by Margot Zemach. Farrar, Straus & Giroux, 1973 (I:8–12 R:6). A Cornish tale resembles "Rumplestiltskin," but the maid makes an agreement with the devil.

French

Brett, Jan. Retold by. *Beauty and the Beast*. Clarion, 1989 (I:8–12 R:6). Tapestries show the real characters.

de Beaumont, Madame. *Beauty and the Beast*. Translated and illustrated by Diane Goode. Bradbury, 1978 (I:8–14 R:7). Lovely illustrations accompany the tale of a girl who is willing to sacrifice her own life for the love of her father.

Hutton, Warwick. Retold by. *Beauty and the Beast*. Atheneum, 1985 (I:9 R:6). Love breaks an evil spell.

Perrault, Charles. *Cinderella*. Illustrated by Marcia Brown. Scribner's Sons, 1954 (I:5–8 R:5). Fine lines suggest the mood of the fairy tale.

———. *Favorite Fairy Tales*. Edited by Jennifer Mulherin. Grosset, 1983 (I:all R:7). An eighteenth-century version includes original illustrations.

———. *The Glass Slipper: Charles Perrault's Tales of Time Past*. Translated by John Bierhorst. Illustrated by Mitchell Miller. Four Winds, 1981 (I:9–12 R:6). This is a new translation of *Histoires ou contes du temps passé*.

———. *Histories or Tales of Past Times*. Garland, 1977 (I:10+ R:6). This is a reprint of the 1729 London edition.

———. *Puss in Boots*. Illustrated by Marcia Brown. Scribner's Sons, 1952 (I:5–8 R:5). A faithful cat helps his master.

———. *The Sleeping Beauty*. Translated and illustrated by David Walker. Crowell, 1976 (I:8–14 R:6). A beautifully illustrated book resembles the stage setting for an opera or ballet.

———. *Tom Thumb*. Retold and illustrated by Lidia Postma. Schocken, 1983 (I:6–9 R:6). Detailed illustrations accompany the classic tale.

German

de Regniers, Beatrice Schenk. *Red Riding Hood*. Illustrated by Edward Gorey. Atheneum, 1972 (I:4–8 R:2). A verse format of the story is based on the version by the Brothers Grimm.

Galdone, Paul. *Hansel and Gretel*. McGraw-Hill, 1982 (I:5–7 R:3). The folktale is appropriate for younger children.

———. *Little Red Riding Hood*. McGraw-Hill, 1974 (I:4–8 R:4). Large, colorful pictures retell the Grimms' folktale.

Grimm, Brothers. *The Bremen Town Musicians*. Retold and illustrated by Ilse Plume. Doubleday, 1980 (I:5–8 R:5). Soft, color illustrations show animals going through the forest.

———. *The Bremen Town Musicians*. Illustrated by Josef Palecek. Picture Book Studio, 1988 (I:3–6 R:4). This version contains large, colorful illustrations.

———. *Cinderella*. Illustrated by Nonny Hogrogian. Greenwillow, 1981 (I:6–12 R:6). This is an attractive version of the German tale.

———. *The Complete Brothers Grimm Fairy Tales*. Edited by Lily Owens. Avenel, 1981 (I:all R:7). The tales were previously published in *Grimms' Household Tales*.

———. *The Devil with the Three Golden Hairs*. Retold and illustrated by Nonny Hogrogian. Knopf, 1983 (I:5–9 R:7). A boy completes a quest to earn the king's daughter for his bride.

———. *Favorite Tales from Grimm*. Retold and illustrated by Mercer Mayer. Four Winds, 1982 (I:7–10 R:6). This book contains twenty illustrated stories.

———. *The Fox and the Cat: Animal Tales from Grimm*. Translated by Kevin Crossley-Holland and Susan Varley. Illustrated by Susan Varley. Lothrop, Lee & Shepard, 1986 (I:9+ R:6). This is an anthology of animal folktales.

———. *The Golden Goose*. Illustrated by Diane Paterson. Troll, 1981. A younger son's generosity wins him a princess.

———. *Hansel and Gretel*. Illustrated by Anthony Browne. Watts, 1982 (I:9–12 R:5). Illustrations show a contemporary setting that should be interesting for a comparative study.

———. *Hansel and Gretel*. Illustrated by Susan Jeffers. Dial, 1980 (I:5–9 R:6). The illustrations with strong lines and a magnificent gingerbread house should appeal to readers.

———. *Hansel and Gretel*. Retold by Rika Lesser. Illustrated by Paul O. Zelinsky. Dodd, Mead, 1984 (I:all R:6). Full-page illustrations depict a dark forest of an earlier time.

———. *Hansel and Gretel*. Translated by Anthea Bell. Illustrated by Otto S. Svend. Larousse, 1983 (I:6–9 R:7). This is an English translation of the folktale published in Denmark.

———. *Little Red Cap*. Translated by Elizabeth Crawford. Illustrated by Lisbeth Zwerger. Morrow, 1983 (I:4–7 R:4). The folktale tells about a deceitful wolf.

———. *Little Red Riding Hood*. Retold and illustrated by Trina Schart Hyman. Holiday House, 1983 (I:6–9 R:7). Richly detailed page borders add to this attractive version.

———. *The Musicians of Bremen*. Translated by Anne Rogers. Illustrated by Otto S. Svend. Larousse, 1974 (I:4–8 R:6). An old dog, donkey, cat, and rooster decide to become musicians.

———. *Rapunzel: From the Brothers Grimm*. Retold by Barbara Rogasky. Illustrated by Trina Schart Hyman. Holiday House, 1982 (I:6–9 R:6). The forest setting seems right for a girl imprisoned in a high tower.

———. *Rumpelstiltskin*. Retold and illustrated by Paul O. Zelinsky. Dutton, 1986 (I:all R:6). A miller's daughter spins gold with the help of a supernatural being.

———. *The Seven Ravens*. Translated by Elizabeth Crawford. Illustrated by Lisbeth Zwerger. Morrow, 1981 (I:6–9 R:6). A girl frees her brothers from an enchantment.

———. *The Six Swans*. Illustrated by Adrie Hospes. McGraw-Hill, 1973 (I:7–12 R:5). A sister saves six brothers enchanted by their evil stepmother.

———. *The Sleeping Beauty*. Illustrated by Warwick Hutton. Atheneum, 1979 (I:7–12 R:6). Watercolors illustrate a story of magic and enchantment.

———. *Snow White and the Seven Dwarfs*. Translated by Randal Jarrell. Illustrated by Nancy Ekholm Burkert. Farrar, Straus & Giroux, 1972 (I:7–12 R:6). The illustrations were carefully researched by the artist to show the Black Forest and German heritage.

———. *The Traveling Musicians*. Illustrated by Hans Fischer. Harcourt Brace Jovanovich, 1955 (I:7+ R:6). Animals save their lives by singing.

———. *The Twelve Dancing Princesses*. Illustrated by Errol LeCain. Viking, 1978 (I:7–12 R:7). Twelve princesses mysteriously dance holes in their shoes every night.

———. *The Twelve Dancing Princesses*. Retold by Marianna Mayer. Illustrated by Kinuko Craft. Morrow, 1989 (I:8+ R:5). Beautiful paintings accompany the tale.

———. *The Twelve Dancing Princesses and Other Tales from Grimm*. Illustrated by Lidia Postma. Dial, 1986 (I:9–12 R:5). This is an anthology of German tales.

———. *The Water of Life*. Retold by Barbara Rogasky. Illustrated by Trina Schart Hyman. Holiday House, 1986 (I:4–9 R:3). A quest leads the youngest son to a princess.

———. *The Wolf and the Seven Little Kids*. Translated by Anne Rogers. Illustrated by Otto S. Svend. Larousse, 1977 (I:4–8 R:4). Seven little goats have a conflict with a wolf when their mother leaves the house.

Grimm, Wilhelm. *Dear Mili*. Translated by Ralph Manheim. Illustrated by Maurice Sendak. Farrar, Straus & Giroux, 1988 (I:all R:6). The story was found in a letter written in 1816.

Marshall, James. *Red Riding Hood*. Dial, 1987 (I:3–8 R:5). Cartoonlike illustrations develop a humorous text.

Hispanic

See Chapter 11.

Jewish

Singer, Isaac Bashevis. *The Golem*. Illustrated by Uri Shulevitz. Farrar, Straus & Giroux, 1982 (I:8+ R:5). This is another version of a Jewish folktale.

———. *Mazel and Shlimazel, or the Milk of the Lioness*. Illustrated by Margot Zemach. Farrar, Straus & Giroux, 1967 (I:8–12 R:4). Mazel, the spirit of good luck, and Shlimazel, the spirit of bad luck, have a contest.

———. *When Shlemiel Went to Warsaw & Other Stories*. Illustrated by Margot Zemach. Farrar, Straus & Giroux, 1968 (I:8–12 R:4). This is a collection of both folktales and original stories.

Zemach, Margot. *It Could Always Be Worse*. Farrar, Straus & Giroux, 1977 (I:5–9 R:2). A small hut seems larger when all the animals are removed.

Norwegian

Asbjörnsen, Peter Christian, and Jorgen E. Moe. *Norwegian Folk Tales*. Illustrated by Erik Werenskiold and Theodor Kittelsen. Viking, 1960 (I:6–10 R:3). This is a collection of thirty-five Norwegian folktales.

———. *The Three Billy Goats Gruff*. Illustrated by Marcia Brown. Harcourt Brace Jovanovich, 1957 (I:3–7 R:5). Goats prance across the pages of this favorite tale for telling.

Booss, Claire, ed. *Scandinavian Folk & Fairy Tales*. Avenel, 1984 (I:10+). A large adult collection of tales from Norway, Sweden, Denmark, Finland, and Iceland will provide sources for storytelling.

Galdone, Paul. *The Three Billy Goats Gruff*. Seabury, 1973 (I:5–8 R:5). A picture storybook tells about three billy goats who defeat the troll who lives under the bridge.

Hague, Kathleen, and Michael Hague. *East of the Sun and West of the Moon*. Harcourt Brace Jovanovich, 1980 (I:7–9 R:5). A maiden lives in the castle of an enchanted white bear.

Haviland, Virginia. *Favorite Fairy Tales Told in Norway*. Illustrated by Leonard Weisgard. Little, Brown, 1961 (I:6–10 R:4). This collection includes "The Princess on the Glass Hill," "Why the Sea Is Salt," "The Three Billy Goats Gruff," "Taper Tom," "Why the Bear Is Stumpy-Tailed," "The Lad and the North Wind," and "Boots and the Troll."

Magnus, Erica. Adapted by. *Old Lars*. Carolrhoda, 1984 (I:4–7 R:3). This is a humorous Norwegian folktale about an old man who goes up the mountain to load wood.

Mayer, Mercer. *East of the Sun and West of the Moon*. Four Winds, 1980 (I:8–10 R:4). This is a beautifully illustrated version of the Asbjörnsen and Moe tale.

Willard, Nancy. *East of the Sun & West of the Moon: A Play*. Illustrated by Barry Moser. Harcourt Brace Jovanovich, 1989 (I:all). This retelling uses both narrative and poetry.

Russian

Afanasev, Aleksandr Nikolaevich. *Russian Folk Tales*. Translated by Robert Chandler. Illustrated by Ivan I. Bilibin. Random House, 1980 (I:8–12 R:7). Seven memorable tales were collected by the nineteenth-century folklorist.

Bain, R. Nisbet, ed. *Cossack Fairy Tales and Folktales*. Illustrated by E. W. Mitchell. Core Collection, 1976 (I:9+ R:7). Twenty-seven western Ukrainian folktales are reprinted from an 1894 edition.

Daniels, Guy. *The Peasant's Pea Patch*. Illustrated by Robert Quackenbush. Delacorte, 1971 (I:5–9 R:4). A merry Russian tale tells about a poor peasant who tries to protect his pea patch.

Fonteyn, Margot. *Swan Lake*. Illustrated by Trina Schart Hyman. Harcourt Brace Jovanovich, 1989 (I:all R:6). This is a retelling of the opera.

Helprin, Mark. *Swan Lake*. Illustrated by Chris Van Allsburg. Houghton Mifflin, 1989 (I:all R:6). This is a retelling of the opera.

Isele, Elizabeth. Retold by. *The Frog Princess*. Illustrated by Michael Hague. Crowell, 1984 (I:6–10 R:4). A czar's son marries the enchanted Vasilisa the Wise.

Kismaric, Carole. *The Rumor of Pavel and Paali: A Ukrainian Folktale*. Illustrated by Charles Mikolaycak. Harper & Row, 1988 (I:6–9 R:6). In the battle between good and evil, evil wins first but good finally overcomes.

McCurdy, Michael. *The Devils Who Learned to Be Good*. Little, Brown, 1987 (I:6–9 R:6). An old soldier outwits several devils in this Russian folktale.

Mikolaycak, Charles. Retold by. *Babushka*.Holiday House, 1984 (I:6–9 R:7). An old woman leaves gifts as she searches for the Christ Child.

Otsuka, Yūzō. *Suho and the White Horse: A Legend of Mongolia*. Adapted from Ann Herring's translation. Illustrated by Suekichi Akaba. Viking, 1981 (I:5–8 R:6). In a tale about good versus evil, a herdsman's horse is killed because of a nobleman's greed.

Pushkin, Alexander. *The Tale of Czar Saltan or the Prince and the Swan Princess*. Translated by Patricia Tracy Lowe. Illustrated by I. Bilibin. Crowell, 1975 (I:8–12 R:6). The czar marries the youngest daughter, but her sisters trick her into exile.

———. *The Tale of the Golden Cockerel*. Translated by Patricia Tracy Lowe. Illustrated by I. Bilibin. Crowell, 1975 (I:8–12 R:6). A czar fails to keep his promise to a sorcerer.

Ransome, Arthur. *The Fool of the World and the Flying Ship*. Illustrated by Uri Shulevitz. Farrar, Straus & Giroux, 1968 (I:6–10 R:6). A simple lad overcomes obstacles to wed the czar's daughter.

———. *Old Peter's Russian Tales*. Jonathan Cape, 1916, 1985 (I:7+ R:6). This is a collection of tales.

Sherman, Josepha. *Vassilisa the Wise: A Tale of Medieval Russia*. Illustrated by Daniel San Souci. Harcourt Brace Jovanovich, 1988 (I:8+ R:6). A clever woman outwits a prince and saves her husband.

Silverman, Maida. Retold by. *Anna and the Seven Swans*. Illustrated by David Small. Morrow, 1984 (I:6–9 R:6). Anna searches for her brother, who was taken by Baba Yaga.

Other Folktales

Aardema, Verna. *Why Mosquitoes Buzz in People's Ears: A West African Tale*. Illustrated by Leo and Diane Dillon. Dial, 1975 (I:5–9 R:6). A cumulative African folktale tells the humorous reason for mosquitoes' buzzing.

Baker, Olaf. *Where the Buffaloes Began*. Illustrated by Stephen Gammell. Warne, 1981 (I:8 R:7). Illustrations with soft, irregular shapes add power to a Native American legend.

Blair, Walter. *Tall Tale America: A Legendary History of Our Humorous Heroes*. Illustrated by Glen Rounds. Coward, McCann, 1944 (I:8–12 R:5). This is a collection of exaggerated tales.

Carew, Jan. *The Third Gift*. Illustrated by Leo and Diane Dillon. Little, Brown, 1974 (I:7+ R:7). A beautifully illustrated tale tells how the Jubas gained the gifts of work, beauty, imagination, and faith.

Chase, Richard. Retold by. *The Jack Tales*. Illustrated by Berkeley Williams, Jr. Houghton Mifflin, 1943 (I:all R:5). This collection of tales is from the southern Appalachians.

Day, Edward C. *John Tabor's Ride*. Illustrated by Dirk Zimmer. Knopf, 1989 (I:8+ R:5). This text is a retelling of a tall tale.

Galdone, Paul. *The Amazing Pig: An Old Hungarian Tale*. Houghton Mifflin, 1981 (I:5–8 R:3). In this humorous tale, a king promises his daughter in marriage to any man who tells him something he cannot believe.

Ginsburg, Mirra. *Two Greedy Bears*. Illustrated by Jose Aruego and Ariane Dewey. Macmillan, 1976 (I:3–6 R:4). In this Hungarian tale, two greedy bears fight over cheese, but a fox solves the problem by eating the cheese.

Haley, Gail E. *Jack and the Bean Tree*. Crown, 1986 (I:4–10 R:5). This is an Appalachian variant of "Jack and the Beanstalk."

Harris, Joel Chandler. *Told by Uncle Remus*. McClure, Philips & Co., 1905 (I:all R:4). More adventures of Brer Rabbit are told.

———. *Uncle Remus and His Friends*. Houghton Mifflin, 1892 (I:all R:4). Tales are told of Brer Rabbit's adventures.

Haviland, Virginia. *Favorite Fairy Tales Told in Italy*. Illustrated by Evaline Ness. Little, Brown, 1967 (I:6–10 R:4). This is a fine source of Italian folktales.

Highwater, Jamake. *Anapao: An American Indian Odyssey.* Illustrated by Fritz Scholder. Lippincott, 1977 (I:12+ R:6). Anapao journeys across the history of Native American traditional tales in order to search for his destiny.

Hodges, Margaret. Retold by. *The Fire Bringer: A Paiute Indian Legend.* Illustrated by Peter Parnall. Little, Brown, 1972 (I:7–10 R:6). Coyote leads the Paiutes on a dangerous quest for fire.

Hooks, William H. *Moss Gown.* Illustrated by Donald Carrick. Clarion, 1987 (I:8+ R:5). This Cinderella-type folktale is from eastern North Carolina.

Jaquith, Patricia. *Bo Rabbit Smart for True: Folktales from the Gullah.* Illustrated by Ed Young. Philomel, 1981 (I:all R:6). These four tales are from islands off the Georgia coast.

Kellogg, Stephen. Retold by. *Johnny Appleseed.* Illustrated by Stephen Kellogg. Morrow, 1988 (I:6–9 R:6). This version of the tall tale is highly illustrated.

———. *Paul Bunyan.* Retold by. Morrow, 1984 (I:6–9 R:7). This version of the tall tale is highly illustrated.

Kurtycz, Marcos, and Ana Garcia Kobeh. *Tigers and Opossums: Animal Legends.* Translated by Felicia Hall. Little, Brown, 1984 (I:all R:8). These are animal tales from Mexico.

Martin, Eva. Retold by. *Canadian Fairy Tales.* Illustrated by Laszlo Gal. Douglas & McIntyre, 1984 (I:7–10 R:4). Twelve traditional tales reflect the Canadian influence on the French, Irish, and British oral traditions.

Toye, William. *The Loon's Necklace.* Illustrated by Elizabeth Cleaver. Oxford University Press, 1977 (I:all R:5). This tale explains how the loon received the lovely shell markings around its neck and across its wings.

FABLES

Aesop. *Aesop's Fables.* Retold by Anne Terry White. Illustrated by Helen Siegle. Random House, 1964 (I:6–10 R:3). Forty of Aesop's fables are told in story format.

———. *Aesop's Fables.* Illustrated by Heidi Holder. Viking, 1981 (I:9–12 R:7). Nine fables are illustrated with full-color paintings.

———. *Aesop's Fables.* Selected and illustrated by Michael Hague. Holt, Rinehart & Winston, 1985 (I:9–12 R:7). Thirteen fables are illustrated with full-page paintings.

———. *Aesop's Fables.* Translated by Sir Roger L'Estrange. Illustrated by Percy J. Billinghurst. Gallery, 1984 (I:9+). This is a reissue of the seventeenth-century translation.

———. *Aesop's Fables.* Illustrated by Charles Santore. Jelly Bean, 1988 (I:all R:6). Twenty-four fables are accompanied by large illustrations.

———. *Aesop's Fables.* Retold by Tom Paxton. Illustrated by Robert Rayevsky. Morrow, 1988 (I:all). The fables are retold in verse form.

———. *Aesop's Fables.* Illustrated by Fulvio Testa. Barron's, 1989 (I:all R:5). Twenty fables are in this collection.

Bierhorst, John. *Doctor Coyote: A Native American Aesop's Fables.* Illustrated by Wendy Watson. Macmillan, 1987 (I:all R:5). This is a fable from the Indians of Mexico.

Caldecott, Randolph. *The Caldecott Aesop: A Facsimile of the 1883 Edition.* Doubleday, 1978 (I:all R:7). This is a reproduction of the earlier Aesop's fables retold and illustrated by Caldecott.

Cauley, Lorinda Bryan. Retold by. *The Town Mouse and the Country Mouse.* Putnam, 1984 (I:6–8 R:5). This is a picture storybook version of the fable.

Stevens, Janet. Retold by. *The Tortoise and the Hare.* Holiday House, 1984 (I:6–8 R:3). This is a picture storybook version of the Aesop fable.

———. *The Town Mouse and the Country Mouse.* Holiday House, 1987 (I:6–8). This is a highly illustrated version of the Aesop fable.

MYTHOLOGY

Greek and Roman Myths

Barth, Edna. *Cupid and Psyche.* Illustrated by Ati Forberg. Seabury, 1976 (I:7–12 R:6). Princess Psyche is loved by Cupid but hated by Venus, the goddess of love.

Bulfinch, Thomas. *A Book of Myths.* Illustrated by Helen Sewell. Macmillan, 1942, 1964 (I:10+ R:6). A collection of Greek myths is written in short-story format.

———. *Myths of Greece & Rome.* Penguin, 1981 (paperback) (I:10 R:8). This is a good source for the myths.

Colum, Padraic. *The Golden Fleece and the Heroes Who Lived Before Achilles.* Illustrated by Willy Pogany. Macmillan, 1921, 1949, 1962 (I:9+ R:6). Jason and the Greek heroes search for the Golden Fleece.

Coolidge, Olivia. *Greek Myths.* Illustrated by Edouard Sandoz. Houghton Mifflin, 1949 (I:10+ R:7). This is an excellent collection of myths.

D'Aulaire, Ingri, and Edgar Parin D'Aulaire. *D'Aulaires' Book of Greek Myths.* Doubleday, 1962 (paperback, 1980) (I:8+ R:6). This collection of tales is about gods, goddesses, and heroes.

Evslin, Bernard. *Hercules.* Illustrated by Jos A. Smith. Morrow, 1984 (I:9 R:6). These are tales of a great hero.

Fisher, Leonard Everett. *The Olympians: Great Gods and Goddesses of Ancient Greece.* Holiday, 1984 (I:8 R:3). Brief biographies accompany large illustrations.

———. *Theseus and the Minotaur.* Holiday House, 1988 (I:8–12 R:6). Theseus defeats the monster in this heroic tale.

Gates, Doris. *The Golden God: Apollo.* Illustrated by Constantinos CoConis. Viking, 1973 (I:9+ R:6). This is a story of Apollo and his associations with other gods and goddesses.

———. *Lord of the Sky: Zeus.* Illustrated by Robert Handville. Viking, 1972 (I:10+ R:7). The myths center on Zeus.

———. *Two Queens of Heaven: Aphrodite and Demeter.* Illustrated by Trina Schart Hyman. Viking, 1974 (I:9+ R:5). A group of myths tells the exploits of Aphrodite and Demeter.

———. *The Warrior Goddess: Athena.* Illustrated by Don Bolognese. Viking, 1972 (I:9+ R:6). This book tells the exploits of the goddess Athena, Zeus's daughter.

Hamilton, Virginia. *In the Beginning: Creation Stories from Around the World.* Illustrated by Barry Moser. Harcourt Brace Jovanovich, 1988 (I:all R:6). Creation stories come from many cultures.

Hutton, Warwick. Retold by. *Theseus and the Minotaur.* Macmillan, 1989 (I:7–12 R:6). This is the Greek myth in which the hero kills the Minotaur.

Kingsley, Charles. *The Heroes.* Mayflower, 1980 (I:8+ R:6). These tales are of Greek heroes.

McDermott, Gerald. *Daughter of the Earth: A Roman Myth.* Delacorte, 1984 (I:8–12 R:6). A highly illustrated version tells of Pluto's kidnapping of Persephone.

———. *Sun Flight.* Four Winds, 1980 (I:all R:6). Daedalus, the master craftsman, and his son construct wings in an attempt to escape from Crete.

Richardson, I. M. *The Adventures of Hercules.* Illustrated by Robert Baxter. Troll, 1983 (I:9 R:6). The Roman hero performs twelve labors.

———. *Demeter and Persephone, The Seasons of Time*. Illustrated by Robert Baxter. Troll, 1983 (I:9 R:6). The Greek myth tells about Hades, Persephone, and Demeter.

———. *Prometheus and the Story of Fire*. Illustrated by Robert Baxter, Troll, 1983 (I:9 R:6). A Greek myth tells how Prometheus gave mortals fire.

Serraillier, Ian. *A Fall from the Sky*. Illustrated by William Stobbs. Walck, 1966 (I:10+ R:6). Daedalus is punished by the loss of his son.

———. *The Way of Danger: The Story of Theseus*. Illustrated by William Stobbs. Walck, 1963 (I:10+ R:5). The son of the king of Athens kills the Minotaur and rescues Theseus from the underworld.

Norse Myths and Epics

Colum, Padraic. *The Children of Odin: The Book of Northern Myths*. Illustrated by Willy Pogany. Macmillan, 1920, 1984 (I:9+ R:6). This book contains thirty-five tales.

Coolidge, Olivia E. *Legends of the North*. Illustrated by Edouard Sandoz. Houghton Mifflin, 1951 (I:9–14 R:6). This book contains the northern legends and the tales from the sagas.

Crossley-Holland, Kevin. Retold by. *Beowulf*. Illustrated by Charles Keeping. Oxford, 1982 (I:9+ R:4). This is a highly illustrated narrative version of the epic.

———, ed. *The Faber Book of Northern Legends*. Illustrated by Alan Howard. Faber & Faber, 1983 (I:9+ R:6). This is a collection of Norse myths, Germanic heroic legends, and Icelandic sagas.

D'Aulaire, Ingri, and Edgar Parin D'Aulaire. *Norse Gods and Giants*. Doubleday, 1967 (I:8–12 R:6). A collection of Norse tales includes explanations about creation and tales of Thor, Odin, and Loki.

Harrison, Michael. *The Curse of the Ring*. Illustrated by Tudor Humphries. Oxford University Press, 1987 (I:9+ R:6). This book contains a retelling of the Norse Ring saga.

LEGENDS

Bawden, Nina. *William Tell*. Illustrated by Pascale Allamand. Lothrop, Lee & Shepard, 1981 (I:6–9 R:5). In this tale, the fourteenth-century Swiss patriot inspires his people to fight for their freedom.

Brown, Marcia. *Backbone of the King: Story of Pakáa and His Son Ku*. University of Hawaii Press, 1966 (I:10+ R:5). A boy helps his father regain his noble position.

Cole, Joanna. *A Gift from Saint Francis*. Illustrated by Michele Lemieux. Morrow, 1989 (I:7+ R:6). This text tells about the first creche.

Hastings, Selina. *Sir Gawain and the Green Knight*. Illustrated by Juan Wijngaard. Lothrop, Lee & Shepard, 1981 (I:9–12 R:4). One of King Arthur's knights is challenged by a giant adversary.

———. *Sir Gawain and the Loathly Lady*. Illustrated by Juan Wijngaard. Lothrop, Lee & Shepard, 1985 (I:10+ R:6). This is an elaborately illustrated version of one of the Arthurian tales.

Hodges, Margaret. *Saint George and the Dragon*. Illustrated by Trina Schart Hyman. Little, Brown, 1984 (I:all R:7). An English legend is adapted from Edmund Spenser's *The Faerie Queene*.

McKinley, Robin. *The Outlaws of Sherwood*. Greenwillow, 1988 (I:10+ R:7). The author interprets the Robin Hood legend.

Middleton, Haydn. *Island of the Mighty: Stories of Old Britain*. Illustrated by Anthea Toorchen. Oxford University Press, 1987 (I:9+ R:6). This is a collection of Celtic tales.

Miles, Bernard. *Robin Hood: His Life and Legend*. Illustrated by Victor G. Ambrus. Hamlyn, 1979 (I:8–12 R:7). This is a highly illustrated version of the English legend.

Pyle, Howard. *The Merry Adventures of Robin Hood*. 1883. Reprint by Scribner's Sons, 1946 (I:10–14 R:8). This is Pyle's original, longer version of Robin Hood's adventures.

———. *Some Merry Adventures of Robin Hood*. Scribner's Sons, 1954 (I:8–12 R:7). Twelve stories were selected from the original version of Robin Hood.

———. *The Story of the Champions of the Round Table*. Scribner's Sons, 1905; reissued 1968 (I:12+ R:8). Four books include "Story of Lancelot" and "Book of Sir Tristram."

———. *The Story of King Arthur and His Knights*. Scribner's Sons, 1903; reissued 1978 (I:12+ R:8). This is a reissue of the classic.

———. *The Story of King Arthur and His Knights*. Scribner's Sons, 1933 (I:12+ R:8). This is the story of how Arthur becomes king of England, establishes the Round Table, and performs heroic deeds.

Riordan, James. *Tales of King Arthur*. Illustrated by Victor G. Ambrus. Rand McNally, 1982 (I:9–12 R:6). New illustrations accompany a classic legend about the English hero.

Seredy, Kate. *The White Stag*. Viking, 1937, 1965 (I:10–14 R:7). This is the story of the Hun-Magyar migration into what became Hungary.

Sutcliff, Rosemary. *The Light Beyond the Forest*. Dutton, 1981 (I:10+ R:7). This book tells of the quest for the Holy Grail.

———. *The Road to Camlann: The Death of King Arthur*. Illustrated by Shirley Felts. Dutton, 1982 (I:10+ R:7). Mordred attempts to destroy the kingdom by exposing Queen Guinevere and Sir Lancelot.

———. *The Sword and the Circle: King Arthur and the Knights of the Round Table*. Dutton, 1981 (I:10+ R:7). Thirteen stories are associated with King Arthur.

7

Modern Fantasy

TIME, SPACE, AND PLACE

INVOLVING CHILDREN IN MODERN FANTASY

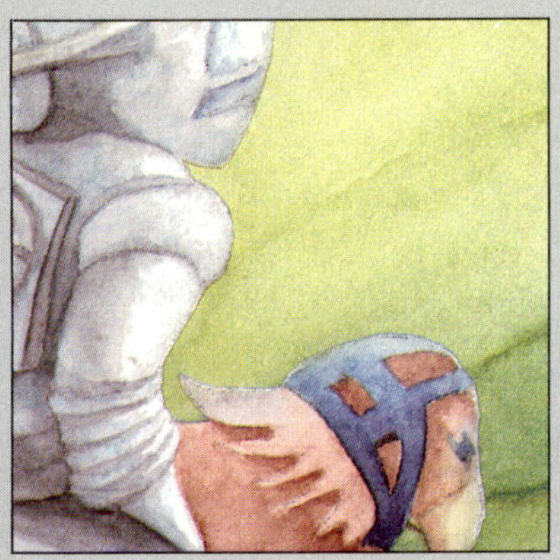

Time, Space, and Place

WHEN CHILDREN ESCAPE INTO BEATRIX Potter's world, they enter the intriguing sphere of fantasy. With the following rhythmical words from *The Tailor of Gloucester,* one of the most popular authors of modern fantasy takes her readers into a time and setting where the impossible becomes convincingly possible:

> In the time of swords and periwigs and full-skirted coats with flowered lappets—when gentlemen wore ruffles, and gold-laced waistcoats of paduasoy and taffeta—there lived a tailor in Gloucester. (p. 11)

Authors create modern fantasy by altering one or more characteristics of everyday reality. They may create entirely new worlds, as J. R. R. Tolkien does Middle Earth in *The Hobbit,* or they may give their characters extraordinary experiences in the real world, as Margaret J. Anderson does in *In the Keep of Time*. A realistic character may go down a rabbit hole and enter another domain, as in Lewis Carroll's *Alice's Adventures in Wonderland,* or nonrealistic characters, such as Mary Norton's little people in *The Borrowers,* may exist in an otherwise realistic setting. In one way or another, however, an author of fantasy permits readers to enter imaginative realms of possibility. More than one fourth of the sixty-three books listed by the Children's Literature Association in *Touchstones: A List of Distinguished Children's Books* (3) are modern fantasy.

This chapter discusses various types of modern fantasy for children. It stresses the ways in which modern authors of fantasy literature follow in the footsteps of the anonymous storytellers who created and transmitted the traditional fantasies of oral literature. It also suggests criteria for evaluating modern fantasy and recommends numerous outstanding fantasy stories that children enjoy.

EVALUATING MODERN FANTASY

Like all authors of fiction, authors of high-quality modern fantasy use basic literary elements to create stories that are interesting, engrossing, and believable. In evaluating modern fantasy for children, you should use the criteria recommended in Chapter 3, while considering the special uses of literary elements that the fantasy genre requires. Consider the following questions when selecting modern fantasy to share with children:

1 Is every action consistent with the framework developed by the author?

2 How does the author's use of characterization allow children to suspend disbelief? Do characters begin in a real world before they travel to the world of fantasy? Does a believable character accept a fanciful world, characters, or happenings? Does the author use an appropriate language or create a believable language consistent with the story?
3 Does the author pay careful attention to the details in the setting? If the author develops several time periods, are the settings authentic and integral to the story?
4 Is the theme worthwhile for children?
5 Does the author encourage readers to suspend disbelief by developing a point of view that is consistent in every detail, including sights, feelings, and physical reactions?

Many books of modern fantasy admirably satisfy these criteria and provide great enjoyment to children and adults alike.

Suspending Disbelief: Plot

A story may seem believable if it begins in a realistic context and then moves into the realm of fantasy. In "The Chronicles of Narnia," C. S. Lewis develops normal human characters who visit a realistic English home and enter into childhood games familiar to most children. When these realistic characters confront the fantastic and believe it, readers believe it too. Likewise, Margaret Anderson's characters in *In the Keep of Time* have a strong foundation in reality before they enter their time-warp fantasies, encouraging readers' belief.

When an author develops a logical framework, and develops characters' actions consistently within this framework, there is an internal consistency in the story. This consistency is important. If, for example, animals supposedly live and behave like animals, they should *consistently* do so unless the author carefully develops when they change, why they change, and how they change.

Suspending Disbelief: Characterization

Of course, the character from whose point of view a story is told must be believable for readers to suspend disbelief. Whether an author humanizes animals and inanimate objects, gives supernatural beings human traits, or places realistic human characters into fantastic situations, the characters in a fantasy story must be internally coherent as well as accessible to the readers.

Language is one way that authors of fantasy can make characters believable. In *The Hobbit* and *The Lord of the Rings,* for example, J. R. R. Tolkien creates distinct languages for different groups of characters. Ruth Noel (19), in her evaluation of Tolkien's use of language, concludes that the musical flow of Elfish words and names implies that the Elves are noble people and that they love beauty and music. In contrast, the guttural Dwarfish, which sounds less familiar to English-speaking readers, indicates that the Dwarfs themselves are different from humans and Elves. Likewise, the croaked curses of the Orcs establish them as a coarse, cruel, unimaginative people, and the prolonged chants of the Ents demonstrate their peaceful life in the forest. David Rees (20) states that Joan Aiken has a similar talent for characterization through language because in such fantasies as *The Wolves of Willoughby Chase,* she is able to create "the dialects, vocabulary, and speech rhythms of various periods in history" (p. 42).

Creating a World: Setting

The magical settings of traditional tales let children know that anything is possible in those environments. Writers of modern fantasy may also create worlds in which unusual circumstances are believable, or they may combine reality and fantasy as characters or stories go back and forth between two worlds. In either case, if the story is to be credible, the author must develop the setting so completely that readers can see, hear, and feel it.

The settings for Mary Norton's "Borrowers" books, described through the eyes of little people, are integral to each story. The inside of a cottage drain becomes both an escape route and an antagonist in *The Borrowers Afloat*. Readers experience a new world as they vicariously join the Borrowers inside the drain: "There were other openings as they went along, drains that branched into darkness and ran away uphill. Where these joined the main drain, a curious collection of flotsam and jetsam piled up over which they had to drag the soap lid. . .the air from that point onwards, smelled far less strongly of tea leaves" (p. 105).

The setting in the drain changes from a fairly calm escape route to one filled with drumming noises and fright as a bath drain opens. Norton describes an antagonistic setting:

> A millrace of hot scented water swilled through her clothes, piling against her at one moment, falling away

the next. Sometimes it bounced above her shoulders, drenching her face and hair; at others it swirled steadily about her waist and tugged at her legs and feet. (p. 110)

Norton provides so much detail in her description of this setting that readers can see the contents of the inside of the drain as if they too were only six inches tall, can smell the soap and tea leaves deposited in the drain, and can hear the changing sounds of water echoing through the drainage system or gushing down in thundering torrents.

Other authors create convincing new worlds as characters go from realistic to fantasy settings. In *Alice's Adventures in Wonderland,* by Lewis Carroll, Alice begins her adventures on a realistically peaceful river bank in nineteenth-century England, then travels down a rabbit hole into a unique world quite different from her normal one, which Carroll describes in great detail from her viewpoint.

In Janet Lunn's *The Root Cellar,* twelve-year-old Rose goes down into a root cellar on an old dilapidated farm in twentieth-century Canada. When she leaves the root cellar, she enters a nineteenth-century world in which the farm is prosperous. The people in that earlier time are engrossed by the approaching American Civil War. Believable descriptions of the same setting in two different centuries are important to the story. Lunn develops an authentic Civil War setting by describing the sights, sounds, feelings, and concerns that the main character experiences as she travels throughout the northeastern United States to find a boy who has not returned from the war. Authors whose characters travel in time warps must create believable, authentic settings for two time periods.

Jane Yolen uses a similar approach in *The Devil's Arithmetic*. After a contemporary girl steps through a door and finds herself in a Jewish village in the 1940s, the sights, sounds, conflicts, and concerns become those of people living in a death camp during the Holocaust.

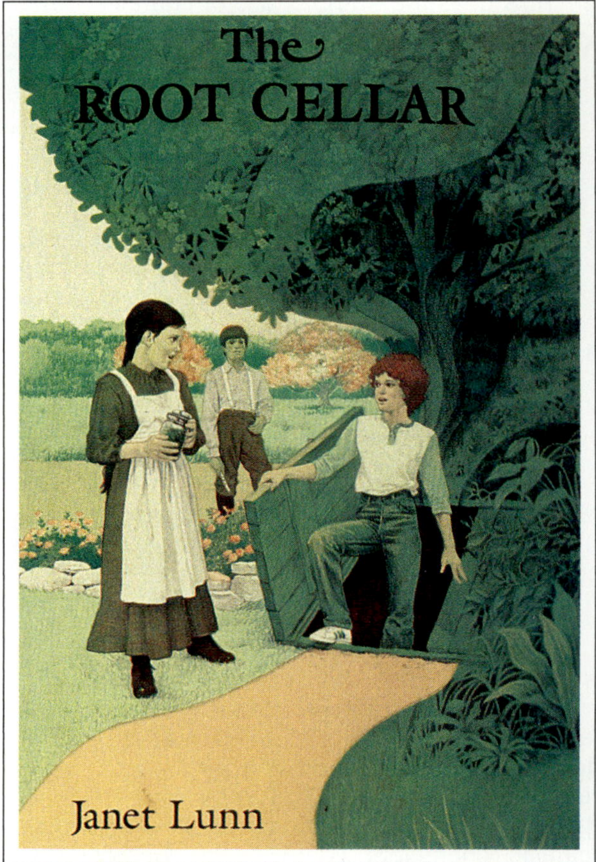

Detailed descriptions of the same setting in two different centuries provide an authentic background for this story. (Illustration by Ruth Sanderson from *The Root Cellar,* by Janet Lunn. Copyright © 1981 Charles Scribner's Sons. Reprinted with the permission of Charles Scribner's Sons.)

Universality: Themes

Memorable modern fantasies develop themes related to universal values, desires, struggles, and emotions. Ned Hedges (10) concluded that classic fantasies for children tend to affirm specific human values and condemn specific human weaknesses. The constant battle between good and evil, the need for faith and perseverance in the face of obstacles, the importance of personal and social responsibility, and the power of love and friendship are important themes in works of modern fantasy ranging from George MacDonald's Victorian story *At the Back of the North Wind* to Madeleine L'Engle's contemporary books of science fiction. Children easily identify with such themes, especially when an author develops them within the framework of consistently believable plots, characterizations, settings, and points of view.

Suspending Disbelief: Point of View

Rebecca J. Lukens (14) says:

If fantasy is to be successful, we must willingly suspend disbelief. If the story's characters, conflict, and theme seem believable to us, we find it plausible and even natural to know the thoughts and feelings of animal characters or tiny people. In fact, the story may be so good that we wish it were true. . . .This persuasion that the writer wishes to bring about—persuasion that 'what if' is really 'it's true'—is most successful when the writer is consistent about point of view. (p. 108)

The point of view of a story is determined by the author's choice of the person telling it. A story could be told quite differently from the perspective of a child, a mother, a wicked witch, an animal or supernatural beast, or an objective observer. Authors of fantasy must decide which point of view best facilitates a believable telling of a story, then sustain that point of view in order to persuade readers to keep suspending disbelief in the fantastic elements of the story.

The Borrowers, by Mary Norton, seems believable because most of this story about "little people" is told from the viewpoint of Arrietty, who is only six inches tall. The little people's family sitting room seems authentic because the reader sees, through Arrietty's eyes, the postage-stamp-sized portraits on the walls, a work of art created by a pillbox that is supporting a chess piece, and a couch made from a human's padded trinket box. Even the reaction to a miniature book that is Arrietty's diary is dealt with through the physical capabilities of a miniature person: "Arrietty braced her muscles and heaved the book off her knees, and stood upright on the floor" (p. 20). Readers are ready to believe the story because the author describes sights, feelings, and physical reactions as if a six-inch-tall person were actually living through the experience.

In *The Tale of Peter Rabbit,* Beatrix Potter creates believable situations by telling the story from both Peter Rabbit's point of view and the first-person point of view of the storyteller, who occasionally interjects comments such as "I am sorry to say that Peter was not very well during the evening." In this case, the authoritative, realistic voice of the storyteller reassures the reader that the fantastic events being described are normal and understandable.

Perry Nodelman (18) emphasizes the need for an author to consider both the storyteller and the audience when creating a credible fantasy. Nodelman says:

Only by ignoring the fact that it is fantastic, by pretending to be a true story about a real world shared by characters in the story, the storyteller, and the people who hear the story, can a fantasy establish its credibility and work its magic on those who actually hear it. (p. 16)

BRIDGES BETWEEN TRADITIONAL AND MODERN FANTASY

In many ways, modern fantasy stories are direct descendants of the folktales, fables, myths, and legends of the oral tradition. Tales about talking animals, wise and foolish humans, supernatural beings, heroic adventurers, and magical realms are as popular with children and adults today as they were hundreds of years ago. Many authors of modern fantasy have drawn upon themes, motifs, settings, and characterizations common in traditional literature. Of course, in the distant past, people believed that the content of some fairy tales, myths, and legends had basis in fact, while most readers of modern fantasy only suspend their disbelief in extraordinary beings and events. Still, to entice their readers into out-of-the-ordinary experiences, authors of modern fantasy play their roles similar to those of storytellers of old, who enchanted live audiences with tales that had been orally transmitted over generations. The bridges between traditional fantasy and modern fantasy are evident in many contemporary tales of wonder, but they are especially strong in literary folktales, allegories, and tales about mythical quests and conflicts.

Literary Folktales

In the past hundred years or so, some authors of fantasy have deliberately attempted to replicate the "Once upon a time" of traditional folktales, with their dark forests, castles, princesses and princes, humble people of noble worth, and "happily ever afters." The traditional theme that goodness is rewarded and evil is punished is common in literary folktales, as are motifs involving magic. Dorothy De Wit (5) compares, for example, the magic of smallness in the traditional tale "Tom Thumb" with that in Hans Christian Andersen's literary folktale "Thumbelina" and the magic sleep in the folktale "Snow White and the Seven Dwarfs" with that in Washington Irving's *Rip Van Winkle*.

Like many folktales, *Melisande,* a literary folktale by E. Nesbit, includes a curse placed on a princess by an evil fairy. *The Magic Fan,* by Keith Baker, includes a magical object that guides a boy's actions, and these actions eventually save the boy's village.

Hans Christian Andersen. Charles Perrault is usually credited with publishing the first chil-

Characteristics of the traditional tale are found in this story about a girl who increases in size. (From *Melisande* by E. Nesbit, illustrated by P. J. Lynch. Copyright, 1989. Illustrations copyright 1989 by P. J. Lynch. Reprinted by permission of Harcourt Brace Jovanovich, Inc.

dren's book of fairy tales, but Hans Christian Andersen is credited with writing, a century later, the first fairy tale for children. While Perrault wrote down stories from the oral tradition, Andersen created new stories for theater audiences and readers. Zena Sutherland, Dianne L. Monson, and May Hill Arbuthnot (22) point out that although Andersen's first stories for children were "elaborations of familiar folk and fairy tales,. . .he soon began to allow his imagination full rein in the invention of plot, the shaping of character, and the illumination of human condition. These later creations, solely from Andersen's fertile imagination, are called literary fairy tales, to distinguish them from the fairy tales of unknown origin, those created by common folk. Andersen's work served as inspiration for other writers" (p. 228).

Andersen's "The Wild Swans" is a literary fairy tale quite similar to the Grimms' traditional tale "The Six Swans." Both stories involve enchantment by an evil stepmother and the courage and endurance of a young girl who is willing to suffer in order to free her brothers.

Experts in children's literature believe that some of Andersen's other literary fairy tales are based on his own life. For example, Andersen's unpleasant experiences in school, where the teacher poked fun at a poor boy's lack of knowledge, large size, and looks, may have inspired his story "The Ugly Duckling." Lorinda Bryan Cauley's illustrations for a book-length version of this story show the transformation of the ugly duckling into the most beautiful swan in the garden lake. Cauley's realistic and humorous pictures portray the duckling's agony in the barnyard, where every animal seems to show contempt for him. Children can follow, in pictures and text, the sorrow felt by the duckling and then his realization that he is not something to be pitied. They can observe his head emerging from under his wing, not in conceit, but in wonder, as he senses his transformation.

Nancy Ekholm Burkert has beautifully illustrated two of Andersen's stories that reflect the beauty of natural life versus the heartbreak associated with longing for mechanical perfection or metallic glitter. *The Nightingale* tells of a Chinese emperor who turned from the voice of a faithful nightingale to a jeweled, mechanical bird. He learns, however, that only the real, unjeweled bird's song can bring comfort and truth. *The Fir Tree* is the story of a little fir tree who learns only after he is taken from the forest the significance of what he has lost. Alison Claire Darke's illustrations for *The Nightingale* may be compared with Burkhert's illustrations. Both illustrators emphasize the beauty of the Chinese setting.

Illustrator Susan Jeffers and author Amy Ehrlich have combined their talents to create three beautiful versions of Andersen's tales. Jeffers's finely detailed drawings suggest fantasy settings in *Thumbelina* and *The Wild Swans*. Her illustrations for and Amy Ehrlich's retelling of *The Snow Queen* may be contrasted with two versions of the same tale, one retold by Naomi Lewis and illustrated by Errol LeCain and the other retold by Naomi Lewis and illustrated by Angela Barrett.

Michael Hague, Kay Nielson, and Edward Ardizzone are among those who have illustrated collections of Andersen's tales for adults to read aloud to children or for children to read independently. *Michael Hague's Favorite Hans Christian Andersen Fairy Tales* includes nine stories in large print. More extensive collections include *Hans Andersen: His Classic Fairy Tales,* illustrated by Michael Foreman.

Jane Yolen. Jane Yolen uses folk themes, such as the power of kindness and the madness of pride, to weave original stories. She also discusses the conquest of fear. Her settings, language, and characters are similar to those in the best traditional tales. The five tales in *The Girl Who Cried Flowers* take place in magical realms, such as "on the far side of yesterday," "far to the North, where the world is lighted only by the softly flickering snow," and ancient Greece. The main characters

A

B

A, Finely detailed lines enhance the dreamlike quality of the fairy tale setting. Excerpted from *The Wild Swans,* retold by Amy Ehrlich, illustrated by Susan Jeffers. Illustrations copyright © by Susan Jeffers. Used by permission of the publisher Dial Books for Young Readers. *B,* The fragile beauty of a forest scene is shown in the artist's delicate use of line, illustrations from *The Nightingale* by Hans Christian Andersen, translated by Eva Le Gallienne, illustrated by Nancy Ekholm Burkert. Pictures copyright © 1985 by Nancy Ekholm Burkert. By permission of Harper & Row, Publishers, Inc.

ISSUE

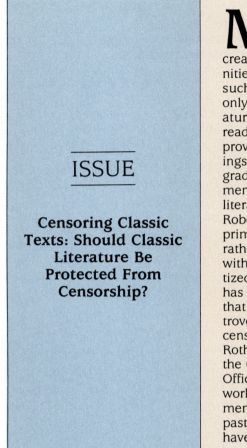

Censoring Classic Texts: Should Classic Literature Be Protected From Censorship?

MANDATES FOR LITERature-based language arts curricula are increasing in states and communities across the nation. States such as California[1] have not only mandated the use of literature in language arts and reading classes, they have also provided recommended readings for kindergarten through grade eight. These recommended readings include many literary classics. According to Robert Rothman,[2] this use of primary sources of literature rather than the use of texts with "laundered" and "sanitized" vocabularies and plots has results in school materials that some people consider controversial and that they want to censor. To clarify this issue, Rothman quotes the director of the California State Education Office of Curriculum Framework and Textbook Development, Glen Thomas: "Unlike the past, when publishers might have kept such material out of textbooks for fear of offending a potential customer, the new literature policy encourages the use of classic texts. Moreover, such literature is exempt from California regulations governing the social content of classroom materials. . . .In our view, classic literature has to be viewed differently. Content that twentieth-century Americans may regard as offensive may reflect the historical context of the time." (p. 5).

Many of the selections discussed in this chapter are classics. As you read this literature, consider the advantages and disadvantages of using classic literature with children. Should classic literature be protected from censorship?

[1]California State Department of Education. *Recommended Readings in Literature: Kindergarten through Grade Eight*. Sacramento, Calif.: State Department of Education, 1986.

[2]Rothman, Robert. "Experts Warn of Attempts to Censor Classic Texts." *Education Week*. February 21, 1990, 5.

also have traditional qualities. Silent Bianca, for example, is a strange and beautiful girl. Her face is as pale as the snow and her hair is as white as a moonbeam. She is not only beautiful but also wise. She does not speak as others do, however; her sentences must be plucked out of the air and her fragile words must be warmed by the hearth fire before they can be heard. A king who seeks a wife both beautiful and wise hears of Bianca and sends his unhappy counselors, who want a girl of noble birth, to bring her to his castle. The king creates an obstacle to measure the wisdom of both Silent Bianca and his arguing counselors. Silent Bianca proves her wisdom, tricks the king's guards, and marries the king. They live happily ever after, with the king spending many hours by the hearthstone listening to the counsel of his wise and loving queen.

Yolen uses the noble quest theme and the legendary characters of traditional literature to create a humorous story in *The Acorn Quest*. This gentle spoof on King Arthur and the knights of the Round Table has animal characters who somewhat resemble their traditional human counterparts: King Earthor, Sir Runsalot, and Wizard Squirrelin. The characters frequently quarrel, and they have difficulty focusing on the problem of probable famine. The plot develops around their quest for a golden acorn at the edge of the world. On the journey, they confront a traditional enemy, a dragon, and the human enemy, greed.

Yolen's *The Faery Flag: Stories and Poems of Fantasy and the Supernatural* is a collection of stories that includes themes and motifs from traditional folktales and ancient myths. For example, "The Faery Flag" develops a theme of love between a human and a supernatural being. The human crosses a bridge into the Land of Faerie and is bewitched by one of the inhabitants. "The Foxwife" includes transformations from human to fox to human. "Words of Power" develops the importance of signs, the power of chants, the quest for identity, a temptation that is really a test, and the ultimate ability to transform oneself into an eagle and soar with the wind.

Religious and Ethical Allegory

Religious themes provide strong links between traditional and modern fantasy. According to Bruno Bettelheim (1), "Most fairy tales originated in periods when religion was a most important part of life; thus, they deal, directly or by inference, with religious themes" (p. 13). Traditional tales from around the world reflect the religions prominent in their times and places of origins, including Islam, Buddhism, and Judaism, to name but a few.

Some European folktales, such as the German "Our Lady's Child," directly refer to the Roman Catholic beliefs of the Middle Ages. In this tale recorded by the Brothers Grimm, a young girl becomes mute when she disobeys the Virgin Mary and then lies about what she has done. After suffering severe ordeals, she desires only to confess her sin, and the Virgin Mary rewards her confession by renewing her power of speech and granting her happiness. Other European folktales and legends develop less explicit religious themes by using allegory, or prolonged metaphors. Characters representing goodness or wisdom must confront and overcome characters representing evil or foolishness.

In our more secular age, as Bettelheim (1) points out, "these religious themes no longer arouse universal and personally meaningful associations" in the majority of people, as they once did. However, modern authors of fantasy still create religious and ethical allegories. Some authors actually replicate the heroic humans, witches, personified animals, and magical settings of traditional literature. Others use characters and settings consistent with their own times. Readers may respond to these stories on different levels, since they are both religious allegories and tales of enchantment and high adventure.

George MacDonald. The strongly moralistic atmosphere of Victorian England and training as a Congregational minister influenced a writer who used allegorical fantasy to portray and condemn the flaws in his society. Cynthia Marshall (15) states that George MacDonald's concern for distinguishing good from evil leads to "moralizing interventions" (p. 61) in books, such as *At the Back of the North Wind*. MacDonald's *At the Back of the North Wind,* first published in 1871 and reissued in 1966, is the story of Diamond, the son of a poor coach driver. Diamond lives two lives: the harsh existence of impoverished working-class Londoners, and a dreamlike existence in which he travels with the North Wind, who takes him to a land of perpetual flowers and gentle breezes, where no one is cold or sick or hungry.

MacDonald uses the North Wind, a beautiful woman with long flowing hair, to express much of his own philosophy. "Good people see good things; bad people, bad things" (p. 37), she tells Diamond, whom MacDonald describes as a good boy, "God's baby." When Diamond questions her reality, she says, "I think. . .that if I were only a dream, you would not have been able to love me so. You love me when you are not with me, don't you?" (p. 363). Diamond clings to the back of the North Wind. With her streaming hair enfolding him, they fly to a land where it is always May. Diamond

The flowing lines of the North Wind seem to enfold little Diamond. (Illustration by E. H. Shepard from *At the Back of the North Wind,* by George MacDonald. Children's Illustrated Classics series. Reprinted with permission of J. M. Dent & Sons, Ltd.)

ISSUE

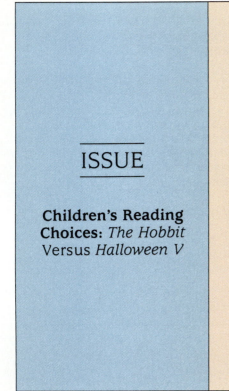

Children's Reading Choices: *The Hobbit* Versus *Halloween V*

A NATIONAL SURVEY OF children's reading choices published in *Booklist*[1] presents concerns, thought-provoking messages, reasons for satisfaction, and reasons for dissatisfaction. Of the fifty most popular titles in the survey, eleven are modern fantasy, thirty-one are realistic fiction, two are poetry, three are picture storybooks, two are historical fiction, and one is traditional literature. The top ten books include two selections from modern fantasy: E. B. White's *Charlotte's Web* and Roald Dahl's *Charlie and the Chocolate Factory*. Other choices in the top fifty are J. R. R. Tolkien's *The Hobbit,* Madeleine L'Engle's *A Wrinkle in Time,* Beverly Cleary's *The Mouse and the Motorcycle,* C. S. Lewis's *The Lion, the Witch, and the Wardrobe,* and Roald Dahl's *James and the Giant Peach*. Although these books are found on almost all recommended lists, comments made by librarians and teachers who took part in the survey should cause you to reflect upon the need to lead children to high-quality literature.

The author of the *Booklist* article, Barbara Elleman, compares the 1982 Chosen-by-Children list with the 1982 juvenile best-seller list issued by Dalton Bookstores. Only three titles appeared on both lists. The Dalton list included Disney, Sesame Street, Strawberry Shortcake, and Smurf spin-offs. Therefore, Elleman concluded that children purchase the Dalton books without the guidance of teachers and librarians. She makes the following points in

returns home from that visit, but the end of the story suggests further allegorical implications:

> I walked up the winding stair, and entered his room. A lovely figure, as white and almost as clear as alabaster, was lying on the bed. I saw at once how it was. They thought he was dead. I knew that he had gone to the back of the North Wind. (p. 378)

C.S. Lewis. A professor of medieval and Renaissance literature at Cambridge University, C. S. Lewis used his interest in theology and his knowledge about medieval allegory, classical legend, and Norse mythology to create a highly acclaimed and popular fantasy saga. "The Chronicles of Narnia" (winner of the Carnegie Medal for best children's books), beginning with *The Lion, the Witch and the Wardrobe* and ending seven books later with *The Last Battle,* develop marvelous adventure stories interwoven with Christian allegory. Children can enjoy the series for its high drama alone, or they can read it for its allegorical significance.

While *The Lion, the Witch and the Wardrobe* is the first book in the series, *The Magician's Nephew* informs readers how the saga began and how the passage between the magical world of Narnia and Earth was made possible. The tree grown from the magical Narnia apple has blown over, and its wood is used to build a large wardrobe. This is the same wardrobe through which the daughters of Eve and the sons of Adam (*The Lion, the Witch and the Wardrobe*) enter into the kingdom, meet the wicked White Witch, and help the great lord-lion Aslan defeat the powers of evil.

In *The Lion, the Witch and the Wardrobe,* Aslan gives his life to save Edmund, who has betrayed them all. Aslan, however, rises from the dead and tells the startled, bereaved children that the deeper magic before the dawn of time has won:

> It means that though the witch knew the Deep Magic, there is a magic deeper still which she did not know. Her knowledge goes back only to the dawn of Time. But if she could have looked a little further back, into the stillness and the darkness before Time dawned, she

the article, reflecting conclusions reached by participants in the survey:

1 The authors on the Chosen-by-Children list are generally respected authors. Several have won awards for literary merit.
2 Libraries that promote children's book interests contain such authors as Tolkien and L'Engle. Therefore, it appears that children can be led to good literature.
3 Choices from the Chosen-by-Children list may reflect only what is being read in classrooms and not actual preferences.
4 Many spin-offs from television shows, such as "Battlestar Galactica," and films, such as *King Kong,* are favorites with children.
5 Junior-high students frequently prefer adult horror novels, such as *Halloween V*.
6 Popularity does not always mean high-quality literature.
7 Certain categories of literature are missing from the Chosen-by-Children list, including nonfiction, most classics, and fairy tales (except "Cinderella").

Are these points reasons for satisfaction or dissatisfaction with classroom and library literature programs? As you consider the implications of the preceding points, also consider the implications of the following comment by one of the adults who took part in the survey:

This survey dramatized for me the tremendous power a teacher has to raise and broaden tastes and cultural value among her students. Thirty minutes a week in the library can supplement, enrich, and stimulate a good classroom program; it cannot adequately nourish a poor one. Children who are required to read challenging books (yet encouraged to select them according to their own tastes) learn the joys of literature. Those who aren't led (or pushed) through that door may never open it on their own. (p. 508)

[1]Elleman, Barbara, "Chosen by Children." *Booklist* 79 (December 1, 1982): 507–509.

would have read there a different incantation. She would have known that when a willing victim who has committed no treachery was killed in a traitor's stead, the Table would crack and Death itself would start working backward (pp. 132–33).

From Aslan, the children learn that after they have once been crowned, they will remain kings and queens of Narnia forever.

The remaining books in the chronicle tell other fantastic tales of adventure in which the characters overcome evil. The final Christian allegory is contained in the last book of the series, *The Last Battle*. Here, the children are reunited with Aslan after their death on earth and discover "for them it was only the beginning of the real story. All their life in this world and all their adventures in Narnia had only been the cover and the title page: now at last they were beginning Chapter One of the Great Story which no one on earth has read: in which every chapter is better than the one before" (p. 184). The stories in the chronicles of Narnia are filled with adventures and characters that appeal to children. There are magical spells, centaurs, dwarfs, unicorns, ogres, witches, and minotaurs. Throughout the stories, characters strive to meet high ideals and recognize the importance of faith.

Mythical Quests and Conflicts

Quests for lost or stolen objects of power, descents into darkness to overcome evil, and settings where lightning splinters the world and sets the stage for battle between two opposing forces are found in traditional myths, legends, and modern fantasy. Some authors of modern fantasy borrow magical settings and characters from traditional tales of heroism, while others create new worlds of enchantment. Modern stories may contain some threads of the allegory that characterizes many traditional tales—such as the English legends about King Arthur, his knights of the Round Table, and the quest for the Holy Grail. Most modern fantasies about mythical quests and conflicts, however, emphasize adventure. Their characters acquire new knowledge and learn honorable uses of personal power.

Mythical elements are found in both Grace Chetwin's *The Riddle and the Rune* and O. R. Melling's *The Singing Stone*. Chetwin's protagonist, Gom, leaves his mountain home to seek Harga, his mother, who is one of the greatest wizards in the world. In traditional fashion, he must solve a riddle in order to find her. Along the way, he is helped by Harga's rune, a magic charm worn around his neck since birth; the Wind, who steers him on his course; a horn that can be blown in time of need; a dog; and a horse. Chetwin's antagonists symbolize evil. For example, a half-bird and half-human predator represents the powers of evil.

In O. R. Melling's *The Singing Stone,* the plot revolves around a quest for four treasures of power that can revive an ancient Irish people: the Spear of Lug, the Cauldron of the Dagda, the Sword of War, and the Stone of Destiny. The objects of power are reminiscent of those in other heroic fantasies. Druids and antlered Sentinels try to keep the heroines from completing their quest.

Naomi Lewis's translation of *Proud Knight, Fair Lady: The Twelve Lais of Marie de France* includes heroic characters who usually have unfailing valor. There are also objects of power, tests of faith, and high purposes.

James Berry's *Magicians of Erianne* draws on the Arthurian legends. Dragon's blood, objects of power, and traveling spirits are found in Diana Wynne Jones's *The Lives of Christopher Chant*.

Sheila Egoff (6) states that epic, or heroic, fantasies, especially those related to "the Arthurian legends and the Welsh tales of the Mabinogion form the largest cauldron of story into which modern fantasists have dipped" (p. 6). Other popular fantasy sources include *Beowulf, Child Roland of the Dark Tower,* and Scandinavian myths and legends. According to Egoff, the resulting fantasies of such authors as J. R. R. Tolkien, Susan Cooper, and Lloyd Alexander are not retellings of the original. Instead, the authors "use both the matter and structure of legend to infuse their works with the epic quality of the original—its emotional impact and grand design" (p. 7).

J. R. R. Tolkien. Destiny, supernatural immortals, evil dragons, and rings of power are found in J. R. R. Tolkien's popular stories. According to Ruth S. Noel (19), Tolkien's writings "form a continuation of the mythic tradition into modern literature. . . . In no other literary work has such careful balance of mythic tradition and individual imagination been maintained" (pp. 6–7). This balance between myth and imagination is not accidental in Tolkien's writing. Tolkien studied mythology for most of his life; he was a linguistic scholar and professor of Anglo-Saxon literature at Oxford University. His chief interest was the literary and linguistic tradition of the English West Midlands, especially as revealed in *Beowulf* and *Sir Gawain and the Green Knight*. Tolkien respected the quality in myths that allows evil to be unexpectedly averted and good to succeed. He masterfully develops this battle between good and evil in *The Hobbit* and in *The Lord of the Rings,* its more complex sequel. According to Tolkien (23), these stories were at first a philological game in which he invented languages: "The stories were made rather to provide a world for the languages than the reverse. I should have preferred to write in 'Elvish' " (p. 242). This creation of languages

The mythological text and illustrations are strongly interrelated in J. R. R. Tolkien's books. (From *The Hobbit* by J. R. R. Tolkien, illustrated by Michael Hague. Illustrations copyright 1984 by Oak, Ash, & Thorn, Ltd. Reprinted by permission of Houghton Mifflin Company.)

with their own alphabets and rules helps make Tolkien's characters believable.

Careful attention to detail and vivid descriptions of setting in Middle Earth also add credibility to Tolkien's stories. For example, he introduces the reluctant hobbit, Bilbo Baggins, to the challenge of a quest to regain the dwarfs' treasures by using a dwarfs' chant:

> Far over the misty mountains cold
> To dungeons deep and caverns old
> We must away ere break of day
> To find our long-forgotten gold. (p. 37)

As Bilbo, the wizard Gandalf, and the twelve dwarfs proceed over the mountains toward the lair of the evil dragon Smaug, Tolkien describes a lightning that splinters the peaks and rocks that shiver. When Bilbo descends into the mountain dungeons to confront Smaug, Tolkien's setting befits the climax of a heroic quest: Red light, wisps of vapor, and rumbling noises gradually replace the subterranean darkness and quiet. Ahead, in the bottom-most cellar, lies a huge red-golden dragon surrounded by precious gold and jewels. As in traditional tales, the quest is successful, the dragon is slain, and the goblins are overthrown. The hero retains his decency, his honor, and his pledge always to help his friends.

The ring found during the hobbit's quest becomes the basis of the plot in the ring trilogy: *The Fellowship of the Ring, The Two Towers,* and *The Return of the King*. In his foreword to *Fellowship of the Ring,* Tolkien says that he had no intention of writing a story with an inner meaning or message. The story is not meant to be allegorical:

> As the story grew it put down roots (into the past) and threw out unexpected branches; but its main theme was settled from the outset by the inevitable choice of the Ring as the link between it and *The Hobbit*. (p. 6).

Many junior-high and high-school students, college students, and other adults have been brought back into the world of mythology through Tolkien's books.

Lloyd Alexander. The stories that unfold in Lloyd Alexander's mythical land of Prydain reflect Alexander's vivid recollections of Wales, favorite childhood stories, and knowledge of Welsh legends. When Alexander researched the Mabinogion, a collection of traditional Welsh legends, he discovered the characters of Gwydion Son of Don, Arawn Death-Lord of Annuvin, Dallben the enchanter, and Hen Wen the oracular pig (25). In Alexander's outstanding Prydain chronicles these characters become involved in exciting adventures of good versus evil.

Alexander's books take place in a time when fair folk lived with humans, a time of enchanters and enchantments, a time before the passages between the world of enchantment and the world of humans were closed. In the first Prydain chronicle, *The Book of Three,* Alexander introduces the forces of good and evil and an assistant pig-keeper, Taran, who dreams of discovering his parentage and becoming a hero. (Alexander tells readers that all people are assistant pig-keepers at heart because their capabilities seldom match their aspirations and they are often unprepared for what is to happen.)

The forces of good include the enchanter Dallben, who reads the prophecy written in *The Book of Three,* the sons of Don and their leader Prince Gwydion, who in ancient times voyaged from the Summer Country to stand as guardians against the evil Annuvin; and the Princess Eilonwy, descendant of enchanters. They are aided by Hen Wen, a pig who can foretell the future by pointing out ancient symbols carved on letter sticks. The forces of evil are led by a warlord who wants to capture Hen Wen because she knows his secret name. This name is powerful because "once you have the courage to look upon evil, seeing it for what it is and naming it by its true nature, it is powerless against you, and you can destroy it" (p. 209).

Throughout his Prydain series—*The Black Cauldron, The Castle of Llyr, Taran Wanderer,* and *The High King*—Alexander develops strong, believable characters with whom upper-elementary and older children can identify. The world of fantasy becomes relevant to the world of reality. The characters gain credibility through Alexander's history of the people and their long struggle against the forces of evil. Alexander encourages readers to believe in the tangible objects of power because the characters place so much faith in the legend of the sword, the prophecies written in *The Book of Three,* and the fearsome black cauldron.

Alexander's literary style also strengthens the credibility of the fantasy and enhances the plot development and characterization in his other fantasy adventure stories, such as *Westmark, The Kestrel,* and *The Beggar Queen*. In *The Beggar Queen,* Alexander carefully builds a foundation for the action that follows. He develops strong person-against-person, person-against-self, and person-against-society conflicts. He uses ghosts from the

A detailed map helps make the land of Prydain more credible to the reader. (From *The High King*, by Lloyd Alexander. Map by Evaline Ness. Copyright © 1968 by Lloyd Alexander. Copyright © 1968 by Holt, Rinehart and Winston. Reproduced by permission of Holt, Rinehart and Winston, Publishers.)

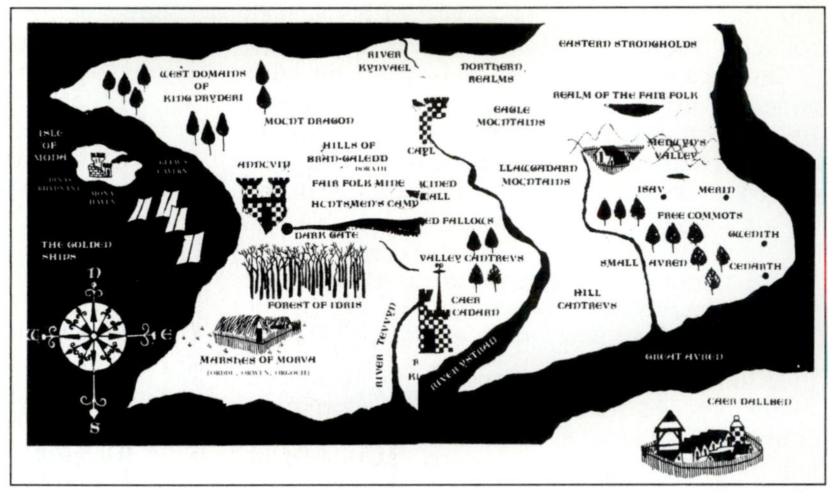

past to introduce the various conflicts and factions; he uses animal symbolism to describe characters; and he concludes each chapter at a point of tension and excitement, foreshadowing the conflict to come.

Ursula K. LeGuin. Somewhere in the land of fantasy lies Earthsea, an archipelago of imaginary islands where wizards cast their spells and people live in fear of fire-blowing winged dragons. Responsible wizards attempt to retain a balance between the forces of good and the forces of evil that seek dominance. Ursula LeGuin helps her readers suspend disbelief through detailed descriptions of Earthsea, its inhabitants, and a culture permeated with magic. LeGuin's series of Earthsea books develops a strong theme about the responsibilities attached to great power by tracing the life of Sparrowhawk from the time he is an apprentice wizard until he is finally the most powerful wizard in the land.

In the first book of the series, *A Wizard of Earthsea,* the young boy has powers strong enough to save his village, but pride and impatience place him in grave danger. A master wizard cautions Sparrowhawk about wanting to learn and use powers of enchantment he is not yet mature enough to understand:

> Have you never thought how danger must surround power as shadow does light? This sorcery is not a game we play for pleasure or for praise. Think of this: that every act of our Art is said and is done either for good, or for evil. Before you speak or do you must know the price that is to pay! (p. 35)

Sparrowhawk, renamed Ged, does not understand the warning. Conflict with another apprentice leads to a duel of sorcery skills, in which Ged calls up a dead spirit and accidentally unleashes an evil being onto the world.

LeGuin's description of the rent in the darkness, the blazing brightness, the hideous black shadow, and Ged's reaction to the beast help convince readers that evil really was released. This belief in unleashed evil is important because the remainder of the book follows Ged as he hunts the shadow-beast across the islands to the farthest waters of Earthsea and develops an understanding that he is responsible for his own actions.

Older and more experienced, Ged understands the power of darkness and light in the *Tombs of Atuan* and *The Farthest Shore*. LeGuin develops a character who has meaning for people living in any time or place. Ged must overcome both personal problems and outside conflicts to reach responsible maturity and to understand the consequences of his actions and the difficulty of attaining true freedom:

> Freedom is a heavy load, a great and strange burden for the spirit to undertake. It is not easy. It is not a gift given, but a choice made, and the choice may be a hard one. The road goes upward towards the light; but the laden traveler may never reach the end of it. (*Tombs of Atuan,* p. 157)

The series ends with *Tehanu: The Last Book of Earthsea.*

Alan Garner. According to John Rowe Townsend (24), Alan Garner was the most influential writer of fantasy in Great Britain of the 1960s. Garner's books are full of magic: the old magic of sun, moon, and blood that survives from crueler times, as well as the high magic of thoughts and spells that checks the old magic and serves as a potent but uncertain weapon against the old evil. Garner's stories transcend time barriers by allowing children from the present to discover objects that contain ancient spells influential in old legends. The ancient masters of good and evil then emerge either to pursue or to safeguard the children.

Garner creates a believable fantasy in *The Weirdstone of Brisingamen* by first placing two realistic characters into a realistic English country setting. He achieves credibility through the reactions of these children as they discover the powers in a tangible object, a tear-shaped piece of crystal that has been handed down over many generations. The plot then revolves around this "weirdstone." It is sought by both the forces of good and the forces of evil. The children, aided by two dwarfs, set out to return the stone to the good wizard who is its guardian. Along the way, however, they encounter evil characters—a shape-changing witch, giant troll women, and a wolf who chases them through underground tunnels and across the countryside. The final confrontation reveals the power of the weirdstone.

Robin McKinley. Magical objects are the focus of quests in Robin McKinley's *The Blue Sword* and *The Hero and the Crown*. McKinley makes *The Blue Sword* believable by depicting a realistic colony called Daria and realistic characters—colonial officials of Her Majesty's government, career army officers—who are unlikely to be influenced by the extraordinary. Fantasy elements enter the story when Harry is kidnapped by the leader of the Hillfolk and taken to the kingdom of Demar. From Harry's point of view, McKinley reveals a people who have the ability to speak in the old tongue, the language of the gods.

In *The Hero and the Crown,* which McKinley describes as a "prequel" to *The Blue Sword,* the power of a magical object is revealed through the sword that brings power from its original owner, Lady Aerin, who was the savior of her people. There is a strong feeling of destiny as the heroine sets forth to regain the objects of power and restore the power to her kingdom. As in many traditional epics, Aerin's quest results in increasingly difficult tests. She proceeds from slaying small dragons to finally overcoming an evil magician. McKinley strongly emphasizes responsibility, as Aerin discovers that even though the price is high, her destiny and her responsibility to her people require this quest.

Susan Cooper. Students of children's literature may identify the influence of English, Celtic, and Welsh legends and myths in Susan Cooper's series of modern fantasies. Her books about the guardians of Light combatting the forces of Darkness contain references to the legend in which King Arthur does not die but lies resting in a place from which he will arise when the need is greatest. According to Celtic tradition, the words on Arthur's tomb mean "Here lies Arthur, King once and King to be."

Richard Cavendish (2) reports that the Welsh version of the legend places Arthur's resting place in a cave in Snowdonia. A similar cave is important in Cooper's *The Grey King,* and Arthur and his knights rise again in *Silver on the Tree* to assist in the final battle against evil. The wizard, Merlin, Arthur's legendary confidant, plays a crucial role throughout Cooper's series. Introduced as Merriman Lyon, Merlin has the ability to suspend the laws of nature and to travel into the past as well as the future. Throughout the series, Merriman retains Merlin's role of representing a profound wisdom from an ancient past that leads the powers of good against the powers of evil.

Legendary objects, places, and occurrences are found throughout the series. For example, the power of a seventh son of a seventh son dominates the characters on heroic quests. Arthur's sword, his ship, and even his dog's name are important in Cooper's books. Quests for the objects of power form a thread of continuity in Cooper's stories. In *Over Sea, Under Stone,* three children visit Cornwall and find an old map that discloses a hidden treasure. This treasure, the Grail, could hinder the forces of Darkness. With the help of the good Old Ones, the children find the Grail, but they lose the manuscript that is the key to its inscriptions.

In *The Dark Is Rising,* the responsibility for continuing the quest falls upon eleven-year-old Will Stanton. While born in twentieth-century England, Will has a special responsibility as the seventh son of a seventh son and the last born of the Old Ones, whose powers can be used against the powers of Darkness. Early in Will's quest, his impatience and ignorance cause him to help the forces of Darkness. He swears that he will never again use his powers unless he knows the consequences. His knowledge increases until he finally understands the magnitude of his powers, and is able to use them successfully:

> Will realized once more, helplessly, that to be an Old One was to be old before the proper time, for the fear he began to feel now was worse than the blind terror he had known in his attic bed, worse than the fear the Dark had put into him in the great hall. This time, his fear was adult, made of experience and imagination and care for others, and it was the worst of all. (p. 127)

Greenwitch, the third book of the series, continues the quest for the Grail and the missing manuscript. *The Grey King* and *Silver on the Tree* complete the series.

Cooper encourages readers to suspend disbelief in her fantasies by developing a strong foundation in the reality of the twentieth century. When her realistic contemporary characters travel into earlier centuries and mythical worlds, her readers follow them willingly and share their quests for greater knowledge. There is a tie, however, between the past and present. For example, in *The Dark Is Rising,* Will goes back into the past to recover the Sign of Fire. When he has fulfilled his quest, there are a great crashing roar, a rumbling, and a growling. Back in the present, thunder is creating earsplitting sounds. The action is believable, and readers feel that the old ways are actually awakening and that the powers live again.

The battle between good and evil is found in literature that bridges traditional and modern fantasy. (From *Hershel and the Hanukkah Goblins* by Eric A. Kimmel, illustrated by Trina Schart Hyman. Reprinted by permission of Holiday House. Text copyright 1989 by Eric A. Kimmel. Illustrations copyright 1989 by Trina Schart Hyman. All rights reserved.)

CATEGORIES OF MODERN FANTASY

Modern fantasies cover a wide range of topics. These topics include articulate animals, toys that come alive, preposterous characters and situations, strange and curious worlds, little people, friendly and frightening spirits, time warps, and science fiction.

Articulate Animals

Concerned rabbit parents worry about what will happen to their family when new folks move into the house on the hill, a mongoose saves his young owner from a deadly cobra, and a mole and a water rat spend an idyllic season floating down an enchanting river. Animals who talk like people but still retain some animal qualities are among the most popular modern fantasy characters. Such authors as Beatrix Potter and Kenneth Grahame have been able to create animal characters who display a balance between animal and human characteristics. This balance is not accidental; many successful authors write from close observations of animal life.

Young children are drawn to the strong feelings of loyalty that the animals in modern fantasies express as they help each other out of dangerous predicaments, stay with friends when they might choose other actions, or protect their human owners while risking their own lives. The memorable animal characters, like all memorable characters in literature, show a wide range of recognizable traits. Children often see themselves in the actions of their animal friends.

Robert O'Brien's *Mrs. Frisby and the Rats of NIMH* is an excellent example of an author's use of believable plot, characters, and setting; interesting theme; and consistent point of view in modern fantasy. This consistency continues in Jane Leslie Conly's sequel, *Racso and the Rats of NIMH,* in which the author, who is the daughter of O'Brien, extends the story. Now, the intelligent rat colony must save their Thorn Valley home from the threat of a dam and the accompanying tourism.

W. J. Corbett's *The Song of Pentecost* and *Pentecost and the Chosen One* are examples of articulate animal books that may be read at two levels: (1) as exciting adventure stories about mice who must move away from the encroaching human environment or die and (2) as allegories of human experience. Beverly Cleary develops humorous animal stories for young children through imaginative and unusual plots. *Ralph and the Motorcycle* and Cleary's other books about a mouse named Ralph are good introductions to modern fantasy.

Ursula K. LeGuin's *Catwings* and *Catwings Return* are also good introductions to fantasy for young children. LeGuin's unique plots introduce a family of kittens whose mother wishes a better life for them than her own city slums. As a result of her dreams, the kittens are born with wings and are able to fly to a safe home in the country. In *Catwings Return,* two of the cats return to the city because they miss their mother. In a satisfying conclusion, they discover and save their sister, who also has wings. Children enjoy reading about the children in the book who lovingly protect and care for the cat family. Dick King-Smith's *Martin's Mice* is another fantasy that develops the need for protection and understanding. Now it is a cat who protects the farm mice from his own predatory family. Through his experiences, Martin discovers the importance of freedom.

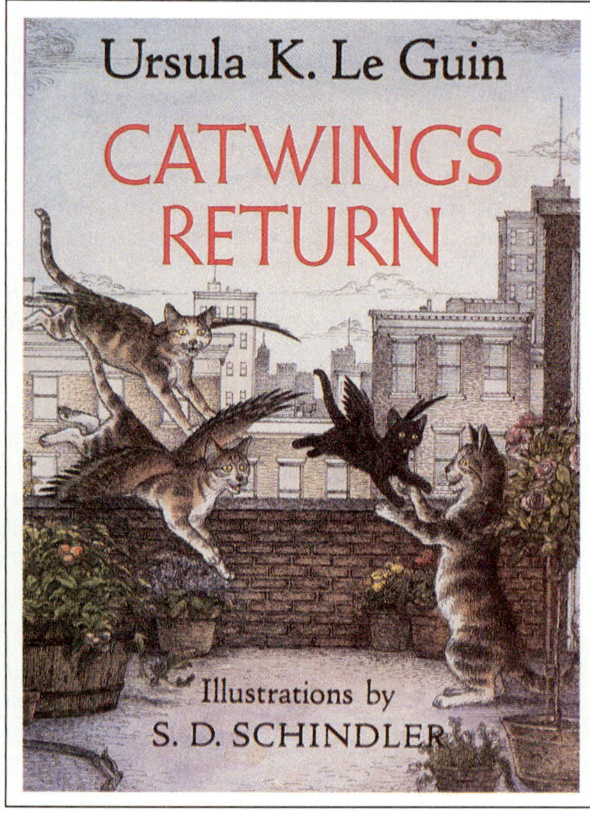

These articulate animals talk like humans but have the additional power of flight. (From *Catwings Return* by Ursula K. Le Guin, illustrated by S. D. Schindler. Copyright © 1989 by Ursula K. Le Guin, illustrations copyright © 1989 by S. D. Schindler. Reprinted by permission of Orchard Books, a division of Franklin Watts, Inc.)

The characterization in Brian Jacques's *Redwall* is enhanced by the author's style. For example, Jacques introduces Matthias, an unlikely and frequently clumsy mouse protagonist, with a description that reveals a great deal about the character's physical and emotional characteristics:

> Matthias cut a comical little figure as he wobbled his way along the cloisters, with his large sandals flip-flopping and his tail peeping from beneath the baggy folds of an oversized novice's habit. He paused to gaze upwards at the cloudless blue sky and tripped over the enormous sandals. Hazelnuts scattered out upon the grass from the rush basket he was carrying. Unable to stop, he went tumbling cowl over tail. (p. 13)

After Matthias lands at the feet of Abbot Mortimer, the author's use of language reinforces the bumbling nature of the apologetic mouse: "Er, sorry, Father Abbot, I tripped, y'see. Trod on my Abbot, Father Habit. Oh dear, I mean. . ." (p. 13).

You may compare the description of Matthias and the description of Cluny, the vicious antagonist:

> Cluny was a bilge rat; the biggest, most savage rodent that ever jumped from ship to shore. He was black, with grey and pink scars all over his heavy vermin-ridden back to the enormous whiplike tail which had earned him his title: Cluny the Scourge! (p. 17)

Thus, Jacques sets the tone for a contest between two opposite characters.

Beatrix Potter. Children of all ages can identify the following sentence as the beginning of an enjoyable story, *The Tale of Peter Rabbit*: "Once upon a time there were four little Rabbits, and their names were—Flopsy, Mopsy, Cotton-tail, and Peter" (p. 3). Beatrix Potter, who wrote so knowledgeably about small animals, spent many

FLASHBACK

BEATRIX POTTER'S ILLUSTRATIONS FOR THE 1902 edition of *The Tale of Peter Rabbit* demonstrate her ability to create animal characters with needs and feelings similar to those of young children. Her detailed drawings reflect her knowledge of animals and the English countryside. *The Tale of Peter Rabbit* was the first in a series of books Potter wrote and illustrated. Potter's other well-known books include *The Tailor of Gloucester* (1902), *The Tale of Squirrel Nutkin* (1903), *The Tale of Benjamin Bunny* (1904), and *The Tale of Mrs. Tittlemouse* (1910).

holidays in the country observing nature, collecting natural objects, and making detailed drawings. Potter had small pets, including a rabbit, a hedgehog, and mice, who later became very real in her illustrated books for children. As an adult, Potter purchased a farm that offered further stimulation for her stories about articulate animals.

Potter's first book, *The Tale of Peter Rabbit,* began as a letter sent to a sick child. When she later submitted the story to a publisher, it was rejected. She did not let this rejection dissuade her; she had the book printed independently. When young readers accepted Peter Rabbit with great enthusiasm, the publisher asked if he might print the book.

Potter's characters may seem real to children because they show many characteristics that children themselves demonstrate. Peter Rabbit, for example, wants to go to the garden so badly that he disobeys his mother. In a vast store of vegetables, happiness changes rapidly to fright as Peter encounters the enemy, Mr. McGregor. Children can sympathize with Peter's fright as he tries unsuccessfully to flee. They can also respond to a satisfying ending, as Peter narrowly escapes and reaches the security of his mother. Children know that such behavior cannot go unpunished. Peter must take a dose of camomile tea to compensate for a stomachache, while his sisters feast on milk and blackberries.

Potter's illustrations, drawn in careful detail, complement the story and suggest the many moods of the main character. Peter stealthily approaches and squeezes under the garden gate. He appears ecstatic as he munches carrots, and hopeless as he reaches the gate in the wall. When Peter discovers that he is too fat to squeeze under the gate, his ears hang dejectedly, a tear trickles down his cheek, one front paw is clenched in fright against his mouth, and his back paws are huddled together. The illustrated moods are so realistic that children feel a close relationship with Peter. *The Tale of Peter Rabbit* is found in a reissue of the 1902 Warne publication, as well as collections such as *A Treasury of Peter Rabbit and Other Stories* and *Tales of Peter Rabbit and His Friends.*

Michael Bond. Paddington Bear is another animal character whose warmth and appeal are related to the author's ability to encourage children to see themselves in the actions of an animal. Unlike Beatrix Potter's Peter Rabbit, who lives in an animal world, Michael Bond's Paddington lives with an English family after the family discovers the homeless bear in Paddington Station. Acceptance of the bear by the family and neighborhood creates a credible and humorous series of stories beginning with *A Bear Called Paddington*.

Bond's Paddington may seem real to children because Paddington displays many childlike characteristics. He gets himself into trouble, and he tries to hide his errors from people who would be disappointed in or disapprove of his actions. Paddington is hard to communicate with when he is in one of his difficult moods, and like a human child, he is often torn between excitement and perplexity. The excitement of preparing the itinerary for a trip in *Paddington Abroad* is balanced by Paddington's trouble in spelling hard words, his difficulty understanding why the bank does not return the same money he put in his savings account, and his inability to read his prepared map. Children in the early elementary grades greatly enjoy these humorous episodes.

Rudyard Kipling. While the majority of articulate animal stories familiar to Americans occur in the woods and farmlands of the United States and Europe, one series uses the jungles of India. Rudyard Kipling spent his early years in Bombay, India, and this time had a great influence on his later writing. He spent much time in the company of Indian *ayahs* (nurses) who told him native tales about the jungle animals. His own young children were the first to hear his most famous stories about the man-cub Mowgli and his brothers, Akela the wolf, Baloo the bear, and Bagheera the panther, published in *The Jungle Book* in 1894.

The story "Mowgli's Brothers" is one of Kipling's most popular. Kipling develops animal characters as diverse as the man-eating tiger Shere Khan, who claims the young Mowgli as his own, and Mother Wolf, who demonstrates her maternal instincts as she protects the man-cub and encourages him to join her own cubs. The law of the jungle is a strong element in the story, as the animals sit in council to decide Mowgli's fate. This story has the flavor of a traditional tale. The suspense rises until old Baloo the bear finally speaks for the man-cub. As in traditional tales about articulate animals, powerful feelings of loyalty grow as Mowgli saves the life of his old friend Akela, the wolf.

The characters, plot, and language of "Rikki-Tikki-Tavi" make it an excellent choice for oral story telling. The wicked cobras Nag and Nagaina live in the garden of a small boy and his parents. They plan a battle against the humans and the heroic mongoose, Rikki-Tikki-Tavi, a hunter with eyeballs of flame and the sworn enemy of all snakes. In keeping with the oral tradition, the action develops rapidly. The boy's loyal mongoose kills Nag. Then, he faces his most deadly peril, a female cobra avenging her mate and protecting her unborn babies. Kipling's language is excellent for oral recitation. As the tension mounts, Rikki-Tikki-Tavi asks:

> What price for a snake's egg? For a young cobra? For a young king-cobra? For the last—the very last of the brood? The ants are eating all the others down by the melon-bed. (p. 117)

A happy-ever-after ending has Rikki-Tikki-Tavi defeating his enemy and remaining on guard so there will not be another threat in the garden.

Humorous incidents and language that is most effective when shared orally are characteristics of Kipling's *Just So Stories*. Young children enjoy the language in such favorite tales as "The Elephant's Child," the story of an adventurous young animal who lives near the banks of the "great, gray-green, greasy Limpopo River."

Kenneth Grahame. Kenneth Grahame first told his stories to his young children; however, scholarly analysis reveals that *The Wind in the Willows* may be read at several levels. For example, Michael Mendelson (16) analyzed the contrast between the values of the dusty road and the riverbank. Peter Hunt (12) analyzed the language and class structure. Richard Gillin (8) searched for evidence of romanticism.

The animals in *The Wind in the Willows* are much more human than are Mowgli's friends in Kipling's jungle (24). Grahame creates characters who prefer the idyllic life and consider work a bore, who long for wild adventures, who demonstrate human frailties through their actions, and who are loyal to friends. The idyllic life is exemplified in the experiences of Mole and Water-Rat as they explore their river world. Grahame introduces his readers to Mole as the scent of spring is penetrating Mole's dark home with a spirit of longing and discontent. Lured out of his hole, Mole observes the busy animals around him and muses that the best part of a holiday is not resting. Instead, it is seeing other animals busy at work. Through detailed description, Grahame communicates this perpetual vacationer's delight and carefree joy to readers:

> He thought his happiness was complete when, as he meandered aimlessly along, suddenly he stood by the edge of a full-fed river. Never in his life had he seen a river before—this sleek, sinuous, full-bodied animal, chasing and chuckling, gripping things with a gurgle and leaving them with a laugh, to fling itself on fresh playmates that shook themselves free, and were caught and held again. All was a-shake and a-shiver—glints and gleams and sparks, rustle and swirl, chatter and

Kipling's young children were the first to hear his stories of articulate animals and a boy raised by the jungle animals. Illustration by W. H. Drake. (From *The Jungle Book* by Rudyard Kipling. Published by Macmillan and Co., 1894. Courtesy of Lilly Library, Indiana University, Bloomington, Indiana.)

bubble. The Mole was bewitched, entranced, fascinated. (p. 6)

Grahame creates credibility for the adventures of his most eccentric character, Toad of Toad Hall, by taking him away from the peaceful surroundings of his ancestral home. In the Wide World, where presumably such adventures could happen, he wrecks cars, is imprisoned, and escapes in a washerwoman's clothing basket. While he is gone, the less desirable animals who live in the Wild Wood, the stoats and the weasels, take over his home. When he returns, Toad's friends—brave Badger, gallant Water-Rat, and loyal Mole—help Toad recapture Toad Hall and tame the Wild Wood. Grahame suggests that a subdued and altered Toad, accompanied by his friends, recaptures his life of contentment along the river, at the edge of the Wild Wood, far away from the Wide World beyond.

Grahame's writing creates strong characters and visual images of the settings. Many children find the text difficult to read, however, so it may be preferable for adults to read this story to children. Young children may become acquainted with the various characters in this book through picture storybooks that are excerpts from chapters in *The Wind in the Willows*. Beverley Gooding has illustrated *The Open Road* and *Wayfarers All: From the Wind in the Willows,* and Adrienne Adams has illustrated *Wind in the Willows: The River Bank*. All three of these books are suitable for young readers.

Robert Lawson. This winner of the Newbery Award, the Caldecott Medal, and the Lewis Carroll Shelf Award has created a believable world in which animals retain their individualized characters. Unlike the river world of Mole in *The Wind in the Willows,* Robert Lawson's animal kingdom is influenced by humans. Like other distinguished authors of articulate animal stories, Lawson spent time closely observing animals (27). In 1936, Lawson built a house called Rabbit Hill in Connecticut. He says that he had wanted to write a story about the animals who ate everything he planted, the deer who trampled his garden, the skunks who upset his garbage pail, and the foxes who killed his chickens. Instead, when he started to write, he found himself growing fond of Little Georgie, a young rabbit, and the other animals on the hill.

The resulting book, *Rabbit Hill,* presents the impact of humans on the animals from the point of view of the animals. Lawson maintains this point of view to create believable characters. The animals on the hill wait expectantly after they learn that new folks are coming. They wonder if this change will bring about a renewal of older and pleasanter days when the fields were planted, a garden cultivated, and the lawns manicured. However, Mother Rabbit fears that the folks will be lovers of shotguns, traps, poison gases, and worst of all, boys.

Lawson centers his book on the exploits of the exuberant Little Georgie, a rabbit who retains his curiosity and love for a good chase even when his father warns him that misbehavior and parental indulgence can have swift and fatal consequences. The animals believe that all will be well when the new owners put up a sign saying "Please drive carefully on account of small animals." Then, Little Georgie has a dreadful experience with a car on the black road, and the folks from the hill take the limp rabbit into the house. Gloom settles over the animals. Is Georgie alive, and, if so, why does he not appear? What terrible experiences are the folks planning for Little Georgie? The animals learn that the new folks are considerate and caring. The story has a satisfactory ending, and the animals pay tribute to their new folks on the hill.

George Selden. Like Robert Lawson, George Selden loves the Connecticut countryside and creates animals with strong and believable personalities. His *The Cricket in Times Square,* however, has an urban setting, the subway station at Times Square. Two animal characters, Tucker Mouse and Harry Cat, are city dwellers. The other animal, Chester Cricket, arrives accidentally, having jumped into a picnic basket in Connecticut and been trapped until he arrived in New York.

Selden tells their story from the point of view of the animals and develops additional credibility by retaining some of each animal's natural characteristics: The city-wise Tucker Mouse lives in a cluttered drainpipe because he enjoys scrounging and does not consider neatness important. Chester Cricket is a natural musician and prefers to play when the spirit moves him rather than when people want to hear him. The plot develops around Chester's remarkable ability to play any music he hears and his need for returning kindness to the poor owner of the newsstand in the subway. Selden concludes his story with a longing that might be felt by anyone taken from his native environment. Chester becomes homesick for autumn in Connecticut and leaves the city to return home. When Tucker asks him how he'll know that he has reached home, Chester reassures him, "Oh, I'll know!. . .I'll smell the trees and I'll feel the air and I'll know" (p. 154).

This is a touching story of friendship, of longing for one's home, and of the love and understanding that can be felt between even a child and a tiny insect. Additional stories about these animals are found in Selden's *Tucker's Countryside, Harry Cat's Pet Puppy,* and *Chester Cricket's Pigeon Ride. Chester Cricket's Pigeon Ride* has a large format and illustrations designed to appeal to young children.

E. B. White. Roger Sale (21) has identified *Charlotte's Web* as "the classic American children's book of the last thirty years" (p. 258), while Rebecca Lukens (14) uses the book as a touchstone, the story around which she develops her critical standards for literature. Therefore, this book is a fitting example for an extended illustration of the techniques an author of fantasy may use to encourage readers to suspend disbelief.

E. B. White introduces his characters within the reality of an authentically described working farm. His human characters have no unusual powers. They do not treat animals like people, and White does not give his animals human characteristics. The harsh reality is that the farmer must keep only animals that can produce a profit. In this setting, Mr. Arable moves toward the hoghouse with an ax in his hand to kill the runt in a newly born litter of six pigs. His daughter, Fern, pleads with him to let her raise the pig. As Wilbur grows, the profitability of the farm again influences Wilbur's fate. Mr. Arable is not willing to provide for Wilbur's growing appetite. Fern again saves Wilbur, but without a hint of fantasy: She sells him to Uncle Homer Zuckerman, who lives within easy visiting distance.

Wilbur's new home also begins on a firm foundation of reality. White describes the barn in which Wilbur will live and the afternoons when Fern visits Wilbur. On an afternoon when Fern does not arrive, White changes the story from reality to fantasy. Wilbur discovers that he can talk. As he realizes this, his barnyard neighbors begin to talk to him. From this point on, White develops the animal characters into distinct individuals, consistent in speech, actions, and appearance.

Wilbur feels lonely, friendless, and dejected. He often complains. He is a character who must be helped by others. When he discovers that he is being fattened to become smoked bacon and ham, he acts nonheroically: He bursts into tears, screams that he wants to live, and cries for someone to save him. Fern does not rescue him this time. Instead, White answers Wilbur's needs by giving him a barnyard friend, Charlotte A. Cavatica, a beautiful gray spider. Charlotte has quiet manners, and she is intelligent and loyal. She reassures Wilbur during their quiet talks, spins the webs that save Wilbur's life, and accompanies him on his trip to the fair.

The character of Templeton, the barnyard rat, is revealed through his convincing actions. He creeps furtively in his search for garbage, talks sneeringly to the barnyard animals, and eats until he gorges himself. White underscores this characterization by describing Templeton as having no morals or decency.

Through the reactions of the farm families, White allows readers to suspend disbelief about the possibility of a spider's spinning a web containing words. When the local residents react in "joyful admiration" and notify their local newspaper (the *Weekly Chronicle*), White's readers tend to believe this could really have happened. Readers can accept even the final, natural death of Charlotte, because life and friendship continue through Charlotte's offspring. Wilbur understands this as he welcomes three of Charlotte's daughters to his home:

> Welcome to the barn cellar. You have chosen a hallowed doorway from which to string your webs. I think it is only fair to tell you that I was devoted to your mother. I owe my very life to her. She was brilliant, beautiful, and loyal to the end. I shall always treasure her memory. To you, her daughters, I pledge my friendship, forever and ever. (p. 182)

You may wish to compare E. B. White's *Charlotte's Web* with Dick King-Smith's believable characters and plot in *Pigs Might Fly*. Like Wilbur, Daggie Dogfoot is the runt of the litter. Unlike Wilbur, Daggie Dogfoot is physically disabled.

Toys

When children play with dolls or have conversations with their stuffed animals and other toys, they demonstrate belief in the human characteristics they give their playthings. An author who tells a story from the point of view of a toy encourages young readers to draw upon their imaginative experiences with toys and to suspend disbelief.

Rumer Godden. Every child who loves dolls knows that a doll is only a thing unless a child loves it. This is also Rumer Godden's philosophy. She writes books about the dolls who live in her own observatory house, and she has her dolls carry on a correspondence with another old family of dolls (4).

Telling *The Dolls' House* from the viewpoint of a doll, Godden creates a believable story about a group of small dolls who long to leave a shoebox and live in their own house. Godden tells her readers:

> It is an anxious, sometimes a dangerous thing to be a doll. Dolls cannot choose; they can only be chosen; they cannot 'do'; they can only be done by; children who do not understand this often do wrong things, and then the dolls are hurt and abused and lost; and when this happens, dolls cannot speak, nor do anything except be hurt and abused and lost. If you have any dolls, you should remember that. (p. 13)

Godden creates dolls who have a range of human characteristics. For example, Mr. and Mrs. Plantagenet are quite ordinary dolls with extraordinary hearts; Tottie is an antique Dutch doll with a warm, friendly character; and Marchpane is an elegant nineteenth-century china doll with a vile disposition. These characteristics play important roles as the dolls express the desire for a new home. When an elegant dollhouse arrives, Marchpane declares that the house is rightfully hers and that the rest of the dolls are her servants. Godden describes the dolls' increasing unhappiness until a tragedy opens the eyes of the two children and the story ends on a note suggesting that justice is related to one's conduct.

Margery Williams. *The Velveteen Rabbit* is told from the viewpoint of a stuffed toy that lives in a nursery and learns to know his owner. Conversations between the stuffed rabbit and an old toy horse are especially effective. They allow Margery Williams to share her feelings about the reality of toys. When the rabbit asks the wise, old Skin Horse what it means to be real, the Skin Horse informs him, "Real isn't how you are made. . . .It's a thing that happens to you. When a child loves you for a long, long time, not just to play with, but REALLY loves you, then you become Real" (p. 17). The horse tells the rabbit that becoming real usually happens after a toy's hair has been loved off, its eyes have dropped out, and its joints have loosened. Then, even if the toy is shabby, it does not mind because it has become real to the child who loves it.

The story develops around the growing companionship between a boy and the toy rabbit. Children's reactions to this story suggest how meaningful the toy-child relationship is. Teachers and librarians describe the concern of young children when the rabbit is placed in the rubbish pile because he spent many hours in bed with the boy when he had scarlet fever. When the nursery fairy appears and turns the toy into a real rabbit, however, children often say that this is the right reward for a toy who has given so much love. These reactions suggest the credibility of a story written from the point of view of a toy. You may wish to compare the versions of this book illus-

Companionship and love between a boy and a toy seem believable in this fantasy. (From *The Velveteen Rabbit,* by Margery Williams. Illustrated by Michael Hague. Illustrations copyright © 1983 by Michael Hague. Reprinted by permission of Henry Holt and Company, Inc.)

trated by William Nicholson (the original edition), Michael Green, Ilse Plume, Allen Atkinson, and Michael Hague.

A. A. Milne. According to his creator A. A. Milne (17), Winnie-the-Pooh does not like to be called a teddy bear because a teddy bear is just a toy; whereas Pooh is alive. The original Pooh was a present to Milne's son, Christopher Robin, on his first birthday. The boy and Pooh became inseparable, playing together on the nursery floor, hunting wild animals among the chairs that became African jungles, and having lengthy conversations over tea. Christopher Robin's nursery contained other "real" animals, including Piglet, Eeyore, Kanga, and Roo. When Milne wrote his stories about Christopher Robin's adventures with all these animals, he was not only thinking about his own son but also remembering himself as a boy.

Winnie-the-Pooh and *The House at Pooh Corner* are filled with stories about Pooh because Pooh likes to hear stories about himself. Milne develops credibility for the actions in his stories by taking Pooh and the others out of the nursery and into the hundred-acre wood, where an inquisitive bear can have many adventures. Several stories suggest Pooh's reality: He climbs trees looking for honey and eats Rabbit's honey when he pays a visit. The text and illustrations leave no doubt that Pooh is a toy, however. No real bear would be so clumsy as to fall from branch to branch or become stuck in Rabbit's doorway. Children may feel a close relationship with Christopher Robin because every time Pooh gets into difficulty the human child must rescue the "silly old bear."

Carlo Collodi. The adventures of a wooden marionette who is disobedient, prefers the joys of playtime to the rigors of school, and finally learns his lesson and wins an opportunity to become a real boy are similar to the experiences of Carlo Collodi, his creator. The Italian author of *Pinocchio* described himself as "the most irresponsible, the most disobedient, and impudent boy in the whole school" (5, p. 74). His story reflects a lesson Collodi learned in school:

> I persuaded myself that if one is impudent and disobedient in school he loses the good will of the teachers and the friendship of the scholars. I too became a good boy. I began to respect the others and they in turn respected me. (p. 76)

Pinocchio's insistence on doing only what he wants leads to a series of adventures: He sells his spelling book instead of attending school, he becomes involved with a devious fox and cat, he goes to a land of perpetual playtime, and he is transformed into a donkey. After Pinocchio learns some bitter lessons, he searches for his creator, Geppetto, who works to restore his health. Pinocchio begins to practice his reading and writing, and eventually becomes a real person. Through the words of the blue fairy, Collodi explains why Pinocchio is rewarded:

> Because of your kind heart I forgive you for all your misdeeds. Boys who help other people so willingly and lovingly deserve praise, even if they are not models in other ways. Always listen to good counsel and you will be happy. (p. 193)

The influence of traditional folktales and fables is evident in Collodi's use of animals with human traits to teach lessons. Magical transformations

ISSUE

Should a Literary Classic Be Rewritten to Conform to Society's Changing Views of Childhood?

IS PINOCCHIO AN EGOTISTICAL and self-centered puppet who cannot anticipate the consequences of his actions? Or is Pinocchio a lovable mischief-maker who is inherently obedient, totally innocent, and thoroughly well-intentioned? Is Geppetto a parent who displays anger, rage, and frustration when his child is disobedient and displays love and sacrifice when the child is in need? Or is Geppetto a parent who displays only love, support, and self-sacrifice?

Richard Wunderlich and Thomas J. Morrissey raise issues related to changing the characters and incidents in Carlo Collodi's *The Adventures of Pinocchio* to meet changing social definitions of childhood.[1] The researchers traced the changing characterizations and incidents found in various editions of *Pinocchio* since it was first published in 1883. For example, Collodi's Pinocchio was a complex figure: He was egotistical, self-centered, intractable, impudent, and rude. In the 1900s, abridged and condensed editions weakened or changed

punish and reward Pinocchio on his path to self-improvement (11).

Preposterous Characters and Situations

Children love exaggeration, ridiculous situations, and tongue-twisting language. Stories that appeal to a sense of humor usually include repetition, plays on words, and clever and original figures of speech. The characters in this section are developed through vivid descriptions of dress, features, or actions.

Floating through the air inside a huge peach propelled by 502 seagulls provides a getaway for an unhappy child in Roald Dahl's *James and the Giant Peach*. Children thoroughly enjoy the freshness and originality of this story. Other enjoyably preposterous journeys occur when a housepainter is granted an unusual wish in *Mr. Popper's Penguins,* by Richard and Florence Atwater; when an eccentric inventor restores an old car in Ian Fleming's *Chitty Chitty Bang Bang;* and when a bed takes flight in Mary Norton's *Bed-Knob and Broomstick*. Pamela L. Travers's preposterous nanny, Mary Poppins, goes on new adventures influenced by traditional myths, legends, and fairy tales in *Mary Poppins in Cherry Tree Lane*.

Carl Sandburg. Readers might expect some unusual characters to be the residents of Rootabaga Country, where the largest city is a village called Liver and Onions. They are usually not disappointed when they hear Carl Sandburg's *Rootabaga Stories*. Told originally to the author's own children, these stories lose part of their humor if they are read rather than heard. The alliteration and nonsensical names are hard for children to read themselves, but they are fun to listen to.

Sandburg begins his ridiculous situation by describing how to get to Rootabaga Country by train: Riders must sell everything they own, put "spot-cash money" into a ragbag, then go to the railroad station and ask for a ticket to the place where the railroad tracks run into the sky and never come back. They will know they have arrived when the train begins running on zigzag tracks, when they have traveled through the country of Over and Under, where no one gets out of the way of anyone else, and when they look out the train windows and see pigs wearing bibs.

The residents of Rootabaga Country have tongue-twisting names, such as Ax Me No Questions, Rags Habakuk, Miney Mo, and Henry Hagglyhoagly and become involved in tongue-twisting situations. For example, when Blixie Bimber puts a charm around her neck, she falls in love with the first man she meets with one *x* in his name (Silas Baxby), then with a man with two *x*'s (Fritz Axanbax), and finally with a man with three *x*'s (James Sixbixdix).

Sandburg's characters often talk in alliteration, repeating an initial sound in consecutive words. When the neighbors see a family selling their possessions, for example, they speculate that the family might be going "to Kansas, to Kokomo, to Canada, to Kankakee, to Kamchatka, to the Chat-

his nature by omitting or cutting episodes. By the 1930s, Pinocchio's mischief became a series of disconnected pranks that made Pinocchio lovable.

Likewise, the incident in which Pinocchio and Geppetto are swallowed by a large fish has changed with time. In the original, they were swallowed by a shark or dogfish. Later, the creature became a sea monster, a whale, and Monstro the Whale (Walt Disney).

Wunderlich and Morrissey conclude, "[C]hanges in *Pinocchio* manifest changes in the social definition of childhood. And thus a literary classic, written in terms of one perception and rewritten to conform to another" (p. 211). Students of children's literature may read the different versions of *Pinocchio* and consider the inappropriateness or appropriateness of changes that have been made since the original publication. In addition, they may consider Richard Wunderlich's evaluation of three new translations of *Pinocchio*.[2] Which translation is the most appropriate for readers of different ages? Why? Are similar changes found in other children's classics? If changes are apparent, how do the changes influence plot, characterization, and theme?

[1]Wunderlich, Richard, and Morrissey, Thomas J. "The Desecration of Pinocchio in the United States." *The Horn Book* (April 1982): 205–212.

[2]Wunderlich, Richard. "Pinocchio at 104." *Children's Literature* 15 (1987): 186–192.

tahoochee" (p. 6). The stories are brief enough to share with children during a short story time, but the uncommon names and the language require preparation by a storyteller or oral reader.

Astrid Lindgren. In *Pippi Longstocking,* Swedish author Astrid Lindgren creates an unusual and vivacious character, who wears pigtails and stockings of different colors. Lindgren relies on exaggeration to develop a character who is supposedly the strongest girl in the world. Pippi demonstrates her ability when she lifts her horse onto the porch of her house and when in *Pippi in the South Seas,* she saves her playmate Tommy from a shark attack.

Pippi's unconventional behavior and carefree existence appeal to many children. Pippi is a child who lives in a home, all by herself. She sleeps on a bed with her feet where her head should be and decides to attend school because she doesn't want to miss Christmas and Easter vacation. Pippi's adventures continue in *Pippi in the South Seas* and *Pippi on the Run,* which is illustrated with large color photographs.

Strange and Curious Worlds

While on their way to Carl Sandburg's Rootabaga Country, young readers may find themselves falling down rabbit holes or flying off into even stranger and more curious worlds of modern fantasy.

Lewis Carroll. A remarkable realm unfolds when one falls down a rabbit hole, follows an underground passage, and enters a tiny door into a land of cool fountains, bright flowers, and unusual inhabitants. The guide into this world is also unusual: an articulate white rabbit who wears a waistcoat complete with a pocket watch.

Perhaps even more remarkable is the fact that this world of fantasy was created by a man who was dreadfully shy with adults, had a tendency to stammer, and displayed prim and precise habits. Charles Lutwidge Dodgson, better known as Lewis Carroll, was a mathematics lecturer at Oxford University during the sedate Victorian period of English history. Warren Weaver (26) describes the life of this Victorian don:

> Dodgson's adult life symbolized—indeed, really caricatured—the restraints of Victorian society. But he was essentially a wild and free spirit, and he had to burst out of these bonds. The chief outlet was fantasy—the fantasy which children accept with such simplicity, with such intelligence and charm. (p. 16)

Dodgson may have been shy with adults, but he showed a very different personality with children. He kept himself supplied with games to amuse them, made friends with them easily, and enjoyed telling them stories. A story told on a warm July afternoon to three young daughters of the dean of Dodgson's college at Oxford made Lewis Carroll almost immortal. As the children—Alice, Edith, and Lorina Liddell—rested on the riverbank, they asked Dodgson for a story. The result was the remarkable tale that later became *Alice's Adventures in Wonderland*. Even the first line of the story is reminiscent of a warm, leisurely afternoon:

> Alice was beginning to get very tired of sitting by her sister on the bank and having nothing to do: Once or twice she had peeped into the book her sister was reading, but it had no pictures or conversations in it, "And what is the use of a book" thought Alice, "without pictures or conversations?" (p. 9)

From that point on, however, the day enters another realm of experience. Alice sees a strange white rabbit muttering to himself and follows him down, down, down into Wonderland, where the unusual is the ordinary way of life. Drinking mysterious substances changes one's size; strange animals conduct a race with no beginning and no finish that everyone wins; a hookah-smoking caterpillar gives advice; the Dormouse, the March Hare, and the Mad Hatter have a very odd tea party; the Cheshire Cat fades in and out of sight; and the King and Queen of Hearts conduct a ridiculous trial. According to Weaver, the strange adventures have a broad appeal to children everywhere because:

> [S]omething of the essence of childhood is contained in this remarkable book—the innocent fun, the natural acceptance of marvels, combined with a healthy and at times slightly saucy curiosity about them, the element of confusion concerning the strange way in which the adult world behaves, the complete and natural companionship with animals, and an intertwined mixture of the rational and the irrational. For all of these, whatever the accidents of geography, are part and parcel of childhood. (p. 6)

Throughout the book, Alice expresses a natural acceptance of the unusual. When she finds a bottle labeled "Drink Me," she does so without hesitation. When the White Rabbit sends her to look for his missing gloves, she thinks to herself that it is queer to be a messenger for a rabbit, but she goes without question. During her adventures in this strange land she does, however, question her own identity. When the Caterpillar opens their conversation by asking, "Who are you?" Alice replies:

> I—I hardly know, Sir, just at present—at least I know who I was when I got up this morning, but I think I must have been changed several times since then. . . .I can't explain myself. I'm afraid, Sir, because I'm not myself, you see. (p. 23)

Lewis Carroll's language is appealing to children, especially if an adult reads the story to them, but children have difficulty reading the story for

A tea party with unusual guests adds to Alice-in-Wonderland's confusion. (From *The Nursery "Alice"*, by Lewis Carroll. Illustrated by John Tenniel. Published by Macmillan Publishing Co., 1890, 1979.)

themselves, and some of the word plays are difficult for them to understand. Carroll's version of the story for young children, *The Nursery "Alice,"* is written as though the author were telling the tale directly to children:

> This is a little bit of the beautiful garden I told you about: You see Alice had managed at last to get quite small, so that she could go through the little door. I suppose she was about as tall as a mouse, if it stood on its hind legs; so of course this was a very tiny rose-tree: and these are very tiny gardeners. (p. 41)

Carroll is noted for his nonsense words as well as for his nonsensical situations. He claimed that even he could not explain the meanings of some words. Myra Cohn Livingston (13) quotes a letter in which Carroll explains at least some words in his popular poem "Jabberwocky":

> I am afraid I can't explain "vorpal blade" for you—nor yet "tulgey wood:" but I did make an explanation once for "uffish thought"—It seems to suggest a state of mind when the voice is gruffish, the manner roughish, and the temper huffish. Then again, as to "burble"; if you take the three verbs, "*b*leat," "m*ur*mur" and "war*ble*," and select the bits I have underlined, it certainly makes "burble": though I am afraid I can't distinctly remember having made it that way.

The appeal of Carroll's nonsensical characters and fantasy, both to himself and to children, may be explained in a quote from a letter he wrote in 1891:

> In some ways, you know, people that don't exist are much nicer than people that do. For instance, people

that don't exist are never cross: and they never contradict you: and they never tread on your toes! Oh, they're ever so much nicer than people that do exist!

James Barrie. *Peter Pan,* the classic flight of James Barrie's imagination into Never Land, was first presented as a play in 1904. Barrie begins his fantasy in the realm of reality, describing the children of Mr. and Mrs. Darling in their nursery as their parents prepare to leave for a party. When the parents leave the house, the world of fantasy immediately enters it in the form of Peter Pan and Tinker Bell, who are looking for Peter's lost shadow. Thus begins an adventure in which the Darling children fly, with the help of fairy dust, to Never Land, the kingdom that is "second to the right and then straight on till morning" (p. 31).

In Never Land, they meet the lost boys, children who have fallen out of their baby carriages when adults were not looking, and discover that there are no girls in Never Land because girls are too clever to fall out of their baby carriages. Along with Peter Pan, who ran away from home because he didn't want to grow up, the children have a series of adventures in Mermaids' Lagoon with the fairy Tinker Bell and against their archenemy, Captain Hook, and his pirates. The children finally decide to return home and accept the responsibility of growing up.

Barrie's description of Mermaids' Lagoon encourages readers to visualize this fantasy land:

If you shut your eyes and are a lucky one, you may see at times a shapeless pool of lovely pale colours suspended in the darkness; then if you squeeze your eyes tighter, the pool begins to take shape, and the colours become so vivid that with another squeeze they must go on fire. But just before they go on fire you see the lagoon. This is the nearest you ever get to it on the mainland, just one heavenly moment; if there could be two moments you might see the surf and hear the mermaids singing. (p. 111)

Barrie's settings and characters seem real. They may seem especially real to children who do not wish to grow up. The reader who does not want to take on the responsibility of adulthood may sympathize with the adult Wendy, who longs to accompany Peter Pan but cannot. The book closes on a touch of nostalgia, as Peter Pan returns to claim each new generation of children who are happy and innocent.

Little People

Traditional folktales and fairy tales describe the kingdoms of small trolls, gnomes, and fairies; Hans Christian Andersen wrote about tiny Thumbelina, who sleeps in a walnut shell; and J. R. R. Tolkien created a believable world for the hobbit. Contemporary authors of fantasy also satisfy children's fascination with people who are a lot like them, only much smaller.

Carol Kendall. In *The Gammage Cup,* Carol Kendall creates a new world, the Land between the Mountains, in which little people in the valley of the Watercress River live in twelve serene towns with names like Little Dripping, Great Dripping, and Slipper-on-the-Water. Kendall gives credibility to this setting by tracing its history, carefully describing its buildings, and creating inhabitants who have lived in the valley for centuries.

The valley has two types of residents. The Periods display smug conformity in their clothing, their insistence on neat houses, and their similar attitudes and values. In contrast, the five Minnipins—whom the Periods refer to as "Oh Them"—insist upon being different. Gummy roams the hills rather than working at a suitable job; Curley Green paints pictures and wears a scarlet cloak; Walter the Earl digs for ancient treasure; Muggles refuses to keep her house organized; and Mingy questions the rulers' authority.

The conflict between the two sides reaches a climax when the five Minnipins refuse to conform to one standard and decide that they would rather outlaw themselves, leave their homes, and become exiles in the mountains than conform to the Periods' wishes. However, Kendall allows nonconformity to save the valley; the Minnipins discover the ancient enemy, the Mushrooms, or Hairless Ones, who have tunneled a way into the valley through an old gold mine. The five exiles rally the villagers and lead the Periods in a glorious victory over the enemy. At this point, the exiles return to their homes as heroes.

Kendall uses similar techniques to encourage readers to suspend disbelief in *The Firelings.* She creates myths, tall tales, and a history engraved on Story Stones; she describes the Firelings' government; and she portrays a convincing setting on the slope of Belcher, a volcano that serves as the focus of a plot about sacrifice and escape. It is interesting to compare the themes, characterizations, and detailed histories and settings in Kendall's two books about little people.

Mary Norton. The little people in Mary Norton's stories do not live in an isolated kingdom of their own. Instead, they are found in "houses which are old and quiet and deep in the country—and where the human beings live to a routine. Routine is their safeguard. They must know which rooms are to be used and when. They do not stay long where there are careless people, or unruly children, or certain household pets" (p. 9). In *The Borrowers,* Norton persuades readers to suspend disbelief by developing a foundation in reality. She describes an old country house in detail, including a clock that has not been moved for over eighty years. Realistic humans living in the house see and believe in the little people.

Norton makes her stories more believable by describing the setting and the fearsome normal-sized people through the eyes of the Clock family, who are only six inches tall. The Clocks' size forces them to lead precarious lives. They borrow their food and furnishings from the human occupants of the house.

Norton further encourages readers to suspend disbelief through the effort made to catch the little people. *The Borrowers* reaches an exciting climax as the housekeeper vows to have the borrowers exterminated by all available means: The ratcatcher arrives, complete with dogs, rabbit snares, sacks, spade, gun, and pickax. When a human boy takes an ax and desperately tries to dislodge the grating from the brick wall so that the little people can escape, readers have no doubt that those extraordinary beings are waiting in the shadows for his aid.

The Borrowers Afloat, The Borrowers Aloft, and *The Borrowers Avenged* continue the Clocks' adventures in fields and hedgerows. Sights, sounds, smells, and experiences seem original and authentic as readers look at the world from this unusual perspective.

Spirits Friendly and Frightening

Most children love good ghost stories or tales about beings from the spirit realm, whether frightening or friendly. Authors who write about these subjects may develop elements from folklore and the historic past. Older children who enjoy stories about ghosts and goblins like the suspense and humor of Mollie Hunter's *The Wicked One*. They also like Peter Fleischman's three short tales of the supernatural in *Graven Images*. Fleischman's tales are successful because they build upon suspenseful turns of events, human folly, and comic mishaps.

In a ghost story, Mary Downing Hahn helps present-day characters deal with their problems. In *Wait till Helen Comes,* Hahn's characters overcome their resentment against their stepfather and stepsister when they help the stepsister overcome her fascination with a ghost who is trying to lure the girl to her death. In *Ghost Abbey,* by Robert Westall, an abbey plays two different roles: (1) it protects those who care for it and (2) it threatens those who harm it. In *Whispers From the Dead,* by Joan Lowery Nixon, the ghost of a murdered character helps solve a mystery and prevent a second murder.

Patricia Wrightson develops a contest of wills between an elderly woman and an otherworld creature in *A Little Fear*. The conflict occurs when the Njimbin, an otherworld creature who can influence nature, challenges old Mrs. Tucker by trying to force her from her cottage in rural Australia. Wrightston's strong female character finally outwits the ancient being. *Balyet,* also by Wrightson, centers on another aboriginal spirit. In *Balyet,* the conflict is between an older woman, a girl, and the spirit.

Demonic forces, incantations, and vanishing humans provide the suspense in *The Spell of the Sorcerer's Skull* by John Bellair. In *Mean Jake and the Devils,* William Hooks tells the story of a contest of wits between three devils (Big Daddy Devil, Devil Junior, and Baby Deviline) and Mean Jake, who is forced to wander the swamps because he is not allowed to enter either heaven or hell. The witty dialogue creates more humor than fright during the contest.

Sam McBratney also uses humorous incidents in *The Ghosts of Hungryhouse Lane*. In this story, three children try to outwit three ghosts who live in their home. In a satisfying ending, the children discover the needs of the ghosts.

Lucy Boston. The winner of the Lewis Carroll Shelf Award for *The Children of Green Knowe,* Lucy Boston uses her own historic manor house at Hemingford Grey near Cambridge, England, as the setting for her stories. The house and the way of life past generations experienced in it provided Boston with ideas for a series of stories written about an old manor house and the friendly presences who return there from generations past.

The first book of a series, *The Children of Green Knowe,* introduces the house, its owner Mrs. Oldknowe, her great-grandson Tolly, and the children who have previously lived in the house.

Boston describes the house through the eyes of Tolly, a lonely, shy boy who comes to live in this old house with furnishings similar to those found in a castle. The past comes alive for Tolly as children who have lived there in previous generations come back to play with each other and bring vitality to the house and gardens. Readers are not surprised by these actions because Great-grandmother Oldknowe expects the children to return and enjoys having them visit. Boston allows readers to learn more about the people in the past through the stories Mrs. Oldknowe tells Tolly.

Other books in this series include *The Treasure of Green Knowe, The River at Green Knowe, A Stranger at Green Knowe,* and *An Enemy at Green Knowe.* In all of the stories, ancestors return because someone wanted to keep their memories alive.

Joan Phipson. In Joan Phipson's *The Watcher in the Garden,* a garden has a benevolent power of its own. It provides refuge from destructive spirits, protects itself and an old blind man who owns and loves it, and attracts and heals an emotionally disturbed teenage girl named Kitty. The garden croons over Kitty, encourages her to lose her unhappy identity, and smooths away the stress of living. Thus, it changes her life.

Phipson develops the growing importance of the garden as a sanctuary for Kitty:

> She felt herself being pulled back again. The garden had begun to grow as an idea in her mind, too, as an alternative world that she could inhabit when her day-to-day existence became too hard to bear. (p. 27)

As Kitty becomes more involved with the garden and protecting the blind man from outside forces, she begins to believe in the power of the garden.

Time Warps

Children who read stories based on time-warp themes discover that there are more things in this world than progress and theories about the future. Time-warp stories encourage children to consider what might have happened in their own towns or geographic locations hundreds of years ago, as well as what the future might hold in centuries to come. Symbols and tangible objects unite past, present, and future, as believable characters travel to a distant past or see a future yet to materialize. Unlike many of the modern fantasies that bridge the world between old and new fantasy, time-warp stories focus on human development rather than the forces of good and evil. The problems are solved by the characters, not by supernatural powers.

Detailed descriptions of a farm and countryside in the twentieth century and during the American Civil War create a believable story in Janet Lunn's time-warp fantasy *The Root Cellar.* In this book, the problems that an unhappy orphan confronts in both the present and the past encourage her personal development. Time-warp experiences help children overcome problems related to growing up and to family in Ruth Park's *Playing Beatie Bow* and Cynthia Voigt's *Building Blocks.*

Belinda Hurmence uses a historical time and person-against-society conflict to help her protagonist understand a conflict that influenced her family. In *A Girl Called Boy,* the author develops vivid descriptions of slavery in 1853 by having a contemporary girl go back in time and live through these experiences. Jane Yolen uses a similar approach in *The Devil's Arithmetic.* In this book, a contemporary Jewish girl faces the Holocaust. Both books are believable because the authors develop historical backgrounds that are authentic and characters who are changed by their experiences.

Margaret J. Anderson. History is not just royalty, palaces, and famous people. Margaret J. Anderson's characters and settings are believable. They help readers understand changes that take place over time. Love, understanding, and friendship, even across years, are strong themes in Anderson's stories.

Anderson's *In the Keep of Time, In the Circle of Time,* and *The Mists of Time* take place in Scotland. In each book, tangible objects have an aura that seems to transcend time, and each story contains some occurrence that allows a change to take place. In *In the Keep of Time,* the ancient Smailholm Tower, a border keep built when Scotland was at war with England, allows children access to the past and future. In this story, a child is touched by a person from another time and a key glows when the moment is right for the children to walk through a door and enter another time period. In *The Circle of Time,* the same tower and the Stones of Arden, an ancient circle of twelve-foot-high stones, create the opportunity for another journey in time. In this story, a dense fog encircles the stones when the children are taken into the future. The trilogy concludes in *The Mists of Time,* which is set in the twenty-second century.

Andre Norton. Interests in history, legend, science, and helping children overcome problems are evident in Andre Norton's popular fantasies, which include both time warps and science fiction. Norton uses time-warp stories effectively to help her characters conquer personal problems in their modern lives: They go back in time and successfully overcome a problem, and the experience gives them the courage to face a crisis in their own times. Strong values from the past help the modern children shape their destinies.

Norton creates credibility by establishing a strong foundation in modern reality before allowing her characters to enter a time warp. In *Red Hart Magic,* two unrelated children, Chris and Nan, resent their parents' marriage, and the problem increases when the parents travel on business and leave the children with an aunt. The children are unhappy with each other and with schoolmates who try to bully them. Then, Chris finds a perfect miniature of an old English inn in a Salvation Army store. When he brings it home, he and Nan discover that they have shared a most unusual dream. Did they dream it, or did they actually go back to the inn during the time of Henry VIII? Did they save a priest from discovery and imprisonment?

The children dream their way back to the inn three times during different periods in English history. The experiences develop the children's confidence, and they use values developed in their experiences to help them solve contemporary problems. Their greatest accomplishment is deciding that attempts to make a real family are worthwhile.

In *Lavender Green Magic,* a father is missing in Vietnam, and three children must live with unknown grandparents and attend a school where they are the only black children in their classes. A dream pillow embroidered with two mysterious patterns and an overgrown maze planted in 1683 transport the children back into colonial America. There they solve the mystery of an ancient curse, discover that good is stronger than evil, find a way to save their grandparents' home, and resolve their own discontent. Norton's stories tie the past with the present because they stress overcoming personal problems.

David Wiseman. Educator and historian David Wiseman combines his knowledge of Cornwall in England and the burial ground at the mining parish of Gwennap to create a time-warp story with a fast plot, memorable characters, and authentic setting. In *Jeremy Visick,* Wiseman develops credibility by placing the story in a contemporary setting, where a lively, naughty, likable, and moody twelve-year-old boy, Matthew, is drawn to an old cemetery and a tombstone inscribed with the words, "And to Jeremy Visick, aged twelve years, whose body still lies in Wheal Maid" (p. 14).

Wiseman ties the plot into Cornish mining history. A neighbor describes the old mines and the disasters that took place over one hundred years ago, and a history assignment requires students to investigate the Cornish family whose men were killed in the accident. Detailed descriptions of Matthew's interactions with the earlier family, the mine shaft as it would have appeared, the terror created by the accident, and Matthew's frantic search for an escape route from the nineteenth-century accident create a credible and exciting time-warp story.

In *Thimbles,* an interest in family history provides the framework that allows a young girl to move across time to 1819. Two thimbles that she finds in her grandmother's trunk link the times in this story. When the girl finds herself back in the earlier time, she is using one of the thimbles to finish a cap of liberty for a protest march demanding the right to vote. Wiseman's detailed historical settings and his recreation of the issues of the time create a believable time-warp fantasy. Like many other authors of time-warp fantasies, Wiseman uses the past to help contemporary characters in their personal and social development.

Science Fiction

Writers of science fiction rely on hypothesized scientific advancements and imagined technology to create their plots. In order to achieve credibility, they provide detailed descriptions of this technology, portray characters who believe in the technology or the results of the technology, and create a world where science interacts with every area of society. Like other modern fantasies, science fiction relies on an internal consistency among plot, characters, and setting to encourage readers' suspension of disbelief. Science fiction written for young children often emphasizes the adventure associated with traveling to distant galaxies or encountering unusual aliens. Stories for older readers often hypothesize about the future of humanity and stress problem solving in future societies.

Critics do not agree on the identity of the first science fiction novel. Margaret P. Esmonde (7) identifies Mary Godwin Shelley's *Frankenstein*, published in 1817, as the earliest science fiction story because the protagonist is a scientist, not a wizard, and the central theme is the proper use of knowledge and the moral responsibility of a scientist for his discovery.

Roland J. Green (9) traces the emergence of the popularity of science fiction from the mid-1800s through the present explosion of interest. Jules Verne published the first major science fiction novel, *Five Weeks in a Balloon*, in 1863. Verne focused that book and later famous books enjoyed by older children and adults, such as *Twenty-Thousand Leagues Under the Sea*, on technology and invention but did not develop a society around them. Later in the nineteenth century, H. G. Wells began writing science fiction novels, such as *War of the Worlds*, that had a strong influence on the genre. According to Green, the writings of Wells differed from those of Jules Verne in that they included the systematic "extrapolation of social trends to create a detailed picture of a future society, revolutionary inventions, interplanetary warfare, and time travel" (p. 46).

After World War I, as technology advanced at an even faster pace, science fiction writing was influenced by the growth of magazines, such as *Amazing Stories*. John W. Campbell, Jr.'s, editorship of *Astounding Science Fiction*, beginning in 1938, was highly influential. Campbell insisted that the authors of stories he published develop strong characters, plausible science and technology, and logical speculation about future societies. He encouraged such talented science fiction writers as Robert A. Heinlein and Isaac Asimov.

In the 1960s, an increasing number of authors began to write science fiction stories. These stories were more suited to older children and young adults than to young children because the plots often relied on a developed sense of time, place, and space. Science fiction became a topic of interest for university and high-school courses. The media were extremely influential during this period. The movie *2001: A Space Odyssey* and the television program "Star Trek" created a devoted science fiction audience and suggested the imaginative potential of science fiction subjects. In the 1970s and 1980s, audiences flocked to such pictures as *Star Wars* and *E.T.* Young people today read and reread the paperback versions of these movies. Many writers are creating high-quality science fiction for young people.

Madeleine L'Engle. Do we all need each other? Is every atom in the universe dependent on every other? Questions like these confront Madeleine L'Engle's characters as they travel the cosmos, face the problem of being different, fight to overcome evil, understand the need for all things to mature, and discover the power of love.

It is interesting to note L'Engle's thoughts about herself as she wrote *A Wrinkle in Time*:

> I was trying to discover a theology by which I could live, because I had learned that I cannot live in a universe where there's no hope of anything, no hope of there being somebody to whom I could say, "Help"! (p. 254)

In *A Wrinkle in Time* L'Engle creates characters who are different from the people around them but have high intelligence and strong bonds of love and loyalty to one another. Meg Murry and Charles Wallace are the children of eminent scientists. Meg worries about the way the people in their town make fun of her brother as backward and strange. Her father consoles her by telling her that her brother is doing things in his own way and time. In fact, Charles Wallace has very special powers: He can probe the minds of his mother and sister, and he is also extremely bright.

L'Engle's development of the characters provides a realistic foundation for the science fiction fantasy that follows. The children discover that their scientist father is fighting the "dark thing"—a thing so evil that it could overshadow a planet, block out the stars, and create fear beyond the possibility of comfort. The children travel in the fifth dimension to a far-distant planet, where their father has been imprisoned by the evil power of "It." L'Engle states that this villain is a naked brain because "the brain tends to be vicious when it's not informed by the heart" (28, p. 254). The heart proves more powerful than the evil It in this story: Meg's ability to love deeply saves her father and Charles.

The battle against evil continues in *A Wind in the Door*, in which Charles appears to be dying. In *A Swiftly Tilting Planet*, readers discover the climactic purpose of Charles's special abilities. L'Engle creates a realistic foundation for the science fiction when fifteen-year-old Charles and his father construct a model of a tesseract, a square squared and then squared again, which is considered the dimension of time. Because Charles and his father can construct the tesseract, readers feel that the story must be true.

Another credible character adds realism to the story: The president of the United States asks for

THROUGH THE EYES OF AN AUTHOR

The Search for Truth

Recipient of the Newbery Medal and the Louis Carroll Shelf Award, MADELEINE L'ENGLE discusses stories as vehicles of truth and scientific theories in science fiction.

LONG AGO WHEN I WAS just learning to read, and the world was (as usual) tottering on the brink of war, I discovered that if I wanted to look for the truth of what was happening around me, and if I wanted to know what made the people tick who made the events I couldn't control, the place to look for that truth was in story. Facts simply told me what things were. Story told me what they were about, and sometimes even what they meant. It never occurred to me then, when I was little, nor does it now, that story is more appropriate for children than for adults. It is still, for me, the vehicle of truth.

As for writing stories for children, whether it's fantasy or "slice-of-life" stories, most people are adults by the time they get published. And most of us adults who are professional writers are writing for ourselves, out of our own needs, our own search for truth. If we aren't, we're writing down to children, and that is serving neither children, nor truth.

I'm sometimes asked, by both children and their elders, why I've written approximately half of my books for children, and I reply honestly that I've never written a book for children in my life, nor would I ever insult a child by doing so. The world is even more confused now than it was when I first discovered story as medium for meaning, and story is still, for me, the best way to make sense out of what is happening, to see "cosmos in chaos" (as Leonard Bernstein said). It is still the best way to

help. Elements of traditional fantasy enter this science fiction story in the form of an ancient rune designed to call the elements of light and hold back evil and a unicorn that aids Charles in a perilous journey. In all of her books, L'Engle emphasizes the mystery and beauty of the cosmos and the necessity of maintaining a natural balance in the order of the universe.

Anne McCaffrey. In Anne McCaffrey's *Dragonsong,* Pern is the third planet of Rukbat, a golden G-type star in the Sagittarian sector. When a wildly erratic bright red star approaches Pern, spore life, which proliferates at an incredible rate on the red star's surface, spins into space and falls in thin threads toward Pern's hospitable earth. The spore life is not hospitable to life on Pern, however; it destroys all living matter. In order to counteract this menace, the colonists enlist a life form indigenous to the planet. These creatures, called dragons, have two remarkable characteristics: (1) they can travel instantly from place to place by teleportation and (2) they can emit flaming gas when they chew phosphine-bearing rock. When guided by dragonriders, they can destroy the spore before it reaches the planet.

In this setting, a young girl fights for her dream to become a harpist. Because her father believes that such a desire is disgraceful for a female and forbids her to play her music, Menolly runs away and makes friends with the dragons. After a series of adventures in both *Dragonsong* and *Dragonsinger,* Menolly learns that she need no longer hide her skill or fear her ambitions:

> The last vestige of anxiety lifted from Menolly's mind. As a journeyman in blue, she had rank and status enough to fear no one and nothing. No need to run or hide. She'd a place to fill and a craft that was unique to her. She'd come a long, long way in a sevenday. (*Dragonsinger,* p. 264)

Monica Hughes. The role of free choice, the importance of truth, and the consequences of intolerance and superstition are themes in the science fiction trilogy of Monica Hughes. Beginning in *The Keeper of the Isis Light,* Hughes creates Isis, a harsh planet that holds a lighthouse designed to guide colonists from Earth. The planet's only inhabitants are Olwen, the orphaned daughter of the original lighthouse keepers, and Guardian, an indestructible robot. Over the years, Guardian has made adaptations in Olwen's body to

keep hope alive, rather than giving in to suicidal pessimism.

Books of fantasy and science fiction, in particular, are books in which the writer can express a vision, in most cases a vision of hope. A writer of fantasy usually looks at the seeming meaninglessness in what is happening on this planet, and says, "No, I won't accept that. There has got to be some meaning, some shape and pattern in all of this," and then looks to story for the discovery of that shape and pattern.

In my own fantasies I am very excited by some of the new sciences; in *A Wrinkle in Time* it is Einstein's theories of relativity, and Planck's Quantum theory; tesseract is a real word, and the theory of tessering is not as far fetched as at first it might seem. If anyone had asked my grandfather if we'd ever break the sound barrier, he'd have said, "Of course not." People are now saying "Of course not" about the light barrier, but, just as we've broken the sound barrier, so, one day, we'll break the light barrier, and then we'll be freed from the restrictions of time. We will be able to tesser.

In *A Wind in the Door*, I turn from the macrocosm to the microcosm, the world of the cellular biologist. Yes, indeed, there are mitochondria, and they live within us; they have their own DNA, and we are their host planet. And they are as much smaller than we are as galaxies are larger than we are. How can we—child or adult—understand this except in story?

Concepts which are too difficult for adults are open to children, who are not yet afraid of new ideas, who don't mind having the boat rocked, or new doors opened, or mixing metaphors! That is one very solid reason my science fiction/fantasy books are marketed for children; only children are open enough to understand them. Let's never underestimate the capacity of the child for a wide and glorious imagination, an ability to accept what is going on in our troubled world, and the courage to endure it with courage, and respond to it with a realistic hope.

allow her to survive the ultraviolet light and thin air on Isis.

Conflict develops as Guardian tries to protect Olwen from the reactions and the prejudices of new settlers, who are unable to accept her because of the adaptations. Hughes explores both the need to be accepted by others and the intolerance of humans to people who do not conform to accepted standards. In a strong conclusion, Olwen discovers that she is not willing to pay the price necessary for acceptance.

The Guardian of Isis is set several decades into the future. Hughes explores the consequences of living in a community where science and invention are considered harmful and where taboos and superstitions rule people's lives. The wisdom of Olwen and Guardian helps a young, questioning inhabitant realize that "it is the damage of today that we must repair, and then slowly build a better way of living. But not by looking back" (p. 122).

The final book in the trilogy by Hughes, *The Isis Pedlar*, explores what happens when an unscrupulous trickster lands on a planet where naive people are in an agricultural phase of social development. The people, who have feared technology and invention and who have developed strong taboos and superstitions, are very susceptible to the lies and greed created by the trickster. In the end, however, the wisest of the people discover, "[O]ur destiny is our own and we'll work it out without interference" (p. 113). The themes in Hughes's books are popular in much of science fiction.

In *Devil on My Back*, Monica Hughes introduces the question of what happens to people who reside in domed cities created to protect them from the terrible Age of Confusion. In this book, the year is 2147, one hundred and fifty years after the domed cities have been created. The society has become computerized and has been stratified because the favored have had access to knowledge from a central computer. In *The Dream Catcher*, also by Hughes, the society is psychic, having a mind meld that forms a powerful web of thought. In many ways, the mind meld is just as controlling as machines, because there is no room for individual thought.

John Christopher. The future world that John Christopher envisions in *The White Mountains* is quite different from the world hoped for by people today. In Christopher's future, people have lost

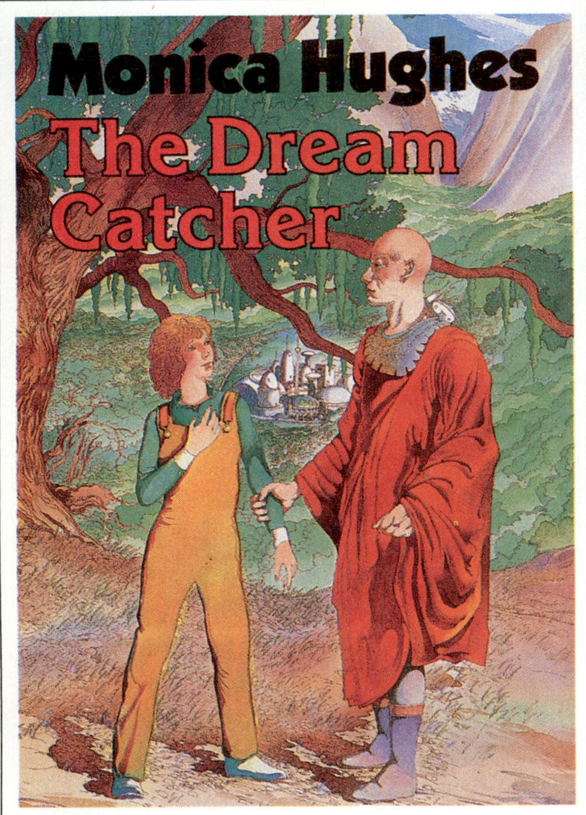

Conflict in this science fiction story develops around mind versus machine. (From *The Dream Catcher* by Monica Hughes, copyright © 1987. Reprinted by permission of Atheneum Publishers.)

their free will, and machines called Tripods have taken over. These machines maintain control through a capping ceremony that places a steel plate on the skull, making the wearer docile and obedient. Fourteen-year-old Will Parker, who is angered by the prospect of an inescapable voice inside his head, discovers that a colony of free people lives in the White Mountains, which are far to the south. Will escapes with two other young people, but the Tripods follow them. Throughout Will's adventures, Christopher emphasizes the importance of free will. Will discovers that freedom and hope are the most important luxuries in life.

In *The City of Gold and Lead* and *The Pool of Fire,* the free humans plan battle against the Tripods and then defeat them. Yet, quarreling factions defeat Will's attempts to plan for new unity among the victorious humans. Christopher's stories are exciting, but they are also sober reminders of what could happen if humanity allows itself to lose the battle for free will.

Suggested Activities for Adult Understanding of Modern Fantasy

- ☐ Read Hans Christian Andersen's "The Wild Swans." Compare the plot, characterization, and setting with the Grimms' "The Six Swans." What are the similarities and differences?
- ☐ Choose a book written from the point of view of someone who is different from a normal person. What techniques does the author use to encourage readers to suspend disbelief and consider the possibility that the story could happen?
- ☐ Discuss C. S. Lewis's "The Chronicles of Narnia" with another adult who has read the books and with a child who has read them. What are the differences, if any, in the interpretations of the two people?
- ☐ After reading J. R. R. Tolkien's *The Hobbit* or *The Lord of the Rings,* identify common elements and symbols in Tolkien's work and mythology. Consider the use of fate, subterranean descents, denial of death, mortals and immortals, supernatural beings, and power granted to objects.
- ☐ Authors who write believably about articulate animals balance reality and fantasy by allowing the animals to talk but still retain some animal characteristics. Choose an animal character such as Beatrix Potter's Peter Rabbit, Little Georgie from Robert Lawson's *Rabbit Hill,* or Mole from Kenneth Grahame's *The Wind in the Willows*. What human characteristics can you identify? What animal characteristics can you identify? Has the author developed a credible character? Why or why not?
- ☐ This text discusses Susan Cooper's use of English, Celtic, and Welsh legends and myths in her fantasies. After reading Pat O'Shea's *The Hounds of the Morrigan,* investigate and identify elements from Irish legends and myths.

References

1 Bettelheim, Bruno. *The Uses of Enchantment: The Meaning and Importance of Fairy Tales*. New York: Knopf, 1976.

2 Cavendish, Richard, ed. *Legends of the World*. New York: Schocken Books, 1982.

3 Children's Literature Association. *Touchstones: A List of Distinguished Children's Books*. Lafayette, Ind.: Purdue University; Children's Literature Association, 1985.

4 Commire, Anne. *Something About the Author: Facts and Pictures About Contemporary Authors and Illustrators of Books for Young People*. Detroit: Gale, 1971.

5 De Wit, Dorothy. *Children's Faces Looking Up: Program Building for the Storyteller*. Chicago: American Library Association, 1979.

6 Egoff, Sheila A. *Worlds Within: Children's Fantasy from the Middle Ages to Today*. Chicago: American Library Association, 1988.

7 Esmonde, Margaret P. "Children's Science Fiction." In *The First Steps: Best of the Early ChLA Quarterly*, compiled by Patricia Dooley. Lafayette, Ind.: Purdue University; Children's Literature Association, 1984.

8 Gillin, Richard. "Romantic Echoes in the Willow." *Children's Literature* 16 (1988): 169–174.

9 Green, Roland J. "Modern Science Fiction and Fantasy: A Frame of Reference." *Illinois School Journal* 57 (Fall 1977): 45–53.

10 Hedges, Ned Samuel. "The Fable and the Fabulous: The Use of Traditional Forms in Children's Literature." Lincoln: University of Nebraska, 1968, University Microfilm No. 68–18,020.

11 Heins, Paul. "A Second Look: The Adventures of Pinocchio." *The Horn Book* (April 1982): 200–204.

12 Hunt, Peter. "Dialogue and Dialectic: Language and Class in *The Wind in the Willows*." *Children's Literature* 16 (1988): 159–168.

13 Livingston, Myra Cohn. *Poems of Lewis Carroll*. New York: Crowell, 1973.

14 Lukens, Rebecca J. *A Critical Handbook of Children's Literature*. Glenview, Ill.: Scott, Foresman, 1986.

15 Marshall, Cynthia. "Allegory, Orthodoxy, Ambivalence: MacDonald's *The Day Boy and the Night Girl*." *Children's Literature* 16 (1988): 57–75.

16 Mendelson, Michael. "*The Wind in the Willows* and the Plotting of Contrast." *Children's Literature* 16 (1988): 125–144.

17 Milne, A. A. *The Christopher Robin Story Book*. New York: Dutton, 1966.

18 Nodelman, Perry. "Some Presumptuous Generalizations About Fantasy." In *The First Steps: Best of the Early ChLA Quarterly*, compiled by Patricia Dooley. Purdue University; Children's Literature Association, 1984, 15–16.

19 Noel, Ruth S. *The Mythology of Middle Earth*. Boston: Houghton Mifflin, 1977.

20 Rees, David. "The Virtues of Improbability: Joan Aiken." *Children's Literature in Education* 19 (Spring 1988): 42–54.

21 Sale, Roger. *Fairy Tales and After: From Snow White to E. B. White*. Cambridge, Mass.: Harvard University Press, 1978.

22 Sutherland, Zena, Dianne L. Monson, and May Hill Arbuthnot. *Children and Books*. Glenview, Ill.: Scott, Foresman, 1986.

23 Tolkien, J. R. R. *Fellowship of the Ring*. Boston: Houghton Mifflin, 1965.

24 Townsend, John Rowe. *Written for Children*. New York: Lippincott, 1975.

25 Tunnell, Michael O., and James S. Jacobs. "Alexander's Chronicles of Prydain: Twenty Years Later." *School Library Journal* 34 (April 1988): 27–31.

26 Weaver, Warren. *Alice in Many Tongues*. Madison, Wis.: University of Wisconsin, 1964.

27 Weston, Annette H. "Robert Lawson: Author and Illustrator." *Elementary English* 47 (January 1970): 74–84.

28 Wintle, Justin, and Emma Fisher. *The Pied Pipers: Interviews with the Influential Creators of Children's Literature*. New York: Paddington Press, 1974.

Involving Children in Modern Fantasy

HELPING CHILDREN RECOGNIZE, UNDERSTAND, AND ENJOY ELEMENTS IN FANTASY

INTERPRETING MODERN FANTASY THROUGH PUPPETRY

INTERPRETING MODERN FANTASY THROUGH ART

DEVELOPING A FANTASY INTEREST CENTER: A MODERN FANTASY WEB

INVOLVING CHILDREN WITH SCIENCE FICTION

USING ONE BOOK OF MODERN FANTASY

YOU CAN EXTEND THE MAGIC THAT CHILdren gain from modern fantasy by providing varied opportunities to interact with the plots, characters, and settings of such stories. Thus, you should give children opportunities to understand elements in fantasy, interpret modern fantasy through puppetry and art, develop a fantasy interest center, and make connections between science and science fiction and between social studies and science fiction.

HELPING CHILDREN RECOGNIZE, UNDERSTAND, AND ENJOY ELEMENTS IN FANTASY

Fantasy is a worthy genre of literature for all children. It challenges the intellect, reveals insights, stimulates the imagination, and nurtures the affective domain. However, many children have difficulty comprehending modern fantasy. Unlike realistic fiction, which mirrors a more or less real world, modern fantasy presents an altered picture.

Authors often enrich their fantasies with allegory, irony, figurative language, and traditional elements. Such elements may increase the appreciation of the stories for gifted children but cause confusion for less able readers. Susan Swanton's (14) survey of the literary choices of gifted students supports this contention. Gifted students indicated that they liked science fiction and fantasy because of the challenges they presented. While almost half of the books preferred by gifted students were classified as modern fantasy (29 percent science fiction, 18 percent other fantasy), none of the top choices of other students were similarly classified. Because modern fantasy can be pleasurable for all readers, the difference in the reading preferences is unfortunate.

With detailed illustrations and simple plots, picture books can help children understand the more complex elements found in modern fantasy. Picture books can stimulate discussion, illuminate meanings, and form bridges between illusion and understanding. Chart 7–1 identifies elements in modern fantasy and selections that develop and illustrate the elements. The picture books include both modern fantasy and traditional tales (see the Children's Literature for Chapter 6 for the traditional tales). Have the children read and discuss the picture books in each category before they read and discuss the fantasy. After children can recognize the literary elements in the picture

CHART 7–1
Books for helping children understand modern fantasy

Elements	Picture Books	Modern Fantasy
Allegory	Holder's *Aesop's Fables* Lobel's *Fables*	Lewis's "Chronicles of Narnia" Corbett's *The Song of Pentecost*
Irony	Oakley's *The Church Mice in Action* Gage's *Cully, Cully and the Bear*	Brittain's *The Wish Giver*
Figurative language	Lewin's *Jafta* and *Jafta's Mother*	Brittain's *The Wish Giver* and *Dr. Dredd's Wagon of Wonders*
Folklore elements		
Power in tangible objects	Marshak's *The Month Brothers*	Lunn's *The Root Cellar*
A quest	Severo's *The Good-Hearted Youngest Brother*	Cooper's *Seaward*
	Hodges's *Saint George and the Dragon*	McKinley's *The Hero and the Crown*
Magical powers	Grimms' *The Devil with the Three Golden Hairs*	McKinley's *The Blue Sword*
Transformations	Andersen's *The Wild Swans*	Alcock's *The Stone Walkers*
	Williams's *The Velveteen Rabbit*	Cooper's *Seaward*
Punishment for misused ability	Van Allsburg's *The Wreck of the Zephyr*	Brittain's *The Wish Giver*

books, they find it easier to identify similar elements in the fantasy sections.

For example, illustrated fables with animal characters who talk, behave like humans, and possess human traits provide excellent examples of allegory. A background in fables can help older children answer the following questions after they read W. J. Corbett's *The Song of Pentecost*: What does the title mean? Why is the leader of the mice named Pentecost? What allegorical implications are found in the author's characterizations, settings, problems, resolutions of problems, and morals?

Each of the other picture books in Chart 7–1 illustrates an important element in fantasy. For example, Hugh Lewin's highly illustrated *Jafta* and *Jafta's Mother* are excellent sources for showing figurative language. Lewin describes and illustrates Jafta's feelings by comparing them to the feelings and actions of animals in Jafta's African environment. The double-spread illustrations show both the boy and the particular animal demonstrating such actions as skipping (like a spider), stamping (like an elephant), and grumbling (like a warthog). In the modern fantasy *The Wish Giver,* Bill Brittain also uses figurative language to suggest character traits and to enhance the rural setting.

Older students may discover the mythological and legendary foundations of Tolkien's modern fantasy by tracing the important motifs found in J. R. R. Tolkien's *The Hobbit* back to Norse myths and legends. Have older students identify the elements and motifs in Padraic Colum's *The Children of Odin,* Kevin Crossley-Holland's *The Faber Book of Northern Legends* and *The Norse Myths,* and Michael Harrison's *The Curse of the Ring*. Children who identify the important motifs in Colum's *The*

Children of Odin will discover that there is a constant battle between forces of good and evil for the control of humanity, that the remote past is considered a golden age, that there is a magical significance for runes, that the ring is a symbol of power, that a dragon must be slain, that promises are contracts that must be kept, that fate governs the lives of all beings, that tricksters may help or hinder, and that heroes frequently make personal sacrifices for common good. (See chapter 6.)

In addition to identifying the important motifs in *The Children of Odin,* older students should identify quotes that show these elements are important. For example, the following are a few of the quotes that show that Norse mythology includes a constant battle between good and evil: "Always there had been war between the Giants and the Gods—between the Giants who would have destroyed the world and the Gods who would have protected the race of men and would have made the world more beautiful" (p. 6), the dwarf Brock's bargain with Loki was an evil bargain and "all its evil consequences you must bear" (p. 42), and "East of Midgard there was a place more evil than any region in Jotunheim. It was Jarnid, the Iron Wood. There dwelt witches who were the most foul of all witches. The son of the most evil witch would be the wolf who would swallow up the Moon and stain the heavens and earth with blood" (p. 168).

After Norse mythology, have students identify similar elements in *The Hobbit* and provide evidence for those elements. For example, the battle between good and evil is important in *The Hobbit,* as the following examples show: The evil goblins battle against the good dwarfs, Bilbo verbally battles against the Gollum, the evil forces lie to the east, evil wolves threaten the dwarfs, Bilbo battles against the dragon Smaug, evil Smaug battles the Lake Men, and the battle of the Five Armies shows good and evil forces.

INTERPRETING MODERN FANTASY THROUGH PUPPETRY

Young Hans Christian Andersen's favorite toys were a puppet theater and puppets. Eva Moore's *The Fairy Tale Life of Hans Christian Andersen* (9) describes the five-year-old Hans watching his father put on puppet plays, the eight-year-old Hans creating his own plays and sewing clothes for the puppets, and the seventeen-year-old Hans putting on puppet shows for the children of Copenhagen. Throughout Moore's book, readers sense how important puppets and the interactions between puppets and fantasy were to Andersen's development.

People throughout history have enjoyed interaction between puppet and puppeteer. Puppets were found in Egyptian tombs; they were part of rituals in ancient Greece and Japan; and Punch and Judy shows in England were very popular. Any viewer of television who watches the "Muppets," "Sesame Street," or "Mr. Rogers" can attest to the current popularity of puppets. Muppet characters, such as Miss Piggy and Kermit the Frog, have even been interviewed on newscasts.

Stories That Stimulate Puppetry

Geraldine Siks (13) develops a strong case for nurturing children's imaginations through puppets. She says, "[A] well-planned puppetry project, by its very nature, can serve as an introduction to all the arts, not as separate entities, but as an integrated whole" (p. 177). Siks believes that puppetry projects should start with existing stories to provide the foundation of plot and character upon which to develop a puppet play. She envisions a logical progression, beginning with nursery rhymes; progressing to folktales, fairy tales, and modern fantasy; moving to contemporary stories; and ending with original scripts.

Nancy E. Briggs and Joseph A. Wagner (1) identify the following characteristics of stories that are appropriate inspirations for puppetry:

1. The structure of a story should be clear and understandable.
2. A story should contain action that can be shown through the movements and voices of puppet characters. (Facial expressions are not possible with puppets.)
3. The pace of a story should be rapid.
4. A story should be one that children want to repeat; it should be well liked and easily understood.
5. The characters of a story should present challenging, imaginative subjects for puppet construction, but they should not be impossible to construct.
6. A story should require that no more characters appear at one time than the stage can accommodate. (Three to five puppeteers are usually all that will fit comfortably behind a stage without having the stage collapse or the players get in one another's way.)

In addition, if you wish to use sets, a story should require only a few simple ones. There is always a

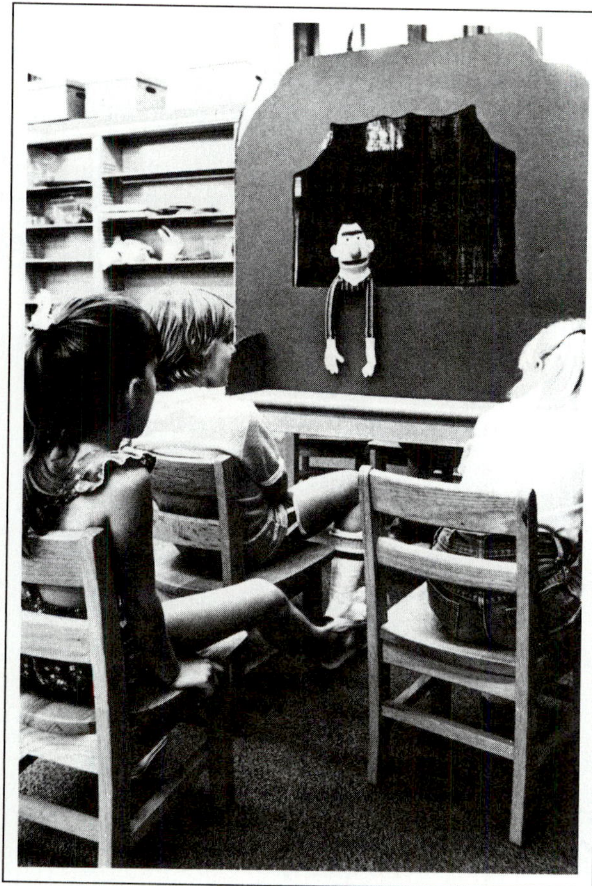

A simple stage and puppets may increase children's enjoyment of literature.

danger in puppetry that children will become so engrossed in making the puppets and the sets that they will run out of time for the actual objectives of the puppet production.

Children who have had considerable experience with listening to stories told or read by adults often have many ideas about stories to use in puppet presentations. However, you may find it helpful to share some appropriate stories with children and then let the children select a story to share with an appreciative audience of their peers.

Children and adults find many modern fantasy stories or particular scenes appropriate and enjoyable for puppetry productions. Young elementary students enjoy creating the Beatrix Potter stories as puppet productions. The interactions and adventures of Mother Rabbit, Flopsy, Mopsy, Cottontail, Peter, and Mr. McGregor make satisfying puppet plays that let children take different roles. In a Beatrix Potter festival, one group of children put on *The Tale of Peter Rabbit,* while another group portrayed the adventures of Benjamin Bunny and Peter as they went back to the garden to retrieve Peter's coat and ran into the cat. A third group depicted the confrontation between Nutkin the squirrel and Old Brown the owl. Stories from *Winnie-the-Pooh* are also enjoyable for puppetry. Because there are a number of Pooh stories, children can use their puppets to create several different plots.

Hans Christian Andersen's fantasies—such as "The Emperor's New Clothes," "The Princess and the Pea," and "The Tinderbox"—are enjoyable sources for lower- and middle-elementary puppeteers. The humorous characters and settings in Carl Sandburg's *Rootabaga Stories* are fun to create as puppets and sets, as well as to present as puppet plays. Children find that such characters as Jason Squiff, with his popcorn hat, popcorn mittens, and popcorn shoes, and Rags Habakuk, with a blue rat on each shoulder, encourage them to create new situations.

Middle- and upper-elementary students have recreated many scenes from L. Frank Baum's *The Wizard of Oz*. They have shown Dorothy and Toto's whirling through the air and landing in Oz, Dorothy's saving the Scarecrow, the meeting with the Tin Woodman and the Cowardly Lion, the journey through the deadly poppy field, their arrival in the Emerald City, the interview with the wizard, and the exciting encounters with the Wicked Witch of the West.

Adults and children can find more ideas for appropriate puppetry stories by reading various books on puppetry plays. For example, Lewis Mahlmann and David Cadwalader Jones's *Puppet Plays for Young Players* (6) contains adaptations of twelve plays, including "The Princess and the Pea," "Pinocchio," "The Tinderbox," "Alice's Adventures in Wonderland," and "The Wizard of Oz," as well as several traditional fairy tales. Mahlmann and Jones have adapted eighteen additional stories in *Puppet Plays from Favorite Stories* (7). This collection contains both traditional and modern fantasy selections.

Puppet Creation

The four major types of puppets are (1) hand puppets, (2) rod puppets, (3) shadow puppets, and (4) marionettes. The professional puppeteer or college student who is investigating puppetry may create and use a wide variety of marionettes and other complex puppets. However, young children have better results creating and working simple puppets. Hand puppets are usually considered ideal for beginning puppeteers because they are the easiest to construct and control.

Hand puppets range from stockings or paper sacks placed over the hand to puppets with heads constructed from papier-mâché. A paper-bag puppet is easy and quick to construct. To make this puppet, draw features directly on the bag, allowing the mouth opening to fall on the fold of the bag, or cut features from construction paper and glue them onto the bag. You can use such objects as buttons, yarn, felt, and pipe cleaners to add features to paper-bag puppets.

Paper plates also provide material for puppets that are easy for children to construct and manip-

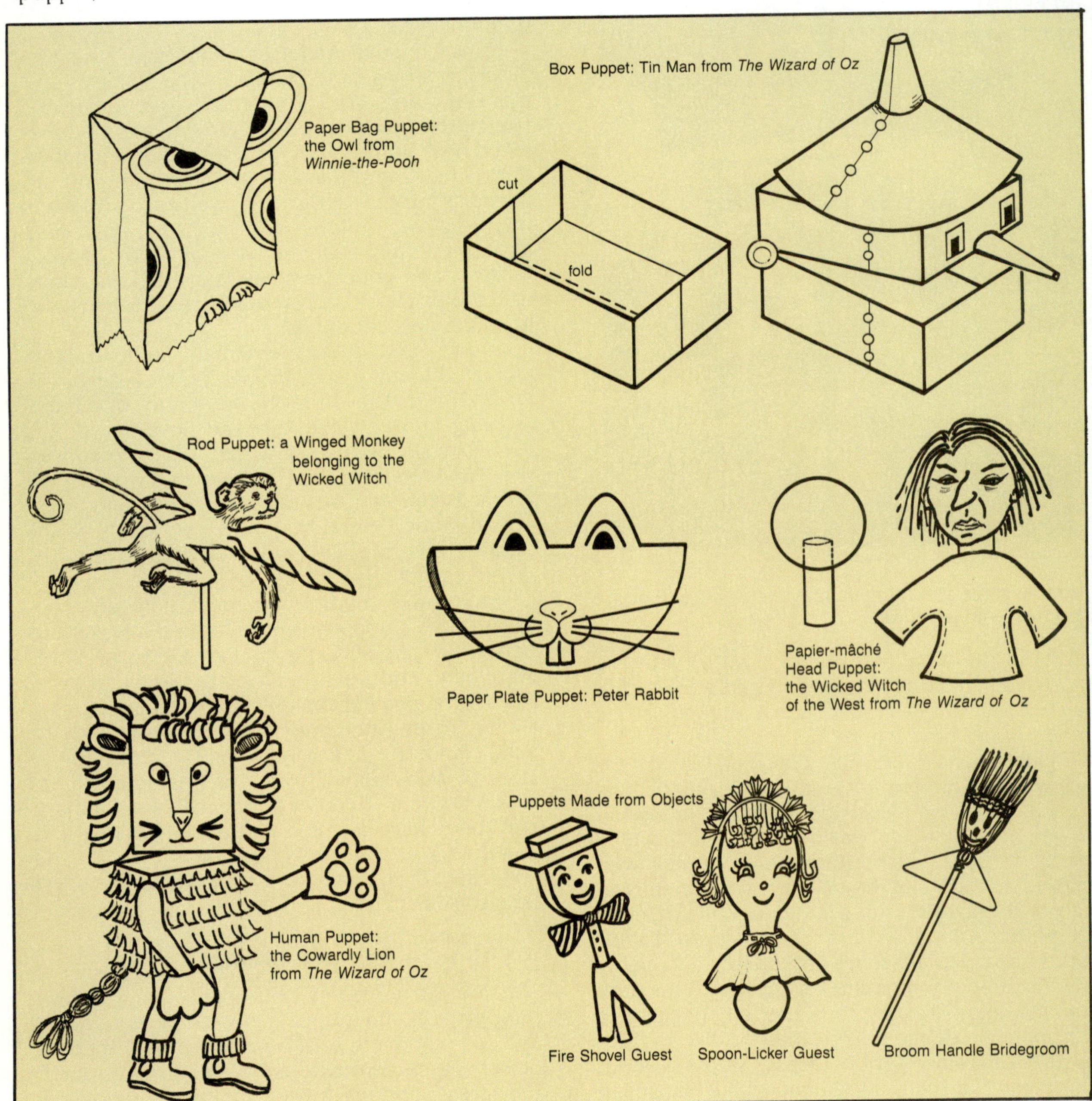

FIGURE 7–1
Puppets that children can make

ulate. Fold the paper plate in half and add features to it. This folding allows the child to manipulate the puppet's speaking action. Glue on cut paper for ears and pipe cleaners for whiskers.

Turn boxes of various sizes into hand puppets. To form the base of a puppet, cut a box on the sides and fold it, then add features to the box to create the desired character.

Puppets with papier-mâché heads can be given features that look real. To form a head, use a plastic foam ball, a crumpled newspaper ball, or an inflated balloon as a base. Before adding the papier-mâché to the base, place a cardboard tube from paper toweling into the center of the neck. This tube should be wide enough to hold one or two fingers. Then cut newspaper or toweling into small pieces or strips, dip the strips into thinned wallpaper paste or glue, and apply them over the form until you have formed the desired features. After the head has dried, paint additional features onto the head and add hair. Then, cut, sew, or glue together a simple garment to fit over the hand.

Very simple puppets can be constructed by cutting characters from construction paper or cardboard and attaching the figures to sticks. A child maneuvers the puppet by grasping the lower end of the rod and moving it across the stage. (See Figure 7–1.)

Children can actually become human puppets by constructing cardboard shapes or designing boxes large enough to cover their bodies to represent characters from modern fantasies. Sometimes stories suggest other objects that can be turned into puppets. One group of children created puppets for Carl Sandburg's "The Wedding Procession of the Rag Doll and the Broom Handle and Who Was in It." One child turned a broom into a puppet who was ready for a wedding. He added facial features to a broom, attached a coat hanger just below the face, and placed a shirt and jacket over the coat hanger. The bottom of the broom handle became the stick by which the puppet was maneuvered. A fireplace shovel, tablespoons, dishpans, frying pans, and striped bibs were also turned into puppets. After the children made their puppets and recreated the wedding procession, they created other situations in which their characters played major roles.

Children as Puppeteers

Preparing for a puppet presentation when literature is the stimulus is similar to preparing for other types of creative dramatizations. George Merten (8) recommends that a story be read several times, until the players feel they know it thoroughly. He suggests that the children develop a mental image of the characters, their personalities, and their quirks. The children should consider the relationships among characters. Next, the children should improvise each segment while an adult considers where and when the scene takes place, who is in the scene, what happens in the scene, how the scene moves forward, and the objective of the scene.

George Latshaw (4) believes that the players should go through a three-step improvisation. First, they should pantomime the scene. Then, they should repeat the same scene but add sounds that express the characters' feelings (yawns, giggles, gasps). Finally, they should improvise using dialogue. The resulting puppet play should be believable to both the actors and the audience.

Children usually enjoy giving a puppet production several times so that they can play different parts or all of the children who made a certain puppet character can play that particular part. Many stories have several different scenes. Thus, children become involved in the production as both players and audience.

Teachers, librarians, and other adults who work with children find that children will turn many favorite stories into puppet productions if they are given opportunities to create puppets and even simple stages on which to perform. Many productions are very informal, with one or two children putting on a play for their own enjoyment. Whether the production is two children behind a living room sofa or a group of fifth graders staging a more elaborate story for classmates or parents, a magical quality usually transforms the children into storybook characters.

INTERPRETING MODERN FANTASY THROUGH ART

The strange and curious worlds, imaginary kingdoms, animal fantasy, and preposterous situations found in modern fantasy lend themselves to artistic interpretations. Betty Coody (2) says:

> [C]reative art-literature experiences occur in the classroom when boys and girls are moved by a good story well told or read, when art materials are made available, and when time and space are allowed for experimenting with the materials. (p. 92)

Note, however, that art should allow children to expand their enjoyment of a story through self-expression; it should not be forced following the reading of every story.

Modern fantasy selections that can stimulate artistic interpretations range from books that interest preschool children through books appropriate for upper-elementary and middle-school children. You can explore a wide variety of art media in relation to modern fantasy selections, as well as to other literary genres.

Murals and Friezes

Mural and frieze interpretations of literature encourage children to work in a group in order to create a large picture. A mural is usually made by designing and creating a picture on a long piece of paper placed on the floor or long tables so that children can work together on it. A frieze is similar to a mural, but it consists of a long narrow border or band of paper that stretches across a wall or around a room.

Have the children plan the content of a mural and decide the responsibilities of each individual. Let the children create drawings on the mural with paints, chalk, or crayons. Finally, let the children add objects cut out of construction paper on top of background paintings. Place the finished mural on a large bulletin board or whole sections of a wall or hallway. Murals can depict one setting suggested by a book or can be divided into segments to illustrate different parts of a story.

Stories with vivid settings are enjoyable sources of mural subjects for young children. Beatrix Potter's *The Tale of Squirrel Nutkin* contains a description of the island in the middle of the lake where the squirrels go to gather nuts. Children have created murals showing a large lake surrounded by a woods, with a tree-covered island in the center. The largest tree is the hollow oak tree, the old brown owl's home. Because the story takes place in the autumn, have children create trees and bushes covered with shades of red, gold, and orange. On the lake, have them paint squirrels sailing toward the island on rafts. One group of children gathered real acorns, autumn leaves, and twigs to add to the mural. Other stories that suggest scenic murals include scenes in the hundred-acre wood in A. A. Milne's *Winnie-the-Pooh;* the river world of Mole, the Wild Wood, and Toad's home at Toad Hall in Kenneth Grahame's *The Wind in the Willows;* and the barnyard world of E. B. White's *Charlotte's Web.*

Children have also drawn in large mural format to show the travels of various characters in stories. They have illustrated Little Georgie's journey as he travels across the countryside in search of Uncle Analdas's home in chapters three and four of Robert Lawson's *Rabbit Hill.* Little Georgie travels to the Twin Bridges, walks briskly down the Hill, moves quietly past the home of the Dogs of the Fat-Man-at-the-Crossroads, runs happily across the High Ridge, leaps over Deadman's Brook, and eventually finds Uncle Analdas's disorderly burrow. Children may also create murals to contrast the city and rural settings found in Ursula K. LeGuin's *Catwings* and *Catwings Return.*

An illustration of an actual frieze of richly carved people and animals that decorated Greek architecture often interests children and helps them create their own friezes depicting the important characters and events in a story. After reading Carl Sandburg's *Rootabaga Stories,* one group of children created a humorous frieze. They showed the train and its occupants traveling toward Rootabaga Country through the land of Over and Under, the country of balloon pickers, and the country of circus clowns; the tracks running in zigzags in the land where pigs wear bibs; and the final destination of the village of Liver and Onions. The characters and their adventures found in J. R. R. Tolkien's *The Hobbit* and Lloyd Alexander's Prydain chronicles are fine inspirations for other friezes by older children.

Collages, Montages, and Mosaics

Three types of art involve gluing other materials onto flat surfaces. All three are also enjoyable ways to interpret literature. A collage is a picture made by pasting different shapes and textures of materials onto a surface (see Figure 7–2). Collect many materials—including newspapers, lace paper doilies, velvet, burlap, felt, satin, yarn, aluminum foil, rope, buttons, toothpicks, twigs, bark, corrugated paper, tissue paper, and paints—so that children have many things to choose from to achieve the desired effects when they are creating collages.

Young children like working with texture and then feeling the results of the different materials on their collages. Beatrix Potter's *The Tale of Peter Rabbit and Other Stories* is an enjoyable inspiration for collage interpretations. Some young children created Peter by cutting a jacket out of material and shoes out of construction paper, then adding a cotton-ball tail and string whiskers. They portrayed him in a gooseberry net made from string or nylon netting and had him peering

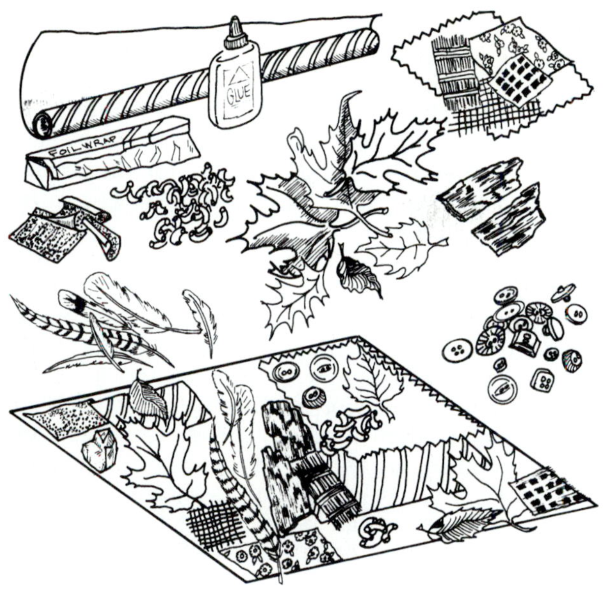

FIGURE 7–2
Collage

forlornly at a scarecrow complete with brass-buttoned jacket, hanging shoes, and three-dimensional lettuce plants. Russell Erickson's various Warton the Toad books, Roald Dahl's *James and the Giant Peach*, Jane Yolen's *The Girl Who Cried Flowers* and *The Faery Flag: Stories and Poems of Fantasy and the Supernatural*, and Keith Baker's *The Magic Fan* are other excellent inspirations for collage.

A montage is a composite picture created by bringing together into a single composition a number of different pictures or parts of pictures and arranging them to form a blended whole. Children can create a montage by cutting pictures from magazines or other sources and then mounting them so that the surfaces overlap. The pictures and their arrangement may suggest feelings, themes, moods, or concepts. They may be abstract in nature or rely on concrete symbols. Montage may be the first art form some children experience that is not necessarily realistic. Through montage, however, children find that they can select and rearrange pictures and parts of pictures to express their feelings.

E. B. White's *Charlotte's Web* has stimulated the creation of montage. Throughout the book, Templeton the rat is portrayed as an animal who "had a habit of picking up unusual objects around the farm and storing them in his home" (p. 45). He collected delectable food scraps: part of a ham sandwich, a chunk of Swiss cheese, and a wormy apple core. Children have developed a montage that suggests the essence of the material objects Templeton prizes.

After reading Ian Fleming's *Chitty Chitty Bang Bang*, children created a montage of antique cars and a candy factory. Older children have created more complex themes. They have used the montage process to suggest the battles between good and evil in J. R. R. Tolkien's *The Hobbit* and *The Lord of the Rings* and in Lloyd Alexander's Prydain chronicles. They have created montages of symbols representing past, present, and future inspired by the time-warp fantasies of Margaret J. Anderson and others. They have used montage to create worlds of friendly ghosts, such as those found in Lucy Boston's *The Children of Green Knowe*, and of less benevolent spirits, such as Mollie Hunter's *The Wicked One*.

A mosaic is a design or picture that results from gluing small objects of different colors onto a surface. Children can select a favorite character from literature; draw the character on a surface of heavy paper, cardboard, or wood; select appropriate small objects to fill in the lines—such as seeds, stones, or small bits of paper; place glue inside the shape; and then attach the objects to the surface. They may fill in the background with color or drawings if they wish. Favorite characters for this activity include Margery Williams's *The Velveteen Rabbit*, A. A. Milne's characters in *Winnie-the-Pooh*, and Lewis Carroll's characters in *Alice's Adventures in Wonderland*.

Papier-Mâché

Children enjoy creating sculptures of their favorite animal or human characters in books that they read. Papier-mâché characters are created by covering lightweight structural forms with strips of newspaper or paper toweling that have been dipped into thinned wallpaper paste. Children can make the structural forms by inflating balloons of appropriate size, wadding and taping newspapers into desired shapes, selecting plastic containers that resemble the desired shapes, forming the shapes from clay, or developing wire or wire-mesh constructions. All of these techniques are described in step-by-step detail in Whitman's *A Whitman Creative Art Book, Papier-Mâché* (15).

The statues in the queen's courtyard in C. S. Lewis's *The Lion, the Witch and the Wardrobe* are interesting subjects for papier-mâché treatments, as are Rudyard Kipling's Mowgli, Rikki-Tikki-Tavi, and other characters in *The Jungle Books* and animal characters in the *Just So Stories*. Children's favorite articulate animals provide lively subjects for papier-mâché.

Shadowboxes

Many stories lend themselves to miniature recreations of settings inside boxes or framed on shelves. Stories about small people or dolls, such as Mary Norton's *The Borrowers* or Rumer Godden's *The Dolls' House* are obvious sources of inspiration for such shadowboxes or dioramas. Children of many ages, and adults as well, are often fascinated by miniatures.

Children enjoy collecting small items around their own homes, such as spools, thimbles, bottle caps, and boxes and then turning them into furniture for Norton's Clock family. After reading *The Dolls' House,* children may wish to learn more about the elegant dollhouse described in the book and then choose and recreate a favorite room from the house. Books such as Barbara Farlie and Charlotte L. Clarke's *All About Doll Houses* (3) illustrate many kinds of dollhouses, period rooms, furniture, and accessory projects. Children can see, for example, how a bead from a broken necklace can be turned into a lamp and how a round bottle top can be turned into a teapot.

Robert O'Brien's *Mrs. Frisby and the Rats of NIMH* can inspire children to recreate the inside of the laboratory, the rats' new colony in Thorn Valley, and other scenes. The strange and curious world of Lewis Carroll's *Alice's Adventures in Wonderland* provides many exciting scenes for dioramas, such as Alice's tea party with the Mad Hatter. James Barrie's Never Land in *Peter Pan* provides other rewarding subjects for dioramas, including the Darling children's nursery and Captain Hook's ship.

These scenes are merely suggestive of the many interpretations that children can attempt in using literature to stimulate artwork. For many children, art interpretation allows interaction with their favorite characters in new ways. As suggested earlier, however, children do not need to interpret all of their reading with art projects. For young children, art should be an enjoyable extension of a story, not a general assignment. Classrooms and homes that provide rich backgrounds of art materials will encourage children to create many interpretations of their favorite storybook settings and characters.

DEVELOPING A FANTASY INTEREST CENTER: A MODERN FANTASY WEB

University students in children's literature classes can use the webbing process suggested by Donna Norton (11) to identify topics related to a central theme or subject, identify children's books related to the topic, and then develop activities that stimulate children to interact with the characters and situations in these books. One group chose

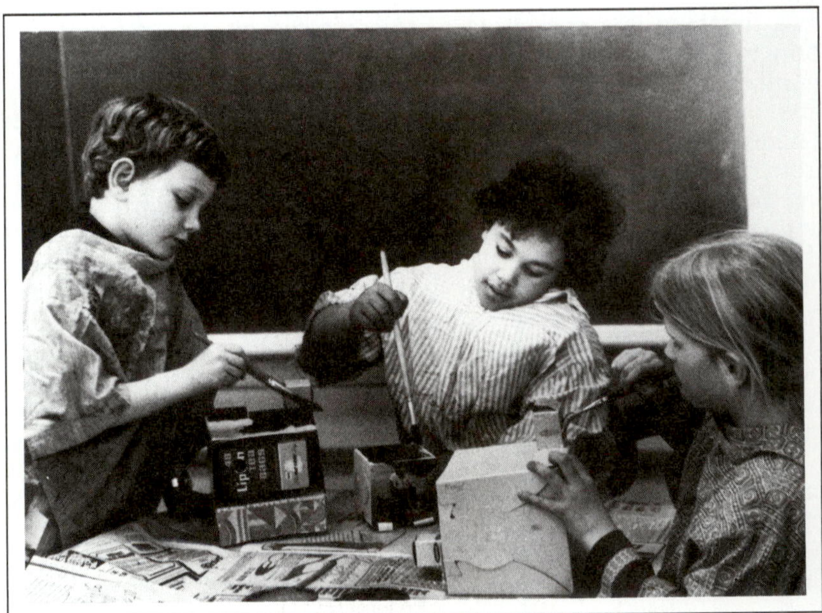

Children are creating settings for dioramas out of boxes and paint.

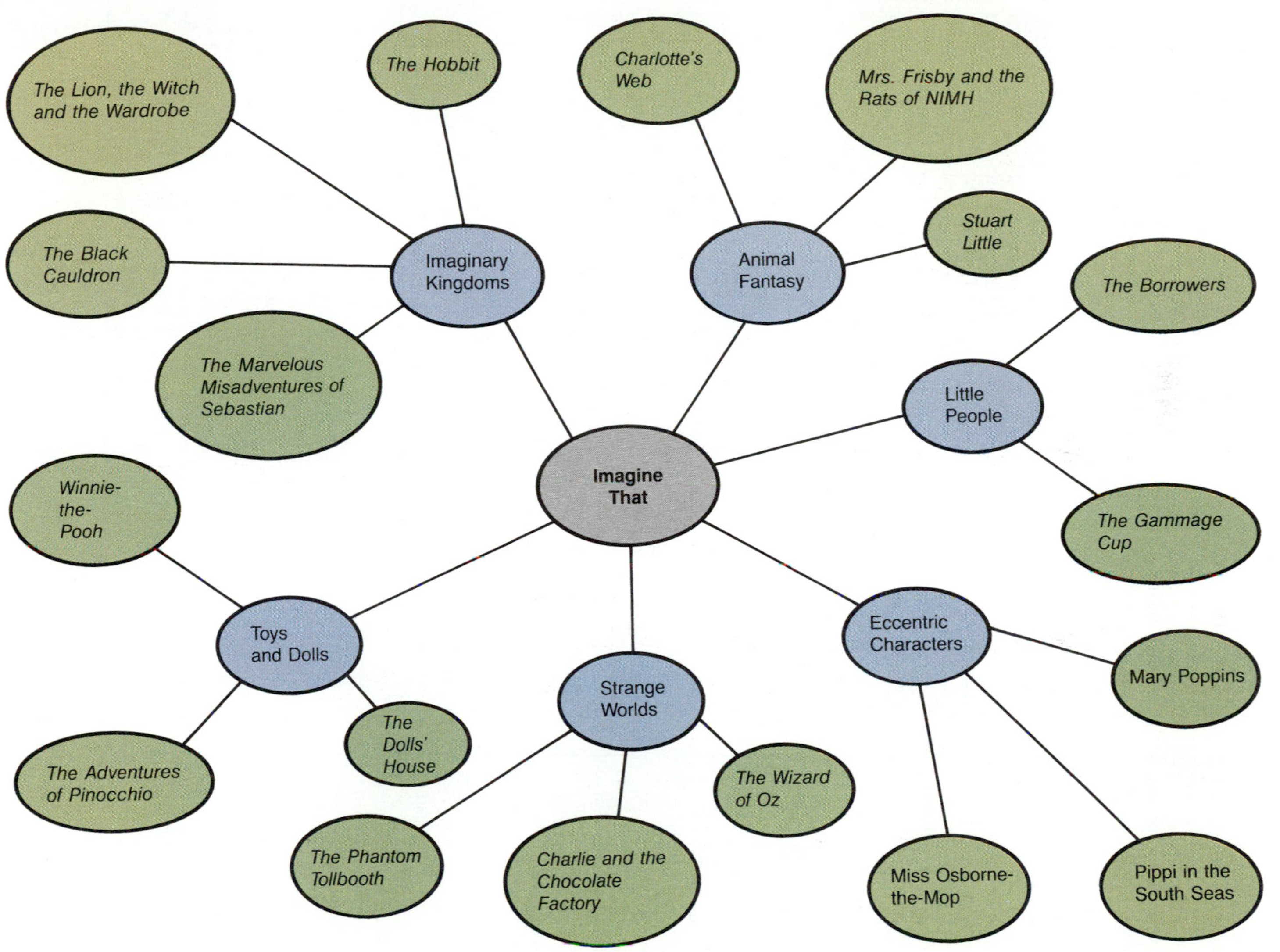

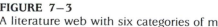

FIGURE 7–3
A literature web with six categories of modern fantasy

IMAGINARY KINGDOMS

The Lion, the Witch and the Wardrobe by C. S. Lewis.

It's true! A wardrobe leads to another land called Narnia, a land where it always snows but it's never Christmas. Peter, Susan, Edmund, and Lucy discover Narnia and must help break the wicked Snow Queen's spell. The centaurs, beavers, unicorns, and talking horses depend on the Pevensie children and on Aslan, the noble lion.

EXAMPLES OF ACTIVITIES

Pretend you are Edmund's shadow. You are right there with him in all his adventures. You hear what he says and you know how he feels. Write a character sketch about Edmund from the viewpoint of his shadow. Include the things he does and why you, his shadow, think he does them. How and why does Edmund change? How do you feel about being his shadow? What would you say if you could talk?

With a group of classmates who have read this book, act out "what happened about the statues" for the rest of the class. Refer to chapter sixteen for this exciting adventure.

Choose your favorite part in *The Lion, the Witch and the Wardrobe* (about three pages). Practice reading it; when you are ready, record your selection. Following your recording, tell why this was your favorite part in the book. After everyone is finished, we will all listen to the tapes of *The Lion, the Witch and the Wardrobe.*

Create and construct a box movie using ten scenes in proper sequence from *The Lion, the Witch and the Wardrobe.* Write an accompanying script to narrate the movie. Present your movie to the class.

ANIMAL FANTASY

Mrs. Frisby and the Rats of NIMH by Robert O'Brien

"You must go, Mrs. Frisby," said the owl, "to the rats under the rosebush. They are not, I think like other rats."

The rats under the rosebush are *not* like other rats. Mrs. Frisby, a mouse, did go to the rats for help, and she did discover their secret. Mrs. Frisby found rats that could read, use machines, and plan a self-supporting rat society. She also found rats that were in great danger. Could tiny Mrs. Frisby help them? Read the book and find out for yourself.

EXAMPLES OF ACTIVITIES

The publisher is searching high and low—it doesn't know what to do. The public is going wild and wants a sequel to *Mrs. Frisby and the Rats of NIMH.* Please help this publisher. Write to the publisher, and tell the editor why you should write *Mrs. Frisby and the Rats of NIMH, Part II.* In your letter tell what you would include in your story. (Compare your ideas with Jane Leslie Conly's *Racso and the Rats of NIMH.)*

Choose a friend who has read Charlotte's Web. Pretend that you are Nicodemus and your friend is Charlotte. Have a conversation in which you tell each other what it is like to live the life of a rat or a spider. Tell about your best friends, your adventures, and the advantages and disadvantages of being the kind of creature you are. During your conversation, tell each other why you think humans dislike spiders and rats.

Pretend that you are a mouse or a rat. Somehow you have found your way into Ms. *(teacher's name)*'s classroom. You have never seen anything like it. Write about your adventures as you journey through the classroom and meet the people or objects in the room.

STRANGE WORLDS

The Phantom Tollbooth by Norton Juster

Inside the mysterious package that Milo found in his room was what looked like a genuine turnpike tollbooth. But Milo was in for an even bigger surprise when he drove his small electric car through the tollbooth gate. Suddenly, he found himself in The Lands Beyond, the enchanted home of some of the craziest creatures ever imagined. As Milo traveled through this confusing world, he was joined by an ill-mannered little Humbug and a ticking watchfob named Tock. The three characters found themselves drawn into a chain of adventures that led them closer and closer to the forbidden Mountains of Ignorance and black-hearted demons that awaited them there.

EXAMPLES OF ACTIVITIES

Pretend that you are Milo: you just can't believe that you have found The Lands Beyond. You don't want to forget this crazy world that is so different from the one that you know. There must be a way to record your adventures. You decide to keep a diary. Write seven entries in your diary telling about different adventures in the enchanted and confusing world of The Lands Beyond. In your final entry, include any important lessons that you have learned. Bind your entries together and design a cover for your diary.

Choose a friend who has also read *The Phantom Tollbooth* and together prepare a debate to present to the class. One of you is a faithful citizen of Dictionopolis and the other is from Digitopolis. Each of you must try to convince the class that your kingdom is better. Tell the class about the advantages of living where you live and the disadvantages of living in the other place. Defend your own kingdom so that your classmates will choose to live there.

FIGURE 7–4
Motivational paragraphs and activities for three categories of modern fantasy

this technique to help formulate and develop a children's literature interest center for the middle-elementary grades around the central subject "Imagine That."

After choosing their subject, the university students identified six major categories of modern fantasy that would be appropriate for their "Imagine That" theme. Next, they identified children's modern fantasy selections suitable for each category. In order to satisfy the interests and reading needs of different students, they identified books that were on several different reading levels or that, like *Pinocchio,* had been published in various versions with different levels of reading difficulty. Following their search of the literature, they completed a literature web by identifying the books they would use (see Figure 7–3).

With these books in hand and the web developed, the group divided its responsibilities. Each student wrote motivational paragraphs to introduce the books, to captivate children's interests, and to encourage the children to read the books. Next, the students developed four or five different activities to encourage children to interact with each book, including art interpretations, creative dramatics, oral discussions, and creative writings. The students shared their paragraphs and activities in order to receive feedback from each group member. They placed the motivational paragraphs and directions for the suggested activities on large cards and put them into an attractive fantasy-land interest center complete with the books, necessary materials, and room to display the completed activities. Examples of motivational paragraphs and book-related activities developed around three of the six categories in the literature web of interest are shown in Figure 7–4.

Because several students were student teaching at the time, they placed an interest center in their classrooms and shared it with children. The students who developed and used the literature interest centers with children found that other children in a class wanted to read books because of the interest and the activities that the center generated. The teachers led or motivated some activities, while the children did others independently.

INVOLVING CHILDREN WITH SCIENCE FICTION

Science fiction stories have inspired children to become scientists and writers. Scientist Carl Sagan (12), of the popular "Cosmos" television series, credits the science fiction stories of H. G. Wells with stimulating his boyhood dreams of flying to the moon and Mars and with eventually leading him to become an astronomer. Robert Goddard, the inventor of modern rocketry, read *War of the*

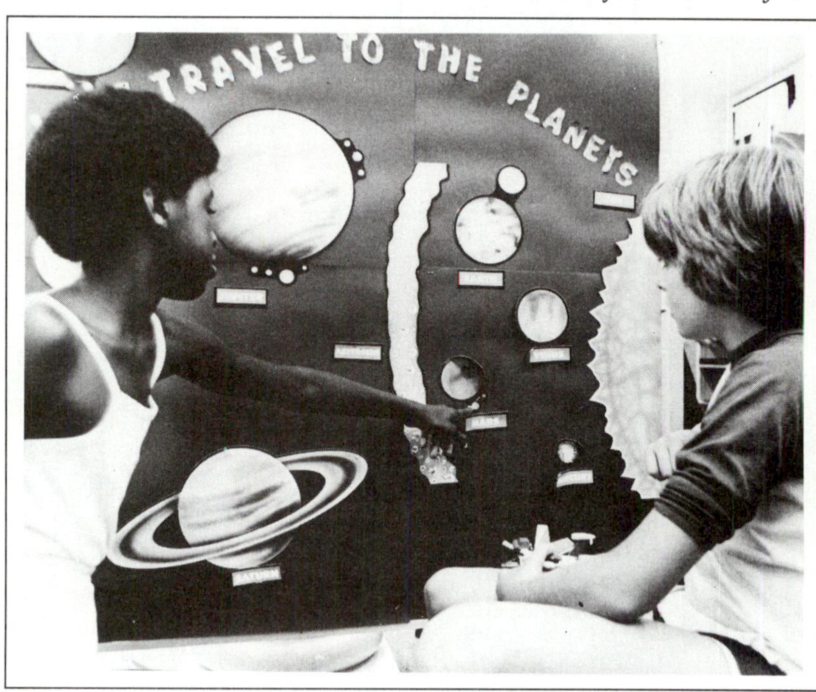

For these children, there is a close relationship between science fiction and astronomy.

CHART 7–2

Books, discussion topics, and activities relating to science and science fiction

Astronomy and Science Fiction	Changes in Natural Events or Environments That Could Affect the Future of Earth or Another Planet	Influences of Inventions, Machines, and Computers
Science Fiction to Share with Children 1 Cameron, Eleanor. *The Wonderful Flight to the Mushroom Planet.* With the help of a friend, two boys construct a spaceship and travel to a strange planet. 2 Engdahl, Sylvia Louise. *This Star Shall Abide.* A boy learns the secrets of his planetary civilization. 3 Marzollo, Jean, and Marzollo, Claudio. *Jed's Junior Space Patrol: A Science Fiction Easy-to-Read.* This intergalactic adventure includes robots and telepathic creatures. (See chapter twelve for nonfiction books about planets and space flights.) *Discussion Topics and Related Activities* 1 Have the children discuss the possibility of living in a space colony. How would colonists control their environment? How would they communicate with other colonies? How would they travel between colonies? During the discussions, encourage the children to let their imaginations soar. Also, have them consider scientific principles and the ways authors of science fiction stories solve these problems. Discuss films and television programs as well. 2 Because many science fiction stories take place on other planets, have the children consider the possibilities of discovering a new planet. Share excerpts from nonfictional books that discuss searching for new planets. 3 Use the discussion on astronomers' searching for new planets to lead to a discussion about NASA's 430-foot-long orbiting space telescope. 4 Use the latest discoveries about the characteristics of other planets and the sun, as discovered by Voyagers 1 and 2 explorations of the solar system and orbiting telescope, to stimulate discussions about science fiction and about how these characteristics would affect possible life on the planets or the development of space colonies.	*Science Fiction to Share with Children* 1 Doyle, Arthur Conan. *The Lost World.* People on earth discover a lost land in which prehistoric animals still live. 2 Hamilton, Virginia. *Dustland.* The air in a future earth time supports only dust and mutant animals and humans. 3 McCaffrey, Anne. *Dragonsong, Dragonsinger,* and *Dragonquest.* Colonists on Perm create a life form to destroy the spore life that invades the planet and has the ability to destroy all living matter. 4 Snyder, Zilpha Keatley. *Below the Root.* A thirteen-year-old survivor of a society that has experienced devastating destruction sets out to discover a civilization that supposedly lives underground. *Discussion Topics and Related Activities* 1 Have the children discuss what could happen on earth if prehistoric animals were discovered and then began to multiply rapidly. Have the children consider competition for food, the eating habits of various prehistoric animals, conditions necessary for rapid reproduction, and possible consequences for plants, smaller animals, and human life. Also, have the children consider what could happen if species that are now considered endangered were to multiply rapidly. What changes in the environment might account for the reversal? What would be the consequences for other life? 2 Several science fiction books develop plots around consequences of changes in the earth because of pollution and overpopulation. Have the children develop discussions and writings around nonfictional books on pollution and overpopulation. 3 Have the children consider various environmental problems on earth today or problems that could develop due to litter from disabled space ships or other space-traveling vehicles, such as Voyager I. Through discussions, have the children try to predict and provide various solutions to these problems.	*Science Fiction to Share with Children* 1 Christopher, John. *The White Mountains.* A futuristic mechanized society forms the setting for the story. 2 Hamilton, Virginia. *The Gathering.* A computer programmed by survivors helps rehabilitate a wasteland. 3 Hughes, Monica. *Devil on My Back* and *The Dream Catcher.* A rigid class system is imposed on society by the computer and mind meld. 4 Watson, Simon. *No Man's Land.* A mechanized world causes a boy to rebel. *Discussion Topics and Related Activities* 1 Have the children consider changes that have occurred in the world over the last one hundred years due to inventions, such as airplanes, automobiles, calculators, computers, and even light bulbs. Encourage the children to speculate about a world without these inventions and a world in which any of these inventions could become too powerful. 2 Have the children make their own inventions, draw and create models of them, describe the purposes and advantages of their inventions, share them with other children, and speculate what might happen if their inventions became too powerful. 3 Robots such as R2D2 and C3PO in *Star Wars* also fascinate children. Have the children design their own robot models, describe capabilities of the robots, and contemplate what other worlds or earth might be like if robots were plentiful or if they became more powerful than their human inventors.

Worlds by Wells. Stories about the space traveler Buck Rogers influenced George Lucas, the creator of the movies *Star Wars* and *The Empire Strikes Back*. Science fiction provides enjoyment but it can also stimulate interaction between science fiction and science or social studies.

Interactions Between Science and Science Fiction

Many science fiction books are based on scientific principles and can be used as springboards for discussions involving creative thinking, critical thinking and reinforcement of scientific facts. Children can sharpen their research skills by verifying scientific information in fantasies. Children also can enhance their appreciation and evaluation of settings in science fiction by discussing various books. Interaction between science and science fiction is highly motivating for gifted and talented students.

Several children's literature students and upper-elementary and middle-school teachers have developed activities that stress interaction between the science curriculum and science fiction. One class of teachers was stimulated by the suggestions of Dorothy Zjawin (16), who recommended different ways to encourage interaction between science and science fiction. The class divided into small groups, each of which chose the study of astronomy; the human body; inventions; or changes in nature, including environmental problems, weather, ecosystems, or time. Next, the groups identified science fiction books that could be shared orally with children or displayed in the library for children to read independently. Then, the groups investigated the science curriculum and discovered science-related materials, scientific principles, and topics in current science magazines that could stimulate interest in upper-elementary students. Finally, the groups shared their activities with children. Chart 7–2 contains examples of books, discussion topics, and related activities that proved rewarding.

Interaction Between Social Studies and Science Fiction

Science fiction relates to not only scientific principles and technology but also the possible impacts of technological changes, such as mechanization, space travel, and life on other planets, upon people and societies. Because science fiction is of high interest to many upper-elementary students, you can use it to help relate activities to meet the following four motivational recommendations for social studies recommended by John P. Lunstrum and Bob L. Taylor (5):

1 Use materials and approaches that are responsive to and built on student interests.
2 Design and/or use strategies that demonstrate the relevance of the reading task in social studies, focusing on the study and discussion of controversy and the clarification of values.
3 Help students who have negative attitudes toward reading in the social studies and little confidence in their ability to experience success in this area.
4 Encourage students to use language activities, such as role-playing games and listening more effectively. Arouse curiosity about the communication process, of which reading is an integral part, and develop interpersonal communication skills. (p. 21)

Alan Myers's recommendations for using science fiction in social studies classrooms correspond with many of the motivational recommendations of Lunstrum and Taylor. Myers says that science fiction has an important position in social studies classes because "broad themes like the nature of government, the merits of different types of social organization, racial hatred, poverty, and exploitation in unfamiliar contexts" (p. 183) can stimulate debate that is unhindered by children's stereotypes. Myers also suggests that through science fiction children acquire a sense of the relationship between cause and effect, and in so doing, they can begin to grasp the sweep of history that is important to any study of social studies.

Many science fiction books lend themselves to debates on issues related to society and social studies. Classroom teachers have successfully used the issues and books in Chart 7–3 to motivate children to consider different viewpoints during social studies classes.

Because science fiction stories often describe futuristic cities on earth or other inhabited planets, they can inspire children to create their own model cities. Children can consider what a city of the future would look like and how it would function if they could build it any way that they wished. One sixth-grade class designed such a city. The children researched known design possibilities and used their imaginations.

For the project, the children investigated energy-efficient buildings, transportation systems, sanitation systems, and suburban/urban growth before they began to build. They chose high-rise office and apartment buildings for their efficient use of urban space. For energy efficiency and beauty, their suburban homes were partially or

CHART 7–3
Issues and books to motivate children to consider different viewpoints

Issue: *People who differ from those around them are often misunderstood, feared, and even hated. This treatment is inconsistent with the prevalent belief that fellowship and love are essential if society is to survive. How should people deal with those who are different? What could happen if fellowship and love are not emphasized by society?*

Science Fiction to Share with Children

1 Hughes, Monica. *The Keeper of the Isis Light.* Settlers from earth do not accept the physical adaptations made by another human being who has learned to survive on the harsh planet of Isis.
2 Key, Alexander. *Escape to Witch Mountain.* Two children from another planet have strange powers. As they search for their identities, they must outwit sinister forces who would like to use their powers.
3 L'Engle, Madeleine. *A Wrinkle in Time.* People fear and whisper about Charles Wallace because he is different from the other children in the town. He can communicate without speaking.

Issue: *Should society allow its members to have free will? What could happen if people do not strive to retain freedom of choice?*

Science Fiction to Share with Children

1 Christopher, John. *The White Mountains.* People in the twenty-first century are controlled by machines called Tripods. When human members of the society reach the age of fourteen, steel plates are inserted into their skulls so that they can be controlled by the state.
2 Christopher, John. *The City of Gold and Lead.* Will tries to discover the secrets of the Tripod culture by spying inside the major Tripod city.
3 Chistopher, John. *The Pool of Fire.* People try to set up a new government after defeating the Tripods; dissident groups, however, cannot agree on a unified approach.
4 Hughes, Monica. *The Guardian of Isis* and *The Isis Pedlar.* These books explore the role of free choice within a society that fears science and invention.

totally below ground and had solar collectors. Shopping centers used below- and above-ground space, and they utilized light shafts to bring in light for plants and people. The children's transportation included clean, electric mass transit; computerized road systems for private cars to ensure safe, steady traffic; and moving sidewalks. Their sanitation system used a three-phase treatment process that produced drinkable water, and their power plant incinerated garbage to provide recycled power. The children planned museums and recreational facilities, including parks, trees, and an arboretum in their city. They considered the issues of controlling growth, providing an ideal number of people for their city, and satisfying their city's future energy needs.

Children can think about the impact on their own lives and society if an alien people landed on earth or if space exploration discovered life forms on other planets. Through role playing, they can imagine a first meeting, ways they might communicate, and ways humans and aliens could function together without destroying either culture. Television programs such as "Star Trek" can lead to the issue of interfering with another culture. Children can consider the possibility of the earth's being invaded or colonized by aliens who are far superior intellectually to people on earth or a space exploration's discovering human life forms who have not progressed as far as the earth's civilization.

Children can discuss the impact of various environments on space travelers who are trying to colonize them. Children can construct whole new environments in their classrooms. They can design settings that include atmosphere, plants, animals, and land characteristics; create new languages; develop communication systems; and suggest fine arts possibilities.

USING ONE BOOK OF MODERN FANTASY

Teachers and librarians can develop numerous enjoyable activities around one book of modern fantasy. Madeleine L'Engle's *A Wrinkle in Time*, for example, is a popular science fiction book. It has a plot, characters, settings, and themes that stimulate discussion, artwork, and creative dramatization. Many outstanding books can serve as bases for such activities. Therefore, you may wish to use the suggestions related to L'Engle's book as guidelines for activities in connection with other books.

Oral Discussion

Some of the suggestions for discussion of L'Engle's text involve questions that require children to consider information presented at different points in the text and then to integrate this information. Leading a discussion, you may wish to interject appropriate text passages as the children consider their answers. Listen to the children's responses and, if appropriate, ask divergent questions. Divergent questions encourage more than one "correct" answer. Let the children verbalize different interpretations of the story. Encourage the children to consider their own experiences and reactions and thus to interact with the text.

Your discussion of L'Engle's text can focus on plot, characterization, setting, theme, and style, too. The following questions and suggestions are listed in the order of the material in the book (which is indicated by page or chapter references). If you wish to focus on plot, characterization, setting, theme, or style at one time, group the following suggestions accordingly:

1. *Characterization*. What did Meg's father mean when he told Meg not to worry about Charles Wallace because "he does things in his own way and in his own time"? Was her father right? What exceptional behavior does Charles Wallace display? Why is Charles Wallace considered strange by the villagers? Why doesn't he want the people in the village to know his real capabilities? (chapter 2)
2. *Plot Development*. Tesseract is mentioned in several places in the book. Present ideas about what students think is meant by a tesseract. For example, Mrs. Whatsit informs Mrs. Murry that there is such a thing as a tesseract (p. 21). Mrs. Murry tells the children that she and their father used to have a joke about a concept called tesseract (p. 23). The term *tesseract* is described as traveling in the fifth dimension—going beyond the fourth dimension to the fifth dimension. The five dimensions are described as first, a line; second, a flat square; third, a cube; fourth, time; and fifth, the square of time, a tesseract in which people can travel through space without going the long way around (p. 76).
3. *Style: Emotional Response to Language*. Throughout the book, L'Engle makes associations between smells and emotions. Discuss some of these associations: Mrs. Whatsit's statement that she found Charles Wallace's house by the smell; and then her reaction in which she describes how lovely and warm the house is inside (p. 17); or the delicate fragrance that Meg smells when the gentle beast with tentacles relieves her of her pain (p. 175). Express your associations between smells and emotions.
4. *Theme*. Mrs. Who tells Meg that if she wants to help her father, she will need to stake her life on the truth. Mrs. Whatsit agrees and tells the children that their father is staking his life on the truth. What do Mrs. Who and Mrs. Whatsit mean by their remarks (p. 92)? How does Mrs. Whatsit stake her life in the battle against evil (p. 92)?
5. *Characterization, Theme*. Throughout the book, L'Engle develops descriptions and associations around "It." Discuss these associations and meanings:

   p. 72 — "It" is described as a dark thing that blotted out the stars, brought a chill of fear, and is the evil their father is fighting.

p. 88 It is described as evil; It is the powers of darkness. It is being fought against throughout the universe. The great people of the earth who have fought against It include Jesus, Leonardo da Vinci, Michelangelo, Madame Curie, Albert Einstein, and Albert Schweitzer. Discuss how these people fought against darkness, and identify other people who fought or are fighting against darkness.

p. 108 It makes its home in Camazotz, the most oriented city on the planet, the location of the Central Intelligence Center.

p. 118 The man is frightened about the prospect of being sent to It for reprocessing.

p. 141 It sometimes calls itself "The Happiest Sadist."

p. 158 It is a huge brain.

p. 170 Meg feels iciness because she has gone through the dark thing.

6 *Characterization, Plot Development*. Mrs. Whatsit gives each child a talisman to strengthen the child's greatest ability: for Calvin, it is the ability to communicate with all kinds of people; for Meg, it is her faults; and for Charles Wallace, it is the resilience of his childhood (p. 100). How do the children use these abilities throughout the story in their fight against It and in their endeavors to free Mr. Murry? Which ability is most important? Why?

7 *Characterization, Theme, Setting*. Why did L'Engle introduce Camazotz by showing the children skipping and bouncing in rhythm, identical houses, and women who opened their doors simultaneously (p. 103)? Why is the woman so frightened about an Aberration? What eventually happened to the Aberration? What is the significance of these actions?

8 *Characterization, Theme*. Compare the people living in Camazotz with Meg, Charles Wallace, and Calvin. How do you account for these differences (p. 118)? Could the people living in a city on earth become like the people in Camazotz? Why or why not? Why does the man at Central Intelligence Center tell the children that life will be easier for them if they don't fight It? What would happen if everyone took the man's suggestion (p. 121)? What are the consequences of allowing someone to accept all the pain, the responsibility, and the burdens of thought and decision? Would this be good or bad? Give a reason for your answer.

9 *Plot Development*. What is Meg's reason for saying the periodic table of elements when she is standing before It (p. 161)?

10 *Characterization, Plot Development, Theme*. What characteristics does Meg have that make her the only one who is able to go back to Camazotz and try to save Charles from the power of It (p. 195)? What is the only weapon that Meg has that It does not possess (p. 203)? How does Meg use this weapon to free Charles Wallace? Do any people ever use this weapon? Has anyone here ever used this weapon? Is it a weapon for good or for bad?

Artwork

Art activities accompanying *A Wrinkle in Time* can stimulate children's interpretations of setting and characterization. Ideally, children can demonstrate their divergent thinking as they interpret the author's descriptions. Following are several suggestions for art interpretations:

1 *Characterization*. Mrs. Whatsit goes through several different transformations in the course of the book. Encourage your students to illustrate these transformations. Suggestions include Mrs. Whatsit's appearance as a plump, tramplike character in her blue and green paisley scarf, red and yellow flowered print, red and black bandanna, sparse grayish hair, rough overcoat, shocking pink stole, and black rubber boots (pp. 16–17). Readers then see her transformed from this comical character into a beautiful winged creature with "wings made of rainbows, of light upon water, of poetry" (p. 64). Readers also discover that Mrs. Whatsit had been a star who gave her life in the battle against It (p. 92).

2 *Setting*. The medium is able to show the children visions through her globe. Ask your students to pretend to be sitting before a magical globe and to draw either the series of visions that the children see or the visions that people would like to see if they could ask the globe to show them anything.

3 *Setting*. Meg, Mr. Murry, and Calvin travel to a planet inhabited by creatures with four arms and five tentacles attached to each hand. The

planet also has a different appearance from Earth or Uriel. Ask your students to create a shadowbox showing the inhabitants and their planet.

Creative Dramatization

Creative drama allows children to interact with the characters in a story, interpret aspects of plot development, and express their reactions to the author's style. Following are several suggestions for creative dramatizations:

1 *Characterization*. Have your students role-play Mrs. Whatsit's first visit to Charles Wallace's home and Meg's and Mrs. Murry's reactions to her.

2 *Setting, Style*. Use Chapter 4 to create a Reader's Theater presentation for upper-elementary classes. Have your students accompany their oral readings with music that depicts the mood as Meg describes the light disappearing (p. 56); the sensations of moving with the earth (p. 58); leaving the silver glint of autumn behind and arriving in a golden field filled with light, multicolored flowers, singing birds, and an air of peace and joy (pp. 59—61); the transformation of Mrs. Whatsit into a beautiful winged creature with a voice as warm as a woodwind, with the clarity of a trumpet, and the mystery of an English horn; and ascending into the atmosphere to observe the moon and then seeing the dark ominous shadow that brought a chill of fear—the dark thing that their father was fighting.

3 *Style*. Have your students pantomime the passages on pages 56 and 57, when Meg experiences the black thing, complete with darkness, the feeling of her body's being gone, legs and arms tingling, traveling through space, and reuniting with Charles and Calvin on Uriel.

4 *Theme*. Have your students debate the argument between Meg and It, talking through Charles Wallace, found on page 160. Have them consider the question, and encourage one group to take It's view—like and equal are the same thing; people will be happy if they are alike—while another group argues Meg's point—like and equal are two different things; people cannot be happy if they are the same.

5 *Characterization, Plot Extension*. Have your students pretend that the story continues and role-play the scene in the kitchen after Mr. Murry, Charles Wallace, Meg, and Calvin return home. What would they say to Mrs. Murry and the two boys? What would Mrs. Murry and the boys say to them?

Many science fiction books encourage creative thinking and imagination. If science fiction can inspire children as it did Carl Sagan, then it can open new universes for other children.

Suggested Activities for Children's Appreciation of Modern Fantasy

☐ Develop a story-hour program that includes several short stories, a major story, and connecting materials appropriate for sharing with a designated group of children. Decide on a unifying theme within a modern fantasy topic. Combine modern fantasy and traditional literature.

☐ Using the criteria for selecting effective stories for puppetry, compile a list of stories or scenes from longer stories that might be appropriate for children's puppetry productions. After sharing the stories with the children, encourage the children to select one to develop as a puppetry presentation. Help them decide on the types of puppets they will create, and interact with them as they pantomime the story, express the characters' feelings, and add dialogue to their production.

☐ With a peer group, investigate one of the methods for artistic interpretation discussed in this chapter—mural, frieze, collage, montage, mosaic, papier-mâché, or shadowbox. Demonstrate the use of the method to the rest of the class.

☐ Share a modern fantasy selection that lends itself to artistic interpretations. Interact with a group of children as they interpret the story through a mural, frieze, collage, montage, mosaic, papier-mâché, or shadowbox. How did various children decide to interpret the story? Did they interact with the plot, characters, or setting? Did they account for all three aspects of the story? Did they develop a mood, or did they create concrete images? Encourage the children to tell about their artistic interpretations.

☐ With a peer group, develop a modern fantasy web of interest around children's literature. For example, develop webs around such topics as "Travels in Time, Space, and Imagination" or "Animals as People." Identify books appropriate for the topics. Develop an introduction for each book to stimulate interest in the book. Suggest activities to encourage children to interact with the stories in a variety of ways.

- ☐ Search the science curriculum for topics that relate to science fiction. Identify appropriate children's science fiction for one of the topics. Develop an oral discussion lesson to share with children. In the lesson, suggest discussion questions and issues to stimulate creative and critical thinking. Relate the science content to the science fiction story.
- ☐ Choose a science fiction book and develop an in-depth plan for sharing the book with children. In the plan, include discussion questions, activities that relate to science or social studies, creative dramatizations, artistic interpretations, and creative writing suggestions.

References

1 Briggs, Nancy E., and Joseph A. Wagner. *Children's Literature Through Storytelling and Drama*. Dubuque, Iowa: Brown, 1979.

2 Coody, Betty. *Using Literature with Young Children*. Dubuque, Iowa: Brown, 1979.

3 Farlie, Barbara L., and Charlotte L. Clarke. *All About Doll Houses*. New York: Bobbs-Merrill, 1975.

4 Latshaw, George. *Puppetry, the Ultimate Disguise*. New York: Rosen, 1978.

5 Lunstrum, John P., and Bob L. Taylor. *Teaching Reading in the Social Studies*. Newark, Del.: International Reading Association, 1978.

6 Mahlmann, Lewis, and David Cadwalader Jones. *Puppet Plays for Young Players*. Boston: Plays, 1974.

7 Mahlmann, Lewis, and David Cadwalader Jones. *Puppet Plays from Favorite Stories*. Boston: Plays, 1977.

8 Merten, George. *Plays for Puppet Performance*. Boston: Plays, 1979.

9 Moore, Eva. *The Fairy Tale Life of Hans Christian Andersen*. Illustrated by Trina Schart Hyman. New York: Scholastic, 1969.

10 Myers, Alan. "Science Fiction in the Classroom." *Children's Literature in Education* 9 (Winter 1978): 182–187.

11 Norton, Donna E. "A Web of Interest." *Language Arts* 54 (November 1977): 928–932.

12 Sagan, Carl. *Cosmos*. Public Broadcasting System, October 26, 1980.

13 Siks, Geraldine. *Drama with Children*. New York: Harper & Row, 1977.

14 Swanton, Susan. "Minds Alive: What and Why Gifted Students Read for Pleasure." *School Library Journal* 30 (March 1984): 99–102.

15 *A Whitman Creative Art Book, Papier-Mâché*. Racine. Wis.: Whitman, 1967.

16 Zjawin, Dorothy. "Close Encounters of the Classroom Kind." *Instructor* 87 (April 1978): 54–57.

CHILDREN'S LITERATURE

Aiken, Joan. *The Wolves of Willoughby Chase*. Illustrated by Pat Marriott. Doubleday, 1963 (I:7–10 R:5). An English country house is the setting for a Victorian melodrama.

Alcock, Vivien. *The Monster Garden*. Delacorte, 1988 (I:9+ R:5). A being is created from materials taken from a science laboratory.

———. *The Stone Walkers*. Delacorte, 1981 (I:9+ R:5). Statues come to life in a British fantasy.

Alexander, Lloyd. *The Beggar Queen*. Dutton, 1984 (I:10+ R:7). This is the climax to the Westmark trilogy.

———. *The Black Cauldron*. Holt, Rinehart & Winston, 1965 (I:10+ R:7). Taran and his companions seek to find and destroy the evil cauldron.

———. *The Book of Three*. Holt, Rinehart & Winston, 1964 (I:10+ R:5). This is the first of the Prydain chronicles.

———. *The Castle of Llyr*. Holt, Rinehart & Winston, 1966 (I:10+ R:5). The adventure increases when Princess Eilonwy is abducted by the forces of evil.

———. *The First Two Lives of Lukas-Kasha*. Dutton, 1978 (I:8–10 R:3). Lukas, a carpenter's apprentice, is conjured into a strange land, where he is known as the king.

———. *The High King*. Holt, Rinehart & Winston, 1968 (I:10+ R:5). This is the final book in the Prydain chronicles.

———. *The Kestrel*. Dutton, 1982 (I:10+ R:7). The characters in Westmark face war and corruption.

———. *The Marvelous Misadventures of Sebastian*. Dutton, 1970 (I:10+ R:6). A young musician living in the eighteenth century has a series of adventures.

———. *Taran Wanderer*. Holt, Rinehart & Winston, 1967 (I:10+ R:5). This is the fourth book of the Prydain chronicles.

———. *The Town Cats and Other Tales*. Illustrated by Laszlo Kubinyi. Dutton, 1977 (I:8–12 R:6). In eight tales, cats succeed in outwitting humans.

———. *Westmark*. Dutton, 1981 (I:10+ R:7). Moral dilemmas and high adventure combine to give a story of good versus evil.

———. *The Wizard in the Tree*. Illustrated by Laszlo Kubinyi. Dutton, 1975 (I:10+ R:6). Mallory, a kitchen maid, encounters Arbican, a wizard, and her life is changed forever.

I = Interest by age range.
R = Readability by grade level.

Allard, Harry. *Bumps in the Night*. Illustrated by James Marshall. Doubleday, 1979 (I:5–8 R:3). In a book for young children, Dudley Stork is frightened when he hears bumps at night.

Andersen, Hans Christian. *The Emperor's New Clothes*. Retold by Anne Rockwell. Translated by H. W. Dulcken. Illustrated by Anne Rockwell. Harper & Row, 1982 (I:6–9 R:6). Everyone except a child is afraid to tell the emperor the truth about his clothes.

———. *The Fir Tree*. Illustrated by Nancy Ekholm Burkert. Harper & Row, 1970 (I:7–10 R:6). The little tree yearns for a different life and realizes too late that he should have enjoyed the beautiful forest.

———. *Hans Andersen: His Classic Fairy Tales*. Translated by Erik Haugaard. Illustrated by Michael Foreman. Doubleday, 1974 (I:7–10 R:7). This collection contains eighteen Andersen tales.

———. *Michael Hague's Favorite Hans Christian Andersen Fairy Tales*. Illustrated by Michael Hague. Holt, Rinehart & Winston, 1981 (I:5–8 R:7). A collection of nine stories is printed in fairly large type.

———. *The Nightingale*. Illustrated by Alison Clair Darke. Doubleday, 1989 (I:6–12 R:5). The illustrations, which show a Chinese court setting, surround the text.

———. *The Nightingale*. Translated by Eva Le Gallienne. Illustrated by Nancy Ekholm Burkert. Harper & Row, 1965 (I:all R:7). The emperor learns to value the real nightingale more than a jeweled mechanical bird.

———. *The Red Shoes*. Translated by Anthea Bell. Illustrated by Chihiro Iwasaki. Neugebauer, 1983 (I:6–10 R:5). A girl must dance as punishment for her pride.

———. *The Snow Queen*. Retold by Amy Ehrlich. Illustrated by Susan Jeffers. Dial, 1982 (I:6–9 R:6). Detailed line drawings suggest a wintry world.

———. *The Snow Queen*. Adapted by Naomi Lewis. Illustrated by Errol LeCain. Viking, 1979 (I:6–9 R:6). An icy Snow Queen is shown against a dark blue background.

———. *The Snow Queen*. Adapted by Naomi Lewis. Illustrated by Angela Barrett. Holt, Rinehart & Winston, 1988 (I:6–9 R:6). The illustrations in this version are interesting for comparisons.

———. *The Steadfast Tin Soldier*. Illustrated by Thomas DiGrazia. Prentice-Hall, 1981 (I:6–8 R:6). The toy soldier falls in love with a paper ballerina.

———. *The Swineherd*. Translated by Anthea Bell. Illustrated by Lisbeth Zwerger. Morrow, 1982 (I:8–10 R:6). A princess does not merit the love of a prince.

———. *Thumbelina*. Retold by Amy Ehrlich. Illustrated by Susan Jeffers. Dial, 1979 (I:6–8 R:6). In a beautifully illustrated version, a girl is only one inch tall.

———. *The Ugly Duckling*. Retold and illustrated by Lorinda Bryan Cauley. Harcourt Brace Jovanovich, 1979 (I:6–8 R:2). An ostracized duckling turns into a beautiful swan.

———. *The Wild Swans*. Retold by Amy Ehrlich. Illustrated by Susan Jeffers. Dial, 1981 (I:7–12 R:7). Finely detailed illustrations develop a fantasy setting.

Anderson, Margaret J. *In the Circle of Time*. Knopf, 1979 (I:9+ R:5). Two children find themselves in twenty-second-century Scotland.

———. *The Druid's Gift*. Knopf, 1989 (I:9+ R:5). The characters interact with ancient cultures.

———. *In the Keep of Time*. Knopf, 1977 (I:9+ R:6). Children step first into the past of the Middle Ages and then into the twenty-second century.

———. *The Mists of Time*. Knopf, 1984 (I:9+ R:5). A story set in twenty-second-century Scotland concludes the trilogy.

Atwater, Richard, and Florence Atwater. *Mr. Popper's Penguins*. Illustrated by Robert Lawson. Little, Brown, 1938 (I:7–11 R:7). Excitement develops when Captain Cook, an Antarctic penguin, is sent to a quiet, dreaming house painter who longs for adventure.

Baker, Keith. *The Magic Fan*. Harcourt Brace Jovanovich, 1989 (I:5–8 R:4). A Japanese man saves his village when he is guided by a magic fan.

Barber, Antonia. *The Enchanter's Daughter*. Illustrated by Errol LeCain. Farrar, Straus & Giroux, 1987 (I:6–9 R:5). This story contains many folktale elements.

Barrie, James. *Peter Pan*. Illustrated by Nora S. Unwin. Scribner's Sons, 1911, 1929, 1950 (I:8–10 R:6). Wendy, Michael, and John accompany Peter Pan to Never Land.

Baum, L. Frank. *The Wizard of Oz*. Illustrated by W. W. Denslow. Reilly, 1956 (I:8–11 R:6). This book contains many illustrations of the original 1900 edition.

———. *The Wizard of Oz*. Illustrated by Michael Hague. Holt, Rinehart & Winston, 1982 (I:8–11 R:6). This is a newly illustrated version of Oz.

Bellairs, John. *The Spell of the Sorcerer's Skull*. Dial, 1984 (I:8–12 R:4). A professor disappears and a boy fights evil forces.

Berry, James R. *Magicians of Erianne*. Harper & Row, 1988 (I:10+ R:6). This story contains Arthurian elements.

Bond, Michael. *A Bear Called Paddington*. Illustrated by Peggy Fortnum. Houghton Mifflin, 1960 (I:6–9 R:4). This book begins a series of adventures after a bear joins a human family.

———. *Paddington Abroad*. Illustrated by Peggy Fortnum. Houghton Mifflin, 1972 (I:6–9 R:4). Paddington plans the family vacation.

———. *Paddington at Large*. Illustrated by Peggy Fortnum. Houghton Mifflin, 1963 (I:6–9 R:4). Paddington has another series of humorous adventures.

———. *Paddington Helps Out*. Illustrated by Peggy Fortnum. Houghton Mifflin, 1961 (I:6–9 R:4). The bear's actions provide humorous episodes.

———. *Paddington Marches On*. Illustrated by Peggy Fortnum. Houghton Mifflin, 1965 (I:6–9 R:4). The bear's adventures continue.

———. *Paddington on Screen*. Illustrated by Barry Macey. Houghton Mifflin, 1982 (I:6–9 R:4). This is part of the series of bear stories.

———. *Paddington Takes the Air*. Illustrated by Peggy Fortnum. Houghton Mifflin, 1971 (I:6–9 R:4). This book tells more about Paddington.

Bond, Nancy. *A String in the Harp*. Atheneum, 1976 (I:10+ R:8). The key to a harp allows Peter to experience events in Taliesin's life.

Boston, Lucy M. *The Children of Green Knowe*. Illustrated by Peter Boston. Harcourt Brace Jovanovich, 1955 (I:8–12 R:6). An old English house, a great-grandmother, and children who lived in the house during past generations make life happy again for a lonely boy.

———. *An Enemy at Green Knowe*. Illustrated by Peter Boston. Harcourt Brace Jovanovich, 1964 (I:8–12 R:6). A psychology researcher and an evil spirit threaten the existence of Green Knowe.

———. *The River at Green Knowe*. Illustrated by Peter Boston. Harcourt Brace Jovanovich, 1959 (I:8–12 R:6). Ancestors from the past visit Green Knowe again.

———. *A Stranger at Green Knowe*. Illustrated by Peter Boston. Harcourt Brace Jovanovich, 1961 (I:8–12 R:6). An escaped gorilla seeks sanctuary at Green Knowe.

———. *The Treasure of Green Knowe*. Illustrated by Peter Boston. Harcourt Brace Jovanovich, 1958 (I:8–12 R:6). Tolly finds a treasure hidden in his great-grandmother's house.

Bowkett, Stephen. *Gameplayers*. Victor Gollancz, 1989 (I:10+ R:6). A boy goes back and forth between fantasy and reality.

Brittain, Bill. *The Devil's Donkey*. Illustrated by Andrew Glass. Harper & Row, 1981 (I:9–12 R:5). A boy is changed into a donkey when he comes under the spell of Old Magda.

———. *Dr. Dredd's Wagon of Wonders*. Illustrated by Andrew Glass. Harper & Row, 1987 (I:9–12 R:6). A power struggle results between a boy with rainmaking power and Dr. Dredd.

———. *The Wish Giver*. Illustrated by Andrew Glass. Harper & Row, 1983 (I:8–12 R:5). Three children have surprising experiences when their wishes are granted.

Cameron, Eleanor. *The Wonderful Flight to the Mushroom Planet*. Illustrated by Robert Henneberger. Little, Brown, 1954 (I:8–10 R:4). Two boys construct and fly a spaceship.

Carroll, Lewis. *Alice's Adventures in Wonderland*. Illustrated by S. Michelle Wiggins. Ariel/Knopf, 1983 (I:8+ R:6). Double-page illustrations accompany the classic.

———. *Alice's Adventures in Wonderland*. Illustrated by Justin Todd. Crown, 1984 (I:8+ R:6). Photographs of Alice Liddell provided models for Todd's depiction of Alice.

———. *Alice's Adventures in Wonderland*. Illustrated by John Tenniel. Macmillan, 1866; Knopf, 1984 (I:8+ R:6). This is a facsimile edition.

———. *Through the Looking-Glass, and What Alice Found There*. Illustrated by John Tenniel. Macmillan, 1872; Knopf, 1984 (I:8+ R:6). This is a facsimile edition.

———. *Alice's Adventures in Wonderland*. Illustrated by John Tenniel. Macmillan, 1865, 1963 (I:all R:6). The classic tale begins as Alice falls down a rabbit hole.

———. *Alice's Adventures in Wonderland, Through the Looking Glass, and the Hunting of the Snark*. Illustrated by Sir John Tenniel. Chatto, Bodley Head & Jonathan Cape, 1982 (I:all R:6). This reissue of the classic stories celebrates Carroll's 150th anniversary.

———. *The Nursery "Alice."* Illustrated by John Tenniel. Macmillan, 1890, 1979 (I:6–10 R:5). Lewis Carroll prepared a version of *Alice's Adventures in Wonderland* for young children.

Chetwin, Grace. *The Riddle and the Rune*. Bradbury, 1987 (I:9+ R:6). A boy must answer a riddle as part of a dangerous quest.

Christopher, John. *The City of Gold and Lead*. Macmillan, 1967 (I:10+ R:6). In this science fiction story, Will wins an athletic contest so that he may go to the city of the Tripods.

———. *The Pool of Fire*. Macmillan, 1968 (I:10+ R:6). The Tripods are finally defeated, but Will's plans for world unity are hindered by quarreling factions among the people.

———. *The White Mountains*. Macmillan, 1967 (I:10+ R:6). A boy questions the Tripods' control over humans.

Cleary, Beverly. *The Mouse and the Motorcycle*. Illustrated by Louis Darling. Morrow, 1965 (I:7–11 R:3). Ralph makes friends with a boy who owns a toy motorcycle.

———. *Ralph S. Mouse*. Illustrated by Paul O. Zelinsky. Morrow, 1982 (I:7–11 R:3). Ralph finds himself in school.

———. *Runaway Ralph*. Illustrated by Louis Darling. Morrow, 1970 (I:7–11 R:3). Ralph is an unusual mouse who rides a motorcycle and doesn't like his life in an old hotel.

Cohen, Daniel. *The Restless Dead: Ghostly Tales from Around the World*. Dodd, Mead, 1984 (I:9+ R:7). This is a collection of eleven ghost stories.

Collodi, Carlo. *The Adventures of Pinocchio: Tale of a Puppet*. Translated by M. L. Rosenthal. Illustrated by Troy Howell. Lothrop, Lee & Shepard, 1983 (I:9+ R:7). This is a newly translated version of the classic.

———. *The Adventures of Pinocchio*. Illustrated by Naiad Einsel. Macmillan, 1892, 1963 (I:7–12 R:7). A disobedient marionette eventually learns to be a real boy.

———. *The Adventures of Pinocchio*. Retold by Neil Morris. Illustrated by Frank Baber. Rand McNally, 1982 (I:7–12 R:7). This is a recent version of the classic story.

———. *The Adventures of Pinocchio*. Illustrated by Roberto Innocent. Knopf, 1988 (I:4–12 R:7). This is a nicely illustrated version.

Cooper, Susan. *The Dark Is Rising*. Illustrated by Alan E. Cober. Atheneum, 1973 (I:10+ R:8). The last of the Old Ones goes on a quest to overcome the forces of evil.

———. *Greenwitch*. Atheneum, 1974 (I:10+ R:8). The quest continues for the key to the inscriptions on the Grail.

———. *The Grey King*. Atheneum, 1975 (I:10+ R:8). Will Stanton sets out on a dangerous quest to regain the golden harp.

———. *Over Sea, Under Stone*. Illustrated by Margery Gill. Harcourt Brace Jovanovich, 1965 (I:10+ R:8). Three children go on a quest for the Grail.

———. *Seaward*. Atheneum, 1983 (I:10+ R:5). A boy and a girl face perils as they travel from the real world into a complex world filled with good and evil.

———. *Silver on the Tree*. Atheneum, 1977, 1980 (I:10+ R:8). The final battle between the forces of good and evil takes place.

Corbett, W. J. *Pentecost and the Chosen One*. Delacorte, 1987 (I:9+ R:6). This is a sequel to *The Song of Pentecost*.

———. *The Song of Pentecost*. Illustrated by Martin Ursell. Dutton, 1983 (I:9+ R:6). The Pentecost mouse leads his followers to safety in an allegorical tale.

Cresswell, Helen. *Moondial*. Macmillan, 1987 (I:8–12 R:5). The moondial in an English garden provides the force for a time-warp experience.

Dahl, Roald. *James and the Giant Peach*. Illustrated by Nancy Ekholm Burkert. Knopf, 1961 (I:7–11 R:7). A boy's unhappiness changes when a peach grows large enough for him to enter.

Dickinson, Peter. *A Box of Nothing*. Delacorte, 1985 (I:8+ R:5). A ten-year-old is in a strange land created from junk.

———. *Eva*. Delacorte, 1989 (I:10+ R:6). In a future world, a girl lives in a chimpanzee's body after an accident.

Dillon, Barbara. *What's Happened to Harry*. Illustrated by Chris Conover. Morrow, 1982 (I:9–12 R:5). Hepzibah the Hateful lures Harry into her kitchen on Halloween and transforms him into a poodle.

Doyle, Arthur Conan. *The Lost World*. Random House, 1959 (I:10+ R:7). Prehistoric animals live in a hidden land.

Engdahl, Sylvia Louise. *This Star Shall Abide*. Illustrated by Richard Cuffari. Atheneum, 1972 (I:10+ R:6). A boy in the future learns about his planet.

Erickson, Russell E. *A Toad for Tuesday*. Illustrated by Lawrence DiFiori. Lothrop, Lee & Shepard, 1974 (I:6–9 R:4). An owl captures Warton, but Warton becomes his friend rather than his dinner.

Fleischman, Paul. *Graven Images*. Illustrated by Andrew Glass. Harper & Row, 1982 (I:10+ R:6). This book contains three stories of the supernatural.

Fleming, Ian. *Chitty Chitty Bang Bang*. Illustrated by John Burmingham. Random House, 1964 (I:7–11 R:6). A restored car has remarkable properties.

Garfield, Leon. *The Empty Sleeve*. Delacorte, 1988 (I:10+ R:6). A ghost story is set in early England.

Garner, Alan. *Elidor*. Walck, 1967 (I:10+ R:7). Four children explore an old church in England and are drawn into a world in the grip of an evil power.

———. *The Owl Service*. Walck, 1968 (I:10+ R:5). The discovery of an old set of dishes decorated with an owl pattern marks the beginning of some strange events.

———. *The Weirdstone of Brisingamen*. Walck, 1969 (I:10+ R:5). Two modern English children discover the truth about an ancient legend as they battle witches, troll women, and wolves.

Gerstein, Mordicai. *The Mountains of Tibet*. Harper & Row, 1987 (I:6–8 R:4). Elements of Asian folklore occur in this story of reincarnation.

Godden, Rumer. *The Dolls' House*. Illustrated by Tasha Tudor. Viking, 1947, 1962 (I:6–10 R:2). Three dolls want a home of their own.

———. *The Mousewife*. Illustrated by Heidi Holder. Viking, 1982 (I:7–10 R:3). A mousewife wishes for adventure, and a turtledove longs for freedom.

Grahame, Kenneth. *The Open Road*. Illustrated by Beverley Gooding. Scribner's Sons, 1979 (I:7–10 R:7). This book is based on a chapter from *The Wind in the Willows*.

———. *Wayfarers All: From the Wind in the Willows*. Illustrated by Beverley Gooding. Scribner's Sons, 1981 (I:7–10 R:7). This is a picture book version of one of the original chapters.

———. *The Wind in the Willows*. Illustrated by E. H. Shepard. Scribner's Sons, 1908, 1940 (I:7–12 R:7). Mole, Water-Rat, and Toad of Toad Hall have a series of adventures along the river, on the open road, and in the wild wood.

Hahn, Mary Downing. *Wait till Helen Comes*. Clarion, 1986 (I:8–12 R:5). A ghost from the 1800s haunts a young child.

Hamilton, Virginia. *Dustland*. Greenwillow, 1980 (I:10+ R:7). The psychic unit travels into a future time, when earth supports only dust and mutant forms of animal and human life.

———. *The Gathering*. Greenwillow, 1981 (I:10+ R:7). The psychic friends go into a domed city of the future.

———. *Justice and Her Brothers*. Greenwillow, 1978 (I:10+ R:7). Justice and her brothers have psychic powers.

———. *The Magical Adventures of Pretty Pearl*. Harper & Row, 1983 (I:10+ R:5). Pretty Pearl comes to earth to help former slaves journey from Georgia to Ohio.

Hooks, William H. *Mean Jake and the Devils*. Illustrated by Dirk Zimmer. Dial, 1981 (I:9–12 R:6). Three stories tell about how Mean Jake outwits Big Daddy Devil, Devil Junior, and Baby Deviline.

Howe, James. *The Celery Stalks at Midnight*. Illustrated by Leslie Morrill. Atheneum, 1983 (I:8–10 R:5). This animal fantasy is a sequel to *Bunnicula* and *Howliday Inn*.

Hughes, Monica. *Devil on My Back*. Atheneum, 1985 (I:9+ R:6). A person-against-society conflict in science fiction.

———. *The Dream Catcher*. Atheneum, 1987 (I:9 R:6). The author speculates about social and political changes in 2147 A.D.

———. *The Guardian of Isis*. Atheneum, 1984 (I:9+ R:8). This is a sequel to *The Keeper of the Isis Light*.

———. *The Isis Pedlar*. Atheneum, 1983 (I:9+ R:8). This is the final story in a science fiction trilogy.

———. *The Keeper of the Isis Light*. Atheneum, 1984 (I:9+ R:8). The first book in a trilogy is set on a distant planet.

———. *Ring-Rise Ring-Set*. Watts, 1982 (I:9+ R:6). A science fiction novel portrays life after a great climatic change.

Hunter, Mollie. *The Mermaid Summer*. Harper, 1988 (I:10+ R:6). In a Scottish fantasy, two children gain three wishes from a mermaid.

———. *The Wicked One*. Harper & Row, 1977 (I:10+ R:7). A hot-tempered Scotsman and a Grollican have an adventure filled with suspense and humor.

Hurmence, Belinda. *A Girl Called Boy*. Houghton Mifflin. 1982 (I:10+ R:6). A black girl goes back in time to 1853 and experiences slavery.

Jacobs, Paul Samuel. *Born to Light*. Scholastic, 1988 (I:10+ R:5). Extraterrestrial beings are found in this science fiction.

Jacques, Brian. *Redwall*. Philomel, 1986 (I:10+ R:7). Matthias, a young mouse, seeks the legendary sword of Martin the Warrior.

Jones, Diana Wynne. *The Lives of Christopher Chant*. Greenwillow, 1988 (I:10+ R:6). A fantasy tells about a boy who can traverse other worlds.

Juster, Norton. *The Phantom Tollbooth*. Illustrated by Jules Feiffer. Random House, 1961 (I:9+ R:8). Milo enters a tollbooth and finds himself in the Kingdom of Wisdom.

Kendall, Carol. *The Firelings*. Atheneum, 1982 (I:10+ R:6). A world of little people live on the edge of a volcano.

———. *The Gammage Cup*. Illustrated by Erik Blegvad. Harcourt Brace Jovanovich, 1959 (I:8–12 R:4). The peaceful existence of a land inhabited by little people is challenged by five nonconformists and an outside enemy.

Key, Alexander. *Escape to Witch Mountain*. Illustrated by Leon B. Wisdom, Jr. Westminster, 1968 (I:8–12 R:6). Two children search for others like themselves after a sinister man tries to use their powers.

———. *The Forgotten Door*. Westminster, 1965 (I:8–12 R:6). A boy from another planet is not understood by people.

King-Smith, Dick. *Harry's Mad*. Illustrated by Jill Bennett. Crown, 1987 (I:8–12+ R:7). Harry inherits a very unusual parrot.

———. *Martin's Mice*. Illustrated by Jez Alborough. Crown, 1989 (I:8–12 R:6). An animal fantasy explores animal nature and freedom.

———. *The Mouse Butcher*. Illustrated by Margot Apple. Viking, 1982 (I:9–12 R:6). An animal fantasy explores what happens when cats are isolated on an island.

———. *Pigs Might Fly*. Illustrated by Mary Rayner. Viking, 1982 (I:9–12 R:6). The runt of the litter helps his fellow pigs in their time of need.

Kipling, Rudyard. *The Elephant's Child*. Illustrated by Lorinda Bryan Cauley. Harcourt Brace Jovanovich, 1983 (I:5–7 R:7). This is a highly illustrated version of one of the *Just So Stories*.

———. *The Jungle Book*. Doubleday, 1894, 1964 (I:8–12 R:7). A collection of jungle stories includes "Mowgli's Brothers," "Tiger-Tiger!" "Rikki-Tikki-Tavi," and "Toomai of the Elephants."

———. *Just So Stories*. Doubleday, 1902, 1907, 1952 (I:5–7 R:5). This is a collection enjoyed by young children.

———. *Just So Stories*. Illustrated by Victor G. Ambrus. Rand McNally, 1982 (I:5–7 R:5). The classic stories are newly illustrated.

Langton, Jane. *The Astonishing Stereoscope*. Illustrated by Erik Blegvad. Harper & Row, 1971 (I:10+ R:7). Edward and Eleanor discover that they can enter the world of pictures inside the stereoscope.

Lawson, Robert. *Ben and Me*. Little, Brown, 1939 (I:7–11 R:6). The autobiography of Benjamin Franklin's friend, Amos Mouse.

———. *Rabbit Hill*. Viking, 1944 (I:7–11 R:7). The animals on the hill wait expectantly for the new folks.

LeGuin, Ursula K. *Catwings*. Illustrated by S. D. Schindler. Watts, 1988 (I:3–8 R:4). Four winged kittens escape from the city slums.

———. *Catwings Return*. Illustrated by S. D. Schindler. Watts, 1989 (I:3–8 R:4). Two winged cats return to their city home.

———. *The Farthest Shore*. Illustrated by Gail Garraty. Atheneum, 1972 (I:10+ R:6). Ged, the Archimage of Roke, is placed in final combat against an evil wizard.

———. *Tehanu: The Last Book of Earthsea*. Atheneum, 1990 (I:10+ R:6). This book concludes the stories of Earthsea.

———. *Tombs of Atuan*. Illustrated by Gail Garraty. Atheneum, 1971, 1980 (I:10+ R:5). Ged, the wizard, comes to the Tombs of Atuan seeking the missing half of the Ring of Erreth-Akbe.

———. *A Wizard of Earthsea*. Illustrated by Ruth Robbins. Parnassus, 1968 (I:10+ R:6). Young Sparrowhawk shows great powers of enchantment.

L'Engle, Madeleine. *A Swiftly Tilting Planet*. Farrar, Straus & Giroux, 1978 (I:10+ R:7). Charles Wallace travels a perilous journey through time to keep a mad dictator from destroying the world.

———. *A Wind in the Door*. Farrar, Straus & Giroux, 1973 (I:10+ R:7). Strange beings come to enlist the children's aid in the galactic fight against evil.

———. *A Wrinkle in Time*. Farrar, Straus & Giroux, 1962 (I:10+ R:5). A search for Meg and Charles's father takes them across the galaxy into combat with an evil darkness that is threatening the cosmos.

Lewis, C. S. *The Last Battle*. Illustrated by Pauline Baynes. Macmillan, 1956. The final book of Narnia sees Aslan lead his people into paradise.

———. *The Lion, the Witch and the Wardrobe.* Illustrated by Pauline Baynes. Macmillan, 1950 (I:9+ R:7). Four children enter the magical kingdom of Narnia through a wardrobe.

———. *The Magician's Nephew.* Illustrated by Pauline Baynes. Macmillan, 1955 (I:9+ R:7). This sixth book in the chronicles explains how Aslan created Narnia.

———. *Prince Caspian, the Return to Narnia.* Illustrated by Pauline Baynes. Macmillan, 1951 (I:9+ R:7). The prince leads his army of talking beasts against the Telmarines.

———. *The Silver Chair.* Illustrated by Pauline Baynes. Macmillan, 1953 (I:9+ R:7). The children complete Aslan's mission.

———. *The Voyage of the Dawn Treader.* Illustrated by Pauline Baynes. Macmillan, 1952 (I:9+ R:7). Lucy and Edmund are reunited with King Caspian of Narnia.

Lewis, Naomi, trans. *Proud Knight, Fair Lady: The Twelve Lais of Marie de France.* Viking/Kestrel, 1989 (I:10+ R:6). This text includes stories of love, honor, and chivalry.

Lindgren, Astrid. *Pippi in the South Seas.* Illustrated by Louis S. Glanzman. Viking, 1959 (I:7–11 R:5). Pippi continues her hilarious adventures on a South Seas island.

———. *Pippi Longstocking.* Illustrated by Louis S. Glanzman. Viking, 1950 (I:7–11 R:5). Pippi does some very unusual things, such as scrubbing the floor with brushes tied onto her feet.

———. *Pippi on the Run.* Photographs by Bo-Erik Gyberg. Viking, 1971, 1976 (I:6–10 R:3). Large color photographs accompany the story of Pippi, the strongest girl in the world.

Lunn, Janet. *The Root Cellar.* Scribner's Sons, 1983 (I:10+ R:4). A girl has a time-warp experience that sends her back to Canada in the 1860s.

McBratney, Sam. *The Ghosts of Hungryhouse Lane.* Illustrated by Lisa Thiesing. H. Holt, 1989 (I:7–10 R:4). Children discover that their new home has ghosts.

McCaffrey, Anne. *Dragonquest.* Ballantine, 1981 (I:10+ R:6). This book contains continued adventures on a distant planet.

———. *Dragonsinger.* Atheneum, 1977 (I:10+ R:6). Menolly studies under the masterharper of the planet Pern.

———. *Dragonsong.* Atheneum, 1976 (I:10+ R:6). The planet Pern must be protected from spores that can destroy all living matter.

MacDonald, George. *At the Back of the North Wind.* Illustrated by Arthur Hughes. Dutton, 1871, 1966 (I:10+ R:6). In an allegorical story, a poor boy travels to back of the North Wind.

———. *The Princess and the Goblin.* Illustrated by Nora S. Unwin. Macmillan, 1872, 1951 (I:10+ R:9). Princess Irene discovers her fairy godmother spinning magical thread.

McKinley, Robin. *The Blue Sword.* Greenwillow, 1982 (I:10+ R:7). A girl discovers her mysterious powers and her heritage.

———. *The Hero and the Crown.* Greenwillow, 1984 (I:10+ R:7). Aerin faces the forces of evil during her quest for the crown.

Mahy, Margaret. *The Changeover.* Atheneum, 1984 (I:10+ R:7). A girl discovers her supernatural powers and saves her brother.

Marzollo, Jean, and Claudio Marzollo. *Jed's Junior Space Patrol: A Science Fiction Easy-to-Read.* Illustrated by David S. Rose. Dial, 1982 (I:6–8 R:1). Robots and telepathic animals add to the space adventure.

Melling, O. R. *The Singing Stone.* Viking/Kestrel, 1986 (I:8+ R:6). A quest is set in ancient Ireland.

Milne, A. A. *The House at Pooh Corner.* Illustrated by Ernest H. Shepard. Dutton, 1928, 1956 (I:6–10 R:3). Pooh builds a house.

———. *Winnie-The-Pooh.* Illustrated by Ernest H. Shepard. Dutton, 1926, 1954 (I:6–10 R:5). Pooh has adventures with his nursery friends and Christopher Robin.

Nesbit, E. *Melisande.* Illustrated by P. J. Lynch. Harcourt Brace Jovanovich, 1989 (I:7+ R:6). A princess must overcome a curse.

Nixon, Joan Lowery. *Whispers from the Dead.* Delacorte, 1989 (I:10+ R:6). A girl receives messages from a murder victim.

Norton, Andre. *Lavender Green Magic.* Illustrated by Judith Gwyn Brown. Crowell, 1974 (I:9–12 R:6). A magic dream pillow and a maze planted in the 1600s lead three children back to a time when people believed in witches.

———. *Red Hart Magic.* Illustrated by Donna Diamond. Crowell, 1976 (I:9–12 R:4). A miniature inn permits time travel.

Norton, Mary. *Bed-Knob and Broomstick.* Illustrated by Erik Blegvad. Harcourt Brace Jovanovich, 1943, 1971 (I:7–11 R:6). An old brass bed becomes a flying machine.

———. *The Borrowers.* Illustrated by Beth and Joe Krush. Harcourt Brace Jovanovich, 1952, 1953 (I:7–11 R:3). Three little people survive by borrowing items from the human household above.

———. *The Borrowers Afield.* Illustrated by Beth and Joe Krush. Harcourt Brace Jovanovich, 1955 (I:7–11 R:4). The Clock family leaves their home under the floorboards and escapes into the fields.

———. *The Borrowers Afloat.* Harcourt Brace Jovanovich, 1959 (I:7–11 R:4). The fantasy about little people continues.

———. *The Borrowers Aloft.* Harcourt Brace Jovanovich, 1961 (I:7–11 R:4). These are additional tales about small people in a normal world.

———. *The Borrowers Avenged.* Illustrated by Beth and Joe Krush. Harcourt Brace Jovanovich, 1982 (I:7–11 R:4). This is a new book in the borrowers series.

Oakley, Graham. *The Church Mice in Action.* Atheneum, 1982 (I:5–10 R:7). The church mice enter Sampson in a cat show in this picture storybook.

O'Brien, Robert C. *Mrs. Frisby and the Rats of NIMH.* Illustrated by Zena Berstein. Atheneum, 1971 (I:8–12 R:4). A group of superior rats escape from a laboratory.

O'Shea, Pat. *The Hounds of the Morrigan.* Holiday House, 1986 (I:10+ R:6). Irish traditional literature influences this modern fantasy.

Park, Ruth. *Playing Beatie Bow.* Atheneum, 1982 (I:10+ R:6). A girl from Sydney, Australia, travels in time back to the 1870s.

Phipson, Joan. *The Watcher in the Garden.* Atheneum, 1982 (I:10 R:7). A garden has a strange influence on an old man, a girl, and a disruptive boy.

Potter, Beatrix. *The Tailor of Gloucester, from the Original Manuscript.* Warne, 1969, 1978 (I:5–9 R:8). This text is illustrated with Potter's original drawings.

———. *The Tale of Peter Rabbit.* Warne, 1902. This is the original tale of the mischievous rabbit.

———. *Tales of Peter Rabbit and his Friends.* Chatham, 1964 (I:3–9 R:6). The collection includes thirteen tales accompanied by Potter's illustrations.

———. *A Treasury of Peter Rabbit and Other Stories.* Avenel, 1979 (I:3–7 R:6). A collection of favorite stories includes "Peter Rabbit," "Benjamin Bunny," "Squirrel Nutkin," "Two Bad Mice," and "Jeremy Fisher."

Rodgers, Mary. *Summer Switch.* Harper & Row, 1982 (I:8–12 R:6). A father and son switch identity in this humorous fantasy.

Rodowsky, Colby F. *The Gathering Room.* Farrar, Straus & Giroux, 1981 (I:10+ R:7). Spirits of people buried in the cemetery are friends of a nine-year-old boy.

Sandburg, Carl. *Rootabaga Stories.* Illustrated by Maud and Miska Petersham. Harcourt Brace Jovanovich, 1922, 1950 (I:8–11 R:7). This is a series of short nonsense stories.

———. *Rootabaga Stories.* Illustrated by Michael Hague. Harcourt Brace Jovanovich, 1922, 1988 (I:8–11 R:7). This is a newly illustrated text.

Selden, George. *Chester Cricket's Pigeon Ride.* Illustrated by Garth Williams. Farrar, Straus & Giroux, 1981 (I:6–9 R:4). Chester goes on a night tour of Manhattan because he misses his country home.

———. *The Cricket in Times Square.* Illustrated by Garth Williams. Farrar, Straus & Giroux, 1960 (I:7–11 R:3). Chester the cricket accidentally finds himself in a subway station below Times Square.

———. *Harry Cat's Pet Puppy.* Farrar, Straus & Giroux, 1975 (I:7–11 R:3). Harry experiences problems after he adopts a dog.

———. *Tucker's Countryside.* Farrar, Straus & Giroux, 1969 (I:7–11 R:3). The friends come to Connecticut to help Chester save the meadow.

Sleator, William. *Interstellar Pig.* Dutton, 1984 (I:10 R:8). A game becomes a real experience in a science fiction story.

Snyder, Zilpha Keatley. *Below the Root.* Illustrated by Alton Raible. Atheneum, 1975 (I:9–12 R:6). A girl searches for a civilization underground.

Tolkien, J. R. R. *Farmer Giles of Ham.* Illustrated by Pauline Baynes. Houghton Mifflin, 1978 (I:7–10 R:6). Farmer Giles becomes a hero when he accidentally fires his blunderbuss into a giant's face.

———. *Fellowship of the Ring.* Houghton Mifflin, 1967 (I:12+ R:8) This is part of a trilogy enjoyed by older readers.

———. *The Hobbit.* Houghton Mifflin, 1938 (I:9–12 R:6). Bilbo Baggins, a hobbit, joins forces with thirteen dwarfs in their quest to overthrow the evil dragon.

———. *The Lord of the Rings.* Houghton Mifflin, 1974 (I:12+ R:8). This is part of a trilogy enjoyed by older readers.

———. *The Return of the King.* Houghton Mifflin, 1967 (I:12+ R:8). This is part of a trilogy enjoyed by older readers.

Travers, Pamela L. *Mary Poppins.* Illustrated by Mary Shepard. Harcourt Brace Jovanovich, 1934, 1962 (I:7–11 R:7). An unusual nanny arrives with the east wind and changes the life of the Banks family.

———. *Mary Poppins in Cherry Tree Lane.* Illustrated by Mary Shepard. Delacorte, 1982 (I:7–11 R:7). The nanny returns to give the Banks children a magical happening in the park on Midsummer Eve.

Van Allsburg, Chris. *The Wreck of the Zephyr.* Houghton Mifflin, 1983 (I:5–8 R:6). This is a picture storybook fantasy in which a boy tries to become a great sailor.

Voigt, Cynthia. *Building Blocks.* Atheneum, 1984 (I:9 R:7). A time-warp experience helps a boy understand his father.

Watson, Simon. *No Man's Land.* Greenwillow, 1976 (I:10+ R:6). Mechanization in the twenty-first century causes a boy to rebel.

Westall, Robert. *Ghost Abbey.* Scholastic, 1989 (I:10+ R:6). The abbey protects those who care for it and threatens those who would harm it.

White, E. B. *Charlotte's Web.* Illustrated by Garth Williams. Harper & Row, 1952 (I:7–11 R:3). Charlotte, with the help of Templeton the rat, saves Wilbur's life and creates a legend.

———. *Stuart Little.* Illustrated by Garth Williams. Harper & Row, 1945 (I:7–11 R:6). Mrs. Little's second son is quite different from the rest of the family: He is a mouse.

Williams, Margery. *The Velveteen Rabbit.* Illustrated by Allen Atkinson. Knopf, 1984 (I:6–9 R:5). This is another newly illustrated version of the 1922 classic.

———. *The Velveteen Rabbit.* Illustrated by Michael Hague. Holt, Rinehart & Winston, 1983 (I:6–9 R:5). The drawings emphasize the boy.

———. *The Velveteen Rabbit.* Illustrated by Ilse Plume. Godine, 1982 (I:6–9 R:5). This book contains new illustrations with a classic tale.

———. *The Velveteen Rabbit: Or, How Toys Become Real.* Illustrated by Michael Green. Running Press, 1982 (I:6–9 R:5). Drawings in brown tones create a newly illustrated version of the story.

———. *The Velveteen Rabbit: Or How Toys Become Real.* Illustrated by William Nicholson. Doubleday, 1958 (I:6–9 R:5). A toy rabbit is given life after his faithful service to a child.

Wiseman, David. *Jeremy Visick.* Houghton Mifflin, 1981 (I:10+ R:4). A contemporary Cornish boy goes back in time to discover the location of a boy lost in a mine accident.

———. *Thimbles.* Houghton Mifflin, 1982 (I:10+ R:4). Two thimbles in an old family trunk provide the ties when a girl goes back in time.

Wisniewski, David. *The Warrior and the Wise Man.* Lothrop, Lee & Shepard, 1989 (I:6–10 R:4). An original story contains Japanese folklore elements.

Wrightson, Patricia. *A Little Fear.* Hutchinson, 1983 (I:9 R:6). An old woman outwits the Njimbin, a creature from Australian folklore.

———. *Balyet.* McElderry, 1989 (I:10+ R:6). An aboriginal spirit, an older woman, and a girl share an experience.

Yolen, Jane. *The Acorn Quest.* Illustrated by Susanna Natti. Crowell, 1981 (I:7–10 R:6). The quest is for a golden acorn that could end the famine for the animals.

———. *The Devil's Arithmetic.* Viking/Kestrel, 1988 (I:8+ R:5). In a time-warp story, a Jewish girl finds herself in World War II.

———. *Dragon's Blood.* Delacorte, 1982 (I:10+ R:5). On the planet Austar IV, a boy raises a dragon to be a fighter.

———. *The Faery Flag: Stories and Poems of Fantasy and the Supernatural.* Watts, 1989 (I:7–10 R:6). This text includes fifteen selections.

———. *The Girl Who Loved the Wind.* Illustrated by Ed Young. Crowell, 1972 (I:7–10 R:6). The wind visits a girl and sings to her about life.

———. *The Girl Who Cried Flowers.* Illustrated by David Palladini. Crowell, 1974 (I:7–10 R:6). Five original fairy tales tell about giants, miraculous abilities, and wisdom that overcomes adversity.

———. *The Hundredth Dove and Other Tales.* Illustrated by David Palladini. Crowell, 1977 (I:7–10 R:6). This book contains seven original fairy tales.

———. *Neptune Rising: Songs and Tales of the Undersea Folks.* Illustrated by David Weisner. Philomel, 1982 (I:7–10 R:6). This is a collection of stories about undersea beings.

———. *The Robot and Rebecca and the Missing Owser.* Illustrated by Lady McCrady. Knopf, 1981 (I:8–10 R:5). The year is 2121 and Rebecca's three-legged pet is missing.

8

Poetry

RHYTHMIC PATTERNS OF LANGUAGE

INVOLVING CHILDREN IN POETRY

Rhythmic Patterns of Language

THE VALUES OF POETRY FOR CHILDREN

WHAT POETRY IS

CHARACTERISTICS OF POEMS THAT CHILDREN PREFER

CRITERIA FOR SELECTING POETRY FOR CHILDREN

ELEMENTS OF POETRY

FORMS OF POETRY

POETS AND THEIR POEMS

ACCORDING TO EVE MERRIAM (21), POetry is "Rainbow Writing" because it colors the human mind with the vast spectrum of human experience:

Rainbow Writing

Nasturtiums with
their orange cries
flare like trumpets;
their music dies.

Golden harps
of butterflies;
the strings are mute
in autumn skies.

Vermillion chords,
then silent gray;
the last notes of
the song of day.

Rainbow colors
fade from sight,
come back to me
when I write.

Eve Merriam
Rainbow Writing, p. 3

Just as a rainbow inspires an awe of nature, so too may a poem inspire an awe for words and the expression of feelings. Poetry often has a musical quality that attracts children and appeals to their emotions. The poet's choice of words can suggest new images and create delightful word plays.

Many poems allow children to see or feel with fresh insights. The first section of this chapter discusses the values of poetry, the characteristics of poems that children prefer, criteria for selecting poetry, elements of poetry, and forms of poetry. It concludes with a discussion of children's poets and the poems they write to create magical worlds for their youthful readers.

THE VALUES OF POETRY FOR CHILDREN

Children can share feelings, experiences, and visions with poets. Poetry also brings new understandings of the world. It encourages children to play with words and realize the images that are possible when words are chosen carefully. Through poetry, children may discover the power of words, a power that the poet can release. Poet Lillian Moore (23) describes this power when she relates her reactions to the poetry of Valerie Worth. She states that she "felt a delicious shock, a pleasure at the clarity with which real things were seen" (p. 470). She continues to compare reading poetry to taking a field trip with binoculars that allow readers to look in new ways at the details of the world, at the bugs, the earthworms, and the dandelions.

Rumer Godden (11) equates giving a child a love of poetry to giving a child the ability to enjoy life. She states:

> To give a child a love of poetry is like installing a spring or fountain of perpetual private refreshment—and not only refreshment; a love and understanding of poetry brings a perception, a sort of sixth sense that makes its possessor quick to life—quick in the sense of being very much alive—quick to the world around him; it rescues him from dullness, gives him a sense of form, a mental discipline, and because it is limitless it will grow as he grows. (p. 306)

Poet Charles Causley (22) emphasizes the illuminating quality of poetry. He believes that one of the values of poetry is that a poem may suggest something different each time it is read.

During a stimulating address to the International Reading Association, Jean Le Pere (16) identified six reasons for sharing poetry with children. First, poetry provides enjoyment. Young children begin to discover the enjoyment in poetry by hearing and sharing nonsense poems, Mother Goose rhymes, and tongue twisters. They grow into poetry through story poems, such as those written by A. A. Milne, and they gradually discover the many exciting forms available to the poet. Second, poetry provides children with knowledge about concepts in the world around them: size, numbers, colors, and time. Third, because precise and varied words play such important roles in poetic expression, poetry encourages children to appreciate language and expand their vocabularies. Horses not only run, they clop; kittens jump, but they also pounce; and the moon may be not only bright but also a silver sickle. Fourth, poetry helps children identify with people and situations. With Robert Louis Stevenson, they go up in a swing; with Robert Frost, they share a snowy evening in the woods; and with Karama Fufuka, they brag, "My Daddy Is a Cool Dude." Fifth, poetry expresses moods familiar to children and helps children understand and accept their feelings. Other children empathize with the child in Charlotte Zolotow's "Nobody Loves Me." Sometimes, it seems as if nobody loves the speaker, and sometimes it seems as if everybody loves him—feelings common to all children. Finally, poetry grants children insights into themselves and others, developing their sensitivity to universal needs and feelings. Through poems written by other children, as well as by adults, children discover that others have feelings similar to their own.

WHAT POETRY IS

What is this literary form that increases enjoyment, develops appreciation for language, and helps children gain insights about themselves? Poetry is not easily defined; it is not easily measured or classified. There is no single accepted definition of poetry. Some definitions specify the characteristics of poetry, including the poetic elements and the functions of words, while other definitions emphasize the emotional impact of poetry. Try to develop your own definition of poetry as you read the following definitions by poets, critics, and children. Author Rumer Godden (11) states, "[T]rue poetry, even in its smallest shape, should have form, meter, rhythm bound into a whole with words that so match and express its subject they seem inevitable" (p. 310).

Critic Patrick Groff (12) maintains that poetry for children is writing that, in addition to using the mechanics of poetry, transcends literal meaning. He explains:

> The use of original combinations of words is probably the easiest, the best, and the most obvious way to write poetry that transcends the literal and goes beyond a complete or obvious meaning. Consequently, in poetry a word has much more meaning than a word in prose. In the former the emphasis is connotative rather than denotative. Words possess suggested significance apart from their explicit and recognized meanings. It is the guessing element that requires the reader to go below the surface of words, to plumb their literal meanings. Figurative language most often provides the guessing element. (p. 185)

Emotional and physical reactions defined poetry for poet Emily Dickinson, who related poetry to a feeling: If she read a book that made "her body so cold no fire could warm" her, she knew it was poetry; if she felt physically as if the top of her head were taken off, she also knew it was poetry.

Judson Jerome (14) contends that poetry is words performed. He stresses that meaning cannot be separated from the sounds of words. As visual shape is important to the sculptor or the painter, tonal shape is important to the poet. Jerome compares the work of the poet to the composition of a musician; in both forms, total quality is essential.

Lee Bennett Hopkins's (13) interviews with poets in *Pass the Poetry, Please!* include numerous and varied definitions of poetry. Various poets express such phrases as "music of words," "celebration of life," and "revelation of feelings." David McCord (19) expresses these feelings about poetry when he states:

> Poetry is so many things besides the shiver down the spine. It is a new day lying on an unknown doorstep. It is *Peer Gynt* and *Moby-Dick* in a single line. It is the best translation of words that do not exist. It is hot coffee dripping from an icicle. It is the accident involving sudden life. It is the calculus of the imagination. It is the finishing touch to what one could not finish. It is a hundred things as unexplainable as all our foolish explanations. (p. 7)

Poet Harry Behn (2) reports a thought-provoking example of what children think poetry is or is not. When he asked children to tell him what poetry should be, one boy replied, "Anything that recites nicely without people. . . .People are stories. A poem is something else. Something way out. Way out in the woods. Like Robert Frost waiting in a snowstorm with promises to keep" (p. 159). Other answers suggest a wide range of definitions of poetry, such as, "A poem should be about animals, what you feel, springtime, something funny, anything you see and hear, anything you can imagine. Anything. Even a story!" (p. 159).

Author Margaret Mahy presents a definition of poetry in her short story, "The Cat Who Became a Poet," found in *Nonstop Nonsense*. After the cat cannot stop himself from speaking in poetic form, he thinks, "I became a poet through eating the mouse. Perhaps the mouse became a poet through eating seeds. Perhaps all this poetry stuff is just the world's way of talking about itself" (p. 19). Following the cat's rendition of a poem that tricks a dog, the cat concludes, "If only he knew. I wasn't meaning to praise him. Poetry is very tricky stuff and can be taken two ways." (p. 19).

Overall, the various definitions of poetry highlight the importance of original combination of words, distinctive sound, and emotional impact. Visual element is also significant in poetry. Some poems are like paintings; they must be seen to be appreciated. Poets may use shape and space to increase the impact of their words. They may group lines into stanzas, use open spaces to emphasize words, capitalize important words, or arrange a whole poem to suggest the subject matter.

The essential elements of poetry must be savored to be enjoyed. Like painting or sculpture, poetry cannot be experienced rapidly. It must be read slowly, even reread several times to immerse its readers or listeners in its sounds and imagery. In other words, children must have time to see, hear, and feel the world of the poet.

CHARACTERISTICS OF POEMS THAT CHILDREN PREFER

Consider children's individual interests when choosing poetry for them. Samuel French Morse (25) believes that when children honestly judge what speaks to their imaginations, their judgments must be respected. Even though children's interests and experiences vary widely, students of children's literature will discover valuable information in the research into children's poetry choices. Several researchers have identified poems that children enjoy and analyzed the subjects and elements in these poems.

Carol Fisher and Margaret Natarella (7) examined poetry preferences in the first through the third grades. They found that children preferred narrative poems and limericks, poems about strange and fantastic events, traditional poems, and poems that rhymed or used alliteration and onomatopoeia to create sound patterns.

Ethel Bridge (3) investigated children's poetry preferences in the middle grades and concluded that both girls and boys like poems related to their experiences and interests, humorous poems, and poems with elements of rhythm and rhyme. Because children's interests vary so widely, she concluded, poetry selections are difficult to categorize according to grade level.

Karen Sue Kutiper (15) surveyed preferences of students in the seventh, eighth, and ninth grades. She concluded that these students prefer rhyme, humorous narrative, and content based on familiar experiences.

Ann Terry (27) investigated the poetry preferences of children in the fourth, fifth, and sixth grades. She also analyzed poetic elements in the poems the children preferred. She concluded that:

1. Children's enthusiasm for poetry declines as children advance in the elementary grades.
2. Children respond more favorably to contemporary poems than to traditional ones.
3. Children prefer poems dealing with familiar and enjoyable experiences.
4. Children enjoy poems that tell a story or have a strong element of humor.
5. Children prefer poems that feature rhythm and rhyme.

6 Among the least popular poems are those that rely too heavily on complex imagery or subtly implied emotion.
7 The majority of teachers in the fourth, fifth, and sixth grades pay little attention to poetry, seldom read it to children, and do not encourage them to write their own poems.

When Terry analyzed the forms of poetry children preferred or disliked, she concluded that narrative poems and limericks were among the most preferred, while haiku and free verse were among the least popular. Her content analysis showed that the most popular poems were humorous, even nonsensical, about familiar experiences or animals.

Both Bridge and Terry stress that adults should provide children with many experiences with poetry and include a wide range of poetry. Terry also recommends that books on poetry be made accessible to children, that listening centers include tapes and records of poetry, and that a rich poetry environment be used to stimulate children to write their own poetry.

One reason for the narrow range of poems that children enjoy may be that adults infrequently share poetry with children. The enjoyment of poetry, like the enjoyment of other types of literature, can be increased by an enthusiastic adult who reads poetry to children. Because Terry's research indicates that teachers of older children seldom use poetry with them, enthusiasm for poetry must first be stimulated among teachers themselves.

The need for and the advantages of longer interactions with poetry are indicated by an analysis of poetry included in the International Reading Association's Children's Choices. Sam Sebesta (26) reports that "serious poetry, blank and free verse, and extended imagery—all qualities that children disapproved of in other preference studies—are present on the lists of Children's Choices" (p. 67). For example, children liked serious traditional poems, such as Robert Frost's "Stopping by Woods on a Snowy Evening" and the poems in Arnold Adoff's *My Black Me: A Beginning Book of Black Poetry*. They liked the personified desert in Byrd Baylor's *The Desert Is Theirs*. They chose Arnold Adoff's free verse *Tornado!*, and the imagistic poems about everyday things in Valerie Worth's *More Small Poems*. In addition, Sebesta found that the number of poetry books included in children's literary preferences implied a greater affection for poetry than was found in many previous studies.

Sebesta's conclusions about the reasons for the discrepancies between the previous studies and the Children's Choices provide valuable insights for anyone responsible for selecting and sharing poetry. First, unlike many of the research studies that present poetry in a brief fashion, the poetry on the Children's Choices is available in the classroom and is shared with children over a two- to six-week period. Second, unlike most of the studies that present poetry orally, the poetry on the Children's Choices includes books that emphasize the visual impact of poetry. The selections frequently develop unique arrangements on the page, and the illustrations arouse the readers' interests and feelings. Third, recent developments in teaching poetry emphasize both the study of the structure of poetry and the readers' responses to poetry. A merger of the two approaches may expand the range of poetry that children enjoy.

CRITERIA FOR SELECTING POETRY FOR CHILDREN

The following criteria for selecting poetry for children are compiled from recommendations by Leonard Clark (4), Patrick Groff (12), Harry Behn (2), Samuel Morse (25), Myra Cohn Livingston (17), Kinereth Gensler and Nina Nyhart (10) and Rumer Godden (11).

1 Poems that are lively, with exciting meters and rhythms, are most likely to appeal to young children.
2 Poems for young children should emphasize the sounds of language and encourage play with words.
3 Sharply cut visual images and words used in fresh, novel manners allow children to expand their imaginations and see or hear the world in a new way.
4 Poems for young children should tell simple stories and introduce stirring scenes of action.
5 The poems selected should not have been written down to children's supposed level.
6 The most effective poems allow children to interpret, to feel, and to put themselves into the poems. They encourage children to extend comparisons, images, and findings.
7 The subject matter should delight children, say something to them, enhance their egos, strike happy recollections, tickle their funny bones, or encourage them to explore.
8 Poems should be good enough to stand up under repeated readings.

THROUGH THE EYES OF A POET

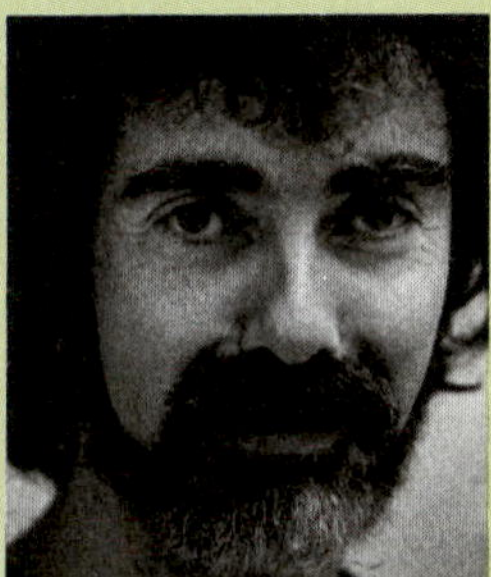

Poetry Doesn't Have to Be Boring!

Creator of strange beasts and fanciful worlds of humorous incidents, JACK PRELUTSKY shares his views on making poetry exciting.

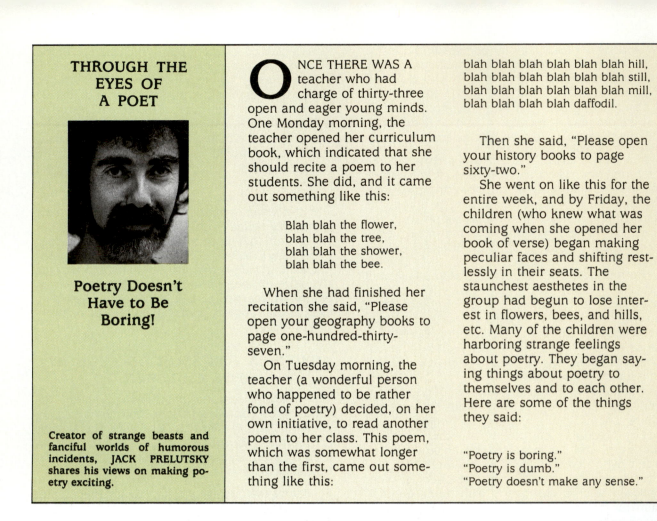

ONCE THERE WAS A teacher who had charge of thirty-three open and eager young minds. One Monday morning, the teacher opened her curriculum book, which indicated that she should recite a poem to her students. She did, and it came out something like this:

Blah blah the flower,
blah blah the tree,
blah blah the shower,
blah blah the bee.

When she had finished her recitation she said, "Please open your geography books to page one-hundred-thirty-seven."

On Tuesday morning, the teacher (a wonderful person who happened to be rather fond of poetry) decided, on her own initiative, to read another poem to her class. This poem, which was somewhat longer than the first, came out something like this:

blah blah blah blah blah blah hill,
blah blah blah blah blah blah still,
blah blah blah blah blah blah mill,
blah blah blah blah daffodil.

Then she said, "Please open your history books to page sixty-two."

She went on like this for the entire week, and by Friday, the children (who knew what was coming when she opened her book of verse) began making peculiar faces and shifting restlessly in their seats. The staunchest aesthetes in the group had begun to lose interest in flowers, bees, and hills, etc. Many of the children were harboring strange feelings about poetry. They began saying things about poetry to themselves and to each other. Here are some of the things they said:

"Poetry is boring."
"Poetry is dumb."
"Poetry doesn't make any sense."

Both Rumer Godden (11) and Charles Causley (22) emphasize that a good poem need not be understood all at once. Godden states that a good poem "has a mysterious capacity for growing, unfolding more and more of itself in the mind, and very soon a child whose ear is tuned, mind made alert, is ready to go beyond children's poets and the lively, quickly assimilable poems—far, far beyond" (p. 310).

ELEMENTS OF POETRY

Poets use everyday language in different ways to encourage readers to see familiar things in new lights, to draw on their senses, and to fantasize. Poets also use certain devices to create medleys of sounds, suggest visual interpretations, and communicate messages. The criteria for selecting poetry for children suggest the importance of such poetic elements as rhythm, rhyme and other sound patterns, repetition, imagery, and shape in the creation of poetry.

Rhythm

The word *rhythm,* is derived from the Greek *rhythmos,* meaning to flow. In poetry, this flowing quality refers to the movement of words in the poem. Stress, and the number and pattern of syllables direct the feelings expressed in a poem. Many poems have a definite, repetitive cadence, or meter, with certain lines containing a certain number of pronounced beats. For example, limericks have a strict rhythmic structure easily recognizable even when one is hearing them in a foreign language. Free verse, however, usually has a casual, irregular rhythm similar to that of everyday speech.

Poets use rhythm for four specific purposes. First, they use rhythm to increase enjoyment in hearing language. Young children usually enjoy

"Poetry is about things that don't interest me."
"I hate poetry."

Once there was another teacher with a class of thirty-three young students. She was also a wonderful person with a fondness for poetry. One Sunday evening, she opened her curriculum book and saw that a unit of poetry was scheduled for the next day's lesson. "Hmmmmmm," she mused. "Now what poem shall I share with them tomorrow?" After giving it some careful thought, she settled on a poem about a silly monster, which the poet had apparently created out of whole cloth, and which she thought might stimulate her pupils' imaginations. "Hmmmmmm," she mused again. "Now how can I make this poem even more interesting?" She deliberated a bit more and, in the course of memorizing the poem, came up with several ideas. The next morning, this is what happened:

"Children," she said. "Today is a special day. It is the first day of silly monster week, and to honor the occasion, I am going to share a silly monster poem with you." She held up a small tin can, and continued. "The monster lives in this can, but I am not going to show it to you yet, because I would like you to imagine what it looks like while I'm reciting the poem."

She then recited the poem, and upon reaching the last word in the last line, suddenly unleashed an expanding snake from the can. The children reacted with squeals of mock terror and real delight. Then they asked her to recite the poem again, which she did. Afterward, she had them draw pictures of the silly monster. No two interpretations were alike.

The drawings were photographed and later presented in an assembly as a slide show, with the children reciting the poem in chorus. She shared a number of other poems during "silly monster week," always showing her honest enthusiasm and finding imaginative methods of presentation. She used masks, musical instruments, dance, sound-effects recordings, and clay sculpture. The children grew so involved that she soon was able to recite poems with no props at all. At the end of the week, these are some of the things her students said about poetry:

"Poetry is exciting."
"Poetry is fun."
"Poetry is interesting."
"Poetry makes you think."
"I love poetry."

the repetitive cadences of nursery rhymes, chants, and nonsensical verses. Rhythm encourages children to join in orally, experiment with language, and move with it. Second, poets use rhythm to highlight and emphasize specific words. Poets often use stress to suggest the importance of words. Third, poets use rhythm to create dramatic effects. Irregular meter or repeatedly stressed words may immediately attract listeners' or readers' attention. Fourth, poets use rhythm to suggest mood. For example, a rapid rhythm can suggest excitement and involvement, while a slow, leisurely rhythm can suggest laziness and contemplation. David McCord uses rhythm to suggest the sounds a stick might make if a child dragged it along a fence. Rhythm in the following poem emphasizes specific words, attracts and holds attention, and suggests a certain mood.

The Pickety Fence

The pickety fence
The pickety fence
Give it a lick it's
The pickety fence
Give it a lick it's
A clickety fence
Give it a lick it's
A lickety fence
Give it a lick
Give it a lick
Give it a lick
With a rickety stick
Pickety
Pickety
Pickety
Pick

David McCord
Far and Few: Rhymes of the Never Was and Always Is, p. 7

Kinereth Gensler and Nina Nyhart (10), who have used poetry to stimulate feeling of involvement in children, suggest that the rhythm of a poem works particularly well when it reinforces the content of the poem. Consider, for example,

Robert Louis Stevenson's "From a Railway Carriage." The rhythm suggests the dash and rattle of a train as it crosses the country. One can easily imagine oneself peering out the window as the scenery rushes by.

From a Railway Carriage

Faster than fairies, faster than witches,
Bridges and houses, hedges and ditches;
And charging along like troops in a battle,
All through the meadows the horses and cattle:
All of the sights of the hill and the plain
Fly as thick as driving rain;
And ever again, in the wink of an eye,
Painted stations whistle by.

Here is a child who clambers and scrambles,
All by himself and gathering brambles;
Here is a tramp who stands and gazes;
And here is the green for stringing the daisies!
Here is a cart run away in the road
Lumping along with man and load;
And here is a mill and there is a river:
Each a glimpse and gone forever!

Robert Louis Stevenson
A Child's Garden of Verses, 1883

Many more poems that stimulate a sense of rhythm are found in Lillian Morrison's anthology *Rhythm Road: Poems to Move To*. This collection is divided according to such areas as "Poems to Dance To," "Poems to Ride To," and "Active Entertainments."

Rhyme and Other Sound Patterns

Sound is an important part of the pleasure of poetry. One of the ways that a poet can emphasize sound is rhyming. Many beloved traditional poems for children—such as Edward Lear's "The Owl and the Pussy-Cat"—use careful rhyme schemes. The twenty-five most preferred poems in Ann Terry's (27) study of children's poetry preferences contain rhyming patterns.

Rhyming words may occur at the ends of lines and within lines. Poets of nonsense verse even create their own words to achieve humorous, rhyming effects. Consider, for example, Zilpha Keatley Snyder's use of rhyme in "Poem to Mud." The end rhymes—*ooze–slooze, crud–flood,* and *thickier–stickier,*—suggest visual and auditory characteristics of mud. The internal rhymes—*fed–spread, slickier–stickier–thickier*—create a tongue-twisting quality.

Poem to Mud

Poem to mud—
Poem to ooze—
Patted in pies, or coating the shoes.
Poem to slooze—
Poem to crud—
Fed by a leak, or spread by a flood.
Wherever, whenever, whyever it goes,
Stirred by your finger, or strained by your toes,
There's nothing sloopier, slipperier, floppier,
There's nothing slickier, stickier, thickier,
There's nothing quickier to make grown-ups sickier,
Trulier coolier,
Than wonderful mud.

Zilpha Keatley Snyder
Today Is Saturday, pp. 18–19

Poets also use alliteration, the repetition of initial consonants or groups of consonants, to create sound patterns. In "The Tutor," Carolyn Wells uses repetition of the beginning consonant *t* to create a humorous poem about a teacher trying to teach "two young tooters to toot." "The Tutor" is one of the poems selected by Isabel Wilner for *The Poetry Troupe,* a collection of over two hundred poems that children have selected for reading aloud. Mary Ann Hoberman's four-line poem "Gazelle," also in Wilner's collection, contains fifteen words beginning with *g*. If a poem contains a great deal of alliteration, a tongue twister results.

Assonance, the repetition of vowel sounds, is another means of creating interesting and unusual sound patterns. Jack Prelutsky uses the frequent repetition of the long *e* sound in the following poem.

Don't Ever Seize a Weasel by the Tail

You should never squeeze a weasel
for you might displease the weasel,
and don't ever seize the weasel by the tail.

Let his tail blow in the breeze;
if you pull it, he will sneeze,
for the weasel's constitution tends to be a little frail.

Yes the weasel wheezes easily;
the weasel freezes easily;
the weasel's tan complexion rather suddenly turns pale.

So don't displease or tease a weasel,
squeeze or freeze or wheeze a weasel
and don't ever seize a weasel by the tail.

Jack Prelutsky
A Gopher in the Garden and Other Animal Poems, p. 19

The sounds of some words suggest the meanings that they are trying to convey. The term *onomatopoeia* refers to words that imitate the actions or sounds with which they are associated. Words such as *plop, jounce,* and *beat* may suggest to children the loud sound of rain hitting the concrete in Aileen Fisher's "Rain."

Young children who like to experiment with language may develop their own nonsense words that suggest to them certain sounds or meanings. In Kinereth Gensler and Nina Nyhart's (10) *The Poetry Connection,* two poems written by second graders incorporate onomatopoeic language. One boy uses consecutive letter *d*'s to suggest that rain sounds like a machine gun. A girl uses repetitive words—*lip–lap* and *slip–slap*—to suggest sounds of a waterfall.

Eve Merriam effectively uses onomatopoeia in her poem "Owl," found in *Halloween ABC*. Merriam's repeated use of "who" sounds like the subject of her poem. One of her poems, "Weather," found in Beatrice Schenkde Regniers's *Sing a Song of Popcorn,* begins with "Dot a dot dot" and continues with words like "spack a spack speck" to sound like rain.

Repetition

Poets frequently use repetition to enrich or emphasize words, phrases, lines, or even whole verses in poems. David McCord uses considerable repetition of whole lines in "The Pickety Fence," and Lewis Carroll uses repetition to accent his feelings about soup.

Beautiful Soup

Beautiful Soup, so rich and green,
Waiting in a hot tureen!
Who for such dainties would not stoop?
Soup of the evening, beautiful Soup!
Soup of the evening, beautiful Soup!
  Beau—ootiful Soo—oop!
  Beau—ootiful Soo—oop!
Soo—oop of the e—e—evening,
  Beautiful, beautiful Soup!

Beautiful Soup! Who cares for fish,
Game, or any other dish?
Who would not give all else for two
Pennyworth only of beautiful Soup?
  Beau—ootiful Soo—oop!
  Beau—ootiful Soo—oop!
Soo—op of the e—e—evening,
  Beautiful, beauti—FUL SOUP!

Lewis Carroll
Alice's Adventures in Wonderland, 1865

"Beautiful Soup" is another favorite for oral reading; children find that they can recreate that marvelous sound of rich, hot soup being taken from the spoon and placed into their mouths.

Lullabies shared with young children are often enhanced by repetition. Christina G. Rossetti's "Lullaby" uses repetition to suggest a musical quality.

Lullaby

  Lullaby, oh, lullaby!
Flowers are closed and lambs are sleeping;
  Lullaby, oh, lullaby!
Stars are up, the moon is peeping;
  Lullaby, oh, lullaby!
While the birds are silence keeping,
  (Lullaby, oh, lullaby!)
Sleep, my baby, fall a-sleeping,
  Lullaby, oh, lullaby!

Christina Rossetti
Sing-Song, 1872

Young children enjoy the numerous poems that contain repetition in Jane Yolen's *The Three Bears Rhyme Book*. Poems that are especially strong in repetition include "Three Bears Walking," "Photographs," "Bears' Chairs," and "Poppa Bear's Hum."

The cumulative illustrations reinforce the repetitive lines of the poetry and suggest a cumulative arrangement for choral speaking. (Illustration by Anita Lobel, from *The Rose in My Garden* by Arnold Lobel. Illustration copyright © 1984 by Anita Lobel. By permission of Greenwillow Books, a division of William Morrow and Company, Inc.)

Imagery

Imagery is a primary element in poetry. It encourages children to see, hear, feel, taste, smell, and touch the worlds created by poets. We have already seen how rhythm, sound patterns, and repetition cause readers to experience what poets describe. Poets also use figurative language (language with nonliteral meanings) to clarify, add vividness, and encourage readers to experience things in new ways. Several types of figurative language are used in poetry. This discussion looks at metaphor, simile, personification, and hyperbole.

Metaphors are implied comparisons between things that have something in common but are essentially different. Metaphors highlight certain qualities in things to make readers see them in new ways. In the introduction to *Flashlight and Other Poems,* Judith Thurman uses metaphor when she asserts that a "poem is a flashlight, too: the flashlight of surprise. Pointed at a skinned knee or at an oil slick, at pretending to sleep or at kisses, at balloons, or snow, or at the soft, scary nuzzle of a mare, a poem lets us feel and know each in a fresh, sudden and strong light" (28, Introduction). Thurman demonstrates her command of metaphor when she compares the Milky Way to thick white breath in cold air or clay to a clown without bones. In "Spill," Thurman compares a flock of flying sparrows to loose change spilling out of a pocket.

Spill

the wind scatters
a flock of sparrows—
a handful of small change
spilled suddenly
from the cloud's pocket

Judith Thurman
Flashlight and Other Poems, p. 16

While metaphors are implied comparisons, similes are direct comparisons between things that have something in common but are essentially different. The comparisons made by similes are considered direct because the word *like* or *as* is included in the comparison. In "The Path on the Sea," a thirteen-year-old Russian child uses simile to capture the mystery and allure of moonlight on the ocean. Notice the use of the word *like* in the first line. What are the commonalities between a silver sickle and a new moon?

The Path on the Sea

The moon this night is like a silver sickle
Mowing a field of stars.
It has spread a golden runner
Over the rippling waves.
With its winking shimmer
This magic carpet lures me
To fly to the moon on it.

Inna Miller in
The Moon Is Like a Silver Sickle,
Miriam Morton, ed., p. 28

Insightful comparisons can develop what Judson Jerome (14) describes as meaning that transcends words. Poetic imagery can open the minds of children to new worlds and can allow children to ascend to different levels of consciousness.

Personification allows poets to give human emotions and characteristics to inanimate objects, abstract ideas, and nonhuman living things. For example, personification is an important element in Byrd Baylor's poetry about Native Americans and Native American legends. In *Moon Song,* Baylor personifies the moon as a mother who gives birth to Coyote Child, wraps him in her magic, caresses him with pale white mist, and shines on him with love. In Jamake Highwater's *Moonsong Lullaby,* the moon "sings," "smiles," "caresses," and "watches over us." In Myra Cohn Livingston's "Moon," found in her *Space Songs,* the moon "remembers" and "thinks" about space explorers. Kaye Starbird uses personification in the following poem to encourage readers to visualize a wind with human characteristics.

The Wind

In spring, the wind's a sneaky wind,
A tricky wind,
A freaky wind,
A wind that hides around the bends
And doesn't die, but just pretends;
So if you stroll into a street
Out of a quiet lane,
All of a sudden you can meet
A smallish hurricane.

And as the grown-ups gasp and cough
Or grumble when their hats blow off,
And housewives clutch their grocery sacks
While all their hairdos come unpinned. . .
We kids—each time the wind attacks—
Just stretch our arms and turn our backs,
And then we giggle and relax
And lean against the wind.

Kaye Starbird
The Covered Bridge House and Other Poems, p.11

Hyperbole is exaggeration that creates specific effects. John Ciardi's humorous "Mummy Slept Late and Daddy Fixed Breakfast" says that a waffle is so tough that it cannot be dented by a hacksaw.

Mummy Slept Late and Daddy Fixed Breakfast

Daddy fixed the breakfast.
He made us each a waffle.
It looked like gravel pudding.
It tasted something awful.

"Ha, ha," he said, "I'll try again.
This time I'll get it right." But what I got was in between
Bituminous and anthracite.

"A little too well done? Oh well,
I'll have to start all over."
That time what landed on my plate
Looked like a manhole cover.

I tried to cut it with a fork:
The fork gave off a spark.
I tried a knife and twisted it
into a question mark.

I tried it with a hack-saw.
I tried it with a torch.
It didn't even make a dent.
It didn't even scorch.

The next time Dad gets breakfast
When Mommy's sleeping late,
I think I'll skip the waffles.
I'd sooner eat the plate!

John Ciardi
You Read to Me, I'll Read to You, p. 18

Many of the poems in Shel Silverstein's *Where the Sidewalk Ends* also include exaggeration.

Shape

Poets may place their words on pages in ways designed to enhance meaning and to create greater visual impact. Word division, line division, punctuation, and capitalization can add emphasis to a poem's content, as when Lewis Carroll writes about "Beau—ootiful Soo—oop!"

The shape of a poem may represent the thing or the physical experience the poem describes. In Regina Sauro's "I Like to Swing," the poem becomes wider and wider toward the bottom as the sweep of the swing becomes wider and wider. In "Seals," by William Jay Smith (anthologized in Stephen Dunning, Edward Lueders, and Hugh Smith's excellent *Reflections on a Gift of Watermelon Pickle. . .and Other Modern Verse*), the poem forms the shape of a supple seal that is reinforced by an accompanying photograph of a seal. Several of the poems in Myra Cohn Livingston's *Space Songs* are shaped like objects in space. For example, "Moon" looks like a crescent, "Meteorites" has a tail, and "Satellites" looks like a mechanical object. Children enjoy discovering that shape may be related to the meaning of a poem and experimenting with shape in their own poetry writing.

FORMS OF POETRY

Some children do not believe that they are reading a poem unless the lines rhyme. While adults should not spend time with young children analyzing the form of a poem, children should realize that poetry has many different forms and that as poet Amy Lowell (18) once remarked, "every form is proper to poetry" (p. 7).

Children should be encouraged to write their own poetry. When they write poetry, they enjoy experimenting with different forms. For such experiments, however, they must be immersed in poetry and led through many enjoyable experiences with poems. This section takes a brief look at various forms of poetry, including lyric, narrative, ballad, limerick, concrete, free verse, and haiku.

Lyric Poetry

According to Northrop Frye, Sheridan Baker, and George Perkins (8), a lyric poem is "a poem, brief and discontinuous, emphasizing sound and picture imagery rather than narrative or dramatic movement. Lyrical poetry began in ancient Greece in connection with music, as poetry sung, for the most part, to the accompaniment of a lyre" (p. 268). The epic poems of the Greeks were narratives emphasizing heroic deeds. Now, as in the past, lyric poems emphasize musical, pictorial, and emotional qualities. The musical roots of lyric poetry are indicated by the fact that the words of songs are now termed *lyrics*.

Poet Jose Garcia Villa's (5) description of poetry emphasizes the importance of a lyrical quality. According to Villa, a poem must be magical, must be musical, and must fly like a bird. Many of the poems discussed in this chapter have a lyrical quality.

Children's early experiences with poetry may be through Mother Goose rhymes sung to music and traditional lullabies sung at bedtime. Consider the melody associated with the words in the following traditional lullaby.

Hush, Little Baby

Hush, little baby, don't say a word,
Mama's going to buy you a mocking bird.
And if that mocking bird don't sing,
Mama's going to buy you a diamond ring.
And if that diamond ring turns to brass,
Mama's going to buy you a looking glass.
And if that looking glass gets broke,
Mama's going to buy you a billy goat.
And if that billy goat won't pull,
Mama's going to buy you a cart and bull.
And if that cart and bull turn over,
Mama's going to buy you a dog named Rover.
And if that dog named Rover won't bark,
Mama's going to buy you a horse and cart.
And if that horse and cart fall down,
You'll still be the sweetest little baby in town.

Traditional poem

Dan Fox's *Go in and out the Window: An Illustrated Songbook for Young People* contains numerous traditional lyrics. Ashley Bryan's *I'm Going to Sing: Black American Spirituals* and John Langstaff's *What a Morning! The Christmas Story in Black Spirituals* show the emotional power associated with some lyrics.

Children's favorite storybook characters make up verses and sing their poems—as does A. A. Milne's Winnie-the-Pooh, for example. Many poets write poems that have singing qualities. Jack Prelutsky's anthology *The Random House Book of Poetry for Children* contains, for example, Lois Lenski's "Sing a Song of People," which recreates the tempo of people traveling through a city. John Ciardi's "The Myra Song," captures the personality of a little girl who enjoys singing, skipping, chattering, and playing. William Blake's "Introduction to 'Songs of Innocence'" has its piper of "happy songs/Every child may joy to hear."

Narrative Poetry

Poets may be expert storytellers. When a poem tells a story, it is narrative poetry. With rapid action and typically chronological order, story poems have long been favorites of children. They are excellent for increasing children's interest in, and appreciation of, poetry. Robert Browning's "The Pied Piper of Hamelin," first published in 1882, contains many of the characteristics that make narrative poems appealing to children. The actions of the villainous rats, for example, are easy to visualize.

Rats!
They fought the dogs, and filled the cats,
And bit the babies in the cradles,
And ate the cheeses out of the vats,
And licked the soup from the cook's own ladles,
Split open the kegs of salted sprats,
Made nests inside men's Sunday hats,
And even spoiled the women's chats
By drowning their speaking
With shrieking and squeaking
In fifty different sharps and flats.

The plot develops rapidly, as the townspeople approach the mayor and the town council demanding action. Into this setting comes the hero.

And in did come the strangest figure!
His queer long coat from heel to head
Was half of yellow and half of red;
And he himself was tall and thin,
With sharp blue eyes, each like a pin,
And light, loose hair, yet swarthy skin,
No tuft on cheek nor beard on chin,
But lips where smiles went out and in—
There was no guessing his kith and kin!
And nobody could enough admire
The tall man and his quaint attire:

With rapidity, the council offers the stranger a thousand gilders to rid the town of its rats, and the piper places the pipe to his lips. At this point, the tempo of the poem resembles the scurrying of rats.

And out of the house the rats came tumbling.
Great rats, small rats, lean rats, brawny rats,
Brown rats, black rats, gray rats, tawny rats,
Grave old plodders, gay young friskers,
Fathers, mothers, uncles, cousins,
Cocking tails and pricking whiskers,
Families by tens and dozens,
Brothers, sisters, husbands, wives—
Followed the piper for their lives.
From street to street he piped advancing,
And step for step they followed dancing,

Robert Browning
The Pied Piper of Hamelin, 1882

After the efficient disposal of the rats comes the confrontation, when the mayor refuses to pay the thousand gilders. In retribution, the piper puts the pipe to his lips and blows three notes. At this point, the tempo of the poem resembles the clapping of hands and the skipping of feet. Every child in the town merrily follows the piper through a wondrous portal into the mountain.

Other narrative poems long popular with children include Clement Moore's "A Visit from St. Nicholas" (now better known as "The Night Before Christmas"), which has been produced as books illustrated by Tomie dePaola and by Tasha Tudor; Lewis Carroll's delightful "The Walrus and the

FLASHBACK

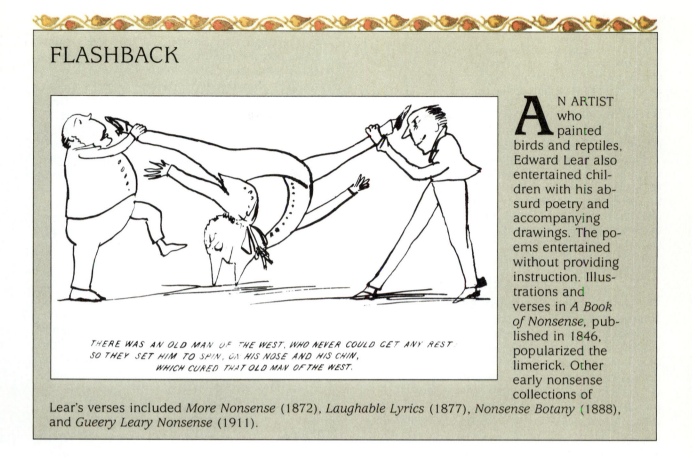

THERE WAS AN OLD MAN OF THE WEST, WHO NEVER COULD GET ANY REST;
SO THEY SET HIM TO SPIN, ON HIS NOSE AND HIS CHIN,
WHICH CURED THAT OLD MAN OF THE WEST.

AN ARTIST who painted birds and reptiles, Edward Lear also entertained children with his absurd poetry and accompanying drawings. The poems entertained without providing instruction. Illustrations and verses in *A Book of Nonsense,* published in 1846, popularized the limerick. Other early nonsense collections of Lear's verses included *More Nonsense* (1872), *Laughable Lyrics* (1877), *Nonsense Botany* (1888), and *Gueery Leary Nonsense* (1911).

Carpenter," in which some young oysters go for a walk on the beach with one hungry animal and one hungry human; and Henry Wadsworth Longfellow's romantic dramas from early American history, "The Song of Hiawatha" and "Paul Revere's Ride."

Many contemporary poets—including John Ciardi, Jack Prelutsky, and Beatrice Curtis Brown—also write narrative poems. Their topics are both nonsensical and realistic. Several contemporary poets have written highly illustrated narrative poems. In *The Voyage of the Ludgate Hill: Travels with Robert Louis Stevenson,* Nancy Willard uses the poetic form to retell Stevenson's adventures on a tramp steamer. Her fanciful narrative poem explores what might have happened if Stevenson had interacted with the animals in the cargo hold. Roy Gerrard's *Sir Francis Drake & His Daring Deeds* tells a lively story about the explorer. Gerrard's *Sir Cedric* is a heroic tale of Cedric the Good and Matilda the Pure.

Julia Fields's *The Green Lion of Zion Street* follows the exploits of a group of urban children while they wait for a bus on a foggy morning. In epic fashion, the children decide to challenge their fears and approach the dangerous lion that crouches "Fierce/Smirking/Vain" on Zion Street. Thankfully, they are able to walk through the frightening mists, face the lion, and laugh at their fears. After all, the scowling lion is made of stone.

Ballads

The ballad is a form of narrative folk song developed in Europe during the Middle Ages. Minstrels and bards (*bard* is the Welsh word for poet) sang the tales of legend or history, often accompanying themselves on stringed instruments. Modern poets have used the ballad form for poems they intend to be read rather than sung. However, traditional ballads are part of the oral literary heritage of European culture, passed on by word of mouth.

Action, usually heroic or tragic, is the focus of such traditional ballads as "Tom Dooley" and "Barbara Allen." Cecil Day-Lewis (6), says:

The meter is simple because the ballads were composed by simple people, and often members of the audience liked to make up additional stanzas. It is a fast-moving meter because a ballad generally had quite a long story to tell, and it was necessary to keep it on the go so that listeners shouldn't get bored. (p. 57)

Day-Lewis compares ballads to movies because both are highly dramatic and both rely on fast-paced incidents and dialogue.

Salt-Sea Verse, compiled by Charles Causley, contains a number of sea ballads. Among the most famous is Samuel Taylor Coleridge's "The Rime of the Ancient Mariner." Gene Kemp's anthology *Ducks and Dragons: Poems for Children* contains a variety of English, Scottish, and American ballads that children enjoy reading or hearing read aloud.

Limericks

The short, witty poems called limericks are popular with children. Four of the best-liked poems in Ann Terry's (27) study of children's poetry preferences are limericks. All limericks have the same basic structure and rhythm: They are five-line poems in which the first, second, and fifth lines rhyme and have three pronounced beats each, and the third and fourth lines rhyme and have two pronounced beats each. The limerick form was popularized by Edward Lear in the nineteenth century. Following is an example of humorous verse from Lear's *A Book of Nonsense*.

There was an Old Man with a beard,
Who said, "It is just as I feared!—
Two Owls and a Hen,
Four Larks and a Wren
Have all built their nests in my beard."

Edward Lear
A Book of Nonsense, 1846

Children enjoy the visual imagery this poem creates. They can see and laugh at the predicament of having all those fowl nesting in a beard. They also enjoy reciting the definite rhythm and rhyme found in the limerick.

David McCord (19), who has written numerous contemporary limericks himself, says that for a limerick to be successful, it must have perfect rhyming and flawless rhythm. McCord's amusing limericks in his *One at a Time: Collected Poems for the Young* illustrate the author's ability to play with words and the sounds of language. These limericks may also stimulate children to experiment with language by writing their own limericks.

Concrete Poems

Concrete means something that can be seen or touched, something that is physically real. When a poet emphasizes the meaning of a poem by shaping it into the form of a picture, concrete poetry results. Robert Froman's poem "Dead Tree," from *Seeing Things: A Book of Poems,* is lettered in the shape of a dead tree trunk. Mary Ellen Solt was inspired to create both a poem and a picture about the promise of spring in a forsythia bush. Children should turn this poem on its side to read the thoughts of the author.

Children find concrete poetry exciting to look at. Observing concrete objects and writing picture poems about them also stretches children's imaginations.

Free Verse

Free verse is characterized by little or no rhyme, and rhythm similar to everyday speech. Skateboards are popular with children, who experience the movement in the following poem by Lillian Morrison even though it has little rhyme and no repetitive meter.

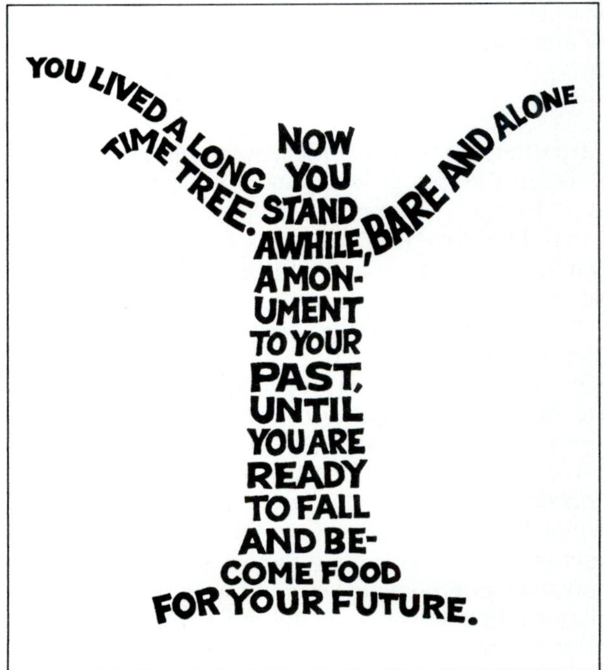

"Dead Tree" (From Robert Froman, "Dead Tree." *Seeing Things: A Book of Poems*. New York: Crowell, 1974, p. 9)

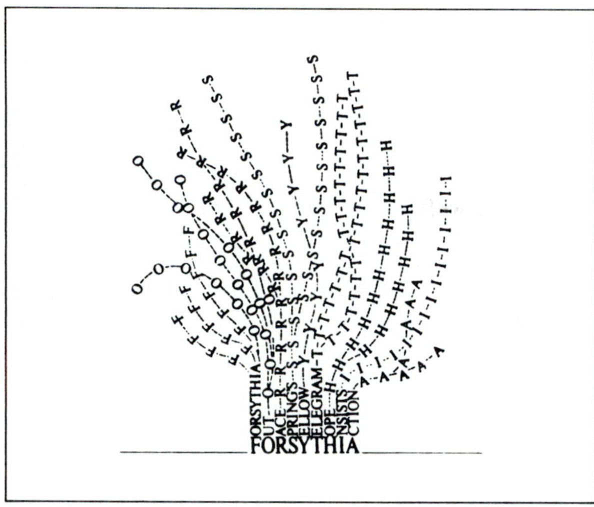

"Forsythia" (From Mary Ellen Solt, ed. "Forsythia." *Concrete Poetry: A World View*. Bloomington, Ind.: Indiana University Press.)

The Sidewalk Racer
or
On the Skateboard

Skimming
an asphalt sea
I swerve, I curve, I
sway; I speed to whirring
sound an inch above the
ground; I'm the sailor
and the sail; I'm the
driver and the wheel
I'm the one and only
single engine
human auto
mobile.

Lillian Morrison
The Sidewalk Racer and Other Poems of Sports and Motion, p. 12

Haiku

Haiku is a very old form of Japanese poetry. A haiku has three lines. The first line has five syllables, the second line has seven, and the final line has five. According to Ann Atwood (1), a modern writer of haiku, the seventeen syllables of a haiku are valuable discipline that ideally results in a poem that is "both simple and profound, constructive and expansive, meticulously descriptive yet wholly suggestive" (introduction, unnumbered). Such a poem must be savored, not read hurriedly.

Poets of haiku link themselves with nature and the cycle of the seasons. The following example of Atwood's haiku accompanies a photograph of a beach scene, in which a stream of water is placing its mark upon the land.

A blank page of sand—
at the water's cutting edge
the pattern shaping.

Ann Atwood
Haiku: The Mood of Earth, p. 4, unnumbered

Haiku by the great Japanese poet Issa, among other geniuses of this art, illustrate how this ancient form of verse has been used to express feelings, experiences, and vision in just the right words. Poems by Issa and important information about his life are included in Richard Lewis's *Of This World: A Poet's Life in Poetry*. Ann Atwood's haiku are collected in her *Haiku: The Mood of the Earth* and other books.

POETS AND THEIR POEMS

To share poetry with children, adults have many classic and contemporary poems from which to select. Poets who write for children use subject matter of interest to children. Children's poets write humorous poems; nature poems; poems that encourage children to identify with characters, situations, and locations; poems that suggest moods and feelings; animal poems; and poems about witches and ghosts. Although these categories sometimes overlap and some poets write about many different topics, many children's poets focus on certain subjects and types of poetry.

Nursery Rhymes, Nonsense, and Humor: Poems for Starting Out Right

Nursery rhymes are among the best-known literature in America and are the first form of poetry that most children experience (see Chapter 5). Rumer Godden (11) maintains that children should be introduced to poetry through nursery rhymes because "nursery rhymes are true poems, poetry with all its gifts of language, rhythm, and unexpectedness" (p. 309).

According to Nicholas Tucker (29), nursery rhymes are appropriate to share with young children because they are based on easily memorized rhymes and rhythms that help young children master speech. The rhymes encourage children to respond orally as they join in with the rhyme, answer a question formulated by the rhyme, or provide a missing word suggested by the rhyme. Tongue twisters and alliteration expand children's delight in the sounds of language and teach them that words can be manipulated in playful ways. Tucker maintains that characters found in nursery rhymes have important links with children's imaginative life and with antiquity. Children also find bonds with other children when they share nursery rhymes.

Mother Goose rhymes such as *Songs from Mother Goose,* compiled by Nancy Larrick, are appropriate for stimulating an interest in poetry. The collection of Iona and Peter Opie in *Tail Feathers from Mother Goose* is especially appealing for slightly older children because it contains rhymes that are not commonly found in many collections. Jack Prelutsky's anthology *Read-Aloud Rhymes for the Very Young* includes poems that have many of the characteristics of nursery rhymes. Consequently, the poems form a natural bridge to other types of poetry.

Research has shown that children particularly like poetry that tickles their funny bones. Jean Le Pere (16) as well as Cornelia Meigs and Elizabeth Nesbitt (20) believe that nonsense rhymes are logical successors to Mother Goose rhymes for enjoyably introducing children to poetry. According to Meigs, the nonsense poems of such great poets as Edward Lear and Lewis Carroll are ideal: They suggest spontaneous fun through emphatic, regular rhythms that are heightened by alliteration. Nonsense verses convey absurd meanings or even no meanings at all.

Humorous poetry, while closely related to nonsense poetry, deals with amusing happenings that might actually befall a person or an animal. Numerous contemporary poets also write nonsensical or humorous verse to entice children into the fun and life-enriching world of poetry.

The idiosyncrasies of *Jonathan Bing* create a humorous book of verse by Beatrice Curtis Brown. In these poems, Jonathan Bing visits the king, displays his manners, does arithmetic, reads a book, dances, catches tea, and finally moves away. All of poor old Jonathan's actions, however, are a little different from what might be expected. Samuel Marshak's *The Pup Grew Up* presents the comical dilemma of a lady's placing a Pekingese on a train and collecting a Great Dane when she gets off the train. The poem, written by a famous Russian poet, is a subtle dig at bureaucracy.

An early love of William Blake's *Songs of Innocence* and *Songs of Experience* inspired Nancy Willard's *A Visit to William Blake's Inn: Poems for Innocent and Experienced Travelers*. The nonsense and lyric poems in the book, evocatively illustrated by Alice and Martin Provensen, present an odd assortment of guests and workers at the inn, including a rabbit that makes the bed and two dragons that bake the bread. "The Man in the Marmalade Hat Arrives" shows another of the guests.

> The man in the marmalade hat
> arrived in the middle of March,
> equipped with a bottle of starch
> to straighten the bends in the road, he said.
> He carried a bucket and mop.
> A most incommodious load, he said,
> and he asked for a room at the top.
>
> Now beat the gong and the drum!
> Call out the keepers
> and waken the sleepers.
> The man in the marmalade hat has come!
>
> The man in the marmalade hat
> bustled through all the rooms,
> and calling for dusters and brooms
> he trundled the guests from their beds,
> badgers and hedgehogs and moles.
> Winter is over, my loves, he said.
> Come away from your hollows and holes.
>
> Now beat the gong and the drum!
> Call out the keepers
> And waken the sleepers.
> The man in the marmalade hat has come!
>
> Nancy Willard
> *A Visit to William Blake's Inn,* p. 22

William Cole's *Poem Stew* includes humorous poems. Jill Bennett's collection of poems, *Tiny Tim: Verses for Children,* includes a variety of jingles and other humorous poems. Bryan Holme's *A Present of Laughter: Wit and Nonsense in Pictures and Verse* is a large collection of English nonsense verse. Two larger anthologies contain sections of nonsense poetry. Jack Prelutsky's *The Random House Book of Poetry for Children* contains a section titled "Nonsense! Nonsense!" Beatrice Schenk de Regniers's *Sing a Song of Popcorn: Every Child's Book of Poems* includes poems categorized "Mostly Nonsense."

Edward Lear. Edward Lear, introduced earlier as the popularizer of the limerick form, had many loyal friends among the leaders and creative artists of Great Britain in the nineteenth century.

He was welcomed into their homes and became an "Adopty Duncle" to their children, for whom he wrote and illustrated the nonsense verses collected in *A Book of Nonsense* and *Nonsense Songs and Stories*: limericks, narrative poems, tongue twisters, and alphabet rhymes.

Lear's nonsense poems can be found in many anthologies. They have also been illustrated in single editions by several well-known illustrators. *Hilary Knight's The Owl and the Pussy-Cat* is an excellent choice for young children. The highly illustrated text begins with a fantasy situation and presents the poem as a story told by Professor Comfort. A careful search of the illustrations reveals numerous references to Lear's works and interests. *The Scroobious Pip*, illustrated by Nancy Ekholm Burkert, is a longer, more complex poem that was discovered after Lear's death and completed by Ogden Nash. Older children and adults enjoy this poem and the beautiful illustrations as they speculate about the nature of the Scroobious Pip.

Lewis Carroll. Carroll's works are historical milestones of children's literature. His nonsense verses are found in *Alice's Adventures in Wonderland* and *Through the Looking Glass*. One of Carroll's most famous poems is "Jabberwocky," from *Through the Looking Glass*, which introduces the marvelous nonsense words *brillig, slithy toves*, and *borogoves*. This poem has been published as a lovely book illustrated by Jane Breskin Zalben.

A large collection of Carroll's poems, along with illustrations by John Tenniel, Harry Furniss, Henry Holiday, Arthur B. Frost, and Carroll himself, can be found in Myra Cohn Livingston's compilation of *Poems of Lewis Carroll*. This book also provides considerable information about the poet, who was a mathematician named Charles Lutwidge Dodgson.

Laura E. Richards. Contemporary children may be surprised to discover that a well-known author of nonsense poetry is the daughter of Julia Ward Howe, who wrote a beautiful but somber poem, "The Battle Hymn of the Republic." Like Lear and Carroll, Richards has shared marvelous words and sounds with children. There are *wizzy wizzy woggums, ditty dotty doggums*, and *diddy doddy dorglums*. There are *Rummy-jums, Viddipocks*, and *Orang-Outang-Tangs*. Richards's collection *Tirra Lirra, Rhymes Old and New* contains many rhymes that emphasize the sound of language and encourage children to play with words. One of her best-loved nonsense poems follows.

Eletelephony

Once there was an elephant,
Who tried to use the telephant—
No! No! I mean an elephone
Who tried to use the telephone—
(Dear me! I am not certain quite
That even now I've got it right.)

Howe'er it was, he got his trunk
Entangled in the telephunk;
The more he tried to get it free,
The louder buzzed the telephee—
(I fear I'd better drop the song
Of elephop and telephong!)

Laura E. Richards
Tirra Lirra, Rhymes Old and New, p. 31

Shel Silverstein. One of the most popular children's poets, Shel Silverstein writes much nonsense and humorous poetry. Librarians report that Silverstein's *Where the Sidewalk Ends* and *A Light in the Attic* are in considerable demand by young readers. Improbable characters and situations in *A Light in the Attic* include a Quick-Digesting Gink, Sour Ann, and a polar bear in the Frigidaire. Silverstein covers slightly more realistic topics in poems like "The Boa Constrictor," from *Where the Sidewalk Ends*. In this poem, the narrator describes the experience of being swallowed by a boa constrictor. Children enjoy dramatizing this popular action poem.

Consider Silverstein's use of rhythm, rhyme, sound patterns, and repetition in "Ickle Me, Pickle Me, Tickle Me Too."

Ickle Me, Pickle Me, Tickle Me Too

Ickle Me, Pickle Me, Tickle Me too
Went for a ride in a flying shoe.
"Hooray!"
"What fun!"
"It's time we flew!"
Said Ickle Me, Pickle Me, Tickle Me too.

Ickle was captain, and Pickle was crew
And Tickle served coffee and mulligan stew
As higher
And higher
And higher they flew,
Ickle Me, Pickle Me, Tickle Me too.

Ickle Me, Pickle Me, Tickle Me too,
Over the sun and beyond the blue.
"Hold on!"
"Stay in!"

"I hope we do!"
Cried Ickle Me, Pickle Me, Tickle Me too.

Ickle Me, Pickle Me, Tickle Me too
Never returned to the world they knew,
And nobody
Knows what's
Happened to
Dear Ickle Me, Pickle Me, Tickle Me too.

Shel Silverstein
Where the Sidewalk Ends, pp. 16–17

Jack Prelutsky. The world created by Prelutsky's nonsense and humorous poetry for children could be described as the kingdom of immortal zanies. Within the pages of *The Queen of Eene,* children will find preposterous characters, such as peculiar Mister Gaffe, Poor Old Penelope, Herbert Glerbertt, and the Four Foolish Ladies, (Hattie, Harriet, Hope, and Hortense).

Rolling Harvey down the Hill describes the humorous experiences of a boy and his four friends. In *The Sheriff of Rottenshot,* eccentric characters include Philbert Phlurk, Eddie the spaghetti nut, and a saucy little ocelot. *The Baby Uggs Are Hatching* contains poems about oddly named creatures, such as sneepies and slitchs. Humorous poems written by "Anonymous" make up the text in Prelutski's *Poems of A. Nonny Mouse.* Another unusual individual is Pumberly Pott's unpredictable niece, described in the following poem.

Pumberly Pott's Unpredictable Niece

Pumberly Pott's unpredictable niece
declared with her usual zeal
that she would devour by piece after piece,
her uncle's new automobile.

She set to her task very early one morn
by consuming the whole carburetor;
then she swallowed the windshield, the headlights and horn,
and the steering wheel just a bit later.

She chomped on the doors, on the handles and locks,
on the valves and the pistons and rings;
on the air pump and fuel pump and spark plugs and shocks,
on the brakes and the axles and springs.

When her uncle arrived she was chewing a hash
made of leftover hoses and wires
(she'd just finished eating the clutch and the dash
and the steel-belted radial tires).

"Oh what have you done to my auto," he cried.
"You strange unpredictable lass"
"The thing wouldn't work, Uncle Pott," she replied,
and he wept, "It was just out of gas."

Jack Prelutsky
The Queen of Eene, pp. 10–11

William Jay Smith. Smith's *Laughing Time* contains many funny and entrancing poems, including limericks similar to those of Edward Lear. Smith's poem about escape to a strange land illustrates the spirit of fun that makes his poetry appealing to children.

The Land of Ho-Ho-Hum

When you want to go wherever you please,
Just sit down in an old valise,
And fasten the strap
Around your lap,
And fly off over the apple trees.

And fly for days and days and days
Over rivers, brooks, and bays
Until you come
To Ho-Ho-Hum
Where the Lion roars, and the Donkey brays.

Where the unicorn's tied to a golden chain,
And Umbrella Flowers drink the rain.
After that,
Put on your hat,
Then sit down and fly home again.

William Jay Smith
Laughing Time, p. 8

John Ciardi. Two books by a poet who has been both a professor of English and a columnist for *Saturday Review World* are written with a simple vocabulary to appeal to children with beginning reading skills: Ciardi's *I Met a Man* and *You Read to Me, I'll Read to You*. In the second book, Ciardi tells readers, "All the poems printed in black, you read to me," and "All the poems printed in blue, I'll read to you." This collection contains the popular "Mummy Slept Late and Daddy Fixed Breakfast." Other popular poems in this book tell about such characters as Change McTang McQuarter Cat and Arvin Marvin Lillisbee Fitch.

Ciardi's *The Hopeful Trout and Other Limericks* contains numerous poems about funny situations that are enhanced by tongue-twisting sounds. However, some of Ciardi's poems are better understood by older children. Poems by Ciardi often contain satirical observations about human behavior or problems of society, and the humorous poems in *Doodle Soup* tend to be caustic.

N. M. Bodecker. Poems suggesting that children should wash their hands with number-one dirt, shampoo their hair with molasses, and rinse off in cider are welcomed by young readers. Bodecker uses word play in "Bickering" to create humorous verse enjoyed by older children.

Bickering

The folks in Little Bickering
they argue quite a lot.
Is tutoring in bickering
required for a tot?
Are figs the best for figuring?
Is pepper ice cream hot?
Are wicks the best for wickering
a wicker chair or cot?
They find this endless dickering
and nonsense and nit pickering
uncommonly invigor'ing
I find it downright sickering!
You do agree!

N. M. Bodecker
Hurry, Hurry Mary Dear, p. 13

In *Hurry, Hurry Mary Dear,* the title poem depicts a harassed woman who is told to pick apples, dill pickles, chop trees, dig turnips, split peas, churn butter, smoke hams, stack wood, take down screens and put up storm windows, close shutters, stoke fires, mend mittens, knit sweaters, and brew tea. This might not be so bad, but the man who is giving the orders sits in a rocking chair all the time. Finally, Mary has enough: She places the teapot carefully on the demanding gentleman's head.

Nature Poems

Like children, poets have marveled at the opening of the first crocus, seen new visions in a snowflake, or stopped to watch a stream of crystal-clear water tumbling from a mountaintop. They have understood that people should feel reverence and respect for nature. Such reverence and respect require special ways of hearing as well as special ways of looking.

Charlotte Zolotow's poetry is about childhood experiences and nature. Two different editions of Zolotow's *River Winding* provide for interesting comparisons of the effects of illustrations. Children may enjoy evaluating the illustrations by Regina Shekerjian (1970 edition) and by Kazue Mizumura (1978 edition). The poem "Change" demonstrates how Zolotow is able to bring nature and children's experiences together in poetry.

Change

The summer
still hangs
heavy and sweet
with sunlight
as it did last year.

The autumn
still comes
showering gold and crimson
as it did last year.

The winter
still stings
clean and cold and white
as it did last year.

The spring
still comes
like a whisper in the dark night.

It is only I
who have changed.

Charlotte Zolotow
River Winding, p. 5 (1978 ed.)

The ancient stories of Native Americans provide the inspiration for Jamake Highwater's *Moonsong Lullaby*. Notice the images in the following excerpt from the longer poem:

Listen carefully, child.
The singing is everywhere.
The dark trees,
the clouded sky,
the mountains,
the grasslands all echo
the Moon's mellow music
until the last long whisper
that brings the dawn.

Jamake Highwater
Moonsong Lullaby, unnumbered

Nature also provides the focus for many of the selections included in John Bierhorst's *The Sacred Path: Spells, Prayers & Power Songs of the American Indians*.

Nature poems frequently stimulate artists to create the settings described by poets. Ed Young illustrated Robert Frost's poem "Birches." Marcia Brown illustrated a series of "Mostly Weather" poems in de Regniers's *Sing a Song of Popcorn: Every Child's Book of Poems*. Wendell Minor's illustrations for Diane Siebert's *Mojave* illuminate the desert landscape and his illustrations in *Heartland* illuminate the land and people of the Midwest. Many of the poems that are enhanced with artwork from the Metropolitan Museum of Art in Kenneth Koch and Kate Farrell's *Talking to the*

Sun, an anthology, are nature poems. Such illustrated versions help children discover new ways to look at nature.

Aileen Fisher. Fisher's poetry communicates the excitement and wonder of discovering nature. Her vision is fresh and full of the magic possible when a person really looks at the natural world. Fisher creates images that are real to children and that may encourage children to extend these images to other observations. In her poems about insects, found in *When It Comes to Bugs*, and her poems about seasons and rabbits, found in *Listen, Rabbit* and *Rabbits, Rabbits*, Fisher encourages readers to closely observe nature.

In Fisher's poems about winter, evergreens after a snowfall wear woolly wraps, snow fills the garden chairs with teddy bears, and footsteps go so quietly the observer thinks they are asleep. Fisher's "Frosted-Window World" allows children to visit winter's house by going inside a frosted windowpane.

Frosted-Window World

The strangest thing,
the strangest thing
came true for me today:
I left myself beneath the quilt
and softly slipped away.

And do you know
the place I went
as shyly as a mouse,
as curious as a cottontail,
as watchful as a grouse?
Inside the frosted windowpane
(it's rather puzzling to explain)
to visit Winter's house!

How bright it was.
How light it was.
How white it was all over,
with twists and turns
through frosted ferns
and crusted weeds and clover,
through frost-grass
reaching up to my knees,
and frost-flowers
thick on all the trees.

The brightest sights,
the whitest sights
kept opening all around,
for everything
was flaked with frost,
the plants, the rocks,
the ground,
and everything was breathless-still
beneath the crusty rime—
there wasn't any clock to tick
or any bell to chime.
Inside the frosted windowpane
(it's rather puzzling to explain)
there wasn't any Time.

How clear it was.
How queer it was.
How near it was to heaven!
Till someone came
and called my name
and said, "It's after seven!"
And heaven vanished like an elf
and I whisked back, inside myself.

Aileen Fisher
In One Door and out the Other: A Book of Poems, pp. 59–60

Byrd Baylor. The closeness between the land and the creatures who live upon it is strikingly presented in Baylor's poetry. Baylor tells readers that they must learn *The Other Way to Listen* if they are to be fortunate enough to hear corn singing, wildflower seeds bursting open, or a rock murmuring to a lizard. Nature will not talk to people if people feel superior, the old man in the poem teaches the child. A person must respect every aspect of nature, humble as well as grand, but must begin with the small things: one ant, one horned toad, one tree. In several of Baylor's books, Peter Parnall's sensitive illustrations are attuned to both nature and Baylor's words.

The poems in *Desert Voices* are written from the viewpoints of various inhabitants of the desert, animal and human. In *The Desert Is Theirs*, a poem about Native Americans, the poetry and accompanying illustrations develop the theme that the land is meant to be shared; it belongs to not only people but also spiders, scorpions, birds, coyotes, and lizards. This beautifully illustrated poem tells how Earthmaker created the desert, Spider People sewed the sky and earth together, and Elder Brother taught the people to live in the sun and touch the power of the earth. Readers discover that the Papagos know how to share the earth. Notice how Baylor develops the close relationship between people and nature through terms such as *brother* and actions that emphasize respect.

Papagos try
not to anger
their animal brothers.

They don't
step on
a snake's track
in the sand.

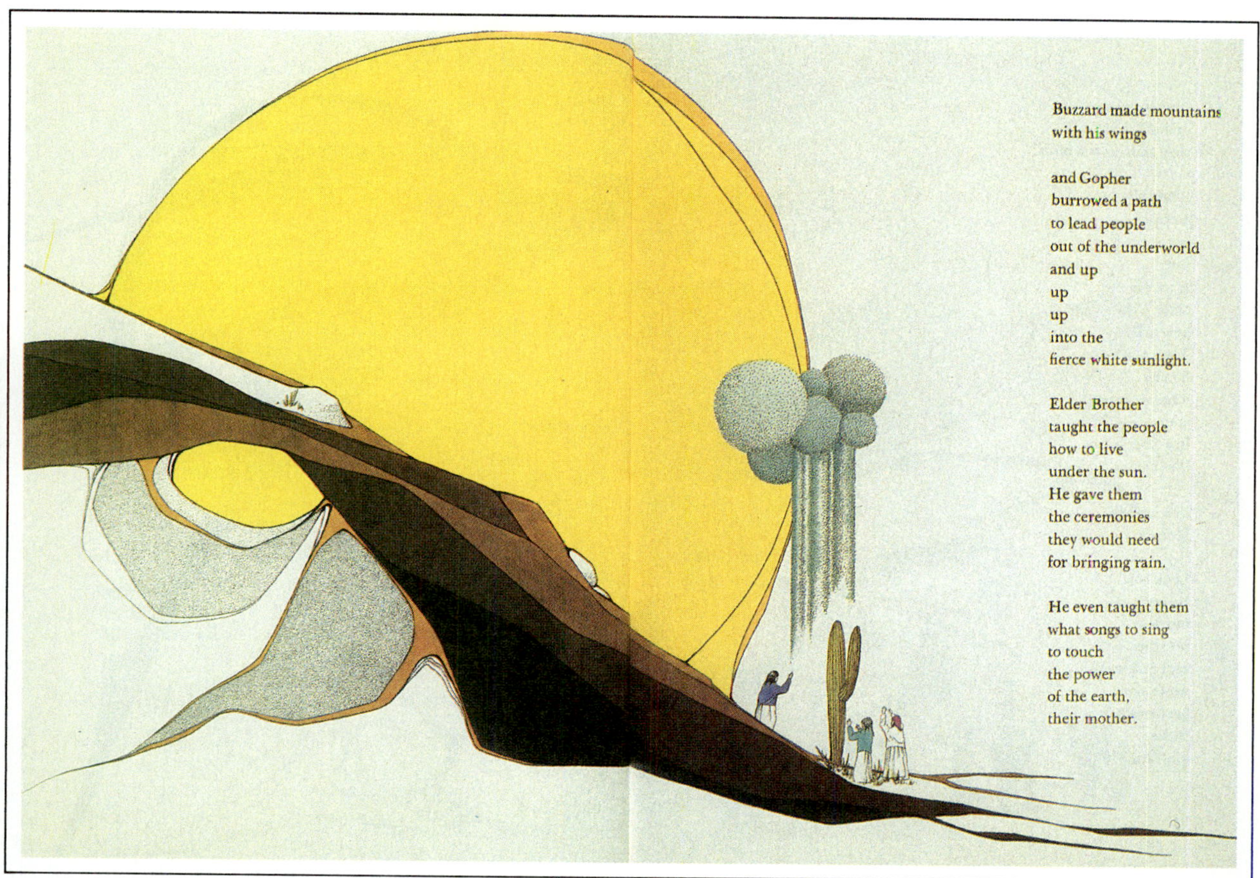
Buzzard made mountains
with his wings

and Gopher
burrowed a path
to lead people
out of the underworld
and up
up
up
into the
fierce white sunlight.

Elder Brother
taught the people
how to live
under the sun.
He gave them
the ceremonies
they would need
for bringing rain.

He even taught them
what songs to sing
to touch
the power
of the earth,
their mother.

Flowing lines in the illustrations create the mood for poems about the desert. (From Byrd Baylor, *The Desert Is Theirs*. Text copyright © 1975 by Byrd Baylor; illustrations copyright © 1975 by Peter Parnall. Reprinted with the permission of Charles Scribner's Sons.)

They don't disturb
a fox's bones.
They don't shove
a horned toad
out of the path.

They know
the land belongs
to spider and ant
the same as it does
to people.

They never say,
"This is my land
to do with as I please."
They say,
"We share. . .
we only share."

Byrd Baylor
The Desert Is Theirs, p. 15 unnumbered

Paul Fleischman. Sound and motions in nature are strongly depicted in Paul Fleischman's *Joyful Noise: Poems for Two Voices* and *I am Phoenix: Poems for Two Voices*. The texts are designed to be read aloud by two readers, one taking the left side, the other taking the right side. The poems are read from top to bottom, with some parts solo and some parts duet. For example, read aloud the poem, "Cicadas" with another reader in Figure 8–1. Notice the effect created by the solo parts and the two voices.

Characters, Situations, and Locations

Poems about experiences that are familiar to children make up a very large category of poetry for children. Familiar experiences may be related to friends or family, may tell about everyday

FIGURE 8–1
"Cicadas" (From Paul Fleischman. "Cicadas." *Joyful Noise: Poems for Two Voices*. Text © 1988 by Paul Fleischman. Illustrations © by Eric Beddows. All selections reprinted by permission of Harper & Row Publishers, Inc., p. 26)

Cicadas	
Afternoon, mid-August	
Two cicadas singing	Two cicadas singing
	Air kiln-hot, lead-heavy
Five cicadas humming	Five cicadas humming
Thunderheads northwestward	
Twelve cicadas buzzing	Twelve cicadas buzzing
	Up and down the street
the mighty choir's	the mighty choir's
assembling	assembling
Shrill cica-	
das	Ci-
droning	cadas
	droning
	in the elms
Three years	*Three years*
spent underground	
	among the roots
in darkness	in darkness
Now they're breaking ground	
	and climbing up
	the tree trunks
splitting skins	
and singing	and singing
	Jubilant
rejoicing	cicadas
	pouring out their
fervent praise	fervent praise
	for heat and light
their hymn	their hymn
sung to the sun	
Cicadas	Cicadas
whin-	whining
ing	ci-
	cadas
	whirring
whir-	
ring	ci-
	cadas
	pulsing
pulsing	
chanting from the treetops	chanting from the treetops
sending	
forth their	sending
booming	forth their
boisterous	booming
joyful noise!	joyful noise!

occurrences, or may provide insights into children's environments.

My Daddy Is a Cool Dude, by Karama Fufuka, presents the experiences of a child who lives in an urban black community. Children can identify with Fufuka's descriptions of good times and bad: celebration of family holidays, pride felt in a new baby, wanting a bicycle but needing new shoes, listening to neighbors fighting, or watching an ambulance take away Jerry Lee's big brother who "o-deed." Fufuka (9) says about her writing:

> In writing these poems I have gone back to my childhood and relived the experiences of those years of growing and learning. I have tried to deal here with both the positive and negative aspects of life which constitute reality for a child in the urban black community today.

I have tried to do so with the honesty of a child and I hope that adult readers of my poems will work to change those negative images for the sake of the children who will inherit our tomorrows. (p. 9)

In contrast, Eloise Greenfield illuminates life in the Bahamas in *Under the Sunday Tree*. The poems in this book develop positive images of life. Jo Carson's *Stories I Ain't Told Nobody Yet* is a collection of poetry written by people from the Appalachian region of the United States.

Both realistic and fanciful experiences related to growing up contribute the subjects for X. J. Kennedy's poems in *The Forgetful Wishing Well: Poems for Young People*. Developing an understanding of poetry provides the motivation for the poems in Kennedy's anthology *Knock at a Star: A Child's Introduction to Poetry*. The poems in the text are organized to help readers understand types and elements of poetry.

The excitement of skateboarding, running in a women's 400-meter race, and riding the surf is found in Lillian Morrison's *The Sidewalk Racer and Other Poems of Sports and Motion*. Morrison (24) says that she enjoys writing this kind of poetry because she loves rhythms, "the body movement implicit in poetry, explicit in sports. I have always believed that the attempt to achieve excellence in either of these fields is both noble and exciting. And there are emotions connected with sports, sometimes a kind of transcendence and beauty one wants to catch. One turns naturally to poetry to express these things" (p. 63). R. R. Knudson and May Swenson's *American Sports Poems* is a large anthology that includes poems about both specific sports and well-known athletes.

Sylvia Cassedy's *Roomrimes* explores various types of human and animal rooms. Cassedy's vivid language takes readers from an attic, where shadows stand "like flowers pressed against a page," to a zoo, where the caribou and shrew gaze at you.

Myra Cohn Livingston. Whether about whispers that are tickling children's ears or celebration of such holidays as Thanksgiving, Christmas, and Martin Luther King Day, Livingston's verses create images and suggest experiences to which children can relate. One child felt his mouth puckering as he read Livingston's poem about learning to whistle.

I Haven't Learned to Whistle

I haven't learned to whistle.
I've tried—
But if there's anything like a whistle in me,
It stops
Inside.

Dad whistles.
My brother whistles
And almost everyone I know.

I've tried to put my lips together with wrinkles,
To push my tongue against my teeth
And make a whistle
Come
Out
Slow—

But what happens is nothing but a feeble gasping
Sound
Like a sort of sickly bird.

(Everybody says they never heard
A whistle like *that*
And to tell the truth
Neither did I.)

But Dad says, tonight, when he comes home,
He'll show me again how
To put my lips together with wrinkles,
To push my tongue against my teeth,
To blow my breath out and really make a whistle.

And I'll *try!*

Myra Cohn Livingston
O Sliver of Liver, p. 12

In additional poems, Livingston deals with characters, situations, and locations. Livingston's books of poems include *Celebrations, Sea Songs, Sky Songs, Space Songs,* and *Up in the Air*.

Valerie Worth. In *More Small Poems,* Valerie Worth poetically describes looking at a moth's wing through a magnifying glass, observing a kitten with a stiffly arched back, and seeing fireworks in the night sky. Something as simple as taking off one's shoes becomes a sensual experience for Worth, as in the following poem:

Barefoot

After that tight
Choke of sock
And blunt
Weight of shoe,

The foot can feel
Clover's green
Skin
Growing,

And the fine
Invisible
Teeth
Of gentle grass,

And the cool

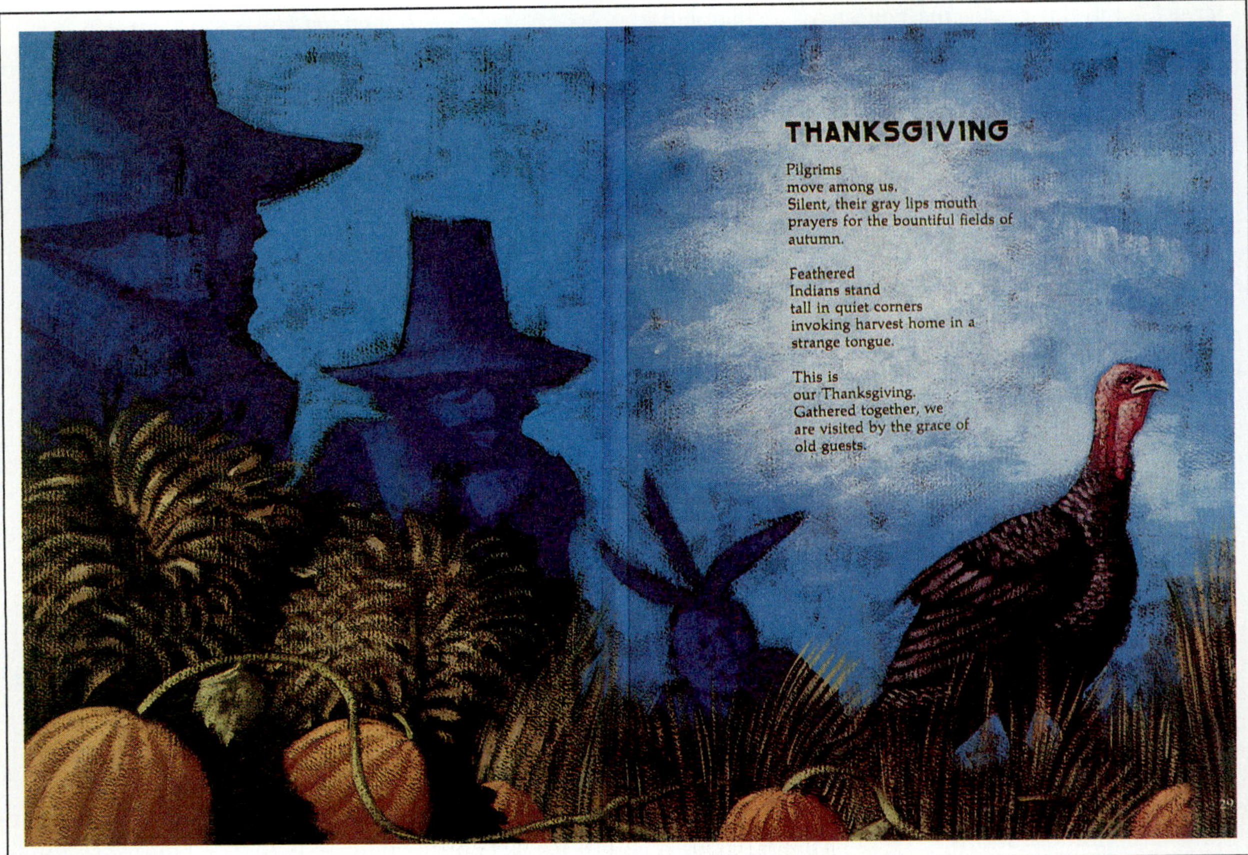

THANKSGIVING
Pilgrims
move among us.
Silent, their gray lips mouth
prayers for the bountiful fields of
autumn.
Feathered
Indians stand
tall in quiet corners
invoking harvest home in a
strange tongue.
This is
our Thanksgiving.
Gathered together, we
are visited by the grace of
old guests.

Illustrations enhance the mood of the various holidays. (Illustration copyright © 1985 by Leonard Everett Fisher. Reprinted from *Celebrations* by Myra Cohn Livingston by permission of Holiday House.)

Breath
Of the earth
Beneath.

Valerie Worth
Still More Small Poems, p. 13

In the poems of Valerie Worth, common things in the worlds of children contain magical qualities. In *Still More Small Poems,* Worth sees common objects with uncommon insights: grandmother's door with the fancy glass pattern, a kite riding in the air, and rags that are no longer faithful pajamas but crumpled cloths used to wash windows. The poems from all four of Valerie Worth's series of small poems appear in *All the Small Poems*.

Kaye Starbird. Children's honest reactions to such experiences as a friend's keeping them waiting once too often, and enduring an obnoxious girl at summer camp are found in Starbird's *The Covered Bridge House and Other Poems*. The poem about the summer camp experience, "Watch Out," describes the exasperation of one girl at Camp Blue Sky when another girl pulls a series of pranks. Starbird's poetry can also be a lesson to teachers, as when she suggests what should not be done when teaching spelling.

The Spelling Test

One morning in a spelling test
The teacher said to Hugh:
"I have a word for you to spell
The word is 'kangaroo.' "
But Hugh was puzzled by the word
Which wasn't one he knew,
So, when he wrote it on the board,
He printed "hannagrue."

"No, No! Go take your seat again,"
The teacher said to Hugh,

"And take along this copy card.
The card says 'kangaroo,'
Then get your pencil out," she said,
"And get your notebook, too.
And write the word a hundred times
And tell me when you're through."

So Hugh did just exactly what
The teacher told him to,
And, when he handed in his work,
The teacher said to Hugh:
"I hope you know your spelling now."
And Hugh said, "Yes, I do,"
Then—walking bravely to the board—
He printed "kannagrue."

Kaye Starbird
The Covered Bridge House and Other Poems, p. 17

David McCord. The poetic genius of McCord has won him numerous honors, including the Sarah Josepha Hale Medal, a Guggenheim Fellowship, and, in 1977, the first national award for excellence in children's poetry awarded by the National Council of Teachers of English. Clifton Fadiman (19) said, "David McCord stands among the finest of living writers of children's verse. He is both an acrobat of language and an authentic explorer of the child's inner world" (coverleaf).

One at a Time: Collected Poems for the Young contains over two hundred of McCord's poems: favorite chants, such as "Song of the Train," alphabet verses, riddles, poetic conversations, and numerous poems about animals, children's experiences, nature, and nonsense. The last section of the book, "Write Me Another Verse," attempts to show readers how to write different poetry forms, including the ballad, the tercet, the villanelle, the clerihew, the cinquain, and the haiku. Earlier in the book, McCord gives directions for writing the couplet (two-line verse), the quatrain (four-line verse), the limerick (five-line verse), and the triolet (eight-line verse).

McCord's skill in using shape to enhance meaning is illustrated in the following poem.

The Grasshopper

Down
a
deep
well
a
grasshopper
fell.

By kicking about
He thought to get out.
He might have known better,
For that got him wetter.

To kick round and round
Is the way to get drowned,
And drowning is what
I should tell you he got.

But
the
well
had
a
rope
that
dangled
some
hope.
And sure as molasses
On one of his passes
He found the rope handy
And up he went, *and he*

it
up
and
it
up
and
it
up
and
it
up
went

And hopped away proper
As any grasshopper.

David McCord
One at a Time: Collected Poems for the Young pp. 28–30

Moods and Feelings

Children can learn through poets' descriptions of everyday life, dreams, and nostalgia that others experience many moods and feelings like their own. Arnold Adoff's *All the Colors of the Race* contains poems written from the viewpoint of a girl who has black and white parentage. The poems reflect her thoughts and moods as she contemplates her heritage and other experiences in her life. Adoff's *Sports Pages* presents the exhilarations and the disappointments expressed by young athletes.

The moods associated with the various interactions between two brothers form the themes in Richard J. Margolis's *Secrets of a Small Brother*. These poems reveal a range of feelings, including jealousy, anger, love, and compassion.

A bedtime fantasy forms the setting for the adventures in David McPhail's *The Dream Child*. McPhail's selection of incidents in the world of

A dream-like mood is captured in the illustrations for a lullaby. (From *The Dream Child* by David McPhail. Copyright © 1985 by David McPhail. By permission of E. P. Dutton, Inc.)

Dream Child and Tame Bear creates a happy and dreamlike mood. Adventures that could be frightening or disruptive end with discord transformed into harmony. Other moods and feelings related to nighttime, bedtime, and happy dreams are the focus of Nancy Larrick's colorfully illustrated anthology *When the Dark Comes Dancing: A Bedtime Poetry Book,* Thomas Hood's *Before I Go to Sleep,* and Kay Chorao's anthology *The Baby's Bedtime Book,* in which a full-page painting accompanies each selection. Fantastic events in a dream world create a happy, imaginative setting in Nancy Willard's *Night Story*.

Moods and feelings in poems for older students are found in two anthologies by Paul B. Janeczko. *Going over to Your Place: Poems for Each Other* includes over one hundred poems dealing with love and loss. *The Music of What Happens: Poems That Tell Stories* includes poignant poems about such emotional experiences as killing a rabbit or reading a grandfather's last letter.

Langston Hughes. Although Hughes is not considered primarily a children's poet, his poetry explores human feelings, asks difficult questions, and expresses hopes and desires that are meaningful to readers of any age. Some of his poems—such as "Merry-Go-Round"—can be used to help children understand and identify with the feelings and experiences of black people in earlier eras of American history. In another poem, Hughes provides vivid descriptions of what life would be like without dreams.

Dreams

Hold fast to dreams
For if dreams die
Life is a broken-winged bird
That cannot fly.

Hold fast to dreams
For when dreams go
Life is a barren field
Frozen with snow.

Langston Hughes
The Dream Keeper, 1932, 1960

The photograph that accompanies "Dreams" in the anthology *Reflections on a Gift of Watermelon Pickle. . .and Other Modern Verse,* edited by Dunning, Lueders, and Smith, shows a solitary dried weed surrounded by ice crystals. When this poem was shared with a group of fifth graders, one of the students reminded the class that dreams do not need to die: Like the weed, they can be reborn in the spring.

Cynthia Rylant. Moods and feelings related to growing up form the unifying theme in Rylant's *Waiting to Waltz: A Childhood.* Rylant's poems paint word pictures of a young girl feeling pride in her small town, pondering the relationships within the town, and revealing the experiences that influence her own maturation. In "Teenagers," for example, Rylant explores the longings of a child who is too big for some things and not big enough for others.

Teenagers

Watching the teenagers
in Beaver
using hairspray and
lipstick.
Kissing at ballgames.
Going steady.
And wanting it fast,
wanting it now.
Because all my pretend
had to be hidden.
All my games
secret.
Wanting to be a wide-open child
but too big,
too big.
No more.
Waiting to shave
and wear nylons
and waltz.
Forgetting when
I was last time
a child.
Never knowing
when it
ended.

Cynthia Rylant
Waiting to Waltz: A Childhood, p. 44

Animals in Poetry

Animals, whether teddy bears, cuddly puppies, purring kittens, or preposterous beasts of imagination, hold special places in the hearts of both children and adults. Therefore, it is not surprising that many poets write about animals. In *Feathered Ones and Furry*, Aileen Fisher shares with children her love for all types of animals, including the furry.

The Furry Ones

I like
the furry ones—
the waggy ones
the purry ones
the hoppy ones
that hurry,

The glossy ones
the saucy ones
the sleepy ones
the leapy ones
the mousy ones
that scurry,

The snuggly ones
the huggly ones
the never, never
ugly ones. . .
all soft
and warm
and furry.

Aileen Fisher
Feathered Ones and Furry, p. viii

The best-known collection of cat poems by a single author is probably T. S. Eliot's *Old Possum's Book of Practical Cats*. These poems, which were composed for Eliot's godchildren, are full of vivid language, interesting characterizations, and lyrical quality, as revealed when the poems were set to music in the Broadway show, *Cats*. In the following excerpt from "Macavity: The Mystery Cat," notice how Eliot captures the illusive nature of cats.

Macavity: The Mystery Cat

Macavity's a Mystery Cat: he's called the Hidden Paw—
For he's the master criminal who can defy the Law.
He's the bafflement of Scotland Yard, the Flying Squad's despair:
For when they reach the scene of crime—*Macavity's not there*!

Macavity, Macavity, there's no one like Macavity,
He's broken every human law, he breaks the law of gravity.
His powers of levitation would make a fakir stare,
And when you reach the scene of crime—*Macavity's not there*!
You may seek him in the basement, you may look up in the air—
But I tell you once and once again, *Macavity's not there*!

Macavity's a ginger cat, he's very tall and thin;
You would know him if you saw him, for his eyes are sunken in.
His brow is deeply lined with thought, his head is highly domed;
His coat is dusty from neglect, his whiskers are uncombed.
He sways his head from side to side, with movements like a snake;
And when you think he's half asleep, he's always wide awake.

Macavity, Macavity, there's no one like Macavity,
For he's a fiend in feline shape, a monster of depravity.
You may meet him in a by-street, you may see him in the square—
But when a crime's discovered, then *Macavity's not there*!

He's outwardly respectable. (They say he cheats at
 cards.)
And his footprints are not found in any file of Scotland
 Yard's.
And when the larder's looted, or the jewel-case is rifled,
Or when the milk is missing, or another Peke's been
 stifled,
Or the greenhouse glass is broken, and the trellis past
 repair—
Ay, there's the wonder of the thing! *Macavity's not there*!

And when the Foreign Office find a Treaty's gone astray,
Or the Admiralty lose some plans and drawings by the
 way,
There may be a scrap of paper in the hall or on the
 stair—
But it's useless to investigate—*Macavity's not there*!
And when the loss has been disclosed, the Secret
 Service say:
'It *must* have been Macavity!'—but he's a mile away.
You'll be sure to find him resting, or a-licking of his
 thumbs,
Or engaged in doing complicated long division sums.

Macavity, Macavity, there's no one like Macavity,
There never was a Cat of such deceitfulness and suavity.
He always has an alibi, and one or two to spare:
At whatever time the deed took place—MACAVITY
 WASN'T THERE!
And they say that all the Cats whose wicked deeds are
 widely known
(I might mention Mungojerrie, I might mention Griddle-
bone)
Are nothing more than agents for the Cat who all the
time
Just controls their operations: the Napoleon of Crime!

T. S. Eliot
Old Possum's Book of Practical Cats, p. 37.

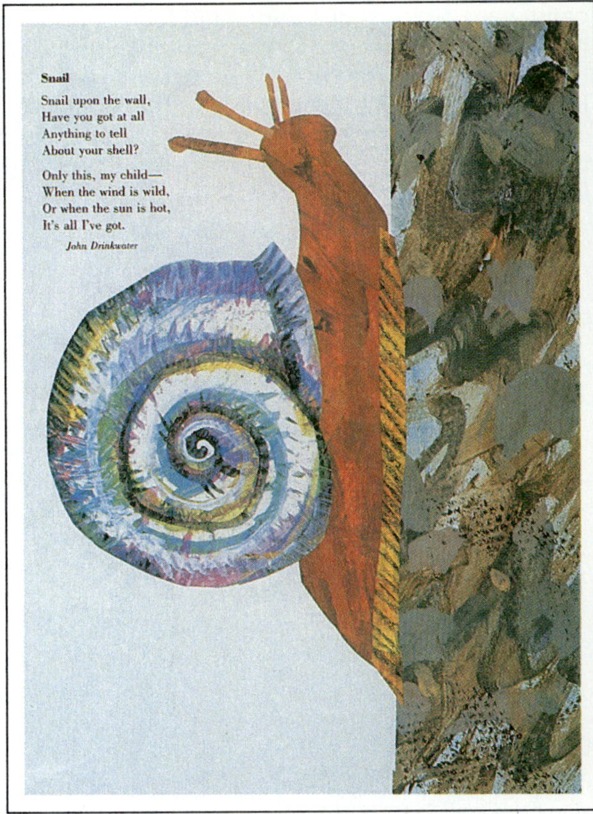

Eric Carle's collage illustrations add to the beauty in a poetry collection about animals. (From *Eric Carle's Animals Animals*. Illustrations copyright © 1989 by Eric Carle. Reprinted by permission of Philomel Books. *Snail* by John Drinkwater, © 1929. Reprinted by permission of Samuel French, Inc.)

Anthologies of animal poems include Lee Bennett Hopkins's *My Mane Catches the Wind: Poems About Horses,* which describes the birth of a colt and the beauty of a stallion. It also has other poems that appeal to horse lovers. Animals and other experiences associated with the circus are the subject of poems in Hopkins's *Circus! Circus!* Laura Whipple's *Eric Carle's Animals, Animals,* an anthology, includes poems about a variety of animals. Carle's collage illustrations are vivid. Myra Cohn Livingston's *Cat Poems* explores all types of cats, from T. S. Eliot's humorous "The Song of the Jellicles" to Karla Kuskin's sad remembrances of a lost cat, "In August Once."

Students of children's literature should compare the impact of the illustrations in two poetry collections about dinosaurs. They can compare the mood of the poems and the influence of Arnold Lobel's watercolor illustrations that accompany Jack Prelutsky's poems in *Tyrannosaurus Was a Beast: Dinosaur Poems* with the influence of Murray Tinkelman's black-and-white illustrations in Lee Bennett Hopkins's *Dinosaurs*.

Witches and Ghosts

Haunted houses, ghostly appearances, mysterious happenings, and diabolic demons are found in Eve Merriam's *Halloween ABC*. The spooky nature of the poems is intensified by Jane Smith's dark, dramatic illustrations. Notice how Merriam uses repetition, alliteration, and vivid imagery to capture the essence of a witch.

Witchery

Which, which,
which witchery?
Nectar of nightshade
or venom of bee?

Which, which,
which woeful bane?
Juice of the hemlock
or brimstone with rain?

Which, which,
which plaguey pox?
Soup bowls of toadstools
or mouse broth in crocks?

Which, which,
which should we choose?
Buckets of slimy
or barrels of ooze?

Which wicked wickedness,
which will we serve?
Well, which pretty poison
do you deserve?

Eve Merriam
Halloween ABC, unnumbered

Alfred Noyes's classic poem *The Highwayman* provides a ghostly conclusion to a tale of love, horror, and unselfish motives. Charles Keeping's black-and-white illustrations reinforce the drama in this poem for older readers. Prior to death, the characters are sketched in black. Following death, the horseman becomes a predominantly white figure, who rides through ghostly trees, approaches the old inn door, and finds the landlord's daughter, who is now a ghostly figure herself.

Other vivid poems about ghoulies, ghosties, and graveyards are found in Daisy Wallace's collection, *Ghost Poems*, illustrated by Tomie dePaola. The world of spirits and eerie images is also evoked by Blaise Cendrars's words and Marcia Brown's illustrations in *Shadow*. Cendrar's carefully chosen words suggest a shadow that prowls, mingles, watches, spies, and sprawls in silence. Brown's collages reinforce this ghostly world. Several more ghostly poems are found in the section of poems titled "Spooky Poems" in *Sing a Song of Popcorn: Every Child's Book of Poems* by de Regniers, Moore, White, and Carr.

Suggested Activities for Adult Understanding of Poetry

- ☐ Read a poem that relies heavily on rhyming elements. Find the location of the rhyming words (at the ends of lines, at the beginnings of the lines, and within the lines). Read the poem orally. What feelings do the rhyming elements suggest?
- ☐ Look through an anthology of poetry and find some poems that rely on sound patterns to create excitement. Prepare for oral presentation a poem that relies on alliteration (the repetition of initial consonant sounds) or assonance (the repetition of vowel sounds). Share the poem orally with a peer group.
- ☐ Locate several poems that develop images literally and several poems that develop images figuratively. Is there a difference in your interest in the two types of imagery? Share the poems with a child. Does the child respond in the same ways to these types?
- ☐ Compile a list of similes and metaphors found in a poem. What images does the poet suggest? Is simile or metaphor more effective or more easily visualized in word pictures than are realistic words?
- ☐ Compare the subject matter of limericks written by Edward Lear with the subject matter of limericks written by such contemporary poets as N. M. Bodecker and William Jay Smith. How are they similar? How do they differ?
- ☐ Read several collections of haiku. Based on your reading, tell what Ann Atwood meant when she said that haiku is "begun by the writer and completed by the reader."
- ☐ Select and read several poems by one poet of humorous verse—such as Edward Lear, Lewis Carroll, Laura E. Richards, Jack Prelutsky, Shel Silverstein, William Jay Smith, John Ciardi, or N. M. Bodecker. What poetic elements does the poet use? What subjects does the poet write about?
- ☐ Compare the content and style of a poet who wrote humorous verse in the nineteenth century (such as Lewis Carroll or Edward Lear) with those of a contemporary author (such as Jack Prelutsky or N. M. Bodecker). What are the similarities and differences between the writers in the two time periods?

References

1 Atwood, Ann. *Haiku: The Mood of Earth*. New York: Scribner's Sons, 1971.

2 Behn, Harry. *Chrysalis, Concerning Children and Poetry*. New York: Harcourt Brace Jovanovich, 1968.

3 Bridge, Ethel Brooks. "Using Children's Choices of and Reactions to Poetry as Determinants in Enriching Literary Experience in the Middle Grades." Philadelphia: Temple University, 1966. University Microfilm No. 67–6246.

4 Clark, Leonard. "Poetry for the Youngest." In *Horn Book Reflections*, edited by Elinor Whitney Field. Boston: Horn Book, 1969.

5 Cowen, John E. "Conversations with Poet Jose Garcia Villa on Teaching Poetry to Children." In *Teaching Reading Through the Arts,* edited by John E. Cowen. Newark, Del.: International Reading Association, 1983, pp. 78–87.

6 Day-Lewis, Cecil. *Poetry for You*. New York: Oxford, 1947.

7 Fisher, Carol, and Margaret Natarella. "Young Children's Preferences in Poetry: A National Survey of First, Second, and Third Graders." *Research in the Teaching of English* 16 (December 1982): 339–354.

8 Frye, Northrop, Sheridan Baker, and George Perkins. *The Harper Handbook to Literature*. New York: Harper & Row, 1985.

9 Fufuka, Karama. *My Daddy Is a Cool Dude*. New York: Dial, 1975.

10 Gensler, Kinereth, and Nina Nyhart. *The Poetry Connection: An Anthology of Contemporary Poems with Ideas to Stimulate Children's Writing*. New York: Teachers & Writers, 1978.

11 Godden, Rumer. "Shining Popocatapetl: Poetry for Children." *The Horn Book* (May/June 1988): 305–314.

12 Groff, Patrick. "Where Are We Going with Poetry for Children?" In *Horn Book Reflections,* edited by Elinor Whitney Field. Boston: Horn Book, 1969.

13 Hopkins, Lee Bennett. *Pass the Poetry, Please!* New York: Harper & Row, 1987.

14 Jerome, Judson. *Poetry: Premeditated Art*. Boston: Houghton Mifflin, 1968.

15 Kutiper, Karen Sue. "A Survey of the Adolescent Poetry Preferences of Seventh, Eighth, and Ninth Graders." University of Houston: Ed.D. Dissertation, 1985. DAI 47:451–452A.

16 Le Pere, Jean. "For Every Occasion: Poetry in the Reading Program." Albuquerque, N. Mex.: Eighth Southwest Regional Conference, International Reading Association, 1980.

17 Livingston, Myra Cohn. "Not the Rose. . ." In *Horn Book Reflections,* edited by Elinor Whitney Field. Boston: Horn Book, 1969.

18 Lowell, Amy. *Poetry and Poets*. New York: Biblo, 1971.

19 McCord, David. *One at a Time: Collected Poems for the Young*. Boston: Little, Brown, 1977.

20 Meigs, Cornelia, and Elizabeth Nesbitt. *A Critical History of Children's Literature*. New York: Macmillan, 1969.

21 Merriam, Eve. *Rainbow Writing*. New York: Atheneum, 1976.

22 Merrick, Brian. "With a Straight Eye: An Interview with Charles Causley." *Children's Literature in Education* 19 (Winter 1988): 123–135.

23 Moore, Lillian. "A Second Look: Small Poems." *The Horn Book* (July/August 1988): 470–473.

24 Morrison, Lillian. *The Sidewalk Racer and Other Poems of Sports and Motion*. New York: Lothrop, Lee & Shepard, 1977.

25 Morse, Samuel French. "Speaking of the Imagination." In *Horn Book Reflections,* edited by Elinor Whitney Field. Boston: Horn Book, 1969.

26 Sebesta, Sam. "Choosing Poetry." In *Children's Choices,* edited by Nancy Roser and Margaret Frith. Newark, Del.: International Reading Association, 1983.

27 Terry, Ann. *Children's Poetry Preferences: A National Survey of Upper Elementary Grades*. Urbana, Ill.: National Council of Teachers of English, 1974.

28 Thurman, Judith. *Flashlight and Other Poems*. New York: Atheneum, 1976.

29 Tucker, Nicholas. "Why Nursery Rhymes?" In *Children and Literature: Views and Reviews,* edited by Virginia Haviland. Glenview, Ill.: Scott, Foresman, 1973.

Involving Children in Poetry

KNOWLEDGE ABOUT CONCEPTS, APPRECIation for language, empathy with characters and situations, insights about oneself and others, self-expression, and enjoyment are all values of poetry for children. Unfortunately, research has supported Jon E. Shapiro's (17) assertion that "poetry has often been the most neglected component of the language arts curriculum" (p. 91). Over 75 percent of the middle-elementary teachers in Ann Terry's (20) study of children's poetry preferences read poetry to their children less than once a month. This finding may also relate to the fact that the children in Terry's study reported a decreased interest in poetry as they progressed through the elementary grades. Gwendda McKay (12) reported a similar finding in Australia. She concluded that children at all levels heard stories daily, whereas poetry received little attention.

Shapiro maintains that adults' own lack of interest in poetry causes them to neglect it in the classroom. The only way for adults to feel comfortable sharing poetry with children is to read poetry written by many fine authors and thus discover a new or revitalized delight in poetry.

John Gough (4) argues that the anthology format of many poetry collections discourages enjoyment. Individual poems are presented in isolation, rather than in a continuity that sustains interest. Gough believes that appreciation of poetry should be carefully developed and nurtured through a logical sequence: nursery rhymes and songs; rhymed stories, such as Dr. Seuss's *The Cat in the Hat;* narrative poems that are highly but carefully illustrated; stories, such as A. A. Milne's *Winnie-the-Pooh,* in which characters, adventures, and poems are strongly interrelated; narrative poems that give contextual support to the poetry; and then a coherent, related sequence of poems by one poet, in which the poems encourage the readers to understand the personality of the poet and to appreciate the poems.

Rumer Godden (3) stresses that children can be enticed with good poetry. She believes that children should proceed from singing and saying nursery rhymes to exploring lively poems that emphasize movement and rhythm, such as Stevenson's "Windy Nights," to hearing and reading small anthologies of poems to sharing poetry in which poets tell stories, such as Browning's "The Pied Piper of Hamelin," Rossetti's "Goblin Market," Noyes's "The Highwayman," and Scott's "Lochinvar."

University students in this author's classes often say that their aversion to poetry stems from the way it was presented in their elementary, middle-school, and high-school classrooms. They fondly remember the rhymes and jingles shared in kindergarten and first grade, but the pleasant associations are undercut by later forced memorization of poems and exercises in which everyone had to agree with the teacher's analysis of a poem. One student recalled her feelings of terror every Friday when she had to recite a memorized poem in front of the class and then had points deducted from her presentation for each error she made.

Other university students, however, describe more positive memories of poetry in their elementary classrooms. The students remembered teachers who spontaneously shared a wide variety of poetry with their classes; who encouraged students to write poems and share them with an appreciative audience; and who had their students experiment with choral readings of poetry, sometimes accompanied by rhythm instruments. One student remembered a teacher who always had a poem to reflect the mood of a gentle rain, a smiling jack-o-lantern, or a mischievous child. Another remembered going outside on a warm spring day, looking at the butterflies and wildflowers in a meadow, listening to the world around her, sharing her feelings with the class, and then writing a poem to express the promise of that beautiful day. Yet another remembered a librarian who always included poetry in story-hour presentations.

After university students explore the various ways of sharing poetry with children, many of them sadly conclude that something was left out of their own educations. This section considers some ways that you may encourage children to enjoy and experience poetry by listening to poetry, moving to poetry, using poetry as the basis for creative dramatizations, developing choral speaking, combining music and poetry, combining art and poetry, and writing poetry themselves.

LISTENING TO POETRY

Poetry is meant to be read, reread, and shared. The sounds, the rhythms, the vivid words, and the unexpected phrases lend themselves to oral reading. Research shows that poetry is rarely shared with children, and even when poetry is shared, it is often isolated from other experiences. Poet Lee Bennett Hopkins (8) argues that poetry may be disliked by children because it is frequently taught as an isolated unit instead of shared at appropriate times throughout the day. Hopkins maintains that poetry deserves to be added to the total curriculum, not limited to the language arts. Hopkins provides the following guidelines for reading poetry orally to children, whether you are a parent, teacher, or librarian:

1 Before reading a poem aloud, read it aloud several times by yourself to get the feel of the words and rhythm. Know the poem well. Mark the words and phrases you would like to emphasize, and then you will read it exactly as you feel it.
2 Follow the rhythm of the poem, reading it naturally. The physical appearance of most poems on the printed page dictates the rhythm and the mood of the words. Some poems are meant to be read softly and slowly; others must be read at a more rapid pace.
3 Make pauses that please you—pauses that make sense. Some poems sound better when the lines are rhythmically strung together. Sometimes great effects can be obtained by pausing at the end of each line. Many of the poems by E. E. Cummings and William Carlos Williams convey greater mood when they are read by pausing at the end of each short line, as though you were saying something yourself for the first time, thinking of a word or words that will come from your tongue next. . . .
4 When reading a poem aloud, speak in a natural voice. Don't change to a high-pitched or bass-pitched tone. Read a poem as though you were telling the children about a new car, or a television program you saw last night. Again, you must be sincere. A poem must interest you as well as be one that you feel is right for your children.
5 After a poem is read, be quiet. Don't feel trapped into asking children questions such as "Did you like it?" Most girls and boys will answer yes—even if they didn't like it—because you selected and read it. And what if they didn't like it? By the time you begin finding out the reasons, the poem is destroyed and half of the class will see why they, too, shouldn't like it anymore (pp. 16–17).

MOVING TO POETRY

The rhythms, sounds, characters, and images in many poems encourage physical responses from children. An observer of children in a playground is likely to see two children swinging a rope while a third child jumps to the rhythm and the actions described in a chant such as the following:

Teddy bear, teddy bear, turn around.
Teddy bear, teddy bear, touch the ground.
Teddy bear, teddy bear, close your eyes.
Teddy bear, teddy bear, be surprised.
Teddy bear, teddy bear, climb up the stairs.
Teddy bear, teddy bear, say your prayers.

Teddy bear, teddy bear, turn out the light.
Teddy bear, teddy bear, say good night.

In a similar way, children may be inspired to move when you slowly read a poem aloud. Valerie Worth's *More Small Poems* provides children with an opportunity to become a "Kitten," arching their backs, dancing sideways, tearing across the floor, crouching against imagined threats, and pouncing with claws ready; or to become "Fireworks," exploding in the air, billowing into bright color, and spilling back down toward earth in waterfalls. They can be spectacular in a much quieter way as a "Soap Bubble" that bends into different shapes, rises shimmering into the air, then pops and disappears. Worth's *Still More Small Poems* encourages children to experience the free flight of a "Kite" as the wind tears it from a hand and sends it soaring; to become a "Mushroom" pushing up through the soil; or to go "Barefoot," as their feet emerge from choking socks and they feel cool clover and gentle blades of grass between their toes.

Sports enthusiasts can move to poetry that emphasizes the movements and tensions of various sports. Edwin Hoey's "Foul Shot" and Eve Merriam's "Cheers," both found in Stephen Dunning, Edward Lueders, and Hugh Smith's *Reflections on a Gift of Watermelon Pickle. . .and Other Modern Verse,* inspire children to recreate the rhythms and tensions of a basketball game and the sounds and feels of cheerleaders at a football game. Several poems in R. R. Knudson and May Swenson's *American Sports Poems* lend themselves to acting out through movement. Joseph Colin Murphy's "The Skydivers" encourages children to experience the feel of wind, Arnold Adoff's "Point Guard" simulates passing and scoring, and Maxine Kumin's "400-Meter Freestyle" explores the excitement of a swimming match.

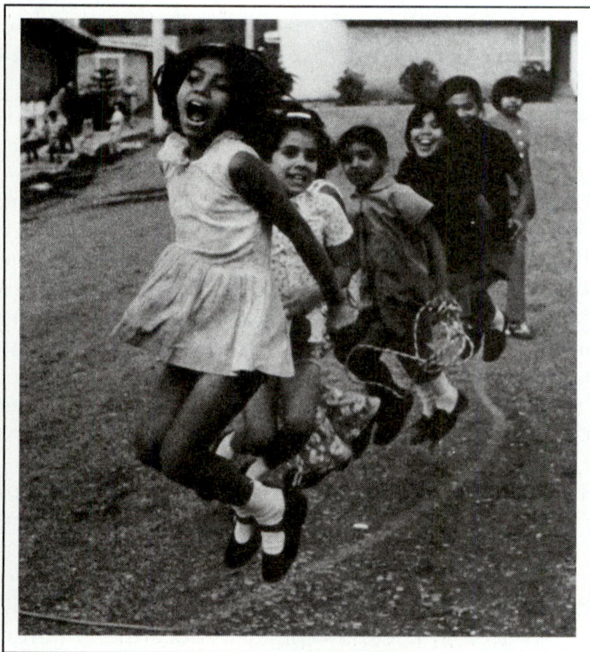

Children respond to the rhythm in a jumping-rope chant.

Poetry anthologies, especially if they group poems according to theme, provide numerous opportunities for moving to poetry. For example, Jack Prelutsky's anthology *The Random House Book of Poetry for Children* allows children to become Stanley Kunitz's "The Waltzer in the House" and William Jay Smith's "Seal." Many of the poems in Lillian Morrison's *Rhythm Road: Poems to Move To* stimulate movement. The poems in this collection are divided according to subjects, such as "Poems to Dance To," "Poems to Work To," "Watching Water," and "The Feel of Sports." The grouping allows students to move to similar topics and to compare the feelings and the movements created by several poets.

DRAMATIZING POETRY

One of the values of poetry for children noted by Jean Le Pere (10) is encouragement to identify with characters and situations. Ann Terry (20) discovered that narrative poems are among children's favorite poems. Creative dramatizations enhance children's enjoyment of the situations found in poetry (6).

Clement C. Moore's narrative poem "A Visit from St. Nicholas" (now familiarly known as "The Night Before Christmas") suggests several scenes to dramatize. Children can prepare for the Christmas celebration by trimming the tree and decorating the room. They can imagine the sugarplum dreams and act them out. They can reenact the father's response to hearing the clatter of hoofs. They can be reindeer pulling the loaded sleigh or St. Nicholas as he comes down the chimney, fills the stockings, and then bounds up the chimney and drives out of sight.

The poem has many other dramatic possibilities. Children have created the dialogue for an imaginary meeting between the father and St.

ISSUE

Analyzing Poetry: Help or Hindrance?

WILL CHILDREN ENJOY and understand poetry more if they analyze the meaning and meter, identify figurative language, and define terminology and poetic devices? The activities suggested in basal readers that include poetry and in literature anthologies designed to be shared with children frequently suggest such analysis. Teachers or librarians may ask children to read or listen to a poem to identify the author's meaning and theme, locate the similes and metaphors, or identify the rhyming schemes. Adults encourage such activities in the belief that analyzing poetic devices improves children's understanding, enjoyment, and writing of poetry.

Louise M. Rosenblatt takes a contrasting viewpoint.[1] She maintains that reading poetry should be an aesthetic experience in which children focus upon cognitive and affective elements, such as sensations, images, feelings, and ideas that allow them to have a "lived-through" experience. She believes that focusing children's attention on analysis is detrimental when children have not yet had many opportunities to experience poetry on their own terms. Adults should first encourage children to savor what they visualize, feel, think, and enjoy while hearing or reading poetry.

Myra Cohn Livingston also dislikes analysis.[2] She states that she is unhappy when authors of basal readers use her poem "Whispers" to teach about rhyming words or punctuation, or to ask such questions as "What color is a whisper?"

[1]Rosenblatt, Louise M. "What Facts Does This Poem Teach You?" *Language Arts* 57 (April 1980): 386–394.

[2]Livingston, Myra Cohn. "An Unreasonable Excitement." *The Advocate* (Spring 1983).

Nicholas or the children and St. Nicholas. What would they say to each other? How would they act? If the children could ask St. Nicholas questions, what would they ask? If St. Nicholas could ask questions, what would he want to know? Children have imagined themselves as St. Nicholas going into many homes on Christmas Eve. What was the most unusual experience they had? They have imagined themselves going back to St. Nick's workshop at the North Pole. What kind of a welcome did they receive?

Adults have used the nonsensical situations found in Jack Prelutsky's poems in *The Queen of Eene* to stimulate humorous dramatizations. One group, for example, dramatized the conversation and actions of the four foolish ladies, (Hattie, Harriet, Hope, and Hortense) as they roped a rhinoceros and took him to tea. Then, the group imagined and acted out other predicaments that could have been created by the actions of the foolish ladies. "Gretchen in the Kitchen," stimulates spooky witch scenes at Halloween. The quarts of curdled mud, salted spiders, ogre's backbone, and dragon's blood provide a setting appealing to children who are preparing to be spooks, witches, and black cats.

Other poems can be used to stimulate creative dramatizations, including the following:

1 "The Pied Piper of Hamelin," by Robert Browning, located in numerous sources, including Iona and Peter Opie's *The Oxford Book of Children's Verse*. The piper lures rats to their deaths. Then, after the mayor refuses to pay for his services, the piper entices the children of the town to follow him to a strange land.
2 "Hurry, Hurry Mary Dear," from N. M. Bodecker's book of the same title. A harassed woman

follows the directions of a demanding man until she has finally had enough.

3 "The Adventures of Chris," by David McCord, found in *One at a Time: Collected Poems for the Young*. A toad and a boy discuss arithmetic, spelling, and what not to miss on earth.
4 *Sir Cedric,* by Roy Gerrard. Cedric the Good, Black Ned, and Matilda the Pure have knightly adventures.
5 *Sir Francis Drake & His Daring Deeds,* by Roy Gerrard. This explorer has numerous adventures that can stimulate dramatizations.
6 *Night Story,* by Nancy Willard. A small boy has a series of adventures in dreamland.
7 *The Voyage of the Ludgate Hill: Travels with Robert Louis Stevenson,* by Nancy Willard. Travelers on a steamship interact with the animals in the cargo hold.
8 *A Visit to William Blake's Inn: Poems for Innocent and Experienced Travelers,* by Nancy Willard. Many unusual characters, such as the man in the marmalade hat, visit the inn. The characters and incidents can stimulate many dramatizations.

DEVELOPING CHORAL SPEAKING

Choral speaking, the interpretation of poetry or other literature by two or more voices speaking as one, is a group activity that allows children to experience, enjoy, and increase their interest in rhymes, jingles, and other types of poetry. During a choral-speaking or choral-reading experience, children discover that speaking voices can be combined as effectively as singing voices. Young children who cannot read can join in during repeated lines or can take part in rhymes and verses they know from memory; older children can select anything suitable within their reading ability. Choral speaking is useful in a variety of situations: library programs, classrooms, and extracurricular organizations.

Increasing children's enjoyment of poetry and other literature, not developing a perfect performance, is the main purpose for using choral speaking with elementary children. Allow children to enjoy the experience and experiment with various ways of interpreting poetry. Donna Norton (13) suggests the following guidelines for encouraging children to interact in choral arrangements:

1 When selecting materials for children who cannot read, choose poems or rhymes that are simple enough to memorize.
2 Choose material of interest to children. Young children like nonsense and active words; consequently, humorous poems are enjoyable first experiences and encourage children to have fun with poetry.
3 Select poems or nursery rhymes that use refrains, especially for young children. Refrains are easy for nonreaders to memorize and result in rapid participation from each group member.
4 Let children help select and interpret the poetry. Have them experiment with the rhythm and tempo of a poem, improvise the scenes of the selection, and try different voice combinations and various choral arrangements before they decide on the best structure.
5 Let children listen to each other as they try different interpretations within groups.

Barbara McIntyre (11) maintains that adults should also understand the different phases through which children should be guided in their choral interpretations of poetry. First, because young children delight in the rhythm of nursery rhymes, encourage them to explore the rhythm in poetry. They can skip to the rhythm of "Jack and Jill," clap to the rhythm of "Hickory Dickory Dock," and sway to the rhythm of "Little Boy Blue." They can sense fast or slow, happy or sad rhythms through their bodies. They can explore rhythm and tempo as they "hoppity, hoppity, hop" to A. A. Milne's poem "Hoppity" (found in *When We Were Very Young*).

Second, encourage children to experiment with the color and quality of voices available in the choral-speaking choir. McIntyre says that children do not need to know the meaning of *inflection* (rise and fall within a phrase), *pitch levels* (change between one phrase and another), *emphasis* (pointing out of the most important word), and *intensity* (loudness and softness of voices), but adults must understand these terms so that they can recommend exciting materials that allow children to try different interpretations. Third, encourage children to understand and experiment with different types of choral arrangements, such as refrain, line, antiphonal or dialogue, cumulative, and unison arrangements.

Refrain Arrangement

In this type of arrangement, an adult or a child reads or recites the body of a poem, and the other children respond in unison when a refrain or chorus is repeated. Poems such as Maurice Sendak's *Pierre: A Cautionary Tale,* Lewis Carroll's "Beautiful Soup," and Jack Prelutsky's "The Yak" have lines that seem to invite group participation. A nursery rhyme that encourages young children to participate is "A Jolly Old Pig."

Leader: A jolly old pig once lived in a sty,
And three little piggies she had,
And she waddled about saying,
Group: "Grumph! grumph! grumph!"
Leader: While the little ones said,
Group: "Wee! Wee!"
Leader: And she waddled about saying,
Group: "Grumph! grumph! grumph!"
Leader: While the little ones said,
Group: "Wee! Wee!"

The poetic retelling of "The Fox and the Grapes" in Tom Paxton's version of *Aesop's Fables* contains lines in parentheses, such as "(A very high tree, Yes, a very high tree.)" that encourage group responses. Paxton's *Belling the Cat and Other Aesop's Fables* provides additional enjoyable sources for choral speaking.

Line Arrangement

To develop a line arrangement, have one child or a group of children read the first line, another child or group read the next line, a third child or group read the next line, and so forth. Continue this arrangement with a different child or different group reading each line until the poem is finished. Use a familiar nursery rhyme to introduce this arrangement, such as:

Child 1 or Group 1: One, two, buckle my shoe;
Child 2 or Group 2: Three, four, shut the door;
Child 3 or Group 3: Five, six, pick up sticks;
Child 4 or Group 4: Seven, eight, lay them straight;
Child 5 or Group 5: Nine, ten, a good fat hen.

Enjoyable poems for line-a-child arrangements include Zilpha Keatley Snyder's "Poem to Mud," Laura E. Richards's "Eletelephony," and Jack Prelutsky's "Pumberly Pott's Unpredictable Niece."

Antiphonal, or Dialogue, Arrangement

This arrangement highlights alternate speaking voices. Boys' voices may be balanced against girls' voices, or high voices may be balanced against low voices. Poems such as "Eskimo Chant," found in *The New Wind Has Wings: Poems from Canada* compiled by Mary Alice Downie and Barbara Robertson, encourage children to respond in either joyful or fearful voices. Poems with question-and-answer formats or other dialogue between two people are obvious choices for antiphonal arrangements. Such poems as Kaye Starbird's "The Spelling Test" and the nursery rhyme "Pussy-Cat, Pussy-Cat" are enjoyable in dialogue arrangements. Paul Fleischman's *I Am Phoenix: Poems for Two Voices* includes poems about birds. Fleischman's *Joyful Noise: Poems for Two Voices* allows children to experiment with sounds and movements of insects. The poems are written to be read by more than one person. Children also enjoy chorally reading the lyrics from folk songs. The words of "Yankee Doodle," for example, can be used with one group of children reading each verse and another group responding with the chorus. Many traditional songs are found in Dan Fox's *Go in and out the Window: An Illustrated Songbook for Young People*.

The words from the folk song "A Hole in the Bucket," present a dialogue between Liza and Henry:

Boys: There's a hole in the bucket, dear Liza, dear Liza,
There's a hole in the bucket, dear Liza, There's a hole.
Girls: Well, fix it, dear Henry, dear Henry, dear Henry.
Well, fix it, dear Henry, dear Henry, go fix it.
Boys: With what shall I fix it, dear Liza, dear Liza?
With what shall I fix it, dear Liza, with what?
Girls: With a straw, dear Henry, dear Henry, dear Henry.
With a straw, dear Henry, dear Henry, with a straw.
Boys: But the straw is too long, dear Liza, dear Liza.
But the straw is too long, dear Liza, too long.
Girls: Then cut it, dear Henry, dear Henry, dear Henry.
Then cut it, dear Henry, dear Henry, then cut it.
Boys: Well, how shall I cut it, dear Liza, dear Liza?
Well, how shall I cut it, dear Liza, well, how?
Girls: With a knife, dear Henry, dear Henry, dear Henry.
With a knife, dear Henry, dear Henry, with a knife.
Boys: But the knife is too dull, dear Liza, dear Liza.
But the knife is too dull, dear Liza, too dull.
Girls: Then sharpen it, dear Henry, dear Henry, dear Henry.
Then sharpen it, dear Henry, dear Henry, then sharpen it.
Boys: With what shall I sharpen it, dear Liza, dear Liza?
With what shall I sharpen it, dear Liza, with what?
Girls: With a whetstone, dear Henry, dear Henry, dear Henry.
With a whetstone, dear Henry, dear Henry, with a whetstone.
Boys: But the whetstone's too dry, dear Liza, dear Liza.
But the whetstone's too dry, dear Liza, too dry.

Girls: Then wet it, dear Henry, dear Henry, dear Henry.
Then wet it, dear Henry, dear Henry, then wet it.
Boys: With what shall I wet it, dear Liza, dear Liza?
With what shall I wet it, dear Liza, with what?
Girls: With water, dear Henry, dear Henry, dear Henry.
With water, dear Henry, dear Henry, with water.
Boys: Well, how shall I carry it, dear Liza, dear Liza?
Well, how shall I carry it, dear Liza, how?
Girls: In a bucket, dear Henry, dear Henry, dear Henry.
In a bucket, dear Henry, dear Henry, in a bucket.
Boys: But there's a hole in the bucket, dear Liza, dear Liza.
There's a hole in the bucket, dear Liza, a hole.

Cumulative Arrangement

A crescendo arrangement may be used effectively to interpret a poem that builds to a climax. Have the first group read the first line or verse; the first and second groups read the second line or verse; the first, second, and third groups read the third line or verse; and so forth, until the climax. Then, have all of the groups read together.

Edward Lear's "The Owl and the Pussy-Cat" may be read in a cumulative arrangement by six groups; John Ciardi's "Mummy Slept Late and Daddy Fixed Breakfast" is also fun for six groups to develop into a climax, as Daddy's waffles become impossible to eat. Other poems appropriate for cumulative reading include Arnold Adoff's *The Cabbages Are Chasing the Rabbits* and Arnold Lobel's *The Rose in My Garden*. The nursery rhymes "There Was a Crooked Man" and "This Is the House That Jack Built" are also enjoyable.

Group 1: This is the house that Jack built.
Group 1,2: This is the malt
That lay in the house that Jack built.
Group 1,2,3: This is the rat that ate the malt,
That lay in the house that Jack built.
Group 1,2,3,4: This is the cat,
That killed the rat, that ate the malt,
That lay in the house that Jack built.
Group 1,2,3,4,5: This is the dog,
That worried the cat,
That killed the rat, that ate the malt,
That lay in the house that Jack built.
Group 1,2,3,4,5,6: This is the cow with the crumpled horn,
That tossed the dog, that worried the cat,
That killed the rat, that ate the malt,
That lay in the house that Jack built.

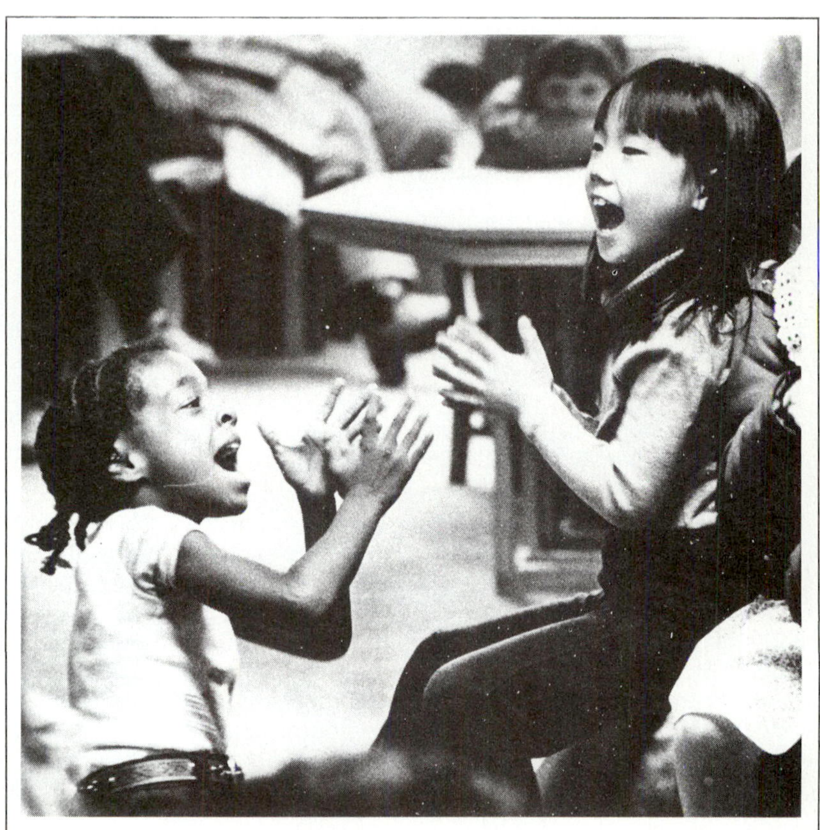

Music encourages additional enjoyment of poetry.

Group 1,2,3, 4,5,6,7:	This is the maiden all forlorn. That milked the cow with the crumpled horn, That tossed the dog, that worried the cat, That killed the rat, that ate the malt, That lay in the house that Jack built.
Group 1,2,3, 4,5,6,7,8:	This is the man all tattered and torn, That kissed the maiden all forlorn, That milked the cow with the crumpled horn, That tossed the dog, that worried the cat, That killed the rat, that ate the malt, That lay in the house that Jack built.
Group 1,2,3, 4,5,6,7,8,9:	This is the priest all shaven and shorn, That married the man all tattered and torn, That kissed the maiden all forlorn, That milked the cow with the crumpled horn, That tossed the dog, that worried the cat, That killed the rat, that ate the malt, That lay in the house that Jack built.
Group 1,2,3, 4,5,6,7,8,9, 10:	This is the cock that crowed in the morn, That waked the priest all shaven and shorn, That married the man all tattered and torn, That kissed the maiden all forlorn, That milked the cow with the crumpled horn, That tossed the dog, that worried the cat, That killed the rat, that ate the malt, That lay in the house that Jack built.
Group 1,2,3, 4,5,6,7,8,9, 10,11:	This is the farmer that sowed the corn, That kept the cock that crowed in the morn, That waked the priest all shaven and shorn, That married the man all tattered and torn, That kissed the maiden all forlorn, That milked the cow with the crumpled horn, That tossed the dog, that worried the cat, That killed the rat, that ate the malt, That lay in the house that Jack built.

As a variation, develop a reverse arrangement. Have all groups begin together; then, with each subsequent line or verse, have a group drop out until only one group remains. This arrangement works well with such poems as Barbara Kunz Loots's "Mountain Wind" and James Reeves's "The Wind." Both poems begin with louder expressions and end in silence or quiet. These poems are found in Jack Prelutsky's *The Random House Book of Poetry for Children*.

Unison Arrangement

In this arrangement, the entire group or class reads or speaks a poem together. This arrangement is often the most difficult to perform, because it tends to create a singsong effect. For this reason, shorter poems, such as Myra Cohn Livingston's "O Sliver of Liver," Lillian Morrison's "The Sidewalk Racer" or "On the Skateboard," and Judith Thurman's "Campfire," are appropriate.

Additional Suggestions

Fran Tanner (19) recommends that older children experiment with the effects of grouping their voices according to resonance, with light, medium, and dark voices. Through experimentation, children discover that light voices may effectively interpret happy, whimsical, or delicate parts; medium voices may add to descriptive and narrative parts; and dark voices may interpret robust and tragic material. Tanner recommends the following classic poem for such an experiment.

The Brook

(light)	I slip,
(medium)	I slide,
(dark)	I gloom,
(medium)	I glance.
	Among my skimming swallows;
(light)	I make the netted sunbeams dance
	Against my sandy shallows.
(dark)	I murmur under moon and stars
	In brambly wildernesses;
(medium)	I linger by my shingly bars,
(light)	I loiter round my cresses;
(medium)	And out again I curve and flow
	To join the brimming river,
(dark)	For men may come
(dark and medium)	and men may go,
(all)	But I go on forever.

Alfred, Lord Tennyson

The poems in a single poetry collection may be read, discussed, and developed into various choral-speaking arrangements. For example, this activity could accompany Nancy Larrick's anthology, *When the Dark Comes Dancing: A Bedtime Poetry Book*. The poems might be presented in the following ways: Martin Brennan's "Benue Lullaby," refrain; Margaret Wise Brown's "Little Donkey Close Your Eyes," line-a-group; Arthur Guiterman's "Nocturne," antiphonal between lighter voices and heavier voices; Felice Holman's "Night Sounds," antiphonal between male and female voices; Sabine Baring-Gould's "Now the Day Is Over," reverse cumulative; Vachel Lindsay's "The Moon's the North Wind's Cooky," reverse cumulative followed by cumulative; Myra Cohn Livingston's "The Night," unison; and Eve Merriam's "Lullaby," unison.

COMBINING MUSIC AND POETRY

The rhythms of music and poetry naturally complement each other. Rhythm instruments, including sticks, bells, tambourines, and blocks, allow children to emphasize the rhythm of a poem and interpret its mood. A group of six-year-olds, for example, thoroughly enjoyed accompanying David McCord's "The Pickety Fence" (from *Far and Few: Rhymes of the Never Was and Always Is*) with their rhythm band sticks. They experimented with the sticks until they sounded like the striking of a picket fence by a child with a stick. They recorded the poem and its accompaniment, and they were pleased with the sound interpretation.

Many old ballads and chants have been passed down through the generations in the form of folk songs. They may be listened to, read in choral arrangements, sung, or accompanied by movements, improvisations, and rhythm instruments.

Ruth Crawford Seeger's *American Folk Songs for Children—In Home, School, and Nursery School* (16) presents words, music, and suggestions for interpreting rhythms and lyrics. The suggestions result from extensive use of the materials with young children. The following suggestions are taken from Seeger's (pp. 35–38) recommendations for sharing songs with young children.

1 Sing the song at its natural speed. Allow children to experience the impression of the song as a whole rather than analyzing the song.
2 Do not let the songs drag. Most of the songs were originally sung at lively speeds and with strong metrical accents.
3 Sit directly with the children when presenting and singing the songs.
4 Allow the children to listen and then interpret the songs at their own leisure.
5 Many folk songs make excellent rhythm band music. Encourage the children to accompany some of the songs with rhythm instruments.
6 Repeat a song many times, especially when using the songs for rhythmic activities.
7 Include both action songs and listening songs when planning the activities for a session. The different needs and moods of the children should be considered when making the selections.
8 Do not hurry when moving from one song or activity to another; children frequently derive pleasure from savoring a favorite song or interpreting a song in several different ways. Very young children may need several repetitions before they feel confident enough to join into an activity.
9 Have confidence. Be ready with a few songs that draw the children together if there is a need to bring younger children back into the group.
10 Listen to the children. Wait, watch, and be ready for them to interpret the words or music. Keep your eyes and attention on the children, not on an instrument or printed page. Be sensitive to signals from the children, even small movements, that give you clues about what the children need or want to do next.

Some of Lewis Carroll's nonsense poetry has been set to music by Don Harper in *Songs from Alice*. The music is included in Harper's text so that the words can be sung or an accompaniment can be played for choral renditions. Colorful, humorous illustrations make this an enjoyable book to share with children. Ashley Bryan's *I'm Going to Sing: Black American Spirituals* and Dan Fox's *Go in and out the Window: An Illustrated Songbook for Young People* also include musical arrangements.

Ruth Crawford Seeger (16) suggests that ballads as well as folk chants and songs be grouped in order to immerse children in a total experience with a subject. For example, children who are fascinated by trains can experience a sequence progressing from the laying of the tracks through meeting someone at the station. This sequence might include the following railroad-related activities as you read the songs or the children sing them. The music to the songs is found in Seeger's *American Folk Songs for Children—In Home, School, and Nursery School* and other folk song collections.

1 *"This Old Hammer."* Tracks were laid across America by railroad gangs who were hitting

their hammers to the beat of work songs. While you read the song or the children sing the words ("This old hammer shine like silver,/ Shine like gold, boys,/Shine like gold"), have the children pretend to be hammering the tracks in place to the rhythm of the words or music.

2 *"John Henry."* Have the children pretend to pick up their twelve-pound hammers and compete with the steam drill to the rhythm of this tribute to a famous steel-driving man.

3 *"The Train Is A-Coming."* Have the children pretend to be engines, passenger cars, coal-cars, flatcars, boxcars, and a caboose as they move to the words: "The train is a-coming, oh yes." You can change the words so that each child is identified, through repetitive verses, as part of the train.

   Jamie is the engine, oh yes,
   Jamie is the engine, oh yes.
   Jamie is the engine, Jamie is the engine,
   Jamie is the engine, oh yes.

   through

   Mary is the caboose, oh yes,
   Mary is the caboose, oh yes,
   Mary is the caboose, Mary is the caboose,
   Mary is the caboose, oh yes.

   Similarly, children can become the different workers on the train, as each child selects an occupation and then improvises words to suggest the part:

   Betsy is the engineer, oh yes,
   Betsy is the engineer, oh yes,
   Betsy is the engineer, Betsy is the engineer,
   Betsy is the engineer, oh, yes.

4 *"The Little Black Train."* Have the children continue their train movements, keeping their "wheels a-moving and rattling through the land" around curves and up long hills "a-whistling and a-blowing, and straining every nerve."

5 *"When the Train Comes Along."* To dramatize this song, have part of the group be the train arriving and the remainder at the station to meet the train.

COMBINING ART AND POETRY

There is a close relationship between artist and poet: Both see the world in unique ways. Through words, poets create vivid landscapes, illuminate experiences, and reveal characterizations. They focus interest on small details or search for grand patterns in the universe. Artists use paints and brushes to accomplish the same goals.

Poetry frequently motivates artists to create pictorial visions of a poet's world. Kenneth Sterck (18) states that he decided to study the landscapes and figures in Walter De la Mare's poetry because of "the number of illustrators, including Heath Robinson, Rowland Emett, and Edward Ardizzone," who were drawn to the "evident pictorial quality" (p. 17) of De la Mare's poems.

The same pictorial qualities may be used to stimulate children's interest in exploring artists' interpretations of poetry or in creating their own artistic interpretations. The numerous illustrated versions of poems lend themselves to this first type of activity. For example, children may compare Errol Le Cain's and Susan Jeffers's illustrations for Henry Wadsworth Longfellow's "Hiawatha." After they read or listen to the poem, have them speculate about what attracted the artists' interests, why the artists interpreted the poems in certain ways and what visions the artists were trying to reveal.

Explore several poetry books in which both the poems and the illustrations have won awards or recognition. Have the children consider the close relationships between the poems and illustrations in *A Visit to William Blake's Inn: Poems for Innocent and Experienced Travelers;* a book for which Nancy Willard won the Newbery Medal for the poetry and Alice and Martin Provensen won the Caldecott Honor award for the illustrations. Likewise, Eve Merriam's poetry in *Halloween ABC* was chosen for the Fanfare list and Lane Smith's illustrations were on the New York Times Best Illustrated Children's Books of the Year list.

Close exploration of two books helps children see how different well-known artists interpreted the poetry. Beatrice Schenk de Regniers's *Sing a Song of Popcorn: Every Child's Book of Poems* was illustrated by nine Caldecott Medal artists. Iona and Peter Opie's *Tail Feathers from Mother Goose: The Opie Rhyme Book* was illustrated by sixty artists. These illustrations show children that poetry is very personal. Artists' interpretations vary a great deal. You may make another interesting comparison because Regniers's text is an American publication while the Opies' text is a British publication.

In two publications by the Metropolitan Museum of Art, the editors paired poetry and art works. Both of these texts can lead to spirited discussions about the relationships between art and poetry. Both *Talking to the Sun: An Illustrated Anthology of Poems for Young People,* selected by Kenneth Koch and Kate Farrell, and *Go in and out the Window: An Illustrated Songbook for Young People,* selected by Dan Fox, combine poetry and works of art that are found in the Metropolitan Museum of Art. Both texts provide information on the art.

Illustrated texts that show close collaboration between poets and artists are worthy of examination. For example, poet Myra Cohn Livingston and artist Leonard Everett Fisher have collaborated on several texts, including *Space Songs, Sky Songs,* and *Sea Songs*. Have students discuss the impact of the two art forms. Then, have the students illustrate their own favorite poems or even write and illustrate their own creations.

WRITING POETRY

Research into the development of the writing process of children, which was conducted by Donald Graves (5), George Hillocks (7), and Beatrice Furner (2), suggests that adults should work with children during the writing process rather than after the materials are completed. Current research emphasizes phases in the writing process that encourage students to explore, plan, draft, and revise. For example, Proett and Gill (14) report a sequence of events and recommend activities from experiences at the Bay Area Writing Project and the University of California. These educators sequence the process according to activities that should be done (a) before the students write (content and idea building through observing, remembering, imagining, experiencing, logging, reading, brainstorming, listing, dramatizing, developing details, and structuring), (b) while the students write (developing rhetorical stance and linguistic choices by deciding voice, audience, purpose, form, word choice, figurative language, structure, and syntax), and (c) after the students write (encouraging revision and highlighting by sharing with editing groups, raising questions, expanding, clarifying, proofreading, sharing, reading, and publishing). The various areas are certainly crucial to poetry writing. By reading or listening to poetry, children obtain motivational and observational opportunities to develop their awareness and stimulate their imaginations. Children require opportunities to incubate and clarify ideas, to compose and revise their poetry, and to share their poetry with an appreciative audience. To share poetry writing experiences with children, use the sequence in Chart 8–1, adapted from research by Donna Norton (13).

CHART 8–1
An instructional sequence for poetry writing

I. Motivation
   A. Ongoing activities
   B. Everyday experiences
   C. New, adult-introduced experiences
II. Oral exchange of ideas
   A. Questions and answers to extend stimulation activities
   B. Brainstorming of subjects, vocabulary, images, and such
   C. Idea clarifications
III. Transcription
   A. Individual dictation of poems to adults
   B. Individual writing
   C. Teacher interaction to help development
   D. Adult assistance when required
   E. Revision and editing through small-group interaction and teacher interaction during individual writing
IV. Sharing
   A. Reading of the poetry to a group
   B. Audience development
   C. Permanent collections
   D. Poetry extensions, if desired, to poetry dramatizations, choral reading, art interpretations, and so forth
V. Post-transcription
   A. Permanent writing folders
   B. Writing conferences
   C. Modeling of the writing process

Motivations

The three categories of motivational activities outlined in Chart 8–1 suggest that numerous topics can stimulate the writing of poetry. Many activities already occurring in classrooms, libraries, or extracurricular organizations are natural sources of topics for self-expression through poetry. For example, while teaching a social studies unit a second-grade teacher showed a film about farm life. The teacher encouraged the children to observe the characteristics and actions of the farm animals and then to write about them in poetic form. A Girl Scout leader encouraged children to describe and write about their feelings following a soccer game. A librarian asked children to write their own color poems after they had heard Mary O'Neill's poems about colors in *Hailstones and Halibut Bones*.

Gerald Duffy (1) identified frequent sharing of poetry as effective in motivating children to write poetry. University students have used both poetry written by adult authors and poetry written by children as ways of stimulating children to write their own poems. For example, they have used Kenneth Koch's *Wishes, Lies, and Dreams* (9), reading the poems under a certain topic to children and then using the suggestions developed by Koch to encourage the children to write their own poems. Several of the categories include experiences that are common to children but allow the children to think of these experiences in new ways. A third-grade teacher encouraged his students to consider the wishes they might make if they had the opportunity and then asked them to write a poem expressing those wishes. The following is an example of a third grader's wishes.

I wish I had a puppy,
  not a dog, a puppy
  not a cat, a puppy
  not a kitten, a puppy.
I wish I was rich
  not poor, but rich
  not a little bit of money, a lot
  so I'm really rich.
I wish I had a Genie
  not a pony, a Genie
  not a pig, a Genie
  not a pig or a pony
  a Genie.
I wish I could
have anything
  know anything
  be anything
  see anything
  and do anything
  I wish.

Eight-year-old

Many adults encourage children to write poetry by introducing them to experiences that allow the children to nurture their awareness and their observational powers. The children may go for a walk in a flower-strewn park or meadow, listen to the noises around them, smell the air in spring, touch trees and flowers, describe their sensations with new feelings, and then write poems about their experiences. The following poem resulted from a sixth grader's visual experiences out-of-doors.

Woodland

Cool crisp air calls me
Late September afternoon
Crimson, gold, green, rust
Falling leaves whisper softly
Come look, what's new in the woods?

Eleven-year-old

Even the sun's shining through a window can be used to inspire a poem.

The Sunshine

The sunshine entered the morning
And birds began to sing.
The sunshine entered the clouds
And a rainbow appeared.
The sunshine entered the afternoon
And made the evening clear.
Your smile entered the room
And sunshine entered my heart.

Eleven-year-old

Other activities found to be successful stimuli for poetry include listening to music, becoming involved in art projects, closely observing and touching objects, considering the various uses for unique objects, and looking at and discussing pictures. One girl described very well how music affected her.

A Song

Something I want to say
But haven't got the words
To say what I feel
The music makes it easy
The music sets me free.

Nine-year-old

A sixth-grade teacher found music to be especially stimulating for her students. She says, "We spent several sessions writing to music such as *Icarus* by Winter Consort and *Night on Bald Mountain* by Mussorgsky. The children let their imaginations soar, they visualized the images created by the music, and wrote their impressions. They especially enjoyed sharing their impressions with each other" (personal communication to author).

A class of older students studied possible relationships between art and poetry. First, the students viewed and discussed art chosen from the Metropolitan Museum of Art to illustrate the poems in Kenneth Koch and Kate Farrell's anthology *Talking to the Sun*. The students shared their feelings about the art, the poetry, and the appropriateness or inappropriateness of the matches between the art and poetry. Then, the students wrote their own poems about their moods and feelings, the settings in the paintings, or the characters in the paintings. The purpose for this activity was to enhance the enjoyment of the viewing and the writing, not to create literal interpretations of the artworks.

Oral Exchanges of Ideas

During an oral exchange of ideas, encourage children to think aloud about a subject. For example, through brainstorming, children may gain many ideas from each other and look at old ideas in new ways. Susan Nugent Reed (15) describes how a poet in the schools, Bill Wertheim, encouraged discussion before writing:

> The figure of a skeleton in one of the classrooms evolved into a lesson about death. Wertheim wrote, "The discussion went from Halloween to skeletons, to fear of skeletons, to monsters, to dying: loss of something and/or someone we love. How it feels to die, how it feels to lose someone you care about." He indicated that the topic first was discussed aloud, then later on paper. For those children who preferred an alternative topic, he suggested writing about coming back to life. Wertheim said it was the most touching lesson he had ever taught and that some children cried. This led to a discussion about crying, trust, and kindness. He took this opportunity to express the idea that "crying is OK, even for boys." He said that the children were kind and supportive of one another. (p. 110)

During an outside observational session, have children look at clouds and share their impressions, describe the ways the light filters through the leaves, or close their eyes and describe the sounds they hear. The librarian who encouraged children to write color poems after listening to Mary O'Neill's poems in *Hailstones and Halibut Bones* asked the children to observe the colors around them. They searched for objects that reminded them of the colors in the poems and talked about their moods as reflected by colors. For example, brainstorming the color white produced some of the following associations: snowflakes, winter silence, puffy clouds, a wedding veil, the flash of winning, a frost-covered window, quivering vanilla pudding, heaps of popcorn, a plastered wall, apple blossoms, pale lilac blossoms, sails skimming across a lake, a forgotten memory, fog rising from a marsh, a polar bear, and a gift wrapped in tissue paper. After this experience, the children began to look at common objects and feelings with new awareness.

Transcriptions

You can help young children compose by taking dictation. Encourage the children to tell you their thoughts while you write them down. Parents indicate that even very young children enjoy seeing their creative jingles, rhymes, and poems in print. Children enjoy playing with language and feeling the tickle of new ways of expression falling off their tongues.

One university student found it meaningful that her mother had kept a notebook of her early experiences writing poetry. Another university student, who had had several poems published, felt that his early spontaneous poetry, written down by his mother, had stimulated his desire to become a professional writer. Parents who have been successful in this type of dictation have been careful not to force dictation upon a child or criticize any thoughts or feelings expressed. The experiences have been warm, trusting relationships, in which children discover that their thoughts can be written down and saved for themselves and for sharing with others.

When children have mastered the mechanics of writing, they usually write their own poems. However, when working with them, continue to interact with them as they progress with their writing. Encourage them to reread their poems aloud, ask questions to help clarify a problem or an idea, or answer questions pertaining to spelling and punctuation.

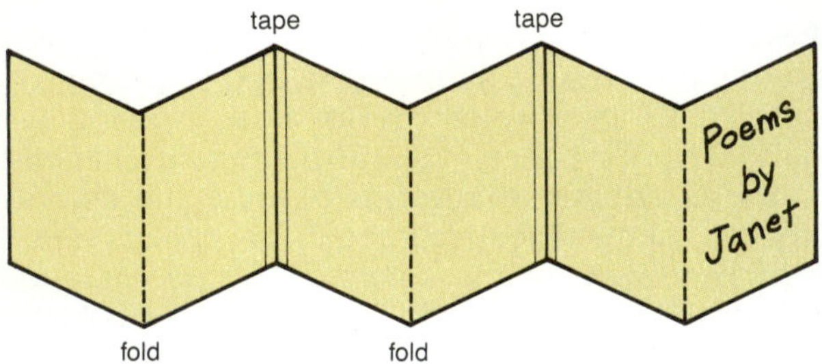

FIGURE 8–2
An accordion-pleated poem book

Sharing

The ideal way to share poetry is to read it to an appreciative audience. Consequently, many adults encourage children to share their creations with others. Attractive bulletin boards of children's poems may also stimulate children to read one another's poems and write more poems.

Children enjoy making permanent collections of their poems. One teacher had each child develop an accordion-pleated poem book (see Figure 8–2). To construct their books, the children folded large sheets of heavy drawing paper in half, connected several sheets with tape, and printed an original poem and an accompanying illustration on each page.

Other classes have made their own books by constructing covers in various appropriate shapes, cutting paper to match the shapes, and binding the covers and pages together. A group of second graders placed Halloween poems inside a jack-o-lantern book, fourth graders wrote city poems inside a book resembling a skyscraper, and third graders placed humorous mythical animal poems inside a book resembling a beast from Dr. Seuss (see Figure 8–3). Although it is not necessary to extend writing of poetry to other activities, children often enjoy using their own poetry for choral reading, art interpretations, or dramatizations.

FIGURE 8–3
Shapes of various poetry books

Various Forms of Poetry

Many children enjoy experimenting with writing different types of poems, such as limericks, cinquains, and diamantes. Limericks, for example, were among the poetry most enjoyed by children in Ann Terry's (20) study of children's poetry preferences. David McCord's *One at a Time: Collected Poems for the Young* describes the content and form of limericks and provides examples that you can share with children. You can use the nonsense limericks of Edward Lear, N. M. Bodecker, and William Jay Smith to stimulate these five-line poems. Follow this form: Lines 1, 2, and 5 rhyme and have a three-beat rhythm; lines 3 and 4 rhyme and have a two-beat rhythm. Brainstorming words that rhyme helps children complete their rhyming lines. After reading and listening to a number of limericks, a sixth grader wrote about and illustrated the following predicament.

> There once was a girl named Mandy
> Whose hair was dreadfully sandy
> She never did wash it
> Instead she did frost it
> The icing made Mandy smell dandy
>
> Eleven-year-old

Cinquains are another form of poetry having specific structural requirements. These poems help children realize that descriptive words are important when expressing feelings in poetry and that rhyming words are not necessary. A cinquain uses the following structure.

Line 1: One word for the title.
Line 2: Two words that describe the title.

Line 3: Three words that express action related to the title.
Line 4: Four words that express a feeling about the title.
Line 5: One word that either repeats the title or expresses a word closely related to the title.

Brainstorming descriptive words and action words adds to children's enjoyment in writing and sharing their cinquains. The following cinquains were written by middle-school children.

Tree

Huge, woody
Expanding, reproducing, entertaining
Leaves are colorfully crisp
Oak

Eleven-year-old

Lasagna

Hot, delectable
Steaming, bubbling, oozing
Always great on Fridays
Paisans

Eleven-year-old

A diamante is a diamond-shaped poem. Poems written in the diamante format progress from one noun to a final noun that contrasts with the first noun. Because this form is more complex than the cinquain, you should describe each line and draw a diagram of the diamante to assist children in seeing the relationships among the lines. The diamante has the following structure.

Line 1: One noun.
Line 2: Two adjectives that describe the noun.
Line 3: Three words that express action related to the noun.
Line 4: Four nouns or a phrase that expresses a transition in thought between the first noun and the final contrasting noun.
Line 5: Three words that express action related to the contrasting noun.
Line 6: Two adjectives that describe the contrasting noun.
Line 7: One contrasting noun.

Diagramming this type of poem as follows is also helpful:

noun

describing describing
action action action
transition nouns or phrase
action action action
describing describing
noun

Children find it helpful to brainstorm suggestions for contrasting nouns to form the framework for the ideas developed in a diamante. One teacher brainstormed with upper-elementary students and developed the following contrasts.

sun—moon	summer—winter
tears—smiles	war—peace
day—night	sky—ground
young—old	love—hate
life—death	angel—devil
happy—sad	darkness—light
friends—enemies	boredom—excitement
man—woman	dreams—reality

Next, the group wrote its own poetry. The following poems were created by this experience.

Light

Beautiful, bright
Seeing, glistening, refreshing
Light is sometimes blinding
Groping, cautioning, frightening
Evil, insecure
Dark

Ten-year-old

Friends

Happiness, security
Understanding, caring, laughing
Reaching out your hand
Hating, hurting, fighting
Silence, tension
Enemies

Ten-year-old

Suggested Activities for Children's Appreciation of Poetry

- ☐ Develop a card file of poetry that is appropriate to use with children. Type the poems on cards using a primary-type typewriter. On the back of each card, list several suggestions for sharing the poem with children. Put the cards into a logical categorization.
- ☐ Ask some children to tell their favorite jumping-rope chants. Collect as many of these chants as possible. Share any new chants with other children. Ask them why they like and remember such chants.
- ☐ Select a series of poems that encourage physical responses from children. Share the poems with a group of children or a peer group. Include poems that encourage children to move through the air, mimic the

movements of an animal, or become something other than themselves.

- ☐ Select a poem or a series of poems that encourage creative dramatizations. Plan the steps needed to encourage children to interpret the poetry.
- ☐ Select poems that can be interpreted through choral-speaking arrangements: refrain, line, antiphonal, cumulative, and unison. Share the poems with a group of children or a peer group.
- ☐ Using Seeger's recommendations for sharing songs with children, select several songs for an appropriate age group. Share the songs with children or a peer group. Evaluate the group's response to them.
- ☐ Compile a bibliography of poems that can be used to enhance an art and poetry connection. Stipulate how you would use each selection.
- ☐ Following an instructional sequence for poetry writing, develop a lesson plan designed to stimulate children's writing of poetry.

References

1 Duffy, Gerald G. "Crucial Elements in the Teaching of Poetry Writing." In *The Language Arts in the Middle School*, edited by Martha L. King, Robert Emans, and Patricia J. Cianciolo. Urbana, Ill.: National Council of Teachers of English, 1973.

2 Furner, Beatrice A. "Creative Writing Through Creative Dramatics." *Language Arts* 50 (March 1973): 405–408.

3 Godden, Rumer. "Shining Popocatapetl: Poetry for Children." *The Horn Book* (May/June 1988): 305–314.

4 Gough, John. "Poems in a Context: Breaking the Anthology Trap." *Children's Literature in Education* 15 (Winter 1984): 204–210.

5 Graves, Donald. *Writing: Teachers and Children at Work*. Exeter, N.H.: Heinemann, 1988.

6 Heinig, Ruth Beall, and Lyda Stillwell. *Creative Dramatics for the Classroom Teacher*. Englewood Cliffs, N.J.: Prentice-Hall, 1974.

7 Hillocks, George. *Research on Written Composition: New Directions for Teaching*. Urbana, Ill.: National Conference on Research in English, 1986.

8 Hopkins, Lee Bennett. *Pass the Poetry Please!* New York: Harper & Row, 1987.

9 Koch, Kenneth. *Wishes, Lies, and Dreams*. New York: Vintage Books/Chelsea House, 1970.

10 Le Pere, Jean. "For Every Occasion: Poetry in the Reading Program." Albuquerque, N. Mex.: Eighth Southwest Regional Conference, International Reading Association, 1980.

11 McIntyre, Barbara M. *Creative Drama in the Elementary School*. Itasca, Ill.: Peacock, 1974.

12 McKay, Gwendda. "Poetry and the Young Child." *English in Australia* (June 1986): 52–58.

13 Norton, Donna. *The Effective Teaching of Language Arts*. Columbus, Ohio: Merrill, 1989.

14 Proett, Jackie, and Kent Gill. *The Writing Process in Action: A Handbook for Teachers*. Urbana, Ill.: National Council of Teachers of English, 1986.

15 Reed, Susan Nugent. "Career Idea: Meet the Poet at His Craft." In *Using Literature and Poetry Affectively*, edited by Jon E. Shapiro. Newark, Del.: International Reading Association, 1979.

16 Seeger, Ruth Crawford. *American Folksongs for Children—In Home, School, and Nursery School*. New York: Doubleday, 1948.

17 Shapiro, Jon E. ed. *Using Literature and Poetry Affectively*. Newark, Del.: International Reading Association, 1979.

18 Sterck, Kenneth. "Landscape and Figures in the Poetry of De la Mare." *Children's Literature in Education*. 19 (Spring 1988): 17–31.

19 Tanner, Fran. *Creative Communication: Projects in Acting, Speaking, Oral Reading*. Pocatello, Idaho: Clark, 1979.

20 Terry, Ann. *Children's Poetry Preferences: A National Survey of the Upper Elementary Grades*. Urbana, Ill.: National Council of Teachers of English, 1974.

CHILDREN'S LITERATURE

Adoff, Arnold. *All the Colors of the Race.* Illustrated by John Steptoe. Lothrop, Lee & Shepard, 1982. A girl from a mixed racial parentage reflects on tolerance.

———. *Birds: Poems.* Illustrated by Troy Howell. Lippincott, 1982. Thirty poems are about birds.

———. *The Cabbages Are Chasing the Rabbits.* Illustrated by Janet Stevens. Harcourt Brace Jovanovich, 1985. A cumulative poem was developed on the idea of role reversals.

———. *Eats Poems.* Illustrated by Susan Russo. Lothrop, Lee & Shepard, 1979. Poems celebrate a love affair with food.

———. *Greens.* Illustrated by Betsy Lewin. Lothrop, Lee & Shepard, 1988. Poems explore the various items and feelings associated with the color green.

———. *My Black Me: A Beginning Book of Black Poetry.* Dutton, 1974. This is a collection of black poetry.

———, ed. *The Poetry of Black America: Anthology of the 20th Century.* Harper & Row, 1973. This text includes over three hundred poems by black poets.

———. *Sports Pages.* Illustrated by Steve Kuzma. Lippencott, 1986. This text includes poems about experiences of athletes.

———. *Tornado!* Illustrated by Ronald Himler. Delacorte, 1977. Vivid words make this poem enjoyable.

Aesop. *Aesop's Fables.* Retold by Tom Paxton. Illustrated by Robert Rayevsky. Morrow, 1988. This is a poetic version of the fables.

———. *Belling the Cat and Other Aesop's Fables.* Retold by Tom Paxton. Illustrated by Robert Rayevsky. Morrow, 1990. Additional fables are written in rhyme.

Atwood, Ann. *Fly with the Wind, Flow with the Water.* Scribner's Sons, 1979. Haiku poems about things in nature that swing, soar, leap, run, tumble, swirl, flutter, and float are accompanied by color photographs.

———. *Haiku: The Mood of Earth.* Scribner's Sons, 1971. Beautiful photographs accompany haiku nature poems.

Baylor, Byrd. *The Desert Is Theirs.* Illustrated by Peter Parnall. Scribner's Sons, 1975. A poem stresses the love the Papago Indians have for their desert home.

———. *Moon Song.* Illustrated by Ronald Himler. Scribner's Sons, 1982. A Pima Indian legend, in poetic text, tells how Coyote was born and survived.

———. *The Other Way to Listen.* Illustrated by Peter Parnall. Scribner's Sons, 1978. You have to be patient to hear cactuses blooming and rocks murmuring, but it's worth it.

Baylor, Byrd, and Peter Parnall. *Desert Voices.* Scribner's Sons, 1981. Ten creatures from the desert give their viewpoints on their surroundings.

Bechely, Paddy, ed. *Drumming in the Sky: Poems from 'Stories and Rhymes.'* Illustrated by Priscilla Lamont. British Broadcasting, 1981. The poems are selected from the BBC Radio series.

Bennett, Jill, ed. *Days Are Where We Live and Other Poems.* Illustrated by Maureen Roffey. Lothrop, Lee & Shepard, 1982. Poems for very young children cover such subjects as playing, eating, and walking.

———. *Tiny Tim: Verses for Children.* Illustrated by Helen Oxenbury. Delacorte, 1982. This book contains a variety of poems, including jingles and humorous poems.

Bierhorst, John, ed. *The Sacred Path: Spells, Prayers & Power Songs of the American Indians.* Morrow, 1983. This collection is from sources across North America.

Blegvad, Lenore, ed. *The Parrot in the Garret: And Other Rhymes About Dwellings.* Illustrated by Erik Blegvad. Atheneum, 1982. Twenty-five rhymes stress dwellings and their inhabitants.

Bodecker, N. M. *Hurry, Hurry Mary Dear.* Atheneum, 1976. A collection of forty-three humorous poems is accompanied by pen sketches.

———. *Let's Marry Said the Cherry.* Atheneum, 1974. A collection of nonsense poems relies heavily upon word play.

———. *A Person from Britain Whose Head Was the Shape of a Mitten and Other Limericks.* Dent, 1980. This is a collection of absurd limericks.

Brooks, Gwendolyn. *Bronzeville Boys and Girls.* Illustrated by Ronni Solbert. Harper & Row, 1956. This book explores children and their feelings.

Brown, Beatrice Curtis. *Jonathan Bing.* Illustrated by Judith Gwyn Brown. Lothrop, Lee & Shepard, 1978. This is a humorous poem.

Browning, Robert. *The Pied Piper of Hamelin.* Illustrated by Kate Greenaway. Warne Classic, 1888. This reissue of the original poem has delightful illustrations of children by Greenaway.

Bryan, Ashley. *I'm Going to Sing: Black American Spirituals*. Vol. 2. Atheneum, 1982. This text includes musical arrangements.

Burkert, Nancy Ekholm. *Valentine and Orson*. Farrar, Straus & Giroux, 1989. A tale of twins separated at birth is told in poetry.

Carroll, Lewis. *The Hunting of the Snark*. Illustrated by Helen Oxenbury. Watts, 1970. Large, colorful illustrations accompany Carroll's poem.

———. *Jabberwocky*. Illustrated by Jane Breskin Zalben. Warne, 1977. This picture interpretation of Carroll's poem is in watercolors.

———. *Poems of Lewis Carroll*. Selected by Myra Cohn Livingston. Crowell, 1973. This collection of poems is from *Alice's Adventures in Wonderland* and *Through the Looking-Glass*.

———. *Songs from Alice*. Music by Don Harper. Illustrated by Charles Folkard. Holiday House, 1979. Carroll's nonsense poems are set to music and humorously illustrated.

Carson, Jo, ed. *Stories I Ain't Told Nobody Yet*. Watts, 1989. This anthology includes a collection of poems written by people in Appalachia.

Cassedy, Sylvia. *Roomrimes*. Illustrated by Michele Chessare. Crowell, 1987. Alphabetically arranged poems take readers through different types of rooms.

Causley, Charles, ed. *Salt-Sea Verse*. Illustrated by Antony Maitland. Kestrel, Puffin, 1981. This anthology of poems is about the sea.

Cendrars, Blaise. *Shadow*. Translated and illustrated by Marcia Brown. Scribner's Sons, 1982. An eerie poem talks about the world of spirits.

Chorao, Kay. *The Baby's Bedtime Book*. Dutton, 1984. This is a collection of lullabies.

Ciardi, John. *Doodle Soup*. Illustrated by Merle Nacht. Houghton Mifflin, 1985. This is a collection of humorous poems.

———. *The Hopeful Trout and Other Limericks*. Illustrated by Susan Meddaugh. Houghton Mifflin, 1989. This text includes humorous limericks.

———. *I Met a Man*. Illustrated by Robert Osborn. Houghton Mifflin, 1961. A controlled vocabulary creates poetry for beginning readers.

———. *You Read to Me, I'll Read to You*. Illustrated by Edward Gorey. Lippincott, 1962. Poems for a child to read are followed by poems for an adult to read.

Cole, William, ed. *Beastly Boys and Ghastly Girls*. Illustrated by Tomi Ungerer. World, 1964. This is a book of humorous poems.

———, ed. *The Birds and the Beasts Were There*. Illustrated by Helen Siegl. World, 1963. This is a collection of real and fantasy animal poems.

———, ed. *Poem Stew*. Illustrated by Karen Ann Weinhaus. Lippincott, 1981. This collection of humorous poems is related to food.

de Regniers, Beatrice Schenk, Eva Moore, Mary Michaels White, and Jean Carr. *Sing a Song of Popcorn: Every Child's Book of Poems*. Scholastic, 1988. An anthology of poems is illustrated by nine Caldecott Medal artists.

Downie, Mary Alice, and Barbara Robertson, eds. *The New Wind Has Wings: Poems from Canada*. Illustrated by Elizabeth Cleaver. Oxford University Press, 1984. This is a collection of poems.

Dunning, Stephen, Edward Lueders, and Hugh Smith, eds. *Reflections on a Gift of Watermelon Pickle. . .and Other Modern Verse*. Lothrop, Lee & Shepard, 1967. An anthology of 114 poems is accompanied by photographs.

Eliot, T. S. *Old Possum's Book of Practical Cats*. Illustrated by Edward Gorey. Harcourt Brace Jovanovich, 1939, 1967, 1982. This book includes such poems as "Mr. Mistofelees," "The Rum Tum Tugger," and "Macavity: The Mystery Cat."

Ferris, Helen, ed. *Favorite Poems Old and New*. Doubleday, 1957. This is an anthology.

Field, Eugene. *Wynken, Blynken and Nod*. Illustrated by Susan Jeffers. Dutton, 1982. The classic poem appears in a newly illustrated edition.

Fields, Julia. *The Green Lion of Zion Street*. Illustrated by Jerry Pinkney. Macmillan, 1988. In this poem, children conquer their fears.

Fisher, Aileen. *Feathered Ones and Furry*. Illustrated by Eric Carle. Crowell, 1971. Fifty-five poems are about furry animals and feathery birds.

———. *In One Door and Out the Other: A Book of Poems*. Illustrated by Lillian Hoban. Crowell, 1969. A collection of poems tells about childhood experiences.

———. *Listen, Rabbit*. Illustrated by Simeon Shimin. Crowell, 1964. These verses follow a boy through the seasons as he tries to befriend a rabbit.

———. *Rabbits, Rabbits*. Illustrated by Gail Nieman. Harper & Row, 1983. These poems tell about rabbits during different times of the year.

———. *When it Comes to Bugs*. Illustrated by Chris and Bruce Degen. Harper & Row, 1986. This text includes eighteen poems about bugs.

Fleischman, Paul. *I Am Phoenix: Poems for Two Voices*. Illustrated by Ken Nutt. Harper & Row, 1985. Poems about birds are designed to be read by two readers.

———. *Joyful Noise: Poems for Two Voices*. Illustrated by Eric Beddows. Harper & Row, 1988. Poems written in two parts are designed to be read concurrently by two readers.

Fox, Dan, ed. *Go in and out the Window: An Illustrated Songbook for Young People*. Metropolitan Museum of Art and Holt, Rinehart & Winston, 1987. This is a beautifully illustrated collection of songs.

Froman, Robert. *Seeing Things: A Book of Poems*. Crowell, 1974. Several concrete poems are in this collection.

Frost, Robert. *Birches*. Illustrated by Ed Young. Holt, Rinehart & Winston, 1988. This is a highly illustrated version of Frost's classic poem.

———. *Stopping by Woods on a Snowy Evening*. Illustrated by Susan Jeffers. Dutton, 1978. Large pictures illustrate Frost's poem.

Fufuka, Karama. *My Daddy Is a Cool Dude*. Illustrated by Mahiri Fufuka. Dial, 1975. Twenty-seven poems tell about life in an urban black community as seen through the experience of a child.

Gerrard, Roy. *Sir Cedric*. Farrar, Straus & Giroux, 1984. The heroic deeds of a bold knight are told in poetic form.

———. *Sir Francis Drake: His Daring Deeds*. Farrar, Straus & Giroux, 1988. This poem tells about the exploits of the explorer.

Greenfield, Eloise. *Nathaniel Talking*. Illustrated by Jan Gilchrist. Black Butterfly Children's Books, 1989. The life of a nine-year-old is told in rap and verse.

———. *Under the Sunday Tree*. Illustrated by Amos Ferguson. Harper & Row, 1988. Poems explore life in the Bahamas.

Harrison, Michael, and Christopher Stuart-Clark, eds. *The New Dragon Book of Verse*. Oxford University Press, 1983. An anthology of classic and contemporary poetry is categorized according to subject.

Highwater, Jamake. *Moonsong Lullaby*. Photographs by Marcia Keegan. Lothrop, Lee & Shepard, 1981. A poem is inspired by ancient Native American stories.

Holman, Felice. *The Song in My Head*. Illustrated by Jim Spanfeller. Scribner's Sons, 1985. This is a collection of whimsical poetry.

Holme, Bryan, ed. *A Present of Laughter: Wit & Nonsense in Pictures & Verse*. Viking, 1982. This is an anthology of English nonsense verse.

Hood, Thomas. *Before I Go to Sleep*. Illustrated by Mary Jane Begin-Callanan. Putnam, 1990. Nighttime verse is by Thomas Hood.

Hopkins, Lee Bennett, ed. *Circus! Circus!* Illustrated by John O'Brien. Knopf, 1982. Circus poems are by such poets as Jack Prelutsky and Beatrice Schenk de Regniers.

———, ed. *Click, Rumble, Roar*. Photographs by Anna Held Audette. Crowell, 1987. This text includes eighteen poems about machines.

———, ed. *Dinosaurs*. Illustrated by Murray Tinkelman. Harcourt Brace Jovanovich, 1987. Eighteen poems are about dinosaurs.

———, ed. *My Mane Catches the Wind: Poems About Horses*. Illustrated by Sam Savitt. Harcourt Brace Jovanovich, 1979. Twenty-two poems about horses are written by different poets.

———, ed. *Surprises*. Illustrated by Megan Lloyd. Harper & Row, 1984. This is a collection of easy-to-read poems.

———, ed. *The Sky is Full of Song*. Illustrated by Dirk Zimmer. Harper & Row, 1983. This text arranges poems by season.

Hughes, Langston. *The Dream Keeper*. Knopf, 1932, 1960. This is a collection of poems by the black poet.

———. *Selected Poems of Langston Hughes*. Knopf, 1942, 1959. Many poems relate to Hughes's black heritage.

Hughes, Shirley. *Out and About*. Lothrop, Lee & Shepard, 1988. Poems follow a child and her infant brother through the seasons.

Hughes, Ted. *Under the North Star*. Illustrated by Leonard Baskin. Viking, 1981. These poems are about northern animals.

Janeczko, Paul B., ed. *Going over to Your Place: Poems for Each Other*. Bradbury, 1987. A collection of poems explores the feelings of young adults.

———, ed. *The Music of What Happens: Poems That Tell Stories*. Watts, 1988. A collection of poems tells about serious occurrences in the lives of young adults.

———. *Postcard Poems: A Collection of Poetry for Sharing*. Bradbury, 1979. This book contains one hundred poems, each brief enough to write on a postcard and share with a friend.

Kemp, Gene, ed. *Ducks and Dragons: Poems for Children*. Illustrated by Carolyn Dinan. Faber & Faber, 1980; Puffin, 1983. This is an anthology of poems about seasons, reality, animals, fantasy, fear, and old songs.

Kennedy, X. J. *Did Adam Name the Vinegarroon?* Illustrated by Heidi Johanna Selig. Godine, 1982. Poems tell about unusual animals.

———. *The Forgetful Wishing Well: Poems for Young People*. Illustrated by Monica Incisa. Atheneum, 1985. A collection of poems tells about meaningful experiences.

———, and Dorothy M. Kennedy, eds. *Knock at a Star: A Child's Introduction to Poetry*. Illustrated by Karen Ann Weinhaus. Little, Brown, 1982. The anthology is organized to help children understand poetry.

Kipling, Rudyard. *Gunga Din*. Illustrated by Robert Andrew Parker. Harcourt Brace Jovanovich, 1987. The poem is set in nineteenth century India.

Knudson, R. R., and May Swenson, eds. *American Sports Poems*. Watts, 1988. An anthology of poems is about sports and athletes.

Koch, Kenneth, and Kate Farrell, eds. *Talking to the Sun*. Metropolitan Museum of Art/Holt, Rinehart & Winston, 1985. Reproductions from the Metropolitan Museum illustrate this anthology.

Lalicki, Barbara, ed. *If There Were Dreams to Sell*. Illustrated by Margot Tomes. Lothrop, Lee & Shepard, 1984. The poems follow an alphabetical format.

Langstaff, John, ed. *What a Morning! The Christmas Story in Black Spirituals*. Illustrated by Ashley Bryan. Macmillan, 1987. Black spirituals and illustrations tell the Christmas story.

Larrick, Nancy, ed. *Songs from Mother Goose*. Illustrated by Robin Spowart. Harper & Row, 1989. A collection of nursery rhymes is accompanied by music.

———, ed. *When the Dark Comes Dancing: A Bedtime Poetry Book*. Illustrated by John Wallner. Philomel, 1982. This poetry is to be read aloud at bedtime.

Lawrence. D. H. *Birds, Beasts and the Third Thing*. Selected and illustrated by Alice and Martin Provensen. Viking, 1982. Twenty-three poems focus on Lawrence's "Delight of Being Alone."

Lear, Edward. *A Book of Bosh*. Compiled by Brian Alderson. Penguin, 1982. This is a collection of Lear's poetry.

———. *The Complete Nonsense Book*. Dodd, Mead, 1946. This book includes *A Book of Nonsense*, originally published in 1846, and *Nonsense Songs and Stories*, originally published in 1871.

———. *Hilary Knight's The Owl and the Pussy-Cat*. Illustrated by Hilary Knight. Macmillan, 1983. Knight creates a fantasy around Lear's poem.

———. *The Nonsense Books of Edward Lear*. New American Library, 1964. These nonsense poems are still enjoyed by children.

———. *Nonsense Omnibus*. Warne, 1943. Original illustrations and verses are from four of Lear's collections.

Lear, Edward, and Ogden Nash. *The Scroobius Pip*. Illustrated by Nancy Ekholm Burkert. Harper & Row, 1968. A beautifully illustrated picture book is about the wondrous animal that is neither fish nor fowl, insect nor beast.

Lewis, Richard. *Of This World: A Poet's Life in Poetry*. Photographs by Helen Buttfield. Dial, 1968. This book includes poems by the Japanese poet Issa and information about his life.

Little, Jean. *Hey World, Here I Am!* Illustrated by Sue Truesdell. Harper & Row, 1989. Poems and short stories are told from a teenage girl's viewpoint.

Livingston, Myra Cohn, ed. *Cat Poems*. Illustrated by Trina Schart Hyman. Holiday House, 1987. Nineteen poems are about cats.

———. *Celebrations*. Illustrated by Leonard Everett Fisher. Holiday House, 1985. A collection of sixteen poems is about holidays.

———, ed. *Christmas Poems*. Illustrated by Trina Schart Hyman. Holiday House, 1984. This is an anthology of eighteen Christmas poems.

———. *A Circle of Seasons*. Illustrated by Leonard Everett Fisher. Holiday House, 1982. Poems are about the four seasons.

———. *O Sliver of Liver*. Illustrated by Iris Van Rynbach. Atheneum, 1979. This book contains a variety of poems, including cinquains, haiku, and poems about nature, holidays, daily life, human relationships, and emotions.

———. *Sea Songs*. Illustrated by Leonard Everett Fisher. Holiday House, 1986. A collection of poems is about the sea.

———. *Sky Song*. Illustrated by Leonard Everett Fisher. Holiday House, 1983. Poems are about the sky.

———. *Space Songs*. Illustrated by Leonard Everett Fisher. Holiday House, 1988. These poems are about elements in space.

———, ed. *Thanksgiving Poems*. Illustrated by Stephen Gammell. Holiday House, 1985. This book contains contemporary and traditional holiday poems.

———. *Up in the Air*. Illustrated by Leonard Everett Fisher. Holiday House, 1989. This poem portrays experiences associated with looking out of airplane windows.

———, ed. *Why Am I So Cold? Poems of the Unknowable*. Atheneum, 1982. These are poems about ghosts and monsters.

Lobel, Arnold. *The Rose in My Garden*. Illustrated by Anita Lobel. Greenwillow, 1984. A cumulative poem traces the flowers in the garden.

———. *Whiskers and Rhymes*. Greenwillow, 1985. These are rhyming poems for young children.

Longfellow, Henry Wadsworth. *Hiawatha*. Illustrated by Susan Jeffers. Dutton, 1983. Hiawatha's boyhood is illustrated in detailed artwork.

———. *Hiawatha*. Illustrated by Keith Mosely. Putnam, 1988. This is an abridged, pop-up version of the poem.

———. *Hiawatha's Childhood*. Illustrated by Errol LeCain. Farrar, Straus & Giroux, 1984. This winner of the 1985 Greenaway Medal provides a mystical setting.

———. *Paul Revere's Ride*. Illustrated by Paul Galdone. Crowell, 1963. The classic poem is illustrated for younger children.

Loveday, John, ed. *Over the Bridge: An Anthology of New Poems*. Illustrated by Michael Foreman. Kestrel, Penguin, 1981. An anthology of poetry is by British poets.

McCord, David. *Away and Ago: Rhymes of the Never Was and Always Is*. Illustrated by Leslie Morrill. Little, Brown, 1974. Poems are about familiar places, objects, and experiences.

———. *Far and Few: Rhymes of the Never Was and Always Is*. Illustrated by Henry B. Kane. Little, Brown, 1952. This book includes the popular nonsense poems found in "Five Chants."

———. *One at a Time: Collected Poems for the Young*. Illustrated by Henry B. Kane. Little, Brown, 1977. A large collection of poems is on many subjects.

McPhail, David. *The Dream Child*. Dutton, 1985. The poetic text follows a child's imaginative journey.

Mahy, Margaret. *Nonstop Nonsense*. Illustrated by Quentin Blake. Macmillan, 1989. This text contains nonsense poetry as well as short stories.

Margolis, Richard J. *Secrets of a Small Brother*. Illustrated by Donald Carrick. Macmillan, 1984. The poems are written from a younger brother's perspective.

Marshak, Samuel. *The Pup Grew Up*. Translated by Richard Pevear. Illustrated by Vladimir Radunsky. H. Holt, 1989. Translated from Russian, this poem develops a comical incident on a train.

Merriam, Eve. *Halloween ABC*. Illustrated by Lane Smith. Macmillan, 1987. This is a collection of spooky Halloween poems.

———. *Rainbow Writing*. Atheneum, 1976. This poetry is designed to color our minds with the vast spectrum of human experience.

———. *A Word or Two with You: New Rhymes for Young Readers*. Illustrated by John Nez. Atheneum, 1981. Seventeen poems emphasize rhyming and word play.

Milne, A. A. *When We Were Very Young*. Illustrated by Ernest H. Shepard. Dutton, 1961. Delightful poems are about Winnie-the-Pooh and the hundred-acre wood.

———. *Winnie-the-Pooh*. Illustrated by Ernest H. Shepard. Dutton, 1954. This is the classic story, with poems, about Christopher Robin's friend, the bear.

———. *The World of Christopher Robin*. Illustrated by E. H. Shepard. Dutton, 1958. Poems tell about a boy and his toy animal friends.

Moore, Clement. *The Night Before Christmas*. Illustrated by Tomie dePaola. Holiday House, 1980. Large, brightly colored illustrations appear in picture-book format.

———. *The Night Before Christmas*. Illustrated by Tasha Tudor. Rand McNally, 1975. This book contains large illustrations of the popular Christmas poem.

Moore, Lilian, ed. *Go with the Poem*. McGraw-Hill, 1979. Ninety poems are written by outstanding twentieth-century poets.

———. *See My Lovely Poison Ivy*. Illustrated by Diane Dawson. Atheneum, 1975. Poems are about witches, ghosts, goblins, bats, and monsters.

———. *Something New Begins*. Atheneum, 1982. This book contains fifteen new poems as well as selections from her previous poems.

Morrison, Lillian, ed. *Rhythm Road: Poems to Move To*. Lothrop, Lee & Shepard, 1988. An anthology of poems is divided according to motion responses.

———. *The Sidewalk Racer and Other Poems of Sports and Motion*. Lothrop, Lee & Shepard, 1977. Poems are about sports, including surfing, tennis, boxing, football, skateboarding, and baseball.

Morton, Miriam, ed. *The Moon Is Like a Silver Sickle: A Celebration of Poetry by Russian Children*. Illustrated by Eros Keith. Simon & Schuster, 1972. This is a collection of ninety-two poems written by Russian children.

Noyes, Alfred. *The Highwayman*. Illustrated by Charles Keeping. Oxford University Press, 1981. A story poem is about a highwayman who risked his life every evening to visit the innkeeper's daughter.

———. *The Highwayman*. Illustrated by Gilbert Riswold. Prentice-Hall, 1969. The story poem is illustrated.

O'Neill, Mary. *Hailstones and Halibut Bones*. Illustrated by Leonard Weisgard. Doubleday, 1961. Poems describe the basic colors.

Opie, Iona, and Peter Opie, eds. *The Oxford Book of Children's Verse*. Oxford University Press, 1984. This anthology includes poems from the medieval period through the twentieth century.

———. *Tail Feathers from Mother Goose*. Little, Brown, 1988. A large collection of verses is illustrated by various artists.

Pomerantz, Charlotte. *If I Had a Paka: Poems in Eleven Languages*. Illustrated by Nancy Tafuri. Greenwillow, 1982. Poems rely on foreign words.

Pooley, Sarah, ed. *A Day of Rhymes*. Knopf, 1988. A collection of sixty-one poems and fingerplays is for preschool children.

Prelutsky, Jack. *The Baby Uggs Are Hatching*. Illustrated by James Stevenson. Greenwillow, 1982. Humorous poems are about Grebles, Sneepies, and Slitchs.

———. *A Gopher in the Garden and Other Animal Poems*. Illustrated by Robert Leydenfrost. Macmillan, 1966, 1967. Humorous poems are about animals.

———. *The Headless Horseman Rides Tonight*. Illustrated by Arnold Lobel. Greenwillow, 1980. Twelve scary poems are about giants, banshees, poltergeists, and zombies.

———. *Poems of A. Nonny Mouse*. Knopf, 1989. This is a collection of humorous poetry.

———. *The Queen of Eene*. Illustrated by Victoria Chess. Greenwillow, 1978. Fourteen humorous poems have funny illustrations.

———, ed. *The Random House Book of Poetry for Children*. Illustrated by Arnold Lobel. Random House, 1983. An anthology of over five hundred poems is divided according to themes.

———, ed. *Read-Aloud Rhymes for the Very Young*. Illustrated by Marc Brown. Knopf, 1986. An attractive collection of poems stresses vivid language.

———. *Rolling Harvey down the Hill*. Illustrated by Victoria Chess. Greenwillow, 1980. Humorous poems are about the adventures of five boys.

———. *The Sheriff of Rottenshot*. Illustrated by Victoria Chess. Greenwillow, 1982. Humorous poems use strong rhyming patterns.

———. *Tyrannosaurus Was a Beast: Dinosaur Poems*. Illustrated by Arnold Lobel. Greenwillow, 1988. Fourteen poems are about characteristics of dinosaurs.

Richards, Laura E. *Tirra Lirra, Rhymes Old and New*. Illustrated by Marguerite Davis. Little, Brown, 1955. Over one hundred humorous poems include "Eletelephony" and "Bobbily Boo and Wollypotump."

Rossetti, Christina. *Goblin Market*. Illustrated and adapted by Ellen Raskin. Dutton, 1970. This is a picture-book version of the poem originally published in 1862.

———. *Sing-Song*. Illustrated by Arthur Hughes. Routledge, 1872. This is a classic poem.

Rylant, Cynthia. *Waiting to Waltz: A Childhood*. Illustrated by Stephen Gammell. Bradbury, 1984. This is a collection of poems about growing up in a small Appalachian town.

Seeger, Ruth Crawford. *American Folksongs for Children—In Home, School, and Nursery School*. Illustrated by Barbara Cooney. Doubleday, 1948. This book contains words and music to numerous folksongs, plus suggestions for using them with young children.

Sendak, Maurice. *Pierre: A Cautionary Tale*. Harper & Row, 1962. A boy learns that he should sometimes care.

Seuss, Dr. *The Cat in the Hat*. Random House, 1957. This is an illustrated humorous poem.

Siebert, Diane. *Heartland*. Illustrated by Wendell Minor. Crowell, 1989. The poem and illustrations describe the Midwest.

———. *Mojave*. Illustrated by Wendell Minor. Crowell, 1988. This poem and the illustrations show the landscape and the inhabitants of the Mojave Desert.

Silverstein, Shel. *A Light in the Attic*. Harper & Row, 1981. Humorous poems tell about such situations as the polar bear in the Frigidaire.

———. *Where the Sidewalk Ends*. Harper & Row, 1974. This is a collection of humorous poems.

Skofield, James. *Nightdances*. Illustrated by Karen Gundersheimer. Harper & Row, 1981. A boy and his parents go outside on a moonlit night.

Smith, William Jay. *Laughing Time*. Illustrated by Juliet Kepes. Little, Brown, 1955. Humorous poems tell about animals and people.

Snyder, Zilpha Keatley. *Today Is Saturday*. Illustrated by John Arms. Atheneum, 1969.

Solt, Mary Ellen, ed. *Concrete Poetry: A World View*. Indiana University Press, 1980. This text includes poetry written in forms that relate to the meanings.

Starbird, Kaye. *The Covered Bridge House and Other Poems*. Illustrated by Jim Arnosky. Four Winds, 1979. Thirty poems tell about childhood experiences, such as jumping rope, hopping after falling on a ski slope, and wondering why no one can get rags from ragweed.

Stevenson, Robert Louis. *A Child's Garden of Verses*. Longmans, Green 1885. This is a classic book of poetry.

Thurman, Judith. *Flashlight and Other Poems*. Illustrated by Reina Rubel. Atheneum, 1976. Poems describe such familiar things as balloons, closets, and going barefoot.

Van Vorst, M. L. *A Norse Lullaby*. Illustrated by Margot Tomes. Lothrop, Lee, & Shepard, 1988. A mother and children wait for Father to return on a wintry night.

Viorst, Judith. *If I Were in Charge of the World and Other Worries: Poems for Children and Their Parents*. Illustrated by Lynne Cherry. Atheneum, 1981. The poems are about everyday situations that frustrate.

Wallace, Daisy. *Fairy Poems*. Illustrated by Trina Schart Hyman. Holiday House, 1980. A collection of poems is about leprechauns and fairies.

———. *Ghost Poems*. Illustrated by Tomie dePaola. Holiday House, 1979. A collection of seventeen poems is about ghosts.

Westcott, Nadine Bernard. *Peanut Butter and Jelly: A Play Rhyme*. Dutton, 1987. The text includes suggested hand and body actions.

Whipple, Laura, ed. *Eric Carle's Animals, Animals*. Illustrated by Eric Carle. Philomel, 1989. This text includes an anthology of poems about animals.

Willard, Nancy. *Night Story*. Illustrated by Ilse Plume. Harcourt Brace Jovanovich, 1986. A small boy has an adventure in dreamland.

———. *A Visit to William Blake's Inn: Poems for Innocent and Experienced Travelers*. Illustrated by Alice and Martin Provensen. Harcourt Brace Jovanovich, 1981. Poems describe a menagerie of guests.

———. *The Voyage of the Ludgate Hill: Travels with Robert Louis Stevenson*. Illustrated by Alice and Martin Provensen. Harcourt Brace Jovanovich, 1987. A poem tells about Stevenson's adventures on a cargo steamer.

Wilner, Isabel, ed. *The Poetry Troup: An Anthology to Read Aloud*. Scribner's Sons, 1977. An anthology of over two hundred poems is selected for reading aloud.

Worth, Valerie. *All the Small Poems*. Illustrated by Natalie Babbitt. Farrar, Straus & Giroux, 1987. This is a collection of Worth's previously published "Small Poems."

———. *More Small Poems*. Illustrated by Natalie Babbitt. Farrar, Straus & Giroux, 1976. Ordinary objects, such as acorns, soap bubbles, and Christmas lights, are the subjects of short poems.

———. *Still More Small Poems*. Illustrated by Natalie Babbitt. Farrar, Straus & Giroux, 1978. Twenty-five poems are about such ordinary objects as doors, rocks, slugs, and mushrooms.

Yolen, Jane, ed. *The Lullaby Songbook*. Illustrated by Charles Mikolaycak. Harcourt Brace Jovanovich, 1986. This is a collection of lullabies from various cultures.

———. *The Three Bears Rhyme Book*. Illustrated by Jane Dyer. Harcourt Brace Jovanovich, 1987. Fifteen poems are about the three bears and Goldilocks.

Zolotow, Charlotte. *River Winding*. Illustrated by Kazue Mizumura. Crowell, 1978. Poems for young children paint images of things seen and remembered.

———. *River Winding*. Illustrated by Regina Shekerjian. Abelard-Schuman, 1970. These poems are for young children.

GIL
FATY
LEGO

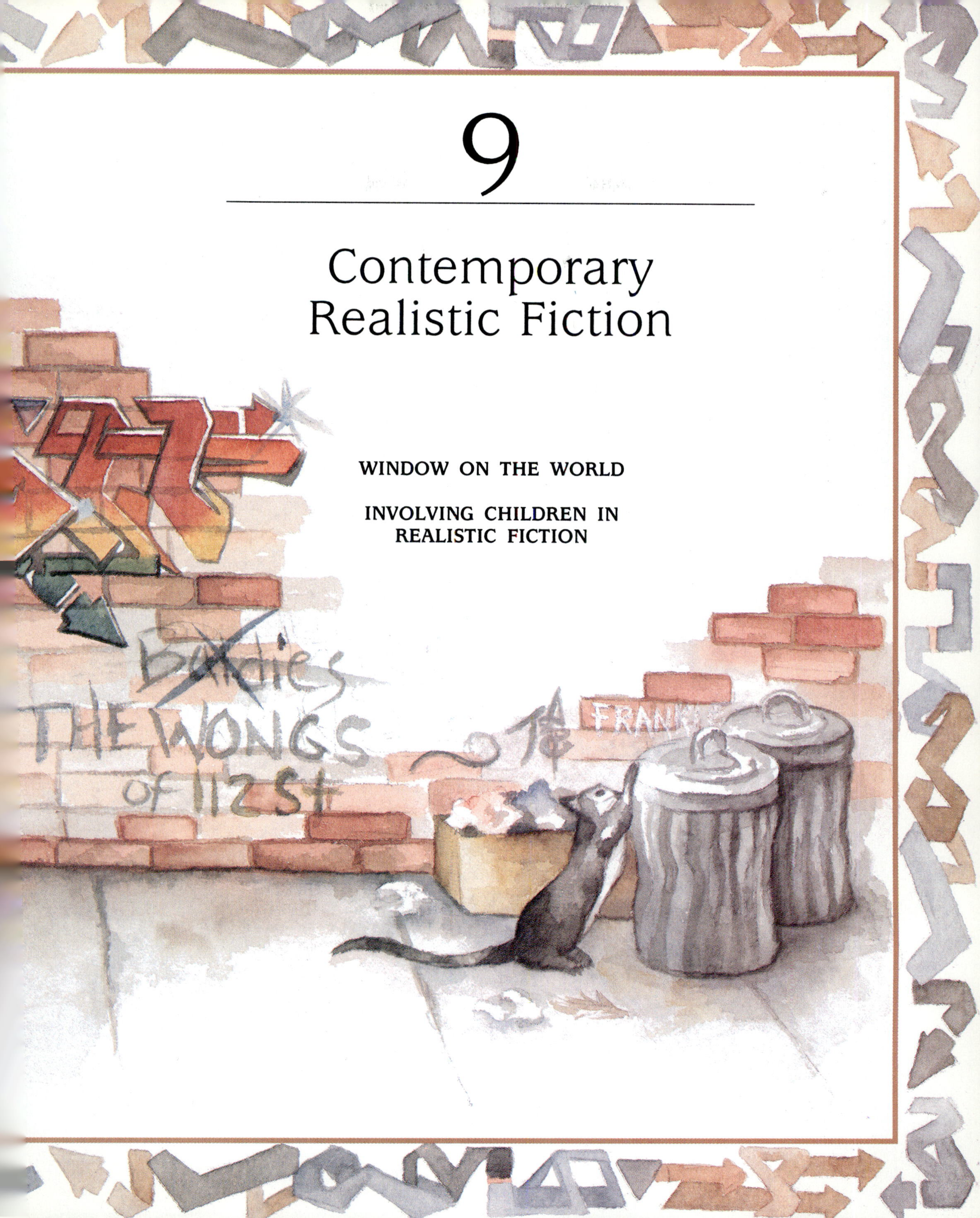

9

Contemporary Realistic Fiction

WINDOW ON THE WORLD

INVOLVING CHILDREN IN REALISTIC FICTION

Window on the World

WHAT CONTEMPORARY REALISTIC FICTION IS

VALUES OF REALISTIC FICTION

HOW REALISTIC FICTION HAS CHANGED

NEW REALISM AND THE PROBLEM NOVEL

CONTROVERSIAL ISSUES

GUIDELINES FOR SELECTING CONTROVERSIAL FICTION

CRITERIA FOR EVALUATING REALISTIC FICTION

LITERARY ELEMENTS

SUBJECTS IN REALISTIC FICTION

ANIMAL STORIES, MYSTERIES, SPORTS STORIES, AND HUMOR

NEW TERMINOLOGY ENTERS THE DISCUSsion of children's books as you leave the realm of Mother Goose, most picture storybooks, traditional literature, and modern fantasy. Such terms as *relevant books, extreme realism, problem novel,* and *everyday occurrences* are found in critiques and discussions of contemporary realistic fiction.

While some of the books in this genre are among the most popular with older children, they are also among the most controversial. Interest groups, educators, and parents criticize and debate the value of some realistic stories for children. Many adults are concerned about such issues as censorship, sexism, violence, alienation from society, racism, and promiscuity. This chapter discusses what contemporary realistic fiction is, why it should be shared with children, how realistic fiction has changed, issues related to realistic fiction, and criteria for evaluating realistic fiction.

WHAT CONTEMPORARY REALISTIC FICTION IS

The term *contemporary realistic fiction* implies that everything in a realistic story—including plot, characters, and setting—is consistent with the lives of real people in our contemporary world. The word *realistic* does not mean that the story is true, however; it means only that the story could have happened.

Use of the words *realistic* and *fiction* together is confusing to some children, who have trouble distinguishing contemporary realistic fiction from modern fantasy or from stories that really happened. Certainly authors of modern fantasy attempt to make their stories realistic in the sense that they try to create believable plots, characters, and settings; make their stories as internally consistent as possible; and ground their stories in familiar reality before introducing elements of fantasy. Contemporary realistic fiction, however, requires that plots focus on familiar, everyday problems, pleasures, and personal relationships and that characters and settings seem as real as the contemporary world we know. The supernatural has no part in such stories, except occasionally in the beliefs of realistic human characters.

Two popular animal stories demonstrate the differences between modern fantasy and contemporary realistic fiction. These differences are summarized in Chart 9–1. In Beatrix Potter's fantasy,

CHART 9–1
Differences between modern fantasy and contemporary realistic fiction

	Modern Fantasy	Contemporary Realistic Fiction
Creating believable stories	Authors must encourage readers to suspend disbelief	Authors may rely on "relevant subjects," everyday occurrences, or extreme realism
Plot Development	Conflict may be against supernatural powers Problems may be solved through magical powers	Conflict develops as characters cope with such problems as growing up, survival, family discord, and inner city tensions Antagonists may be self, other family members, society, or nature
Characters	Personified toys, little people, supernatural beings, real people who have imaginary experiences, animals who behave like people	Characters who act like real people Animals who always behave like animals
Setting	Past, present, or future Imaginary world May travel through time and space	Contemporary world as we know it

The Tale of Peter Rabbit, Peter talks, thinks, acts, and dresses like an inquisitive, sometimes greedy, sometimes frightened human child who needs his mother's love and care. While the story's garden setting is realistic, Peter's home is furnished with human furniture. In this fantasy, conflict develops because Peter demonstrates believable childlike desires.

In contrast, the three animals in Sheila Burnford's *The Incredible Journey* retain their animal characteristics as they struggle for survival in a realistically depicted Canadian wilderness. A trained hunting dog leads his companions across the wilderness; An English bulldog, who is a cherished family pet, seeks people to give him food; and a Siamese cat retains her feline independence. Conflict in this realistic story develops as the animals become lost and face problems while trying to return to their home. Burnford does not give them human thoughts, values, or other human characteristics. The characters and settings are not only believable; they are also completely realistic by the standard of what we know and expect in our everyday world.

VALUES OF REALISTIC FICTION

One of the greatest values of realistic fiction for children is that many realistic stories allow children to identify with characters of their own age who have similar interests and problems. Children like to read about people they can understand. Thus, their favorite authors express a clear understanding of children. For example, one girl said about Judy Blume's *Are You There God? It's Me, Margaret,* "I've read this book five times; I could be Margaret."

Realistic fiction can help children discover that their problems and desires are not unique and that they are not alone in experiencing certain feelings and situations. Children who are unhappy about their physical appearance may identify with Constance Greene's *The Unmaking of Rabbit,* for example, or children who are having preadolescent anxieties, especially about boy-girl relationships, may find a comrade in Phyllis Naylor's *Alice in Rapture, Sort Of.* The young characters in these books face and overcome their problems while remaining true to themselves.

Realistic fiction also extends children's horizons by broadening their interests, allowing them to experience new adventures, and showing them different ways to view and deal with conflicts in their own lives. They can vicariously live a survival adventure and mature in the process as they read Scott O'Dell's *Island of the Blue Dolphins,* for example, or experience the death of a father in Vera and Bill Cleaver's *Where the Lilies Bloom.*

According to Joanne Bernstein (3), reading about children who are facing emotional problems can help other children discharge repressed emotions and cope with fear, anger, or grief. For example, books about divorce or abuse may help children cope with a traumatic period in their lives. In Beverly Cleary's *Dear Mr. Henshaw,* readers discover that parents as well as children are hurt by divorce. Children may realize the consequences of wife and child abuse by reading Betsy Byars's *Cracker Jackson*. (*A word of caution*: realistic fiction should *not* be used to replace professional help in situations that warrant such intervention. Children experiencing severe depression, anger, or grief may require professional help.) Many of the books discussed in this chapter can stimulate discussion and help children share their feelings and solve their problems. Of course, realistic fiction also provides children with pleasure and escape. Realistic animal stories, sports stories, mysteries, and humorous stories are enjoyable getaways for young people.

HOW REALISTIC FICTION HAS CHANGED

Synonyms for *realistic* include other adjectives, such as *lifelike, genuine,* and *authentic*. Of course, what people consider lifelike depends upon the social context. What seems realistic to us might seem fantastic to people in different societies or other eras.

In the Victorian era of the late nineteenth and early twentieth centuries, realistic fiction emphasized traditional family roles and ties in warm, close, and stable family units that lived in one place for generations; strict roles for males and females, stressing higher education and careers for males and wifehood and motherhood for females; respect for law and adult authority; strong religious commitment; duty to educate, Christianize, or care for the poor; and problems related to overcoming sinfulness and becoming good.

Realistic fiction continued to emphasize many of these values well into the second half of the twentieth century, although the literature began to depict both female and male children gaining more independence. The characters in realistic children's fiction were usually white, middle-class, and members of stable families consisting of a father, a mother, and their children. Nontraditional families and family disturbances were virtually unrepresented in this literature.

Beginning roughly in the 1960s, however, the content of contemporary realistic fiction became more diverse—no doubt reflecting the increasingly diverse and complex social life in the United States and elsewhere. Contemporary realistic stories for children depict some unhappy and unstable families, single-parent families, and families in which both parents work outside the home. Career ambitions are not as confined to traditional gender roles as they were in the past. Children often have considerable responsibility and independence. Fear of or disrespect for law and authority is more common. Education and religion receive less stress. Ethnic and racial minorities are more in evidence, and in general, people's economic, emotional, and social problems receive more emphasis.

John Rowe Townsend (33) is among the researchers who have pointed out the striking contrasts between children's realistic fiction of the 1950s and the late 1960s. The 1950s was one of the quietest decades in children's literature: In keeping with traditional values, children were pictured as part of a stable community: Grandparents were wise, parents were staunch and respected, and childhood was happy and secure. In contrast, children's literature of the late 1960s implied an erosion of adult authority and an apparent widening of the generation gap. It was no longer self-evident that parents knew best and that children could be guided into accepting the established codes and behavior.

In a study of themes found in contemporary realistic fiction published in the late 1970s, Jane M. Madsen and Elaine B. Wickersham (23) found that popular themes for young children were overcoming fear and meeting responsibility and that stories about problems related to adoption, divorce, disabilities, and minority social status were more common than in the past. In the 1980s, contemporary realistic fiction for older children often depicted children overcoming family and personal problems as they confronted quarreling or divorcing parents, deserting or noncaring parents, cruel foster families, conflicts between personal ambitions and parental desires, and death of loved ones. Discovery of self and development of maturity as children face and overcome their fears are other popular themes in stories written for older children. Such stories often stress the importance of self-esteem and being true to oneself.

NEW REALISM AND THE PROBLEM NOVEL

New realism is the term Shelton L. Root (27) applies to certain segments of contemporary realistic fiction. He describes new realism as "that fiction for young readers which addresses itself to personal problems and social issues heretofore considered taboo for fictional treatment by the general public, as enunciated by its traditional spokesmen: librarians, teachers, ministers, and others. The new realism is often graphic in its language and always explicit in its treatment" (p. 19).

Some literary critics question the merit of at least portions of this new realism. Sheila Egoff (11), for example, applauds realistic novels that have strong literary qualities, including logical flow of narrative, delicate complexity of characterization, insights that convey the conduct of life as characters move from childhood to adolescence and to adulthood, and a quality that touches both the imagination and the emotions. In an outstanding realistic novel, says Egoff, conflict is integral to the plot and characterization; its resolution has wide implications growing out of the personal vision or experience of the writer. In contrast, Egoff maintains, conflict in a problem novel stems from the writer's social standards more than from personal feelings and emotions. The author's intentions may be good, but in an effort to make a point or argue a social position, the author creates a cardboard story instead of one that really comes alive. The conflict is specific rather than universal and narrow rather than far-reaching in its implications.

Egoff identifies other typical characteristics of the problem novel:

1 Concern is with externals, with how things look rather than how things are. The author begins with a problem rather than with a plot or characters.
2 The protagonist is burdened with anxieties and grievances that grow out of alienation from the adult world.
3 The protagonist often achieves temporary relief through association with an unconventional adult from outside the family.
4 The narrative is usually in the first person, and its confessional tone is self-centered.
5 The vocabulary is limited, and observation is restricted by the pretense that an ordinary child is the narrator.
6 Sentences and paragraphs are short, the language is flat, without nuance, and the language may be emotionally numb.
7 Inclusion of expletives seems obligatory.
8 Sex is discussed openly.
9 The setting is usually urban.

Jack Forman (13) adds that in contrast to the fully developed characterizations in books of literary quality, many topical novels "are peopled with characters who are more mouthpieces of a particular point of view than fully developed protagonists" (p. 470). Beverly Cleary (9) further articulates the difference between stories that focus on problems and stories that focus on people:

> I'm more interested in writing about people than problems. *Dear Mr. Henshaw* [the winner of the 1984 Newbery Medal] is about a boy that had a problem, not a problem that had a boy. I don't search for a new problem. (p. 1F)

Educators and critics of children's literature in the mid-1980s disagreed, however, about how prominent new realism and problem novels actually are in contemporary realistic fiction for children. Such critics as Bertha M. Cheatham (7) maintained that novels "mirroring real-life situations and tackling controversial subjects (drugs, sex, suicide) are increasing in numbers" (p. 25), while such critics as Marilyn F. Apseloff (1) saw "a definite swing away from the serious 'new realism' which dominated the lists half a decade ago" (p. 32) in the United States, Europe, and Japan. Apseloff noted an apparently increasing demand for adventure stories, humorous stories, and realistic fiction of high literary quality.

Nancy Vasilakis (35) maintains that in the late 1960s taboos began "falling like dominoes. . . . No subject was too lurid, no language too explicit, and no outlook too bleak"; but by the mid-1980s "librarians were questioning the existence of too many books that are poorly written, dishonest, and manipulative, simply because they are destined to be popular" (p. 768). Vasilakis concludes that controversial books are no longer automatic best-sellers. Instead, "the fear of censorship, concern over declining standards, and the economic recession of the early eighties forced publishers and librarians alike, after the first few tremors, to hunker down and become more discriminating in their choices of what to publish and what to buy" (p. 769).

Today's students of children's literature are living in an interesting era of book publishing for children. They have the opportunity to analyze new books of contemporary realistic fiction and contemplate the different directions that authors may choose to pursue.

CONTROVERSIAL ISSUES

Barbara Feldstein (12) identifies the major controversies in children's books as political views that differ from that of a censor, treatment of minorities, stereotyped roles of women, problems of contemporary society, and profane language. When any of these subjects are in books, we may expect to have varied reactions. The degree to which realistic fiction should reflect the reality of the times leads to controversy as writers create characters who face problems relating to sexism, sexuality, violence, and drugs. There is no simple solution: What one group considers controversial, another does not. Realistic fiction has resulted in more controversy and calls for censorship than has any other genre. Therefore, educators must be aware of some concerns in this area of literature, including sexism, sexuality, violence, profanity, and family problems.

Sexism

The following position statement by the Association of Women Psychologists (2) stresses dangers to both females and males when they are expected to live up to the traditional roles created by society and reflected in literature:

> Psychological oppression in the form of sex role socialization clearly conveys to girls from the earliest ages that their nature is to be submissive, servile, and repressed, and their role is to be servant, admirer, sex object and martyr. . . .The psychological consequences of goal depression in young women. . .are all too common. In addition, both men and women have come to realize the effect on men of this type of sex role stereotyping, the crippling pressure to compete, to achieve, to produce, to stifle emotion, sensitivity and gentleness, all taking their toll in psychic and physical traumas.

Feldstein (12) brings this issue into current times by stating:

> Over the past twenty years, no doubt as a result of the efforts of feminist groups, there has been an increase in the number of positive role models in children's literature. Nonetheless, there are still objections to passive female characters who do not take control over their own destiny. (p. 140)

The controversial issue of sexism in children's literature involves not only exclusion of females from many children's books but also the stereotyped roles in which children's books often depict females. Female characters are often shown as homemakers or employees in "feminine" occupations. Often, female characters are passive, docile, fearful, and dependent. Children's books do not necessarily depict the roles of homemakers and of employees in traditionally female occupations in a condescending or demeaning light, but the implication that these are the *only* roles open to females is harmful to the girls and boys who read these stories.

People concerned with sexism have evaluated the roles of males and females in children's literature and the elementary classrooms. The evaluations are usually harshly critical of the negative forces of sex-role stereotyping. Ramona Frasher (14), for example, reviewed research on sexism and sex-role stereotyping in children's literature and identified some trends. In Newbery Award-winning books published prior to the 1970s, male main characters outnumbered female main characters by about three to one. In addition, negative comments about females and stereotyping were common. Frasher's analysis of Newbery Award winners published between 1971 and 1980 showed the ratio of male characters to female characters was about equal. In addition, female characters tended to be portrayed with more positive and varied personality characteristics, and they exhibited a greater variety of behaviors.

Even though these changes reflect a heightened sensitivity to feminist concerns, Frasher's article identifies three areas still of major concern: (1) changes are found predominantly in books written for children in middle- and late-childhood years, (2) the rush to respond to criticism resulted in too many examples of poor or marginal literature, and (3) until more authors are able to write with ease about both sexes engaged in a broad scope of activities and exhibiting a range of characteristics, children's literature will remain stereotyped. Frasher's conclusion emphasizes the need for critical evaluation in this area:

> The number of books accessible to children is immense; it will take many years of publishing quality nonsexist literature to insure that a random selection is as likely to be nonstereotyped as it is to be stereotyped. (p. 77)

Educators, psychologists, and other concerned adults also criticize the sexism and sex-role stereotyping in realistic picture books. In an earlier study, Aileen Pace Nilsen (24) analyzed the role of females in eighty Caldecott Medal winners and honor books. She chose picture books because illustrated books are "the ones influencing children at the time they are in the process of developing their own sexual identity. Children decide very early in life what roles are appropriate to male and female" (p. 919). Of the books that were realistic (as compared with fantasy), she found fewer stories having girls as the leading characters. She also compared the number of girl- and boy-centered stories over a twenty-year period; the percentage of girl-centered stories had decreased from a high of 46 percent in 1951–1955 to a low of 26 percent in 1966–1970.

Nilsen does not recommend that children not read these books, but she does suggest that they be provided with equally interesting books that have female main characters. She also recommends that artists become aware of the stereotypes they can perpetuate in illustrating books. She points out that in Ezra Jack Keats's *Goggles,* Peter's sister sits on the sidewalk beside a baby and draws pictures while the boys' excitement rages around her. Likewise, in *A Tree Is Nice,* the boys are pictured in the upper branches of the trees, while the girls are pictured sitting in the lowest branches, waving to boys climbing trees, or sprinkling plants with a watering can.

Many female protagonists in books for older children behave in ways quite different from those of the heroines of traditional literature. They reflect the fairly recent realization that females are also *heroes,* with considerable intellectual, emotional, and physical potential in their actions. Some of the most memorable girl characters—including Karana in Scott O'Dell's *Island of the Blue Dolphins,* Queenie in Robert Burch's *Queenie Peavy* (who insisted that she would grow up to be a doctor, not a nurse), Harriet in Louise Fitzhugh's *Harriet the Spy,* and even Jo in Louisa May Alcott's Victorian novel, *Little Women*—are believable and exciting because they do not follow stereotypic behavior patterns.

Nontraditional behaviors can, of course, also result in controversy; women's roles and women's rights are political issues. Advocates express strong opinions on both sides. One of the areas that illustrates women's changing roles is the portrayal of the minor characters in stories. Mothers may be sports writers, as in Ellen Conford's *The Revenge of the Incredible Dr. Rancid and His Youthful Assistant, Jeffrey;* photographers who travel on assignments and join peace marches accompanied by their daughters, as in Norma Klein's *Mom, the Wolf Man and Me;* book illustrators who travel on consulting contracts, as in Lois Lowry's *Anastasia on Her Own;* and authors whose children consider them eccentric, as in Patricia MacLachlan's *The Facts and Fictions of Minna Pratt*. Recent books suggest that the roles of males and females may be changing, as increasingly varied occupations and behavior patterns are found in the books. Teachers, librarians, and parents should be aware, however, that not all people look on these changes favorably.

Sexuality

Today is a time of increasing sophistication and frankness about sexuality; television programs and movies portray sexual relationships that would not have been shown to earlier generations of adults, let alone children. Premarital and extramarital sex, sexual development, homosexual experiences, and sex education are controversial topics in children's literature.

Several books written for older children describe nontraditional living situations in which a child's mother lives with a male friend. In Stuart Buchan's *When We Lived with Pete,* Tommy and his mother live with a man who is not ready to get married.

In Norma Klein's more controversial *Mom, the Wolf Man and Me,* Theodore spends weekends with Brett's mother, which leads eleven-year-old Brett to ask her mother if she is having sexual relations with him. This results in a frank discussion about sexual intercourse. As might be expected, this book has met with varying reactions. John M. Kean and Carl Personke (20) point out that numerous children today are living in one-parent households and that such children should have opportunities to read about "a warm home environment that differs from the usual pattern" (p. 334). In contrast, several librarians and literature professors at one reading conference (29) reported receiving many negative comments from parents and college students about the sexual discussions and the unconventional life-styles described in Klein's book.

Cynthia Rylant's *A Kindness,* written for a teenage audience, explores a fifteen-year-old boy's feelings and reactions when his single mother becomes pregnant and decides to keep the baby. At first, the boy feels threatened because his relationship with his mother changes. Later, however, he feels a close, loving relationship with the new baby girl.

Books describing children's concerns about their developing sexuality may also be controversial. For example, Judy Blume's popular *Are You There God? It's Me, Margaret* has been reviewed favorably as a book that realistically conveys preadolescent girls' worries over menstruation and body changes. Yet in 1981, this book was one of several taken from library shelves and burned because some adults viewed it as a negative influence on children. In that same year, the national television news showed angry adults criticizing the morality of this book, as well as many others, and the resulting flames of protest.

The results of a censorship survey may surprise many students of children's literature. Ken Donelson (10) reports that Judy Blume, with five titles and thirty-three protests, is the second most widely protested author. (John Steinbeck, with seven titles and forty-five protests, is the most widely protested author.) In addition to *Are You There God? It's Me, Margaret,* Blume's *Then Again, Maybe I Won't; Deenie; Forever; It's Not the End of the World,* and *Blubber* have been strongly criticized or censored because of their sexual content or strong language.

Violence

Television, movies, and books have been accused of portraying too much violence. Children's cartoons are often criticized for their excessive violence. Children's books become the object of controversy when they portray what some people define as inappropriate behavior or excessive violence. Many realistic books containing violence have inner-city settings. For example, Frank Bonham's *Durango Street* describes the hero's bid for survival in a world of grim gang violence and drugs, a world where he could be used for "bayonet practice." Drugs also play a significant role in Walter Dean Myers's *It Ain't All for Nothin'!* and *Scorpions*. Some people believe that children should read about the reality of drugs in the world around them, while others believe that the minds of children should not be contaminated by the mention of drugs.

Profanity

Profanity and other language objectionable to some people are also controversial. What is considered objectionable has changed over the years, however. Mary Q. Steele (31) describes her own experiences with writing. In the 1950s, editors deleted "hecks" and "darns" from manuscripts written for children, but now, a more permissive climate encourages authors to write relevant dialogue. Ken Donelson's (10) survey on censorship reports that a committee unsuccessfully challenged the placement of Katherine Paterson's *The Great Gilly Hopkins* in an elementary library because the author used language that the committee members considered objectionable.

In 1990, a teacher in Donna Norton's Children's Literature class successfully met a challenge to Paterson's *Bridge to Terabithia.* A parent wanted the book removed from the class reading list because of mild profanity. The teacher successfully defended the book for literary merit, especially the importance of themes.

Family Problems and Other Controversial Issues

Strong young protagonists in contemporary novels frequently overcome obstacles related to family problems caused by adult family members. The antagonists are frequently adults who have less than desirable qualities. The lack of strong adult role models in many contemporary books is also controversial. For example, Robert Unsworth (34) praises the fully developed fathers in several recently published books, but he also states, "The bad news is the portrayal of that Dad at home. A grander group of adulterers, philanderers, child abusers, wife-beaters, drunks, and all-around ne-er-do-wells hasn't been seen since the fall of Rome" (p. 48).

In her review of Brock Cole's *The Goats,* Anita Silvey (30) states, "Like all powerful books, *The Goats* will repel some readers and attract others. Critics of the book are concerned with the absence of positive adult characters—as was the case with *Harriet the Spy*—and the change in the young protagonists from innocents to thieves" (p. 23). Silvey goes on to praise the book, saying that the publication of the novel "signifies that we are still creating children's books that affirm the human spirit and the ability of the individual to rise above adversity" (p. 23). Other issues that can become controversial in children's books include viewpoints on war and peace, religion, death, and racial matters. (Chapter 11 discusses critics' concerns about books related to Black Americans, Hispanics, Native Americans, and Asian Americans.)

ISSUE

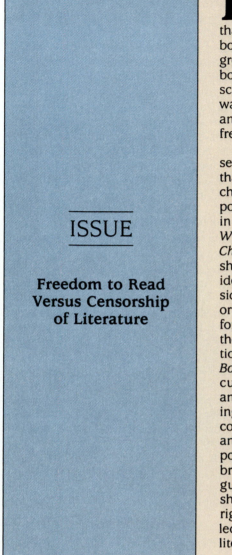

Freedom to Read Versus Censorship of Literature

RESEARCH ARTICLES, such as those written by Ken Donelson,[1] show that censorship of children's books is increasing. Organized group efforts are focusing on both children's literature and school textbooks. Some groups want considerable censorship and some groups advocate freedom of choice.

Patrick Shannon[2] identifies several positions on censorship that are currently influencing children's literature. First is the position on censorship reflected in Mel and Norma Gabler's *What Are They Teaching Our Children?*[3] This type of censorship encourages parents to identify materials that they consider antifamily, anti-Christian, or anti-American, and then to force objectionable books off the shelves. Second is the position expressed in Cal Thomas's *Book Burning.*[4] Thomas accuses librarians, publishers, and school officials of censoring Christian and traditional content from school curricula and library shelves. Third is the position of the American Library Association,[5] which argues for the end of all censorship of books, for the readers' right to choose, and for the selection of books to be based on literary merit. Fourth is the position of the Council on Interracial Books for children,[6] which objects to the biases in school textbooks. This group recommends that selection of library books be based on social concerns for equality and justice as well as for literary merit.

In all likelihood, the issue of censorship will continue through the 1990s, as concerned adults on both sides of the question argue whether literature and educators should indoctrinate the mores and morals of a community or expand the ideas and understandings of children through exposure to and discussion of a variety of books and ideas.

[1]Donelson, Ken. "Almost 13 Years of Book Protests—Now What?" *School Library Journal* 31 (March 1985): 93–98.

[2]Shannon, Patrick. "Overt and Covert Censorship of Children's Books." *The New Advocate* 2 (Spring 1989): 97–104.

[3]Gabler, Mel, and Norma Gabler. *What Are They Teaching Our Children?* Wheaton, Ill.: Victor, 1985.

[4]Thomas, Cal. *Book Burning.* Westchester, Ill.: Crossways, 1983.

[5]American Library Association. "The Freedom to Read." *Bill of Rights.* Chicago, Ill.: American Library Association, 1972.

[6]Council on Interracial Books for Children. *Human (and Anti-Human) Values in Children's Books.* New York: Council on Interracial Books for Children, 1976.

GUIDELINES FOR SELECTING CONTROVERSIAL FICTION

The question of how "realistic" realistic fiction should be is answered differently by various groups. Historically, schools and the literature that children read in them have often been under the pressures of censorship, as different groups have tried to impose their values on all children. While modern censors might laugh at the literary concerns of the Puritans, there is still concern over appropriate subjects for children's literature. When children's books explore sexuality, violence, moral problems, racism, and religious beliefs, they are likely to be thought objectionable by those who believe that children should not be exposed to such ideas.

Teachers and librarians need to be knowledgeable about their communities, subjects that may prove controversial, and the merits of controversial books they would like to share with children. John M. Kean and Carl Personke (20) say:

> [E]ven though educators attempt to avoid controversy by selecting only 'safe' books that they believe won't offend anyone, someone is likely to be offended. . . . Everybody has a value position that he considers important and that he thinks the schools ought to perpetuate for his children and for other people's children. When educators have an empathetic understanding of the community, they will be better able to work with parents—helping parents to view the wide range of books that are appropriate for children, rather than telling them which are the 'right' materials. (p. 340)

Day Ann K. McClenathan (22) suggests that wholesale avoidance of books containing controversial topics, in addition to encouraging overt censorship, is inappropriate because (1) books about relevant sociological or psychological problems can give young people opportunities to grow in their thinking processes and to extend their experiences; (2) problems in books can provide some children with opportunities for identification and allow others opportunities to empathize with their peers; (3) problems in books invite decisions, elicit opinions, and afford opportunities to take positions on issues.

Given the controversial issues and the need for books that are relevant to the interests, concerns, and problems of today's children, you should consider some guidelines when choosing realistic fiction for children. Day Ann K. McClenathan provides a useful guide for selecting books that might be considered controversial. Following is a summary of her guidelines:

1. Know exactly what might be considered controversial. This means you have to really read the book. You can't rely on the opinion of someone else or even on a good review. As a member of a school and a community, you must be able to appraise specific content. What might offend in one community would go unnoticed or unchallenged in another.
2. Ascertain the author's point of view and weigh the power of the positive influence against exposure to a theme some people perceive negatively. For example, if an author writes about the drug culture but events in the story clearly point up harmful effects of drug use, then you may miss an opportunity for healthy shaping of attitudes.
3. Apply literary criteria to the selection of library books in such ways that vulnerability to the arguments of would-be censors is at least partially reduced by the obvious overall quality of book choices. Occasionally, teachers and librarians select books of inferior quality because they deal with topics having a high interest for middle grade or older children. This sometimes happens with books involving experimentations with sex. The information in such books may be harmless (or even useful), but the books may fall short of accepted literary criteria. If a book is then targeted because it offends community groups, it will be difficult to defend, and having it in your school collection will suggest that considerations other than literary quality determine choices. In addition, examine books that attempt to counter stereotypes for what can be thought of as the overcorrection syndrome. Sometimes, in a passion to change images, authors work too hard on issues and neglect plot and characterization.
4. Know and be able to explain your purpose in using a particular book. Have answers ready to the following questions:
   a. Will the topic be understood by the group with which I intend to use the book?
   b. What merits of this particular book have influenced me to use it rather than another book of comparable literary, sociological, or psychological importance?
   c. Is the book an acceptable model in terms of writing style and use of language?
   d. Are my objectives in using this book educationally defensible (for example, presentation or clarification of information, extension of experiences, refinement of attitudes, promotion of reading habits)?
5. In order to clarify and maintain your objectivity, review and be prepared to discuss both sides of the censorship question.

CRITERIA FOR EVALUATING REALISTIC FICTION

In addition to the basic literary criteria, high-quality contemporary realistic fiction should satisfy the following requirements, as suggested by Sheldon Root (27), and previous discussions in this chapter:

1. The content should be honestly presented; sensationalizing and capitalizing on the novelty of a subject should be avoided.
2. A story should expose personal and social values central to our culture, at the same time revealing how overt expression of those values may have changed.

3. The story should allow readers to draw personal conclusions from the evidence; the author should respect the readers' intelligence.
4. The author should recognize that today's young readers are in the process of growing toward adult sophistication.
5. The language and syntax should help reveal the background and the nature of characters and situations.
6. The author should write in a hopeful tone; a story should communicate in an honest way that there is hope in this world.
7. Children's literature should reflect sensitivity to the needs and rights of girls and boys without preference, bias, or negative stereotypes. Males should be allowed to show emotions, and females should be able to demonstrate courage and ambition. Girls and boys should not be denied access to certain occupations because of their sex. Children should sense that they can be successful in many occupations.
8. If violence is included in a story, the author should treat the subject appropriately. Does the author give the necessary facts? Are both sides of the conflict portrayed fully, fairly, and honestly? Is the writing developed with feeling and emotion? Does the author help children develop a perspective about the subject?
9. A story should satisfy children's basic needs and provide them with increased insights into their own problems and social relationships.
10. A story should provide children with enjoyment.

LITERARY ELEMENTS

Contemporary realistic fiction should meet the basic literary criteria discussed in Chapter 3. A conflict that could really occur in our contemporary world should be integral to the plot, characterization, setting, and theme. In realistic contemporary settings, authors should thoroughly develop internal and external conflicts as well as characters so that readers can understand the characters' responses. In this section, consider how several authors develop credible stories through their depiction of conflict, their characterization, their style, and their themes.

Plot

The conflicts at the center of plots in contemporary realistic fiction may arise from external forces, as the characters try to overcome problems related to families, peers, or the society around them; or they may arise as the characters try to overcome problems related to inner conflicts. However, internal conflicts often result from conflict with external forces. Consequently, person-against-self conflicts are common in contemporary realistic fiction.

As in traditional literature, conflict in contemporary realistic fiction may involve protagonists in quests (17). Caron Lee Cohen (8) identifies four major components in the development of person-against-self conflicts: (1) problem, (2) struggle, (3) realization, and (4) achievement of peace or truth. She says:

> The point at which the struggle wanes and the inner strength emerges seems to be the point of self-realization. That point leads immediately to the final sense of peace or truth that is the resolution of the quest. The best books are those which move readers and cause them to identify with the character's struggle. (p. 28)

Of course, if readers are to understand the conflict and empathize with characters' responses, the characters themselves must be convincingly developed. The pressures they experience and the motives they act upon must be very clear. According to Hazel Rochman (26), the age of protagonists in realistic fiction for older children is not so important as the authors' convincing depictions of common hopes, fears, and important choices.

As an example of credible conflict, consider the person-against-self conflict that Paula Fox develops in *One-Eyed Cat*. Fox sets the stage for the forthcoming conflict by describing an incident in which Uncle Hilary gives Ned a loaded Daisy air rifle for his eleventh birthday. Ned's father, the Reverend Wallace, forbids his son to use the gun until he is at least fourteen. Instead of hiding the gun, Ned's father takes it to the attic, where it can easily be found. A conflicting relationship of trust is developed as Ned considers, "The painful thing was that, though Ned didn't always trust his father, his father trusted him, and that seemed to him unfair, although he couldn't explain why it was so" (p. 40).

Ned cannot resist the temptation of the gun, and fires it, shooting a wild stray cat. The person-against-self conflict deepens as Fox vividly describes Ned's fear and accompanying guilt when he sees the "gap, the dried blood, the little worm of mucus in the corner next to the cat's nose where the eye had been" (p. 70). The author's choice of metaphor explains Ned's emotional response as "the gun was like a splinter in his mind" (p. 90). Ned's quest becomes to save the wild cat from sickness and starvation during the approaching winter. It also becomes a quest to overcome his sense of guilt and remorse and to tell the truth about what has happened.

Fox's novel follows Cohen's four major components. The problem results because Ned betrays his parent's trust; the struggle continues as Ned feels increasingly guilty because of his lies as he tries to save the wounded animal; the point of self-realization begins when Ned feels relief as he confesses his guilt to a critically ill older neighbor; and peace and truth finally result on a moonlit night when Ned confesses his actions to his mother after they see a one-eyed cat and kittens emerging from the woods. In a satisfying conclusion, Ned and his mother exchange revealing confessions.

This book may be successful because the conflict appeals to more than one age or ability group. Most readers can empathize with the desire to commit a forbidden action and the terror of possible consequences. More mature readers can appreciate the psychological portrayal of a boy as he successfully accomplishes a hurdle in the maturation process.

Marion Dane Bauer's *On My Honor* develops a person-against-self conflict that is similar to the conflict in *One-Eyed Cat*. Consequently, the two books provide excellent comparisons. For example, the problem results for Bauer's character, Joel, because Joel betrays his parents' trust and swims with his friend in a treacherous river. The struggle continues as Joel feels increasing guilt, tries not to accept his friend's disappearance and probable death, and blames his father for allowing the two boys to go on a bike ride in the first place. The point of self-realization begins when Joel admits that Tony drowned and realizes that his father is not the cause of his problem. Although the seriousness of the problem does not allow complete resolution, peace and truth begin after Joel sobbingly tells his father the whole truth. One of Bauer's themes, we have to live with our choices, is revealed when Joel's father says, "But, we all made choices today, Joel. You, me, Tony. Tony's the only one who doesn't have to live with his choice" (p. 88). Claudia Lepman-Logan (21) maintains that books with such strong moral choices are excellent because "Young readers need books that do more than entertain them. Books like *On My Honor* use readers as active participants, drawing them in on both emotional and intellectual levels" (p. 110).

Characterization

The characterization of Ned in Fox's *One-Eyed Cat* is an integral part of the conflict. For example, Fox describes Ned's actions, clarifies his response to his parents and to the wounded cat, and reveals his thoughts during his traumatic experiences. Readers know Ned intimately. They understand his hopes, his fears, his past, his present, and his relationships with his parents.

Complex characterizations that lead to self-discovery and personal relationships are also important in Cynthia Voigt's books about the Tillerman family. In *Homecoming,* Voigt focuses on the children's experiences after their emotionally ill mother deserts them. In the sequel, *Dicey's Song,* Voigt focuses on four children and their grandmother: a young girl who is trying to hold her family together, a learning-disabled girl who has a gift for music, a gifted boy who tries to hide his giftedness because he does not want to be different, a younger brother who strikes out in anger, and a grandmother whom the townspeople consider eccentric.

In *A Solitary Blue,* Voigt focuses on Jeff Greene, a friend of Dicey Tillerman, as he faces his mother's desertion and his father's inability to interact on a personal basis. In *Sons from Afar,* Voigt continues the story of the Tillerman family, as James and Sammy search for the father who deserted them. Although the boys do not discover the father of their dreams, they do develop understanding of and appreciation for their close family relationships. In all of Voigt's books, as in Fox's *One-Eyed Cat,* readers discover that the protagonists have many-sided personalities like their own. Readers come to know these characters intimately, sharing their hopes, fears, pasts, and presents.

Throughout her books, Voigt effectively uses symbolism in her characterizations. Her use of symbolism associated with the blue heron is especially meaningful in *A Solitary Blue*. Consider the implications for Jeff's character in the following examples. When Jeff has low self-esteem, he views the heron as a creature that occupies "its own insignificant corner of the landscape in a timeless, long-legged solitude" (p. 45). Later, when Jeff feels angry, broken, and bruised due to his mother's behavior, he again views the heron;

"'Just leave me alone,' the heron seemed to be saying. Jeff rowed away, down the quiet creek. The bird did not watch him go" (p. 91). Finally, when Jeff discovers that he is a worthwhile person, he realizes that the solitary heron reminds him of his best friend, Dicey Tillerman. When Dicey laughingly states that she was thinking that the bird reminded her of Jeff, Jeff is flattered by the comparison. Jeff knows that he, like the heron, is a "rare bird," with staying power and a gentle spirit.

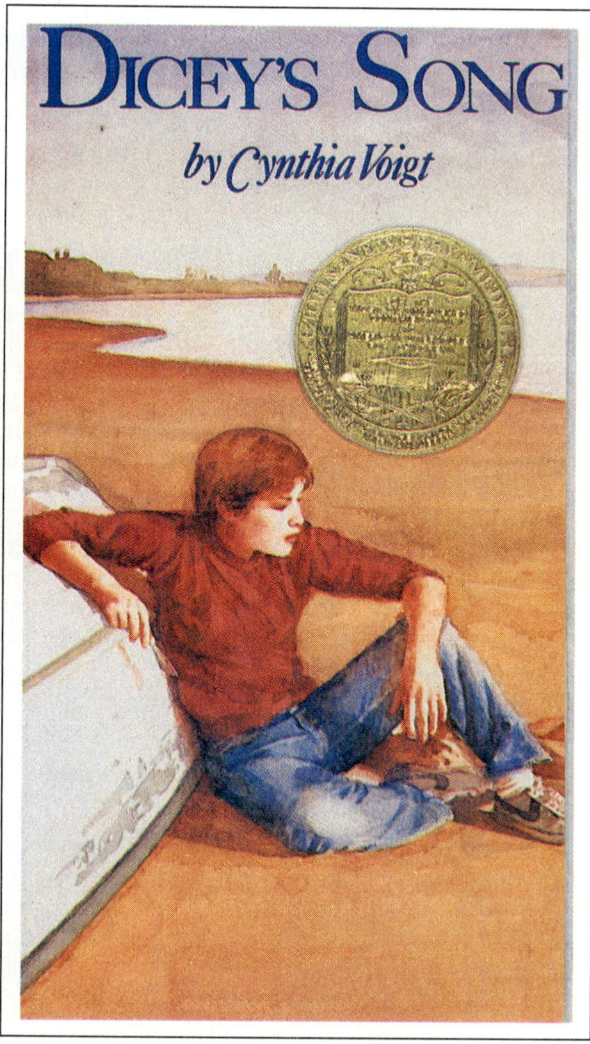

Symbolism enhances characterization as a girl makes discoveries about herself. (Illustration by James Shefcik from *Dicey's Song* by Cynthia Voigt is used by permission of Atheneum Publishers. Illustrations copyright © 1982 James Shefcik.)

The synthesis of symbolism and character traits is equally important in *Dicey's Song*. For example, a careful tracing of musical selections, including the title, shows that the author uses music to develop characterization and to illustrate changes in personal development. Likewise, a dilapidated boat and a tree provide important symbolic meanings.

Norma Fox Mazer also synthesizes symbols and characters in *After the Rain*. Mazer uses the symbolism of rain at the end of the book both to reveal and to review Rachel's changing feelings for her grandfather, Izzy. For example, after Izzy's death, Mazer states:

> Then, behind her closed eyes, she sees a road, a narrow sandy road with tall trees on both sides, and she sees herself walking down this road in the rain. . .dark, blue-green of the trees. . .hard, dark lines of water sleeting down. . .nothing else exists but the wet road, the trees lashed by wind, and herself, a solitary figure walking in the rain (p. 267).

Later, Rachel uses these words when talking about Izzy to her brother Jeremy:

> 'Anyway, I'm glad that I finally ______,' she begins, and then she can't say it, can't say she's finally glad she got to know him. The sky is clear and cloudless, the trees are blazing purely with autumn color, but she is all at once in a storm. Hard rain again, this time with thunder and lightening. This time, not grief but anger. Anger at Izzy, hard strikes of anger splitting the blue sky she's created out of their feeling for each other. Anger for all those years he let slip by when they could have been knowing each other, when she could have loved him so much. (p. 278)

After Rachel has spent days searching for and finally finding Izzy's handprint and initials on the bridge he helped construct, "They are here now she thinks, and they will still be here years from now, when she, herself, is old. And then, though today the whole sky is covered by gray clouds, for a moment she feels the sun on her head, as warm as a loving hand" (p. 288). Mature readers enjoy the development of and the interactions with such characters as Dicey, Jeff, and Rachel. The symbolism makes the reading experience even more vivid and meaningful.

Style

An effective literary style greatly enhances plot and characterization in realistic fiction. Vivid descriptions, believable dialogue, symbolism, figures of speech, and other stylistic techniques subtly provide readers with in-depth understanding of characters and situations. In *Dicey's Song,* for example, Cynthia Voigt develops a synthesis of symbols and character traits; allusions to familiar music are among Voigt's symbolic means of emphasizing changes in the character's personal development.

Authors' styles of writing can develop descriptions that appeal to the senses, that awaken readers to the emotional impact of situations, and that suggest the moods. These moods in contemporary realistic fiction range from terror to humor. Consider, for example, how Tormod Haugen uses short, choppy sentences and descriptive words to create the image of *The Night Birds,* the birds that Jake believes live in his closet and that symbolize a seven-year-old boy's conflicts and inner terrors:

> The night birds. He remembered the first time they were there. But in a way they'd been there as long as he could remember. Suddenly one night he'd woken up. Something had woken him. Then he heard them. Buzzing in the air from all sides. He saw them too. Like black shadows, even blacker than the night. They popped out of the dark and just were there. Big, flapping wings with feathers that made a rushing sound. Red, staring eyes. As if they had fire in them. And beaks that were open, big and dangerous. They wanted to peck at him. Closer and closer, thousands of them. The night was full of birds. The darkness was nothing but birds. His room was bursting with birds. They wanted to get him. He screamed and got under the quilt. The first birds struck the bed with their claws and tried to pull off his quilt. He heard the birds scream, loud and shrill. Louder than he could. (p. 34)

Other authors use language to create humorous moods. Humor is an important element in Beverly Keller's *No Beasts! No Children!* In a tale about family adjustment following divorce, Keller develops humor through irony and descriptions of preposterous situations. First, there is the irony of the divorce itself. The children's father is a marriage counselor who is trying to find himself. Second, there are preposterous situations caused by three mischievous children, three huge dogs, an extremely strict housekeeper who dislikes animals, a landlord who dislikes both dogs and children, and a mule with white stripes.

In *Anastasia on Her Own,* Lois Lowry does not rely on descriptions of preposterous situations to develop humor. Instead, she highlights the humor in a realistic contemporary situation. Two busy professional parents are trying to manage a household and raise two children, and an enthusiastic, determined young protagonist believes that housekeeping can be easy if the family can only develop and closely follow a nonsexist household schedule. An unexpected consulting contract temporarily removes Anastasia's mother from the household and allows Anastasia an opportunity to test her theories.

Lowry develops humor by contrasting Anastasia's dream world with the world of reality; by describing the consequences when a naive, but determined, young girl approaches household tasks that are beyond her ability; and by describing the consequences of unexpected interruptions. Chapter one, for example, contains Anastasia's full-page schedule, which details hourly tasks from 7:00 A.M. to 8:00 P.M. In contrast, the eighth schedule in the book reads simply:

> Housekeeping Schedule
> Aftermath
> Clean up. For hours and hours and hours.
> Cry. (p. 122)

There is the humor in contrasts between young Anastasia's fantasy dreams of her first date and the actuality of thirteen-year-old Steve Harvey: "She had envisioned someone tall and handsome—someone who looked a lot like Lawrence Olivier in Wuthering Heights—maybe wearing a tuxedo and holding a corsage in his hand" (p. 113). Instead, Steve wears a sweatshirt bearing the words PSYCHOTIC STATE, discusses chicken pox scabs, stuffs peanuts into his mouth, talks with his mouth full, and tells her that her first attempt at adult entertaining was horrible. Well-written stories of this sort, with convincingly developed plots and characterizations, make many books of contemporary realistic fiction highly popular with children.

SUBJECTS IN REALISTIC FICTION

The literary techniques that authors use to develop credible realistic fiction are discussed further in the following sections of the text. In order to assist educators in recommending or choosing specific books for children, these sections emphasize personality and social development in children. The various subject matters within the genre of contemporary realistic fiction encompass a wide range of themes.

Family Life

The family stories of the late 1930s through the early 1960s depict some of the strongest, warmest family relationships in contemporary realistic fiction for children. Today's children still enjoy the warmth and humor represented by the families in Elizabeth Enright's *Thimble Summer,* Eleanor Estes's *The Moffats,* Sydney Taylor's *All-of-a-Kind Family,* and Madeleine L'Engle's *Meet the Austins.* The actions of the characters suggest that security is gained when family members work together, that each member has responsibility to other members, that consideration for others is desirable, and that family unity and loyalty can overcome hard times and peer conflicts.

Since the early 1960s, many changes have taken place in the characterizations of the American family in realistic fiction. Authors writing in the 1970s, 1980s and 1990s often focused on the need to overcome family disturbances, as children and adults adjusted to new social realities. Death of one or both parents, foster families, single-parent families, children of unmarried females, the disruptions caused by divorce and remarriage, and child abuse are some of the issues related to children and their families that now appear in contemporary realistic fiction for children.

Such literature may help children realize that many family units other than the traditional one are common and legitimate in our society today. Children may also see that problems often can be solved if family members work together. Even when depicting the most disturbing of relationships, authors of realistic fiction may show a strong need for family unity and a desire to keep at least some of the members together.

Authors of realistic stories about family disturbances use several literary techniques to create credible plots and characters. Often, they look at painful and potentially destructive situations and feelings that are common in society today. These situations are usually familiar to readers, who may have experienced similar situations, who may have known someone who had such experiences, or who may fear that they will have similar experiences. Authors often tell such stories from the perspective of a child or children involved. First-person or limited omniscient point of view from a child's perspective can successfully depict characters' emotional and behavioral reactions as the children first discover a problem, experience a wide range of personal difficulties and emotions when they try to change or understand the situation, and finally arrive at acceptance of the situation.

The characterization may portray the vulnerability of the characters, create sympathy for them, and describe how they handle jolting disruptions and personal discoveries that affect their lives. Symbolism and allusion may emphasize conflicts and characters. Authors often use characters' reactions to change, trouble, and new discoveries to trace the development of better relationships with others or positive personal growth.

Some authors, however—such as those trying to make a point about child abuse—use specific situations or discoveries to allow children to escape from all reality. A family member may be the antagonist in these realistic stories about family life, or the antagonist may be an outside

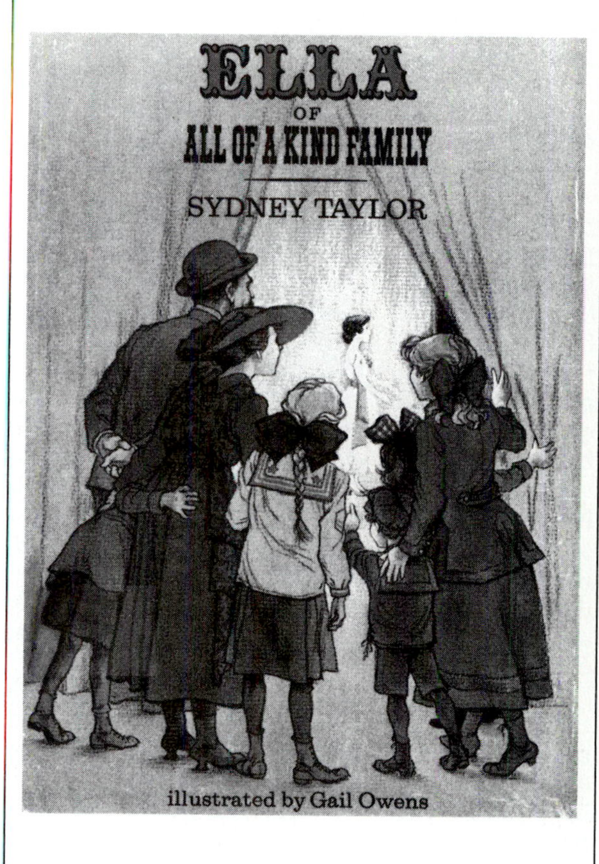

Sydney Taylor creates family stories that show warmth, humor, and strong family relationships. (Cover illustration by Gail Owens. From *Ella of All-of-a-Kind Family,* by Sydney Taylor. Copyright © 1978 by Sidney Taylor. Illustrations copyright © 1978 by Gail Owens. Reprinted by permission of the publisher, E. P. Dutton.)

force, such as death of a parent, divorce, or moving to a new location. To relieve the impact of painful situations, authors may add humor to their characterizations or plots. Humor can make situations bearable, create sympathy for characters, or clarify the nature of confrontations.

Divorce and Remarriage. In Peggy Mann's *My Dad Lives in a Downtown Hotel,* Joey experiences a series of strong emotional reactions to his parents' divorce. First, he believes the separation is his fault. Mann develops the strength of these feelings through Joey's actions. Joey makes out a list of promises he will keep if his father returns and delivers them to his father. When his promises have no effect on the situation, Joey's emotional reactions change. Joey goes through a period of hating his father and feeling confused. Mann suggests that Joey accepts the change in his family life when he can enjoy being with his father during their Sunday visits. A popular theme in stories about divorce is acceptance of oneself and the changes in one's life.

In *Dear Mr. Henshaw,* Beverly Cleary effectively uses letters and diary entries written by her sixth-grade hero, Leigh Botts, to develop believable characters and plot and to show changes in Leigh as he begins to accept the actuality of his parents' divorce. As a classroom assignment, Leigh sends his favorite author a list of ten questions. Mr. Henshaw answers Leigh's questions and sends Leigh a list of ten questions that he wants Leigh to answer about himself.

At first, Leigh refuses to answer the questions. Then, his mother insists that because Mr. Henshaw answered Leigh's questions, Leigh must answer Mr. Henshaw's questions. The answers to the questions allow Cleary an opportunity to provide important background information and to reveal Leigh's feelings about himself, his family, and his parents' divorce. Eventually, Leigh begins to write a diary—both because Mr. Henshaw suggests it and because Leigh's mother refuses to fix the television.

By midpoint in the book, the diary entries begin to change and Leigh realizes changes in his own character:

> I don't have to pretend to write to Mr. Henshaw anymore. I have learned to say what I think on a piece of paper. And I don't hate my father either. I can't hate him. Maybe things would be easier if I could. (p. 73)

The entries seem believable because Cleary includes both humorous and painful experiences that are important in Leigh's life.

In *The Animal, the Vegetable, and John D. Jones,* author Betsy Byars focuses on the reactions of three children to painful changes in the family. Clara and Deanie's father asks the widow he loves and her son to share a summer vacation with him and his daughters. The two sisters, who had been experiencing sibling rivalry, confront an outside antagonist in the person of a boy named John D. Jones. Byars describes him as a worthy opponent: He is bright, sophisticated, and conceited. John D. is writing a book of advice for his inferiors, who incidentally, are all other children. John D. is also vulnerable, however, and perhaps sensitive. His book is about functioning in a hostile world.

Byars describes a series of incidents that emphasize the parents' dilemma, imply their inability to handle the situation, and create sympathy for the characters. Whenever the adults plan a happy excursion, something goes wrong. At a cookout, the only edible hamburger falls in the sand, and during a visit to an amusement park Clara escapes her family only to become sick after riding the Space Cyclone and then seeing John D. with a huge sundae. Although Byars's descriptions are humorous, the story contains some hostile undercurrents. Byars uses a near tragedy to focus the attention of the characters on the importance of others. The themes of the story are that we all need other people in our lives and we need to work at interpersonal relationships. The reactions of the characters indicate that the characters have learned a great deal about interpersonal relationships.

In Carol Lea Benjamin's *The Wicked Stepdog,* twelve-year-old Lou is afraid of losing her father's love when he presents her with a new stepmother and a new "stepdog." Benjamin's first-person narrative from Lou's viewpoint emphasizes Lou's sometimes painful and sometimes humorous reactions to her changed family. Lou's changing responses to her stepmother's golden retriever symbolize her gradual acceptance of new circumstances. At first, she hates to walk the dog, but by the end of the story, when she meets a boy who also walks a dog, stepdog-walking has become one of Lou's favorite pastimes.

Ann Fine develops the importance of understanding the feelings of others and accepting changes in one's life in *My War with Goggle-Eyes.* Fine's heroine tries to help another girl accept a possible stepfather by telling her own story, in which the girl tries to sabotage her mother's boyfriend every time he tries to gain her acceptance. The ending shows that understanding is possible.

Single-Parent Families. Single-parent families have always existed, but recent realistic fiction for children portrays such families more often, and sometimes more candidly, than did most realistic fiction in the past. In contemporary novels for children, some of the families are doing quite well, while others face serious problems due to the lack of emotional and economic support from a mother or a father.

A family's struggle to survive without one parent is popular in contemporary realistic fiction. Authors may suggest that the experience strengthens the children in the family or that the experience causes so many difficulties that the children find coping impossible. In Vera and Bill Cleaver's *Where the Lilies Bloom,* a fourteen-year-old girl experiences conflict between her desire to keep a promise she made to her dying father and her developing realization that she must break that promise in order to ensure her family's survival.

Although Mary Call's father dies quite early in the plot, the Cleavers characterize him plausibly, as a person who lives by a strong moral and family code. He demands that his daughter take pride in the family name, instill that pride in her brothers and sisters, and hold the family together without accepting charity. Later, this promise becomes a crucial element of the plot and in Mary Call's character development. The authors develop a believable and interesting conflict as Mary Call tries to do as her father demanded, but gradually realizes that she must accept help if she is to gain the knowledge she needs and improve her family's welfare.

This story lacks sentimentality. Mary Call recognizes her father's weaknesses and eventually realizes that his judgment about his oldest daughter and the despised neighbor, Kaiser Pease, was in error. The Cleavers lighten the almost insurmountable odds against survival by adding touches of humor. This is especially true in the sequel, *Trial Valley,* as a more mature Mary Call copes with both family problems and suitors. (You may find it interesting to compare the characteristics of this contemporary female protagonist with the Victorian female protagonist in Charlotte Yonge's *The Daisy Chain.*)

Jenny Davis's *Good-Bye and Keep Cold* begins with death and continues with making adjustments in a single-parent family. Edda, a girl in the

A child leaves her own harsh reality for a make-believe dollhouse world. (From *The Bears' House,* by Marilyn Sachs, Copyright © 1971 by Marilyn Sachs. Reprinted by permission of Doubleday & Company, Inc.)

Kentucky mining area, first faces her father's accidental death in a strip mine and then grows up as her mother and younger brother must also face the traumatic changes in their lives. Davis uses nature to introduce the conflicting emotions. On the day of the funeral, young Edda retreats to Heaven, the favorite forest sanctuary of Edda and her father. The conflict and grief build as she first watches the glasslike water splash and glide over flat rocks and then:

> Suddenly there were birds screaming overhead, loud, horrible screams, like people in pain. I started screaming back at them. . . .Mama was sleeping in her dark room up at the house, and Daddy was dead. There was no one to stop me, and that in itself made it all the more frightening and necessary to do. (p. 22)

Davis's story follows a family's healing process and deals with mature problems. Analyze the symbolic meaning of Davis's title which is based on Robert Frost's poem, "Good-bye and Keep Cold." Consider the meaning for Edda in the final paragraph. What does Edda mean when she thinks to herself:

> Mama walked off from the people who raised her and never looked back. I don't want to do that. But I do want to be free of them, want them in perspective, want myself apart. I need to shake them loose, let go. Charlie says everybody has to raise their parents. Is that true? He says the time comes for all of us when we have to kiss them good-bye and trust them to be okay on their own. I've done the best I could with mine. Good-bye, you all, and good luck. Good-bye and keep cold. (p. 210)

In Marilyn Sachs's *The Bears' House,* detailed portrayal of a harsh reality gives the plot and the protagonist's responses full credibility. Five children live in a crowded apartment, their mother is emotionally disturbed, and their father deserts the family. The children's distrust of the adult world is expressed through their fears of being placed in foster homes and their lies to their social worker. Sachs contrasts the harsh reality of nine-year-old Fran Ellen's life with the beautiful make-believe place of her fantasies. When Fran Ellen sits in front of the dollhouse in her fourth-grade classroom, she can visit the Bear family and sit on Pappa Bear's lap when she feels unhappy. The conclusion of the story illustrates that contemporary realistic fiction may not have a happy-ever-after ending: Fran Ellen withdraws into her make-believe world, where she has found a way to survive in frightening and bewildering circumstances.

In *The Night Swimmers,* Betsy Byars uses a painful and possibly destructive situation to highlight a young girl's personal and social development and her acceptance of difficult discoveries. Retta's mother has died. She and her younger brothers are being reared by their father, who works nights and is more concerned about developing his career as a singer/composer than about attending to his children. Byars chronicles Retta's personal growth by describing her feelings after her mother's death, the moment when she understands her father's career goals (in reaction to her mother's death he composed a hit song but did not pay attention to the children), her changing feelings as she tries to be a mother to her two younger brothers, and her final realization that she must accept her father as he is, not as she would like him to be.

Byars uses humor to highlight some of the situations and to look at the painful moments. Retta discovers how a mother should act by observing mothers in the supermarket and she gains cooking skills by watching television commercials. The reactions of Retta and her younger brother, Roy, to their own final discoveries may be the most poignant moments in the book. Roy discovers that the Bowlwater Plant is not the enormous and wondrous vegetation of his imagination. Instead, it is a smelly and ugly chemical factory. Retta realizes that their father is so obsessed with stardom that he cannot relate to his children as she would like. Roy expresses their discoveries effectively when he compares swallowing a hard truth about life with Popeye's swallowing his spinach: Both experiences make you stronger.

Authors who place their protagonists in single-parent families frequently develop plots in which the characters go through unusual circumstances to learn about themselves or their parents. For example, in *The Moonlight Man,* Paula Fox places Catherine in the summer care of her father. As Catherine goes through a series of adventures with her novelist father, who is often intoxicated, she learns to accept his foibles and discovers characteristics about her mother and herself that she had never realized. By the end of the story, she realizes that it is sometimes very difficult to love someone, but we may still love someone if we dislike him. This theme is reinforced when Catherine realizes:

> She had disliked her father that day. Yet she loved him. She went to bed and hit the pillow hard. Love, love, love, everyone was always saying. As though it were the

easiest thing! The words she had shouted at him in the swing came back to her. Her father had been right; she hadn't known she had it in her to be so mean. (p. 149)

Many of the stories written about single-parent families develop themes in which children become stronger as they make discoveries about themselves and the adults in their lives. As in *The Moonlight Man,* some protagonists learn to accept the foibles of separated fathers or mothers and even grow closer to their parents. These stories depict changes from the realistic fiction of the 1950s. The family structures, life-styles, values, and problems reflect contemporary concerns and issues.

Child Abuse and Foster Homes. As reflected in children's literature, the adult world may provide cruel experiences rather than happy and secure environments for development. The American Library Association's bibliography of literature related to child abuse includes thirty-nine titles that reflect chronic child abuse, relating to violence, sexual harassment, or neglect. According to Betsy Hearne (16):

> Some of the books are grim, but most offer the hope or outright assertion that children can break out of tormenting situations through determined, independent actions. Sharing these books with children encourages exactly the kind of awareness that might help a victim of child abuse or help a friend help out. (p. 1261).

Marion Dane Bauer explores the sinister side of foster care in *Foster Child*. Twelve-year-old Renny is placed in a foster home when her great-grandmother becomes too ill to care for her. Her foster father, Pop Beck, expresses sexual interest in the girls who are staying at his farm. Readers realize the danger in this situation when Renny and her friend run away and try to live in the great-grandmother's empty house.

Incest, possibly the most harmful father-daughter relationship, is the focus in Katherine Martin's *Night Riding*. Martin tells the story through the viewpoint of Prin, a girl who befriends a new neighbor. Through her interactions with the new girl, Prin discovers child abuse.

More hopeful treatments of foster care and child abuse appear in Patricia MacLachlan's *Mama One, Mama Two,* a picture storybook that depicts the warm, loving relationship between a foster mother and her foster child, and in Betsy Byars's *Cracker Jackson,* in which an eleven-year-old boy manages to convince adults that his former babysitter and her daughter are being abused by the husband and father. As in her other books, Byars uses humor and compassion to lighten the fear in the situation. As you read Bauer's *Foster Child,* MacLachlan's *Mama One, Mama Two,* and Byars's *Cracker Jackson,* consider each author's possible purpose. Consider, too, how each author develops plots, characters, settings, and themes. In addition, consider the possible responses of young readers.

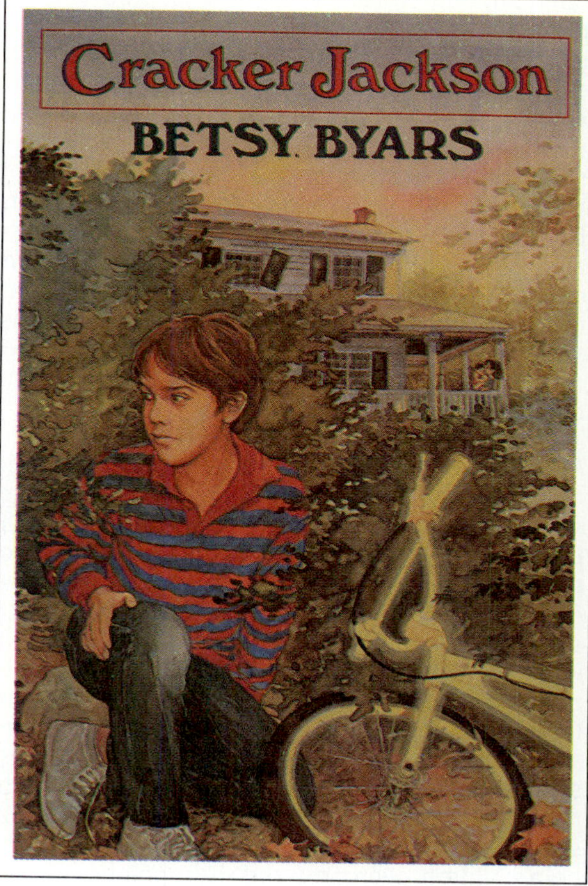

Humor and compassion lighten a story about child abuse. (From *Cracker Jackson* by Betsy Byars. Jacket illustration by Diane de Groat. Text copyright © Betsy Byars, 1985. Jacket illustration copyright © Viking Penguin, Inc., 1985. Reprinted by permission of Viking Penguin Inc.)

Growing Up

Children face numerous challenges as they venture from the family environment and begin the often difficult process of growing up. Forming and maintaining relationships with peers is one important task. In addition, children may need to overcome emotional problems, to develop or recover self-esteem, and to identify their roles in their widening world. As children grow older, they may feel self-conscious about their changing bodies and developing sexuality. They must confront other facts of life as well, including survival and the inevitability of death. Books that explore children's concerns can stimulate discussion with children who are facing these same concerns. Such books also let children know that they are not alone and that other children experience and overcome the same problems.

Peer Relationships. Children, like adults, need the shared understanding, pleasure, challenge, sense of equality, and security that friendship with peers provides. Peer relationships involve many of the joys and sorrows with which children become familiar in family life, but they also expand understandings of other people and the world in ways that familiar family ties cannot. Contemporary realistic fiction portrays children who are forming friendships with peers much like themselves in certain ways and with peers who at first seem strange. Books that explore the meaning of real friendship and suggest that best friends should support, rather than hurt, each other may help children overcome the disappointment that results when friends move or may stimulate a discussion about the meaning of friendship.

Authors often develop conflict in stories about interpersonal relationships by using person-against-self or person-against-person conflicts. In credible person-against-self conflicts, authors enable readers to identify inner conflicts and to understand why the characters have the conflicts, how the characters handle the conflicts, and what things cause the conflicts to be resolved. Resolutions should not be contrived; they should appear as natural outcomes. Contrived endings result when authors try too rapidly or too conveniently to create happy endings for serious and hurtful situations.

In credible person-against-person conflicts, authors develop both believable protagonists and believable opposing forces that serve as antagonists. Readers need to understand why conflicts occur between the forces. Do differences in values, personalities, or character traits cause conflict? An author's development of character should reflect such differences and encourage readers to understand why the characters act and react as they do. The conflicts authors identify and the ways that the characters overcome these conflicts usually communicate unifying themes about interpersonal relationships. The most successful themes develop naturally, as readers glimpse truths about friendship and life in general from the actions of the characters. The least successful themes are created solely for didactic purposes.

A person-against-self conflict and carefully developed character create a credible plot in E. L. Konigsburg's *Jennifer, Hecate, Macbeth, William McKinley, and Me, Elizabeth*. Konigsburg encourages readers to understand Elizabeth's inner conflict and need for a friend by emphasizing her shyness. She is a new girl in school, she goes to school alone, and she is afraid she will cry when she walks into her classroom. Elizabeth's shyness and need for a friend are reemphasized through her responses when she meets Jennifer, a very imaginative girl. At first, Elizabeth complies with Jennifer's demands and suggestions even when she does not want to do what her new friend asks of her. Later, as she gains confidence in herself, Elizabeth becomes assertive. Her inner conflict is resolved when the friends no longer need the support of the game in which they pretend to be witch and assistant witch. Then, they can be just good friends and act as equals.

Mary Stolz develops person-against-society conflict as well as person-against-self conflict in *Cider Days*. The person-against-self conflict develops as Polly faces loneliness after her best friend moves and then learns to respect the courage of a new friend. The person-against-society conflict develops when Polly tries to make friends with a new neighbor, a Mexican girl named Consuela. Stoltz encourages readers to glimpse conflicts caused by racial bias by describing the reactions of several classmates to Consuela and Consuela's responses to them.

In *The Robbers*, Nina Bawden creates effective characters and emphasizes important aspects of plot development by contrasting the life-styles of two children—one who has lived in the security of his grandmother's apartment in a castle and one who is knowledgeable in the ways of the London streets. When nine-year-old Philip moves to London, life is difficult because his schoolmates tease him about his princely manners and they physically attack him. His outlook changes, however, when he becomes friends with Darcy, whose

FLASHBACK

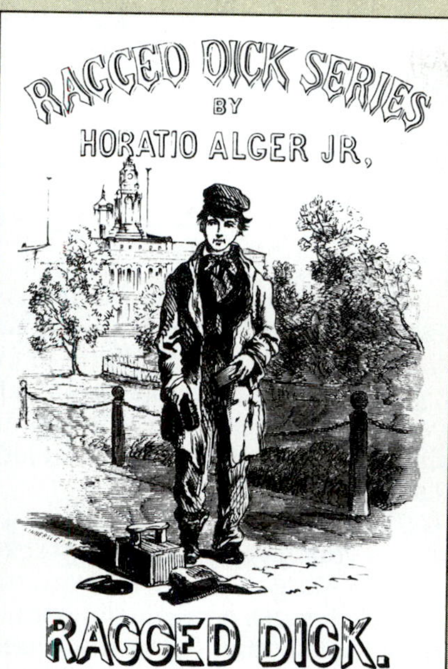

THE RAGGED DICK SERIES, PUBLISHED IN 1868, TOLD of the sad plight of children who tried to survive in a city without family or friends. They often worked long hours in factories or on farms. Many died. Horatio Alger, Jr. wrote the series in the hope that readers would be sympathetic to the cause of poor children and the Children's Aid Society. Since 1854, the society has been finding homes for abandoned children.

Horatio Alger's *Frank's Campaign* (1864) was the first of a series of books in which poor American youths went from rags to riches. Other books by Alger that have a similar theme include *Fame and Fortune* (1868), *Sink or Swim* (1870), *Strong and Steady* (1871), *Brave and Bold* (1874), *Risen from the Ranks* (1874), and *From Farm Boy to Senator; Being the History of the Boyhood and Manhood of Daniel Webster* (1882).

crippled father was a canal worker. As the two become close friends, Philip discovers that not all people live in his secure, protected world.

Older students may enjoy comparing this book by an English author with books on friendship by American authors. They will discover that the English characters reflect greater concern for class distinctions and express feelings of inevitability because of class.

The consequences of being different, having unusual responsibilities, and needing friendship and understanding are effectively developed in Janet Taylor Lisle's *Afternoon of the Elves*. Even though the two main characters are almost opposite in backgrounds and personalities, they are drawn together by Sara-Kate's insistence that she has an elfin village in her backyard. By working together in the village, Hillary gains new respect for Sara-Kate's differences and independence. Hillary discovers that Sara-Kate is responsible for nursing an invalid mother and holding the family together. Hillary concludes, "Perhaps being hungry and cold and angry and alone didn't mean you couldn't still be an elf. In fact, maybe those were exactly the things elves always were" (p. 119).

Stories about growing up frequently deal with problems associated with moving to new locations. Barbara Park's *The Kid in the Red Jacket* explores the problems faced by a fifth-grade boy when he moves to a different city. Making life more difficult for him is the first-grade girl who lives across the street and wants to be his best friend. Park uses a humorous approach to reveal many of the fears and problems associated with making new friends. In *The Broccoli Tapes,* Jan Slepian uses the concept of sending tapes from Hawaii back to friends in Boston to reveal a twelve-year-old girl's experiences as she adjusts to being away from her friends. In *Next-Door Neighbors,* Sarah Ellis's heroine discovers that new neighbors may help make a move bearable when her minister father is transferred to a new location in Western Canada.

Physical Changes. In order to develop credible problems, authors who write about physical maturity often describe embarrassing physical characteristics and explore ways that the characters, friends, and family members respond to the characteristics. The stories may depict both person-against-self and person-against-person conflicts. Person-against-person conflicts include peer victimization of a main character, with the story told from the viewpoint of either the victimized child or a child who is part of the peer group. In the case of a main character who is part of a victimizing peer group, the author may develop the consequences of peer victimization by having the peer group turn against the main character. Some problems have simplistic or humorous resolutions, while other resolutions are complex and express the extreme sensitivity of children as they experience changes in their bodies and increased self-consciousness about their appearance as they grow up.

Constance C. Greene uses two different approaches to develop and resolve the conflicts in *The Ears of Louis* and *The Unmaking of Rabbit*. In *The Ears of Louis,* a boy responds to the jeers of "Elephant Boy," "Dumbo," and "Stay out of the wind or you will sail to Alaska" by taping his ears to the sides of his head and wearing a football helmet to try to reduce their size. Because he has a supportive next-door neighbor and a best friend who believes that ears are a sign of character, Louis's emotional problems are not severe. However, Greene resolves Louis's problem with an overly simplistic solution: When the older boys learn that Louis can play football, they are impressed by his ability and no longer tease him.

In *The Unmaking of Rabbit,* the solution cannot be so simple, because Greene creates more conflict for Paul, an eleven-year-old boy who lives with his grandmother. His peers tease him about his father who deserted him and his mother who visits him infrequently. They also taunt him about his big ears, pink nose, and a tendency to stutter. Although Paul has a loving and supportive grandmother, he longs for close relationships with friends. The author reveals Paul's true character when Paul has the opportunity to gain the friends he desires. This is a difficult decision, however, because the overtures are from a gang of boys who want him to help them break the law. Greene convinces readers that Paul has made an important discovery about himself and suggests his appropriate handling of an important moral issue when he decides that a clear conscience is worth more than friends. The resolution of the conflict in this story is more interesting, emotionally satisfying, and true to life than the resolution of Louis's conflict because Paul faces so many more conflicts.

Self-consciousness about small size causes problems with self-esteem for eleven-year-old Jeffrey in Ellen Conford's *The Revenge of the Incredible Dr. Rancid and His Youthful Assistant, Jeffrey*. Jeffrey believes that in real life the little guy is always physically whipped:

> One of those harsh realities of life you have to face when you're built like me, you're going to spend most of your free time wishing you were built like Clint Eastwood, and the rest of your free time being scared of guys who are. (p. 5)

To make matters worse, Jeffrey's mother is the first female sports editor in the county and his father is very self-confident. The bully in Jeffrey's life is a sixth grader who is twice his size. Conford reveals a great deal about Jeffrey's true character when the bully picks on his only friend and Jeffrey steps in to resolve the problem.

In *Are You There God? It's Me, Margaret,* Judy Blume explores a young girl's developing sexuality. Eleven-year-old Margaret has many questions about the physical changes occurring in her body, including breast development and the onset of menstruation. This topic is also found in Norma Klein's *Tomboy*. Unlike Margaret, ten-year-old Toe does not look forward to bodily changes. While Margaret feared she might be the last girl in her group to menstruate, Toe fears that she is the first. She believes that if her friends discover her secret, they will not allow her to join the Tomboy Club. She does not believe that a girl mature enough to have a baby can be a tomboy. Toe discovers that the physical changes she fears are also happening to her best friend, and the two girls decide to abandon the club. These books discuss a topic that is very serious to girls who are approaching physical maturity.

Emotional Changes. Books that develop plots around emotional maturity—and physical maturity as well—differ in several important ways from the realistic fiction of the past. For example, several authors imply that parents are ineffective in helping a child cope with emotional changes and problems, are unavailable, or are unable to understand the child. Current realistic fiction often suggests that a person outside the family, an understanding grandparent or a knowledgeable friend, is the most important influence in a child's discovery of self—in contrast to the literature of the past, in which strong parents and caring brothers and sisters provide necessary support.

Unlike many family stories in the past, current books also suggest that children have numerous problems as they struggle toward emotional maturity.

Children confront a wide range of emotional issues while growing up. For example, in Lois Lowry's *Anastasia Krupnik,* a ten-year-old girl begins to overcome her desire to be the center of attention and her jealousy when she is able to place her family's new baby on her list of loves instead of her list of hates.

In *Bingo Brown and the Language of Love,* Betsy Byars uses lists to reveal a boy's growth, self-realization, and emotional maturity. For example, early in the novel, Bingo's lists include "Trials of Today" but no "Triumphs of Today." By the end of the novel, the trials are listed as "none!" and the triumphs include entries such as the following: "Attaining the mainstream of life and despite the unexpected strength of the current, not paddling in panic for shore" (p. 125). Through his summer ordeals and his reactions to a girlfriend who has moved, Bingo discovers that he can successfully face life. Lois Lowry's *Your Move, J. P.!* follows a seventh grader who is hopelessly in love.

In *Sydney, Herself,* Colby Rodowsky develops themes related to the importance of self-awareness through creative writing assignments. As a result of keeping a writing journal, Sydney learns to accept her heritage and respect her mother's needs.

The main character in Phyllis Reynolds Naylor's *Alice in Rapture, Sort Of* faces emotional changes caused by boy-girl relationships. Alice and her father live through what the father refers to as the summer of the first boyfriend. Naylor's figurative language effectively introduces the emotional conflict: The summer "stretched out before me like a roller coaster. I didn't want to go off, but I was terrified of what was over the next hill" (p. 2). By the end of the story, Alice concludes that it is more enjoyable to have male friends than boyfriends. In this humorous story, Naylor explores fears and issues associated with relationships, peer pressures, and growing up.

The boy in Jean Little's *Different Dragons* has more serious fears to overcome, including fear of darkness, thunderstorms, and dogs. When the boy visits his aunt, he makes some amazing discoveries about his father's and his brother's fears. A growing relationship with a dog, however, allows him to overcome his fears.

In Katherine Paterson's *Come Sing, Jimmy Jo,* painful shyness causes person-against-self conflict, and the demands of a gifted but often selfish family create person-against-person conflicts for a gifted eleven-year-old boy. Paterson explores a young singer's fears after he reluctantly joins his Appalachian family's musical group and moves away from the protection of his beloved grandmother. Paterson describes changes in attitudes toward his gift in Jamie's changing responses to the audiences. Jamie proceeds from being a frightened boy who feels sick when he plays in front of people; to a bewildered boy who believes that his father, but not his mother, will protect him from the aggressive fans; to an entertainer who accepts his gift and discovers pleasure in sharing music. Readers can identify with Paterson's character because his fears about growing up and the changes that he faces are universal.

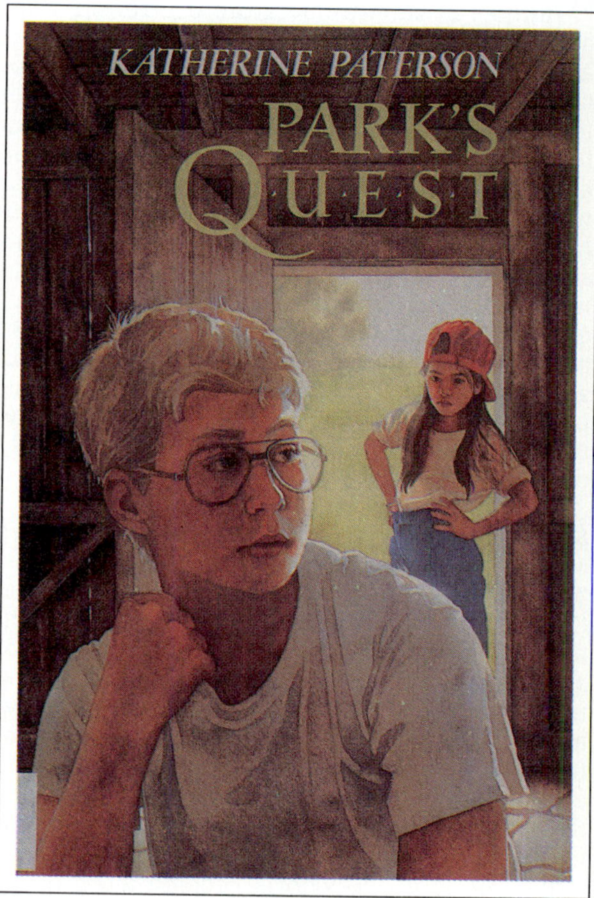

Paterson develops strong characterization in her novels. (From *Park's Quest* by Katherine Paterson, jacket illustration by Ellen Thompson. Copyright © 1988 by Katherine Paterson. Reprinted by permission of the publisher, Lodestar Books, an affiliate of Dutton Children's Books, a division of Penguin Books USA, Inc.)

Cynthia Rylant's *A Fine White Dust* explores equally traumatic person-against-self conflicts as Pete, a thirteen-year-old boy, becomes involved with an unscrupulous traveling evangelist and struggles to understand his own religious beliefs. In a strong conclusion, Pete discovers that "the Preacher Man is behind me. But God is still right there, in front" (p. 106).

Survival

Physical and emotional survival are fundamental challenges for all humans. Confrontations with dangers in nature, society, or oneself require and, ideally, develop strength of character in young people and adults. The strong personalities in survival literature are especially popular with older children, who enjoy adventure stories.

Authors of survival literature use several literary techniques to create credible plots and characters. Person-against-nature, person-against-society, and person-against-self conflicts are often the stimuli for complex and exciting plots. Authors may develop forceful natural or social settings as antagonists in stories, clarifiers of conflicts, or means of developing desired moods. Style is also important in survival literature. Careful word selection, imagery, and rhythm patterns can heighten the emotional impact and credibility of adventures outside the realms of experience of most readers. Authors of survival literature usually rely on consistent point of view—often first-person or limited omniscient—to encourage the readers to identify with and believe in the protagonists and their experiences.

Surviving in Nature. In Jean Craighead George's *My Side of the Mountain,* Sam Gribley leaves his home in New York City to live off the land in the Catskill Mountains. George tells part of the story in the form of Sam's diary, which adds a sense of authenticity to the story and creates the feeling that the readers are sharing an autobiographical account of Sam's experiences. Detailed descriptions of Sam's preparing and storing food, tanning and sewing a deerhide suit, and carving and firing the interior of his home in a hemlock tree are told in a matter-of-fact manner, which resembles the writing of someone who is keeping a log of his experiences and observations. The detailed descriptions of wild edible plants and important survival techniques also suggest to readers that Sam prepared carefully for his experiment in the wild. George creates other exciting survival-in-nature stories in *Julie of the Wolves,* as a thirteen-year-old girl lost in the arctic tundra develops a friendship with wolves, and in *River Rats, Inc.,* in which two boys rafting on the turbulent Colorado River become lost in the Grand Canyon and must improvise food and shelter.

The consistent first-person point of view used by Scott O'Dell in *Island of the Blue Dolphins* creates a plausible plot, main character, and setting. When Karana, a young Indian girl who survives years alone on a Pacific Island, tells readers, "I will tell you about my island," readers visualize the important features from her viewpoint and believe the description. When she says, "I was afraid," the fear seems real. Later, her discovery of her brother's body justifies her fear.

Paulsen develops strong person-versus-nature and person-versus-self conflicts in *Hatchet*. (Jacket cover by Neil Waldman from *Hatchet* by Gary Paulsen. Copyright © 1987 by Neil Waldman.)

This first-person viewpoint increases the readers' belief in her personal struggles as she is torn between two forces. Will she adhere to the tribal law that prohibits women from making weapons? Or will she construct the weapons that will probably mean the difference between her life or death? Her inner turmoil heightens the suspense, as suggested by the following quote:

> Would the four winds blow in from the four directions of the world and smother me as I made the weapons? Or would the earth tremble, as many said, and bury me beneath its falling rocks? Or, as others said, would the sea rise over the island in a terrible flood? Would the weapons break in my hands at the moment when my life was in danger, which is what my father had said? (p. 54)

Other major decisions are also more meaningful because they are told through Karana's point of view. When she decides to take a tribal canoe and sail in the direction her people sailed, readers believe her turmoil as the canoe begins to leak and she must again make a difficult decision: Should she go back and face loneliness or go on and face probable disaster? Karana decides to return to her island and make it as much of a home as she can.

O'Dell emphasizes the small details of days filled with improving shelter, finding food, and hiding supplies against the possibility of her Aleut enemies' returning to the island. Karana's need for companionship is shown when she cannot kill the leader of the wild dogs after wounding him. Instead, she takes him to her shelter, cares for him, and names him Rontu. Returned to health, Rontu becomes her constant companion and defender. After Rontu's death, Karana tames another dog, who eventually sails with her to the mainland when her long years on the island are finally over.

The credibility of Gary Paulsen's survival story, *Hatchet,* is enhanced because Paulsen carefully documents Brian's problem-solving approaches. Each time that Brian faces a critical, often life-and-death problem, Paulsen reveals Brian's reasoning processes. Brian thinks about the pros and cons of various actions. For example, Brian thinks through the various actions he could take after the pilot has a heart attack and he realizes that he is alone (pp. 17–30), the reasons he should have no fear of the bear and return to the raspberry patch (p. 75), the reasons a water animal would come up to the sand (pp. 98–99), a way to create a weapon to effectively catch fish (pp. 111–115), ways to capture birds for meat (pp. 140–141), and a way to make a craft and reach the plane after a tornado reveals the location of the plane (pp. 166–183). Memories of books he has read or television programs he has seen frequently help him solve what otherwise would be impossible problems.

Paulsen encourages readers to understand both the gravity and the consequences of many of the problems by using contrasts. For example, Brian compares his experiences in the wilderness with experiences he has had at home. Readers understand that the search for and the storage of food is more than a simple trip to the grocery store; unlike Brian's home experiences, the actions in the wilderness are life-and-death matters.

Surviving Inner-City Reality. Dangerous, polluted, and economically deprived inner cities are the environments in which many American children face the challenges of growing up. Several authors of realistic fiction portray the problems of overcoming poverty, gang violence, and living without the security of strong, supportive family. It is easy to rely on sensationalism for plot development in such stories, and numerous authors do. However, Virginia Hamilton and Walter Dean Myers, for example, create inner-city stories with literary merit.

One of the strongest inner-city stories is Virginia Hamilton's *The Planet of Junior Brown*. Hamilton's memorable characters enliven a complex story about friendship, loyalty, and learning to live together. The three main characters, all outcasts, live on the fringe of busy New York City. Junior Brown is a talented pianist who should be recognized for his skill, but the fact that he weighs almost three hundred pounds causes people to leave him alone. Consequently, he feels ugly and is afraid of being trapped in small spaces. Buddy Clark is an intelligent street boy who has lived on his own since the age of nine. The third outcast is Mr. Pool, a former teacher, who is a school custodian.

Mr. Pool feels that tough black children who know the city streets should be given opportunities to learn, but the rigid school regime causes him to lose heart, give up his teaching job, and move to the school basement. In this basement, however, Mr. Pool has a secret room where he can teach Junior Brown and Buddy Clark. Hamilton uses the symbolism associated with the word *planet* to develop each character's place in the story. Junior Brown's planet is an artistic creation that hangs suspended from metal rods and spherical tracks attached to the ceiling of the hidden room. While the children in the rooms above go through their normal days, the three outcasts build their solar system, create their planets, and learn about science and each other.

Buddy Clark's planet is not a work of art and science; it is the frightening inner-city reality of homeless boys, hunger, and survival. On his planet, this strong character first learns about personal survival from an experienced street survivor called a "planet leader." Then, Buddy becomes a leader with a planet and inhabitants of his own to train and supervise. Buddy spends part of his time in one world, as the protector and companion of Junior Brown, and the rest of his time in another world, where he takes care of children and works to feed and clothe them. Hamilton develops a strong theme as Buddy Clark takes the other outcasts to his own planet in the basement of a deserted house and shares with them his own views of life:

> "We are together," Buddy told them, "because we have to learn to live for each other. . . .If you stay here, you each have a voice in what you will do here. But the highest law for us is to live for one another. I can teach you how to do that." (p. 210)

Walter Dean Myers's *It Ain't All for Nothin'* also depicts two different worlds. One is the secure world of twelve-year-old Tippy's religious, caring grandmother; the other is the violent world of crime and his father's neglect. Tippy begins to live more in the second world when his grandmother becomes crippled by arthritis and can no longer care for herself or her grandson. The boy is frightened and angered by his father's use of drugs and his keeping of stolen goods and guns in the apartment. In a need to forget, Tippy begins to drink. Life becomes frightening; his father is involved in a robbery, during which one of his friends is wounded. Myers emphasizes Tippy's inner conflicts between the world of his grandmother and the world of his father when Tippy debates his own actions. Myers suggests hope for Tippy when the boy decides to tell an older friend about the problems in his father's apartment, informs the police, and decides that his life will not be like his father's.

In *Scorpions,* Myers creates a less hopeful and more tragic ending. Conflict begins when Jamal's older brother, who is in jail, wants Jamal to take over leadership of a gang. Jamal is torn between worry over his mother, who works too hard, and indecision over his role in the gang. Jamal's person-against-self conflict increases when he is given a gun. Should he keep it even though his best friend warns him against having a gun? Should he use it to make his position strong within the gang? Should he use it to frighten a bully at school who has always tormented him? When the gun is used at the end of the story, Myers shows the tragic consequences of Jamal's decision. Because of the gun, Jamal loses his best friend. Readers of this story will understand the author's theme: There is danger when people are involved with violent gangs, drugs, and guns.

Surviving in a Dangerous World. A new type of survival literature is emerging in both American and British children's literature: realistic fiction that mirrors international headlines about new dangers in our modern age. In the person-against-society conflicts of this survival literature, the protagonists are usually innocent children and the antagonists are terrorist groups, oppressive military governments, mass violence, and nuclear accidents.

In Susan Lowry Rardin's *Captives in a Foreign Land,* six children are kidnapped while accompanying their parents to a conference in Rome and are transported to a remote Middle Eastern desert. Rardin explains that she wrote the book in order to explore how American young people would respond to a situation in which the usual American support systems were nonexistent. The children's interactions with their kidnappers reveal the kidnappers' reasons for their actions and their attitudes toward Americans. The survival plot develops and the characters change as the children realize that they must plan and execute their own liberation.

Rosemary Harris's *Zed* is a more complex story. Eight years after Thomas was held hostage by terrorists, his teacher asks him to write his remembrances. Harris focuses on a boy's changing perceptions of both victims and terrorists as they are confined together for four days in a London office. In addition to experiencing irrevocable changes in himself, Thomas witnesses courage, cowardice, cruelty, and kindness in his own family members and members of the terrorist group.

Terrorists also create the person-against-society conflicts in Gillian Cross's *On the Edge*. In this book, the hostage is the kidnapped son of a journalist. Cross explores important choices. For the mother, it is complying with the terrorists' demands for the release of her son versus revealing information that could save the life of a world

Gang violence and guns create conflict in this inner-city setting. (Cover art: Copyright © 1988 by Bradford Brown from *Scorpions* by Walter Dean Myers, copyright © 1988 by Walter Dean Myers. Reprinted by permission of Harper & Row, Publishers, Inc.)

leader and destroy the assassination plot of the terrorists. For the son, it is what to do with the last few moments of his life.

James Watson's *Talking in Whispers,* a 1983 British Carnegie Honor book for older children, is a survival story in which the main character is hunted by the security forces of a South American government that denies basic human rights.

In Lois Duncan's *Don't Look Behind You,* a family is threatened by hired assassins. Duncan develops the frightening adjustments that the family must make when it is placed under the federal witness security program. Older readers will understand the conflicts of the teenage girl who tries to salvage parts of her former life.

The antagonists in Louise Moeri's *Downwind* are an accident at a nuclear power plant and the fear and violence that result as people try to flee. Moeri's book stresses the dangers of nuclear power and the need to make important decisions if the world is to be saved.

Dealing with Death

Part of growing up is realizing and gradually accepting the fact of death. An increasing number of realistic fiction stories develop themes related to the acceptance of death and the overcoming of emotional problems following the death of a loved one. As might be expected, different authors treat the subject differently. Treatments also depend on the developmental levels of their intended readers.

Differences in cause of conflict, resolution of conflict, and depth of emotional involvement are apparent in books of realistic fiction about death. Consider how several authors develop these areas in books written for younger readers, preadolescents, and teenagers. For comparative purposes, consider Charlotte Graeber's *Mustard* and Eve Bunting's *The Empty Window* written for younger readers; Constance C. Greene's *Beat the Turtle Drum* and Peggy Mann's *There Are Two Kinds of Terrible* written for ten- to twelve-year-olds; Richard Peck's *Remembering The Good Times* and Judy Blume's *Tiger Eyes* written for readers in their early teens; and Robert Cormier's *The Bumblebee Flies Anyway* written for teenagers and young adults.

In Charlotte Graeber's *Mustard,* a book for young children, members of a family share the sorrow following a fourteen-year-old cat's heart attack and their decision to let the veterinarian help the cat die in peace. Graeber looks at the importance of a pet to a young boy and encourages readers to understand the boy's relationship to the cat by describing the boy's disbelief in the cat's ailments and his reactions after the pet dies. When Alex and his father go to the pet shelter to donate some of Mustard's things, Alex declines the offer of a kitten because he does not have room at the moment for anything but memories of Mustard. In another year, he may be ready for a pet, he says. This resolution encourages readers to understand that healing takes time, memories are worth retaining, and family members can help each other in times of sadness.

Eve Bunting's *The Empty Window,* a picture storybook, explores a boy's feelings of fear, guilt, and sadness as he faces the death of his best friend. The boy, C. G., realizes he has been afraid to see his dying friend, Joe, when he recognizes that the time spent in capturing a wild parrot who lived in the tree outside his friend's window was an excuse for not visiting him. Joe teaches C. G. something about the meaning of life when he thanks him for the parrot but asks him to release it because "once the parrots were free and then someone caught them and caged them, but they go free again. That's why I like them" (unnumbered). Bunting also makes an important point about people who are critically ill. C. G. realizes that although Joe is dying, he has not changed. They can still sit and talk as they did before.

Stories written for ten- through twelve-year-olds have more fully developed characters and deal with more difficult emotions, those related to adjusting to the death of a family member. Constance C. Greene's *Beat the Turtle Drum* develops the basis for a girl's reactions to her sister's accidental death by describing the warm relationship between ten-year-old Joss and her twelve-year-old sister, Kate. Kate believes that her parents prefer her younger sister. After Joss dies as a result of a fall from a tree, Kate faces both the sorrow of losing a sister and the inner conflict resulting from her belief that her sister was the favorite. Greene encourages readers to glimpse Kate's inner turmoil when she finally admits her feelings to an understanding relative, who responds:

> I bet Joss would've felt the same way. If it'd been you, she might've said the same thing. And both of you would've been wrong. I think when a child dies, it's the saddest thing that could ever happen. And the next saddest is the way the brothers and sisters feel. They feel guilty, because they fought or were jealous or lots of things. And here they are, alive, and the other one is dead. And there's nothing they can do. It'll take time, Kate. (p. 105)

Kate gradually understands that overcoming her grief and conflicting emotions will take more than a moment but that she will receive pleasure from her memories of Joss.

In *There Are Two Kinds of Terrible,* Peggy Mann compares a boy's emotions when he breaks his arm and his emotions when his mother dies of cancer. Robbie can recover from the first kind of terrible, but the second kind is irreversible. Still, his mother's death actually brings him closer to his distant father, who is suffering intense grief, too.

The believable characters in Richard Peck's *Remembering the Good Times* help readers in their teens identify with this story about the suicide of a best friend. Peck first carefully develops the distinct personalities of two boys and a girl in their junior-high years. Kate is involved with people and believes in herself; Buck does not know which group he belongs with; and Trav is angry, unsure of himself, and afraid of the future. Peck develops the main person-against-self conflict by describing Trav's increasing fears as he discusses current events and as he reacts to evidence that he is expected to grow up to be like his successful parents. Trav becomes angry when he feels that he is not being prepared for the realities of life.

Peck develops a strong relationship among the three friends. After Trav's suicide, Kate admonishes herself because she did not notice the little things that should have warned them about Trav's approaching suicide. Peck explores various responses to Trav's death, as high-school administrators blame the parents, the parents blame the school, a knowledgeable older friend states the community's responsibility, and Kate and Buck discover that they can remember the good times of their friendship.

The causes of the conflict in Blume's story for older readers, *Tiger Eyes,* are the sudden, violent death of a parent and a society that creates such violence. Blume develops a person-against-self conflict as a teenage girl, Davey, tries to adjust emotionally and physically to the death of her father, who was a robbery victim. Blume also develops a person-against-society conflict as the characters respond to and reflect about a society in which there are violent death, vandalism, excessive teenage tension, and powerful weapons. Blume's characterization encourages readers to understand Davey's turmoil. Blume shows Davey's emotional ties with her father, Davey's physical reactions when she faces her peers (she faints at school but cannot tell the nurse her problem), Davey's need for a quiet place to reflect, Davey's interactions with a man who is dying from cancer and an uncle who will not allow her to take chances but designs weapons at Los Alamos; and Davey's interactions with two friends who are also facing inner conflicts. The resolutions of the conflicts require considerable time, but Davey can finally face what happened, tell new friends how her father died, and consider her own future.

The setting in *The Bumblebee Flies Anyway,* Robert Cormier's psychological novel for teenagers and young adults, is a terminal care facility in which a sixteen-year-old boy, Barney, realizes that his treatment is only experimental and that he is actually dying. Cormier uses symbolism to convey Barney's feelings about being a terminally ill guinea pig: The complex is a facility for experimental medicine; "the Handyman" is a doctor who treats the patients and creates illusions; "the merchandise" is special medicines, chemicals, and drugs that are calculated to produce expected responses; and "the bumblebee" is a sportscar in a junkyard that at first appears to be shining and new but is actually only a cardboard mockup of reality.

These stories about death deal with irreversible problems that are difficult to accept and resolve. Consequently, the responses of individual children to the books may be very personal. An eight-year-old said he felt better after reading *The Empty Window* because he had a friend who was very ill, and he was pleased that someone else felt as he did. An eleven-year-old, however, began to read *Two Kinds of Terrible* and then could not finish it. She said that she did not want to read a book that reminded her that her mother might die.

Several responses by fourteen-year-olds to *Tiger Eyes* demonstrate how personal the reactions to realistic fiction can be. One reader said, "This is not a good book to read in class. You need to be by yourself so you can cry if you want to." Another child said, "It's great. You get into the story and forget everything. I was afraid Davey was going to kill herself, but I thought, Judy Blume wouldn't kill her main character." A third reader said that the story was sad but its moral was happy: "Take a chance on your talents; planning someone's life for them doesn't make them happy; it's always better to face the truth rather than run from it; life is a great adventure; you can't go back in time. So pick up the pieces and move ahead; and some changes happen down inside of you and only you know about them." These responses indicate that a fourteen-year-old grasped many of the complex themes Blume wove into her novel. It is also interesting to note that the themes the reader identified are positive rather than negative.

People as Individuals, not Stereotypes

Stereotypical views of males and females, the disabled, and the elderly are becoming less prevalent than they once were in children's literature. Chapter 11, "Multicultural Literature," also discusses contemporary realistic fiction that portrays racial and ethnic minorities in unstereotyped ways.

Males and Females. Publishers are becoming sensitive to the need for literature that does not portray either sex in stereotypic roles. For example, since 1981, the Houghton Mifflin Publishing Company (19) has had guidelines for eliminating sex stereotypes in materials it publishes. Following are several guidelines:

1 Published materials should balance female and male protagonists and female and male contributors to society, and should present females and males in a variety of jobs. Stories should suggest that both females and males can prepare for and succeed in a variety of occupations.

2 Literature should recognize that males and females share the same basic emotions, personality traits, and capabilities. Both sexes should be portrayed in active pastimes and in solitary pursuits.

3 Sensitivity, taste, and nonstereotypic images should be employed in humor used to characterize the sexes.

4 Literature should present a broad range of historical references to women, including women whose contributions are well-known and less well-known.

5 Where appropriate, literature should include reference to legal, economic, and social issues related to women.

6 Historical books should include coverage of the roles and activities of women in past centuries.

As the roles of females in our society shift away from the stereotypes of the past, female characters in children's literature reflect these changes. Contemporary realistic fiction contains more girls who are distinct individuals. Girls may be brave, they may be tomboys, and they may be unorthodox. Mothers in realistic fiction are also taking on different roles. Often, they work outside the home; they may even have jobs more demanding than those of their husbands. Whatever roles females in recent realistic fiction play, the female characters are quite different from the female characters in earlier children's literature, even literature of the fairly recent past.

Consider, for example, the popular contemporary character Ramona, created by Beverly Cleary. Stories of her exploits span the years from the early 1950s into the 1980s. In *Henry and Beezus,* published in 1952, readers discover that the girls, Beezus and Ramona, are considered worthy playmates *even* by an active boy, such as Henry Huggins. These thoughts at least imply that active pastimes are not usually considered appropriate for girls; girls may not be considered creative playmates.

In later books, however, Ramona comes into her own. In *Ramona the Pest* (1968), she is not the stereotypic quiet girl; instead, she is the "worst rester" in kindergarten. By the time *Ramona and Her Father* was published in the late 1970s, the roles in her family have changed: Her father loses his job and stays home, while her mother returns to work on a full-time basis. Ramona humorously tries to help her father through this change in his life. *Ramona and Her Mother* explores a working mother's life as viewed by her seven-year-old daughter. By 1981, *Ramona Quimby, Age 8* is helping her family while her father returns to college. The Ramona books are popular with children who enjoy reading about the exploits of a spunky, humorous girl.

Louise Fitzhugh's hero in *Harriet the Spy* is an eleven-year-old girl whom other characters describe as exceptional, intelligent, and curious. Harriet's actions support these descriptions, as she hides in her secret places, observes her neighbors and classmates, and writes down her observations. The extent of this popular character's resourcefulness and self-confidence is revealed when her classmates find her notebook and organize "The Spy Catcher Club." Harriet uses all of her considerable creativity to devise a plan that will convince her friends to forgive her. She is far from the fainting female of most traditional literature and Victorian fiction, who must be rescued from her failures by the males in the story. She is even able to return to her real loves, spying and writing. More tales about Harriet are found in *The Long Secret* and *Sport*.

The exuberant, precocious protagonist in Vera and Bill Cleaver's *Lady Ellen Grae* does not accept the feminine role her father and society expect of her. The Cleavers describe first Ellen Grae's unrestricted life with her artist father and then her reactions when he wants her to leave her beloved Thicket, Florida, live with her aunt in Seattle, and learn to be a "lady." At this point, Ellen strongly presents her personal philosophy:

> I've found, that most things are simply a matter of mental reconciliation, because the mind is elastic—it stretches and can be pulled this way and that. The trick is not to flinch from it. If you do you're a goner before you get started. Mentally, I've reconciled myself to a thousand things: school, being a girl, collard greens, baths. . .But Seattle? Oh, no. No, sir, I, Ellen Grae Derryberry, do not reconcile to things like Seattle. I like it here and here I intend to stay until it's time for me to hop into my grave. (p. 19)

Although the Cleavers develop a plot that allows Ellen Grae to return to her father, she also discovers that there are many things that she doesn't know. Because she doesn't like to be ignorant about anything, she decides that she will learn about them on her own. The Cleavers at least imply that Ellen may discover many dimensions of womanhood and not just the confining one she has pictured.

E. L. Konigsburg's *From the Mixed-Up Files of Mrs. Basil E. Frankweiler* is another book of realistic fiction in which a female protagonist belies the traditional stereotypes about passive femininity. Claudia Kincaid leads her brother in running away from home and hiding out in the Metropolitan Museum of Art. When the two children are given one hour to search the files and discover the answer to a mystery involving a statue of an angel, Claudia tells her impatient brother that five minutes of planning are worth fifteen minutes of haphazard looking. Her techniques prove successful, and they discover the answer to the statue's authenticity.

Stereotyped views of males are also changing in our society and children's literature. In Katherine Paterson's *Bridge to Terabithia,* for example, a boy hates football, aspires to be an artist, and feels pressured by his father's traditionally masculine expectations of him. Although the father is afraid that Jess is becoming a "sissy," Jess finds support for being his true self in a strong friendship with the story's other protagonist, a girl named Leslie, who is also a nonconformist in their rural community.

One outstanding book of realistic fiction from the mid-1960s portrays the wider options for males that are becoming more prevalent in children's literature today. In Maia Wojciechowska's *Shadow of a Bull,* the son of a famous and supposedly fearless bullfighter learns that a male doesn't have to prove his manliness through acts of physical daring or violence. Manolo's village expects him to follow in his dead father's footsteps. As the men of the village begin training him in the art of bullfighting, Manolo believes he is a coward because he has no interest in being a bullfighter. Manolo eventually learns that in order to be truly brave he must be true to himself and not attempt to satisfy others' expectations. The author effectively resolves Manolo's person-against-self conflict when Manolo tells the waiting crowd in the bullring that he prefers medicine to bullfighting.

The Physically Different or Disabled. Most children and adults dislike to stand out in a crowd because of their appearance or physical capabilities. They may also feel discomfort when they see someone who does not conform to the customary standards of how a person should look or who is physically disabled. Children's realistic fiction is becoming increasingly sensitive to the importance of overcoming cruel or condescending stereotypes.

In *Blubber*, Judy Blume shows how peer cruelty to the physically different can have negative consequences for all concerned. Classmates torment a girl they consider grossly overweight. A strong peer leader manipulates her friends into composing a list entitled "How to Have Fun with Blubber" and forces the girl herself to make self-demeaning statements, such as "I am Blubber, the smelly whale of class 206" (p. 72). The main character realizes the crushing impact of what she has done when she tries to stop the cruelty and her classmates then turn on her.

In *Please Don't Tease Me. . .*, Jane M. Madsen and Diane Bockoras relate the true story of a child whose body is swollen from eukocytoclastic angiitis. The authors' theme of needing understanding and friendship may be so compelling because Bockoras is telling her own story.

Authors who develop realistic plots around credible characters who have physical disabilities often describe details related to a disability, the feelings and experiences of the disabled person, and the feelings and experiences of family members and others who interact with the character. Accurate, honest, and sensitive books provide physically disabled children with characters and situations close to their own experiences. Well-written books also help other children empathize with and gain understanding of the physically disabled. While adults should evaluate such books by literary standards, they should also evaluate them by their sensitivity. Mary Sage (28) recommends the following criteria when evaluating books concerning the disabled.

1 The author should deal with the physical, practical, and emotional manifestations of the disabling condition accurately but not didactically.
2 Other characters in the story should behave realistically as they relate to the disabled individual.
3 The story should provide honest and workable advice to the disabled character about his or her condition and potential for the future.

The resolution of conflict can be a special concern in realistic fiction dealing with physical disabilities. Does the author concoct a happy ending because he or she believes all children's stories should have happy endings, or does the resolution of conflict evolve naturally and honestly? Through fiction that honestly deals with handicaps, readers can empathize with children who are courageously overcoming their problems and with their families, who are facing new challenges. Writers of such literature often express the hope that their stories will encourage positive attitudes toward the physically disabled. As mainstreaming brings more disabled children into regular classrooms, this goal becomes more important for both children and adults.

Stories set in different historical periods often reflect changing attitudes about physical disabilities and provide bases for discussion with children. Julia Cunningham's story of a mute boy in *Burnish Me Bright* takes place in a French village of the past. The boy encounters prejudice, misunderstanding, fear, and even hostility. Monsieur Hilaire, a retired performer who befriends the boy and brings him into his world of pantomime, clarifies the reasons behind society's prejudice:

> These people you have known are no worse than the others that walk the world but they share with the others a common enemy, and the enemy is anyone who is different. They fear the boy who can't speak, the woman who lives by herself and believes in the curative power of herbs, the man who reads books instead of going to the café at night, the person like me who has lived in the distant differences of the theater. They are not willing to try to understand, so they react against them and occasionally do them injury. (p. 18)

Ellen Howard sets *Edith Herself* in the pioneer America of the 1890s. The girl, Edith, faces her own fears and the ignorance of others who do not understand her epileptic seizures. The story may seem realistic because the experience happened to a relative of the author. Carol Carrick's *Stay away from Simon* shows the damage inflicted on a mentally disabled boy in the early 1800s. Both texts develop strong themes about the consequences of prejudice caused by ignorance.

In Larry Callen's *Sorrow's Song,* nondisabled people have quite different reactions to a modern-day girl who is mute. Sorrow's best friend, a boy named Pinch, sees her this way: "She is so smart, I don't even like to think about it. She knows words I never heard of. But Sorrow can't use words the way most people can. Sorrow can't talk" (p. 5). Her teacher defends Sorrow and challenges a man who thinks her condition is tragic: "Sorrow Nix is more normal than the two of us. Don't you do anything that will make her feel otherwise" (p. 56). Pinch's mother considers Sorrow someone special and compares her to a weeping willow, which she considers a friendly tree.

Callen, however, does not imply that Sorrow is always happy. Callen draws parallels between Sorrow's special needs and the needs of an injured whooping crane. When the crane flies away to live its own life, there is a strong feeling that Sorrow has won her own conflict. The author develops a strong theme about individual abilities and not judging people by outward appearances.

In *From Anna,* Jean Little develops a credible perspective on visual impairment by describing a girl's frightening experiences when letters are blurred, look the same, or even appear to jiggle across the page. In *Mine for Keeps,* Jean Little explores the conflicting emotions of a child with cerebral palsy.

The physically disabled include those whose mental capacities are not up to the social norm. Authors who write plausible books about the relationships between mentally disabled children and their normal siblings often portray the conflicting emotions of normal characters who experience both protective feelings and feelings of anger toward a disabled child. In Betsy Byars's *The Summer of the Swans,* Sara is a normal teenager who is discontented with her looks, sometimes miserable for no apparent reason, and often frustrated with her mentally retarded brother as she cares for him.

Byars encourages readers to understand and empathize with Charlie's gentle nature. He is fascinated by the swans who glide silently across the lake, but he becomes confused and terrified when he follows the swans and becomes lost. During a frantic search for Charlie, Sara forgets her personal miseries. When the siblings are reunited, Sara discovers that she feels better about herself and life in general than she had before. Vera and Bill Cleaver's *Me Too* portrays the protective relationship of a twelve-year-old girl with her mentally retarded twin.

Elizabeth Laird's *Loving Ben* develops two lives for Anna, her life at school with friends and her life at home with Ben, a hydrocephalic infant. In this book, Anna's love for her little brother changes her life.

Virginia Euwer Wolff's *Probably Still Nick Swansen* develops a many-sided character, Nick, who faces the realities of his learning disability. The author explores the similarities between sixteen-year-old Nick and other teens as well as individual differences among the students in Nick's special education class. In a strong ending, Nick learns to accept himself.

The Elderly. When children's literature students evaluate the characterizations of elderly people in children's books, they often discover stereotypes. Denise C. Storey (32) describes a study in which fifth-grade children analyzed the elderly characters found in books from their classroom library. The children concluded that (1) some elderly people lead boring, lonely lives where nothing changes; (2) grandparents in books look older than their own grandparents; (3) the elderly do not work, have fun, or do anything exciting; (4) young people are mean to elderly people; (5) book characters do not want to listen or talk to the elderly; (6) some elderly people are mean, crabby, overly tidy, fussy, and unfair; (7) the elderly like to remember the good old days or dream of better times; and (8) there are few happy books about the elderly.

Some authors of contemporary realistic fiction are exploring the problems related to old age with greater sensitivity than authors expressed in books of the past. When evaluating books dealing with the elderly, you should select books that show elderly people in a wide variety of roles. Close experiences between grandparents and grandchildren are common in books for young children, such as Tomie de Paola's *Nana Upstairs & Nana Downstairs* and Sharon Bell Mathis's *The Hundred Penny Box*. Books for older children often stress the worthwhile contributions that are still being made by the elderly, the warm relationships that can develop between grandparents and grandchildren, and a desire of elderly people to stay out of nursing homes. Some books are very serious; others develop serious themes through humorous stories.

Eleanor Clymer's *The Get-Away Car* should appeal to children because it includes humor, mystery, and adventure. Clymer depicts a resourceful, energetic woman who is granddaughter

Maggie's idea of a perfect grandmother because she lives by the motto "Fun first, work later." Other children in their tenement support Grandma's philosophy and join in the outings and fun.

All goes well until Maggie's Aunt Rubey decides that Grandma is not capable of taking care of a young girl. Aunt Rubey's solution is to put Grandma into a home for the elderly and have Maggie move in with Aunt Rubey. While Aunt Rubey is trying to change their lives, Grandma and the children decide to borrow a car and run away to Cousin Esther's home in upstate New York. Along the way, they have many adventures. The story has a satisfying ending. The children solve the mystery of the old black car, a way is found for Cousin Esther to restore her formerly beautiful home, and Grandma convinces everyone that she is capable of looking after her granddaughter.

Kidnapping Mr. Tubbs is a more complex book. In it, author Don Schellie explores the feelings of the young and the elderly and develops the theme that people of all ages make contributions. Mr. Tubbs, a nearly one-hundred-year-old cowboy, lives in a nursing home and has neither freedom nor a relative who cares for him. His friends are a teenage volunteer and A. J., the grandson of the man who shares his room. The young people "snatch" Mr. Tubbs out of the rest home to satisfy his wish to visit the ranch in northern Arizona where he worked as a cowboy, the place that gave him happy memories. Schellie uses discoveries during the trip to reveal lessons learned by young and old. Mr. Tubbs discovers that many places he remembers have changed for the worse, and A. J. realizes that he has always avoided becoming involved with the elderly because he fears they will die like his early childhood friend. A. J. expresses one of the story's major themes when he tries to convince Mr. Tubbs that he is not worthless, but very much needed by his young friend.

The growing relationships and understandings between a girl and her grandfather form the basis for Norma Fox Mazer's *After the Rain*. At first, Rachel resents the time she is asked to spend with her ailing grandfather, but she mourns the loss of their precious moments together after his death. Well-developed characters help readers understand the needs of the two different generations and the changes that can result because people learn to understand each other.

Other outstanding books about the elderly and young people who love and respect them include Betsy Byars's *The House of Wings*, Vera and Bill Cleaver's *Queen of Hearts*, and Gary and Gail Provost's *David and Max*. With their diverse, nonstereotyped depictions of elderly people, such books provide discussion materials that encourage older children to explore the roles of elderly people in literature and their own feelings about the elderly.

Mazer develops a believable relationship between grandfather and granddaughter (From *After the Rain* by Norma Fox Mazer, copyright 1987 by Norma Fox Mazer. Reprinted by permission of Morrow Junior Books [A Division of William Morrow & Co.].)

ANIMAL STORIES, MYSTERIES, SPORTS STORIES, AND HUMOR

Animals

The animals in contemporary realistic fiction are quite different from the animals in traditional literature and modern fantasy. In traditional literature and modern fantasy, animals talk and act like people or have other magical powers. The animals in realistic fiction have a strong sense of reality and sometimes tragedy. Realistic animal stories place specific demands upon authors. When evaluating realistic animal stories for children, you should consider the following questions.

1 Does the author portray animals objectively, without giving them human thoughts or motives?
2 Does the behavior of the animal characters agree with information provided by knowledgeable observers of animals and authorities on animal behavior?
3 Does the story encourage children to respond to the needs of animals or the needs of people to love animals without being too sentimental or melodramatic?

Authors who write credible animal stories often depict warm relationships between children and pets. The conflict in such stories usually occurs when something happens to disrupt the security of a pet's life. The antagonist may be a physical change in the animal, an environment different from the pet's secure home, or a human character whose treatment of the animal is cruel or even life threatening. Detailed descriptions of physical changes, settings that become antagonists, or cruel human characters may encourage children to understand the vulnerability of animals to such forces.

Credible stories about wild animals usually reflect considerable research about animal behavior and natural habitats. Conflict may arise when animals face natural enemies, when humans take them from natural surroundings and place them in domestic environments, or when humans hunt or trap them.

Some authors use animal-against-society or animal-against-person conflicts to develop strong themes advocating protection of animals. Other themes stress the human development made possible by human interaction with animals. Many authors stress the positive consequences of loyalty and devotion between humans and animals.

Consider, for example, the various techniques used by Theodore Taylor in *The Trouble with Tuck*. Taylor first develops a believably close relationship between Helen and her golden Labrador. Helen's love for Tuck and her family's devotion to the dog are strengthened by two incidents in which Tuck saves Helen from harm or possible death. The reactions of the family members when the veterinarian declares that Tuck is going blind and cannot be helped reflect their devotion to the dog and make plausible their acceptance of Helen's resolution of the problem. She calls a trainer for Seeing Eye dogs and makes an appointment for her parents without telling the trainer that the blind individual is a dog.

Although the trainer's initial reaction is negative, the family is finally offered an older Seeing Eye dog whose master has died. Taylor describes Helen's trials and frustrations as she tries to train Tuck to follow the seeing eye dog. After weeks of disappointment, she is rewarded when Tuck accepts and follows the older dog. This story, based on a true incident, emphasizes determination, loyalty, and self-confidence that may develop because of animal and human interaction.

A classic book with a notable dog as the main character is Jack London's *Call of the Wild,* first published in 1903. This story depicts life in the Klondike during the Alaskan gold rush. London develops a credible story of transformation as Buck progresses from a docile pet to a rugged work dog and finally to an animal who is inescapably drawn by the wild cries of the wolf pack. London develops these remarkable changes in Buck by providing details of his life before and after he is stolen from his home in California and brought, raging and roaring, to face the primitive law of the Klondike. Buck changes as he reacts to a beating and the fierce fangs of fighting dogs, but he retains his spirit. While crossing the countryside in a dogsled harness, his long-suppressed instincts come alive.

This is also the story of strong bonds between dog and human. After a succession of sometimes cruel owners, Buck is purchased by kind John Thornton. Buck apparently feels an adoration for John that causes him continually to return from his wilderness treks until the terrible day when he returns to camp to find that John has been killed. Only then are the bonds between man and dog broken, allowing Buck to roam with the wolf pack:

> His cunning was wolf cunning, and wild cunning; his intelligence shepherd intelligence and St. Bernard intelligence; and all this, plus an experience gained in the fiercest of schools, made him as formidable a creature as any that roamed the wild. (p. 114)

Other well-known books about dogs that have been popular in the last few decades include Jim Kjelgaard's *Big Red,* in which a mountain boy raises a dog that wins a prize in a big-city dog show; Fred Gipson's *Old Yeller,* the story of a boy and his dog in the Texas hill country of the 1860s;

and Sheila Burnford's *The Incredible Journey,* an outstanding realistic story about a Labrador retriever, an English bull terrier, and a Siamese cat that travel 250 miles through the Canadian wilderness in search of their human family. A more recent realistic story, Helen Griffiths's *Running Wild,* portrays the problems that result when domesticated pets are allowed to live in the wilds, as abandoned puppies become a pack of mature dogs that kill livestock and terrorize farmers in a mountainous region of Spain.

Horse stories also have qualities that make them marvelous for children. The horses and their owners, or would-be owners, usually have devoted relationships. Often the little horse, who may have been laughed at or scorned, becomes the winner of a race and begins a famous line of horses. Sadness in many of these stories results when both horse and owner must overcome severe obstacles and even mistreatment.

Two outstanding authors of horse stories are Marguerite Henry and Walter Farley. Henry's stories reflect research and knowledge about horses and their trainers, and several of them report the history of a breed of horses. One memorable story narrates the ancestry of Man o' War, the greatest racehorse of his time. In *King of the Wind,* readers travel back two hundred years to the royal stables of a sultan of Morocco, where Agba, a young horse tender, has a dream of glory for a golden Arabian stallion with a white chest.

The story travels from Morocco to France as the Sultan sends six of his best horses to King Louis XV, who rejects the horses, which have become thin from their voyage. Agba and the once-beautiful Sham are handed over to several degrading and even cruel masters before the English Earl of Godolphin discovers their plight and takes them home with him. In England, Agba's dream and promise to the horse come true. Three of the golden Arabian's offspring win various important races. When the great Arabian horse, renamed The Godolphin Arabian, stands before royalty, Agba's thoughts flash back to the promise he made in Morocco:

> "My name is Agba. Ba means father. I will be a father to you, Sham, and when I am grown I will ride you before the multitudes. And they will bow before you, and you will be the king of the Wind. I promise it." He had kept his word! (p. 169)

Other enjoyable books by Marguerite Henry include *Justin Morgan Had a Horse,* the story of the Morgan horse; *Black Gold,* the story of a racehorse and the jockey who brings her to winning form; *Misty of Chincoteague,* the story of the small, wild descendants of the Spanish horses shipwrecked off the Virginia coast; and *San Domingo: The Medicine Hat Stallion,* a story of a Nebraska frontier boy and his affection for an unusual horse. All of Henry's stories reflect an understanding of horses and the people who feel loving attachments to them.

A beautiful black stallion and his descendants are the chief characters in a series of books written by Walter Farley. The first, *The Black Stallion,* introduces a beautiful wild horse that is being loaded, unwillingly, onto a large ship. On this same ship is Alec Ramsay, who understands and loves horses. The two are brought together as the ship sinks, and the black horse pulls Alec through the waves to a small deserted island. Friendship develops as the two help each other survive, and Alec discovers the joy of racing on the back of the amazing horse.

After they are rescued, Alec's friend realizes what a remarkable horse he has and they secretly train the horse for a race between the two fastest horses in the United States. In an exciting climax, the unknown horse wins the race. This story has also been written as a picture storybook illustrated with color photographs from the movie of the same name. Questions about the black stallion's heritage are answered in Farley's *The Black Stallion Returns*. Many other stories in Farley's series examine the great horse and his notable and courageous descendants.

Helen Griffiths relies on a detailed setting and background information on horses and bullfighting to develop a plausible story in *The Dancing Horses,* set in post-Civil War Spain. The need for taking responsibility for the animals in one's care is emphasized in Lynn Hall's *Danza!,* whose human protagonist is a Puerto Rican boy.

Several of the books already discussed stress the vulnerability of animals to changes in their environments or to humans who interfere with their way of life. In *The Wheel on the School,* Meindert DeJong explores the impact of negative environmental change and positive human intervention on birds. DeJong introduces several issues related to storks through the questions and investigations of six school children and their teacher in a Dutch fishing village. After they ask "Why didn't the storks come to Shora?" they explore the various reasons for the missing storks: The roofs are too steep, there are no trees, there are too many storms, and there is too much salt spray. A plausible situation develops because the children take the problem seriously and work to rectify it. Their honest concern suggests to readers that this matter should be of interest to others. The author also suggests that every effort counts; the children must overcome many obstacles, but a stork family finally accepts the wheel on the schoolhouse roof.

Jean Craighead George explores the problems that result when wild creatures are tamed in *The Cry of the Crow*. Mandy Tressel's family in the piney woods of the Florida Everglades kills crows to save their strawberry crop. Mandy, however, secretly feeds and tames a young crow, the only survivor of her younger brother's gun blast. As Mandy raises the crow, Nina Terrance, she discovers that the crow can imitate some human speech. When wild crows try to lure Nina away from her human friend, Mandy, knowing that she should encourage the bird to return to the wild, asks her mother's advice. George develops the girl's inner conflicts when she ignores her mother's warnings and decides to keep the bird. George also explores the controversy related to taming wild creatures through the neighbors' mixed reactions to the crow; some threaten to poison her, some are intrigued by her speech, and others want to put her in a cage as a tourist attraction. The return home of Mandy's young brother brings the conflict to a climax. When he repeats the same words he said as he killed the crow family, the crow attacks his face. George suggests Mandy's feelings as she is torn between her love for her pet and her brother: "I'll never feed her again. Mommy was right. She'd be gone now, far, far away, if I hadn't been selfish and dumb. . . .If she hurts you, I'll never forgive myself" (p. 142). When Nina again attacks the boy, Mandy makes the difficult decision that the crow must be killed, and the children realize that they are both responsible for Nina's death.

Mysteries

Footsteps on a foggy night, disappearing people, mysterious strangers, and unusual occurrences woven together into exciting, fast-paced plots create mystery stories that appeal to older children. One eleven-year-old girl, an avid reader of mysteries, listed the following four characteristics that make a mystery exciting for her: (1) it should have an exciting plot that holds the interest of readers, (2) it should contain suspense, (3) it should have enough clues to allow readers to follow the action, and (4) the clues should be written in such a way that readers can try to discover "who done it." In answer to the question, "What has caused your interest in mysteries?" she replied that she had read Donald J. Sobol's *Encyclopedia Brown* in third grade and enjoyed trying to follow the clues. She said that her favorite suspense story was Virginia Hamilton's *The House of Dies Drear,* a tale about the Underground Railroad.

The best-known mysteries for young readers are probably contained in Donald J. Sobol's *Encyclopedia Brown* series. In each of the books, ten-year-old Leroy Brown helps his father, the police chief of Idvalle, solve crimes by figuring out the clues. For example, in *Encyclopedia Brown Tracks Them Down,* Leroy solves the case of a missing ambassador by reviewing the gifts presented to him at a birthday party. In another case in that book, Leroy solves the riddle of a flower can and discovers the identity of the boy who stole an 1861 Confederate coin worth $5,000. *Encyclopedia Brown Sets the Pace* contains ten more cases in which young readers can try to identify a thief or solve the problem of a bully who picks on smaller children. Sobol provides readers with the solutions and the reasoning behind them.

A mystery associated with a possible killing provides the suspense and the conflict in Robbie Branscum's *The Adventures of Johnny May*. In addition to the mystery, a person-against-self conflict develops as a young girl believes she has witnessed a killing. The possible killer is Homer, a gentle, friendly man who would not even kill a deer or hurt an animal. The possible victim is a hateful, bitter man. Johnny May's personal conflict increases when she does not report her suspicions. With the aid of three friends, Johnny May searches for clues that will both prove Homer's innocence and relieve Johnny May's conscience.

In *Roscoe's Leap,* Gillian Cross enhances mysterious elements by building suspense. Cross introduces fragments of memory that bring back feelings of terror in the protagonist. For example, Cross develops suspense associated with believable fear when Stephen hears words that trigger memories:

> "Take them to see the Collection."
>
> In Stephen's memory, something huge and dark moved suddenly out of the shadows. A pain along the side of his head and voices shouting and someone—himself?—screaming and screaming and screaming. . . . (p. 28)

The author gradually introduces new memories until the mystery of the French Terror is solved.

Powers of observation play important roles in the mysteries of Robert Newman, two of which are set in the London of Sherlock Holmes's time. *The Case of the Baker Street Irregular* and *The Case of the Vanishing Corpse* include suspense, sinister characters who must be outwitted, and several mysteries that seem not to be related but actually are.

Ellen Raskin's several books challenge readers to join often preposterous characters in working out puzzle clues. These clues include word puzzles, a series of obscureiy written messages, and even observations gained through reading. *The Mysterious Disappearance of Leon (I Mean Noel)* is a humorous word puzzle, a game about names, liberally sprinkled with clues. As the story of Leon and Little Dumpling, the heirs to Mrs. Carillon's Pomato Soup fortune, proceeds, Raskin informs readers that there is a very important clue in a particular section or that they should mark the locations of Leon's fourteen messages because they contain important clues. Noel's final words, for example, as he bobs up and down in the water cause Little Dumpling years of searching. What is meant by "Noel glub C blub all. . .I glub new. . ."?

In *Figgs & Phantoms,* the clue Raskin provides is "the bald spot." This clue eventually helps Mona Figg discover whether she has or has not actually visited Capri, the Figg family's idea of a perfect heaven. Raskin's *The Westing Game* includes many clues that must be worked through before the teams of players solve the mystery.

Zilpha Keatley Snyder's mysteries involve kidnapping, complex games, and mysterious secret environments. In *The Famous Stanley Kidnapping Case,* masked strangers kidnap five unusual children who accompany their parents to Italy. In *The Egypt Game,* six children create an ancient Egyptian world in an abandoned storage yard and solve a murder mystery. Numerous clues and mounting tension create a fast-moving plot in Barbara Corcoran's *You're Allegro Dead,* in which two twelve-year-old girls encounter a mysterious intruder and a kidnapping instead of the summer camp activities they expected.

Mysteries provide escape and enjoyable reading through their plots and suspense. They allow children to become involved in the solutions through clues and character descriptions. They also suggest that children themselves—if they are observant, creative, and imaginative—can solve mysteries.

Sports

Sports stories rate highly with children who are sports enthusiasts. Some quite reluctant readers will finish a book about their favorite sport or sports hero. The majority of these stories are about boys, however, and few authors yet write about girls who enjoy participating in sports. Many stories deal with the ideal of fair play, the values of sports, the overcoming of conflicts between fathers and sons, and the overcoming of fears connected with sports. Unfortunately, many of the stories are didactic and have familiar plot lines and stock characters.

Authors who write about baseball often imply that the sport has therapeutic values. Often, the emphasis in these books is on the role baseball can play in helping children overcome problems at home, develop new friendships, face physical disabilities, or feel accomplishment. Matt Christopher's *The Fox Steals Home,* for example, tells the story of troubled Bobby Canfield as he faces his parents' divorce and the prospect of his father's taking a job far from home. His father and his grandfather have coached him and nicknamed him "Fox." His proudest moment comes when he steals home and demonstrates to his father what a good player he has become.

Likewise, in *Hang Tough, Paul Mather,* Alfred Slote writes about a leukemia victim whose greatest interest is baseball. The boy must face the knowledge that he has a short time to live and that his parents are trying to prevent him from playing to protect him. However, an understanding doctor helps him play his last season with dignity and courage. In *The Trading Game,* Slote builds his plot around a ten-year-old boy who matures during his interactions with his grandfather. His grandfather is a former baseball player.

In *Herbie Jones and the Monster Ball,* Suzy Kline humorously develops a story about a young boy who hates baseball until his uncle coaches a baseball team for eight- and nine-year-olds. The book does not stereotype girls, who play on the team. The boy's older sister also gives him baseball lessons.

Football is both the major interest and the cause of conflict between a father and son in Matt Christopher's *Football Fugitive*. Larry Shope loves football and longs for his father to leave his law

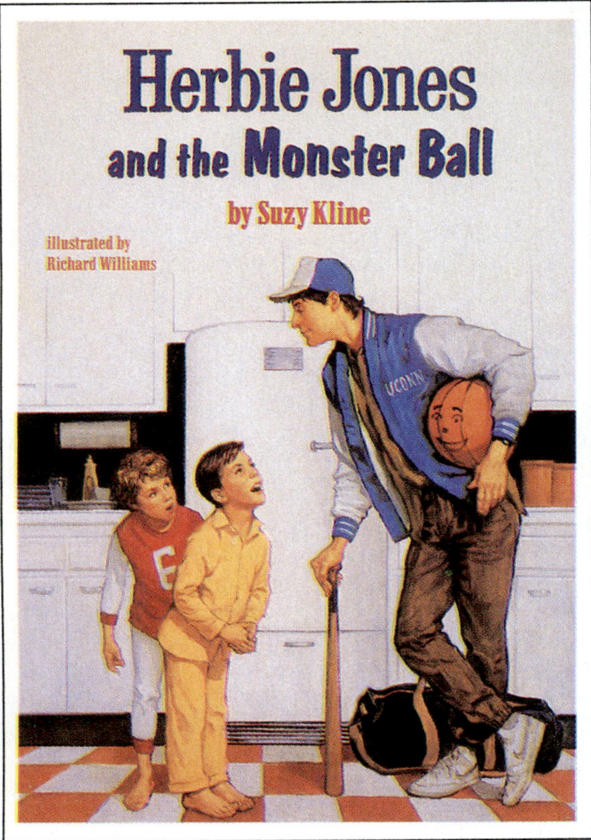

Humor is added to a story about a reluctant ballplayer from *Herbie Jones and the Monster Ball* by Suzy Kline, illustrations by Richard Williams, copyright © 1988 by Richard Williams. Reprinted by permission of G. P. Putnam's Sons.)

practice long enough to watch him play. Larry and his father become closer when Mr. Shope provides legal assistance for a professional football star.

Christopher's *Face-Off* describes Scott Harrison's love for hockey and the fear of being struck in the face that keeps him from playing his best, to his teammates' disgust. Christopher's *The Twenty-One-Mile Swim* describes a marathon swim that results when the son of Hungarian immigrants is teased about his small size and his inadequate swimming skills. Christopher's *Dirt Bike Racer* looks at boys and their minibikes.

Frank Bonham's *The Rascals from Haskell's Gym* is one of the few sports stories with female heroes. Sissy Benedict is a gymnast who becomes involved in the competition between the Butterflies Gymnastics Club and their arch rivals, Haskell's Raskells. Another story about girls in sports is K. M. Peyton's *The Team,* in which Ruth Hollis joins an English Pony Club team, prepares her horse for competition, and enters cross-country races. This book is enjoyable for young riders who have experienced the same thrill during a competitive race.

Humor

Humorous stories, whether involving figures of fantasy or realistic people living in our contemporary world, are among children's favorites. Authors who write about humorous situations that could happen to real people (these situations and characters may stretch probability) allow children to understand that life can be highly entertaining and that it is not always serious. Writers may encourage readers to laugh at themselves and at numerous human foibles. Humorous situations and characters may highlight real problems and make reading about them palatable.

Authors of humorous realistic fiction use many of the sources of humor discussed in Chapter 5—word play, surprise and the unexpected, exaggeration, and ridiculous situations. For example, authors may use a play on words or ideas to create humorous situations or clarify characters' feelings. Consider Betsy Byars's *The Cybil War,* an entertaining story about a fifth-grade boy who has a crush on a girl. The war develops as Cybil Ackerman responds in various ways to Simon's advances, which are intentionally misinterpreted by his best friend.

Beverly Cleary uses a twist on the words of a familiar television commercial to create a funny incident in *Ramona Quimby, Age 8*. When Ramona gives her book report, she presents it in the style of a television commercial. Her statement, "I can't believe I read the whole thing," causes a hilarious reaction among her classmates. In *The One in the Middle Is the Green Kangaroo,* Judy Blume uses a humorous analogy to clarify a middle child's feelings: "He felt like the peanut butter part of a sandwich squeezed between Mike and Ellen" (p. 7).

Exaggeration provides humor in Helen Cresswell's various books in the Bagthorpe saga. The series, including *Ordinary Jack, Absolute Zero, Bagthorpes Unlimited, Bagthorpes v. the World,* and *Bagthorpes Abroad,* presents the talented and eccentric Bagthorpes, who feel that life is a hilarious challenge. For example, when Uncle Parker wins a Caribbean cruise as a prize in a slogan-writing contest, the competitive Bagthorpes begin to enter every contest imaginable. The result is chaos as the prizes start arriving.

In *Bagthorpes Unlimited*, the family attempts immortality by creating the great Bagthorpe daisy chain, a chain of daisies 4,750 feet long, containing 22,000 daisies, that they hope will place them in the *Guinness Book of World Records*. The fame they earn is not, however, what Mr. Bagthorpe envisioned. Instead of being interviewed as a serious writer for a story in the *Sunday Times*, he is photographed on his front lawn surrounded by daisies and enthusiastic chain weavers.

In *Bagthorpes v. the World*, Mr. Bagthorpe is still feeling the trauma of having his one chance at national acclaim whisked away from him. Creswell suggests his frame of mind: "It needed only the slightest nudge, he felt, to topple the balance of his mind and send it plummeting into full-scale schizophrenia or paranoia" (p. 18). The nudge that creates chaos in this episode is the arrival of a bank statement showing that he is overdrawn at the bank by billions.

In addition to plots filled with humorous exaggerated incidents, the Bagthorpe saga recreates a family that is overflowing with loyalty and happiness. Children enjoy reading about a family that includes an eccentric grandmother, a precocious and unpredictable cousin, and assorted aunts and uncles. One fourth grader expressed her hope that Helen Cresswell would write more books about the Bagthorpes because her books make children laugh.

Judy Delton's *Angel's Mother's Wedding* continues the adventures of warm, humorous Angel O'Leary. Delton develops both humor and vivid characters by describing Angel's worries and imaginings. Misunderstandings provide a series of humorous incidents when five-year-old Rudy, Angel's brother, tries to give his new father a red paint job for a wedding present and then enacts how he believes a ring bearer should perform at the wedding.

Judy Blume uses a surprising and unexpected situation in *Tales of a Fourth Grade Nothing*, in which a humorous conflict between two brothers is brought to a climax when the younger boy swallows the older brother's pet turtle. An unexpected situation provides humor in Lois Lowry's *Anastasia on Her Own* when a naive cook, trying to prepare a gourmet dinner, asks for and receives cooking advice from a stranger who is calling to sell tap dancing lessons. In *Anastasia's Chosen Career*, Lowry uses excerpts from Anastasia's own writings to show a humorous attitude and indicate plot changes. The writings are taken from a school assignment about careers. An unexpected situation in Anne Fine's *Alias Madame Doubtfire* occurs when an ex-husband disguises himself as a cleaning woman and baby-sitter in his ex-wife's house.

In Sheila Greenwald's *Give Us a Great Big Smile, Rosy Cole*, several ridiculous situations develop when an author and photographer who is writing successful information books that chronicle his nieces' accomplishments turns to Rosy, who has no accomplishments except her definite inability to play the violin. Greenwald's book is characteristic of many realistic humorous stories about people. Although most of the incidents are humorous, the actions of the characters reflect and highlight human foibles, and the main characters learn something about themselves as they experience situations that are more humorous to readers than to them.

Suggested Activities for Adult Understanding of Realistic Fiction

- ☐ Sexism in literature, including the harmful sex-role socialization resulting from female- and male-role stereotyping, is a major concern of many educators and psychologists. In a school, public, or university library, choose a random sampling of children's literature selections. If these books were the only sources of information available about male and female roles, what information would be acquired from the books and their illustrations? Is this information accurate?
- ☐ Read an earlier study that analyzes realistic fiction, such as Gloria Toby Blatt's "Violence in Children's Literature: A Content Analysis of a Select Sampling of Children's Literature and a Study of Children's Responses to Literary Episodes Depicting Violence." (5); Carolyn Wilson Carmichael's "A Study of Selected Social Values as Reflected in Contemporary Realistic Fiction for Children" (6); Ann E. Hall's "Contemporary Realism in American Children's Books" (15); Alma Cross Homeze's "Interpersonal Relationships in Children's Literature from 1920 to 1960" (18); or Judith Ann Noble's "The Home, the Church, and the School as Portrayed in American Realistic Fiction for Children 1965–1969" (25). Read a sampling of the most current literature. How does this literature compare with the earlier findings?
- ☐ Compile an annotated bibliography of books that show both girls and boys in nontraditional

THROUGH THE EYES OF AN AUTHOR

The Laughter of Children

BEVERLY CLEARY, recipient of the Laura Ingalls Wilder Award, the Newbery Award, and many children's choice awards, discusses the importance of humor in children's realistic fiction.

ALTHOUGH FOR OVER thirty years I have been absorbed in stories that spring from the humor of everyday life, I try not to think about humor while writing, because of the sound advice given me by my first editor Elisabeth Hamilton, whom I met after writing *Henry Huggins* & *Ellen Tebbits*. In discussing writing for children, I happened to mention humor. Elisabeth, a forceful woman, interrupted. "Darlin'," she said, "don't *ever* analyze it. Just do it." I have followed her advice. While I am writing, if I find myself thinking about humor and what makes a story humorous, I am through for the day; and that chapter usually goes into the wastebasket, for spontaneity has drained out of my work. Although introspection is valuable to every writer, I find that analyzing my own work is harmful because it makes writing self-conscious rather than intuitive. When I am not writing, however, I find myself mulling over the subject of humor, my kind of humor, and why so many children find it funny.

As a child I would have agreed that humor is "what makes you laugh." I could not find enough laughter in life or in books, so the stories I write are the stories I wanted to read as a child in Portland, Oregon—humorous stories about the problems which are small to adults but which loom so large in the lives of children, the sort of problems children can solve themselves. I agree with James Thurber's statement: "Humor is the best that lies closest to the familiar, to that part of the familiar which

sex roles. What is the greatest strength or weakness of each book?

- ☐ Compare the professional roles of fathers and mothers in literature published in the 1970s, 1980s, and 1990s with the professional roles of fathers and mothers in literature published in earlier periods. Do the later books illustrate the changing family roles of both males and females? Is there conflict in a story if roles are reversed? How is this conflict handled?
- ☐ Interview children's librarians in public or school libraries. Ask them to state the guidelines used by the library when selecting books considered controversial for children. What are the issues, if any, that they feel are relevant in the community? Can they identify any books that have caused controversy in the libraries? If there are such books, how did they handle the controversy?
- ☐ Many realistic fiction stories deal with the problems that children must face and overcome when they experience separation from a friend, a neighborhood, or a parent, or they face the ultimate separation caused by death. Choose one area and read several books that explore the problem, and recommend books to share with younger children and books more appropriate for older children. Explain your decisions. Annotated bibliographies such as those found in Joanne E. Bernstein's *Books to Help Children Cope with Separation and Loss* (4) and "Bibliotherapy: How Books Can Help Young Children Cope" (3) may be helpful in the search.
- ☐ Read a survival story, such as Jean Craighead George's *My Side of the Mountain* or Scott O'Dell's *Island of the Blue Dolphins*. What writing style or technique does the author use that allows readers to understand the awesome power of natural enemies?
- ☐ Compare the characteristics of a specific type of animal in a modern fantasy story with the characteristics of the same type of animal in a realistic animal adventure story.

is humiliating, distressing, even tragic. . . .There is always a laugh in the utterly familiar."

My first book, *Henry Huggins,* a group of short stories about the sort of children I had known as a child, was written with a light heart from memories of Portland. As I wrote I discovered I had a collaborator, the child within myself—a rather odd, serious little girl, prone to colds, who sat in a child's rocking chair with her feet over the hot air outlet of the furnace, reading for hours, seeking laughter in the pages of books while her mother warned her she would ruin her eyes. That little girl, who has remained with me, prevents me from writing down to children, from poking fun at my characters, and from writing an adult reminiscence about childhood instead of a book to be enjoyed by children. And yet I do not write solely for that child; I am also writing for my adult self. We are collaborators who must agree. The feeling of being two ages at one time is delightful, one that surely must be a source of great pleasure to all writers of books enjoyed by children.

By the time I had published five books, several things had happened which forced me to think about children and humor: I had children of my own, twins—a boy and a girl; reviews said my books were hilarious or genuinely funny; a textbook of children's literature said my books were to be read "purely for amusement"; and enough children had written to me to give me some insight into their thoughts about my books.

One phrase began to stand out in these letters from children. Letter after letter told me my books were "funny and sad." Until these letters arrived, I had not thought of *Henry Huggins* as sad. The words, at that time never used by adults in reference to my books, began to haunt me. Funny and sad, or even funny and tragic, describes my view of life. To borrow another phrase from James Thurber, I had chosen "reality twisted to the right into humor rather than to the left into tragedy"—for that is my nature. I feel that comedy is as illuminating as tragedy—more so for younger readers who may be frightened or discouraged by tragedy in realistic fiction.

Abridged from "The Laughter of Children," *The Horn Book* (October 1982): 555–564. Copyright © 1982 by Beverly Cleary.

References

1 Apseloff, Marilyn F. "New Trends in Children's Books from Europe and Japan." *School Library Journal* 32 (November 1985): 30–32.

2 Association of Women Psychologists. "Statement Resolutions and Motions." Miami, Fla.: American Psychological Association Convention, September 1970.

3 Bernstein, Joanne E. "Bibliotherapy: How Books Can Help Young Children Cope." In *Children's Literature: Resource for the Classroom,* edited by Masha Kabakow Rudman. Norwood, Mass.: Christopher Gordon, 1989, 159–173.

4 ———. *Books to Help Children Cope with Separation and Loss*. New York: Bowker, 1977.

5 Blatt, Gloria Toby. "Violence in Children's Literature: A Content Analysis of a Select Sampling of Children's Literature and a Study of Children's Responses to Literary Episodes Depicting Violence." East Lansing, Mich.: Michigan State University, 1972. University Microfilm No. 72–29,931.

6 Carmichael, Carolyn Wilson. "A Study of Selected Social Values as Reflected in Contemporary Realistic Fiction for Children." East Lansing, Mich.: Michigan State University, 1971. University Microfilm No. 71–31.

7 Cheatham, Bertha M. "News of '85: SLJ's Annual Roundup." *School Library Journal* 32 (December 1985): 19–27.

8 Cohen, Caron Lee. "The Quest in Children's Literature." *School Library Journal* 31 (August 1985): 28–29.

9 Connell, Christopher. "Middle-Class Housewife Writes High-Class Children's Tales." Bryan-College Station *Eagle* (March 28, 1984): 1F.

10 Donelson, Ken. "Almost 13 Years of Book Protests—Now What?" *School Library Journal* 31 (March 1985): 93–98.

11 Egoff, Sheila. "The Problem Novel." In *Only Connect: Readings on Children's Literature,* edited by Sheila Egoff, G. T. Stubbs, and L. F. Ashley. Toronto: Oxford University Press, 1980.

12 Feldstein, Barbara. "Selection as a Means of Diffusing Censorship." In *Children's Literature: Resource for the Classroom,* edited by Masha Kabakow Rudman. Norwood, Mass.: Christopher Gordon, 1989, 139–158.

13 Forman, Jack. "Young Adult Books: Politics—The Last Taboo." *Horn Book* 61 (July/August 1985): 469–471.

14 Frasher, Ramona. "A Feminist Look at Literature for Children: Ten Years Later." In *Sex Stereotypes and Reading: Research and Strategies*. edited by E. Marcia Sheridan. Newark: International Reading Association, 1982.

15 Hall, Ann E. "Contemporary Realism in American Children's Books." *Choice* (November 1977): 1171–1178.

16 Hearne, Betsy. "Contemporary Issues—Child Abuse." *Booklist* 81 (May 1, 1985): 1261–1262.

17 Henke, James T. "Dicey, Odysseus, and Hansel and Gretel: The Lost Children of Voigt's *Homecoming*." *Children's Literature in Education* 16 (Spring 1985): 45–52.

18 Homeze, Alma Cross. "Interpersonal Relationships in Children's Literature from 1920 to 1960." University Park, Pa.: Pennsylvania State University, 1963. University Microfilm No. 64–5366.

19 Houghton Mifflin Company. *Eliminating Stereotypes, School Division Guidelines*. Boston: Houghton Mifflin, 1981.

20 Kean, John M., and Carl Personke. *The Language Arts: Teaching and Learning in the Elementary School*. New York: St. Martin, 1976.

21 Lepman-Logan, Claudia. "Books in the Classroom: Moral Choices in Literature." *The Horn Book* (January/February 1989): 108–111.

22 McClenathan, Day Ann K. "Realism in Books for Young People. Some Thoughts on Management of Controversy." In *Developing Active Readers: Ideas for Parents, Teachers, and Librarians*, edited by Dianne L. Monson and Day Ann K. McClenathan. Newark, Del.: International Reading Association, 1979.

23 Madsen, Jane M., and Elaine B. Wickersham. "A Look at Young Children's Realistic Fiction." *The Reading Teacher* 34 (December 1980): 273–279.

24 Nilsen, Aileen Pace. "Women in Children's Literature." *College English* 32 (May 1971): 918–926.

25 Noble, Judith Ann. "The Home, the Church, and the School as Portrayed in American Realistic Fiction for Children 1965–1969." East Lansing, Mich.: Michigan State University, 1971. University Microfilm No. 31, 271.

26 Rochman, Hazel. "Young Adult Books: Childhood Terror." *The Horn Book* 61 (September/October 1985): 598–602.

27 Root, Shelton L. "The New Realism—Some Personal Reflections." *Language Arts* 54 (January 1977): 19–24.

28 Sage, Mary. "A Study of the Handicapped in Children's Literature." In *Children's Literature, Selected Essays and Bibliographies*, edited by Anne S. MacLeod. College Park, Md.: University of Maryland College of Library and Informational Services, 1977.

29 Sam Houston Area Reading Conference, Sam Houston State University, February 1981.

30 Silvey, Anita. "The Goats." *The Horn Book* (January/February 1988): 23.

31 Steele, Mary Q. "Realism, Truth, and Honesty." *The Horn Book* 46 (February 1971): 17–27.

32 Storey, Denise C. "Fifth Graders Meet Elderly Book Characters." *Language Arts* 56 (April 1979): 408–412.

33 Townsend, John Rowe. *Written for Children: An Outline of English-Language Children's Literature*. New York: Lippincott, 1974.

34 Unsworth, Robert. "Welcome Home. . .I Think." *School Library Journal* 35 (May 1988): 48–49.

35 Vasilakis, Nancy. "Young Adult Books: An Eighties Perspective." *The Horn Book* 61 (November/December 1985): 768–769.

IF REALISTIC FICTION IS TO OFFER CHILDREN opportunities to identify with others, extend their horizons, and gain personal insights, then adults who work with children must be aware of a wide range of realistic fiction and activities that encourage this growth. It is not necessary, or even advisable, to attach literature-related activities to all realistic fiction that children read, but some activities are appropriate for this genre. This section considers how realistic fiction may be used to stimulate role playing that strengthens understanding of the world and offers suggestions for handling real problems.

This section also takes an in-depth look at the development of children's literature units that stress the themes of island survival and survival in mountains, canyons, and tundra. In addition to activities and discussions that stress the influence of settings upon the conflicts in stories, a unit relates literature to the science curriculum through activities that increase understanding of geography and botany.

This section also stresses how literature can be used to develop an appreciation for the contributions of females and an understanding of the various roles that both males and females can play in life. The section concludes with questioning strategies that can accompany realistic fiction or any other genre of literature.

Involving Children in Realistic Fiction

USING REALISTIC FICTION DURING ROLE PLAYING AND BIBLIOTHERAPY

Role playing is a creative dramatics activity in which children consider a problem and possible actions of people in reaction to the problem, and then act out the situation as they believe it might unfold in real life. Laurie and Joseph Braga (5) give several reasons for encouraging role playing with children. First, they stress that role playing helps young children develop an understanding of the world around them. Second, the Bragas suggest that role playing enhances children's understanding of various ways to handle common problems. Children can play the roles of the people concerned, switch roles to develop understanding of other points of view, and talk about what happened, why it happened, and what they think should be done. The Bragas believe that adults can learn a great deal about children as they listen to the children's responses during role-playing activities and follow-up discussions.

Literature can be the stimulus for involving children in activities that satisfy the purposes of role playing. Realistic picture books about doctors, dentists, and other neighborhood helpers can be used to encourage young children to act out the roles of adults with whom they come in contact. Such role playing can decrease the fears of children by allowing them to experience a role before facing a real situation. Books about families encourage children to role-play interactions between different members of a family, nuclear or extended.

The plots in realistic fiction provide many opportunities for children to role-play problems. Zena Sutherland and May Hill Arbuthnot (17) recommend that literature selected for stimulating, thought-provoking problem situations should (1) contain characters who are well developed and have clearly defined problems, (2) have plots that contain logical stopping places so that children can role-play the endings, (3) include problems, such as universal fears and concerns, that allow children to identify with the situations, and (4) present problems that help children develop their personal value systems.

In role playing, you may either choose stories in which problems are developed to certain points and then have children role-play the unfinished situations, or have children role-play various solutions to problems after they have read or listened to the whole stories.

Fannie and George Shaftel (16) recommend certain steps in guiding older children in a literature-related role-playing experience. First, introduce and read the story problem to the children. During the introduction, help the children think about the situation and how it might be solved. Second, encourage the children to describe the characters in the story. Then, have the children choose parts for the first role-playing situation. Third, discuss the responsibility of the audience, suggest observations that children could make, and encourage the children to consider the reasonableness of the solution. Fourth, have the players discuss what they will do during the role-playing activity. Fifth, have the children role-play the problem situation, with each participant playing the role of the character he or she has chosen to represent. Sixth, when the role playing is over, lead the audience and the characters in discussing the actions, consequences, and possible alternative behaviors of the characters. Seventh, have children reenact the role-playing situation using the new actions and solutions suggested during the discussion. Eighth, again lead a discussion of the different solutions to the problem. Finally, have the children assess the possible outcomes of each portrayal and draw conclusions about the best way or ways to handle the problem.

The books of realistic fiction discussed in this chapter offer considerable stimulus for role-playing situations. Because the books are categorized according to their content, you may refer to this chapter when searching for specific situations connected with family life, peer relationships, individuality, and so forth. The following books also contain problem situations that adults have used to stimulate children's role-playing experiences in connection with family life:

Family Life

1. Responsibility toward family members and friends: *The Moffats,* by Eleanor Estes. Rufus's friend Hughie feels unhappy during the first day of school. In fact, Hughie runs away, causing Rufus to follow him and persuade him to return. Ask children to pretend they are Rufus and Hughie. If they were Rufus, what arguments would they use to persuade Hughie to stay in school or return to school?
2. Responsibility toward family members: *Meet the Austins,* by Madeleine L'Engle. The Austin parents include their children in many important family discussions and stress the importance of sharing family responsibilities. Ask children to pretend that they are family members and role-play what they believe is meant by responsibility toward the family. The conflicts between Maggy and various Austin family members are also useful for role playing.

Family Disturbances

1. Problems related to accepting parents' divorce and discovering oneself: *Dear Mr. Henshaw,* by Beverly Cleary. Ask children to pretend that they are either Leigh Botts or Mr. Henshaw. It is March 31, five months after the two people started their correspondence. The two characters are taking part in a conversation. What information did they learn about each other? How did the writing experience affect either of their lives? How would Leigh Botts change the answers to any of the questions that he answered in his letters dated between November 20 and November 27? What advice would they give to each other?
2. Problems connected with surviving without a parent: *Mama,* by Lee Bennett Hopkins. Ask

children how they could convince Mama that they love her for herself and not for the stolen gifts she brings them.

Interpersonal Relationships

1 The loss of a friend and the meaning of friendship: *A Secret Friend,* by Marilyn Sachs. Encourage children to empathize with Jessica as she tries to regain Wendy's friendship. What would they do and say in that situation?

2 Being accepted by others: *Please Don't Tease Me. . .,* by Jane M. Madsen and Diane Bockoras. Use the authors' discussion questions to highlight this true story about feelings. *Edith Herself,* by Ellen Howard. Encourage children to empathize with Edith's need to have friends who are "sticking up for me" (p. 110).

3 Relationships with the elderly: *How Does It Feel to Be Old?,* by Norma Farber. Ask children to think about all of the good and bad things suggested in the book that relate to growing old. Have them role play a situation revolving around each person who might have a conversation with Grandmother about the positive side of becoming older.

Physical Maturity

1 Overcoming problems related to physical characteristics: *The Ears of Louis* by Constance C. Greene. Encourage children to empathize with Louis's feelings about his big ears. How would he react to taunts of "Elephant Boy"? Ask them to role-play scenes between Louis and his best friend, Louis and his friendly neighbor, Louis and his classmates, and Louis and the older boys who want him to join them for a football game.

2 Overcoming problems related to physical characteristics: *Blubber,* by Judy Blume. Encourage children to role-play episodes of insensitivity between children and the girl who is overweight.

Such stories allow children to empathize with characters who have problems that many children in elementary school experience. Through role playing, children may discover ways to handle problems and increase their sensitivity to the problems of others.

In addition to understandings gained through role playing, students gain understandings through discussions about books in which characters make moral choices. After reading Marion Dane Bauer's *On My Honor* with sixth- and seventh-grade students, Claudia Lepman-Logan (9) states:

> [I] was astonished at the response it provoked. I had thought that using a book with a moral choice as its theme might stimulate some interesting discussions, but I was quite unprepared for the intense and lively debates that engaged even the most passive students. . . .Throughout the reading of the book my students found themselves comparing and contrasting their own inclinations with Joel's motivations. The element of uncertainty is stretched out until the ending, which, interestingly enough, did not bring a close to either the events in the book or to our discussions. By following Joel's inner turmoil readers had to decide whether his final decision was indeed believable. (p. 108)

Lepman-Logan extended the initial discussion by asking her students to consider the choices that writers face when they resolve the problems they create. Students who wanted more details to accompany *On My Honor* created additional dialogues among characters and explored further consequences that might result for the characters. Additional books that have moral choices and endings that lead to further consequences for the characters include Paula Fox's *One-Eyed Cat,* Walter Dean Myers's *Scorpions,* Gillian Cross's *On the Edge,* Cynthia Rylant's *A Fine White Dust,* Stephanie S. Tolan's *A Good Courage,* and Brock Cole's *The Goats.*

In recent years, librarians and educators have recommended reading and interacting with particular books as ways for individuals to gain insights into their own problems. According to the *Dictionary of Education* by Carter Good (8), bibliotherapy is the "use of books to influence the total development, a process of interaction between the reader and literature which is used for personality assessment, adjustment, growth, clinical and mental hygiene purposes; a concept that ideas inherent in selecting reading material can have a therapeutic effect upon the mental or physical ills of the reader" (p. 58). By this definition, everyone can be helped through reading; bibliotherapy is a process in which every literate person participates at some time.

According to Joanne Bernstein (3), bibliotherapy is gaining insights from reading fiction or nonfiction that lead to self-examination. Bernstein suggests that to use books to help children gain insights into their own lives and to help them identify with others you must (1) know how and when to introduce the materials, (2) be sufficiently familiar with the materials, and (3) know each child's particular need.

Bernstein stresses that if you are using books to help children cope with their problems, you should not force the books upon them. Instead, you should provide a selection of materials from which the children can choose and then be patient until the children are ready to use them. After a child has read a book, be available for discussion or, more important, for listening. During a discussion, let children talk about the actions and feelings of the characters in the story, suggest areas in which they agree and disagree with the characters, consider the consequences of the characters' actions, and talk about other ways that a problem might be approached.

Many books provide additional resources for those who are interested in bibliotherapy. Bernstein's book contains a bibliography of adult references pertaining to bibliotherapy and an extensive annotated bibliography of children's books that deal with accepting a new sibling; going to a new school; getting used to a new neighborhood; coping with death, divorce, desertion, serious illness, and displacement due to war; and dealing with foster care, stepparents, and adoption.

ANALYZING CHILDREN'S RESPONSES TO LITERATURE

Your use of realistic fiction and other types of books for role playing and bibliotherapy will be more effective if you have a general understanding of children's responses to literature. Louise Rosenblatt (13) states that a literature selection "should not be thought of as an object, an entity, but rather as an active process lived through during the relationship between a reader and a text" (p. 12). Readers bring past experiences, present interests, and expectations that influence the reading process. Consequently, different readers often read and interpret the same piece of literature in different ways. Arthur Applebee (1) emphasizes that the stories children hear lead them to make expectations about what a story should be and about what new stories will be like.

Studies of children's oral and written responses to literature analyze the types of comments that children make when they retell a selection or talk about a story. In a review of children's responses to literature, Alan C. Purves and Dianne L. Monson (12) identify characteristic responses of children in different grades. For example, children up to the third grade tend to respond to and retell literal aspects of a story. In addition to literal responses, fourth- and fifth-grade students tend to elaborate on their responses by placing themselves in the roles of the characters, comparing themselves to the characters and talking about their personal reactions. By sixth grade, students begin to emphasize and interpret characterizations. In seventh and eighth grades, interpretations increase and evaluations frequently emphasize meaning and understanding. Eighth-grade students begin to look for hidden or deeper meanings in stories.

Working with children and literature, you can learn a great deal about children's responses to literature by analyzing what children choose to say or write about when they discuss literature. Purves and Monson recommend a classification system to use when analyzing children's comments about literature. See Chart 9–2.

USING CHILDREN'S INTEREST IN SURVIVAL TO MOTIVATE READING AND INTERACTION WITH LITERATURE

Many realistic fiction adventure stories portray physical survival and increased emotional maturity of the main characters. The plots and strong characterizations in this type of realistic fiction encourage children to live the adventures vicariously. When the physical characteristics described in the stories cause major conflicts, these characteristics may help children understand the importance of setting. University students have used interest in physical and emotional survival to develop stimulating literature-related activities to share with children.

Two very interesting instructional activities developed by university students and then shared with classrooms of children centered on the survival theme. One group developed an in-depth literature unit around physical and emotional survival on islands. Another group chose physical and emotional survival on mountains, in canyons, and on arctic tundra. Each group used the webbing process to organize its units.

Island Survival

The university students who chose the island survival theme identified the following books for

CHART 9–2
Classifying children's comments about books

Type of Response	Examples
Descriptive	Retelling the story, naming the characters, listing the media used in illustration.
Analytic	Pointing to the uses of language, structure, point-of-view, in the work.
Classificatory	Placing the work in its literary historical context.
Personal	Describing the reader's reactions to the work and the emotions and memories that have been evoked.
Interpretive	Making inferences about the work and its parts, relating the work to some way of viewing phenomena (e.g., psychology).
Evaluative	Judging the work's merit on personal, formal, or moral criteria.

Note: From Alan C. Purves and Dianne L. Monson. *Experiencing Children's Literature.* Glenview, Ill.: Scott, Foresman, 1984, p. 143.

ability to survive physically and grow in maturity because of the experiences:

Island of the Blue Dolphins, by Scott O'Dell
Call It Courage, by Armstrong Sperry
The Cay, by Theodore Taylor
The Swiss Family Robinson, by Johann David Wyss

The group read the books and identified the central themes and the main areas that challenged the physical survival: characteristics of the natural environment, including climatic conditions of the islands caused by their geographical locations, and survival needs related to other human needs. This central theme and six subtopics associated with survival were identified in the first phase of the "Survival on Islands" web (see Figure 9–1). During the next phase, the group identified subjects related to each subtopic on the web. The group developed the extended web shown in Figure 9–2.

After finishing the webs, the group planned activities to help children learn the importance of setting, realize that setting may cause major conflicts, and understand each identified physical survival topic. The university students also identified topics related to an upper-elementary science curriculum. They used interesting literature to increase children's understanding of scientific principles, and they developed activities to stimulate oral language, written language, and artistic interpretations of the plots and characters.

The examples in Chart 9–3 are taken from the physical survival activities developed around Scott O'Dell's *Island of the Blue Dolphins*. Several activities are included for each main subtopic in the web to allow you to visualize the types of physical survival activities that are possible in the classroom. Many of these activities are also appropriate for discussion in the library. The university students developed similar activities around each island survival book. Their discussions and activities stressed the importance of setting in devel-

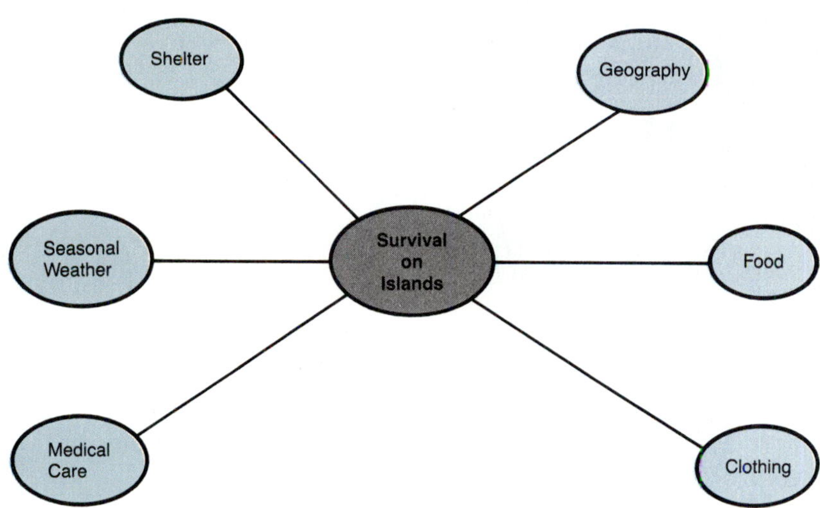

FIGURE 9–1
Island survival web, first phase

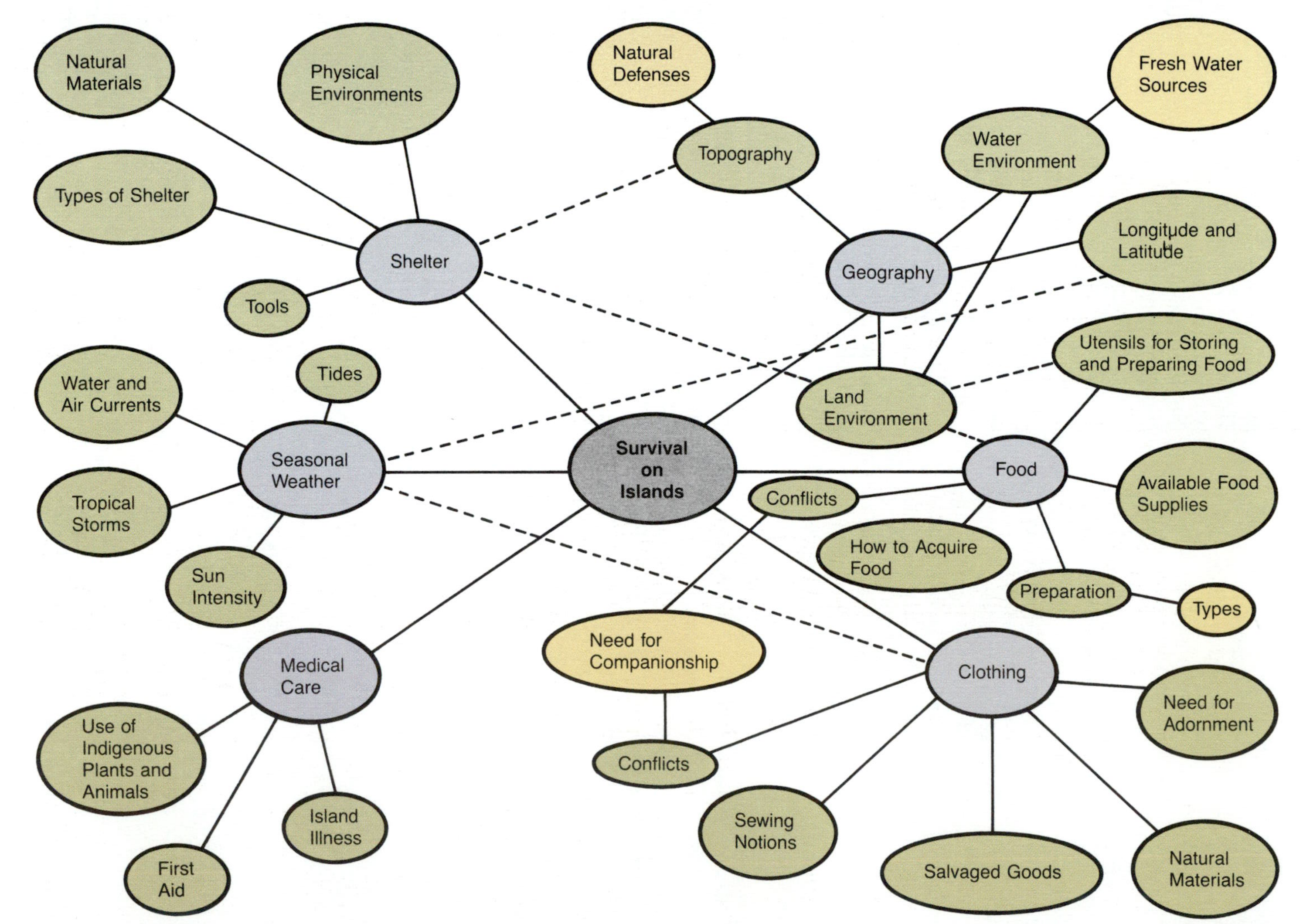

FIGURE 9–2
Extended island survival web

oping the conflict and the effects upon the growth of the characters as they overcame problems connected with setting or loneliness. The students also compared the various characters, their settings, and the physical and emotional strategies that led to survival.

In a final activity, the university students set up an elementary-school classroom as an island. They divided the children into groups according to shelter, food, clothing, geography, medical care, and seasonal weather. For Island Day, the elementary-school children chose and developed activities that represented their areas of interest. The children constructed shelters in which they located various interest centers. The children shared tool-making and cooking experiences. Art and science displays depicted weather, geography, clothing, food, and shelter. A special demonstration showed possible medical care for island survival. While learning about the impact of setting upon characters in survival literature, the children also discovered much about their own environments and how they might conquer their own worlds.

Survival in Mountains, Canyons, and Tundra

Three books by Jean Craighead George stimulated interesting discovery activities related to survival. First, *My Side of the Mountain* portrays survival in the mountains of the northeastern United States. Second, *River Rats, Inc.* portrays survival in a canyon in the southwestern United States. Third, *Julie and the Wolves* portrays survival on the arctic tundra. The stories also stress emotional and personal maturation.

After developing webs similar to the ones developed for island survival, upper-elementary students compared the three different settings according to their geographical locations, topography, longitude and latitude, and physical environments; their natural food supplies; the clothing they required; medical care required and how characters in the books solved this problem; seasonal changes in weather that influenced the characters' actions; and the types of shelters the characters made out of natural materials. The students compared the actions of the main characters in each story and identified the different ways that the characters responded to personal and environmental problems. One class developed a large chart (see Chart 9–4) that helped define these differences.

The descriptions of edible foods and their growing locations found in *My Side of the Mountain* and *River Rats, Inc.* related to topics studied in the science curriculum. To highlight these relationships, students reviewed the environmental implications of vegetation that grew along the water and in the desert regions described in *River Rats, Inc.* They identified the edible plants that characters found in each location and the procedures that the characters used to prepare and store the foods. For example, page 70 in *River Rats, Inc.* lists the following water-loving plants that created either a beautiful "Inner Kingdom" or, equally important, nourishing foods: cottonwoods, watercress, cattails, monkey flowers, maidenhair fern, wild garlic, and Indian vine.

In *My Side of the Mountain,* the students identified the larger trees that covered the slopes of a northeastern mountain: hemlock, oak, walnut, and hickory. They located references to plants that grew next to springs decorated with "flowers, ferns, moss, weeds—everything that loved water" (p. 30). Then, students followed the searches in the book for edible food, the steps in preparing the food, and methods of storing the food. Plant foods included hickory nuts and salt from hickory limbs (p. 23), apples (p. 24), walnuts, cattails, arrowleaf (p. 24), bulbs of dogtooth violets (pp. 27–28), dandelion greens (p. 28), strawberries (p. 35), wild garlic, jack-in-the-pulpit roots (p. 45), daisies, inner bark from the poplar tree, acorns (p. 62), sassafras roots (p. 66), pennyroyal, winterberry leaves (p. 67), arrowleaf bulbs, cattail tubers, bulrush roots, and wild onions (p. 81).

Referring to Laurence Pringle's *Wild Foods: A Beginner's Guide to Identifying, Harvesting and Preparing Safe and Tasty Plants from the Outdoors* (11) and Euell Gibbons's *Stalking the Wild Asparagus* (7), students investigated the wild plants mentioned in *My Side of the Mountain,* read suggestions for identifying and preparing them, compared these suggestions with the ways that the book's main character identified and prepared them, and identified which plants might be found near their own homes. (Warnings were also stressed; many wild plants are dangerous to eat. Therefore, the teacher recommended that the children not eat any plant unless they were accompanied by someone who knew exactly which plants were safe and which were dangerous.)

Because cattails were mentioned in both books and were available near the school, the students gathered them and tried grinding them into flour.

CHART 9–3
Physical survival activities developed around Scott O'Dell's *Island of the Blue Dolphins*

I. Seasonal weather
   A. Karana's life revolves around the seasons; she calculates time and the jobs she must do according to the seasons. Identify the island seasons, the characteristics, and the reasons for Karana's total involvement in the seasons. O'Dell's text provides many clues to seasonal weather: The flowers are plentiful in the spring because of heavy winter rains; in the spring, the birds leave the island and fly to the north; Karana gathers food for the winter; seasonal storms have winds and high waves.
   B. On a large mural, draw the Island of the Blue Dolphins, depicting the different seasons and weather conditions described in the book.
   C. Pretend to be Karana and write a diary. Include five entries from each season on the island. In the entries, describe seasonal weather and activities during that season.

II. Medical care
   A. *Use of indigenous plants and animals:* In the wilderness, accidents or illnesses are dangerous; there are no doctors or drugstores. Read page 96 to find out what Karana used on Rontu's wound. Find this plant (coral bush) in a reference book and consider why it would help Rontu's wound.
   B. *First aid and use of indigenous plants and animals:* Pretend that you and your family are isolated on an island in the Pacific. Consider the minor illnesses or accidents that could easily occur while on the island. For example, sunburn is common in warm climates. Other problems might include poisonous stings, broken legs, stomach upsets, headaches, and wounds. Research some plants, herbs, and other first aid resources that might be found on the island. Make an illustrated island survival book for medical care. Include drawings of plants, their medical properties, and sketches of first aid measures. After this is finished, consider Karana's personal medical needs and how she handled her problems.

III. Clothing
   A. *Natural materials:* Karana and her people lived on an island where the only sources of clothing were natural materials, plant and animal, found on the island or in the sea. What garments did Karana make for herself? What natural materials did she use? Divide into groups and investigate the procedures Karana would need to use and the time that would be involved in making a skirt from yucca fibers, a belt or a pair of sandals from sealskin, an otter cape, or a skirt of cormorant skins. (Even the needle and thread were made from natural sources.) After describing the natural materials and the procedures, discuss the importance of obtaining clothing in an isolated area and the influence that the need to obtain clothing has on the actions of the characters.

      Consider how your life is different because clothing and materials for clothing are easy to obtain. In your environment, identify natural materials that you could use for clothing and consider what you would need to do to make clothing from them. If possible, try making a garment from natural materials.
   B. *Adornment:* Karana and the women of her island wanted flowers and jewelry that would improve their appearance. Consider why Karana found satisfaction in making a flower wreath for her hair and for Rontu's neck. Investigate the types of flowers that Karana might have used to make her wreath. If possible, make your own flower wreaths using flowers in your own locality.

      Karana was also fond of jewelry. Consider the implications of Karana's spending five nights to make a circlet of abalone shells as a present for the Aleut girl, Tutok. Examine jewelry made from seashells. If possible, make your own jewelry from seashells. This can also be an opportunity for investigating the types of seashells that might be available on Karana's island.

IV. Food
   A. *Available food supplies:* List the foods Karana ate in the story. References are made to the scarlet apples that grow on cactus bushes (tunas) and foods from the sea, such as abalones and scallops. Research the possible sources that might be available on a Pacific island. Investigate several cookbooks and make an Island of the Blue Dolphins cookbook using the foods and seasonings Karana might find.
   B. *Utensils for storing and preparing food:* How did Karana fix her food? Where did she store the food to preserve it and protect it from animals? Karana had to make all of the utensils and storage containers for her food and water. Draw or make a list of five things Karana had to make in order to cook or store her food. Tell or show how she made these utensils or storage containers. Why was it important that Karana create each item? What could have happened if she had not created ways to store food? What impact did preparing and storing food have on her use of time and the plot of the story?

CHART 9–3 cont.
Physical survival activities developed around Scott O'Dell's *Island of the Blue Dolphins*

C. *How to acquire food:* Women in Karana's village were forbidden to make weapons. What is the significance for Karana when in spite of her fear, she makes weapons to protect herself and to obtain food? Why did she think of destructive winds when she considered the advisability of making weapons? Draw several weapons that Karana created, explain how she made them, and identify the natural resources she used.

D. *How to acquire food and available food supplies:* Rontu and Karana encounter and later hunt a devilfish. From the description on pages 103–104 and 118–124, try to determine another name for a devilfish. Use reference books and pay close attention to the details. Why did Karana spend her whole winter crafting a special kind of spear to hunt the devilfish?

E. *Conflicts between food or clothing sources and need for companionship:* A conflict arises for Karana when she begins to make friends with some animals on the island. What is the significance of her statement on page 156 that she would never kill another otter, seal, cormorant, or wild dog? Debate this issue as it could relate to your own life. (Another topic for debate is the destruction of animals, such as the sea otter. Karana decided to stop killing the otters even for a cape and would not tell the white men where the otters were located. Investigate the controversy connected with killing or saving the sea otter and then, taking pro and con positions, debate the issue.)

V. Geography

A. *Topography:* Based on Karana's description of the Island of the Blue Dolphins in chapter two and other parts of the book, make a map of the island. The map should include a scale and symbols. To make the scale, you must determine the equivalent length of a league. In her descriptions of where the sun rises and sets, Karana has given the north, south, east, and west directions. Place these symbols on the map. Chart the wind directions on the map. (The island is two leagues long and one league wide. A league is equivalent to about three miles. The island looks like a dolphin lying on its side. The tail points toward sunrise, which is east, and the nose points toward sunset, which is west.)

B. *Physical environment, longitude and latitude:* The Island of the Blue Dolphins is real. On a large map or atlas that shows the California coastline, find San Nicolas, which is located about seventy-five miles southwest of Los Angeles. Identify the longitude and latitude of the island. What is the effect of this longitude and latitude upon the island? Compare a description of San Nicolas in a reference book with the description of the island in the story. Are there any similarities or differences?

If someone were marooned on an island, what longitude and latitude would that person choose in order to have a natural environment most advantageous to survival? Write a short story describing the setting and how one would survive on the island.

C. *Topography, physical environment:* Several geographical terms are used in *Island of the Blue Dolphins.* Following is a list of some of these terms. To develop an understanding of the geography of the island, define each term as used in the story, find pictures illustrating each term, and draw examples of the terms as they looked on Karana's island. Try to see each one through Karana's eyes. What was the significance of each feature for Karana's survival?

mesa	cliffs	ravine
harbor	canyon	spring
cove		

VI. Shelter

A. *Types of shelters:* In her struggles for survival, Karana constructed both a fenced-in house (pp. 74–76) and a cave dwelling (p. 89). Reread the descriptions of each house and consider Karana's needs when she constructed these shelters. What was the advantage of each type of shelter? How did each shelter relate to the natural materials found upon the island, the physical environment of the island, and the tools that Karana had available for her use? Why did the need for shelter play such an important part in the development of the story and in the use of Karana's time and energy? Choose one of her island shelters and build a model of the shelter.

B. *Natural Materials:* Look at our own environment. If people were isolated in their physical environments without the houses and other buildings they have now, what types of natural shelter would they construct? Write a short story describing the decision-making processes that people use as they think about the types of shelter they will construct. In this story, consider the need for protection against weather changes, natural predators that might harm individuals or take their food supplies, the topography of the land that could be used to advantage, the proximity of the shelter to life-sustaining food and water supplies, and the availability of building materials and tools needed for construction. Build a model of this shelter.

CHART 9–4
Comparison of three different survival settings

	Catskill Mountains	Southwest Canyon	Arctic Tundra
Geography			
Topography			
Longitude and latitude			
Physical environment			
Fresh water sources			
Food			
Available supplies			
How to acquire food			
How to create utensils			
Food preparation			
Clothing			
Requirements related to environment			
Natural materials			
Sewing notions			
Medical Care			
Major concerns			
First aid			
Use of indigenous plants and animals			
Seasonal Weather			
Sun intensity			
Seasonal storms			
Air currents			
Shelter			
Requirements due to weather			
Requirements due to topography			
Natural materials			
Types of shelter tools			

They also followed Laurence Pringle's suggestions for boiling cattail rhizomes and using them as a potato substitute. This experience increased their empathy for the characters in the book, who had to work hard to survive on natural foods. The children related their research on natural foods and their preparation to the climatic conditions, geographical locations, and amount of water available for plants in both *River Rats, Inc.* and *My Side of the Mountain*. Gary Paulsen's *Hatchet* may be used for a similar activity. The main character in *Hatchet* must survive in the Canadian wilderness.

USING WEBBING IN GUIDED DISCUSSIONS

The webbing techniques used in the preceding survival activities may also be used to show the plot, conflict, characterization, setting, and theme of realistic fiction, and other literature. Webbing is a visual way that encourages oral discussions. My own research (10) with fifth- through eighth- grade students shows that webbing is one of the most effective ways to help students understand important characteristics of a story. Webbing also helps students increase their appreciation of literature and improve their reading and writing competencies.

Prior to the webbing experience, introduce the literary elements of plot (including conflict), characterization, setting, and theme by reading and discussing folktales with the children. Then draw simple webs that include each of these components. Lead discussions that help students identify the important characteristics being placed on the web.

This use of webbing can be applied, for example, to Byrd Baylor's *Hawk, I'm Your Brother,* a contemporary realistic story about a Native American boy's dreams of flying like a hawk. (Chapter eleven discusses using this book to develop an understanding of author's point of view.) First, introduce the story. As part of the introduction, draw the beginning of the web on the board, placing *Hawk, I'm Your Brother* in the center circle and extending the terms *setting, characterization, conflict, plot development,* and *themes* from that center. Next, read the story to the students, asking them to listen for the various categories. After the story is completed, lead a discussion in which the students fill in the various categories on the web. As you complete the web on the board, have the students copy the web onto their own papers. If necessary, reread parts of the story to help the students consider what information should be placed on the web. Figure 9–3 provides an example of a relatively simple web that sixth-grade students developed. Some webs become quite large. Some may cover several chalkboards.

In another class period following the development of the web, have the students write their own

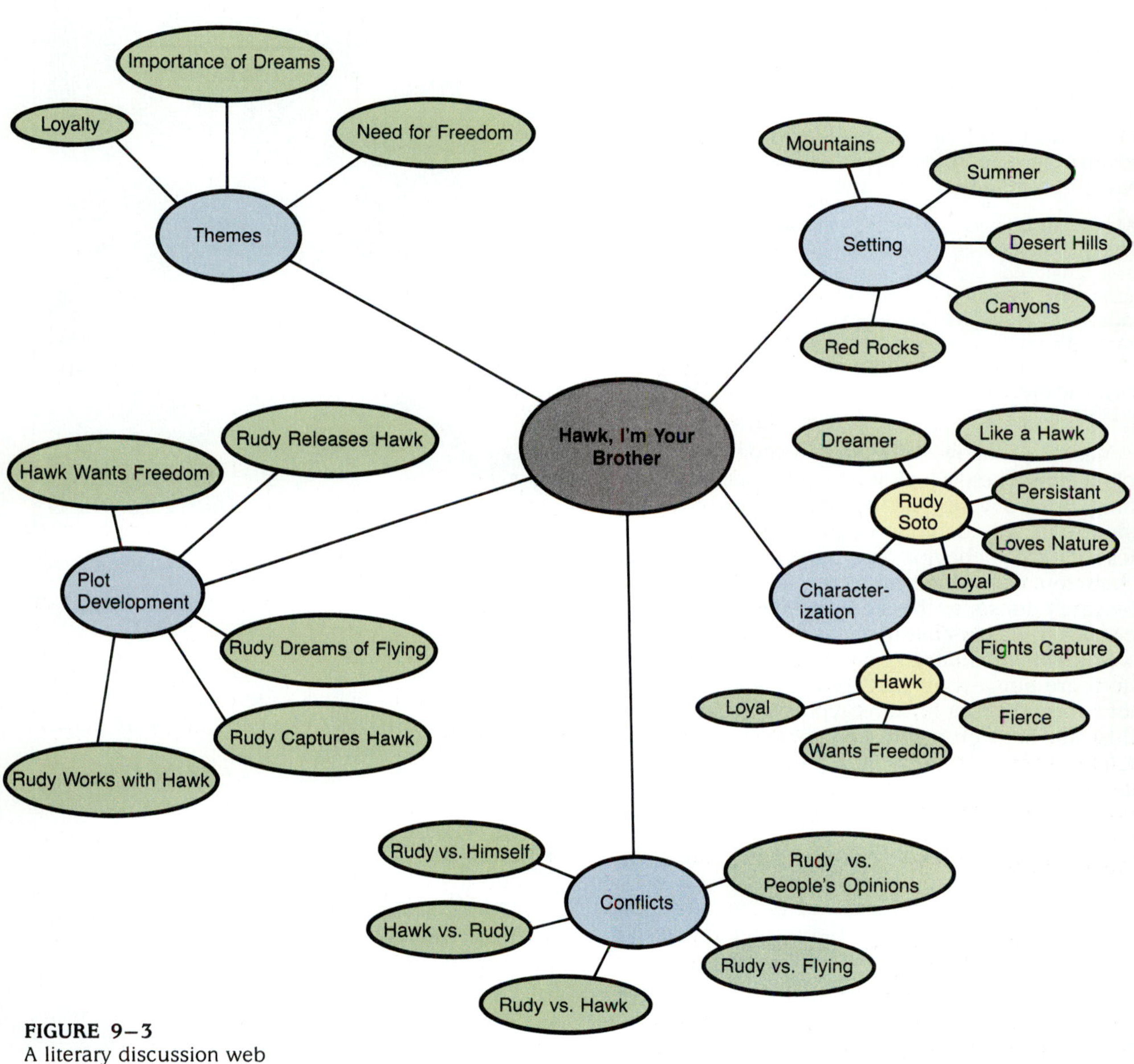

FIGURE 9–3
A literary discussion web

stories about the book. Have them use the information on the web to help them construct their stories.

Other types of charting are also effective in discussions about books. Mary G. Flender (6) provides charts that depict book covers, plot discussions, character attributes, themes, stylistic details, and connections between books.

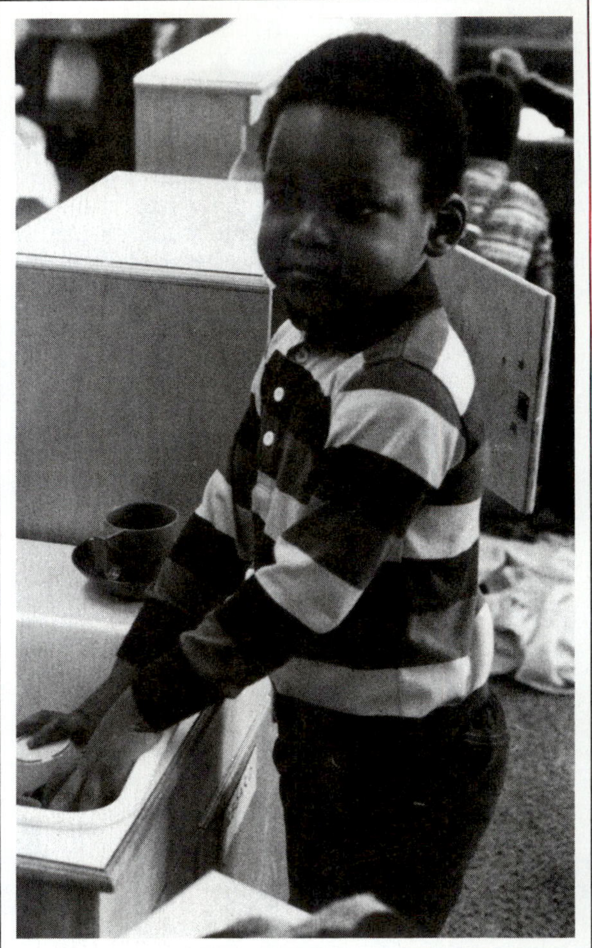

Nonstereotypic realistic fiction can help children overcome sex stereotypes.

DEVELOPING AN APPRECIATION FOR INDIVIDUALS: IMPROVING SELF-ESTEEM AND UNDERSTANDING

Researchers and writers in educational publications have found that until quite recently, children's textbooks lacked sufficient portrayals of positive female roles. Myra Pollack Sadker and David Miller Sadker (15) say:

> [A] growing body of research. . .attests to loss of female potential as girls go through school, and many writers have analyzed the way sex stereotyping occurs in classrooms across the country—from sexist teaching patterns to segregated activities. One key way that girls learn to undervalue themselves is through the books they read. When children open elementary school texts, they read most often about the activities and adventures of boys. (p. 231)

Masha Kabakow Rudman (14) concludes that "clinical psychologists have regularly defined anything but conventional gender role behavior as abnormal. This definition extends to characteristics beyond behavior and indicates that male characters are valued far above female" (p. 101). Research attests to the stereotyping of males and females found in children's literature.

Students of children's literature have identified literature suggesting that females and males do not necessarily act in stereotypic ways. Books that illustrate nonstereotypic behavioral patterns can help teachers, librarians, and parents who wish to combat stereotypes. Following are several examples.

1. Both girls and boys can overcome great struggles in nature and survive.
   Female: Scott O'Dell's *Island of the Blue Dolphins,* Jean Craighead George's *Julie of the Wolves*.
   Male: Armstrong Sperry's *Call It Courage,* Gary Paulsen's *Hatchet*.
2. Both young girls and young boys can be brave and intelligent.
   Female: Beverly Cleary's *Ramona The Brave*.
   Male: Eleanor Schick's *Joey on His Own*.
3. Girls can be independent and take care of their younger siblings or pets.
   Female: E. L. Konigsburg's *From the Mixed-up Files of Mrs. Basil E. Frankweiler* and Theodore Taylor's *The Trouble with Tuck*.
4. Both girls and boys can be intelligent and curious.
   Female: Louise Fitzhugh's *Harriet the Spy*.
   Male: Donald J. Sobol's *Encyclopedia Brown Sets the Pace*.
5. Boys can express feelings of fear; facing death is not the only way to demonstrate courage.
   Male: Maia Wojciechowska's *Shadow of a Bull* and Jean Little's *Different Dragons*.

These books have led to interesting discussions and comparisons. Children have learned that both boys and girls can demonstrate a wide range of acceptable behaviors—or have read stories that verified what their own experience has already taught them about the full range of feelings and behaviors available to girls and boys.

DEVELOPING QUESTIONING STRATEGIES

Not all literature selections should be accompanied by questioning. Nevertheless, librarians and teachers responsible for encouraging children to think about and react to literature in a variety of ways find a framework helpful for designing questions that assist children in examining certain aspects of a story and questions that require higher-level thought processes. Teachers and librarians who wish to develop such questioning strategies will find assistance in taxonomies of reading comprehension, such as those developed by Benjamin Bloom (4) and Thomas C. Barrett (2). For example, Barrett identifies four levels of reading comprehension: (1) literal recognition or recall, (2) inference, (3) evaluation, and (4) appreciation.

Questions related to levels of reading comprehension can be developed in relation to realistic fiction, such as Katherine Paterson's *Jacob Have I Loved,* which is used in the following extended examples. Paterson's book is appropriate for the upper-elementary and middle-school grades. The following questions only suggest the types of questions that might be developed around any book. A librarian or teacher might choose to focus upon only a few of these questions. The questions simply illustrate a variety of examples from each subsection of the taxonomy. They are not meant to suggest that every question must be discussed.

Literal Recognition

Literal recognition requires children to identify information provided in the literature. You may require children to recall the information from memory after reading or listening to a story or to locate information while reading a literature selection. Literal-level questions, such as the following often use such words as *who, what, where, when,* and *how*:

1 *Recall of details*: Where does the story *Jacob Have I Loved* take place? When does the story take place? Who are the characters in the story?
2 *Recall of sequence of events*: What was the sequence of events that led Louise to believe that Caroline was the favored child in the family? What was the sequence of events that caused Louise to move from an island to a mountain community?
3 *Recall of comparisons*: Compare the author's physical descriptions of Louise and Caroline. Compare the way Louise thought the family treated her with the way she thought they treated her twin sister, Caroline.
4 *Recall of character traits*: Describe Louise's response to the story about the birth of the twins, Louise and Caroline. How does Grandma respond to Caroline, to Louise, to Captain Wallace, to her son, and to her daughter-in-law?

Inference

When children infer an answer to a question, they go beyond the information the author provides and hypothesize about such things as details, main ideas, and cause-and-effect relationships. Inference is usually considered a higher-level thought process; the answers are not specifically stated within the text. Examples of inferential questions include the following:

1 *Inferring supporting details*: At the end of *Jacob Have I Loved,* Joseph Wojtkiewicz says, "God in heaven's been raising you for this valley from the day you were born." What do you believe he meant by this statement?
2 *Inferring main idea*: What do you believe is the theme of the book? What message do you think the author was trying to express to the reader?
3 *Inferring comparisons*: Think about the Captain Wallace, who is such a part of Louise's story. Compare that character with the one who left the island when he was a young man. How do you believe they are alike and how do you believe they are different?
4 *Inferring cause-and-effect relationships*: If you identified any changes in Captain Wallace, what do you believe might have caused them? Why do you believe Louise dreamed about Caroline's death? Why do you believe that Louise felt wild exultation and then terrible guilt after these dreams?
5 *Inferring character traits*: What do you believe caused Louise to change her mind about

wanting Hiram Wallace to be an islander who escaped rather than a Nazi spy? What is Louise saying about herself when she emphasizes the word *escaped*? Why do you believe Louise became so upset whenever she was called "Wheeze"? Why do you think Louise was so upset when Call invited Caroline to join them during their visit to the captain? At the end of the book, after Louise has delivered twins to a mountain family, she becomes very anxious over the healthier twin. Why do you think she gave this advice, "You should hold him. Hold him as much as you can. Or let his mother hold him" (p. 215)? What does this reaction say about Louise's own character and the changes in character that took place in her lifetime?

6 *Inferring outcomes*: There were several places in the book when the action and outcome of the story would have changed if characters had acted in different ways. Have students read or listen to the book up to a certain point. At various points, ask students to predict the outcomes. For example:
   - **a** At the end of chapter four, a mysterious man leaves the boat and walks alone toward an abandoned house. Who do you think he is? How do you think this man will influence the story?
   - **b** At the end of chapter twelve, Caroline finds and uses Louise's hidden hand lotion. What do you think will happen after Louise angrily breaks the bottle and runs out of the house?
   - **c** At the close of chapter fourteen, the captain has offered to send Caroline to Baltimore to continue her musical education. How do you think Caroline, her parents, and Louise will react to this suggestion?
   - **d** At the end of chapter seventeen, Louise and the captain are discussing what she plans to do with her life. Louise responds that she wants to become a doctor but cannot leave her family. Knowing Louise and her family, how do you think the story will end?

Evaluation

Evaluative questions require children to make judgments about the content of the literature by comparing it with external criteria, such as what authorities on a subject say, or internal criteria, such as experience or knowledge. The following are examples of evaluative questions:

1 *Judgment of adequacy or validity*: Do you agree that Louise in *Jacob Have I Loved* would not have been accepted as a student in a medical college? Why or why not? This story took place in the 1940s; would the author have been able to include the same scene between a woman and a university advisor if the story had taken place in the 1990s? Why or why not?

2 *Judgment of appropriateness*: What do you think the author meant by the reference to the quote, "Jacob have I loved, but Esau have I hated." How does this biblical line relate to the book? Do you think it is a good title for the book? Why or why not?

3 *Judgment of worth, desirability, or acceptability*: Was Louise right in her judgment that her parents always favored Caroline? What caused her to reach her final decision? Do you believe Louise made the right decision when she left the island? Why or why not?

Appreciation

Appreciation of literature requires a sensitivity to the techniques that authors use in order to have emotional impact on their readers. Questions can encourage children to respond emotionally to the plot, identify with the characters, react to an author's use of language, and react to an author's ability to create a visual image through word choices in the text. The following are examples of questions to stimulate appreciation:

1 *Emotional response to plot or theme*: How did you respond to the plot of *Jacob Have I Loved*? Did the author hold your interest? If so, how? Do you believe the theme of the story was worthwhile? Why or why not? Pretend you are either recommending this book for someone else to read or recommending that this book not be read; what would you tell that person?

2 *Identification with characters and incidents*: Have you ever felt, or known anyone who felt, like thirteen-year-old Louise or her twin sister, Caroline? What caused you or the person to feel that way? How would you have reacted if you had been thirteen-year-old Louise? How would you have reacted if you had been Caroline? Pretend to be a grown-up Louise in chapter eighteen talking with your mother about leaving the island. What emotions do you think your mother would feel when you responded, "I'm not going to rot here like

Grandma" (p. 200)? How would you feel when she told you, "I chose to leave my own people and build a life for myself somewhere else. I certainly wouldn't deny you that same choice. But. . .oh, Louise, we will miss you, your father and I" (p. 201)?

3 *Imagery*: How did the author encourage you to see the relationship between the island setting and changes in Louise's character over her lifetime?

4 *Appreciative comprehension and identification with characters and incidents*: Have you ever felt or known anyone who felt like thirteen-year-old Louise when she listened to the story about her birth and thought, "I felt cold all over, as though I was the newborn infant a second time, cast aside and forgotten" (p. 15)? How would you have reacted if you had been Louise and had heard this story repeatedly? What do you think could make you feel cold all over if you were Caroline and heard this story?

Suggested Activities for Children's Appreciation of Realistic Fiction

☐ Using the criteria for selecting appropriate literature for role playing, develop a file of stories that have problem situations appropriate for elementary-school children. Include stories that can be used by reading to a certain point and allowing children to role-play possible solutions, as well as stories that are more appropriate for role playing after an entire story has been read. Choose a role-playing situation and lead a role-playing activity with either a group of children or a peer group.

☐ Listen to several children tell you about a book they have read. Analyze the children's responses using Chart 9–2, "Classifying Children's Comments About Books."

☐ Choose a survival book related to the survival on islands webs. Develop instructional activities for the book to correspond with the webs. Suggested books include *Call It Courage*, *The Cay*, *The Swiss Family Robinson*, *My Side of the Mountain*, *River Rats, Inc.*, and *Julie of the Wolves*.

☐ Review the stories in a basal reader, and evaluate their content according to stereotypic roles for either males or females. Assume that some corrective action is required if a balanced portrayal of contributions of males and females is to occur, and identify several children's literature selections that could be used to balance a viewpoint. How could the literature be used in an instructional setting?

☐ Identify a list of children's literature sources that show many behavioral patterns for boys and girls, men and women.

☐ Develop a bibliography of books that illustrate nonstereotypic behavioral patterns in boys and girls. Write a short summary to describe the behavioral patterns that are shown in each book.

☐ Choose a realistic fiction book other than *Jacob Have I Loved*. Develop questioning strategies that follow a taxonomy of comprehension, such as that developed by Thomas C. Barrett or Benjamin Bloom.

References

1 Applebee, Arthur S. "Children and Stories: Learning the Rules of the Game." *Language Arts* 56 (September 1979).

2 Barrett, Thomas C. "Taxonomy of Reading Comprehension." In *Reading 360 Monograph*. Lexington, Mass.: Ginn, 1972.

3 Bernstein, Joanne. *Books to Help Children Cope with Separation and Loss*. 2nd ed. New York: Bowker, 1983.

4 Bloom, Benjamin. *Taxonomy of Educational Objectives*. New York: Longman, 1956.

5 Braga, Laurie, and Joseph Braga. *Learning and Growing: A Guide to Child Development*. Englewood Cliffs, N.J.: Prentice-Hall, 1975.

6 Flender, Mary G. "Charting Book Discussions: A Method of Presenting Literature in the Elementary Grades." *Children's Literature in Education* 16 (Summer 1985): 84–92.

7 Gibbons, Euell. *Stalking the Wild Asparagus*. New York: McKay, 1962, 1970.

8 Good, Carter. *Dictionary of Education*. New York: McGraw-Hill, 1969, 1973.

9 Lepman-Logan, Claudia. "Books in the Classroom: Moral Choices in Literature." *The Horn Book*. (January/February 1989): 108–111.

10 Norton, Donna E. "The Expansion and Evaluation of a Multiethnic Reading/Language Arts Program Designed for 5th, 6th, 7th, and 8th Grade Children." Meadows Foundation Grant, No. 55614, A Three Year Longitudinal Study. Texas A&M University, 1984–1987.

11 Pringle, Laurence. *Wild Foods: A Beginner's Guide to Identifying, Harvesting and Preparing Safe and Tasty Plants from the Outdoors*. Illustrated by Paul Breeden. New York: Four Winds, 1978.

12 Purves, Alan C., and Dianne L. Monson. *Experiencing Children's Literature*. Glenview, Ill.: Scott, Foresman, 1984.

13 Rosenblatt, Louise. *The Reader, the Text, and the Poem: The Transactional Theory of the Literary Work*. Carbondale, Ill.: Southern Illinois Press, 1978.

14 Rudman, Masha Kabakow. *Children's Literature: An Issues Approach*. 2d ed. New York: Longman, 1984.

15 Sadker, Myra Pollack, and David Miller Sadker. *Now upon a Time: A Contemporary View of Children's Literature*. New York: Harper & Row, 1977.

16 Shaftel, Fannie R., and George Shaftel. *Role-Playing for Social Values: Decision-Making in the Social Studies*. Englewood Cliffs, N.J.: Prentice-Hall, 1967.

17 Sutherland, Zena, and May Hill Arbuthnot. *Children and Books*. Glenview, Ill.: Scott, Foresman, 1986.

CHILDREN'S LITERATURE

Amdur, Nikki. *One of Us*, Illustrated by Ruth Sanderson. Dial, 1981 (I:9–12+ R:5). A blind boy and caring for a rabbit help a girl adjust to a new school.

Bauer, Marion Dane. *Foster Child*. Seabury, 1977 (I:12+ R:6). A foster child suffers child abuse.

———. *On My Honor*. Clarion, 1986 (I:10+ R:4). A strong person-against-self conflict results when a friend drowns in a river.

Bawden, Nina. *Kept in the Dark*. Lothrop, Lee & Shepard, 1982 (I:10+ R:7). A psychological thriller results when a previously unknown relative returns.

———. *The Outside Child*. Lothrop, Lee & Shepard, 1989 (I:10+ R:6). A thirteen-year-old girl discovers that her father has a second family.

———. *The Peppermint Pig*. Lippincott, 1975 (I:9–12 R:6). A family moves to rural Norfolk, England.

Baylor, Byrd. *Hawk, I'm Your Brother*. Illustrated by Peter Parnall. Scribner's Sons, 1976 (I:all R:6). Rudy Soto would like to glide through the air like a hawk.

Benjamin, Carol Lea. *The Wicked Stepdog*. Crowell, 1982 (I:9–12 R:4). A twelve-year-old girl fears she is losing her father's love when he remarries.

Blume, Judy. *Are You There God? It's Me, Margaret*. Bradbury, 1970 (I:10+ R:6). Eleven-year-old Margaret wonders about the changes that are occurring in her body.

———. *Blubber*. Bradbury, 1974 (I:10+ R:4). The children in the fifth grade start a campaign against a heavier girl in the class.

———. *Deenie*. Bradbury, 1973 (young adult).

———. *Forever*. Bradbury, 1975 (young adult).

———. *It's Not the End of the World*. Bradbury, 1972 (young adult).

———. *The One in the Middle Is the Green Kangaroo*. Illustrated by Amy Aitken. Bradbury, 1981 (I:6–9 R:2). A middle child gains self-esteem when he gets a part in a play.

———. *Otherwise Known as Sheila the Great*. Dutton, 1972 (I:9–12 R:6). Ten-year-old Sheila experiences an exciting summer.

———. *Tales of a Fourth Grade Nothing*. Illustrated by Roy Doty. Dutton, 1972 (I:7–12 R:4). Peter's problem is his two-year-old brother, Fudge.

———. *Then Again, Maybe I Won't*. Bradbury, 1971 (young adult).

I = Interest by age range.
R = Readability by grade level.

———. *Tiger Eyes*. Bradbury, 1981. (I:12+ R:7). A fifteen-year-old girl faces violence and fear.

Bonham, Frank. *Durango Street*. Dutton, 1965 (I:12+ R:5). Gang violence is realistically portrayed as two inner-city gangs cut out their territories.

———. *The Rascals from Haskell's Gym*. Dutton, 1977 (I:10+ R:6). Two gymnastic teams compete in this story about girls' sports.

Branscum, Robbie. *The Adventures of Johnny May*. Illustrated by Deborah Howland. Harper & Row, 1984 (I:8–12 R:6). A girl solves a mystery and provides Christmas for her grandparents.

Brooks, Bruce. *The Moves Make the Man*. Harper & Row, 1984 (I:10+ R:7). Basketball develops understanding between a black and a white boy.

Buchan, Stuart. *When We Lived with Pete*. Scribner's Sons, 1978 (I:12+ R:6). Tommy Bridge makes the final move that gives him the family he wants.

Bunting, Eve. *The Empty Window*. Illustrated by Judy Clifford. Warne, 1980 (I:7–10 R:3). A boy captures a wild parrot to give to his best friend, who has only a short time to live.

Burch, Robert. *Queenie Peavy*. Illustrated by Jerry Lazare. Viking, 1966 (I:10+ R:6). A strong female character longs for the day when her father will return from jail, but then she discovers his true nature.

Burnford, Sheila. *The Incredible Journey*. Illustrated by Carl Burger. Little, Brown, 1960, 1961 (I:8+ R:8). Three animals travel through 250 miles of Canadian wilderness.

Byars, Betsy. *After the Goat Man*. Illustrated by Ronald Himler. Viking, 1974 (I:9–12 R:7). An overweight boy meets a man who is trying to protect his home from an advancing interstate highway.

———. *The Animal, the Vegetable, and John D. Jones*. Illustrated by Ruth Sanderson. Delacorte, 1982 (I:9–12 R:5). Three children come into conflict when their single parents share a vacation.

———. *Beans on the Roof*. Illustrated by Melodye Rosales. Delacorte, 1988 (I:9–12 R:5). Members of a family try to write roof poems.

———. *Bingo Brown and the Language of Love*. Viking, 1989 (I:10+ R:5). A fifth-grade boy experiences his first crush.

———. *The Burning Questions of Bingo Brown*. Viking Kestrel, 1988 (I:10+ R:6). A boy searches for answers to confusing questions.

———. *Cracker Jackson*. Viking, 1985 (I:10+ R:6). An eleven-year-old boy tries to save his former baby-sitter from abuse by her husband.

———. *The Cybil War*. Illustrated by Gail Owens. Viking, 1981 (I:9–12 R:6). Two fourth graders battle for a girl's affections.

———. *The 18th Emergency*. Illustrated by Robert Grossman. Viking, 1973 (I:8–12 R:3). Problems arise from insulting the biggest boy in school.

———. *Good-bye, Chicken Little*. Harper & Row, 1979 (I:10+ R:7). Jimmy feels guilty because he thinks he didn't try hard enough to keep his uncle from walking across thin ice.

———. *The House of Wings*. Illustrated by Daniel Schwartz. Viking, 1972 (I:8–12 R:3). A transformation takes place as Sammy, with the help of a blind crane, learns to love his grandfather.

———. *The Night Swimmers*. Illustrated by Troy Howell. Delacorte, 1980 (I:8–12 R:5). An older sister tries to care for her brothers while her father works nights.

———. *The Summer of the Swans*. Illustrated by Ted CoConis. Viking, 1970 (I:8–12 R:4). A mentally disabled boy goes out alone in search of the wild swans.

Callen, Larry. *Sorrow's Song*. Little, Brown, 1979 (I:8–10 R:3). A young girl who cannot talk cares for a wounded whooping crane.

Cameron, Eleanor. *Julia's Magic*. Illustrated by Gail Owens. Dutton, 1984 (I:9–12 R:5). Julia causes difficulty when she breaks a perfume bottle.

———. *That Julia Redfern*. Illustrated by Gail Owens. Dutton, 1982 (I:9–12 R:5). A book about Julia is based on experiences when she was younger.

Carrick, Carol. *The Accident*. Illustrated by Donald Carrick. Seabury, 1976 (I:5–8 R:4). Christopher experiences a series of emotions after his dog is killed.

———. *Stay Away from Simon*. Clarion, 1985 (I:7–10 R:3). A mentally retarded boy helps two children discover that disabled people have great worth.

Christopher, Matt. *Dirt Bike Racer*. Illustrated by Barry Bomzer. Little, Brown, 1979 (I:10+ R:4). Twelve-year-old Ron Baker restores a minibike.

———. *Face-Off*. Illustrated by Harvey Kidder. Little, Brown, 1972 (I:8–12 R:4). Scott Harrison must overcome a tremendous fear about a hockey player.

———. *Football Fugitive*. Illustrated by Larry Johnson. Little, Brown, 1976 (I:9–12 R:6). Larry wishes his father would take an interest in football.

———. *The Fox Steals Home*. Illustrated by Larry Johnson. Little, Brown, 1978 (I:8–12 R:6). Baseball helps a boy overcome his worries about his parents' divorce.

———. *The Twenty-One-Mile Swim*. Little, Brown, 1979 (I:10+ R:5). A boy of small stature decides that he will swim the twenty-one miles across a lake.

Cleary, Beverly. *Dear Mr. Henshaw*. Illustrated by Paul O. Zelinsky. Morrow, 1983 (I:9–12 R:5). Corresponding with an author helps a boy overcome problems related to his parents' divorce.

———. *Henry and Beezus*. Illustrated by Louis Darling. Morrow, 1952 (I:7–10 R:6). Henry and the girl he finds least obnoxious have a humorously good time.

———. *Muggie Maggie*. Illustrated by Kay Life. Morrow, 1990 (I:7–10 R:5). A third grader decides that she does not want to learn cursive writing.

———. *Mitch and Amy*. Illustrated by George Porter. Morrow, 1967 (I:7–10 R:6). A humorous story is about everyday experiences.

———. *Ramona and Her Father*. Illustrated by Alan Tiegreen. Morrow, 1977 (I:7–10 R:6). Ramona tries to help her father through a trying period after he has lost his job.

———. *Ramona and Her Mother*. Illustrated by Alan Tiegreen. Morrow, 1979 (I:7–10 R:6). Ramona's mother goes to work.

———. *Ramona the Brave*. Illustrated by Alan Tiegreen. Morrow, 1975 (I:7–10 R:6). Ramona has many difficulties until she finally wins a truce with the first-grade teacher.

———. *Ramona the Pest*. Illustrated by Louis Darling. Morrow, 1968 (I:7–10 R:4). Ramona enters kindergarten and spreads exasperation into a wider sphere.

———. *Ramona Quimby, Age 8*. Illustrated by Alan Tiegreen. Morrow, 1981 (I:7–10 R:6). Ramona faces new challenges when her father returns to college.

Cleaver, Vera, and Bill Cleaver. *I Would Rather Be a Turnip*. Lippincott, 1971 (I:11+ R:6). Changes occur in twelve-year-old Annie's life when her illegitimate nephew comes to live with her family.

———. *Lady Ellen Grae*. Illustrated by Ellen Raskin. Lippincott, 1968 (I:8–12 R:6). An eleven-year-old tomboy goes to Seattle so she can learn to be a lady.

———. *A Little Destiny*. Lothrop, Lee & Shepard, 1979 (I:12+ R:6). When Lucy decides to avenge her father's death, she discovers that her destiny is a matter of her own choosing.

———. *Me Too*. Lippincott, 1973 (I:10–14 R:7). Lydia tries to educate her mentally disabled sister so that she will not be different.

———. *Queen of Hearts*. Lippincott, 1978 (I:11+ R:6). Twelve-year-old Wilma makes discoveries about herself and her grandmother.

———. *Trial Valley*. Lippincott, 1977 (I:11+ R:5). In a sequel to *Where the Lilies Bloom*, Mary Call struggles to keep the family together.

———. *Where the Lilies Bloom*. Illustrated by Jim Spanfeller. Lippincott, 1969 (I:11+ R:5). Four children hide their father's death so that they can remain together.

Clymer, Eleanor. *The Get-Away Car*. Dutton, 1978 (I:8–12 R:3). In a humorous story, a resourceful grandmother solves her granddaughter's problems and her own problems.

Cole, Brock. *The Goats*. Farrar, Straus & Giroux, 1987 (I:10+ R:5). A boy and a girl survive a camp experience in which they are humiliated by their peers.

Conford, Ellen. *The Revenge of the Incredible Dr. Rancid and His Youthful Assistant, Jeffrey*. Little, Brown, 1980 (I:10+ R:4). A small, skinny boy discovers a way to become a superhero and overcome the class bully.

Corcoran, Barbara. *The Potato Kit*. Atheneum, 1989 (I:10+ R:6). A girl from a poor rural family spends the summer with a wealthier family.

———. *You're Allegro Dead*. Atheneum, 1981 (I:10+ R:5). Twelve-year-old friends encounter a mystery at a summer camp.

Cormier, Robert. *The Bumblebee Flies Anyway*. Pantheon, 1983 (I:14+ R:6). A sixteen-year-old boy faces illness in a terminal care facility.

Cresswell, Helen. *Absolute Zero: Being the Second Part of the Bagthorpe Saga*. Macmillan, 1978 (I:8–12 R:6). The Bagthorpes began competing in their efforts to win contests.

———. *Bagthorpes Abroad*. Macmillan, 1984 (I:8–10 R:6). The family vacations in a dilapidated, maybe ghostly, house in Wales.

———. *Bagthorpes Unlimited.* Macmillan, 1978 (I:8–12 R:6). The Bagthorpes try to set a new world record.

———. *Bagthorpes v. the World: Being the Fourth Part of the Bagthorpe Saga.* Macmillan, 1979 (I:8–12 R:6). An overdraft notice from the bank sends the Bagthorpes into a chaotic survival campaign.

———. *Ordinary Jack.* Macmillan, 1977 (I:8–12 R:6). This is the first book in the series about the humorous Bagthorpes.

Cross, Gillian. *A Map to Nowhere.* Holiday House, 1989 (I:10+ R:5). A boy decides if he should betray his friend.

———. *On the Edge.* Holiday House, 1985 (I:10+ R:5). This is a gripping story of kidnapping and terrorism.

———. *Roscoe's Leap.* Holiday House, 1987 (I:10+ R:6). This mystery is about a collection of windup toys.

Cunningham, Julia. *Burnish Me Bright.* Illustrated by Don Freeman. Pantheon, 1970 (I:8–12 R:8). A mute boy in a French village is taught to pantomime by a retired actor and then is persecuted by the villagers.

———. *Come to the Edge.* Pantheon, 1977 (I:12+ R:7). In a psychological story, a fourteen-year-old boy must discover the will to love.

———. *Dorp Dead.* Illustrated by James Spanfeller. Pantheon, 1965 (I:11+ R:7). In a complicated psychological novel, an eleven-year-old orphan faces evil.

———. *The Silent Voice.* Dutton, 1981 (I:10+ R:8). A teenage mute boy is helped by a group of Parisian performers and a famous mime.

Davis, Jenny. *Good-bye and Keep Cold.* Orchard, 1987 (I:12+ R:6). A girl looks back on the traumatic years after her father's death in a mining accident.

DeJong, Meindert. *Shadrach.* Illustrated by Maurice Sendak. Harper & Row, 1953 (I:8–10 R:4). A boy in the Netherlands tries to sneak away from his protective mother and grandmother.

———. *The Wheel on the School.* Illustrated by Maurice Sendak. Harper & Row, 1954 (I:10+ R:6). The children of Shora, Netherlands, make a home for storks.

Delton, Judy. *Angel's Mother's Wedding.* Houghton Mifflin, 1987 (I:7–10 R:4). Angel worries that her mother is not taking the upcoming wedding seriously enough.

de Paola, Tomie. *Nana Upstairs & Nana Downstairs.* Putnam, 1973 (I:3–7 R:6). A boy has two beloved grandmothers.

Desbarats, Peter. *Gabrielle and Selena.* Illustrated by Nancy Grossman. Harcourt Brace Jovanovich, 1968 (I:5–8 R:4). This is a story of interracial friendship.

Dicks, Terrance. *The Baker Street Irregulars in the Case of the Blackmail Boys.* Elsevier/Nelson, 1981 (I:10+ R:6). London youngsters outwit criminals.

———. *The Baker Street Irregulars in the Case of the Cinema Swindle.* Elsevier/Nelson, 1981 (I:10+ R:6). A boy uses techniques developed by Sherlock Holmes to solve a mystery.

———. *The Baker Street Irregulars in the Case of the Cop Catchers.* Dutton, 1982 (I:10+ R:6). The amateur detectives solve the case of the disappearance of a police sergeant.

———. *The Baker Street Irregulars in the Case of the Crooked Kids.* Elsevier/Nelson, 1981 (I:10+ R:6). Youthful detectives capture a ring of juvenile thieves.

———. *The Baker Street Irregulars in the Case of the Ghost Grabbers.* Elsevier/Nelson, 1981 (I:10+ R:6). A haunted house provides the setting.

Domke, Todd. *Grounded.* Knopf, 1982 (I:9–12 R:5). A sixth grader involves his classmates in a play so that he can earn money to build a glider.

Dubellar, Thea. *Maria.* Translated by Anthea Bell. Illustrated by Mance Post. Morrow, 1982 (I:9–12 R:5). A girl retains her sense of self even though she experiences many family problems.

Duncan, Lois. *Don't Look Behind You.* Delacorte, 1989 (I:12+ R:6). A family must move when the father is threatened.

Ellis, Sarah. *Next-Door Neighbors.* Macmillan, 1990 (I:10+ R:5). A girl has difficulty making friends her own age when she moves.

Enright, Elizabeth. *Thimble Summer.* Holt, Rinehart & Winston, 1938, 1966 (I:7–12 R:5). Nine-year-old Garnet spends the summer on her Wisconsin farm.

Estes, Eleanor. *The Moffats.* Illustrated by Louis Slobodkin. Harcourt Brace Jovanovich, 1941 (I:7–10 R:4). The happy Moffat children experience a series of adventures.

Farber, Norma. *How Does It Feel to Be Old?.* Illustrated by Trina Schart Hyman. Dutton, 1979 (I:5–8 R:2). A grandmother tells her granddaughter about the good and bad experiences related to growing old.

Farley, Walter. *The Black Stallion.* Illustrated by Keith Ward. Random House, 1944 (I:8+ R:3). The black stallion saves Alec's life.

———. *The Black Stallion Picture Book.* Photographs furnished by United Artists. Random House, 1979 (I:6–8 R:2). This is a picture storybook version of *The Black Stallion.*

———. *The Black Stallion Returns.* Random House, 1945, 1973 (I:8+ R:3). Alec learns the history of the horse and finds himself in the center of a blood feud and an important race.

Fassler, Joan. *Howie Helps Himself.* Illustrated by Joe Lasker. Whitman, 1974 (I:4–8 R:2). A child with cerebral palsy tries very hard to move his wheelchair by himself.

Fine, Anne. *Alias Madame Doubtfire.* Little, Brown, 1988 (I:9+ R:5). A father in disguise becomes babysitter and cleaning woman in the home of his ex-wife.

———. *My War with Goggle-Eyes.* Little, Brown, 1989 (I:11+ R:6). A girl tries to sabotage her mother's boyfriend.

Fitzhugh, Louise. *Harriet the Spy.* Harper & Row, 1964 (I:8–12 R:3). Eleven-year-old Harriet keeps a notebook of observations about people.

———. *The Long Secret.* Harper & Row, 1965 (I:8–12 R:3). This is a sequel to *Harriet the Spy.*

———. *Sport.* Delacorte, 1979 (I:8–12 R:3). When eleven-year-old Sport inherits $20 million, his mother appears and tries to get the money.

Fox, Paula. *The Moonlight Man.* Bradbury, 1986 (I:12+ R:5). A girl makes discoveries about herself and her father after her parents' divorce.

———. *One-Eyed Cat.* Bradbury, 1984 (I:10+ R:5). An eleven-year-old boy shoots a cat and then must face his guilt.

———. *The Village by the Sea.* Watts, 1988 (I:10+ R:6). A girl discovers human foibles when she stays with an aunt while her father has surgery.

George, Jean Craighead. *The Cry of the Crow.* Harper & Row, 1980 (I:10+ R:5). Mandy must make a choice when her pet crow attacks her brother.

———. *Julie of the Wolves.* Illustrated by John Schoenherr. Harper & Row, 1972 (I:10+ R:7). An Eskimo girl lost on the North Slope of Alaska survives with the help of wolves.

———. *My Side of the Mountain.* Dutton, 1959 (I:10+ R:6). Sam Gribley creates a home inside a rotted-out tree.

———. *River Rats, Inc.* Dutton, 1979 (I:10+ R:7). Two boys must survive with the help of a wild boy, a canyon, and the desert beyond.

Gerson, Corinne. *Son for a Day*. Illustrated by Velma Ilsley. Atheneum, 1980 (I:7–11 R:4). In a humorous story, a boy joins divorced fathers who bring their children to the zoo.

Gipson, Fred. *Curly and the Wild Boar*. Illustrated by Ronald Himler. Harper & Row, 1979 (I:10+ R:7). Curly is determined to kill the wild boar that smashed his prize melon.

———. *Old Yeller*. Illustrated by Carl Burger. Harper & Row, 1956 (I:10+ R:6). Old Yeller is bitten by a rabid wolf as he saves the lives of those he loves.

Graeber, Charlotte. *Mustard*. Illustrated by Donna Diamond. Macmillan, 1982 (I:7–10 R:4). A boy faces the death of his beloved fourteen-year-old cat.

Greenberg, Jan. *The Iceberg and Its Shadow*. Farrar, Straus & Giroux, 1980 (I:9–14 R:6). This story of peer manipulation and victimization is similar to Judy Blume's *Blubber*.

Greene, Constance. *Al(exandra) the Great*. Viking, 1982 (I:8–12 R:3). A girl's vacation plans are changed when her mother gets pneumonia.

———. *Beat the Turtle Drum*. Illustrated by Donna Diamond. Viking, 1976 (I:10+ R:7). After an accident, the family must cope with Joss's death.

———. *The Ears of Louis*. Illustrated by Nola Langner. Viking, 1974 (I:8–12 R:3). Louis tries many solutions to his big ears before he discovers that he has many desirable characteristics and skills.

———. *The Unmaking of Rabbit*. Viking, 1972 (I:10+ R:5). Eleven-year-old Paul is teased about his big ears and his stuttering.

Greenwald, Sheila. *Give Us a Great Big Smile, Rosy Cole*. Little, Brown, 1981 (I:8–10 R:4). Rosy's uncle decides that he will base a book on his niece and her violin.

Griffiths, Helen. *The Dancing Horses*. Holiday House, 1982 (I:10+ R:6). A poor boy struggles to realize his dreams in post-Civil War Spain.

———. *Running Wild*. Illustrated by Victor Ambrus. Holiday House, 1977 (I:10+ R:6). A boy discovers tragic results when two dogs grow wild in the forest.

Haas, Jessie. *Keeping Barney*. Greenwillow, 1982 (I:9–12 R:5). A girl gets a chance to care for a horse and tries to win his devotion.

Hall, Lynn. *Danza!* Scribner's Sons, 1981 (I:10–14 R:5). A boy's care for a horse helps his personal development in a story set in Puerto Rico.

———. *In Trouble Again, Zelda Hammersmith?* Harcourt Brace Jovanovich, 1987 (I:8–12 R:3). Five humorous episodes are about a fourth-grade girl.

Hamilton, Virginia. *The House of Dies Drear*. Macmillan, 1968 (I:11+ R:4). In a suspenseful story, a family lives in a home that was once a station on the Underground Railroad.

———. *The Planet of Junior Brown*. Macmillan, 1971 (I:12+ R:6). Three outcasts from society create their own world in a secret basement room.

Harris, Rosemary. *Zed*. Farber & Farber, 1982 (I:12+ R:7). An eight-year-old boy is held by terrorists in London.

Haugen, Tormod. *The Night Birds*. Translated from the Norwegian by Sheila La Farge. Delacorte, 1982 (I:10+ R:3). A seven-year-old boy faces real and imagined terrors.

Hautzig, Esther. *A Gift for Mama*. Illustrated by Donna Diamond. Viking, 1981 (I:8–10 R:4). Sarah mends clothing to earn money for a Mother's Day gift.

Henry, Marguerite. *Black Gold*. Illustrated by Wesley Dennis. Rand McNally, 1957 (I:8–12 R:6). This is the history of a great racing horse named Black Gold and the trainer and jockey who loved him.

———. *Justin Morgan Had a Horse*. Illustrated by Wesley Dennis. Rand McNally, 1954 (I:8–12 R:6). This is the story of how Little Bub inherited the name of his owner Justin Morgan.

———. *King of the Wind*. Illustrated by Wesley Dennis. Rand McNally, 1948, 1976 (I:8–12 R:6). This is the story of the great Godolphin Arabian who was the ancestor of Man o' War.

———. *Misty of Chincoteague*. Illustrated by Wesley Dennis. Rand McNally, 1947, 1963 (I:8–12 R:6). Misty is the descendant of the Spanish horses that swam to Assateague Island after a shipwreck.

———. *San Domingo: The Medicine Hat Stallion*. Illustrated by Robert Lougheed. Rand McNally, 1972 (I:9–14 R:4). A boy's greatest joy is his foal with the markings believed sacred by the Indians.

Hopkins, Lee Bennett. *Mama*. Knopf, 1977 (I:7–10 R:6). A boy worries about his mother and tries to change her.

Howard, Ellen. *Edith Herself*. Atheneum, 1987 (I:7–10 R:4). A girl with epilepsy learns to value herself in the 1890s.

Hughes, Dean. *Family Pose*. Atheneum, 1989 (I:10+ R:6). An orphan boy discovers a new family among hotel workers.

Hunt, Irene. *Up a Road Slowly*. Follett, 1966 (I:11+ R:7). This is the story of a girl's life and the influence of an aunt with whom she stays after her mother dies.

Hurwitz, Johanna. *Russell and Elisa*. Illustrated by Lillian Hoban. Morrow, 1989 (I:3–8 R:3). Six stories tell about a brother and sister.

Keller, Beverly. *No Beasts! No Children!* Lothrop, Lee & Shepard, 1983 (I:8–12 R:4). A father, his children, and their pets cope by themselves.

Kjelgaard, Jim. *Big Red*. Illustrated by Bob Kuhn. Holiday House, 1945, 1956 (I:10+ R:7). Danny trains a champion Irish setter.

Klein, Norma. *Mom, the Wolf Man and Me*. Pantheon, 1972 (I:12+ R:6). Eleven-year-old Brett loves her life with her lively unwed mother.

———. *Tomboy*. Four Winds, 1978 (I:9–12 R:4). Ten-year-old Antonia doesn't want to grow up and experience the changes that naturally happen to a girl.

Kline, Suzy. *Herbie Jones and the Monster Ball*. Illustrated by Richard Williams. Putnam, 1988 (I:8+ R:4). A boy learns to play baseball when his uncle is the coach.

Konigsburg, E. L. *About the B'nai Bagels*. Atheneum, 1969 (I:8–12 R:7). Mark Setzer has special problems with his little league baseball team: His mother is the manager, and his brother is the coach.

———. *From the Mixed-up Files of Mrs. Basil Frankweiler*. Atheneum, 1967 (I:9–12 R:7). Eleven-year-old Claudia and her younger brother run away to the Metropolitan Museum of Art.

———. *(George)*. Atheneum, 1970, 1980 (I:10+ R:7). This is a story about a multiple personality and how the differences were resolved.

———. *Jennifer, Hecate, Macbeth, William McKinley, and Me, Elizabeth*. Atheneum, 1967, 1976 (I:8–12 R:4). Elizabeth becomes an apprentice witch in this story of interracial friendships.

———. *Journey to an 800 Number*. Atheneum, 1982 (I:10+ R:7). A boy learns to appreciate his father when he spends the summer with him.

———. *Throwing Shadows*. Atheneum, 1979 (I:11+ R:7). A collection of five short stories is about people making discoveries about themselves.

Laird, Elizabeth. *Loving Ben*. Delacorte, 1988 (I:11+ R:6). A hydrocephalic child changes the lives of the members of a family.

L'Engle, Madeleine. *Meet the Austins*. Vanguard, 1960 (I:10+ R:6). The six Austins have a family filled with spontaneous love, understanding, and personal discipline.

Lisle, Janet Taylor. *Afternoon of the Elves*. Watts, 1989 (I:10+ R:5). Two very different girls become friends as they work on a miniature village.

Little, Jean. *Different Dragons*. Illustrated by Laura Fernandez. Viking, 1986 (I:8–10 R:4). A boy overcomes his fear of dogs.

———. *From Anna*. Illustrated by Joan Sandin. Harper & Row, 1972 (I:8–12 R:5). Nine-year-old Anna lives in a world blurred by poor eyesight until she is placed in a special class.

———. *Mine for Keeps*. Illustrated by Lewis Parker. Little, Brown, 1962 (I:8–12 R:4). A girl crippled by cerebral palsy leaves the security of a home for the physically disabled and returns to her family.

London, Jack. *Call of the Wild*. Photographs by Seymour Linden. Harmony, 1903, 1977 (I:10+ R:5). This is the classic story of a brave dog and the Klondike gold rush.

Lowry, Lois. *All About Sam*. Illustrated by Diane deGroat. Houghton Mifflin, 1988 (I:8–12 R:5). This story is about Anastasia's little brother.

———. *Anastasia Again!* Illustrated by Diane deGroat. Houghton Mifflin, 1981. (I:8–12 R:6). Anastasia must adjust to living in the suburbs.

———. *Anastasia at Your Service*. Illustrated by Diane deGroat. Houghton Mifflin, 1982 (I:8–12 R:6). An older Anastasia becomes a household servant rather than a companion to a rich woman.

———. *Anastasia Krupnik*. Houghton Mifflin, 1979 (I:8–12 R:6). Ten-year-old Anastasia forms a hate list and a love list and discovers that eventually all of the items are on one list.

———. *Anastasia on Her Own*. Houghton Mifflin, 1985 (I:8–12 R:4). In a humorous tale, Anastasia takes over housekeeping when her mother leaves for a consulting job.

———. *Anastasia's Chosen Career*. Houghton Mifflin, 1987 (I:10+ R:6). Anastasia has humerous experiences when she takes a modeling course.

———. *The One Hundredth Thing About Caroline*. Houghton Mifflin, 1983 (I:8–12 R:3). An eleven-year old retaliates when she thinks she is to become the victim of murder.

———. *Rabble Starkey*. Houghton Mifflin, 1987 (I:10+ R:6). Set in an Appalachian town, a twelve-year-old girl learns to value a different type of family.

———. *Your Move, J. P.!* Houghton Mifflin, 1990 (I:10+ R:6). A seventh grader experiences feelings of love.

McDonnell, Christine. *Don't Be Mad, Ivy*. Illustrated by Diane deGroat. Dial, 1981 (I:6–9 R:3). A young girl overcomes everyday problems connected with home and school.

McGraw, Eloise Jarvis. *The Money Room*. Atheneum, 1981 (I:10+ R:6). The mystery of possible hidden money adds to a tale of family survival after a father's death.

MacLachlan, Patricia. *The Facts and Fictions of Minna Pratt*. Harper & Row, 1988 (I:7–12 R:4). A girl learns to appreciate herself and her family.

———. *Mama One, Mama Two*. Illustrated by Ruth Lercher Bornstein. Harper & Row, 1982 (I:4–8 R:3). A child has a happy foster home experience.

Madsen, Jane M., and Diane Bockoras. *Please Don't Tease Me. . . .* Illustrated by Kathleen T. Brinko. Judson, 1983 (I:6–9 R:6). A physically disabled girl asks for understanding.

Mann, Peggy. *My Dad Lives in a Downtown Hotel*. Illustrated by Richard Cuffari. Doubleday, 1973 (I:7–10 R:4). A boy experiences many emotions as he discovers that his parents are divorcing.

———. *There Are Two Kinds of Terrible*. Doubleday, 1977 (I:10+ R:5). A boy must face his mother's death.

Martin, Katherine. *Night Riding*. Knopf, 1989 (I:12+ R:6). A girl becomes friends with a neighbor who is being abused by her father.

Masterman-Smith, Virginia. *The Great Egyptian Heist*. Four Winds, 1982 (I:10+ R:5). Mystery surrounds diamonds found in an Egyptian coffin.

Mathis, Sharon Bell. *The Hundred Penny Box*. Puffin, 1986 (I:6–9 R:3). A boy loves to hear his aunt tell stories about each penny in a box.

Mauser, Pat Rhoads. *A Bundle of Sticks*. Illustrated by Gail Owens. Atheneum, 1982 (I:9–12 R:5). An eleven-year-old is humiliated by a bully and takes self-defense lessons.

Mayne, William. *Gideon Ahoy!* Delacorte, 1989 (I:11+ R:6). A twelve-year-old girl helps her brain-damaged and deaf older brother.

Mazer, Norma Fox. *After the Rain*. Morrow, 1987 (I:12+ R:5). A fifteen-year-old girl faces her grandfather's death.

Moeri, Louise. *Downwind*. Dutton, 1984 (I:10+ R:7). A twelve-year-old boy and his family escape a possible radiation leak at a nuclear power plant.

Myers, Walter Dean. *It Ain't All for Nothin'*. Viking, 1978 (I:10+ R:4). A boy's life changes drastically when he enters his father's world of crime and neglect.

———. *Scorpions*. Harper & Row, 1988 (I:10+ R:5). A boy becomes involved with a gang, and his best friend tries to stop his actions.

Naylor, Phyllis Reynolds. *Alice in Rapture, Sort Of*. Atheneum, 1989 (I:10+ R:5). A girl discovers that it is better to be friends with a boy than to have a boyfriend.

Neville, Emily. *It's Like This, Cat*. Illustrated by Emil Weiss. Harper & Row, 1963 (I:8–12 R:6). David Mitchell has two best friends, an older boy and a stray tomcat.

Newman, Robert. *The Case of the Baker Street Irregular*. Atheneum, 1978 (I:10+ R:6). Kidnappings, bombings, and the mystery of the identity of Andrew's mother bring Andrew and Sherlock Holmes together.

———. *The Case of the Vanishing Corpse*. Atheneum, 1980 (I:10+ R:6). A series of incidents bring Andrew into contact with Constable Wyatt.

O'Dell, Scott. *Island of the Blue Dolphins*. Houghton Mifflin, 1960 (I:10+ R:6). Twelve-year-old Karana survives alone for eighteen years before a ship takes her to the California mainland.

Park, Barbara. *Don't Make Me Smile*. Knopf, 1981 (I:9–12 R:5). A ten-year-old boy reacts to his parents' divorce.

———. *The Kid in the Red Jacket*. Knopf, 1987 (I:7–11 R:3). A ten-year-old boy faces humorous problems when he moves.

———. *Maxie, Rosie, and Earl—Partners in Crime*. Knopf, 1990 (I:8–12 R:5). A humorous story about three children who constantly get into trouble.

Paterson, Katherine. *Bridge to Terabithia*. Illustrated by Donna Diamond. Crowell, 1977 (I:10–14 R:6). Two nonconformists create their own magical realm.

———. *Come Sing, Jimmy Jo*. Dutton, 1985 (I:10+ R:4). An eleven-year-old boy makes self-discoveries through his musical gift.

———. *The Great Gilly Hopkins*. Crowell, 1978 (I:10+ R:6). A rebellious girl tries to adjust to abandonment and foster homes.

———. *Jacob Have I Loved*. Crowell, 1980 (I:10+ R:7). A twin feels that her sister has deprived her of parental affection and schooling.

Paulsen, Gary. *Dancing Carl*. Bradbury, 1983 (I:10+ R:4). Two boys learn to respect a war veteran who had a traumatic experience.

———. *Hatchet*. Bradbury, 1987 (I:10+ R:6). A thirteen-year-old boy learns personal and physical survival in the Canadian wilderness.

Peck, Richard. *Remembering the Good Times*. Delacorte, 1985 (I:12+ R:4). A strong friendship develops among three students until one takes his own life.

Peyton, K. M. *The Team*. Crowell, 1976 (I:10+ R:5). A girl joins a pony club.

Phipson, Joan. *Hit and Run*. Atheneum, 1985 (I:10+ R:6). A survival story is set in Australia.

Powell, Randy. *My Underrated Year*. Farrar, Straus, & Giroux, 1988 (I:10+ R:5). A boy discovers that a girl is one of his greatest competitors in sports.

Provost, Gary, and Gail Levine-Provost. *David and Max*. Jewish Publication Society, 1988 (I:10+ R:6). A twelve-year-old boy remembers the summer before his grandfather died.

Rabe, Berniece. *The Balancing Girl*. Illustrated by Lillian Hoban. Dutton, 1981 (I:7–9 R:4). A physically disabled girl proves she is a capable person.

Rardin, Susan Lowry. *Captives in a Foreign Land*. Houghton Mifflin, 1984 (I:10+ R:6). Six American children are held hostage.

Raskin, Ellen. *Figgs & Phantoms*. Dutton, 1974 (I:10+ R:5). An unusual family is constantly searching for Capri, their idea of heaven.

———. *The Mysterious Disappearance of Leon (I Mean Noel)*. Dutton, 1971 (I:10+ R:5). A word puzzle is used to solve the mystery of the disappearing Leon.

———. *The Westing Game*. Dutton, 1978 (I:10+ R:5). Sixteen heirs are invited to solve a riddle.

Reuter, Bjarne. *Buster's World*. Translated by Anthea Bell. Dutton, 1989 (I:8+ R:5). The main character copes with an alcoholic father.

Riskind, Mary. *Apple Is My Sign*. Houghton Mifflin, 1981 (I:9–12 R:5). A deaf boy goes to a school for the deaf in the early 1900s.

Robertson, Keith. *In Search of a Sandhill Crane*. Illustrated by Richard Cuffari. Viking, 1973 (I:10+ R:7). Link Keller searches the Michigan wilderness in order to photograph sandhill cranes.

Rodowsky, Colby. *Sydney, Herself*. Farrar, Straus & Giroux, 1989 (I:12+ R:6). A writing assignment helps a girl make discoveries about herself.

Roy, Ron. *Where's Buddy?* Illustrated by Troy Howell. Houghton Mifflin, 1982 (I:9–12 R:5). A diabetic boy becomes lost when his older brother does not look after him.

Rylant, Cynthia. *A Fine White Dust*. Bradbury, 1986 (I:11+ R:6). A thirteen-year-old boy faces challenges about his religious beliefs.

———. *A Kindness*. Orchard, 1988 (I:12+ R:6). A teenage boy faces his mother's pregnancy in their single-parent home.

Sachs, Marilyn. *The Bears' House*. Illustrated by Louis Glanzman. Doubleday, 1971 (I:8–11 R:6). An unhappy fourth grader tries to cope with a sick mother and desertion by her father.

———. *A Secret Friend*. Doubleday, 1978 (I:8–12 R:4). Two best friends break their relationship after many years.

Schellie, Don. *Kidnapping Mr. Tubbs*. Four Winds, 1978 (I:12+ R:7). Two young people help an old cowboy who lives in a nursing home visit the ranch that had been important to him.

Schick, Eleanor. *Joey on His Own*. Dial, 1982 (I:5–7 R:2). A young boy's pride increases when he goes to the grocery store by himself.

Shreve, Susan. *Family Secrets: Five Very Important Stories*. Illustrated by Richard Cuffari. Knopf, 1979 (I:8–10 R:7). A collection of five stories tells about five different family problems.

Slepian, Jan. *The Broccoli Tapes*. Philomel, 1989 (I:10+ R:6). Twelve-year-old Sara sends tapes from Hawaii back to her friends in Boston.

Slote, Alfred. *Hang Tough, Paul Mather*. Lippincott, 1973 (I:9–12 R:3). Baseball helps Paul Mather face his death when he discovers that he has an incurable blood disease.

———. *The Trading Game*. Lippencott, 1990 (I:10+ R:4). A ten-year-old boy grows up as he interacts with baseball and his grandfather.

Smith, Doris Buchanan. *Kelly's Creek*. Illustrated by Alan Tiegreen. Crowell, 1975 (I:7–10 R:4). A boy with a learning disability discovers that he has special skills.

Smith, Janice Lee. *The Show-and-Tell War*. Illustrated by Dick Gackenbach. Harper & Row, 1988 (I:7–9 R:4). This is a series of humorous stories.

Snyder, Zilpha Keatley. *The Changeling*. Illustrated by Alton Raible. Atheneum, 1970 (I:10+ R:7). Martha tells about her friendship with a girl who is very different from her own family.

———. *The Egypt Game*. Illustrated by Alton Raible. Atheneum, 1967 (I:10+ R:6). A group of sixth-grade children recreate the land of ancient Egypt.

———. *The Famous Stanley Kidnapping Case*. Atheneum, 1979 (I:10+ R:7). Kidnappers hold children for ransom in a deserted basement.

Sobol, Donald J. *Encyclopedia Brown Sets the Pace*. Illustrated by Ib Ohlsson. Scholastic/Four Winds, 1982 (I:7–10 R:5). This book contains a new series of cases to solve.

———. *Encyclopedia Brown Tracks Them Down*. Illustrated by Leonard Shortall. Crowell, 1971 (I:7–10 R:3). Clues and solutions make it possible for children to solve mysteries.

Sperry, Armstrong. *Call It Courage*. Macmillan, 1940 (I:9–13 R:6). A Polynesian boy travels alone in an outrigger canoe.

Staples, Suzanne Fisher. *Shabanu: Daughter of the Wind*. Knopf, 1989 (I:12+ R:6). A girl in Pakistan asserts her independence.

Stolz, Mary. *Cider Days*. Harper & Row, 1978 (I:8–12 R:6). A satisfying story tells about friendship between children who have different personalities and backgrounds.

———. *Ferris Wheel*. Harper & Row, 1977 (I:8–12 R:6). Polly Lewis is unhappy when her best friend moves away.

———. *What Time of Night Is It?* Harper & Row, 1981 (I:10+ R:6). Three children face problems when their mother leaves home.

Taylor, Sydney. *All-of-a-Kind Family*. Illustrated by Helen John. Follett, 1951 (I:7–10 R:4). Five girls live with their parents on New York's East Side in 1912.

———. *Ella of All-of-a-Kind Family*. Illustrated by Gail Owens. Dutton, 1978 (I:10+ R:5). Ella is grown-up and must decide whether or not she wants a singing career.

Taylor, Theodore. *The Cay*. Doubleday, 1969 (I:10+ R:6). A blind American boy is stranded on a Caribbean cay with a West Indian.

———. *The Trouble with Tuck*. Doubleday, 1981 (I:6–9 R:5). Based on a true incident, the story follows a girl as she trains a blind Labrador to follow a guide dog.

Tolan, Stephanie S. *A Good Courage*. Morrow, 1988 (I:12+ R:6). A boy and his mother enter a commune only for the boy to discover dangers within the cult.

Vogel, Ilse Margaret. *My Summer Brother*. Harper & Row, 1981 (I:9–12 R:4). A nine-year-old expresses feelings about mother-daughter rivalry and her first crush.

Voigt, Cynthia. *Dicey's Song*. Atheneum, 1982 (I:10+ R:5). Dicey brings her brothers and sister to their grandmother's house after their mother abandons them.

———. *Homecoming*. Atheneum, 1981 (I:10+ R:5). The children survive as they try to reach their grandmother.

———. *A Solitary Blue*. Atheneum, 1983 (I:10+ R:6). A boy develops a loving relationship with his father after he faces his mother's desertion.

———. *Sons from Afar*. Atheneum, 1987 (I:10+ R:6). The youngest Tillerman brothers search for their father.

Watson, James. *Talking in Whispers*. Victor Gollancz, 1983 (I:12+ R:7). In a political thriller, a boy survives against an oppressive military government.

Wojciechowska, Maia. *Shadow of a Bull*. Illustrated by Alvin Smith. Atheneum, 1964 (I:10+ R:5). Manolo discovers that true bravery is not always in the bullring.

Wolff, Virginia Euwer. *Probably Still Nick Swansen*. Holt, Rinehart & Winston, 1988 (I:10+ R:6). A learning-disabled boy learns to accept himself and his sister's death.

Wyss, John David. *The Swiss Family Robinson*. Illustrated by Lynd Ward. Grosset & Dunlap, 1949 (I:10+ R:6). In a classic story, a family is shipwrecked.

10

Historical Fiction

THE PEOPLE AND THE PAST COME ALIVE

INVOLVING CHILDREN IN HISTORICAL FICTION

The People and the Past Come Alive

VALUES OF HISTORICAL FICTION FOR CHILDREN

USING LITERARY ELEMENTS TO EVALUATE HISTORICAL FICTION

HISTORICAL AUTHENTICITY

A CHRONOLOGY OF HISTORICAL FICTION

THE THREAD OF PEOPLE'S LIVES WEAVES through the past, the present, and into the future. Many Americans have a deep desire to trace their roots—here in this hemisphere or back to Europe, Asia, or Africa. What did their ancestors experience? Why did their ancestors travel to North America? What were their ancestors' personal feelings and beliefs? What was life like for the settlers who pioneered the American frontier and for the native North Americans who greeted them? Did people of the past have the same concerns as people of the present do? Can their experiences suggest solutions for today's problems?

Through the pages of historical fiction, the past becomes alive. It is not just dates, accomplishments, and battles; it is people, famous and unknown. This chapter discusses the values of historical fiction for children, criteria for evaluating historical fiction, some specific demands on the authors of historical fiction, and examples of historical fiction written about different time periods. Books of historical fiction are linked to a short discussion of events in the time period they reflect, in the hope that this chronological framework will give readers a better understanding of the sweep of history as portrayed in these books.

VALUES OF HISTORICAL FICTION FOR CHILDREN

Children cannot actually cross the ocean on the *Mayflower* and see a new world for the first time, or experience the arrival of the first Europeans on their native shores, or feel the consequences of persecution during World War II. They can imagine all these experiences, however, through the pages of historical fiction. With Patricia Clapp's *Constance: A Story of Early Plymouth,* they can imagine they are standing on the swaying deck of the *Mayflower* and seeing their new home. While reading Scott O'Dell's *The Feathered Serpent,* they can imagine they are witnessing Montezuma's tragic encounter with the Spanish conquistador Hernando Cortés. With a twelve-year-old girl in Els Pelgrom's *The Winter When Time Was Frozen,* they can imagine they are given sanctuary in the home of a Dutch farm family during World War II.

As children relive the past vicariously, they read for enjoyment. Tales based on authentic historical settings or episodes are alive with adventures that appeal to many children. They may follow the adventures of a young girl living on the Wisconsin frontier in Carol Ryrie Brink's *Caddie Woodlawn.*

They may follow the adventures of a girl in Victorian London as she interacts with people in the sinister opium trade and conducts a quest for a missing ruby in Philip Pullman's *The Ruby in the Smoke*. They may follow the adventures of Jeff Bussey in Harold Keith's *Rifles for Watie* as he tries to find information behind enemy lines during the Civil War. They may follow a family as the family prepares for an 1890s Christmas celebration in Virginia Hamilton's *The Bells of Christmas*.

Children who read historical fiction gain an understanding of their own heritage. The considerable research that precedes the writing of an authentic historical story enables an author to incorporate information about the period naturally into the story. Children gain knowledge about the people, values, beliefs, hardships, and physical surroundings common to a period. They discover the events that preceded their own century and made the present possible. Through historical fiction, children can begin to visualize the sweep of history. As characters in historical fiction from many different time periods face and overcome their problems, readers may discover important universal truths, identify feelings and behaviors that encourage them to consider alternative ways to handle their own problems, empathize with viewpoints that are different from their own, and realize that history consists of many people who have learned to work together.

The journal of the National Council for the Social Studies, *Social Education* (11), maintains that an emphasis on human relations is a primary criterion for selecting notable books. Through historical fiction, children can discover that in all times, people have depended upon one another and have had similar needs. They learn that when human relationships deteriorate, tragedy usually results. Historical fiction allows children to judge relationships and realize that their present and future are linked to the actions of humans in the past. Outstanding books of historical fiction for children satisfy what Joan W. Blos (1, p. 375) believes is a primary role of literature: "tying together the past, the present, and the promise of the future" in ways that "confirm human bonds."

USING LITERARY ELEMENTS TO EVALUATE HISTORICAL FICTION

When evaluating historical fiction for children, adults must be certain that a story adheres to the criteria for excellent literature discussed in chapter three. Historical fiction must also satisfy special requirements in terms of setting, characterization, plot development, and theme.

The following questions summarize the criteria that adults should consider (in addition to considerations of literary quality raised in chapter three) when evaluating historical fiction for children:

1 Do the characters' experiences, conflicts, and resolutions of conflicts reflect what is known about the time period?
2 Do the characters' actions express values and beliefs that are realistic for the time period?
3 Is the language authentic for the period without relying on so many colorful terms or dialects that the story is difficult to understand?
4 Is the setting authentic in every detail?
5 Are details integrated into the story so that they do not overwhelm the reader or detract from the story?
6 If the setting is the antagonist, are the relationships between characters and setting clearly developed?
7 Is the theme worthwhile?
8 Does the style enhance the mood and clarify the conflicts, characterizations, settings, and themes?

Plot

Credible plots in historical fiction emerge from authentically developed time periods. The experiences, the conflicts, and the resolutions of conflicts must reflect the times—whether the antagonist is another person, society, nature, or internal dilemmas faced by the protagonist. Conflict in historical fiction often develops when characters leave their environments and move into more alien ones. Authors may highlight the problems, the cultures, or diverse values of time periods by exploring the conflicts developed because of characters' inner turmoil or societal pressures.

In Ann Schlee's *Ask Me No Questions* the protagonist's person-against-self conflict develops after she moves from London to avoid a cholera epidemic in 1848. While living with her aunt and uncle, Laura uncovers a neighbor's sinister activities. Although the neighbor is supposedly training children acquired from the workhouses, Laura discovers that the children are starving and ill. Schlee develops a person-against-self conflict as Laura faces a moral dilemma. Should she help the children even if she must steal food from her own relatives and then lie about her actions? This story, which is based on a true incident, seems believable because of Schlee's believable descriptions of Laura's discoveries—for example, children eating pig slop in her aunt's barn. Schlee's descriptions of Laura's formidable aunt, with her strong Victorian attitudes toward children, illuminate reasons for Laura's conflict.

Scott O'Dell develops credible person-against-self conflict in *The Captive*. In this book, a young Jesuit seminarian faces moral dilemmas when he leaves his Spanish homeland in the early 1500s and accompanies an expedition to the Americas. O'Dell describes the Jesuit's faith and his desire to bring Christianity to the native Maya of New Spain, his turmoil when he discovers the real motives behind the Spaniards' actions, his refusal to betray the native people, his pondering over his inability to change them, and his justification for his own grasping for power by impersonating a Mayan god. The various characterizations help readers understand both good and bad human motives.

Circle of Fire, by William H. Hooks, explores the moral dilemmas created by prejudice. Hooks's story takes place in North Carolina in the 1930s. In this story, a white boy and his two black friends try to prevent a Ku Klux Klan attack on Irish gypsies. Hooks develops additional believable personal conflict when the eleven-year-old boy discovers that his father, whom he loves and respects, is probably involved in the Klan.

These stories also develop plausible person-against-society conflicts. The conflict in *Ask Me No Questions* is credible because Ann Schlee convincingly develops Victorian attitudes about children that on the one hand are sentimental and protective and on the other hand allow poor children to work hard and go hungry. The conflict in *The Captive* develops because of human greed and the Spaniards' socially supported prejudice against non-Europeans, which O'Dell compellingly portrays. Likewise, the conflict in *Circle of Fire* develops because of social prejudice.

Authors who develop credible person-against-society conflicts must describe the values and beliefs of the time period or the attitudes of a segment of the population so that readers understand the nature of the antagonist. In Kathryn Lasky's *The Night Journey*, deadly anti-Semitism is the antagonist that forces a Jewish family to plan and execute a dangerous flight from czarist Russia. The plot seems more credible because a modern-day family in this book believes that these memories would be so painful that the great-grandmother should not be encouraged to remember her own experiences. In Carolyn Reeder's *Shades of Gray*, a boy who is orphaned by the Civil War learns to live with his uncle who has pacifist convictions. To make a believable plot, the author must develop the values and beliefs that cause societal conflicts.

Well-developed person-against-self and person-against-society conflicts help readers understand the values expressed during a time period and the problems, moral dilemmas, and social issues faced by the people. Authors often use these conflicts and their resolutions to develop themes in historical fiction.

Characterization

The actions, beliefs, and values of characters in historical fiction must be realistic for the time period. Authors of historical novels admit that it is sometimes difficult not to give their historical characters contemporary actions and values. Geoffrey Trease (14), author of several historical novels, encountered this problem when he wanted a girl in a story about the Roman Empire to meet a boy and form a friendship. His research showed that Roman citizens kept their daughters in seclusion and would never have allowed them to associate with a noncitizen's child. He admits that he had to search a long time for a twist in the plot that would resolve this dilemma. Trease believes that "history has all the raw material the novelist needs" (p. 27). Consequently, if authors know their job, they will not need to alter facts. At the same time, Trease believes that the concerns of characters in historical fiction should be relevant to contemporary readers, and he carefully selects historical periods, people, and events to have modern-day significance.

Choosing the main and supporting characters can cause additional problems. Hester Burton (3) says that she never uses a famous person as the pivotal character in her stories and never develops dialogue for a famous person unless she has documentary evidence that the character actually carried on such a conversation or would have held those specific sentiments. She feels that creating a historical situation that includes a fictional character is legitimate, but she does not believe in leading a famous person on a fictional adventure. Many authors of historical fiction apparently agree with Burton. Numerous books use fictional characters in historical settings. In Esther Forbes's *Johnny Tremain*, for example, a fictional silversmith's apprentice is the pivotal character, while

THROUGH THE EYES OF AN AUTHOR

Making the Past Come Alive

Graduate of Columbia University's School of Journalism and author of books set in an earlier America, PATRICIA CLAPP discusses the importance of experiencing with and reacting to the protagonists in historical fiction.

As the writer of historical novels, the most rewarding comment I can receive from a young reader is "I felt as if I was there!" Then I know that the book has achieved what I worked for, an immediacy and realism that make the past as alive to the reader as the present in which he lives.

I can only create that immediacy and realism by being there myself. I don't mean checking out the location by visiting the place, although I do that too, whenever I can. I mean feeling the emotions, smelling the air, tasting the food, wearing the clothes—being there. That probably explains why most of my books are written in the first person. I become Constance Hopkins, or Elizabeth Blackwell, or Deborah Sampson, or Mary Warren, and write the story as I live it.

This is not to say that months of research don't precede every book. They do, and I love every minute of them. But what I absorb must become a natural part of the narrative, not paragraphs of exposition which most young people skip over as quickly as possible. For example, there is no need to describe the pastry of the 1780s by giving the recipe for Maid of Honor Tarts when Deborah Sampson makes them. It is enough to mention the succulent ingredients, the sugar and butter, the ground almonds and sherry wine, the currant preserves spread in the bottoms of the patty pans. The reader knows as well as Deborah and I how delicious they will taste.

The same holds true with physical responses. I must be there, experiencing and reacting with my protagonist. When Deborah sits alone by a campfire, weeping as she tries to pry a British musket ball from her shoulder with her army jackknife, we suffer together because we are one. When Mary Warren is caught in the thick web of 17th century superstition she struggles with terrified helplessness, and I struggle with her. When Constance Hopkins seeks escape from the confusion in her heart by walking deep into the Plymouth woods and hacking fiercely at small branches to be used for kindling, kicking them into a pile, feeling her hair caught and tumbled by encroaching twigs, I feel the same sting of cold pine-scented air on my face and the same quick rushing of blood as the axe bites into the wood.

It is an exciting way to live: to move back to whatever era interests me, to live there and then, to know the people and their problems and triumphs. My world is wide and timeless. There is a brief but difficult transition when I cover my typewriter, push my chair back, and return to what some people refer to as "the real world," but there is always the knowledge that I can, at will, retreat into some long-ago time. When a young person tells me "I felt as if I was really there," I know I have taken him traveling with me.

Paul Revere and Samuel Adams are background characters.

Authors develop characterization through dialogue, thoughts, actions, and descriptions. While all of these need to appear authentic, the speech of the characters and the language characteristic of a period can cause problems for writers of historical fiction. For example, Harold Keith wanted one of his characters in *The Obstinate Land* to speak with a dialect: "Mattie Cooper's Arkansas dialect was hard to pin down until I had the good fortune to discover old files of the magazine *Dialect Notes,* containing several studies by Dr. J. W. Carr, associate professor of English and Modern Languages at the University of Arkansas, 1901–06" (7, author's notes). This study provided Keith with the words and the pronunciations necessary to develop a character whose speech was realistic for the time and the location. Authors of children's historical fiction must be careful, however, not to use so many colorful terms from a period that the story is difficult for young readers to comprehend.

Literature critic Rebecca Lukens (9) stresses the importance of believable characters in helping readers understand the differences and similarities between people in different times and places. Readers must believe that the characters in historical fiction are human beings like themselves.

Setting

Because historical fiction must be authentic in every respect, the careful development of setting for a certain time period is essential. Historical fiction author Leon Garfield states that "historical fiction more than any other kind of fiction must be rooted in a particular place and time" (4, p.736) A setting this important to a story is called an integral setting.

Rebecca Lukens (9) says that an integral setting must be described in details so clear that readers understand how the story is related to a time and place. This is of particular concern in historical fiction written for children, because children cannot draw on memory for historical periods. A writer must provide images of the setting through vivid descriptions that do not overpower plot and characterization.

When writing lengthy books for older children, authors have more time to develop settings in which the actions and characters are influenced by both time and place. The setting in historical fiction may guide readers into the plot, encourage them to feel the excitement of a time period, and create visual images that encourage them to accept a character's experiences.

Setting plays the role of antagonist in many stories about exploration and pioneering. For example, in Honore Morrow's *On to Oregon!,* sleet storms, rugged mountains, swift streams, and natural predators act as antagonists. Monroe's descriptions leave little doubt that the children are confronting a beautiful but awesome adversary.

Setting may also be the antagonist in a story set in a city. In *Anna, Grandpa, and the Big Storm,* Carla Stevens develops the 1888 blizzard in New York City into an antagonist.

Authors of historical fiction sometimes contrast settings in order to develop the conflict. This technique is used in both Ann Petry's *Tituba of Salem Village* and Elizabeth George Speare's *The Witch of Blackbird Pond*. Both authors have taken protagonists from the warm, colorful Caribbean and placed them in the bleak, somber surroundings of a Puritan village. Time and place then

The illustrations reflect a happy setting in an Appalachian mountain community. (From *When I Was Young in the Mountains,* by Cynthia Rylant, illustrated by Diane Goode. Illustrations © 1982 by Diane Goode. Reprinted by permission of the publisher, E. P. Dutton, Inc.)

influence how other characters react to these protagonists and how these characters respond to their new environments.

Some settings in historical fiction create happy, nostalgic moods. In Cynthia Rylant's picture storybook *When I Was Young in the Mountains,* the illustrations and the text allow readers to glimpse a girl's happy years of growing up in the Appalachian mountains of Virginia. This peaceful setting includes swimming holes, country stores, and family evenings on the porch. The illustrations help integrate the details of the time period into the story.

Esther Forbes integrates many details of colonial life into the setting of her story for older readers, *Johnny Tremain*. The sights, sounds, and smells of revolutionary Boston are woven into the characters' daily routines. Readers know that Johnny sleeps in a loft, wears leather breeches and a coarse shirt, likes the bustling wharf, and is proud of his work in the silversmith's shop.

Forbes also used historical research when creating an authentic setting for her Pulitzer Prize-winning fictional biography *Paul Revere and the World He Lived In*. In *Winding Valley Farm: Annie's Story,* Anne Pellowski combines Polish customs and rural farming practices to create the feeling of an ethnic community during the early 1900s.

Theme

Themes in historical fiction, as in any literature, should be worthwhile and as relevant in today's society as they were in the historical periods being represented. Many books of historical fiction have themes that have been relevant throughout human history. The search for freedom is a theme in literature about all time periods. For example, Rosemary Sutcliff's *Blood Feud* tells about tribal Britons who are confronting the invading Vikings. Her *Frontier Wolf* tells about tribal Britons who are confronting Roman armies. Both books develop stories in which searching for freedom is a primary goal. Elizabeth Yates's *Amos Fortune, Free Man* tells about an African slave searching for freedom in colonial Boston.

Love of the land and the independence it provides are powerful themes in books about the westward expansion of European settlers in North America and about the Native Americans they displaced. Europeans leave relatives and established communities to face unknown dangers and acquire homesteads. Native Americans first attempt to share their beloved natural environment with the new arrivals, then find themselves being pushed out of their homes. Children in both groups inherit their parents' dreams and fight to retain the land.

Themes of loyalty and honor are also common in stories about all time periods. People are loyal to friends and family members, following them on difficult quests and avenging their deaths or dishonor. They are loyal to their principles and defend them. Many books of historical fiction for children stress the cruelty and futility of war, even when adherence to loyalty and honor have helped cause the conflict. Novels about war in various historical periods often develop the theme of overcoming injustice. They also show ways in which people on both sides of a conflict have much in common. The beliefs of nonviolent people such as the Quakers are the bases of themes in some historical novels. Many themes are relevant to human understanding, whether the stories in which they are developed take place in ancient Rome or contemporary America.

Style

An author's style influences the mood in historical fiction. For example, the repetition of the line "When I was young in the mountains" in Cynthia Rylant's text helps create a warm, nostalgic mood in which harmful occurrences seem improbable. Brett Harvey introduces her mostly happy pioneer adventure, *Cassie's Journey: Going West in the 1860s* with a description that suggests anticipation and security: "We're on our way to California! I'm riding up high with Papa, and the wind is rocking the wagon. When I look back I can see a long line of wagons curling behind us like a snake in the dust" (unnumbered).

In contrast, notice how Patricia MacLachlan's introduction to *Sarah, Plain and Tall* suggests that the story will be about a family, but also that some unhappiness may have entered that family's life:

> "Did Mama sing every day?" asked Caleb. "Every-single-day?" He sat close to the fire, his chin in his hand. It was dusk, and the dogs lay beside him on the warm hearthstones. "Every-single-day," I told him for the second time this week. For the twentieth time this month. The hundredth time this year? And the past few years? (p. 3)

If a historical fiction has elements of suspense and adventure, the introduction frequently hints at the intrigue to follow. Leon Garfield's *The December Rose* and Philip Pullman's *The Ruby and the Smoke* develop mystery and adventure in Victorian England. Notice how Garfield introduces his mystery in a style that hints at intrigue:

> Although the day was warm and sunny, she was dressed entirely in black. . .which served to set off the extreme pallor of her complexion and the brilliancy of her eyes. Her name was Donia Vassilovas. She was known as an enemy of the country and a grave risk to the security of the state. (p. 5)

In a fast-paced plot, Barnacle, a chimney sweep, accidentally lands in the midst of a conspiracy, grabs an important clue, and becomes a hunted individual.

Pullman uses a similar technique to introduce his novel about the sinister opium trade and the quest for a missing ruby:

> On a cold, fretful afternoon in early October, 1872, a hansom cab drew up outside the offices of Lockhart and Selby, Shipping Agents, in the financial heart of London, and a young girl got out and paid the driver. She was a person of sixteen or so—alone, and uncommonly pretty. . . .Her name was Sally Lockhart; and within fifteen minutes she was going to kill a man. (p. 3)

Various forms of figurative language may clarify the conflicts, characters, settings, and themes in historical fiction. Use of figurative language is especially powerful when the author's choice of language provides insights into time, place, and conflict. For example, Rudolf Frank in *No Hero for the Kaiser* creates vivid images of World War I settings. In the following example, notice how Frank makes readers understand both the physical and psychological settings and introduces the antiwar theme through his choice of words:

> The distant thud of cannon came closer, like a thunderstorm brewing. And as if the storm had already broken, women, boys, girls, and soldiers began to rush around in confusion; trumpets sounded, and suddenly the Russians had swept out of the village like the wind. Now they were firing down from the low hills into the village. It sounded like the high-pitched whine of mosquitoes as they fly past your ear looking for a place to settle and bite: zzzzzz—a thin, sharp noise, full of sly malice. Jan knew that any one of these invisible whining bullets could kill man or beast on the spot. A dreadful feeling! But there was worse to come. (p. 2)

Allusions in historical fiction frequently provide insights into plots and characters. These same allusions, however, may require interpretation for less knowledgeable readers. For example, Frank uses allusions to the biblical flood, Napoleon, the skull of an African sultan, and the Maid of Orleans. Some of these allusions are explained in the text, while others are not. In *The True Story of Spit MacPhee,* a story set in Australia in the 1920s, James Aldridge uses an unexplained allusion when Old Fyfe, the Scottish grandfather, looks at his grandson's friend, Sadie, and says with a grim laugh, "How are ye dressed, Jean Armour, aye sae clean and neat" (p. 37). This allusion depicts character and possible conflict when readers understand that the grandfather is referring to poet Robert Burns's first real love. It is interesting to identify such allusions in historical fiction.

HISTORICAL AUTHENTICITY

The need for authentic historical detail places special demands on authors of historical fiction. Some authors actually lived through the experiences they write about or knew someone who lived through them. Other authors write about historical periods far removed from their personal experiences. To gather their data, they must rely on sources of information far different from the people who remember vividly the people and the minute details of a historical period.

Laura Ingalls Wilder, the author of the "Little House" books, lived in the big woods of Wisconsin, traveled by covered wagon through Kansas, lived in a sod house in Minnesota, and shared her life with Pa, Ma, Mary, and Carrie when they finally settled in South Dakota. Wilder's books sound as if they were written immediately after an incident occurred, but Wilder actually wrote the stories describing her life from 1870 through 1889 much later, between 1926 and 1943. Authors who write about their own past experiences need to have both keen powers of observation and excellent memories in order to share the details of their lives with others.

Predominantly happy experiences in the past may be easy to remember. For authors who write about painful experiences in their own lives, however, the doors of memory may be more difficult to open. Johanna Reiss found herself remembering things she had preferred to forget when she began writing the story of her experiences as a Jewish child hidden by Dutch gentiles during the Holocaust and World War II. According to the publishers of *The Upstairs Room,* Reiss (12) "did not set out to write a book about her experiences during the Second World War; she simply wanted to record them for her two daughters, who are now about the age she was when she went to stay with the Oastervelds" (p. 197). When she started to write, Reiss began remembering experiences that she had never talked about with anyone because they were too painful. To reinforce her memory, she took her children back to Usselo, Holland, where she visited the Dutch family who had protected her and looked again at the upstairs room and the closet in which she had hidden from the Nazis.

Authors such as Carol Ryrie Brink write about relatives' experiences. In *Caddie Woodlawn,* Brink recreates the story of her grandmother and her grandmother's family. In her author's note to the book, Brink (2) tells how she lived with her grandmother and loved to listen to her tell stories about her pioneer childhood:

> It was many years later that I remembered those stories of Caddie's childhood, and I said to myself, "If I loved them so much perhaps other children would like them too." Caddie was still alive when I was writing, and I sent letters to her, asking about the details that I did not remember clearly. She was pleased when the book was done. "There is only one thing that I do not understand," she said. "You never knew my mother and father and my brothers—how could you write about them exactly as they were?" "But, Gram," I said, "You told me." (p. 283)

Of course modern authors have no first-hand experience of some earlier times and cannot even talk to someone who lived during certain historical periods, so they must use other resources in researching their chosen time periods. Hester Burton (3), a well-known writer of historical fiction with British settings, says:

> Ideally I should be so knowledgeable that I have no need to turn to a book of reference once I have actually started writing the book. I should be able to see clearly in my mind's eye the houses in which my characters live, the clothes they wear, and the cars and carriages and ships in which they travel. I should know what food they eat, what songs they sing when they are happy, and what are the sights and smells they are likely to meet when they walk down the street. I must understand their religion, their political hopes, their trades and—what is most important—the relationships between different members of a family common to their particular generation. (p. 299)

To acquire this much knowledge about a time period demands considerable research. Some authors have chosen to research and write about one period; others have written books covering many different time periods. Rosemary Sutcliff has written several outstanding books of historical fiction, and John Townsend (13) says that in the area of serious historical novels, Sutcliff stands above the rest. Sutcliff reveals her thorough knowledge of certain historical periods in both the stories themselves and her introductions to them. In her introduction to *Song for a Dark Queen,* for example, she outlines the historical events that influence the incidents in the book, describes how her plot arose out of reading certain scholarly works about the culture of the period, then lists the sources that provided her with background information for the story.

Kathryn Lasky reveals the influence of extensive research in her author's note for *Beyond the Divide*. Lasky says she based the book in part on Theodora Kroeber's biography of the last Yahi Indian, *Ishi: The Last of His Tribe* and in part on J. Goldsborough Bruff's journal that describes his own experiences during the gold rush. Lasky (8) describes her own discoveries about the West:

> Mrs. Kroeber's story was the first true western tale I had ever read. This was not the West of television, nor was the gold rush the one written about in my school books. The bad guys were worse than I had ever imagined, and the greed for gold was pernicious and deadly to the human spirit. People did not just rob, they killed, and on occasion massacred. The conditions of survival were the most arduous imaginable, but there was one emigrant whose spirit was left miraculously intact. (p. 253)

These discoveries, characterizations, settings, and themes are apparent in her historical novel.

Lois Lowry based *Number the Stars* on the experiences of the Danish Resistance. Lowry reveals that she was determined to tell the story of the Danish people and the Danish Resistance after seeing a photograph of Kim Malthe-Bruun and reading about his helping Jewish residents of Denmark. The Nazis captured and executed this resistance leader when he was only twenty-one.

Reading about any of the well-known authors of historical fiction whose books are noted for authentic backgrounds reveals that authors first spend hundreds of hours researching county courthouse records and old letters, newspapers, and history books; conducting personal interviews; and visiting museums and historical locations. Authors must then write stories that develop believable plots, characters, and settings without sounding like history textbooks. In doing so, they must carefully consider the many conflicting points of view that surround particular events. Writing excellent historical fiction is a very demanding task.

A CHRONOLOGY OF HISTORICAL FICTION

In sharing historical fiction with children, you must understand at least some of the history of a time period in order to evaluate stories reflecting that period. Following a three-year study, Donna Norton (10) found that the understanding, evaluation, and utilization of historical fiction of students in children's literature courses improved if the students discussed books of historical fiction in a chronological order, briefly identified the actual historical happenings in each time period, identified major themes in literature written about a specific period (although of course some books have more than one theme), discussed the implications of recurring themes, identified how authors develop believable plots for a time period, and discussed the modern significance of the literature. To assist in the study of historical fiction, this chapter discusses books of historical fiction in an order similar to the one used during Norton's study. Ideally, this framework will assist you as you discuss the literature in children's literature classes and undertake individual studies of historical fiction for children. Chart 10–1 presents a simple chronology of Western and North American history and the main themes developed in books in each period.

Ancient Times Through the Middle Ages

Western culture began over 5,000 years ago in the ancient Sumerian and Egyptian societies of the Middle Eastern "cradle of civilization." Absolute

CHART 10–1
Eras and themes in historical fiction

Date	Period	Themes
3000 B.C.	*Ancient Times Through the Middle Ages*	Loyalty is one of the noblest human traits. Ignorance, prejudice, and hatred can have destructive consequences for all concerned. Hatred, not people, is the great enemy. Love is stronger than hatred and prevails through times of great trouble. People will always search for freedom and riches. Courage is more important than physical strength. A physical disability does not reduce a person's humanity. People can overcome their handicaps.
A.D. 1492	*Changes in the Old World and Discovery of the New*	Greed is a strong motivational force and can have destructive consequences. Moral dilemmas must be faced and resolved. People will face severe hardships to acquire the political and religious freedom they desire. People must work together if they are to survive. Overcoming problems can strengthen character. War creates tragedy. Life is more than physical survival. Land is important: People will endure numerous hardships to acquire land for personal reasons or for the glory of their country.
1692	*The Salem Witch-Hunts*	Prejudiced persecution of others is a frightening and destructive social phenomenon. People seek freedom from persecution. Moral obligations require some people to defend the rights of others.

CHART 10–1 cont.
Eras and themes in historical fiction

Date	Period	Themes
1776	*The American Revolution*	Freedom is worth fighting for.
		Strong beliefs require strong commitments.
1780	*Early Expansion of the United States and Canada*	Friendship and faith are important.
		People long for their own land and the freedom that ownership implies.
		People will withstand considerable hardships to retain their dreams.
		Strong family bonds help physical and spiritual survival.
		Prejudice and hatred are destructive forces.
		The greatest strength comes from within.
		Moral obligations require personal commitment.
1861	*The Civil War*	War creates tragedy.
		Moral obligations must be met even if one's life or freedom is in jeopardy.
		Moral sense does not depend on skin color, but on what is inside a person.
		People should take pride in themselves and their accomplishments.
		Prejudice and hatred are destructive forces.
		People search for freedom.
		Personal conscience may not allow some people to kill others.
		Strong family ties help people persevere.
1860s	*The Western Frontier*	People have moral obligations that must be met.
		People have strong dreams of owning land.
		Families can survive if they work together.
		People need each other and may work together for their mutual good.
		Battles can be won through legal means rather than through unlawful actions.
		Hatred and prejudice are destructive forces.
		Without spiritual hope, people may lose their will to live.
1900	*The Early Twentieth Century*	People will strive for survival of the physical body and the human spirit.
		Prejudice and discrimination are destructive forces.
		There is a bond between people who experience injustice.
		Monetary wealth does not create a rich life.
1939	*World War II*	People will seek freedom from religious and political persecution.
		Prejudice and hatred are destructive forces.
		Moral obligation and personal conscience are strong forces.
		Freedom is worth fighting for.
		Family love and loyality help people endure catastrophic experiences.

rulers directed vast numbers of slaves in constructing temples and pyramids in honor of themselves and their gods. In 332 B.C., Alexander the Great conquered most of the Middle East. Two hundred years later, the great military might of the Romans was creating an empire that eventually surrounded the Mediterranean Sea and covered most of Europe for hundreds of years. As the Roman Empire became larger, encompassing many different cultures and geographical areas, Roman rule became harsher and harsher.

In pre-Roman times, various Celtic peoples, including the Britons and Gaels, inhabited the British Isles. These people lived in tribes ruled by chiefs and often warred with one another over land and people. In 55 B.C., Julius Caesar failed in an attempt to add present-day England and Scotland to the Roman Empire. One hundred years later, Emperor Claudius succeeded in annexing Britain. Roman legions were left behind to subdue the people and keep peace among the tribes.

The Roman dominance lasted throughout Europe until about A.D. 410, when fierce tribes of Teutonic peoples from northern Europe invaded and sacked Rome, beginning the long medieval period in European history that has sometimes been called the Dark Ages. In their great ships, Vikings from Norway were led by people such as Eric the Red. The Vikings raided the coasts of Europe and demonstrated their remarkable seafaring skills by exploring Greenland and Iceland. In about A.D. 1000, Norse explorers under Leif Ericson's command crossed the Atlantic Ocean and stayed briefly in a place in North America they called "Vinland."

Teutonic Saxons and Angles from the continent invaded and settled Britain. The once-unified Roman empire dissolved into many small domains ruled by competing feudal lords and the warrior nobility that served them in ongoing battles. The lords lived in fortified castles surrounded by cottages and fields in which enslaved peasants produced food and wealth for them. Constant warfare and rampant disease, such as the plague (also known as the Black Death), ravaged the developing towns of England, France, and elsewhere. The strong Christian beliefs of the Middle Ages led to the construction of magnificent cathedrals and to crusades in which Christian warriors attempted to capture Jerusalem for the Roman Catholic Church, which still survived in splendor and power after the fall of Rome.

Authors who write historical fiction about the ancient world and medieval times in Europe often tell their stories from the viewpoint of slaves or other people subjugated by the powerful. Other authors represent the perspectives of the mighty, such as Romans and Vikings, and show the ways in which all people have certain desires and fears in common and confront similar problems. Through these various perspectives, authors of historical fiction for children encourage young readers to imagine and empathize with the personal and social conflicts of people in the distant past. Strong themes emerge as the characters fight for their beliefs and personal freedoms, follow their dreams, struggle with moral dilemmas, or overcome prejudices or self-doubts that could destroy them.

In *The Bronze Bow,* Elizabeth George Speare focuses upon Israel during Roman rule. She portrays the harshness of the Roman conquerors by telling the story through the eyes of a boy who longs to avenge the death of his parents. (His father was crucified by Roman soldiers, and his mother died from grief and exposure.) Daniel bar Jamin's bitterness intensifies when he joins a guerrilla band and nurtures his hatred of the Romans. His person-against-self conflict comes to a turning point when he almost sacrifices his sister because of his hatred. The author encourages readers to understand Daniel's real enemy. When Daniel talks to Jesus, both Daniel and the reader realize that hatred, not Romans, is the enemy. In fact, the only thing stronger than hatred is love. The author shows the magnitude of Daniel's change when at the close of the story he invites a Roman soldier into his home.

Rosemary Sutcliff uses a real British mystery twenty centuries old as the basis for her historical novel *Sun Horse, Moon Horse*. The magical Uffington White Horse has raced across the Berkshire Downs in England for over two thousand years. What force, in approximately 100 B.C., motivated the carving of this beautiful animal into the hillside? What sculptor could create an earthen horse alive with movement and power? Sutcliff's novel about the Iceni, a tribe of early Britons before the Roman invasion, presents her version of how this horse, still visible today, came to be carved into the high downs.

Sutcliff's theme, that people will search for freedom, is developed through a comparison of the peaceful existence of the Iceni before their capture to the time of their subjugation by another tribe covetous of the Iceni's land and horses. An Iceni boy's strong desire for freedom for his people, combined with his artistic talent, gives the tribe their chance for liberation. The boy agrees to complete the carving of the conquering tribe's sun-horse symbol if, after he has completed the carving, his people can go free. He does not only carve the symbol of his enemies, however; he also carves the moon horse, symbol of his own tribe. His final actions express the depth of his tribal loyalty, desire for his tribe's freedom, and belief in the symbolism of the moon horse: Upon completion of the moon-horse carving, he asks that his own life be sacrificed upon the horse to give it necessary life and strength. Sutcliff reaffirms the tribe's loyalty to and admiration for the boy through the feelings expressed by the new leader:

> Heart-brother. . .wait for me in the Land of Apple Trees. Whether it be tomorrow, or when I am Lord of many spears in the north, and too old to sit a horse or lift a sword, wait for me until I come. And do not be forgetting me, for I will not forget you. (p. 106)

The Iceni tribe's futile effort to stem the tide of Roman conquest is the subject of Sutcliff's *Song for a Dark Queen*. The year is A.D. 62, over 150 years after the Iceni left the Berkshire Downs in search of new horse runs. The leading character is a queen rather than a male chieftain. (The Iceni leadership did not go from father to son, but down the "moonside," from mother to daughters). Through descriptions of the queen's early training and her reactions when her tribe is conquered by the Romans, Sutcliff shows readers the basis for the Iceni's belief in their strong female leader. She has been trained from early childhood to lead men in battle, and she heads a revolt that almost succeeds in overpowering the Roman rule and defending the ancient tribal culture. Her efforts fail, however. The Romans overpower the Iceni and place them firmly under Roman dominance. Sutcliff emphasizes her theme about the importance of freedom to the Iceni by describing how the queen decides to sacrifice her life rather than be a captive. In books about the Roman legions, such as *Frontier Wolf* and *Lantern Bearers,* Sutcliff develops believable characters whose desires and actions express such timeless themes as loyalty, honor, desire for freedom, and self-sacrifice.

Authors who write about the Viking period develop both honorable heroes who strive for human freedom and evil men who kill and enslave. Vivid descriptions are important for these characterizations. Sutcliff's description of the approaching Vikings is especially effective in *Blood Feud* because it is told from the viewpoint of Jestyn, an English boy who believes terrible stories about the Vikings:

> The men who stood there glancing me over were the true Viking kind that I had heard of in stories and been told to pray God I might never see in life. Men with grey ring-mail strengthening their leather byrnies, iron-bound war-caps, long straight swords. One had a silver arm-ring, one had studs of coral in the clasp of his belt, one wore a rough wolf-skin cloak. (p. 14)

Sutcliff's vivid descriptions help readers understand Jestyn's reactions to being purchased for six gold pieces and a wolf skin and to wearing the hated thrall ring of a slave. When Jestyn concludes that his master is a good man, readers are encouraged to believe in his worth. The remainder of the book stresses the themes of honor toward parents and loyalty between friends as the Viking and his now-loyal friend search for the murderer of the Viking's father.

The settings in historical fiction about the Vikings often stress the importance of the sea. The sea is not usually an antagonist in these stories, since it enables the Vikings to gain riches and expand their world. In Erik Christian Haugaard's *Hakon of Rogen's Saga,* the sea is the road that leads everywhere, the reality from which a young Viking boy's dreams are made. Haugaard develops a fast-paced plot. The enemies of Hakon's father attack, and Hakon is left to the mercies of an uncle who wishes to steal his birthright. Fleeing for his life, Hakon hides in a cave, where he ponders his feelings about courage, strength, and freedom. He realizes that if he can be alone without fear, no one can call him weak, even if he is not yet strong enough to wield a sword. The actions of a few loyal comrades and of a freed slave help him recapture Rogen, his island home, and his birthright. The author emphasizes through Hakon's thoughts and actions that freedom is the greatest birthright that anyone can have. When Hakon assumes rule of the island, his people swear loyalty to him, and he declares, "I swear that on Rogen shall rule only justice. That no man shall fear his tongue nor his thought, but each man shall live in peace" (p. 113).

While the Vikings were roaming the seas, knights in armor all across Europe were challenging one another over land and power, and humble people were working in the fields of nobles or serving the mighty in the great halls of castles. In *The Door in the Wall,* Marguerite DeAngeli uses an English castle and its surroundings as the settings for her story about ten-year-old Robin, who is

FLASHBACK

THE HISTORICAL NOVEL BECAME POPULAR IN THE 1800s with the publication of stories by Sir Walter Scott and Charlotte Yonge. Scott's story of medieval English life, *Ivanhoe* (1820), was often used as a school assignment for older children. Other popular books by Scott included *The Lady of the Lake* (1810), *Waverly: Or, 'Tis Sixty Years Since* (1814), *Rob Roy* (1818), and *Tales of the Crusaders* (1825). Yonge's historical books included *The Little Duke* (1854), *Richard the Fearless* (1856), and *The Lances of Lynwood* (1855). Her series of "Cameos from History" (1850s–1890s), published in *The Monthly Packet,* offered vicarious adventure, relaxation, and sense of history to Victorian children.

expected to train for knighthood. The plot has an unusual twist when Robin is stricken with a mysterious ailment that paralyzes his legs. The door in the title of the story becomes symbolic. A monk gives unhappy Robin difficult advice: "Thou hast only to follow the wall far enough and there will be a door in it" (p. 16).

This symbol is very important in the story. DeAngeli develops the plot by tracing Robin's search for his own door and the preparation necessary to find it. The monk helps Robin by guiding his learning, encouraging him to carve and to read, and expressing the belief that Robin's hands and mind, if not his legs, must be taught because they represent other doors in the wall. Robin worries that as a disabled person who walks with crutches he will be useless as a knight. His father's friend, Sir Peter, reassures him by saying that if a person cannot serve in one way, another means of serving will present itself. Sir Peter is proven correct when Welsh forces attack the castle. Robin proves his worth to himself and the castle by escaping the enemy sentry and obtaining help from the neighboring castle.

DeAngeli encourages readers to understand the importance of accepting people for what they are, rather than rejecting them because of physical disability, when Robin's father congratulates him:

> The courage you have shown, the craftsmanship proven by the harp, and the spirit in your singing all make so bright a light that I cannot see whether or not your legs are misshapen. (p. 120)

Many children enjoy this beautiful story about a child who finds a door in his wall. One girl said that it was her favorite book because she liked the way Robin overcame his problem and was happy with his life. The theme is especially appropriate for teaching positive attitudes about the physically disabled.

More severe problems related to living with a disabling condition in medieval Europe appear in Gloria Skurzynski's *Manwolf*. The author builds a plot around the symptoms of a rare skin disease—hair grows on skin exposed to the sun, and scarring creates an animal appearance—and a superstitious people's prejudice against and fear of anyone who has this disease. The belief in werewolves and the personal tragedy that results from such a belief are shown by the attacks on a young boy and by his mother's attempts to protect him. The lifelong battle against prejudice is suggested by the mask the father wears to hide his own features from the superstitious people.

The following themes are expressed in historical fiction about ancient and medieval times. Students of children's literature may wish to consider how these themes relate to specific happenings in the time periods. Are any of these themes significant in our modern-day world?

1 Loyalty is one of the noblest human traits.
2 Ignorance, prejudice, and hatred can have destructive consequences for all concerned.
3 Hatred, not people, is the great enemy.
4 Love is stronger than hatred and prevails through times of great trouble.
5 People will always search for freedom and riches.
6 Courage is more important than physical strength.
7 A physical disability does not reduce a person's humanity.
8 People can overcome their handicaps.

Changes in the Old World and Discovery of the New

By the fifteenth century, Europe had entered the Renaissance, a time of cultural rebirth and great social change. Large cities were bustling with trade, and middle-class merchants attained more social prominence. New forms of Protestant Christianity were arising out of medieval Catholicism and challenging the religious and political power of the established church. In Germany, Johann Gutenberg was inventing the printing press, which William Caxton soon used to publish the first printed books in England. Great artists such as Michelangelo and William Shakespeare began to raise the visual arts and literature to new heights of creative glory, inspired by the rediscovery of ancient Greek and Roman culture. Ordinary people were expecting and demanding greater economic, political, and religious freedom. Explorers were sailing off to prove their belief that the world was round and then to acquire great riches in the New World, which they discovered in the Western Hemisphere.

The arrival of Christopher Columbus on a Caribbean island in 1492 was soon followed by conquest of ancient Maya and Aztec cultures in Central America by Spanish explorers. By the late sixteenth and the early seventeenth century, colonies were springing up along the Atlantic coast of North America. People followed their lust for wealth and adventure or their desire for freedom from the religious persecution and political conflicts that were occurring in England and elsewhere.

Strong person-against-self conflicts, settings that depict Mayan and Aztec cultures, and themes that illustrate the human consequences of greed are found in Scott O'Dell's historical novels based on the Spanish conquest of Mexico in the early 1500s. O'Dell's *The Captive, The Feathered Serpent,* and *The Amethyst Ring* focus not so much on events of the time as on the moral dilemmas a young priest faces in the New World.

A young, idealistic Jesuit seminarian, Julián Escobar, leaves his secure home in Spain and joins an expedition to Central America, inspired by the prospect of saving the souls of native peoples in New Spain. During the long voyage across the Atlantic, he begins to realize that the Spanish grandee leading the expedition actually intends to exploit and enslave the Mayas and the Aztecs, rather than convert them to Christianity.

Later, Julián questions whether he has the spirit or the patience to spread the Christian faith within cultures so different from his own. O'Dell explores changes in Julián by stressing the changing conflicts in Julián's life: Should he take on the role of the Mayas' mythical Kukulcán in order to save his own life and make his views palatable to people with their own ancient beliefs? Should he advise attacking a neighboring city before his own Mayan city is attacked? How should he respond to the Mayan rites of sun worship? Why does God permit both good and evil? Julián's defense of his inability to change the Mayas and of his own eventual grasping for power demonstrate changes in his character. In *The Feathered Serpent,* for example, he thinks back to Augustine's teachings and concludes that evil exists because God wills it. Therefore, idol worship and human sacrifice are beyond his control. Julián does admit, however, that this argument may only be a defense of his own actions.

O'Dell's descriptions of Mayan and Aztec cities and temples and other aspects of their cultures encourage readers to understand that an advanced civilization inhabited the Americas long before European exploration and settlement. Readers may also ponder the right of one culture to destroy another culture whose citizens worship different gods and possess riches desired by a foreign power.

In 1620, the *Mayflower* brought the first group of settlers to New England. The Pilgrims made no easy conquest of the wilderness. Their sponsors in England did not provide enough supplies, their first winter was filled with sickness and starvation, and the new settlers were apprehensive about the native peoples who lived beyond their settlement.

Authors who write about the settlement of Plymouth colony often look at the reasons for leaving England and the hardships faced by the Pilgrims. In *Constance: A Story of Early Plymouth,* for example, Patricia Clapp tells the story of the early settlement of New England from the viewpoint of a fourteen-year-old girl. Because she did not want to leave her cherished London, Constance's first view of the new world from the deck of the *Mayflower* is an unpleasant one. Clapp encourages readers to understand the various viewpoints of the Pilgrims by contrasting Constance's view of a bleak and unfriendly land with the excitement and anticipation expressed by her father, William Bradford, John Alden, and Miles Standish.

Clapp's vivid descriptions of Constance's first encounter with Samoset, a Native American, her feelings of resentment about doing "womanly" tasks, and her grief when she sees friends struggle and die during the first long winter encourage readers to understand the many facets of Constance's character. Clapp demonstrates the changes in Constance's feelings toward America when, six years after her first disappointing view of New England, she and her new husband decide to begin their life together in the new world. Through her story, readers understand that people will accept hardships to acquire political and religious freedom. They also discover the importance of working together for survival.

Arnold Lobel's *On the Day Peter Stuyvesant Sailed into Town,* a picture storybook for young children, humorously brings the colonial setting of New Amsterdam to life. When Stuyvesant arrived on the shores of present-day New York in 1647, he found a town near collapse. The streets were reverting to weeds and were littered with garbage, animals ran freely, houses were falling into disrepair, and the walls of the fort were crumbling. Stuyvesant considered this abominable and quickly told the settlers to improve their town. He was so successful that within the next ten years the town had doubled in size and had become as neat as any Dutch community in Europe. The pictures in this book help children visualize the sailing ships, colonial dress and homes, and Dutch windmills.

While early colonists in North America were struggling to survive, ominous clouds were gathering over England. Conflict between Catholic King Charles I and the staunchly Protestant Parliament led to war in 1642. Authors who place their settings in England during this time frequently develop themes related to the tragedy of war. The character development often explores the influences that shape a person's growing awareness of the reality of war.

One of the strongest leaders to emerge during the English Civil War was Oliver Cromwell, an ordinary man but a great military organizer. In Erik Christian Haugaard's historical fiction set during this period, a young boy in the book *A Messenger for Parliament* and then in *Cromwell's Boy* discovers the tragic reality of war. After eleven-year-old Oliver's mother dies, he follows his ne'er-do-well father into war. Haugaard effectively encourages readers to understand Oliver's changing feelings as he talks to other boys about the glory of war and describes it in terms of a game. When the boys joke about taking swords and money from dead soldiers, Oliver begins to see warfare in a new light:

> Till now I had not thought that the taking of a sword or a dagger on the battlefield would mean robbing the dead. Though I had seen the sacking of Worcester, war seemed to me still a game. Jack's words made me feel the fear I had not felt before. It came creeping like the shadows of twilight. (p. 64)

Oliver matures rapidly in this harsh time. He is finally given the responsibility of getting a message through to Cromwell. After long days of walking and danger, he reaches Cromwell's home and delivers the message. Cromwell is pleased with young Oliver's bravery and tells him that with allies such as Oliver on its side, Parliament has nothing to fear. Oliver has made a true friend, and Cromwell asks him to be his personal messenger.

In *Cromwell's Boy,* Oliver is a much older thirteen. He rides a horse well, does not divulge secrets, and looks inconspicuous. His ability to serve Cromwell extends beyond messages. Oliver goes into the dangerous stronghold of the king's army as a spy. Haugaard suggests the lessons that Oliver has learned and develops an important theme by using a flashback in which Oliver remembers his youthful experiences:

> In my youth there was little time for dreams. Life challenged me early. The leisure to reflect was not my lot; tomorrow was ever knocking on the door of today with new demands. It made me resourceful and sharpened my wit, but the purpose of life must be more than just to survive. You must be able—at least for short moments—to hold your precious soul in your hands and to contemplate that gift with love and understanding. (p. 1)

Consider the following themes developed in historical fiction about the age of cultural and social change in Europe and about early European settlement of the Western Hemisphere. Why and how are they related to specific happenings in the time periods? Do these themes have relevance in other periods of history? Do they have relevance for us today?

1 Greed is a strong motivational force and can have destructive consequences.
2 Moral dilemmas must be faced and resolved.
3 People will face severe hardships to acquire the political and religious freedom they desire.
4 People must work together if they are to survive.
5 Overcoming problems can strengthen character.
6 War creates tragedy.
7 Life is more than physical survival.
8 Land is important: People will endure numerous hardships to acquire land for personal reasons or for the glory of their country.

The Salem Witch-Hunts

Belief in witchcraft was a common superstition in medieval Europe. Thousands of religious and political nonconformists, independent thinkers and artists, mentally ill persons, and other unusual people seemed to threaten the established social order. Such people were accused of witchcraft and burned at the stake. Belief in witchcraft continued even in the relatively more enlightened sixteenth and seventeenth centuries and crossed the Atlantic with the first settlers of North America.

In the New England colonies of the late 1600s, strict Puritan religious beliefs governed every aspect of social life. Any kind of nonconformity was viewed as the work of the devil. The famous witch-hunts of 1692 in Salem, Massachusetts, began when a doctor stated that the hysterical behavior of several teenage girls was due to the "evil eye." Within six months, twenty persons had been sentenced to death and one hundred and fifty had been sent to prison.

Boston minister Cotton Mather was one of those who preached the power of the devil and the need to purge the world of witchcraft. People charged with witchcraft were pardoned in 1693 when Sir William Phipps, royal governor of the Massachusetts Bay Colony, said that the witch-hunt proceedings were too violent and not based upon fact. Belief in witchcraft faded in the 1700s as new scientific knowledge began to explain previously frightening phenomena.

The conflict in stories set in this short period of American history is usually person-against-society. Authors often place their characters in a hostile environment, where their usual behaviors create suspicion. For example, is a person a witch because he or she brews tea from herbs to give to the ill? Does spinning thread faster and better prove a person is a witch? Does speaking to a cat indicate witchcraft? These are the charges that face the protagonist in Ann Petry's *Tituba of Salem Village*.

Contrasts in setting suggest the drama that follows. Petry describes two slaves who are living in comparative freedom by a sparkling sea on the coral-encrusted coastline of Barbados. Tituba and her husband lose their fairly permissive owner in Barbados and in his place acquire a solemn, dark-clothed minister from Boston. Even their first meeting is ominous: Tituba backs away from a tall, thin shadow that blots out the sun and covers her body. The setting changes rapidly from the tropical home to a dark ship that is taking the slaves to New England.

Petry completes the change in setting when she describes the minister's house in Salem. Rotten eggs on the doorstep of the gloomy, neglected building greet Reverend Parris, his family, and the two slaves to their new home. Soon, people in the town are muttering threats, teenage girls are becoming hysterical, and townspeople are testifying that Tituba can transform herself into a wolf or travel without her body. Tituba's crime is not witchcraft. Instead, she is not only a strange black person in a predominantly white community but also a more capable and intelligent person than many of the people around her.

This book develops insights into the consequences of inhumanity, regardless of time or place. Readers are encouraged to see and feel danger in mass accusations and a fear in people to defend what they know is right. Compare Petry's characterization and plot development with Patricia Clapp's in *Witches' Children: A Story of Salem,* which relates the Salem experience through the eyes of a bound girl.

The free white protagonist in Elizabeth George Speare's *The Witch of Blackbird Pond* comes from Barbados, but Kit's life is quite different from Tituba's. Contrasts between the people in Kit's early childhood environment and the people in New England encourage readers to anticipate the conflict. On Barbados, Kit was raised by a loving grandfather, who encouraged her to read history, poetry, and plays.

After the death of her grandfather, Kit travels to New England to live with her aunt. Several experiences on the ship suggest that her former life-style will not be appropriate for her new world. For example, when Kit tries to discuss Shakespeare with a fellow passenger, he is shocked because a girl should not read such things: "The proper use of reading is to improve our sinful nature, and to fill our minds with God's holy word" (p. 28). An even harsher response occurs after she jumps into a harbor and swims to rescue a child's doll. (The Puritans believe that only guilty people are able to stay afloat.)

When Kit's actions in the Puritan village remain consistent with her earlier behavior, she raises the suspicions of the townspeople: She wears colorful clothes that she brought from Barbados; she teaches children to read by writing frivolous verses, such as "Timothy Cook, jumped over the brook;" she has children act out stories from the Bible; and she becomes friendly with Hannah Tupper, a Quaker, who the villagers believe is a witch. When sickness breaks out in the town, the people believe they are bewitched and blame Hannah. Kit risks her life to warn her friend, and they escape before Hannah's cottage is burned by angry men.

Kit's action incurs the wrath of the settlement, and she is arrested for witchcraft. The charges brought against her are similar to those brought against Tituba. Unlike Tituba, however, Kit has friends and family who stand by her and assist in her acquittal. She learns that it is important to choose your friends and then stand by them.

The protagonists in Petry's and Speare's books have courage, high spirit, and honor in trying circumstances. Both remain true to their beliefs, even when faced with hostility and superstition. They cry out against the injustices around them. Because of their actions, a few people realize the consequences of blind fear and hatred.

Consider the following themes developed in historical fiction about the Salem witch-hunts. What consequences of inhumanity and persecution are developed in other time periods? What historical events coincide with such persecution?

1 Prejudiced persecution of others is a frightening and destructive social phenomenon.
2 People seek freedom from persecution.
3 Moral obligations require some people to defend the rights of others.

The American Revolution

The inhabitants of the thirteen American colonies founded by the British came from different countries and had differing sympathies and practices. They did, however, have several strong antagonisms in common. They shared a fear of the native peoples of North America; they went through a period when they shared a dread of French conquest; and they came to conflict with their ruler, the British crown. Although British subjects, the colonists had no elected representatives in the British Parliament that made decisions affecting their lives. For example, the colonists were allowed to buy tea, a popular beverage, only from the British East Indian Company, and Parliament levied a heavy tax on that tea. By the mid-eighteenth century, an accumulation of such injustices united colonists from New Hampshire to Georgia in opposition to their common oppressor across the Atlantic.

A series of demands made by the British government hastened the uniting of the colonies. In 1765, Britain tried to raise money by passing the Stamp Act, which placed a tax on all paper used in the colonies and declared all unstamped documents to be legally void. Then, the British demanded that British soldiers in the colonies be quartered by the colonists themselves. In 1773, when several British ships bearing tea arrived in Boston Harbor, the Bostonians would not accept the shipment. They refused to pay taxes without the right to vote for those who would represent them. Colonists disguised as Indians boarded the ships and dumped the tea into the harbor. The British Parliament responded by closing Boston Harbor, blocking it from trade. The sympathies of many colonists were in accord with the goal of independence from Great Britain.

Samuel Adams and others like him rallied the colonists in support of this cause. The Declaration of Independence and the long years of the Revolutionary War soon followed—an exciting time in American history. We are all familiar with the famous leaders of this period, but as Elizabeth Yates (15) points out, many other Americans whose names we do not know played dynamic roles in creating a new nation:

> Those who lived in small towns and villages and on distant farms, who thought and talked about events and made their feelings known: men who left their stock and crops and marched off to fight because they were convinced of the rightness of the stand that had been made, women who took over the work of the farms along with the care of their homes and families. Their names made no news. They did no particular acts of heroism, except as the living of each day was heroic in itself. Hard work they knew well, and hardship they could endure. Giving their lives or living their lives, they were as much the foundation of the new nation as were those whose names have long been known. (p. 6)

While famous people are found in the backgrounds of much historical fiction about the American Revolution that has been written for children, everyday people are the heroes of most of these books. In general, two types of stories are written about the revolutionary period: (1) tales about those who defend the home front while others go off to war and (2) tales about males and females who become actively involved in the war itself.

The best-known children's story about this period is Esther Forbes's *Johnny Tremain*. Forbes creates a superbly authentic setting. Paul Revere and Samuel Adams play important parts in the story, but a silversmith's apprentice named Johnny and other boys like him are the heroes. Through Johnny's observations, actions, and thoughts, Forbes emphasizes the issues of the times, the values of the people, and the feelings about freedom. Johnny discovers the political thinking of the time when he hears a minister preach sermons filled with anger against taxation without representation, delivers messages for the secret anti-British Boston Observers, and rides for the Boston Committee of Correspondence.

Forbes's writing style creates believable action and dialogue, as in this excerpt from a speech calling the rebels to action:

> Friends! Brethren! Countrymen! That worst of Plagues, the detested tea shipped for this Port by the East Indian Company, is now arrived in the Harbour: the hour of destruction, of manly opposition to the machinations of Tyranny, stares you in the Face; Every Friend to his Country, to Himself, and to Posterity, is now called upon to meet. (p. 107)

Johnny is one of the "Indians" who throw the tea into Boston Harbor. He experiences the anger and resulting unity when British troops close the harbor. He is there when British troops and colonial rebels clash at Concord. Unhappily, he is also there when his best friend dies. He makes the discovery that a sixteen-year-old is considered a boy in times of peace but a man in times of war. As a man, he has the duty to risk his life for what he believes.

Most school children know about Paul Revere's ride, but Gail E. Haley has chosen a not-so-famous ride to share with younger readers in *Jack Jouett's Ride*. This ride takes place in 1781 and is a deed of daring equal to that of Paul Revere. This time, a young rider discovers that British troops are riding toward Charlottesville, Virginia, to capture Thomas Jefferson, Patrick Henry, and other leaders of the Revolution. Jack saddles his horse, moves into the night, and rides across meadows and thickets to spread the alarm. The picture storybook, with its vivid illustrations and simple language, appeals to young children and helps them grasp the flavor of historic events.

Consider the themes and the historical facts from this period. Why do you think the following themes are developed in the literature? How and why are these themes similar to or different from themes in stories about other wartime periods?

1 Freedom is worth fighting for.
2 Strong beliefs require strong commitments.

Early Expansion of the United States and Canada

As more and more settlers came to America, a need for additional land became evident. Many settlers headed away from the Atlantic coastline into the rolling, tree-covered hills to the west, north, and south. These settlers had something in common: With considerable courage, they sought freedom and land. Some settlers developed friendly relationships with the Native Americans*; others experienced hostilities. It was not uncommon for settlers to be captured by Indians and taken into their tribes, sold as slaves, or held for

*This book primarily uses the term *Native Americans* to denote the people historically referred to as *American Indians*. The term *Indian* is sometimes used interchangeably with *Native Americans* and in some contexts is used to name certain tribes of Native Americans.

ransom. Many abductions, however, were in retaliation for settlers' attacks.

Stories about early pioneer expansion are popular with children, who enjoy vivid characters and rapid action. The young characters may be popular with children because they often show extraordinary courage and prove they can be equal to adults. Many of the stories depict strong family bonds. Vivid descriptions of the new land encourage readers to understand why a family is willing to give up a secure environment to live on a raw and dangerous frontier. Person-against-nature conflicts often appear in these stories. Person-against-self conflicts occur as characters face moral dilemmas, such as racial prejudice.

Alice Dalgliesh's *The Courage of Sarah Noble* is an excellent story for young children. (According to the author, Sarah did exist.) Dalgliesh encourages readers to visualize the courage that even an eight-year-old can demonstrate when she accompanies her father to their new land in Connecticut. On their journey through the wilderness, Sarah often remembers her mother's words: "Keep up your courage, Sarah Noble!" (p. 2). She says these words when the wolves howl in the forest, when she is surrounded by strange Indian children, and when her father leaves her with friendly Indians so that he can travel back to Massachusetts. This is a story of friendship and faith as well as courage. The need to help others is one of its main themes: Sarah and her father help each other and develop strong ties with members of an Indian family, who invite Sarah to stay with them, make her deerskin moccasins, and treat her like a daughter.

Themes of friendship, faith, moral obligation, working together, and love for land are all found in Elizabeth George Speare's *The Sign of the Beaver*. The Maine wilderness in the 1700s can be either an antagonist or a friend. Matt, the thirteen-year-old main character, faces a life-and-death struggle when his father leaves him alone to guard their frontier cabin through the winter. Without food or a gun, Matt confronts a harsh natural environment, fear of the local Indians, and the possibility that he may never see his parents again. In spite of his people's own conflicts about the ways white settlers are changing their land, a Penobscot boy befriends Matt and teaches him how to survive.

The frontier of human understanding rather than the frontier of physical expansion is the setting for Carol Carrick's *Stay Away from Simon!* Attitudes toward and fears about a mentally retarded boy provide the conflict in this story set on Martha's Vineyard in the 1830s. The author

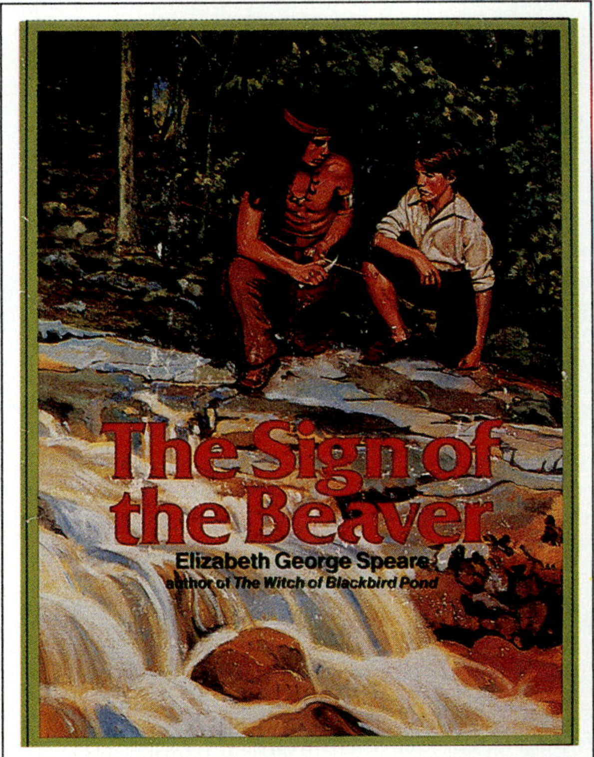

Survival and friendship are important in this story set in the 1700s. (From *The Sign of the Beaver,* by Elizabeth George Speare. Copyright © 1983 by Elizabeth George Speare. By permission of Dell Publishing Company.)

creates believable fear and misunderstanding as two children, Lucy and Josiah, risk getting lost in a snowstorm to avoid walking on the road with Simon. The author encourages readers to understand how ridiculous these fears are by developing Simon as a caring individual who leads the children to safety.

The need to believe in oneself and the importance of retaining and respecting one's own beliefs are themes developed in Janet Lunn's person-against-society and person-against-self conflicts set in Hawthorn Bay, Ontario. Lunn's *Shadow in Hawthorn Bay,* winner of the Canadian children's literature award, follows fifteen-year-old Mary Urquhart as she leaves her Scottish highlands on the shores of Loch Ness to try to find and help her cousin in Canada. Lunn introduces Mary's special powers as she tends sheep in Scotland and hears her cousin Duncan calling her to come to him. She does not consider this unusual, even though Duncan is over three thousand miles away. Her actions and the belief of her Scottish family make her ability to see into the future believable. This same ability, referred to as second sight, causes her considerable conflict as she interacts with a society that not only does not believe in her powers but also fears and distrusts her special abilities.

Lunn develops a related person-against-self conflict as Mary fights her powers and the consequences of her visions. As part of this inner conflict, she must overcome her fear of going into the forest, her fear of the black water, and her belief that something evil is trapped in the bay. Mary overcomes her fears and gains the insight she needs to believe in herself and her powers. With this realization, Lunn develops the theme of the book: It is important to keep your beliefs and ways.

Joan W. Blos's *A Gathering of Days: A New England Girl's Journal, 1830–32* is the fictional journal of a thirteen-year-old girl on a New Hampshire farm. Blos (1) says that she tried to develop three types of truthfulness: "the social truthfulness of the situation, the psychological

ISSUE

Unbalanced Viewpoints in Historical Fiction

REPORTING OF HISTORY may change depending upon the viewpoint of an author. This is also true in the writing of historical fiction. Too many frontier books are told from the perspective of the white settlers rather than from the perspective of the Native Americans. In this context, some critics fear that children will not realize the hardships experienced by the Native Americans or the contributions that the Native Americans made. Stories from the perspective of the white settlers emphasize kidnappings of white children, attacks on wagon trains by warring tribes, the burning of white settlements, and rescues of settlers by soldiers. Many frontier heroes created their reputations as Indian fighters.

Some critics believe that historical fiction about the settlement of North America should include more stories told from the native perspective. These stories might include kidnappings of Indian children by white settlers or emphasize the reasons for the kidnappings of white children. The stories might portray the numerous peaceful tribes, who lived in harmony with settlers. They might emphasize the diversity of the Native American cultures. Students of children's literature should consider the viewpoints of authors and the consequences of unbalanced narratives of other time periods, including narratives about early explorers, the Roman invasion of Britain, religious freedom and the settlement of America, the Revolutionary War, the Civil War, and World War II.

In addition to evaluating the balance in historical fiction, students should be encouraged to evaluate and authenticate the historical accuracy in historical fiction. This need is highlighted by the findings of *The Nation's Report Card.*[1] The latest study reported that fourth, eighth, and twelfth grade students, "have a limited grasp of U.S. history." In addition, the study calls for assignments that encourage "thoughtful analytical essays" (p. 4). Evaluating and authenticating the historical accuracy in historical fiction and in historical biography would be one way to encourage thoughtful analytical essays.

[1]Knight-Ridder News Service. "Most Students Have Limited Grasp of History, Study Finds." Bryan, College Station: *Eagle* (April 3, 1990):1–4.

truthfulness of the characters, and the literary truthfulness of the manner of telling" (p. 371). Consequently, the characters are similar to those who stare from New England portraits. Likewise, the tone of the story is similar to *Leavitt's Almanac,* written for farmers, with the form and style found in journal writings of that period.

Both Elizabeth George Speare's *Calico Captive* and Lois Lenski's *Indian Captive: The Story of Mary Jemison* are stories about white girls captured by native tribespeople. Both girls face difficult conflicts and harsh circumstances, but their experiences eventually cause them to question their former prejudices. Speare's Miriam learns more about the Indians from Pierre, a *coureur des bois.* Mary Jemison, after much inner turmoil, finally decides that the Seneca are her people:

> At that moment she saw Old Shagbark looking at her, his brown eyes overflowing with kindness and understanding. He knew how hard it was for her to decide. . . .She saw the Englishman, too. His lips were smiling, but his eyes of cold gray were hard. Even if she were able to put all her thoughts into words, she knew he would never, never understand. Better to live with those who understood her because they loved her so much, than with one who could never think with her, in sympathy, about anything. . . .Squirrel Woman's scowling face and even Gray Wolf's wicked one no longer held any terrors, because she understood them. (p. 268)

Books written from Native American viewpoints describe the harmful influences of an expanding white population. In *Sweetgrass,* a winner of the Canadian Library Association's Book of the Year Award, Jan Hudson focuses on a young Blackfoot girl's struggle for maturity as she faces a life-and-death battle in 1837. Smallpox, the "white man's sickness," results in hunger and death. The themes in *Sweetgrass* are that it is important to honor moral obligation toward others and that it is important to retain one's dreams.

Hudson employs figurative language that involves signs and omens that are meaningful to the characters and that reinforce themes related to retaining one's identity and meeting obligations toward family members. For example, the main character considers the importance of her name. She believes that it is appropriate because sweetgrass is "ordinary to look at but it's fragrant as the spring" (p. 12). Later, her grandmother tells her that sweetgrass has the power of memories. As Sweetgrass considers her future, readers discover that she is joyfully approaching womanhood. She says, "I felt mightier than a brave. . . .I felt I was holding the future like summer berries in my hands" (p. 26). Instead of allowing the signs and omens to control her life, Sweetgrass uses them to overcome taboos and to help her family in a time of great trouble. She decides, "I would make Father do what I wanted. I would find the signs, the power to control my own days. I would make my life be what I wanted" (p. 15).

The themes in books of historical fiction about the early expansion of the United States vary considerably. Consider the following themes. Why do you think that authors who write stories about this period chose them? How do these themes compare to themes found in different time periods? Are the themes significant today?

1 Friendship and faith are important.
2 People long for their own land and the freedom that ownership implies.

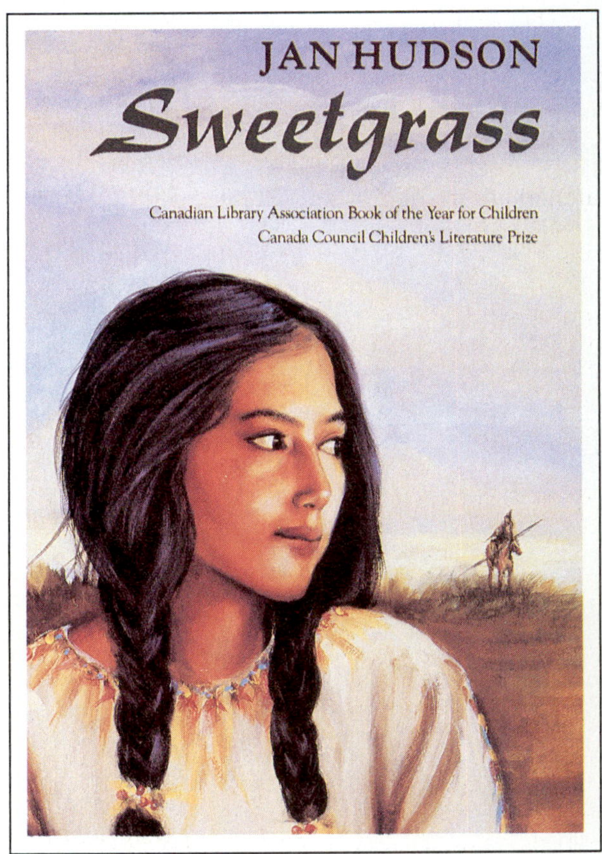

The language and setting reflect the Blackfoot culture. (From *Sweetgrass* by Jan Hudson, copyright © 1989. Illustration copyright © 1989 by Jan Spivey Gilchrist. Reprinted by permission of Philomel Books, a Division of the Putnam & Grosset Group.)

3. People will withstand considerable hardships to retain their dreams.
4. Strong family bonds help physical and spiritual survival.
5. Prejudice and hatred are destructive forces.
6. The greatest strength comes from within.
7. Moral obligations require personal commitment.

The Civil War

In the early centuries of American history, white slave traders brought hundreds of thousands of black Africans to this continent in chains and sold them on auction blocks as field workers, house servants, and skilled craftspeople. Many people in both the North and the South believed that slavery was immoral. Although unable to pass laws against it, they assisted slaves in their flight toward Canada and freedom.

Helping runaway slaves was a dangerous undertaking, especially after the passage of the Fugitive Slave Act in 1850 made it a crime. Handbills offering rewards for the return of certain slaves added to the danger by urging slave catchers to hunt for any suspected runaways. Because of the dangers and the need for secrecy, an illicit network of people dedicated to assisting fugitive slaves linked the North and South. Free people led the fugitives from one safe hiding place to another on each part of their journey along the Underground Railroad to Canada.

Conflicts between northern and southern interests that had emerged during the Constitutional Convention increased in the 1850s and led to the outbreak of the Civil War in 1861. The United States was torn apart. In some cases, relatives were on opposite sides of the conflict and faced one another on the battlefields of Bull Run and Gettysburg.

Strong drama emerges from this historical period. Some authors examine slavery and the experiences of slaves during captivity or as fugitives seeking freedom. Other authors examine the impact of the Civil War on young soldiers or on the people who remained at home. Person-against-society and person-against-self conflicts are common in historical fiction covering this period, as some characters confront prejudice and hatred and others wrestle with their consciences and discover the tragedy associated with slavery and war. Authors who create credible plots consider not only the historical events but also the conflicting social attitudes of the times. The themes developed in this literature reflect a need for personal freedom, ponder the right of one person to own another, consider the tragedies of war, and question the killing of one human by another.

The attitudes expressed toward blacks create special problems for authors who write about slavery. How accurately should historical fiction reflect the attitudes and circumstances of the times? Should authors use terms of the period that are considered insensitive and offensive today? For example, in their authors' note to *Jump Ship to Freedom,* James and Christopher Collier consider use of the word *nigger*. Although the word is considered offensive today, would avoiding it in a novel about slavery distort history? The Colliers chose to use the term in order to illustrate their main character's change in attitude as he develops self-respect and self-confidence and to highlight the social attitudes of the other characters in the book.

In *Jump Ship to Freedom,* those who use the word *nigger* express racial bias toward blacks, and those who do not are concerned with the rights and self-respect of all humans. Consider, for example, how the slave Daniel uses the word. At first he refers to himself as a nigger. He considers himself unintelligent, inferior to whites, and unable to think of himself as a person. He allows other people's opinions to reinforce these beliefs. Self-realization develops slowly. Daniel discovers that he can develop and carry out a plan to recover his father's confiscated funds and free himself, associate with people who consider him capable and slavery immoral, meet his moral obligations to his mother, and fight for his rights. After he makes these personal discoveries, he refuses to call himself nigger.

A slave ship in which human cargo are chained together in cramped quarters provides the setting for Paula Fox's *The Slave Dancer*. The story is told from the point of view of a thirteen-year-old white boy from New Orleans who is kidnapped by slave traders to play his fife on their ship. When the ship reaches Africa, Jessie learns about the trade in human "Black Gold" and discovers that in their greed for trade goods, African chiefs sell their own people and people kidnapped from other tribes. For four long nights, longboats bring their cargoes to the slave ship: men and women who are half-conscious from the pressure of bodies and bruised by ankle shackles. The detailed descriptions of the conditions on the ship are believable. Jessie describes the holds as pits of misery, is horrified by the low regard for human life, and is shocked when prisoners who die are thrown overboard. Jessie learns the reason for having him aboard when slaves are dragged on deck and forced to dance. A dead or weak slave cannot be sold for profit, and the slave traders believe that dancing keeps their bodies strong.

This book has stirred considerable controversy. Some have criticized the fact that the slaves in the book are not treated like human beings or even given names. Many college students, however, say that while reading *The Slave Dancer,* they realized for the first time the true inhumanity of slavery. Fox reveals the impact of the experience on Jessie by flashing ahead in time to Jessie's memories:

> At the first note of a tune or a song, I would see once again as though they'd never ceased their dancing in my mind, black men and women and children lifting their tormented limbs in time to a reedy martial air, the dust rising from their joyless thumping, the sound of the fife finally drowned beneath the clanging of their chains. (p.176)

A book written for young children explains the purposes of the Underground Railroad. F. N. Monjo's *The Drinking Gourd* tells of a family that is part of the Underground Railroad and the role of that family in helping a fugitive slave family escape. Even though this is an easy-to-read book, it illustrates the importance of one family's contributions. The dialogue between father and sons discloses the purpose of the railroad. Young readers also experience excitement and danger as Tommy accompanies his father and an escaping black family on the next part of their journey.

The impact of the Civil War on free whites in the United States is the subject of several novels in which idealistic young men come to realize that war is not simply a glamorous time of brass bands and heroic battles led by banner-carrying leaders. Stories about fighting soldiers often show men realizing the true horrors of war. Janet Hickman's *Zoar Blue* depicts the emotional effects of war when the younger members of the Separatists, a nonviolent religious group in Zoar, Ohio, defy their elders and enlist in the Union Army. Hickman encourages children to understand the person-against-society and person-against-self conflicts that these young men experience as they struggle to maintain personal values out of step with the times. They feel loyalty to their country and are moved by Abraham Lincoln's call for troops, but the teachings of their church stress that people of conscience do not fight each other. Outsiders not of their faith taunt them about playing tunes on a piano while "braver" men play tunes on cannons.

When the young men finally join the army, they continue to feel conflict about killing other people. They long for the simplicity and stability of their home community in the days before they had to face such dilemmas:

> He had learned the Principles too well, perhaps. A Separatist could not murder any enemy, much less, one supposed, a countryman. How was it possible to follow the Principles and be a soldier too? There was no way to make sense between the war and such arguments. He had tried. (p. 54)

Hickman gives further depth to the story by developing the perspective of the nonfighting residents of Zoar—their physical sacrifices and their grief for their sons—and by showing the changes in the soldiers after they return home.

One of the finest books to depict the wartime hardships and conflicts of family members who remain at home is Irene Hunt's *Across Five Aprils*. The beginning conflict is effectively introduced as members of a family in southern Illinois debate the issues related to the Civil War and choose their allegiances: Matt Creighton, the head of the family, argues that a strong union must be main-

Fugitive slaves follow the Underground Railroad to freedom. (Illustration (pp. 34–35) from *The Drinking Gourd,* by F. N. Monjo. Pictures by Fred Brenner. An I CAN READ History Book. Pictures copyright © 1970 by Fred Brenner. Reprinted by permission of Harper & Row, Publishers, Inc.)

tained; the majority of his sons agree with him, but one son argues that people in the South should be able to live without northern interference.

Hunt develops a strong personal conflict as Jethro, the youngest son, is emotionally torn between two beloved brothers, one who joins the Union Army and another who fights for the Confederacy. The consequences of hatred are illustrated when young toughs burn the Creightons' barn and put oil into their well because of the family's divided allegiances. Hunt allows readers to glimpse a different view of people when neighbors guard the farm, help put in the crops, and rebuild the barn.

This is the touching story of a heroic family overcoming problems at home and awaiting news of fighting sons. In spite of disagreement, the Creightons maintain strong family ties. When the son fighting for the South learns that one of his brothers was killed at Pittsburgh Landing, he sends a message to his mother that he was not in that battle and did not fire the bullet that killed his brother. This story helps children understand the real tragedy of the Civil War: Brothers fought against brothers and neighbors against neighbors.

Consider the following themes developed by authors who write about slavery and the Civil War. Why are so many of the themes related to overcoming great personal and social conflicts? How do these themes relate to the events and values of the times? Are they appropriate for the time period? What other time periods, if any, reflect similar themes, and what do they have in common with the Civil War period? Are any of these themes significant in contemporary life and literature?

1 War creates tragedy.
2 Moral obligations must be met even if one's life or freedom is in jeopardy.
3 Moral sense does not depend on skin color, but on what is inside a person.
4 People should take pride in themselves and their accomplishments.
5 Prejudice and hatred are destructive forces.
6 People search for freedom.
7 Personal conscience may not allow some people to kill others.
8 Strong family ties help people persevere.

The Western Frontier

The American frontier was extending further and further west in the 1800s. White Americans were giving up their settled towns and farms in the East to make their fortunes in unknown territories. Former slaves saw the frontier as a place to make a new start in freedom, and Asian immigrants to the West Coast moved inland to work on the railroads that were beginning to span the Great Plains. The Homestead Act of 1862 promised free land to settlers willing to stake their claims and develop the land. Stories of rich earth in fertile valleys caused families to travel thousands of miles over prairies and mountains to reach Oregon. Others dreamed of rich prairie land that did not need to be cleared of rocks or timber, and covered wagons carried many settlers into the Oklahoma Territory.

Whether the pioneers stopped in the Midwest or went along the Oregon Trail, the journey was perilous. They fought nature as they battled blizzards, dust storms, mountain crossings, and swollen rivers. They fought people as they met unfriendly Native Americans, outlaws, and cattle ranchers who did not want them to farm. Some demonstrated noble human qualities as they helped each other search for new land and made friends with the Native Americans they encountered. Others demonstrated greed and prejudice in their interactions with other pioneers and Native Americans.

Native peoples themselves were experiencing a time of considerable trauma as outsiders invaded their ancient territories, staking claims to land that had once been without ownership or boundaries and killing the buffalo and other wild animals on which the people relied for sustenance. The American government had begun its campaign to relocate Native Americans onto reservations that were minuscule in size and resources compared with the rich stretches of prairie and mountain that had long been the native people's domain.

This period of American history—with its high hopes, dangers, triumphs, and tragic conflicts—still captures the imagination of Americans. Stories about pioneer America are popular with children, as exemplified by the continuing interest in such books as Laura Ingalls Wilder's "Little House" series. Historical fiction for children includes three general types of stories about this period: (1) adventure stories in which the characters cross the prairies and mountains, (2) stories about family life on pioneer homesteads, and (3) stories about interactions between Native Americans and pioneers or Native Americans and military forces.

Authors who write about crossing the continent explore people's reasons for moving and their strong feelings for the land. Self-discovery may occur in young characters as they begin to understand their parents' motivations and values. Detailed descriptions allow readers to understand the awesome continent as both inspiration and antagonist. Stories set on homesteads often develop warm family relationships as families seek to achieve their dreams. Like earlier stories about Native Americans and colonial settlers, these Native American and pioneer stories include tales of captive children and stories that depict the harsh treatment of Native Americans by white people as they alter a traditional way of life.

Moving West. Barbara Brenner's *Wagon Wheels* is an enjoyable book for young readers. Based on fact, it tells about a black pioneer family that leaves Kentucky after the Civil War and moves to Kansas to receive land under the Homestead Act. The family develops a friendly relationship with members of an Indian tribe, without whose help they would have starved. Young children enjoy the story because it shows that pioneer children were courageous: Three boys survive a prairie fire and travel over one hundred miles to join their father. This is one of the few books written about blacks as a part of the frontier experience.

Two other books written for younger children follow pioneer families as they journey westward. Brett Harvey's *Cassie's Journey: Going West in the 1860s* develops the dangers and hardships as well as the close relationships of pioneers traveling from Illinois to California. The illustrations reinforce the need to work together if the families are to survive. Kerry Lydon's *A Birthday for Blue* reveals how a pioneer boy spends his seventh birthday traveling westward by covered wagon.

Honore Morrow tells the story of earlier pioneers to the far West in *On to Oregon!,* a book for older children. Morrow's novel about pioneers from Missouri in the 1840s is more than an adventure story about crossing the continent; it is also a psychological story about the challenge of surviving in harsh circumstances. After his parents die on the trail, thirteen-year-old John Sager becomes head of the family and leads his brothers and sisters on to Oregon over a thousand miles of treacherous mountains, canyons, and rivers. The people in the wagon train do not want responsibility for the Sager children and plan to send them back East. The author shows the strength of the father's dream by describing John's actions.

John refuses to forfeit his father's dream; he works out a scheme so that the people think he and his siblings will be traveling with Kit Carson. The children secretly pack their goods on oxen and head out on the lonely trail. The awesome natural environment becomes the chief antagonist against which the children must struggle before reaching a warm, gentle valley in the Oregon of their dreams. Morrow looks at the contributions of people who made westward expansion possible. Consider, for example, the possible impact of the author's closing statements:

> You and I will never hear that magic call of the West, "Catch up! Catch up!" We never shall see the Rockies framed in the opening of our prairie schooner and tingle with the knowledge that if we and our fellow immigrants can reach the valleys in the blue beyond the mountains and there plow enough acreage, that acreage will belong forever to America. (p. 235)

Kathryn Lasky's *Beyond the Divide,* a story of survival set in the ruggedness of the far West just before the Civil War, develops strong themes related to the destructive nature of greed and prejudice and the constructive power of dreams, hope, and moral obligations. Louise Moeri effectively develops similar themes in *Save Queen of Sheba,* as twelve-year-old King David and his young sister Queen of Sheba (named after biblical characters) survive a Sioux raid and set out alone across the prairie in hope of finding the wagons that separated from their portion of the wagon train. Moeri effectively demonstrates the strength of King David's feeling of responsibility by developing his varied emotional responses during several emotionally and physically draining experiences. For another view of the western trails, young children enjoy Sibyl Hancock's *Old Blue,* based on a true incident involving a boy who went on a cattle drive in 1878. The hero of the story is actually an intelligent steer who can find the right direction even in a storm.

Pioneer Family Life. Many stories about pioneer life depict the power of a family that is working to conquer outside dangers and build a home filled with love and decency. One author in particular has enabled children to vicariously experience family life on the frontier. Laura Ingalls Wilder, through her "Little House" books, recreated the world of her own frontier family from 1870 through 1889. The "Little House" books have sold in the millions and received literary acclaim. A popular television series introduced the Ingalls family to millions of new friends.

The first book, *Little House in the Big Woods*, takes place in a deep forest in Wisconsin. Unlike those in many other pioneer stories, this setting is not antagonistic. Although the woods are filled with bears and other wild animals, the danger never really enters the log cabin in the clearing. Any potential dangers are implied through Pa's stories about his adventures in the big woods, told in a close family environment inside the cabin. Other descriptions of family activities also suggest that the environment, while creating hard work for the pioneer family, is not awesome or dangerous. The family clears the land, plants and harvests the crops, gathers sap from the sugar bush, and hitches up the wagon and drives through the woods to Grandpa's house.

Wilder focuses upon the interactions of the family members with one another. Pa's actions, for example, imply that he is a warm, loving father. After working all day, he has time to play the fiddle, play mad dog with the children, and tell stories. Likewise, Ma takes care of the physical needs of the children but also helps them create paper dolls. The impact of what it means to live in the relative isolation of the frontier where a family must be self-sufficient is also implied through the children's actions and thoughts: They feel secure when the attic is hung with smoked hams and filled with pumpkins, they are excited when they get new mittens and a cloth doll for Christmas, and they are astonished when they visit a town for the first time and see a store filled with marvelous treasures.

In other "Little House" books, Laura and her family leave the big woods of Wisconsin to live in the prairie states: Kansas, Minnesota, and South Dakota. The children go to a one-room school, build a fish trap, have a grasshopper invasion, worry when Pa must walk three hundred miles to find a job, and live through a blizzard. Wilder's description of the winter in *Little Town on the Prairie* encourages modern-day children to share the experience:

> All winter long, they had been crowded in the little kitchen, cold and hungry and working hard in the dark and the cold to twist enough hay to keep the fire going and to grind wheat in the coffee mill for the day's bread. All that long, long winter, the only hope had been that sometime winter must end, sometime blizzards must stop, the sun would shine warm again. (p. 3)

When Laura gets her first job in the little town of De Smet, South Dakota, she earns twenty-five cents a day and her dinner for sewing shirts. Unselfishly, she saves this money to help send her sister Mary to a college for the blind in Vinton, Iowa. The series ends with stories about Laura's experiences as a school teacher, her marriage to Almanzo Wilder, and their early years together on a prairie homestead. One reason that children like these books so much is the feeling of closeness they have with Laura.

Carol Ryrie Brink's *Caddie Woodlawn* presents another loving frontier family. The time and setting are similar to those of the first "Little House" book: the last half of the nineteenth century in Wisconsin. In fact, the real Caddie, Brink's grandmother, lived approximately thirty miles north of where Laura Ingalls Wilder was born. Caddie is a warm-hearted, brave, rambunctious girl who loves to play in the woods and along the river with her brothers. She is also a friend of Native Americans in the area.

In one dramatic situation, Caddie jumps on a horse and rides through the night woods to warn her friend, Indian John, about a plot by some settlers to attack John's people. Caddie's experiences differ from present-day ones, but her worries about growing up are similar to those of any girl, no matter when she lives. With Caddie, children know that everything will be all right:

> When she awoke she knew that she need not be afraid of growing up. It was not just sewing and weaving and wearing stays. It was a responsibility, but, as Father spoke of it, it was a beautiful and precious one, and Caddie was ready to go and meet it. (p. 251)

Patricia MacLachlan's *Sarah, Plain and Tall* is a more recently published book about pioneer family life. In this book for younger readers, MacLachlan develops the strong need for a loving mother and a happy family life and introduces the children's need for singing in the home by contrasting the singing that took place before the mother's death with the quiet, sad atmosphere that dominates life after the mother's death. The father's needs are revealed through his actions: He places an advertisement for a wife in an eastern newspaper, in response to which "plain and tall" Sarah enters the family's life.

The children's need for a mother and a happy home is reflected in their desire for singing, in their rereading of Sarah's letters until the letters are worn out, their desire to be perfect for Sarah, their frightened reactions when Sarah misses the sea, their trying to bring characteristics of the sea into their prairie farm, and their complete happiness when they realize that Sarah will stay on the prairie. MacLachlan's characterization of Sarah reveals a strong, loving, independent pioneer woman who discovers that her love for her new family is stronger than her feelings of loneliness for the sea. Like Wilder's and Brink's, MacLachlan's characters may seem real because she drew them from her own family history.

Ellen Howard's *Edith Herself* is another book in which the author draws characterizations and conflict from family history. The experiences, however, involve prejudice and fear. Misunderstandings and fear about epilepsy create person-against-society and person-against-self conflicts in Howard's story set in rural America of the 1890s. The plot follows Edith as she leaves a loving home after her father's death and moves into the sterner environment of her older sister's family. At the same time, Edith experiences her first epileptic seizure. Howard reflects both the ignorance of the society and the fear of people who face circumstances that they do not understand. Howard creates a strong character, who overcomes her own fears, attends school, and learns to believe in herself. These actions emphasize the need to believe in oneself.

Other outstanding books about pioneer family life include Scott O'Dell's *Carlota,* the story of the strong and independent daughter of a Spanish landholder in early California, and Ann Nolan Clark's *Year Walk*, in which a Spanish Basque boy develops self-understanding on a western sheep ranch.

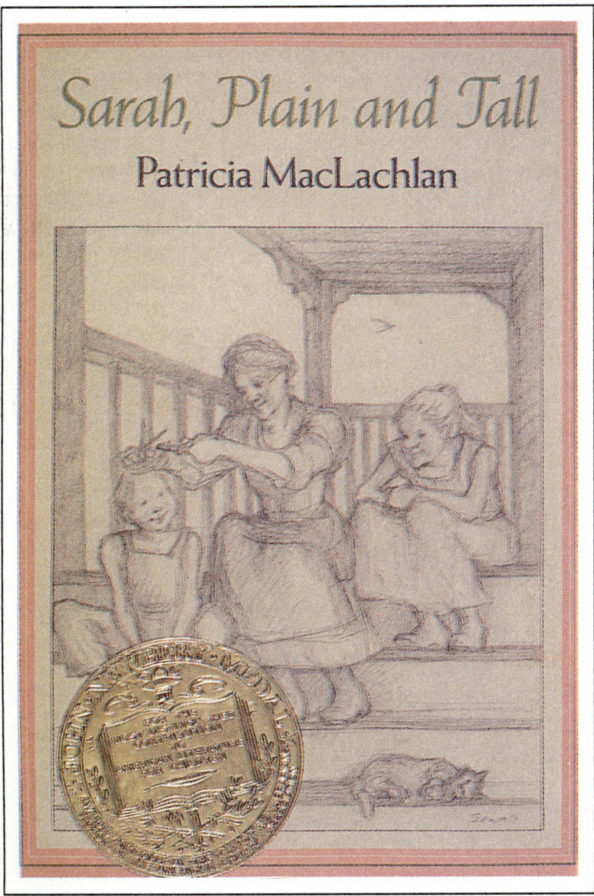

The need for warm family relationships provides the focus for this frontier story. (Jacket art by Marsha Sewall from *Sarah, Plain and Tall,* by Patricia MacLachlan. Jacket art copyright © 1985 by Marcia Sewall. Reprinted by permission of Harper & Row, Publishers, Inc.)

Pioneers and Native Americans. The West Texas frontier of the 1860s provides the setting for Patricia Beatty's *Wait for Me, Watch for Me, Eula Bee*. The story tells of the capture of two farm children by Comanche and Kiowa Indians, the subsequent escape of the older boy, the changing loyalties of the very young girl as she learns to love her Comanche foster parent, and her rescue by her brother. Beatty's descriptions of camp life, food, travel, and behavior create a vivid picture of the period. Her author's notes list the sources for her information on Comanche and Kiowa tribes and their treatment of captives.

While Beatty's descriptions and characterizations depict the Comanche as leading a harsh life built on raiding and warfare, they also depict the value that the Comanche place on children. The developing love between the little girl and her Comanche foster parent exemplifies a warm, loving relationship. Sadness in this book stems from the tragic results of the lack of understanding of two cultures.

A true story from the 1850s is the basis for Evelyn Sibley Lampman's *White Captives*. White men in the Southwest came upon some Tonto Apache women and children who were berry picking, killed the women, and took two girls as slaves. One of the captured girls escaped and took the news back to the Apache, who sent out a raiding party to avenge the deaths of the women. The raiding party killed most members of the Oatman family, who were traveling alone, but like the white men, took two girls of the family captive.

Lampman's retelling of this story contains considerable information about the Native American viewpoint and way of life. The girls were slaves for two different tribes, the nomadic Apache, who

ISSUE

Should Historical Fiction Reflect the Attitudes of the Time Period?

SHOULD HISTORICAL FICtion reflect the attitudes and circumstances of the times? Or should historical fiction reflect the changing attitudes toward people of all races? These issues become especially critical when historical fiction is reviewed by literary critics and various interest groups.

Sounder, by William H. Armstrong, is an example of historical fiction that has been both acclaimed for literary merit and criticized for its portrayal of a black family. Literary acclaim is exemplified in the awarding of the Newbery medal in 1970. However, *Sounder* has been denounced by some critics because they believe it emasculates the black man and destroys the black family by showing it as spiritless and submissive rather than actively fighting injustice. In contrast, other critics maintain that the book authentically depicts the poverty, ignorance, and attitudes of the times; consequently, the family members acted in the only way possible.

A similar debate centers on the depiction of black characters in Paula Fox's 1973 Newbery Medal winner *The Slave Dancer*. Students of children's literature should consider this issue and the implications for writers, publishers, and selectors of literature when they read historical fiction that depicts black Americans, Asian Americans, and Hispanic Americans.

were hunters, and the Mohave, who were farmers. Lampman effectively brings Native American spiritual beliefs into the story through Mohave religious beliefs and ceremonies, such as rituals that preceded the planting of crops.

Like most white settlers, the Oatman girls are shocked to discover that Native Americans have moral principles and spiritual beliefs similar to their own. The Mohave belief in a great flood and the finding of sanctuary at the top of a sacred mountain is similar to the biblical story of Noah. Lampman informs readers that after the older girl's rescue (her sister died in captivity), this girl told her story to a minister named Stratton. His book, *Captivity of the Oatman Girls, Being an Interesting Narrative of Life among the Apache and Mohave Indians,* published in 1857, sold over 25,000 copies. "In a small way," says Lampman, "the book probably did as much to turn public sentiment against the Indians as *Uncle Tom's Cabin* did against. . .slavery" (p. 177). *White Captives,* written over one hundred years later, presents a fairer view of hardworking Native Americans and the reasons behind their hostility toward white settlers.

A tragic period in Navaho history, 1863–1865, is the setting for Scott O'Dell's *Sing down the Moon*. The story of the three-hundred-mile forced march that culminates in holding Navahos prisoner at Fort Sumner, New Mexico, is told through the viewpoint of a Navaho girl, Bright Morning. O'Dell effectively uses both descriptions of physical settings and characterizations to depict a human tragedy. The Navahos are forced to leave their home, the beautiful Canyon de Chelly, with its fruit trees, green grass, sheep, and cool water, for the harsh windswept landscape around Fort Sumner.

The greatest tragedy does not result from the loss of their home, however, but from the loss of their spiritual hope. Still, Bright Morning does not give up her dream of returning to her beautiful canyon, and O'Dell creates a thought-provoking, bittersweet ending. Bright Morning and her husband escape from the U.S. Army and return to her hidden valley. It is as she remembers it: The blossoms are on the trees, a sheep and a lamb are grazing on the green land, and the tools she hid from the soldiers are waiting. However, a menacing shadow looms over their happiness. Readers cannot forget that the Navaho family is hiding from the soldiers they saw on the horizon.

Many authors who write about the pioneer period stress the quest for and love of land and the conflicts between different cultures. Consider the following themes developed in historical fiction about pioneer America. How do the themes correspond with historical events? What other periods have similar themes? What are the similarities between times with similar themes?

1 People have moral obligations that must be met.
2 People have strong dreams of owning land.
3 Families can survive if they work together.
4 People need each other and may work together for their mutual good.
5 Battles can be won through legal means rather than through unlawful actions.
6 Hatred and prejudice are destructive forces.
7 Without spiritual hope, people may lose their will to live.

The Early Twentieth Century

Recent books of historical fiction with settings in the early 1900s often depict social conflicts and the Great Depression, which began in 1929. These stories stress both physical and spiritual survival as people strive to maintain pride and independence. Strong person-against-society and person-against-self conflicts develop as people experience or express racial prejudice and face financial hardships.

Even though Patricia Beatty's *Sarah and Me and the Lady from the Sea* takes place in 1894, the father's bankruptcy caused by a flood is as devastating as the financial hardships caused by the Depression. Beatty shows the importance of family unity and a bond between people who are facing hardships. Beatty humorously contrasts the life of a wealthy family before and after the bankruptcy. For example, a family who has always had servants must learn to cook on a wood-burning stove, dress poultry, and wash clothes. At first, Beatty's characters reflect prejudices against those who have less social standing than themselves. However, these people show the characters how to survive without servants and to enjoy their new life.

Felice Holman's *The Wild Children* is set in Russia in 1917–1921, the time following the Bolshevik Revolution. The main characters are children who are left homeless because their parents are either dead or imprisoned. The antagonist is a society that fears political freedom. Holman's vivid descriptions of the living conditions of the children and their fear of authority create a believable antagonist. The children's struggle for survival and their need for each other emphasize that love and loyalty help people endure and survive catastrophic experiences.

In *No Hero for the Kaiser,* Rudolph Frank develops a strong antiwar theme through the author's depictions of the World War I setting and person-against-society conflict. For example, the author suggests the destructive nature of war when he compares the peaceful Polish hamlet before and after the desolation caused by war. Person-against-society conflict is enhanced through both the main character's conflict with the German officers and the foot soldiers' conflicts as they follow orders while dreaming of homes and families. Frank characterizes soldiers who are caught up in actions that are not of their doing. The final actions of the main character are especially effective in supporting the antiwar theme. When the supreme commander wants to honor Jan and make him a symbol for the war effort, Jan disappears, even though he is giving up personal glory. Frank develops the importance of this action through the words of one of Jan's friends:

> Then Father Distelmann stood up, looked around the circle of his friends, and spoke slowly, "I knew him from the very beginning, isn't that right, Hottenrot, when we were advancing near Lodz. He always showed us the right way, always the right way. . . .I believe he's done the same thing this time." (p. 220)

The impact of the antiwar theme is strengthened when readers discover that this book was banned by Hitler.

Mildred D. Taylor's *Roll of Thunder, Hear My Cry* explores both the subtle and the explicit racial prejudice many white Americans expressed toward black Americans in the early twentieth century. Consider, for example, the subtle discrimination developed by Taylor. Cassie and her brother, who live in rural Mississippi, excitedly await their new schoolbooks, only to receive badly worn, dirty castoffs from the white elementary school. When Cassie's brother looks at the inside cover of his book, he sees that on its twelfth date of issue—to him—it is described as being in very poor condition and the race of the student is listed as "nigra."

The warm family life of the children gives them the strength to confront such discrimination. First, they refuse the books. Then, they create a minor accident for the bus driver, who consistently and intentionally splashes the black children's clothes with dirty water as he drives the white children to

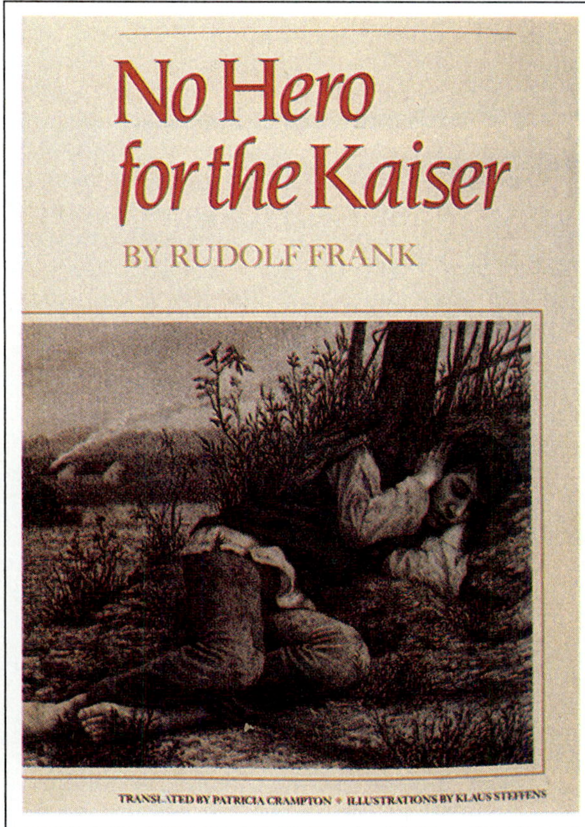

Historically accurate settings add to this World War I story. (From *No Hero for the Kaiser* by Rudolf Frank, translated from the 1931 edition by Patricia Crampton, copyright 1986. Illustrated by Klaus Steffens. Reprinted by permission of Lothrop, Lee & Shepard.)

their separate school. (There is no bus service for the black school.) After the children secretly deepen one of the puddles in the road, the bus breaks an axle and its riders must walk.

Other expressions of racism portrayed in this book are far less subtle, however, and they include the family's experiences with night riders and cross burnings. Understandably, the family feels fear as well as humiliation and indignation. In a sequel to this book, *Let the Circle Be Unbroken,* Taylor helps readers see how the estrangement of white and black people from each other results from ingrained social prejudices. The family in *Roll of Thunder, Hear My Cry* owns its own land, the mother has graduated from a teacher's college, and the children consistently attend school. The family experiences injustice, but a loving environment helps protect and strengthen the members.

The experiences in William H. Armstrong's *Sounder* are harsher and filled with tragedy. An early twentieth-century family of black sharecroppers lives in one of numerous ramshackle cabins scattered across the vast fields of the white landlord. When the poverty-stricken father steals a ham to feed his hungry family, he is handcuffed, chained, and taken to jail. The futility of protest is suggested as Sounder, the family's faithful coon dog, tries to save the father and is wounded by the white sheriff's shotgun.

Comparisons between the two incidents are developed as both the father and Sounder are gone: the father to jail and then to a succession of chain gangs, and Sounder to the woods to heal his wounds. A strong bond between man and dog is implied as Sounder returns, a crippled remnant of his former self. He does not bark until the father returns home, himself crippled by a dynamite blast in the prison quarry. The two old friends are physically and emotionally tired and have only a short life together. The final vision of the two friends is one of remembered strength, as the son, grown to manhood, recalls his father and the faithful dog as they were before the tragic happenings:

> The pine trees would look down forever on a lantern burning out of oil but not going out. A harvest moon would cast shadows forever of a man walking upright, his dog, bouncing after him. And the quiet of the night would fill and echo again with the deep voice of Sounder, the great coon dog. (p. 116)

Critics of *Sounder* believe that, because the dog is the only character in the book with a name, the book implies that the characters need not be respected as human beings. Critics also object to the black family's being characterized as submissive and spiritless. Others argue that the family should be nameless because the tragedy depicted in the story was one shared by many poor black sharecroppers during that period. In the latter view, tragedy is seen as a strong bond between all people who experience injustice. Readers may consider both viewpoints and form their own evaluations of *Sounder*.

In *Circle of Fire,* William H. Hooks also explores the consequences of hatred and prejudice. The setting is North Carolina in the 1930s. The conflict is between the Ku Klux Klan and a group of Irish gypsies. Hooks creates a believable person-against-society conflict by telling the story through the viewpoint of an eleven-year-old boy who befriends the gypsies. Readers may wish to consider an assertion Hooks makes in his end note:

> The Ku Klux Klan grows and expands, reaching even into the alien territory of the North. *Circle of Fire,* set in the 1930s, is about the turbulent drama that occurred when someone dared step outside that "rightful place." These same events could happen today. (p. 147)

The consequences of social injustice and the conflict between classes shape Harry Kullman's *The Battle Horse*. In this story set in 1930s Stockholm, the characters find that they must reexamine their own motives as a consequence of a game in which the knights are the rich preppies and the horses are the poor public school children. Kullman concludes on a strong theme for social equality:

> One day we horses will travel over the Seven Seas like Gulliver and we won't carry the rich and powerful on our backs any more. We'll take control of our lives and everybody will have the same opportunities and the same rights in our kingdom, the Kingdom of the Horses, and there won't be any words for lying or deceit, no words for violence or war, no words for rich or poor. (p. 183)

The conflict in James Aldridge's *The True Story of Spit MacPhee* is a society-against-society conflict developed around a 1928 Adoption of Children Act in Australia that required religious matching of children and adoptive parents.

Franklin D. Roosevelt's fireside chats, a father who mends his shoes with folded paper, and a twelve-year-old's dreams of having her own suitcase contribute to Constance C. Greene's convincing portrayal of the Depression era in *Dotty's Suitcase*. Greene depicts the pressures of hard times by describing Dotty's friend's family which must move to find work, the experiences of a man who loses both wealth and family because of the crash of the stock market in 1929, and the worries of children and adults about the cost of food. Dotty longs to escape from the Depression by obtaining a suitcase and traveling with money she hopes to acquire. Her true character is exposed when she finds the money and the suitcase and gives the money to her friend's family. Dotty discovers that she is rich compared with her friend. She has enough to eat, her father has a job, and she has a radio.

The importance of personal dreams to uphold the human spirit, the detrimental and strengthening consequences of physical and personal hardships, and the sustaining power of love are themes that Crystal Thrasher develops in *A Taste of Daylight*. Thrasher encourages readers to understand the magnitude of the Depression by portraying the problems that a country family faces after they move to the city. Contrasts between rural and urban survival problems, descriptions of physical scars related to manual labor, and responses of characters that enhance family survival create a believable story. Personal dreams and contrasts between rural and city life are also used to develop understandings in George Ella Lyon's *Borrowed Children*. Some of a girl's dreams come true when she leaves her Kentucky home to visit relatives in Memphis. The girl also makes discoveries that allow her to understand her family.

The themes developed in historical fiction set in the early twentieth century highlight both negative and positive human attitudes and values. Consider the following themes found in the literature. How do the themes relate to the historical events? Are these themes found during any other time period in historical fiction?

1 People will strive for survival of the physical body and the human spirit.
2 Prejudice and discrimination are destructive forces.
3 There is a bond between people who experience injustice.
4 Monetary wealth does not create a rich life.

World War II

In 1933, Adolf Hitler took power in Germany, and Germany resigned from the League of Nations. In 1935, Hitler reintroduced conscription of German soldiers and recommended rearmament, contrary to the Treaty of Versailles. Along with a rapid increase in military power came an obsessive hatred of the Jewish people. In March 1938, Hitler's war machine began moving across Europe. Austria was occupied, and imprisonment of Jews began. World War II became a reality when the Germans invaded Poland on September 1, 1939.

The 1940s saw the invasions of Norway, Belgium, and Holland; the defeat of the French army; and the heroic evacuation of British soldiers from Dunkirk. From the start of the invasions through the defeat of Hitler's forces in 1945, these years have inspired many tales of both sorrow and heroism.

Authors who write children's historical fiction set in World War II often focus on the experiences of Jewish people in hiding and concentration camps, the experiences of Japanese Americans in internment centers in the United States, or the perseverance of people in occupied lands. Because some of these stories are written by people who lived similar experiences, the stories tend to be emotional. The authors often create vivid conflicts. Authors explore the consequences of war and prejudice by having characters ponder why their lives are in turmoil, by describing the characters' fears and their reactions to their situations and to one another, and by revealing what happens to the characters or their families as a result of war. As might be expected, the themes of these stories include the consequences of hatred and prejudice, the search for religious and personal freedom, the role of conscience, and obligation toward others.

Some other World War II stories have adventurous plots. For example, Marie McSwigan's *Snow Treasure* is based on a true incident in 1940, in which $9 million in Norwegian gold bullion (thirteen tons) is slipped past Nazi sentries and shipped to Baltimore. The unusual twist is that children on sleds get the bullion past the Nazi troops to a boat hidden in a fiord. Children enjoy this story because it demonstrates how important the work of even young children can be when they work together to preserve their country.

The struggle for freedom and the differences between freedom and tyranny are the major themes developed in Barbara Gehrts's story set in World War II Germany, *Don't Say a Word*. The title reflects the need for secrecy in Hitler's Germany and infers the chilling consequences to German citizens who oppose Hitler. The actions of the characters develop the importance of the title and the struggle for freedom. For example, the characters warn each other about the dangers of poking fun at the fuhrer, worry about the consequences of the father's possible secret involvement with anti-Hitler factions, and fear a later request for secrecy when the father is arrested by the Gestapo. The title is reinforced through a stranger's refusal to speak to the mother in front of the children: "There are certain things that one should really not speak of at all. One extra pair of ears is already too many, not to mention three pairs" (p. 105). Gehrts provides historical background and authenticity by quoting from Hitler's speeches.

Marian Bauer explores the far-reaching effects of war on human emotions in *Rain of Fire*. After World War II, twelve-hear-old Steve first feels great pride in his veteran brother, Matthew, but when Matthew doesn't live up to Steve's heroic expectations, Steve's feelings slowly change to confusion and hostility. Only after a near tragedy does Matthew share with Steve his experiences in Hiroshima, Japan, helping Steve to understand his brother's reluctance to talk about war. Bauer develops the turning point in Steve's feelings as Steve tries to convince Matthew that he must share those experiences so that tragedies like Hiroshima cannot happen again.

The Holocaust. The Nazis' terrible crimes against Jewish people are familiar to adults and children alike. Stories about the Holocaust help children sense the bewilderment and terror of a time when innocent people were the subject of irrational hatred and persecution.

Johanna Reiss tells a fictional version of her own life in *The Upstairs Room*. Reiss allows readers to glimpse varying consequences of prejudice and hatred as a young girl, Johanna, hears news of the war and asks why Hitler hates her people. The girl is barred from restaurants and the public school, and she learns that many Jewish people are being taken to forced-labor camps. Reiss depicts the obligations of one human to another when a Dutch family offers, in spite of great danger, to hide Johanna and her sister on their farm. The farmer builds a secret space in an upstairs closet to provide a hiding place for the two girls. At first, Johanna does not understand why she and her sister must hide, but gradually, she realizes their serious predicament, as word of the Holocaust spreads.

In several scenes, Reiss's style and first-person point of view create the breathless fear of the children. For example, as the children hide in the cramped closet:

> Footsteps. Loud Ones. Boots. Coming up the stairs. Wooden shoes. Coming behind. Sini put her arms around me and pushed my head against her shoulder. Loud voices. Ugly ones. Furniture being moved. And Opoe's protesting voice. The closet door was thrown open. Hands fumbled on the shelves. Sini was trembling. She tightened her arms around me. I no longer breathed through my nose. Breathing through my mouth made less noise. (p. 149)

The girls and the family protecting them are brave during this unsuccessful search by Nazi troops. The story ends happily, as Canadian troops liberate the town and at last, Johanna and her sister may leave their room. This is a powerful story of the experiences of common people during the German occupation. (Some adults have criticized this book because of realistic dialogue, in which members of the farm family use swear words.)

Trust in and loyalty toward a parent are strong motivational forces in Uri Orlev's story of survival set in the Jewish ghetto of Warsaw, Poland. *The Island on Bird Street* chronicles Alex's experiences as he turns a bombed-out building into a refuge while he waits for his father's return. Surrounded by houses emptied of food, Alex feels that his refuge is similar to the desert island in his favorite book, *Robinson Crusoe*. Orlev develops the symbolism of a lonely island, on which Alex, like Robinson Crusoe, must learn how to survive, and the terrifying historical background of the Holocaust, in which Alex witnesses the capture of his Jewish family and friends, experiences fear and loneliness, and nurses a resistance fighter's wounds. The book concludes on a note of hope.

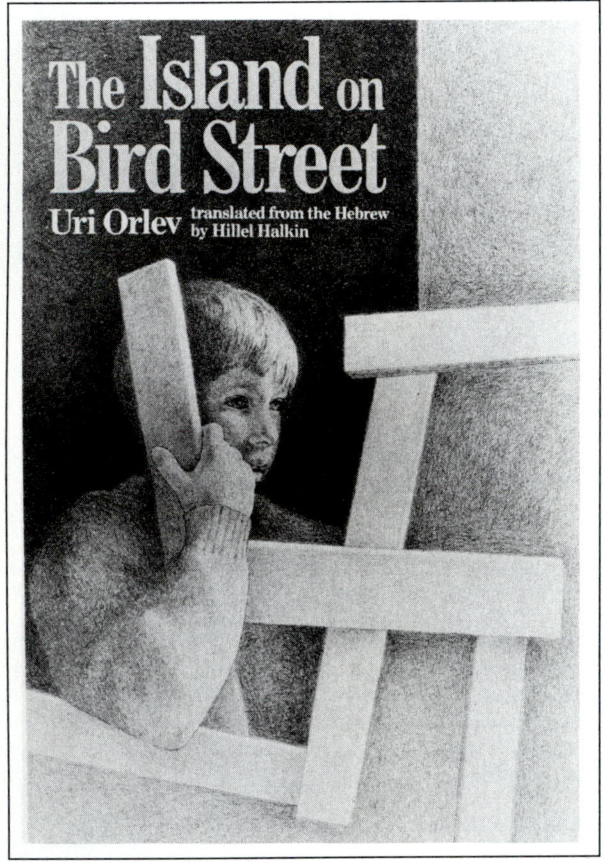

Symbolic and historical settings are integral to a story set in the Warsaw ghetto. (Jacket illustration copyright © 1984 by Jean Titherington from *The Island on Bird Street* by Uri Orlev. Reprinted by permission of Houghton Mifflin Company.)

Alex's father returns, finds Alex where he promised to wait, and takes Alex to the forest to be with the partisans who are resisting the Nazis.

In *When Hitler Stole Pink Rabbit,* Judith Kerr uses personal experiences to provide details about a Jewish family that flees Germany just before the Nazis can arrest her father. Another family escapes in Sonia Levitin's *Journey to America*. In both books, the families show courage in times of great danger. Although they must leave their possessions and friends behind, the families feel that everything will be all right if the family can be together. Levitin extends the experiences of her family in *Silver Days*. In the latter book, Levitin develops the problems of living as refugees in America during World War II. This girl and her family face poverty and try to retain their roots.

Other books about the Holocaust include Aranka Siegal's *Upon the Head of the Goat: A Childhood in Hungary 1939–1944,* which chronicles a nine-year-old girl's experiences from the time she hears about Hitler until her family boards a cattle train to Auschwitz. Benjamin Tene's *In the Shade of the Chestnut Tree* is about the Warsaw ghetto. Lois Lowry's *Number the Stars* is about the Danish endeavor to move Jewish residents to Sweden and safety. After reading such stories, children often are concerned about the implications of not acting when other people are unjustly accused of crimes. Some books, such as Jane Yolen's *The Devil's Arithmetic,* discussed in chapter 7, have accurate historical settings. Even though its time-warp elements make it a fantasy, the book is historically correct.

Internment of Japanese Americans. The Jewish people weren't the only ones to live through persecution and fear during World War II. Many children are surprised to read stories about the American treatment of Japanese Americans during World War II. Two books by Yoshiko Uchida tell about a Japanese American family's experiences after the bombing of Pearl Harbor. (Although the stories are fictional, they are based on what happened to Uchida and her family.)

In *Journey to Topaz,* the police take away Yuki's father, a businessman in Berkeley, California, and send Yuki, her mother, and her older brother to a permanent internment center in Utah, called Topaz. Uchida creates vivid pictures of the internment camp. She describes, for example, latrines without doors, lines of people waiting to use them, and the wind blowing across the desert into the barracks. The fear of the interned people and their

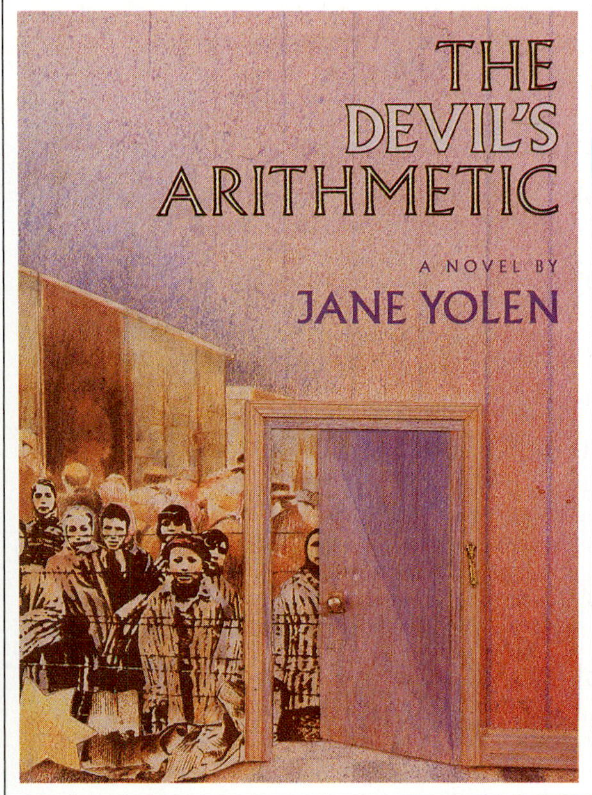

A time-warp experience develops a girl's understanding of the Holocaust. (From *The Devil's Arithmetic* by Jane Yolen, copyright 1988. Reprinted by permission of Viking Penguin, Inc.)

wardens climaxes when the grandfather of Yuki's best friend goes searching for arrowheads and is shot by a guard who believes he is trying to escape. Family members experience conflicting feelings when Yuki's brother, wishing to prove his loyalty to America, joins an army unit composed of Japanese Americans.

Yuki's story continues in *Journey Home,* in which the family returns to Berkeley, only to discover distrust, difficulty finding work, and anti-Japanese violence. The family feels hope and strength more than bitterness, however. Yuki discovers that coming home is having everyone she cares about around her.

The themes in children's historical fiction with settings during World War II resemble themes found during other times of great peril. Consider the following themes. How do they relate to historical events? What are characteristics of other historical periods that have similar themes?

1. People will seek freedom from religious and political persecution.
2. Prejudice and hatred are destructive forces.
3. Moral obligation and personal conscience are strong forces.
4. Freedom is worth fighting for.
5. Family love and loyalty help people endure catastrophic experiences.

Suggested Activities for Adult Understanding of Historical Fiction

- ☐ Find an example of historical fiction written for beginning readers and another written for older readers. Compare the settings. Are they both integral settings? If the book written for younger children does not provide as many details as the one for older children, has the author used any other medium to relate details to the readers? For example, compare Arnold Lobel's setting in *On the Day Peter Stuyvesant Sailed into Town* with Esther Forbes's setting in *Johnny Tremain.*
- ☐ Locate a story in which the setting takes on the role of antagonist (for example, Honore Morrow's *On to Oregon!*). How has the author developed the setting as the antagonist? How do the characters overcome the obstacles of nature? What happens to the characters as they face and overcome the antagonist?
- ☐ Writers of historical fiction often place famous persons into the backgrounds of their stories but make the pivotal character fictional. Read a story such as Erik Christian Haugaard's *Cromwell's Boy* and compare the roles of the little-known eleven-year-old Oliver Cutter with the well-known Oliver Cromwell. Why did the author choose a little-known person as the main character?
- ☐ Writing an excellent historical fiction novel requires considerable research by an author. Choose several authors of historical fiction and investigate the sources they used.
- ☐ Read the acceptance speech of an author of historical fiction who has been awarded the Newbery Medal (1). What were the author's reasons for choosing to write about that period in history? Does the author discuss the sources used?
- ☐ Using Chart 10–1, "Eras and Themes in Historical Fiction," make a list of historical

literature that develops each theme during a selected time period.

- ☐ Read an article on literature with wartime settings, such as Barbara Harrison's "Howl Like the Wolves" (5) or Winfred Kaminski's "War and Peace in Recent German Children's Literature" (6). Summarize the points made by the author and provide your reactions to the article.

References

1 Blos, Joan W. "Newbery Medal Acceptance." *The Horn Book* 56 (August 1980): 369–377.

2 Brink, Carol Ryrie. *Caddie Woodlawn*. Illustrated by Trina Schart Hyman. New York: Macmillan, 1935, 1973.

3 Burton, Hester. "The Writing of Historical Novels." In *Children and Literature: Views and Reviews*, edited by Virginia Haviland. Glenview, Ill.: Scott, Foresman, 1973, 299–304.

4 Garfield, Leon. "Historical Fiction for Our Global Times." *The Horn Book* (November/December 1988): 736–742.

5 Harrison, Barbara. "Howl Like the Wolves." *Children's Literature* 15 (1987): 67–90.

6 Kaminski, Winfred. "War and Peace in Recent German Children's Literature." *Children's Literature* 15(1987): 55–66.

7 Keith, Harold. *The Obstinate Land*. New York: Crowell, 1977.

8 Lasky, Kathryn. *Beyond the Divide*. New York: Macmillan, 1983.

9 Lukens, Rebecca J. *A Critical Handbook of Children's Literature*. Glenview, Ill.: Scott, Foresman, 1986.

10 Norton, Donna E. "A Three-Year Study Developing and Evaluating Children's Literature Units in Children's Literature Courses." Paper presented at the College Reading Association, National Conference, Baltimore, Md., October, 1980.

11 "Notable Children's Trade Books in the Field of Social Studies." *Social Education* 42 (April 1978): 318–321.

12 Reiss, Johanna. *The Upstairs Room*. New York: Crowell, 1972.

13 Townsend, John Rowe. *Written for Children*. New York: Lippincott, 1974.

14 Trease, Geoffrey. "The Historical Story: Is It Relevant Today?" *The Horn Book* (February 1977): 21–28.

15 Yates, Elizabeth. *We, the People*. Illustrated by Nora Unwin. Hanover, N.H.: Regional Center for Educational Training, 1974.

CHILDREN CAN LEARN TO LOVE AND RE-spect history when they vicariously share the experiences of a character with whom they identify. Surrounding themselves with the flavor and spirit of an historical period, they also visualize how people are affected by the times in which they live. Anne Troy (16) says that for children, "history is one of the areas where fiction seems to be preferable and many times nearly replaces textbooks" (p. 473). Historical fiction helps children acquire the idea that history is people rather than merely a series of events, says Troy.

Troy suggests that adults can bring history to life by guiding children toward individual reading selections, reading historical fiction aloud to students, encouraging dramatic presentations of short scenes from favorite books, and using literature in pleasant ways to develop attitudes and general concepts about history. She warns that this should be done with great care, without pressure or preaching, so that the literature does not become "too much of a teaching-learning medium which could turn children off to all literature for fun" (p. 474).

A writer of historical fiction, Geoffrey Trease (15), makes a strong case for using the genre to add new meaning and excitement to social studies:

> So even in the context of social studies, the historical story has an important part to play, and it would be wasteful not to utilize all that the writer has so painstakingly researched and made available to children in an attractive form. (p. 28)

Thus, historical fiction allows children to learn about the continuity of events, understand human relationships, and immerse themselves in the settings characteristic of specific times.

Another author of historical fiction, Alberta Wilson Constant (14), stresses the desirability of allowing children to be immersed in a book:

> One of the best things that you can do for children is to teach them how to escape into a book. Let them be for a while somebody else. Let them stand with their feet on the cobblestones of Paris with Jean Valjean and hear the pursuing steps of police inspector Javert; let them walk into the jungle of Mowgli and hear the cry of their hero the panther and the long howl of the mother wolf. Show them how to mount the winged horse Pegasus and let him carry them away. He will bring them back safely. They'll be better, and they'll be stronger for the journey. (p. 23)

Constant believes that it is equally important for children to be immersed in the American past, as

Involving Children in Historical Fiction

LOOKING AT COLONIAL TIMES

LOOKING AT PIONEER AMERICA

LOOKING AT AMERICAN HISTORY IN FOLK SONGS

they feel the joy and challenge of new frontiers and the pride of self-sufficiency.

Joan Aiken (1) emphasizes that writers must develop within children an awareness of the past, an appreciation for the past, and a feeling of indebtedness toward the past. Aiken believes that as children begin to value and appreciate the contributions of people before their own times, they may realize that they also have obligations to future generations.

Hazel Rochman (11) states that she uses a subject or theme, such as war or survival, to interest readers and "to bring in a variety of reading levels, genres, and cultures; to appeal to a wide range of reading interests and to push readers a little beyond where they might go on their own" (p. 32). Rochman maintains that historical fiction is an excellent genre for interesting and exciting readers.

LOOKING AT COLONIAL TIMES

Celebrations throughout the United States commemorated the bicentennial of our country in 1976. The bicentennial stimulated interest in searching for our roots and learning more about the early colonial days and the Revolutionary War. Carol Gay (8), says that the important task of sharing a sense of the colonial past with children can be effectively approached through the following activities: (1) sharing with children the same stories that colonial children read, (2) encouraging children to take a penetrating look at a historical figure, and (3) inviting students to compare the values and problems of colonial times with those of contemporary times. While these activities would be meaningful for any time period, this section considers some ways to accomplish each of these goals with historical fiction related to colonial days.

Books Read by Colonial Children

What books were available to children in the North American colonies of the 1600s and 1700s? What books did they read at school and at home? One of the books most commonly referred to in colonial literature and used in colonial education was the hornbook. (Reproductions are available through The Hornbook, Inc., Boston, Massachusetts.) The original hornbooks were thin pieces of three-by-five inch wood onto which tacks attached a printed paper covered with a transparent sheet of yellowish horn. Hornbooks contained the alphabet, vowel-consonant and consonant-vowel combinations, the Lord's Prayer, and sometimes Arabic numerals. They were designed to teach a colonial child to read and spell.

Another book mentioned often in the literature of colonial times is *The New-England Primer*. (This primer came out in many editions over the years and is available in a reissued text.) The chapbooks popular in England were also found in the colonies. Some of these had didactic messages; others contained entertaining traditional tales, such as "Tom Thumb," "Reynard the Fox," "Jack the Giant Killer," and "Robin Hood." These stories are available today. An influential book written during the seventeenth century was John Bunyan's *Pilgrim's Progress*. Both children and adults enjoyed following Christian on his perilous journey as he searched for salvation.

Other popular books of colonial times that contemporary children may enjoy include *Babes in the Woods* (reissued in Frederick Warne's edition of Randolph Caldecott's *Picture Book No. 1*), John Newbery's *The History of Little Goody Two Shoes,* and Daniel Defoe's *Robinson Crusoe*. Reading from these books or listening to stories read from them allows children to develop close relationships with characters from the past. Children

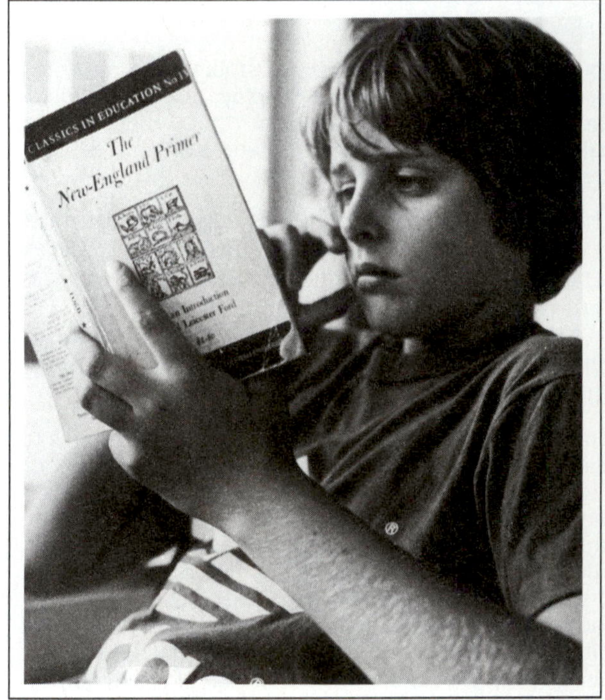

A boy learns about colonial children by reading a book read by children in the 1600s.

are excited to discover that today they are fascinated by the same plots and characters that fascinated children over two hundred years ago. *Fifteen Centuries of Children's Literature: An Annotated Chronology of British and American Works in Historical Context* by Jane Bingham and Grayce Scholt (3) is an excellent resource for locating books that were published during a specific time period.

Historical Figures

Older-elementary and middle-school children can learn about the process of scholarly research used by historical novelists or biographers when they recreate a day in the life of famous American colonists or Native Americans of the period, such as Benjamin Franklin, Pocahontas, George Washington, Betsy Ross, Abigail Adams, or Paul Revere. While many books of historical fiction develop fictional stories about unknown people, many also refer to famous people and leaders. For example, Esther Forbes's *Johnny Tremain* includes frequent mention of well-known figures during the American Revolution. Children can do research on these historical figures because considerable information about them is available.

The first step is to identify a figure about whom there is sufficient source material. With the person selected, break the class into smaller research groups, each to work on a different aspect in the person's life. Next, have the children accumulate as many reference materials as possible. Biographies, information about the person's home, speeches or writings by the person, reproductions of newspapers available at that time, and the weather conditions for the period (listed in almanacs) are valuable resources. Have each group develop a composite picture of what the historical figure did during the chosen period; this should include possible thoughts, writings, actions, associations, and concerns.

Carol Gay (8) says that children should gain two values from this activity. First, they should experience such an intimate look at a day from the past that the person and place come alive for them. Second, they should gain an awareness about how research uncovers the past.

Values and Problems of Colonial Times

Historical fiction set in colonial times presents problems and their associated values. Stories related to the early colonial period stress a search for religious and political freedom, as the colonists fight the tyranny of a hated government and brave the frequent miseries associated with starting over in a new land. The colonists face danger, disease, and even starvation in order to fulfill their dream. In some books, such as Patricia Clapp's *Constance: A Story of Early Plymouth*, people also make personal adjustments as they long to return to a beloved home, battle the role mandated by their society, and finally discover love for their new land.

Much historical fiction set in the Revolutionary War period stresses the battle for freedom, as well as the tragedy of war and the personal and emotional problems associated with people who follow their consciences during wartime. Some books that develop similar problems and values have settings in different time periods. Students may discuss these problems and values, then compare and relate them to current experiences. A few examples of historical fiction that may be used to stimulate such discussion follow.

- ☐ People need political and religious freedom, and they will go through many hardships in search of freedom. *Colonial Times*: Patricia Clapp's *Constance: A Story of Early Plymouth;* Elizabeth George Speare's *The Witch of Blackbird Pond*. *Czarist Russia*: Kathryn Lasky's *The Night Journey*. *World War II*: Dale Fife's *Destination Unknown;* Aranka Siegal's *Upon the Head of the Goat: A Childhood in Hungary 1939–1944;* Yoshiko Uchida's *Journey Home*.
- ☐ Sometimes people must fight or risk freedom to save what they believe in. *Colonial Times*: Esther Forbes's *Johnny Tremain*. *Post-Revolutionary Times*: James and Christopher Collier's *Jump Ship to Freedom*. *Civil War*: Irene Hunt's *Across Five Aprils*. *World War II*: Marie McSwigan's *Snow Treasure*.
- ☐ War and hatred are destructive forces. *Colonial Times*: Patricia Clapp's *I'm Deborah Sampson: A Soldier of the Revolution*. *English Civil War*: Erik Christian Haugaard's *Cromwell's Boy*. *Civil War*: Janet Hickman's *Zoar Blue*. *World War II*: Johanna Reiss's *The Upstairs Room;* Uri Orlev's *The Island on Bird Street*.

When children see and discuss the relationships among values that have been held across historical periods, they begin to realize that these values are also important today.

Creative Dramatizations

Many exciting dramas unfold in the pages of historical fiction written about the colonial period, especially about Revolutionary War days. Jone Wright and Elizabeth Allen (19) describe a creative dramatization in which a group of sixth graders reenacted Paul Revere's ride. The children added an interesting dimension to this activity with comparative dramatizations: One group dramatized Henry Wadsworth Longfellow's poem "Paul Revere's Ride," while the second dramatized the ride as told by Jean Fritz in *And Then What Happened, Paul Revere?* (chapter twelve) and Louis Wolfe in *Let's Go with Paul Revere* (18). The second group also verified additional facts about Revere's ride by reading a magazine article (2). After the group members read and discussed their sources, they pantomimed various actions and planned the scenes they wanted to include. The poetry group included the following:

1 Paul's talking to his friends about hanging the signal lights.
2 Paul's rowing alone across the river.
3 Paul's waiting on the opposite shore for the signal to be hung.
4 Paul's galloping alone through the countryside: 12:00 P.M., Medford; 1:00 A.M., Lexington; 2:00 A.M., Concord.
5 Paul's galloping on through the night.

The authentic sources group included the following:

1 Patriots' giving the signal.
2 Patriots' rowing Revere across the river.
3 Paul Revere's warning patriots at Cambridge and Concord.
4 British soldiers' capturing and releasing Paul Revere.

After the two dramatizations, the children discussed the differences between the two presentations and drew some interesting conclusions about the romanticizing of history and the researching of historical data.

With words like the following in Esther Forbes's *Johnny Tremain,* the colonists were told that they must rally to the cry for freedom if they wanted to repeal the hated taxation-without-representation laws: "The worst of Plagues, the detested tea shipped for this Port by the East Indian Company, is now arrived in the Harbour" (p. 107). The scene is another natural subject for creative dramatizations. The following scenes depicting the Boston Tea Party could be dramatized from *Johnny Tremain*:

1 Samuel Adams's asking the printer to duplicate the placard announcing the tea shipment.
2 Johnny Tremain's going from house to house, using the secret code, notifying the Observers about a secret meeting.
3 The meeting of the Observers and reaching a decision about the tea.
4 The meeting in front of Old South Church, with Josiah Quincy's talking to the crowd and Samuel Adams's giving the message that the tea would be dumped.
5 The colonists' throwing the tea into Boston Harbor.

The Salem Witch-Hunts

Incidents of unreasonable fears and unjustified persecutions appear throughout history. The historical fiction books written about the late 1600s provide stimulating sources for oral discussion, creative dramatizations, clarification of values, writing, understanding of setting and characterization, and comparing of literary works that develop similar themes. Ann Petry's *Tituba of Salem Village* is about an enslaved black woman and Elizabeth George Speare's *The Witch of Blackbird Pond* is about a free teenaged white girl. Both protagonists experience the impact of witch-hunts and unjustified persecution. These stories are excellent for discussion and comparison. Chart 10–2 presents the discussion and learning possibilities that a sixth-grade teacher mapped for using these two books with her students.

Compare the themes of fear and unjustified persecution in *Tituba in Salem Village* and *The Witch of Blackbird Pond* with those set in other time periods, such as (1) suspicion toward and the persecution of the Navaho Indians in Scott O'Dell's *Sing Down the Moon* and (2) suspicion toward and persecution of gypsies in William Hooks's *Circle of Fire*.

Compare the suspicion toward and persecution of Jewish people during World War II in the following books: Johanna Reiss's *The Upstairs Room,* Esther Hautzig's *The Endless Steppe: A Girl in Exile,* Judith Kerr's *When Hitler Stole Pink Rabbit,* Sonia Levitin's *Journey to America,* Aranka Siegal's *Upon the Head of the Goat: A Childhood in Hungary 1939–1944,* Uri Orlev's *The Island on Bird Street,* and Lois Lowry's *Number the Stars*. Compare the suspicion toward and persecution of people who are different in Janet Lunn's *Shadow in*

CHART 10–2
Comparing Ann Petry's *Tituba of Salem Village* and Elizabeth George Speare's *The Witch of Blackbird Pond* for sixth graders

Dramatization

Tituba of Salem Village

1 Dramatize the family's approaching the gloomy house in Salem Village and meeting Goody Good.
2 Recreate the scene in which the children bring in the fortune-telling cards and try to convince Tituba to read their fortunes.
3 Dramatize the court scene, including the witnesses against Tituba and the appearance of Samuel Conklin, who comes to her defense.
4 Interview Tituba, her husband, the minister, Betsy, Abigail, and Samuel Conklin. How does each describe the experiences leading up to the trial? How do they feel about the results of the trial? Are they pleased when Tituba is freed?

The Witch of Blackbird Pond

1 Dramatize Kit's first meeting with her relatives.
2 Recreate the dame's school and Kit's providing instruction for her six students.
3 Role-play the conversations between Kit and the Quaker woman, Hannah Tupper, who lives in the meadow.
4 Dramatize the scenes during which Kit is accused of witchcraft, is taken prisoner to the shed, stands trial for witchcraft, and is freed because Prudence demonstrates her reading skills.

Characterization

Tituba of Salem Village

How does each of the following people see Tituba and feel about her:

1 Her former owner on Barbados?
2 The minister?
3 The minister's wife?
4 Betsy or Abigail?
5 Dr. Griggs?
6 A resident of Salem Village?
7 Samuel Conklin?
8 Tituba herself?

The Witch of Blackbird Pond

How does each of the following people see Kit and feel about her:

1 Kit's grandfather?
2 Matthew Wood?
3 Aunt Rachel?
4 Reverend Gershom Bulkeley?
5 William Ashby?
6 Judith or Mercy?
7 Goodwife Cruff?
8 Hannah Tupper?
9 Nat Eaton?
10 Kit herself?

Setting

1 Compare the jewellike setting of Barbados with Tituba's description of the house in Salem and Kit's description of the colorless Puritan village.
2 Why did both authors choose to take their heroines from tropical islands to very different locations?
3 What might have happened in each story if Kit and Tituba had remained in Barbados?

Values Clarification

Tituba of Salem Village

1 Why did Tituba's former owner decide to sell her two dear companions? Do you believe her reason was good? Why or why not?
2 Why do you believe that Abigail encouraged the other girls to try to put Betsy into a trance?
3 What special skills did Tituba have that made her different from the people in Salem Village? Why would the people hate and fear her?
4 Why do you believe that the minister did not come to Tituba's defense or pay her jail fees?
5 Why was Samuel Conklin the only one to come to Tituba's defense? How did he demonstrate his faith in her?

The Witch of Blackbird Pond

1 Why did Kit's grandfather want her to read and discuss plays? Why do you think the Puritans reacted so differently to her desire to read such material?
2 Why do you believe that Kit enjoyed going to the meadow and visiting Hannah Tupper? Why were the villagers afraid of both the meadow and Hannah Tupper?
3 What makes Hannah Tupper different from the villagers? Why would people fear her?
4 What made Kit Tyler different from the villagers? Why would people fear her?
5 What was the difference between the way Goodwife Cruff felt about her daughter Prudence and the way Kit felt about Prudence? Who was right?

CHART 10–2 cont.
Comparing Ann Petry's *Tituba of Salem Village* and Elizabeth George Speare's *The Witch of Blackbird Pond* for sixth graders

Tituba of Salem Village	The Witch of Blackbird Pond
	6 How would Prudence's life have been different if Kit had not helped Prudence? Why do you think Kit didn't speak out in court about Prudence, even if her answer might have helped her own case? 7 Why do you believe Kit's friend, "dear dependable William," did not come to her defense at the trial? Why did Nat Eaton risk his own liberty to testify for her?
Personal Response 1 How would you have felt if you had been Tituba and had been forced to leave your homeland? What would your reaction have been to your new family and the people of the village? 2 Have you ever known anyone or read about anyone who was feared or disliked because that person was different from others? Has this ever happened to you? When? Who helped you when you needed help?	1 If you had been Kit, would you have risked your safety to help both Hannah Tupper and Prudence Cruff? Why or why not? 2 Have you ever felt like Kit? When?
3 Compare both books. Which story did you like better? Why? 4 Were you satisfied with the ending of each story? Why or why not? If you could change either story, how would you change it? 5 Do you believe that a story about personal persecution could be written about a person today? What would be the cause of the persecution? How might the person solve his or her problem?	
Writing 1 Pretend that you are either Tituba or Kit. Choose a period of time from the story and write your experiences in a journal format. 2 Pretend to be someone living in Salem Village who has relatives in England. Write a letter to these relatives telling them about what has been happening in Salem. 3 Pretend to be a twentieth-century writer developing a script for a television "You Are There" program. Write the script for a reenactment of the trial of either Tituba or Kit.	

Hawthorn Bay, Carol Carrick's *Stay Away from Simon!*, and Ellen Howard's *Edith Herself*.

LOOKING AT PIONEER AMERICA

Most children are fascinated with the time in American history when courageous adults and children were struggling across the country on foot, on horseback, or in covered wagons. They like to hear about children who rode on canal barges, floated on rafts down the Ohio, or traveled on steamboats down the Mississippi. They also enjoy vicariously experiencing the frontier years after the covered wagons were unloaded and families began their new lives in sod houses or log cabins.

Teachers of social studies find this period exciting. They use the fiction of the pioneer period to help children develop closer ties with the past, understand the physical environment of the time, and discover the links between the pioneer past and the present. Ways of developing these understandings range from sharing an individual story with children to developing total units that encourage children to identify with the period through music, art, stories, games, foods, values, home remedies, and the research of historic characters.

In order to immerse children in the physical environment of the time and to stimulate their curiosity, show them objects that were important, for both survival and pleasure, to a pioneer family: quilts, tools (hammer, nails, spade, hoe, grindstone), tallow candles, lengths of cotton cloth, wooden buckets, iron pots, skillets, earthenware jugs, tin lanterns, dried herbs, food (a barrel of flour; yeast; dried beans, peas, and corn; salt; sugar; dried apples; a slab of bacon), seed corn, cornhusk dolls, a china-head doll, a yoke, a churn, a spinning wheel, a fiddle, a log cabin (made from Lincoln Logs), and pictures of pioneers. Accompany these objects by displays of historical fiction, books that pioneer children might have read, and books about pioneer art, music, and crafts.

One teacher introduced some third-grade students to the pioneer period by dressing in pioneer style, greeting the students at the classroom door, and taking them on a classroom tour. By enthusiastically presenting artifacts, the teacher excited the children and made them want to know more.

Values from the Past

Children can learn about the past and relate it to the present when they identify the values held and problems overcome by people living in pioneer America. Children can compare these values and problems and the solutions of problems, as depicted in historical fiction, with those of today. The pioneer period is filled with stories that stress love of the land and the need for positive relationships among family members, neighbors, pioneers, and Native Americans, including the struggle for survival and the need for bravery. The following experiences encourage children to clarify their own values as well as those of others.

Love of the Land. Pioneers were drawn to the West because of the opportunity to own rich farmland. Some people left their homes in the East when their land no longer produced good crops. Others traveled to the West because they wanted more room or fewer neighbors. Still others acquired the free land provided under the Homestead Act (see Figure 10–1). After children have read one of the books that place this strong emphasis on the land (such as Honore Morrow's *On to Oregon!;* Barbara Brenner's *Wagon Wheels;* and Harold Keith's *The Obstinate Land*), ask them to identify the reasons of the pioneers for moving

The pioneer setting in historical fiction seems real when children reenact chores.

Rich Prairie Land Yours For Improvement
160 Acres of Public Land
FREE to Anyone Over 21
Who Will Live On The Land For Five Years

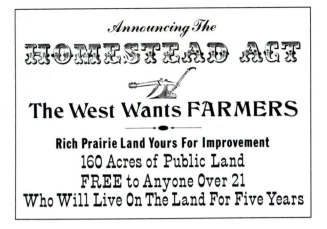

FIGURE 10–1
A poster for the Homestead Act

and conflicts that family members felt when they were deciding whether or not to move.

At this point, use role playing to help clarify the attitudes of pioneer family members. Ask the students to imagine that the year is 1866. The Civil War ended the year before. They are living on a small New England farm. They are sitting with their immediate family and their visiting aunt and uncle at the evening meal. Their aunt begins excitedly talking about an article in the paper telling how many people are going west to claim free land provided under the Homestead Act of 1862. Their aunt and uncle are ready to sell their farm, pack a few belongings, and travel to the West in a covered wagon. The aunt wants her brother's family to join them. Suggest that the students role-play the reactions of the different family characters and decide whether or not they should go. Based on characteristics found in historical fiction stories, the characters might express these concerns:

Mother: She knows that her husband wants to own a better farm, but her family lives in the East and she doesn't want to leave it. In addition, she has lost one child, who is buried on the old farm. She is also concerned about living on the frontier away from a church, a school, and the protection of close neighbors.

Father: He is unhappy with his rocky farm and the poor production it has provided. He has dreamed of a farm with rich soil to produce better crops and support his family.

Twelve-Year-Old Daughter: She is filled with the excitement of a new adventure. She wants to see new lands and Indians. In addition, she is not displeased with the prospect of leaving school for a while.

Seven-Year-Old Son: The farmhouse is the only home he has ever known; his best friend and his relatives live in the surrounding countryside. He'd love to see some Indians and he wants to please his father but he doesn't know what to expect in a land that far from home.

Have the students consider each person's arguments and decide if they would have moved to a new land. Have the students continue by talking about what they would take with them if they decided to homestead.

Finally, draw the discussion into the present time. Do people still have a strong loyalty to the land? Do they want to own their own land? Encourage the students to provide reasons for their arguments. Place the desire for unspoiled land as well as adventure into a modern framework by having students pretend their families are moving to a wilderness area in Alaska. Why would they want to move? Why would they not want to move? What problems do they think they would encounter before moving? How would they solve them? What problems would they encounter in the Alaskan wilderness? How would they solve them? Finally, do they believe that these problems and their solutions are similar to those experienced by pioneers?

Human Relations. Many stories about pioneer days present different ways of dealing with Native Americans and diverse attitudes toward them. The only solution many books give is a battle between the Native Americans and whites. In contrast, Alice Dalgliesh's *The Courage of Sarah Noble* presents a family who settles on land for which the native people have been given a fair price, with the provision that they retain their right to fish in the river. Sarah's parents believe that all people must be treated fairly. Encourage children to discuss the reasons for various actions, the beliefs of the pioneers, and the consequences.

After children have read the "Massacre" and "Ambassador to the Enemy," chapters in Carol Ryrie Brink's *Caddie Woodlawn,* ask them to discuss the decision made by the settlers to attack the Indians because they thought the Indians were going to attack them. Why did the settlers reach their decision? Was it accurate? Why or why not?

Then, ask the students to place themselves in Caddie's role. If they were Caddie, would they have warned the Indians? Why or why not? What might have been the results if Caddie had not made her evening ride?

Finally, bring the discussion to contemporary times. Ask the students if there are times when people today might decide to act out of fright rather than out of knowledge. What events would they consider important enough to risk their own safety?

Books about pioneers also include many stories about need to help others. Neighbors and family members help each other and provide moral support during times of crisis. The "Little House" series, by Laura Ingalls Wilder, contains many incidents of family support and working with neighbors. *Sarah, Plain and Tall* by Patricia MacLachlan emphasizes the need for a mother and wife in pioneer times. Encourage children to discuss the values of positive human relationships during both pioneer and contemporary times.

The Pioneer Environment

Pioneer stories are rich in descriptions of the homes, crafts, store goods, food, transportation, books, and pleasures of the pioneers.

Amusements of the Pioneer Family. Allowing children to take part in the same experiences that entertained pioneer children is a good way to help them feel closer to their counterparts in the past. For example, Laura Ingalls Wilder's *Little House in the Big Woods* describes happy moments that can be recreated with children:

1. For a special birthday treat, Pa played and sang "Pop Goes the Weasel" for Laura. Some of her happiest memories were related to Pa's fiddle. Other songs mentioned in the book are "Rock of Ages" (the fiddle could not play weekday songs on Sunday) and "Yankee Doodle."
2. The family traveled through the woods to a square dance at Grandpa's house. At the dance, the fiddler played and the square-dance caller called the squares for "Buffalo Gals," "The Irish Washerwoman," and "The Arkansas Traveler."
3. After the day's work was finished, Ma would sometimes cut paper dolls for the girls out of stiff white paper and make dresses, hats, ribbons, and laces out of colored paper.
4. In the winter evenings, Laura and Mary begged Pa to tell them stories. He told them about "Grandpa and the Panther," "Pa and the Bear in the Way," "Pa and the Voice in the Woods," and "Grandpa's Sled and the Pig." Enough details are included in these stories so that they can be retold to children.

A School Day with the Pioneer Family. A day in school for pioneer children (if a school was available) was quite different from a contemporary school day. Historical fiction and other sources provide enough information about schools attended, books read, and parables mem-

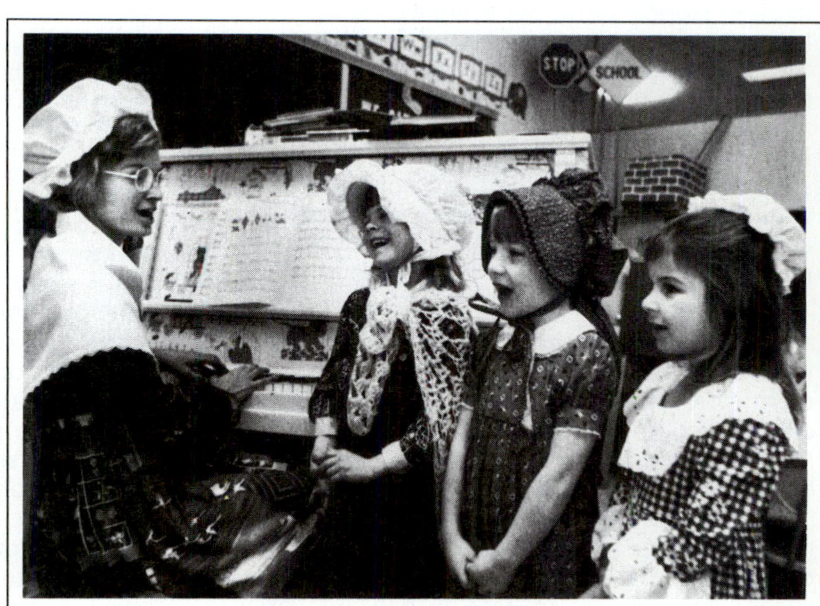

These children recapture the feeling of pioneer America by singing the folk songs that were common during the time.

orized to interest children and recreate a school day that emphasizes spelling, reading, and arithmetic.

Modern children may be surprised that Ma in Laura Ingalls Wilder's *On the Banks of Plum Creek* considered three books on the subjects of spelling, reading, and arithmetic among her "best things" and gave them solemnly to the girls with the advice that they care for them and study faithfully. Likewise, Fritz in Harold Keith's *The Obstinate Land* sold his most prized possession to pay for the schooling of his brother and sister. In addition, these children had to ride sixteen miles on one pony every day in order to get to and from school.

A number of early textbooks and other stories have been reissued in their original form and can be shared with children. For example, children can read the rhyming alphabet; practice their letters; and learn to read words of one, two, three, four, and five syllables from the *New England Primer* (5).

Pioneer children also read and wrote maxims to practice their handwriting or as punishment for bad behavior. Joan W. Blos's *A Gathering of Days: A New England Girl's Journal, 1830–32* tells of this experience in the 1830s and lists some maxims that were written, such as—

> Speak the truth and lie not.
> To thine own self be true.
> Give to them that want.

Additional methods of instruction are described in other stories. Carol Ryrie Brink's *Caddie Woodlawn* describes an 1860 method for memorizing the multiplication tables; the children sang them to the tune of "Yankee Doodle." Recreating a typical school day during which children read from the primer, recite and copy parables, have a spelling bee, and sing their multiplication tables would help them visualize the pioneer child's life and develop an understanding that education was considered important in earlier times.

A Day in the General Store. The country store was very different from the contemporary department store or large shopping mall. It fascinated children, however, just as malls create excitement in today's children. Laura Ingalls Wilder's first experience in a general store is described in *Little House in the Big Woods*. This store included bright materials, kegs of nails, kegs of shot, barrels of candy, cooking utensils, plowshares, knives, shoes, and dishes. In fact it had just about everything.

A source of information about the kinds of materials that might be available to a pioneer family in the late 1800s is a reissue of an early Sears, Roebuck and Company catalogue (13). Through these pages, children can acquire an understanding of the merchandise available and the fashions of the day. They can use the information found in such sources either to recreate a child-sized general store in one corner of the room or create miniature stores in boxes.

While people may not keep the following kind of a work schedule today, the daily activities of the pioneer family associated with the house and other outside responsibilities are of interest to children.

Pioneer Chores

Wash on Monday
Iron on Tuesday
Mend on Wednesday
Churn on Thursday
Clean on Friday
Bake on Saturday
Rest on Sunday

Preparing food is mentioned in many stories. Because pioneer families could not go to the local store for supplies, they needed to prepare their own. Churning butter is one activity that children enjoy. A simple recipe for butter that children can make easily follows:

½ pint whipping cream
¼ teaspoon salt
Pint jar with tight cover

Pour the ½ pint of whipping cream into the pint jar. Seal the cover tightly onto the jar. Shake the jar until the cream turns to butter. Remove the lid, pour off the liquid, and work out any excess liquid. Add salt and stir it into the butter. Remove the butter from jar and shape it.

According to Laura in *Little House in the Big Woods,* Ma was not always satisfied with white butter. Children may wish to experiment with the technique Ma used to add a yellow color to the butter. She rubbed a carrot over a pan that had nail holes punched across the bottom. She placed the soft, grated carrot into a pan of milk, then warmed the mixture and poured it into a cloth bag. When she squeezed the bag, bright yellow milk ran from the cloth and was added to the cream in the churn (p. 30).

Because pioneer families had no refrigerators or freezers, they had to find other ways to preserve their foods. If they lived in the North, they used nature's icebox in the winter. In Joan W. Blos's *A*

Gathering of Days: A New England Girl's Journal, 1830–32, children read about chopping off a frozen wedge of soup and heating it in the kettle. Other stories describe the feeling of well-being when the pantry, shed, attic, and cellar were filled with food. In contrast, people experienced great concern when only seed corn remained between the family and starvation.

Children learn about different ways that the pioneers preserved fruits and vegetables by reading Eliot Wigginton's *The Foxfire Book* (17). Children enjoy drying their own apples and then having them for a special snack. Other books in this series provide details for many additional pioneer activities.

The people in pioneer fiction become alive for children who cannot actually live on a prairie homestead. Children can sing the same songs pioneer children sang, dance to the music of a pioneer fiddle, listen to the pioneer storyteller, imagine they attend a pioneer school, imagine they go to the general store, and do the chores of the homestead.

Trails in Westward Expansion

Deep ruts across a sea of prairie grass, markers along river crossings, and scars created by oxen hooves sliding down the rock sides of canyons were the pioneer equivalent of modern interstate highways. Like highways, these trails were important for moving people and commerce across the country; without them, the West could not have been opened for expansion. It is hard to imagine a thousand men, women, and children with two hundred covered wagons following such rough trails across prairies, deserts, and mountains to reach California or Oregon.

Children can discover additional information about the trails referred to in books of historical fiction by reading Bruce Grant's *Famous American Trails* (10). They can discuss the purpose for the trails (such as cattle drives, wagon trails, fast movement of mail), the locations of the trails, the physical hardships found along the trails, forts built along the trails, and distances covered by the trails. They can draw a large map of the United States, place on it the major westward trails, and then trace, using different colored pencils, the routes taken by pioneers in various books of historical fiction. The following books provide enough descriptions of locations to be of value in this activity:

1. Alice Dalgliesh, *The Courage of Sarah Noble*. Westfield, Massachusetts, to New Milford, Connecticut, by foot and horse backpack, 1707.
2. Brett Harvey, *Cassie's Journey: Going West in the 1860s*. Map shows trail from Independence, Missouri, to Sacramento, California.
3. Evelyn Sibley Lampman, *White Captives*. Illinois to Santa Fe Pass, by wagon train; divided as some went to Salt Lake City, Utah, and others traveled south to Socorro on the Rio Grande, 1851.
4. Honore Morrow, *On to Oregon!* Missouri to Oregon by covered wagon, horse, and foot, 1844.
5. Laura Ingalls Wilder, "Little House" books: Pepin, Wisconsin, to Kansas, to Minnesota, and to Dakota Territory near De Smet by covered wagon, 1870s.

Research Skills

Many historical fiction books describe the sources used by the authors to develop the settings and authenticity of periods. Encouraging children to choose a specific time period and location and then discover as much as possible about the people and their times will help the children develop respect for research skills and gain new insights.

In one class, children researched their own small city during the late 1800s. The group investigated documents at the historical society; searched old newspapers; found old family albums, journals, and letters; searched documents at the courthouse; interviewed people whose relatives had lived in the town during that time; read references to discover information about fashions, transportation, and food; and located buildings that would have existed during that time. After they had gathered this information, they pretended that they were living a hundred years earlier and wrote stories about themselves. The stories contained only authentic background information.

Additional Activities

Have children pretend that they are newspaper reporters sent from an eastern paper to discover what living on the frontier is really like. Encourage them to write news stories to send back to the newspaper. In addition, have them pretend that they can take tintype pictures to accompany their stories; have them draw pictures of the scenes they would like to photograph.

Many pioneers moved to the West because they received encouraging letters from friends and relatives. Have children write letters to friends or relatives telling the Easterners why they should or should not sell all their property and move to ______.

Several books of historical fiction, such as Joan W. Blos's *A Gathering of Days: A New England Girl's Journal, 1830–32* are written in journal format. Have children select a character from a historical fiction story and write several journal entries for a specific period in the story.

Many scenes from historical fiction about the pioneer period can be dramatized. The experiences of Alice Dalgliesh's Sarah Noble in playing and living with the Indian family when her father leaves her to return for his wife are interesting to dramatize.

A Culminating Activity

Children enjoy sharing their knowledge about pioneer days with their parents or other children. A class can plan a pioneer day in which children display pioneer objects, food, arts, and crafts; demonstrate songs or dances learned; and share information gained, creative writing completed, and art projects made during their study of pioneer life and historical fiction.

LOOKING AT AMERICAN HISTORY IN FOLK SONGS

Folk songs, like historical fiction, present a panorama of American history, creating a picture of the common people during different periods. The books discussed in this chapter often refer to characters who are listening to, singing, or playing music. Several songs have already been suggested as means of making the pioneer period come alive for today's children.

One very exciting historical unit used with children combined folk music, historical fiction, and social studies. Singing or square dancing to the music of the times allowed the children to share an experience that was similar to that of the characters in the books they were reading. The words of the songs helped convey the essence of certain periods.

Chart 10–3 lists folk songs from different historical periods. The folk songs in the chart, and information about the historical struggles of the times, can be found in the following books: C. A. Browne's *The Story of Our National Ballads* (4), Edith Fowke and Joe Glazer's *Songs of Work and Protest* (6), Tom Glazer's *A New Treasury of Folk Songs* (9), and Carl Sandburg's *The American Songbag* (12). Dan Fox's *Go In and Out the Window* (7) combines folk songs and art from the Metropolitan Museum of Art.

The teacher who developed this historical song and literature unit with fourth-grade children

CHART 10–3
Folk songs

1754 and 1776	"Yankee Doodle"—symbolic of the struggle for freedom.
1796–1800	"Jefferson and Liberty"—Jefferson pledged to repeal the Sedition Act.
Early 1800s	"Blow Ye Wings in the Morning"—whaling industry along the eastern seaboard.
1825–1913	"Low Bridge Everybody Down"—mule drivers on the Erie Canal.
1841–1847	"Patsy Works on the Railroad"—Irish workers completing railroad in eastern United States.
1850s	"Sweet Betsy from Pike"—taking a covered wagon to California.
1850s	"Go Down Moses"—freedom song of the black slaves.
1850s	"Oh, Freedom"—freedom song of the black slaves.
1859	"John Brown's Body"—attack on garrison at Harper's Ferry to capture arms and liberate slaves.
1861	"The Battle Hymn of the Republic"—Julia Ward Howe watched the campfires of the Union Army.
1872	"John Henry"—a steel-driving man drilling the Big Bend Tunnel on the Chesapeake and Ohio Railroad.
1888	"Drill, Ye Tarriers, Drill"—dynamiters blasting their way through the mountains as the railroads crossed the continent.
1870–1890	"The Old Chisholm Trail"—herding cattle from San Antonio, Texas northward.
1897	"Hallelujah, I'm a Bum"—hoboing on the open road.
Early 1900s	"Sixteen Tons"—coal mining song.

used the following time periods: Revolutionary War, early expansion, Civil War, and pioneer America. He collected many books at different levels of reading ability. Some he shared orally with the group; others the children read themselves. Esther Forbes's Johnny Tremain provided the major emphasis for the Revolutionary War period. Books of historical fiction related to the early expansion period included Honore Morrow's *On to Oregon!* and Joan Blos's *A Gathering of Days: A New England Girl's Journal, 1830–32.* Books related to the Civil War period included Harold Keith's *Rifles for Watie,* Janet Hickman's *Zoar Blue,* and Irene Hunt's *Across Five Aprils.* Books about pioneer America included Carol Ryrie Brink's *Caddie Woodlawn,* all of Laura Ingalls Wilder's "Little House" series, and Patricia MacLachlan's *Sarah, Plain and Tall.*

In addition to books of historical fiction, the teacher used biographies of famous people from the time period and other informational books about the period from the Revolutionary War through the days of pioneer America. The students involved themselves in history; they sang the songs of the people, acted out scenes from the stories, made artifacts such as cornhusk dolls, wrote creative stories, and investigated the historical periods.

One day, the children sat in a circle on the floor and sang folk songs from the Civil War period. After they sang each song, some children pretended to be slaves, seeking freedom by way of the Underground Railroad; Separatists in Ohio deciding if they should or should not fight in the Civil War; and different members of the Creighton family, who were home from the war, sharing their experiences from Irene Hunter's *Across Five Aprils.* Both the teacher and the children thoroughly enjoyed the experience and gained considerable information about their American heritage and literature reflecting this heritage. When evaluating their experience, the children indicated that they had never had such an enjoyable time learning social studies. The characters of the past actually lived for these children, as they discovered the pleasures that may be gained from reading.

Suggested Activities for Children's Appreciation of Historical Fiction

- ☐ Historical fiction provides a means of translating the information found in sterile textbooks into vivid spectacles of human drama. Choose a social studies or history text appropriate for children of a certain age, list the content and time periods covered in the text, and identify historical fiction to stimulate children's interest and understanding of that content or time period.
- ☐ With a group of children or a peer group, compare the information found in a textbook (see the first activity) with the background information discovered in the books of historical fiction. Do the two sources agree? If they do not, research other sources in order to discover which is correct. If they do agree, discuss which sources more vividly describe history and what makes those sources more meaningful.
- ☐ One value of reading historical fiction is the development of an understanding that certain human qualities persist through each century and tie the past to the present. Use Chart 10–1, "Eras and Themes in Historical Fiction," and share literature from several periods with children. Lead a discussion that helps the children identify the human values expressed in those time periods. Allow the children to discuss whether these values are still accepted by people today and whether the values will still be important in the next century. Ask the children why or why not.
- ☐ Discussions of controversial issues create springboards that allow children to become involved in stimulating debates. Historical fiction has numerous characters who take stands on controversial issues. The plots of many historical fiction stories are based on issues considered controversial during a time period. Identify several books from a time period and find paragraphs that state these issues. Develop a list of provocative questions to use when sharing this material with children. For example, in the Revolutionary War period, some literary characters believed that freedom was worth fighting for, no matter what the consequences, others believed that the colonies should stay loyal to England, and still others felt that all killing was wrong.
- ☐ Encourage children to select one controversial issue found in historical fiction, pretend to be on the side of one group or another in the story, do additional research on the issue, and take part in a debate.
- ☐ In order to discover how vividly a setting can be presented in historical fiction, allow chil-

dren to draw detailed pictures after they have read or listened to a story. To increase their appreciation of the settings described in some books, ask the children to draw the setting described in an excellent historical book as well as a setting that is inadequately described. Discuss the differences for the readers and for the writer. Which one is more meaningful to readers? Which one is more demanding on the author? Why?

- ☐ Select a scene from historical fiction that has both memorable characters and an exciting plot. With a group of children or peers, develop the scene into a creative dramatization.
- ☐ Select folk songs that were popular during a specific period in history. Listen to and read the words and sing the songs. What conflicts, problems, or values do the lyrics present? Are the same themes found in historical fiction of that time period?

References

1 Aiken, Joan. "Interpreting the Past." *Children's Literature in Education* 16 (Summer 1985): 67–83.

2 Armstrong, O. K. "The British Are Coming! Great Moments in U.S. History." *Reader's Digest* 106 (April 1975): 187–198.

3 Bingham, Jane, and Grace Scholt. *Fifteen Centuries of Children's Literature: An Annotated Chronology of British and American Works in Historical Context*. Westport, Conn.: Greenwood, 1980.

4 Browne, C. A. *The Story of Our National Ballads*. Edited by Willard Heaps. New York: Crowell, 1960.

5 Ford, Paul Leicester. *The New-England Primer*. New York: Columbia University, Teachers College, 1962.

6 Fowke, Edith, and Joe Glazer. *Songs of Work and Protest*. New York: Dover, 1973.

7 Fox, Dan. *Go in and out the Window: An Illustrated Songbook for Young People*. New York: The Metropolitan Museum of Art and H. Holt, 1987.

8 Gay, Carol. "Children's Literature and the Bicentennial." *Language Arts* 53 (January 1976): 11–16.

9 Glazer, Tom. *A New Treasury of Folk Songs*. New York: Bantam Books, 1961.

10 Grant, Bruce. *Famous American Trails*. Chicago: Rand McNally, 1971.

11 Rochman, Hazel. "Booktalking: Going Global." *The Horn Book* (January/February 1989): 30–35.

12 Sandburg, Carl. *The American Songbag*. New York: Harcourt Brace Jovanovich, 1927.

13 *Sears, Roebuck and Co., Consumers Guide: 1900*. Reprint. Northfield, Ill.: DBI Books, 1970.

14 Toothaker, Roy E. "A Conversation with Alberta Wilson Constant." *Language Arts* 53 (January 1976): 23–26.

15 Trease, Geoffrey. "The Historical Story: Is It Relevant Today?" *The Horn Book* (February 1977): 21–28.

16 Troy, Anne. "Literature for Content Area Learning." *The Reading Teacher* 30 (February 1977): 470–474.

17 Wigginton, Eliot. *The Foxfire Book*. Doubleday, 1972.

18 Wolfe, Louis. *Let's Go with Paul Revere*. Putnam, 1964.

19 Wright, Jone P., and Elizabeth G. Allen. "Sixth-Graders Ride with Paul Revere." *Language Arts* 53 (January 1976): 46–50.

CHILDREN'S LITERATURE

Aiken, Joan. *Bridle the Wind*. Delacorte, 1983 (I:9+ R:4). A thirteen-year-old boy in the 1820s rescues another boy from hanging and then helps him escape into Spain.

———. *The Teeth of the Gale*. Harper & Row, 1988 (I:9+ R:6). Set in Spain in the late 1820s, this is a sequel to *Bridle the Wind*.

Aldridge, James. *The True Story of Spit MacPhee*. Viking Kestrel, 1986 (I:10+ R:6). An Australian story is set in the late 1920s.

Armstrong, William H. *Sounder*. Illustrated by James Barkley. Harper & Row, 1969 (I:10+ R:6). A black sharecropper's family experiences prejudice.

Avi. *The Fighting Ground*. Lippincott, 1984 (I:10+ R:6). A thirteen-year-old boy experiences the reality of war during the American Revolution.

Bauer, Marian. *Rain of Fire*. Clarion, 1983 (I:10+ R:7). A twelve-year-old boy discovers the complexity and the cruel reality of war.

Beatty, Patricia. *Eight Mules from Monterey*. Morrow, 1982 (I:10+ R:6). The Ashmores cross the California mountains in 1916.

———. *Sarah and Me and the Lady from the Sea*. Morrow, 1989 (I:10+ R:6). A family learns self-reliance following the father's business failures.

———. *Wait for Me, Watch for Me, Eula Bee*. Morrow, 1978 (I:12+ R:7). Two white children are taken captive by Indians and the girl grows to trust an Indian brave.

Benchley, Nathaniel. *Bright Candles: A Novel of the Danish Resistance*. Harper & Row, 1974 (I:12+ R:7). The text highlights the courage of the Danes during World War II.

Blos, Joan W. *A Gathering of Days: A New England Girl's Journal, 1830–32*. Scribner's Sons, 1979 (I:8–14 R:6). This book tells a thirteen-year-old girl's experiences on a farm.

Brenner, Barbara. *Wagon Wheels*. Illustrated by Don Bolognese. Harper & Row, 1978 (I:6–9 R:1). An easy-to-read story is about a real pioneer family.

Brink, Carol Ryrie. *Caddie Woodlawn*. Illustrated by Trina Schart Hyman. Macmillan, 1935, 1963, 1973 (I:8–12 R:6). Twelve-year-old Caddie lives with her family on the Wisconsin frontier in 1864.

Carrick, Carol. *Stay Away from Simon!* Illustrated by Donald Carrick. Clarion, 1985 (I:7–10 R:3). A mentally retarded boy and a snowstorm help two children realize that disabled people can have great worth.

Clapp, Patricia. *Constance: A Story of Early Plymouth*. Lothrop, Lee & Shepard, 1968 (I:12+ R:7). This is the story of the first few years of the Plymouth Colony.

———. *I'm Deborah Sampson: A Soldier in the War of the Revolution*. Lothrop, Lee & Shepard, 1977 (I:9+ R:6). Deborah disguises herself as a man and fights in the Revolutionary War.

———. *Witches' Children: A Story of Salem*. Lothrop, Lee & Shepard, 1982 (I:10+ R:7). A bound girl tells about the hysteria that takes over Salem in 1692.

Clark, Ann Nolan. *Year Walk*. Viking, 1975 (I:10+ R:7). A Spanish Basque sheepherder takes his sheep across the desert into the high country.

Cleaver, Vera, and Bill Cleaver. *Dust of the Earth*. Lippincott, 1975 (I:11+ R:6). The text is set in the Dakotas in the 1920s.

Collier, James, and Christopher Collier. *Jump Ship to Freedom*. Delacorte, 1981 (I:10+ R:7). A slave obtains his freedom and that of his mother.

Conrad, Pam. *My Daniel*. Harper & Row, 1989 (I:10+ R:5). A grandmother relives her life on a pioneer Nebraska farm as she takes her grandchildren on a tour through the Natural History Museum.

Crofford, Emily. *A Matter of Pride*. Illustrated by Jim La Marche. Carolrhoda, 1981 (I:9–12 R:6). A ten-year-old girl tells about the Depression on an Arkansas cotton plantation.

Dalgliesh, Alice. *The Courage of Sarah Noble*. Illustrated by Leonard Weisgard. Scribner's Sons, 1954 (I:6–9 R:3). In 1707, Sarah keeps up her courage as she and her father go through the wilderness.

DeAngeli, Marguerite. *The Door in the Wall*. Doubleday, 1949 (I:8–12 R:6). Robin overcomes a mysterious ailment in England during the time of Edward III.

Fife, Dale. *Destination Unknown*. Dutton, 1981 (I:10+ R:6). A twelve-year-old boy stows away on a Norwegian fishing boat in 1940 and sails to safety in America.

I = Interest by age range.
R = Readability by grade level.

Fleischman, Paul. *Coming-and-Going Men: Four Tales*. Illustrated by Randy Gaul. Harper & Row, 1985 (I:10+ R:6). The text includes four short stories set in Vermont in 1800.

———. *Path of the Pale Horse*. Harper & Row, 1983 (I:10+ R:6). A fourteen-year-old boy helps a doctor treat yellow fever in Philadelphia in 1793.

Forbes, Esther. *Johnny Tremain*. Illustrated by Lynd Ward. Houghton Mifflin, 1943 (I:10–14 R:6). A silversmith's apprentice lives through prerevolutionary days and early wartime in Boston.

Fox, Paula. *The Slave Dancer*. Illustrated by Eros Keith. Bradbury, 1973 (I:12+ R:7). In 1840, a fife player experiences the misery of the slave trade.

Frank, Rudolf. *No Hero for the Kaiser*. Translated by Patricia Crampton. Illustrated by Klaus Steffens. Lothrop, Lee & Shepard, 1986 (I:10+ R:7). The author develops an antiwar theme.

Garfield, Leon. *The December Rose*. Viking/Kestrel, 1986 (I:10+ R:7). A mystery is set in Victorian London.

Gehrts, Barbara. *Don't Say a Word*. Translated by Elizabeth Crawford. Macmillan, 1987 (I:12+ R:6). A family discovers the dangers of World War II.

Gray, Elizabeth Janet. *Adam of the Road*. Illustrated by Robert Lawson. Viking, 1942, 1970 (I:8–12 R:6). A young minstrel has many adventures in the England of 1294.

Greene, Constance C. *Dotty's Suitcase*. Viking, 1980 (I:8–12 R:4). During the Depression, a twelve-year-old girl longs to acquire a suitcase and travel to exotic places.

Haley, Gail E. *Jack Jouett's Ride*. Viking, 1973, 1976 (I:6–10 R:4). A picture storybook tells the tale of Jack Jouett as he rides to warn patriots that the British are coming.

Hamilton, Virginia. *The Bells of Christmas*. Illustrated by Lambert Davis. Harcourt Brace Jovanovich, 1989 (I:8+ R:5). A prosperous Black family experiences Christmas in Ohio in the 1890s.

Hancock, Sibyl. *Old Blue*. Illustrated by Erick Ingraham. Putnam, 1980 (I:7–9 R:3). This book is based on historical information about a lead steer on a trail drive in 1878.

Harvey, Brett. *Cassie's Journey: Going West in the 1860s*. Illustrated by Deborah Kogan Ray. Holiday House, 1988 (I:7–9 R:3). A young girl describes her experiences on a wagon train.

Haugaard, Erik Christian. *Cromwell's Boy*. Houghton Mifflin, 1978 (I:11+ R:5). Oliver is a messenger for Oliver Cromwell and Parliament.

———. *Hakon of Rogen's Saga*. Illustrated by Leo and Diane Dillon. Houghton Mifflin, 1963 (I:9–12 R:6). A Viking flees from his wicked uncle before his loyal followers help him regain his birthright.

———. *A Messenger for Parliament*. Houghton Mifflin, 1976 (I:11+ R:7). In 1641, a boy follows the Parliamentary army and is responsible for sending an important message to Cromwell.

Hautzig, Esther. *The Endless Steppe: A Girl in Exile*. Harper Junior Books, 1968 (I:12+ R:7). In a true story, a Jewish girl and her parents are exiled to Siberia during World War II.

Hickman, Janet. *Zoar Blue*. Macmillan, 1978 (I:9–14 R:4). The young men of a nonviolent Zoar, Ohio, religious group fight in the Civil War.

Hoguet, Susan Ramsay. *Solomon Grundy*. Dutton, 1986 (I:6+). A nursery rhyme forms the structure for a highly illustrated story about a nineteenth-century family.

Holman, Felice. *The Wild Children*. Scribner's Sons, 1983 (I:10+ R:4). A group of homeless children strive to survive during the Bolshevik Revolution.

Hooks, William H. *Circle of Fire*. Atheneum, 1983 (I:10+ R:6). A boy and his friends try to prevent a Ku Klux Klan attack.

Howard, Ellen. *Edith Herself*. Atheneum, 1987 (I:7–10 R:4). A girl with epilepsy learns to value herself in the 1890s.

Hudson, Jan. *Sweetgrass*. Tree Frog, 1984, Philomel, 1989 (I:10+ R:4). A young Blackfoot girl grows up during the winter of a smallpox epidemic in 1837.

Hunt, Irene. *Across Five Aprils*. Follett, 1964 (I:10+ R:7). Jethro Creighton must become the man of the family when his brothers go to war and his father has a heart attack.

Keith, Harold. *The Obstinate Land*. Crowell, 1977 (I:12+ R:7). In 1893, thirteen-year-old Fritz Romberg and his family move to the Oklahoma prairie.

———. *Rifles for Watie*. Crowell, 1957 (I:12+ R:7). A Civil War story involves a Cherokee raider.

Kerr, Judith. *When Hitler Stole Pink Rabbit*. Coward, McCann, 1972 (I:8–12 R:3). Anna and her family escape from Hitler's Germany.

Kinsey-Warnock, Natalie. *The Canada Geese Quilt*. Illustrated by Leslie W. Bowman. Dutton, 1989 (I:8+ R:5). Set in 1940s Vermont, a girl and her grandmother make a quilt.

Kullman, Harry. *The Battle Horse*. Bradbury, 1981 (I:10+ R:8). In 1930s Stockholm, children play a game between rich and poor.

Lampman, Evelyn Sibley. *White Captives*. Atheneum, 1975 (I:11+ R:7). The Native American viewpoint in a story about two captives of the Apache.

Lasky, Kathryn. *Beyond the Divide*. Macmillan, 1983 (I:9+ R:6). In 1849, a fourteen-year-old girl accompanies her father across the continent.

———. *The Night Journey*. Illustrated by Trina Schart Hyman. Warne, 1981 (I:10+ R:6). A nine-year-old girl learns about her great-grandmother's escape from Czarist Russia in 1900.

Lenski, Lois. *Indian Captive: The Story of Mary Jemison*. Stokes, 1941 (I:10+ R:7). A captive white girl decides to stay with the Senecas.

Levitin, Sonia. *Journey to America*. Illustrated by Charles Robinson. Atheneum, 1970 (I:12+ R:6). A Jewish family escapes from Nazi Germany.

———. *Silver Days*. Atheneum, 1989 (I:12+ R:6). Here are additional experiences of the family introduced in *Journey to America*.

Lobel, Arnold. *On the Day Peter Stuyvesant Sailed into Town*. Harper & Row, 1971 (I:4–8 R:3). A picture storybook tells about the New Amsterdam colony.

Longfellow, Henry Wadsworth. *Paul Revere's Ride*. Illustrated by Adrian J. Iorio and Frederick J. Alford. Houghton Mifflin (I:8+). This is the classic poem.

Lowry, Lois. *Number the Stars*. Houghton Mifflin, 1989 (I:10+ R:6). In Copenhagen, the Danes try to save their Jewish citizens in 1943.

Lunn, Janet. *Shadow in Hawthorn Bay*. Scribner's Sons, 1986 (I:10+ R:5). A girl with second sight experiences prejudice in Canada in the 1800s.

Lydon, Kerry Raines. *A Birthday for Blue*. Illustrated by Michael Hayes Albert. Whitman, 1989 (I:5–8 R:4). A pioneer boy spends his seventh birthday in a covered wagon.

Lyon, George Ella. *Borrowed Children*. Watts, 1988 (I:10+ R:5). This story is set in Kentucky during the Depression.

MacLachlan, Patricia. *Sarah, Plain and Tall*. Harper & Row, 1985 (I:7–10 R:3). A frontier family longs for a new mother.

McSwigan, Marie. *Snow Treasure*. Illustrated by Mary Reardon. Dutton, 1942 (I:8–12 R:4). This is a retelling of a real adventure against the Nazis in World War II Norway.

Moeri, Louise. *Save Queen of Sheba*. Dutton, 1981 (I:10+ R:5). A twelve-year-old boy and his young sister cross the prairie alone after their wagon train is attacked.

Monjo, F. N. *The Drinking Gourd*. Illustrated by Fred Brenner. Harper & Row, 1970 (I:7–9 R:2). An "I can read" history book about the Underground Railroad.

Morrow, Honore. *On To Oregon!* Illustrated by Edward Shenton. Morrow, 1926, 1948, 1954 (I:10+ R:6). Children travel alone to Oregon in 1844.

O'Dell, Scott. *The Amethyst Ring*. Houghton Mifflin, 1983 (I:10+ R:6). This is the final story of Julián Escobar.

———. *The Captive*. Houghton Mifflin, 1979 (I:10+ R:6). A young Spanish seminarian witnesses the exploitation of the Mayas during the 1500s.

———. *Carlota*. Houghton Mifflin, 1977 (I:9+ R:4). A Spanish girl fights beside her father during the Mexican War.

———. *The Feathered Serpent*. Houghton Mifflin, 1981 (I:10+ R:6). This is a sequel to *The Captive*.

———. *Sing Down the Moon*. Houghton Mifflin, 1970 (I:10+ R:6) This is the forced march of the Navajo from a young girl's perspective.

Orlev, Uri. *The Island on Bird Street*. Translated by Hillel Halkin. Houghton Mifflin, 1984 (I:10+ R:6). A twelve-year-old Jewish boy survives in the Warsaw ghetto.

Pelgrom, Els. *The Winter when Time Was Frozen*. Rudnik, Maryka, & Rudnik, 1980 (I:8–12 R:5). A World War II story is set in Holland.

Pellowski, Anne. *Winding Valley Farm: Annie's Story*. Illustrated by Wendy Watson. Philomel, 1982 (I:9–12 R:6). A Polish community lives in rural Wisconsin during the early 1900s.

Petry, Ann. *Tituba of Salem Village*. Crowell, 1964 (I:11+ R:6). A talented slave becomes part of the famous Salem witch trials.

Phelan, Mary Kay. *The Story of the Louisiana Purchase*. Illustrated by Frank Aloise. Crowell, 1979 (I:12+ R:7). In 1803, the territory of a young nation was doubled.

Pople, Maureen. *The Other Side of the Family*. Holt, Rinehart & Winston, 1986 (I:10+ R:5). A girl is sent from England during World War II to spend time with her Australian grandmother.

Pullman, Philip. *The Ruby in the Smoke*. Knopf, 1985 (I:10+ R:6). A girl is involved in a mystery in Victorian London.

Reeder, Carolyn. *Shades of Gray*. Macmillan, 1989 (I:10+ R:6). Set in the Civil War, a boy encounters pacifism.

Reiss, Johanna. *The Upstairs Room*. Crowell, 1972 (I:11+ R:4). This is the true story of a Jewish girl's experience hiding from the Nazis.

Rylant, Cynthia. *When I Was Young in the Mountains*. Dutton, 1982 (I:4–9 R:3). This book contains memories of Appalachia.

Sandin, Joan. *The Long Way to a New Land*. Harper & Row, 1981 (I:7–9 R:3). A Swedish family emigrates to America in 1868.

Schlee, Ann. *Ask Me No Questions*. Holt, Rinehart & Winston, 1982 (I:10+ R:6). Laura faces moral issues related to feeding hungry children in 1848 London.

Siegal, Aranka. *Grace in the Wilderness: After the Liberation, 1945–1948*. Farrar, Straus & Giroux, 1985 (I:10+ R:7). This is a sequel to *Upon the Head of the Goat*.

———. *Upon the Head of the Goat: A Childhood in Hungary 1939–1944*. Farrar, Straus & Giroux, 1981 (I:10+ R:7). Nine-year-old Piri experiences the Holocaust.

Skurzynski, Gloria. *Manwolf*. Houghton Mifflin, 1981 (I:10+ R:7). A boy's rare disease causes people in medieval Poland to believe he is a werewolf.

Smucker, Anna Egan. *No Star Nights*. Illustrated by Steve Johnson. Knopf, 1989 (I:5–8 R:4). The text and illustrations show growing up in a West Virginia steel-mill town.

Speare, Elizabeth George. *The Bronze Bow*. Houghton Mifflin, 1961 (I:10+ R:6). A boy's hatred of the Romans is affected after he meets Jesus.

———. *Calico Captive*. Illustrated by W. T. Mars. Houghton Mifflin, 1957 (I:10+ R:6). White people are forced to march north to Indian territories in Canada.

———. *The Sign of the Beaver*. Houghton Mifflin, 1983 (I:8–12 R:5). A boy survives in a frontier cabin after an Indian friend teaches him survival techniques.

———. *The Witch of Blackbird Pond*. Houghton Mifflin, 1958 (I:9–14 R:4). A flamboyant girl is accused of witchcraft in colonial New England.

Stevens, Carla. *Anna, Grandpa, and the Big Storm*. Illustrated by Margot Tomes. Houghton Mifflin, 1982 (I:6–9 R:3). Seven-year-old Anna experiences a blizzard in New York City in 1888.

Stolz, Mary. *Pangur Ban*. Illustrated by Pamela Johnson. Harper & Row, 1988 (I:10+ R:6). In ninth-century Ireland, a boy learns to draw in a monastery and must save his works from Viking invaders.

Sutcliff, Rosemary. *Blood Feud*. Dutton, 1976. An English boy is carried away in a Viking raid and sold into slavery.

———. *The Eagle of the Ninth*. Illustrated by C. Walter Hodges. Walck, 1954 (I:11+ R:8). A Roman officer's son discovers the mystery of his father's legion.

———. *Frontier Wolf*. Dutton, 1981 (I:10+ R:8). A Roman centurion leads a band of British warriors.

———. *The Lantern Bearers*. Illustrated by Charles Keeping. Walck, 1959 (I:11+ R:7). The Saxons invade Roman Britain.

———. *The Silver Branch*. Illustrated by Charles Keeping. Walck, 1958 (I:10+ R:8). Two Romans uncover a plot to overthrow the emperor.

———. *Song for a Dark Queen*. Crowell, 1978 (I:10+ R:6). The queen of a tribe of Britains leads the fight against the Roman armies.

———. *Sun Horse, Moon Horse*. Illustrated by Shirley Felts. Dutton, 1978 (I:10+ R:6). A boy saves his people from slavery in pre-Roman Britain.

Taylor, Mildred D. *Let the Circle Be Unbroken*. Dial, 1981 (I:10 R:6). This is a sequel to *Roll of Thunder, Hear My Cry*.

———. *Roll of Thunder, Hear My Cry*. Illustrated by Jerry Pinckney. Dial, 1976 (I:10+ R:6). A black family suffers prejudice in rural Mississippi.

Tene, Benjamin. *In the Shadow of the Chestnut Tree*. Translated by Reuben Ben-Joseph. Illustrated by Richard Sigberman. Jewish Publication Society, 1981 (I:10+ R:6). This is a story about growing up in Warsaw during the years before World War II.

Thrasher, Crystal. *A Taste of Daylight*. Atheneum, 1984 (I:10+ R:7). During the Depression, a girl and her family move from the country to the city.

Trease, Geoffrey. *Saraband for Shadows*. Macmillan, 1982 (I:10+ R:7). In the time of Charles I, the hero uncovers a plot to murder his friend.

Treece, Henry. *Viking's Dawn*. Illustrated by Christine Price. Criterion, 1956 (I:10–14 R:7). Harold joins the crew of the Viking ship *Nameless*.

Uchida, Yoshiko. *Journey Home*. Illustrated by Charles Robinson. Atheneum, 1978 (I:10+ R:5). In a sequel to *Journey to Topaz*, twelve-year-old Yuki and her parents return to California and try to adjust.

———. *Journey to Topaz*. Illustrated by Donald Carrick. Scribner's Sons, 1971 (I:10+ R:5). A Japanese-American family is held in an internment camp in Utah during World War II.

Wilder, Laura Ingalls. *By the Shores of Silver Lake*. Illustrated by Garth Williams. Harper & Row, 1939, 1953 (I:8–12 R:6). The Ingalls move again to the Dakota territory.

———. *The First Four Years*. Illustrated by Garth Williams. Harper & Row, 1971 (I:8–12 R:6). Laura and Almanzo spend their first four years of marriage on a South Dakota homestead.

———. *Little House in the Big Woods*. Illustrated by Garth Williams. Harper & Row, 1932, 1953 (I:8–12 R:6). This is the first in a series of books about a loving pioneer family.

———. *Little House on the Prairie*. Illustrated by Garth Williams. Harper & Row, 1935, 1953 (I:8–12 R:8). The Ingalls family moves to Kansas.

———. *Little Town on the Prairie*. Illustrated by Garth Williams. Harper & Row, 1941, 1953 (I:8–12 R:8). Laura has her first job.

———. *The Long Winter*. Illustrated by Garth Williams. Harper & Row, 1940, 1953 (I:8–12 R:6). A blizzard causes the Ingalls family great discomfort.

———. *On the Banks of Plum Creek*. Illustrated by Garth Williams. Harper & Row, 1937, 1953 (I:8–12 R:6). The Ingalls family moves to Minnesota.

———. *These Happy Golden Years*. Illustrated by Garth Williams. Harper & Row, 1943, 1953 (I:8–12 R:6). Laura becomes a teacher and meets her future husband.

Yates, Elizabeth. *Amos Fortune, Free Man*. Illustrated by Nora S. Unwin. Dutton, 1950 (I:10+ R:6). An African enslaved by white traders is educated by his Quaker owner in Boston.

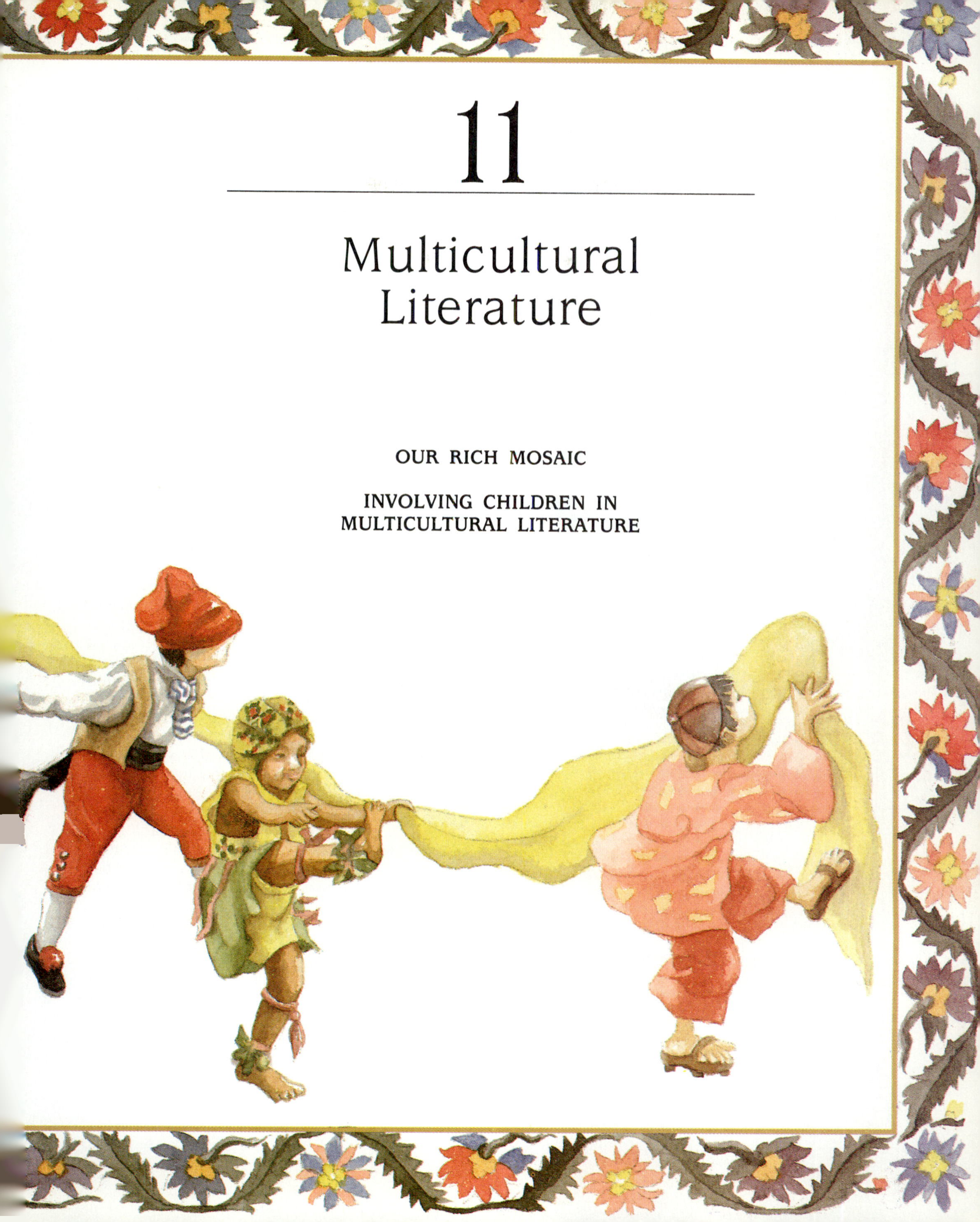

11

Multicultural Literature

OUR RICH MOSAIC

INVOLVING CHILDREN IN MULTICULTURAL LITERATURE

Our Rich Mosaic

A HEIGHTENED SENSITIVITY TO THE NEEDS of all people in American society has led to the realization that reading and literature programs for children should include literature by and about members of all cultural groups. Literature is appropriate for building respect across cultures, sharpening sensitivity toward the common features of all individuals, and improving the self-esteem of people who are members of racial and ethnic minority groups. Educators such as Eileen Tway (32) argue, "[I]n a country of multicultural heritage, children require books that reflect and illuminate that varied heritage" (p. 109). Bruce Sealey (28) emphasizes that education should encourage children to accept and be sensitive to cultural diversity, to understand that similar values frequently underlie different customs, to have quality contact with people from other cultures, and to role-play experiences involved with other cultures. David Piper (25) recommends using traditional stories and fables from various cultural sources and focusing on children's cultural backgrounds. Educators and critics of children's literature maintain that children should be exposed to multicultural literature that heightens respect for the individuals, as well as the contributions and the values of cultural minorities.

Many of the multicultural literature programs that have met these goals have accomplished them through preservice or in-service education of teachers and librarians. Such education stressed evaluating, selecting, and sharing multicultural literature (23). The tasks related to developing such programs are enormous. Universities are beginning to require courses that include selecting and using multicultural literature. Until all educators have been trained in this way, school districts must provide in-service instruction so that teachers and librarians can select and use materials that will create an atmosphere of respect for all children. One of the most formidable tasks is becoming familiar with the available literature and other teaching materials. Library selection committees, teachers, and administrators must all become involved in this process.

This chapter is not intended to isolate the literature and contributions of racial and ethnic minorities from other literature discussed in this book. Instead, it tries to place multicultural literature in a context helpful to librarians, teachers, and parents who wish to select and share such materials with children or develop multicultural literature programs.

WHAT MULTICULTURAL LITERATURE IS

Multicultural literature is literature about racial or ethnic minority groups that are culturally and socially different from the white Anglo-Saxon majority in the United States, whose largely middle-class values and customs are most represented in American literature. Although, of course, ethnic diversity in the United States is extremely great, multicultural literature is usually viewed as literature about Black Americans; Native Americans*; Hispanic Americans, including Mexican Americans, Puerto Ricans, Cuban Americans and others of Spanish descent or cultural heritage; and Asian Americans, including Chinese Americans, Japanese Americans, Korean Americans, Vietnamese Americans and others.

VALUES OF MULTICULTURAL LITERATURE

Many of the goals for multicultural education can be developed through multicultural literature. For example, Rena Lewis and Donald Doorlag (21) state that multicultural education can restore cultural rights by emphasizing cultural equality and respect, enhance the self-concepts of students, and teach respect for various cultures while teaching basic skills.

The goals for multicultural education are matched closely by values of multicultural literature for children who are members of a racial or ethnic minority and for children who are not. Through multicultural literature, children who are members of racial or ethnic minority groups realize that they have a cultural heritage of which they can be proud, and that their culture has made important contributions to the United States and to the world. Pride in their heritage helps children who are members of minority groups improve their self-concepts and develop cultural identity. Learning about other cultures allows children to understand that people who belong to racial or ethnic groups other than theirs are real people, with feelings, emotions, and needs similar to their own—individual human beings, not stereotypes. Through multicultural literature, children discover that while not all people may share their personal beliefs and values, individuals can and must learn to live in harmony. Through multicultural literature, children of the majority culture learn to respect the values and contributions of minority groups in the United States and the values and contributions of people in other parts of the world. In addition, children broaden their understanding of history, geography, and natural history as they read about cultural groups living in various regions of their country and the world. The wide range of multicultural themes also helps children develop an understanding of social change. Finally, reading about members of minority groups who have successfully solved their own problems and made notable achievements helps raise the aspirations of children who belong to a minority group.

*This book primarily uses the term *Native Americans* to denote the people historically referred to as *American Indians*. The term *Indian* is sometimes used interchangeably with *Native American* and in some contexts is used to name certain tribes of Native Americans.

IMAGES OF RACIAL AND ETHNIC MINORITIES IN THE PAST

Only recently have Americans begun to realize that certain books—because of their illustrations, themes, characterizations, and language—can perpetuate stereotypes and result in psychological damage or discomfort for children. In the late 1940s, Americans began to express publicly their growing objections to the use of certain stereotypes in literature. In 1965, Nancy Larrick's article, "The All-White World of Children's Books" (see flashback), had considerable impact because her research showed both that there was a lack of books about minorities and that stereotypes were found in the few available books. Many changes in American social life and literature have occurred since then, but further improvements are needed.

Author Eloise Greenfield (13) is even harsher in her criticism of authors who perpetuate racism and stereotypes in literature. She states that books that express racism or negative attitudes toward any group "constrain rather than encourage human development. To perpetuate these attitudes through the use of the written word constitutes a gross and arrogant misuse of talent and skill" (p. 19).

Through their selection of books and instructional materials, some educators continue to communicate negative messages about minorities to children. Bettye I. Latimer (20) makes a strong criticism of this continuing tendency in education: "If your bulletin boards, your models, and your authority lines are White, and I am Black, Latino or

FLASHBACK

"Why are they always *white* children?"

The question came from a five-year-old Negro girl who was looking at a picturebook at the Manhattanville Nursery School in New York. With a child's uncanny wisdom, she singled out one of the most critical issues in American education today: the almost complete omission of Negroes from books for children. Integration may be the law of the land, but most of the books children see are all white.

But the impact of all-white books upon 39,600,000 white children is probably even worse. Although his light skin makes him one of the world's minorities, the white child learns from his books that he is the kingfish. There seems little chance of developing the humility so urgently needed for world cooperation, instead of world conflict, as long as our children are brought up on gentle doses of racism through their books.

THE ADJACENT EXCERPT FROM THE SEPTEMber 11, 1965, issue of *Saturday Review* (p. 63) is from one of the early and often-quoted articles that criticized the omission of black characters in books for children: Nancy Larrick's "The All-White World of Children's Books" reported the results of a study that analyzed trade books for children published over a three-year period in the 1960s. Most books published during that time showed blacks outside the continental United States or before World War II—only four fifths of 1 percent of the books told stories about contemporary black Americans. Most books that included black characters depicted them as slaves, sharecroppers, or other menial workers. Larrick's article in a prestigious publication may have had considerable impact on future publications for children.

Native American, then you have telegraphed me messages which I will reject" (p. 156). Latimer maintains that white children are taught a distorted image of American society and are not prepared to value American society's multiracial character because they are surrounded with literature and other instructional materials that either present minorities stereotypically or make minorities invisible by omitting them entirely. Latimer also stresses that because of the comparatively small number of books written about members of racial and ethnic minorities, well-meaning librarians, teachers, and other adults are likely to accept any book that describes or pictures members of minority groups, without carefully evaluating the stories and the stereotypes they might be fostering. She believes that adults who work with children and literature should reeducate themselves to the social values that books pass on to children. To do this, adults must learn to assess books written about children from all ethnic backgrounds.

Black Americans

Several researchers have investigated images of Black Americans in children's literature, focusing on stereotypes, attitudes white characters express toward black characters, and the importance of black characters in the literature. Dorothy May Broderick (3), for example, analyzed American children's literature published between 1827 and 1967. She reports that the personal characteristics of black people portrayed in these books suggested that black people (1) are not physically attractive, (2) are musical, (3) combine religious fervor with superstitious beliefs, (4) are required to select life goals that benefit black people, and (5) are dependent upon white people for whatever good things they could hope to acquire. Broderick concluded that in the 140-year period she studied, black children would find little in literature to enhance pride in their heritage and that if these books were white children's only contacts with black people, white children would develop a sense of superiority.

Beryle Banfield (1) reviewed stereotypes found in pre-Civil War literature and found that stories set in the plantation South of the 1800s depicted slavery as idyllic, pastoral, and beneficial for the slave. In addition, these books frequently suggested that the slaves were so contented on the plantation that they were wretched when they tried to survive as free people.

In investigating whether or not changes in attitudes toward black people had occurred in more recent times, Julia Ann Carlson (5) compared American children's literature of the 1930s with that of the 1960s. She discovered that considerable changes in the depiction of black characters occurred between the two time periods. Although 15 percent of the books from the earlier period mentioned black characters, these characters tended to be stereotyped. Only 10 percent of the books in the later period mentioned black characters at all, but when they did, they tended to present black people as individuals with either a racial problem or a universal problem. In 1973, Betty M. Morgan (22) reported that the number of books with black people as the main characters has increased markedly in recent years. In this chapter we discuss numerous selections of excellent Black American literature that do not perpetuate stereotypes from the past.

Native Americans

Native Americans fared no better than Black Americans in the literature of the past, and they still suffer from stereotyping in children's books. According to Mary Gloyne Byler (4):

> There are too many books featuring painted, whooping, befeathered Indians closing in on too many forts, maliciously attacking "peaceful" settlers or simply leering menacingly from the background; too many books in which white benevolence is the only thing that saves the day for the incompetent childlike Indian; too many stories setting forth what is "best" for American Indians. (p. 28)

Researchers analyzing the images of Native Americans in children's literature have identified many negative stereotypes in a large percentage of the literature. According to Laura Herbst (17), three of the most common stereotypes characterize Native Americans as (1) savage, depraved, and cruel; (2) noble, proud, silent, and close to nature; or (3) inferior, childlike, and helpless. Terms and comparisons suggesting negative and derogatory images often reinforce such stereotypes. A white family, for example, may be said to consist of a husband, a wife, and a child; members of Native American families, in contrast, may be called bucks, squaws, and papooses. White authors often dehumanize Native Americans by comparing them to animals. Even Native American language is often described as "snarling," "grunting," or "yelping." *The Matchlock Gun,* by Walter Edmonds, compares the nameless Indians to trotting dogs, sniffing the scent of food. Often Native American characters are depersonalized by not being given names, which implies that they are not individuals, or even full-fledged human beings.

In addition to stereotypes about Native American people, Laura Herbst identifies three stereotypical ways in which Native American culture has been portrayed in children's literature. First, culture may be depicted as inferior to the white culture. The author may treat the abandonment of the Native American way of life as an improvement. Native American characters are often depicted making this gain by going to white schools or taking on the values of the white culture, leaving their culture and even their people behind. A common theme in such literature is that white people must be responsible for remaking Native Americans.

Second, the culture may be depicted as valueless, and thus not worthy of respect. The rich diversity of spiritual beliefs and ceremonies, moral values, artistic skills, and the life-styles in Native American cultures may be ignored in favor of depicting violence as the chief Native American value. Authors may be ignorant of the fact that Native American peoples have many different cultures.

Third, the culture may be depicted as quaint or superficial, without depth or warmth. White characters in children's literature of the past commonly ridicule or scorn customs that have spiritual significance to Native Americans. They disparage sacred ceremonies, medicine men, ancient artifacts, and traditional legends as belonging to "heathen savages." Any of these three stereotypical portrayals of a culture is offensive. More current books, however, especially those written by Native American authors or other authorities on Native American culture, are sensitive to the heritage and individuality of the native peoples of North America.

Hispanic Americans

Betty M. Morgan (22) concluded that the number of children's books with members of minority groups as main characters has increased since World War II, but she also found that this is true only for books about either Black Americans or Native Americans. Far fewer children's books have Hispanic Americans or Asian Americans as the main characters.

Both the lack of children's literature about people of Hispanic descent and heritage and the negative stereotypes found in some of the literature have been criticized. At one children's literature conference, Mauricio Charpenel (6), consultant to the Mexican Ministry of Education, reported that very few stories are written for or about Mexican or Mexican American children. He was especially concerned about poetry: While Latin American writers publish beautiful poetry, the poems are not shared with Mexican American children in the United States. Both teachers and librarians at the conference expressed concern for literature that would appeal to Hispanic American children and create positive images of their heritage.

The Council on Interracial Books for Children (7) has been critical of the depictions of Mexican Americans in children's literature. After analyzing two hundred books, the council concluded that little in the stories would enable children to recognize a culture, a history, or a set of life circumstances. The council criticized the theme of poverty that recurs as if it is a "natural facet of the Chicano condition" (p. 57) and the tendency for Mexican American problems to be solved by the intervention of Anglo Americans. The council also felt that Mexican Americans' problems had been treated superficially in the books it studied: For example, many books suggest that if children learn English, all of their problems will be solved.

Even fewer books are being written about Puerto Rican Americans, Cuban Americans, and the many new Americans from Central American countries. The majority of books about Puerto Ricans, for example, lack literary merit and overuse a New York City ghetto setting.

Asian Americans

Since few books about Asian Americans have been published for children, researchers who have tried to evaluate books about Asian Americans have had little to study. In 1976, the Asian American Children's Book Project (8) identified sixty-six books with Asian American central characters, and most of these books were about Chinese Americans. The members of the project concluded that with only a few exceptions the books were grossly misleading. They presented stereotypes suggesting that all Asian Americans look alike, choose to live in "quaint" communities in the midst of large cities, and cling to "outworn, alien" customs. The project also criticized the books because they tended to measure success by the extent to which Asian Americans have assimilated white middle-class values and because they implied that hard work, learning to speak English, and keeping a low profile would enable Asian Americans to overcome adversity and be successful.

Stereotypes of Asian characters change slowly. Bu Kun-yu (18) identifies past stereotypes of Chinese people and contrasts these stereotypes with current attitudes:

> For hundreds of years, Chinese people have been described as diligent, conservative, obedient. In the wake of modernization, the three traditional words seem inappropriate. Today's students' slogan is: "Be a pioneer of reform, not a lamb of the traditional education system." Thus, three new words are used to describe the demands of modern society: *practical, efficient,* and *adventurous.* (p. 378)

It will be interesting to analyze current Chinese literature for evidence of these more modern characterizations.

EVALUATING MULTICULTURAL LITERATURE

To develop positive attitudes about and respect for individuals in all cultures, children need many opportunities to read and listen to literature that presents accurate and respectful images of everyone. Because few children's books in the United States are written from the perspective of racial or cultural minorities and because many stories perpetuate negative stereotypes, you should carefully evaluate books containing nonwhite characters. Outstanding multicultural literature meets the literary criteria applied to any fine book, but other criteria apply to the treatment of cultural and racial minorities. The following criteria related to literature that represents Black Americans, Native Americans, Hispanic Americans, and Asian Americans reflect the recommendations of the Children's Literature Review Board (19), Anna Lee Stensland (30), and the Council on Interracial Books for Children (7, 8):

1 Are Black, Native, Hispanic, and Asian Americans portrayed as unique individuals, with their own thoughts, emotions, and philosophies, rather than as representatives of particular racial or cultural groups?
2 Does a book transcend stereotypes in the appearance, behavior, and character traits of its nonwhite characters? Does the depiction of nonwhite characters and life-styles lack any implication of stigma? Does a book suggest that all members of an ethnic or racial group live in poverty? Are the characters from a variety of socioeconomic backgrounds, educational levels, and occupations? Does the author avoid depicting Asian Americans as workers in restaurants and laundries, Hispanic Americans as illegal aliens or unskilled laborers, Native Americans as bloodthirsty warriors, Black Americans as menial service employees, and so forth? Does the author avoid the "model minority" and "bad minority" syndrome? Are nonwhite characters respected for themselves, or must they display outstanding abilities to gain approval from white characters?
3 Is the physical diversity within a particular racial or cultural minority group authentically portrayed in the text and the illustrations? Do nonwhite characters have stereotypically exaggerated facial features or physiques that make them all look alike?
4 Will children be able to recognize the characters in the text and the illustrations as Black, Hispanic, Asian, or Native American and not mistake them for white? Are people of color shown as gray—that is, as simply darker versions of Caucasian-featured people?
5 Is the culture of a racial or ethnic minority group accurately portrayed? Is it treated with respect, or is it depicted as inferior to the majority white culture? Does the author believe the culture worthy of preservation? Is the cultural diversity within Black American, Asian American, Hispanic American, and Native American life clearly demonstrated? Are the customs and values of those diverse groups accurately portrayed? Must nonwhite characters fit into a cultural image acceptable to white characters? Is a nonwhite culture shown in an overly exotic or romanticized way instead of being placed within the context of everyday activities familiar to all people?
6 Are social issues and problems related to minority group status depicted frankly and accurately, without oversimplification? Must characters who are members of racial and cultural minority groups exercise all the understanding and forgiveness?
7 Do nonwhite characters handle their problems individually, through their own efforts or with the assistance of close family and friends, or are problems solved through the intervention of whites?
8 Are nonwhite characters shown as the equals of white characters? Are some characters placed in submissive or inferior positions? Are white people always the benefactors?
9 Is a nonwhite character glamorized or glorified, especially in biography? (Both excessive praise and excessive deprecation of nonwhite characters result in unreal and unbalanced characterizations.) If the book is a biography, are both the personality and the accomplishments of the main character shown in accurate detail and not oversimplified?
10 Is the setting of a story authentic, whether past, present, or future? Will children be able to recognize the setting as urban, rural, or fantasy?
11 If a story deals with factual information or historical events, are the details accurate?
12 If the setting is contemporary, does the author accurately describe the situations of nonwhite people in the United States and elsewhere today?
13 Does a book rectify historical distortions and omissions?
14 If dialect is used, does it have a legitimate purpose? Does it ring true and blend in naturally with the story in a nonstereotypical way, or is it simply used as an example of substandard English? If non-English words are used, are they spelled and used correctly?
15 Is offensive or degrading vocabulary used to describe the characters, their actions, their customs, or their life-styles?

16 Are the illustrations authentic and nonstereotypical in every detail?

17 Does a book reflect an awareness of the changing status of females in all racial and cultural groups today? Does the author provide role models for girls other than subservient females?

BLACK AMERICAN LITERATURE

Many fine books of traditional literature, contemporary realistic fiction, and nonfiction reflect the heritage and modern-day experiences of Black Americans. Reading these enjoyable and well-written books will help children from all racial and cultural backgrounds identify with and appreciate the dreams, problems, and cultural contributions of black people on this continent.

Traditional Literature

Traditional folk literature, the tales originally handed down through centuries of oral storytelling, includes many of the stories children most enjoy. Through reading African and Black American traditional tales, children discover a rich literary heritage, gain a respect for the creativity of the people who originated the stories, develop an understanding of the values of the originators, and share enjoyable experiences that have entertained others in centuries past. Modern writers of contemporary realistic fiction about black people often have their characters tell African tales in order to develop closer relationships to and understanding of the African heritage. Other authors write original modern fantasies based on African elements. The beliefs and values found in Black folklore are found in both poetry and contemporary stories; therefore, it is important to begin a study of Black literature with an introduction to the traditional literature.

Traditional Black literature includes folktales that are indigenous to various countries on the African continent, African folk literature that was transported to one of the Caribbean islands and then altered in the new setting, and folk literature that originated in the American South. This final category includes many tales based on African themes and motifs or altered to meet the needs of southern black storytellers.

African Tales. Africa has a long and rich history of oral literature. In 1828, the first known collection of African tales was published for European audiences. This collection, *Fables Sénégalaises Recueillies de l'Oulof,* was translated into French by le Bon Roger, the French Commandant of Senegal. More collections appeared as administrators, traders, and missionaries collected traditional African stories for various purposes. A brief review of these purposes shows how important an understanding of folklore is considered if we are to understand the people. Daniel Crowley (9) states:

> Linguists collected tales as samples of language usage, teachers as a means of inculcating local languages, missionaries to study local values and beliefs, African elites in pursuit of vindication against colonialism, diffusionists in the search of distribution patterns on which to base migration theories, litterateurs and journalists looking for "authentic" themes. . . .(p. 11)

The collection of authentic folklore and artistic representations by ancient peoples is considered so important that Leo Frobenius and Douglas Fox (11) state in the introduction to *African Genesis,* "Every fact, object, and belief which can help us to understand the growth of human culture should be recorded and indexed for use. . . .We will find that there are peoples of whom we do not know enough, and so it will be necessary to send out expeditions to find and gather the material we lack" (p. 16). This is also a worthy attitude for students of children's literature, who can analyze the folklore to make discoveries about the types of stories represented, as well as the values, beliefs, and cultural patterns reflected in the ancient tales. Like other traditional lore, African folklore reveals ancient beliefs in the origins of the natural and tribal worlds and certain physical and spiritual traits. Some tales explore societal problems and provide possible solutions.

Several myths from Virginia Hamilton's *In the Beginning: Creation Stories from Around the World* explore the origins of the natural world. For example, in "Spider Ananse Finds Something: Wulbarie the Creator," a myth from West Africa, Ananse brings the sun, moon, and darkness to earth. Unfortunately, he also causes blindness to come upon some of the people. The theme that weakness can overcome strength is developed as trickster Ananse outwits the more powerful sky god. In "Man Copies God: Nyambi the Creator," a myth from Zambia, Nyambi creates animals and man but is unhappy when man tries to copy god or disobeys his instructions. Consequently, Nyambi climbs into the sky and vanishes from earth. The only sign that god is still in the sky is the sun that rises every morning. The theme in this tale is that humans are at odds with the will of god. Gerald McDermott's *Anansi the Spider: A Tale from the Ashanti* reveals how Nyame, the god of all things, comes to Anansi's aid and places the moon in the sky for all to see. Anansi (or Ananse)* is a popular figure in African folklore. His shrewd and cunning behavior allow him to succeed against great odds or cause him to have tremendous difficulties.

Explanations for the ways in which animals and people acquired certain physical and spiritual traits are popular subjects in African tales. For example, Barbara Knutson's *Why the Crab Has No Head,* a tale from Zaire, shows two characteristics. First, Crab has no head because his pride offended the creator. Second, Crab walks sideways because he is filled with embarrassment instead of pride. A need to humble individuals who express excessive pride is a common theme in African folklore. Two tales in Ashley Bryan's *Beat the Story-Drum, Pum-Pum* are characteristic of explanation stories. "How Animals Got Their Tails" reveals not only how animals received their individual tails but also why there is animosity between rabbits and foxes. "Why Bush Cow and Elephant Are Bad Friends" reveals why animals fight in the bush. Verna Aardema's *Why Mosquitoes Buzz in People's Ears* explains why mosquitoes are noisy. Written as a cumulative tale, it is excellent for sharing orally with children. It suggests a rich language heritage and a respect for storytelling.

African tales in which people are the major characters frequently both reveal societal problems and provide solutions for the problems. Mabel Ross and Barbara Walker (27) state, "The measure of a narrator's skill is indicated in the degree to which he can leave with the listener a valid key to acceptable moral and social behavior, a guide to the making of a responsible choice, within the framework of his own culture" (p. 236). Acceptable moral and social behaviors are revealed in several folktales. For example, Verna Aardema's *Bringing the Rain to Kapiti Plain* shows that individuals have obligations for the betterment of the people, the environment, and the animals that provide their welfare. Ashley Bryan's "The Husband Who Counted the Spoonfuls," found in *Beat the Story-Drum, Pum-Pum,* develops a need for stability in marital relationships.

Ann Grifalconi's *The Village of Round and Square Houses* reveals how a social custom began. In this case, a volcanic eruption in the distant past leaves only two houses within the village: one round and one square. To meet the needs of the village, the women and children move into the round house while the men stay in the square house. According to the tale, the custom continues today because people "live together peacefully here—Because each one has a place to be apart, and a time to be together. . . .'And that is how our way came about and will continue—Til Naka speaks again!' " (unnumbered).

As you read collections of African folktales for children, notice how most of the values and beliefs identified by Ross and Walker in their adult collection are also found in folktales published for children: the importance of maintaining friendship, a need for family loyalty, the desirability of genuine hospitability, the use of wit and trickery in unequal relationships, a strict code for ownership and borrowing, gratitude for help rendered, high risk in excessive pride, care for the feelings of those in authority, respect for individuality, and appropriate awe of the supernatural. Notice that individuals who adhere to these values and beliefs are frequently rewarded, while individuals who reject the values and beliefs are usually punished. For example, traditional values reflected in the folklore of several African cultures are found in Harold Courlander's *The Crest and the Hide: And Other African Stories of Heroes, Chiefs, Bards, Hunters, Sorcerers, and Common People*. This collection of twenty tales from such cultures as the Ashanti, the Yoruba, the Swahili, and the Zulu emphasizes the values of wisdom, friendship, love, and heroism, as well as some behaviors that are not respected, such as foolishness and disloyalty.

Several beautifully illustrated books contain single African folktales retold for children of all ages. Jan Carew's *The Third Gift* suggests the traditional values respected by the Jubas as they acquire the most important gifts that can be given. According to this lovely legend, "in long-time past days" the Jubas were threatened with extinction when the prophet Amakosa gathered his people and led them to the base of a tall mountain. He told them that when he was gone, the young men should climb the Nameless Mountain and the one who could climb the highest and bring back a gift of wonders would be the new leader. One young man reached the top and returned with the gift of work; he ruled for a long time and his people prospered.

When it was time for that ruler to die, the young men again went to the mountain top to seek a gift,

*Variant spellings (*Ananse* or *Anansi*) exist for this character.

THROUGH THE EYES OF A STORYTELLER

The Oral Tradition: People to People, Voice to Voice

ASHLEY BRYAN defines himself first and foremost as a painter, but anyone who has ever heard him tell a story or recite a poem, would argue that he is also a premier storyteller. A true Renaissance man, Bryan is the author/illustrator of several books of tales from motifs discovered in African and Caribbean cultures. He has also collected and illustrated books of African American Spirituals. Bryan was selected by the American Library Association to give the prestigious May Arbuthnot lecture in 1990.

THE ORAL TRADITION IN literature is not exotic or something found only in pre-literate societies. Just listening to people is listening to their stories. While many tales are presented in circumstances where the wise elders answer the questions of children, the oral tradition is not limited to that. All life experience is rich, whether it is children talking to other children on the playground or families talking around the dinner table. The oral tradition will never die, even in this age of television and videocassettes, because each family has its own oral tradition.

Whenever I speak to an audience, I remind listeners that they have an intrinsic art that they have spent years preparing to share with me—the art of listening. My art of storytelling is exchanged for their art of listening. And, believe me, there is excitement generated in that exchange!

I set aside the months of February to June each year to visit schools across the country. When I enter some schools, especially those with older students, I can see that some administrators and teachers fear for me, as I am armed only with the art of poetry. However, I always count on the courtesy and decency of the audience. When they find out how much the poetry means to me, the audience shares that.

Poetry always reminds me that language is man's greatest invention. The poet is more aware than most people of the wonder and mystery of language. Poetry deals with emotions, an area we are most ashamed of as human beings. But it is the emotion of poetry that allows it to reach out and touch the minds and hearts of the listeners in a way that no other medium can.

For this reason, I always begin each storytelling session by reciting a variety of poems written by black poets. I give most of my talks to adults. It is the adults who ask me to come and speak to the children. I try to prepare a range of material that cuts across all ages.

I believe if something is beautiful, it is for everyone. Beauty has no age restrictions. When I watch the evening sky from my island home in Maine, I ask myself, is this sunset meant for a certain age group? I think not.

Also, I never consider limiting the words I choose to tell my stories because children may not understand them. Children are always interested in what the voice is doing and children want to stretch. Whether or not they under-

and the one destined to rule returned with the gift of beauty. During his reign, the Juba country became very beautiful. When young men climbed the mountain for the third time, the gifts brought back were the most important of all, fantasy, imagination, and faith; "So, with the gifts of Work and Beauty and Imagination, the Jubas became poets and bards and creators, and they live at the foot of Nameless Mountain to this day" (p. 32).

Carew's *Children of the Sun* tells a tale about the birth of the sun's twin boys, one rebellious and haughty, the other obedient and gentle. The first son attempts greatness, disobeys his father, and is destroyed. The second chooses to be a good man rather than a great one and eventually brings peace and harmony, the most respected social values, to human beings. Rosa Guy's retelling of *Mother Crocodile,* a folktale from Senegal, also stresses that the knowledge and advice of elders is important and should be taken seriously.

stand a poem completely, even young children will attend to it.

I choose the words of poetry for my stories, too, using the tools of close rhyme, rhythm, repetition, and alliteration. I spend months and years preparing stories and poems. I need that time to make the story or the poem truly mine. I always encourage teachers to allow their students three to four weeks to prepare to recite a poem. No poem should ever be read aloud "cold."

By allowing students time to investigate and play with the language of the poem, one automatically sets up a spirit of cooperation in the classroom. By the time children are asked to recite the poem, they can do so with confidence because now they know all the words and can read with expression.

I like my school visits to be a reminder that reading aloud should be an integral part of the entire school year, no matter what the age of the students. No one is "too old" to be read to, or to be told a story. No one is too young to tell a story that he or she has practiced.

Children always ask me how old I am. I tell them I am four. I tell them I am six. I tell them I am ten. I am forty-six, and I am sixty-four. I ask them to choose the age they want me to be. Invariably, young children will decide and be satisfied that I am four or six, close to their own age.

When I visit schools, I am often treated to wonderful performances of my stories, acted out by the children. It is important that the performance that I see not be the *only* performance. If students have taken time to prepare, they should be allowed to perform again and again. Why not repeat the story to another group a week later? Why not perform again in a month? That way the story will always be truly theirs to own, and there will not be that "emotional letdown" that often occurs after a single performance. Children will also learn each performance can be special. Each time one can embellish a story, and it will grow richer through the retelling.

It is so important to be rooted in who you are, and then all flows naturally from this source. I have always been a teacher. And, I have always earned money to meet my responsibilities from areas other than my art. I write for myself. Since I don't sign contracts before I begin working on a project, I can be patient with a project and release it only when I feel it is ready. That way, my publisher can *choose* to accept my work. I am always prepared to take the work back.

The stories I write often evolve from very spare motifs, sometimes only four or five lines from an ancient journal. I sometimes play with a story for up to ten years before I will focus on it and make it a book.

My challenge is to open up the story from the printed word and try to match the expressive style of illustration to the story itself. That is why I don't use just a single artistic medium or style. When I wanted to concentrate on the movement in the illustrations in *The Dancing Granny,* I used the brushstroke style of painting from the Japanese and Chinese traditions. The characters needed to tumble around the pages. Bright, fresh watercolors captured the mood I wanted to create in *Turtle Knows Your Name*. My current project is a child's book of spirituals. This time I am working with African textile and quilt patterns.

I hope that you will help the art of storytelling flourish in your own way—people to people, voice to voice.

Drawn from an interview, March 30, 1990, by Linda James Scharp

Aardema's *Who's in Rabbit's House?* is an unusual and humorous Masai tale about tricky animals. This tale is written in the form of a play performed by villagers for their fellow townsfolk. In this tale, Caterpillar, who is smaller, slower, and weaker than any of the other animals (including Rabbit, Jackal, Leopard, Elephant, and Rhinoceros), must use wit and trickery to correct the imbalance. In addition, repetition of words adds to the vivid descriptions, and the dialogue suggests the richness of African language. The jackal trots off *kpata, kpata,* the leopard jumps *pa, pa, pa,* and the frog laughs *dgung, dgung, dgung*. This is an excellent tale to stimulate creative dramatizations by children, who enjoy repeating the sound effects and dialogues out loud and creating masks of the various animals.

Another folktale rich in the language of the African storyteller is Gail E. Haley's *A Story, a Story*. This tale about Ananse, the spider man, repeats key words to make them stronger, as Ananse's wit helps him overcome serious difficulties. Ananse seeks stories from the powerful sky god, and the god laughs: "How can a weak old man like you, so small, so small, so small, pay my price?" (p. 6, unnumbered). Ananse fools the god and is able to capture the leopard-of-the-terrible-teeth; Mmboro the hornet who stings like fire; and Mmoatia, the fairy whom people never see. As a reward for these gifts, the sky god gives Ananse the stories that previously belonged only to the god. From this tale, children can understand the importance of storytelling on the African continent as well as recognize the occurrences in which wit and trickery may be legitimately used in African folklore. John Steptoe's *Mufaro's Beautiful Daughters: An African Tale* shows the importance of kindness and generosity toward others and the harmful results of greed and selfishness.

Traditional African folklore elements are found in Mildred Pitt Walter's original tale *Brother to the Wind*. The story, set in Africa, reflects a boy's quest as he searches for Good Snake, the mythical being who is able to grant wishes; as he carefully follows Good Snake's directions; and as he astounds doubting villagers with his ability to fly. (Comparisons may be made between *Brother to the Wind* and the Native American contemporary tale, *Hawk, I'm Your Brother,* by Byrd Baylor. Although one tale is fantasy and one tale is realistic, both tales emphasize similar themes, develop comparable quests, and portray characters whose strong desires control their actions.)

These beautifully expressed and illustrated traditional African tales represent some of the strongest and most noble values attributed to humanity: love of beauty, humor, work, imagination, and perseverance in attaining peace and harmony. Children discover that there are pride and hope in being black, as well as pleasure in the richness of cultural heritage.

American Tales. New folktales developed when Africans became slaves in North America, as Virginia Hamilton (14) points out in her introduction to *The People Could Fly: American Black Folktales*:

Folklore elements and important themes are developed in this southern tale. (From *The Talking Eggs: A Folktale from the American South* retold by Robert D. San Souci, pictures by Jerry Pinkney. Pictures copyright © 1989 by Jerry Pinkney. Reprinted by permission of the publisher, Dial Books for Young Readers.)

Out of the contacts the plantation slaves made in their new world, combined with memories and habits from the old world of Africa, came a body of folk expression about the slaves and their experiences. The slaves created tales in which various animals. . .took on characteristics of the people found in the new environment of the plantation. (p. x)

For example, the favorite Brer Rabbit, who was small and apparently helpless when compared with the more powerful bear and fox, was smart, tricky, and clever, and usually won out over larger and stronger animals. The slaves, who identified with the rabbit, told many tales about his exploits.

Hamilton's collection of tales is divided into four parts: (1) animal tales, (2) extravagant and fanciful experiences, (3) supernatural tales, and (4) slave tales of freedom. The collection provides sources for listening, discussing, and comparing. For example, readers can compare the folklore elements, plot development, and themes in Hamilton's "The Beautiful Girl of the Moon Tower," a folktale from the Cape Verde Islands, and Elizabeth Isele's retelling of the Russian tale "The Frog Princess."

Another group of tales that incorporate characters and language from a new environment into the stories recalled from the African homeland is found in Priscilla Jaquith's *Bo Rabbit Smart for True: Folktales from the Gullah*. The text contains four stories collected from black people living on islands off the coasts of Georgia and South Carolina. The storytellers, whose ancestors came from Angola and the Bahamas, still speak with a lilt similar to calypso, using words from Africa and Elizabethan England and dialect from the British provinces. Language and subject matter in these tales reflect changes in folktales as people added elements of their life-styles while retaining important elements from the past.

The most famous collection of Black American folktales originating in the southern United States are the stories originally collected and retold by Joel Chandler Harris's "Uncle Remus" in the late nineteenth century. Again, we meet that "monstrous clever beast," Brer Rabbit, who always survives by using his cunning against stronger enemies. William J. Faulkner's *The Days When the Animals Talked* (10) presents background information on Black American folktales about animals. Faulkner tells how the tales were created and what their significance is in American history.

Two authors, Van Dyke Parks and Julius Lester, have adapted highly acclaimed versions of the Uncle Remus stories originally written down by

The illustrations and storytelling style combine to provide an enjoyable retelling of the Brer Rabbit tale. (From *Jump Again! More Adventures of Brer Rabbit,* adapted from Joel Chandler Harris's tales by Van Dyke Parks, illustrated by Barry Moser. Copyright © 1987 by Van Dyke Parks, illustrations copyright © 1987 by Pennyroyal Press, Inc. Reprinted by permission of Harcourt Brace Jovanovich, Publishers.)

Joel Chandler Harris. The combination of Parks's text and Barry Moser's illustrations for *Jump! The Adventures of Brer Rabbit* and *Jump Again! More Adventures of Brer Rabbit* form highly readable and visually satisfying experiences. It is interesting to analyze the animal characters and consider the social impact of slavery as depicted in the stories, to identify values that are similar to those found in African tales, to compare similar tales found in other cultures or in other versions of the Uncle Remus stories, and to consider the impact of the authors' styles.

For example, Brer Rabbit is considered a character who can use his head, outdo and outwit all other creatures, and rely on trickery if necessary. In this role, Brer Rabbit uses trickery if he is in conflict with bigger and more powerful characters, but Brer Rabbit also represents what happens

ISSUE

Controversy Surrounding One Book About Black People

Controversy surrounds Margot Zemach's 1982 book, *Jake and Honeybunch Go to Heaven,* a traditional tale with a "green pastures" depiction of heaven and black characters. The *New York Times Book Review* found literary merit in the story. Public school library selection committees in Chicago, San Francisco, and Milwaukee, however, rejected the book as lacking literary merit and/or containing racial stereotyping. The March 1983 issue of *American Libraries*[1] focused on this controversy, presenting both positive and negative points of view.

After reading the book, students of children's literature may decide which of the following viewpoints reflect their own beliefs and opinions:

1 "The book is offensive and degrading, wholly inappropriate for children whether they be black or white" (p. 130).

2 "I regret that a discussion between a library and a publisher on the merits of a book has become a library selection issue debated in the public press" (p. 131).

3 "The prejudice in this book is against portraying blacks in children's books in any but the most positive way; it is appropriate, too, to portray blacks in a realistic way using valid sources" (p. 131).

4 "Do some librarians seriously assert they will not purchase such material for children at least because that time in history is viewed as repellent? If so, isn't that like saying we

when folks "who are full of conceit and proudness are going to get it taken out of them. Brer Rabbit did get caught up with once, and it cooled him right off" (*Jump,* p. 19). Notice how both of these values are also found in African folklore. In addition the tales reflect changes caused by the new environment as the storytellers are influenced by the impact of slavery and European colonization and the need to protect their families and develop friendships that are tempered with distrust.

Symbolism, onomatopoeia, and personification add to Parks's storytelling style. For example, Parks uses symbolic meaning to contrast the length of night and day in *Jump!*: "When the nights were long and the days were short, with plenty of wood on the fire and sweet potatoes in the embers, Brer Rabbit could outdo all the other creatures" (p. 3). Onomatopoeia is used to imitate actions as Brer Rabbit relies on his "lippity-clip and his blickety-blick" (p. 3). Personification is found in descriptions of nature: "Way back yonder when the moon was lots bigger than he is now. . ." (p. 3).

You may make interesting comparisons within and across cultures. For example, compare the stories retold in Parks's version, stories retold in Lester's *The Tales of Uncle Remus: The Adventures of Brer Rabbit,* and stories in earlier versions retold by Joel Chandler Harris. Make cross-cultural comparisons by analyzing "Brer Rabbit Finds His Match" (*Jump!*) with the Aesop fable, "The Tortoise and the Hare."

Stories such as these Brer Rabbit tales are filled with symbolism and alternate meanings. For example, in *The Adventures of High John the Conqueror,* Steve Sanfield states:

> The slaves often told stories about Brer Rabbit, about how, through his cunning and his tricks, he would overcome all the might and power and meanness of Brer Fox and Brer Bear and Brer Wolf. Whites would hear those stories and think, "Oh, isn't that cute, little Brer Rabbit fooling big Brer Bear." But when the slaves told and heard them, they heard them differently. They saw themselves as Brer Rabbit and the slaveholders as Brer Wolf and Brer Fox, and the only way to defeat all that power and brute force was to be just a little bit more clever. (p. 5)

have no past?" (p. 131).

5 "The shallow treatment of the story, the illustrations, the demeaning style of the writing brought a terrible sense of deja vu" (p. 131).

6 "Any library or any children's department of a library has the right to select or reject materials based on that library's selection policy. The operative question here is one raised in a news program on the Public Broadcasting Service (PBS): What do you think of the notion that the publisher is charging censorship in order to sell books over librarians' protests?" (p. 132).

Denise Wilms[2] identified secondary controversies surrounding this book: "While the book's art and story are sound, its depiction of a certain segment of black culture will stir controversy. . . .In addition, its lighthearted view of heaven may be an affront to some groups who see heaven in a more somber light" (p. 619).

Beryle Banfield and Geraldine L. Wilson[3] identified and criticized symbolic misrepresentations and distortions in *Jake and Honeybunch Go to Heaven*. Banfield and Wilson state, "Significantly the book misrepresents the unique, culturally distinctive view of spiritual life held by people of African descent. . . .Zemach has not used one culturally authentic clue about heaven as understood by generations of black people" (pp. 197–198). Banfield and Wilson conclude their article with a comparison of the cultural symbols as presented in *Jake and Honeybunch Go to Heaven* with the African American perspective of those same symbols.

[1]Brandehoff, Susan E. "Jake and Honeybunch Go to Heaven: Children's Book Fans Smoldering Debate," *American Libraries* 14 (March 1983): 130–132.

[2]Wilms, Denise. "Focus: Jake and Honeybunch Go to Heaven." *Booklist* 79 (January 1, 1983): 619.

[3]Banfield, Beryle, and Geraldine L. Wilson. "The Black Experience Through White Eyes—The Same Old Story Again." In *The Black American in Books for Children: Readings in Racism*, edited by Donnarae MacCann and Gloria Woodard. Metuchen, NJ: Scarecrow, 1985: 192–207.

There are distinct oral storytelling styles in Black American folktales. Current retellers of these tales frequently mention the influence of storytellers in their own youth. For example, Patricia McKissack introduces *Flossie & the Fox* by telling readers:

> Here is a story from my youth, retold in the same rich and colorful language that was my grandfather's. He began all his yarns with questions. "Did I ever tell you 'bout the time lil' Flossie Finley come out the Piney Woods heeling a fox?" I'd snuggle up beside him in the big porch swing, then he'd begin his tale. . . .(unpaged author's note)

Interestingly, Julius Lester also introduces *The Tales of Uncle Remus: The Adventures of Brer Rabbit* with the information that his most "lasting memories of my grandmother are of her telling me stories. . . .My favorites, and I'm sure they were hers as well, were the Brer Rabbit stories" (p. vii). Look for, compare, and analyze the influence of the storyteller's style in these selections. Robert D. San Souci's *The Talking Eggs* is adapted from a Creole folktale collected in Louisiana. The tale shows that kindness is a respected value, while greed is not rewarded.

John Henry, a real person and the great black hero of American folklore, is characterized as a "steel-driving" man. Ezra Jack Keats has written and illustrated an attractive edition of John Henry's story, *John Henry: An American Legend*. "Born with a hammer in his hand," the folklore version of John Henry accomplishes seemingly impossible tasks, such as turning a huge broken paddle wheel and saving a ship from sinking, laying more railroad track than many men combined, hammering out a dangerous dynamite fuse and saving the men from a cave-in, and challenging and beating a steam drill in a race until he finally dies "with his hammer in his hand." The large, colorful illustrations in Keats's book suggest the power and heroism of this American legend.

Stories of another folk hero are retold by Steve Sanfield in *The Adventures of High John the Conqueror*. High John is similar to Brer Rabbit because he uses cleverness to outwit his more powerful adversary, the Old Master. The themes in these stories show that human spirit cannot be taken away even if people are living in the worst conditions. Sanfield's text includes factual information that helps readers understand and interpret the tales.

Black spirituals provide another source for understanding the values in the Black American folktales. Black spirituals provide the text to accompany Ashley Bryan's colorful illustrations in John Langstaff's *What a Morning! The Christmas Story in Black Spirituals*. The format of the book includes a colorful illustration and appropriate biblical text followed by the words and music for the accompanying spiritual. Two other sources for Black spirituals are Bryan's *I'm Going to Sing: Black American Spirituals,* volumes one and two.

Fiction

Fiction written about black characters differs depending on the age of the intended audience. Books for younger readers emphasize the universal needs of children. Books for children in the middle-elementary grades emphasize searching for the past and understanding one's ancestry. In books for older children, the characters often face severe personal and social conflicts.

Books for Young Children. Fictional stories about Black Americans written for young children mainly depict black children facing situations and problems common to all young children: overcoming jealousy, adjusting to a new baby, expressing a need for attention, experiencing rivalry with siblings, developing personal relationships, and overcoming family problems. Children from all ethnic backgrounds can realize from these books that black children have the same needs, desires, and problems that other children have and solve their problems in similar ways.

John Steptoe's *Stevie* tells about Robert, a happy young boy who is the center of his mother's attention until his mother begins to care for another child, whose mother works. Steptoe's illustrations and text portray the increasing tension: Toys are broken, and the younger child insists on having his own way. After Stevie moves away, however, Robert remembers the good times they had together and decides that Stevie was "a nice little guy," just like a little brother. This warm story demonstrates a universal emotion.

The varying interactions between a father and his two sons are featured in Steptoe's *Daddy Is a Monster. . .Sometimes*. While the father is nice most of the time, he can turn into a monster with "teeth comin' out his mouth" when his sons fight over the teddy bear, play with their food at a restaurant, are extra messy or noisy, or have an accident in the house. Daddy concludes, "I'm probably a monster daddy when I got monster kids." This book has been praised for the strong father-son relationships it develops; too often, literature about black families shows children who have no father.

The subjects in Steptoe's books for young children could be any children who have problems at home, are jealous of another child, or have a father who is sometimes unhappy with their behavior. However, the language and the illustrations make them black experiences. According to Karen Johnson, in "A Call for Help: Exploring the Black Experience in Children's Books" by Jane Granstrom and Anita Silvey (12), "The thing about *Stevie* that makes it black is the language. There is a cadence to the way this language is written" (p. 102). The dialect in Steptoe's books meets the criteria for multicultural literature because it rings true and blends in naturally with the story.

Warm relationships between young children and elderly people are depicted in Sharon Bell Mathis's *The Hundred Penny Box,* in which Michael makes friends with his Great-great-aunt Dew and learns about the box in which she keeps a penny for every year of her life, and in Valerie Flournoy's *The Patchwork Quilt,* the story of a developing relationship between a grandmother and granddaughter. The books develop strong themes about intergenerational love and respect and the importance of shared memories, which both the hundred penny box and the patchwork quilt contain. "It's my old cracked-up, wacky-dacky box with the top broken," says Michael's Aunt Dew. "Them's my years in that box. . . .That's me in that box" (p. 19). A grandfather and his grandson share stories and develop a closer relationship in Mary Stolz's *Storm in the Night*.

Juanita Havill's *Jamaica's Find* has a universal theme related to the actions one should take after finding a lost object. In a warm text, Jamaica discovers that the toy dog she finds in the park is not hers to keep. She is actually happy only when she helps the rightful owner retrieve the toy. In *Cherries and Cherry Pits,* by Vera Williams, a young girl draws pictures and uses her imagination to tell stories about people who love to eat cherries. The final pages reveal how she would acquire enough of her favorite fruit. She would save and bury the pits, tend the sprouts, nurture the trees, share the crop, and again save and bury

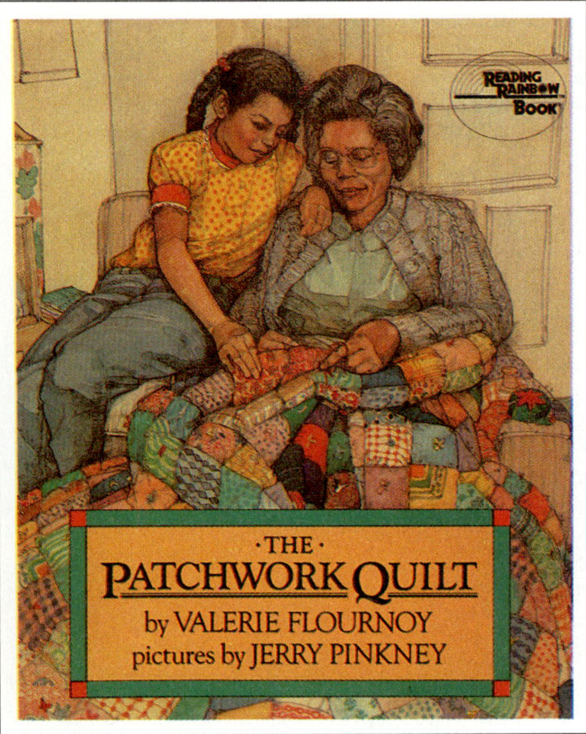

Love and respect are essential emotions in a story that develops a relationship between two generations. (From *The Patchwork Quilt*, by Valerie Flournoy, pictures copyright © 1985 by Jerry Pinkney. Reproduced by permission of the publisher, Dial Books for Young Readers.)

the pits until the block was covered with a forest of cherry trees. Imagination and desire to win a cakewalk combine to make a girl try to capture the wind as her dancing partner in Patricia McKissack's *Mirandy and Brother Wind*. The story may be so believable because the author was influenced by a picture of her grandparents after they won a cakewalk.

In *Nettie Jo's Friends*, McKissack's heroine seeks help from various animals in order to make a dress for a beloved doll. This warm story, in which Nettie Jo discovers that being generous helps her accomplish her goal, appeals to young readers.

Happy childhood memories create warm characters in Elizabeth Fitzgerald Howard's *Chita's Christmas Tree* and Angela Johnson's *Tell Me a Story, Mama*. Howard's story takes place in Baltimore at the turn of the century. It is based on the life of the author's cousin, who was the daughter of one of the first black doctors in Baltimore. In Johnson's story, a young girl asks for and listens to stories about her mother when the mother was a young girl.

Hugh Lewin's *Jafta* and three other books about a black South African boy bring warm cross-cultural experiences to young American children. Lewin's use of figurative language is especially good for aiding children's language development. Lewin describes Jafta in terms of the animals in Jafta's world. When Jafta is happy he purrs like a lion or laughs like a hyena; when he is cross he stamps like an elephant or grumbles like a dog. Chapters 4 and 5 discuss several other picture storybooks about Black people for young readers—including Ezra Jack Keats's stories about inner-city children and Arnold Adoff's story about an interracial family, *Black Is Brown Is Tan*.

Books for Children in the Middle-Elementary Grades. Many stories about black people for children in the middle-elementary grades are written by authors—black and white—who are sensitive to the black experience. Some themes—such as the discovery of oneself, the need to give and receive love, the problems experienced when children realize that the parents they love are getting a divorce, and the fears associated with nonachievement in school—are universal and suggest that all children may have similar needs, fears, and problems. Other themes, such as searching for one's roots in the African past, speak of a special need by black children to know about their ancestry.

Virginia Hamilton's *Zeely* is a warm, sensitive story about an imaginative girl who makes an important discovery about herself and others when she and her brother spend the summer on their Uncle Ross's farm. Elizabeth is not satisfied with the status quo; she calls herself Geeder, renames her younger brother Toeboy, renames her uncle's town Crystal, and calls the asphalt highway Leadback. Hamilton enhances the story as the imaginative Geeder sees her uncle's neighbor, Miss Zeely Tayber. Hamilton describes Zeely's appearance in detail: She is a thin and stately woman over six feet tall, with a calm and proud expression, skin the color of rich Ceylon ebony, and the most beautiful face Geeder has ever seen. When Geeder discovers a photograph of a Watusi queen who looks exactly like Zeely, she decides that Zeely must have royal blood.

Geeder is swept up in this fantasy and shares her beliefs with the village children. Then Zeely helps Geeder make her greatest discovery. As they talk, Geeder realizes that dreaming is fine, but being yourself is even better. This realization causes her to see everything in a new way. She realizes that Zeely is indeed a queen, but not like the ones in books, with their servants, kingdoms, and wealth: Zeely is queen because she is a self-loving person who always does her work better than anybody else. Geeder realizes that what a person is inside is more important than how a person looks or what a person owns. When Hamilton shares Geeder's final thoughts about her wonderful summer and her discovery that even stars resemble people, readers understand just how much wisdom she has gained:

> Some stars were no more than bright arcs in the sky as they burned out. But others lived on and on. There was a blue star in the sky south of Hesperus, the evening star. She thought of naming it Miss Zeely Tayber. There it would be in Uncle Ross' sky forever. (p. 121)

Like Geeder, ten-year-old James in Paula Fox's *How Many Miles to Babylon?* dreams of African royalty. James, however, believes that he himself must be a long-lost prince, whose ancestors had been chained and marched across the land to boats that took them to slavery in a new country. James even fantasizes that, instead of being ill and taken to the hospital, his mother has traveled to Africa to plan for his celebrated return. He goes to the basement of a dilapidated house to dress and dance like the African princes in photographs, but instead, he encounters a harsh reality.

James learns and accepts the truth about himself when a gang of boys kidnaps him and forces him to help in stealing valuable dogs to earn reward money. When the gang takes him to a deserted amusement park, James sees the Atlantic Ocean for the first time and realizes that his gravely ill mother could not have crossed such a fearsome body of water. Fox encourages readers to understand the strength of James's character and his ability to face reality by describing James's thoughts and actions when he plots his escape. James does not merely look out for his own safety; instead, he feels obligated to take the dogs with him and return them to their owners. When James returns home, he knows he is not a prince, but he also knows that he is a strong person in his own right, a person who can solve his own problems.

Another book that explores a character's personal discovery and strength of character is *Sister,* by Eloise Greenfield. (Eloise Greenfield has won several awards for her contributions to children's literature, including the Irma Simonton Black Award and a citation from the Council on Interracial Books for Children.) Sister, whose real name is Doretha, keeps a journal in which she records the hard times—and the good times that "rainbowed" their way through those harder times. Doretha's memory book helps her realize "I'm me." The words of the school song sung in *Sister* are characteristic of the themes found in this and other books by Greenfield:

> We strong black brothers and sisters
> Working in unity,
> We strong black brothers and sisters,
> Building our community,
> We all work together, learn together
> Live in harmony
> We strong black brothers and sisters
> Building for you and for me. (p. 69)

Mildred Taylor's *The Gold Cadillac* is a fictionalized story based on Taylor's painful memories. Taylor develops a story about family unity and the consequences of racial prejudice. The prejudice occurs in 1950, when a northern black family buys a gold Cadillac and tries to drive to Mississippi. For the first time, the children experience segregation and racial hostility. As in other books by Taylor, the theme shows that family love and unity help them overcome such terrible experiences.

Books for Older Children. Outstanding realistic fiction written for older children is characterized by both strong characters and strong themes. The themes in these stories include searching for freedom and dignity, learning to live together, tackling problems personally rather than waiting for someone else to do so, survival of the body and the spirit, and the more humorous problems involved in living through a first crush.

Virginia Hamilton has written several fine novels that older children find engrossing. In her suspenseful contemporary story *The House of Dies Drear,* she skillfully presents historical information about slavery and the Underground Railroad through the conversations of a black history professor and his son who are interested in the history of the pre-Civil War mansion they are about to rent. (Compare Hamilton's presentation of information about slavery with Belinda Hurmence's time travel fantasy about slavery in *A Girl Called Boy*.) Hamilton provides details for a setting that seems perfect for the mysterious occurrences that begin soon after the family arrives:

> The house of Dies Drear loomed out of mist and murky sky, not only gray and formless, but huge and unnatu-

ral. It seemed to crouch on the side of a high hill above the highway. And it had a dark, isolated look about it that set it at odds with all that was living. (p. 26)

Thomas's father tells him about the wealthy abolitionist Dies Drear, who built the house and helped many slaves on their way toward freedom. Hamilton hints at the suspense to follow as Thomas learns that Dies Drear and two escaped slaves were murdered and that rumors say the abolitionist and the slaves haunt the old house and the hidden tunnels below. Mystery fans will enjoy this fast-paced book. In a sequel, *The Mystery of Drear House,* Hamilton answers questions that students may have after reading *The House of Dies Drear*. In the sequel, the characters protect the treasure accumulated by Dies Drear from nature and from the thieving Darrows.

In *Junius Over Far,* Hamilton combines a search for a lost heritage with a sense of mystery. Hamilton reveals the close relationship between fourteen-year-old Junius and his grandfather Jackaro through Junius's actions. Fantasy, folklore, and American history are interwoven in Hamilton's *The Magical Adventures of Pretty Pearl*. After Pearl arrives on earth from Mount Highness in Africa, she and a spirit travel among the slaves in colonial Georgia and, following the Civil War, help former slaves journey from Georgia to Ohio. Through her interactions with the human characters, Pearl discovers both sorrow and joy. Hamilton's rich language and style add to the enjoyment. For example, she uses these words to express Pearl's feelings:

Oh, life is a toil and love is a trouble,
And beauty will fade and riches will flee.
Oh, pleasures they dwindle and prices they double.
And nothing is as I could wish it to be (p. 26).

Hamilton writes about the black experience with a universal appeal that speaks to readers of any heritage. Another of Hamilton's strong characters learns that choice and action lie within his power in *M. C. Higgins, the Great*. In this story, the enemy is the spoil heap remaining from strip mining of the mountains, an oozing pile that threatens to swallow a boy's home and even his mother's beloved sunflower.

In *Scorpions,* Walter Dean Myers's characters face person-against-society conflicts created by the contemporary world of drug dealers and gangs. They also face person-against-self conflicts created by inner fears and consequences related to owning a gun. The characters of Mama and her younger son Jamal are especially strong. Myers develops Mama's character through numerous contrasts. For example, when Mama thinks about her older son, who is in jail for robbery, she remembers looking at him as a baby and feeling great expectations because "You got a baby and you hope so much for it. . . ." (p. 54). Later, Mama is torn between her need to help this older son and to protect her younger children. Myers develops this inner conflict as Mama discusses her problems with her minister:

"And I know they convicted him of taking somebody's life, but that don't mean he ain't my flesh and blood." The minister replies: "Sometimes the herbs we take are bitter, sister, but we got to take them anyway. . . . [Y]ou got to hold your family here together too. We can't let the bad mess up the good." (p. 153)

In Jamal, the younger son, Myers develops a character who is tortured by his feelings of being weak and small. In the beginning of the story, Jamal thinks about all the people who make him feel this way, such as the big kids who laugh at him, the teachers who make him stand in class, and the shop owners who yell at his Mama "because there wasn't anything he could do to stop them. Not by himself, not while he was small and not as tough as they were" (p. 22). Later, Myers contrasts Jamal's earlier fears with his changing feelings after obtaining a gun:

Jamal thought about Randy being scared up in the prison and him being scared down here in Harlem. For a while he hadn't been scared. When he had had the gun in the storeroom, he hadn't been scared. Even when they had gone to the crack house looking for Mack, he hadn't been scared. Maybe, he thought, you got messed up easily when you had a gun, but at least you weren't scared. (p. 204)

In a tragic ending, Jamal discovers the consequences of having the gun and makes an even greater personal discovery. There was "the part of him, a part that was small and afraid, that still wanted that gun" (p. 214). This poignant story reveals the complex problems facing two generations of people who are fighting for personal and family survival in a dangerous world.

A rural story for older children is much lighter in tone than the previously discussed books. Bette Greene's humorous *Philip Hall Likes Me. I Reckon Maybe* is set in Arkansas. The eleven-year-old main characters are Philip Hall, the smartest boy in the class, and Beth Lambert, the girl who has her first crush. Greene creates considerable humor as Beth tries to maneuver herself and Philip into shared experiences. She is a little suspicious that he may not be the smartest child in the class: She may be letting him win. The two work together to solve the mystery of her father's missing turkeys, but they are in direct competition when each of them raises a calf to show at the annual county fair. When Beth's calf wins, Philip's first reaction is shame; then he feels the unfamiliar emotions related to losing. Beth solves their problem when she invites him to be her partner in the square-dancing contest; as friends and partners, they can win or lose together. Philip finally admits what Beth has been longing to hear: "Sometimes I reckon I likes you, Beth Lambert" (p. 135).

Chapter 10 discussed other stories about Black Americans for older children, including Mildred D. Taylor's *Roll of Thunder, Hear My Cry* and James and Christopher Collier's *Jump Ship to Freedom.* Books such as Joyce Hansen's *Which Way Freedom* are based on historical information about Black Americans who participated in the Civil War. The characters in all these stories meet the criteria for outstanding characterization in literature: They are memorable individuals and they are real people who face the best and the worst that life offers. They are portrayed with dignity and without stereotype. As in the literature for young readers, the stories reflect varied settings and socioeconomic levels. The main character may be the child of a highly educated college professor or the child of a destitute sharecropper. The realistic stories for older readers do, however, reflect a harsh realism in the Black American experience, whether in the past or in contemporary life. Some of these stories—such as Virginia Hamilton's *The Planet of Junior Brown* and Walter Dean Myers's *Scorpions* —portray an economically disadvantaged inner-city existence and problems of survival very different from those of the middle-class experience. However, children in the stories reflect pride in their individuality and in their decisions to be themselves. The courage and determination of the characters are inspirational to all.

Nonfiction

Because two of the strongest purposes for sharing literature by and about Black Americans with children are to raise the aspirations of black children and to encourage understanding of Black American experience by nonblack children, biographies should be important in a multcultural literature program. Biographies of black leaders and artists tell children about contributions to American society and the problems overcome.

Several biographies for children portray the life of nineteenth-century freedom fighter Frederick Douglass. For example, Lillie Patterson's *Frederick Douglass: Freedom Fighter* is a dramatic encounter with Douglass's life in slavery, protest against slavery, escape from the slave owners and then slave hunters, work on the Underground Railroad, and championing of the rights of not only black people but also the Chinese, the Irish, and females. Douglas Miller's *Frederick Douglass and the Fight for Freedom* covers similar events, and makes an interesting comparative study. Miller, a professor of American history, includes a valuable list of additional readings and discusses some of the problems in previous biographies.

Virginia Hamilton's *Anthony Burns: The Defeat and Triumph of a Fugitive Slave* covers the life of a slave who is less well-known than Frederick Douglass. However, the escape of Burns to Boston, his arrest, and trial had considerable impact on the abolitionists and advanced the antislavery movement. (See chapter 12 for a discussion of Hamilton's biography.)

James T. DeKay's *Meet Martin Luther King, Jr.* stresses the magnitude of King's work and his reasons for fighting against injustice. Lillie Patterson's *Martin Luther King, Jr. and the Freedom Movement* begins with an account of the 1955–1956 Montgomery, Alabama, bus boycott and Martin Luther King, Jr.'s involvement in the boycott. Patterson then explores King's earlier background and discovers some of the influences that caused King to become a leader in the boycott and the civil rights movement. James Haskins's *The Life and Death of Martin Luther King, Jr.* presents a stirring account of both King's triumphs and tragedies. Eloise Greenfield's *Rosa Parks* focuses on the life of the seamstress in Montgomery who refused to give up her seat on the bus. Arnold Adoff's *Malcolm X* stresses how and why Malcolm X urged Black Americans to be proud of their heritage and themselves. Patricia McKissacks's *Jesse Jackson* focuses on the accomplishments of the first black man to run for President of the United States.

Although many biographies chronicle the lives of civil rights leaders, other biographies reveal the lives of industrial leaders. A current biography reports the life of a little-known individual who revolutionized the shoe industry. Barbara Mitchell's *Shoes for Everyone: A Story About Jan Matzeliger* tells the story of the man in the 1800s who invented the shoe-lasting machine and made affordable shoes possible. Mitchell looks at Matzeliger's love of machinery and the persistence needed for him to realize his dream. Mitchell also shows how difficult it was for a black worker to live and work in the years just after the Civil War.

Three books reflect the contributions of Black Americans to the fine arts. Ashley Bryan's *I'm Going to Sing: Black American Spirituals, Volume Two* includes words and music that help children understand the importance of the spiritual to American heritage. The contributions of black people to the American theater are stressed in James Haskins's *Black Theater in America*. Haskins traces the American theater from minstrel shows through contemporary protest plays and drama, highlighting black writers, actors, and musicians. Ossie Davis effectively uses the poetry of Langston Hughes to create a play about the well-known black poet in *Langston: A Play*. Glennette Tillie Turner's *Take a Walk in Their Shoes* includes short biographies of fourteen Black Americans. The text includes skits that can be performed by children.

Patricia and Frederick McKissack focus attention on the contributions of Black Americans in the labor movement. Their *A Long Hard Journey: The Story of the Pullman Porter* chronicles the struggle for Black Americans to form a union for railroad porters.

Several picture books for children of all ages show different aspects of the African heritage. Nonny Hogrogian's illustrations let children share the beautiful and varied sights seen by an African child in Leila Ward's *I Am Eyes, Ni Macho*. The title of the book means "I am awake"; it also means "I am eyes." Long-necked giraffes amble through tall grass, elands and elephants stroll across the land, camels rest in a desert oasis, birds soar above Mt. Kilimanjaro, colorful flamingos stand in a pond, and butterflies flutter through the air.

Leo and Diane Dillon's beautiful illustrations and Margaret Musgrove's text in *Ashanti to Zulu* portray the customs of twenty-six African peoples. This unusual alphabet book reinforces the understanding that the African continent has a rich heritage of culture and tradition. Veronica Freeman Ellis's *Afro-Bets First Book About Africa* includes considerable information about African history.

The books discussed in this chapter have broad appeal for children and a wide range of content. The emergence of outstanding authors who write about the black experience with sensitivity and honesty has provided more excellent books about Black Americans than are available about other minorities in the United States. When shared with children, such books contribute toward positive self-images and respect for individuals across cultures. They also do much to lessen the negative stereotypes of black people common in American literature of the past.

NATIVE AMERICAN LITERATURE

The copyright dates listed in the annotated bibliography at the end of this chapter show that the majority of recommended books about Native Americans have been published relatively recently. Few copyright dates precede the 1970s, which indicates a recent increase in the number of books written from a Native American perspective. Many of these books are beautifully illustrated traditional tales, and several have won the Caldecott Medal. Some are written by Native Americans themselves; others have been written by non–Native American writers, such as anthropologist Joyce Rockwood, who have used their knowledge of native cultures to create authentic portrayals of the Native American past.

The lovely poetry written by Byrd Baylor and the tales she has collected increase understanding of Native American values and heritage. There are still too few stories with contemporary settings and Native American main characters, however. Consequently, most children have few opportunities to read about Native American children facing the problems of today.

Traditional Tales

Native American tales show that the North American continent had traditional tales that were centuries old before the European settlers arrived. Traditional Native American tales make up a heritage that all North Americans should take pride in and pass on to future generations. In his collection of traditional Native American tales, *Anpao: An American Indian Odyssey*, Jamake Highwater compares the teller of Native American folktales to a weaver whose designs are the threads of his or her personal saga, as well as the history of his or her people. These stories of the Native American oral tradition have been passed from one generation to the next and often mingled with tales from other tribes. Says Highwater:

> They exist as the river of memory of a people, surging with their images and their rich meanings from one place to another, from one generation to the next—the tellers and the told so intermingled in time and space that no one can separate them. (p. 239)

Highwater recounts the task of preserving and transmitting traditional stories described by the Santee Dakota, Charles Eastman. Writing of his own boyhood, Eastman said that very early in life, Indian boys assumed the task of preserving and transmitting their legends. In the evening, a boy would listen as one of his parents or grandparents told a tale. Often, the boy would be required to repeat the story the following evening. The household became his audience and either criticized or applauded his endeavors.

Highwater has combined a number of traditional Indian tales in *Anpao: An American Indian Odyssey*. The story begins "In the days before the people fled into the water. . .[when] there was no war and the people were at peace" (p. 15). During this time, Anpao travels across the great prairies, through deep canyons, and along wooded ridges in search of his destiny. Along the way, he observes the cultures and customs of many different tribes. His odyssey illustrates the diversity of the land, life-styles, and history found within the Indian cultures of North America.

Native American traditional literature provides an excellent source for identifying and understanding tribal traditional values and beliefs. Several sources provide documentation for traditional Native American values and beliefs. For example, *Human Behavior and American Indians,* by Hanson and Eisenbise (15), documents tribal traditional values and compares them to urban industrial values. *The Journal of American Indian Education* (29) identifies North American Indian cultural values and compares them to the values of the dominant non-Indian culture. The Coalition of Indian Controlled School Boards (26) identifies traditional Lakota values and compares them to non-Lakota values. This last source is especially valuable when analyzing the traditional literature of the Northern Plains Indians.

A review of these sources indicates that many of the traditional values, such as living in harmony with nature, viewing religion as a natural phenomenon closely related to nature, showing respect for wisdom gained through age and experience, acquiring patience, and emphasizing group and extended family needs rather than individual needs, are also dominant themes in the traditional tales from various tribal regions. As you read various Native American traditional tales, see if you can identify these important values.

For example, living in harmony with nature is a dominant theme in Tomie dePaola's retelling of the Comanche tale, *The Legend of the Bluebonnet*. The theme is developed when selfishly taking from the land is punished by drought, while unselfishly giving of a prized possession is rewarded with bluebonnets and rain. The name change in the main character as she goes from She-Who-Is-Alone to One-Who-Dearly-Loved-Her-People supports the emphasis on extended family rather than the individual.

Paula Underwood Spencer's *Who Speaks for Wolf* develops the importance of living in harmony with nature through a "Native American Learning Story," told to the author by her Oneida father, Sharp-Eyed Hawk. The story chronicles the experiences of the Oneida as they move to a new location, only to discover that they have failed to consider the rights of the animals. The tale ends as the wise storyteller gazes slowly around the council circle and asks the ancient question:

> Tell me now my brothers
> Tell me now my sisters
> Who speaks for Wolf? (p. 40)

The strong interactions between buffalo and Great Plains Indians are developed in both Olaf Baker's *Where the Buffalos Begin* and Paul Goble's *Buffalo Woman*. In *Where the Buffalos Begin,* Stephen Gammell's marvelous black-and-white drawings capture the mythical lake where the buffalo, after their birth, surge out of the water, rampage across the prairie, and eventually save Little Wolf's people from their enemies. In traditional tales from the Great Plains, the buffalo people frequently save those who understand and respect them. Goble's tale ends with why the relationship between the Great Plains Indians and the Buffalo is so important:

> The relationship was made between the People and the Buffalo Nation; it will last until the end of time. It will be remembered that a brave young man became a buffalo because he loved his wife and little child. In return the Buffalo People have given their flesh so that little children, and babies still unborn, will always have meat to eat. It is the Creator's wish. (unnumbered)

Showing respect for animals, keeping one's word, and listening to elders are interrelated themes in Frank Cushing's "The Poor Turkey Girl," found in *Zuni Folk Tales*. In this Cinderella-type tale, a Zuni maiden who cares for the turkeys is helped to go to a festival by the old Gobbler and the other turkeys. When the girl does not heed the old Gobbler's admonition and return on time to feed the turkeys, she loses everything because:

> After all, the gods dispose of men according as men are fitted; and if the poor be poor in heart and spirit as well as in appearance, how will they be aught but poor to the end of their days? Thus shortens my story. (p. 64)

Traditional tales of legendary heroes reflect many important values and beliefs of the people. These legendary heroes may have many of the same characteristics found in heroic tales from other cultures. For example, like Beowulf in the Norse legend, an Inuit hero shows bravery, honor, and a willingness to avenge wrongs. In the introduction to one of the tales included in *Stories from the Canadian North,* Muriel Whitaker states:

> [I]n order to understand fully the ending of 'The Blind Boy and the Loon,' one must realize that the Eskimo hero was predominantly an avenger. Just as the spirits of weather, thunder, lightning, and the sea took vengeance on those who mistreated them, so too was the mortal here expected to have the will and the power to exact retribution for evil. (p. 20)

Legends from the Northwest coasts of the United States and Canada emphasize heroes who venture onto the unpredictable sea and overcome perils associated with the ocean wilderness. Christie Harris's *The Trouble with Adventurers* includes tales with representative themes. For example, "The Bird of Good Luck" shows that fame can arouse envy; "How Raven Gets the Oolikan" suggests that the deeds of heroes are not always to be admired; "Revenge of the Wolf Prince" suggests that heroes do not always survive to enjoy a happy-ever-after future; and "Ghost Canoe People" shows that heroes often need supernatural help but that supernatural beings may not be inclined to offer assistance. Harris's *Mouse Woman and the Vanished Princesses* is a collection of tales about how the supernatural Mouse Woman helps the daughters of chiefs who find themselves tricked by evil supernatural beings. Additional tales from British Columbia are found in *Kwakiutl Legends,* retold by Chief James Wallas.

Native North Americans, like people everywhere, evolved mythology that explained the origins of the universe and natural phenomena. According to Virginia Haviland (16), Native Americans believed in "supernatural forces and their legends told of culture heroes and shape-shifters who used magic. Animals had power to turn into people and people into animals. The animal stories, like animal folklore of many other countries, are often humorous, and the characters are accomplished tricksters" (p. 13).

Native Americans, Native Canadians, and the Inuit peoples developed a rich heritage of traditional myths and legends. John Bierhorst (2) identifies the following four categories found in Native American mythology: (1) myths that emphasize "setting the world in order," in which the world is created out of or fashioned from the chaos of nature; (2) myths that emphasize "family drama" by centering on various conflicts and affinities rising out of the kinship unit; (3) myths that emphasize "fair and foul," such as the trickster cycle tales in which the hero progresses from a character of utter worthlessness to one that displays a gradual understanding of social virtue; and (4) myths that emphasize "crossing the threshold" by depicting the passage from unconsciousness to consciousness, the ordeal of puberty, the passage into and out of the animal world, the passage into and out of death, and the transition from nature to culture. In a book for adults, *Red Swan: Myths and Tales of the American Indians,* Bierhorst presents and discusses examples of these various categories of myths. Notice that Bierhorst's categories are also found in single stories and anthologies that include several tales passed down in tribes across the North American continent.

Setting-the-World-in-Order Tales. Traditional tales that emphasize setting the world in order tell about creating the earth and various animal and plant life. Earth-diver type myths are found in the literature of numerous North American Indians. For example, one of the tales in *The Adventures of Nanabush: Ojibway Indian Stories,* compiled by Emerson and David Coatsworth, tells how Nanabush, a very powerful Ojibway spirit, created the world. In this flood and creation story, the Serpent People cause the water to rise in retaliation for Nanabush's destruction of two of their people. Anticipating their reactions, Nanabush builds a large raft, places it on top of a mountain, and invites the animals to join him as the water rises. After they float on the raft for a month without sighting land, Nanabush realizes that the old world has been submerged forever. In order to get substance to create a new world, Nanabush sends animals to the old world to retrieve mud. The muskrat returns with a few particles of sand, out of which Nanabush forms a tiny globe. After

Nanabush breathes life into the globe, he places it on the water next to the raft and commands it to grow. The globe revolves until it is large enough to contain Nanabush and all the animals.

Similar earth-diver myths are found in the literature of numerous North American Indians. Virginia Hamilton includes two additional earth-diver myths in *In the Beginning: Creation Stories from Around the World*: (1) "Turtle Dives to the Bottom of the Sea: Earth Starter the Creator," a Maidu tale from California, and (2) "The Woman Who Fell from the Sky: Divine Woman the Creator," a Huron myth from the northeastern United States. Hamilton's collection also includes a Blackfoot myth in which Na'pi, or Old Man the Creator, travels around the world creating people and animals and an Eskimo myth in which Raven, a trickster god, travels around the world instructing people in how to live.

Native American tales, such as Barbara Esbensen's *The Star Maiden,* account for the creation of plant life. In this lyrical rendition of an Ojibway tale, Star Maiden and her sisters leave their home in the sky and become the beautiful star-shaped water lilies.

Family Drama Tales. Family drama tales focus on various family needs and conflicts, such as learning from elders, providing protection, obtaining food, and overcoming problems, including rivalry and aggression. The family in these stories may be the smaller tribal unit or the greater cosmos. If the tale deals with the greater world family, the storyteller may refer to Earth as mother, Sky as father, and humanity as children. Many of these stories reveal tribal standards.

Several tales in Jean Monroe and Ray Williamson's *They Dance in the Sky: Native American Star Myths* illustrate universal family concerns and appropriate behaviors. For example, "Bright Shining Old Man," an Onondaga tale from New York, shows that children will be punished if they ignore the warnings of their elders. In "The Little Girl Who Scatters the Stars," a tale from the Cochita Pueblo in New Mexico, a girl cannot overcome her curiosity. It is a universal family tale. In it, "Our Mother" tells the people that they are all brothers and sisters and instructs them to live as one large family.

Trickster Tales. Trickster tales reveal both good and bad conduct. John Bierhorst (2) states, "[T]he trickster tale affords the narrator an opportunity to flirt with immoral or antisocial temptations" (p. 6) in humorous ways. Trickster characters are found throughout North America. On the northwestern coast of the Pacific Ocean, the trickster is called Raven. Coyote, who may be a creator or a trickster, is a popular character in the plains. Iktomi is the Sioux name for trickster.

In *Iktomi and the Boulder: A Plains Indian Story,* Paul Goble describes the fair and foul side of Iktomi, who is "beyond the realm of moral values. He lacks all sincerity. Tales about Iktomi remind us that unsociable and chaotic behavior is never far below the surface. We can see ourselves in him. Iktomi is also credited with greater things: in many of the older stories, the Creator entrusts him with much of Creation. People say that what seem to be the 'mistakes' and 'irrational' aspects of Creation, such as earthquakes, floods, disease, flies, and mosquitos, were surely made by Iktomi" (introduction). In Goble's version of the Sioux tale, conceited Iktomi first gives his blanket to a boulder and then deceitfully takes the blanket back when he needs it for protection. Iktomi then uses trickery to save himself from the angry boulder. Even though he eventually wins the confrontation, he is frightened and momentarily humbled by his experience. Goble's *Iktomi and the Berries* provides another humbling experience for the trickster character.

Threshold Tales. Numerous Native American tales depict crossing various thresholds. Transformations that allow characters to go into and out of the animal world are especially popular in stories retold for children. Both Elizabeth Cleaver's *The Enchanted Caribou* and Paul Goble's *Buffalo Woman* use transformations to show the bond between Native Americans and animals. In a retelling of an Inuit tale, Cleaver emphasizes the bond between the Inuit and the white caribou. Goble's retelling of a tale from the Great Plains reflects a strong bond between the humans and the buffalo herds, a bond that was essential if both the people and the buffalo were to prosper.

In Goble's *Beyond the Ridge,* the main character goes from the land of the living to the spirit world. In this story, an elderly Plains Indian experiences the afterlife as believed by her people. On her way, she discovers Owl Maker. The spirits of individuals who have led good lives pass Owl Maker to the right, toward Wanagiyata, Land of Many Tipis. However, Owl Maker pushes the spirits of those who have led bad lives to the left, along a short path where they fall off, landing back on earth to wander for a time as ghosts.

Combination Tales. Many traditional tales have elements that include several of the folklore types. For example, John Bierhorst's *The Ring in the Prairie: A Shawnee Legend* has elements related to fair and foul tricksters, to crossing thresholds, and to family drama. First, the Shawnee hunter plays the trickster as he turns himself into a mouse and creeps close to a beautiful young woman who descends from the sky. Then, he returns to his human form and captures his heart's desire. The tale contains several crossing-the-threshold experiences. The hunter passes into and out of the animal world before he and his family are permanently transformed into animals. His captured bride crosses from the world of the star people to the world of humans and back to the world of the star people before she is permanently transformed into a white hawk. The story also reflects strong family ties. The hunter mourns the loss of his wife and son and then goes on a difficult quest so that he can be reunited with his family.

Songs and Poetry

Songs, chants, and poems are very important in the various Native American cultures. Many poems express reverence for creation, nature, and beauty. Native Americans created poetry for a purpose; they believed there was power in the word. Songs were often part of ceremonial rituals, with their symbolism portrayed through dance.

The beauty of both ancient Native American poetry and contemporary poetry about Native American experiences can be shared with children. An interesting resource book that shares the music of Native Americans with children of many cultures is John Bierhorst's *A Cry from the Earth: Music of the North American Indians*. According to Bierhorst, native peoples throughout North America shared a belief in the supernatural power of music to cure disease, bring rain, win a lover, or defeat an enemy.

Many Native Americans today sing the songs for pleasure and to express pride in their heritage. Bierhorst's book contains words and music for many songs, including songs of prayer, magic, and dreams, songs to control the weather, and music to accompany various dances. There are greeting songs, love songs, a Hopi flute song, a Hopi sleep song, a Cherokee lullaby, and a Kwakiutl cradlesong. Music, words, and dance steps are included so that children can recreate, experience, and respect this musical heritage.

The wide range of subjects around which songs were created suggests a Native American heritage that is richly various. Bierhorst's anthology *The Sacred Path: Spells, Prayers and Power Songs of the American Indians* is organized according to themes. An introduction, a glossary, and a list of notes and sources add authenticity and additional information.

Byrd Baylor has expressed her love and concern for the Native American peoples and the land of the Southwest in a series of books written in poetic form. One of them ponders the secrets of prehistoric people as seen through their drawings on pottery. In *When Clay Sings*, the designs on ancient shards of pottery created by the Anasazi, Mogollon, Hohokam, and Mimbres cultures of the Southwest are the models for Bahti's illustrations and suggest the inspiration for Baylor's poetry. According to Baylor:

> Indians who find this pottery today say that everything has its own spirit—even a broken pot. . . .They say that every piece of clay is a piece of someone's life. They even say it has its own small voice and sings in its own way. (cover summary)

Poetry selections by Byrd Baylor and Jamake Highwater reflect foundations in traditional beliefs and mythological references. For example, Baylor's *The Other Way to Listen* and *The Desert Is Theirs* communicate to young readers the Native American closeness to nature. Peter Parnall's illustrations suggest the majesty of the desert and the respect of the Papago Indians for it. In *Moon Song*, Baylor presents a why tale in poetic form. She develops the closeness in nature between Moon and coyotes. Highwater's *Moonsong Lullaby* has foundations in traditional beliefs. The poem develops respect for nature, close relationships with animals, respect for older people, and belief in ancient knowledge.

Mythological references also abound in the poetry by Highwater and Baylor. For example, in *Moonsong Lullaby*, animals give their lives to the people who respect them, holy people have special powers, and Moon is wife to Sun. Baylor's *A God on Every Mountain Top: Stories of Southwest Indian Sacred Mountains* retells legends and myths in poetic form. In it are the tales of creation, protection, and spirits that are also found in the Native American traditional literature from the Southwest. Virginia Driving Hawk Sneve's collection, *Dancing Teepees: Poems of American Indian Youth,* includes poems from various tribes, such as the Hopi, the Zuni, and the Lakota Sioux. The poems vary from the words of heroes, such as Black Elk, to the prayers of ancient peoples to the writings of contemporary tribal poets.

Poetic texts reinforce the desirable understanding that Native American peoples have diverse cultures and great artistic traditions.

Historical Fiction

Themes and conflicts in historical fiction about Native Americans often emphasize the survival of the body or the spirit. Some authors emphasize periods in history in which contact with white settlers or cavalry resulted in catastrophic changes. Others emphasize growing interpersonal relationships between Native American and white characters. Four award-winning books provide examples for these two types of historical fiction.

Scott O'Dell's Newbery honor book, *Sing Down the Moon,* focuses on the mid-1860s, when the U.S. Cavalry forced the Navaho to make the three-hundred-mile Long Walk from their beautiful and productive home in Canyon de Chelly to stark Fort Sumner. O'Dell effectively develops the resulting conflict through descriptions of the contrasting settings. He provides detailed descriptions of the Canyon de Chelly, a place of miracles. This idealistic setting does not last. It is followed by horror as Colonel Kit Carson's soldiers first destroy the Navaho's crops and livestock in the canyon, then force the Navaho to walk through desolate country to a setting that is unconducive to physical or spiritual survival. Fifteen hundred Navaho die, and many others lose their will to live. O'Dell's protagonist, a Navaho woman named Bright Morning, retains an inner strength based on hope for the future. While she is a captive, she hoards food and plans for the day when she and her husband will return to their canyon.

Jan Hudson's *Sweetgrass* is a story of a Blackfoot girl who survives a smallpox epidemic in the 1830s. Even though the girl does not interact with white characters, she battles the disease brought to her people. Hudson, the author of this Canadian Library Association Book of the Year Award winner, writes about native peoples with sensitivity. (See chapter 10 for a discussion of *Sweetgrass.*)

Farley Mowat's Canadian Library Association Book of the Year, *Lost in the Barrens,* takes place in the twentieth century in a remote arctic wilderness, hundreds of miles from the nearest town. The two main characters are Awasin, a Woodland Cree, and Jamie, a white Canadian orphan who moves north to live with his uncle. The setting becomes an antagonist for both boys when they accompany the Crees on a hunting expedition and then become separated from the hunters. Mowat provides vivid descriptions of searching for food and preparing for the rapidly approaching winter. Through long periods of isolation, the boys develop a close relationship and an understanding of each other. Elizabeth George Speare's Newbery Honor Book, *The Sign of the Beaver,* focuses on the friendship between a Native American boy and a white boy in the Maine wilderness of the 1700s. (See chapter 10 for a discussion of *The Sign of the Beaver.*)

Joyce Rockwood, an anthropologist, uses her knowledge of Cherokee culture to write a lighter, more humorous story about a young Cherokee boy in 1750. In *Groundhog's Horse,* Creek Indians steal Groundhog's horse and leave a message signifying that they have taken it to Rabbit-town. Even worse, the Cherokee warriors do not consider Groundhog's horse important enough to retrieve. Instead of being able to go on the trail after his horse with a loud whoop, Groundhog decides he must "sneak away like a weasel" and find his horse himself. He stealthily plans his trip and "with bravery fluttering faintly in his heart," approaches the sleeping Rabbit-town and the house in front of which his horse Midnight is hobbled. Surprisingly, he finds not only the horse, but also another young Cherokee boy captured by the Creeks and adopted into a family to replace their own son.

After a series of adventures, Groundhog's horse finds the way home, and the boys are reunited with their anxious families. Rockwood weaves tradition and history naturally into the story, but the overwhelming feeling is one of human relationships and the personalities of the characters. Unlike many Native American characters in children's literature of the past, these Indians laugh and have distinctly individual personality traits and desires. Children can learn a great deal about Cherokees, as well as enjoy a humorous adventure.

Through all these stories, children can experience Native American characters who have personal thoughts and emotions and live within a family as well as within a tribe. In addition, children will begin to understand the impact of white people on the Native American way of life. (Additional historical stories are discussed in chapter 10.)

Contemporary Realistic Fiction

Little contemporary realistic fiction for children focuses on Native Americans. In the books that are available, Native Americans often express conflict between the old ways and the new ones. Characters must decide whether to preserve their heritage or abandon it. Many of these stories allow Native Americans to honor the old ways but live with the new ones. Some stories show life on modern reservations; others depict families who have left the reservation to live in cities. The needs of all individuals are shown: Characters search for their identities or express a desire for love. The Native American characters often express hostility toward white characters who have been unfair to them, but some stories develop strong friendships between people from different backgrounds.

Like other contemporary realistic fiction for younger children, stories about Native Americans for younger audiences frequently develop themes related to love and family relationships. Jean Speare's *A Candle for Christmas,* a story set in the Canadian Northwest, tells a story of love and family unity. In this story, a boy hopes that his parents will return home in time for Christmas. The candle that he leaves on the porch plays a major role in helping his parents return.

Knots on a Counting Rope, by Bill Martin, Jr., and John Archambault, is a poetic story about a blind boy's birth and his later preparation for a horse race. The title symbolizes the passage of time and the boy's growing confidence. The authors use a storytelling style that goes back and forth between the grandfather's telling the story and the boy's interjecting his own ideas, as shown in the following examples:

> Then what happened, Grandfather?
> Just as I was born. . .
> tell me that part.
>   It was strange. . .strange.
>   Just as you came forth
>   and made your first cry,
>   the wind stopped howling
>   and the storm was over. . . .
>   (p. 8, unnumbered)

This style lends itself to choral reading between two groups or a reader's theatre portrayal between two voices.

A strong, loving relationship between a Navaho girl and her grandmother provide the foundation in Miska Miles's *Annie and the Old One.* The conflict in the story develops because Annie does not want to accept the natural order of aging and death. In an effort to hold back time, Annie tries to prevent her grandmother from completing the rug she is weaving because her grandmother has said, "My children, when the new rug is taken from the loom, I will go to Mother Earth" (p. 15). The author emphasizes the way that Annie's inner conflict ends and the theme that we are all part of nature emerges when Annie finally realizes:

> [T]he cactus did not bloom forever. Petals dried and fell to earth. She knew that she was a part of the earth and the things on it. She would always be a part of the earth, just as her grandmother had always been, just as her grandmother would always be, always and forever. And Annie was breathless with the wonder of it. (p. 41)

Annie's actions show that she has accepted nature's inevitable role. Annie picks up the weaving stick and begins to help her grandmother complete the rug.

Need to live in harmony with nature is the theme in another book for younger readers. The conflict occurs in White Deer of Autumn's *Ceremony—In the Circle of Life* because Little Turtle cannot accept the terrible environmental destruction that surrounds him in his city environment. Through a vision, the author allows Little Turtle to learn about the wisdom and knowledge of his ancestors. This contemporary story is closely related to traditional values and beliefs. Little Turtle discovers the importance of the nuclear family as found in Mother Earth, Grandmother Moon, and Father Sky. He discovers that the Circle of Life requires listening to Mother Earth if people are to prosper. Daniel San Souci's illustrations show the symbolic importance of the four directional parts of the circle and help readers understand these traditional beliefs. Conflicts between traditional Native American values and the values of the white culture are found in many of the contemporary books.

Symbolism, ancient traditions, and person-against-self conflicts are important elements in three books written for children of different ages. In *The Scared One,* a book for young children, Dennis Haseley develops a survival story about a boy whose ancient heritage helps him face and overcome fear and ridicule. In Jean Craighead George's *The Talking Earth,* a book for middle-elementary readers, a Seminole girl who lives on the Big Cypress Reservation questions the traditions of her people.

Jamake Highwater's *Legend Days,* a book for older readers, may require several readings for students to appreciate the author's use of symbolism, traditional values, and tribal customs. You may discuss possible meanings of the book's title and trace the legend days motif throughout the story. Omens, powers, visions, and close relationships with animals and nature are important in the plot and character development of this book. For example, Highwater compares Amana's physical development with the rhythms of nature: "Like the springtime berries, she felt ripe and whole. Like the little rivers, her blood flowed rich and warm from its winter's sleep" (p. 22). Many of Amana's inner conflicts result because she is both a warrior and a woman. She wants to be a warrior and not a woman. Through her story, readers discover the impact of both a dream and European civilization on her life. Amana's story continues into the present in *The Ceremony of Innocence* and *I Wear the Morning Star,* parts two and three of Highwater's Ghost Horse Cycle.

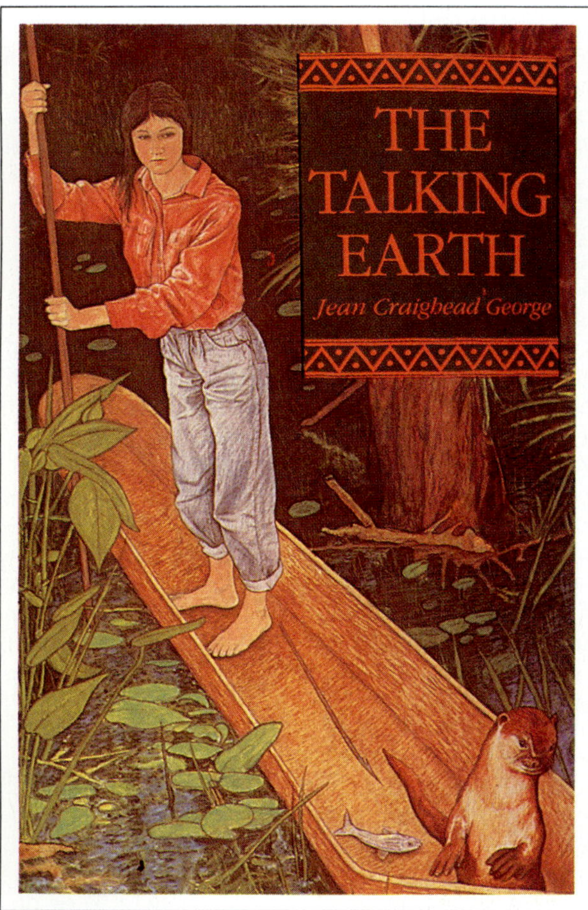

A contemporary Seminole girl searches for her legendary heritage. (Jacket art by Bob Marstall from *The Talking Earth* by Jean Craighead George. Jacket art copyright © 1983 by Bob Marstall. Reprinted by permission of Harper & Row, Publishers, Inc.)

Authors of contemporary stories about Native Americans frequently develop understandings about the past to help their characters respect their heritage. For example, in *High Elk's Treasure,* Virginia Driving Hawk Sneve ties the past to the present with a flashback to the year 1876, when the Sioux were taken to the reservation following the defeat of General Custer at the Battle of the Little Big Horn. One hundred years later, High Elk's descendants excitedly discover a pictograph of the Battle of the Little Big Horn. This pictograph is later authenticated by an expert from the university. Sneve develops a strong feeling for the past and pride in Native American heritage throughout this book. In *Bearstone,* Will Hobbs uses an ancient turquoise bear to help a Ute Indian boy clarify his beliefs and overcome his personal problems.

Three stories with Eskimo protagonists show the range of subjects and conflicts that are covered in contemporary literature. In Jean Craighead George's *Water Sky* a boy from Massachusetts journeys to Barrow, Alaska, in search of his uncle. The conflict between cultures is reinforced by the boy's mother, who does not want Lincoln to make this journey. During his quest, Lincoln lives at a whaling camp, where he learns to understand and respect his Eskimo heritage. Throughout this story, George combines vivid settings and information about Eskimo values and beliefs.

In Gary Paulsen's *Dogsong,* Russel, a contemporary Eskimo boy, leaves the mechanized world in which his people hunt seal and caribou by snowmobiles to discover the ways and beliefs that were there in the days of dogsleds. Russel's mentor is an elderly Eskimo who believes that the Eskimo people have lost the songs that made the whales and other animals come to the people in times of need. Russel's search for his own song takes him on a 1,400 mile dogsled trek across the isolated ice and tundra. In a traditional manner, dreams and visions become part of the learning experience. In a dream, Russel goes back in time, faces his fear, kills a mammoth, and sings a song in exultation. Through his ordeal with nature, Russel discovers the power of the old Eskimo ways.

In Scott O'Dell's *Black Star, Bright Dawn,* an Eskimo girl drives a dogsled team in the Iditarod Trail Sled Race from Anchorage to Nome. Through her experiences, the girl learns to depend on her dogs and herself. In addition, she discovers the strength in her Eskimo heritage, values, and beliefs. Realistic fictional stories portray some conflicts in contemporary Native American children's lives, as well as some resolutions that reflect strong self-esteem and respect for an ancient heritage.

Nonfiction

Authors of informational books about Native Americans for young children often use illustrated texts to encourage identification with traditional ways of life and cultural contributions made by Native Americans. Authors of informational books for older readers often stress history, the struggle for survival, and various contemporary conflicts.

In *Before Columbus,* a book for young children, Muriel Batherman uses information revealed by archaeological explorations to discuss the daily life of native North Americans in pre-European times. The text and illustrations depict dwellings, clothes, tools, and customs.

Native peoples of the Western Hemisphere gave the world a very important food product. Aliki's *Corn Is Maize: The Gift of the Indians* traces the history of corn in the text and illustrations, from five-thousand-years-old tiny ears of corn recently discovered in a cave in Mexico, through improvement of corn into the large ears grown today. Children discover how corn is planted, cultivated, harvested, and manufactured into many different products. Illustrations show how native peoples of Mexico and North America cultivated and used corn and depict their introducing it to Christopher Columbus and the Pilgrims. Alice Hermina Poatgieter's *Indian Legacy: Native American Influences on World Life and Culture* explores broader contributions of North and South American native peoples to modern life, including agriculture, art, and democratic attitudes.

Paul Goble's *Death of the Iron Horse* and Russell Freedman's *Buffalo Hunt* provide historical perspectives. Goble uses an actual incident in 1867, when a Union Pacific train was derailed by the Cheyenne. In his fictionalized story, Goble shows that the Cheyenne fought the encroaching white culture by attacking the railroad. Freedman shows the importance of the buffalo to the Indians living on the Great Plains. His text includes descriptions of the hunts, attitudes of the Indians toward the buffalo, and consequences to the Indians when the white culture all but eliminated the buffalo. The text is illustrated with reproductions of paintings by such artists as George Catlin and Karl Bodmer, who actually saw the buffalo hunts. The titled and dated illustrations add considerable interest to the text.

Current books of nonfiction for older children commonly emphasize Native American struggles for survival against overwhelming odds when Europeans began claiming the continent. The turbulent years between 1866 and 1895 are the focus of historian Albert Marrin's *War Clouds in the West: Indians & Cavalrymen, 1860–1890*. The text discusses various Native American peoples and their struggles to retain their ways of life. Maps, early photographs, archive illustrations, and references provide additional source materials.

Brent Ashabranner's *Morning Star, Black Sun: The Northern Cheyenne Indians and America's Energy Crisis* traces the history of the Northern Cheyenne through their early migrations into Montana to their recent conflicts with power and mining companies. Through the depiction of a century-old struggle, Ashabranner characterizes the Northern Cheyenne as people who have strong traditional values, such as respect for the land and animals, regard for bravery and wisdom, and reverence for religious principles.

In *To Live in Two Worlds: American Indian Youth Today,* Ashabranner's interviews with Native American young people, both on reservations and in urban environments, show that some young Native Americans experience confusion and conflict as they try to adjust to the dominant white culture. Others experience cultural security as they develop confidence in their own heritage. The final chapter focuses on René Cochise, the great-great-great granddaughter of the famous Apache leader Cochise. She grew up on a reservation and now works in Washington, D.C. She says:

> I don't know yet what the Washington experience will mean to me. I've met Indians here, ones who have worked here a long time, who don't seem like Indians, not like the ones in New Mexico. I don't think that would happen to me, no matter how long I stayed away. I have the language of my tribe. I have the religion. I have the years of growing up on the land inside me. I have lived the customs of my people. I know who I am. No matter where I am, I am an Apache. (p. 145)

Arlene Hirschfelder's *Happily May I Walk: American Indians and Alaska Natives Today* is a comprehensive text. It discusses such contemporary topics as tribal governments, education, economic life, and organizations. It includes photographs, further reading lists, and an index. A map of Native American lands and communities helps readers find locations identified in the text.

Biographies

Biographies are important reading for children because they encourage high aspirations and respect for the social contributions of outstanding people. However, there are even fewer biographies about Native Americans than there are about Black Americans.

Several biographies look at famous Native Americans who interacted with white settlers of this continent. For example, *Sacajawea, Wilderness Guide,* by Kate Jassem, is the biography of the Shoshone woman who guided the Lewis and Clark expedition across the Rocky Mountains to the Pacific Ocean. This book is appropriate for young readers.

Conflicts between worlds provide numerous opportunities for character and plot development in Jean Fritz's *The Double Life of Pocahontas*. Fritz effectively develops a character who is torn between loyalty to her father's tribe and to her new friends in the Jamestown colony. As in her other biographies, Fritz documents her historical interpretations. Notes, a bibliography, an index, and a map add to the authenticity.

Russell Freedman's *Indian Chiefs* includes short biographies about Red Cloud, Satanta, Quanah Parker, Washakie, Joseph, and Sitting Bull. The text is supported with photographs, a bibliography, and an index. Dorothy Moorison's *Chief Sarah: Sarah Winnemucca's Fight for Indian Rights* is one of the strongest biographies of this period. Moorison develops conflicts through contrasts when she describes Sarah's confusion:

> The whites killed—but they had made her well. They took the Indians' meadows—but gave them horses and presents. They burned stores of food—but they gave food, too. Would she ever understand these strange people who were overrunning the land? (p. 31)

Moorison shows Sarah's battle for retention of Paiute culture when she describes Sarah's dream:

> All this time Sarah had been lecturing and saving every penny, for she had another dream—of a school for Indian children, taught by Indians themselves, a school that would train its students as teachers for their own people. Up to then, Indian schools, both private and under the Bureau, had been taught and managed by white people who tried to 'civilize' the students by wiping out native language and culture. Sarah, however, was sure her people's culture was worth preserving. (p. 149)

Additional literature about Native Americans may be found in Anna Lee Stensland's *Literature by and About the American Indian* (30). (Additional Native American biographies are discussed in Chapter 12.)

HISPANIC AMERICAN LITERATURE

Most children's books about Hispanic Americans depict people of Mexican or Puerto Rican heritage, although the United States population contains numerous other Hispanic groups. People of Hispanic descent are the largest minority group in the United States, but relatively few children's books have been written about them. There is also an imbalance in the types of stories available. Award-winning picture storybooks about Hispanic Americans tend to examine Christmas celebrations. Award-winning novels are about a small segment of the Hispanic American population, the sheepherders of Spanish Basque heritage, whose ancestors emigrated to parts of North America before those parts came under United States control. Although folktales and poetry are available for adults, a shortage of children's literature exists.

Many books for children about Hispanic Americans develop strong connections between the people and their religious faith. Celebrations, such as La Posada, suggest this cultural heritage. The respect for freedom is stressed through the celebration of Cinco de Mayo. Spanish vocabulary is also interspersed throughout many stories, allowing children to associate with a rich language heritage. (Misspelled and incorrectly used Spanish words have appeared all too often in this type of book, however. These errors have, understandably, caused criticism.) Several books are more factual, presenting the Spanish heritage that existed on the North American continent long before the United States became a nation. These stories suggest that Americans with Spanish ancestry have a heritage worthy of respect and of sharing with others.

Folklore

The wide cultural areas for Hispanic folklore include Mexico, South and Central America, Cuba, and the American Southwest. The folklore incorporates pre-Spanish tales of the Aztecs, Maya, and Incas. The Spaniards colonized the earlier populations, and different groups, such as the Apache and Pueblo Indians, interacted. As in other cultures, there are myths that explain (*ejemplo*), as well as folktales and fairy tales (collectively called *cuento*).

Many of the early Aztec and Mayan tales were recorded for European audiences by Spaniards in the sixteenth century. Others were written down by Aztecs who learned to read and write in the Texcoco Seminary. These tales were illustrated in pictographic forms on codices and provide many of the sources used by current folklorists and retellers of the tales. Carleton Beals's *Stories Told by the Aztecs: Before the Spaniards Came* includes myths about the three Aztec gods: (1) Quetzalcoattl, the Plumed Serpent, who drove out earlier animal gods and led the Toltecs in central Mexico; (2) Tezcatlipoca, the Black Mirror that Smokes, who led the Chichimeca, or Stone Men; and (3) Huitzilopochtli, the Aztec war god, also known as Mexitli, who was considered the greatest god. Mexitli is so important that Mexico City is named after him. John Bierhorst's *The Hungry Woman: Myths and Legends of the Aztecs* provides additional sources for Aztec traditional tales.

Tales in John Bierhorst's *The Monkey's Haircut and Other Stories Told by the Maya,* collected from the Maya in Guatemala and southeastern Mexico, indicate many of the traditional Mayan values and cultural characteristics. For example, the extensive use of riddles in the folklore shows that the people value cleverness. In "Rabbit and Coyote," double meanings allow Rabbit to dupe Coyote and escape from his cage. The plot of "Tup and the Ants" hinges on a pun. Cultural characteristics are shown in other tales, such as "The Mole Catcher," in which a husband must pay a price for his wife through a bride service.

Values and beliefs from numerous Hispanic cultures are reflected in *The King of the Mountains: A Treasury of Latin American Folk Stories* collected by M. A. Jagendorf and R. S. Boggs. This collection contains stories from twenty-six countries. Stories such as the Mexican "The Sacred Drum of Tepozteco" show that wisdom, understanding, and virtuous living are respected values because they lead to rewards. In contrast, attacking a revered king and putting on a display for the sake of appearance only are despised actions because they lead to punishment.

Additional Mexican folktales are found in Francisco Hinojosa's *The Old Lady Who Ate People,* a collection of frightening stories from Mexico.

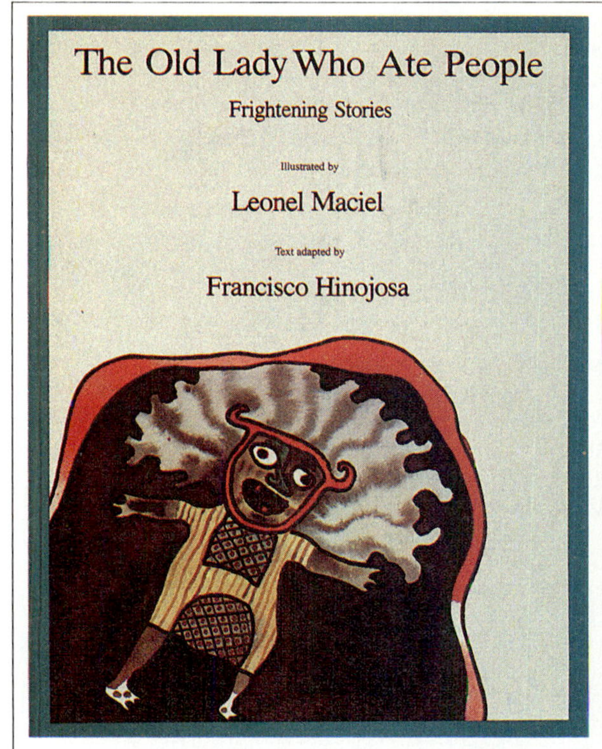

The illustrations enhance the frightening quality of these folktales. (From *The Old Lady Who Ate People,* illustrated by Leonel Maciel. Copyright © 1981 by Organización Editorial Novaro, S.A.)

Mexican *pourquoi* tales collected in Marcos Kurtycz and Ana Garcia Kobeh's *Tigers and Opossums* tell why the hummingbird is richly dressed, how the opossum got his tail, and how the tiger got his stripes.

Legends and myths from South America are found in two collections by John Bierhorst. *Black Rainbow: Legends of the Incas and Myths of Ancient Peru* includes an introduction to the people and their culture, a selection of traditional tales, notes on sources, and a glossary of terms. *The Mythology of South America* provides considerable scholarly background and selections that reflect creation of the world and the origins of civilization as well as the conflicts between people. Bierhorst divides the stories and the discussions according to Greater Brazil, Guiana, Brazilian Highlands, Gran Chaco, Far South, Northwest, and Central Andes. Extensive notes on sources and references add to the text.

Many of the folktales from Mexico, South and Central America, and Hispanic cultures in the United States reflect a blending of cultures as stated in the introduction to José Griego y Maestas's and Rudolfo A. Anaya's *Cuentos: Tales from the Hispanic Southwest*:

> The stories also reflect a history of thirteen centuries of cultural infusing and blending in the Hispan mestizaje, from the Moors and Jews in Spain, to the Orientals in the Philippines, Africans in the Caribbean, and the Indians in America—be they Aztec, Apache or Pueblo. (p. 4)

For example, "The Man Who Knew the Language of the Animals," a folktale found in *Cuentos: Tales from the Hispanic Southwest,* is based on a Moorish tale from "A Thousand and One Nights." The tale is also similar to Verna Aardema's African tale, *What's So Funny, Ketu?* Differences between the African and Hispanic tales reflect cultural values. The main character in the Hispanic tale portrays a stronger masculine role.

The illustrations provide a southwestern setting for this variant of *Aesop's Fables*. (From *Dr. Coyote: A Native American Aesop's Fables* retold by John Bierhorst. Illustrated by Wendy Watson. Text © 1987 by John Bierhorst. Illus. copyright © 1987 by Wendy Watson. Reprinted by permission from Macmillan Publishing Co.)

John Bierhorst's retelling of *Doctor Coyote: A Native American Aesop's Fables* also indicates cultural infusion. Bierhorst identifies the text as Mexican in origin and shows the strong Spanish-Aztec connection. It is interesting to compare these fables with Aesop's fables and with coyote trickster tales.

Bierhorst's *Spirit Child: A Story of the Nativity* shows the infusion of Christian and Aztec beliefs. The text and Barbara Cooney's illustrations depict an Aztec setting for the birth of the Christ child, and extensive Aztec beliefs are infused. Likewise, various versions of "The Virgin of Guadalupe" represent what Richard M. Dorson (24) describes as "the merger of Spanish-Catholic and Aztec Indian heritages that produced Mexican folk nationalism" (p. xvi).

Tomie de Paola's retelling of *The Lady of Guadalupe,* a Mexican tale, develops a strong connection between the people and their religious faith. According to legend, the Lady of Guadalupe, now the patron saint of Mexico, appeared to a poor Mexican Indian on a December morning in 1531. Juan Diego, "He-who-speaks-like-an-eagle," was walking toward the Church of Santiago when he saw a hill covered with a brilliant white cloud. Out of the cloud came a gentle voice calling Juan's name and telling him that a church should be built on that site so that the Virgin Mary could show her love for Juan's people, the Indians of Mexico. On Juan's third visit to the bishop, he was believed because he brought with him a visual sign from the Lady of Guadalupe: His rough cape had been changed into a painting of the lady. The church was built on the location, and the cape with its miraculous change was placed inside the structure. De Paola says that he has had a lifelong interest in the legend of the Lady of Guadalupe. His drawings, based on careful research, depict the dress and architecture of sixteenth-century Mexico.

Two traditional tales adapted by Harriet Rohmer originate with the Miskito Indians of Nicaragua. *The Invisible Hunters* reflects the impact of European cultures on the Miskito people. The three hunters are punished when they break their promise and forsake their people. European traders influence the hunters' actions and create and expand their greed. *Mother Scorpion Country* is a tale of love. In this tale, a husband tries to accompany his wife into the land of the dead. According to the author's notes, "the compassionate figure of Mother Scorpion reflects a pre-Christian matriarchal past" (p. 32).

Both of Rohmer's texts include information about the author's research. For example, Rohmer began her research for *The Invisible Hunters* in anthropological archives, visited the Miskito communities in the company of an Afro-Indian Catholic priest, learned more details of the story from an elder Miskito Catholic deacon, and finally met a Miskito Bishop of the Moravian Church, who provided many additional details. During this final contact, Rohmer was told, "According to the stories I heard as a child the Dar has a voice. I can take you to people who say they have heard that voice" (p. 31). Likewise, in *Mother Scorpion Country,* Rohmer traces the story to the endeavors of a young Moravian minister who recorded the stories and customs of the Miskito Indians in the early 1900s.

Several Hispanic folktales have universal themes and elements that are similar to European folktales. For example, Pura Belpré's *The Rainbow-Colored Horse,* a Puerto Rican tale, includes motifs found in tales from other cultures. Two "superior" sons cannot solve a problem (the fields are mysteriously trampled), the quietest and gentlest son solves the problem (a rainbow horse is in the field), the youngest son is granted three wishes if he will not capture the horse, a king offers his daughter's hand in marriage to anyone who can meet a challenge (while riding a horse at full gallop, the winner must toss balls into the princess's lap), and the supernatural horse makes it possible for the hero to pass the test. The tale suggests a universality in folktales and the people who tell them and enjoy them. The Spanish names and the inclusion of Spanish phrases evoke a strong Spanish heritage.

Verna Aardema's *The Riddle of the Drum: A Tale From Tizapán, Mexico* translates a folktale with universal motifs. A king with a marriageable daughter challenges suitors to a task. On the way to the palace, the suitor meets four people with exceptional skills. The king adds additional tasks after the first task is completed, and the suitor's extraordinary abilities allow him to win the princess. The tale also reflects a strong Spanish heritage, respect for the language, and beauty in architecture and costumes. The names are Spanish, counting is in Spanish, the foods are Mexican, and Tony Chen's illustrations depict early Mexican culture. Aardema includes a pronunciation guide for Spanish words and a glossary of their meanings.

Picture Storybooks

Listening to and saying rhymes from various cultures encourage children to interact with language as well as to discover the joy in language and in word play. Margot Griego's *Tortillitas Para Mama and Other Spanish Nursery Rhymes,* Lulu Delacre's *Arroz Con Leche: Popular Songs and Rhymes from Latin America,* and Isabel Schon's *Doña Blanca and Other Hispanic Nursery Rhymes and Games* are written in both English and Spanish. These texts provide sources for sharing literature in either language.

My Song Is a Piece of Jade: Poems of Ancient Mexico in English and Spanish, adapted by Toni de Gerez, includes poems from the Toltec people of ancient Mexico. These poems, written in Spanish and English, reveal many of the values and beliefs of the Toltec, who admired storytelling, learning, and art. For example, the true storyteller, according to Toltec tradition, considered language noble and boldly used words of joy. In contrast, the bad storyteller was careless and said useless words without dignity. Likewise, the true doctor was wise, gave life, understood herbs, and experimented. Through the poems that give advice to sons or daughters, readers discover gender values considered important in the culture.

Deborah Lattimore's *The Flame of Peace: A Tale of the Aztecs* is a literary fairy tale based on the Aztec nine evil lords of darkness and the god of peace. Lattimore uses information from Aztec myth and hypothesizes about what might have caused the Alliance of Cities during the time of Itzcoatl. In the resulting story, a young boy uses his wits against the evil lords and brings peace to the cities. The illustrations reflect Aztec settings and characters.

Richard Garcia's *My Aunt Otilia's Spirits,* a fictional story set in contemporary San Francisco, includes elements of the supernatural. Garcia bases the story on a visit from a Puerto Rican relative. Consider the interrelationships among reality and fantasy as Garcia describes the story in the endnotes:

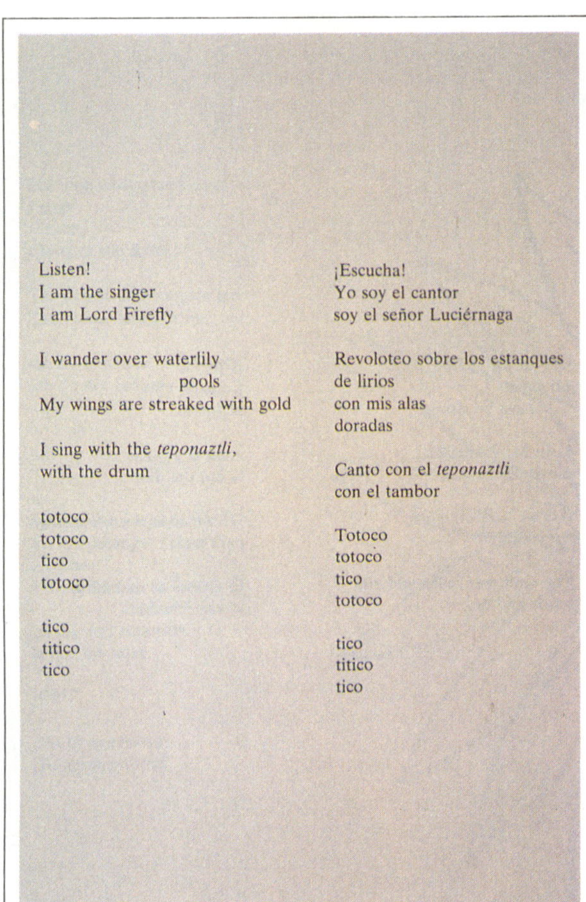

Listen! I am the singer I am Lord Firefly	¡Escucha! Yo soy el cantor soy el señor Luciérnaga
I wander over waterlily pools My wings are streaked with gold	Revoloteo sobre los estanques de lirios con mis alas doradas
I sing with the *teponaztli*, with the drum	Canto con el *teponaztli* con el tambor
totoco totoco tico totoco	Totoco totoco tico totoco
tico titico tico	tico titico tico

The ancient Mexican source for the poetry is reinforced through the illustrations in *My Song is a Piece of Jade: Poems of Ancient Mexico in English and Spanish* adapted by Toni de Gerez, illustrated by William Stark. (Copyright © 1981, English translation copyright © 1984 by Organización Editorial Novaro, S. A. Reprinted by permission of Little, Brown and Company.)

Like all stories, this one is based on a kernel of fact—that is that my Aunt Otilia was accompanied by bed shakings and wall knockings wherever she went. However, this was not regarded as unusual in my family, or a cause for much concern. The supernatural had a natural place in our life. Most of the time we ignored it—sometimes it meant something—as in the case of an omen or a dream. We had a large and well-worn copy of an old dream book—and this was often consulted in the morning if a dream seemed significant. . . .And those who had died were never thought of as being very far away—and were often spoken to as if they were in the room. (p. 24)

Leo Politi has written and illustrated a number of award-winning picture storybooks about Mexican American children living in southern California. His *Song of the Swallows* tells the story of a young boy whose dear friend is the gardener and bell ringer at the mission of San Juan Capistrano. Politi shares Mexican American history with readers as the gardener tells Juan the story of the mission and of *las golondrinas,* the swallows who always return to the mission in the spring, on Saint Joseph's Day, and remain there until late summer. Politi's illustrations recreate the Spanish architecture of the mission and demonstrate a young boy's love for plants and birds.

In *The Nicest Gift,* Carlitos lives with his family and his dog, Blanco, in the barrio of East Los Angeles. He accompanies his mother as she goes to the *mercado* (the marketplace) to buy foods and other goods for the Christmas holiday. Unhappily,

Blanco is lost at the market. The best gift occurs on Christmas Eve, when Blanco finds Carlitos. This book is filled with Spanish terms associated with La Posada, a celebration associated with Christmas.

Marie Hall Ets and Aurora Labastida's *Nine Days to Christmas: A Story of Mexico* tells of a kindergarten child who is excited because she is going to have her own special Christmas party, complete with a piñata. In the midst of numerous other everyday activities, Ceci chooses her piñata at the market, fills it with toys and candy, and joins the La Posada procession. After Ceci sees her beautiful piñata being broken at the party, she is unhappy until she sees a star in the sky that resembles her piñata. Children relate to the girl's feelings and learn about the Mexican celebration of Christmas when they read this book. This story depicts a middle-class family that lives in an attractive city home. Children can see that poverty is not the condition of all people with a Spanish heritage.

Historical and Contemporary Realistic Fiction

Only a few books of historical and contemporary realistic fiction for children portray Hispanic Americans in suitably positive ways or as the main characters. Marian L. Martinello and Samuel P. Nesmith's *With Domingo Leal in San Antonio 1734* takes a documentary approach to Hispanic American history and life in the United States. Published by the University of Texas Institute of Texas Cultures at San Antonio, this carefully researched book depicts a day in the life of a young Spanish boy who travels with his family from the Canary Islands through Mexico to the Villa de San Fernando on the banks of the Rio San Antonio de Padua in present-day Texas. This historical novel can strengthen children's understanding of a lengthy Hispanic heritage in the southwestern United States. It also demonstrates that people of Spanish ancestry were living on the North American frontier before English-speaking settlers tried to claim it.

Another book of historical fiction depicting the early Spanish presence in western North America is Scott O'Dell's *Carlota*. In this story set in Spanish California in the mid-1800s, O'Dell explores the conflicts that occur between people who expect females to play a traditionally feminine role and others who encourage a different type of behavior. Carlota is the strong and independent daughter of Don Saturnino, a native Californian whose ancestors came from Spain. Her father supports her brave and adventurous inclinations.

Even though her grandmother deplores such behavior, Carlota rides a black stallion around the ranchero at top speed, races horses with neighbors, brands cattle, and eventually joins her father and other men in ambushing Americans who are trying to annex California for the United States. When Carlota wounds a young American soldier, her feelings of compassion overcome her sense of obedience to her father, and she nurses the wounded man back to health on the ranchero. Her strength of character is ultimately demonstrated when she manages the ranchero after her father's death. Like other memorable heroes in literature, Carlota grows in self-understanding and inner strength.

Joseph Krumgold's . . . *And Now Miguel,* based on a full-length documentary film feature, is the story of the Chavez family, which has been raising sheep in New Mexico since before their region became part of the United States. Their ancestors raised sheep in Spain. Krumgold tells the story from the viewpoint of the middle child, Miguel, who unlike his older brother, is too young to get everything he wants and unlike his younger brother, is too old to be happy with everything he has. Miguel has a secret wish to accompany the older family members when they herd the sheep to the summer grazing land in the Sangre de Cristo Mountains. With the help of San Ysidro, the patron saint of farmers, Miguel strives to make everyone see that he is ready for this responsibility. When he is allowed to accompany his elders on the drive and reaches the summer camp, he feels pride in his family's traditions and in his own accomplishments:

> In this place many men named Chavez had come. Those I could remember, and then my grandfather as well. And my father, Blas, and my uncles, Eli and Bonifacio. And my brothers, Blasito and Gabriel. And now, watching the shining world as I knew it would look when I came to this place, I stood, Miguel. (p. 244)

Krumgold visited the real Miguel and his family when the film was produced. Krumgold celebrated Saints' Day with them and observed all the important functions of a sheep ranch. He grew to know a closely knit family with a heritage going back to ancient Spain.

The eight-year-old in Nicholasa Mohr's *Felita* has lived in her Puerto Rican neighborhood of New York City for as long as she can remember. Mohr depicts the reasons for Felita's great love of her neighborhood. When Felita walks down the street, she can greet everyone by name. Her dearest friends live in the apartments on the block, and her grandmother, Abuelita, lives nearby. Conflict results when Felita's father decides that the family must move to a neighborhood where the schools are better and the threats of gang violence are fewer. In the new neighborhood, Anglo children call Felita names, tear her clothes, and tell her to move away. Felita's mother is shocked by the attitudes of the children and tells Felita that she must not hate, because that could make her as mean inside as the people who are attacking her:

> Instead you must learn to love yourself. This is more important. To love yourself and feel worthy, despite anything they might say against you and your family! That is the real victory. It will make you strong inside. (p. 39)

When violence against the family continues and no neighbors offer help, Felita's family moves back to the old neighborhood. Felita experiences anger, sorrow, and humiliation, but she finally regains her feeling of self-worth. With her grandmother's help, Felita returns to her happy, lively self, secure in the surroundings of her warm, loving family and friends. Perhaps the neighborhood and the people in *Felita* seem so real because Mohr herself was born and grew up in a similar neighborhood in New York City.

Mohr's *Going Home* provides additional adventures for Felita. Twelve-year-old Felita finds that she must face and overcome new person-against-self and person-against-society conflicts. During a trip to visit relatives in Puerto Rico, Felita finds that she is the object of attack because she is the gringa and not accepted by some of the Puerto Rican girls.

Readers may compare Mohr's *Going Home* setting with the setting in *Danza!*, by Lynn Hall. Hall's story takes place on a farm in Puerto Rico and emphasizes the interaction between Paulo, a Puerto Rican boy, and Danza, a Paso Fino stallion. Hall develops strong characters with believable emotions and actions.

Nonfiction

High-quality informational books about Hispanic Americans include books on history, geography, culture, and people. For example, several recently published books look at the discoveries about and the accomplishments of the ancient native cultures of the Western Hemisphere. Carolyn Meyer and Charles Gallenkamp's *The Mystery of the Ancient Maya* provides a thoroughly documented presentation of Mayan history and accomplishments. The writing style of the Gallenkamps creates interest in the subject, and early photographs and drawings add to the authenticity. Likewise, Anne Millard's *The Incas* emphasizes the achievements of ancient civilizations through carefully documented texts. Information about various geographic locations in Hispanic America are available in Pat Hargreaves's *The Caribbean and Gulf of Mexico,* Patricia Maloney Markun's *Central America and Panama,* and Edmund Lindop's *Cuba*.

While the majority of books about Spanish American celebrations for young children concentrate on the Christmas holidays, Cinco de Mayo, the commemoration of the Mexican army's defeat of the French army on May 5, 1862, is also a major holiday for Mexican Americans. June Behrens's *Fiesta!* is an informational book describing the modern-day celebration of this holiday. Photographs show a Mexican American festival in which music is played by a mariachi band, costumed dancers perform traditional Mexican dances, and young and old enjoy the celebration. Photographs also show children at school as they learn about and participate in the Cinco de Mayo activities. The book closes with a message from the author, who suggests that Americans of all heritages have become good amigos.

Information on the history and contributions of Puerto Ricans, Mexican Americans, and Cubans is discussed in Milton Meltzer's *The Hispanic Americans*. Meltzer explores Spanish influences resulting from exploration and colonization. Then he considers the development of the political, economic, and cultural status of Hispanic Americans. Meltzer's chapter on the harmful influences of racism provides thought-provoking discussion material for older children.

Two nonfiction books provide information about Hispanic children and families. Tricia Brown's *Hello, Amigos!* is a photo essay for younger children. It chronicles a special day in the life of six-year-old Frankie Valdez, a Mexican American boy whose family lives in San Francisco's Mission District. Fran Ortiz's photographs show the boy as he goes to school, attends classes, plays with friends, reacts to a classroom birthday cake, goes to the boys' club, and shares his birthday celebration with his family. In a book for older children, *Children of the Maya: A Guatemalan*

ISSUE

Are Children's Books Still Perpetuating Negative Stereotypes of Hispanic Americans?

LACK OF CHILDREN'S LITerature about Hispanic Americans and Hispanic cultures and the negative stereotypes found in the available literature are often criticized. In a 1981 issue of *Top of the News,* Isabel Schon[1] contends that the "overwhelming majority of recent books incessantly repeat the same stereotypes, misconceptions, and insensibilities that were prevalent in the books published in the 1960s and the early 1970s" (p. 79). Schon supports this contention by reviewing books published in 1980 and 1981 that develop the stereotypes of poverty, distorted and negative narratives about pre-Columbian history, and simplistic discussions of serious Latin American problems.

In this review, Schon contrasts two books about pre-Columbian cultures. The first, Brenda Ralph Lewis's *Growing Up in Aztec Times*[2] is cited as a book that perpetuates a lack of appreciation for the culture and uses stereotypic phrases, such as "behaved like barbarians" and "ferocious nature." In contrast, Elizabeth Gemming's *Lost City in the Clouds: The Discovery of Machu Picchu*[3] describes Hiram Bingham's discovery of the spectacular monuments and achievements of the Incas. This book portrays the achievements of a people and accurately records historical incidents. Schon ends her article with a plea that young readers in the United States be exposed to more distinguished books about Hispanic peoples and cultures rather than to books that perpetuate misconceptions and negative impressions.

Although Schon expressed her concern in the early 1980s, the concern continues. Donna Norton[4] analyzed various multicultural books according to both quality and retention in print. Norton discovered that many of the Hispanic books did not remain in print. This is of considerable concern because the few good books may not be available when parents, schools, and libraries wish to order them. In addition, the lack of books remains a top concern in the 1990s. The list of "Notable Children's Books, 1990" contains no examples of Hispanic literature.[5]

[1]Schon, Isabel. "Recent Detrimental and Distinguished Books About Hispanic People and Cultures." *Top of the News* 38 (Fall 1981): 79–85.

[2]Lewis, Brenda Ralph. *Growing Up in Aztec Times*. North Pomfret, Vt.: Batsford, 1981.

[3]Gemming, Elizabeth. *Lost City in the Clouds: The Discovery of Machu Picchu*. New York: Coward, 1980.

[4]Norton, Donna E. "The Rise and Fall of Ethnic Literature." National Conference of Teachers of English, Phoenix, Ariz., March 1986.

[5]The 1990 Children's Notable Book Committee. "Notable Children's Books, 1990," *Booklist* 86 (March 15, 1990): 1474, 1476, 1478, 1479.

Indian Odyssey, Brent Ashabranner portrays the hardships, struggles, and courage of a group of Guatemalan refugees who live in Indiantown, Florida. Paul Conklin's photographs show people involved in all aspects of their culture. The book includes a list of facts about Guatemala, a bibliography, and an index.

ASIAN AMERICAN LITERATURE

Few highly recommended books for children represent an Asian American perspective. Folktales from several Asian countries can help Asian American children and children from other ethnic backgrounds appreciate the traditional values and creative imagination of Asian peoples (see Chapter 6). Folktales, such as those found in *The Rainbow People,* retold by Laurence Yep, are especially good because they were collected from Chinese Americans living in California. The widest range of Asian American experiences in current children's literature is found in the works of Laurence Yep, who writes with sensitivity about Chinese Americans who, like himself, have lived in San Francisco, California. His characters overcome the stereotypes associated with literature about Asian Americans, and his stories integrate information about Chinese cultural heritage into the everyday lives of the people involved. Yep has received the International Reading Association's 1976 Children's Book Award and a Newbery Honor Book award.

Yep's *Dragonwings,* set in 1903 San Francisco, is based on a true incident in which a Chinese-American built and flew an airplane. The characters are strong people who retain their values and respect for their heritage while adjusting to a new country. The "town of the Tang people" is eight-year-old Moon Shadow's destination when he leaves his mother in the Middle Kingdom (China). He is filled with conflicting emotions when he first meets his father in the country some call the "Land of the Demons," and others call the "Land of the Golden Mountain." The Tang men in San Francisco give Moon Shadow clothing and things for the body, but his father gives him a marvelous, shimmering kite shaped like a butterfly, a gift designed to stir the soul. Moon Shadow joins his father in his dream to build a flying machine. Motivated by the work of Orville and Wilbur Wright, Moon Shadow's father builds an airplane, names it *Dragonwings,* and soars off the cliffs overlooking San Francisco Bay. Having achieved his dream, he decides to return to work so his wife can join him in America.

In the process of the story, Moon Shadow learns that his stereotype of the white demons is not always accurate. When he and his father move away from the Tang men's protection, Moon Shadow meets and talks to his first demon. Instead of being ten feet tall, with blue skin and a face covered with warts, she is a petite woman who is very friendly and considerate. As Moon Shadow and his father get to know this Anglo-Saxon woman and her family, they all gain respect for each other. When they share knowledge, the father concludes: "We see the same thing and yet find different truths."

Readers also discover that many stereotypes about Chinese Americans are incorrect. This book is especially strong in its coverage of Chinese traditions and beliefs. For example, readers learn about the great respect Chinese Americans feel for the aged and the dead. Family obligations do not end when a family member has retired or died. As Moon Shadow seeks to educate his white friend about the nature of dragons, readers discover traditional Chinese tales about a benevolent and wise dragon who is king among reptiles and emperor of animals. Readers realize the strong value of honor as they join the doubting Tang men who come to pull *Dragonwings* up the hill for its maiden voyage. They do not come to laugh at or

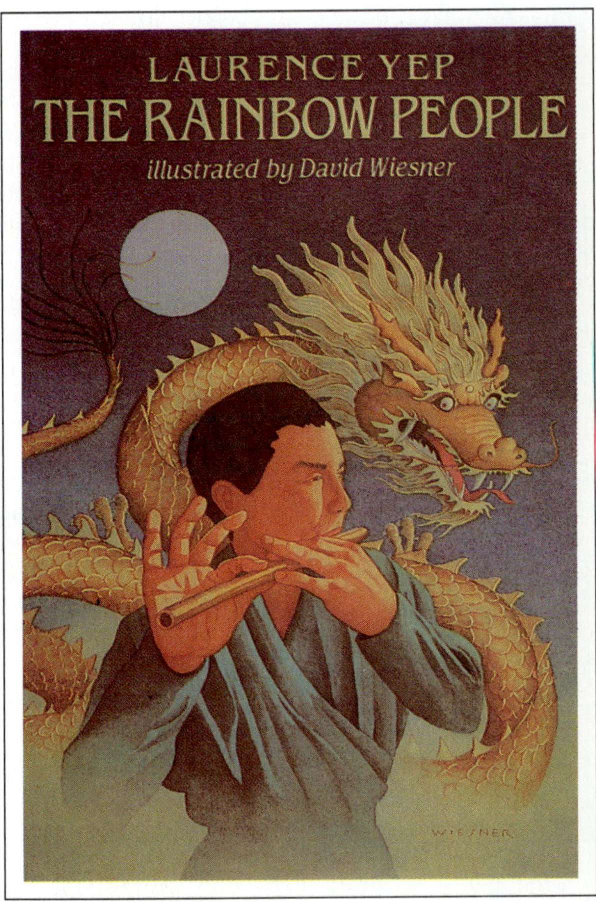

These tales were collected from Chinese Americans. (From *The Rainbow People* by Laurence Yep, illustrated by David Wiesner. Jacket copyright © 1989 by David Wiesner. Reprinted by permission of Harper & Row, Publishers.)

applaud a heroic venture. Instead, they come to share in their friend's perceived folly. If the Tang men laugh at Moon Shadow's father, they laugh at a strong body of people who stand beside each other through times of adversity and honor. Children who read this story learn about the contributions and struggles of the Chinese Americans and the prejudice that they still experience.

Other excellent books by Yep include *The Serpent's Children,* a story set in a time when China was battling both Manchu and British domination; *Child of the Owl,* in which young Casey discovers that she knows more about racehorses than about her own Chinese heritage; and *Sea Glass,* in which a boy deals with the unhappy experience of leaving Chinatown and learning to live in a non-Chinese community. The protagonists in all of these books are distinct and believable individuals, far from the conventional stereotypes about Asian people.

Paul Yee's *Tales from Gold Mountain: Stories of the Chinese in the New World* includes eight stories about Chinese immigrants in the United States and Canada. It is interesting to compare Yee's stories with the experiences developed in Yep's *Dragonwings* and the following book, written about contemporary experience.

Betty Bao Lord, the author of *In the Year of the Boar and Jackie Robinson,* created a story that reflects her own experiences and beliefs. Like her protagonist Shirley Temple Wong, Lord was a Chinese immigrant to America. Lord says:

> Many feel that loss of one's native culture is the price one must pay for becoming an American. I do not feel this way. I think we hyphenated Americans are doubly blessed. We can choose the best of both. (unnumbered)

In 1947, Shirley discovers that she can adore baseball, the Brooklyn Dodgers, and Jackie Robinson and still maintain the bond of family and the bond of culture.

In *Chin Chiang and the Dragon's Dance,* Ian Wallace creates a satisfactory conclusion for a person-against-self conflict. Young readers can understand Chin Chiang's conflict. He has practiced for and dreamed of dancing the dragon's dance on the first day of the Year of the Dragon. The time arrives, but he runs away because he fears he will not dance well enough to make his grandfather proud. With the help of a new friend, Chin Chiang discovers that his dream can come true. Full-page watercolor paintings capture the beauty of the celebration and depict Asian influences on the city of Vancouver.

The setting of Ann Nolan Clark's *To Stand Against the Wind* is wartime Vietnam. As the story begins, eleven-year-old Elm, a refugee living in America, is helping his grandmother, older sister, and uncle prepare for the traditional Day of the Ancestors, when those who have recently died are honored and remembered. As the head of the household, Elm must record the family history and tell his descendants about a country they may never know. His thoughts go back, and he remembers the beautiful countryside of the Mekong River delta that was his ancestors' home for uncounted centuries. Clark describes Elm's memories and compares them with the last time he saw his village, with its buildings burned, its ground bulldozed, and its dikes destroyed.

Elm remembers his father, who loved the land, and the American reporter who often visited them to learn about the Vietnamese. As the war progresses in Elm's memories, he recalls the male members of his family going off to fight, the reporter's description of the fall of Saigon, and the terrible day when his village was accidentally bombed by American planes. His mother, his father, his grandfather, his brother, and his friend the reporter are dead. Elm and his remaining family travel to America, where they are sponsored by a church group. This realistic story about a sad chapter in the life of a people concludes as Elm tries to express his memories. The only words that seem appropriate, however, are from a proverb that his father taught him: "It takes a strong man to stand against the wind" (p. 132).

Huynh Quang Nhuong's *The Land I Lost: Adventures of a Boy in Vietnam* is also a story of pre-war Vietnam. In this story, Nhoung takes readers back to a time of family and village experiences. Traditions and beliefs are important elements in the stories of both Nhuong and Clark.

Adjusting to a new culture and developing understanding of oneself and others are problems faced by many new Americans. Two books about Vietnamese children may help children who are adjusting to new situations and new cultures. Michele Surat's *Angel Child, Dragon Child* is a contemporary realistic story about a young Vietnamese girl's difficulties developing associations with her classmates after her family moves to the United States. In Marylois Dunn's *The Absolutely Perfect Horse,* both the adoption of a Vietnamese boy and the arrival of a new baby create family difficulties. In a book about a Chinese girl written for younger children, Ellen Levin's *I Hate English!*, the author explores personal conflicts as the heroine refuses to speak English after she arrives from Hong Kong. A sympathetic teacher helps the girl through these frustrating experiences. The plots, characters, and themes in these books may encourage discussion and promote understanding.

The importance of even small cultural artifacts, such as eating utensils, stimulates humorous plot developments in Ina R. Friedman's *How My Parents Learned to Eat*. Friedman suggests the solution to a problem on the first page of this picture storybook: "In our house, some days we eat with chopsticks and some days we eat with knives and forks. For me, it's natural" (p. 1, unnumbered). The remainder of the story tells how an American sailor courts a Japanese girl, and each secretly tries to learn the other's way of eating. The couple reaches a satisfactory compromise because each person still respects the other's culture.

The harsh consequences of war for Japanese Americans provide the subject of Daniel Davis's *Behind Barbed Wire: The Imprisonment of Japanese Americans During World War II*. In this informational book, Davis explores United States government actions against Japanese Americans during World War II. Davis focuses upon the denial of civil rights to an American minority and wonders if similar action could happen today.

If children are to learn about the cultural heritage and the contributions of Asian American people, as well as discover the similarities between Asian and non-Asian Americans, more high-quality literature about Asian Americans is needed. Because biographies and autobiographies are especially good for raising children's aspirations and enhancing understanding about the contributions and problems of individuals, multicultural literature programs need biographies of Asian Americans.

Suggested Activities for Adult Understanding of Multicultural Literature

- ☐ Collect several examples of children's literature written before 1960 that contain black characters. Compare these books with books written after 1975. Using the evaluative criteria for multicultural literature, compare the images of black people reflected in the literature of the two time periods.
- ☐ Bettye I. Latimer (20) surveyed trade books published in the mid-1960s and the 1970s and concluded that about 1 percent of the books involved black characters. Choose a recent publication date, and select books that have been chosen as the best books of the year by the School Library Journal Book Review Editors or some other group that selects outstanding books. Tabulate the number of books that are about Black Americans, Native Americans, Hispanic Americans, and Asian Americans. What percentage of the books selected as outstanding literature include characters who are members of minority groups?
- ☐ Many African tales have characteristics, such as repetition of words, that make them appealing for oral storytelling. Select several traditional African tales and identify the characteristics that make them appropriate for storytelling or oral reading.
- ☐ Choose one of the cultural groups discussed in the chapter. Read a number of myths, legends, and folktales from that culture. Summarize the traditional beliefs and values. Provide quotations from the tales to show the beliefs and values. Try to identify those same beliefs and values in other genres of literature depicting the same culture. What conclusions can you reach about the importance of traditional literature?
- ☐ Read James M. Taggart's "'Hansel and Gretel' in Spain and Mexico" (31). How are the versions the same? How are they different? How do the versions compare with the Grimms' version? Why are the versions different? How does each version relate to traditional cultural values?
- ☐ Choose an outstanding author, such as Virginia Hamilton or Laurence Yep, and read several books by that author. What makes the plot and the characters memorable? What are the themes in the writer's work? Is there a common theme throughout the writing?
- ☐ With a group of your peers, choose an area of literature discussed in this chapter. Select five books that develop the values of multicultural literature discussed in this chapter. Also select five books that do not develop the same values. Share the books and your rationales for selecting them with the rest of the class.

- ☐ Compare the characterizations of Native Americans in children's literature published before 1960 with the characterizations of Native Americans in books published after 1975. How would readers describe Native Americans, if this literature were their only contact with Native Americans? Has there been a change in characterizations between the literature of the two periods?
- ☐ The Children's Literature Review Board does not recommend several books listed in Betty I. Latimer's *Starting Out Right: Choosing Books About Black People for Young Children* (19) because of stereotypes, unacceptable values, or terms used in relationship to the characters. Read one of these books, such as David Arkin's *Black and White,* Florine Robinson's *Ed and Ted,* Shirley Burden's *I Wonder Why,* Anco Surany's *Monsieur Jolicoeur's Umbrella,* May Justus's *New Boy in School,* or William Pappas's *No Mules*. Are the review board's recommendations accurate in your opinion? Why or why not?
- ☐ Several classics, or old standards, in children's literature have been praised by some but criticized by others. In the area of literature referring to black experiences, Marguerite De Angeli's *Bright April* has been criticized because of the way April is subjected to prejudice and because of the prescribed formula for success that the story implies. Likewise, Ingrid and Edgar D'Aulaire's *Abraham Lincoln* has been criticized for overromanticizing Lincoln's life and depicting both black and Native American people as the "white man's burden." Read one of these books. Discuss your reactions with your peers.

References

1 Banfield, Beryle. "Racism in Children's Books: An Afro-American Perspective." In *The Black American in Books for Children: Readings in Racism,* edited by Donnarae MacCann and Gloria Woodard. Metuchen, N.J.: Scarecrow, 1985.

2 Bierhorst, John, ed. *The Red Swan: Myths and Tales of the American Indians*. New York: Farrar, Straus & Giroux, 1976.

3 Broderick, Dorothy May. *The Image of the Black in Popular and Recommended American Juvenile Fiction, 1827–1967*. New York: Columbia University, 1971. University Microfilm No. 71–4090.

4 Byler, Mary Gloyne. "American Indian Authors for Young Readers." In *Cultural Conformity in Books for Children,* edited by Donnarae MacCann and Gloria Woodard. Metuchen, N.J.: Scarecrow, 1977.

5 Carlson, Julia Ann. *A Comparison of the Treatment of the Negro in Children's Literature in the Periods 1929–1938 and 1959–1968*. Storrs, Conn.: University of Connecticut, 1969. University Microfilm No. 70–1245.

6 Charpenel, Mauricio. "Literature About Mexican American Children." College Station, Tex.: Texas A&M University, Children's Literature Conference, 1980.

7 Council on Interracial Books for Children. "Chicano Culture in Children's Literature: Stereotypes, Distortions and Omissions." In *Cultural Conformity in Books for Children,* edited by Donnarae MacCann and Gloria Woodard. Metuchen, N.J.: Scarecrow, 1977.

8 Council on Interracial Books for Children. "Criteria for Analyzing Books on Asian Americans." In *Cultural Conformity in Books for Children,* edited by Donnarae MacCann and Gloria Woodard. Metuchen, N.J.: Scarecrow, 1977.

9 Crowley, Daniel. Foreword to *"On Another Day. . ." Tales Told Among the Nkundo of Zaire,* collected by Mabel Ross and Barbara Walker. Hamden, Conn.: Archon, 1979.

10 Faulkner, William J. *The Days When the Animals Talked*. Illustrated by Troy Howell. Chicago: Follett, 1977.

11 Frobenius, Leo, and Douglas Fox. *African Genesis*. Berkeley, Calif.: Turtle Island for the Netzahualcoyal Historical Society, 1983.

12 Granstrom, Jane, and Anita Silvey. "A Call for Help: Exploring the Black Experience in Children's Books." In *Cultural Conformity in Books for Children,* edited by Donnarae MacCann and Gloria Woodard. Metuchen, N.J.: Scarecrow, 1977.

13 Greenfield, Eloise. "Writing for Children—A Joy and a Responsibility." In *The Black American in Books for Children: Readings in Racism,* edited by Donnarae MacCann and Gloria Woodard. Metuchen, N.J.: Scarecrow, 1985.

14 Hamilton, Virginia. *The People Could Fly: American Black Folktales*. New York: Knopf, 1985.

15 Hanson, W. D., and M. O. Eisenbise. *Human Behavior and American Indians*. Rockville, Md.: National Institute of Mental Health, 1983. ERIC Document Reproduction Service, ED 231-589.

16 Haviland, Virginia. *North American Legends*. New York: Collins, 1979.

17 Herbst, Laura. "That's One Good Indian: Unacceptable Images in Children's Novels." In *Cultural Conformity in Books for Children,* edited by Donnarae MacCann and Gloria Woodard. Metuchen, N.J.: Scarecrow, 1977.

18 Kun-yu, Bu. "Between Two Cultures." *Social Education* 52 (September 1988): 378–383.

19 Latimer, Bettye I. *Starting Out Right: Choosing Books About Black People for Young Children*. Madison, Wis.: Wisconsin Department of Public Instruction, 1972, Bulletin No. 2314.

20 Latimer, Bettye I. "Telegraphing Messages to Children About Minorities." *The Reading Teacher* 30 (November 1976): 151–156.

21 Lewis, Rena, and Donald Doorlag. *Teaching Special Students in the Mainstream*. 2d ed. Columbus, Ohio: Merrill, 1987.

22 Morgan, Betty M. *An Investigation of Children's Books Containing Characters from Selected Minority Groups Based on Specified Criteria*. Carbondale, Ill.. Southern Illinois University, 1973. University Microfilm No. 74–6232.

23 Norton, Donna E. "The Expansion and Evaluation of a Multi-Ethnic Reading/Language Arts Program Designed for 5th, 6th, 7th, and 8th Grade Children." Meadows Foundation Grant No. 55614, A Three Year Longitudinal Study, Texas A&M University, 1984–1987.

24 Paredes, Américo. *Folktales of Mexico*. Chicago: University of Chicago Press, 1970.

25 Piper, David. "Language Growth in the Multiethnic Classroom." *Language Arts* 63 (January 1986): 23–26.

26 Ross, A. C., and D. Brave Eagle. *Value Orientation—A Strategy for Removing Barriers*. Denver, Colo.: Coalition of Indian Controlled School Boards, Inc., 1975. ERIC Document Reproduction, ED 125-811.

27 Ross, Mabel, and Barbara Walker. *"On Another Day. . ." Tales Told Among the Nkundo of Zaire*. Hamden, Conn.: Archon, 1979.

28 Sealey, D. Bruce. "Measuring the Multicultural Quotient of a School." *TESL Canada Journal/Revue TESL Du Canada* 1 (March 1984): 21–28.

29 Spang, A. "Counseling the Indian." *Journal of American Indian Education* 5 (1965): 10–15.

30 Stensland, Anna Lee. *Literature by and About the American Indian*. Urbana Ill.: National Council of Teachers of English, 1979.

31 Taggart, James M. "'Hansel and Gretel' in Spain and Mexico." *Journal of American Folklore* 99 (1986): 435–460.

32 Tway, Eileen. "Dimensions of Multicultural Literature for Children." In *Children's Literature: Resource for the Classroom,* edited by Masha Kabakow Rudman. Christopher-Gordon, 1989, 109–138.

EDUCATORS ARE CONCERNED ABOUT THE quality and the quantity of multicultural materials available for sharing with children. They are also concerned about the teaching strategies used in developing understanding of and positive attitudes toward various cultural groups. Across the decades, educators have called for more involvement with multicultural concepts. For example, in the 1970s, Gwendolyn Baker (2) argued that little planning had been given to the process of multicultural education. She maintained that both college students and teachers required training in the concepts to be developed, the objectives to be achieved, the knowledge about various cultures, and the integration of multicultural concepts at all levels of education.

By 1989, other educators were equally critical of the quality of multicultural education. For example, Cathy Roller (29) argued, "[R]eading instruction as presently delivered has, probably unintentionally, been instrumental in perpetuating and maintaining our class- and race-stratified society" (p. 492). Educators such as D. Bruce Sealey (31) were also critical of current instructional practices. They emphasized that instruction should encourage students to accept and be sensitive to cultural diversity, to understand that similar values frequently underlie different customs, to have quality contact with people from other cultures, and to role-play experiences in order to involve students with other cultures.

Many educators during the 1980s recommended using multicultural literature and literature-related activities to improve children's understandings. For example, Eileen Tway (35) maintained that multicultural literature and literature-related activities are essential in the classroom because they meet the needs of children and help them understand themselves and others. Likewise, David Piper (27) recommended using the traditional stories and fables from various cultural sources and creating awareness of different language and cultural backgrounds.

This section considers many types of activities that can heighten the positive values of excellent multicultural literature. Many of the teaching models and instructional ideas evolved from Donna Norton's (19–22) research experiences during the past ten years. These experiences included different approaches with undergraduate and graduate classes, research in elementary and middle school classes, multicultural literature evaluations, and multicultural-literature-curriculum and in-service activities development.

Involving Children in Multicultural Literature

DEVELOPING AN APPRECIATION FOR BLACK AMERICAN CULTURE

DEVELOPING AN APPRECIATION FOR NATIVE AMERICAN CULTURE

DEVELOPING AN APPRECIATION FOR HISPANIC AMERICAN CULTURE

DEVELOPING AN APPRECIATION FOR ASIAN AMERICAN CULTURE

RECOGNIZING SIMILARITIES

Research and experience as well as a search through the scholarly literature support a sequence of study in multicultural literature that proceeds from the ancient literature of a culture to the contemporary literature. For example, both Franchot Ballinger (3) and Michael Dorris (11) recommend a sequence of study of Native American literature that begins with a study of broad oral traditions, narrows to specific tribal experiences as expressed in mythology, continues with biographical and autobiographical study of specific cultural areas, and concludes with a study of contemporary Native American literature. Dorris supports this sequence because:

> To investigate any Native American literature one must examine its evolution and development through time; one must know something of the language—its rules, its implied world view—of its creation; one must know something of the culture's history of contacts with other peoples, both Native American and Euro-American; and one must know something of the modern social setting of the culture. (p. 157)

The sequence of study used in Chart 11–1 modifies the Ballinger and Dorris models and emphasizes literature written for children. This study is a five-phase approach. It begins with a broad awareness of myths, legends, and folktales from one cultural group (for example, Native American). Then, it narrows to the myths, legends, and folktales of one or two tribal or cultural areas (for example, Native American myths and legends from the Plains Indians or Indians of the Northwest Coast). It proceeds to autobiographies, biographies, and other informational literature about an

CHART 11–1
Sequence for multicultural literature study

Phase I: Traditional Literature (Generalizations and Broad Views)

A. Identify distinctions among folktales, myths, and legends.
B. Identify ancient stories that have common features and that are found in many regions.
C. Identify types of stories that dominate a subject.
D. Summarize the nature of oral language, the role of traditional literature, the role of an audience, and the literary style.

Phase II: Traditional Tales from One Area (Narrower View)

A. Analyze traditional myths and other story types and compare findings with those in Phase I.
B. Analyze and identify values, beliefs, and themes in the traditional tales of one region.

Phase III: Historical Nonfiction

A. Analyze nonfiction for the values, beliefs, and themes identified in traditional literature.
B. Compare adult autobiographies and children's biographies (if possible).
C. Compare information in historical documents with autobiographies and biographies.

Phase IV: Historical Fiction

A. Evaluate historical fiction according to the authenticity of the conflicts, characterizations, settings, themes, language, and traditional beliefs and values.
B. Search for the role of traditional literature in historical fiction.
C. Compare historical fiction with autobiographies, biographies, and historical information.

Phase V: Contemporary Literature

A. Analyze the inclusion of any beliefs and values identified in traditional literature and nonfictional literature
B. Analyze contemporary characterizations and conflicts.
C. Analyze the themes and look for threads that cross the literature.

earlier time in history, continues with historical fiction, and concludes with literature written for children by authors whose work represents that cultural group and contemporary time.

Follow the total sequence with one cultural group before proceeding to another cultural group. As you work through each phase, you are developing understandings that build upon each other. For example, after students can identify the traditional values and beliefs of the people as represented in their folktales, myths, and legends, they will find it easier to identify values and beliefs in historical nonfiction. They can use the knowledge gained from analyzing historical nonfiction, including autobiographies and biographies, to evaluate the appropriateness and authenticity of historical fiction and contemporary literature. As you proceed through the study, make cross-cultural comparisons. This series of activities can easily take the form of a unit.

DEVELOPING AN APPRECIATION FOR BLACK AMERICAN CULTURE

As educators help students to develop an appreciation of the culture of Black Americans, they may encourage the students to read a number of literature selections. Students can appreciate and understand the various genres of literature. Educators may use the following activities to develop higher comprehension abilities in literature-based reading programs and to add understanding to other areas of the curriculum, such as social studies.

Phase One: Traditional Literature

Before beginning a study of the folktales, myths, and legends from Africa, discuss the importance of the oral tradition in transmitting the beliefs and values of people. Make sure that students know the background of the oral tradition and that tales were handed down for many generations before they were transcribed into written form. Also show and discuss a map of the African continent so that students understand the diversity of locations for folklore.

To help students understand the power and importance of using oral language to transmit cultural information, begin with a study of African folklore. Emphasize the power of oral storytellers and the impact of the language. Share with students that ancient Africans depended on oral storytellers to keep alive the cultural past. Storytellers chanted and sang, interacted with the audience, and acted out story elements. The art of storytelling was so highly valued that storytelling competitions were held to encourage the most vivid and entertaining stories. Tell the students that they will be listening to oral storytellers, identifying oral storytelling styles, and creating their own storytelling experiences.

Storytelling. Begin this enjoyable study by investigating how authentic storytellers selected their stories, what story openings were found in African folklore, what styles were common in storytelling, and how storytellers ended their stories.

Story Selections. Descriptions of storytellers from West Africa provide ideas for selecting a story from a number of possibilities. During her travels through Africa in the nineteenth century, Mary Kingsley (17) discovered story minstrels who carried nets resembling fishing nets that contained such objects as bones, feathers, and china bits. When a listener chose an object, the storyteller would tell a story about it. Another interesting technique required storytellers to wear hats with articles suspended from the brims. A listener again would select an intriguing item, and the story would begin.

Teachers and librarians can easily use these techniques to help children select the story or stories to hear and to stimulate their interest. Cardboard cutouts, miniature objects, or real things that suggest a character or animal in a story can be chosen. Chart 11–2 gives examples of objects and the stories they represent.

Story Openings. Storytellers from several African countries introduce stories by calling out sentences that elicit responses by the audiences. For example, Philip Noss (23) relates that the following is a common story starter from Cameroon:

Storyteller: Listen to a tale! Listen to a tale!
Audience: A tale for fun, for fun.
Your throat is a gong, your body a locust; bring it here for me to roast!
Storyteller: Children, listen to a tale,
a tale for fun, for fun.

If an adult or a child prefers to use an opening statement and response in an African language, the following Hausa opening from Nigeria, identified by A. J. Tremearne (34), can be used:

Storyteller: Ga ta, ga ta nan.
(See it, see it here.)

CHART 11–2
Introducing traditional tales with objects

	Object	Association	Traditional Tales
1	A flower	A flower is a gift of beauty.	Jan Carew, *The Third Gift*
2	A cardboard rainbow	Pia is trying to bring harmony to human world, while his mother weaves curtains from rainbows.	Jan Carew, *Children of the Sun*
3	A rabbit and a hut	Someone has taken possession of rabbit's house.	Verna Aardema, *Who's in Rabbit's House?*
4	A mosquito	The mosquito was not always noisy.	Verna Aardema, *Why Mosquitoes Buzz in People's Ears*
5	A crab	Pride causes Crab to be left without a head.	Barbara Knutson, *Why the Crab Has No Head*
6	A box containing stories	How did stories come to earth?	Gail Haley, *A Story, A Story*
7	Round and square houses	Why do men live in square houses and women live in round houses?	Ann Grifalconi, *The Village of Round and Square Houses*

Audience: Ta zo, muii.
(Let it come, for us to hear.)

If the stories are from the West Indies, one of the introductions identified by Elsie Clews Parsons (25) would be appropriate:

(1) Once upon a time, a very good time
Not my time, nor your time, old people's time
(2) Once upon a time, a very good time
Monkey chew tobacco and spit white lime

These openings can be used with any of the traditional African tales previously described, or they can be used to introduce a series of folktales. For example, Verna Aardema's humorous *Who's in Rabbit's House* seems particularly appropriate for an introduction stressing a tale for fun. An enjoyable series of folktales might include "why" tales such as Aardema's *Why Mosquitoes Buzz in People's Ears* and Ashley Bryan's *The Cat's Purr* and "Why Frog and Snake Never Play Together" in *Beat the Story-Drum, Pum-Pum*. Another series might include hero or trickster tales.

Storytelling Styles. Listening to Ashley Bryan's tape, *The Dancing Granny and Other African Stories* (7), is an excellent way to introduce storytelling styles. Students may listen to the tape and then describe this very vivid style. Have them search other sources for descriptions of storytelling styles. They will discover that the style of the traditional African storyteller, still found in many African countries today, can be characterized as a lively mixture of mimicking dialogue, body action, audience participation, and rhythm. Storytellers mimic the sounds of animals, change their voices to characterize both animal and human characters, develop dialogue, and encourage their listeners to interact with the story. Usually, they also add musical accompaniment with drums or other rhythm and string instruments such as thumb pianos. Anne Pellowski (26) says that music and rhythm are important additions to African storytellers:

> Taken as a whole, all storytelling in Africa, whether folk, religious, or bardic, whether in prose or poetry, seems to be strongly influenced by music and rhythm. It is rare to find stories that do not have some rhythmical or musical interlude or accompaniment, using either the voice, body parts, or special instruments. (p. 116)

Because children enjoy interacting with storytellers and interpreting tempos with drums or other musical instruments, such additions to storytelling can increase appreciation and understanding of traditional African tales. Stories such as Aardema's *Why Mosquitoes Buzz in People's Ears* and *Who's in Rabbit's House?,* with their strong oral language patterns and varied animal characterizations, can effectively introduce traditional African style.

Story Endings. Just as African storytellers use interesting story beginnings, they also often use certain types of story endings. If the story was dramatic, it could end with the Hausa *Suka zona* (they remained) or the Angolan *Mahezu* (finished).

If the story was an obvious exaggeration from the West Indies, the storyteller might choose this ending:

> Chase the rooster and catch the hen
> I'll never tell a lie like that again.

Storytellers from the West Indies also provide an appropriate ending for humorous folktales:

> They lived in peace, they died in peace
> And they were buried in a pot of candle grease.

A folktale from the West Indies, such as Ashley Bryan's retelling of *Turtle Knows Your Name,* would be appropriate. Bryan's rhythmic language makes this tale an enjoyable choice for an oral experience.

Children enjoy recreating the atmosphere of traditional African tales. Black American children take special pride in the stories and the exciting ways they can be presented to an audience. Both adults and children can tell them and then discuss the traditional African approaches to storytelling and ways that these approaches enhanced the enjoyment for both storyteller and listeners. After the stories are told, students may read them constantly. Donna Norton (19) found that elementary children enjoy the folktales and their enrichment through traditional means of storytelling. Conclude by asking students to identify and summarize the oral language styles that are found in traditional African folklore.

Values and Beliefs. After students have considered the impact of the language on the folklore of Africa, ask them to read numerous examples of folklore from Africa to identify values and beliefs found in the tales. Several approaches may be used to help students identify values and beliefs. Because themes are closely related to values and beliefs, students may search for themes in the folklore. Asking students to provide support for the themes helps them develop higher comprehension and cognitive skills as they provide evidence for their statements.

In the following example, the themes in John Steptoe's *Mufaro's Beautiful Daughters: An African Tale* also show values and beliefs. First, help students search for themes by asking them to listen to or to read the story and ask themselves: What is the author trying to tell me that would make a difference in my life? How do I know that the author is telling me _____? Remind the students that proof of theme may include many elements in the story, such as the characters' actions, the characters' thoughts, the interaction of characters as shown through dialogue, the rewards and punishments that end the story, a statement of theme by the author, and illustrations.

Next, read *Mufaro's Beautiful Daughters* as students listen to answer the first question: What is the author trying to tell me that would make a difference in my life? After you complete the story, ask the students to provide at least two important themes in this book. They may say, for example, greed and selfishness are harmful, or bad, personal characteristics and that kindness and generosity are beneficial, or good, personal characteristics. The wording of these themes will differ depending on the age level of the students.

Reread *Mufaro's Beautiful Daughters,* asking the students to identify support for each theme within the tale. Remind them of the different ways that authors develop and support a theme. As support for "greed and selfishness are harmful personal characteristics," students may identify some of the following examples:

1 Illustrations show bad-tempered girl (illustrations).
2 Manyara tries to trick her sister so only Manyara will visit the king (actions).
3 Greed causes Manyara to leave the village secretly (actions).
4 Manyara refuses to give a hungry boy food and responds, "I have brought only enough for myself" (actions and dialogue).
5 Manyara shows anger when she says, "Out of my way, boy!" (actions and dialogue).
6 Manyara refuses to take advice from an older woman (actions that show disrespect for older people).
7 Manyara sees a monster snake with five heads (punishment as part of the ending).
8 Manyara becomes a servant to her sister, the queen (punishment as part of the ending).
9 Greed is punished (represented by the ending).

As support for "kindness and generosity are beneficial personal characteristics," students may identify some of the following examples:

1 Nyasha sings while she works, causing people to think that her singing makes the plants bountiful (actions).
2 Nyasha is kind to a garden snake (actions).

3 Nyasha does not complain because she is considerate of her father's feelings (actions and the author tells us).
4 Illustrations show Nyasha as a happy, thoughtful girl (illustrations).
5 Nyasha gives food to a hungry boy; she says, "You must be hungry," . . .and handed him a yam she had brought for her lunch (actions and dialogue).
6 Nyasha takes advice from the older woman (actions show respect for older people).
7 Nyasha bravely approaches the chamber in which she is to meet the king (actions).
8 Nyasha sees a little snake and then the king (reward as part of the ending).
9 Nyasha proves herself to be both most worthy and most beautiful (ending).
10 Kindness and generosity are rewarded as Nyasha becomes queen (reward as ending).

After completing this activity, ask the students to identify any additional values and beliefs that they discovered. For example, in addition to admiring generosity and kindness and disrespecting greed and selfishness, the African people represented in this tale value the advice of older people and consider worthiness to be more important than beauty. Again, students should support these values and beliefs with evidence from the tale.

Charting answers to questions related to folk characteristics is another technique that helps students identify values in folklore (21). First, discuss various ways in which students can identify traditional values found in folklore. For example, they can read the folklore to discover answers to each of the following questions:

1 What reward or rewards are desired?
2 What actions are rewarded or admired?
3 What actions are punished or despised?
4 What rewards are given to the heroes, the heroines, or the great people in the stories?
5 What are the personal characteristics of the heroes, the heroines, or the great people in the stories?

Next, print each of these questions on a chart. Allow room to include several African tales. When students read various African tales, have them use the chart to identify and discuss traditional values and beliefs.

Introduce the first book on the chart, Gail Haley's *A Story, a Story*. It is advisable to complete the first example together. Ask the students to listen carefully so that they will be able to answer the questions and identify the values on the chart. After reading *A Story, a Story* aloud, ask the students to identify the answers to the questions and place them on the proper location on the chart. Chart 11–3 shows the results of this activity using *A Story, a Story* and Jan Carew's *The Third Gift* and *Children of the Sun*. For the additional books in this example, use a similar listening, listing, and discussing procedure, or have the students read these books independently and then discuss their results.

After each reading activity, discuss the values and beliefs that are developed in the story. Ask the students to notice ways that some of the values and beliefs express the importance of oral language discussed earlier. Ask the students to notice how the theme in *Mufaro's Beautiful Daughters: An African Tale* is similar to that in *Children of the Sun*. Read as many African tales as possible to find additional values and beliefs and to discover common values and beliefs in various folklore selections.

Notice that within these tales are many trickster tales. Tricksters may win or lose. Explain to students that in folklore, trickery is often considered necessary to create a balance. Consequently, students should consider what forces are out of balance. Trickster tales, such as the Ananse tales, are among the most enjoyable folktales from Africa. Consequently, a trickster characters festival allows children to extend, summarize, and apply their knowledge of language, values, and beliefs in folklore.

Trickster Characters Festival. Many folktales from West Africa include a character called Ananse, the spider, or Kwaku (Uncle) Ananse. He is the main hero in a series of stories from the Ashanti people. In these stories, animals speak and act as humans. These stories usually teach a moral or account for the origin of things. According to Harold Courlander (10), Ananse is also a cultural hero. Ananse is often a buffoon, who is endlessly preoccupied with outwitting the creatures of the field and forest, people, and even the deities. He is an adversary in endless contests with his community. He is shown with a range of personalities: sympathetic, wise, cunning, predatory, greedy, gluttonous, and unscrupulous. Moral teachings in many of his defeats suggest that he was humiliated or punished because of unacceptable behavior. As a cultural hero, some of his

CHART 11–3
Values identified in African folklore

Questions for Values	A Story, a Story	The Third Gift	Children of The Sun
What reward is desired?	Stories from the powerful sky god	The gift of wonders for people threatened with extinction	Peace and harmony
What actions are rewarded or admired?	Outwitting the leopard, the hornet, and the fairy	Climbing the highest mountain and using gifts wisely	Being good and searching for peace and harmony
What actions are punished or despised?	—	—	Disobeying one's father, haughtiness, and rebelliousness
What rewards are given to heroes, heroines, or great people?	Oral stories to delight the people	The gifts of work, beauty, and imagination, as well as leadership of people	Patience and life
What are the personal characteristics of heroes, heroines, or great people?	Intelligence and verbal ability (in the small old man)	Verbal ability (in poets and bards), imagination (in creators), as well as intelligence and the desire to serve (in leaders)	Goodness, patience, the desire to serve, and humanity

escapades result in creating a natural phenomenon, such as the moon, or beginning institutions, traditions, or customs. Ananse has frequent encounters with the Sky God, Nyame, and the earth deity, Aberewa.

According to Gerald McDermott, in his introduction to *Anansi the Spider: A Tale from the Ashanti,* the Ashanti people have a long-established culture:

> The Ashanti have had a federation, a highly organized society, for over four hundred years. Still, today as long ago, the Ashanti are superb artisans. They excel as makers of fine metal work and as weavers of beautiful silk fabric. Into this fabric they weave the rich symbols of their art and folklore—Sun, Moon, Creation, Universe, the Web of the Cosmos, and Anansi, the Spider. (p. i)*

Because the Ananse tales and Ashanti proverbs incorporate many traditional African values—wit, strength, verbal ability, achievement, and a distinctive personality—they are excellent means of stimulating discussions and enjoyment. The following ideas were developed with fourth-grade students who enjoyed the Ananse and other trickster stories so much that they created a festival and shared some of the exciting activities, artwork, creative writing, and knowledge of Ashanti culture.

The first Ananse tale shared with the group was Gail E. Haley's *A Story, a Story* (the book that created the interest in reading additional Ananse stories), which tells how the spider stories of Africa were created. After reading the story, the children talked about the importance of storytelling, the beauty of the repetitive language that allowed them to visualize an Ananse who was "so small, so small, so small" and a leopard so powerful that he had to be tied "by his foot, by his foot, by his foot, by his foot." The teacher shared the fact that African storytellers often repeated words to make them stronger. The class also discussed the descriptive language connected with the names of animals, such as the leopard "of-the-terrible-teeth." Finally, they discussed the wit, verbal ability, and trickery suggested by Ananse's actions in trapping the animals and acquiring the box of stories from Nyame, the Sun God.

The next series of stories shared were those in Joyce Cooper Arkhurst's *The Adventures of Spider: West African Folktales*. The book was introduced in this way:

*Variant spellings (*Ananse* or *Anansi*) exist for this character.

In the book, *A Story, a Story,* you learned how Ananse was given all the stories by the Sky God. This book contains some of the stories that are said to have been stories of Ananse the spider. In this book, however, he is just called Spider.

Then, the teacher wrote on the chalkboard the titles of the Ananse stories found in the book:

"How Spider Got a Thin Waist"
"Why Spiders Live in Ceilings"
"How Spider Got a Bald Head"
"How Spider Helped a Fisherman"
"Why Spiders Live in Dark Corners"
"How the World Got Wisdom"

After the children discussed the probable contents of the listed stories and decided which story they wanted to share through dramatization or other visual approach, the teacher divided the class into five groups of five children. Methods of dramatizing the stories included pantomime, a puppet show, a play, a reader's theater, a flannelboard story, and a box movie theater. The children in each group read their stories (each group read the stories orally because there were not enough books for each child to have a copy) and decided how they would share their stories with their audience. The children's activities for the next few class sessions revolved around preparing puppets, flannelboard characters, and so forth, and practicing the stories. The teacher went from group to group, giving assistance when required. Each group presented its story to the rest of the class. After each presentation, the teacher led a discussion in which the children considered the characters, the moral suggested, and the traditional values found in the story. Gerald McDermott's *Anansi the Spider: A Tale from the Ashanti* stimulated the creation of a mural that depicted the six wondrous deeds performed by Ananse's sons—See Trouble, Road Builder, River Drinker, Game Skinner, Stone Thrower, and Cushion—as they tried to save their father from a terrible danger.

In order to show where the Ananse tales originated, the children made a large map of Africa and identified the areas in West Africa where the Ashanti live. They also showed the movement of the tales from Africa to America. During the discussion of the movement of Ashanti traditions to the United States, several children showed an interest in learning more about these people.

The children shared Margaret Musgrove's *Ashanti to Zulu: African Traditions* in order to observe the cultures of the various African peoples and compare them with the Ashanti culture. The children described what they saw in each picture: beautiful designs in fabrics, intricate jewelry, clothing, animals, artifacts, and characteristics of geography. They also shared pictures from other sources.

The teacher chose Ashanti proverbs from Harold Courlander's *A Treasury of African Folklore* (10). The teacher led a discussion, and the children talked about the fact that many cultures have wise sayings that have been passed down from generation to generation. They listed some of the proverbs they knew and discussed the meaning of each. Then the teacher introduced some Ashanti proverbs:

Only birds of the same kind gather together.
Regrets are useless.
A man with no friends has no one to help him up.

Finally, the teacher had the students discuss the meanings of the Ashanti proverbs and list similar proverbs from their own families.

The children also wrote their own Ananse stories. They read Ananse stories from other African peoples, such as "The Foolish Boy" in Ashley Bryan's *Lion and the Ostrich Chicks, and Other African Folk Tales* (Hausa tales), and compared these Ananse stories to the stories they had read earlier. In addition, the children read other African trickster tales, such as those found in Bryan's *Lion and the Ostrich Chicks,* and they compared the roles of such trickster characters as Hare to Ananse. (Stories with a rabbit character as the trickster are important because they are similar to Brer Rabbit in the American tales read during Phase Two.)

The children took part in a creative dramatics activity motivated by the trickster Frog in Verna Aardema's Masai tale *Who's in Rabbit's House?* They also compared contemporary writings about animal characters that are given human characterizations with the Ananse characters. Examples include Snoopy and Woodstock in the "Peanuts" cartoons, Heathcliff, and Winnie-the-Pooh.

On the day of the festival, the children invited their parents into a room decorated with their Ashanti projects. The parents observed the creative dramatizations, read the writings, saw the artwork, and listened to other information that the children had discovered about the Ashanti culture, Ananse the Spider, and tricksters.

Before leaving Phase One, teachers may review discoveries about oral storytelling and summarize the values and beliefs that they and the students discovered in reading African folklore.

Phase Two: Folklore of the American South

Black American folktales and legends include many of the values and characteristics of the African tales. The resulting tales combine a past culture, a new environment, and new experiences. Many of the traditional values, including love for language, respect for wit, hospitality, generosity, gratitude, and reverence for elderly people, are also found in Black American folklore. During Phase Two, teachers may identify the philosophy, values, and beliefs of the people as reflected in Black American folklore. Students can identify similarities between the African folklore and the American folklore. Teachers may also help students identify any differences that reflect the new environment and experiences.

Begin the study by sharing and discussing the stories found in Virginia Hamilton's *The People Could Fly: American Black Folktales*. Identify the types of tales, such as animal tales, supernatural tales, and slave tales of freedom. As you continue your study, encourage your students to identify values, beliefs, and language styles. Use the same techniques that encouraged students to search for values, beliefs, and themes in African folklore. For example, trace themes in several Black American folktales and compare those themes with the themes found in African folklore. Develop charts that are similar to Chart 11–3. Analyze numerous Black American folktales and compare the values. Read Black American folktales aloud. Are there any similarities in language style? Identify stories that have similar story structures and discuss the similarities but also consider why there might be differences. In addition to Hamilton's book, the following texts are excellent sources of tales: Julius Lester's *The Tales of Uncle Remus: The Adventures of Brer Rabbit, More Tales of Uncle Remus: Further Adventures of Brer Rabbit, His Friends, Enemies, and Others,* and *The Knee-High Man and Other Tales;* Van Dyke Parks's adaptation of Joel Chandler Harris's tales in *Jump! The Adventures of Brer Rabbit* and *Jump Again! More Adventures of Brer Rabbit;* Patricia McKissack's *Flossie & the Fox;* Priscilla Jaquith's *Bo Rabbit Smart for True;* and Steve Sanfield's *The Adventures of High John the Conqueror.*

Activities developed around John Henry, the tall tale hero, provide opportunities for creative dramatizations, discussions about values, learning about history, and writing. As a poem, a song, or a longer narrative, the tale can stimulate many creative activities. Because there are several versions of the John Henry tale, compare the books, poem, and song. Is the story the same in each version? Are the illustrations alike or different? Which version is the most effective? Why?

Teachers have used the tale in its various forms with children in all of the elementary grades. In the lower grades, children can listen to the story and discuss the large illustrations in the picture book *John Henry,* by Ezra Jack Keats. The language of the book makes pleasant listening while children discover that American folk heroes are from different ethnic backgrounds. Through the story and pictures, children can gain an understanding of tall tales and the actions that heroes are supposed to perform. Discuss other folk heroes, such as Davy Crockett and Paul Bunyan. Have the children compare the remarkable feats of each hero and decide how much of each hero's story is exaggerated.

In poetic form, John Henry makes a good choral presentation. Classes have tried the poem as a refrain in which a leader reads the opening lines of each verse and the class enters in on each of the repetitive lines, such as "He laid down his hammer and he died." Each verse can also be read in a cumulative arrangement, in which one group begins the first verse, the second joins the second verse, and a third joins the third verse. This arrangement continues until the poem is complete.

Older children may want to learn more about the history of the railroad, the laying of tracks by work gangs, and the ways in which the steam drill changed railroad construction. One group, for example, investigated the purposes of work songs and identified songs sung by railroaders and other types of workers. These work songs or chants were done as choral readings while the group pantomimed the actions of a work gang. One such chant used by Black Americans laying track has a line chanted by the leader while the crew rests. It is followed by a response while the crew works in unison. The "shack-a-lack-a" response is an imitation of the sound made by the pieces of track as they are pushed into line with long metal poles:

Leader: Oh boys, can't you line her?
Gang: shack-a-lack-a
Leader: Oh boys, can't you line her?
Gang: shack-a-lack-a

Leader: Oh boys, can't you line her?
Gang: shack-a-lack-a
Leader: Every day of the week we go linin' track.

Work songs from different periods in American history are also excellent sources of information about our country's history and its people.

Teachers can encourage creative writing as children write their own work chants and tall tales. One class pretended that John Henry was a contemporary hero and wrote about the heroic deeds he could do if he lived in their lifetime. Stories described him saving the nuclear reactor at Three Mile Island, rescuing people from the upper floors during a hotel fire, and completing work on a superhighway or a skyscraper. Illustrations accompanying the stories showed John Henry as a strong man who was also concerned with the lives of the people around him.

Other classes have used tales about John Henry to stimulate creative drama. Scenes from John Henry's life that are good for this purpose include the following:

1 John Henry's birth, when the moon stood still and went backward, the stars stood still and went backward, and a mighty river flowed uphill.
2 John Henry's early life. (One class speculated about what extraordinary things he might have done as a child.)
3 John Henry's saving a riverboat from sinking.
4 John Henry's work on the railroads, the tunnel cave-in, and his saving of men's lives.
5 The race between John Henry and the steam drill.

As a conclusion to Phase Two, summarize the likeness and differences between African and Black American folklore. Identify stories that have close similarities, and consider any reasons for similarities. Also consider reasons for the differences within the tales.

Phase Three: Historical Nonfiction

By this time, students should have gained considerable understanding that they can use as they read, analyze, and evaluate both nonfictional and fictional literature. During Phase Three, have students read, discuss, and evaluate nonfictional literature that reflects a historical perspective. For example, as students read biographies and autobiographies, have them analyze the inclusion of values, beliefs, and philosophies found in the traditional literature. Have the students read a number of sources, evaluate the authenticity of historical information, and identify historical happenings that influenced the culture. Include other types of nonfictional informational texts so that students may critically evaluate the authenticity of historical settings, happenings, and sources of conflict.

Use Chart 11–4 to help students as they proceed with this evaluation. Note, however, that the material included in Chart 11–4 is only a partial listing of the information that may be included. Notice a continuity within the literature of the language style, theme, and values found in earlier traditional literature. Also notice that the sources of conflict are authentic for this time period. The students who evaluated *Amos Fortune,* however, concluded after reading other nonfictional sources that many of the horrors of the period were not included in this biography. Additional biographies that are excellent for analyzing during Phase Three include Lillie Patterson's *Frederick Douglass: Freedom Fighter,* Douglas Miller's *Frederick Douglass and the Fight for Freedom,* and Virginia Hamilton's *Anthony Burns: The Defeat and Triumph of a Fugitive Slave*. Milton Meltzer's *The Black Americans: A History in Their Own Words, 1619–1983* provides an excellent source for shorter autobiographical sketches and information.

Phase Four: Historical Fiction

During Phase Four, students read, analyze, and evaluate historical fiction and fiction with historical backgrounds according to credibility of conflict, believability of characterization, authenticity of setting, authenticity of traditional beliefs expressed by the characters, appropriateness of themes, and appropriateness of the author's style. Understandings gained from the previously studied biographies, autobiographies, and informational books are especially important during Phase Four. For example, if students have read a number of biographies and other nonfictional texts about the time of slavery, then they can analyze a fictional book, such as Belinda Hurmence's *A Girl Called Boy*. Even though there is a time-warp experience in this story, the major portion of the story is set in North Carolina in the 1850s. Students can evaluate the authenticity of the 1850s North Carolina plantation setting. Also, they can use the knowledge that they gained while reading biographies of this time period to analyze the credibility of the conflict. Students can provide

CHART 11–4
Analyzing historical biography and autobiography

Literature	Evidence of Philosophy, Values, Beliefs, and Language from Phases One and Two	Sources of Conflict	Historical Happenings and Evaluations
Yates's *Amos Fortune: Free Man.*	African story told by Amos is in the style of African storytellers, using repetition, chants, and audience participation. *Theme:* Freedom is important. *Values:* Work, family, retribution, generosity, love of nature.	Person against society, as Amos fights mistreatment, injustice, and separation. Person against self, as Amos considers consequences of his actions.	New Hampshire, 1725–1801. Blacks are taken from Africa and sold as slaves. The horrors of the slave block are avoided in the text, so acceptance of the situations may be too easy.
Ferris's *Go Free or Die: A Story of Harriet Tubman.*	*Themes:* Freedom is worth risking one's life. We must help others obtain their freedom. *Values:* Obligations to family and people, wit, trickery when needed for balance, responsibility, and gratitude.	Person against society, as Harriet fights to free Blacks and to combat injustice.	America, mid-1800s to the end of the Civil War. This story is based on facts related to slavery, the Underground Railroad, the 1850 Fugitive Slave Act, and the 1863 Emancipation Proclamation. Tubman freed more than three hundred slaves in ten years.

evidence for answers to the following questions: Is the setting authentic for a plantation that included numerous slaves? If the setting is authentic, what makes it authentic? What proof do you have that this setting is or is not authentic? Does the plot parallel stories of actual slaves? How? Is the person-against-society conflict as believable as are the conflicts in biographies and autobiographies? What are the comparisons? Why is the conflict believable? How does the author develop believable characters?

Relate instances of characterization with examples from biographies and autobiographies. Are any of the traditional beliefs, themes, and language styles that were found during Phases One and Two also found in this book? Which ones? How are these beliefs developed in the story? Are any of the themes identified in biographies also found in this book? If so, how does the author develop these themes? Do you believe that the themes are appropriate for this story? Why or why not? Is the author's style appropriate for the story? Why or why not? Find examples of author's style that you think are either very good or inappropriate. What, if any, is the relationship of this book to the findings from Phases One, Two, and Three of this study? Defend your answer.

Numerous books may be used for Phase Four. Additional books with historical settings about slavery include N. Monjo's *The Drinking Gourd,* Paula Fox's *Slave Dancer,* and James Collier's *Jump Ship to Freedom.* Mildred Taylor's family survival stories set in the 1900s, *The Gold Cadillac, Roll of Thunder, Hear My Cry,* and *Let the Circle Be Unbroken,* provide excellent sources for analysis and comparison. The strong themes related to family, physical, and spiritual survival have threads that may be traced to the earlier studies.

Phase Five: Contemporary Literature

During the final phase, students read, analyze, and evaluate contemporary literature, including poetry, fiction, and biography. Have the students search for continuity within the literature as reflected in the images, themes, values, and sources of conflict. Also, have them reflect on changes that have taken place. For example, ask the students to read the poetry of Langston Hughes, Gwendolyn Brooks, and Tom Feelings. Poetry selections such as Hughes's "Dreams" and "Merry-Go-Round" should have special significance because the students should understand both the pain of prejudice and the joy of life experienced by people earlier in American history. They also should gain respect for the poets who created such vivid images within their poems.

Some books are especially good for relating the past and the present. For example, ask students to read such contemporary realistic fiction selections as Sharon Bell Mathis's *The Hundred Penny Box* and Virginia Hamilton's *The House of Dies Drear*. The students should understand Mathis's characterization when Aunt Dew excitedly says, "18 and 74. Year I was born. Slavery over! Black men in Congress running things. They was in charge. It was the Reconstruction" (p. 26). In Hamilton's book, they should understand the pride in the Black family as it tries to unravel a mystery related to a home on the Underground Railroad.

Strong family relationships and respect for elders are found in books that span all five phases of this study. Ask students to search for support for these themes in such books as Valerie Flournoy's *The Patchwork Quilt,* Elizabeth Fitzgerald Howard's *Chita's Christmas Tree,* Lucille Clifton's *Everett Anderson's Goodbye,* Mildred Pitts Walter's *Justin and the Best Biscuits in the World,* and Mary Stolz's *Storm in the Night*. Likewise, pride in heritage and strength in character are frequent themes and values. Ask the students to trace these themes and values in books such as Eloise Greenfield's *Sister* and Virginia Hamilton's *Zeely* and *Junius over Far*.

Finally, ask the students to read biographies of contemporary black people, such as Martin Luther King, Jr., Barbara Jordan, Malcolm X, Langston Hughes, and Arthur Mitchell. Ask them to search for sources of conflict, characterizations, values, and themes. Is there any evidence of continuity within the literature? If so, what aspects are also found in the other phases?

Comparisons between the more historical biographies and the contemporary biographies are especially interesting. Biographies lend themselves to numerous activities in the curriculum. The following activities show how a study of biographies may be included in history, science, literature, reading, art, music, and sports:

1 Have the children search the literature and develop a timeline illustrating the contributions of famous Black Americans in history. Develop the timeline on a bulletin board and display literature selections that tell about the people.
2 Ask the children to share their reactions after reading a biography about Martin Luther King, Jr. Have them interview parents and other adults about the goals of the late civil rights leader.
3 After reading a biography, perform "A Day in the Life of ______ ."
4 Share literature written by black authors. Discuss the contributions and styles of such authors as John Steptoe, Sharon Mathis, Eloise Greenfield, and Virginia Hamilton.
5 After reading biographies or stories about black musicians, share and discuss their music.
6 Read biographies of black athletes and discuss records set or other contributions.
7 After reading literature about the contributions and lives of Black Americans, create a "What's My Line" game in which a panel of children asks questions while another group answers.
8 Using a "Meet the Press" format, ask children to take roles of famous Black Americans or reporters who interview them. Prepare for the session by reading literature.

Similar activities can highlight the contributions of Native Americans, Hispanics, and Asian Americans. However, before proceeding to the literature of another cultural group, review what the students have learned from this five-phase study. Review the evidence of both continuity and change. What do the students know about the literature of the Black culture that will make a difference in their lives?

DEVELOPING AN APPRECIATION FOR NATIVE AMERICAN CULTURE

To study Native American cultures, use many of the same techniques that you used for Black American culture. Begin with Native American folklore, in general. Then, narrow the study to the folklore of specific peoples. Proceed to historical nonfiction. Follow historical nonfiction with historical fiction, and end with contemporary literature.

Phase One: Native American Folklore

Before beginning a study of Native American culture, show and discuss a map of the North American continent to show students the diversity of locations for Native American peoples. John Bierhorst's *The Mythology of North America* (5) includes a useful map of North American mythological regions. Have students begin their study of Native American folklore with an investigation of the oral language.

Storytelling. Native American storytellers, like African storytellers, developed definite styles in their storytelling over centuries of oral tradition. Storytelling was an important part of early Indian life, and stories were carefully passed down from one generation to the next. It was quite common for Indians to gather around a fire or sit around their homes while listening to stories. The storytelling sessions often continued for long periods of time, with each person telling a story. Children have opportunities to empathize with members of Native American culture when they take part in storytelling activities that closely resemble the original experience.

Story Openings. Several collectors of Native American tales and observers of Native American storytellers have identified characteristic opening sentences that may be used when presenting Native American stories to children. Franc Newcomb (18), for example, found that many Navaho storytellers opened their stories with one of the following tributes to the past:

> In the beginning, when the world was new
> At the time when men and animals were all the same and spoke the same language

A popular beginning with the White Mountain Apache was "long, long ago, they say."

Have the children search through stories from many Native American tribes and discover how interpreters and translators of traditional Indian folktales introduced their stories. Have the children investigate further and find the exact story openers a certain tribe would be likely to use so that they can use those openings when telling stories from that tribe.

Storytelling Styles. The storytelling styles used by various Indians of North America were quite different from the styles for African storytellers. Melville Jacobs (16) describes the storytelling style of Northwest Indians as being terse, staccato, and rapid. It was usually compact, with little descrip-

Children enjoy listening to a Native American storyteller.

tion, although storytellers might use pantomime and gestures to develop the story. Gladys Reichard (28) found that the Coeur d'Alene Indians used dramatic movements to increase the drama of their tales.

The listening styles of the Native American audiences were also quite different. Native American children were expected to be very attentive and not interrupt the storyteller. Their only response might be the Hopi's repetition of the last word in a sentence, or the Crow's responsive *E!* (yes) following every few sentences. According to Byrd Baylor (4), this response was a sign that the audience was attentive and appreciative. Children in classroom and library story times may also enjoy using these signs to show that they are listening.

Morris Opler (24) discovered an interesting detail about Jicarilla Apache storytellers that can be used to add authenticity and cultural understanding to Native American storytelling. Storytellers gave kernels of corn to children during story time. Because corn was very important, it was believed that if children ate the corn during the storytelling they would remember the content and the importance of the stories.

Story Endings. Melville Jacobs (16) says that Clackama Indians ended many stories by telling an epilogue about an Indian's metamorphosis into an animal, bird, or fish. Most of the stories also had a final ending that meant "myth, myth" or "story, story." Jicarilla Apache storytellers sometimes ended their stories by giving gifts to the listeners because they had stolen a night from their audience.

Teachers and librarians have found that adding authentic storytelling techniques increases understanding and respect for a cultural heritage and stimulates discussions about traditional values. Before leaving this portion of Phase One ask students to summarize what they have learned about Native American folklore styles.

Types of Tales. Collect as many examples of North American Indian folklore as possible. Have the students use these tales to categorize stories that meet Bierhorst's story types found in Native American folklore: (1) setting-the-world-in-order tales, (2) family drama tales, (3) trickster tales, and (4) threshold tales. Chart 11–5 includes examples of literature that may be used for this purpose. Before leaving Phase One, summarize your generalizations about Native American folklore and review your discoveries about oral storytelling.

CHART 11–5
Literature for a study of Native American folklore

Setting the World in Order
Coatsworth's *The Adventures of Nanabush: Ojibway Indian Stories*
Esbensen's *The Star Maiden*
Hamilton's "Turtle Dives to the Bottom of the Sea" in *In the Beginning: Creation Stories from Around the World*
Monroe and Williamson's *They Dance in the Sky: Native American Star Myths*

Family Drama
Metayler's *Tales from the Igloo*
Monroe and Williamson's *They Dance in the Sky: Native American Star Myths*
Spencer's *Who Speaks for Wolf*

Tricksters
Anderson's *Trickster Tales from Prairie Lodgefires*
Goble's *Iktomi and the Boulder: A Plains Indian Story*
Harris's *Mouse Woman and the Vanished Princesses*
Robinson's *Raven the Trickster*

Thresholds
Bierhorst's *The Ring in the Prairie: A Shawnee Legend*
Cleaver's *The Enchanted Caribou*
Goble's *Buffalo Woman*

Phase Two: Folklore from Specific Peoples

During Phase Two, the emphasis narrows to the folklore of one or two Native American peoples. If the students work well in groups, the teacher may choose several tribal regions and allow each group to do an in-depth study of the folklore of that region. For example, there are many stories from the Plains Indians, from the Southwest Pueblo peoples, and from Indians of the Pacific Northwest. Students can search for similarities in story types found in Phase One and analyze the literature for values and beliefs of the specific people. Have them consider the importance of variants in the story types and search for cultural and geographical reasons for these variants.

Locate as many folktales, myths, and legends as possible from the specific regions to be studied. Several documented sources of Native American traditional values will be useful as the students search for evidence of those values. For example, Hanson and Eisenbise's *Human Behavior and*

CHART 11–6
Folklore sources for a study of literature from the Great Plains, the Southwest, and the Northwest

Great Plains	Southwest	Northwest
Baker's *Where the Buffalos Begin*	Baylor's *A God on Every Mountain Top*	Harris's *The Trouble with Adventurers*
Bierhorst's *The Ring in the Prairie*	Cushing's *Zuni Folk Tales*	Harris's *Mouse Woman and the Vanished Princesses*
de Paola's *The Legend of the Bluebonnet*	Baylor's *Moon Song*	Bierhorst's *The Girl Who Married a Ghost*
Goble's *Buffalo Woman*		Wallas's *Kwakiutl Legends*

American Indians (15) documents traditional values and compares them to urban industrial values. Ross and Brave Eagle (30) identify traditional Lakota values. These Lakota values are especially important if the students are reading and analyzing literature from various Great Plains peoples.

Numerous collections of folklore contain selections from various tribal areas. These sources include Monroe and Williamson's *They Dance in the Sky: Native American Star Myths,* Virginia Haviland's *North American Legends,* and Virginia Hamilton's *In the Beginning: Creation Stories from Around the World*. Chart 11–6 presents a few additional sources of folklore from the Great Plains, the Southwest, and the Northwest. Students should summarize the values, beliefs, and themes found in the traditional literature of a specific people and compare the types of stories found in Phase One and Phase Two. (Use similar techniques to help students discover themes and values like those developed under Phases One and Two of Black literature.)

As the conclusion of Phase Two, have older students analyze Jamake Highwater's *Anpao: An American Indian Odyssey*. This story combines a number of traditional Native American tales.

Phase Three: Historical Nonfiction

As in the study of Black literature, students' previous knowledge should help them evaluate the inclusion of accurate values, beliefs, and philosophies in historical nonfiction. Students may read a number of sources to evaluate the authenticity of historical information and to identify the historical happenings that influenced the culture. Have the students develop a chart similar to Chart 11–4. This time the sources should be Native American biographies and autobiographies from the particular region that the students are studying.

Historical literature frequently includes considerable personal conflict. The individuals must overcome problems because of differences between their own Native American beliefs and values and those of the Euro-American culture. As part of the Phase Three study, have the students search for evidence of such conflicts. Are the beliefs, values, customs, and religion in conflict with the different culture? As might be expected, adult autobiographies reflect considerable cultural conflict. Using data from a study of adult autobiographies, students may analyze what percentage of their biographies correspond with the findings from adult texts. See Chart 11–7 for a calculation from a study by Donna Norton (20).

Students may also search for the development of conflicts caused by differences of opinion over land. For example, does the biographer emphasize conflicts because the people were displaced? Is the impoverishment of the people of considerable concern? Or does the biographer emphasize the emergence of leaders who try to regain or keep the land? Students may compare the types of conflicts found in children's biographies with the types of conflicts found in adult autobiographies.

CHART 11–7
Percentages of adult autobiographies that include conflicts caused by cultural beliefs

Tribal Location	Beliefs	Values	Customs	Religion
Great Plains	46%	85%	54%	85%
Great Basin	50	50	50	—
Southwest	50	75	50	63

CHART 11–8
Percentages of adult autobiographies that deal with conflicts over land

Tribal Location	People Displaced	People Impoverished	Leaders Emerging
Great Plains	61%	77%	38%
Great Basin	100	100	50
Southwest	50	25	38

Chart 11–8 identifies conflicts found in adult texts.

This comparison encourages students to consider the credibility of biographies from different regions. Nonfictional sources, such as Albert Marrin's *War Clouds in the West: Indian & Cavalrymen, 1860–1890,* Russell Freedman's *Buffalo Hunt,* and Hermina Poatgieter's *Indian Legacy: Native American Influences on World Life and Culture* provide historical perspectives. Byrd Baylor's *When Clay Sings* provides a poetic telling of the ancient way of life of Native Americans living in the Southwest desert.

Phase Four: Historical Fiction

If students are examining literature from the Great Plains, Jan Hudson's *Sweetgrass* is excellent for analyzing historical fiction according to authenticity of setting, credibility of conflict, believability of characterization, authenticity of traditional beliefs, appropriateness of themes, and the author's style. The setting is among the Blackfoot people in southern Canada. The conflict develops a person-against-society problem. European expansion and smallpox cause the Native American characters to face disruption of their lives. The person-against-self conflicts result when characters must overcome differences in belief systems or taboos to survive within their cultures. Without an understanding of Blackfoot values and beliefs, these conflicts would not seem believable. *Sweetgrass* is especially effective for showing students that language should reflect the people, the setting, and the time period. Students should consider the effectiveness of the figurative language and prairie symbolism to describe characters, setting, and conflict.

In Paul Goble's *Beyond the Ridge,* students should discover a belief in the afterlife as experienced by an elderly Indian woman from the Great Plains. This belief is also found in traditional literature.

The following example shows how the teacher can present a historical fiction text from the Southwest. Scott O'Dell's *Sing Down the Moon* is based on a tragic time in Navaho history, spanning 1863 to 1865. The story begins during a beautiful spring in Canyon de Chelly. Life seems promising. Then, the United States government sends Colonel Kit Carson to the canyon to bring the Navahos to Fort Sumner, New Mexico. In order to force the Indians' surrender, the troops destroy the crops and livestock, then drive the Navahos to the fort. This three-hundred-mile journey is known as *The Long Walk*. While at Fort Sumner, more than fifteen hundred Indians died, and many others lost their will to live.

The creation stories of the Navahos refer to creating the mountains as "singing up the mountains." Ask students: What is the significance of Scott O'Dell's title *Sing Down the Moon?* What happened to the Navaho way of life during the years depicted in the story? Why did the government force the Indians to leave their home? If people today were Navahos living at that time, how might they feel? How might a soldier feel?

When it was time for Bright Morning to become a woman, the tribe prepared for the Womanhood Ceremony. Students can investigate the ceremonies celebrated by Navaho Indians. In groups, students may demonstrate one ceremony to the rest of the class and explain its purpose.

When Tall Boy was wounded, Bright Morning rode to the village to get the Medicine Man. The Medicine Man used the juice of mottled berries to treat his wound. Many medicine men effectively used herbs and berries to cure the sick. Students may use resource materials such as Joe Graham's *Grandmother's Tea, Mexican Herbal Remedies* (13). Students may research various plants that might cure illness. Many of these herbs and plants have significant pharmacological value. Identify the plants that have the greatest value and the illnesses they can cure. Discuss the importance of medicine men, the reasons they were respected within the tribe, and what knowledge was required.

Tall Boy made a lance to use against the Long Knives. The only materials he had to work with were those available in nature. Students may investigate other weapons and tools that Native Americans used, review how the people made the weapons and tools, and draw a picture of each.

In *Sing Down the Moon,* Bright Morning steps on a spear and breaks it when her son reaches out toward a young lamb. Discuss the symbolic meaning of this action.

Many clues in *Sing Down the Moon* suggest the environment in which Bright Morning and her tribe live. For example, O'Dell develops a visual image as he describes the canyons: "The stone walls of the canyons stand so close together that you can touch them with your outstretched hand" (p. 1). He describes the rain through Bright Morning's thoughts: "At first it was a whisper, like a wind among the dry corn stalks of our cornfield" (p. 2). Even the streams are suggested to have a voice of their own: "The stream sounded like men's voices speaking" (p. 53). These descriptions of the environment also suggest characteristics of the Navahos' environment, as well as their respect for nature, and whether they were a hunting or a farming tribe.

Discuss the significance of the descriptions in O'Dell's language. How does the author feel about the Navaho? Students may search for other visual language in the book that describes the various environments experienced by the Navahos as they leave their canyon and go to Fort Sumner. Compare the canyon environment with that at Fort Sumner and draw pictures of both locations.

For creative writing, have the students describe two environments, one that is lovely and enjoyable to live in and one that is not. Have them draw a picture illustrating each and describe the pictures using language that will allow someone else to visualize them. Before completing Phase Four, ask the students to summarize their findings and to trace any threads that continue through Phases One to Four.

Phase Five: Contemporary Literature

Contemporary Native American poetry is especially rich in symbolism and mythological references. Allow students to discover the close relationships between the folklore read in Phases One and Two and contemporary texts. For example, ask students to read Jamake Highwater's *Moonsong Lullaby* and identify mythological references, personification of nature, and foundations in traditional beliefs. A cognitive web such as Figure 11–1 is an excellent way to help students identify relationships.

Read the poem *Moonsong Lullaby* for the enjoyment of the words and the imagery. Draw a web on the board with the title in the center and the circled topics extending from the center. Tell the students that *Moonsong Lullaby* shows very close relationships between nature and the people. Ask the students to identify evidence of these close relationships through such topics as the personification of nature, mythological references within the poem, and foundations on traditional beliefs. Tell the students that they will need to use the knowledge that they acquired about Native American peoples in the previous phases of their study. After the students have completed the web, have them analyze the appropriateness of the language for a Native American poem that emphasizes traditional beliefs. If the students are studying the Southwest, Byrd Baylor's poem about the Papago Indians, *The Desert Is Theirs,* is an excellent choice for a similar activity.

Several contemporary fiction books are interesting for analysis and comparison. For example, younger students may search for any evidence of continuity in the writings of Virginia Driving Hawk Sneve while older students analyze Jamake Highwater's *Legend Days, The Ceremony of Innocence,* and *I Wear the Morning Star*. White Deer of Autumn's contemporary story *Ceremony—In the Circle of Life* provides an excellent text for comparing the values in realistic fiction and folklore. For example, ask the students to compare *Ceremony* and *The Legend of the Bluebonnet*. Chart 11–9 compares these books. Have the students discuss the results of the comparison and consider the reasons for the similarities between the values in the traditional tale and the contemporary story.

Byrd Baylor's contemporary story from the Southwest, *Hawk, I'm Your Brother,* is another excellent choice for comparative studies. Through this book, students can visualize the close relationships between a Native American boy and a hawk. There are also frequent references to dreams of flying and ancient knowledge. In addition to identifying relationships between traditional folklore and contemporary stories, you may use *Hawk, I'm Your Brother* to help children recognize differences in the author's point of view and to motivate the writing of a story from another point of view. (See chapter 9 for a literary web of this book.) Such activities help students analyze the characterizations within the book. Use the

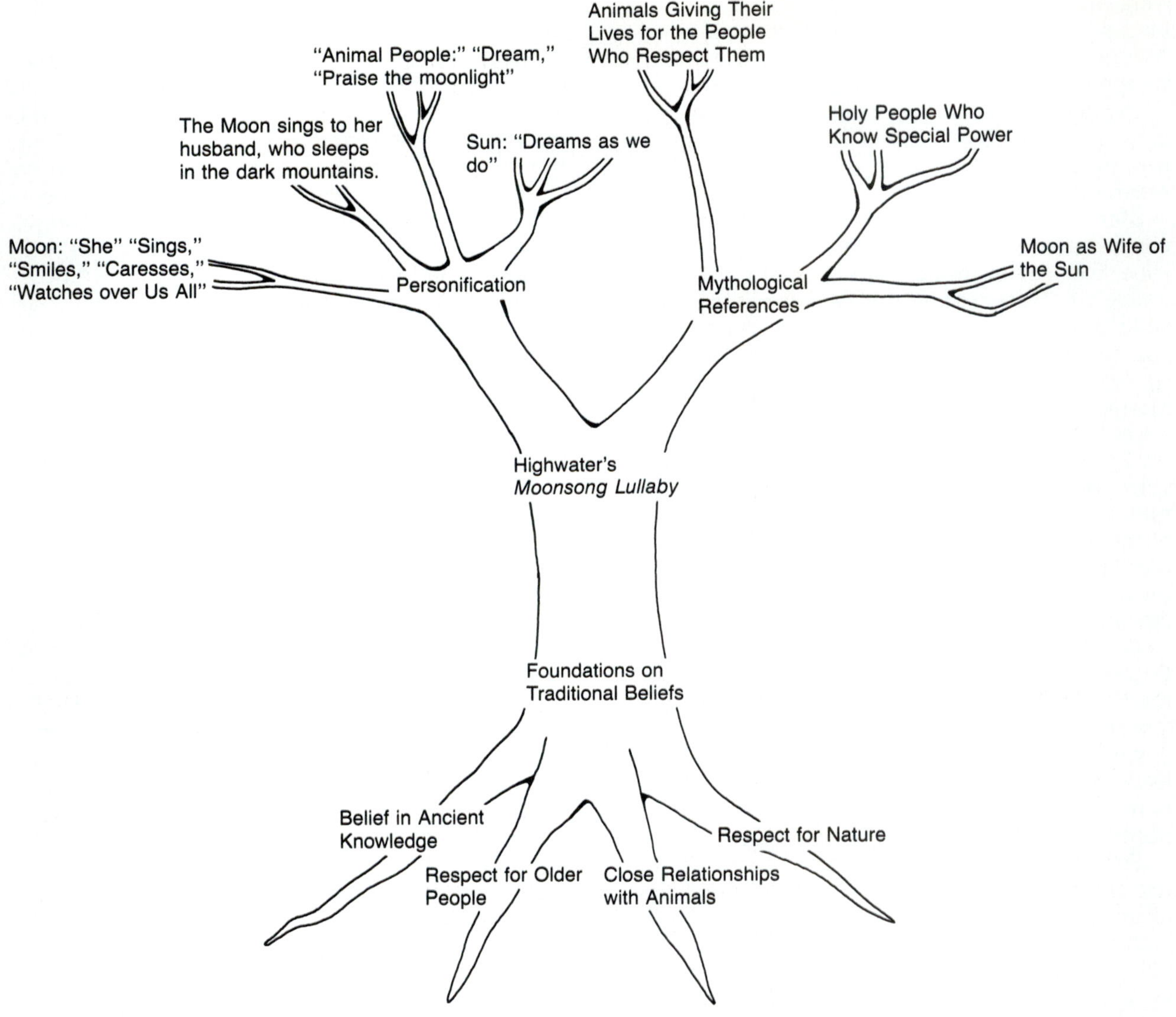

FIGURE 11–1
Relationships between folklore and Jamake Highwater's *Moonsong Lullaby*

following instructional sequence for developing understanding of point of view:

1 Introduce the story and tell the students that they will be listening to a story in which the author describes and develops the hero's aspirations. Ask the students to consider how they would feel as Rudy Soto. Also, ask them to consider the feelings and desires of the hawk.
2 After reading *Hawk, I'm Your Brother* aloud, lead a discussion in which the students characterize Rudy and the hawk, and identify the major sequence of events leading up to Rudy's decision to release the hawk.
3 Ask the students to consider the significance of the title of the book. Why did Baylor choose *Hawk, I'm Your Brother*? Is it an accurate description of Rudy Soto's relationship to the hawk? How are Rudy and the hawk alike? How are they different? Why did Rudy release the hawk? How do you think Rudy felt after releasing the hawk? How do you think the hawk felt after being released? What would

CHART 11–9
A comparison of values in traditional and contemporary Native American literature

Comparisons	Traditional Folklore *The Legend of the Bluebonnet*	Contemporary Fiction *Ceremony—In the Circle of Life*
What is the problem?	Drought and famine that are killing the Comanche	Destruction of the land by humans
What reward is desired?	To end the drought and famine To save the land and people	To comfort and honor Mother Earth To teach humans about Mother Earth
What actions (or values) are rewarded or admired?	Sacrifice to save the land and tribe Belief in the Great Spirit	Honor and care for Mother Earth Living in harmony with nature Knowledge, truth, and belief
What actions are punished or despised?	Selfishness Taking from Earth without giving back	Pollution and destruction of Mother Earth
What rewards are given?	Bluebonnets, as a sign of forgiveness Rain to end the drought A name change	A living pipe to symbolize the vision of Mother Earth New strength, knowledge, and understanding
What are the personal characteristics of heroes, heroines, or great people?	Unselfish love of the people and land Respect for the Great Spirit Willingness to sacrifice to benefit others	Love of animals and the land Respect for the Star Spirit and the ways of the people Desire for knowledge and truth

you have done if you were Rudy Soto? How would you react if you were the hawk?

4 Tell the students that an incident may be described in different ways by several people who have the same experience. The details that characters describe, the feelings they experience, and their beliefs in the right or wrong of an incident may vary. Consequently, the same story could change drastically, depending on the point of view of the storyteller. Ask the students to tell you whose point of view Baylor develops in *Hawk, I'm Your Brother*. How did they know that the story was told from Rudy Soto's point of view? Then ask the students to consider how the story might be written if the author chose the hawk's point of view.

5 Ask the students to imagine that they are the hawk that Rudy captured. Have them write a story about what happened to them, beginning from the time of the capture from the nest high on Santos Mountain.

As a conclusion to Phase Five, summarize the findings and the threads discovered across the ages of literature. Review examples of continuity and evidence of change. What do the students know about the literature of Native Americans that will make a difference in their lives?

DEVELOPING AN APPRECIATION FOR HISPANIC AMERICAN CULTURE

Hispanic literature and culture are very complex. This complexity results from the infusion of numerous influences. Jose Griego y Maestas and Rudolfo A. Anaya (14) reinforce the importance of the traditional literature in understanding the culture and show the complexity of such a study: The tales "are a great part of the soul of our culture, and they reflect the values of our forefathers. . . .The stories reflect a history of thirteen centuries of infusing and blending from the Moors and Jews in Spain, to the orientals in the Philippines, Africans in the Caribbean, and the Indians in America—be they Aztec, Apache or Pueblo" (p. 4). The choices of Hispanic literature are also considerable. This chapter includes the ancient literature of the Aztecs and Maya, proceeds to the more recent folklore of Mexico and America, and then concludes with contemporary Hispanic American poetry and fiction.

Phase One: Ancient Aztec and Mayan Folklore

Ancient folklore was first recorded for European audiences by the Spaniards in the sixteenth century. Introduce the folklore by showing students a map of Mexico and Central America that indicates locations of Aztec and Mayan peoples, such as those found in various adult sources, including *Atlas of Ancient America,* by Michael Coe, Dean Snow, and Elizabeth Benson (9); *The Maya,* by Michael Coe (8); and *The King Danced in the Marketplace,* by Frances Gillmor (12). These texts are also excellent sources for additional information about these ancient cultures.

Myths found in Carleton Beals's *Stories Told by the Aztecs: Before the Spaniards Came* allow students to identify characteristics of Aztec folklore and to discover the importance of the three gods that dominate much of the mythology and other literature: "(1) Quetzalcoatl, the Plumed Serpent, who drove out earlier animal gods and led the Toltecs in the Central Valley of Mexico; (2) Tezcatlipoca, the Black Mirror that Smokes, leader of the Chichimeca, or Stone Men; (3) and Huitzilopochtli, the Left-legged Hummingbird, the Aztec war god also known as Mexitli, Heart of the Maguey, after whom modern Mexico is named" (p. 10). John Bierhorst's *The Hungry Woman: Myths and Legends of the Aztecs* is another source for Aztec literature.

After students read or listen to some of the Aztec tales and look at Aztec art in such sources as the *Atlas of Ancient America,* have them analyze the inclusion of Aztec tales and art in Deborah Nourse Lattimore's *The Flame of Peace: A Tale of the Aztecs.* Lattimore states that she combined "the known elements and the lively, authentic art with some educated guesses based on my research and knowledge of the period—to create a story with pictures that I hope will satisfy those two most critical audiences: scholars and children" (end cover). Students should use their own research abilities to decide if she reached her goal. What evidence do they have that Lattimore based her story on research and knowledge?

John Bierhorst's *The Monkey's Haircut and Other Stories Told by the Maya* provides a source for students to identify characteristics of and values in Mayan folklore. For example, have students search for stories that have the following values and characteristics identified by Bierhorst: (1) cleverness, as shown by stories that include riddles, puns, double meanings and tricksters; (2) culture, such as paying a bride service and being godparents; (3) corn and farming practices.

Students should search for characteristics and values in other tales from before interaction with the Spanish culture. They will discover many of the values previously discussed. In addition, they will find stories that reflect such values as need to sacrifice for the betterment of the group and the worthiness of bravery and honor. Good choices for this activity include Francisco Hinojosa's *The Old Lady Who Ate People,* Harriet Rohmer and Dorminster Wilson's *Mother Scorpion Country,* Marcos Kurtycz and Ana Garcia Kobeh's *Tigers and Opossums: Animal Legends,* and Vivien Blackmore's *Why Corn Is Golden: Stories About Plants.*

Ask the students to use all of the information they have gained from a study of ancient folklore to analyze and interpret Toni de Gerez's adaptation of the ancient Toltec poem, *My Song Is a Piece of Jade.* Ask the students to identify the values, characters, and mythological references that they discover in the folklore. Ask them to identify any additional information that the poetry reveals about the culture. Also, ask them to consider how and why a study of the mythological foundations of the people has made this poem more interesting and understandable. Before leaving Phase One, have the students summarize their findings.

Phase Two: Stories that Reflect Interaction with Other Cultures

Many of the values, beliefs, and characteristics of ancient literature are found in more recent traditional literature. The most dramatic difference coincides with the arrival of Cortés and the Spanish. A considerable body of folklore reflects the interactions between the ancient peoples and Christianity. Some tales show the clash of cultural values while others reflect stories that changed because of the settings. Teachers should choose tales according to the appropriateness for the ages of their students. For example, tales that reflect interactions between the people and Christianity include Tomie de Paola's *The Lady of Guadalupe* and John Bierhorst's translation of *Spirit Child: A Story of the Nativity. The Invisible Hunters,* by Harriet Rohmer, Octavio Chow, and Morris Vidaure, may help students understand what happens when cultures clash.

The impact of Spanish culture is found in Verna Aardema's *The Riddle of the Drum: A Tale from Tizapan, Mexico.* Changes due to place are easy to identify in Bierhorst's retelling from an Aztec manuscript, *Doctor Coyote: A Native American Aesop's Fables.* Students may identify the relationships with the earlier Aesop and the trickster characters of Indian lore.

Jose Griego y Maestas and Rudolfo A. Anaya's *Cuentos: Tales from the Hispanic Southwest* includes numerous tales that are valuable for Phase Two. For example, students enjoy comparing one of the tales, "The Man Who Knew the Language of the Animals," with Verna Aardema's African tale, *What's So Funny, Ketu?* They can identify the similarities and differences and note ways in which the differences reflect cultural differences.

Older students may compare the "Hansel and Gretel" variants from Spain and Mexico found in James M. Taggart's article, "'Hansel and Gretel' in Spain and Mexico" (33). Have them compare these versions with the Grimms' tales. These variants are more complex and include changes in the tales due to male or female storytellers.

Before leaving Phase Two, have the students summarize similarities and differences between Phases One and Two and consider reasons for the stories to be either alike or different.

Phase Three: Historical Nonfiction

Several books can help students understand the Aztecs and Maya. For example, Cottie Burland's *An Aztec Town* provides background information and drawings of different parts of a city. Albert Marrin's *Aztecs and Spaniards: Cortés and the Conquest of Mexico* describes the culture and the conquest. *The Mystery of the Ancient Maya,* by Carolyn Meyer and Charles Gallenkamp, explores the ancient culture. Jamake Highwater's *Journey to the Sky* follows John Stephens and Frederick Catherwood as they search for the Maya kingdom. Albert Prago's *Strangers in Their Own Land: A History of Mexican-Americans* traces the history of Mexican-Americans and explores reasons for difficulties that Mexican-Americans face today.

Phase Four: Historical Fiction

An understanding of history is important for students to analyze historical fiction about the Spanish conquest. Older students may read and analyze the historical accuracy and trace the traditional beliefs in such books as Scott O'Dell's *The Captive, The Feathered Serpent,* and *The Amethyst Ring*. In *The King's Fifth,* O'Dell accompanies Coronado's army as it searches for the golden cities of the Southwest.

Ann Nolan Clark's historical fiction provides gentler sources for analysis. For example, *Secret of the Andes* is an Inca story that reveals the importance of respecting elders, giving and sharing oneself, and making discoveries. *Year Walk,* also by Clark, is based on the experiences of Basque sheepherders who settled in America.

Phase Five: Contemporary Literature

Of the groups studied thus far, there are fewer contemporary Hispanic literature selections available for children. Likewise, contemporary study may require broadening the base of Hispanic literature to include authors of Cuban or Puerto Rican ancestry. Authors who may be analyzed include Pura Belpre, Nicole DeMessieres, Francisco Hinojosa, Nicholasa Mohr, Sandra Cisneros, and Richard García.

Many stories, such as Cisneros's *The House on Mango Street,* express the pain and fear of the characters as they struggle to find themselves in a world that is often alien. In books such as Nicholasa Mohr's *Going Home,* students may analyze the forces that cause an American girl from Puerto Rican ancestry not to be accepted by Puerto Rican girls.

The Newbery Medal winner, *. . .And Now Miguel,* by Joseph Krumgold, includes many cultural values and beliefs. In addition, the book provides insights into a young boy's development. The following example shows how the teacher might share and discuss this book.

Ask students if there has ever been anything they wanted to do very badly but were told by their parents that they couldn't do until they were older. Talk about some of the things the students mention. Discuss the possible reasons they would have to be older to do those things. Then explain that this book is about a twelve-year-old boy who wants something and that the story is about how he goes about getting what he wants.

The book can be read aloud to children or individually by children, if there are enough copies. If each child has a copy, read the beginning of a chapter aloud and have the students read the remainder of the chapter silently.

Chapter one describes the setting of the story in detail. Prepare a map of New Mexico showing the Sangre de Cristo Mountain Range, the Rio Grande River, the city of Taos, and the San Juan mountain range. Show the cliffs of the San Juan range going down to the Rio Grande. Have the children locate and label each detail on the map. Then have them trace the migration of the sheep as described by Miguel in chapter one. The beginning chapters also mention the following landforms: cliff, mountain, mesa, plain, canyon, and arroyo. Collect pictures to show examples of each type of landform. Discuss characteristics of each picture and ways the characteristics relate to the section in the story.

In chapter two, Miguel says that he must take his winter clothes to wear in the mountains even though it will be summer. Have the children speculate about the reasons for the differences between the temperature on the plain and in the mountains. Using reference books, have a group of children find the temperature ranges for New Mexico. Have them check other areas where there is a plain and there are nearby mountains. Have them check differences in temperature according to elevation. Lead them into a generalization on the effect of elevation on temperature and on Miguel's plans.

Miguel comes from a large, multigenerational family. Starting with Grandfather Chavez, have the children make a genealogical chart of the Chavez family. Then have them make charts of their own families.

The life of the Chavez family revolves around the life cycle of the sheep. Review the cycle with the children: winter on the mesa, back to the ranch in early spring for the birth of the lambs and the shearing, and into the mountains for the summer. Discuss the importance of sheep to the Chavez family and the ways in which the sheep influence the life-style and desires of each family member.

Ask the children to imagine they are Miguel and are planning their trip into the mountains. They will be gone all summer, so they must take everything with them. Have them list everything they will need and defend the reasons they would use valuable space on the pack mule to take each item. In addition, ask the children to pretend they are Miguel and use a dairy format to write their feelings and experiences as they try to convince the family that they are old enough to accompany the men to the summer pasture.

Mutual cooperation within the family is an important value stressed in the book. Discuss how each family member contributes to the family's welfare.

Another value is the strong integration of religious beliefs into daily life. There are references to this value throughout the book, but it is particularly strong beginning with chapter eight, in which Miguel explains about San Ysidro to the readers. Grandfather Chavez is the embodiment of the values, whereas Eil has seemingly rejected the religious values. Ask the students to identify values, beliefs, and themes in . . . *And Now Miguel* that are similar to the values, beliefs, and themes discovered in other Hispanic literature. Ask the students to account for any similarities and differences.

Conclude the study of Hispanic literature with an analysis of biographies. A few examples include Betty Lou Phillips's *The Picture Story of Nancy Lopez,* Maurice Roberts's *Henry Cisneros: Mexican American Mayor,* and Clarence M. White's *Cesar Chavez: Man of Courage*.

DEVELOPING AN APPRECIATION FOR ASIAN AMERICAN CULTURE

Because there are so many different Asian groups, a thorough study would require investigating the

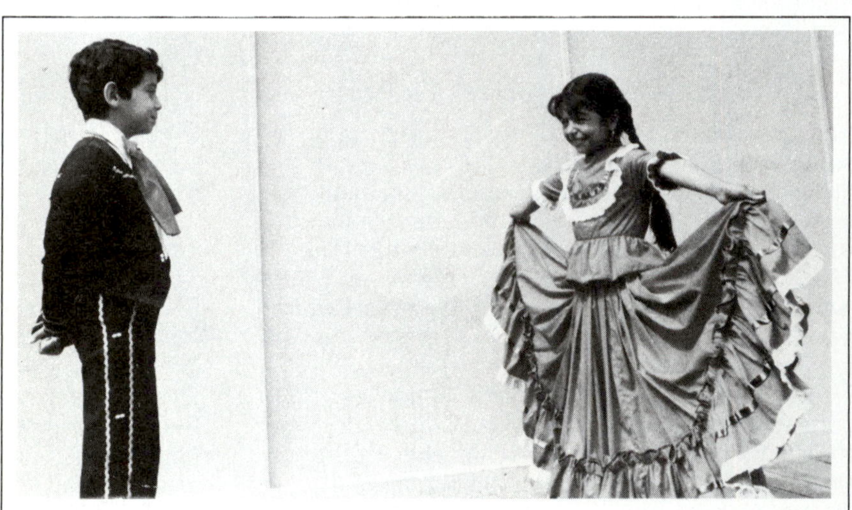

Children learn about Hispanic customs and traditional celebrations by taking part in dramatizations

A child learns to value the contributions of a culture different from his own.

folklore from Japan, China, Vietnam, and other Eastern countries and then extending that analysis into historical and contemporary works. (See chapter 6 for a unit that emphasizes developing understandings of the Chinese culture.) Such an investigation is much too extensive for this chapter. However, if you are planning such a study, the writings of the following authors will be beneficial: Sumiko Yogawa, Taro Yashima, Laurence Yep, Yoshiko Uchida, Yozo Otsuki, He Liyi, Huynh Quang Nhuoung, Shizuye Takashima, and Toshi Maruki.

Traditional Tales

A Japanese style of storytelling that is especially interesting to children is the *kamishibai*—an outdoor form of storytelling with pictures. Although it is not so old as the African and Native American techniques discussed earlier, it is different from either the African or the Native American traditions.

Story Opening. Keigo Seki (32) identifies an opening sentence that is often used in Japanese storytelling. The following opening can add an authentic flavor to storytelling in classrooms, especially if the storyteller begins the story in Japanese:

Mukashi, mukash (Long, long ago)
Aro tokoro ni (In a certain place)

Storytelling Style. Kamishibai was performed by men who had a collection of about four stories that were illustrated on cards and shown in a wooden boxholder resembling a miniature stage. The stories were illustrated on a series of picture cards and then placed in a wooden holder about one foot high and eighteen inches wide. The front of the theater had flaps that opened to reveal the stage. The cards fit into a slot in the side of the box. The storyteller pulled the sequentially placed cards out of the box. The text was written on the back of the card that preceded the picture that was currently showing on the stage. (The title was the first card removed and placed in the back of the box; the text that accompanied the next picture was on the back of the title card. This procedure continued with each card as the story unfolded in pictures and words.)

Anne Pellowski (26) describes how influential kamishibai storytelling has been in Japan:

> Considering the impact that the kamishibai had on children's literature and the fact that the same publishers who produced the cards were also later producing children's books, it is no wonder that one of the most popular formats for children's picture books in Japan is the horizontal style reminiscent of the kamishibai. (p. 145)

A Japanese Kamishibai Presentation

A kamishibai storytelling experience with its boxholder and picture cards is an enjoyable way for children to illustrate a story, retell the story, and also experience the way in which Japanese children enjoy folktales. One group of children created a kamishibai theater out of a heavy cardboard box. First, they cut a viewing opening in the front of the box. Next, they cut flaps that could open and close across the front of the stage and attached them to the front sides of the box so the flaps could be in either an open or a closed position. Then they cut openings in the sides of the box so that the cards could be placed inside. They placed identical openings on either side so that the openings would provide support for the pictures viewed on the stage. They made the side openings a little taller than the front openings so that each card would be framed by the center stage.

Next, they cut tagboard cards to fit inside the theater. The cards were a few inches wider than the theater so that the storyteller could grasp them easily and remove them at the proper time. They were also slightly shorter than the side opening so they would go in and out easily (see Figure 11–2).

The group chose a Japanese folktale, Arlene Mosel's *The Funny Little Woman,* to illustrate on the kamishibai picture cards. The group liked the story and wanted to illustrate the characters, including the wicked Oni (demons who live in underground caverns) and the old woman they kidnap and force to cook for them. The children selected the scenes they wanted to illustrate, selected from this list the scene or scenes each one would draw (the original kamishibai presentations usually ranged from six to twenty scenes), and completed the drawings. They put the cards into sequence, including a title card for an introduction. Then, like authentic *kamishibai* storytellers, they wrote the dialogue for each card on the back of the card preceding it. They placed the cards in the theater and told the story to an

FIGURE 11–2
A kamishibai theater

appreciative audience. (As they removed each card, they placed it at the back of the box, so the storytellers would have their cues in front of them.)

This activity is especially appropriate for small groups, because each group can select a particular Japanese tale, prepare it for presentation, and present the story to the other groups. In that way, children can be both storytellers and audience. Momoko Ishii's *The Tongue-Cut Sparrow* is another story excellent for kamishibai presentations.

RECOGNIZING SIMILARITIES

One value of sharing multicultural literature with children is increasing the understanding of the children that those who belong to groups other than their own are real people, with feelings, emotions, and needs similar to theirs. Elaine M. Aoki (1) says that literature can contribute to children's development of values. Consequently, she feels that adults must lead children in active discussions about those values. She says that this discussion should not be a didactic lesson, but it should help children gain positive attitudes toward all people. She identifies two steps that should be included in such discussion. First, children can take the viewpoint of a character in a story. When they are that character, they can consider what they would have done under similar circumstances and how they would have felt. Second, children can search for elements within the story that are related to their own experiences. They can identify times when they had feelings or needs like those the characters in the story express.

Many multicultural books, especially those written for young children, have themes suggesting that children everywhere have more similarities than differences. These books can stimulate discussions in which children relate similar experiences they have had, tell how they handled similar problems, suggest how they would feel if they had a similar experience, or relate ways they might respond to similar circumstances. For example, after reading John Steptoe's *Stevie,* children can talk about how they would feel if a younger child came to their room and broke their toys, how they would solve this problem if they were Stevie, and the feelings they might experience if the child were no longer there. They can discover from discussing Valerie Flournoy's *The Patchwork Quilt* that love between grandparents and grandchildren is universal.

Many books for older readers also suggest universal needs and emotions. The following books can be used to stimulate discussions on the topics suggested:

1. *Experiencing prejudice creates strong emotions*: Laurence Yep's *Dragonwings* (Chinese American), Nicholasa Mohr's *Felita* (Puerto Rican), Scott O'Dell's *Sing Down the Moon* (Native American), and Mildred Taylor's *Roll of Thunder, Hear My Cry* (Black American).
2. *All people have dreams that influence their lives*: Laurence Yep's *Dragonwings* and *Sea Glass* (Chinese American), Joseph Krumgold's *. . .And Now Miguel* (Spanish American-Basque), Virginia Driving Hawk Sneve's *High Elk's Treasure* (Native American), Paula Fox's *How Many Miles to Babylon?* (Black American).
3. *Discovering one's own heritage brings pride*: Laurence Yep's *Child of the Owl* (Chinese American), Brent Ashabranner's *To Live in Two Worlds: American Indian Youth Today* (Native American), and Virginia Hamilton's *Zeely* (Black American).
4. *People can have strong feelings of love toward older family members*: Ann Nolan Clark's *To Stand Against the Wind* (Vietnamese), Miska Miles's *Annie and the Old One* (Native American), Sharon Bell Mathis's *The Hundred Penny Box* (Black American), and Valerie Flournoy's *The Patchwork Quilt* (Black American).

Suggested Activities for Children's Appreciation of Multicultural Literature

- ☐ Choose African, Native American, or Asian traditional tales. Prepare a story opening, storytelling style, and story ending that reflect the authentic traditional presentation of the tales. Share the stories with a group of children or a peer group.
- ☐ Choose an African people other than the Ashanti. Suggest stories and other learning experiences that would allow children to develop an appreciation for the culture.
- ☐ Search a social studies or history curriculum and identify Black Americans, Native Americans, Hispanic Americans, or Asian Americans who have made contributions during the time periods or subjects being studied. Identify literature selections that include additional

information about those individuals and their contributions.

- ☐ Develop a time line showing the chronology of famous Black Americans, Native Americans, Hispanic Americans, and Asian Americans. Identify literature that may be used with the time line.
- ☐ Develop a "What's My Line" program, a roundtable discussion, or a "Meet the Press" activity that stresses the contributions of famous Black Americans, Native Americans, Hispanic Americans, or Asian Americans.
- ☐ Choose a Native American story and develop a series of discussion questions that would allow children to gain insights into the culture portrayed in the book.
- ☐ Choose an Asian culture and develop a five-phase study that proceeds from traditional literature to contemporary Asian-American literature.

References

1 Aoki, M. Elaine. "Are You Chinese? Are You Japanese? Or Are You Just a Mixed-Up Kid?—Using Asian American Children's Literature." *The Reading Teacher* 34 (January 1981): 382–385.

2 Baker, Gwendolyn C. "The Role of the School in Transmitting the Culture of All Learners in a Free and Democratic Society." *Educational Leadership* 36 (November 1978): 134–138.

3 Ballinger, Franchot. "A Matter of Emphasis: Teaching the 'Literature' in Native American Literature Courses." *American Indian Culture and Research Journal* 8 (1984): 1–12.

4 Baylor, Byrd. *And It Is Still That Way*. New York: Scribner's Sons, 1976.

5 Bierhorst, John. *The Mythology of North America*. New York: Morrow, 1985.

6 Bierhorst, John, ed. *The Red Swan: Myths and Tales of the American Indians*. New York: Farrar, Straus & Giroux, 1976.

7 Bryan, Ashley. *The Dancing Granny and Other African Stories*. New York: Caedmon, 1985.

8 Coe, Michael. *The Maya,* 3d ed. New York: Thames & Hudson, 1984.

9 Coe, Michael, Dean Snow, and Elizabeth Benson. *Atlas of Ancient America*. New York: Facts on File, 1986.

10 Courlander, Harold. *A Treasury of African Folklore*. New York: Crown, 1975.

11 Dorris, Michael. "Native American Literature in an Ethnohistorical Context." *College English* 41 (October 1979): 147–162.

12 Gillmor, Frances. *The King Danced in the Marketplace*. Salt Lake City: University of Utah Press, 1977.

13 Graham, Joe. *Grandmother's Tea: Mexican Herbal Remedies*. San Antonio: Institute of Texan Cultures, 1979.

14 Griego y Maestas, Jose, and Rudolfo A. Anaya. *Cuentos: Tales from the Hispanic Southwest*. Santa Fe: Museum of New Mexico, 1980.

15 Hanson, W. D., and M. D. Eisenbise. *Human Behavior and American Indians*. Rockville, Md.: National Institute of Mental Health, 1983. ERIC Document Reproduction, ED 231-589.

16 Jacobs, Melville. *The Content and Style of an Oral Literature: Clackamas Chinook Myths and Tales*. Chicago: University of Chicago Press, 1959.

17 Kingsley, Mary. *West African Studies*. 3d ed. New York: Barnes & Noble, 1964.

18 Newcomb, Franc J. *Navajo Folk Tales*. Santa Fe: Museum of Navajo Ceremonial Art, 1967, xvi.

19 Norton, Donna E. "The Expansion and Evaluation of a Multiethnic Reading/Language Arts Program Designed for 5th, 6th, 7th, and 8th Grade Children." Meadows Foundation Grant No. 55614, A Three Year Longitudinal Study, Texas A&M University, 1984–1987.

20 ———. "The Intrusion of an Alien Culture: The Impact and Reactions as Seen Through Biographies and Autobiographies of Native Americans." *Vitae Scholasticae* 6 (Spring 1987): 59–75.

21 ———. *Language Arts Activities for Children*. 2d ed. Columbus, Ohio: Merrill, 1985.

22 ———, and James F. McNamara. *An Evaluation of the Multicultural Reading/Language Arts Program for Elementary and Junior High School Students*. College Station, Tex.: Texas A&M University, 1988.

23 Noss, Philip A. "Description in Gbaya Literary Art." In *African Folklore,* edited by Richard Dorse. Bloomington, Ind.: Indiana University Press, 1972.

24 Opler, Morris Edward. *Myths and Tales of the Jicarilla Apache Indians*. Memoirs 31. New York: American Folklore Society, 1938.

25 Parsons, Elsie Clews. *Folktales of Andros Island, Bahamas*. New York: American Folklore Society, 1918.

26 Pellowski, Anne. *The World of Storytelling*. New York: Bowker, 1977.

27 Piper, David. "Language Growth in the Multiethnic Classroom." *Language Arts* 63 (January 1986): 23–36.

28 Reichard, Gladys A. *An Analysis of Coeur d'Alene Indian Myths*. Philadelphia: American Folklore Society, 1974.

29 Roller, Cathy. "Classroom Interaction Patterns: Reflections of a Stratified Society." *Language Arts* 66 (September 1989): 492–500.

30 Ross, A. C., and D. Brave Eagle. *Value Orientation—A Strategy for Removing Barriers*. Denver, Colo.: Coalition of Indian Controlled School Boards, 1975. ERIC Document Reproduction, ED 125–811.

31 Sealey, D. Bruce. "Measuring the Multicultural Quotient of a School." *TESL Canada Journal/Revue TESL Du Canadan* 1 (March 1984): 21–28.

32 Seki, Keigo, ed. *Folktales of Japan*. Translated by Robert J. Adams. Chicago: University of Chicago, 1963, xv.

33 Taggart, James. "'Hansel and Gretel' in Spain and Mexico." *Journal of American Folklore* 99 (1986): 435–460.

34 Tremearne, A. J. *Hausa Superstitions and Customs: An Introduction to the Folklore and the Folk*. London: Frank Cass, 1970.

35 Tway, Eileen. "Dimensions of Multicultural Literature for Children." In *Children's Literature: Resource for the Classroom,* edited by Masha Kabakow Rudman. Needham Heights, Mass.: Christopher-Gordon, 1989, 109–138.

CHILDREN'S LITERATURE

ASIAN AMERICAN LITERATURE

Asian Culture Centre for UNESCO. *Folktales from Asia for Children Everywhere*. 3 vols. Weatherhill, 1976, 1977 (I:8–12 R:6). The folktales come from many Asian countries.

Carrison, Muriel. *Cambodian Folk Stories from the Gatiloke*. Tuttle, 1987 (I:8+ R:7). A collection of tales originated in the teachings of Buddhist monks.

Clark, Ann Nolan. *To Stand Against the Wind*. Viking, 1978 (I:11+ R:4). An eleven-year-old Vietnamese boy's memories return to the beautiful land of his birth before it was destroyed by war.

Conger, David. *Many Lands, Many Stories: Asian Folktales for Children*. Illustrated by Ruth Ra. Tuttle, 1987 (I:8+ R:5). Fifteen folktales are identified by their countries of origin.

Davis, Daniel. *Behind Barbed Wire: The Imprisonment of Japanese Americans During World War II*. Dutton, 1982 (I:10+ R:7). Actions are taken against Japanese Americans.

Dunn, Marylois, and Ardath Mayhar. *The Absolutely Perfect Horse*. Harper & Row, 1983 (I:9+ R:6). A horse helps family members, including an adopted Vietnamese boy, understand their values.

Friedman, Ina R. *How My Parents Learned to Eat*. Illustrated by Allen Say. Houghton Mifflin, 1984 (I:6–8 R:3). A humorous story is about eating with chopsticks or with knives and forks.

Hyun, Peter, ed. *Korea's Favorite Tales and Lyrics*. Illustrated by Dong-il Park. Tuttle/Seoul International, 1986 (I:5–10 R:6). This is a collection of folktales, poems, and stories.

Ishii, Momoko. *The Tongue-Cut Sparrow*. Translated by Katherine Paterson. Illustrated by Suekichi Akaba. Dutton, 1987 (I:7–10 R:6). A kind man and a greedy wife receive quite different rewards.

Levin, Ellen. *I Hate English!* Illustrated by Steve Bjorkman. Scholastic, 1989 (I:6–9 R:4). A girl from Hong Kong is helped by a sympathetic teacher.

Lord, Bette Bao. *In the Year of the Boar and Jackie Robinson*. Illustrated by Marc Simont. Harper & Row, 1984 (I:8–12 R:4). Developing a love for baseball helps a Chinese girl make friends in America.

Mosel, Arlene. *The Funny Little Woman*. Illustrated by Blair Lent. Dutton, 1972 (I:6–8 R:6). In a Japanese folktale, a woman steals a magic paddle.

Nhuong, Huynh Quang. *The Land I Lost: Adventures of a Boy in Vietnam*. Illustrated by Vo-Dinh Mai. Harper & Row, 1982 (I:8–12 R:6). The author tells about his boyhood experiences in Vietnam.

Surat, Michele Maria. *Angel Child, Dragon Child*. Illustrated by Vo-Dinh Mai. Carnival/Raintree, 1983 (I:6–8 R:4). A young Vietnamese child learns to adjust to her American home.

Wallace, Ian. *Chin Chiang and the Dragon's Dance*. Atheneum, 1984 (I:6–9 R:6). A boy dreams of dancing on the first day of the Year of the Dragon.

Yagawa, Sumiko. *The Crane Wife*. Illustrated by Suekichi Akabas. Morrow, 1981 (I:all R:6). A traditional Japanese tale depicts the consequences of greed.

Yee, Paul. *Tales from Gold Mountain: Stories of the Chinese in the New World*. Macmillan, 1990 (I:10+ R:5). Eight original stories are based on the experiences of Chinese immigrants.

Yep, Laurence. *Child of the Owl*. Harper & Row, 1977 (I:10+ R:7). Casey learns to respect her heritage and to look deep inside herself.

———. *Dragonwings*. Harper & Row, 1975 (I:10+ R:6). In 1903, eight-year-old Moon Shadow helps his father build a flying machine.

———. *Mountain Light*. Harper & Row, 1985 (I:10+ R:6). This story is set in China and California in the 1850s.

———. *The Rainbow People*. Illustrated by David Wiesner. Harper & Row, 1989 (I:8+ R:5). This text includes Chinese folktales that were collected from Asian Americans.

———. *Sea Glass*. Harper & Row, 1979 (I:10+ R:6). Craig faces problems as he tries to make his father understand his desires.

———. *The Serpent's Children*. Harper & Row, 1984 (I:10+ R:6). In nineteenth-century China, a girl finds that she has strength to protect her family.

BLACK AMERICAN LITERATURE

Aardema, Verna. *Bringing the Rain to Kapiti Plain: A Nandi Tale*. Illustrated by Beatriz Vidal. Dial, 1981 (I:5–8). This is a cumulative tale from Kenya.

———. *What's So Funny, Ketu?* Illustrated by Marc Brown. Dial, 1982 (I:all R:4). This is a tale from Sudan.

I = Interest by age level.
R = Readability by grade level.

———. *Who's in Rabbit's House?* Illustrated by Leo and Diane Dillon. Dial, 1977 (I:7+ R:3). A Masai folktale is illustrated as a play performed by villagers wearing masks.

———. *Why Mosquitoes Buzz in People's Ears*. Illustrated by Leo and Diane Dillon. Dial, 1975 (I:5–9 R:6). An African folktale explains why mosquitoes buzz.

Adoff, Arnold. *Black Is Brown Is Tan*. Harper & Row, 1973 (I:5–7). A story in poetic form is about an integrated family.

———. *Malcolm X*. Crowell, 1970 (I:7–12 R:5). This is a biography of the black leader.

———, ed. *The Poetry of Black America: Anthology of the 20th Century*. Harper & Row, 1973. This text includes over six hundred poems by black poets.

Arkhurst, Joyce Cooper. *The Adventures of Spider: West African Folktales*. Illustrated by Jerry Pinkney. Little, Brown, 1964 (I:7–12 R:6). This is a collection of West African folk tales.

Bryan, Ashley. *Beat the Story-Drum, Pum-Pum*. Atheneum, 1980 (I:6+ R:5). This is a collection of tales.

———. *I'm Going to Sing: Black American Spirituals*, Vol. 2. Atheneum, 1982 (I:all). Words, music, and illustrations present a black experience.

———. *Lion and the Ostrich Chicks, and Other African Folk Tales*. Atheneum, 1986 (I:6+ R:5). This is a collection of folktales.

———. *Turtle Knows Your Name*. Atheneum, 1989 (I:6+ R:5). This folktale is from the West Indies.

Campbell, Barbara. *A Girl Called Bob and A Horse Called Yoki*. Dial, 1982 (I:9–12 R:5). An eight-year-old girl saves a horse from the glue factory.

Carew, Jan. *Children of the Sun*. Illustrated by Leo and Diane Dillon. Little, Brown, 1980 (I:8+ R:6). Twin boys, the children of the sun, search the world to discover the values they wish to live by.

———. *The Third Gift*. Illustrated by Leo and Diane Dillon. Little, Brown, 1974 (I:7+ R:7). A beautifully illustrated tale tells how the Jubas gained the gifts of work, beauty, imagination, and faith.

Clifton, Lucille. *Everett Anderson's Goodbye*. Illustrated by Ann Grifalconi. Holt, Rinehart & Winston, 1983 (I:6–9). Written in poetic form, the story describes a boy's pain after his father's death.

Collier, James, and Christopher Collier. *Jump Ship to Freedom*. Delacorte, 1981 (I:10+ R:7). A slave acquires his freedom and that of his mother.

Courlander, Harold. *The Crest and the Hide: And Other African Stories of Heroes, Chiefs, Bards, Hunters, Sorcerers, and Common People*. Illustrated by Monica Vachula. Coward, McCann, 1982 (I:8+ R:5). Twenty tales are from the Ashanti, Swahili, Lega, Tswana, and Yoruba cultures of Africa.

Davis, Ossie. *Langston: A Play*. Delacorte, 1982 (I:10+ R:5). Scenes from Langston Hughes's life are presented in play format.

DeKay, James T. *Meet Martin Luther King, Jr*. Illustrated by Ted Burwell. Random House, 1969 (I:7–12 R:4). This biography stresses the magnitude of Martin Luther King's work and the reasons he fought against injustice.

Desbarats, Peter. *Gabrielle and Selena*. Illustrated by Nancy Grossman. Harcourt Brace Jovanovich, 1968 (I:5–8 R:4). A black girl and a white girl share a close friendship.

De Trevino, Elizabeth Borton. *I, Juan de Pareja*. Farrar, Straus & Giroux, 1965 (I:11+ R:7). The story is based on the true characters of the seventeenth-century Spanish painter Velazquez and his black African slave, Juan de Pareja.

Ellis, Veronica Freeman. *Afro-Bets First Book About Africa*. Just Us Books, 1990 (I:8–12 R:5). The text includes a natural, social, and political history of Africa.

Feelings, Muriel. *Jambo Means Hello: Swahili Alphabet Book*. Dial, 1974 (I:all). A beautiful book uses the Swahili alphabet.

———. *Moja Means One: Swahali Counting Book*. Illustrated by Tom Feelings. Dial, 1971 (I:all). A beautiful book uses Swahili numbers.

Ferris, Jeri. *Go Free or Die: A Story of Harriet Tubman*. Carolrhoda, 1988 (I:7+ R:4). The biography describes Tubman's experiences during slavery and the Underground Railroad.

Flournoy, Valerie. *The Patchwork Quilt*. Illustrated by Jerry Pinkney. Dial, 1985 (I:5–8 R:4). Constructing a quilt brings a family together.

Fox, Paula. *How Many Miles to Babylon?* Illustrated by Paul Giovanopoulos. White, 1967 (I:8+ R:3). Ten-year-old James discovers the truth about who he really is when he is abducted by a gang of boys.

———. *Slave Dancer*. Illustrated by Eros Keith. Bradbury, 1973 (I:12+ R:7). In 1840, a fife player experiences the misery of the slave trade.

Fufka, Karama. *My Daddy Is a Cool Dude*. Illustrated by Mahiri Fufka. Dial, 1975 (I:7–9). This is an inner-city story told in poetry form.

Greene, Bette. *Philip Hall Likes Me. I Reckon Maybe*. Illustrated by Charles Lilly. Dial, 1974 (I:10+ R:4). Beth Lambert experiences her first crush.

Greenfield, Eloise. *Nathaniel Talking*. Illustrated by Jan Gilchrist. Black Butterfly Children's Books, 1989 (I:all). A boy's life is revealed through rap and verse.

———. *Paul Robeson*. Illustrated by George Ford. Crowell, 1975 (I:7–10 R:4). This text highlights the achievements and struggles of an artist and leader.

———. *Rosa Parks*. Illustrated by Eric Marlow. Crowell, 1973 (I:7–10 R:4). This biography is about the woman who refused to give up her bus seat in Montgomery, Alabama.

———. *Sister*. Illustrated by Moneta Barnett. Crowell, 1974 (I:8–12 R:5). Thirteen-year-old Doretha reviews the memories written in her journal.

———. *Under the Sunday Tree*. Illustrated by Amos Ferguson. Harper & Row, 1988 (I:all). Poetry is about the Bahamas.

Grifalconi, Ann. *The Village of Round and Square Houses*. Little, Brown, 1986 (I:4–9 R:6). A why story is from Cameroon.

Guy, Rosa. *Mother Crocodile*. Illustrated by John Steptoe. Delacorte, 1981 (I:5–9 R:6). A folktale from Senegal, West Africa, stresses that elders' advice should be heeded.

Haley, Gail E. *A Story, a Story*. Atheneum, 1970 (I:6–10 R:6). An African tale tells about a spider man's bargain with Sky God.

Hamilton, Virginia. *Anthony Burns: The Defeat and Triumph of a Fugitive Slave*. Knopf, 1988 (I:10+ R:6). This is the life of the escaped slave, whose trial caused riots in Boston.

———. *The Bells of Christmas*. Illustrated by Lambert Davis. Harcourt Brace Jovanovich, 1989 (I:8+ R:5). A prosperous black family experiences Christmas in Ohio in the 1890's.

———. *The House of Dies Drear*. Illustrated by Eros Keith. Macmillan, 1968 (I:11+ R:4). A contemporary, suspenseful story tells about a family who is living in a home that was a station on the Underground Railroad.

———. *Junius over Far*. Harper & Row, 1985 (I:10+ R:5). A boy discovers his heritage when he goes to a Caribbean island looking for his grandfather.

———. *M. C. Higgins, the Great*. Macmillan, 1974 (I:12+ R:4). M. C. dreams of fleeing from the danger of a strip mining spoil heap, but he decides to stay and build a wall to protect his home.

———. *The Magical Adventures of Pretty Pearl*. Harper & Row, 1983 (I:10+ R:5). A god-child disguises herself as a human and helps poor black people.

———. *The Mystery of Drear House*. Greenwillow, 1987 (I:11+ R:5). This is a sequel to *The House of Dies Drear*.

———, retold by. *The People Could Fly: American Black Folktales*. Illustrated by Leo and Diane Dillon. Knopf, 1985 (I:9 R:6). A collection of tales is told by or adapted by Black Americans.

———. *The Planet of Junior Brown*. Macmillan, 1971 (I:12+ R:6). Three outcasts from society create their own world in a secret basement room in a schoolhouse.

———. *Paul Robeson: The Life and Times of a Free Black Man*. Harper & Row, 1974 (I:10+ R:7). This is a biography of a football player, singer, and actor.

———. *The Time-Ago Tales of Jahdu*. Illustrated by Nonny Hogrogian. Macmillan, 1969 (I:6–11 R:3). Four stories tell about a powerful, mischievous being.

———. *Zeely*. Illustrated by Symeon Shimin. Macmillan, 1967 (I:8–12 R:4). Geeder is convinced that her tall, stately neighbor is a Watusi queen.

Hansen, Joyce. *Which Way Freedom*. Walker, 1986 (I:10+ R:6). This novel is based on historical accounts of black involvement in the Civil War.

Harris, Joel Chandler. *Jump! The Adventures of Brer Rabbit*. Adapted by Van Dyke Parks. Illustrated by Barry Moser. Harcourt Brace Jovanovich, 1986 (I:all R:4). Five Brer Rabbit stories include "The Comeuppance of Brer Wolf," "Brer Fox Goes Hunting But Brer Rabbit Bags the Game," "Brer Rabbit Finds His Match," "Brer Rabbit Grossly Deceives Brer Fox," and "The Moon in the Millpond."

———. *Jump Again! More Adventures of Brer Rabbit*. Adapted by Van Dyke Parks. Illustrated by Barry Moser. Harcourt Brace Jovanovich, 1987 (I:all R:4). Five Brer Rabbit stories include "Brer Rabbit, He's a Good Fisherman," "The Wonderful Tar-Baby Story," "How Brer Weasel Was Caught," "Brer Rabbit and the Mosquitos," and "Brer Rabbit's Courtship."

———. *More Tales of Uncle Remus: Further Adventures of Brer Rabbit, His Friends, Enemies, and Others*. Retold by Julius Lester. Dial, 1988 (I:all R:4). This book contains additional tales.

———. *The Tales of Uncle Remus: The Adventures of Brer Rabbit*. Retold by Julius Lester. Illustrated by Jerry Pinkney. Dial, 1987 (I:all R:4). This book contains forty-eight Brer Rabbit tales.

Haskins, James. *Black Theater in America*. Crowell, 1982 (I:10+ R:7). This book stresses contributions of Black people to the theater.

———. *The Life and Death of Martin Luther King, Jr.* Lothrop, Lee & Shepard, 1977 (I:10+ R:7). This biography covers the life of the Civil Rights leader.

Havill, Juanita. *Jamaica's Find*. Illustrated by Anne Sibley O'Brien. Houghton Mifflin, 1986 (I:2–6 R:2). A girl discovers how good it feels to return a lost possession.

Howard, Elizabeth Fitzgerald. *Chita's Christmas Tree*. Illustrated by Floyd Cooper. Bradbury, 1989 (I:4–8 R:3). In early Baltimore, a family prepares for Christmas.

Hurmence, Belinda. *A Girl Called Boy*. Houghton Mifflin, 1982 (I:10+ R:6). A black girl goes back in time to 1853 and experiences slavery.

Jaquith, Priscilla. *Bo Rabbit Smart for True: Folktales from the Gullah*. Illustrated by Ed Young. Philomel, 1981 (I:all R:6). Four tales from the islands off the Georgia coast.

Johnson, Angela. *Tell Me a Story, Mama*. Illustrated by David Soman. Watts, 1989 (I:3–8 R:4). This is a picture book in which a mother tells stories about her childhood.

Keats, Ezra Jack. *John Henry: An American Legend*. Pantheon, 1965 (I:6–9 R:4). This is a picture storybook of the tall tale about the baby who grew up to be a steel-driving man.

Knutson, Barbara, retold by. *Why the Crab Has No Head*. Carolrhoda, 1987 (I:all R:4). This is a why tale from Zaire.

Langstaff, John. *What a Morning! The Christmas Story in Black Spirituals*. Illustrated by Ashley Bryan. McElderry, 1987 (I:all). Five spirituals focus attention on the Christmas story.

Lester, Julius. *How Many Spots Does a Leopard Have?* Illustrated by David Shannon. Scholastic, 1989 (I:all R:4). Folktales in this collection reflect both African and Jewish traditions.

———. *The Knee-High Man and Other Tales*. Illustrated by Ralph Pinto. Dial, 1972 (I:all R:4). These six Black folktales are from the southern United States.

Lewin, Hugh. *Jafta*. Illustrated by Lisa Kopper. Carolrhoda, 1983 (I:3–7 R:6). A young South African boy is compared to the animals in his environment.

———. *Jafta and the Wedding*. Illustrated by Lisa Kopper. Carolrhoda, 1983 (I:3–7 R:6). Pictures show a village wedding celebration.

———. *Jafta's Father*. Illustrated by Lisa Kopper. Carolrhoda, 1983 (I:3–7 R:6). Jafta's father plays with him when he returns to the village.

———. *Jafta's Mother*. Illustrated by Lisa Kopper. Carolrhoda, 1983 (I:3–7 R:6). Jafta's mother is compared to the South African environment.

Little, Lessie Jones. *Children of Long Ago*. Illustrated by Jan Spivey Gilchrist. Philomel, 1988 (I:all). Poems tell about growing up in the rural South.

McDermott, Gerald. *Anansi the Spider: A Tale from the Ashanti*. Holt, Rinehart & Winston, 1972 (I:7–9). This is a colorfully illustrated African folktale.

McKissack, Patricia. *Flossie & the Fox*. Illustrated by Rachel Isadora. Dial, 1986 (I:3–8+ R:3). This is a tale of the rural South.

———. *Jesse Jackson*. Scholastic, 1989 (I:8+ R:5). A biography of the political leader emphasizes his accomplishments.

———. *Mirandy and Brother Wind*. Illustrated by Jerry Pinkney. Knopf, 1988 (I:4–9 R:5). A girl enters a cakewalk contest.

———. *Nettie Jo's Friends*. Illustrated by Scott Cook. Knopf, 1989 (I:3–8 R:3). Animal friends help a young girl find a needle so she can make a dress for her doll.

———, and Frederick McKissack. *A Long Hard Journey: The Story of the Pullman Porter*. Walker, 1989 (I:10+ R:6). A history of the porters who formed the first Black American-controlled union.

Mathis, Sharon Bell. *The Hundred Penny Box*. Illustrated by Leo and Diane Dillon. Viking, 1975 (I:6–9 R:3). Young Michael loved to hear his elderly aunt tell the story of each penny that stood for her one hundred years.

Meltzer, Milton. *The Black Americans: A History in Their Own Words, 1619–1983*. Crowell, 1984 (I:10+ R:6). This book provides information for political and social history.

———. *Langston Hughes: A Biography*. Crowell, 1968 (I:10+ R:6). This is a biography of a writer and poet.

Miller, Douglas. *Frederick Douglass and the Fight for Freedom*. Facts on File, 1988 (I:10+ R:6). The black leader escaped slavery to become a political leader.

Mitchell, Barbara. *Shoes for Everyone: A Story About Jan Matzeliger*. Carolrhoda, 1986 (I:10+ R:6). A biography tells about the man who invented the shoe-lasting machine.

Monjo, N. *The Drinking Gourd*. Illustrated by Fred Brenner. Harper & Row, 1970 (I:7–9 R:2). This is an "I Can Read" history book about the Underground Railroad.

Musgrove, Margaret. *Ashanti to Zulu: African Traditions*. Illustrated by Leo and Diane Dillon. Dial, 1976 (I:7–12 R:6). Traditions of twenty-six African peoples are presented in alphabetical order.

Myers, Walter Dean. *Scorpions*. Harper & Row, 1988 (I:11+ R:5). A boy faces problems with a gang.

Patterson, Lillie. *Frederick Douglass: Freedom Fighter*. Garrard, 1965 (I:6–9 R:3). This is a biography of a great Black American leader.

———. *Martin Luther King, Jr. and the Freedom Movement*. Facts on File, 1989 (I:10+ R:6). This book chronicles King's nonviolent struggles against segregation.

Petry, Ann. *Harriet Tubman: Conductor on the Underground Railroad*. Crowell, 1955 (I:10+ R:6). This is a biography of a woman who led over three hundred slaves to freedom.

Sanfield, Steve. *The Adventures of High John the Conqueror*. Illustrated by John Ward. Watts, 1989 (I:8+ R:4). This text includes a collection of sixteen southern folktales.

Stanley, Diane, and Peter Vennema. *Shaka: King of the Zulus*. Illustrated by Diane Stanley. Morrow, 1988 (I:6–10 R:6). This is a picture biography.

Steptoe, John. *Daddy Is a Monster. . . Sometimes*. Lippincott, 1980 (I:4–7 R:3). Two children remember the times when their daddy gets angry and takes on his monster image.

———. *Mufaro's Beautiful Daughters: An African Tale*. Lothrop, Lee & Shepard, 1987 (I:all R:4). An African folktale has some Cinderella elements.

———. *Stevie*. Harper & Row, 1969 (I:3–7 R:3). Robert is unhappy when Stevie plays with his toys and wants his own way.

Stolz, Mary. *Storm in the Night*. Illustrated by Pat Cummings. Harper & Row, 1988 (I:4–9 R:4). A young boy and his grandfather experience a storm.

Taylor, Mildred. *The Gold Cadillac*. Illustrated by Michael Hays. Dial, 1987 (I:8–10 R:3). A Black family experiences racial prejudice when it tries to drive an expensive car into the segregated South.

———. *Let the Circle Be Unbroken*. Dial, 1981 (I:10+ R:6). This is a sequel to *Roll of Thunder, Hear My Cry*.

———. *Roll of Thunder, Hear My Cry*. Dial, 1976 (I:10+ R:6). A black Mississippi family in 1933 experiences humiliating and frightening situations but retains its pride.

Tobias, Tobi. *Arthur Mitchell*. Illustrated by Carol Byard. Crowell, 1975 (I:7–9 R:5). This is a biography of the founder of Dance Theatre of Harlem.

Turner, Glennette Tilley. *Take a Walk in Their Shoes*. Cobblehill Books, 1989 (I:8+ R:4). The text includes short biographies and skits of fourteen Black Americans.

Wagner, Jane. *J. T.* Photographs by Gordon Parks, Jr. Dell, 1969 (I:7–11 R:6). Ten-year-old J. T. discovers himself as he cares for a battered cat and interacts with people in his inner-city neighborhood.

Walter, Mildred Pitts. *Brother to the Wind*. Illustrated by Diane and Leo Dillon. Lothrop, Lee & Shepard, 1985 (I:all R:3). An African boy wishes to fly.

———. *Justin and the Best Biscuits in the World*. Illustrated by Catherine Stock. Lothrop, Lee & Shepard, 1986 (I:7–10 R:5). A young black boy spends time on his grandfather's ranch.

Ward, Leila. *I Am Eyes, Ni Macho*. Illustrated by Nonny Hogrogian. Greenwillow, 1978 (I:3–7 R:1). An African child wakes to the marvelous sights of her land.

Weik, Mary Hays. *The Jazz Man*. Illustrated by Ann Grifalconi. Atheneum, 1966 (I:7–10 R:6). When the Jazz Man moves into the apartment with the wonderful yellow walls, life seems to change for a crippled boy living in Harlem.

Williams, Vera B. *Cherries and Cherry Pits*. Greenwillow, 1986 (I:3–8 R:3). A girl uses her magic marker to tell stories about people who like cherries.

Yates, Elizabeth. *Amos Fortune, Free Man*. Illustrated by Nora S. Unwin. Dutton, 1950 (I:10+ R:6). An African becomes a slave in Boston.

HISPANIC AMERICAN LITERATURE

Aardema, Verna. *The Riddle of the Drum: A Tale from Tizapán, Mexico*. Illustrated by Tony Chen. Four Winds, 1979 (I:6–10 R:3). The man who marries the king's daughter must guess the kind of leather in a drum.

Ashabranner, Brent. *Children of the Maya: A Guatemalan Indian Odyssey*. Photographs by Paul Conklin. Dodd, Mead, 1986 (I:10+ R:7). Photographs and text depict the life of Guatemalan refugees.

Beals, Carleton. *Stories Told by the Aztecs: Before the Spaniards Came*. Illustrated by Charles Pickard. Abelard, 1970 (I:10+ R:7). A collection of tales has footnotes and a bibliography.

Behrens, June. *Fiesta!* Photographs by Scott Taylor. Children's Press, 1978 (I:5–8 R:4). This book contains photographs of the Cinco de Mayo fiesta.

Belpré, Pura. *Once in Puerto Rico*. Illustrated by Christine Price. Warne, 1973 (I:8–12 R:5). This is a collection of Puerto Rican tales.

———. *The Rainbow-Colored Horse*. Illustrated by Antonio Martorell. Warne, 1978 (I:6–10 R:5). Three favors granted by a horse allow Pio to win the hand of the Don Nicanor's daughter.

Bierhorst, John, ed. *Black Rainbow: Legends of the Incas and Myths of Ancient Peru*. Farrar, Straus & Giroux, 1976 (I:10+ R:7). These are twenty traditional tales.

———. *Doctor Coyote: A Native American Aesop's Fables*. Illustrated by Wendy Watson. Macmillan, 1987 (I:all). A fable is from Indians of Mexico.

———, ed. *The Hungry Woman: Myths and Legends of the Aztecs*. Morrow, 1984 (I:12+ R:6). The tales include creation myths and legends about the conquest.

———, ed. *The Monkey's Haircut and Other Stories Told by the Maya*. Illustrated by Robert Andrew Parker. Morrow, 1986 (I:8+ R:6). This book contains twenty-two tales.

———. *The Mythology of South America*. Morrow, 1988 (I:12+ R:7). This is a good resource for information.

———, trans. *Spirit Child: A Story of the Nativity*. Illustrated by Barbara Cooney. Morrow, 1984 (I:8–12 R:6). Pre-Columbian illustrations accompany an Aztec story.

Blackmore, Vivien. *Why Corn Is Golden: Stories About Plants*. Illustrated by Susana Martinez-Ostos. Little, Brown, 1984 (I:all R:5). This book contains folklore about corn.

Brown, Tricia. *Hello Amigos!* Photographs by Fran Ortiz. Holt, Rinehart & Winston, 1986 (I:3–8 R:3). Photographs accompany a boy on his sixth birthday.

Burland, Cottie. *An Aztec Town*. Hutchinson, 1980 (I:all R:5). This is a highly illustrated version of how a town might have appeared.

Cisneros, Sandra. *The House on Mango Street*. Arte Publico, 1983 (I:12+ R:7). A girl records her feelings about the world.

Clark, Ann Nolan. *Secret of the Andes*. Illustrated by Jean Charlot. Viking, 1952, 1980 (I:8+ R:5). A boy learns about the traditions of his Inca ancestors.

———. *Year Walk*. Viking, 1975 (I:10+ R:7). A Spanish Basque sheepherder faces loneliness as he takes his 2,500 sheep across the desert into the high country.

De Gerez, Toni. *My Song Is a Piece of Jade: Poems of Ancient Mexico in English and Spanish*. Illustrated by William Stark. Little, Brown, 1981 (I:all). Ancient Mexican poems are written in English and Spanish.

Delacre, Lulu. *Arroz con Leche: Popular Songs and Rhymes from Latin America*. Scholastic, 1989 (I:all). This text includes a variety of songs and poems.

DeMessieres, Nicole. *Reina the Galgo*. Dutton, 1981 (I:10+ R:6). An eleven-year-old girl describes her experiences living in Peru.

de Paola, Tomie. *The Lady of Guadalupe*. Holiday House, 1980 (I:8+ R:6). This is a traditional Mexican tale.

Ets, Marie Hall, and Aurora Labastida. *Nine Days to Christmas: A Story of Mexico*. Illustrated by Marie Hall Ets. Viking, 1959 (I:5–8 R:3). Ceci is going to have her first Posada with her own piñata.

Garcia, Richard. *My Aunt Otilia's Spirits*. Illustrated by Robin Cherin and Roger Reyes. Children's Press, 1987 (I:5–8 R:2). An aunt from Puerto Rico with magical powers visits her family in the United States.

Griego y Maestas, José, and Rudolfo A. Anaya. *Cuentos: Tales from the Hispanic Southwest*. Illustrated by Jaime Valdez. Museum of New Mexico, 1980 (I:9+ R:5). This is a collection of tales.

Griego, Margot C. *Tortillitas Para Mama and Other Spanish Nursery Rhymes*. Illustrated by Barbara Cooney. Holt, Rinehart & Winston, 1981 (I:3–7). Nursery rhymes appear in Spanish and English.

Hall, Lynn. *Danza!* Scribner's Sons, 1981 (I:10+ R:6). A boy and his horse share life on a farm in Puerto Rico.

Hargreaves, Pat. *The Caribbean and Gulf of Mexico*. Silver Burdett, 1980 (I:10+ R:6). This book contains informational photographs and text.

Highwater, Jamake. *Journey to the Sky*. Crowell, 1978 (I:12+ R:7). Two men search for the Mayan kingdom.

Hinojosa, Francisco, adapted by. *The Old Lady Who Ate People*. Illustrated by Leonel Maciel. Little, Brown, 1984 (I:all R:6). These four frightening folktales are from Mexico.

Jagendorf, M. A., and R. S. Boggs. *The King of the Mountains: A Treasury of Latin American Folk Stories*. Vanguard, 1960 (I:9+ R:6). This is a collection of tales from twenty-six countries.

Krumgold, Joseph. . . *.And Now Miguel*. Illustrated by Jean Charlot. Crowell, 1953 (I:10+ R:3). Miguel Chavez is a member of a proud sheep-raising family.

Kurtycz, Marcos, and Ana Garciá Kobeh. *Tigers and Opossums: Animal Legends*. Little, Brown, 1984 (I:all R:8). These animal tales are from Mexico.

Lattimore, Deborah. *The Flame of Peace: A Tale of the Aztecs*. Harper & Row, 1987 (I:all R:6). This story is based on Aztec mythology.

Lindop, Edmund. *Cuba*. Watts, 1980 (I:10+ R:6). This book contains history, geography, and current information.

Mangurian, David. *Children of the Incas*. Macmillan, 1979 (I:7–12 R:3). Photographs and text tell about a boy in Peru.

Markun, Patricia Maloney. *Central America and Panama*. Watts, 1983 (I:10+ R:6). This book is about the geography, history, economics, and politics of the area.

Marrin, Albert. *Aztecs and Spaniards: Cortés and the Conquest of Mexico*. Atheneum, 1986 (I:12+ R:7). This book is a history of the Aztecs and tells about the influence of Cortés.

Martinello, Marian L., and Samuel P. Nesmith. *With Domingo Leal in San Antonio 1734*. The University of Texas, Institute of Texas Cultures at San Antonio, 1979 (I:8+ R:4). This book tells the results of research investigating the lives of Spanish settlers who arrived in Texas in the 1730s.

Meltzer, Milton. *The Hispanic Americans*. Photographs by Morrie Camhi and Catherine Noren. Crowell, 1982 (I:9–12 R:6). Puerto Ricans, Chicanos, and Cubans have influenced America.

Meyer, Carolyn, and Charles Gallenkamp. *The Mystery of the Ancient Maya*. Atheneum, 1985 (I:10 R:8). This book tells about early explorers and discoveries.

Millard, Anne. *The Incas*. Illustrated by Richard Hook. Warwick, 1980 (I:10+ R:6). Text and illustrations show the accomplishments of the Incas.

Mohr, Nicholasa. *El Bronx Remembered: A Novella and Stories*. Harper & Row, 1975 (I:10+ R:6). Twelve short stories are set in the inner city.

———. *Felita*. Illustrated by Ray Cruz. Dial, 1979 (I:9–12 R:2). Felita is unhappy when her family moves to a new neighborhood.

———. *Going Home*. Dial, 1986 (I:10+ R:6). Twelve-year-old Felita spends the summer with relatives in Puerto Rico.

———. *Nilda*. Harper & Row, 1973 (I:10+ R:6). This is the story of a Puerto Rican girl living in Harlem during the 1940s.

O'Dell, Scott. *The Amethyst Ring*. Houghton Mifflin, 1983 (I:10+ R:6). This is the final story of Julian Escobar.

———. *The Captive*. Houghton Mifflin, 1979 (I:10+ R:6). A young Spanish seminarian witnesses the exploitation of the Maya during the 1500s.

———. *Carlota*. Houghton Mifflin, 1981 (I:10+ R:6). A high-spirited Spanish-American girl fights beside her father during the days of the Mexican War in early California.

———. *The Feathered Serpent*. Houghton Mifflin, 1981 (I:10+ R:6). This book is a sequel to *The Captive*.

———. *The King's Fifth*. Houghton Mifflin, 1966 (I:10+ R:6). Esteban de Sandoval accompanies Coronado's army in search of the cities of gold.

Phillips, Betty Lou. *The Picture Story of Nancy Lopez*. Messner, 1980 (I:8+ R:4). This is the biography of a professional golfer.

Politi, Leo. *The Nicest Gift*. Scribner's Sons, 1973 (I:5–8 R:6). Carbitos lives in the barrio of East Los Angeles with his family and his dog Blanco.

———. *Song of the Swallows*. Scribner's Sons, 1949 (I:5–8 R:4). Juan lives in Capistrano, California. Excellent illustrations show Spanish architecture.

Prago, Albert. *Strangers in Their Own Land: A History of Mexican-Americans*. Four Winds, 1973 (I:10+ R:7). This book traces both the history and the difficulties of Mexican-Americans.

Roberts, Maurice. *Henry Cisneros: Mexican American Mayor*. Children's Press, 1986 (I:8+ R:5). This is the biography of a former mayor of San Antonio.

Rohmer, Harriet, Octavio Chow, and Morris Viduare. *The Invisible Hunters*. Illustrated by Joe Sam. Children's Press, 1987 (I:all R:5). A tale reflects the impact of European traders.

———, and Dornminster Wilson. *Mother Scorpion Country*. Illustrated by Virginia Steams. Children's Press, 1987 (I:all R:4). A Central American tale is written in both English and Spanish.

Rutland, Jonathan. *Take a Trip to Spain*. Watts, 1980 (I:6–10 R:3). This book contains color photographs of Spain.

Schon, Isabel, ed. *Doña Blanca and Other Hispanic Nursery Rhymes and Games*. Denison, 1983 (I:4–8). Nursery rhymes are presented in English and Spanish.

Soto, Gary. *Baseball in April and Other Stories*. Harcourt Brace Jovanovich, 1990 (I:11+ R:6). This is a collection of stories about Mexican-American Youth in California.

White, Clarence. *Cesar Chavez, Man of Courage*. Garrard, 1973 (I:8+ R:5). This is a biography of a political leader.

NATIVE AMERICAN LITERATURE

Aliki. *Corn Is Maize: The Gift of the Indians*. Crowell, 1976 (I:6–8 R:2). This is a history of corn, how it grows, and how it was first used.

Anderson, Bernice G. *Trickster Tales from Prairie Lodgefires*. Illustrated by Frank Gee. Abingdon, 1979 (I:all R:5). Tales come from the Blackfoot, Kiowa, Crow, Ponca, Dakota, and Cheyenne.

Ashabranner, Brent. *To Live in Two Worlds: American Indian Youth Today*. Photographs by Paul Conklin. Dodd, Mead, 1984 (I:10+ R:7). Indian youth tell about their lives.

———. *Morning Star, Black Sun: The Northern Cheyenne Indians and America's Energy Crisis*. Photographs by Paul Conklin. Dodd, Mead, 1982 (I:10+ R:7). This book traces the history of the Northern Cheyenne and discusses the fight to save their lands.

Baker, Betty. *Rat Is Dead and Ant Is Sad*. Illustrated by Mamoru Funai. Harper & Row, 1981 (I:6–8 R:2). This is a cumulative Pueblo Indian tale.

Baker, Olaf. *Where the Buffaloes Begin*. Illustrated by Stephen Gammell. Warne, 1981 (I:all R:6). A story tells about the lake where the buffaloes were created.

Batherman, Muriel. *Before Columbus*. Houghton Mifflin, 1981 (I:6–9 R:5). Illustrations and text present information about North American inhabitants revealed from archaeological explorations.

Baylor, Byrd. *The Desert Is Theirs*. Illustrated by Peter Parnall. Scribner's Sons, 1975. (I:all). The life of the Papago Indians is captured in illustrations and text.

———. *A God on Every Mountain Top: Stories of Southwest Indian Mountains*. Illustrated by Carol Brown. Scribner's Sons, 1981 (I:6–10 R:5). Southwest Indian folktales tell about the sacred mountains.

———. *Hawk, I'm Your Brother*. Illustrated by Peter Parnall. Scribner's Sons, 1976 (I:all). Rudy Soto would like to glide through the air like a hawk, wrapped up in the wind.

———. *Moonsong*. Illustrated by Ronald Himler. Scribner's Sons, 1982 (I:all). Written in poetic style, this Pima Indian tale tells how coyote was born of the moon.

———. *The Other Way to Listen*. Illustrated by Peter Parnall. Scribner's Sons, 1978. (I:all). If one listens carefully, nature is heard.

———. *When Clay Sings*. Illustrated by Tom Bahti. Scribner's Sons, 1972 (I:all). A poetic telling of the ancient way of life is stimulated by designs on prehistoric Indian pottery found in the Southwest desert.

Bierhorst, John. *A Cry from the Earth: Music of the North American Indians*. Four Winds, 1979 (I:all). This is a collection of Indian songs of North America.

———. *The Ring in the Prairie, a Shawnee Legend*. Illustrated by Leo and Diane Dillon. Dial, 1970 (I:all R:6). One of the most skilled Indian hunters discovers a mysterious circle in an opening in the forest.

———, ed. *The Sacred Path: Spells, Prayers, and Power Songs of the American Indians*. Morrow, 1983 (I:8+). This is a collection of poems, prayers, and songs.

———, ed. *The Whistling Skeleton: American Indian Tales of the Supernatural*. Illustrated by Robert Andrew Parker. Four Winds, 1982 (I:10+ R:6). Nine mystery tales are told by nineteenth-century storytellers.

Bulla, Clyde Robert, and Michael Syson. *Conquista!* Illustrated by Ronald Himler. Crowell, 1978 (I:6–10 R:2). A story tells how a young Native American boy might have experienced his first horse at the time of Coronado.

Cleaver, Elizabeth. *The Enchanted Caribou*. Atheneum, 1985 (I:6–10 R:6). This is an Inuit tale of transformation.

Coatsworth, Emerson, and David Coatsworth, eds. *The Adventures of Nanabush: Ojibway Indian Stories*. Illustrated by Francis Kagige. Atheneum, 1980 (I:8+ R:6). Sixteen tales are told by Ojibway tribal elders.

Curtis, Edward S. *The Girl Who Married a Ghost and Other Tales from the North American Indian*, edited by John Bierhorst. Four Winds, 1978 (I:9+ R:5). The tales are from the Plains, California, the Northwest, the Southwest, and Alaska.

Cushing, Frank Hamilton. *Zuni Folk Tales*. University of Arizona Press, 1901, 1986. An adult source contains many tales that may be retold to or read by older students.

de Paola, Tomie. *The Legend of the Bluebonnet*. Putnam, 1983 (I:all R:6). In a Comanche tale, unselfish actions are rewarded.

Esbensen, Barbara Juster, ed. *The Star Maiden*. Illustrated by Helen K. Davie. Little, Brown, 1988 (I:all). A poetic Ojibway tale tells about creation of water lilies.

Freedman, Russell. *Buffalo Hunt*. Holiday House, 1988 (I:8+ R:6). Illustrations and text show the importance of the buffalo to Great Plains Indians.

———. *Indian Chiefs*. Holiday House, 1987 (I:10+ R:6). Here are short biographies of six Indian chiefs.

Fritz, Jean. *The Double Life of Pocahontas*. Illustrated by Ed Young. Putnam, 1983 (I:8–10 R:7). A biography of Pocahontas focuses on her involvement with two cultures.

George, Jean Craighead. *The Talking Earth*. Harper & Row, 1983 (I:10+ R:6). An Indian girl tries to discover her heritage.

———. *Water Sky*. Harper & Row, 1987 (I:10+ R:6). A boy discovers his Eskimo heritage.

Goble, Paul. *Beyond the Ridge*. Bradbury, 1989 (I:all R:5). An elderly Indian woman from the Great Plains experiences death and goes to the afterlife.

———. *Buffalo Woman*. Bradbury, 1984 (I:all R:6). A bond between animals and humans is developed in a tale from the Great Plains.

———. *Death of the Iron Horse*. Bradbury, 1987 (I:8+ R:5). This story is based on an incident in 1867, when a Union Pacific frieght train was derailed by Cheyenne Indians.

———. *The Gift of the Sacred Dog*. Bradbury, 1980 (I:all R:6). The Sioux tale tells how the horse was given to the people.

———. *The Girl Who Loved Wild Horses*. Bradbury, 1978 (I:6–10 R:5). A picture storybook tells about an Indian girl's attachment to horses.

———. *Iktomi and the Berries*. Watts, 1989 (I:4–10 R:4). Iktomi is a trickster character from the Lakota Sioux.

———. *Iktomi and the Boulder: A Plains Indian Story*. Orchard, 1988 (I:4–10 R:4). This trickster tale is good for choral arrangements.

Hamilton, Virginia. *In the Beginning: Creation Stories from Around the World*. Illustrated by Barry Moser. Harcourt Brace Jovanovich, 1988 (I:all R:5). The creation stories come from many cultures.

Harris, Christie. *Mouse Woman and the Vanished Princesses*. Illustrated by Douglas Tait. Atheneum, 1976 (I:10+ R:6). The six tales come from the northwestern coast of North America.

———. *The Trouble with Adventurers*. Illustrated by Douglas Tait. Atheneum, 1982 (I:10+ R:6). A collection of stories was drawn from the Northwest Coast tribes.

Haseley, Dennis. *The Scared One*. Illustrated by Deborah Howland. Warne, 1983 (I:5–8 R:6). A Native American boy faces and overcomes fear and ridicule.

Haviland, Virginia. *North American Legends*. Illustrated by Ann Stugnell. Philomel, 1979 (I:8+ R:6). This is a large collection of Native American, Black, and European variants and tall tales.

Highwater, Jamake. *Anpao: An American Indian Odyssey*. Illustrated by Fritz Scholder. Lippincott, 1977 (I:12+ R:5). Anpao journeys across the history of Native American traditional tales in order to search for his destiny.

———. *The Ceremony of Innocence*. Harper & Row, 1985 (I:12+ R:6). This is part two of the Ghost Horse Cycle.

———. *I Wear the Morning Star*. Harper & Row, 1986 (I:12+ R:6). This is part three of the Ghost Horse Cycle.

———. *Legend Days*. Harper & Row, 1984 (I:12+ R:6). A Northern Plains Indian is the focus of this part one of the Ghost Horse Cycle.

———. *Moonsong Lullaby*. Photographs by Marcia Keegan. Lothrop, Lee & Shepard, 1981 (I:all). Color photographs show the animals and activities as the moon watches.

Hirschfelder, Arlene. *Happily May I Walk: American Indians and Alaska Natives Today*. Scribner's Sons, 1986 (I:10+ R:6). An informational book is about such topics as reservations, performing artists, and sports.

Hobbs, Will. *Bearstone*. Atheneum, 1989 (I:10+ R:6). A troubled Ute boy is helped by an elderly rancher.

Hudson, Jan. *Sweetgrass*. Tree Frog, 1984 (I:10+ R:4). A Blackfoot girl grows up during the winter of a smallpox epidemic in 1837.

Jassem, Kate. *Sacajawea, Wilderness Guide*. Illustrated by Jan Palmer. Troll Associates, 1979 (I:6–9 R:2). This is an illustrated biography of the Shoshone woman who guided the Lewis and Clark expedition.

Luenn, Nancy. *Nessa's Fish*. Atheneum, 1990 (I:4–8 R:4). An Inuit girl and her grandmother go on an ice fishing expedition.

Marrin, Albert. *War Clouds in the West: Indians & Cavalrymen, 1860–1890*. Atheneum, 1984 (I:10+ R:6). This is a history of the conflict for the West.

Martin, Bill, and John Archambault. *Knots on a Counting Rope*. Holt, Rinehart & Winston, 1987 (I:all). A poetic story is about a blind boy's horse race as told by his grandfather.

Metayer, Maurice, ed. *Tales from the Igloo*. Illustrated by Agnes Nanogak. Hurtig, 1972 (I:all R:5). This is a collection of Copper Eskimo tales.

Miles, Miska. *Annie and the Old One*. Illustrated by Peter Parnall. Little, Brown, 1971 (I:6–8 R:3). Annie's love for her Navaho grandmother causes her to prevent the completion of a rug that she associates with the probable death of her grandmother.

Monroe, Jean Guard, and Ray A. Williamson. *They Dance in the Sky: Native American Star Myths*. Illustrated by Edgar Stewart. Houghton Mifflin, 1987 (I:10+ R:7). A collection of tales is from different peoples.

Morrison, Dorothy Nafus. *Chief Sarah: Sarah Winnemucca's Fight for Indian Rights*. Atheneum, 1980 (I:10+ R:6). Sarah was a leader of the Paiute people.

Mowat, Farley. *Lost in the Barrens*. Illustrated by Charles Geer. McClelland & Stewart, 1966, 1984 (I:9+ R:6). A Cree Indian boy and his friend are lost in northern Canada.

O'Dell, Scott. *Black Star, Bright Dawn*. Houghton Mifflin, 1988 (I:8+ R:6). An Eskimo girl enters the Iditarod Trail Sled Dog Race in Alaska.

———. *Sing Down the Moon*. Houghton Mifflin, 1970 (I:10+ R:6). A young Navaho girl tells of the 1864 forced march of her people.

Paulsen, Gary. *Dogsong*. Bradbury, 1988 (I:10+ R:6). An Eskimo boy journeys 1,400 miles by dogsled as he crosses the ice.

Poatgieter, Alice Hermina. *Indian Legacy: Native American Influences on World Life and Culture*. Messner, 1981 (I:10+ R:7). This book discusses Native North and South American contributions to democratic attitudes, agriculture, and culture.

Prusski, Jeffrey. *Bring Back the Deer*. Illustrated by Neil Waldman. Harcourt Brace Jovanovich, 1988 (I:6+ R:5). A Native American boy discovers the values of respect, wisdom, and patience.

Robbins, Ruth. *How the First Rainbow Was Made*. Parnassus, 1980 (I:6–9 R:6). A California Indian tale tells how Coyote got the Old Man Above to make the first rainbow.

Robinson, Gail. *Raven the Trickster: Legends of the North American Indians*. Illustrated by Joanna Troughton. Atheneum, 1982 (I:8–12 R:6). The nine tales are from the Northwest Indian tribes.

Rockwood, Joyce. *Groundhog's Horse*. Illustrated by Victor Kalin. Holt, Rinehart & Winston, 1978 (I:7–12 R:4). A young Cherokee boy's horse is stolen by the Creeks in 1750.

Sneve, Virginia Driving Hawk, selected by. *Dancing Teepees: Poems of American Indian Youth*. Illustrated by Stephen Gammell. Holiday House, 1989 (I:all). This is a collection of ancient and contemporary poems.

———. *High Elk's Treasure*. Illustrated by Oren Lyons. Holiday House, 1972 (I:8–12 R:6). A dream beginning in the autumn of 1876 is renewed in the 1970s when Joe High Elk's family expands the herd of palomino horses.

———. *Jimmy Yellow Hawk*. Illustrated by Oren Lyons. Holiday House, 1972 (I:6–10 R:5). Awarded first prize in its category by the Council on Interracial Books for Children, this story is about a contemporary Sioux boy who lives on an Indian reservation in South Dakota.

———. *When Thunder Spoke*. Illustrated by Oren Lyons. Holiday House, 1974 (I:8–12 R:4). A fifteen-year-old Sioux boy experiences conflict between the old ways and the new.

Speare, Elizabeth George. *The Sign of the Beaver*. Houghton Mifflin, 1983 (I:8–12 R:5). A white boy survives through the help of a Native American friend.

Spear, Jean. *A Candle for Christmas*. Illustrated by Ann Blades. Macmillan (I:3–8 R:3). A young boy lights a candle to help his parents find their way home.

Spencer, Paula Underwood. *Who Speaks for Wolf*. Illustrated by Frank Howell. Tribe of Two Press, 1983 (I:all R:5). This is a Native American learning story.

Steptoe, John. *The Story of Jumping Mouse*. Lothrop, Lee & Shepard, 1984 (I:all R:4). This is a Great Plains Indian legend.

Toye, William. *The Loon's Necklace*. Illustrated by Elizabeth Cleaver. Oxford, 1977 (I:all R:5). This tale explains how the loon received the lovely shell markings around its neck and across its wings.

Wallas, James. *Kwakiutl Legends*. Recorded by Pamela Whitaker. Hancock House, 1981 (I:all R:4). Tales from British Columbia are told by Chief Wallas of the Quatsino tribe.

Whitaker, Muriel, ed. *Stories from the Canadian North*. Illustrated by Vlasta van Kampen. Hurtig, 1980 (I:12+ R:7). This is a collection of short stories.

White Deer of Autumn. *Ceremony—In the Circle of Life*. Illustrated by Daniel San Souci. Raintree, 1983 (I:all R:5). A nine-year-old boy discovers his ancestors' beliefs.

12

Nonfiction: Biographies and Informational Books

FROM WHO'S-WHO TO HOW-TO

INVOLVING CHILDREN IN NONFICTIONAL LITERATURE

From Who's-Who to How-To

BIOGRAPHIES

INFORMATIONAL BOOKS

CURIOSITY AND THE DESIRE TO MAKE discoveries about the world strongly motivate children to read. Books of nonfiction encourage children to look at the world in new ways, to discover laws of nature and society, and to identify with people different from themselves.

BIOGRAPHIES

Many children who read well-written biographies feel as if the biographical subjects become personal friends. Often, these children carry with them into adulthood a love of nonfiction that portrays the lives of interesting people with whom they can identify and from whom they can learn. Biography offers children the high adventure and engrossing drama that fiction also supplies, but it also offers the special satisfaction of knowing that the people and events described are "really real."

Writers of biographies have a vast pool of real people from which to choose. There are brave men and women who conquer seas, discover new continents, and explore space. There are equally brave and intelligent women and men who fight discrimination, change lives through their ministering or inventions, and overcome handicaps in their efforts to achieve. The ways in which writers of children's literature choose to portray these figures, however, change with historical time periods.

Changing Ideas About Biographies for Children

A brief review of biographies for children shows that the authors of biographies have been influenced by social attitudes toward children and attitudes about appropriate content. Children's biographies written in the seventeenth through the nineteenth centuries in Europe and North America were affected by the didactic themes of the Puritan era, the Victorian emphasis on duty to God and parents, the values associated with the American frontier, and the belief that children should be educated in a highly structured environment. In addition, early biographers believed that children's biographies should be tools for religious, political, or social education. Emulation of biographical heroes was considered desirable (18). Consequently, many pre-twentieth century biographies reflected the belief that literature should save children's souls. Jon Stott (21) concludes that this time produced numerous "biographies of good little children who died early and went to

Heaven and of bad little children who died early and went to Hell" (p. 177). For example, in 1671, leading Puritan writer James Janeway published a series of stories about children who died at an early age after leading saintly lives.

In the mid-1800s, the religious zeal of many early Americans was replaced by concern for the nation and the acquisition of the "American dream." Salvation was no longer the primary goal. The supreme achievements were acquisition of power, fame, and wealth. Consequently, biography changed from a religious tool to a political tool.

The early twentieth century brought new insights into child development. The developing science of psychology emphasized the vulnerability of youth and a need for protective legislation. Religious training placed less emphasis on sinfulness and more emphasis on moral development and responsibility toward others. In keeping with these ideas, biographers also protected children from the indiscretions of biographical subjects. Because idealized heroes were still believed to be desirable and necessary, biographers avoided areas concerning sensitive political beliefs and private lives. Taboos imposed by society included infamous people, unsavory or undistinguishing actions, and controversial subjects.

Furthermore, in the early 1900s, as in earlier periods of American history, the contributions of female and nonwhite Americans were either not highly regarded or were considered too controversial. Traditional social patterns kept most women and members of minority groups out of the positions of power and the fame that produced what American society considered the most appropriate subjects of biography. Consequently, few biographies dealt with women, Black Americans, Native Americans, and members of other ethnic and racial minorities.

Biographies of most political leaders published through the 1960s continued to present role models for political and social instruction. Omissions and distortions allowed biographers to stress important contributions and highlight dates of accomplishment. Biographers still did not explore motives. Literary critic Margery Fisher (8) maintains that biographies for children were controlled by an establishment that exercised a powerful invisible influence.

In an effort to increase the ability of children to empathize with political heroes, biographers writing for young readers often focused on the boyhood years of their characters. Still, these biographers tended to glorify the individuals. For example, the titles of several biographies published by Bobbs-Merrill before 1980 indicated the accomplishments that the subjects would achieve: *Thomas Paine: Common Sense Boy* and *John D. Rockefeller: Boy Financier*.

During the late 1960s and the 1970s, traditional social, family, and personal values were changing. The new openness was reflected in fiction for children. In addition, the previous instructional uses of, and role models in, children's biography were challenged. Some literary critics, educators, and authors of children's biographies maintained that idealizing subjects distorted not only history but also development. According to this argument, if prominent men and women were shown in favorable lights only, children would assume that because they themselves make errors, they could never be great. In an effort to overcome past shortcomings in biographies for children, Marilyn Jurich (15) advocated a greater variety in the choice of subjects—including great people who were not famous, ordinary people, and antiheroes—as well as a fuller and more honest treatment of all subjects. Biographer Russell Freedman (10) summarizes the changes when he concludes:

> The hero worship of the past has given way to a more realistic approach, which recognizes the warts and weaknesses that humanize the great. And fictionalization has become a naughty word. Many current biographies for children adhere as closely to documented evidence as any scholarly work. And the best of them manage to do so without becoming tedious or abstract or any less exciting than the most imaginative fictionalization. (p. 447)

As with realistic fiction, educators, authors, publishers, and parents today have different opinions about what the content of children's biographies should be. Jean Fritz (12), a well-known author of historical biographies for young children, says:

> Biographies have for the most part lagged behind other types of children's literature, bogged down, for one thing, by didacticism. Famous men and women must be shown in their best colors so children can emulate them. The idea of emulation has been a powerful factor in determining the nature of biography for children; you see the word over and over again in textbooks and courses of study. And I think it has done great harm in distorting history and breeding cynicism; the great men are all gone, the implication is. Because history is old, educators are often guilty of simply repeating it instead of taking a fresh look at it. Because it is complicated,

THROUGH THE EYES OF AN AUTHOR

On Writing Biography

JEAN FRITZ, biographer of early American patriots, creates believable characters by admitting their foibles as well as their strengths.

THE REASON FOR WRITING biography for children is the same as for writing biography for adults: to explore human behavior; to come to grips with specific characters interrelating with their specific times. This is not as obvious as it sounds. It was once a commonly held assumption (one that still persists in some quarters) that biographies written for children should portray idealized heroes and heroines, models held up by the adult world to inspire children to attain virtue and, by implication, its concomitant rewards. Furthermore, according to some educators, the motivation of characters should not be examined, only their deeds.

Such an approach, it seems to me, is dull, unrealistic, and unfair. Children look for clues to life. They want the truth, they need the truth, and they deserve it. So I try to present characters honestly with their paradoxes and their complexities, their strengths and their weaknesses. To do this, I involve myself in as much research as I would if I were writing a biography for adults. Contrary to what I call "old-fashioned" biography for children, I do not invent dialogue. I use dialogue only when I can document it. If the text is meaty enough, I do not think that children need facts dressed up in fictional trimmings. Indeed, children welcome hard, specific facts that bring characters to life—not only the important facts but those small vivid details that have a way of lighting up an event or a personality. Had I been present, for instance, to hear Patrick Henry give his famous "liberty or death" speech, I would certainly have been impressed by his dramatic oratory, but I would also have remembered the man in the balcony who became so excited, he spit a wad of tobacco into the audience below. The trivial and the significant generally travel hand in hand and indeed I suspect that most people find that memory of trivial off-the-record detail serves to nail down memory itself. I think of history and biography as *story* and am convinced that the best stories are the true ones.

they tend to simplify by watering down material for children, whereas children need more meat rather than less, but selected for their own interests. This, of course, involves original research, a great deal of it, which twenty years ago, I think was rather rare in children's biographies. (p. 125)

Biographies now develop many sides of a person's character—as well as people who are female and nonwhite, like many young readers themselves. Readers may discover, through the work of such authors as Jean Fritz, that the heroes of biography were real people who, like other humans, often demonstrated negative qualities. In fact, a biographical subject who is a believable human being may be easier for children to emulate than a subject who is not.

Gertrude B. Herman (13) relates changing understanding of biography to children's stages of personal development. She maintains that until children are about eight years old, they have difficulty stepping out of their own time and space to explore the lives of real people whom they most likely can never meet. Herman believes that children in the fourth through sixth grades read biographies with increasing understanding and self-identification, as long as the books are about people they are interested in and the authors have written to hold the children's interest. In adolescence, says Herman, children are—

finally ready for causes. . .and for all those fascinating persons who are not necessarily models of perfection, but who are human beings through whose doubts and triumphs, courage or villainy, victories or defeats, young people may try on personalities, life styles, and modes of thought and commitment. It is in investigating, in shifting and winnowing facts and ideas, in empathizing with the deeds and sufferings of others that growth is helped along—intellectual, emotional, and spiritual growth. It is through this integrative function that biography and autobiography, honesty presented with literary and artistic merit, can make important contributions to self-integration and social realization. The testimony of many individuals over many years supports a conviction that young people have much to gain from reading about real human beings in all their complexity, with all their sometimes troubled lives. (p. 88)

Evaluating Biographies

Like other literature, biographies should be evaluated according to the criteria for good literature. They should carefully avoid negative stereotypes based on gender, race, ethnicity, and physical ability. With regard to literary elements, the development of characterization is of primary concern, and authors of biography must place special emphasis on accuracy of detail and use sound research methods. Adults who select biographies for children should be concerned with the accuracy of the information, the worthiness of the subject, and the balance between fact and story line.

Characterization. Margaret Fleming and Jo McGinnis (9) compare the artistry required in the writing of a good biography to the artistry required in the painting of a portrait; the "style and setting only enhance the portrayal of the subject. The development of character is the primary focus" (p. xi). Like other authors, biographers have a responsibility to portray their subjects three-dimensionally. Unlike authors of fiction, biographers are restricted from inventing characters and indicating unsupported thoughts and actions.

Elizabeth Robertson and Jo McGinnis (19) provide a guideline for evaluating characterization:

In biography, the writer can only infer from the actions of the subject and other characters what might be going on in the person's head. Look for evidence that the biographer is overstepping the bounds of scholarly writing in this respect. (p. 19)

Robertson and McGinnis recommend that readers analyze the supporting characters in a biography and the influence of these characters on the main character by answering the following questions:

Who are the people who most influenced the life of the subject? How important were these people in the development of the subject's character? Were they positive or negative influences? How are they developed as characters? What differences are there between a fictional development of character and this non-fictional work? How would life for the subject have been different if these influences had not been present? (p. 19)

Another way to analyze the characterization in a biography, according to Robertson and McGinnis, is to examine the biographical subject by analyzing the subject's thoughts about himself or herself as reflected in autobiographies, journals, essays, speeches, and letters. Does the subject perceive himself or herself in a way different from that developed by the biographer? What might account for differences in characterization?

Factual Accuracy. Comparisons between biographies for children and biographies for adults and between biographies and reference books often reveal differences in basic facts. Ann W. Moore (16) reports:

[E]rrors in contemporary children's biographies fall into one of the following three categories: (1) inaccuracies in numbers, dates, and names, items easily checked in reference books or authorized and/or reputable adult titles; (2) incomplete, unclear, or misleading statements caused by attempts at simplification; and (3) patently false, incorrect information. (p. 34)

Moore emphasizes the need for writers and publishers to improve the accuracy of biographies for children and for reviewers to check the facts against reputable sources. Biographies have a special responsibility to be accurate and authentic in characters and settings. The task is so important and demanding that May Hill Arbuthnot and Dorothy M. Broderick (1) say that biographers "should be prepared to spend months, and probably longer, in study and research before touching the typewriter" (p. 225). Extensive research should use recent scholarly works and historical materials that indicate what the subjects and others of the time actually said and wrote.

Any search for accuracy should include a wide range of sources. For example, Russell Freedman (10), author of the 1988 Newbery Award winner *Lincoln: A Photobiography,* stresses the importance of visiting original sites and studying original materials. Freedman states:

> There's something magic about being able to lay your eyes on the real thing—something you can't get from your reading alone. As I sat at my desk in New York City and described Lincoln's arrival in New Salem at the age of twenty-two, I could picture the scene in my mind's eye, because I had walked down those same dusty lanes, where cattle still graze behind split-rail fences and geese flap about underfoot. When I wrote about Lincoln's morning walk from his house to his law office in downtown Springfield, I knew the route because I had walked it myself. (p. 449)

Frank J. Dempsey (5) verifies Freedman's research in Springfield, Illinois, when he describes Freedman's fervor for on-site research. Other authors often mention research in historical societies, newspaper records, diaries, and letters. Often, they visit actual locations. Even simple biographies for young children must be authentic in the illustrations, as well as in the text, because young children acquire considerable knowledge about a time or a setting from the illustrations rather than from detailed descriptions.

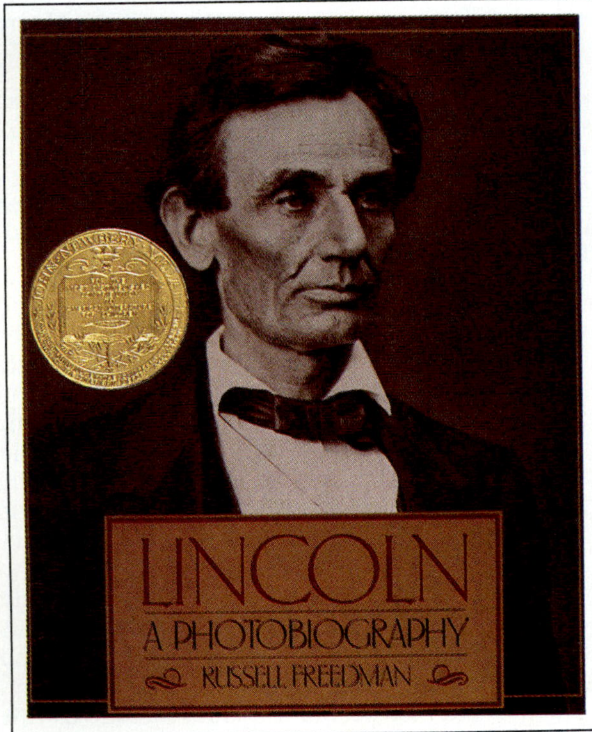

Russell Freedman develops a carefully documented biography in his book, *Lincoln: A Photobiography,* copyright © 1987. Illustration reprinted by permission of Clarion Books a Houghton Mifflin Company.

It is helpful if a biographer includes a bibliography. Freedman includes "A Lincoln Sampler" (a listing of quotes from Lincoln's speeches), "In Lincoln's Footsteps" (a listing of historical sites), and "Books About Lincoln" (a listing of additional sources). Both Milton Meltzer's *Benjamin Franklin: The New American* and Virginia Hamilton's *Anthony Burns: The Defeat and Triumph of a Fugitive Slave* include extensive listings of the primary sources used by the authors.

According to biographer Olivia Coolidge (4), authors of biographical literature must also distinguish fact from judgment. Coolidge says:

> [A] good biography is also concerned with the effect its hero has on other people, with environment and background, with the nature of. . .achievements, and their value. I find that I examine facts in all these and many other spheres before I form judgments and that it needs great care to do what sounds quite easy, namely to distinguish a fact from a judgment. (p. 146)

Coolidge concludes her concern over fact and judgment by saying:

> It simply seems that I need to know everything possible—because knowledge may affect judgment or because I am not yet really certain what I shall use or omit. In other words, I find it necessary to have a habit of worrying about facts, small or large, because my buildings are made up of these bricks, stones, or even pebbles. (p. 148)

Worthiness of Subject. The subject of a biography should be worth reading about, just as she or he should be worthy of the meticulous research and time that the author spent in writing. Has the subject made a significant impact on the world—for good or for ill—that children should be aware of? Will children have a better understanding of the complexities of human nature after they have read the biography? Will they discover that history is made up of real people when they read the book? Will they appreciate the contributions of their ancestors or their heritage through the life of the person in the biography?

The subjects of biography and autobiography need not be famous, infamous, or outstanding in a worldly sense in order for their lives to communicate important lessons about people and society. The subjects should be portrayed in believable ways, however. Whether a notable personage or an unsung hero of everyday life, the person upon whom a biographer focuses should have a many-faceted character, just like the people children know. Jean Fritz, for example, has written a series of historical biographies suggesting that leaders of the American Revolution were very human. Fritz portrays Patrick Henry as a practical joker who did not appreciate school in his youth, and Samuel Adams as a man who was not afraid to speak out against the British but who refused to ride a horse.

Whereas Fritz's biographies emphasize the lives of well-known people, John Jakes's *Susanna of the Alamo* develops a story line around unsung heroes. Jakes characterizes a brave woman whose life is spared by Santa Anna, the Mexican general, so that she can take a message to Sam Houston.

Balance Between Fact and Story Line. Writers of biographies for children must balance the requirement for accuracy with the requirement for a narrative that appeals to children. For example, authors may emphasize humorous facts as they develop plots and characters that present information in story formats. A poor balance between fact and story line may cause problems for young readers. Children have difficulty evaluating differences between fiction and nonfiction. Jean Fritz's (11) foreword to her own fictionalized autobiography, *Homesick: My Own Story,* clarifies differences between fiction and biography:

> Since my childhood feels like a story, I decided to tell it that way, letting the events fall as they would into the shape of a story, lacing them together with fictional bits, adding a piece here and there when memory didn't give me all I needed. I would use conversation freely, for I cannot think of my childhood without hearing voices. So although this book takes place within two years from October 1925 to September 1927, the events are drawn from the entire period of my childhood, but they are all, except in minor details, basically true. The people are real people; the places are dear to me. But most important, the form I have used has given me the freedom to recreate the emotions that I remember so vividly. Strictly speaking, I have to call this book fiction, but it does not feel like fiction to me. It is my story, told as truly as I can tell it. (unnumbered foreword)

Writers of biographies for older children usually include considerable factual detail. For example, in a note to *Under a Strong Wind: The Adventures of Jessie Benton Frémont,* Dorothy N. Morrison states that whenever she uses quotation marks, "the enclosed words are taken exactly from some primary source. As with my other biographies, I have not made up anything—conversations, characters, or incidents" (unnumbered author's note). Morrison effectively uses facts from books, manuscripts, and periodicals. In addition, she portrays her characters in lively and believable ways. She presents the facts so that they do not overshadow her style and characterizations.

In his note on sources in *Benjamin Franklin: The New American,* Milton Meltzer stipulates that he uses quoted passages from Franklin's own writings. He does, however, modernize "them as to spelling, capitalization, punctuation, and paragraphing. This, only to make Franklin more easily accessible to today's readers, in preference to preserving the eighteenth-century modes" (p. 280). This type of information allows readers to evaluate the appropriateness of changes.

Biographical Subjects

The subjects of biographies and autobiographies for children range from early European explorers and rulers to American space travelers and ordinary people of today. Political leaders rise to eminence in times of need, and social activists speak out against oppression. Great achievers make contributions in science, art, literature, and sports. Common people express uncommon courage in their daily struggle for survival.

Explorers of Earth and Outer Space. People who question existing boundaries and explore the unknown fascinate children and adults alike, and they are the subjects of numerous biographies. The consequences of the quest of Columbus are familiar to every schoolchild and are portrayed in many biographies of the discoverer of America. These biographies differ in literary style, focus, amount of detail, and development of character. Consequently, they are good for evaluation and comparison.

Alice Dalgliesh's simple, highly illustrated picture book, *The Columbus Story,* is characterized by short sentences and repetitive language. For example, Dalgliesh uses the following words to introduce readers to the growing desire of Columbus to go to sea:

> Mystery, danger, adventure—what exciting words! Christopher wanted more than ever to be a sailor. The wind that ruffled his red hair seemed to call to him, "Come, come, come!" The waves that lapped the wharves said it over and over. (p. 3 unnumbered)

Dalgliesh focuses on three incidents in Columbus's life: (1) his unsuccessful pleas to the king of Portugal, (2) his successful pleas to the queen of Spain, and (3) his first voyage to America. This simpler version does not develop the problems

ISSUE

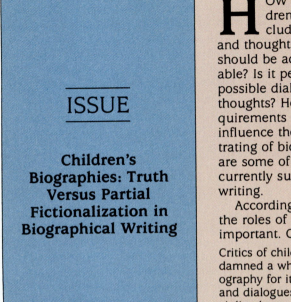

Children's Biographies: Truth Versus Partial Fictionalization in Biographical Writing

HOW MUCH OF A CHILDren's biography, including the dialogue and thoughts of the characters, should be actual and verifiable? Is it permissible to create possible dialogues and thoughts? How should the requirements of younger readers influence the writing and illustrating of biographies? These are some of the questions that currently surround biographical writing.

According to Linda Girard,[1] the roles of fact and fiction are important. Girard states:

> Critics of children's books have damned a whole generation of biography for its made-up scenes and dialogues and called for a disciplined return from fancy to fact. But does invented dialogue necessarily make bad biography? And should biography return to pure fact? (p. 465)

Girard follows this question with examples from Jean Fritz's biographies. Girard claims that Fritz has brought truth back to biography but "with some stretchers," such as "invented dialogue, indirect discourse, interior monologue, and attribution" (p. 469).

Jean Fritz[2] provides her viewpoints for facts versus fiction by stating:

> My facts are my stepping stones, and it seems a very small step to go from Sam Houston's political and emotional stress at the time of the revival meeting to the fact that "his heart welled up and he knew he was ready." . . . Well, I don't make up facts, but at the same

and disappointments that later plagued Columbus.

Ingri and Edgar Parin D'Aulaire's *Columbus,* written for slightly older children, includes details that develop a character quite different from the Columbus in the Dalgliesh version. Additional information enables children to visualize an explorer who did not recognize the magnitude of his discovery and who considered himself a failure because he had not reached the Far East. The D'Aulaires say:

> Old and tired, Columbus returned to Spain from his fourth and last voyage. While he was searching in vain, the Portuguese had found the seaway to the East by sailing south around Africa. Now Columbus stood in the shadow. (p. 54)

The focus of Piero Ventura's *Christopher Columbus,* based on the text by Gian Paolo Ceserani, is a pictorial account of Columbus's adventures. Detailed drawings depict the city of Genoa, the fleet sailing from Palos, the interior of the Santa Maria, typical clothing worn by each crew member, the Bahamas as they looked in 1492, an Indian village on the coast of Cuba, the plants discovered in the new world, and the fort built by the crew. David Goodnough's *Christopher Columbus* emphasizes the early seafaring years of Columbus and the efforts of Columbus to persuade Portuguese and Spanish royalty to back his exploration and first voyage.

Jean Fritz's *Where Do You Think You Are Going, Christopher Columbus?* is written in a light style that appeals to many children. Through use of detailed background information, Fritz creates a lively history inhabited by realistic people. For example, Columbus's sponsor, Queen Isabella of Spain, "was so religious that if she even found Christians who were not sincere Christians, she had them burned at the stake. (Choir boys sang during the burning so Isabella wouldn't have to hear the screams.)" (p. 17). Fritz ends her book with additional historical notes and an index of people and locations discussed in the book.

The life of another explorer who took to the sea to prove his theories—this time in the twentieth century—is portrayed in *Thor Heyerdahl: Viking Scientist* by Wyatt Blassingame. Heyerdahl believed strongly that islands in the Pacific Ocean had been populated by pre-Columbian native peoples of South America. His critics maintained that the balsa rafts used by the traditional pre-

time I have no desire to write in a factual style. Nonfiction can be told in a narrative voice and still maintain its integrity. The art of fiction is making up facts; the art of nonfiction is using facts to make up a form. Incidentally, I really do not use quotation marks unless I have a source. (p. 759)

Diane Stanley[3] discusses issues related to writing and illustrating biographies for younger readers. In comparing these biographies to biographies written for older audiences, Stanley states:

Usually the scope is narrower, allowing more room for rich detail, and these books are lavishly illustrated in color. The message they convey is that history is just another fascinating story—as enjoyable to read as a fairy tale. (p. 209)

Stanley uses her own experiences in writing and illustrating *Peter the Great* and *Shaka, King of the Zulus* to highlight her problems and concerns. For example, Stanley discusses the constraints of length, the exclusion of details inappropriate or boring for younger readers, the need to balance the virtues and vices of the subjects, and the research that allows the illustrations to go beyond the written text.

After reading several biographies for younger and older audiences, identify issues that surround the writing of each type of book. How should the facts be presented in biographical writing? How does the author's style influence the readability of the text? What are the words and the techniques that biographers use to let the readers know that the dialogue is factual or fictional? (For example, a biographer may use quotations to show that the dialogue is taken from a source or terms such as *perhaps* to let readers know that the text is based on conjecture.) Are these techniques appropriate?

[1]Girard, Linda. "The Truth with Some Stretchers." *The Horn Book* (July/August 1988): 464–469.

[2]Fritz, Jean. "Biography: Readability Plus Responsibility." *The Horn Book* (November/December 1988): 759–760.

[3]Stanley, Diane. "Picture Book History." *The New Advocate* 1 (Fall 1988): 209–220.

Columbians would have become waterlogged and would have sunk long before they could have reached their destination. Heyerdahl built a balsa raft, *Kon Tiki* (named after an ancient Polynesian god), and with five friends, Heyerdahl successfully sailed 4,000 miles from Peru to the Polynesian islands of the South Pacific.

Blassingame uses background information to show what caused Heyerdahl to become interested in the origins of the early inhabitants of the Polynesian islands and why he believed they came from South America. Trade winds and currents move from east to west; words like *Tiki* are common to both natives of Peru and native Polynesians; similar stone terraces are found in both locations; and the skulls of Polynesians are long, similar to those of the South Americans, rather than round like those of Asian people. Children can vicariously accompany the crew of the *Kon Tiki* on the perilous voyage through storms and pounding waves.

In the fifteenth and sixteenth centuries, astronomers, such as Nicolaus Copernicus and Galileo Galilei, shared and proved the belief of Christopher Columbus that the world is round. Through their explorations of the stars—by means of mathematical equations, naked-eye observations, and the earliest telescopes—such early explorers of outer space further shook the foundations of European world views. The astronomers discovered that the earth is not only round but also one of numerous planets rotating around the sun and that the sun itself is only one of many astral bodies moving through the universe. In a time when the church insisted that the earth was the stationary center of the one solar system created by God, these beliefs were radical.

In *Galileo and the Magic Numbers,* Sidney Rosen suggests a reason for Galileo's questioning of established "truth" by describing the influence of Galileo's father, who taught him: "Do not be afraid to challenge authority at any time, if a search for truth is in question. This is not the easy path in life, but it is the most rewarding" (p. 50). Because of Rosen's detailed descriptions, children are able to share Galileo's first look at the craters of the moon through the improved telescope that Galileo invented, Galileo's elation when he confirms the theories of Copernicus, and Galileo's bitterness when he is charged with heresy, forced to recant his position, and imprisoned. Children are encouraged to believe in Galileo's strong will when he swears that "in spite of what they forced me to say, the earth will continue to move on its path about the sun" (p. 205).

The work of Galileo and other astronomers of his time and later centuries helped make today's space exploration possible. Helen L. Morgan's *Maria Mitchell: First Lady of American Astronomy* is a biography of one of the foremost astronomers in American history. Mitchell explored the stars, but she also refused to accept existing boundaries in everyday social life. Mitchell felt strongly about the right to question and the right of women to have equality with men. By becoming an astronomer in the nineteenth century, when females were expected to confine themselves to wifehood and motherhood, Mitchell was an oddity and a social trail-blazer. Morgan presents a person not only on a quest for knowledge about the universe but also on a quest to overcome extreme prejudice against females in higher education and particularly in the sciences. Mitchell's love of astronomy and her strength of character in confronting obstacles are revealed in her reaction to visiting the site of Galileo's trial by the Inquisition in Rome:

> Maria could imagine it all and knew how much it must have hurt Galileo to recant his belief after seeing proofs of it in the heavens. The petty restrictions of his later life, when he was ill and blind, were unpleasant but could not equal the despair he must have known in publicly denying his belief. She felt that she was on sacred ground when she walked near the place where he had suffered. (p. 104)

Morgan describes in detail the criticism that Mitchell received when she upheld Charles Darwin's theory of evolution, the discriminatory treatment of female faculty members at schools where Mitchell taught astronomy, and the bigotry Mitchell confronted when she fought for equal rights for women. Still, Mitchell managed to become and remain both an outstanding scientist, discoverer of a new comet, and advocate of her most cherished values:

> I have so long believed in woman's right to a share in the government that it is like the first axiom I learned in geometry—a straight line is the shortest distance between two points. (p. 123)

Amelia Earhart, by Carol Ann Pearce, is the biography of the first woman to fly across the Atlantic Ocean. In showing the early life of Earhart and Earhart's experiences as an aviator, Pearce shows the role of women during early aviation.

Maria Mitchell's legacy to both American science and American women is evident in Mary Virginia Fox's *Women Astronauts: Aboard the Shuttle*. This book describes the 1983 flight of Sally Ride, the first female American astronaut, and presents brief biographies of eight other female astronauts and numerous photographs.

Michael Collins's *Flying to the Moon and Other Strange Places* is the autobiography of another contemporary space explorer, an astronaut who journeyed aboard Gemini and Apollo. Collins provides photographs of early jets, fighting planes, astronauts in training, and the moon, which should interest children who enjoy reading about space exploration.

Political Leaders and Social Activists. Men and women who have achieved noteworthy political power or who have attempted to bring about social change are common subjects of biography. Often, these public figures are controversial—adored by some, deplored by others. As a result, biographers sometimes create imbalanced portraits of their subjects. Because biographers usually, but not always, choose to write about people they admire, hagiography (literally, "the biography of saints"), rather than objective biography, may result. Even authors who create well-rounded portrayals of political leaders and social activists inevitably express their own perspectives. For example, after reading three books about a certain political leader, one student of children's literature commented that she could have been reading about three different people. Because each author had a specific purpose in writing a biography, characterization of the person, choice of events to discuss, style, and tone created a different bias in readers. If possible, read several biographies of the same person and draw your own conclusions.

The biographer of the following book uses many techniques to make the book an excellent example of biography. Polly Schoyer Brooks uses strong characterizations and vivid settings to capture the people and the times in *Queen Eleanor: Independent Spirit of the Medieval World*. Brooks portrays Eleanor of Aquitaine as she develops from a frivolous, immature girl who acts to satisfy her whims to a mature queen who has a shrewd talent for politics. Brooks uses a variety of techniques to develop colorful characters. Consider, for example, the picture that Brooks paints of Eleanor and her husband, Henry II, through the following comparisons:

> Eleanor gradually restored some measure of peace and order to her duchy, using persuasion where Henry had used force. (p. 100)

While Eleanor had become serene, Henry had become more irascible. (p. 126)

From a queen of the troubadours, who had inspired romance and poetry, she became a queen with as much authority as a king. . . .Henry had been admired and feared; Eleanor was admired and loved. (p. 132)

Brooks includes verses composed about Eleanor to describe the attitudes expressed toward the Queen and reinforce the mood of medieval chivalry. The following lyrics were written by troubadour Bernard de Ventadour and were included as an integral part of the text:

> Lady, I'm yours and yours shall be
> Vowed to your service constantly
> This is the oath of fealty
> I pledged to you this long time past,
> As my first joy was all in you,
> So shall my last be found there too,
> So long as life in me shall last. (p. 107)

Two highly illustrated biographies by Diane Stanley appeal to students in the lower-elementary grades. *Peter the Great* is supported by numerous full-page and half-page illustrations of Russian life in the late 1600s and early 1700s. *Shaka: King of the Zulus* is enhanced by the illustrations that provide valuable details about the setting, Zululand in the early 1800s. The illustrations in both biographies provide background information to help younger readers picture the times, places, and biographical characters.

In *The King's Day: Louis XIV of France,* Aliki uses a similar approach to provide background information to young readers. The detailed illustrations depict the social life and customs found in seventeenth- and eighteenth-century France. Aliki's illustrations include explanatory sentences and legends that help clarify the details found in the pictures.

Founding Fathers and Mothers of America. Jean Fritz's stories about Patrick Henry, Samuel Adams, John Hancock, Benjamin Franklin, James Madison, and Sam Houston seem to come alive through

The illustrations in this biography provide considerable background information. (Reprinted with permission of Four Winds Press, an imprint of Macmillan Publishing Company from *Peter the Great* by Diane Stanley. Copyright, 1986 by Diane Stanley Vennema.)

Fritz's inclusion of little-known information. Through these books, children discover that heroes, like themselves, have fears, display good and bad characteristics, and are liked by some and disliked by others. For example, Fritz adds humor to *Where Was Patrick Henry on the 29th of May?* by developing the theory that unusual things always seemed to happen to Henry on the date of his birth. She characterizes Henry as not only a great patriot but also a practical joker and a person filled with "passion for fiddling, dancing, and pleasantry."

Similar insights enliven Fritz's biographies of other beloved figures from the Revolutionary period. Fritz doesn't limit her writing to supporters of American independence from Great Britain, however. In *Traitor: The Case of Benedict Arnold,* Fritz describes a man who wanted to be a success and a hero. Fritz attracts the readers' interest in Arnold and prepares the readers for the apparently dramatic changes in a man who chose to support the British by suggesting early in the book the complete reversal of Arnold's popularity. In 1777, following Arnold's successes in the assault on Quebec and in the Saratoga Campaign, George Washington called him "the bravest of the brave." But by 1780, after his plot with John Andre to betray the American post at West Point, he was regarded as "the veriest villain of centuries past." The incidents Fritz chooses to include develop many sides of Arnold's character and encourage readers to understand why Arnold joined forces against his country.

In *The Great Little Madison,* Fritz uses jokes that James Madison told on himself and humorous anecdotes to show how Madison overcame his small stature and his weak voice. The early experiences cited by Fritz show why Madison believed in logic, freedom of religion, and the written word.

In *Make Way for Sam Houston,* Fritz uses Houston's belief in destiny to emphasize Houston's interactions with other characters. For example, Houston accepted Andrew Jackson's vision of America because "now he had a picture and words for what he'd call Destiny" (p. 20). Fritz reinforces Houston's belief in destiny by describing Houston's responses each time he saw an eagle, the medicine bird that influenced major decisions in his life.

In *Benjamin Franklin: The New American,* Milton Meltzer carefully introduces readers to the historical background of his biographical character. In the following quotation, notice how Meltzer encourages readers to understand the time and place:

> It is almost three hundred years since Benjamin Franklin was born in Boston. (The date was January 17, 1706.) It is hard to put yourself back in that time and grasp what it was like. About 12,000 people lived in Boston, and in all the English colonies of North America there were only 250,000. (That's about the same as the population of Rochester, New York, today.) Most of the people were clustered around Boston, the Connecticut and Hudson river valleys. . . .They had little connection with one another. Roads were really paths, and bad weather made them almost impassible. (p. 15)

Meltzer develops a many sided character by developing both strengths and weaknesses in Franklin. Meltzer adds credibility to the characterization through numerous quotations drawn from Franklin's writings and speeches.

Meltzer's *George Washington and the Birth of Our Nation* is another carefully researched biography of an American statesman. The text includes maps showing key areas, battles of the Revolutionary period, and territorial lines.

Fiery words and bold actions are not the only forms of patriotism and leadership. Elizabeth Yates's *Amos Fortune, Free Man* depicts a man who advanced freedom. Fortune was an African who was brought to slavery in Boston, learned a trade, and eventually acquired freedom. He represents thousands of unsung heroes of the American Revolution—black and white, male and female. The words on his tombstone, erected in 1801, suggest the fundamental American values Fortune exemplified: ". . .born free in Africa, a slave in America, he purchased liberty, professed Christianity, lived reputably, and died hopefully" (p. 181).

Because of traditional social patterns that kept women out of public life in the eighteenth century, most female Americans of the times were "taking care of the homefront" and have remained anonymous in history. The prominence of the male figures of the period has also cast something of a shadow over the female Americans who were making important contributions to a developing nation. Selma R. Williams's *Demeter's Daughters: The Women Who Founded America 1587–1787* attempts to rectify the oversights of standard American history and biography by providing biographical sketches of several great women of colonial and revolutionary America. This book is appropriate for older children. Although it may be too complex and lengthy to appeal to many, it is a valuable source of material about the role of women in the founding of the United States.

Leaders of a Growing America. As the United States became more confident of itself as a nation, it began to expand its interests overseas. Rhoda Blumberg's *Commodore Perry in the Land of the Shogun* depicts the attempts of the American naval officer Matthew Perry to open Japanese harbors to American trade in 1853. This book, an excellent choice for multicultural studies, strongly emphasizes the dramatic interactions between Perry and the Japanese. Reproductions of the original drawings that recorded the expedition, Japanese scrolls and handbills, and photographs provide documentation and enhance children's understanding of the setting and Japanese culture.

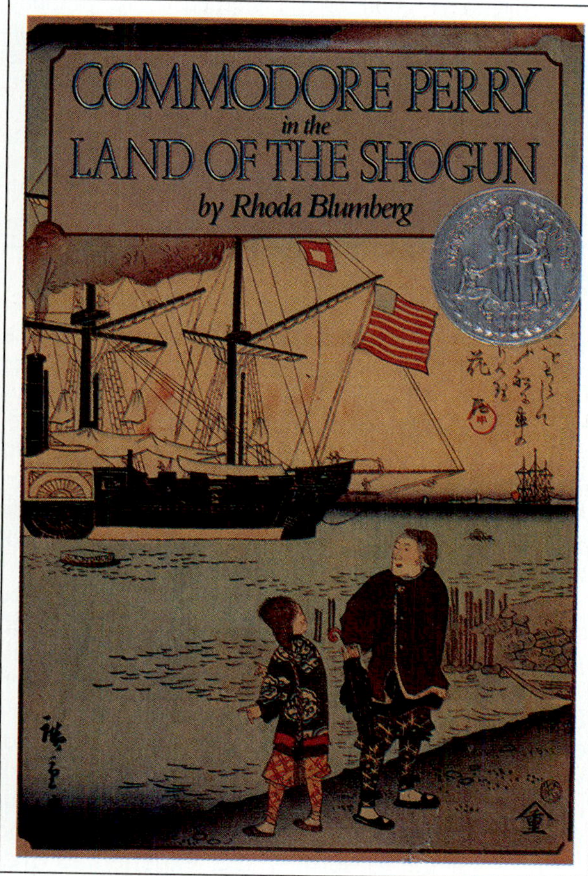

The illustrations reinforce the Japanese setting. (From *Commodore Perry in the Land of the Shogun* by Rhoda Blumberg, copyright © 1985 by Rhoda Blumberg. Reprinted by permission of Lothrop, Lee & Shepard Books a division of William Morrow & Co.

The best-known biographer of Abraham Lincoln is probably Carl Sandburg. His *Abraham Lincoln: The Prairie Years* was the basis for his biography for children, *Abe Lincoln Grows Up*. Through this book, children vicariously share the youth of a great American leader. They discover an impoverished young man of the backwoods who is starved for books, hungry for knowledge, eager to have fun, and ambitious to test himself and his principles in a wider world. Sandburg says:

> It seemed that Abe made the books tell him more than they told other people. . . .Abe picked out questions. . .such as "Who has the most right to complain, the Indian or the Negro?" and Abe would talk about it, up one way and down the other, while they were in the cornfield pulling fodder for the winter. (p. 135)

In the 1988 Newbery Medal winner, *Lincoln: A Photobiography,* Russell Freedman uses numerous techniques that should be considered by students of children's literature. First, Freedman introduces each of the seven chapters with quotations from Lincoln's own writing. For example, Freedman introduces chapter two, "A Backwoods Boy," with this quotation:

> It is a great piece of folly to attempt to make anything out of my early life. It can all be condensed into a simple sentence, and that sentence you will find in Gray's Elegy—"the short and simple annals of the poor." That's my life, and that's all you or anyone else can make out of it. (p. 7)

Second, Freedman clearly separates legend from fact. For example, in chapter three, "Law and Politics," Freedman states:

> He also fell in love—apparently for the first time in his life. Legend tells us that Lincoln once had a tragic love affair with Ann Rutledge, daughter of the New Salem tavern owner, who died at the age of twenty-two. While this story has become part of American folklore, there isn't a shred of evidence that Lincoln ever had a romantic attachment with Ann. Historians believe that they were just good friends. (p. 28)

Third, Freedman supports his text with photographs of various documents of Lincoln's own writing. For example, the text includes a page of Lincoln's autobiographical sketch written in 1859 (p. 6), a page from Lincoln's homemade copybook (p. 13), and a handwritten copy of the Gettysburg Address (p. 103).

Fourth, Freedman includes numerous historical photographs that support the settings and the biographical characters. For example, there are photographs of battlefields and of Lincoln and his family. Fifth, the text includes photographs of authentic posters, newspaper ads, and documents. For example, there is a photograph of the marriage license of Abraham Lincoln and Mary Todd, dated November 4, 1842 (p. 33), a wanted poster for a runaway slave (p. 44), a victory poster from 1860 (p. 62), and a newspaper cartoon from a Baltimore paper (p. 71). Sixth, Freedman supports the text with references to sources for quotations and major speeches, lists of historical sites, sources for additional books about Lincoln, and lists of acknowledgements and picture credits.

Charles Eastman, the most famous Native American of his time, was a Sioux of the Great Plains, born in 1858. Eastman overcame poverty and racial prejudice to become a physician and a crusader for Native American rights. Betsy Lee's *Charles Eastman: The Story of an American Indian* looks at the influences that combined to make Eastman a spokesperson for his people, including the forced migration of the Sioux from Minnesota, Eastman's medical education, and Eastman's efforts to provide medical treatment and better living conditions for the Sioux. Eastman worked to restore broken treaties and to encourage Indians and whites to respect Native American culture. Eventually, says Lee, Eastman's decades of effort bore fruit:

> Charles's message was finally heard, at long last his people would have a voice of their own. Charles Eastman, perhaps more than anyone else, kept Sioux culture and tradition alive during the silent years from 1890 to 1934. Much of what we know today about the American Indian we owe to him. (p. 62)

Numerous biographies of escaped black slaves develop the importance of freedom and the inhumanity of slavery. Virginia Hamilton's *Anthony Burns: The Defeat and Triumph of a Fugitive Slave* is a narrative history of events surrounding the life of Burns as well as a biography. In the research material, however, there existed no day-to-day calendar of the activities and movements of Burns as an ordinary slave child and youth. The life of Burns became well-documented only after Burns's twentieth year, when Burns was hired out to Richmond, Virginia, and carefully began to plan his escape. Because of the lack of documentation, Hamilton draws from supporting factual material to recreate the early life of Burns.

Hamilton uses an interesting technique to allow readers to understand the early life of Burns. After Burns is captured as a fugitive slave, he goes within himself and remembers his happier childhood days. Notice in the following quotation how Hamilton transfers her character from his unhappy days of imprisonment to his memories: "Anthony was not aware Suttle had gone anywhere, for he had left first and gone deep inside himself, to his childhood. These days seemed endless, perfect. There mornings and waking up were the times he could hardly wait for, he loved them so" (p. 7). In a later chapter Hamilton returns to the current world:

> The INNOCENT child of five slipped away. Anthony stirred. Layer by layer, he returned to his miserable time of manhood in the year 1854. He found himself with the ones who had seized him this night on Brattle Street. They had cuffed his hands with irons connected by chains. How had they done that? But I was daydreaming, Anthony thought. He lifted his hands to look at the chains. They felt so heavy, he let them drop. "Wish all this was a dream, like that vision of when I was small," he told himself. It was more like a nightmare. Chains! (p. 19)

When Hamilton refers to a vision and a dream, she gives credibility to her invented dialogues and happenings. Dreams and visions do not always reflect the exact happenings in a person's life. Douglas Miller's *Frederick Douglass and the Fight for Freedom* and John Anthony Scott and Robert Alan Scott's *John Brown of Harper's Ferry* also depict the harshness of slavery and the power of the abolitionists.

Lillian Wald felt a powerful commitment to social change in the late 1800s. Wald defied traditional roles for women by entering the medical profession. In *Lillian Wald of Henry Street*, Beatrice Siegel portrays the strength of Wald's commitment by contrasting the affluence of Wald's Jewish American family with the squalor of New York City's Lower East Side, where immigrants from many lands were living in disease and poverty. Siegel describes the experiences that caused Wald to develop a strong social conscience, defy her family's wishes, train for the nursing profession, and establish the Henry Street Settlement House in order to help impoverished citizens of New York.

Photographs from an earlier time add authenticity to this biography. (From *Lillian Wald of Henry Street*, by Beatrice Siegel. Copyright © 1983 by Beatrice Siegel. Photo courtesy of Visiting Nurse Service of New York.)

Another excellent book about a nineteenth-century American with a strong social conscience is Anne E. Neimark's *A Deaf Child Listened: Thomas Gallaudet, Pioneer in American Education*. For centuries, deaf children had been placed in asylums for the retarded and the insane. Gallaudet, founder of American education specifically for the deaf, helped bring deaf Americans out of their "silent prison."

Twentieth-Century Leaders in America and Abroad. Biographies written for young children and for older children differ in tone, focus, choice of content, amount of detail, and development of character. Because of the range in intended audiences, biographies about political leaders and social activists in the twentieth century provide opportunities to compare the techniques used by the authors and content that they include.

First, consider several "Crowell Biographies" written for young children: Jane Goodsell's *Eleanor Roosevelt,* Ophelia Settle Egypt's *James Weldon Johnson,* and Ruth Franchere's *Cesar Chavez*. The books share several features. The readability levels range from second to fourth grades, indicating that the books are meant for independent reading. The books contain numerous illustrations, and they emphasize very positive characteristics and situations.

Jane Goodsell's *Eleanor Roosevelt* looks at the personality development of Eleanor Roosevelt and the changes that allowed Roosevelt to overcome internal conflicts and eventually become a great contributor to American social life. Goodsell characterizes the young Roosevelt as shy, lonely, and often bored. However, as an adult, Roosevelt gradually became an assistant to her husband in his political career, then a crusader for her own beliefs in social justice and world peace as a worker for the United Nations. Goodsell does not include any materials that hint at the personal unhappiness portrayed in biographies of Eleanor Roosevelt for adults.

Ophelia Settle Egypt forthrightly declares her admiration and affection for the Civil Rights leader, author, and educator in *James Weldon Johnson*. As a child, Egypt says, she felt pride when singing Johnson's "Lift Every Voice and Sing," and she was also "his most ardent fan" when she was a young instructor at Fisk University, where Johnson was a professor. Egypt's words set her tone (the author's attitude toward the character). Egypt's content and descriptions of Johnson also create admiration and affection in readers.

Ruth Franchere's *Cesar Chavez* looks at the Mexican American political leader's struggles to develop the National Farm Workers Association and gain political and economic power for Mexican Americans. Franchere arouses sympathy for Chavez's undertakings by showing pictures of the poor living conditions of a migrant farming family and providing details related to Chavez's schooling. Chavez's family moved so often that Chavez attended thirty-six schools while acquiring an eighth-grade education. Franchere's choice of factual content directs the readers' attention to Chavez's concerns and values. Chavez tries to organize classes where Mexican Americans can learn to read and write English. He works for Mexican American voter registration, and he organizes the 1968 grape boycott in order to demand better pay and living conditions for migrant workers.

Next, consider the biographies of Franklin Roosevelt, Adolf Hitler, Golda Meir, and John F. Kennedy that have been written for older children. Longer format allows authors to include more details and develop more information about the historical periods.

Appropriately enough for an older audience, Barbara Silberdick's *Franklin D. Roosevelt, Gallant President* looks in some detail upon Franklin Roosevelt's ability to overcome physical disabilities during his rise to power. As the title suggests, Silberdick presents Roosevelt in a positive light. She includes no viewpoints that might be considered critical and gives no in-depth look at his private life.

Edward F. Dolan, Jr.'s, biography for older readers, *Adolf Hitler: A Portrait in Tyranny,* follows the belief that children should read about the villains in history as well as the heroes. As reflected in the title, the tone is not affectionate or praising. Instead, Dolan refers to a "frightening period in the past" that should be shared with children so they will be able to recognize dangers in the present and the future. Dolan's characterization includes Hitler's shrewdness in analyzing the German people and his ability to select followers who advocated his viewpoint. Dolan also looks at times when Hitler's rise to power might have been prevented. The details about the Holocaust and Hitler's suicide provide a look at a terrifying period of world history.

Margaret Davidson creates a well-rounded characterization of one of the memorable prime ministers of Israel in *The Golda Meir Story*. For example, Davidson relates experiences in Meir's childhood to her achievements as an adult. However, Davidson does not imply that Meir's private life was always happy. She discusses Meir's marital problems. The nuances of Meir's forceful personality are evident as Meir faces both the problems and the rewards of leading her country during the Yom Kippur war.

Judie Mills's *John F. Kennedy* is a carefully documented biography for older students. This biography includes fifty-four pages of footnotes. Mills does not idolize the president, but she includes his idealism and commitment. She also includes his relationships with various women.

Other sources provide information about political leaders and social activists. Children can verify factual information presented in the biographies or extend an interest by reading more about a particular person. When children do library research, they discover some of the techniques that biographers use. Such investigations may also lead children to outstanding, recently published biographies of other social leaders, such as Lillie Patterson's *Sure Hands, Strong Heart: The Life of Daniel Hale Williams,* a black American physician who worked for interracial hospitals, and *Martin Luther King, Jr. and the Freedom Movement*. (See chapter 11 for a discussion of additional biographies.)

Artists, Scientists, and Sports Figures. Barbara Brenner's *On the Frontier with Mr. Audubon* is based on a diary the naturalist and artist John James Audubon kept in 1820 and 1821, when he and a young assistant, Joseph Mason, traveled down the Mississippi and Ohio Rivers to find and draw birds. Brenner also used information from other writings by Audubon and from Alice Ford's *John James Audubon*. The resulting biography is in the form of a journal that could have been written by the assistant. Brenner says that almost every incident in the book actually happened but that the conversations are fictional, based on the facts found in her research. The book is illustrated with black-and-white photographs of Audubon's work and with photographs from original sources. Photographs show flatboats on the river and people and places discussed in the book.

Color reproductions of art works add considerable interest to Leslie Sills's *Inspirations: Stories About Women Artists.* This biography includes four biographical sketches of contemporary women artists and art works for which they are known.

Margery Facklam's *Wild Animals, Gentle Women* is a collection of short biographical sketches of eleven women who have spent their lives as ethologists studying animal behavior. The book includes Belle Benchley, former director of the San Diego Zoo; Jane Goodall, the scientist who became famous because of her work with chimpanzees; and Karen Pryor, a research scientist who specializes in behavioral studies with porpoises. The last chapter of Facklam's book discusses ethology as a profession and makes suggestions about appropriate education, including developing writing skills, learning photography, learning first aid, as well as becoming involved with Outward Bound or similar programs.

Autobiographies give children insights into the illustrators and authors of children's books. In *Self-Portrait: Erik Blegvad,* the artist reveals the forces that motivated his career. A love of the sea, which he inherited from his father, inspired his early drawings. *Self-Portrait: Margot Zemach,* tells about another award-winning illustrator. Zemach tells how as a child during the Depression, she drew pictures to make herself and others laugh. *Bill Peet: An Autobiography* provides information about the artist's experiences as a Disney cartoonist. Peet worked on such films as *Dumbo* and *Fantasia*. This text is heavily illustrated with Peet's drawings.

My Diary, My World, by Elizabeth Yates, written in journal format, expresses Yates's love for books and writing during a time when women did not have careers. According to the author's notes, the entries in the book were actually written during the years when Yates was growing up. Beverly Cleary's *A Girl from Yamhill: A Memoir* is a chronicle of the early life of the popular realistic fiction author. Numerous photographs should intrigue readers of the "Ramona" series and *Dear Mr. Henshaw*.

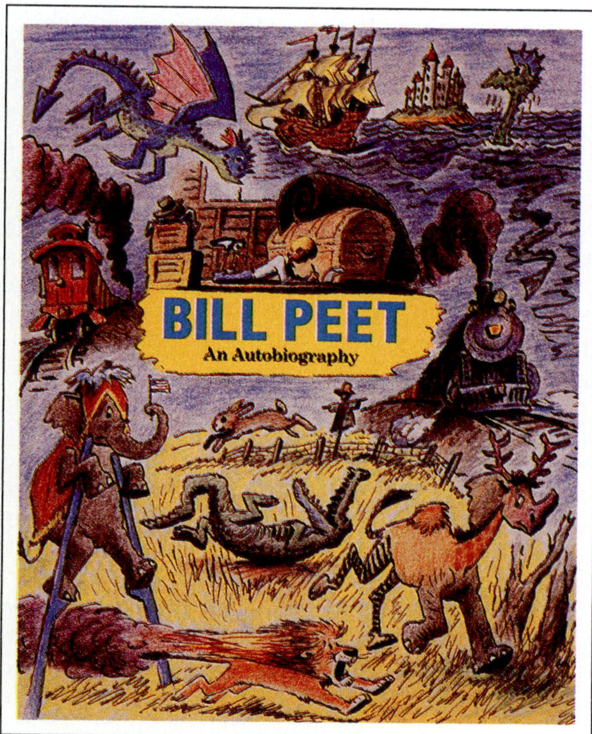

The humorous illustrations show the work of the author. (Jacket illustration from *Bill Peet: An Autobiography* by Bill Peet, copyright © 1989 by Bill Peet. Reprinted by permission of Houghton Mifflin Company.)

In *Starting from Home: A Writer's Beginnings,* author Milton Meltzer clarifies the problems of writing about his own youth. Meltzer states that the book is a combination of fact and fiction because he has changed some names and circumstances "not to avoid the truth, but to capture it" and because "this is my life as I see it now. I can't pretend to know exactly how it was when I was five or fifteen. Inevitably the story is colored by what I have become this many years later" (p. 145). Notice in the following quotation how Meltzer's introduction encourages readers to join in Meltzer's search for identity:

> Who was I? No, I don't mean the man who's writing these words down, but the child who was born soon after the twentieth century began. Was he me? The me I am today? Or someone so different in an early photo that I hardly recognize him: small, skinny, wavy brown hair, green eyes, straight nose, pale skin, thin arms and chest encased in a khaki shirt, and an uneasy smile as he looks into my eyes. That's the boy on the outside. Inside was a being no one knew but himself. And often he was not sure who that was (p. 3).

Whether you read Meltzer's text as autobiography or as fiction, you will receive insights into the life of a prolific author of biographical literature.

Keith Ferrell's *H. G. Wells: First Citizen of the Future* is typical of the books, especially those written for older children, in which Ferrell develops a character with both strengths and weaknesses. Ferrell incorporates the strong social and political views that influenced the life and writing of Wells.

Tobi Tobias's *Arthur Mitchell* is a highly illustrated biography of a famous dancer. This book for young readers describes the experiences of a young black dancer as he tries to enter the world of classical ballet, a field in which few blacks had found acceptance. The author portrays Mitchell's numerous struggles by describing his problems in meeting the demands of ballet at the High School of Performing Arts, the audience prejudice he had to overcome while a dancer with the New York City Ballet, his dancing in a lead role developed especially for him, and his desire to form an all-black classical ballet company where young black dancers could practice and perform. Mitchell's Dance Theatre of Harlem, which began in an empty garage, is now internationally known and provides training for hundreds of black dancers.

The early days of growing up as a child star provide fascinating reading in Lillian Gish's *An Actor's Life for Me!* (as told to Selma Lanes). Gish and Lanes introduce the biography with a humorous incident that attracts the interest of readers and presents a glimpse of both the hard work and the excitement in the theater. Throughout the book, Gish and Lanes use anecdotes to increase interest, add credibility, and characterize both the actress, Lillian Gish, and the supporting characters who influenced her life. Photographs introduce each of the eight chapters, while colored drawings appear within the chapters. The photographs add to the real-life characterizations developed in the biography.

Children who are sports enthusiasts enjoy reading about the people they see on television or those whose records they would like to duplicate. Vernon Pizer's *Glorious Triumphs: Athletes Who Conquered Adversity* is a collection of short biographies about athletes who overcame physical disabilities, reversals, and social obstacles. The book presents such athletes as Barney Rose, 1933 lightweight boxing champion of the world; Ben Hogan, professional golfer; Carole Heiss, Olympic gold medalist; Jerry Kramer, football player for the Green Bay Packers; and Althea Gibson, tennis professional. Howard Liss's *Bobby Orr: Lightning on Ice* presents the life story of an ice hockey great. The book is enhanced with photographs of hockey players.

Anecdotes and photographs add interest and credibility to this biography. (From *An Actor's Life for Me!* by Lillian Gish as told to Selma Lanes. Illustrated by Patricia Lincoln. Copyright © 1987. Reprinted by permission of Viking Publishers.)

Biographies about sports stars may become dated quickly because of rapidly changing stardom and team memberships. Many children who are sports enthusiasts, however, enjoy reading almost everything about their favorite sports heroes—outdated or not.

People Who Have Persevered. Biographies are not always written about famous people or people of great material success. Some excellent biographies and autobiographies portray the courage and perseverance of ordinary people. One such book is David Kherdian's *The Road from Home: The Story of an Armenian Girl*. This story about the author's mother, Vernon Dumehjian, is one of courage, hope, and survival. In 1915, the Turkish government decided to eliminate its Armenian people by deporting them to the Mesopotamian desert or killing them. Vernon spends days in a caravan on the march, days of weakening physical condition, days of not knowing her destination, and days of sadness when family members die from cholera. Days of hope result when Vernon meets kind people who provide her with an education while she waits to return to her home. The security of home does not last long, however, as fighting resumes between Turkey and Greece. When Vernon's aunt is approached by a family whose Armenian American son wants a wife to join him in the United States, Vernon finally finds a means of becoming safe. Children can compare this book and Billi Rosen's *Andi's War*, the story of a girl who survives the Greek civil war, which lasted from 1946 through 1949.

Another author who develops a theme related to the joy and sorrow of being human is Bernard Wolf. His *In This Proud Land: The Story of a Mexican American Family* is the biography of a family rather than an individual—a photographic essay about Texas farmers at home, at work, at play, and traveling to Minnesota to supplement their income by working in the sugar beet fields. The photographs and text show the warm relationships in the Hernandez family. The children work at part-time jobs to help their family financially. In this story, proud people attempt to educate their children and create a better life for them in the midst of difficult circumstances. Wolf ends his story with these words:

> In this proud land there are many Americas. There is an America of inequality and racial prejudice. There is an America of grave poverty, despair, and tragic human waste. And yet because of people like the Hernandez family, there is also an America of simple courage, strength, and hope. (p. 95)

Another book that traces a family's experiences is Eloise Greenfield and Lessie Jones Little's *Childtimes: A Three-Generation Memoir*. In the book's three parts, a black American grandmother, mother, and daughter tell about growing up in time periods ranging from the late 1800s through the 1940s. Both Greenfield and Little are well-known authors of children's books. This book concludes poignantly:

> It's been good, stopping for a while to catch up to the past. It has filled me with both great sadness and great joy. Sadness to look back at suffering, joy to feel the unbreakable threads of strength. Now, it's time for us to look forward again, to see where it is that we're going. Maybe years from now, our descendants will want to stop and tell the story of their time and their place in this procession of children. A childtime is a mighty thing. (p. 175)

The words provide a fitting conclusion to this discussion of biographies written for children. What better purpose is there for sharing biographies with children than allowing them to feel good, to catch up to the past, and to experience the sadness and great joy of other people's lives?

INFORMATIONAL BOOKS

Informational books are available on almost any subject. They are valued by children, teachers, parents, and librarians. The nonfictional nature of the books, however, requires careful evaluation of the contents.

Values of Informational Books

"I am curious." "It is easier to find the answer from reading than it is to ask my teacher." "I want to learn to take better pictures." "I want to learn about a career I might enjoy." "I like reading the books." These reasons were given to this author by children who were asked why they read informational books. The range of answers also reflects the many values of informational books for children. Nonfiction books provide information about hobbies, experiments, the ways in which things work, the characteristics of plants and animals, and many other phenomena in our world.

Gaining knowledge about the world is a powerful reason for reading informational books. Glenn O. Blough (2), a professor of science education and an author of science books for children maintains:

> [T]he fact that information grows and ideas change is no excuse for not expecting children and young people to learn from science. While the great supply of information may be somewhat discouraging, and the fluctuation of ideas disconcerting, neither is an excuse for remaining ignorant of the world we live in, or not understanding the methods by which knowledge grows. (p. 420)

Many recently published books contain information on timely subjects that children hear about on television or radio or read about in newspapers. For example, children excited by NASA's space explorations can consult Seymour Simon's *Jupiter* and *Saturn* for color photographs and information obtained during NASA's Pioneer and Voyager space explorations. Children can extend their knowledge about satellites, space shuttles, and possible space colonies by reading Franklyn M. Branley's *Mysteries of Outer Space*. Likewise, Janet Mohun's *Drugs, Steroids and Sports* contains information about various drug scandals in sports. Laurence Pringle's *Saving Our Wildlife* presents the latest endeavors to save vanishing animals.

Informational books also provide opportunities for children to experience the excitement of new discoveries. For example, Barbara Reid's *Playing with Plasticine* provides detailed directions for making plasticine sculptures. Children open new doors when they follow step-by-step directions for experiments that reinforce scientific principles. Children can discover the importance of fibers and learn how to spin cotton or wool by hand when they follow Vicki Cobb's directions in *Fuzz Does It!* They can make discoveries about surface tension when they follow Seymour Simon's instructions in *Soap Bubble Magic*. They can discover characteristics of the ocean when they follow Simon's directions in *How to Be an Ocean Scientist in Your Own Home*.

Another value of informational books is introduction to the scientific method. Through first-hand experience and reading about the work of scientists, children discover how scientists ob-

Color photographs taken during actual space explorations clarify the content of an informational book. (From *Jupiter* by Seymour Simon. Published by William Morrow & Company, Inc., 1985. Photograph courtesy of NASA.)

serve, compare, formulate and test hypotheses, and draw conclusions or withhold them until they uncover more evidence (2). Children also become familiar with the instruments used by scientists. As children learn about the scientific method, they gain appreciation for the attitudes of the people who use this method. Children discover the importance of careful observation over long periods of time, the need for gathering data from many sources, and the requirement that scientists, whatever their field, make no conclusions before all the data have been collected. For example, in Kathryn Lasky's *Dinosaur Dig,* students follow several families as they are guided by paleontologist, Keith Rigby, on a dig in eastern Montana. In books such as this, readers discover the importance of careful research.

Informational books also encourage self-reliance. One enjoyable discovery can motivate children to make further investigations. Parents and educators need to provide books such as David Macaulay's *The Way Things Work* and Howard Smith's *Small Worlds: Communities of Living Things* to pique children's interest and then help children explore their environment. A high school student who likes to read informational books emphasizes the satisfaction in following his curiosity into broader and deeper exploration:

> I enjoy reading to answer my own curiosity. Fictional books don't have the information that I want. I am more interested in real things. When I was in first grade, astronomy was the first science that interested me; the more I read, the more I learned I didn't know. As I became older I read a lot of books about the stars, space exploration, and theories about the black hole. I discovered that reality is stranger and more exciting than any fiction could be. I could not take fiction and transfer it into the real world; factual books help me learn about the real world.

Informational books can encourage children to develop critical reading and thinking skills. While reading books written on one subject by different authors, children can compare the books to evaluate the objectivity of the various authors and determine the qualifications of the authors to write about the particular subject. They also can check the copyright dates to see if the information is current. For example, children can consider var-

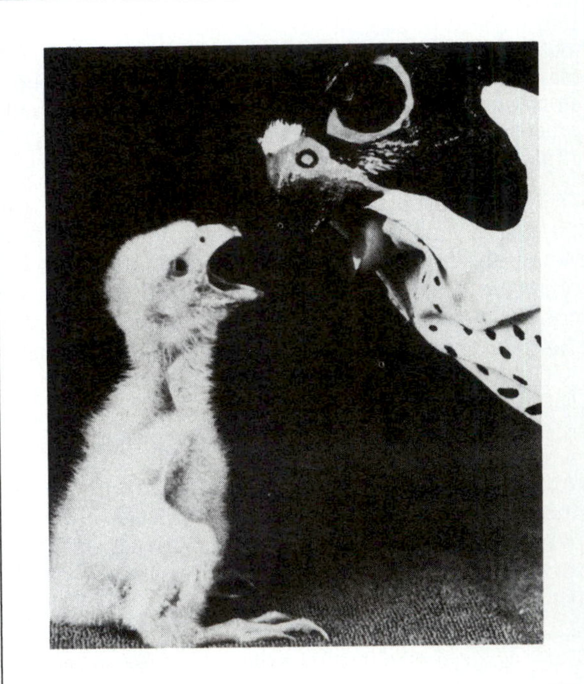

Carefully sequenced photographs show how an endangered species is being helped by science. (From *Saving the Peregrine Falcon,* by Caroline Arnold. Photographs copyright © 1985 by Richard R. Hewett. By permission of Carolrhoda Books, Inc. 241 First Avenue N. Minneapolis, MN 55401.)

FLASHBACK

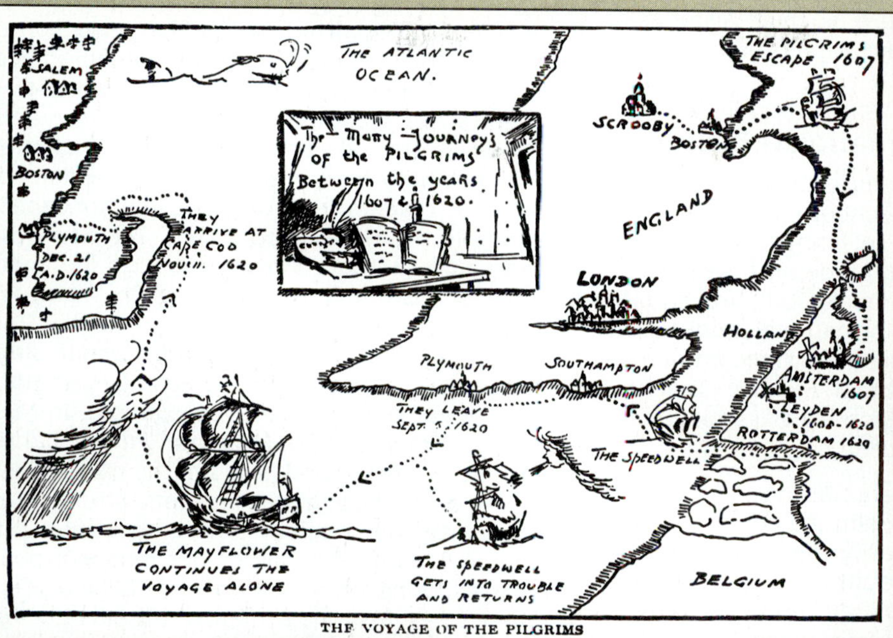

THE VOYAGE OF THE PILGRIMS

THE FIRST Newbery Medal was awarded in 1922 to an informational book that traced the steps in the development of the human race from prehistoric times to the early twentieth century. Hendrik Willem Van Loon's *The Story of Mankind* is also noteworthy because Van Loon dealt with ideas and acts that greatly influenced the human race, rather than focusing primarily on dates and picturesque incidents. At the time of its publication, the book was praised for its comprehensiveness, taste, and humor. The book was credited with changing the writing of informational books; authors were encouraged to write books that presented learning as an exciting process.

ious views on using chimpanzees as experimental subjects in captivity by reading Anna Michel's *The Story of Nim: The Chimp Who Learned Language* and Linda Koebner's *From Cage to Freedom: A New Beginning for Laboratory Chimpanzees*.

Of course, informational books encourage children to stretch their minds. When children read Caroline Arnold's *Saving the Peregrine Falcon,* Dorothy Hinshaw Patent's *The Whooping Crane: A Comeback Story,* or David Cook's *Environment,* they may discover the perilous balance between animals, the environment, and humans and begin to think of ways in which their generation can conserve animals, plants, and other natural resources. Informational books also inform children about values, beliefs, life-styles, and behaviors different from their own.

Many well-written informational books expand children's vocabularies by introducing new words, including technical terms. Meanings of technical terms are often enriched through photographs or detailed illustrations. For example, *Glaciers: Nature's Frozen Rivers* by Hershell H. and Joan Lowery Nixon introduces the term *crevasses* in the text: "The cracks that are found in the ice are called crevasses. They can be very deep and wide and dangerous, or very shallow" (p. 23). A deep crevass is then shown in a photograph on the same page. The definition is followed by a detailed discussion of crevasses.

Books also allow children to look at the world creatively. Anyone who has observed young children playing with a box has seen the creative and imaginative toys they can develop. Flo Ann Hedley Norvell's *The Great Big Box Book* suggests many fascinating toys that can be created out of large boxes and then encourages children to use their imaginations to think of yet more uses for a box.

Finally, do not forget that one of the greatest values in informational books is *enjoyment*. Many children who make new discoveries, become involved in the scientific process, or read because of curiosity are also reading for enjoyment. In fact, enjoyment is often the primary reason children read informational literature, such as histories of the ancient world or photographic essays about animal life.

Evaluating Informational Books

Several science associations concerned with the education of elementary-school children provide valuable guidelines for selecting informational books for children. These guidelines are specifically tailored to science books but are equally valid for all types of informational books. The following guidelines are taken from recommendations made by the National Science Teachers Association (17) and the American Association for the Advancement of Science (22).

1. All facts should be accurate.
2. Stereotypes should be eliminated.
3. Illustrations should clarify the text.
4. Analytical thinking should be encouraged.
5. The organization should aid understanding.
6. The style should stimulate interest.

Accurate Facts. *Does the author have the scientific qualifications to write a book on the particular subject?* Franklyn M. Branley, author of *Mysteries of Outer Space* and over one hundred other scientific books, has a doctorate, is an astronomer emeritus, and is the former chairman of the American Museum-Hayden Planetarium. Many books, however, provide little or no helpful information by which to evaluate the authors' qualifications.

Are facts and theory clearly distinguished? Children should know if something is a fact or if it is a theory that has not been substantiated. For example, in *Changes in the Wind: Earth's Shifting Climate,* Margery and Howard Facklam examine the changing climate. The Facklams begin their exploration of the subject by discussing several theories, such as the possibility of another ice age or global warming. The Facklams carefully separate fact from theory and opinion. As you read the following excerpt, consider why the authors use such terms as *might, if, could,* and *guess*:

> Green plants might even be tapped for energy someday through bioengineering. If a super species of high hydrogen-producing plant could be genetically engineered, it might add to our energy supplies. The EPA closes its report by admitting we can only guess at the results of global warming. (p. 40)

Are significant facts omitted? An author should present enough significant facts to make the text accurate. Specialized books that give complete histories of certain animals are valuable because they help children understand the evolution of a species, as well as its characteristics, and its needs, if any, for protection. Texts that provide historical information should also provide enough facts for readers to understand the concepts. For example, in *Smoke and Ashes: The Story of the Holocaust,* Barbara Rogasky traces the roots of anti-Semitism before presenting the World War II experiences.

Are differing views on controversial subjects presented? Subjects such as ecology and nuclear energy are controversial. For example, in *Nuclear Energy: Troubled Past, Uncertain Future,* Laurence Pringle discusses both sides of the nuclear energy issue even though he presents stronger arguments against nuclear power. A biased author should identify that his or her personal point of view is not necessarily a universally held position. Sometimes, just one sentence will interject author bias into what is an otherwise factual presentation of controversial views. For example, Ann E. Sigford, in *Eight Words for Thirsty,* discusses the needs of farmers for water for irrigation and of townspeople for water, but then she makes this statement:

> Someone has to pay the high cost of desert water, and that someone is the American people. The CAP was born in a time when farming seemed to be the only way a state could be developed. Today, however, farming contributes only about 7 percent of Arizona's income. It does not seem smart to spend so much to earn so little. (p. 77)

History texts should present both sides of controversial issues. For example, David Anderson uses archaeological research to provide new interpretations of the Spanish and English conflict in *The Spanish Armada*. In his carefully researched text, Anderson dispels some previously held beliefs and places blame on both the English and Spanish.

Is the information presented without relying on anthropomorphism? While it is perfectly acceptable for authors of fantasy to write about animals that think, talk, act, and dress like people, authors of informational books should not ascribe human thoughts, motives, or emotions to animals or to plants and other inanimate things (a practice called *anthropomorphism*). A writer of animal information books should describe the animals in terms that can be substantiated through careful observation. For example, in *The Book of the Pig*, Jack Denton Scott describes an incident in which a boar consistently unlatched a gate and took the endangered runt of a litter out into a meadow until it was no longer a runt. Instead of giving human reasons for the pig's actions, Scott states:

> Was the boar Andy exhibiting pig instinct or pig intellect when he "adopted" Sawyer? We don't know, but a five-year research program at the University of Kentucky found that pigs not only are the smartest of all farm animals but are also more intelligent than dogs, mastering any trick or feat accomplished by canines in much shorter time. (p. 31)

Scott continues to describe pigs in terms of information gained from observation and research.

Is the information as up-to-date as possible? Because knowledge in some areas is changing rapidly, copyright dates are very important for certain types of informational books. For example, *Halley's Comet: What We've Learned*, by Gregory Vogt, provides more reliable information than do earlier space books. Likewise, *The News About Dinosaurs*, by Patricia Lauber, compares early beliefs about dinosaurs with the current information.

Attitudes and values also change. Comparing older factual books with more recent ones is one way to illustrate how attitudes and biases change. No educator or publisher today would condone the untrue and highly offensive descriptions of Native Americans presented in *Carpenter's Geographical Reader, North America* (3) published by Frank G. Carpenter in 1898. For example, the following is Carpenter's depiction of the historical background of Native Americans:

> The savage Indians were in former times dangerous and cruel foes. They took delight in killing women and children. They hid behind rocks and bushes to fight. . . .They used tomahawks to brain their victims, and delighted in torturing their captives and in burning them at the stake. (p. 293)

Information about Australian native people is just as biased in Charles Redway Dryer's *Geography, Physical, Economic and Regional* (6), published in 1911, while V. M. Hillyer's 1929 text, *A Child's Geography of the World* (14), says that the most curious animals in Africa are the people. Students of children's literature may not realize how outdated, misinformed, and biased informational books can be until they discover books such as these that influenced the thinking of school children earlier in this century.

Stereotypes. *Does the book violate basic principles against racism and sexism?* As the above examples make clear, informational books, like all books, should lack demeaning racist or sexist stereotypes. Brent Ashabranner's *Morning Star, Black Sun: The Northern Cheyenne Indians and America's Energy Crisis*, for example, meets this criterion. It portrays the Northern Cheyenne as a people with a culture worth preserving, who are striving to overcome their own problems. Compare Ashabranner's description of the Cheyenne Indians and their culture with quotes from the previously discussed *Carpenter's Geographical Reader*. Ashabranner says:

> Although the Cheyenne did not have books, a system of writing, or schools, they had a tribal organization, codes of conduct, and ways of teaching their people that could rival those of any society anywhere. (p. 13)

Later, Ashabranner describes the criteria for selecting Cheyenne leaders:

> Chiefs were chosen for their wisdom, good judgment, and bravery, though they did not necessarily have to be great warriors. They did have to be good-hearted men who were concerned about their people. (p. 14)

Some contemporary books reflect stereotypes through inclusion or exclusion of certain types of people in certain professions. For example, are people of both sexes and various racial and ethnic groups shown in illustrations depicting interest in science or science professions? The illustrations in Judy Cutchins and Ginny Johnston's *Are These Animals Real? How Museums Prepare Wildlife Exhibits* show that both men and women can be interested in the natural sciences.

Illustrations. *Are the illustrations accurate?* Illustrations should be as accurate as the text and add to its clarity. Photographs and drawings should be accompanied by explanatory legends keyed directly to the text to allow children to expand their understanding of the principles or terminology presented. David Macaulay's detailed illustrations in *The Way Things Work* are labeled to clarify concepts. *The Incredible Journey of Lewis & Clark*, by Rhoda Blumberg, includes maps showing both the journey west and the return journey east. Key locations are numbered and keyed to dates and pages of discussion within the text. *Searches in the American Desert,* by Sheila Cowing, includes maps that add to this history of various reasons for going into the desert including search for wealth, flight from persecution, and tests for weapons.

Leonard Everett Fisher (7), writer and illustrator of nonfictional material, states that illustrations should also create historical mood. Fisher says:

> Today what interests me in nonfiction is giving youngsters a visual memory of a fact rather than just the fact. I am trying to present a factual mood. The Tower of London, for instance, is a creepy place, and if I can establish the creepiness of the place so that the youngster gets an unsettled feeling about the tower, then that child is going to have more of an understanding of history than just learning a date. I'm trying to create the emotion of history, the dynamics of history, together with the fact of history. I'm trying to communicate what events in history felt like. These feelings will bring children back to reading information to find out the facts—back to reality! I want to give a sense of history created by the fallible, mortal human beings who made it. (p. 317)

Fisher's illustrations may be found in his texts *The Tower of London, The Great Wall of China,* and *The Wailing Wall.*

Analytical Thinking. *Do children have an opportunity to become involved in solving problems logically?* Many informational books, particularly scientific ones, should encourage children to observe, gather data, experiment, compare, and formulate hypotheses. Informational books should encourage children to withhold judgment until enough data have been gathered or enough facts have been explored. Books that demonstrate scientific facts and principles should encourage children to do more experiments on their own and stress the value of additional background reading. For example, in *How to Be an Ocean Scientist in Your Own Home,* Seymour Simon develops a series of experiments that proceed from "Let's Find Out" to "Here's What You Will Need" to "Here's What to Do." In addition, Simon includes a bibliography of books about the topics.

Organization. *Is the organization logical?* Ideas in informational books should be broken down into easily understood component parts. Authors often use an organization that progresses from the simple to the more complex, or from the familiar to the unfamiliar, or from early to later development. In *Pack, Band, and Colony: The World of Social Animals,* Judith and Herbert Kohl introduce readers to the world of social animals by first telling a story about a boy's experiences with ravens and then describing how his experiences resulted in observations, informal experiments, and library research. Diagrams and recommended experiments increase comprehension of several difficult concepts. Diagrams of blocks and suggestions for manipulation by readers illustrate concepts related to dependence and independence in social animals.

Are organizational aids included? Reference aids such as a table of contents, an index, a glossary, a bibliography, and a list of suggested readings can encourage children to use organized reference skills. While very young children do not need all of these aids, older children find them helpful. For example, in *Farming Today Yesterday's Way,* Cheryl Walsh Bellville uses boldface words in the text to identify the words that are defined in the glossary. In *Commodore Perry in the Land of the Shogun,* Rhonda Blumberg includes a table of contents, notes, information about the illustrations, a bibliography, an index, and five appendices of additional information about the time period.

Style. *Is the writing style lively and not too difficult for children of a certain age to understand?* Kathryn Lasky's *Sugaring Time* is an excellent example of both stimulating literary style and careful documentation. For example, Lasky describes corn snow, large and granular snow crystals, as follows: "When Jonathan skis it sounds as if he is skimming across the thick frosting of a wedding cake" (p. 7). The maple sap "runs like streams of Christmas tinsel" (p. 19). The environment in the sugarhouse is "like sitting in a maple cloud surrounded by the muffled roar of the fire and the bubbling tumble of boiling sap" (p. 34). The photographs reinforce the language, following the family during all aspects of collecting and processing maple syrup.

Comparisons can help clarify complex ideas or startling facts. In *Dinosaurs and Their World,* Laurence Pringle develops comparisons between known objects or animals and unknown animals when he describes dinosaurs:

> Imagine a seventy-foot-long animal weighing more than a dozen elephants. . . .However, not all dinosaurs were huge. Some were only as big as automobiles. Others were as small as rabbits. . . .There were skinny dinosaurs that looked like ostriches. There were armored dinosaurs, built like army tanks. (p. 9)

Authors of credible informational books meet many of these guidelines. Consider in the following sections how authors develop credible books that may stimulate and inform readers.

History and Culture

Informational books about history and culture include books about ancient civilizations as well as more recent ones. The illustrations and photographs in many of the books help children visualize the past.

The Ancient World. Authors who write about the ancient world may develop credible books by citing the latest information gained from their own research or that of others and by describing details so that readers can visualize an ancient world. Because readers cannot verify facts about the ancient world through their own experiences, authors may include drawings that clarify information, or use photographs of museum objects or archaeological sites.

Ancient Mayan and Aztec civilizations in Central America are the subjects of several books. Carolyn Meyer and Charles Gallenkamp create a hint of mystery and excitement in their introduction to *The Mystery of the Ancient Maya*. Consider the development of vivid setting, the motivation of the two explorers, and the sense of discovery and anticipation in the following:

> Two travelers—one American, one English—struggled through the jungle, hacking away the tangled vines with their machetes. New York City, which they had left that fall of 1839, seemed impossibly far away. Since their arrival in Central America the trip had been grueling. In the past few weeks they had endured hunger and had been thrown into a makeshift prison. They had hung on as their mules picked their way along the edges of cliffs. But now, standing on a river bank in Honduras, they felt hopeful again. On the opposite shore they could make out a stone wall, perhaps a hundred feet high but nearly hidden by the thick growth of trees. Maybe this was what they had been searching for—the lost city of Copan. (p. 3)

The book proceeds from a history of the early explorers, to revelations about the Mayan civilization, to disclosures about the Mayan people, and to the unanswered questions that are under investigation. Drawings, photographs, and excerpts from early journals add to the sense of time and place.

Sky Watchers of Ages Past, by Malcolm E. Weiss, discusses the scientific contributions of the ancient Maya and other early civilizations. Weiss introduces readers to the sophisticated astronomy developed by the Anasazi Indians, the Mayan calendar makers of the Yucatan, and Polynesian navigators.

Archaeological investigations in Europe provide the sources for information in Susan Woodford's *The Parthenon*. Woodford's book, part of the Cambridge History Library, presents a detailed account of the building of the Greek Parthenon. The text follows a chronological order beginning in 490 B.C. The discussion extends through current problems caused by air pollution. Labeled drawings, captioned photographs, and detailed descriptions of ancient Greek life and religious practices could expand a study of Greek culture and Greek mythology.

A King's Treasure: The Sutton Ho Ship Burial, by Katherine East, published in association with the British Museum, is based on an archaeological

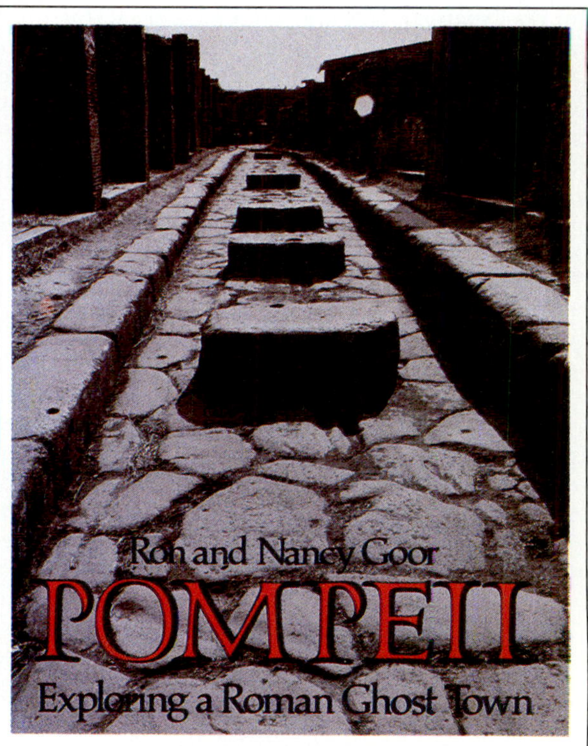

The extensive use of photographs clarifies the text. (Jacket art: copyright © 1986 by Ron Goor from *Pompeii: Exploring a Roman Ghost Town* by Ron and Nancy Goor, (Crowell) copyright © 1986 by Ron and Nancy Goor. Reprinted by permission of Harper & Row, Publishers.)

investigation that uncovered the burial site of an Anglo-Saxon king who lived in seventh-century England. East uses information and artifacts discovered at the site to reconstruct that period in history.

In *Pompeii: Exploring a Roman Ghost Town,* Ron and Nancy Goor use photographs from the archaeological dig to recreate Pompeii before it was destroyed by the eruption of Mt. Vesuvius in A.D. 79. The Goors first introduce the magnitude of the disaster by quoting from a letter that is an eyewitness account about the eruption. In the remainder of the text, the Goors describe the discovery of Pompeii, the probable appearance of the city in A.D. 79, the public and private lives of the people living within the city, and the commercial development of the city. Labeled photographs and drawings clarify the text. Additional information about the process and contributions of archaeology are found in W. John Hackwell's *Digging to the Past: Excavations in Ancient Lands*.

Recent archaeological research adds to David Anderson's development of historical information in *The Spanish Armada*. Anderson uses this information to challenge some previous beliefs. The text includes maps, diagrams, illustrations, photographs, and charts to help readers understand the period in history and comprehend the forces that caused the war between England and Spain.

Readers who enjoy traditional literature and historical fiction set in medieval times and adults who would like to help children recreate medieval festivals should find Sheila Sancha's *The Luttrell Village: Country Life in the Middle Ages* rewarding. The full-page illustrations and accompanying text describe a year in the lives of people who lived in a fourteenth-century Lincolnshire village. The glossary adds to the understanding of the time period. Huck Scarry's pop-up book *Looking into the Middle Ages* will also provoke interest in the subject. David Macaulay's *Castle* and *Cathedral: The Story of Its Construction* include detailed drawings to clarify how castles and cathedrals are constructed. Leonard Everett Fisher's *The Tower of London* uses gray illustrations to add a feeling of ominousness to the surroundings. These books should be helpful to librarians, teachers, and other adults who are interested in giving children a feeling for earlier times and cultures.

Authors may trace the history of a common item to show its importance in diverse cultures and across different time periods. James Cross Giblin uses this approach in *Let There Be Light: A Book About Windows,* in which he traces windows from prehistoric to modern times. Photographs clarify concepts as Giblin proceeds from Blackfoot tipis in America, thatched dwellings in central Africa, and window grilles in ancient Egypt to glass and its use in structures from log cabins to great cathedrals. Colored photographs show examples of beautiful stained glass windows. Giblin uses a similar approach in *From Hand to Mouth: Or, How We Invented Knives, Forks, Spoons, and Chopsticks & Table Manners to Go with Them*. In this text, Giblin also shows that history includes changes in etiquette. Giblin explores the history of table utensils in an often humorous manner.

Piero Ventura's illustrations for Gian Paolo Ceserani's *Grand Constructions* create an architectural bridge between ancient and modern times. This large-format text includes forty-two great architectural wonders, beginning with Stonehenge and concluding with skyscrapers. The large, detailed drawings present a visual history of architectural highlights. A glossary of architectural terms provides helpful information.

History also includes religious traditions. Miriam Chaikin, the author of several books on Jewish holidays, retells the biblical story of Queen Esther and describes the celebration of Purim in *Make Noise, Make Merry: The Story and Meaning of Purim*. A glossary, an index, and a list of additional readings are excellent additions.

Informational books may dramatize content and present concepts through moveable pages. From *Leonardo da Vinci,* by Alice and Martin Provensen. Copyright © 1984 by Alice and Martin Provensen. Reprinted by permission of Viking Penguin Inc.

Archaeologist and anthropologist Brian M. Fagan's *The Great Journey: The Peopling of Ancient America* explores in text and photographs the early people who lived in North America. The text is divided into five parts: (1) ideas, (2) ancestry, (3) the crossing, (4) the first Americans, and (5) the great diversity. In addition to photographs, Fagan uses drawings and maps to clarify concepts. Helen Roney Sattler's *Hominids: A Look Back at Our Ancestors* also uses an anthropological approach to look at early hominids and to research the human family. Christopher Santoro's labeled drawings and maps clarify the concepts developed in Sattler's text. Santoro also provides numerous comparative illustrations to help readers. You may make interesting comparisons between Sattler's text and Joanna Cole's *The Human Body: How We Evolved* as well as Nick Merriman's *Early Humans*.

The Modern World. The factual data in informational books about the modern world may be made credible by citing research, quoting authorities, quoting original sources, and providing detailed descriptions of the setting, circumstances, or situations. Photographs also often add authenticity.

You may discover the impact of photographs and illustrations by comparing two books on historical places written for younger students with two books written for older students. For example, in a book for younger students, *The Great Wall of China,* Leonard Fisher develops a simple text that is extensively illustrated with black-and-white illustrations. The text provides minimal information about the reasons for building the wall and the actual construction of the wall. The illustrations are labeled with Chinese characters that are translated on the final page. Likewise, Karla Kuskin's *Jerusalem, Shining Still* is a highly illustrated book that tells the history of Jerusalem as a storyteller might reveal the battles, the people, and the rebuilding. In both books, the use of illustrations rather than photographs and drawings, and the emphasis on sequence of actions and plot rather than exact historical dates presents the impression of a story rather than a history.

In contrast, Fisher's *The Alamo,* a book for older students, is extensively documented with historical photographs, maps, and paintings supplied by the Daughters of the Republic of Texas Library. Fisher's original drawings are interspersed within the text rather than serving as the only illustrations for the text. Likewise, the changes in *New Providence: A Changing Cityscape* by Renata Von Tscharner and Ronald Fleming are documented with detailed illustrations by Denis Orloff to show how the city changed in time periods labeled 1910, 1935, 1955, 1970, and 1980. Although the text does not include photographs, the illustrations are very realistic.

Orloff's carefully detailed illustrations for *New Providence: A Changing Cityscape* show how important illustrations are in the clarification of text. Likewise, Roxie Munro's almost wordless approach for *The Inside-Outside Book of Washington, D.C.* shows that large, detailed illustrations can provide a great deal of factual information. The only text provided in the book introduces each series of illustrations. Detailed illustrations include the Library of Congress, the Supreme Court of the United States, the National Air and Space Museum, the East Room of the White House, and the Senate Wing of the United States Capitol.

Many informational books about the modern world help children develop an understanding of the varied people on earth, including their struggles and achievements and their impact on history. For example, Suzanne Hilton focuses on the early years of American history in *We the People: The Way We Were 1783–1793*. Hilton creates an authentic and lively history of America by incorporating quotations from primary sources, such as letters, newspapers, and diaries, to clarify the attitudes of the people and the issues of the times. Consequently, this book communicates the fact that history is people rather than dates.

Current historical texts include books related to the writing of the Constitution and the people of that time period. Again, students may make interesting comparisons because two of the books cover similar content but are written for different audiences. Jean Fritz's *Shh! We're Writing the Constitution* is written for younger children. Fritz writes about the constitutional leaders in the lighter, often humorous style found in her biographies.

For example, when Fritz describes one of the debates over a proposal, she compares James Madison's ability at debate to that of a fencer in a duel. She shows Madison controlling the discussion against William Paterson's plan by attacking it from different directions as if dancing about Mr. Paterson's arguments. Madison's thrusts succeed so well, that the plan seems to have nothing left. When delegates vote, Mr. Paterson's plan loses to Mr. Randolph's plan, seven states to three.

Doris and Harold Faber's *We the People: The Story of the United States Constitution Since 1787* is a comprehensive text written for older students. The Fabers begin with the delegation meeting and conclude with the most recent changes in the Constitution. You may compare the description of the debate over the Randolph proposal cited in Fritz's text with the same debate over the Randolph proposal described on pages 23–34 in the Fabers' text. You may wish to consider the differences in style and information, and discuss how those differences relate to the age levels of the children for which the books were written. *The Birth of a Nation: The Early Years of the United States,* also by the Fabers, extends beyond the days of the Constitutional Convention. Milton Meltzer's *The American Revolutionaries: A History in Their Own Words, 1750–1800* provides an excellent source for the original writings of the people who fought in the Revolutionary War or designed the Constitution. The text includes actual letters, diaries, journals, and speeches.

Two excellent books by Rhoda Blumberg present the histories of explorations in more modern times. *Commodore Perry in the Land of the Shogun* follows Commodore Perry as he opens Japan to world trade in the 1850s. The illustrations, which are reproductions of works of William Heine or Eliphalet Brown, Jr. (the official artists on Perry's expedition), add considerable authenticity to the text. *The Incredible Journey of Lewis & Clark* chronicles the 1803–1806 explorations of the Lewis and Clark expedition. Labeled maps and illustrations follow the quest for a water passage to the Pacific Ocean. Extensive notes, sources of illustrations, bibliography, and index add to the usefulness and scholarly feeling of the text.

Robert D. Ballard describes an even more recent exploration in *Exploring the Titanic*. Photographs from the 1912 Titanic are used extensively to show what the boat and interior rooms looked like before the "unsinkable" boat sank. Colored photographs and text then document the finding of the Titanic in 1985 and subsequent exploration of the ship. A glossary of terms and a time line add to the text.

The cry of "Gold!" in 1898 created a great change in a land that previously had been peaceful and isolated, populated by Native Americans, white trappers, and wild animals. Margaret Poynter's *Gold Rush! The Yukon Stampede of 1898* describes the people who abandoned their jobs and businesses in the United States to travel to rugged Alaska. Poynter, whose parents and maternal grandparents were Alaskan pioneers, uses her knowledge of the period to describe those frantic, adventuresome days. Old photographs add authenticity by showing prospectors hitting the trail, panning for gold, sluicing the gold, climbing the Chilkoot Pass in winter, and walking through downtown Skagway in 1898. Students may compare the California gold rush of the mid-1800s with the Alaskan gold rush by reading Rhoda Blumberg's *The Great American Gold Rush.* Blumberg covers the period from 1845 to 1852.

An author's style of writing may entice readers to explore the past. For example, David Weitzman's introduction to *Windmills, Bridges, and Old Machines: Discovering Our Industrial Past* encourages interest and exploration by sounding as if the author is talking to the readers. Weitzman says:

> We're about to take a walk in time, back through the years when America was growing. Along the way we'll be looking for the work of some of America's first builders and engineers, two centuries of canals, windmills, and waterwheels, steam engines and bridges, furnaces and foundries and locomotives, all kinds of wondrous things. . . .The search needn't take us very far. We're sure to find something close by. . .just around the corner, downtown, or just a little farther along a bike trail. (unnumbered introduction)

Other books exploring the industrial past of the United States include E. Boyd Smith's *The Railroad Book,* first published in 1913, and David Macaulay's *Mill,* which describes and illustrates mills as they would have appeared in nineteenth-century New England.

Highly emotional periods in history are difficult to present objectively. Seymour Rossel, however, approaches *The Holocaust* with a historian's detachment. He traces Adolf Hitler's rise to power; describes the harassment, internment, and extermination of many Jewish people; and discusses the Nuremburg trials of the Nazis. Rossel effectively quotes from original sources, such as diaries and letters, to allow readers to visualize the drama and draw their own conclusions.

Barbara Rogasky's *Smoke and Ashes: The Story of the Holocaust* begins with the history of anti-Semitism and proceeds to the 1933–1945 experience. This text shows life in the camps and explores such questions as, Why and how did it happen? and Didn't anyone try to stop the Holocaust? Photographs add to the feeling of tragedy. Milton Meltzer's *Rescue: The Story of How Gentiles Saved Jews in the Holocaust* develops another side of the Holocaust and shows that many people risked their lives to help the Jewish people.

Robert Goldston's *Sinister Touches: The Secret War Against Hitler* looks at people and organizations that struggled against the Nazis between 1939 and 1945. A chronological diary of events precedes each chapter, and numerous quotations from documents and historical figures, a bibliography, and additional suggested reading enhance the book's authenticity. The concluding chapter, "Apocalypse Now," begins with a hypothetical scenario, a description of what might have hap-

ISSUE

Sharing Books About the Nuclear Age

TWO BOOKS THAT EITHER depict nuclear holocaust or provide allegorical interpretations of the arms race are receiving both praise and criticism. Toshi Maruki's *Hiroshima No Pika*[1] is a highly illustrated, picture-storybook depiction of the bombing of Hiroshima. Seuss's *The Butter Battle Book*[2] is a highly illustrated, allegorical fantasy depicting the consequences when opposing forces increase the destructive powers of their weapons.

Praise for these books that actively champion nuclear disarmament is exemplified in reviews in *The New Republic*[3]; and in *Social Education*.[4] For example, in *The New Republic,* Joan Ganz Cooney states that *The Butter Battle Book* "brilliantly dramatized for children the number one issue of the age." The book review subcommittee for the National Council for the Social Studies Book Council identified *Hiroshima No Pika* as an excellent basis for discussions of modern war and nuclear holocaust with children who have intermediate and advanced reading ability. It was selected as a 1983 Notable Children's Trade Book in the Field of Social Studies and was awarded the Ehon Nippon Prize for the most excellent picture book published in Japan.

In contrast to these positive reviews, Richard Elias[5] voices strong concern about sharing such books with elementary-school children. Elias discusses the controversy generated by the nuclear-education movement and asks that librarians consider whether or not a book can help children cope with fear and whether or not children will benefit from the information in the books. Elias argues that both *The Butter Battle Book* and *Hiroshima No Pika* are actually adult books "in masquerade."

You should read the two books, read the reviews of the books, share the books with librarians and other adults, and discuss the positive and negative attributes of each book. Consider Elias's charges. If you believe these books are actually books for adults masquerading as children's books, suggest some reasons why the authors would present their messages in children's-book format. Is this appropriate or inappropriate?

[1]Maruki, Toshi. *Hiroshima No Pika*. Lothrop, 1982.

[2]Seuss, Dr. *The Butter Battle Book*. Random House, 1984.

[3]Cooney, Joan Ganz. *The New Republic* (March 26, 1984).

[4]"Notable Children's Trade Books in the Field of Social Studies." *Social Education* (April 1983): 241–252.

[5]Elias, Richard. "Facts of Life in the Nuclear Age." *School Library Journal* 31 (April 1985): 42–43.

pened if Hitler had won the race for atomic weapons, dropped the atomic bomb on London, and made his demands upon the world.

Readers may compare Robert Goldston's description of atomic warfare with the highly visual and personalized description in Toshi Maruki's *Hiroshima No Pika* (The Flash of Hiroshima), Laurence Pringle's scientific observations in *Nuclear War: From Hiroshima to Nuclear Winter,* and Carl B. Feldbaum and Ronald J. Bee's historical and scientific descriptions in *Looking the Tiger in the Eye*. Through a picture-storybook format, Maruki relates the experiences of seven-year-old Mii on August 6, 1945, as the child and her mother pass by fire, death, and destruction. Maruki, who actively campaigns for nuclear disarmament and world peace, concludes her book on a hopeful note: "It can't happen again if no one drops the bomb" (p. 43, unnumbered). Pringle's text covers the history of nuclear weapons and suggests probable consequences of using them. Feldbaum and Bee's text includes the history of nuclear weapons and discusses decisions made by political, scientific, and military officials.

Daniel S. Davis's *Behind Barbed Wire: The Imprisonment of Japanese Americans During World War II* presents another emotional period in history. This book effectively explores attitudes toward Japanese Americans before and after the attack on Pearl Harbor and the effects of internment on the later lives of Japanese Americans.

Some authors explore various cultures by studying one person or family in depth. Exceptional photographs document the lives of the Tasaday, a Stone-Age Philippino people, in John Nance's *Lobo of the Tasaday*. Once again, by focusing on a child, an author vividly depicts social organization, living conditions, and beliefs.

Books about people from various cultures and about people who have different occupations encourage children to expand their interests and understandings. Sabra Holbrook's *Canada's Kids* relates information about the families, schools, hobbies, and expectations of Canadian children —rural and urban, white and Native Canadian. Maxine P. Fisher's *Women in the Third World* develops personal profiles of women. Lila Perl's *Red Star and Green Dragon: Looking at New China* combines a concise history of China with a description of contemporary China. The photographs of ordinary people help understanding. Excellent supporting information includes a list of important dates, a bibliography, and an index.

Richard Ammon's *Growing Up Amish* explores the social life and customs of an Amish family in Pennsylvania. Photographs, a bibliography, and an index provide useful support. Other books about rural life in the United States are Patricia Demuth's *Joel: Growing Up a Farm Man,* which is about the responsibilities involved in being a farmer in the Midwest, Nancy Price Graff's *The Strength of the Hills: A Portrait of a Family Farm,* which documents the various responsibilities of family members on a Vermont farm, and Cheryl Walsh Bellville's *Farming Today Yesterday's Way,* which shows a twentieth-century farmer using horses and other nonmechanized farming techniques. The books by Demuth and Bellville also use photographs, and they supply considerable detail to help young readers gain a clearer understanding of farm life in America. You may contrast farming and ranching by reading Joan Anderson's *The American Family Farm* and Brent Ashabranner's *Born to the Land: An American Portrait*. Anderson's text is a photo essay of families living in Massachusetts, Georgia, and Iowa. Ashabranner's text is about New Mexico.

Roger Englander, an award-winning producer of opera, effectively used his extensive opera background in *Opera, What's All the Screaming About?* This "guide for the curious listener" traces the development of opera from its beginnings in the European Renaissance to the contemporary musical theater. Of special interest to the novice is Englander's method of depicting the plots of famous operas through newspaper-style headlines:

> LOVERS BURIED ALIVE IN TOMB
> AS JILTED PRINCESS MOURNS
> *Aida*
> Music: Giuseppe Verdi
> Libretto: Antonio Ghislanzoni, in Italian
> First Performed: Cairo, December 24, 1871 (p. 25)

Englander's text includes extensive reference materials; lists of leading composers, librettists, and opera companies; a glossary; a discography; and an index.

Nature

Effective informational books about nature encourage children to understand their own bodies, observe nature, explore the life cycles of animals, consider the impact of endangered species, experiment with plants, understand the balance of the smallest ecosystem, and explore the earth's geology. In order to create effective and credible books, authors must blend fact into narrative. The authors must gain these facts about animals from observation and research. Close-up photography is especially effective in clarifying information and stimulating interest. For example, photographs may illustrate what happens inside an egg or a nest or follow the life cycle of an animal or a plant. Labeled diagrams may clarify text descriptions. Maps may show natural habitats of animals, migration patterns of birds, or locations of earthquakes. If authors present new vocabulary or concepts, they should define the terms, illustrate them with diagrams or photographs, and proceed from known to unknown information. Clearly developed activities that encourage children to observe and experiment can make a book even more useful. A bibliography, an index, and a list of additional readings are helpful, too.

The Human Body. Informational books about the human body are especially interesting to readers who are curious about their own bodies and how they function. Books for children about the human body range from overviews to detailed discussions of one aspect of the body, such as the brain or the eyes. Some books also discuss body-related issues, such as the right to live or to die, genetic engineering, and human origins.

Two books on the human body illustrate the importance of labeled diagrams when studying anatomy. Jonathan Miller's *The Human Body* is a fascinating, twelve-page pop-up book. Each double-page spread, along with tabs that simulate functions, explains some part of the human body. Body parts are labeled with numbers and then explained in the captions for the pop-up illustrations. Ruth and Bertel Bruun clarify their longer text, *The Human Body,* with diagrams and drawings that show the interiors of various body regions and the relationships of these regions to each other.

In-depth presentations of specific body parts and functions are found in numerous informational books. For example, Hilda Simon focuses on the miracle of sight in *Sight and Seeing: A World of Light and Color*. Simon clarifies a complex topic through the extensive use of color-coded drawings. Color comparisons clarify corresponding parts of an eye and a camera and differences between human and animal sight. For example, in the chapter on color perception, Simon compares colors of wildflowers as humans see them and as bees might perceive them. Simon's extensive text includes a discussion of special visual adaptations that are unique to some animals. In *The Story of Your Hand,* Alvin and Virginia B. Silverstein use drawings and experiments to focus on the structure and functions of hands.

Alan Nourse's *Your Immune System* discusses the body's immune system and illustrates it with photographs and diagrams. Nourse's writing style heightens interest and understanding. For example, Nourse compares the body's immune system to an army whose soldiers protect the body against alien invaders. Clearly written information about the body's ability to heal various injuries is found in Joanna Cole's *Cuts, Breaks, Bruises and Burns: How Your Body Heals*.

Anecdotes from real case histories increase readers' interest in Margery and Howard Facklam's *The Brain: Magnificent Mind Machine*. Information gained by studying people who have lost various brain functions provides the background information in this text.

Stephen Parker and John Bavosi's *Life Before Birth: The Story of the First Nine Months* is a straightforward discussion of the facts related to the fertilization of the egg, the development and growth of the fetus, and the birth of the baby. The book, which is enhanced with color illustrations adapted from a slide program at the British Museum, concludes with a photograph of a newborn baby. Camilla Jessel develops a broader scope of coverage in *The Joy of Birth: A Book for Parents and Children*. However, Jessel's text emphasizes the mother's physical changes, the birth process itself, and the care of newborn babies. Black-and-white photographs follow the sequence of an actual birth, show the breast-feeding of a baby, and show babies with their families. Dorothy Hinshaw Patent's *Babies!* is for younger children. The text and photographs follow the physical, mental, and social development achieved by babies from birth to age two.

Several informational books for older children provide detailed information about the human species and may encourage further reading and discussion about controversial subjects. In *Human Origins,* anthropologist Richard E. Leakey traces the evolution of humans from early apelike creatures to farmers. Maps, photographs, drawings, and recommendations for further reading clarify this informative text. Contemporary issues related to humanity are the focus in Ann E. Weiss's

THROUGH THE EYES OF AN AUTHOR

Writing Natural History for Young Readers

Naturalist, former war correspondent, spokesman for endangered species, and recipient of numerous awards for outstanding science trade books for children, author JACK DENTON SCOTT discusses his beliefs about writing children's nonfictional books.

DEMANDS ARE PRECISE: Be accurate. Be relaxed; write fluently; never write down to your readers; never try to write up either. Know your audience; also know your subject; but even if you do know it, research it so that you will know perhaps more than you or anyone else will want to know. Put these all together and they may be an axiom for writing nonfiction for your readers.

But there is more: There can be no cloudy language; writing must be simple, crisp, clear. This, in fact, should be a primer for all writing. Children demand the best from a writer. If young readers become bored, confused, puzzled by style, or showered with a writer's self-important, complicated words you've lost readers. Young readers instinctively shy away from the pretentious and the phony.

In the dozen photo-essays that photographer Ozzie Sweet and I have produced for Putnam and our brilliant editor, Margaret Frith, we have worked with one object in mind: Entertain and inform. We believe that children want to learn; and everyone knows that they want to be entertained. We have tried to do this with clarity in words and with dramatic but thoughtfully conceived photographs by perhaps the most talented man with the camera in the U.S.

We have also introduced our series of books to children with a new technique. Action, constant movement, words flowing into photographs, photographs flowing into words, no labored captions, no slowing of pace. Almost a cinematic technique.

Bioethics: Dilemmas in Modern Medicine. Weiss uses case histories of people such as Karen Ann Quinlan to discuss the moral issues related to the right to live or to die, conflicts between medicine and religion, organ transplants, and human experimentation. A bibliography of additional readings provides sources for library research and additional discussion. A series of books provides a history of various drugs and discusses effects of the drugs on the brain and the body, treatments of addicts, and ways to resist peer pressure. David Friedman's *Focus on Drugs and the Brain* discusses the brain and how drugs influence the brain. Friedman distinguishes differences between drugs used for medicine and drugs used for harmful purposes. The remainder of the books emphasize specific drugs and provide clear warnings about the harmful influences of drugs: Catherine O'Neill's *Focus on Alcohol,* Robert Perry's *Focus on Nicotine and Caffeine,* Jeffrey Shulman's *Focus on Cocaine and Crack,* and Paula Klevan Zeller's *Focus on Marijuana.*

Texts on the AIDS virus are available for both younger and older readers. In Rosmarie Hausherr's *Children and the AIDS Virus,* the text and illustrations look at ways that children may or may not get the disease. Hausherr's text is written for two levels of readers. The large print is to be read to or by younger children. The smaller print provides additional information for older children. Susan Kuklin's *Fighting Back: What Some People Are Doing About AIDS* is written for older readers. Kuklin includes the experiences of people who have AIDS and a glossary of terms associated with AIDS.

Animals. Authors who write effectively about prehistoric animals or about modern-day reptiles and amphibians, birds, land invertebrates (earthworms), insects, and mammals must present their facts clearly, and they must not give their animals human qualities and emotions. Because books about animals are popular with many different age groups, authors must consider the readers'

This is difficult, demanding that photographer and writer work closely together.

I, personally, also have the belief that too much weird way-out fiction is pushed at children. (I have nothing against fiction; in fact I also write adult fiction.) But children have their own vivid and creative imaginations that they bring to their reading. One 10-year-old boy wrote me that while he was reading our book, *Canada Geese,* he actually flew south with the geese. I bet he did. I *hope* he did.

Ozzie Sweet and I also object to violence in children's literature; it's boring, it's burdensome, and it's unwanted by children. I write of the free, wild creatures and try to give children straight information that will interest them and educate them, staying away from cuteness or giving animals or birds human traits which, of course, they don't have. There is an entire essay on our shrinking world and what wildlife means to children, wildlife that may not even be around when our readers become adults.

Finally, we believe that children who are forming habits and outlooks that will serve them forever are more important than adult readers and we feel fortunate that we have the opportunity to give them worthwhile subjects to think about. Thus we choose those subjects carefully for our intelligent and demanding audience. Ask any librarian or teacher. They know children's standards better than anyone. And thank God for librarians and teachers! Without them the darkness of ignorance would close in much more quickly than it is doing at present, pushed by television which creates non-readers and a growing careless attitude toward the written word—by adults, of course. Not children. They still are excited about good books and receptive to the well-written word. Ozzie Sweet and I shall continue to try to give them the best we have.

backgrounds as they develop new concepts.

Ancient Reptiles. With scientists as detectives and fossils as clues, twentieth-century children can experience the thrill of investigating the earth's pre-human past. Children often become enthusiastic amateur paleontologists as they learn about dinosaurs in books, study about them in museums, search for fossilized footprints or bones, and make dinosaur models. Books depicting excavation sites such as Caroline Arnold's *Dinosaur Mountain: Graveyard of the Past* and Kathryn Lasky's *Dinosaur Dig* present the work of paleontologists and show the careful work that has provided answers about dinosaurs. Books on dinosaurs range from highly illustrated texts for younger children, such as Russell Freedman's *Dinosaurs and Their Young* and Gail Gibbons's *Dinosaurs,* to texts for older children that provide extensive scientific details, such as Helen Roney Sattler's *Dinosaurs of North America.* Freedman's book explores the significance of a 1978 discovery that raised questions about how these reptiles raised their young. Drawings of both dinosaurs and excavation sites clarify the text. In contrast, Sattler's book is arranged by geologic time periods. It describes the characteristics and habitats of more than eighty types of dinosaurs. Further readings and an index add to the usefulness.

Other books that explore the subject of dinosaurs are Laurence Pringle's *Dinosaurs and People: Fossils, Facts, and Fantasies,* which traces research associated with dinosaurs, David C. Knight's *"Dinosaurs" that Swam and Flew,* which discusses lesser-known reptiles, and William Mannetti's *Dinosaurs in Your Backyard,* which challenges some previous theories about dinosaurs and provides new interpretations suggesting that birds are feathered dinosaurs, dinosaurs may have been warm blooded, and some dinosaurs previously believed to be water inhabitants spent most of the time on land. Mannetti, however, implies that the theories he presents are accepted by all authorities and does not refer to opposing

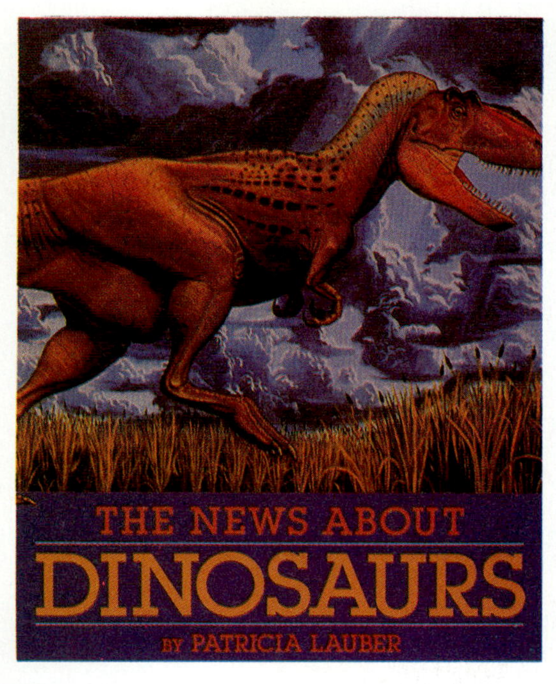

Illustrations and text present old and new information about dinosaurs. (From *The News About Dinosaurs* by Patricia Lauber, copyright © 1989 by Patricia Lauber. Reprinted by permission from Bradbury Press.)

viewpoints or discuss how others have interpreted the same evidence.

Patricia Lauber uses comparisons and contrasts to clarify points in her *Dinosaurs Walked Here and Other Stories Fossils Tell*. For example, Lauber compares photographs of a 315-million-year-old amphibian and a bullfrog to highlight similarities. Likewise, she compares photographs of fossils of the oldest known bird and the skeleton of a barn owl. To illustrate contrasts among animals, Lauber compares photographs showing the teeth of a duckbill, which are meant to grind plants, and the teeth of a tyrannosaurus rex, which are suited for tearing flesh. In *The News About Dinosaurs,* Lauber presents past beliefs as well as the latest information, which often refutes earlier beliefs.

Descriptions of both prehistoric and contemporary animals are included in *Giants of Land, Sea & Air: Past & Present,* by David Peters. This Sierra Club book describes over seventy large animals. All of the illustrations are drawn to the same scale (1 inch = 22 1/2 inches). Some of the pages are foldouts so that the readers may compare the sizes of dinosaurs such as the brachiosaurus and apatosaurus and contemporary mammals such as the sperm whale and the blue whale.

Insects, Spiders, and Snakes. Books for younger children frequently present nature in familiar environments. Bianca Lavies's *Tree Trunk Traffic* presents the various spiders, insects, and other animals that are found in a maple tree during spring and summer. Color photographs add to the visual appeal of the book and encourage the readers to search for inhabitants in the tree and to explore trees in their own neighborhoods. Julie Brinckloe's *Fireflies!* shares a young boy's fascination with the insects as he watches them, captures them in a jar, and then realizes that he must release them or they will die. Molly McLaughlin's *Dragonflies* follows the life cycle of these insects. Photographs of dragonflies resting on hands indicate sizes. Other photographs are magnified to reveal physical characteristics. Lavie's text and illustrations in *Backyard Hunter: The Praying Mantis* follow the life cycle of this interesting insect.

In a book for older readers, *Small Worlds: Communities of Living Things,* Howard Smith introduces readers to the ecosystems in such places as a sand dune, a milkweed plant, and a vacant lot. Smith clarifies difficult words and concepts by highlighting them in boldface print and defining them in a glossary.

Authors of informational books may entice children by presenting challenges or comparisons. In *Someone Saw a Spider: Spider Facts and Folktales,* Shirley Climo compares factual information and spider folklore from various cultures.

Snakes fascinate just about everybody. Patricia Lauber's *Snakes Are Hunters* is an introductory text that is part of the "Let's-Read-and-Find-Out" Science Book series. The text and illustrations describe the physical characteristics of snakes and ways in which snakes hunt their prey. Ginny Johnston and Judy Cutchins's *Scaly Babies: Reptiles Growing Up* uses photographs and text to introduce cobras, boas, lizards, crocodilians, and turtles. The text includes a glossary and an index. In Joanna Cole's *A Snake's Body,* Jerome Wexler's series of photographs shows a python's body as it captures and swallows a chick.

Seymour Simon, who has had over twenty books selected as outstanding Science Trade Books for Children, effectively presents straightforward facts about snakes and dispels some myths about them in *Poisonous Snakes* and *Meet the Giant Snakes*. In the latter book, Simon uses comparisons to clarify: The boa constrictor is as long as a sedan automobile, the African python is as long as a station wagon, and both the anaconda and the reticulated python are as long as a school bus.

Mammals. Jack Denton Scott and photographer Ozzie Sweet have collaborated to give children several outstanding books about mammals. Because their work contains many of the characteristics of outstanding informational books for children, we consider several of the techniques that Scott uses in *The Book of the Pig*. First, Scott skillfully blends facts acquired from animal experts and naturalists and the observations of a pig farmer into the narrative. Consider, for example, Scott's support of the intelligence, cooperativeness, and cleanliness of pigs. Scott provides examples of the adaptability of pigs, research demonstrating the intelligence of pigs and the meanings of the sounds that pigs utter, photographs of pigs walking or playing with people, and proof that young pigs try to keep their farrowing pens clean.

Scott uses frequent comparisons to help readers understand the nature and development of pigs. For example, members of a family that raise pigs "romp with their piglets as they would with puppies" (p. 9). Later, Scott cites research that claims that a newborn "piglet's mobility is equivalent to that of a 2 1/2-year-old child" (p. 20). Scott clarifies the meaning of new vocabulary, such as "the mother, or sow," (p. 15), "giving birth to, or farrowing," (p. 19). Sweet's photographs enhance the text and frequently add warmth and humor. When the text indicates that "pigs really are in clover" (p. 7), a photograph shows piglets in a flower-dappled meadow.

Several books on animals are especially appropriate for young readers because the subjects are familiar. Joanna Cole's *A Cat's Body* explores characteristic cat behaviors, such as pouncing, reacting to moving objects, and purring. The text

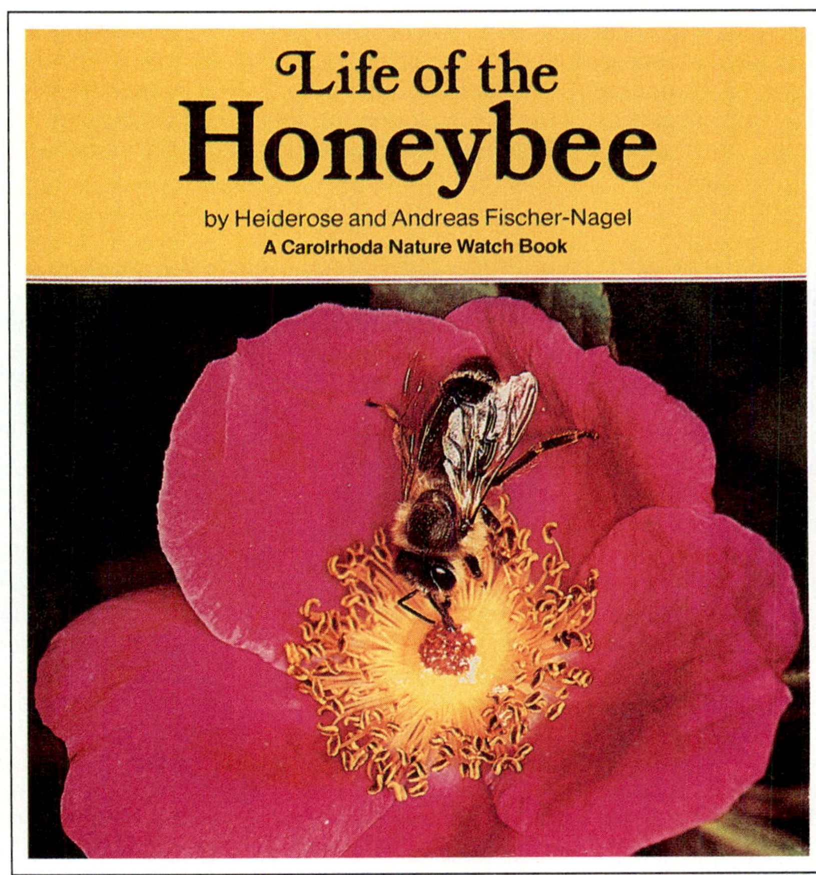

Photographs present the life cycle of the honeybee and add important information. (From *Life of the Honeybee* by Heiderose and Andreas Fischer-Nagel, © 1986, a Carolrhoda Nature Watch Book published in 1986 and translated from *Im Bienenstock* copyright 1982 by Elise H. Scherer. Reprinted by permission of the publisher, Carolrhoda Books, Inc., 241 First Avenue North, Minneapolis, MN 55401.)

and photographs may encourage children to observe their own pets. In *My Puppy Is Born,* Cole presents the birth of miniature dachshund puppies. Jerome Wexler's photographs show the pregnant dog going into her box, the emergence of the first puppy, born inside a sac, and the mother tearing the sac and licking the puppy. The book follows the growth of the puppies during their first eight weeks, as they are unable to see or hear, as they nurse, and then as they open their eyes and take their first steps.

Illustrated books about familiar animals enhance younger children's observational and descriptive abilities. Such books include Lilo Hess's *Diary of a Rabbit;* David McPhail's *Farm Morning,* which accompanies a young girl and her father as they take care of the barnyard animals; zoologist Dorothy Hinshaw Patent's *Farm Animals, The Sheep Book, Thoroughbred Horses* and *Appaloosa Horses;* and Tana Hoban's *A Children's Zoo.*

Millicent Selsam and Joyce Hunt have written several books designed for young children. Both *A First Look at Animals with Horns* and *A First Look at Seals, Sea Lions, and Walruses* answer simple questions and encourage readers to observe physical characteristics. In *A First Look at Animals with Horns,* Selsam and Hunt differentiate between goats and sheep by stating, "The horns of sheep sweep down and around" (p. 18), while "[t]he horns of goats sweep up and straight back" (p. 19). Illustrations accompany the text and show these characteristics of sheep and goats. In *Keep Looking!,* Selsam and Hunt encourage readers to search for animals in the yard of a country house.

In another book for young children, *Young Lions* by Toshi Yoshida, the text and illustrations follow three young lions as they move across the African plain. The illustrations show other animals that live in Africa, including water buffaloes, rhinoceroses, and zebras. *Polar Bear Cubs,* by Downs Matthews, includes characteristics of polar bears and adventures typical of cubs. In this book, two cubs explore their arctic home. The color photographs capture the feeling of the far northern landscape as well as provide insight into the lives of animals in the arctic.

Kenneth Lilly's Animals, with text by Joyce Pope, is for older students, although the beautiful animal portraits appeal to all ages. The animals in this text are divided according to their habitat, including hot forests, cool forests, seas and rivers, grasslands, deserts, and mountains. To increase geographic understanding, each double-page spread includes a small map of the world that highlights the location of the animal. The text concludes with a list of facts and figures and an index. Many of the animals included in the text are in danger of extinction.

Wild mammals, their contributions, and their survival are topics common in informational books. Authors may describe the contributions of animals, argue for their protection by means of responsible population control, and use statistics to develop points on survival and to demonstrate the plight of the animal. In *The Kingdom of Wolves,* Scott Barry pleas for protection of the wolf, which he depicts as a powerful, intelligent, social animal that does not deserve the reputation suggested in fairy tales. Scott's argument seems credible because he describes seven years of working with and observing wolves. (Children who have read Jean Craighead George's *Julie of the Wolves* may enjoy reading Barry's description of wolf body language and the lives of wolves on the Alaskan tundra.)

In *Whales, Giants of the Deep,* Dorothy Hinshaw Patent concludes her in-depth discussion of whales with a history of whaling and the consequences of an unregulated industry. While Patent states the arguments against a moratorium on whaling presented by Japan, Norway, and the USSR, she concludes with a strong statement in favor of the moratorium:

> While the whaling nations argue that some whale species are not diminishing and will not become extinct even with continued whaling, conservationists believe that without a ban on commercial whaling, whales will disappear from the Earth. Unfortunately, all nations that kill whales do not belong to the IWC. So even if Norway, Japan, and the U.S.S.R. decide to abide by the IWC moratorium, some whaling may continue. We can only hope that it is not enough to further endanger these magnificent animals. (p. 82)

Other excellent books about wild animals and protection of species include Patent's *Dolphins and Porpoises,* Kay McDearmon's *Rocky Mountain Bighorns,* Barbara Ford's *Alligators, Raccoons, and Other Survivors: The Wildlife of the Future,* and Laurence Pringle's *Feral: Tame Animals Gone Wild* and *Saving Our Wildlife.*

Depending upon their purposes and points of view, authors may approach monkeys, apes, and chimpanzees quite differently. For example, Nina Leen's purpose in *Monkeys* is to provide general information and some consideration of the possible extinction of monkeys. Consequently, she includes a short description of each primate's habitat, use of prehensile tail, preferred foods,

The photographs follow a day in the life of Jane Goodall, the British naturalist. (From *The Chimpanzee Family Book* by Jane Goodall, copyright © 1989 by the Jane Goodall Institute for Wildlife Research, Education and Conservation. Photos copyright © 1989 by Michael Neugebauer. Reprinted by permission of Picture Book Studio.)

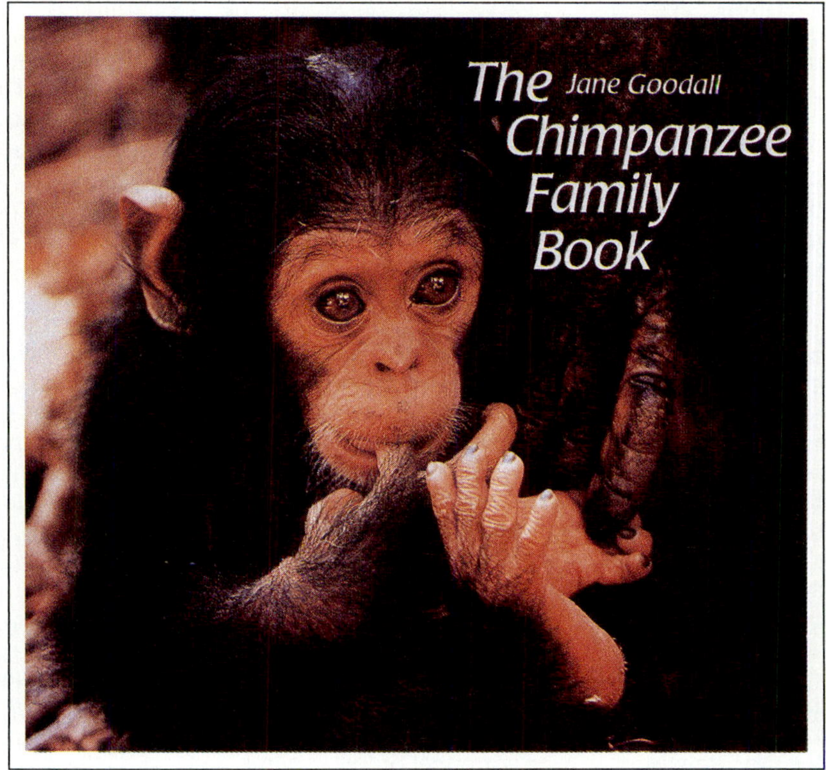

vocalization, sleeping habits, grooming, family relationships, and danger of extinction. Jane Goodall's *The Chimpanzee Family Book* explores chimpanzees in their natural habitat in the Gombe Natural Park, Tanzania. In this text, the natural environment seems to be the only appropriate one.

Anna Michel's *The Story of Nim: The Chimp Who Learned Language* reports Herbert Terrace's research as he tried to teach a chimpanzee to recognize and use words in sign language. Linda Koebner's *From Cage to Freedom: A New Beginning for Laboratory Chimpanzees* presents a more cautious and skeptical view of using chimpanzees for experimental purposes. Her book reports results from a research project that investigated whether formerly caged chimps can learn to survive without humans and eventually breed in their natural environment.

Birds. The topics of informational books about birds range from common barnyard fowl to exotic tropical birds. Through these books, you can observe various techniques that authors use to create interest for young children and ways in which they present concepts new to older children.

In *A First Look at Bird Nests,* a simply written book for young readers, Millicent Selsam and Joyce Hunt describe the nests of common American birds and tell how the nests are built. Selsam and Hunt stimulate the development of observational skills by asking questions and providing puzzles. The answers to the questions are located in the accompanying illustrations.

In *Window into a Nest,* a book for older children, Geraldine Lux Flanagan reveals the stages in chickadee nesting and hatching behavior. The text describes the placement of a concealed camera into an opening in a wooden birdhouse. The photographs clarify behavioral patterns, such as floor hammering before nest building, reactions of alarm when an intruder peers into the house, struggles with straw brought into the home, and the feeding ceremony between male and female. Flanagan's text, a winner of the London Times Educational Supplement Senior Information Book Award shows the careful research that should go into scientific investigation.

Accuracy and observational techniques are also emphasized in Ada Graham's *Six Little Chickadees:*

A Scientist and Her Work with Birds. In *A Bird's Body,* Joanna Cole relies on diagrams and photographs of parakeets and cockatiels to help readers understand flying ability and behavioral characteristics.

Close-up photography is especially effective in books written about evolving embryos. Several books clarify this development by allowing readers to see what happens inside an egg—for example, Hans-Heinrich Isenbart's *A Duckling Is Born.*

Powerful flying birds and exotic water birds have interested a number of eminent researchers, writers, and photographers. Because the birds and their environments may be new to young readers, many books for young children present most of their information through photographs. For example, in Caroline Arnold's *Saving the Peregrine Falcon,* the large photographs alone are sufficient to show scientists raising the endangered birds in captivity, encouraging them to identify with falcons rather than humans, and releasing them into the environment.

Authors of nonfiction informational books frequently focus on endangered species. In *Peeping in the Shell: A Whooping Crane Is Hatched,* Faith McNulty develops the importance of preserving the whooping crane by describing the work of ornithologist George Archibald to produce a healthy whooping crane in captivity. The suspenseful descriptions of the young chick hatching suggest that each action in nature must take place in the proper time. Dorothy Hinshaw Patent's *The Whooping Crane: A Comeback Story* explores attempts to save this bird, which was almost extinct. Peter and Connie Roop's *Seasons of the Cranes* begins in the spring and follows whooping cranes as they mate in northern Canada, raise their young, and migrate to their winter home in Texas. The Roops provide a map to let young readers follow the flyway of the cranes. The Roops also use the familiar to help clarify the unfamiliar. For example, when they describe the crane eggs, they say, "The two eggs, twice as long as chicken eggs, lie side by side in the shallow bowl of bulrushes" (p. 6).

The efforts to save endangered birds or birds that are harmed through human cruelty are also effectively presented in Paula Hendrich's *Saving America's Birds* and in several books written by Jack Denton Scott and illustrated with photographs by Ozzie Sweet, including *Orphans from the Sea,* a compelling book about attempts by the Florida Suncoast Seabird Sanctuary to save the brown pelican. Because Scott includes various theories about birds and describes research, older children learn to distinguish between fact and theory in informational books. For example, Scott presents various theories about the migrating habits of geese in *Canada Geese.* Scott describes studies such as the Stellar-Orientation System, which tested the star-map theory of how the geese find exact locations and follow exact routes year after year.

In *The Book of Eagles,* Helen Roney Sattler looks at several kinds of eagles and dangers to eagles. Numerous illustrations, by Jean Day Zallinger, help readers understand the characteristics of the birds. Maps show specific locations of eagles throughout the world. Sattler also relates unknown content to known and emphasizes cause-and-effect relationships. She says, for example:

> An eagle's wing and tail feathers are incredibly strong. They are made of keratin, the same material as human fingernails. . . .The wings are flatter on the bottom than on the top, like the wings of an aircraft. Small feathers called coverts grow along the forward edges of the wings, making them thicker in front. This causes the air to flow faster over the top, providing lift. (p. 11)

The majority of the animal books discussed here were written by eminent authorities in animal studies. In the introduction to *The Daywatchers,* artist and author Peter Parnall identifies himself as a self-taught rather than a formally educated naturalist. Consequently, he employs his own feelings, memories, experiences, and observations when writing about and illustrating the birds of prey in this large text. Each chapter reveals Parnall's discoveries and his emerging feelings of wonder. The artist's eye, rather than the perfection of a camera, rules the illustrations. Parnall states that he tried to capture a feeling, "not every feather, but the character, the aura, of the creatures, whatever those qualities are that set them apart from the chicken and the mole. Children dream as lions and eagles. I still do" (p. 11). This book might motivate young readers to observe nature and to achieve their own sense of wonder.

Plants. Informational books about plants should develop clear details in logical order, include diagrams and photographs that illustrate terminology, and encourage children to become involved in learning. In *The Amazing Dandelion,* Millicent E. Selsam effectively introduces the considerable reproductive potential of the dandelion by showing two photographs of a field. In one photograph, the field contains a single dandelion plant; a few years later, the field is covered with dandelions. Then, Selsam attracts the readers' attention and speculation as she asks how the dandelion is able to spread so quickly. Why is it one of the most successful plants? The text and photographs answer this question by tracing the life cycle of the dandelion. Several experiments also encourage children to become involved in learning about why the dandelion is so successful in its reproduction.

Other books by Selsam also contain step-by-step directions accompanied by photographs. In *Popcorn,* Selsam describes how to sprout seeds in a glass, transplant them into a garden or container, pollinate the corn, and wait for it to reach maturity. In *Cotton,* a dime next to the first two leaves of a cotton seedling clarifies the size, close-up photographs effectively illustrate the stages in plant development, and labeled photographs and drawings clarify the terminology.

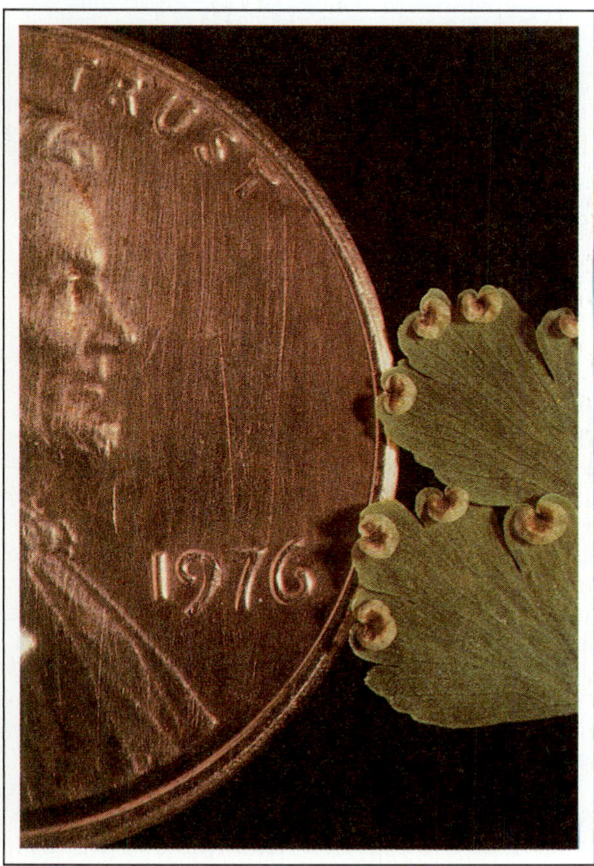

Magnified common objects clarify size concepts. (From *Spore to Spore: Ferns and How They Grow,* by Jerome Wexler. Copyright © 1985 by Jerome Wexler. By permission of Dodd, Mead & Company.)

Another informational book that develops concepts about plants through chronological order and personal experience is Patricia Lauber's *Seeds Pop! Stick! Glide!* Lauber's text and Jerome Wexler's photographs help children understand the many different ways in which seeds travel and disperse. Consider, for example, the presentation of Queen Anne's lace. The text and photographs proceed in chronological order from a plant with many small flowers, to the dried appearance of the plant in early winter, and finally to what happens when the dried plant opens and closes its umbrella. Lauber encourages children to become involved in the discovery process by describing an experiment that they can do to replicate the plant's changes in nature.

The Let's-Read-and-Find-Out Science Book series contains several books that allow children to explore the world of plants. For example, Phyllis S. Busch's *Cactus in the Desert* encourages children to learn about a variety of cacti, from the tall saguaro to the tiniest pincushion. The text emphasizes the ability of cacti to store water and survive in dry climates. In order to help children perceive height and quantity, the illustrations compare the cactus with known quantities: the height of a saguaro cactus is compared to ten people standing on each other's shoulders; the amount of water evaporating from a regular tree is illustrated as being about 320 quarts, compared with less than a glass from a cactus. The book concludes with suggestions of cacti that can be raised at home and recommendations for their care.

Desert Giant: The World of the Saguaro Cactus, by Barbara Bash, is part of the Tree Tales series of Sierra Club Books. This book is written for young readers. It emphasizes that the cactus provides food and shelter for desert inhabitants. Large illustrations show the interior as well as the exterior of the cactus. Labelled drawings clarify flower fertilization and detail seed interiors.

Anita Holmes's *Cactus: The All-American Plant,* written for older readers, describes the major kinds of cacti, discusses the natural surroundings of cacti, and stresses the interdependence of life forms. Like Busch's book for younger readers, Holmes's book encourages her readers to learn more about cacti by following instructions for raising various cacti. Unlike the simpler text, Holmes's text provides an extensive glossary, a bibliography, and information on classification.

Photographs and drawings often clarify books about the complex concepts related to photosynthesis. Masaharu Suzuki's photographs in Sylvia Johnson's *Potatoes* are especially interesting. Colored water produces photographs that clearly illustrate the location of the vascular system in a plant stem and the location of the vascular ring in the potato.

Illustrators of informational books may clarify size by photographing common objects next to a plant or seed. Jerome Wexler uses this technique in *From Spore to Spore: Ferns and How They Grow* to clarify size and to show that the photographs are magnified. A common pin placed next to fern seedlings and a penny shown next to a new leaf illustrate the diminutive sizes. Likewise, a greatly enlarged penny next to two sporangia illustrates the microscopic size of the spores. Without such visual comparisons readers would have difficulty understanding the size perspective.

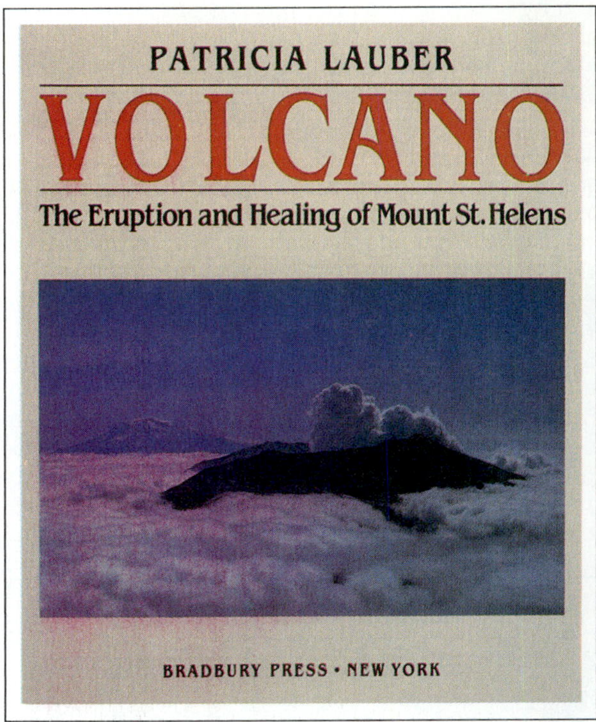

Color photographs show important sequences in the Mount St. Helens eruption. (From *Volcano: The Eruption and Healing of Mount St. Helens* by Patricia Lauber, copyright © 1986. Reprinted by permission of Bradbury Press.)

Geology and Geography. Because children often see the results of earthquakes on television, geology is a subject that interests many children. Seymour Simon's *Danger from Below: Earthquakes—Past, Present, and Future* provides a comprehensive coverage. This book includes a history of devastating earthquakes and ancient people's explanations for them, explanations of the Richter Scale and the Modified Mercali Intensity Scale, discussion of recent discoveries about how and why earthquakes occur, discussion of how scientists are working to monitor the intensity of earthquakes and to predict where and when they will occur; and safety precautions that children should know about. Photographs of actual earthquake damage show the destructive power, and maps illustrate the plates of the earth's crust and identify places where earthquakes are likely to happen.

You may find it interesting to compare Simon's book, which is written for older students, with Hershell and Joan L. Nixon's book, which is for younger students, *Earthquakes: Nature in Motion*. These books provide interesting background information for children who also read Laurence Yep's novel *Dragonwings*, which describes the great San Francisco earthquake of 1906.

Since the eruption of Mount St. Helens, several books emphasizing volcanic activity in North America have appeared. In *The Mount St. Helens Disaster: What We've Learned*, Thomas and Virginia Aylesworth discuss the chronological order of the seismic events that led up to the eruption. The Aylesworths enrich the text with eyewitness accounts, photographs, diagrams, and maps. Patricia Lauber's *Volcano: The Eruption and Healing of Mount St. Helens* is an excellent photographic essay of the eruption and the changes since the eruption. Photographs showing minute changes in time are effective, as are photographs of specific settings taken before and after the eruption. Hershell and Joan Nixon's *Volcanoes: Nature's Fireworks* and Seymour Simon's *Volcanoes* provide sources for studying volcanic eruptions in other parts of the world.

Technical terms in informational books about geology may be difficult for children to understand unless the authors clarify the terms with photographs or drawings. Written descriptions of such terms as *cirques, hanging valleys, stalactites,* and *stalagmites* may prove bewildering to children who have not seen these formations. In Hershell and Joan Nixon's *Glaciers: Nature's Frozen Rivers,* photographs show different classifications of glaciers and illustrate the ability of glaciers to alter land formation in places children might visit, such as Yosemite National Park and Glacier National Park. The Nixons describe the work of glaciologists and give a history of the ice ages, when glaciers covered northern portions of the earth. The book concludes with the modern-day benefits of glaciers from the past and ways in which people are using, or are trying to benefit from, the vast water supply contained in glaciers and icebergs.

Humor provides a strong interest in Joanna Cole's *The Magic School Bus: Inside the Earth*. Dialogue between children is presented in cartoon-type bubbles, while information is presented in both conventional text and examples of reports written by a school class. Magic and learning occur when the teacher drives a bus load of children into the earth, where they learn about rocks and the structure of the earth.

Nayana Currimbhoy's *Living in Deserts: A Cultural Geography* describes desert regions of the world and discusses how deserts affect the lives of the people living in them. Theodore Rees Cheney's *Living in Polar Regions: A Cultural Geography* uses a similar approach for exploring the polar regions. Both texts use an approach that considers: How did the people who live here get here? How did they decide where to settle and how to make a living? How have they influenced their environment (land and climate) and how has it affected them? A major focus of cultural geography is the fit between culture and environment. Both texts include numerous maps and labeled photographs. Ron Hirschi's *Who Lives in. . .the Mountains?* and *Who Lives on. . .the Prairie?* introduce young readers to different geographical regions. Galen Burrell's photographs show the mountains and prairies and the animals that live within these regions.

Discoveries and How Things Work

Some informational books answer children's questions about discoveries of the past and present or provide explanations of how machines work. Authors may clarify their texts through step-by-step directions, carefully labeled diagrams, photographs that illustrate concepts, and content that proceeds from the simple to the complex or from the known to the unknown.

Discoveries. Books about discoveries may describe the basic principles of past discoveries or the latest space or computer technology. Some books combine information about discoveries with experiments designed to help children understand and duplicate earlier experiments. One such book is Seymour Simon's *How to Be an Ocean Scientist in Your Own Home*. Simon first asks a question, such as "How can you make fresh water from seawater?" Then, he presents information in a "Let's Find Out" section. Next, he tells students "Here's What You Will Need," and he provides detailed directions in "Here's What to Do."

Informational books about space and space travel should reflect current knowledge. Copyright dates may therefore be a very important consideration when selecting these books. Franklyn M. Branley, former chairman of the Hayden Planetarium in New York City, emphasizes the expanding nature of knowledge about space in *Saturn: The Spectacular Planet* by pointing out that the Pioneer and Voyager space probes have provided more knowledge than had previously been gathered during the more than three hundred years since Galileo first saw the planet in a telescope. In *Mysteries of Outer Space,* a source of current information, Branley uses a question-and-answer format that progresses from questions about the kinds of space and the characteristics of space to questions about survival in space and uses of space. Branley's other books on space include *Space Colony: Frontier of the 21st Century* and *Halley: Comet 1986*. (Comparisons may be made between Branley's *Halley: Comet 1986,* Isaac Asimov's *Asimov's Guide to Halley's Comet,* and Gregory Vogt's *Halley's Comet: What We've Learned*.)

Patricia Lauber's *Journey to the Planets* contains large black-and-white NASA photographs of the earth and the planets. They clarify an interesting discussion of the search for intelligent life on other planets and the constructions that may indicate intelligent life, even from millions of miles out in space. Seymour Simon has written several readable books that, through words and photographs, take young readers into the far reaches of outer space and explain comets and planets. Simon's *The Long View into Space, The Long Journey from Space, Saturn, Jupiter,* and *Galaxies* provide current information in a simple and illuminating way. For example, in *The Long View into Space,* Simon explains why space distances between earth and the planets are not measured in miles by saying that to measure in miles would be like "trying to measure the distance between New York and London in inches" (p. 4 unnumbered). Necia

Apfel's *Nebulae: The Birth & Death of Stars* uses photographs taken through telescopes at various planetariums and observatories.

Ann Elwood and Linda C. Wood's *Windows in Space* contains two features that should stimulate children's interest: "Questions We Still Cannot Answer" and "Facts About. . . ." The latter feature may help improve readers' cognitive abilities because the authors summarize important facts. Aspiring artists and scientists as well as readers who are curious about spaceships and artists' renditions of various spacecraft will enjoy Don Bolognese's *Drawing Spaceships and Other Spacecraft*. His detailed text and illustrations introduce perspective, tools, and finishing touches.

Questions related to the universe are explored in Roy Gallant's *The Macmillan Book of Astronomy* and James Jespersen and Jane Fitz-Randolph's *From Quarks and Quasars: A Tour of the Universe*. Gallant's text contains a brief account of and statistical information about the sun and the various planets. Color photographs, many obtained from the National Aeronautics and Space Administration, add interest and clarification. You may compare the coverage of the planets in this text with that in Seymour Simon's *Jupiter* and *Saturn*. Jesperson and Fitz-Randolph's text is for older students. It provides an historical perspective on the universe and the scientists who contributed to our knowledge. In *Before the Sun Dies: The Story of Evolution,* Gallant compares the known and unknown to help readers understand the galaxies. The book includes numerous labeled drawings, a glossary of terms, a list of further readings, and an index.

How Things Work. Several informational books respond to children's curiosity about how common home appliances and bigger machines actually work. These books usually contain detailed diagrams or photographs that accompany two or three pages of descriptive text about each item. While the readability and interest levels are usually considered upper-elementary and above, many younger children ask questions about how percolators, dishwashers, or Thermos bottles work. Therefore, parents may find these books helpful when answering the questions of young children. (One mother said that her six-year-old son's favorite book was one containing diagrams of machines at work.)

David Macaulay's *The Way Things Work* includes over three hundred pages of detailed diagrams of almost every conceivable instrument. The text is arranged in four sections, including "The Mechanics of Movement," "Harnessing the Elements," "Working with Waves," and "Electricity & Automation." The book includes a glossary of technical terms and an index. The humorous analogies used throughout the text appeal to many readers.

Ron and Nancy Goor's *In the Driver's Seat* presents an interesting and novel introduction to various motorized vehicles. Each chapter begins with a photograph showing the driver's seat and the instruments the driver uses. The text then tells readers what they would do if they were in that driver's seat. The idea of driving large and complex machines, such as combines, tanks, jets, eighteen-wheel trucks, and trains appeals to many children. *Cars and How They Go* by Joanna Cole explains how the pistons, crankshaft, drive shaft, and axles work interdependently to motorize a car. Gail Gibbons's illustrations and Cole's text clarify a subject that otherwise might be too complex for many elementary children.

Where is the longest, the highest, or the most expensive bridge? What did the first bridge probably look like? Who were the first great bridge builders? What changes have taken place in bridge construction? These are some of the questions answered in Scott Corbett's *Bridges*. Drawings help clarify the terminology and illustrate the kinds of bridges, from early suspension bridges, to Roman arches, to medieval fortified bridges, to covered New England bridges, to railroad trestles, and finally, to the great twentieth-century bridges.

Proceeding from the simple to the complex, an important technique in books that explain concepts, Anne and Scott MacGregor develop concepts related to physical stress and the construction of domes in *Domes: A Project Book*. They begin with simple igloos and proceed to cathedrals. Models for domes and directions for building them encourage children to experiment.

Peter Schaaf's *An Apartment House Close Up* shows photographs of architectural features, typical rooms, elevators, and heating facilities in an apartment house. Photographs in Elinor Horwitz's *How to Wreck a Building* follow the demolition of an elementary school from the time the crane operator's wrecking ball strikes the building until the debris is loaded into dump trucks. Byron Barton's *Airport,* an excellent picture book for young children, answers many questions about airports and airline travel as it follows passengers from their arrival at the airport to boarding the plane.

Authors of informational books often use photographs and text to document—as in Bernard Wolf's *Firehouse,* which documents the work of New York City firefighters. Charlotte Wilcox's *Trash!* follows trash collection and recycling methods. William Jaspersohn's *Magazine: Behind the Scenes at Sports Illustrated* follows the production staff, reporters, and photographers as they prepare a typical weekly issue of *Sports Illustrated.*

Hobbies, Crafts, and How-To Books

One of the main reasons that older elementary-school children give for reading is learning more about their hobbies and interests. Children told one educator who asked them how teachers could improve enjoyment of reading that teachers should ask them about their hobbies and help them find books about them (20). Informational books cover almost every hobby and craft. The more useful books contain clearly written directions, provide guidelines for choosing equipment or other materials, or give interesting background information.

Physical Activities. In addition to a history of tennis, Robert J. Antonacci and Barbara D. Lockhart's *Tennis for Young Champions* provides step-by-step directions and extensive advice for all aspects of the game. Detailed illustrations clarify terms such as *right-hand forehand grip* and *backhand grip.* Both authors are professors of physical education and former tennis champions.

The humorous illustrations in Barbara Isenberg and Marjorie Jaffe's *Albert the Running Bear's Exercise Book* provide detailed directions for exercises that are appropriate for children between the ages of five and nine. Frank and Jan Asch's *Running with Rachel* presents a personalized approach to running by describing how a young girl takes up running after meeting a woman jogging on the road. The book discusses warm-up and cool-down exercises and the importance of wearing the right shoes and eating proper food. Photographs of a young runner illustrate the exercises.

Jim Arnosky, an illustrator for *Rod and Reel* magazine, uses his considerable knowledge of fishing to create a useful book for young people who like to fish. *Freshwater Fish and Fishing* includes clear directions for tying a fly and making lures, detailed illustrations showing types of fish, and advice on how to catch fish.

Jill Krementz, a documentary photographer, has included photographs in several books that she has written about young people who have chosen hobbies that they hope to extend into professional or competitive status sports. The rigorous schedule and dedication needed for success in a sport is shown in *A Very Young Skater* and *A Very Young Rider.* Krementz has also done photo essays on dancers, gymnasts, and circus performers. The pictures effectively present the joys, as well as the day-to-day struggles, of such aspiring athletes and performers. Comparisons may be made between Krementz's *A Very Young Rider* and Lynn Hall's *Tazo and Me,* a documentary of a rider showing a horse.

Creative Arts. Young photographers stimulated by Jill Krementz's beautiful black-and-white photographs can find instructions for photography in Edward E. Davis's *Into the Dark: A Beginner's Guide to Developing and Printing Black and White Negatives.* This book includes information on setting up a home darkroom and step-by-step directions for developing negatives, making contact prints, and printing enlargements.

Clear, detailed drawings that illustrate the points made in the text are important in informational books. Jim Arnosky's *Drawing from Nature* not only provides directions for drawing water, land forms, plants, and animals but also stimulates interest in carefully observing nature and increases understanding of science concepts. The step-by-step pencil sketches illustrate techniques that let artists accurately interpret nature. A careful reading and viewing of this text may encourage children to answer Arnosky's invitation:

> Drawing from nature is discovering the upside down scene through a water drop. It is noticing how much of a fox is tail. Drawing from nature is learning how a tree grows and a flower blooms. It is sketching in the mountains and breathing air bears breathe. . . .I invite you to sharpen your pencils, your eyesight, and your sense of wonder. Turn to a fresh leaf in your drawing pad and come outdoors. (unnumbered foreword)

Arnosky uses a similar technique to illustrate step-by-step drawing techniques in *Drawing Life in Motion* and *Sketching Outdoors in Summer.*

One large box and some imagination can result in a horse, a castle, or even a supermarket when young children follow the step-by-step instructions in Flo Ann Hedley Norvell's *The Great Big Box Book.* Each step in seventeen projects is numbered and illustrated with an accompanying drawing or photograph. Of interest to the slightly older child is Paul Berman's *Make-Believe Empire: A How-to Book*. Simple instructions and accompanying drawings show young construction workers how to build a city from cans, boxes, and wood; how to construct a navy; and how to create their own laws and documents. Barbara Reid's *Playing with Plasticine* provides detailed directions for making plasticine sculptures.

Food. Children who read frontier stories and survival stories may be interested in discovering more about the foods eaten by the characters. Barbara M. Walker's *The Little House Cookbook: Frontier Foods from Laura Ingalls Wilder's Classic Stories* presents frontier foods Wilder wrote about in her "Little House" stories. Walker searched for authentic recipes by reading the writings of Wilder and her daughter Rose, pioneer diaries, and local recipe collections. Her hope in sharing this collection is that children will rediscover basic connections between the foods on the table and the grains in the field and the cows in the pasture, as well as between people in the past and today. Walker uses liberal excerpts from the "Little House" books and the original Garth Williams illustrations in discussing the foods and their preparation.

Readers often ask how the characters in Jean Craighead George's *My Side of the Mountain* and *River Rats, Inc.* could identify and live off the wild foods discussed in the two books. Laurence Pringle's *Wild Foods: A Beginner's Guide to Identifying, Harvesting and Cooking Safe and Tasty Plants from the Outdoors* shows how. Pringle studied wildlife conservation at Cornell University and has been the editor of *Nature and Science,* a children's science magazine published by the American Museum of Natural History. His book discusses common, edible wild plants that are easily identified. Pringle presents the wild plants in the seasonal order in which they appear in nature, spring to winter. He describes the plants and their locations and gives instructions on how to harvest and prepare them. The drawings by Paul Breeden, an artist whose illustrations have appeared in *National Geographic, Audubon,* and *Smithsonian* magazines, are especially effective and clarify differences between edible plants and poisonous plants that resemble them.

Pets. Pets usually interest children. Books such as Rosmarie Hausherr's *My First Kitten* present information about caring for a common pet. *Care of Uncommon Pets,* written by veterinarian William J. Weber, answers questions about handling, housing, feeding, breeding, and caring for more unusual pets. This book should provide valuable information for children who want uncommon pets or for teachers who have small animals in their classrooms.

Harriet Rubins's *Guinea Pigs: An Owner's Guide to Choosing, Raising, Breeding, and Showing* is an in-depth coverage of one pet. Written for older readers, this book discusses breeding, showing, recordkeeping, and experimenting with guinea pigs and gives guidelines for selection and care. A glossary, a bibliography, and an index increase the usefulness of the book. Colleen Stanley Bare's *Guinea Pigs Don't Read Books* is a simpler, highly illustrated book written for younger children.

Many books encourage children to consider new hobbies or to learn more about existing ones. Children discover that some hobbies may even lead to a career.

Suggested Activities for Adult Understanding of Biographies and Informational Books

- ☐ In order to provide accurate information and differentiate fact from opinion, biographers must research many sources. Select a writer of biographies for children and identify the sources the writer used in doing research for a book. Do you believe these sources were sufficient? Why or why not?
- ☐ Choose someone who has had several biographies written about him or her. Read several interpretations of that person's life. Compare the biographies in terms of content, accuracy of information, sources of references indicated by the author, balance of facts with story line for young readers, intended audience for the biography, and author's style.
- ☐ Select a well-known author who has written several biographies for older children, such as Beatrice Siegel, and another biographer who has written several biographies for younger children, such as Jean Fritz. What techniques does each author use in order to write a biography that will appeal to a specific age group?
- ☐ Select a content area, such as science or social studies, that is taught in an elementary- or middle-school grade. From the curriculum,

identify names of men and women who are discussed in that content area. Develop an annotated bibliography of literature on a subject, such as biology, to stimulate interest in the subject and provide additional information about the contributors.

- ☐ Select the work of an outstanding author of informational books for children, such as Millicent E. Selsam, Seymour Simon, or Laurence Pringle. Evaluate the books according to the criteria listed in this chapter. Share with the class the characteristics of the books that make them highly recommended.
- ☐ Select several informational books that include many illustrations. Evaluate the illustrations according to the value of the explanatory legends presented next to the illustrations, the accuracy of the illustrations, and the possibility that the illustrations will stimulate children's interest in the subject.
- ☐ Choose several informational books that encourage logical problem solving. Share the books with a peer group and present rationales for your belief that these books will encourage logical problem solving.
- ☐ Search the elementary social studies or science curriculum for a given grade level. With a peer group, develop an annotated bibliography of informational books that would reinforce the curriculum and stimulate the acquisition of additional information.

References

1 Arbuthnot, May Hill, and Dorothy M. Broderick. *Time for Biography*. Glenview, Ill.: Scott, Foresman, 1969.

2 Blough, Glenn O. "The Author and the Science Book." *Library Trends* 22 (April 1974): 419–424.

3 Carpenter, Frank G. *Carpenter's Geographical Reader, North America*. New York: American Book, 1898.

4 Coolidge, Olivia. "My Struggle with Facts." *Wilson Library Bulletin* 49 (October 1974): 146–151.

5 Dempsey, Frank J. "Russell Freedman." *The Horn Book* (July/August 1988): 452–456.

6 Dryer, Charles Redway. *Geography, Physical, Economic, and Regional*. New York: American Book, 1911.

7 Fisher, Leonard Everett. "The Artist at Work: Creating Nonfiction." *The Horn Book* (May/June 1988): 315–323.

8 Fisher, Margery. "Life Course or Screaming Farce?" *Children's Literature in Education* 7 (Autumn 1976): 108–115.

9 Fleming, Margaret, and Jo McGinnis, eds. *Portraits: Biography and Autobiography in the Secondary School*. Urbana, Ill.: National Council of Teachers of English, 1985.

10 Freedman, Russell. "Newbery Medal Acceptance." *The Horn Book* (July/August 1988): 444–451.

11 Fritz, Jean. *Homesick: My Own Story*. New York: Putnam, 1982.

12 Fritz, Jean. "Making It Real." *Children's Literature in Education* 22 (Autumn 1976): 125–127.

13 Herman, Gertrude B. "'Footprints on the Sands of Time': Biography for Children." *Children's Literature in Education* 9 (Summer 1977): 85–94.

14 Hillyer, V. M. *A Child's Geography of the World*. Illustrated by Mary Sherwood Wright Jones. New York: Century, 1929.

15 Jurich, Marilyn. "What's Left Out of Biography for Children?" *Children's Literature: The Great Excluded* 1 (1972): 143–151.

16 Moore, Ann W. "A Question of Accuracy: Errors in Children's Biographies." *School Library Journal* 31 (February 1985): 34–35.

17 National Science Teachers Association. "Outstanding Science Trade Books for Children in 1985." *Science and Children* (March 1986): 26.

18 Norton, Donna E. "Centuries of Biographies for Childhood." *Vitae Scholasticae* 3 (Spring 1984): 113–129.

19 Robertson, Elizabeth, and Jo McGinnis. "Biography as Art: A Formal Approach." In *Portraits: Biography and Autobiography in the Secondary School*, edited by Margaret Fleming and Jo McGinnis. Urbana, Ill.: National Council of Teachers of English, 1985.

20 Roettger, Doris. "Reading Attitudes and the Estes Scale." Paper presented at the 23rd Annual Convention, International Reading Association, Houston, Texas, 1978.

21 Stott, Jon C. "Biographies of Sports Heroes and the American Dream." *Children's Literature in Education* 10 (Winter 1979): 174–185.

22 Wolff, Kathryn. "AAAS Science Books: A Selection Tool." *Library Trends* 22 (April 1974): 453–456.

Involving Children in Nonfictional Literature

USING BIOGRAPHIES IN CREATIVE DRAMATIZATIONS

COMPARING ATTITUDES AND CHECKING FACTS IN BIOGRAPHIES

INVESTIGATING THE QUALITIES OF WRITERS

ANALYZING LITERARY ELEMENTS IN BIOGRAPHIES

INCORPORATING LITERATURE INTO THE SCIENCE CURRICULUM

CHILDREN OFTEN FIND BIOGRAPHIES AND other informational books more exciting than textbooks. The lively dialogues, the confrontations between people and ideas, and the joys and sorrows in many biographies are natural sources for creative dramatizations and discussions. Thus, you can use biographies to help children understand people of the past and present. With informational books, you also can help children acquire abilities related to the content areas, such as using the parts of a book, locating sources of information, understanding science vocabulary, reading for meaning, evaluating science literature, and applying learning to practical problems.

USING BIOGRAPHIES IN CREATIVE DRAMATIZATIONS

The biographies of significant people of the past and present are filled with lively dialogue, confrontations, and the joys connected with discovery. Consequently, biographies provide many opportunities for children to dramatize the momentous experiences in people's lives. Children can create "You Are There" dramas based on scenes of historical significance. They can also create imaginary conversations between two people from the past or present or from different time periods who had some common traits but were never able to communicate because of time or distance. The following ideas are only samples of the creative dramatizations that can result from using biographies in the classroom.

Jean Fritz's stories of Revolutionary War heroes, with their humorous and human portrayals of the characters, are excellent sources for dramatizations. For example, you can read *Where Was Patrick Henry on the 29th of May?* and ask children how Patrick Henry acted and how they would act if they were Patrick Henry. Then read the story a second time as the children dramatize the story. There is another way to approach this dramatization: after the children listen to or read the book, have them identify and discuss scenes they would like to depict and then act out each one. Children have identified the following scenes as being of special interest in Patrick Henry's life:

1. Going fishing with a pole over his shoulder.
2. Going hunting for deer or opossum, with a rifle in his hands, accompanied by a dog at his heels.
3. Walking barefoot through the woods, then

lying down while listening to the rippling of a creek or the singing of birds and imitating their songs.

4 Listening to rain on the roof, his father's fox horn, and the music of flutes and fiddles.

5 Teaching himself to play the flute when he is recovering from a broken collarbone.

6 Listening to his Uncle Langloo Winston making speeches.

7 Waiting for the school day to end.

8 Playing practical jokes on his friends, including upsetting a canoe.

9 Trying to be a storekeeper without success.

10 Attempting to be a tobacco farmer.

11 Attending court and discovering that he likes to watch and listen to lawyers.

12 Beginning his law practice and not finding many clients.

13 Defending his first big case in court and winning.

14 Arguing against taxation without representation as a member of Virginia's House of Burgesses.

15 Delivering his "give me liberty or give me death" speech at St. John's Church.

16 Governing Virginia.

17 Hearing the news that the Continental army has defeated the English troops at Saratoga, New York.

18 Speaking against the enactment of the Constitution of the United States and for individual and states' rights after the war is over.

19 Retiring on his estate in western Virginia.

These scenes may also be developed into what Ruth Beall Heinig and Lyda Stillwell (3) describe as a sequence game. This game involves careful observation by all players, who must interpret what someone else is doing and according to directions written on their cue cards, stand and perform the next action at the correct time. (Players must be able to read to do this activity.) Develop cue cards for scenes from Patrick Henry's life. The first cue card would look approximately like this:

> *You* begin the game.
>
> Pretend that you are a young, barefoot Patrick Henry happily going fishing with a pole over your shoulder.
>
> When you are finished, sit down in your seat.

The second card would read:

> Cue: Someone pretends to be a young Patrick Henry going fishing with a pole over his shoulder.
>
> You are a young Patrick Henry happily going hunting for deer or opossum, with a rifle in your hands and accompanied by a dog running at your heels.
>
> When you are finished, sit down in your seat.

Place the rest of the scenes, written in a similar manner, on cards. It is helpful if the cue and the directions for the dramatization are written in different colors. Mix the cards and distribute randomly. There should be at least one cue card for each player, but you may add more scenes if a whole class is taking part in the activity. If there are fewer players, you can reduce the number of scenes or give each player more than one cue card. Ask the children to pay close attention and wait for each player to complete the dramatization.

It is helpful if you have a master cue sheet with all of the cues in correct order so that you can help if someone misinterprets a scene, the children seem uncertain, or the group loses its direction. Heinig and Stillwell say that to involve as many children as possible, you may divide large groups into three small groups. Have each small group dramatize a set of identical cue cards independently. Let a child act as leader of each group and follow the master sheet.

Incidents in the lives of other Fritz heroes—described in *Why Don't You Get a Horse, Sam Adams?, The Great Little Madison,* and *What's the Big Idea, Ben Franklin?*—also make enjoyable dramas.

When appropriate, encourage children to pantomime scenes. Children can pantomime the actions of dancers, as in *Arthur Mitchell* by Tobi Tobias; the actions of actors, as in *An Actor's Life for Me!* by Lillian Gish as told to Selma Lanes; the actions of singers as in *Beverly Sills* by Bridget Paolucci; and the actions of a skater, as in *A Very Young Skater* by Jill Krementz.

"You Are There" Dramatizations

Biographies allow children to experience some very exciting moments in history through the emotions, words, and contributions of the people who created those moments. Consequently, reenactments of those scenes can allow children to experience the excitement and realize that history is made up of real people and actual incidents.

A group of seventh graders chose to return in time to Rome in 1632, during the cruel days of the Inquisition. Their "You Are There" drama, based on Sidney Rosen's *Galileo and the Magic Numbers,* began after Galileo had published his *A Dialogue on the Two Great Systems of the World* and was facing an angry Pope Urban. Have children perform the following dramatization.

1 To the audience, an announcer says: "You are there; the year is 1632; Galileo is facing an angry Pope Urban. The Pope's face is reddened in anger, his eyes are flashing venom. He is pounding his fists on the arms of the papal throne. Shouting, he declares:

> That scoundrel! That ingrate! We try to befriend him. And how does he repay us? By doing all this behind our back! Well this time he has gone too far! Let him take care! It is out of our hands now. This is a matter for the Holy Office! (p. 192).

With these words, the slow process of the Inquisition begins. Galileo's enemies are winning, and he is to be charged with heresy."

2 The announcer, the action, and the dialogue go back to Florence. Galileo waits anxiously with his health failing, his fever returning, and his eyesight failing.

3 In October, the Inquisitor of Florence appears at Galileo's door with a summons. Galileo has thirty days in which to appear before the Holy Office in Rome.

4 On April 12, 1633, Galileo is summoned to the Inquisition chambers, where he is exhaustively questioned and threatened with torture for many days. He finally signs a document confessing his wrongdoing; he then feels shame and guilt for his weakness.

5 On June 21, Galileo discovers that signing the document is not sufficient; he is to be tried for heresy before ten cardinals who will be his judges. A bent, graying Galileo is in front of the men dressed in red cloaks and hats, sitting about a great semicircular table. The questioning begins. The judges ask Galileo whether he does, indeed, believe that the earth moves about the sun. Silence hangs over the hall as the judges await Galileo's response.

6 On June 22, 1633, Galileo is dressed in the shirt of penitence, awaiting the verdict of the Inquisition. A hush falls over the hall. Galileo, kneeling before the cardinals, listens to the long document of charges read against him. At last, he hears the words that crush all hope:

> But in order that your terrible error may not go altogether unpunished, and that you may be an example and a warning to others to abstain from such opinions, we decree that your book, *Dialogue on the Two Great Systems of the World,* be banned publicly; also, we condemn you to the formal prison of this Holy Office for an indefinite period convenient to our pleasure. So we, the subscribing and presiding cardinals pronounce! (p. 202)

Galileo and the Magic Numbers contains vividly described settings and characters and enough dialogue that children can develop a realistic "You Are There" drama. With the help of an announcer, the actors can develop the dialogue as they proceed, or they can choose some actual dialogue from the book. The seventh-grade group chose a combination of these two approaches.

You can create a "You Are There" episode around Christopher Columbus's meeting with Queen Isabella, his discovery of America, and his return to the Spanish court. Also, you can create a "You Are There" episode around Benjamin Franklin's testifying before the English Parliament. In *Benjamin Franklin: The New American,* a biography of Benjamin Franklin, Milton Meltzer describes the setting in which 174 questions are asked and answered. Have students research questions and answers concerning the Stamp Act. Another possibility is to have students recreate exciting moments from Virginia Hamilton's *Anthony Burns: The Defeat and Triumph of a Fugitive Slave,* in which the Boston Vigilance Committee defended the rights of Anthony Burns, a fugitive slave.

Imaginary Conversations Between People of Two Time Periods

Children enjoy contemplating what historic personalities might say to each other if they had the opportunity to meet. Because this is impossible except through imagination, children can be motivated to read biographies in order to enter into such conversations. For example, an exciting conversation could result if Maria Mitchell (Helen S. Morgan's *Maria Mitchell, First Lady of American Astronomy*) and Galileo (Sidney Rosen's *Galileo and the Magic Numbers*) could meet. Children can consider what questions each person might ask the other, what interests and viewpoints the two would probably share, and what differences of opinion they might express.

After the children have discussed these points, have them role-play a meeting between these figures. What advice could Galileo have given Mitchell to help her defend her teaching before the Vassar Board of Trustees? Galileo worried about how history would view him. How would Galileo feel about nineteenth-century scientists' views of his work? Let different children present their views through the role-playing format. Then, let the class or group discuss what the most likely responses would be and give reasons for their opinions.

Other historical biographical characters might have stimulating conversations if they could meet with world figures of the 1990s. What views would emerge if Patrick Henry could share his opinions on states' rights and the rights of the individual with the current president of the United States? What would be Amelia Earhart's response to space travel and exploration? What questions would she ask of a contemporary astronaut? What role would she want if she could be involved in the space program? When children read in order to role-play a character's actions, express a character's feelings, or state dialogue that a character might express, they interact with the character on a human level and will often read until they feel empathy with that character and the historic time period.

COMPARING ATTITUDES AND CHECKING FACTS IN BIOGRAPHIES

Elizabeth Robertson and Jo McGinnis (7) recommend that students compare the tone and attitude of a biographer as reflected in a biography about a specific person with the tone and attitude expressed by the biographical subject in his or her own writing. Ann W. Moore (5) recommends that reviewers check the accuracy of facts in juvenile biographies by referring to reputable adult titles and other reference books.

Biographies about Eleanor Roosevelt are excellent sources for comparisons in the classroom. There are numerous children's biographies, including one written by Elliott Roosevelt, reputable adult biographies, and autobiographies written by Eleanor Roosevelt herself. The following books will provide sources for such comparisons. Biographies for children include Jane Goodsell's *Eleanor Roosevelt* and Sharon Whitney's *Eleanor Roosevelt*. A biography for children written by Eleanor Roosevelt's son is Elliott Roosevelt's *Eleanor Roosevelt, with Love*. Biographies for adults include Joseph P. Lash's *Eleanor and Franklin* and *Eleanor: The Years Alone;* Elliott Roosevelt and James Brough's *An Untold Story: The Roosevelts of Hyde Park* and *Mother R: Eleanor Roosevelt's Untold Story;* and Lorena Hickok's *Eleanor Roosevelt: Reluctant First Lady*. Autobiographies include Eleanor Roosevelt's *The Autobiography of Eleanor Roosevelt; On My Own; This I Remember; This Is My Story; Tomorrow Is Now;* and *You Learn by Living*.

INVESTIGATING THE QUALITIES OF WRITERS

What are the qualities that characterize successful writers of children's literature? Is there any way for students to discover these qualities? Are these qualities important in the lives of school children? Patricia J. Cianciolo (1) believes that the words of authors as expressed in their autobiographies, journals, and interviews are excellent for discovering the abilities, attitudes, and character traits of competent writers. Cianciolo analyzed the comments about writing expressed by children's authors Rosemary Sutcliff, Donald Hall, Katherine Paterson, M. E. Kerr, Mollie Hunter, Lois Duncan, Alan Garner, Julia Cunningham, Vera and Bill Cleaver, and Barbara Wersba.

You may have students read some of the sources identified by Cianciolo and read other autobiographies by children's authors, such as Elizabeth Yates's *My Diary, my World* and *My Widening World,* Beverly Cleary's *A Girl from Yamhill: A Memoir,* Milton Meltzer's *Starting from Home: A Writer's Beginnings,* and Bill Peet's *Bill Peet: An Autobiography*. Have the students search for comments that reflect the authors' attitudes about writing. They may find some of the same important abilities, attitudes, and character traits as did Cianciolo.

1. A good writer must be a good reader.
2. A good writer cares intensely about language and is sensitive to it.
3. A good writer is well educated.
4. A good writer is an alert observer.
5. A good writer is a storyteller and enjoys stories told by others.
6. A good writer is a compulsive writer.

After identifying these characteristics of a good writer, lead a discussion in which the students identify the importance of each quality and discuss how these qualities might be used to improve their own writing and reading.

In a related activity, encourage students to read autobiographies or biographies about an author and then read other literary works by the same author. Have the students analyze whether or not there are relationships between the biography and the literary works. Why does an author write about certain subjects? Does the literary work develop the style, the character, the emotions, and the beliefs of the writer? Examples for this activity include Beverly Cleary's *A Girl from Yamhill: A Memoir* and Cleary's various books about Ramona and Henry Huggins or *Dear Mr. Henshaw;* Milton Meltzer's *Starting from Home: A Writer's Beginnings* and any of Meltzer's biographies and informational books; Martin Fido's *Rudyard Kipling: An Illustrated Biography* and Kipling's *Just So Stories* and *The Jungle Books;* Martin Fido's *Oscar Wilde: An Illustrated Biography* and Wilde's *The Happy Prince* and *The Selfish Giant;* and Bill Peet's *Bill Peet: An Autobiography* and any of Peet's humorous fictional books, such as *No Such Thing* and *The Gnats of Knotty Pine.*

ANALYZING LITERARY ELEMENTS IN BIOGRAPHIES

In addition to evaluating the accuracy of characterization in biographies by comparing the characterizations in biographies written by different authors, have students analyze and evaluate plot, setting, and theme in biographies. For example, to analyze plot in biographies have students identify and plot the pattern of action, locate examples of specific types of conflict developed in a biography, analyze why the biographer emphasizes those types of conflict, consider why and how the conflicts relate to the biographer's purpose in writing, and locate examples of ways in which the biographer develops the readers' interest. To evaluate setting in biographies, have students identify the various settings, identify the way the biographer informs the readers about the important details related to the time period, analyze how much influence the setting has on the characterization and plot, find specific locations mentioned in the biography and locate these places on a map, in geography texts, or in other nonfictional sources, evaluate the authenticity of settings by comparing the various nonfictional sources, check the accuracy of dates and happenings in other nonfictional sources, draw a setting as if it were a backdrop for a stage production, and evaluate whether or not there is enough information about setting to complete a drawing. To evaluate theme in biography, have the students find the primary, or main, theme in a biography and several secondary themes. Have the students consider how these themes are integrated into the biography, analyze whether or not the title of the biography reflects the theme, search for evidence of the biographical character's ability to triumph over obstacles, identify and compare the themes developed in several biographies written about the same person, and compare the themes in biographies written for younger children and those written for young adults.

INCORPORATING LITERATURE INTO THE SCIENCE CURRICULUM

Several values of informational books relate to the science curriculum. Interesting books—such as those by Seymour Simon, Millicent Selsam, and Laurence Pringle—allow children to experience the excitement of discovery. Through books such as Simon's *How to Be an Ocean Scientist in Your Own Home,* children can observe, experiment, compare, formulate hypotheses, test hypotheses, draw conclusions, and evaluate their evidence. Children can become directly involved in the scientific method. Through the experiments and information found in many informational books, children can learn about the world of nature. Because many informational books that deal with science subjects have greater depth of coverage than do science textbooks, such informational books are valuable for extending knowledge and understanding.

Illa Podendorf (6) maintains that communication abilities, such as graphing, illustrating, recording, and reporting, are especially important to science. She believes that an author of science information books should use these communication abilities often when writing. She also says:

> At an early age children are able to read and interpret graphs and can present their own ideas and findings in graphic form. A trade book which provides such experiences is a valuable addition to their literature. Any opportunity to help children get experience in interpreting data and making predictions from recorded data should not be overlooked. Such experiences often result in activities in which children can become actively involved. (p. 428)

However, the nature of science materials—with their heavy concentration of facts and details, new scientific principles to be understood, and new technical vocabulary—may cause reading problems for children who are accustomed to the narrative writing style. David L. Shepherd (8) identifies the following three types of reading that students face in the content area of science: (1) science textbooks that tend to be technical and require a careful, slow, and analytical reading; (2) assigned readings in scientific journals, popular science magazines, and books on scientific research that contain many small but important interrelated details that require analytical reading; and (3) nontechnical scientific materials found in biographies of scientists, newspapers, and popular magazines reporting scientific findings that are easier to read and understand.

You can use excellent informational materials on science-related topics to encourage children to develop their abilities to read science-related materials and to understand science-related concepts. This text considers abilities that relate to both literature and the content areas: using the parts of the book, locating sources of information, understanding science vocabulary, reading for exact meaning, evaluating science materials and applying data from reading to practical problems. The specific books mentioned are only examples of the numerous books that can be used in the classroom. You may wish to add other informational books.

Using the Parts of a Book

Science informational books reinforce the ability to use parts of a book, because many books contain a table of contents, a glossary, a bibliography of further readings, and an index. Children can use the table of contents in conjunction with an index to locate specific content. For example:

1. Find the chapter describing fossils and the geological record in Roy A. Gallant's *Before The Sun Dies: The Story of Evolution* (chapter 7, p. 61).
2. Find the chapter about "Survival in Space" in Franklyn M. Blanley's *Mysteries of Outer Space* (chapter 5, p. 36).
3. Find the chapter on "People and Whales" in Dorothy Hinshaw Patent's *Whales: Giants of the Deep* (chapter 5, p. 73).
4. Find the chapter "Bridges" in David Weitzman's *Windmills, Bridges, & Old Machines: Discovering Our Industrial Past* (chapter 11, p. 77).
5. Find the chapter describing damage caused by mudflows in Patricia Lauber's *Volcano: The Eruption and Healing of Mount St. Helens.* (chapter 2, pp. 15–17).

Laurence Pringle's books usually have a glossary of technical terms, an index, and a list of further readings that can provide additional information about a subject. These books can be used to reinforce the importance of each part of the book, the kind of information that is available, and the use of each locational aid. Books that include lists of further reading and biographical sources, such as Rhoda Blumberg's *Commodore Perry in the Land of the Shogun* and James Cross Giblin's *Let There Be Light,* provide opportunities for students to locate additional subjects.

Locating Sources of Information

You can use the lists of references at the back of many informational books to show children how to use a library card catalog for more information. The sources can be found in the library card catalog under an author card, a title card, and a subject card. For example, one additional source listed in Laurence Pringle's *City and Suburb: Exploring an Ecosystem* is Pringle's *Into the Woods: Exploring the Forest Ecosystem*. Children learn and reinforce library location skills by learning how to find this book or other informational books under three types of cards, as shown in Figure 12–1. Children can also discover related reading materials while looking for a particular reference in the card catalog.

Using Science Vocabulary

The glossary in many informational books is also a source of information about the meaning of technical terminology found in the book. Authors such as Caroline Arnold in *Saving the Peregrine Falcon* use boldface type to identify terms that are defined in the glossary. Authors of informational books for children often present the meaning of new words through their context in the text. You should specifically point out this technique to children to help them understand the meanings of words. In *Sight and Seeing: A World of Light and Color,* Hilda Simon uses contextual clues to suggest the meaning of scientific terms. Throughout the book, Simon places new words in italics and defines the words in the context. For example, "Birds of prey are further aided by their unusual powers of *accommodation*. In optical terms, that means an extremely rapid focus adjustment of the lens to different distances" (p. 55).

AUTHOR CARD

QH
541.5
.F6
P74

Pringle, Laurence P.
Into the woods: exploring the forest ecosystem [by] Laurence Pringle. New York, Macmillan [1973]
54 p. illus. 23 cm.
SUMMARY: Explains the interdependency of plants and animals and examines man's role in protecting this ecological balance.
Bibliography: p. 51.

1. Forest ecology--Juvenile literature. I. Title

TITLE CARD

Into the woods: exploring the forest ecosystem

QH
541.5
.F6
P74

Pringle, Laurence P.
Into the woods: exploring the forest ecosystem [by] Laurence Pringle. New York, Macmillan [1973]
54 p. illus. 23 cm.
SUMMARY: Explains the interdependency of plants and animals and examines man's role in protecting this ecological balance.
Bibliography: p. 51.

1. Forest ecology--Juvenile literature. I. Title

SUBJECT CARD

FOREST ECOLOGY--JUVENILE LITERATURE.

QH
541.5
.F6
P74

Pringle, Laurence P.
Into the woods: exploring the forest ecosystem [by] Laurence Pringle. New York, Macmillan [1973]
54 p. illus. 23 cm.
SUMMARY: Explains the interdependency of plants and animals and examines man's role in protecting this ecological balance.
Bibliography: p. 51.

1. Forest ecology--Juvenile literature. I. Title

FIGURE 12–1
Cards in a library card catalog

Authors also clarify the meanings of technical terminology through photographs, diagrams, and charts. Even books written for young children often use labeled drawings to clarify meanings of technical terminology. An illustration by Aliki, in Judy Hawes's *Bees and Beelines,* a Let's-Read-and-Find-Out Science Book, shows the directions a bee moves when flying a "round dance" and a "waggle." This illustration is followed by four pages of drawings that resemble a map of a bee's flying actions when it leaves the hive to search for nectar. Arrows are included in the drawings so that children can follow the bee's movement. When you share the book with children, you should help them to follow the directions of the arrows and tell what is occurring in the drawings.

Millicent Selsam and Joyce Hunt's books for young children, including *A First Look at Caterpillars, A First Look at Animals with Horns,* and *A First Look at Seals, Sea Lions, and Walruses,* discuss specific characteristics that are easy to observe in illustrations. Selsam and Hunt use technical terms frequently and ask children to use their knowledge to answer questions.

Tomie de Paola's *The Cloud Book* presents the technical names for clouds and explains them through the text and humorous illustrations. Drawings show *cirrus, cumulus,* and *stratus* clouds; *cirrocumulus* and *cirrostratus* clouds; *altostratus* and *altocumulus* clouds; and *nimbostratus, stratocumulus,* and *cumulonimbus* clouds. Because many children are curious about the changing cloud formations they see in the sky, you can use this book to introduce the technical terms for the clouds observed. Drawings and bulletin boards on which different types of clouds are labeled are excellent extensions of this knowledge. A bulletin board created to extend the vocabulary in the book might look like one made by a group of fifth-grade children (see Figure 12–2).

Reading for Meaning

A major reason that many students give for reading scientific informational books is to acquire facts; therefore, comprehending the author's meaning is important. Unlike writings that stress make-believe, scientific informational books are based on accuracy. Children often need encouragement to note main ideas and supporting details and to see organization. Reading-methods books usually include several chapters on these comprehension abilities, but a few approaches considered here allow content-area teachers and parents to reinforce and encourage the abilities through informational books.

Noting Main Ideas. Short, fact-filled paragraphs, as well as paragraph and chapter organization, provide considerable materials for content-area teachers who are trying to enhance the ability of children to find main ideas. Because many informational books written for children have a main idea as a topic sentence at the beginning of a paragraph, many teachers have children read a paragraph and then visualize the author's organization of the material according to the main idea and important details. (This technique may also help children evaluate whether the author uses a logical organization.) A typical paragraph may follow this organization:

Main Idea
  Supporting Detail
  Supporting Detail
  Supporting Detail
  Supporting Detail

Seymour Simon's writing tends to follow this structure. Use this diagram with material from *Meet the Giant Snakes* to help children identify the main idea and supporting details and evaluate whether or not the organization is logical. On page 13 of Simon's book is a paragraph that describes how the python, unlike other snakes, cares for its young. If this paragraph were arranged like the above diagram, it would look like this:

A giant python is unusual because the female
  cares for her young.

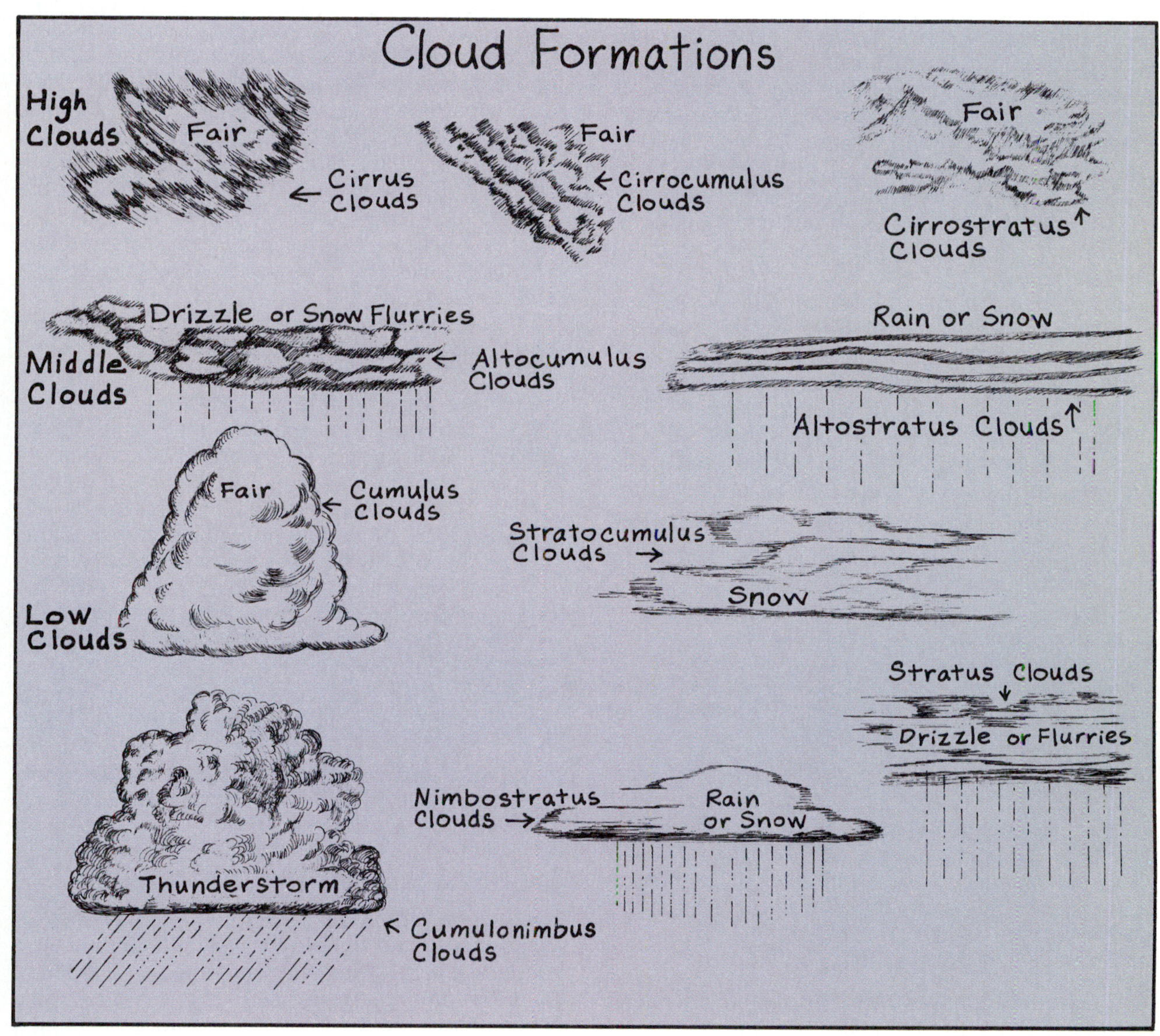

FIGURE 12–2
A bulletin board to extend knowledge about clouds

She pushes her eggs into a pile.
She coils her body around the eggs.
She stays on the nest until the eggs are hatched in about ten weeks.
She leaves her nest only for water.

Children can discover that each of the important details supports the idea that the giant python takes care of her young. This main idea can also be turned into a question. Children can decide if the rest of the paragraph answers these questions: Does the female giant python take care of her young? How does the female giant python take care of her young?

The same book introduces a series of paragraphs by asking the question "How does a giant snake find food to eat?" (p. 15). Each of the succeeding paragraphs answers some question about the giant python's eating habits. Children find that they will get the main idea from the three following pages if they read to answer the introductory question. This should be demonstrated to children so that they can use this important comprehension aid.

Other activities using informational books also stress main ideas. If the informational material contains subheadings, ask children to turn each subheading into a question and read to answer the question. For example, in Martha Brenner's *Fireworks Tonight!,* the author uses subheadings to divide the contents of each chapter. Have the children turn each of the following subheadings into questions and then read to answer those questions:

An American Tradition (Chapter 1)

Triumph and Tragedy on the Fourth
Protective Regulation
Mischief and Misuse
How Safe Are Fireworks?

Noting Supporting Details. In noting main ideas, children also identify supporting details in diagrams and questions. In science informational books, size, color, number, location, and texture are also supporting details. Have the children listen to or read a description from a science informational book and draw a picture that shows the important details. The following descriptions are examples of sources that you can use:

1 The description of *Kon Tiki* found on pages 44–45 in Wyatt Blassingame's *Thor Heyerdahl: Viking Scientist*.
2 The description of leaves found in Laurence Pringle's *Wild Foods: A Beginner's Guide to Identifying, Harvesting and Cooking Safe and Tasty Plants from the Outdoors*—maple leaves (p. 24), cattails (pp. 63–64), and milkweed (pp. 103–104).
3 The descriptions of pueblos of the American Southwest found in James Cross Giblin's *Let There Be Light* (pp. 14–16).

Seeing an Author's Organization. A logical organization of information is often critical in the science content areas. You can use books that emphasize the life cycles of plants and animals, the correct steps to use in following an experiment, or a chain of events to help children increase their ability to note scientific organization and evaluate an author's ability to organize logically. You can also use books that organize content according to subject. For example, discuss why David Macaulay chose the following organizational plan for the relationships among the objects pictured in *The Way Things Work*: (1) the mechanics of movement, (2) harnessing the elements, (3) working with waves, and (4) electricity and automation.

To organize content according to geographic area, on a large world map, mark in different colors the six areas identified in Joyce Pope's *Kenneth Lilly's Animals: A Portfolio of Paintings*. Have students list the characteristics of the areas, the animals in each area, and the characteristics of the animals. The areas are (1) hot forests, (2) cool forests, (3) seas and rivers, (4) grasslands, (5) deserts, and (6) mountains. Have the students search through geography texts to identify additional characteristics of these areas. Ask the students to consider why Pope's organization seems logical. Have them compare the effectiveness of Pope's organization with the organization in three other texts that use maps to identify locations of mammals: John Stidworthy's *The Large Plant-Eaters,* Robin Kerrod's *Primates: Insect-Eaters and Baleen Whales,* and Martyn Bramwell and Steve Parker's *The Small Plant Eaters*.

Evaluating Scientific Materials

Evaluation requires critical thinking abilities. Critical reading and thinking go beyond factual comprehension; they require weighing the validity of facts, identifying the problem, making judgments, interpreting implied ideas, distinguishing fact from opinion, drawing conclusions, determining the adequacy of a source of information, and suspending judgment until all the facts have been accumulated. Helen Huus's (4) list of questions that students should ask about an author and the content of the material can help children evaluate both the author and the content of scientific informational books. For example, students should ask the following questions about the authors:

1 *Why did the author write this book?* Was it to present information? Was it to promote a point of view? Was it to advertise? Was it to propagandize? Was it to entertain?
2 *How competent is the author to write an article on this topic for this purpose?* What is the author's background? What is the author's reputation? Does the author have any vested interests in this topic? What is the author's professional position?

To help children critically evaluate authors of informational books (this list and activity are excellent for all informational books, not just those related to science), provide access to many books by different authors and biographical information about the authors. One teacher of upper-elementary students divided a class into five research groups according to a category of interest each group chose to investigate. The categories included botany, birds, earth and geology, land mammals, and insects.

Next, the teacher had each group use John T. Gillespie and Christine B. Gilbert's *Best Books for Children, Preschool Through the Middle Grades* (2) in order to identify authors who had written at least three books in their chosen category. (As a variation, you may use the annotated bibliography at the end of this chapter.) For example, the group working on botany chose the following authors:

Anne Dowden—Three books
Rose E. Hutchins—Three books
Joan Elma Rahn—Three books
Millicent E. Selsam—Five books

Similarly, the group working on birds selected these authors:

Olive L. Earle—Three books
Roma Gans—Four books
John Kaufman—Four books
Jack Scott—Four books

The group working on earth and geology specified the following authors:

Roma Gans—Four books
Delia Goetz—Five books
Laurence Pringle—Three books

The group working with land mammals chose the following authors:

Gladys Conklin—Four books
Irmengarge Eberle—Four books
Michael Fox—Three books
Russell Freedman—Three books
Alice L. Hopf—Five books
Sylvia Johnson—Three books
Laurence Pringle—Three books
Jack Scott—Three books
Millicent E. Selsam—Five books
Alvin Silverstein—Five books
Seymour Simon—Three books

The group working with insects named these authors:

Gladys Conklin—Eight books
Rose E. Hutchins—Eight books
Robert McClung—Four books

Next, the students found as many of the books as possible in the library, including each author's most recent publications on the subject. The students read the information about the author on the dust jacket or elsewhere in the book and searched for biographical data and magazine or journal articles written by the author. Then, the students evaluated the author's background and read and reread the books, searching for each author's point of view and purpose for writing the book.

After the students had carefully read the books, they evaluated the content of the materials. For this evaluation, the students referred to a list of content suggestions recommended by Helen Huus and developed the following evaluative guide for content.

1 Does the author include all of the necessary facts?
2 Are all of the facts presented accurately?
3 Is the information recent?
4 Are the facts presented logically and in perspective?

The children also read background information in science textbooks, encyclopedias, and magazines or journals. They checked the copyright dates of the materials; scrutinized the photographs, graphs, charts, and diagrams; and tried to evaluate whether the author had differentiated fact from opinion. If the students found that there was more than one viewpoint on the subject, they tried to discover if the author had presented both.

Finally, the groups presented their information on the authors and their books to the rest of the class. The students learned how to critically evaluate informational books and authors. They also learned much about the content area and the procedures that writers of informational books should go through as they research their subjects.

Several authors of science informational books develop themes related to endangered species and ecology. Books with these themes can provide stimulating sources for topics of debate and independent research. Students should use the criteria for evaluating authors and content that were given earlier in this section. In addition, students should test the validity of an argument presented in written materials. Willavene Wolf (9) lists the following steps for testing an argument.

1 Strip the argument of any excess words or sentences.
2 Be sure to identify all the premises upon which an author's conclusion may rest.
3 Determine whether the author is referring to all of a group, some of a group, or none of a group.
4 After stripping the argument to its basic framework, identifying all of the premises (both stated and assumed), and transforming the premises, determine whether the conclusion logically follows from the premises.

Children can independently evaluate whether an author's conclusion is logical and supported by facts. They can also enter into debates, choosing different sides of an issue presented by an author, researching outside sources, and developing contrasting viewpoints. For example, you can use Helen Roney Sattler's *The Book of Eagles* to help students form a debate about the plight of eagles and the role of humans in this plight. After reading Sattler's chapter five, "Humans: Friends or Foes?", have students debate whether humans are doing more to help or to harm eagles. Have the students do additional research related to the issue. Ask: Should farmers be allowed to use certain poisons to kill insects and weeds even though the poisons cause the eggs of eagles to be too thin to hatch? Should stricter pollution standards be made into law because eagles die from eating polluted animals and fish?

Have the students choose sides in these issues, complete additional research, and present their positions in debate format. They may include the following points that show humans as friends of eagles:

1 Scientists are attempting to restore nesting populations to former nesting areas. Scientists are raising eaglets in captivity and then releasing them into natural habitats.
2 Millions of acres of land have been set aside as sanctuaries for eagles.
3 The government grants special licenses to people who care for sick or injured eagles in their homes.
4 Money is being donated for research to help scientists learn more about eagles.
5 Scientists are banding eaglets to help them track the maturing birds and to help them discover information about the eagles.

The following points show humans as foes to eagles:

1 Humans have moved into wilderness areas that were the natural habitats of eagles, cut trees, cleared land, and destroyed the habitats. Most eagles will not nest or hunt in areas occupied by humans.
2 Contaminated food kills eagles because farmers use poisons to kill insects and weeds. The insecticides cause the eggshells to become so thin that the eggs break in the nest.
3 Factories use chemicals that pollute the air and water. Eagles die after they eat animals and fish that have been poisoned.
4 Sheep farmers have shot thousands of eagles because the farmers believed that eagles killed lambs.
5 Sportsmen have killed eagles because the eagles occasionally killed game birds.
6 Accidents kill eagles when they land on power lines and are electrocuted.

Some animals are not endangered because people hunt or poison them. Instead, human pollution or land development has endangered their survival. Books on this subject can spark debates whether the interests of people are in opposition to the interests of animals and whether the protective measures designed for animals also protect humans. Books that you can use for this purpose include Caroline Arnold's *Saving the Peregrine Falcon,* Robert M. McClung's *America's Endangered Birds: Programs and People Working to Save Them,* and the biography *Thor Heyerdahl: Viking Scientist* by Wyatt Blassingame.

Other books about animals that have been endangered include Dorothy Hinshaw Patent's *Whales: Giants of the Deep,* Scott Barry's *The Kingdom of the Wolves,* and Dorothy Hinshaw Patent's *Where the Bald Eagles Gather.*

Applying Data from Reading to Practical Problems

After children have critically evaluated the subjects of water, land, and air pollution discussed in informational books, they may be interested in evaluating the extent of pollution in their own environment. An informational book that can spark this kind of critical evaluation through experimentation and observation is Betty Miles's *Save the Earth! An Ecology Handbook for Kids*. Several projects that appeal to third and fourth graders include planning a new town to make the best possible use of land, recording air pollution by placing several cards covered with a thin layer of petroleum jelly outside in different locations and noting after twenty-four hours the pollution that has collected on the cards, and tracking water pollution in their own neighborhood, town, or city.

This last project reinforces observation, critical evaluation, and graphic interpretation abilities. A fourth-grade class identified various waterways in their town. Then they walked beside several creeks, a lake, a river, and a pond where the students made notes about pollution they found. When the students returned to school, they drew a large map of the waterways and used their notes to mark on the map any pollution they had found. Next, they filled in the type of building or human activity that was near the pollution so that they could more closely evaluate the possible causes of the pollution. When the students discovered a definite problem, they took pictures of the evidence, wrote letters to the newspaper, made "clean up the waterways" posters, and asked people to make pledges to clean up their waterways.

You can encourage children to relate their reading to experiences and observations in their daily lives. In addition, you can help children link new applications of science principles to their previous knowledge. Helen Huus (4) emphasizes the desirability of encouraging children to place new learning into a personal context. According to Huus, a reader

> fails to obtain the greatest pleasure, enjoyment, and even knowledge from his efforts unless, in the doing he gives something of himself. He must amalgamate the total into his own background of information, what the psychologists call his "apperceptive mass," and reorganize his ideas to accommodate his new learnings, his attitudes, or his feelings. In this reorganization, he gains new insights—sees the same things from a different point of view, sees aspects hitherto not noticed, savors the color and texture of a word or phrase, stores away a new visual image, or feels empathy with characters he has previously ignored or misunderstood. (p. 164)

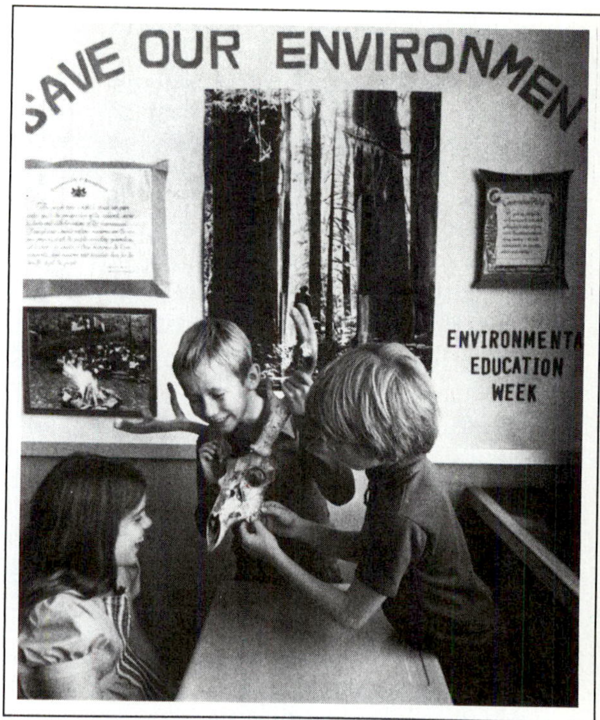

Children apply knowledge gained from informational books during an environmental project.

Deciding whether information about animals is fact or fantasy is another way for children to apply data from reading to a practical problem. You can develop discussions with children that encourage the children to observe and analyze differences in behavior of real animals, behavior of real animals depicted in informational books, and behavior of the same animals depicted in folktales and modern fantasy. For example, you might bring a caged chicken into the classroom for observational purposes. The children could observe the eating, sleeping, moving, and clucking of the chicken. They could also observe the chicken's appearance. Then, the children could compare their factual observations with the presentation of chickens in an informational book such as *The Chicken and the Egg* by Oxford Scientific Films. Finally, the children could consider the behavior of chickens in folktales such as Paul Galdone's *The Little Red Hen*. They might discuss the differences in behavior and identify different purposes for writing and reading the two types of literature. You could stimulate other observations and discussions by comparing students' observations of a caged mouse to the content of an informational book such as *The Small Plant-Eaters* by Martyn Bramwell and Steve Parker and either of Beverly Cleary's fantasies *The Mouse and the Motorcycle* or *Runaway Ralph*.

Suggested Activities for Children's Understanding of Biographies and Informational Books

- ☐ Prepare a sequencing game that identifies both the cue and the directions for a dramatic activity. Share the game with a peer group or a group of children.
- ☐ Select a biographical incident that you believe would make an excellent "You Are There" creative dramatization. Identify the introductory scene and circumstances, the consecutive scenes to be used, the characters to be involved, and the questions to be asked of children while they discuss and develop the drama.
- ☐ Select several biographies written about the same person. Plan a discussion that encourages children to consider the strengths and weaknesses of each biography.
- ☐ Identify the parts of a book that are necessary if children are to use informational materials effectively at a particular grade level. Choose a specific part of a book, such as the table of contents, index, glossary, or bibliography of further readings, and select several informational books that can be used to encourage the development and use of this book aid. Prepare an activity that increases children's understanding of that part of the book.
- ☐ Visit a public library or school library. What reference aids are available to assist children in finding nonfictional materials? Explore the relationship between the author card, the title card, and the subject card in the library card catalog. Is the library information on cards or computerized? Ask librarians how they help children find information.
- ☐ Choose several books by authors who have effectively presented the meanings of new technical terminology through text or photographs, diagrams, and charts. Share the books with a peer group and suggest how you would use the books with children.
- ☐ Search through a science or social studies curriculum to identify the graphic aids that children at a particular grade level are expected to use, understand, or develop themselves. Develop an annotated bibliography of informational books by authors who have included accurate, clear graphic aids. Include page numbers for each aid you identify.
- ☐ Choose a reading-for-meaning requirement for science-related materials. Using a science-related book not discussed in this chapter, develop a lesson to encourage children to note the main idea of a selection, identify supporting details, or note the author's organization.
- ☐ Select an informational book that encourages children to perform an experiment in order to understand a scientific principle. Perform the experiment as directed. Are the directions clearly stated? Should they be modified or clarified for use with children? Make any necessary modifications, and encourage a child to perform the experiment. Follow each step of the experiment and discuss the scientific principle with the child.
- ☐ Develop a lesson that encourages children to critically evaluate what they read, including the author's purpose for writing the book, the author's competence, and the adequacy and accuracy of the content.

References

1 Cianciolo, Patricia J. "Reading Literature, and Writing from Writers' Perspectives." *English Journal* 74 (December 1985): 65–69.

2 Gillespie, John T., and Christine B. Gilbert. *Best Books for Children, Preschool Through the Middle Grades*. New York: Bowker, 1978, 1981.

3 Heinig, Ruth Beall, and Lyda Stillwell. *Creative Dramatics for the Classroom Teacher*. Englewood Cliffs, N.J.: Prentice-Hall, 1974.

4 Huus, Helen. "Critical and Creative Reading." In *Developing Comprehension Including Critical Reading*, edited by Mildred A. Dawson. Newark, Del.: International Reading Association, 1968.

5 Moore, Ann W. "A Question of Accuracy: Errors in Children's Biographies." *School Library Journal* 31 (February 1985): 34–35.

6 Podendorf, Illa. "Characteristics of Good Science Materials for Young Readers." *Library Trends* 22 (April 1974): 425–431.

7 Robertson, Elizabeth, and Jo McGinnis. "Biography as Art: A Formal Approach." In *Portraits: Biography and Autobiography in the Secondary School*, edited

by Margaret Fleming and Jo McGinnis. Urbana, Ill.: National Council of Teachers of English, 1985.

8 Shepherd, David L. *Comprehensive High School Reading Methods,* 3d ed. Columbus, Ohio: Merrill, 1982.

9 Wolf, Willavene. "The Logical Dimension of Critical Reading." In *Developing Critical Reading,* edited by Mildred A. Dawson. Newark, Del.: International Reading Association, 1968.

CHILDREN'S LITERATURE

BIOGRAPHIES

Adolf, Arnold. *Malcolm X*. Crowell, 1970 (I:7–12 R:5). This is a biography of the Black American leader.

Aliki. *The King's Day: Louis XIV of France*. Crowell, 1989 (I:8+ R:6). This biography is a highly illustrated depiction of the social life and customs in France in the seventeenth and eighteenth centuries.

Bains, Rae. *Harriet Tubman: The Road to Freedom*. Illustrated by Larry Johnson. Troll, 1982 (I:8–12 R:4). This is an illustrated version of Tubman's experiences with the Underground Railroad.

Black, Sheila. *Sitting Bull and the Battle of the Little Bighorn*. Illustrated by Ed Lee. Silver Burdett, 1989 (I:10+ R:6). The author traces the controversies over Indian lands and the involvement with the Sioux leader.

Blassingame, Wyatt. *Thor Heyerdahl: Viking Scientist*. Elsevier-Dutton, 1979 (I:8+ R:5). This is the story of the scientist who built and sailed the *Kon Tiki*.

Blegvad, Erik. *Self-Portrait: Erik Blegvad*. Addison-Wesley, 1979 (I:all R:5). A short autobiography is written and illustrated by an artist of children's books.

Blumberg, Rhoda. *Commodore Perry in the Land of the Shogun*. Lothrop, Lee & Shepard, 1985 (I:10+ R:6). In 1853, Perry leads an expedition to open trade with Japan.

Brenner, Barbara. *On the Frontier with Mr. Audubon*. Coward, McCann, 1977 (I:8–12 R:3). In a trip down the Ohio and Mississippi Rivers, John James Audubon and his assistant sketched birds.

Brooks, Polly Schoyer. *Queen Eleanor: Independent Spirit of the Medieval World*. Lippincott, 1983 (I:10+ R:8). This is a biography of the twelfth-century queen.

Cleary, Beverly. *A Girl from Yamhill: A Memoir*. Morrow, 1988 (I:8+ R:5). This popular author tells of her early life through high school.

Collins, Michael. *Flying to the Moon and Other Strange Places*. Farrar, Straus & Giroux, 1976 (I:10+ R:6). This is an autobiography about travel to the moon.

Cooper, Irene. *Susan B. Anthony*. Watts, 1984 (I:10+ R:6). This is a biography of a leader in women's rights.

Cwiklik, Robert. *Sequoyah and the Cherokee Alphabet*. Illustrated by T. Lewis. Silver Burdett, 1989 (I:10+ R:6). This is a biography of the leader who created the first alphabet for a North American tribe.

Dalgliesh, Alice. *The Columbus Story*. Illustrated by Leo Politi. Scribner's Sons, 1955 (I:5–8 R:3). A picture book provides a version of Columbus's first voyage to America.

Dank, Milton. *Albert Einstein*. Watts, 1983 (I:10+ R:7). This biography emphasizes both Einstein's life and discoveries.

D'Aulaire, Ingri, and Edgar Parin D'Aulaire. *Abraham Lincoln*. Doubleday, 1939, 1957 (I:8–11 R:5). This is a book for young children.

———. *Benjamin Franklin*. Doubleday, 1950 (I:8–12 R:6). This is a colorfully illustrated biography.

———. *Columbus*. Doubleday, 1955 (I:7–10 R:5). This is a colorfully illustrated biography.

Davidson, Margaret. *The Golda Meir Story*. Scribner's Sons, 1981 (I:9–12 R:6). This book traces Meir's life through the Yom Kippur war and her tenure as prime minister.

DeKay, James T. *Meet Martin Luther King, Jr.* Illustrated by Ted Burwell. Random House, 1969 (I:7 R:4). This book stresses the magnitude of King's work and his reasons for fighting injustice.

Dolan, Edward F. *Adolf Hitler: A Portrait in Tyranny*. Dodd, Mead, 1981 (I:10+ R:7). This book contains Hitler's rise to power, the days of World War II, the facts of the Holocaust, and Hitler's suicide.

Egypt, Ophelia Settle. *James Weldon Johnson*. Illustrated by Moneta Barnett. Crowell, 1974 (I:5–9 R:3). Johnson was a Black American author, educator, lawyer, and diplomat.

Facklam, Margery. *Wild Animals, Gentle Women*. Illustrated by Paul Facklam. Harcourt Brace Jovanovich, 1978 (I:10+ R:6). This book contains information on the lives of eleven women who have studied animal behavior.

Ferrell, Keith. *H. G. Wells: First Citizen of the Future*. Evans, 1983 (I:12+ R:7). This is a biography of the science fiction writer.

Fido, Martin. *Oscar Wilde: An Illustrated Biography*. Harper & Row, 1987 (I:12+ R:7). This is a biography of an author.

———. *Rudyard Kipling: An Illustrated Biography*. Harper & Row, 1987 (I:12+ R:7). This is a biography of an author.

I = Interest by age range.
R = Readability by grade level.

Ford, Alice. *John James Audubon*. Abbeville Press, 1988 (I:8+ R:5). This is a biography of a naturalist and painter of birds.

Fox, Mary Virginia. *Women Astronauts: Aboard the Shuttle*. Messner, 1984 (I:10+ R:8) This book emphasizes Sally Ride's 1983 flight and includes brief biographies of eight women.

Franchere, Ruth. *Cesar Chavez*. Illustrated by Earl Thollander. Crowell, 1970 (I:7–9 R:4). This is an illustrated biography of Chavez's struggles to improve the pay and living conditions of migrant workers.

Freedman, Russell. *Lincoln: A Photobiography*. Clarion, 1987 (I:8+ R:6). This is a carefully documented life of Abraham Lincoln.

Fritz, Jean. *The Great Little Madison*. Putnam, 1989 (I:9+ R:6). This biography traces the life of the fourth president of the United States.

———. *Make Way for Sam Houston*. Illustrated by Elise Primavera. Putnam, 1986 (I:9 R:6). This is the biography of a nineteenth-century hero.

———. *The Man Who Loved Books*. Illustrated by Trina Schart Hyman. Putnam, 1981 (I:6–9 R:5). This is a highly illustrated biography of Saint Columba, A.D. 521–597.

———. *Stonewall*. Illustrated by Stephen Gammell. Putnam, 1979 (I:10+ R:6). This is a biography of a famous Civil War general, Thomas Jackson.

———. *Traitor: The Case of Benedict Arnold*. Putnam, 1981 (I:8+ R:5). This is the life of the man who chose the British cause in the Revolutionary War.

———. *What's the Big Idea, Ben Franklin?* Illustrated by Margot Tomes. Coward, McCann, 1978 (I:7–10 R:5). This is a biography of the inventor, ambassador, and coauthor of the Declaration of Independence.

———. *Where Do You Think You're Going, Christopher Columbus?* Illustrated by Margot Tomes. Putnam, 1980 (I:7–12 R:5). Fritz's style creates a believable background for the four voyages of Columbus.

———. *Where Was Patrick Henry on the 29th of May?* Illustrated by Margot Tomes. Coward, McCann, 1975 (I:7–10 R:5). This is a humorous telling of incidents in Patrick Henry's youth and political career.

———. *Why Don't You Get a Horse, Sam Adams?* Illustrated by Trina Schart Hyman. Coward, McCann, 1974 (I:7–10 R:5). This is a humorous story about Samuel Adams, his refusal to ride a horse, and his final decision to ride.

———. *Will You Sign Here, John Hancock?* Illustrated by Trina Schart Hyman. Coward, McCann, 1976 (I:7–10 R:5). This book tells of the rise to fame of a charming Revolutionary War hero.

Gish, Lillian, as told to Selma Lanes. *An Actor's Life for Me*! Illustrated by Patricia Lincoln. Viking, 1987 (I:8+ R:6). This is a biography of Gish's childhood years.

Goodnough, David. *Christopher Columbus*. Illustrated by Burt Dodson. Troll Associates, 1979 (I:8–12 R:6). This is an illustrated life story of Columbus.

Goodsell, Jane. *Daniel Inouye*. Crowell, 1977 (I:7–10 R:3). This is a biography of the first Japanese American member of Congress.

———. *Eleanor Roosevelt*. Illustrated by Wendell Minor. Crowell, 1970 (I:7–10 R:2). This book tells of Eleanor's life as a shy child, as well as her years in the White House and her work after her husband's death.

Greenfield, Eloise, and Lessie Jones Little. *Childtimes: A Three-Generation Memoir*. Crowell, 1979 (I:10+ R:5). Three black women tell about their childhood experiences.

Gross, Ruth Belov. *True Stories About Abraham Lincoln*. Illustrated by Jill Kastner. Lothrop, Lee & Shepard, 1990 (I: 7–10 R: 4). The text includes a series of short stories that emphasize aspects of Lincoln's life, especially his early years.

Gutman, Bill. *The Picture Life of Reggie Jackson*. Watts, 1978 (I:5–9 R:2). This is a picture story of the experiences of the baseball player.

Hamilton, Virginia. *Anthony Burns: The Defeat and Triumph of a Fugitive Slave*. Knopf, 1988 (I:10+ R:6). This is the story of the escaped slave whose trial caused riots in Boston.

Hodges, Margaret. *Making a Difference: The Story of an American Family*. Scribner's Sons, 1989 (I:12+ R:6). This is the biography of Mary Sherwood, 1864–1963.

Hyman, Trina Schart. *Self-Portrait: Trina Schart Hyman*. Addison-Wesley, 1981 (I:9–12 R:5). This is the autobiography of an artist.

Jakes, John. *Susanna of the Alamo*. Illustrated by Paul Bacon. Harcourt Brace Jovanovich, 1986 (I:7–12 R:6). A survivor of the Alamo retells the story of the battle.

Kherdian, David. *The Road from Home: The Story of an Armenian Girl*. Greenwillow, 1979 (I:12+ R:6). In 1915, an Armenian girl experiences the horrors of the Turkish persecution of Christian minorities.

Lasker, Joe. *The Great Alexander the Great*. Viking, 1983 (I:6–9 R:6). This is a highly illustrated version of the life of the conqueror.

Lawson, Don. *The Picture Life of Ronald Reagan*. Watts, 1984 (I:6–10 R:5). This is a brief version of Reagan's life from childhood to the presidency.

Lee, Betsy. *Charles Eastman, The Story of an American Indian*. Dillon, 1979 (I:8–12 R:5). Eastman was a famous doctor, writer, and worker for Indian rights.

Lipman, Jean, and Margaret Aspinwall. *Alexander Calder and His Magical Mobiles*. Hudson Hills, 1981 (I:9+ R:6). The text begins with the artist's early work and illustrates his work in wood, bronze, wire, and mobiles.

Liss, Howard. *Bobby Orr: Lightning on Ice*. Illustrated by Victor Mays. Garrard, 1975 (I:8–12 R:4). The hockey star's story begins when he is a young player in Canada.

Marrin, Albert. *Hitler*. Viking, 1987 (I:10+ R:7). This biography emphasizes Hitler's rise to power, his victories, and his final defeat.

———. *Stalin: Russia's Man of Steel*. Viking, 1988 (I:10+ R:7). This biography emphasizes how Stalin shaped Russia.

Meltzer, Milton. *Benjamin Franklin: The New American*. Watts, 1988 (I:10+ R:6). This is a carefully documented biography of an American statesman.

———. *Dorothea Lange, Life Through the Camera*. Viking, 1985 (I:10+ R:5). Lange's photographs increase understanding of the photographer.

———. *George Washington and the Birth of Our Nation*. Watts, 1986 (I:10+ R:6). A comprehensive biography tells of Washington from his birth through his leadership years and his death.

———. *Starting from Home: A Writer's Beginnings*. Viking Kestrel, 1988 (I:10+ R:5). This book tells the early life experiences of the biographical author.

Miller, Douglas. *Frederick Douglass and the Fight for Freedom*. Facts on File, 1988 (I:10+ R:6). This book tells the life of the Black leader who escaped slavery to become a political leader.

Mills, Judie. *John F. Kennedy*. Watts, 1988 (I:12+ R:7). This book tells the life of Kennedy and his family.

Morgan, Helen L. *Maria Mitchell: First Lady of American Astronomy*. Westminster, 1977 (I:12+ R:7). This book covers the years from Mitchell's childhood, when she learns astronomy from her father, through her years as the first woman astronomy professor at Vassar College.

Morrison, Dorothy N. *Under a Strong Wind: The Adventures of Jessie Benton Frémont*. Atheneum, 1983 (I:10+ R:6). This is a biography of the wife of John Charles Frémont.

Myers, Elizabeth. *John D. Rockefeller: Boy Financier*. Bobbs-Merrill, 1973 (I:8+ R:5). This text covers the early life of a financial giant.

———. *Thomas Paine: Common Sense Boy*. Bobbs-Merrill, 1976 (I:8+ R:5). This text covers the early life of a political hero.

Neimark, Anne E. *A Deaf Child Listened: Thomas Gallaudet, Pioneer in American Education*. Morrow, 1983 (I:10+ R: 7). This book traces the life of the founder of American education for the deaf.

Paolucci, Bridget. *Beverly Sills*. Chelsea House, 1990 (I: 12+ R:7). This biography tells about the life of the opera singer.

Patterson, Lillie. *Frederick Douglass: Freedom Fighter*. Garrard, 1965 (I:6–9 R:3). This is the biography of a great Black American leader.

———. *Martin Luther King, Jr. and the Freedom Movement*. Facts on File, 1989 (I:10+ R:6). This book tells of King's nonviolent struggles against segregation.

———. *Sure Hands, Strong Heart: The Life of Daniel Hale Williams*. Illustrated by David Scott Brown. Abingdon, 1981 (I:10+ R:5). This is the biography of a Black physician who worked for interracial hospitals.

Pearce, Carol Ann. *Amelia Earhart*. Facts on File, 1988 (I:8+ R:5). This book tells about the first woman pilot to fly across the Atlantic Ocean.

Peet, Bill. *Bill Peet: An Autobiography*. Houghton Mifflin, 1989 (I:all R:5). This text is highlighted with numerous drawings by Peet.

Pizer, Vernon. *Glorious Triumphs: Athletes Who Conquered Adversity*. Dodd, Mead, 1966, 1968, 1980 (I:12+ R:8). This book includes a collection of brief biographies about sports personalities who have overcome some problem.

Provensen, Alice, and Martin Provensen. *The Glorious Flight Across the Channel with Louis Bleriot, July 25, 1909*. Viking, 1983 (I:all R:4). This is a highly illustrated account of the first flight across the English Channel.

Quackenbush, Robert. *Mark Twain? What Kind of a Name Is That? A Story of Samuel Langhorne Clemens*. Prentice-Hall, 1984 (I:7–10 R:5). Humorous illustrations appeal to younger readers.

Reiss, Johanna. *The Upstairs Room*. Crowell, 1972 (I:11 R:4). This is the story of a Jewish girl's experience in hiding from the Nazis.

Roosevelt, Elliott. *Eleanor Roosevelt, with Love*. Dutton, 1984 (I:10+ R:7). Eleanor's life is told from the viewpoint of her son.

Rosen, Billi. *Andi's War*. Dutton, 1989 (I:12+ R:6). A girl experiences the Greek Civil War, 1946–1949.

Rosen, Sidney. *Galileo and the Magic Numbers*. Illustrated by Harie Stein. Little, Brown, 1958 (I:10+ R:6). A story tells about the astronomer and mathematician who invented the first telescope.

Sandburg, Carl. *Abe Lincoln Grows Up*. Illustrated by James Daugherty. Harcourt Brace Jovanovich, 1926, 1928, 1954 (I:10+ R:6). This book tells about the first nineteen years of Lincoln's life.

———. *Abraham Lincoln: The Prairie Years*. Harcourt Brace Jovanovich, 1926 (I:12+ R:7). This biography covers a portion of Lincoln's life.

Scott, John Anthony, and Robert Alan Scott. *John Brown of Harper's Ferry*. Facts on File, 1988 (I:10+ R:6). This book tells about an abolitionist.

Siegel, Beatrice. *Lillian Wald of Henry Street*. Macmillan, 1983 (I:12+ R:7). Lillian Wald was the founder of the Henry Street Settlement House.

Silberdick, Barbara. *Franklin D. Roosevelt, Gallant President*. Feinberg, 1981 (I:9–12 R:6). This biography focuses upon Roosevelt's accomplishments.

Sills, Leslie. *Inspirations: Stories About Women Artists*. Whitman, 1989 (I:8+ R:5). The text includes biographical sketches of four artists.

Stanley, Diane. *Peter the Great*. Four Winds, 1986 (I:8+ R:7). This is a highly illustrated biography of the emperor of Russia who lived from 1672 to 1725.

———, and Peter Vennema. *Shaka: King of the Zulus*. Illustrated by Diane Stanley. Morrow, 1988 (I:8+ R:5). This is a biography of a Zulu chief who lived from 1787 to 1828.

Tobias, Tobi. *Arthur Mitchell*. Illustrated by Carol Byard. Crowell, 1975 (I:7–9 R:5). This book describes the founder of the Dance Theatre of Harlem.

Ventura, Piero. Based on text by Gian Paolo Ceserani. *Christopher Columbus*. Random House, 1978 (I:all R:6). This is a picture biography of Columbus.

Whitney, Sharon. *Eleanor Roosevelt*. Watts, 1982 (I:10+ R:5). This book follows the life of Roosevelt from childhood through work with the United Nations.

Williams, Selma R. *Demeter's Daughters: The Women Who Founded America, 1587–1787*. Atheneum, 1976 (I:12+ R:7). This book contains biographical sketches of women whose contributions made the settlement of America possible.

Wolf, Bernard. *In This Proud Land: The Story of a Mexican American Family*. Lippincott, 1978 (I:all R:4). Photographs and text follow a family from the Rio Grand Valley to Minnesota for summer employment.

Yates, Elizabeth. *Amos Fortune, Free Man*. Illustrated by Nora S. Unwin. Dutton, 1950 (I:10+ R:6). A man is captured by slave traders in Africa and brought to Boston.

———. *My Diary, My World*. Westminster, 1981 (I:10+ R:5). A journal format covers ages twelve to twenty.

———. *My Widening World*. Westminster, 1983 (I:10+ R:5). A journal format describes the beginning writing career of Yates.

Zemach, Margot. *Self-Portrait, Margot Zemach*. Addison-Wesley, 1978 (I:all R:8). This is an autobiography of an illustrator of children's books.

INFORMATIONAL BOOKS

Ammon, Richard. *Growing Up Amish*. Atheneum, 1989 (I:8+ R:5). Photographs, maps, and drawings depict the Amish in Pennsylvania.

Ancona, George. *Dancing Is*. Dutton, 1981 (I:6–12 R:5). Photographs show and text describes different dances, such as the Highland fling.

Anderson, David. *The Spanish Armada*. Hampstead, 1988 (I:10+ R:6). Maps, charts, and graphs help readers understand this time in history.

Anderson, Joan. *The American Family Farm*. Photographs by George Ancona. Harcourt Brace Jovanovich, 1989 (I:8+ R:5). This text looks at three family farms, in Massachusetts, Georgia, and Iowa.

———. *The First Thanksgiving Feast*. Photographs by George Ancona. Clarion, 1984 (I:6–9 R:6). Photographs from the Plimoth Plantation in Plymouth, Massachusetts, accompany this story of the first Thanksgiving.

Anderson, Madelyn Klein. *Oil in Troubled Waters*. Vanguard, 1983 (I:10+ R:6). This book discusses the effects of oil on marine life.

Antonacci, Robert J., and Barbara D. Lockhart. *Tennis for Young Champions*. Illustrated by Robert Handville. McGraw-Hill, 1982 (I:10+ R:6). This book gives the history of tennis and step-by-step instructions for playing.

Apfel, Necia. *Nebulae: The Birth & Death of Stars*. Lothrop, Lee & Shepard, 1988 (I:6–10 R:5). Photographs from observatories highlight this text.

Ardley, Neil. *Music*. Knopf, 1989 (I:8+ R:6). This history of musical instruments is enhanced by numerous pictures.

Arnold, Caroline. *Dinosaur Mountain: Graveyard of the Past*. Photographs by Richard Hewett. Clarion, 1989 (I:8–12 R:6). Text and photographs depict excavations at Dinosaur National Monument in Utah.

———. *Saving the Peregrine Falcon*. Photographs by Richard R. Hewett. Carolrhoda, 1985 (I:8–12 R:7). This book describes various ways that people are trying to save the falcon from extinction.

Arnosky, Jim. *Drawing from Nature*. Lothrop, Lee & Shepard, 1982 (I:all R:6). This book provides directions for drawing water, land, plants, and animals.

———. *Drawing Life in Motion*. Lothrop, Lee & Shepard, 1984 (I:all R:6). This book provides directions for drawing action in nature.

———. *Freshwater Fish and Fishing*. Four Winds, 1982 (I:8–12 R:5). This book provides information about trout, perch, and pike and how to catch them.

———. *Sketching Outdoors in Summer*. Lothrop, Lee & Shepard, 1988 (I:all R:6). This book provides examples of sketches from nature.

Arthur, Alex. *Shell*. Knopf, 1989 (I:9+ R:6). A highly illustrated reference book examines different types of shells.

Asch, Frank, and Jan Asch. *Running with Rachel*. Photographs by Jan Asch and Robert M. Buscow. Dial, 1979 (I:7–10 R:3). A young girl explains how she became interested in running.

Ashabranner, Brent. *Born to the Land: An American Portrait*. Photographs by Paul Conklin. Putnam, 1989 (I:9+ R:5). The photographs and text depict ranch life in New Mexico.

———. *Morning Star, Black Sun: The Northern Cheyenne Indians and America's Energy Crisis*. Photographs by Paul Conklin. Dodd, Mead, 1982 (I:10+ R:7). This is a history of a tribe and its conflict with mining interests.

Asimov, Isaac. *Asimov's Guide to Halley's Comet*. Walker, 1985 (I:10+ R:6). This book provides detailed information on history, formation, and anecdotes.

Aylesworth, Thomas G., and Virginia Aylesworth. *The Mount St. Helens Disaster: What We've Learned*. Watts, 1983 (I:10+ R:6). This book tells about the environmental effects resulting from the volcanic eruption.

Ballard, Robert D. *Exploring the Titanic*. Scholastic, 1988 (I:8+ R:5). This book tells of the history of the ship and its discovery in the ocean.

Banish, Roslyn. *Let Me Tell You About My Baby*. Harper & Row, 1988 (I:2–6 R:4). An older child tells the story of the new baby.

Bare, Colleen Stanley. *Guinea Pigs Don't Read Books*. Dodd, Mead, 1985 (I:6–9 R:3). Photographs accompany a simple book on the characteristics of guinea pigs.

Barry, Scott. *The Kingdom of Wolves*. Putnam, 1979 (I:9+ R:6). The author pleads for the protection of wolves.

Barton, Byron. *Airport*. Crowell, 1982 (I:3–8). Large illustrations follow passengers as they get ready to board a plane.

Bash, Barbara. *Desert Giant: The World of the Saguaro Cactus*. Sierra Club/Little Brown, 1989 (I:5–9 R:4). The text and illustrations are about the life cycle of the saguaro cactus.

Bellville, Cheryl Walsh. *Farming Today Yesterday's Way*. Carolrhoda, 1984 (I:all R:7). Photographs show and the text describes a farm that uses early methods of farming.

Berger, Melvin. *Germs Make Me Sick!* Illustrated by Marylin Hafner. Crowell, 1985 (I:5–8 R:6). This book tells how viruses affect people.

Bergman, Thomas. *Finding a Common Language: Children Living with Deafness*. Gareth Stevens, 1989 (I:7–12 R:5). This text introduces readers to people who are deaf.

———. *One Day At a Time: Children Living with Leukemia*. Gareth Stevens, 1989 (I:7–12 R:5).

———. *On Our Own Terms: Children Living with Physical Disabilities*. Gareth Stevens, 1989 (I:7–12 R:5). Photographs and text present children with special needs.

———. *Seeing in Special Ways: Children Living with Blindness*. Gareth Stevens, 1989 (I:7–12 R:5).

———. *We Laugh, We Love, We Cry: Children Living with Mental Retardation*. Gareth Stevens, 1989 (I:7–12 R:5).

Berman, Paul. *Make-Believe Empire: A How-to Book*. Atheneum, 1982 (I:8–12 R:6). This book provides directions for creating a city, a navy, and other objects needed for one's own kingdom.

Bester, Roger. *Fireman Jim*. Crown, 1981 (I:5–10 R:4). Photographs and text follow a twenty-four-hour day in the life of a New York City firefighter.

Billings, Charlene. *Scorpions*. Dodd, Mead, 1983 (I:10+ R:7). This book tells about the physiology, life cycle, and behavior of scorpions.

Bitter, Gary G. *Exploring with Computers*. Messner, 1981 (I:4–6 R:5). This book explains the use of computers and encourages readers to become involved in activities, such as reading a punch card.

Blumberg, Rhoda. *Commodore Perry in the Land of the Shogun*. Lothrop, Lee & Shepard, 1985 (I:9+ R:6). The illustrations depicting Japanese life in the nineteenth century add authenticity.

———. *The Great American Gold Rush*. Bradbury, 1989 (I:9+ R:6). The text covers the California Gold Rush from 1848 to 1852.

———. *The Incredible Journey of Lewis and Clark*. Lothrop, Lee & Shepard, 1987 (I:9+ R:6). Maps showing the journey clarify the text.

Bolognese, Don. *Drawing Spaceships and Other Spacecraft*. Watts, 1982 (I:8+ R:6). Detailed illustrations introduce readers to various stages of drawing spaceships.

Bramwell, Martyn, and Steve Parker. *The Small Plant-Eaters*. Facts on File, 1988 (I:8+ R:5). An index, a glossary, and photographs accompany this text.

Branley, Franklyn M. *Halley: Comet 1986*. Illustrated by Sally J. Bensusen. Dutton, 1983 (I:9+ R:6). This book explains the history, composition, and sighting information of Halley's comet.

———. *Mysteries of Outer Space*. Illustrated by Sally J. Bensusen. Dutton, 1985 (I:9+ R:7). A question-and-answer format explores major questions about space.

———. *Saturn: The Spectacular Planet*. Illustrated by Leonard Kessler. Harper & Row, 1983 (I:9+ R:6). The author uses information from the Pioneer and Voyager space explorations.

———. *Space Colony: Frontier of the 21st Century*. Illustrated by Leonard D. Dank. Dutton, 1982 (I:10+ R:6). The author explores the possibilities of space colonies, their functions, and the hazards of living in space.

Brenner, Martha. *Fireworks Tonight!* Hastings, 1983 (I:9+ R:6). This book traces the history of fireworks and discusses types and regulations.

Brinckloe, Julie. *Fireflies!* Macmillan, 1985 (I:5–8 R:3). A young boy catches, watches, and then releases fireflies.

Brown, Laurie Krasny, and Marc Brown. *Dinosaurs Alive and Well! A Guide to Good Health*. Little, Brown, 1990 (I:5–8 R:4). A humorous text provides rules on nutrition, exercise, and cleanliness.

Brown, Marc. *Your First Garden Book*. Atlantic-Little, 1981 (I:5–9 R:4). Over thirty simple projects introduce children to gardening.

———, and Stephen Krensky. *Dinosaurs, Beware!: A Safety Guide*. Little, Brown, 1982 (I:2–5 R:2). Safety rules are presented through humorous pictures.

Bruun, Ruth Dowling, and Bertel Bruun. *The Human Body*. Illustrated by Patricia J. Wynne. Random, 1982 (I:9+ R:6). This book provides an overview of the body systems.

Busch, Phyllis S. *Cactus in the Desert*. Illustrated by Harriet Barton. Crowell, 1979 (I:7–9 R:3). This book discusses a variety of cacti.

———. *The Seven Sleepers: The Story of Hibernation*. Illustrated by Wayne Trimm. Macmillan, 1985 (I:7–9 R:3). This book tells what some northern animals do in the winter.

Cajacob, Thomas, and Teresa Burton. *Close to the Wild: Siberian Tigers in a Zoo*. Photographs by Thomas Cajacob. Carolrhoda, 1986 (I:6–10 R:6). Large color photographs depict life in a natural-habitat zoo.

Carrick, Donald. *Milk*. Greenwillow, 1985 (I:4–8). Large illustrations trace milk from a dairy farm to a grocery store.

Catchpole, Clive. *Desert*. Illustrated by Brian McIntyre. Dial, 1984 (I:6–9 R:3). A highly illustrated book tells about deserts.

———. *Jungles*. Illustrated by Denise Finney. Dial/Dutton, 1984 (I:6–9 R:3). The environment of the jungle is presented in colorful illustrations.

Ceserani, Gian Paolo. *Grand Constructions*. Illustrated by Piero Ventura. Putnam, 1983 (I:all R:7). This history of architecture begins with Stonehenge and concludes with skyscrapers.

Chaikin, Miriam. *Make Noise, Make Merry: The Story and Meaning of Purim*. Illustrated by Demi. Houghton Mifflin, 1983 (I:10+ R:7). This book tells about the history and symbols related to the Jewish holiday.

Cheney, Theodore A. Rees. *Living in Polar Regions: A Cultural Geography*. Watts, 1987 (I:8+ R:4). This book describes characteristics of the polar regions.

Climo, Shirley. *Someone Saw a Spider: Spider Facts and Folktales*. Illustrated by Dirk Zimmer. Crowell, 1985 (I:10+ R:6). The author retells spider folktales and discusses facts about spiders.

Cobb, Vicki. *For Your Own Protection: Stories Science Photos Tell*. Lothrop, Lee & Shepard, 1989 (I:9+ R:5). The photographs reveal health information.

———. *Fuzz Does It!* Illustrated by Brian Schatell. Lippincott, 1982 (I:6–12 R:6). This book tells about various fibers, their sources, and their uses.

———. *Why Can't You Unscramble an Egg? And Other Not Such Dumb Questions About Matter*. Illustrated by Ted Enik. Lodestar, 1990 (I:8–12 R:6). Developed in a question-and-answer format, the text and illustrations answer questions such as "Why does wood burn?"

Cole, Joanna. *A Bird's Body*. Photographs by Jerome Wexler. Morrow, 1983 (I:8–12 R:4). Photographs and diagrams show the anatomy of birds.

———. *Cars and How They Go*. Illustrated by Gail Gibbons. Harper & Row, 1983 (I:6–10 R:4). This is a simplified explanation of how parts of the car function.

———. *A Cat's Body*. Photographs by Jerome Wexler. Morrow, 1982 (I:6–12 R:4). Photographs and text show how a cat responds physically in different moods and activities.

———. *Cuts, Breaks, Bruises and Burns: How Your Body Heals*. Illustrated by True Kelley. Crowell, 1985 (I:8–10 R:4). This book tells how the body heals various injuries.

———. *A Horse's Body*. Photographs by Jerome Wexler. Morrow, 1981 (I:2–6 R:5). The text explains the horse's anatomy.

———. *The Human Body: How We Evolved*. Illustrated by Walter Gaffney-Kessell and Juan Carolos Barberis. Morrow, 1987 (I:10+ R:5). This book traces the development of humans from prehistoric ancestors.

———. *An Insect's Body*. Photographs by Jerome Wexler and Raymond A. Mendez. Morrow, 1984 (I:8–12 R:4). The anatomy of a cricket is explained in text and photographs.

———. *The Magic School Bus: Inside the Earth*. Illustrated by Bruce Degan. Scholastic, 1987 (I:6–8 R:4). This book provides a humorous approach to the study of the Earth.

———. *My Puppy Is Born*. Photographs by Jerome Wexler. Morrow, 1973 (I:7–9 R:2). The text and photographs follow puppies from their birth through their first eight weeks of life.

———. *A Snake's Body*. Photographs by Jerome Wexler. Morrow, 1981 (I:8–10 R:4). Photographs and text present the anatomy of a python.

Cone, Ferne Geller. *Crazy Crocheting*. Illustrated by Rachel Osterlof. Photographs by J. Morton Cone. Atheneum, 1981 (I:9–12 R:5). This book provides instructions for a range of projects, including finger puppets.

Cook, David. *Environment*. Crown, 1985 (I:9+ R:6). This book discusses several ecological systems and endangered species.

Corbett, Scott. *Bridges*. Illustrated by Richard Rosenblum. Four Winds, 1978 (I:10+ R:6). This is a history of bridges and the people who built them.

Costabel, Eva Deutsch. *A New England Village*. Atheneum, 1983 (I:6–10 R:4). The illustrations and text depict rural life in a nineteenth-century New England village.

Cowan, Paul. *A Torah Is Written*. Photographs by Rachel Cowan. Jewish Publication Society, 1986 (I:all R:5). This book describes the process for creating handwritten Torah scrolls.

Cowing, Sheila. *Searches in the American Desert*. Photographs by Walter S. Cowing. Macmillan, 1989 (I:12+ R:7). Maps add clarification to this history of various pilgrimages into the desert.

Currimbhoy, Nayana. *Living in Deserts: A Cultural Geography*. Watts, 1987 (I:10+ R:5). This book describes the climate and resources of desert areas.

Cutchins, Judy, and Ginny Johnston. *Are Those Animals Real? How Museums Prepare Wildlife Exhibits*. Morrow, 1984 (I:9–12 R:4). The text and photographs present steps in taxidermy.

Davis, Daniel S. *Behind Barbed Wire: The Imprisonment of Japanese Americans During World War II*. Dutton, 1982 (I:10+ R:7). This book tells of the internment of Japanese Americans and the ways in which their lives were altered.

Davis, Edward E. *Into the Dark: A Beginner's Guide to Developing and Printing Black and White Negatives*. Atheneum, 1979 (I:10+ R:7). This is an extensive coverage of beginning photography.

Demuth, Patricia. *Joel: Growing Up a Farm Man*. Photographs by Jack Demuth. Dodd, Mead, 1982 (I:9+ R:6). Photographs and text reveal how a thirteen-year-old learns to be a farmer.

de Paola, Tomie. *The Cloud Book*. Holiday House, 1975 (I:6–9 R:4). This book presents ten clouds and tells about their shapes and the ways they forecast weather.

———. *The Popcorn Book*. Holiday House, 1978 (I:3–8 R:5). The illustrations and story present facts about popcorn.

East, Katherine. *A King's Treasure: The Sutton Hoo Ship Burial*. Illustrated by Dinah Cohen. Kestrel, 1982 (I:9+ R:8). The text and illustrations describe the excavation of the burial ground of a seventh-century king.

Elwood, Ann, and Linda C. Wood. *Windows in Space*. Walker, 1982 (I:10+ R:6). This is a history of astronomy and the relationship with space exploration.

Englander, Roger. *Opera, What's All the Screaming About?* Walker, 1983 (I:10+ R:7). This is a listener's guide to opera.

Englebardt, Stanley L. *Miracle Chip: The Microelectronic Revolution*. Lothrop, Lee & Shepard, 1979 (I:10+ R:8). This book tells about the development of the miracle chip used in minicomputers.

Esbensen, Barbara Juster. *Great Northern Diver: The Loon*. Illustrated by Mary Barrett Brown. Little, Brown, 1990 (I:5–8 R:4). In a picture book format, the text and illustrations describe the loon's migrations, habitat, and characteristics.

Faber, Doris, and Harold Faber. *The Birth of a Nation: The Early Years of the United States*. Scribner's Sons, 1989 (I:10+ R:7). This book covers major events in early United States history.

———. *We the People: The Story of the United States Constitution Since 1787*. Scribner's Sons, 1987 (I:10+ R:7). This book discusses the writing of the Constitution and subsequent changes in the Constitution.

Facklam, Margery, and Howard Facklam. *Changes in the Wind: Earth's Shifting Climate*. Harcourt Brace Jovanovich, 1986 (I:10+ R:7). This book, which includes a glossary, a bibliography, and an index, discusses changes in climate.

———. *The Brain: Magnificent Mind Machine*. Harcourt Brace Jovanovich, 1982 (I:10+ R:7). This book discusses brain functions and how they were discovered.

Fagan, Brian M. *The Great Journey: The Peopling of Ancient America*. Thames & Hudson, 1987 (I:10+ R:7). This book tells the history of early people in North America.

Feldbaum, Carl B., and Ronald J. Bee. *Looking the Tiger in the Eye: Confronting the Nuclear Threat*. Harper & Row, 1988 (I:12+ R:7). This book tells the history of nuclear weapons.

Fenner, Carol. *Gorilla, Gorilla*. Illustrated by Symeon Shimin. Random House, 1973 (I:7–10 R:4). This book tells the early life of a gorilla and his capture and confinement in a zoo.

Fischer-Nagel, Heiderose, and Andraes Fischer-Nagel. *Life of the Honey Bee*. Carolrhoda, 1986 (I:6–10 R:6). Close-up photographs show various stages in the honey bee's life cycle.

Fisher, Leonard Everett. *The Alamo*. Holiday House, 1987 (I:8+ R:7). This is a history of the fort in San Antonio, Texas.

———. *The Great Wall of China*. Macmillan, 1986 (I:all R:6). This is a highly illustrated history of the Great Wall.

———. *The Tower of London*. Macmillan, 1987 (I:all R:6). This is a highly illustrated history of the tower.

———. *The Wailing Wall*. Macmillan, 1989 (I:all R:6). This is a highly illustrated history of the Wailing Wall in Jerusalem.

Fisher, Maxine P. *Women in the Third World*. Watts, 1989 (I:12+ R:6). Personal profiles clarify issues and statistics.

Flanagan, Geraldine Lux, and Sean Morris. *Window into a Nest*. Houghton Mifflin, 1975 (I:9+ R:8). This is an excellent, detailed account of the life of a pair of chickadees.

Fleisher, Paul. *Understanding the Vocabulary of the Nuclear Arms Race*. Dillon, 1988 (I:12+ R:7). This book provides definitions of about three hundred terms.

Ford, Barbara. *Alligators, Raccoons, and Other Survivors: The Wildlife of the Future*. Morrow, 1981 (I:9+ R:6). This book tells how animals have survived in spite of human encroachment.

Freedman, Russell. *Dinosaurs and Their Young*. Illustrated by Leslie Morrill. Holiday House, 1983 (I:6–9 R:4). This is a picture book version of discoveries about the duck-billed dinosaurs.

———. *Sharks*. Holiday House, 1985 (I:6–10 R:5). This book tells characteristics, evolution, and types of sharks.

Friedman, David. *Focus on Drugs and the Brain*. Illustrated by David Neuhaus. 21st Century Books, 1990 (I:10+ R:6). The author discusses how drugs affect the brain.

Fritz, Jean. *Shh! We're Writing the Constitution*. Illustrated by Tomie de Paola. Putnam, 1987 (I:7–10 R:5). This is a description of the Constitutional Convention of 1787.

Gallant, Roy A. *Before the Sun Dies: The Story of Evolution*. Macmillan, 1989 (I:10+ R:6). This text presents theories and scientific thinking about the Earth.

———. *The Macmillan Book of Astronomy*. Macmillan, 1986 (I:8+ R:6). This book explores planets and stars.

Gardner, Beau. *Guess What?* Lothrop, Lee & Shepard, 1985 (I:5–8). Silhouettes encourage children to observe and predict.

George, William T. *Box Turtle at Long Pond*. Illustrated by Lindsay Barrett George. Greenwillow, 1989 (I:3–8 R:3). An illustrated book introduces turtles to young children.

Gibbons, Gail. *Beacons of Light: Lighthouses*. Morrow, 1990 (I:7–9 R:4). The illustrations and text present the history of lighthouses.

———. *Dinosaurs*. Holiday House, 1987 (I:4–8 R:3). This is a highly illustrated and simplified text.

Giblin, James Cross. *From Hand to Mouth: Or, How We Invented Knives, Forks, Spoons, and Chopsticks & the Table Manners to Go with Them*. Crowell, 1987 (I:8+ R:6). This is a history of table etiquette.

———. *Let There Be Light: A Book About Windows*. Crowell, 1988 (I:8+ R:6). This is the history of windows.

Goldston, Robert. *Sinister Touches: The Secret War Against Hitler*. Dial, 1982 (I:10+ R:9). This book covers the war years from 1939 to 1945.

Goodall, Jane. *The Chimpanzee Family Book*. Photographs by Michael Neugebauer. Picture Book Studio, 1989 (I:8+ R:5). This book tells about the chimpanzees of Gombe National Park.

Goor, Ron, and Nancy Goor. *In the Driver's Seat*. Crowell, 1982 (I:6–10 R:6). This book gives a driver's view of large vehicles.

———. *Pompeii: Exploring a Roman Ghost Town*. Crowell, 1986 (I:10+ R:7). Photographs enhance a text describing Pompeii as it might have been in A.D. 79.

———. *Shadows: Here, There, and Everywhere*. Photographs by Ron Goor. Crowell, 1981 (I:6–10 R:4). This book experiments with shadows.

Graff, Nancy Price. *The Strength of the Hills: A Portrait of a Family Farm*. Photographs by Richard Howard. Little, Brown, 1989 (I:all R:5). The author documents the work of a Vermont farm family.

Graham, Ada. *Six Little Chickadees: A Scientist and Her Work with Birds*. Photographs by Cordelia Stanwood. Four Winds, 1982 (I:8–12 R:6). This is a story about Cordelia Stanwood's studies of bird life.

Hackwell, W. John. *Digging to the Past: Excavations in Ancient Lands*. Scribner's Sons, 1986 (I:10+ R:9). This book describes archaeological field work and discusses findings.

Hall, Lynn. *Tazo and Me*. Photographs by Jan Hall. Scribner's Sons, 1985 (I:10+ R:6). A photo documentary shows a rider caring for and showing a horse.

Hausherr, Rosmarie. *Children and the AIDS Virus*. Clarion, 1989 (I:7+ R:4). This text includes two levels of information, with large print for younger children and smaller print for older children and adults.

———. *My First Kitten*. Four Winds, 1985 (I:6–9 R:3). This book is about selecting and caring for a kitten.

Hawes, Judy. *Bees and Beelines*. Illustrated by Aliki. Crowell, 1964 (I:4–8 R:3). A Let's-Read-and-Find-Out Science Book explores flight of bees.

Heilman, Joan Rattner. *Bluebird Rescue*. Lothrop, Lee & Shepard, 1982 (I:9–12 R:6). This book gives reasons for decline of the bluebird and suggestions for conservation groups.

Hendrich, Paula. *Saving America's Birds*. Lothrop, Lee & Shepard, 1982 (I:10+ R:6). This book discusses the varied circumstances that result in endangered birds.

Herbst, Judith. *Sky Above and Worlds Beyond*. Atheneum, 1983 (I:9+ R:7). This is an enthusiastic guided tour of space.

Hess, Lilo. *Diary of a Rabbit*. Scribner's Sons, 1982 (I:9–12 R:6). This book provides information on different breeds of rabbits and the care of them, as well as a five-month diary about one rabbit.

Hilton, Suzanne. *We the People: The Way We Were 1783–1793*. Westminster, 1981 (I:10+ R:7). This book explores such subjects as education, living conditions, and culture.

Hirschi, Ron. *Who Lives in. . .the Mountains?* Photographs by Galen Burrell. Putnam, 1989 (I:3–8 R:5). Photographs show mountain scenes and animals.

———. *Who Lives on. . .the Prairie?* Photographs by Galen Burrell. Putnam, 1989 (I:3–8 R:5). Photographs provide an easy introduction to prairie life.

Hirst, Robin, and Sally Hirst. *My Place in Space*. Illustrated by Roland Harvey and Joe Levine. Orchard, 1990 (I:5–8 R:5). Detailed drawings provide a humorous introduction to astronomy.

Hoban, Tana. *A Children's Zoo*. Greenwillow, 1985 (I:2–6). Each photograph is accompanied by a list of three words that describe the animal.

Holbrook, Sabra. *Canada's Kids*. Atheneum, 1983 (I:10+ R:6). This book reflects varied backgrounds of Canadian youth.

Holmes, Anita. *Cactus: The All-American Plant*. Illustrated by Joyce Ann Powzyk. Four Winds, 1982 (I:10+ R:6). This book discusses the environment, the interdependence of life forms, and major cactus types.

Hopf, Alice L. *Bats*. Photographs by Merlin D. Tuttle. Dodd, Mead, 1985 (I:8–12 R:6). The text includes the dangers of pesticides and the loss of habitats.

Horwitz, Elinor Lander. *How to Wreck a Building*. Photographs by Joshua Horwitz. Pantheon, 1982 (I:9–12 R:5). A former student describes the procedures used to demolish an elementary school.

Hunt, Patricia. *Koalas*. Dodd, Mead, 1980 (I:8–10). Photographs depict the life of the koalas.

———. *Tigers*. Dodd, Mead, 1981 (I:8–10 R:4). The Bengal and Siberian tigers are described.

Huntington, Harriet E. *Let's Look at Cats*. Doubleday, 1981 (I:9–12 R:5). Photographs show various members of the cat family.

Isenbart, Hans-Heinrich. *A Duckling Is Born*. Translated by Catherine Edwards Sadler. Photographs by Othmar Baumli. Putnam, 1981 (I:4–8 R:3). This book describes the life cycle of ducks.

Isenberg, Barbara, and Marjorie Jaffe. *Albert the Running Bear's Exercise Book*. Illustrated by Diane de Groat. Houghton Mifflin, 1984 (I:5–9 R:6). This book provides step-by-step directions for exercises.

Jaspersohn, William. *Magazine: Behind the Scenes at Sports Illustrated*. Little, Brown, 1983 (I:10+ R:10). The work associated with publishing a weekly issue is shown in photographs and text.

Jespersen, James, and Jane Fitz-Randolph. *From Quarks to Quasars: A Tour of the Universe*. Atheneum, 1987 (I:10+ R:10). This book describes how scientists have conducted research and contributed to knowledge of the universe.

Jessel, Camilla. *The Joy of Birth: A Book for Parents and Children*. Dutton, 1983 (I:9+ R:6). This book provides an introduction to pregnancy and birth.

Johnson, Neil. *All in a Day's Work: Twelve Americans Talk About Their Jobs*. Little, Brown, 1989 (I:10+ R:6). This book includes first-person reports about jobs and job satisfaction.

Johnson, Sylvia. *Potatoes*. Photographs by Masaharu Suzuki. Lerner, 1984 (I:10+ R:9). This book traces the development of a potato.

Johnston, Ginny, and Judy Cutchins. *Andy Bear: A Polar Cub Grows Up at the Zoo*. Photographs by Constance Noble. Morrow, 1985 (I:9–12 R:6). A young cub is raised by a zookeeper.

———. *Scaly Babies: Reptiles Growing Up*. Morrow, 1988 (I:7+ R:5). Photographs and text cover baby snakes, lizards, crocodilians, and turtles.

Kalb, Jonah, and Laura Kalb. *The Easy Ice Skating Book*. Illustrated by Sandy Kossin. Houghton Mifflin, 1981 (I:7–12 R:5). This book discusses beginning ice skating skills, such as stopping, gliding, and spinning.

Kerrod, Robin. *Primates: Insect-Eaters and Baleen Whales*. Facts on File, 1988 (I:8+ R:5). Photographs, illustrations, a glossary, and an index add to discussions of monkeys, apes, bats, echidnas, platypuses, and whales.

Knight, David C. *"Dinosaurs" That Swam and Flew*. Illustrated by Lee J. Ames. Prentice-Hall, 1985 (I:8–12 R:5). Numerous drawings and lists of museums add to the text.

Koebner, Linda. *From Cage to Freedom: A New Beginning for Laboratory Chimpanzees*. Dutton, 1981 (I:9+ R:5). Scientists follow laboratory chimps after they are released on a Florida island.

Kohl, Herbert. *A Book of Puzzlements: Play and Invention with Language*. Schocken, 1981 (I:10+ R:7). This is a large collection of word games, including anagrams, hieroglyphics, and crossword puzzles.

Kohl, Judith, and Herbert Kohl. *Pack, Band and Colony: The World of Social Animals*. Illustrated by Margaret La Farge. Farrar, Straus & Giroux, 1983 (I:10+ R:9). This book includes wolves, lemurs, and termites.

Krementz, Jill. *A Very Young Rider*. Knopf, 1977 (I:7–12 R:3). Photographs and text describe the preparation of an Olympic hopeful.

———. *A Very Young Skater*. Knopf, 1979 (I:7–12 R:4). Ten-year-old Katherine spends several hours every day preparing for her desired goal of being an accomplished skater.

Kronenwetter, Michael. *Journalism Ethics*. Watts, 1988 (I:12+ R:6). This book examines issues in journalism.

Kuklin, Susan. *Fighting Back: What Some People Are Doing About AIDS*. Putnam, 1989 (I:12+ R:6). This text includes reactions of people who have AIDS.

Kuskin, Karla. *Jerusalem, Shining Still*. Illustrated by David Frampton. Harper & Row, 1987 (I:8+ R:5). Three thousand years of history is told in simple storytelling style.

Lasky, Kathryn. *Dinosaur Dig*. Photographs by Christopher Knight. Morrow, 1990 (I:9+ R:5). Several families are guided on a dig by a paleontologist.

———. *Dollmaker: The Eyelight and the Shadow*. Photographs by Christopher G. Knight. Scribner's Sons, 1981 (I:9+ R:5). A doll that will be a collector's item is described in text and shown in photographs.

———. *Sugaring Time*. Photographs by Christopher Knight. Macmillan, 1983 (I:all R:6). Photographs show and text describes collecting and processing maple sap.

Lauber, Patricia. *Dinosaurs Walked Here and Other Stories Fossils Tell*. Bradbury, 1987 (I:all R:6). This book presents information on how fossils reveal characteristics of the prehistoric world.

———. *Journey to the Planets*. Crown, 1982 (I:8–12 R:4). Photographs and text highlight the prominent features of each planet in our solar system.

———. *The News About Dinosaurs*. Bradbury, 1989 (I:8+ R:6). This book presents new findings about dinosaurs.

———. *Seeds Pop! Stick! Glide!* Photographs by Jerome Wexler. Crown, 1981 (I:8–10 R:4). This book discusses the many ways that seeds travel.

———. *Snakes Are Hunters*. Illustrated by Holly Keller. Crowell, 1988 (I:4–8 R:3). This is an introductory book on snakes.

———. *Volcano: The Eruption and Healing of Mount St. Helens*. Bradbury, 1986 (I:all). Photographs and text follow progress of the eruption.

Lavies, Bianca. *Backyard Hunter: The Praying Mantis*. Dutton, 1990 (I:5–9 R:4). The life cycle is presented in text and illustrations.

———. *Lily Pad Pond*. Dutton, 1989 (I:5–9 R:3). Photographs follow tadpoles and other pondlife.

———. *Tree Trunk Traffic*. Dutton, 1989 (I:5–9 R:3). Wildlife live in an old maple tree.

Lawson, Don. *The Abraham Lincoln Brigade: Americans Fighting Fascism in the Spanish Civil War*. Crowell, 1989 (I:12+ R:7). This is a history of the Spanish Civil War and the impact of Americans.

Leakey, Richard E. *Human Origins*. Dutton, 1982 (I:10+ R:7). This text traces human evolution from man-apes to early farmers.

Leen, Nina. *Monkeys*. Holt, Rinehart & Winston, 1978 (I:7–12 R:5). Photographs show monkeys, apes, and great apes.

Lerner, Carol. *Dumb Cane and Daffodils: Poisonous Plants in the House and Garden*. Morrow, 1990 (I:10+ R:5). Detailed drawings add to the discussion about poisonous plants.

Lewin, Ted. *Tiger Trek*. Macmillan, 1990 (I:10+ R:6). The illustrations take readers on a safari in the Indian jungle.

Linsley, Leslie. *Air Crafts: Playthings to Make and Fly*. Photographs by Jon Aron. Lodestar, 1982 (I:9–12 R:6). This book presents six how-to activities for objects such as a boomerang and a skate sail that can be made to move through the air.

Macaulay, David. *Castle*. Houghton Mifflin, 1978 (I:all R:5). This book describes the construction of a castle.

———. *Cathedral: The Story of Its Construction*. Houghton Mifflin, 1973 (I:all R:5). Detailed drawings show construction of a cathedral.

———. *Mill*. Houghton Mifflin, 1983 (I:9+ R:5). This book discusses the mills of nineteenth-century New England.

———. *The Way Things Work*. Houghton Mifflin, 1988 (I:all R:6). Humorous analogies add to detailed drawings.

McClung, Robert M. *America's Endangered Birds: Programs and People Working to Save Them*. Illustrated by George Founds. Morrow, 1979 (I:9+ R:6). This book discusses six endangered types of birds.

McDearmon, Kay. *Rocky Mountain Bighorns*. Photographs by Valerius Geist. Dodd, Mead, 1980 (I:9+ R:6). Pictures show and text describes bighorn sheep, their habitat and behavior, and the need to protect them.

McDonald, Megan. *Is This a House for Hermit Crab?* Illustrated by S. D. Schindler. Orchard, 1990 (I:3–6). A picture book follows a crab as it looks for a new home.

MacGregor, Anne, and Scott MacGregor. *Domes: A Project Book*. Lothrop, Lee & Shepard, 1982 (I:9+ R:7). This book provides history of domes and models for building one.

McLaughlin, Molly. *Dragonflies*. Walker, 1989 (I:7–12 R:5). The text and photographs show the life cycle of dragonflies.

McNulty, Faith. *Peeping in the Shell: A Whooping Crane Is Hatched*. Harper & Row, 1986 (I:6–12 R:4). This book follows the hatching process.

McPhail, David. *Farm Morning*. Harcourt Brace Jovanovich, 1985 (I:2–5). A young girl and her father explore the barnyard.

Malnig, Anita. *Where the Waves Break: Life at the Edge of the Sea*. Photographs by Jeff Rotman, Alex Kerstitch, and Franklin H. Barnwell. Carolrhoda, 1985 (I:9+ R:6). Color photography enhances a study of marine life.

Mannetti, William. *Dinosaurs in Your Back Yard*. Atheneum, 1982 (I:9+ R:6). This book discusses some new theories about dinosaurs.

Marrin, Albert. *Aztecs and Spaniards: Cortez and the Conquest of Mexico*. Atheneum, 1986 (I:12+ R:7). This history of the Aztecs tells the influences of Cortez.

Maruki, Toshi. *Hiroshima No Pika*. Lothrop, Lee & Shepard, 1982 (I:8–12 R:4). A powerfully illustrated picture book shows the aftereffects of the first atomic bomb.

Math, Irwin. *Wires and Watts: Understanding and Using Electricity*. Illustrated by Hal Keith. Scribner's Sons, 1981 (I:10+ R:10). This book looks at experiments with electricity.

Matthews, Downs. *Polar Bear Cubs*. Photographs by Dan Guravich. Simon & Schuster, 1989 (I:5–10 R:5). The photographs and text follow polar bear cubs as they explore their arctic homes.

Meltzer, Milton, ed. *The American Revolutionaries: A History in Their Own Words, 1750–1800*. Crowell, 1987 (I:10+). This is a collection of letters, diaries, interviews, and speeches.

———. *Rescue: The Story of How Gentiles Saved Jews in the Holocaust*. Harper & Row, 1988 (I:10+ R:7). Non-Jewish individuals helped Jewish people during World War II.

———. *Voices from the Civil War*. Crowell, 1989 (I:10+). Excerpts from speeches, diaries, and letters form this collection.

Merriman, Nick. *Early Humans*. Knopf, 1989 (I:all R:5). The text and photographs present a history of humans.

Meyer, Carolyn, and Charles Gallenkamp. *The Mystery of the Ancient Maya*. Atheneum, 1985 (I:10+ R:8). This book tells about early explorers and discoveries.

Michel, Anna. *The Story of Nim: The Chimp Who Learned Language*. Photographs by Susan Kuklin and Herbert S. Terrace. Knopf, 1980 (I:8+ R:6). A research study resulted in a chimpanzee's learning to identify and use 125 signs in sign language.

Miles, Betty. *Save the Earth! An Ecology Handbook for Kids*. Illustrated by Claire A. Nivola. Knopf, 1974 (I:8+ R:5). Activities are designed to help children explore their environment.

Millard, Anne. *Ancient Egypt*. Illustrated by Angus McBridge, Brian and Constance Dear, and Nigel Chamberlain. Warwick, 1979 (I:9+ R:6). This book provides background information about the Egyptian civilization that lasted from 3118 B.C. to 31 B.C.

Miller, Jonathan. *The Human Body*. Viking, 1983 (I:9+). A pop-up book illustrates the human body.

Miller, Margaret. *Who Uses This?* Greenwillow, 1990 (I:2–5). Readers must turn the page to check if they have identified the correct user of a tool.

Mohun, Janet. *Drugs, Steroids, and Sports*. Watts, 1988 (I:12+ R:6). This book explores abuse of drugs in sports.

Munro, Roxie. *The Inside-Outside Book of Washington, D.C.* Dutton, 1987 (I:all). Illustrations in an almost wordless book show major structures in our capital.

Murphy, Jim. *Tractors: From Yesterday's Steam Wagons to Today's Turbocharged Giants*. Lippincott, 1984 (I:9+ R:6). This is a history of tractors.

Nance, John. *Lobo of the Tasaday*. Pantheon, 1982 (I:9–12 R:5). Photographs and text follow a Filipino boy whose people lived in the Stone Age.

National Geographic Society. *Inventors and Discoverers: Changing Our World*. National Geographic, 1988 (I:10+ R:8). Numerous photographs and illustrations add to the information about inventors.

Nixon, Hershell, and Joan Lowery Nixon. *Earthquakes: Nature in Motion*. Dodd, Mead, 1981 (I:8–10 R:5). This book describes the what, how, and why of earthquakes.

———. *Glaciers: Nature's Frozen Rivers*. Dodd, Mead, 1980 (I:9+ R:6). The text describes and photographs show glacier formation, different types of glaciers, results of glaciers, and use of glaciers for water supplies and electric power.

———. *Volcanoes: Nature's Fireworks*. Dodd, Mead, 1978 (I:7–10 R:5). This book discusses causes of volcanoes.

Norvell, Flo Ann Hedley. *The Great Big Box Book*. Photographs by Richard Mitchell. Crowell, 1979 (I:5–9 R:5). The text provides directions for making playthings out of large boxes.

Nourse, Alan E. *Your Immune System*. Watts, 1982 (I:10+ R:7). This book provides information about lymphatic systems, inoculation, allergic reactions, and research.

O'Connor, Karen. *Homeless Children*. Lucent Books, 1989 (I:10+ R:6). Photographs and text focus on the urban homeless.

O'Neill, Catherine. *Focus on Alcohol*. Illustrated by David Neuhaus. 21st Century Books, 1990 (I:10+ R:6). The author discusses how alcohol effects the body.

Parker, Steve. *Mammal*. Knopf, 1989 (I:8–12 R:7). This heavily illustrated reference book examines the world of mammals.

Parker, Stephen, and John Bavosi. *Life Before Birth: The Story of the First Nine Months*. Cambridge, 1979 (I:9+ R:6). Illustrations are from a British Museum program.

Parnall, Peter. *The Daywatchers*. Macmillan, 1984 (I:9+ R:7). The author uses his own experiences to introduce different birds of prey.

Patent, Dorothy Hinshaw. *Appaloosa Horses*. Photographs by William Munoz. Holiday House, 1988 (I:5–8 R:5). This book explores the origins and characteristics of Appaloosas.

———. *Babies*. Holiday House, 1988 (I:4–8 R:4). This book tells about infants to age two.

———. *Dolphins and Porpoises*. Holiday House, 1987 (I:8–12 R:6). Life cycles and habits are discussed.

———. *Farm Animals*. Photographs by William Munoz. Holiday House, 1984 (I:8–12 R:6). This book discusses different categories of farm animals.

———. *Looking at Dolphins and Porpoises*. Holiday House, 1989 (I:8–12 R:6). This book discusses differences between dolphins and porpoises.

———. *A Picture Book of Cows*. Photographs by William Munoz. Holiday House, 1982 (I:5–8 R:3). This book tells how cows develop and are raised.

———. *The Sheep Book*. Illustrated by William Munoz. Dodd, Mead 1985 (I:9–12 R:6). The text describes raising of and behavior of sheep.

———. *Thoroughbred Horses*. Holiday House, 1985 (I:9–12 R:6). This book covers all aspects of raising and training thoroughbreds.

———. *Whales: Giants of the Deep*. Holiday House 1984 (I:8–12 R:6). This book discusses baleen whales, toothed whales, whale mysteries, and human influences on whales.

———. *Where the Bald Eagles Gather*. Photographs by William Munoz. Clarion, 1984 (I:9–12 R:5). This book describes the habits of America's endangered species.

———. *The Whooping Crane: A Comeback Story*. Photographs by William Munoz. Clarion, 1988 (I:8+ R:6). This book discusses attempts to save the whooping crane.

Perl, Lila. *Red Star and Green Dragon: Looking at New China*. Morrow, 1983 (I:10+ R:6). This book discusses political, social, and economic influences on China.

Perry, Robert. *Focus on Nicotine and Caffeine*. Illustrated by David Neuhaus. 21st Century Books, 1990 (I:10+ R:5). The author focuses on how nicotine and caffeine affect the body.

Peters, David. *Giants of Land, Sea & Air: Past & Present*. Knopf/Sierra Club, 1986 (I:10+ R:10). An illustrated resource describes some of the largest animals.

Petersen, Gwenn Boardman. *Careers in the United States Merchant Marine*. Lodestar, 1983 (I:9+ R:7). This book provides career information and facts about life at sea.

Pettit, Florence H. *The Stamp-Pad Printing Book*. Photographs by Robert M. Pettit. Crowell, 1979 (I:10+ R:6). This book provides directions for carving, printing, and then using a stamp pad to create several projects.

Pope, Joyce. *Kenneth Lilly's Animals: A Portfolio of Paintings*. Illustrated by Kenneth Lilly. Lothrop, Lee & Shepard, 1988 (I:all R:7). Animals are divided according to geographic regions.

Powzyk, Joyce. *Wallaby Creek*. Lothrop, Lee & Shepard, 1985 (I:9+ R:6). Illustrations show Australian animals.

Poynter, Margaret. *Gold Rush! The Yukon Stampede of 1898*. Atheneum, 1979 (I:9+ R:6). The lure of the Yukon gold rush and the people who searched for gold are reported by a descendant of Alaskan pioneers.

Pringle, Laurence. *Animals at Play*. Harcourt Brace Jovanovich, 1985 (I:9–12 R:7). This is an introduction to animal behavior.

———. *City and Suburb: Exploring an Ecosystem*. Macmillan, 1975 (I:9–12 R:7). The author suggests ways to explore a city ecosystem.

———. *Death Is Natural*. Four Winds, 1977 (I:9–12 R:6). Death in nature is an essential part of life.

———. *Dinosaurs and People: Fossils, Facts, and Fantasies*. Harcourt Brace Jovanovich, 1978 (I:9+ R:6). This book describes dinosaurs and traces research.

———. *Dinosaurs and Their World*. Harcourt Brace Jovanovich, 1968 (I:8–12 R:6). Over the previous fifteen years, scientists have discovered what life was like millions of years ago.

———. *Feral: Tame Animals Gone Wild*. Macmillan, 1983 (I:9+ R:7). This book discusses problems related to wild birds, pigs, dogs, cats, burros, and horses.

———. *Into the Woods: Exploring the Forest Ecosystem*. Macmillan, 1973 (I:8–12 R:4). This book explores the energy cycle of forests and encourages readers to respect the valuable ecosystem.

———. *Living in a Risky World*. Morrow, 1989 (I:12+ R:7). People experience difficulties when evaluating risks.

———. *Nuclear Energy: Troubled Past, Uncertain Future*. Macmillan, 1989 (I:10+ R:6). This book provides a history and discusses issues related to nuclear energy.

———. *Nuclear War: From Hiroshima to Nuclear Winter*. Enslow, 1985 (I:12+ R:7). This book tells the history and consequences of nuclear weapons.

———. *Saving Our Wildlife*. Enslow, 1990 (I:10+ R:6). The author describes how people are attempting to save wildlife.

———. *Vampire Bats*. Morrow, 1982 (I:9–12 R:6). Some bats feed on blood rather than insects.

———. *Wild Foods: A Beginner's Guide to Identifying, Harvesting and Cooking Safe and Tasty Plants from the Outdoors*. Illustrated by Paul Breeden. Four Winds, 1978 (I:10+ R:7). This book provides information on identifying safe wild foods and recipes that may be used in their preparation.

Reid, Barbara. *Playing with Plasticine*. Morrow, 1989 (I:8+ R:5). This book gives directions for making plasticine sculptures.

Rogasky, Barbara. *Smoke and Ashes: The Story of the Holocaust*. Holiday House, 1988 (I:10+ R:6). This is a history of the 1933–1945 Holocaust.

Roop, Peter, and Connie Roop. *Seasons of the Cranes*. Walker, 1989 (I:8+ R:5). The text describes the life of the whooping crane by progressing from spring through winter.

Rosenberg, Maxine. *Artists of Handcrafted Furniture at Work*. Photographs by George Ancona. Lothrop, Lee & Shepard, 1988 (I:7+ R:5). Color photographs show artists at work.

Rossel, Seymour. *The Holocaust*. Watts, 1981 (I:9+ R:6). This book examines Germany in the 1930s, Hitler's dictatorship, the Nuremberg trials.

Rubins, Harriet. *Guinea Pigs: An Owner's Guide to Choosing, Raising, Breeding, and Showing*. Illustrated by Pamela Carroll. Lothrop, Lee & Shepard, 1982 (I:9+ R:6). This text includes guidelines for selecting and caring for guinea pigs.

Ryden, Hope. *America's Bald Eagle*. Putnam, 1985 (I:9+ R:6). Numerous photographs illustrate the life cycle of the eagle.

St. George, Judith. *Panama Canal: Gateway to the World*. Putnam, 1989 (I:12+ R:7). This book tells about the building and operating of the canal.

Sancha, Sheila. *The Castle Story*. Crowell, 1982 (I:10+ R:7). A reference includes considerable information about types of castles.

———. *The Luttrell Village: Country Life in the Middle Ages*. Crowell, 1983 (I:10+ R:6). Illustrations and text provide information on fourteenth-century England.

Sattler, Helen Roney. *The Book of Eagles*. Illustrated by Jean Day Zallinger. Lothrop, Lee & Shepard, 1989 (I:8+ R:6). This text presents the behavior and life cycle of eagles.

———. *Dinosaurs of North America*. Illustrated by Anthony Rao. Lothrop, Lee & Shepard, 1981 (I:9+ R:6). In addition to discussions about various dinosaurs, the text includes theories about their extinction.

———. *Hominids: A Look Back at Our Ancestors*. Illustrated by Christopher Santoro. Lothrop, Lee & Shepard, 1988 (I:10+ R:6). This is a history of early hominids.

———. *Train Whistles*. Illustrated by Giulio Maestro. Lothrop, Lee & Shepard, 1985 (I:5–8 R:4). This is a picture-book guide to the meaning of train whistles.

Scarry, Huck. *Life on a Fishing Boat: A Sketchbook*. Prentice-Hall, 1983 (I:8+ R:6). Equipment, daily life, and types of boats are related to commercial fishing.

———. *Looking into the Middle Ages*. Harper & Row, 1985 (I:8–12). A pop-up book shows castles, cathedrals, and villages.

Schaaf, Peter. *An Apartment House Close Up*. Four Winds, 1980 (I:all). Black-and-white photographs show the various parts of an apartment house.

Schmitt, Lois. *Smart Spending: A Young Consumer's Guide*. Scribner's Sons, 1989 (I:12+ R:6). This book explores such topics as comparison shopping.

Scott, Jack Denton. *The Book of the Goat*. Photographs by Ozzie Sweet. Putnam, 1979 (I:9 R:5). The goat is presented as an intelligent and useful animal.

———. *The Book of the Pig*. Photographs by Ozzie Sweet. Putnam, 1981 (I:8–10 R:4). This book tells the characteristics and history of the pig.

———. *Canada Geese*. Photographs by Ozzie Sweet. Putnam, 1976 (I:9+ R:6). This book tells the migration habits of Canada geese as they fly from Canada to their southern feeding area in the Mississippi Valley.

———. *Discovering the American Stork*. Photographs by Ozzie Sweet. Harcourt Brace Jovanovich, 1976 (I:9+ R:7). Photographs show and text describes the habits, habitats, and unique qualities of the American stork.

———. *Discovering the Mysterious Egret*. Photographs by Ozzie Sweet. Harcourt Brace Jovanovich, 1978 (I:9+ R:7). The background history and details of mating, nesting, and feeding are developed through photographs and text.

———. *Little Dogs of the Prairie*. Photographs by Ozzie Sweet. Putnam, 1977 (I:9+ R:6). This text covers the life of the prairie dog and the contributions that it makes to the prairie.

———. *Moose*. Photographs by Ozzie Sweet. Putnam, 1981 (I:8–10 R:5). This book discusses physical characteristics and behavior of moose.

———. *Orphans from the Sea*. Photographs by Ozzie Sweet. Putnam, 1982 (I:8+ R:6). This book tells about the work of the Florida Suncoast Seabird Sanctuary.

Selsam, Millicent E. *The Amazing Dandelion*. Photographs by Jerome Wexler. Morrow, 1977 (I:7–10 R:4). The life cycle of the dandelion is presented in text and photographs.

———. *Cotton*. Photographs by Jerome Wexler. Morrow, 1982 (I:7–10 R:5). This book tells the history, stages in development, and uses of cotton.

———. *How to Be a Nature Detective*. Illustrated by Ezra Jack Keats. Harper & Row, 1958, 1963 (I:5–8 R:4). This book encourages children to identify animals by observing their tracks.

———. *Mushrooms*. Photographs by Jerome Wexler. Morrow, 1986 (I:7–10 R:6). This book tells the history and life cycle of the common edible mushroom.

———. *Plants We Eat*. Photographs by Jerome Wexler. Morrow, 1981 (I:10+ R:5). This book gives the history and development of plants as food.

———. *Where Do They Go? Insects in Winter*. Illustrated by Arabelle Wheatley. Four Winds, 1982 (I:5–10 R:3). This book discusses flies, grasshoppers, and bees.

———, and Joyce Hunt. *A First Look at Animals with Horns*. Illustrated by Harriet Springer. Walker, 1989 (I:5–8 R:3). This book discusses characteristics of animals with horns.

———. *A First Look at Animals that Eat Other Animals*. Illustrated by Harriet Springer. Walker, 1990 (I:5–8 R:3). This introductory book defines carnivores and discusses animal groups.

———. *A First Look at Bird Nests*. Illustrated by Harriet Springer. Walker, 1985 (I:5–8 R:3). This book describes nests of common American birds.

———. *A First Look at Caterpillars*. Illustrated by Harriet Springer. Walker, 1987 (I:5–8 R:3). This book tells the life cycle and habits of the caterpillar.

———. *A First Look at Seals, Sea Lions, and Walruses*. Illustrated by Harriett Springer. Walker, 1988 (I:5–8 R:3). This book tells characteristics of the animals.

———. *Keep Looking!* Illustrated by Normand Chartier. Macmillan, 1989 (I:3–7 R:3). This text encourages readers to find animals in a winter setting.

Shapiro, Mary. *How They Built the Statue of Liberty*. Illustrated by Huck Scarry. Random House, 1985 (I:all). Detailed drawings show development of the statue.

Shemie, Bonnie. *Houses of Snow, Skin, and Bones*. Tundra, 1989 (I:7–12 R:5). Drawings and text present construction of igloos, sod houses, and tents.

Shulman, Jeffrey. *Focus on Cocaine and Crack*. Illustrated by David Neuhaus. 21st Century Books, 1990 (I:10+ R:6). The author discusses how cocaine and crack affect the body.

Silverstein, Alvin, and Virginia B. Silverstein. *The Story of Your Hand*. Illustrated by Greg Wenzel. Putnam, 1985 (I:10+ R:6). This book discusses structures, functions, and experiments.

Simon, Hilda. *Sight and Seeing: A World of Light and Color*. Philomel, 1983 (I:10+ R:9). This book tells how human and animal eyes function.

Simon, Seymour. *Danger from Below: Earthquakes—Past, Present, and Future*. Four Winds, 1979 (I:10+ R:6). Information developed through text, photographs, diagrams, and maps tells where earthquakes occur, why they occur, and how they are measured.

———. *Galaxies*. Morrow, 1988 (I:5–8 R:5). This book examines the Milky Way and other galaxies.

———. *How to Be an Ocean Scientist in Your Own Home*. Illustrated by David A. Carter. Lippincott, 1988 (I:8+ R:5). This book describes twenty-four experiments.

———. *Jupiter*. Morrow, 1985 (I:5–8 R:5). Color photographs from NASA reveal latest knowledge.

———. *Little Giants*. Illustrated by Pamela Carroll. Morrow, 1983 (I:7–12 R:4). Animals that are giants are compared to others of their kind.

———. *The Long Journey from Space*. Crown, 1982 (I:9+ R:6). Old and new photographs trace the history of comets and changes in them.

———. *The Long View into Space*. Crown, 1979 (I:all R:5). A photographic essay depicts the moon, the sun, planets, stars, nebulas, and galaxies.

———. *Meet the Giant Snakes*. Illustrated by Harriet Springer. Walker, 1979 (I:7–10 R:5). This book gives characteristics of pythons and boa constrictors.

———. *Poisonous Snakes*. Illustrated by William R. Downey. Four Winds, 1981 (I:7–10 R:5). This book discusses the important role of poisonous snakes, where they live, and their behavior.

———. *Saturn*. Morrow, 1985 (I:5–8 R:5). Color photographs from NASA add to the information.

———. *The Smallest Dinosaurs*. Illustrated by Anthony Rao. Crown, 1982 (I:5–9 R:6). This book presents seven small members of the Coelurosauria, or hollow, lizard family.

———. *Soap Bubble Magic*. Illustrated by Stella Ormai. Lothrop, Lee & Shepard, 1985 (I:6–9 R:3). This book encourages observation of and experimentation with soap bubbles.

———. *Storms*. Morrow, 1989 (I:8–12 R:5). This book tells about tornadoes, lightning, and storm clouds.

———. *Volcanoes*. Morrow, 1988 (I:8–12 R:5). Full-page photographs show dramatic volcanoes.

Smith, E. Boyd. *The Railroad Book*. Houghton Mifflin 1983 (I:all). A new edition of a book first published in 1913 presents a view of railroads in the early 1900s.

Smith, Howard E. *Small Worlds: Communities of Living Things*. Scribner's Sons 1987 (I:10+ R:7). This book describes the ecosystems of an old house, a sand dune, a tree, etc.

Stidworthy, John. *The Large Plant-Eaters*. Facts on File, 1988 (I:8+ R:5). This book is about large herbivores and marsupials.

Tayntor, Elizabeth, Paul Erickson, and Les Kaufman. *Dive to the Coral Reefs: A New England Aquarium Book*. Crown, 1986 (I:all R:5). Color photographs reveal the beauty of coral reefs.

Tinkelman, Murray. *Rodeo: The Great American Sport*. Greenwillow, 1982 (I:8–12 R:5). Black-and-white photographs illustrate each event in a rodeo.

Van Loon, Hendrik Willem. *The Story of Mankind*. Liveright, 1921, 1984 (I:9+ R:5). This historical informational book was the first Newbery Award winner.

Vogt, Gregory. *Halley's Comet: What We've Learned*. Watts, 1987 (I:12+ R:6). This book gives a history and discusses recent discoveries.

Von Tscharner, Renata, and Ronald Fleming. *New Providence: A Changing Cityscape*. Illustrated by Denis Orloff. Harcourt Brace Jovanovich, 1987 (I:all R:7). This book gives a historical look at a city from 1910 to 1987.

Walker, Barbara M. *The Little House Cookbook: Frontier Foods from Laura Ingalls Wilder's Classic Stories*. Illustrated by Garth Williams. Harper & Row, 1979 (I:8–12 R:7). This book provides authentic pioneer recipes.

Weber, William J. *Care of Uncommon Pets*. Holt, Rinehart & Winston, 1979 (I:all R:5). A veterinarian shares information about caring for rabbits, guinea pigs, hamsters, mice, rats, gerbils, frogs, turtles, snakes, and parakeets.

Weiss, Ann E. *Bioethics: Dilemmas in Modern Medicine*. Enslow, 1985 (I:10+ R:7). Case histories reflect issues such as the right to live or die.

Weiss, Malcolm E. *Sky Watchers of Ages Past*. Illustrated by Eliza McFadden. Houghton Mifflin, 1982 (I:10+ R:6). This is a history of the ancient scientists.

Weitzman, David. *Windmills, Bridges, and Old Machines: Discovering Our Industrial Past*. Scribner's Sons, 1982 (I:10+ R:7). This book traces America's industrial past.

Wexler, Jerome. *From Spore to Spore: Ferns and How They Grow*. Dodd, Mead, 1985 (I:9+ R:5). This book follows the two phases of the fern plant.

White, Jack R. *The Invisible World of the Infrared*. Dodd, Mead, 1984 (I:10+ R:6). This book defines and discusses infrared as used in pictures, cameras, missiles, and lasers.

———. *Satellites of Today and Tomorrow*. Dodd, Mead, 1985 (I:10+ R:6). This book gives a history, and discusses the types and uses of satellites.

Wilcox, Charlotte. *Trash!* Photographs by Jerry Bushey. Carolrhoda, 1988 (I:8–12 R:5). This book is about trash collecting and recycling.

Wolf, Bernard. *Firehouse*. Morrow, 1983 (I:8+ R:7). Photographs show the demanding and dangerous job of New York firefighters.

Woodford, Susan. *The Parthenon*. Cambridge/Lerner, 1983 (I:10+ R:7). Drawings, photographs, and text describe the design, building, and destruction of the Parthenon.

Yoshida, Toshi. *Young Lions*. Philomel, 1989 (I:3–9 R:4). This book is about lion cubs on an African plain.

Zeinert, Karen. *The Salem Witchcraft Trials*. Watts, 1989 (I:12+ R:7). This book is about events at Salem, Massachusetts in 1692.

Zeller, Paula Klevan. *Focus on Marijuana*. Illustrated by David Neuhaus. 21st Century Books, 1990 (I:10+ R:6). The author discusses how marijuana affects the body.

Zomberg, Paul G. *A Look Inside Computers*. Raintree, 1985 (I:10+ R:6). Diagrams and photographs help clarify definitions.

Zubrowski, Bernie. *Messing Around with Water Pumps and Siphons*. Illustrated by Steve Lindblom. Little, Brown, 1981 (I:5–8 R:3). A children's museum activity book encourages children to experiment.

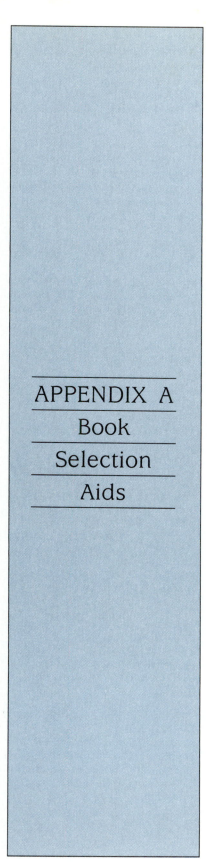

APPENDIX A
Book Selection Aids

BOOKS

A to Zoo: A Subject Access to Children's Picture Books. 2nd ed. Bowker, 1985.

Adventuring with Books: A Booklist for Pre-K–Grade 6, ed. by Mary Jett-Simpson. National Council of Teachers of English, 1989.

"All-Time Bestselling Children's Books". *Publishers Weekly*. October 27, 1989.

American Indian Stereotypes in the World of Children: A Reader and Bibliography, by Arlene B. Hirschfelder. Scarecrow Press, 1982.

Best Books for Children: Preschool Through the Middle Grades, 3rd ed., ed. by John T. Gillespie and Christine B. Gilbert. Bowker, 1985.

The Best in Children's Books: The University of Chicago Guide to Children's Literature 1966–1972, ed. by Zena Sutherland. The University of Chicago Press, 1973.

The Best in Children's Books: The University of Chicago Guide to Children's Literature 1973–1978, ed. by Zena Sutherland. The University of Chicago Press, 1980.

The Best of Children's Books: 1964–1978: with 1979 Addenda, ed. by Virginia Haviland. Library of Congress, 1980.

Bibliography on Disabled Children, Canadian Assoc. of Children's Librarians' Committee on Library Service to Disabled Children. Canadian Library Assoc., 1982.

Black Authors and Illustrators of Children's Books: A Biographical Dictionary. Garland, 1988.

The Black Experience in Children's Books, Barbara Rollock. New York Public Library, 1984.

The Bookfinder: A Guide to Children's Literature About the Needs and Problems of Youth Aged 2–15, Sharon Spredemann Dreyer. American Guidance Service, 1981.

Books Without Bias: Through Indian Eyes. Oyate, 1988.

Books for the Teen Age, 1985 Annual. New York Public Library, 1985.

Books for Today's Young Readers: An Annotated Bibliography of Recommended Fiction for Ages 10–14, comp. by Jeanne Bracken et al. Feminist Press, 1981.

Books in American History: A Basic List for High Schools and Junior Colleges, 2nd ed., ed. by John E. Wiltz and Nancy C. Cridland. Indiana University Press, 1981.

Caldecott Medal Books: 1938–1957, ed. by Bertha Mahony Miller and Elinor Whitney Field. The Horn Book Inc., 1957.

Canadian Books for Young People, 3rd ed., comp. by Irma McDonough. University of Toronto Press, 1980.

Censorship and Selection: Issues and Answers for Schools. American Library Association, 1988.

Children's Authors and Illustrators: An Index to Biographical Dictionaries, 3rd rev. ed., ed. by Adele Sarkissian. Gale, 1981.

Children's Books: Awards and Prizes, comp. by the Children's Book Council (revised periodically).

Children's Books in Print. Bowker (annual).

Children's Books in the Rare Book Division of the Library of Congress: Author-Title and Chronological Catalogs. Rowman and Littlefield, 1975.

Children's Books of International Interest, 3rd ed., ed. by Barbara Elleman. American Library Assoc., 1985.

Children's Books of the Year 1981, Barbara S. Smith. Watts, 1982.

Children's Books of the Year 1982. The Child Study Children's Book Committee. Bank Street College, 1982.

Children's Books Too Good to Miss: Revised Edition 1979, May Hill Arbuthnot, et al. University Press Books, 1980.

A Comprehensive Guide to Children's Literature with a Jewish Theme, Enid Davis. Schocken, 1981.

Easy Reading: Book Series and Periodicals for Less Able Readers, Michael F. Graves, Judith A. Boettcher, and Randall A. Ryder. International Reading Assoc. 1979.

The Elementary School Library Collection, 14th ed., ed. by Louis Winkel. Brodart, 1984.

Eyeopeners! How to Choose and Use Children's Books About Real People, Places, and Things. Viking, 1988.

Folklore: An Annotated Bibliography and Index to Single Editions, comp. by Elsie B. Ziegler. Faxon, 1973.

Fun for Kids: An Index to Children's Craft Books, Marion F. Gallivan. Scarecrow Press, 1981.

The Great Lakes Region in Children's Books: A Selected Annotated Bibliography, ed. by Donna Taylor. Green Oak Press, 1980.

Guide to Reference Books for School Media Centers, 2nd ed., ed. by Christine Gehr Wynar. Littleton, CO.: Libraries Unlimited, 1981.

Guide to Reference Books: Supplement, 9th ed., ed. by Eugene P. Sheehy. American Library Assoc. 1980.

A Hispanic Heritage: A Guide to Juvenile Books About Hispanic People and Cultures, Isabel Schon. Scarecrow Press, 1980.

Hispanic Heritage: Series II, Isabel Schon, Scarecrow Press, 1985.

Index to Fairy Tales, 1949–1972, Including Folklore, Legends and Myths in Collections, comp. by Norma Olen Irland. Faxon, 1973.

Index to Poetry for Children and Young People: 1970–1975, ed. by John E. Brewton, G. Meredith Blackburn, and Lorraine A. Blackburn. Wilson, 1978.

Index to Poetry for Children and Young People: 1976–1981, comp. by John E. Brewton et al. Wilson, 1983.

Indian Children's Books, Hap Gilliland. Billings, Mont.: Montana Council for Indian Education, 1980.

Junior High School Library Catalog, 4th ed., Wilson, 1980 (annual supplements).

Learning About Aging. The National Retired Teachers Assoc. and the American Assoc. of Retired Persons. American Library Assoc., 1981.

Let's Read Together: Books for Family Enjoyment, 4th ed., comp. by Assoc. for Library Service to Children, Let's Read Together Revision Committee. American Library Assoc., 1981.

Literature by and about the American Indian: An Annotated Bibliography, 2nd ed. Anna Lee Stensland. National Council of Teachers of English, 1979.

A Multimedia Approach to Children's Literature: A Selective List of Films, Filmstrips, and Recordings Based on Children's Books., 3rd ed., ed. by Mary Alice Hunt. American Library Assoc., 1983.

Multimedia Library: Materials Selection and Use, James Cabeceiras. Academic Press, 1982.

Museum of Science and Industry Basic List of Children's Science Books. American Library Association, 1988.

Newbery Medal Books: 1922–1955, ed. by Bertha Mahony Miller and Elinor Whitney Field. The Horn Book Inc., 1955.

Newbery and Caldecott Medal Books: 1956–1965, ed. by Lee Kingman. The Horn Book Inc., 1965.

Newbery and Caldecott Medal Books: 1966–1975, ed. by Lee Kingman. The Horn Book Inc., 1975.

Newbery and Caldecott Medal Books, 1976–1985, ed. by Lee Kingman. The Horn Book Inc., 1985.

The New York Times Parent's Guide to the Best Books for Children. Times Books, 1988.

Notable Children's Books, 1940–1970, comp. by Children's Service Division. American Library Assoc., 1977.

Notable Children's Books, 1971–1975, comp. by 1971–75 Notable Children's Books Re-evaluation Committee, Assoc. for Library Service to Children. American Library Assoc., 1981.

A Parents' Guide to Children's Reading, 5th ed., by Nancy Larrick. Westminster Press, 1982.

Reading for Young People: The Great Plains, ed. by Mildred Laughlin. American Library Assoc., 1979.

Reading for Young People: Kentucky, Tennessee, West Virginia, ed. by Barbara Mertins. American Library Assoc., 1985.

Reading for Young People: The Middle Atlantic, ed. by Arabelle Pennypacker. American Library Assoc., 1980.

Reading for Young People: The Midwest, ed. by Dorothy Hinman and Ruth Zimmerman. American Library Assoc., 1979.

Reading for Young People: The Mississippi Delta, ed. by Cora Matheny Dorsett. American Library Assoc., 1984.

Reading for Young People: The Northwest, ed. by Mary Meacham. American Library Association, 1981.

Reading for Young People: The Rocky Mountains, ed. by Mildred Laughlin. American Library Assoc., 1980.

Reading for Young People: The Southeast, ed. by Dorothy Heald. American Library Assoc., 1980.

Reading for Young People: The Southwest, ed. by Elva Harmon and Anna L. Milligan. American Library Assoc., 1982.

Reading for Young People: The Upper Midwest, ed. by Marion F. Archer. American Library Assoc., 1981.

Reference Books for Young Readers: Authoritative Evaluations of Encyclopedias, Atlases, and Dictionaries. Bowker, 1988.

A Reference Guide to Historical Fiction for Children and Young Adults. Greenwood Press, 1987.

A Reference Guide to Modern Fantasy for Children, by Pat Pflieger. Greenwood Press, 1984.

Science Books for Children: Selections from Booklist, 1976–1983, selected by Denise M. Wilms. American Library Assoc., 1985.

Sixth Book of Junior Authors and Illustrators. Wilson, 1989.

Special Collections in Children's Literature, ed. by Carolyn W. Field. American Library Assoc., 1982.

Subject Guide to Children's Books in Print. Bowker (annual).

PERIODICALS CONTAINING INFORMATION ON CHILDREN'S BOOKS

Appraisal: Science Books for Young People. Boston University School of Education.

Book Review Digest. Wilson.

Bookbird. International Board on Books for Young People, International Institute for Children's Literature.

The Booklist. American Library Association.

The Bulletin of the Center for Children's Books. Graduate Library School, University of Chicago Press.

Canadian Children's Literature: A Journal of Criticism and Review. Canadian Children's Literature Assoc., Canadian Children's Press.

Childhood Education. Assoc. for Childhood Education International.

Children's Literature Association Quarterly. Children's Literature Association, Purdue University Press.

Children's Literature in Education. Agathon Press, Inc.

The Horn Book Magazine. Horn Book.

Interracial Books for Children. Council on Interracial Books for Children.

Language Arts. National Council of Teachers of English.

The Lion and the Unicorn. Department of English, Brooklyn College.

Media and Methods. North American Publishing.

The New Advocate. Christopher-Gordon Publishers, Inc.

The New York Times Book Review. New York Times.

Parents' Choice: A Review of Children's Media—Books, Television, Movies, Music, Story Records, Toys and Games. Parents' Choice Foundation.

Phaedrus: An International Journal of Children's Literature Research. Fairleigh Dickinson University.

Previews: Non-Print Software & Hardware News & Reviews. Bowker.

Publishers Weekly. Bowker.

School Library Journal. Bowker.

School Media Quarterly. American Assoc. of School Librarians, American Library Assoc.

Science Books and Films. American Assoc. for the Advancement of Science.

Science and Children. National Science Teachers Assoc.

Teacher. Macmillan Professional Magazines.

Top of the News. Assoc. for Library Service to Children and the Young Adult Services Division, American Library Assoc.

The Web. Center for Language, Literature, and Reading, The Ohio State University.

Wilson Library Bulletin. Wilson.

APPENDIX B

Professional Reading

ADDITIONAL REFERENCES*

Aaron, Shirley L. *A Study of Combined School-Public Libraries*. Chicago: American Library Assoc., 1980. The author discusses the feasibility of combining public and school libraries.

Ash, Russell. *The Life and Times of Paddington Bear*. New York: Viking, 1989. The author discusses the Paddington Bear Series.

Boner, Charles, trans. *Kate Greenaway's Original Drawings for The Snow Queen*. New York: Schocken, 1981.

Bratton, J. S. *The Impact of Victorian Children's Fiction*. Barnes & Noble Imports, 1981. The author explores Victorian literature written for moral instruction.

Butler, Dorothy. *Babies Need Books: How Books Can Help Your Child Become a Happy and Involved Human Being*. New York: Atheneum, 1985. Characteristics of children age one through five are discussed and stories that will stimulate their development are presented.

Butler, Francelia. *Skipping around the World: The Ritual Nature of Folk Rhymes*. Hamden, CT: Shoe String Press, 1988. The author discusses folk rhymes from various cultures.

Butler, Francelia, and Rees, Compton, eds. *Children's Literature*. Vol. 12. New Haven, Conn.: Yale University Press. 1984. Essays on children's literature.

Carpenter, Humphrey and Prichard, Mari. *The Oxford Companion to Children's Literature*. New York: Oxford University Press, 1984. Descriptions of authors, books, characters, and literary terms.

Carr, Jo, comp. *Beyond Fact: Nonfiction for Children and Young People*. Chicago: American Library Assoc., 1982. A collection of previously published essays on nonfiction, science, history, and biography.

Chambers, Nancy, ed. *The Signal Approach to Children's Books*. Metuchen, N.J.: Scarecrow Press, 1981. A collection of articles from the British literature journal are included.

Chester, Tessa Rose. *Children's Books Research: A Practical Guide to Techniques and Sources*. Thimble Press, 1989. The author discusses various approaches for developing research.

Colwell, Eileen. *The Magic Umbrella and other Stories for Telling*. Lawrence, Mass.: Chatto, Bodley Head & Jonathan Cape, 1981. Includes information on how to tell stories to children.

Cope, Dawn, and Cope, Peter. *Humpty Dumpty's Favorite Nursery Rhymes*. New York: Holt, Rinehart & Winston, 1981. Reproductions of nursery rhyme postcards that were popular in the early 20th century.

Coplan, Kate. *Poster Ideas and Bulletin Board Techniques: For Libraries and Schools,* 2nd ed. Dobbs Ferry, N.Y.: Oceana, 1981. Illustrations and directions for developing bulletin boards are developed in school and library settings.

Crane, Walter, *An Alphabet of Old Friends and the Absurd ABC*. New York: Thames & Hudson, 1981. Reproductions of two of Walter Crane's toy books.

Donelson, Kenneth L. and Nilsen, Alleen Pace. *Literature for Today's Young Adults,* 3rd ed. Glenview Ill.: Scott, Foresman, 1989. This is a textbook that includes literature and related issues.

Egoff, Shelia. *Thursday's Child: Trends and Patterns in Contemporary Children's Literature*. Chicago: American Library Assoc., 1981. Includes a series of essays about fantasy, picture books, realistic fiction, and poetry.

Emmens, Carol A., ed. *Children's Media Market Place,* 2nd ed. New York: Neal-Schuman, 1982. This reference includes information about publishers, periodicals, and bookstores.

Engen, Rodney. *Kate Greenaway: A Biography*. New York: Schocken, 1981. A biography of the English artist.

Giblin, James Cross. *Writing Books for Young People*. The Writer, Inc., 1990. The author discusses writing for a young audience.

*These references provide additional adult sources. They are not referenced at the end of the preceding chapters.

Griswold, Jerome. *The Children's Books of Randall Jarrell*. University of Georgia, 1988. The author discusses the children's author and his works.

Hart, Thomas L. *Instruction in School Library Media Center Use [K–12]*, 2nd ed. Chicago: American Library Association, 1985.

Hearne, Betsy, and Kaye, Marilyn, eds. *Celebrating Children's Books: Essays on Children's Literature*. New York: Lothrop, Lee & Shepard, 1981. Text contains twenty-three essays.

Hickman, Janet and Cullinan, Bernice, eds. *Children's Literature in the Classroom: Weaving Charlotte's Web*. Needham Heights, MA: Christopher-Gordon Publishers, 1989. The text includes ideas for using literature.

Jacobs, Joseph, comp. *English Fairy Tales: Being the Two Collections, English Fairy Tales and More English Fairy Tales*. Lawrence, Mass.: Chatto, Bodley Head & Jonathan Cape, 1980. Versions of Jacobs's tales published in the 1890s.

Jagusch, Sybille, ed. *Stepping Away from Tradition: Children's Books of the Twenties and Thirties*. Library of Congress, 1988.

Jenkins, Peggy Davison. *The Magic of Puppetry: A Guide for Those Working with Young Children*. Englewood Cliffs, N.J.: Prentice-Hall, 1980. Illustrations and text present the instructions for making more than forty puppets.

Jenkinson, Edward B. *Censors in the Classroom: The Mind Benders*. Carbondale, Ill.: Southern Illinois University Press, 1979. Reviews censorship cases and discusses factors contributing to censorship.

Keightley, Moy. *Investigating Art: A Practical Guide for Young People*. New York: Facts on File Publications, 1984. A practical guide to art techniques.

Kellman, Amy. *Guide to Children's Libraries & Literature Outside the United States*. Chicago: American Library Assoc., 1982. A helpful location reference for libraries.

Kelly, R. Gordon, ed. *Children's Periodicals of the United States*. Westport, Conn.: Greenwood Press, 1984. A historical guide to periodicals and newspapers.

Kimmel, Margaret Mary and Segel, Elizabeth. *For Reading Out Loud! A Guide to Sharing Books With Children*. New York: Delacorte, 1988. The authors present guidelines for sharing books orally.

Kingman, Lee, ed. *The Illustrator's Notebook*. Boston: The Horn Book Inc., 1985. Children's book artists discuss their philosophies of illustration.

Kingman, Lee; Foster, Joanna; and Lontoft, Ruth Giles; comp. *Illustrators of Children's Books: 1957–1966*. Boston: The Horn Book Inc., 1968. Articles by children's book illustrators of the period.

Kingman, Lee; Hogarth, Grace Allen; and Quimby, Harriet; comp. *Illustrators of Children's Books: 1967–1976*. Boston: The Horn Book Inc., 1978.

Klemin, Diana. *The Illustrated Book: Its Art and Craft*. Greenwich, CT: The Murton Press, 1970. A contemporary survey of the work of 74 children's book artists.

Knox, Rawle, ed. *The Work of E. H. Shepard*. New York: Schocken, 1980. Samples of Shepard's work and an outline of his life are published to celebrate the hundredth anniversary of his birth.

Kohn, Rita T., and Tepper, Krysta A. *Have You Got What They Want? Public Relations Strategies for the School Librarian–Media Specialist*. Metuchen, N.J.: Scarecrow Press, 1982. Discusses various public relations strategies that may be useful to the librarian.

Kulleseid, Eleanor R. and Strickland, Dorothy S. *Literature, Literacy, and Learning: Classroom Teachers, Library Media Specialists, and the Literature-Based Curriculum*. Chicago: American Library Association, 1989. The authors discuss various aspects of literature-based programs.

Lacy, Lyn Ellen. *Art and Design in Children's Picture Books*. Chicago: American Library Association, 1986. An analysis of Caldecott-award-winning illustrations.

Lanes, Selma G. *The Art of Maurice Sendak*. New York: Harry N. Abrams, 1980. In an illustrated text, the author discusses Sendak's books, recurring themes, and early influences on his work.

Leach, Maria, ed. *Funk and Wagnall's Standard Dictionary of Folklore, Mythology, and Legend*. New York: Harper & Row, 1972.

Leland, Nita. *Exploring Color: How to Use and Control Color in Your Paintings*. Cincinnati: North Light (Writer's Digest Books), 1985.
Paintings. Cincinnati: North Light (Writer's Digest Books), 1985.

Linder, Enid and Leslie. *The Art of Beatrix Potter*. New York: Frederick Warren and Co., 1980. Examples of the art of Beatrix Potter.

Livingston, Myra Cohn. *Climb into the Bell Tower: Essays on Poetry*. New York: Harper & Row, 1990. A collection of essays.

Lystad, Mary. *From Dr. Mather to Dr. Seuss: 200 Years of American Books for Children*. Cambridge, Mass.: Schenkman, 1980. The author examines the changing values expressed in children's literature.

Mahony, Bertha E.; Latimer, Louise; and Folmsbee, Beulah; comp. *Illustrations of Children's Books: 1744–1945*. Boston: The Horn Book Inc., 1947. A history of illustration.

Manguel, Alberto and Guadalupi, Gianni. *The Dictionary of Imaginary Places*. New York: Macmillan Publishing Co., 1980.

Moore, Vardine. *The Pleasure of Poetry with and by Children: A Handbook*. Metuchen, N.J.: Scarecrow Press, 1981. Includes poems and suggestions for sharing them with children.

Nickel, Mildred. *Steps to Service: A Handbook of Procedures for the School Library Media Center*. Chicago. American Library Association, 1984.

Opie, Iona Archibald, and Opie, Peter. *A Nursery Companion*. New York: Oxford University Press, 1980. A reproduction of a collection of nineteenth-century alphabets, verses, and grammars.

Opie, Iona Archibald; Opie, Robert; and Alderson, Brian. *The Treasures of Childhood: Books, Toys, and Games from the Opie Collection*. Arcade, 1990. The examples are taken from the collection of early books, toys, and games.

Painter, William M. *Musical Story Hours: Using Music With Storytelling and Puppetry*. Library Professional Publications, 1989. The author provides suggestions for adding music.

Paterson, Katherine. *Gates of Excellence: On Reading and Writing Books for Children,* New York: Lodestar Books, 1981. Includes speeches and book reviews by the Newbery author.

Paulin, Mary Ann. *Creative Uses of Children's Literature*. Hamden, CT; Shoestring Press 1982. Ideas for using books in the library.

Polette, Nancy, and Hamlin, Marjorie. *Exploring Books with Gifted Children*. Littleton, Colo.: Libraries Unlimited, 1980. Units are developed around style, theme, character, and setting in books by L'Engle, Konigsburg, Paterson, Alexander, Lenski, and Cleavers.

Pellowski, Anne. *Hidden Stories in Plants: Unusual and Easy-to-Tell Stories from Around the World together with Creative Things to Do While Telling Them*. New York: Macmillan, 1990.

Potter, Beatrix. *Beatrix Potter's Letters*. New York: Warne, 1989. The text includes letters written by the famous author of *Peter Rabbit*.

Potter, Beatrix. *The Journal of Beatrix Potter, 1881–1897*. New York: Warne, 1989.

Preiss, Byron, ed. *The Art of Leo & Diane Dillon*. New York: Ballantine Books, 1981. Text and illustrations provide a review of the Dillons' works from the 1950s to the present.

Rees, David. *Painted Desert, Green Shade: Essays on Contemporary Writers for Children*. Boston: Horn Book, 1989.

Schwarcz, Joseph H. *Ways of the Illustrator: Visual Communication in Children's Literature*. Chicago: American Library Assoc., 1982. Discusses illustrations in children's books.

Scott, Dorothea Hayward. *Chinese Popular Literature and the Child*. Chicago: American Library Assoc., 1980. Author discusses oral and literary heritage of the Chinese people.

Senick, Gerald, ed. *Children's Literature Review,* Vol. 14. Detroit: Gale Research Co., 1988. This is a collection of reviews, criticism, and commentary on books for children.

Shulevitz, Uri. *Writing with Pictures: How to Write and Illustrate Children's Books*. New York: Waterson-Guptill Publishers, 1985. A well-known illustrator provides a guide for aspiring children's book artists.

Sierra, Judy. *Twice Upon a Time: Stories to Tell, Retell, Act Out and Write About*. Wilson, 1989.

Spiegel, Dixie Lee. *Reading for Pleasure: Guidelines*. Newark, Del.: International Reading Assoc., 1981. Discusses the development of a recreational reading program.

Stewig, John Warren and Sebesta, Sam Leaton. *Using Literature in the Elementary Classroom,* third edition. Urbana, Ill.: National Council of Teachers of English, 1989. The authors present ideas for bringing literature into the classroom.

Trelease, James. *The Read-Aloud Handbook*. New York: Penguin, 1982. Presents practical suggestions for sharing books orally with children.

Tunnell, Michael O. *The Prydain Companion: A Reference Guide to Lloyd Alexander's Prydain Chronicles*. Greenwood, 1989.

Vandergrift, Kay E. *Child and Story: The Literary Connection*. Edited by Jane Anne Hannigan. New York: Neal-Schuman, 1981. Explores literary form, elements of the story, and practical suggestions for using literature.

Van Orden, Phyllis. *The Collection Program in Elementary and Middle Schools: Concepts, Practices, and Information Sources*. Illustrated by William R. Harper. Littleton, Colo.: Libraries Unlimited, 1982. A guide for elementary and middle school libraries.

White, Gabriel. *Edward Ardizzone: Artist and Illustrator*. New York: Schocken, 1980. Text includes samples of Ardizzone's work, discussion of his style, and information about his personal life.

Yolen, Jane. *Touch Magic: Fantasy, Faerie and Folklore in the Literature of Childhood*. New York: Putnam/Philomel, 1981. Yolen stresses the importance of folklore in stimulating children's emotional and intellectual growth.

Zinsser, William, ed. *Worlds of Childhood: The Art and Craft of Writing for Children*. Boston: Houghton, Mifflin, 1990.

APPENDIX C
Book Awards

AWARDS FOR OUTSTANDING CHILDREN'S BOOKS ARE PRESENTED yearly by organizations, publishers, and other interested groups. These awards have multiplied since the instigation of the Newbery Award in 1922. The following lists include the books, authors, and illustrators who have received the Caldecott Medal and honor awards, the Newbery Medal and honor awards, the Children's Book Award, the Hans Christian Andersen International Medal, or the Laura Ingalls Wilder Medal. Following this list are examples of additional awards presented in the United States, Canada, and the United Kingdom. Complete lists of book award winners, including United States, British Commonwealth, and international awards, are found in *Children's Books: Awards and Prizes,* compiled and edited by the Children's Book Council. An annotated bibliography of Newbery and Caldecott books is available in *Newbery and Caldecott Medal and Honor Books,* compiled by Linda Kauffman Peterson and Marilyn Leathers Solt.

CALDECOTT MEDAL AND HONOR AWARDS

The Caldecott awards, named after a British illustrator of children's books, Randolph Caldecott, are granted by the Children's Services Division of the American Library Association. The medal and honor awards are presented annually to the illustrators of the most distinguished picture books published in the United States. The first Caldecott Medal and honor awards were presented in 1938.

1938 *Animals of the Bible* by Helen Dean Fish, ill. by Dorothy P. Lathrop, Stokes

Honor Books: *Seven Simeon: A Russian Tale* by Boris Artzybasheff, Viking; *Four and Twenty Blackbirds: Nursery Rhymes of Yesterday Recalled for Children of Today* by Helen Dean Fish, ill. by Robert Lawson, Stokes

1939 *Mei Li* by Thomas Handforth, Doubleday

Honor Books: *The Forest Pool* by Laura Adams Armer, Longmans; *Wee Gillis* by Munro Leaf, ill. by Robert Lawson, Viking; *Snow White and the Seven Dwarfs* by Wanda Gág, Coward; *Barkis* by Clare Newberry, Harper; *Andy and the Lion: A Tale of Kindness Remembered or the Power of Gratitude* by James Daugherty, Viking

1940 *Abraham Lincoln* by Ingri and Edgar Parin d'Aulaire, Doubleday

Honor Books: *Cock-a-Doodle Doo: The Story of a Little Red Rooster* by Berta and Elmer Hader, Macmillan; *Madeline* by Ludwig Bemelmans, Simon & Schuster; *The Ageless Story,* by Lauren Ford, Dodd

1941 *They Were Strong and Good* by Robert Lawson, Viking

Honor Book: *April's Kittens* by Clare Newberry, Harper

1942 *Make Way for Ducklings* by Robert McCloskey, Viking

Honor Books: *An American ABC* by Maud and Miska Petersham, Macmillan; *In my Mother's House* by Ann Nolan Clark, ill. by Velino Herrera, Viking; *Paddle-to-the-Sea* by Holling C. Holling, Houghton; *Nothing at All* by Wanda Gág, Coward

1943 *The Little House* by Virginia Lee Burton, Houghton

Honor Books: *Dash and Dart* by Mary and Conrad Buff, Viking; *Marshmallow* by Clare Newberry, Harper

1944 *Many Moons* by James Thurber, ill. by Louis Slobodkin, Harcourt Brace Jovanovich

Honor Books: *Small Rain: Verses from the Bible* selected by Jessie Orton Jones, ill. by Elizabeth Orton Jones, Viking; *Pierre Pigeon* by Lee Kingman, ill. by Arnold E. Bare, Houghton; *The Mighty Hunter* by Berta and Elmer Hader, Macmillan; *A Child's Good Night Book* by Margaret Wise Brown, ill. by Jean Charlot, W. R. Scott; *Good Luck Horse* by Chih-Yi Chan, ill. by Plato Chan, Whittlesey

1945 *Prayer for a Child* by Rachel Field, ill. by Elizabeth Orton Jones, Macmillan

Honor Books: *Mother Goose: Seventy-Seven Verses with Pictures* ill. by Tasha Tudor, Walck; *In the Forest* by Marie Hall Ets, Viking; *Yonie Wondernose* by Marguerite de Angeli, Doubleday; *The Christmas Anna Angel* by Ruth Sawyer, ill. by Kate Seredy, Viking

1946 *The Rooster Crows . . .* ill. by Maud and Miska Petersham, Macmillan

Honor Books: *Little Lost Lamb* by Golden MacDonald, ill. by Leonard Weisgard, Doubleday; *Sing Mother Goose* by Opal Wheeler, ill. by Marjorie Torrey, Dutton; *My Mother Is the Most Beautiful Woman in the World* by Becky Reyher, ill. by Ruth Gannett, Lothrop; *You Can Write Chinese* by Kurt Wiese, Viking

1947 *The Little Island* by Golden MacDonald, ill. by Leonard Weisgard, Doubleday

Honor Books: *Rain Drop Splash* by Alvin Tresselt, ill. by Leonard Weisgard, Lothrop; *Boats on the River* by Marjorie Flack, ill. by Jay Hyde Barnum, Viking; *Timothy Turtle* by Al Graham, ill. by Tony Palazzo, Viking; *Pedro, the Angel of Olvera Street* by Leo Politi, Scribner's; *Sing in Praise: A Collection of the Best Loved Hymns* by Opal Wheeler, ill. by Marjorie Torrey, Dutton

1948 *White Snow, Bright Snow* by Alvin Tresselt, ill. by Roger Duvoisin, Lothrop

Honor Books: *Stone Soup: An Old Tale* by Marcia Brown, Scribner's; *McElligot's Pool* by Dr. Seuss, Random; *Bambino the Clown* by George Schreiber, Viking; *Roger and the Fox* by Lavinia Davis, ill. by Hildegard Woodward, Doubleday; *Song of Robin Hood* ed. by Anne Malcolmson, ill. by Virginia Lee Burton, Houghton

1949 *The Big Snow* by Berta and Elmer Hader, Macmillan

Honor Books: *Blueberries for Sal* by Robert McCloskey, Viking; *All Around the Town* by Phyllis McGinley, ill. by Helen Stone, Lippincott; *Juanita* by Leo Politi, Scribner's; *Fish in the Air* by Kurt Wiese, Viking

1950 *Song of the Swallows* by Leo Politi, Scribner's

Honor Books: *America's Ethan Allen* by Stewart Holbrook, ill. by Lynd Ward, Houghton; *The Wild Birthday Cake* by Lavinia Davis, ill. by Hildegard Woodward, Doubleday; *The Happy Day* by Ruth Krauss, ill. by Marc Simont, Harper; *Bartholomew and the Oobleck* by Dr. Seuss, Random; *Henry Fisherman* by Marcia Brown, Scribner's

1951 *The Egg Tree* by Katherine Milhous, Scribner's

Honor Books: *Dick Whittington and His Cat* by Marcia Brown, Scribner's; *The Two Reds* by William Lipkind, ill. by Nicholas Mordvinoff, Harcourt Brace Jovanovich; *If I Ran the Zoo* by Dr. Seuss, Random; *The Most Wonderful Doll in the World* by Phyllis McGinley, ill. by Helen Stone, Lippincott; *T-Bone, the Baby Sitter* by Clare Newberry, Harper

1952 *Finders Keepers* by William Lipkind, ill. by Nicholas Mordvinoff, Harcourt Brace Jovanovich

Honor Books: *Mr. T. W. Anthony Wood: The Story of a Cat and a Dog and Mouse* by Marie Hall Ets, Viking; *Skipper John's Cook* by Marcia Brown, Scribner's; *All Falling Down* by Gene Zion, ill. by Margaret Bloy Graham, Harper; *Bear Party* by William Pène du Bois, Viking; *Feather Mountain* by Elizabeth Olds, Houghton

1953 *The Biggest Bear* by Lynd Ward, Houghton

Honor Books: *Puss in Boots* by Charles Perrault, ill. and tr. by Marcia Brown, Scribner's; *One Morning in Maine* by Robert McCloskey, Viking; *Ape in a Cape: An Alphabet of Odd Animals* by Fritz Eichenberg, Harcourt Brace Jovanovich; *The Storm Book* by Charlotte Zolotow, ill. by Margaret Bloy Graham, Harper; *Five Little Monkeys* by Juliet Kepes, Houghton

1954 *Madeline's Rescue* by Ludwig Bemelmans, Viking

Honor Books: *Journey Cake, Ho!* by Ruth Sawyer, ill. by Robert McCloskey, Viking; *When Will the World Be Mine?* by Miriam Schlein, ill. by Jean Charlot, W. R. Scott; *The Steadfast Tin Soldier* by Hans Christian Andersen, ill. by Marcia Brown, Scribner's; *A Very Special House* by Ruth Krauss, ill. by Maurice Sendak, Harper; *Green Eyes* by A. Birnbaum, Capitol

1955 *Cinderella, or the Little Glass Slipper* by Charles Perrault, tr. and ill. by Marcia Brown, Scribner's

Honor Books: *Book of Nursery and Mother Goose Rhymes,* ill. by Marguerite de Angeli, Doubleday; *Wheel on the Chimney* by Margaret Wise Brown, ill. by Tibor Gergely, Lippincott; *The Thanksgiving Story* by Alice Dalgliesh, ill. by Helen Sewell, Scribner's

1956 *Frog Went A-Courtin'* ed. by John Langstaff, ill. by Feodor Rojankovsky, Harcourt Brace Jovanovich

Honor Books: *Play with Me* by Marie Hall Ets, Viking; *Crow Boy* by Taro Yashima, Viking

1957 *A Tree Is Nice* by Janice May Udry, ill. by Marc Simont, Harper

Honor Books: *Mr. Penny's Race Horse* by Marie Hall Ets, Viking; *1 Is One* by Tasha Tudor, Walck; *Anatole* by Eve Titus, ill. by Paul Galdone, McGraw; *Gillespie and the Guards* by Benjamin Elkin, ill. by James Daugherty, Viking; *Lion* by William Pène du Bois, Viking

1958 *Time of Wonder* by Robert McCloskey, Viking

Honor Books: *Fly High, Fly Low* by Don Freeman, Viking; *Anatole and the Cat* by Eve Titus, ill. by Paul Galdone, McGraw

1959 *Chanticleer and the Fox* adapted from Chaucer and ill. by Barbara Cooney, Crowell

Honor Books: *The House That Jack Built: A Picture Book in Two Languages* by Antonio Frasconi, Harcourt Brace Jovanovich; *What Do You Say, Dear?* by Sesyle Joslin, ill. by Maurice Sendak, W. R. Scott; *Umbrella* by Taro Yashima, Viking

1960 *Nine Days to Christmas* by Marie Hall Ets and Aurora Labastida, ill. by Marie Hall Ets, Viking

Honor Books: *Houses from the Sea* by Alice E. Goudey, ill. by Adrienne Adams, Scribner's; *The Moon Jumpers* by Janice May Udry, ill. by Maurice Sendak, Harper

1961 *Baboushka and the Three Kings* by Ruth Robbins, ill. by Nicolas Sidjakov, Parnassus

Honor Book: *Inch by Inch* by Leo Lionni, Obolensky

1962 *Once a Mouse . . .* by Marcia Brown, Scribner's

Honor Books: *The Fox Went Out on a Chilly Night: An Old Song* by Peter Spier, Doubleday; *Little Bear's Visit* by Else Holmelund Minarik, ill. by Maurice Sendak, Harper; *The Day We Saw the Sun Come Up* by Alice E. Goudey, ill. by Adrienne Adams, Scribner's

1963 *The Snowy Day* by Ezra Jack Keats, Viking

Honor Books: *The Sun Is a Golden Earring* by Natalia M. Belting, ill. by Bernarda Bryson, Holt; *Mr. Rabbit and the Lovely Present* by Charlotte Zolotow, ill. by Maurice Sendak, Harper

1964 *Where the Wild Things Are* by Maurice Sendak, Harper

Honor Books: *Swimmy* by Leo Lionni, Pantheon; *All in the Morning Early* by Sorche Nic Leodhas, ill. by Evaline Ness, Holt; *Mother Goose and Nursery Rhymes* ill. by Philip Reed, Atheneum

1965 *May I Bring a Friend?* by Beatrice Schenk de Regniers, ill. by Beni Montresor, Atheneum

Honor Books: *Rain Makes Applesauce* by Julian Scheer, ill. by Marvin Bileck, Holiday; *The Wave* by Margaret Hodges, ill. by Blair Lent, Houghton; *A Pocketful of Cricket* by Rebecca Caudill, ill. by Evaline Ness, Holt

1966 *Always Room for One More* by Sorche Nic Leodhas, ill. by Nonny Hogrogian, Holt

Honor Books: *Hide and Seek Fog* by Alvin Tresselt, ill. by Roger Duvoisin, Lothrop; *Just Me* by Marie Hall Ets, Viking; *Tom Tit Tot* by Evaline Ness, Scribner's

1967 *Sam, Bangs & Moonshine* by Evaline Ness, Holt

Honor Book: *One Wide River to Cross* by Barbara Emberley, ill. by Ed Emberley, Prentice

1968 *Drummer Hoff* by Barbara Emberley, ill. by Ed Emberley, Prentice

Honor Books: *Frederick* by Leo Lionni, Pantheon; *Seashore Story* by Taro Yashima, Viking; *The Emperor and the Kite* by Jane Yolen, ill. by Ed Young, World

1969 *The Fool of the World and the Flying Ship* by Arthur Ransome, ill. by Uri Shulevitz, Farrar

Honor Book: *Why the Sun and the Moon Live in the Sky: An African Folktale* by Elphinstone Dayrell, ill. by Blair Lent, Houghton

1970 *Sylvester and the Magic Pebble* by William Steig, Windmill

Honor Books: *Goggles!* by Ezra Jack Keats, Macmillan; *Alexander and the Wind-Up Mouse* by Leo Lionni, Pantheon; *Pop Corn and Ma Goodness* by Edna Mitchell Preston, ill. by Robert Andrew Parker, Viking; *Thy Friend, Obadiah* by Brinton Turkle, Viking; *The Judge: An Untrue Tale* by Harve Zemach, ill. by Margot Zemach, Farrar

1971 *A Story—A Story: An African Tale* by Gail E. Haley, Atheneum

Honor Books: *The Angry Moon* by William Sleator, ill. by Blair Lent, Atlantic-Little; *Frog and Toad Are Friends* by Arnold Lobel, Harper; *In the Night Kitchen* by Maurice Sendak, Harper

1972 *One Fine Day* by Nonny Hogrogian, Macmillan

Honor Books: *If All the Seas Were One Sea* by Janina Domanska, Macmillan; *Moja Means One: Swahili Counting Book* by Muriel Feelings, ill. by Tom Feelings, Dial; *Hildilid's Night* by Cheli Duran Ryan, ill. by Arnold Lobel, Macmillan

1973 *The Funny Little Woman* retold by Arlene Mosel, ill. by Blair Lent, Dutton

Honor Books: *Anansi the Spider: A Tale from the Ashanti* adapted and ill. by Gerald McDermott, Holt; *Hosie's Alphabet* by Hosea Tobias and Lisa Baskin, ill. by Leonard Baskin, Viking; *Snow White and the Seven Dwarfs* translated by Randall Jarrell, ill. by Nancy Ekholm Burkert, Farrar; *When Clay Sings* by Byrd Baylor, ill. by Tom Bahti, Scribner's

1974 *Duffy and the Devil* by Harve Zemach, ill. by Margot Zemach, Farrar

Honor Books: *Three Jovial Huntsmen* by Susan Jeffers, Bradbury; *Cathedral: The Story of Its Construction* by David Macaulay, Houghton

1975 *Arrow to the Sun* adapted and ill. by Gerald McDermott, Viking

Honor Book: *Jambo Means Hello: A Swahili Alphabet Book* by Muriel Feelings, ill. by Tom Feelings, Dial

1976 *Why Mosquitoes Buzz in People's Ears* retold by Verna Aardema, ill. by Leo and Diane Dillon, Dial

Honor Books: *The Desert Is Theirs* by Byrd Baylor, ill. by Peter Parnall, Scribner's; *Strega Nona* retold and ill. by Tomie de Paola, Prentice

1977 *Ashanti to Zulu: African Traditions* by Margaret Musgrove, ill. by Leo and Diane Dillon, Dial

Honor Books: *The Amazing Bone* by William Steig, Farrar; *The Contest* retold and ill. by Nony Hogrogian, Greenwillow; *Fish for Supper* by M. B. Goffstein, Dial; *The Golem: A Jewish Legend* by Beverly Brodsky McDermott, Lippincott; *Hawk, I'm Your Brother* by Byrd Baylor, ill. by Peter Parnall, Scribner's

1978 *Noah's Ark* by Peter Spier, Doubleday

Honor Books: *Castle* by David Macaulay, Houghton; *It Could Always Be Worse* retold and ill. by Margot Zemach, Farrar

1979 *The Girl Who Loved Wild Horses* by Paul Goble, Bradbury

Honor Books: *Freight Train* by Donald Crews, Greenwillow; *The Way to Start a Day* by Byrd Baylor, ill. by Peter Parnall, Scribner's

1980 *Ox-Cart Man* by Donald Hall, ill. by Barbara Cooney, Viking

Honor Books: *Ben's Trumpet* by Rachel Isadora, Greenwillow; *The Treasure* by Uri Shulevitz, Farrar; *The Garden of Abdul Gasazi* by Chris Van Allsburg, Houghton

1981 *Fables* by Arnold Lobel, Harper

Honor Books: *The Bremen-Town Musicians* by Ilse Plume, Doubleday; *The Grey Lady and the Strawberry Snatcher* by Molly Bang, Four Winds; *Mice Twice* by Joseph Low, Atheneum; *Truck* by Donald Crews, Greenwillow

1982 *Jumanji* by Christ Van Allsburg, Houghton
Honor Books: *A Visit to William Blake's Inn: Poems for Innocent and Experienced Travelers* by Nancy Willard, ill. by Alice and Martin Provensen, Harcourt Brace Jovanovich; *Where the Buffaloes Begin* by Olaf Baker, ill. by Stephen Gammell, Warner; *On Market Street* by Arnold Lobel, ill. by Anita Lobel, Greenwillow; *Outside Over There* by Maurice Sendak, Harper
1983 *Shadow* by Blaise Cendrars, ill. by Marcia Brown, Scribner's
Honor Books: *When I Was Young in the Mountains* by Cynthia Rylant, ill. by Diane Goode, Dutton; *Chair for My Mother* by Vera B. Williams, Morrow
1984 *The Glorious Flight: Across the Channel with Louis Bleriot* by Alice and Martin Provensen, Viking
Honor Books: *Ten, Nine, Eight* by Molly Bang, Greenwillow; *Little Red Riding Hood* retold and ill. by Trina Schart Hyman, Holiday House
1985 *St. George and the Dragon* retold by Margaret Hodges, ill. by Trina Schart Hyman, Little, Brown
Honor Books: *Hansel and Gretel* retold by Rika Lesser, ill. by Paul O. Zelinsky, Dodd; *Have You Seen My Duckling?* by Nancy Tafuri, Greenwillow; *The Story of Jumping Mouse* by John Steptoe, Lothrop
1986 *The Polar Express* by Chris Van Allsburg, Houghton
Honor Books: *King Bidgood's in the Bathtub* by Audrey Wood, ill. by Don Wood, Harcourt; *The Relatives Came* by Cynthia Rylant, ill. by Stephen Gammell, Bradbury
1987 *Hey, Al* by Arthur Yorinks, ill. by Richard Egielski, Farrar, Straus and Giroux
Honor Books: *Alphabatics* by Suse MacDonald, Bradbury; *Rumpelstiltskin* retold and ill. by Paul O. Zelinsky; *The Village of Round and Square Houses* by Ann Grifalconi, Little, Brown
1988 *Owl Moon* by Jane Yolen, ill. by John Schoenherr, Philomel.
Honor Book: *Mufaro's Beautiful Daughters: An African Tale* by John Steptoe, Lothrop, Lee & Shepard
1989 *Song and Dance Man* by Karen Ackerman, ill. by Stephen Gammell
Honor Books: *The Boy of the Three-Year Nap* by Dianne Snyder, ill. by Allen Say, Houghton Mifflin; *Free Fall* by David Wiesner, Lothrop, Lee & Shepard; *Goldilocks* retold and ill. by James Marshall, Dial; *Mirandy and Brother Wind* by Patricia C. McKissack, ill. by Jerry Pinkney, Knopf
1990 *Lon Po Po: A Red-Riding Hood Story from China* translated and ill. by Ed Young, Philomel
Honor Books: *Bill Peet: An Autobiography* by Bill Peet, Houghton Mifflin; *Color Zoo* by Lois Ehlert, Lippincott; *Hershel and the Hanukkah Goblins* by Eric Kimmel, ill. by Trina Schart Hyman, Holiday House; *The Talking Egg* by Robert D. SanSouci, ill. by Jerry Pinkney, Dial

THE NEWBERY MEDAL AND HONOR AWARDS

The Newbery award, named after the first English publisher of books for children, John Newbery, is granted by the Children's Services Division of the American Library Association. The medal and honor awards are presented annually for the most distinguished contributions to children's literature published in the United States. The first Newbery Medal and honor awards were presented in 1922.

1922 *The Story of Mankind* by Hendrik Willem van Loon, Liveright
Honor Books: *The Great Quest* by Charles Hawes, Little; *Cedric the Forester* by Bernard Marshall, Appleton; *The Old Tobacco Shop: A True Account of What Befell a Little Boy in Search of Adventure* by William Bowen, Macmillan; *The Golden Fleece and the Heroes Who Lived before Achilles* by Padriac Colum, Macmillan; *Windy Hill* by Cornelia Meigs, Macmillan
1923 *The Voyages of Doctor Dolittle* by Hugh Lofting, Lippincott
Honor Books: No record
1924 *The Dark Frigate* by Charles Hawes, Atlantic/Little
Honor Books: No record
1925 *Tales from Silver Lands* by Charles Finger, Doubleday
Honor Books: *Nicholas: A Manhattan Christmas Story* by Anne Carroll Moore, Putnam; *Dream Coach* by Anne Parrish, Macmillan
1926 *Shen of the Sea* by Arthur Bowie Chrisman, Dutton
Honor Book: *Voyagers: Being Legends and Romances of Atlantic Discovery* by Padraic Colum, Macmillan
1927 *Smoky, the Cowhorse* by Will James, Scribner's
Honor Books: No record
1928 *Gayneck, The Story of a Pigeon* by Dhan Gopal Mukerji, Dutton
Honor Books: *The Wonder Smith and His Son: A Tale from the Golden Childhood of the World* by Ella Young, Longmans; *Downright Dencey* by Caroline Snedeker, Doubleday
1929 *The Trumpeter of Krakow* by Eric P. Kelly, Macmillan
Honor Books: *Pigtail of Ah Lee Ben Loo* by John Bennett, Longmans; *Millions of Cats* by Wanda Gág, Coward; *The Boy Who Was* by Grace Hallock, Dutton; *Clearing Weather* by Cornelia Meigs, Little; *Runaway Papoose* by Grace Moon, Doubleday; *Tod of the Fens* by Elinor Whitney, Macmillan
1930 *Hitty, Her First Hundred Years* by Rachel Field, Macmillan
Honor Books: *Daughter of the Seine: The Life of Madame Roland* by Jeanette Eaton, Harper; *Pran of Albania* by Elizabeth Miller, Doubleday; *Jumping-off Place* by Marian Hurd McNeely, Longmans; *Tangle-coated Horse and Other Tales: Episodes from the Fionn Saga* by Ella Young, Longmans; *Vaino: A Boy of New England* by Julia Davis Adams, Dutton; *Little Blacknose* by Hildegarde Swift, Harcourt Brace Jovanovich

1931 *The Cat Who Went to Heaven* by Elizabeth Coatsworth, Macmillan

Honor Books: *Floating Island* by Anne Parrish, Harper; *The Dark Star of Itza: The Story of a Pagan Princess* by Alida Malkus, Harcourt Brace Jovanovich; *Queer Person* by Ralph Hubbard, Doubleday; *Mountains Are Free* by Julia Davis Adams, Dutton; *Spice and the Devil's Cave* by Agnes Hewes, Knopf; *Meggy Macintosh* by Elizabeth Janet Gray, Doubleday; *Garram the Hunter: A Boy of the Hill Tribes* by Herbert Best, Doubleday; *Ood-Le-Uk the Wanderer* by Alice Lide and Margaret Johansen, Little

1932 *Waterless Mountain* by Laura Adams Armer, Longmans

Honor Books: *The Fairy Circus* by Dorothy P. Lathrop, Macmillan; *Calico Bush* by Rachel Field, Macmillan; *Boy of the South Seas* by Eunice Tietjens, Coward; *Out of the Flame* by Eloise Lownsbery, Longmans; *Jane's Island* by Marjorie Allee, Houghton; *Truce of the Wolf and Other Tales of Old Italy* by Mary Gould Davis, Harcourt Brace Jovanovich

1933 *Young Fu of the Upper Yangtze* by Elizabeth Foreman Lewis, Winston

Honor Books: *Swift Rivers* by Cornelia Meigs, Little; *The Railroad to Freedom: A Story of the Civil War* by Hildegarde Swift, Harcourt Brace Jovanovich; *Children of the Soil: A Story of Scandinavia* by Nora Burglon, Doubleday

1934 *Invincible Louisa: The Story of the Author of 'Little Women'* by Cornelia Meigs, Little

Honor Books: *The Forgotten Daughter* by Caroline Snedeker, Doubleday; *Swords of Steel* by Elsie Singmaster, Houghton; *ABC Bunny* by Wanda Gág, Coward; *Winged Girl of Knossos* by Erik Berry, Appleton; *New Land* by Sarah Schmidt, McBride; *Big Tree of Bunlahy: Stories of My Own Countryside* by Padraic Colum, Macmillan; *Glory of the Seas* by Agnes Hewes, Knopf; *Apprentice of Florence* by Ann Kyle, Houghton

1935 *Dobry* by Monica Shannon, Viking

Honor Books: *Pageant of Chinese History* by Elizabeth Seeger, Longmans; *Davy Crockett* by Constance Rourke, Harcourt Brace Jovanovich; *Day on Skates: The Story of a Dutch Picnic* by Hilda Van Stockum, Harper

1936 *Caddie Woodlawn* by Carol Ryrie Brink, Macmillan

Honor Books: *Honk, the Moose* by Phil Stong, Dodd; *The Good Master* by Kate Seredy, Viking; *Young Walter Scott* by Elizabeth Janet Gray, Viking; *All Sail Set: A Romance of the Flying Cloud* by Armstrong Sperry, Winston

1937 *Roller Skates* by Ruth Sawyer, Viking

Honor Books: *Phoebe Fairchild: Her Book* by Lois Lenski, Stokes; *Whistler's Van* by Idwal Jones, Viking; *Golden Basket* by Ludwig Bemelmans, Viking; *Winterbound* by Margery Bianco, Viking; *Audubon* by Constance Rourke, Harcourt Brace Jovanovich; *The Codfish Musket* by Agnes Hewes, Doubleday

1938 *The White Stag* by Kate Seredy, Viking

Honor Books: *Pecos Bill* by James Cloyd Bowman, Little; *Bright Island* by Mabel Robinson, Random; *On the Banks of Plum Creek* by Laura Ingalls Wilder, Harper

1939 *Thimble Summer* by Elizabeth Enright, Rinehart

Honor Books: *Nino* by Valenti Angelo, Viking; *Mr. Popper's Penguins* by Richard and Florence Atwater, Little; *"Hello the Boat!"* by Phyllis Crawford, Holt; *Leader by Destiny: George Washington, Man and Patriot* by Jeanette Eaton, Harcourt Brace Jovanovich; *Penn* by Elizabeth Janet Gray, Viking

1940 *Daniel Boone* by James Daugherty, Viking

Honor Books: *The Singing Tree* by Kate Seredy, Viking; *Runner of the Mountain Tops: The Life of Louis Agassiz* by Mabel Robinson, Random; *By the Shores of Silver Lake* by Laura Ingalls Wilder, Harper; *Boy with a Pack* by Stephen W. Meader, Harcourt Brace Jovanovich

1941 *Call It Courage* by Armstrong Sperry, Macmillan

Honor Books: *Blue Willow* by Doris Gates, Viking; *Young Mac of Fort Vancouver* by Mary Jane Carr, Crowell; *The Long Winter* by Laura Ingalls Wilder, Harper; *Nansen* by Anna Gertrude Hall, Viking

1942 *The Matchlock Gun* by Walter D. Edmonds, Dodd

Honor Books: *Little Town on the Prairie* by Laura Ingalls Wilder, Harper; *George Washington's World* by Genevieve Foster, Scribner's; *Indian Captive: The Story of Mary Jemison* by Lois Lenski, Lippincott; *Down Ryton Water* by Eva Roe Gaggin, Viking

1943 *Adam of the Road* by Elizabeth Janet Gray, Viking

Honor Books: *The Middle Moffat* by Eleanor Estes, Harcourt Brace Jovanovich; *Have You Seen Tom Thumb?* by Mabel Leigh Hunt, Lippincott

1944 *Johnny Tremain* by Esther Forbes, Houghton

Honor Books: *The Happy Golden Years* by Laura Ingalls Wilder, Harper; *Fog Magic* by Julia Sauer, Viking; *Rufus M.* by Eleanor Estes, Harcourt Brace Jovanovich; *Mountain Born* by Elizabeth Yates, Coward

1945 *Rabbit Hill* by Robert Lawson, Viking

Honor Books: *The Hundred Dresses* by Eleanor Estes, Harcourt Brace Jovanovich; *The Silver Pencil* by Alice Dalgliesh, Scribner's; *Abraham Lincoln's World* by Genevieve Foster, Scribner's; *Lone Journey: The Life of Roger Williams* by Jeanette Eaton, Harcourt Brace Jovanovich

1946 *Strawberry Girl* by Lois Lenski, Lippincott

Honor Books: *Justin Morgan Had a Horse* by Marguerite Henry, Rand; *The Moved-Outers* by Florence Crannell Means, Houghton; *Bhimsa, the Dancing Bear* by Christine Weston, Scribner's; *New Found World* by Katherine Shippen, Viking

1947 *Miss Hickory* by Carolyn Sherwin Bailey, Viking

Honor Books: *Wonderful Year* by Nancy Barnes, Messner; *Big Tree* by Mary and Conrad Buff, Viking; *The Heavenly Tenants* by William Maxwell, Harper; *The Avion My Uncle Flew* by Cyrus Fisher, Appleton; *The Hidden Treasure of Glaston* by Eleanore Jewett, Viking

1948 *The Twenty-One Balloons* by William Pène du Bois, Viking

Honor Books: *Pancakes-Paris* by Claire Huchet Bishop, Viking; *Le Lun, Lad of Courage* by Carolyn Treffinger, Abindgon; *The Quaint and Curious Quest of Johnny Longfoot, The Shoe-King's Son* by Catherine Besterman, Bobbs; *The Cow-tail Switch, and Other West African Stories* by Harold Courlander, Holt; *Misty of Chincoteague* by Marguerite Henry, Rand

1949 *King of the Wind* by Marguerite Henry, Rand

Honor Books: *Seabird* by Holling C. Holling, Houghton; *Daughter of the Mountains* by Louise Rankin, Viking; *My Father's Dragon* by Ruth S. Gannett, Random; *Story of the Negro* by Arna Bontemps, Knopf

1950 *The Door in the Wall* by Marguerite de Angeli, Doubleday

Honor Books: *Tree of Freedom* by Rebecca Caudill, Viking; *The Blue Cat of Castle Town* by Catherine Coblentz, Longmans; *Kildee House* by Rutherford Montgomery, Doubleday; *George Washington* by Genevieve Foster, Scribner's; *Song of the Pines: A Story of Norwegian Lumbering in Wisconsin* by Walter and Marion Havighurst, Winston

1951 *Amos Fortune, Free Man* by Elizabeth Yates, Aladdin

Honor Books: *Better Known as Johnny Appleseed* by Mabel Leigh Hunt, Lippincott; *Ghandi, Fighter Without a Sword* by Jeanette Eaton, Morrow; *Abraham Lincoln, Friend of the People* by Clara Ingram Judson, Follett; *The Story of Appleby Capple* by Anne Parrish, Harper

1952 *Ginger Pye* by Eleanor Estes, Harcourt Brace Jovanovich

Honor Books: *Americans Before Columbus* by Elizabeth Baity, Viking; *Minn of the Mississippi* by Holling C. Holling, Houghton; *The Defender* by Nicholas Kalashnikoff, Scribner's; *The Light at Tern Rock* by Julia Sauer, Viking; *The Apple and the Arrow* by Mary and Conrad Buff, Houghton

1953 *Secret of the Andes* by Ann Nolan Clark, Viking

Honor Books: *Charlotte's Web* by E. B. White, Harper; *Moccasin Trail* by Eloise McGraw, Coward; *Red Sails to Capri* by Ann Weil, Viking; *The Bears on Hemlock Mountain* by Alice Dalgliesh, Scribner's; *Birthdays of Freedom, Vol. 1*, by Genevieve Foster, Scribner's

1954 *. . . and now Miguel* by Joseph Krumgold, Crowell

Honor Books: *All Alone* by Claire Huchet Bishop, Viking; *Shadrach* by Meindert DeJong, Harper; *Hurry Home Candy* by Meindert DeJong, Harper; *Theodore Roosevelt, Fighting Patriot* by Clara Ingram Judson, Follett; *Magic Maize* by Mary and Conrad Buff, Houghton

1955 *The Wheel on the School* by Meindert DeJong, Harper

Honor Books: *The Courage of Sarah Noble* by Alice Dalgliesh, Scribner's; *Banner in the Sky* by James Ullman, Lippincott

1956 *Carry on, Mr. Bowditch* by Jean Lee Latham, Houghton

Honor Books: *The Secret River* by Marjorie Kinnan Rawlings, Scribner's; *The Golden Name Day* by Jennie Linquist, Harper; *Men, Microscopes, and Living Things* by Katherine Shippen, Viking

1957 *Miracles on Maple Hill* by Virginia Sorensen, Harcourt Brace Jovanovich

Honor Books: *Old Yeller* by Fred Gipson, Harper; *The House of Sixty Fathers* by Meindert DeJong, Harper; *Mr. Justice Holmes* by Clara Ingram Judson, Follett; *The Corn Grows Ripe* by Dorothy Rhoads, Viking; *Black Fox of Lorne* by Marguerite de Angeli, Doubleday

1958 *Rifles for Watie* by Harold Keith, Crowell

Honor Books: *The Horsecatcher* by Mari Sandoz, Westminster; *Gone-away Lake* by Elizabeth Enright, Harcourt Brace Jovanovich; *The Great Wheel* by Robert Lawson, Viking; *Tom Paine, Freedom's Apostle* by Leo Gurko, Crowell

1959 *The Witch of Blackbird Pond* by Elizabeth George Speare, Houghton

Honor Books: *The Family Under the Bridge* by Natalie Savage Carlson, Harper; *Along Came a Dog* by Meindert DeJong, Harper; *Chucaro: Wild Pony of the Pampa* by Francis Kalnay, Harcourt Brace Jovanovich; *The Perilous Road* by William O. Steele, Harcourt Brace Jovanovich

1960 *Onion John* by Joseph Krumgold, Crowell

Honor Books: *My Side of the Mountain* by Jean George, Dutton; *America is Born* by Gerald W. Johnson, Morrow; *The Gammage Cup* by Carol Kendall, Harcourt Brace Jovanovich

1961 *Island of the Blue Dolphins* by Scott O'Dell, Houghton

Honor Books: *America Moves Forward* by Gerald W. Johnson, Morrow; *Old Ramon* by Jack Schaefer, Houghton; *The Cricket in Times Square* by George Selden, Farrar

1962 *The Bronze Bow* by Elizabeth George Speare, Houghton

Honor Books: *Frontier Living* by Edwin Tunis, World; *The Golden Goblet* by Eloise McCraw, Coward; *Belling the Tiger* by Mary Stolz, Harper

1963 *A Wrinkle in Time* by Madeleine L'Engle, Farrar

Honor Books: *Thistle and Thyme: Tales and Legends from Scotland* by Sorche Nic Leodhas, Holt; *Men of Athens* by Olivia Coolidge, Houghton

1964 *It's Like This, Cat* by Emily Cheney Neville, Harper

Honor Books: *Rascal* by Sterling North, Dutton; *The Loner* by Ester Wier, McKay

1965 *Shadow of a Bull* by Maia Wojciechowska, Atheneum

Honor Books: *Across Five Aprils* by Irene Hunt, Follett

1966 *I, Juan de Pareja* by Elizabeth Borten de Treviño, Farrar

Honor Books: *The Black Cauldron* by Lloyd Alexander, Holt; *The Animal Family* by Randall Jarrell, Pantheon; *The Noonday Friends* by Mary Stolz, Harper

1967 *Up a Road Slowly* by Irene Hunt, Follet

Honor Books: *The King's Fifth* by Scott O'Dell, Houghton; *Zlateh the Goat and Other Stories* by Isaac Bashevis Singer, Harper; *The Jazz Man* by Mary H. Weik, Atheneum

1968 *From the Mixed-Up Files of Mrs. Basil E. Frankweiler* by E. L. Konigsburg, Atheneum

Honor Books: *Jennifer, Hecate, Macbeth, William McKinley, and Me, Elizabeth* by E. L. Konigsburg, Atheneum; *The Black Pearl* by Scott O'Dell, Houghton; *The Fearsome Inn* by Isaac Bashevis Singer, Scribner's; *The Egypt Game* by Zilpha Keatley Synder, Atheneum

1969 *The High King* by Lloyd Alexander, Holt

Honor Books: *To Be a Slave* by Julius Lester, Dial; *When Shlemiel Went to Warsaw and Other Stories* by Isaac Bashevis Singer, Farrar

1970 *Sounder* by William H. Armstrong, Harper

Honor Books: *Our Eddie* by Sulamith Ish-Kishor, Pantheon; *The Many Ways of Seeing: An Introduction to the Pleasures of Art* by Janet Gaylord Moore, World; *Journey Outside* by Mary Q. Steele, Viking

1971 *Summer of the Swans* by Betsy Byars, Viking

Honor Books: *Kneeknock Rise* by Natalie Babbitt, Farrar; *Enchantress from the Stars* by Sylvia Louise Engdahl, Atheneum; *Sing Down the Moon* by Scott O'Dell, Houghton

1972 *Mrs. Frisby and the Rats of NIMH* by Robert C. O'Brien, Atheneum

Honor Books: *Incident at Hawk's Hill* by Allan W. Eckert, Little; *The Planet of Junior Brown* by Virginia Hamilton, Macmillan; *The Tombs of Atuan* by Ursula K. Le Guin, Atheneum; *Annie and the Old One* by Miska Miles, Atlantic-Little; *The Headless Cupid* by Zilpha Keatley Sunder, Atheneum

1973 *Julie of the Wolves* by Jean Craighead George, Harper

Honor Books: *Frog and Toad Together* by Arnold Lobel, Harper; *The Upstairs Room* by Johanna Reiss, Crowell; *The Witches of Worm* by Zilpha Keatley Snyder, Atheneum

1974 *The Slave Dancer* by Paula Fox, Bradbury

Honor Book: *The Dark is Rising* by Susan Cooper, Atheneum

1975 *M.C. Higgins, the Great* by Virginia Hamilton, Macmillan

Honor Books: *Figgs & Phantoms* by Ellen Raskin, Dutton; *My Brother Sam Is Dead* by James Lincoln Collier & Christopher Collier, Four Winds; *The Perilous Gard* by Elizabeth Marie Pope, Houghton; *Philip Hall Likes Me. I Reckon Maybe* by Bette Greene, Dial

1976 *The Grey King* by Susan Cooper, Atheneum

Honor Books: *The Hundred Penny Box* by Sharon Bell Mathis, Viking; *Dragonwings* by Laurence Yep, Harper

1977 *Roll of Thunder, Hear My Cry* by Mildred D. Taylor, Dial

Honor Books: *Abel's Island* by William Steig, Farrar; *A String in the Harp* by Nancy Bond, Atheneum

1978 *Bridge to Terabithia* by Katherine Paterson, Crowell

Honor Books: *Ramona and Her Father* by Beverly Cleary, Morrow; *Anpao: An American Indian Odyssey* by Jamake Highwater, Lippincott

1979 *The Westing Game* by Ellen Raskin, Dutton

Honor Book: *The Great Gilly Hopkins* by Katherine Paterson, Crowell

1980 *A Gathering of Days: A New England Girl's Journal 1830–32* by Joan Blos, Scribner's

Honor Book: *The Road from Home: The Story of an Armenian Girl* by David Kherdian, Greenwillow

1981 *Jacob Have I Loved* by Katherine Paterson, Crowell

Honor Books: *The Fledgling* by Jane Langton, Harper; *A Ring of Endless Light* by Madeleine L'Engle, Farrar

1982 *A Visit to William Blake's Inn: Poems for Innocent and Experienced Travelers* by Nancy Willard, Harcourt Brace Jovanovich

Honor Books: *Ramona Quimby, Age 8* by Beverly Cleary, Morrow; *Upon the Head of the Goat: A Childhood in Hungary, 1939–1944* by Aranka Siegal, Farrar

1983 *Dicey's Song* by Cynthia Voigt, Atheneum

Honor Books: *Blue Sword* by Robin McKinley, Morrow; *Dr. DeSoto* by William Steig, Farrar; *Graven Images* by Paul Fleischman, Harper; *Homesick: My Own Story* by Jean Fritz, Putnam's; *Sweet Whisper, Brother Rush,* by Virginia Hamilton, Philomel.

1984 *Dear Mr. Henshaw* by Beverly Cleary, Morrow

Honor Books: *The Sign of the Beaver* by Elizabeth George Speare, Houghton; *A Solitary Blue* by Cynthia Voigt, Atheneum; *The Wish Giver* by Bill Brittain, Harper

1985 *The Hero and the Crown* by Robin McKinley, Greenwillow

Honor Books: *Like Jake and Me* by Mavis Jukes, Knopf; *The Moves Make the Man* by Bruce Brooks, Harper; *One-Eyed Cat* by Paula Fox, Bradbury

1986 *Sarah, Plain and Tall* by Patricia MacLachlan, Harper

Honor Books: *Commodore Perry in the Land of the Shogun* by Rhoda Blumberg, Lothrop; *Dogsong* by Gary Paulsen, Bradbury

1987 *The Whipping Boy* by Sid Fleischman, Greenwillow

Honor Books: *A Fine White Dust* by Cynthia Rylant, Bradbury; *On My Honor* by Marion Dane Bauer *Volcano: The Eruption and Healing of Mount St. Helens* by Patricia Lauber, Bradbury

1988 *Lincoln: A Photobiography* by Russell Freedman, Clarion

Honor Books: *After the Rain* by Norma Fox Mazer, Morrow; *Hatchet* by Gary Paulsen, Bradbury

1989 *Joyful Noise: Poems for Two Voices* by Paul Fleischman, Harper

Honor Books: *In the Beginning: Creation Stories from around the World* by Virginia Hamilton, Harcourt; *Scorpions* by Walter Dean Myers, Harper & Row

1990 *Number the Stars* by Lois Lowry, Houghton Mifflin

Honor Books: *Afternoon of the Elves* by Janet Taylor Lisle, Orchard; *Shabanu, Daughter of the Wind,* by Susan Fisher Staples, Knopf; *The Winter Room* by Gary Paulsen, Orchard

CHILDREN'S BOOK AWARD

The Children's Book Award is presented annually by the International Reading Association to a children's author whose work shows unusual promise. The award was established in 1975.

1975 *Transport 7-41-R* by T. Degens, Viking

1976 *Dragonwings* by Laurence Yep, Harper

1977 *A String in the Harp* by Nancy Bond, Atheneum

1978 *A Summer to Die* by Lois Lowry, Houghton

1979 *Reserved for Mark Anthony Crowder* by Alison Smith, Dutton

1980 *Words by Heart* by Ouida Sebestyen, Little

1981 *My Own Private Sky* by Delores Beckman, Dutton

1982 *Good Night, Mr. Tom* by Michelle Magorian, Harper

1983 *The Darkangel* by Meredith Ann Pierce, Atlantic/Little

1984 *Ratha's Creature* by Clare Bell, Atheneum

1985 *Badger on the Barge* by Janni Howker, Greenwillow

1986 *Prairie Songs* by Pam Conrad, Harper

1987 *The Line Up Book* by Marisa Russo, (picture book), Greenwillow; *After the Dancing Days* by Marisa Russo, (older readers), Harper

1988 *The Third-Story Cat* by Leslie Baker, (picture book), Little; *Ruby in the Smoke* by Philip Pullman, (older readers), Knopf

1989 *Rechenka's Eggs* by Patricia Polacco (picture book), Philomel. *Probably Still Nick Swanson* by Virginia Euwer Wolff (older readers), H. Holt

1990 *No Star Nights* by Anna Egan Smucker and Steve Johnson, (picture book), Knopf; and *Children of the River* by Linda Crew, (older readers), Delacorte

HANS CHRISTIAN ANDERSEN INTERNATIONAL MEDAL

This international award was established in 1956 by the International Board on Books for Young People. It is presented every two years to a living author and a living artist whose total works have made an outstanding contribution to children's literature. A committee of five members, each from a different country, judges the selections.

1956 Eleanor Farjeon (Great Britain)

1958 Astrid Lindgren (Sweden)

1960 Erich Kästner (Germany)

1962 Meindert DeJong (United States)

1964 René Guillot (France)

1966 Author: Tove Jansson (Finland); Illustrator: Alois Carigiet (Switzerland)

1968 Authors: James Krüss (Germany); Jose Maria Sanchez-Silva (Spain); Illustrator: Jiri Trnka (Czechoslovakia)

1970 Author: Gianni Rodari (Italy); Illustrator: Maurice Sendak (United States)

1972 Author: Scott O'Dell (United States); Illustrator: Ib Spang Olsen (Denmark)

1974 Author: Maria Gripe (Sweden); Illustrator: Farshid Mesghali (Iran)

1976 Author: Cecil Bodker (Denmark); Illustrator: Tatjana Mawrina (Union of Soviet Socialist Republics)

1978 Author: Paula Fox (United States); Illustrator: Svend Otto S. (Denmark)

1980 Author: Bohumil Riha (Czechoslovakia); Illustrator: Suekichi Akaba (Japan)

1982 Author: Lygia Bojunga Nunes (Brazil) Illustrator: Zbigniew Rychlicki (Poland)

1984 Author: Christine Nostlinger (Austria) Illustrator: Mitsumasa Anno (Japan)

1986 Author: Patricia Wrightson (Australia) Illustrator: Robert Ingpen (Australia)

1988 Author: Annie M. G. Schmidt (Netherlands) Illustrator: Dusan Kallay (Czechoslovakia)

1990 Author: Tormod Haugen (Norway); Illustrator: Lisbeth Zwerger (Austria)

LAURA INGALLS WILDER MEDAL

The Laura Ingalls Wilder award, named after the author of the "Little House" series, is presented every five years by the American Library Association, Children's Book Division, to an author or illustrator whose books have made a lasting contribution to children's literature. The award was established in 1954 and is restricted to books published in the United States.

1954 Laura Ingalls Wilder

1960 Clara Ingram Judson

1965 Ruth Sawyer

1970 E. B. White

1975 Beverly Cleary

1980 Theodor Geisel (Dr. Seuss)

1983 Maurice Sendak

1986 Jean Fritz

1989 Elizabeth George Speare

EXAMPLES OF ADDITIONAL BOOK AWARDS FOR CHILDREN'S LITERATURE

Amelia Frances Howard–Gibbon Medal, Canadian Library Association, is awarded annually to a Canadian illustrator for outstanding illustrations in a children's book published in Canada. First presented in 1971.

Boston Globe/Horn Book Awards, Boston Globe, Boston, Mass., are awarded annually, since 1967, to an author of fiction, an author of nonfiction, and an illustrator.

The Canadian Library Awards, Canadian Library Association, are given annually to a children's book of literary merit written by a Canadian citizen and to a book of literary merit published in French. First presented in 1947 (Canadian citizen) and 1954 (French publication).

The Carnegie Medal, British Library Association, is awarded annually, since 1936, to an outstanding book first published in the United Kingdom.

Charles and Bertie G. Schwartz Award, National Jewish Welfare Board, New York, is awarded annually to a book that combines literary merit with an affirmative expression of Jewish thought. Established in 1952.

CIBC Award for Unpublished Writers, Council on Interracial Books for Children, New York, awards the United States writer from a racial minority whose manuscript best challenges stereotypes, supplies role models, and portrays distinctive aspects of a culture. Given for the first time in 1969.

Coretta Scott King Award is made to one black author and one black illustrator for outstandingly inspirational contributions to children's literature. The award was first given in 1970.

Jane Addams Children's Book Award, Jane Addams Peace Association and the Women's International League for Peace and Freedom, New York, is given annually, since 1953, to honor the book that most effectively promotes peace, world community, and social justice.

The Kate Greenaway Medal, British Library Association, is awarded each year to the most distinguished work in illustration first published in the United Kingdom. Established in 1956.

Mildred L. Batchelder Award, American Library Association, Children's Services Division, Chicago, is given annually to the publisher of the most outstanding book originally issued in a foreign language. First awarded in 1968.

National Book Awards, Association of American Publishers, New York, are given annually to United States authors whose books have contributed most significantly to human awareness, national culture, and the spirit of excellence. Established in 1969 (Children's Literature Division).

William Allen White Children's Book Award, William Allen White Library, Kansas State Teachers College, Emporia, Kansas, is given annually, since 1953, to an outstanding children's book selected by Kansas children.

APPENDIX D
Readability

THE BOOKS IN THE ANNOTATED BIBLIOGRAPHIES HAVE BEEN evaluated according to approximate reading levels. This information is important for teachers, librarians, and parents who are interested in selecting or recommending books that children can read independently. Several readability formulas may be used to determine readability levels. The books in this text were evaluated according to the Fry Readability Graph that follows, which calculates a book's reading level by the following method:

1 Select three 100-word passages, one each from the beginning middle, and end of the book. Count proper nouns, initializations, and numerals in these 100-word selections. For example, "We went to the circus in Sarasota, Florida" counts as 8 words.
2 Count the total number of sentences in each 100-word passage. Estimate the number of sentences to the nearest tenth of a sentence. Average the total number of sentences in the beginning, middle, and ending passages so that you have one number to represent the number of sentences per 100 words.
3 Count the total number of syllables in each of the three 100-word passages. You will find it faster to count syllables if you tabulate every syllable over one in each word, then add this number to 100 at the end of the passage. For example:

   1 1 2 1
   Jim was planning to take a camping vacation in the high country.
   (17 syllables)

   Now, find the average total number of syllables for the three 100-word passages.

4 Plot on the graph the average number of sentences per 100 words, and the average number of syllables per 100 words. The example shown below places the reading level of *Stuart Little* at fourth grade, with 9.2 average number of sentences per 100 words and 127 average number of syllables per 100 words.

Source

Stuart Little **(E. B. White)**	**Sentences per 100 words**	**Syllables per 100 words**
100-word sample page 6	6.3	116
100-word sample page 72	10.5	136
100-word sample page 125	10.7	129
Total	27.5	381
Average	9.2	127

Readability formulas assume that shorter sentences and fewer syllables in words result in easier reading materials. In contrast, long sentences and numerous multisyllabic words are thought to be more difficult to read. While this is often true, the adult should be aware that readability formulas do not take into consideration such factors as the difficulty of the concepts presented, or the child's interest in a particular subject. Although readability formulas are useful, they should not be used without examining a book for difficult conceptual content, difficult figurative language, and stylistic or organizational peculiarities that might cause comprehension problems. In addition, the adult should note a book's content and interest value, since a child may be able to read a book that would otherwise be at his frustration level if he is interested in the subject.

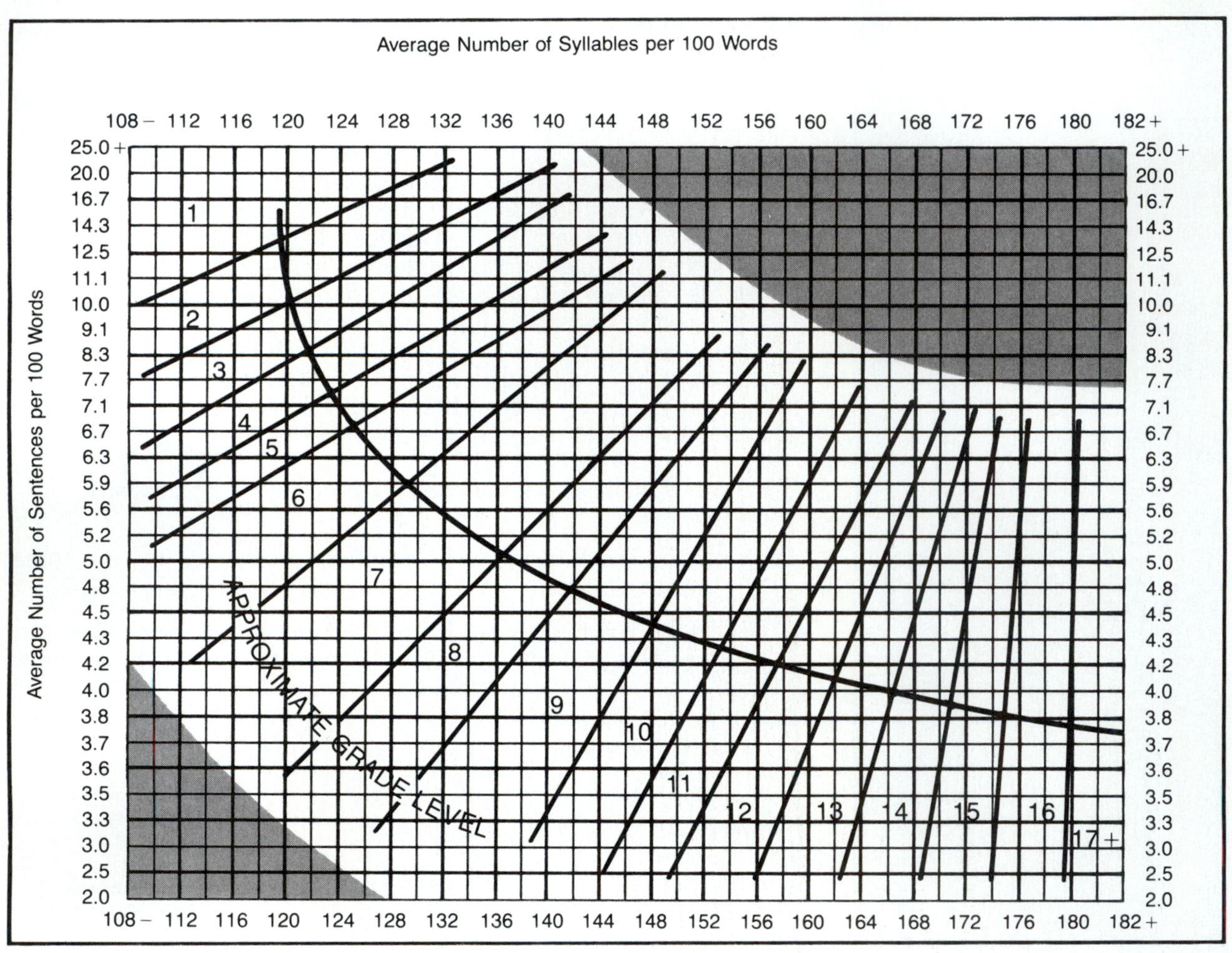

From Edward Fry, "Fry's Readability Graph: Clarifications, Validity, and Extension." *Journal of Reading* 21 (Dec. 1977): 249. The journal is published by the International Reading Association.

APPENDIX E
Publishers and Their Addresses

Abingdon Press
Div. of United Methodist Publishing House
201 Eighth Ave. S.
Nashville, Tenn. 37202

Accent Books
Division of Accent Publications
12100 W. Sixth Ave.
Denver, Colo. 80215

Addison-Wesley Publishing Co., Inc.
Rte. 128
Reading, Mass. 01867

Antioch Publishing Co.
888 Dayton St.
Yellow Springs, Ohio 45387

Arte Publico Press
University of Houston
M.D. Anderson Library, Rm. 2
Houston, Tex. 77204-2090

Associated Features, Inc.
Box 1762, Murray Hill Station
New York, N.Y. 10156

Atheneum Publishers
Subs. of Macmillan Publishing Co.
866 Third Ave.
New York, N.Y. 10022

Avon Books
Div. of The Hearst Corp.
105 Madison Ave.
New York, N.Y. 10016

BackPax International, Ltd.
Box 603
Wilton, Conn. 06897

Baha'i Publishing Trust
415 Linden Ave.
Wilmette, Ill. 60091

Ball-Stick-Bird Publications, Inc.
Box 592
Stony Brook, N.Y. 11790

Bankcroft-Sage Publishing
Box 664
533 8th St., S.
Naples, Fla. 33939

Bantam Books, Inc.
Div. of Bantam Doubleday Dell Publishing
666 Fifth Ave.
New York, N.Y. 10103

Barron's Educational Series, Inc.
250 Wireless Blvd.
Hauppauge, N.Y. 11788

Peter Bedrick Books, Inc.
2112 Broadway, Ste. 318
New York, N.Y. 10023

Bellerophon Books
36 Anacapa St.
Santa Barbara, Calif. 93101

Berkley Publishing Group
Subs. of The Putnam Berkley Publishing Group, Inc.
200 Madison Ave.
New York, N.Y. 10016

Bloch Publishing Co., Inc.
37 W. 26th St., 9th Floor
New York, N.Y. 10010

Bookmakers Guild, Inc.
Subs. of Dakota Graphics, Inc.
9655 W. Colfax Ave.
Lakewood, Colo. 80215

Bradbury Press
Affil. of Macmillan, Inc.
866 Third Avenue
New York, N.Y. 10022

Allen D. Bragdon Publishers, Inc.
Tupelo Rd.
South Yarmouth, Mass. 02664

Broadman Press
Div. of Southern Baptist Convention
Sunday School Board
127 Ninth Ave. N.
Nashville, Tenn. 37234

Brunner/Mazel, Inc.
19 Union Sq. W.
New York, N.Y. 10003

Carolrhoda Books, Inc.
241 First Ave. N.
Minneapolis, Minn. 55401

Chelsea House Publishers
Div. of Main Line Book Co.
95 Madison Ave.
New York, N.Y. 10016

Chicago Zoological Society
3300 Golf Rd.
Brookfield, Ill. 60513

Children's Book Press
1461 Ninth Ave.
San Francisco, Calif. 94122

Children's Division Dial Books for Young Readers
Div. of E. P. Dutton
2 Park Ave.
New York, N.Y. 10016

Children's Press
Subs. of Grolier, Inc.
5440 N. Cumberland Ave.
Chicago, Ill. 60656

The Child's World, Inc.
980 N. McLean Blvd.
Elgin, Ill. 60123

China Books & Periodicals, Inc.
2929 24th St.
San Francisco, Calif. 94110

Cinco Puntos Press
2709 Louisville
El Paso, Tex. 79930

Clarion Books
Div. of Houghton Mifflin Co.
215 Park Ave. S.
New York, N.Y. 10003

Cobblehill Books
Imprint of E. P. Dutton
2 Park Ave.
New York, N.Y. 10016

Cobblesmith
Box 191
RFD 1
Freeport, Me. 04032

Contemporary Books, Inc.
180 N. Michigan Ave.
Chicago, Ill. 60601

David C. Cook Publishing Co.
850 N. Grove Ave.
Elgin, Ill. 60120

CPI (Contemporary Perspectives, Inc.)
145 E. 49th St.
New York, N.Y. 10017

Crabtree Publishing Co.
350 Fifth Ave.
Suite 3308
New York, N.Y. 10118

Crane Publishing Co.
Box 3713
1301 Hamilton Ave.
Trenton, N.J. 08629

Creative Education, Inc.
Box 227
123 S. Broad St.
Mankato, Minn. 56001

Creative Learning Press, Inc.
Box 320
Mansfield Center, Conn. 06250

Daughters of St. Paul
50 St. Paul's Ave.
Jamaica Plain
Boston, Mass. 02130

Dell Publishing Co., Inc.
Subs. of Bantam Doubleday Dell Publishing Group, Inc.
666 Fifth Ave.
New York, N.Y. 10103

Deseret Book Co.
Box 30178
40 E. South Temple
Salt Lake City, Utah 84130

Dial Books for Young Readers
Inprint of Penguin USA
1633 Broadway
New York, N.Y. 10019

Dillon Press, Inc.
242 Portland Ave. S.
Minneapolis, Minn. 55415

Doubleday
Div. of Bantam Doubleday Dell Publishing Group, Inc.
666 Fifth Ave.
New York, N.Y. 10103

Dufour Editions, Inc.
Box 449
Chester Springs, Pa. 19425-0449

E. P. Dutton
Imprint of Penguin USA
2 Park Ave.
New York, N.Y. 10016

Eakin Press
Div. of Eakin Publications, Inc.
Box 90159
Austin, Tex. 78709-0159

Enslow Publishers
Box 777
Bloy St. & Ramsey Ave.
Hillside, N.J. 07205

M. Evans & Co., Inc.
216 E. 49th St.
New York, N.Y. 10017

Evergreen Press
3380 Vincent Rd.
Pleasant Hill, Calif. 94523

Faber & Faber, Inc.
Subs. of Faber & Faber Publishers, Ltd.
50 Cross Street
Winchester, Mass. 01890

Farrar, Straus & Giroux, Inc.
19 Union Sq. W.
New York, N.Y. 10003

The Feminist Press at the City University of New York
311 E. 94th St.
New York, N.Y. 10128

J. G. Ferguson Publishing Co.
200 W. Monroe St.
Chicago, Ill. 60606

Field Publications
Subs. of Field Corporation
245 Long Hill Rd.
Middletown, Conn. 06457

Fleet Press Corp.
160 Fifth Ave.
New York, N.Y. 10010

Four Winds Press
Imprint of Macmillan Publishing Co.
866 Third Ave.
New York, N.Y. 10022

Friendship Press
Subs. of National Council of the Churches of Christ U.S.A.
475 Riverside Dr.
New York, N.Y. 10115

Funk & Wagnalls
Field Publications
70 Hilltop Rd.
Ramsey, N.J. 07446

Galison Books
Subs. of GMG Publishing
25 W. 43rd St.
New York, N.Y. 10036

Gareth Stevens, Inc.
7317 W. Green Tree Rd.
Milwaukee, Wis. 53223

Garrett Educational Corp.
Box 1588
130 E. 13th S.
Ada, Okla. 74820

Gateway Press, Inc.
3167 Kalamazoo Ave. S.E.
Grand Rapids, Mich. 49508

Gessler Publishing Co., Inc.
55 W. 13th St.
New York, N.Y. 10011

The C. R. Gibson Co.
32 Knight St.
Norwalk, Conn. 06856

David R. Godine, Publisher, Inc.
Horticulture Hall
300 Massachusetts Ave.
Boston, Mass. 02115

Golden Books
Div. of Western Publishing Co.
1220 Mound Ave.
Racine, Wis. 53404

Good Books
Subs. of Good Enterprises, Inc.
Main St.
Intercourse, Pa. 17534

Graphic Arts Center Publishing Co.
Box 10306
3019 N.W. Yeon Ave.
Portland, Ore. 97210

Great Northwest Publishing & Distributing Co. Inc.
Box 103902
Anchorage, Alaska 99510

Green Tiger Press, Inc.
Subs. of WJT Enterprises, Inc.
435 Carmel St.
San Marcos, Calif. 92069-4362

Greenwillow Books
Div. of William Morrow & Co., Inc.
105 Madison Ave.
New York, N.Y. 10016

Grey Castle Press
Pocket Knife Sq.
Lakeville, Conn. 06039

Grosset & Dunlap
Member of The Putnam Berkley Group
51 Madison Ave.
New York, N.Y. 10010

Harbinger House
3131 North Country Club, Suite 106
Tucson, Ariz. 85716

Harcourt Brace Jovanovich, Inc.
6277 Sea Harbor Dr.
Orlando, Fla. 32821

Harmony Books
Div. of Crown Publishers, Inc.
225 Park Ave. S.
New York, N.Y. 10003

Harper & Row Publishers, Inc.
10 E. 53rd St.
New York, N.Y. 10022

Harrison House Publishers
1029 N. Utica
Tulsa, Okla. 74110

Hebrew Publishing Co.
Box 020875
100 Water St.
Brooklyn, N.Y. 11202-0019

Heian International, Inc.
Box 1013
Union City, Calif. 94587

Heyday Books
Box 9145
Berkeley, Calif. 94709

Hill & Wang
Div. of Farrar, Straus & Giroux, Inc.
19 Union Sq., W.
New York, N.Y. 10003

Holiday House, Inc.
18 E. 53rd St.
New York, N.Y. 10022

Henry Holt & Co.
115 W. 18th St.
New York, N.Y. 10011

Holt, Rinehart and Winston, Inc.
Subs. of Harcourt Brace Jovanovich, Inc.
6277 Sea Harbor Dr.
Orlando, Fla. 32821

Houghton Mifflin Co.
One Beacon St.
Boston, Mass. 02108

Hunter House, Inc., Publishers
Box 847
428 W. Harrison, Suite 101 C & D
Claremont, Calif. 91711

Huntington House, Inc.
Box 53788
Lafayette, La. 70505

Ideals Publishing Corp.
Subs. of Egmont, Inc., U.S.A., A Gutenberghus Co.
Box 140300, Nelson Place at Elm Hill Pike
Nashville, Tenn. 37214-0300

ISIS Large Print Books
Div. of ABC-CLIO
Box 1911, 130 Cremona Dr.
Santa Barbara, Calif. 93116-1911

Jalmar Press, Inc.
Subs. of B L Winch & Associates
45 Hitching Post Dr., Bldg. 2
Rolling Hills Estates, Calif. 90274-4297

Jewish Publication Society
1930 Chestnut Street
Philadelphia, Pa. 19103-4599

Joy Street Books
Little, Brown & Co., Inc.
34 Beacon St.
Boston, Mass. 02108

Kalimat Press
1600 Sawtelle Blvd., Suite 34
Los Angeles, Calif. 90025

Kane/Miller Book Publishers
Box 529
Brooklyn, N.Y. 11231-0005

Kar-Ben Copies, Inc.
6800 Tildenwood Lane
Rockville, Md. 20852

Alfred A. Knopf, Inc.
Subs. of Random House, Inc.
201 E. 50th St.
New York, N.Y. 10022

KTAV Publishing House, Inc.
Box 6249
900 Jefferson St.
Hoboken, N.J. 07030

Lerner Publications Co.
241 First Ave. N.
Minneapolis, Minn. 55401

Liguori Publications
One Liguori Dr.
Liguori, Mo. 63057

Lion Books Publisher
210 Nelson Rd., Suite B
Scarsdale, N.Y. 10583

Lion Publishing Corp.
Subs. of Lion Publishing PLC
1705 Hubbard Ave.
Batavia, Ill. 60510

J. B. Lippincott Co.
Subs. of Harper & Row, Publishers, Inc.
E. Washington Sq.
Philadelphia, Pa. 19105

Little, Brown & Co., Inc.
Subs. of Time, Inc.
34 Beacon St.
Boston, Mass. 02108

Lodestar Publishing
Imprint of Penguin USA
1633 Broadway
New York, N.Y. 10019

Lothrop, Lee & Shepard Books
Div. of William Morrow & Co., Inc.
105 Madison Ave.
New York, N.Y. 10016

Lynx Books
Div. of Lynx Communications
41 Madison Ave.
New York, N.Y. 10010

McGraw-Hill Book Co.
Div. of McGraw-Hill, Inc.
1221 Avenue of the Americas
New York, N.Y. 10020

Macmillan Publishing Co.
Div. of Macmillan, Inc.
866 Third Ave.
New York, N.Y. 10022

Mage Publishers, Inc.
1032 29th St. N.W.
Washington, D.C. 20007

Marshall Cavendish Corp.
Subs. of Marshall Cavendish, Ltd.
147 W. Merrick Rd.
Freeport, N.Y. 11520

Meadowbrook Press, Inc.
18318 Minnetonka Blvd.
Deephaven, Minn. 55391

Media Projects, Inc.
Rutherford Place
305 Second Ave.
New York, N.Y. 10003

Melius & Peterson, Publishing, Inc.
Div. of Video Resources, Inc.
Box 925, Citizens Bldg.
202 S. Main, Rm. 515
Aberdeen, S.D. 57401

Meriwether Publishing Ltd/Contemporary Drama Service
885 Elkton Dr.
Colorado Springs, Colo. 80907

Mesorah Publications
4401 Second Ave.
Brooklyn, N.Y. 11232

Microsoft Press
Div. of Microsoft Corp.
Box 97017
16011 N.E. 36th Way
Redmond, Wash. 98073-9717

Middle Atlantic Press
Box 945
848 Church St.
Wilmington, Dela. 19899

Modern Publishing
Div. of Unisystems, Inc.
155 E. 55th St.
New York, N.Y. 10022

Joshua Morris Publishing, Inc.
Subs. of Joshua Morris, Inc.
221 Danbury Rd.
Wilton, Conn. 06897

William Morrow & Co., Inc.
Subs. of the Hearst Corp.
105 Madison Ave.
New York, N.Y. 10016

Morrow Junior Books
Div. of William Morrow & Co., Inc.
105 Madison Ave.
New York, N.Y. 10016

National Geographic Society
1145 17th St. N.W.
Washington, D.C. 20036

Thomas Nelson, Inc.
Nelson Place at Elm Hill Pike
Nashville, Tenn. 37214

Network Publications
Div. of ETR Associates
Box 1830
Santa Cruz, Calif. 95061-1830

Oddo Publishing, Inc.
Box 68
Stonybrook Acres
Fayetteville, Ga. 30214

Outlet Book Co.
Div. of Random House, Inc.
225 Park Ave. S.
New York, N.Y. 10003

Oxford University Press, Inc.
200 Madison Ave.
New York, N.Y. 10016

Pantheon Books, Inc.
Div. of Random House, Inc.
201 E. 50th St.
New York, N.Y. 10022

Paraclete Press
Div. of Creative Joys, Inc.
Box 1568
Hilltop Plaza, Rte. 6A
Orleans, Mass. 02653

Parents Magazine Press
Div. of Gruner & Jahr USA, Publishing
685 Third Ave.
New York, N.Y. 10017

Pelican Publishing Co., Inc.
Box 189
1101 Monroe St.
Gretna, La. 70053

Penguin USA
1633 Broadway
New York, N.Y. 10019

Pharos Books
Affil. of United Media
200 Park Ave.
New York, N.Y. 10166

Philomel Books
Member of The Putnam Berkley Group
51 Madison Ave.
New York, N.Y. 10010

Picture Book Studio
Box 9139
10 Central St.
Saxonville, Mass. 01701

Pittenbruach Press
Box 553
15 Walnut St.
Northampton, Mass. 01061

Platt & Munk, Publishers
Div. of Putnam Berkley Group
51 Madison Ave.
New York, N.Y. 10010

Playmore Inc., Publishers
200 Fifth Ave.
New York, N.Y. 10010

Pleasant Co.
8400 Fairway Place
Middleton, Wis. 53562

Prentice-Hall, Inc.
Imprint of Simon & Schuster, Inc.
Englewood Cliffs, N.J. 07632

Price Stern Sloan, Inc.
360 N. LaCienega Blvd.
Los Angeles, Calif. 90048

The Putnam Berkley Group, Inc.
Subs. of MCA
200 Madison Ave.
New York, N.Y. 10016

Raintree Publishers, Inc.
310 Wisconsin Ave.
Milwaukee, Wis. 53203

Random House, Inc.
201 E. 50th St.
New York, N.Y. 10022

Santillana Publishing Co., Inc.
257 Union St.
Northvale, N.J. 07647

Scholastic, Inc.
Subs. of S.I. Holdings, Inc.
730 Broadway
New York, N.Y. 10003

Charles Scribner's Sons
Imprint of Macmillan Publishing Co.
866 Third Ave.
New York, N.Y. 10022

Seventh-Wing Publications
515 E. Washington St.
Colorado Springs, Colo. 80907

Sharon Publications, Inc.
Subs. of Edrei Communications Corp.
1086 Teaneck Rd.
Teaneck, N.J. 07666

The Shoe String Press, Inc.
Box 4327
925 Sherman Ave.
Hamden, Conn. 06514

Simon & Schuster
Subs. of Paramount Communications, Inc.
The Simon & Schuster Bldg.
1230 Avenue of the Americas
New York, N.Y. 10020

Slawson Communications, Inc.
165 Vallecitos de Oro
San Marcos, Calif. 92069

W. H. Smith Publishers, Inc.
Subs. of W. H. Smith Group PLC
112 Madison Ave.
New York, N.Y. 10016

Stemmer House Publishers, Inc.
2627 Caves Rd.
Owings Mills, Md. 21117

Stoneway, Ltd.
Box 548
Southeastern, Pa. 19399

Troll Associates
100 Corporate Dr.
Mahwah, N.J. 07430

Tuffy Books, Inc.
Div. of Grosset & Dunlap, Inc./The Putnam Berkley Group
51 Madison Ave.
New York, N.Y. 10010

Tundra Books of Northern New York
Affil. of Tundra Books (Canada)
Box 1030
Plattsburgh, N.Y. 12901

Charles E. Tuttle Co., Inc.
28 S. Main St.
Rutland, Vt. 05701

Twenty-First Century Books
38 N. Market St.
Frederick, Md. 21701

UAHC Press
Div. of Union of American Hebrew Congregations
838 Fifth Ave.
New York, N.Y. 10021

The Unicorn Publishing House, Inc.
120 American Rd.
Morris Plains, N.J. 07950

Value Communications, Inc.
Subs. of Oak Tree Publications, Inc.
3870 Murphy Canyon, Suite 200
San Diego, Calif. 92123

Viking Penguin
Imprint of Penguin USA
1633 Broadway
New York, N.Y. 10019

Volcano Press, Inc.
Box 270
Volcano, Calif. 95689

Walker & Co.
Div. of Walker Publishing Co., Inc.
720 Fifth Ave.
New York, N.Y. 10019

Frederick Warne & Co., Inc.
Imprint of Penguin USA
1633 Broadway
New York, N.Y. 10019

Warner Books, Inc.
Subs. of Warner Publishing, Inc.
666 Fifth Ave.
New York, N.Y. 10103

Franklin Watts, Inc.
Subs. of Grolier, Inc.
387 Park Ave. S.
New York, N.Y. 10016

Western Publishing Co., Inc.
1220 Mound Ave.
Racine, Wis. 53404

The Westminster Press/John Knox Press
Publications Unit of The Presbyterian Church (U.S.A.)
100 Witherspoon St.
Louisville, Ky. 40202

Albert Whitman & Co.
5747 W. Howard St.
Niles, Ill. 60648

Winston-Derek Publishers, Inc.
1722 West End Ave.
Nashville, Tenn. 37203

Alan Wofsy Fine Arts
401 China Basin St.
San Francisco, Calif. 94107

Word, Inc.
Subs. of Capital Cities/ABC, Inc.
Div. of ABC Publishing
5221 N. O'Connor Blvd., Suite 1000
Irving, Tex. 75039

World Book, Inc.
Subs. of The Scott Fetzer Co.
510 Merchandise Mart Plaza
Chicago, Ill. 60654

Young Discovery Library
217 Main St.
Ossining, N.Y. 10562

Zondervan Publishing House
Div. of Zondervan Corp. & Harper & Row, Publishers, Inc.
1415 Lake Dr. S.E.
Grand Rapids, Mich. 49506

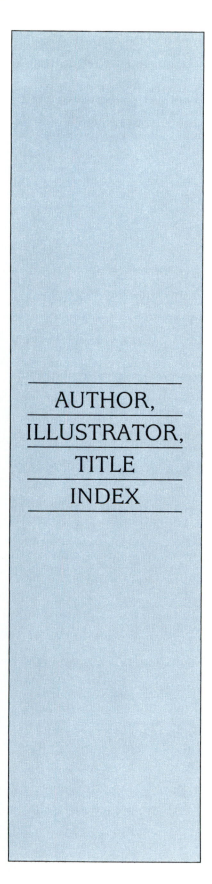

AUTHOR, ILLUSTRATOR, TITLE INDEX

Note: Page numbers in *italics* refer to illustrations.

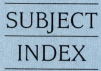

SUBJECT INDEX